Basic Econometrics

Fifth Edition

Damodar N. Gujarati
Professor Emeritus of Economics, United States Military Academy, West Point

Dawn C. Porter
University of Southern California

Boston Burr Ridge, IL Dubuque, IA Madison, WI New York San Francisco St. Louis
Bangkok Bogotá Caracas Kuala Lumpur Lisbon London Madrid Mexico City
Milan Montreal New Delhi Santiago Seoul Singapore Sydney Taipei Toronto

The McGraw·Hill Companies

BASIC ECONOMETRICS
International Edition 2009

Exclusive rights by McGraw-Hill Education (Asia), for manufacture and export. This book cannot be re-exported from the country to which it is sold by McGraw-Hill. This International Edition is not to be sold or purchased in North America and contains content that is different from its North American version.

Published by McGraw-Hill/Irwin, a business unit of The McGraw-Hill Companies, Inc. 1221 Avenue of the Americas, New York, NY 10020.

10 09 08 07 06 05 04
15 14 13 12 11 10
CTP BJE

When ordering this title, use ISBN: 978-007-127625-2 or MHID: 007-127625-4

Printed in Singapore

www.mhhe.com

About the Authors

Damodar N. Gujarati

After teaching for more than 25 years at the City University of New York and 17 years in the Department of Social Sciences, U.S. Military Academy at West Point, New York, Dr. Gujarati is currently Professor Emeritus of economics at the Academy. Dr. Gujarati received his M.Com. degree from the University of Bombay in 1960, his M.B.A. degree from the University of Chicago in 1963, and his Ph.D. degree from the University of Chicago in 1965. Dr. Gujarati has published extensively in recognized national and international journals, such as the *Review of Economics and Statistics,* the *Economic Journal,* the *Journal of Financial and Quantitative Analysis,* and the *Journal of Business.* Dr. Gujarati was a member of the Board of Editors of the *Journal of Quantitative Economics,* the official journal of the Indian Econometric Society. Dr. Gujarati is also the author of *Pensions and the New York City Fiscal Crisis* (the American Enterprise Institute, 1978), *Government and Business* (McGraw-Hill, 1984), and *Essentials of Econometrics* (McGraw-Hill, 3d ed., 2006). Dr. Gujarati's books on econometrics have been translated into several languages.

Dr. Gujarati was a Visiting Professor at the University of Sheffield, U.K. (1970–1971), a Visiting Fulbright Professor to India (1981–1982), a Visiting Professor in the School of Management of the National University of Singapore (1985–1986), and a Visiting Professor of Econometrics, University of New South Wales, Australia (summer of 1988). Dr. Gujarati has lectured extensively on micro- and macroeconomic topics in countries such as Australia, China, Bangladesh, Germany, India, Israel, Mauritius, and the Republic of South Korea.

Dawn C. Porter

Dawn Porter has been an assistant professor in the Information and Operations Management Department at the Marshall School of Business of the University of Southern California since the fall of 2006. She currently teaches both introductory undergraduate and MBA statistics in the business school. Prior to joining the faculty at USC, from 2001–2006, Dawn was an assistant professor at the McDonough School of Business at Georgetown University, and before that was a visiting professor in the psychology department at the Graduate School of Arts and Sciences at NYU. At NYU she taught a number of advanced statistical methods courses and was also an instructor at the Stern School of Business. Her Ph.D. is from the Stern School in Statistics.

Dawn's areas of research interest include categorical analysis, agreement measures, multivariate modeling, and applications to the field of psychology. Her current research examines online auction models from a statistical perspective. She has presented her research at the Joint Statistical Meetings, the Decision Sciences Institute meetings, the International Conference on Information Systems, several universities including the London School of Economics and NYU, and various e-commerce and statistics seminar series. Dawn is also a co-author on *Essentials of Business Statistics,* 2nd edition, McGraw-Hill Irwin, 2008. Outside of academics, Dawn has been employed as a statistical consultant for KPMG, Inc. She has also worked as a statistical consultant for many other major companies, including Ginnie Mae, Inc., Toys R Us Corporation, IBM, Cosmaire, Inc., and New York University (NYU) Medical Center.

For Joan Gujarati, Diane Gujarati-Chesnut,
Charles Chesnut, and my grandchildren,
"Tommy" and Laura Chesnut.

—DNG

For Judy, Lee, Brett, Bryan, Amy, and Autumn Porter.
But especially for my adoring father, Terry.

—DCP

Brief Contents

Contents

CHAPTER 7
Multiple Regression Analysis: The Problem of Estimation 188

CHAPTER 8
Multiple Regression Analysis: The Problem of Inference 233

CHAPTER 9
Dummy Variable Regression Models 277

PART TWO
RELAXING THE ASSUMPTIONS OF THE CLASSICAL MODEL 315

CHAPTER 10
Multicollinearity: What Happens If the Regressors Are Correlated? 320

CHAPTER 11
Heteroscedasticity: What Happens If the Error Variance Is Nonconstant? 365

CHAPTER 12

Autocorrelation: What Happens If the Error Terms Are Correlated? 412

CHAPTER 13

Econometric Modeling: Model Specification and Diagnostic Testing 467

CHAPTER 19
The Identification Problem 689

CHAPTER 20
Simultaneous-Equation Methods 711

CHAPTER 21
Time Series Econometrics: Some Basic Concepts 737

CHAPTER 22
Time Series Econometrics: Forecasting 773

APPENDIX A
A Review of Some Statistical Concepts 801

APPENDIX B
Rudiments of Matrix Algebra 838

Preface

Objective of the Book

The first edition of *Basic Econometrics* was published thirty years ago. Over the years, there have been important developments in the theory and practice of econometrics. In each of the subsequent editions, I have tried to incorporate the major developments in the field. The fifth edition continues that tradition.

What has not changed, however, over all these years is my firm belief that econometrics can be taught to the beginner in an intuitive and informative way without resorting to matrix algebra, calculus, or statistics beyond the introductory level. Some subject material is inherently technical. In that case I have put the material in the appropriate appendix or refer the reader to the appropriate sources. Even then, I have tried to simplify the technical material so that the reader can get an intuitive understanding of this material.

I am pleasantly surprised not only by the longevity of this book but also by the fact that the book is widely used not only by students of economics and finance but also by students and researchers in the fields of politics, international relations, agriculture, and health sciences. All these students will find the new edition with its expanded topics and concrete applications very useful. In this edition I have paid even more attention to the relevance and timeliness of the real data used in the text. In fact, I have added about fifteen new illustrative examples and more than thirty new end-of-chapter exercises. Also, I have updated the data for about two dozen of the previous edition's examples and more than twenty exercises.

Although I am in the eighth decade of my life, I have not lost my love for econometrics, and I strive to keep up with the major developments in the field. To assist me in this endeavor, I am now happy to have Dr. Dawn Porter, Assistant Professor of Statistics at the Marshall School of Business at the University of Southern California in Los Angeles, as my co-author. Both of us have been deeply involved in bringing the fifth edition of *Basic Econometrics* to fruition.

Major Features of the Fifth Edition

Before discussing the specific changes in the various chapters, the following features of the new edition are worth noting:

1. Practically all of the data used in the illustrative examples have been updated.
2. Several new examples have been added.
3. In several chapters, we have included extended concluding examples that illustrate the various points made in the text.
4. Concrete computer printouts of several examples are included in the book. Most of these results are based on **EViews** (version 6) and **STATA** (version 10), as well as **MINITAB** (version 15).
5. Several new diagrams and graphs are included in various chapters.
6. Several new data-based exercises are included in the various chapters.
7. Small-sized data are included in the book, but large sample data are posted on the book's website, thereby minimizing the size of the text. The website will also publish all of the data used in the book and will be periodically updated.

8. In a few chapters, we have included class exercises in which students are encouraged to obtain their own data and implement the various techniques discussed in the book. Some Monte Carlo simulations are also included in the book.

Specific Changes to the Fifth Edition

Some chapter-specific changes are as follows:

1. The assumptions underlying the classical linear regression model (CLRM) introduced in Chapter 3 now make a careful distinction between fixed regressors (explanatory variables) and random regressors. We discuss the importance of the distinction.
2. The appendix to Chapter 6 discusses the properties of logarithms, the Box-Cox transformations, and various growth formulas.
3. Chapter 7 now discusses not only the marginal impact of a single regressor on the dependent variable but also the impacts of simultaneous changes of all the explanatory variables on the dependent variable. This chapter has also been reorganized in the same structure as the assumptions from Chapter 3.
4. A comparison of the various tests of heteroscedasticity is given in Chapter 11.
5. There is a new discussion of the impact of *structural breaks* on autocorrelation in Chapter 12.
6. New topics included in Chapter 13 are *missing data, non-normal error term,* and *stochastic,* or *random,* regressors.
7. A non-linear regression model discussed in Chapter 14 has a concrete application of the Box-Cox transformation.
8. Chapter 15 contains several new examples that illustrate the use of logit and probit models in various fields.
9. Chapter 16 on *panel data regression models* has been thoroughly revised and illustrated with several applications.
10. An extended discussion of Sims and Granger causality tests is now included in Chapter 17.
11. Stationary and non-stationary time series, as well as some of the problems associated with various tests of stationarity, are now thoroughly discussed in Chapter 21.
12. Chapter 22 includes a discussion on why taking the first differences of a time series for the purpose of making it stationary may not be the appropriate strategy in some situations.

Besides these specific changes, errors and misprints in the previous editions have been corrected and the discussions of several topics in the various chapters have been streamlined.

Organization and Options

The extensive coverage in this edition gives the instructor substantial flexibility in choosing topics that are appropriate to the intended audience. Here are suggestions about how this book may be used.

One-semester course for the nonspecialist: Appendix A, Chapters 1 through 9, an overview of Chapters 10, 11, 12 (omitting all the proofs).

One-semester course for economics majors: Appendix A, Chapters 1 through 13.

Two-semester course for economics majors: Appendices A, B, C, Chapters 1 to 22. Chapters 14 and 16 may be covered on an optional basis. Some of the technical appendices may be omitted.

Graduate and postgraduate students and researchers: This book is a handy reference book on the major themes in econometrics.

Supplements

A comprehensive website contains the following supplementary material:

–Data from the text, as well as additional large set data referenced in the book; the data will be periodically updated by the authors.

–A Solutions Manual, written by Dawn Porter, providing answers to all of the questions and problems throughout the text.

–A digital image library containing all of the graphs and figures from the text.

For more information, please go to www.mhhe.com/gujarati5e

Acknowledgments

Since the publication of the first edition of this book in 1978, we have received valuable advice, comments, criticism, and suggestions from a variety of people. In particular, we would like to acknowledge the help we have received from Michael McAleer of the University of Western Australia, Peter Kennedy of Simon Frazer University in Canada, Kenneth White, of the University of British Columbia, George K. Zestos, of Christopher Newport University, Virginia, and Paul Offner, of Georgetown University, Washington, D.C.

We are also grateful to several people who have influenced us by their scholarship. We especially want to thank Arthur Goldberger of the University of Wisconsin, William Greene of New York University, and the late G. S. Maddala. We continue to be grateful to the following reviewers who provided valuable insight, criticism, and suggestions for previous editions of this text: Michael A. Grove at the University of Oregon, Harumi Ito at Brown University, Han Kim at South Dakota University, Phanindra V. Wunnava at Middlebury College, and Andrew Paizis of the City University of New York.

Several authors have influenced the writing of this text. In particular, we are grateful to these authors: Chandan Mukherjee, director of the Centre for Development Studies, Trivandrum, India; Howard White and Marc Wuyts, both at the Institute of Social Studies in the Netherlands; Badi H. Baltagi, Texas A&M University; B. Bhaskara Rao, University of New South Wales, Australia; R. Carter Hill, Louisiana University; William E. Griffiths, University of New England; George G. Judge, University of California at Berkeley; Marno Verbeek, Center for Economic Studies, KU Leuven; Jeffrey Wooldridge, Michigan State University; Kerry Patterson, University of Reading, U.K.; Francis X. Diebold, Wharton School, University of Pennsylvania; Wojciech W. Charemza and Derek F. Deadman, both of the University of Leicester, U.K.; and Gary Koop, University of Glasgow.

A number of very valuable comments and suggestions given by reviewers of the fourth edition have greatly improved this edition. We would like to thank the following:

Valerie Bencivenga
University of Texas–Austin
Andrew Economopoulos
Ursinus College
Eric Eide
Brigham Young University
Gary Ferrier
University of Arkansas–Fayetteville
David Garman
Tufts University
David Harris
Benedictine College
Don Holley
Boise State University
George Jakubson
Cornell University
Bruce Johnson
Centre College of Kentucky
Duke Kao
Syracuse University
Gary Krueger
Macalester College
Subal Kumbhakar
Binghamton University
Tae-Hwy Lee
University of California–Riverside
Solaiman Miah
West Virginia State University
Fabio Milani
University of California–Irvine
Helen Naughton
University of Oregon
Solomon Smith
Langston University
Kay Strong
Bowling Green State University
Derek Tittle
Georgia Institute of Technology
Tiemen Woutersen
Johns Hopkins University

We would like to thank students and teachers all over the world who have not only used this book but have communicated with us about various aspects of the book.

For their behind-the-scenes help at McGraw-Hill, we are grateful to Douglas Reiner, Noelle Fox, and Anne Hilbert.

Finally, but not least important, Dr. Gujarati would like to thank his daughters, Joan and Diane, for their constant support and encouragement in the preparation of this and the previous editions.

Damodar N. Gujarati
Dawn C. Porter

Introduction

I.1 What Is Econometrics?

Literally interpreted, *econometrics* means "economic measurement." Although measurement is an important part of econometrics, the scope of econometrics is much broader, as can be seen from the following quotations:

> Econometrics, the result of a certain outlook on the role of economics, consists of the application of mathematical statistics to economic data to lend empirical support to the models constructed by mathematical economics and to obtain numerical results.[1]

> . . . econometrics may be defined as the quantitative analysis of actual economic phenomena based on the concurrent development of theory and observation, related by appropriate methods of inference.[2]

> Econometrics may be defined as the social science in which the tools of economic theory, mathematics, and statistical inference are applied to the analysis of economic phenomena.[3]

> Econometrics is concerned with the empirical determination of economic laws.[4]

> The art of the econometrician consists in finding the set of assumptions that are both sufficiently specific and sufficiently realistic to allow him to take the best possible advantage of the data available to him.[5]

> Econometricians . . . are a positive help in trying to dispel the poor public image of economics (quantitative or otherwise) as a subject in which empty boxes are opened by assuming the existence of can-openers to reveal contents which any ten economists will interpret in 11 ways.[6]

> The method of econometric research aims, essentially, at a conjunction of economic theory and actual measurements, using the theory and technique of statistical inference as a bridge pier.[7]

[1]Gerhard Tintner, *Methodology of Mathematical Economics and Econometrics,* The University of Chicago Press, Chicago, 1968, p. 74.

[2]P. A. Samuelson, T. C. Koopmans, and J. R. N. Stone, "Report of the Evaluative Committee for *Econometrica,*" *Econometrica,* vol. 22, no. 2, April 1954, pp. 141–146.

[3]Arthur S. Goldberger, *Econometric Theory,* John Wiley & Sons, New York, 1964, p. 1.

[4]H. Theil, *Principles of Econometrics,* John Wiley & Sons, New York, 1971, p. 1.

[5]E. Malinvaud, *Statistical Methods of Econometrics,* Rand McNally, Chicago, 1966, p. 514.

[6]Adrian C. Darnell and J. Lynne Evans, *The Limits of Econometrics,* Edward Elgar Publishing, Hants, England, 1990, p. 54.

[7]T. Haavelmo, "The Probability Approach in Econometrics," Supplement to *Econometrica,* vol. 12, 1944, preface p. iii.

I.2 Why a Separate Discipline?

As the preceding definitions suggest, econometrics is an amalgam of economic theory, mathematical economics, economic statistics, and mathematical statistics. Yet the subject deserves to be studied in its own right for the following reasons.

Economic theory makes statements or hypotheses that are mostly qualitative in nature. For example, microeconomic theory states that, other things remaining the same, a reduction in the price of a commodity is expected to increase the quantity demanded of that commodity. Thus, economic theory postulates a negative or inverse relationship between the price and quantity demanded of a commodity. But the theory itself does not provide any numerical measure of the relationship between the two; that is, it does not tell by how much the quantity will go up or down as a result of a certain change in the price of the commodity. It is the job of the econometrician to provide such numerical estimates. Stated differently, econometrics gives empirical content to most economic theory.

The main concern of mathematical economics is to express economic theory in mathematical form (equations) without regard to measurability or empirical verification of the theory. Econometrics, as noted previously, is mainly interested in the empirical verification of economic theory. As we shall see, the econometrician often uses the mathematical equations proposed by the mathematical economist but puts these equations in such a form that they lend themselves to empirical testing. And this conversion of mathematical into econometric equations requires a great deal of ingenuity and practical skill.

Economic statistics is mainly concerned with collecting, processing, and presenting economic data in the form of charts and tables. These are the jobs of the economic statistician. It is he or she who is primarily responsible for collecting data on gross national product (GNP), employment, unemployment, prices, and so on. The data thus collected constitute the raw data for econometric work. But the economic statistician does not go any further, not being concerned with using the collected data to test economic theories. Of course, one who does that becomes an econometrician.

Although mathematical statistics provides many tools used in the trade, the econometrician often needs special methods in view of the unique nature of most economic data, namely, that the data are not generated as the result of a controlled experiment. The econometrician, like the meteorologist, generally depends on data that cannot be controlled directly. As Spanos correctly observes:

> In econometrics the modeler is often faced with **observational** as opposed to **experimental** data. This has two important implications for empirical modeling in econometrics. First, the modeler is required to master very different skills than those needed for analyzing experimental data. . . . Second, the separation of the data collector and the data analyst requires the modeler to familiarize himself/herself thoroughly with the nature and structure of data in question.[8]

I.3 Methodology of Econometrics

How do econometricians proceed in their analysis of an economic problem? That is, what is their methodology? Although there are several schools of thought on econometric methodology, we present here the **traditional** or **classical** methodology, which still dominates empirical research in economics and other social and behavioral sciences.[9]

[8] Aris Spanos, *Probability Theory and Statistical Inference: Econometric Modeling with Observational Data,* Cambridge University Press, United Kingdom, 1999, p. 21.

[9] For an enlightening, if advanced, discussion on econometric methodology, see David F. Hendry, *Dynamic Econometrics,* Oxford University Press, New York, 1995. See also Aris Spanos, *op. cit.*

Broadly speaking, traditional econometric methodology proceeds along the following lines:

1. Statement of theory or hypothesis.
2. Specification of the mathematical model of the theory.
3. Specification of the statistical, or econometric, model.
4. Obtaining the data.
5. Estimation of the parameters of the econometric model.
6. Hypothesis testing.
7. Forecasting or prediction.
8. Using the model for control or policy purposes.

To illustrate the preceding steps, let us consider the well-known Keynesian theory of consumption.

1. Statement of Theory or Hypothesis

Keynes stated:

> The fundamental psychological law . . . is that men [women] are disposed, as a rule and on average, to increase their consumption as their income increases, but not as much as the increase in their income.[10]

In short, Keynes postulated that the **marginal propensity to consume (MPC),** the rate of change of consumption for a unit (say, a dollar) change in income, is greater than zero but less than 1.

2. Specification of the Mathematical Model of Consumption

Although Keynes postulated a positive relationship between consumption and income, he did not specify the precise form of the functional relationship between the two. For simplicity, a mathematical economist might suggest the following form of the Keynesian consumption function:

$$Y = \beta_1 + \beta_2 X \qquad 0 < \beta_2 < 1 \tag{I.3.1}$$

where $Y =$ consumption expenditure and $X =$ income, and where β_1 and β_2, known as the **parameters** of the model, are, respectively, the **intercept** and **slope** coefficients.

The slope coefficient β_2 measures the MPC. Geometrically, Equation I.3.1 is as shown in Figure I.1. This equation, which states that consumption is linearly related to income, is an example of a mathematical model of the relationship between consumption and income that is called the **consumption function** in economics. A model is simply a set of mathematical equations. If the model has only one equation, as in the preceding example, it is called a **single-equation model,** whereas if it has more than one equation, it is known as a **multiple-equation model** (the latter will be considered later in the book).

In Eq. (I.3.1) the variable appearing on the left side of the equality sign is called the **dependent variable** and the variable(s) on the right side is called the **independent,** or **explanatory,** variable(s). Thus, in the Keynesian consumption function, Eq. (I.3.1), consumption (expenditure) is the dependent variable and income is the explanatory variable.

[10] John Maynard Keynes, *The General Theory of Employment, Interest and Money,* Harcourt Brace Jovanovich, New York, 1936, p. 96.

FIGURE I.1
Keynesian consumption function.

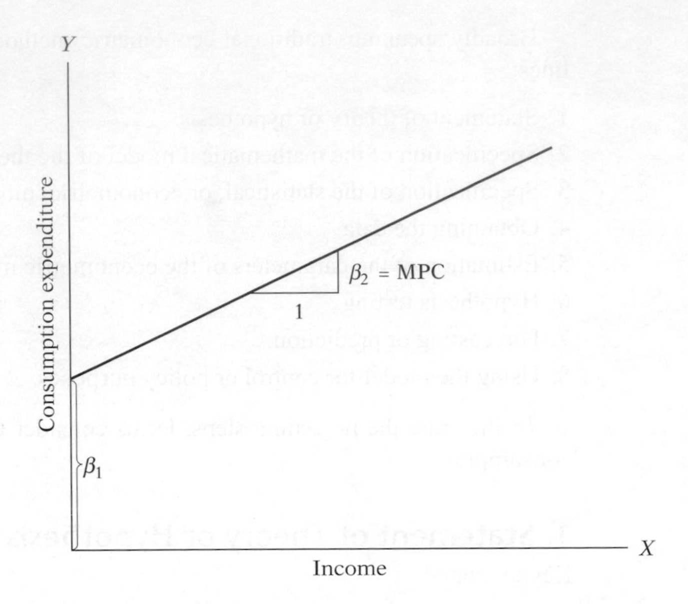

3. Specification of the Econometric Model of Consumption

The purely mathematical model of the consumption function given in Eq. (I.3.1) is of limited interest to the econometrician, for it assumes that there is an *exact* or *deterministic* relationship between consumption and income. But relationships between economic variables are generally inexact. Thus, if we were to obtain data on consumption expenditure and disposable (i.e., aftertax) income of a sample of, say, 500 American families and plot these data on a graph paper with consumption expenditure on the vertical axis and disposable income on the horizontal axis, we would not expect all 500 observations to lie exactly on the straight line of Eq. (I.3.1) because, in addition to income, other variables affect consumption expenditure. For example, size of family, ages of the members in the family, family religion, etc., are likely to exert some influence on consumption.

To allow for the inexact relationships between economic variables, the econometrician would modify the deterministic consumption function in Eq. (I.3.1) as follows:

$$Y = \beta_1 + \beta_2 X + u \tag{I.3.2}$$

where u, known as the **disturbance, or error, term,** is a **random (stochastic) variable** that has well-defined probabilistic properties. The disturbance term u may well represent all those factors that affect consumption but are not taken into account explicitly.

Equation I.3.2 is an example of an **econometric model.** More technically, it is an example of a **linear regression model,** which is the major concern of this book. The econometric consumption function hypothesizes that the dependent variable Y (consumption) is linearly related to the explanatory variable X (income) but that the relationship between the two is not exact; it is subject to individual variation.

The econometric model of the consumption function can be depicted as shown in Figure I.2.

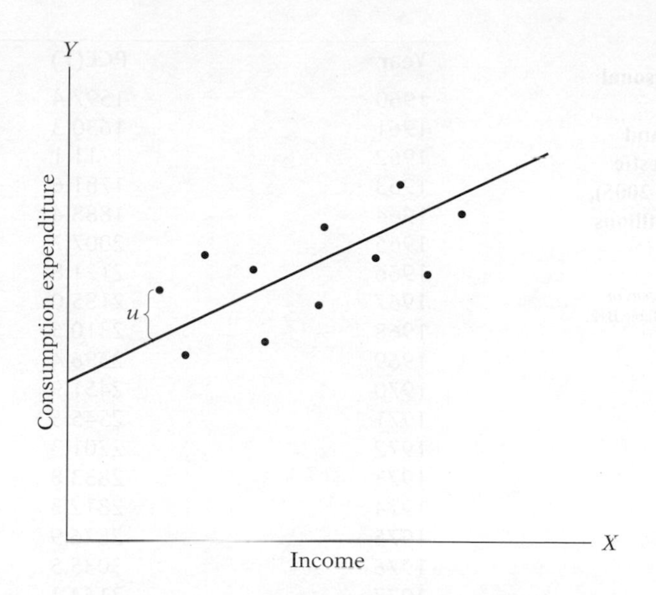

FIGURE I.2 Econometric model of the Keynesian consumption function.

4. Obtaining Data

To estimate the econometric model given in Eq. (I.3.2), that is, to obtain the numerical values of β_1 and β_2, we need data. Although we will have more to say about the crucial importance of data for economic analysis in the next chapter, for now let us look at the data given in Table I.1, which relate to the U.S. economy for the period 1960–2005. The Y variable in this table is the *aggregate* (for the economy as a whole) personal consumption expenditure (PCE) and the X variable is gross domestic product (GDP), a measure of aggregate income, both measured in billions of 2000 dollars. Therefore, the data are in "real" terms; that is, they are measured in constant (2000) prices. The data are plotted in Figure I.3 (cf. Figure I.2). For the time being neglect the line drawn in the figure.

5. Estimation of the Econometric Model

Now that we have the data, our next task is to estimate the parameters of the consumption function. The numerical estimates of the parameters give empirical content to the consumption function. The actual mechanics of estimating the parameters will be discussed in Chapter 3. For now, note that the statistical technique of **regression analysis** is the main tool used to obtain the estimates. Using this technique and the data given in Table I.1, we obtain the following estimates of β_1 and β_2, namely, −299.5913 and 0.7218. Thus, the estimated consumption function is:

$$\hat{Y}_t = -299.5913 + 0.7218X_t \tag{I.3.3}$$

The hat on the Y indicates that it is an estimate.[11] The estimated consumption function (i.e., regression line) is shown in Figure I.3.

[11]As a matter of convention, a hat over a variable or parameter indicates that it is an estimated value.

TABLE I.1
Data on Y (Personal Consumption Expenditure) and X (Gross Domestic Product, 1960–2005), both in 2000 Billions of Dollars

Source: *Economic Report of the President,* 2007, Table B–2, p. 230.

Year	PCE(Y)	GDP(X)
1960	1597.4	2501.8
1961	1630.3	2560.0
1962	1711.1	2715.2
1963	1781.6	2834.0
1964	1888.4	2998.6
1965	2007.7	3191.1
1966	2121.8	3399.1
1967	2185.0	3484.6
1968	2310.5	3652.7
1969	2396.4	3765.4
1970	2451.9	3771.9
1971	2545.5	3898.6
1972	2701.3	4105.0
1973	2833.8	4341.5
1974	2812.3	4319.6
1975	2876.9	4311.2
1976	3035.5	4540.9
1977	3164.1	4750.5
1978	3303.1	5015.0
1979	3383.4	5173.4
1980	3374.1	5161.7
1981	3422.2	5291.7
1982	3470.3	5189.3
1983	3668.6	5423.8
1984	3863.3	5813.6
1985	4064.0	6053.7
1986	4228.9	6263.6
1987	4369.8	6475.1
1988	4546.9	6742.7
1989	4675.0	6981.4
1990	4770.3	7112.5
1991	4778.4	7100.5
1992	4934.8	7336.6
1993	5099.8	7532.7
1994	5290.7	7835.5
1995	5433.5	8031.7
1996	5619.4	8328.9
1997	5831.8	8703.5
1998	6125.8	9066.9
1999	6438.6	9470.3
2000	6739.4	9817.0
2001	6910.4	9890.7
2002	7099.3	10048.8
2003	7295.3	10301.0
2004	7577.1	10703.5
2005	7841.2	11048.6

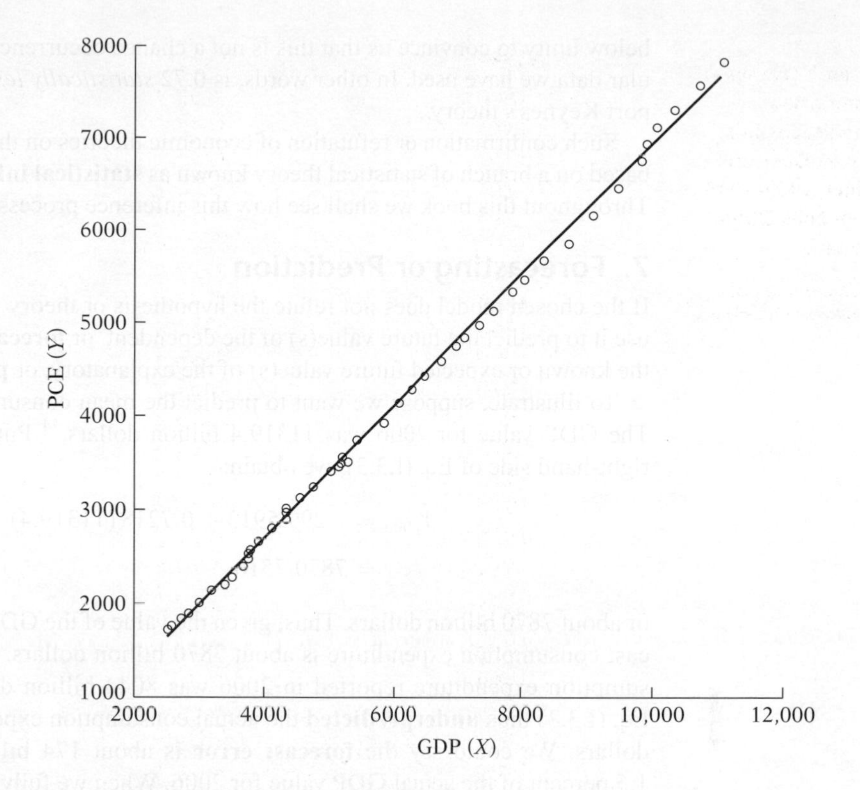

FIGURE I.3 Personal consumption expenditure (Y) in relation to GDP (X), 1960–2005, in billions of 2000 dollars.

As Figure I.3 shows, the regression line fits the data quite well in that the data points are very close to the regression line. From this figure we see that for the period 1960–2005 the slope coefficient (i.e., the **MPC**) was about 0.72, suggesting that for the sample period an increase in real income of one dollar led, *on average*, to an increase of about 72 cents in real consumption expenditure.[12] We say *on average* because the relationship between consumption and income is inexact; as is clear from Figure I.3, not all the data points lie exactly on the regression line. In simple terms we can say that, according to our data, the *average*, or *mean*, consumption expenditure went up by about 72 cents for a dollar's increase in real income.

6. Hypothesis Testing

Assuming that the fitted model is a reasonably good approximation of reality, we have to develop suitable criteria to find out whether the estimates obtained in, say, Equation I.3.3 are in accord with the expectations of the theory that is being tested. According to "positive" economists like Milton Friedman, a theory or hypothesis that is not verifiable by appeal to empirical evidence may not be admissible as a part of scientific enquiry.[13]

As noted earlier, Keynes expected the MPC to be positive but less than 1. In our example we found the MPC to be about 0.72. But before we accept this finding as confirmation of Keynesian consumption theory, we must enquire whether this estimate is sufficiently

[12]Do not worry now about how these values were obtained. As we show in Chapter 3, the statistical method of **least squares** has produced these estimates. Also, for now do not worry about the negative value of the intercept.

[13]See Milton Friedman, "The Methodology of Positive Economics," *Essays in Positive Economics*, University of Chicago Press, Chicago, 1953.

below unity to convince us that this is not a chance occurrence or peculiarity of the particular data we have used. In other words, is 0.72 *statistically less than 1?* If it is, it may support Keynes's theory.

Such confirmation or refutation of economic theories on the basis of sample evidence is based on a branch of statistical theory known as **statistical inference (hypothesis testing).** Throughout this book we shall see how this inference process is actually conducted.

7. Forecasting or Prediction

If the chosen model does not refute the hypothesis or theory under consideration, we may use it to predict the future value(s) of the dependent, or **forecast, variable** Y on the basis of the known or expected future value(s) of the explanatory, or **predictor, variable** X.

To illustrate, suppose we want to predict the mean consumption expenditure for 2006. The GDP value for 2006 was 11319.4 billion dollars.[14] Putting this GDP figure on the right-hand side of Eq. (I.3.3), we obtain:

$$\begin{aligned} \hat{Y}_{2006} &= -299.5913 + 0.7218(11319.4) \\ &= 7870.7516 \end{aligned} \tag{I.3.4}$$

or about 7870 billion dollars. Thus, given the value of the GDP, the mean, or average, forecast consumption expenditure is about 7870 billion dollars. The actual value of the consumption expenditure reported in 2006 was 8044 billion dollars. The estimated model Eq. (I.3.3) thus **underpredicted** the actual consumption expenditure by about 174 billion dollars. We could say the **forecast error** is about 174 billion dollars, which is about 1.5 percent of the actual GDP value for 2006. When we fully discuss the linear regression model in subsequent chapters, we will try to find out if such an error is "small" or "large." But what is important for now is to note that such forecast errors are inevitable given the statistical nature of our analysis.

There is another use of the estimated model Eq. (I.3.3). Suppose the president decides to propose a reduction in the income tax. What will be the effect of such a policy on income and thereby on consumption expenditure and ultimately on employment?

Suppose that, as a result of the proposed policy change, investment expenditure increases. What will be the effect on the economy? As macroeconomic theory shows, the change in income following, say, a dollar's worth of change in investment expenditure is given by the **income multiplier M,** which is defined as

$$M = \frac{1}{1 - \text{MPC}} \tag{I.3.5}$$

If we use the MPC of 0.72 obtained in Eq. (I.3.3), this multiplier becomes about $M = 3.57$. That is, an increase (decrease) of a dollar in investment will *eventually* lead to more than a threefold increase (decrease) in income; note that it takes time for the multiplier to work.

The critical value in this computation is MPC, for the multiplier depends on it. And this estimate of the MPC can be obtained from regression models such as Eq. (I.3.3). Thus, a quantitative estimate of MPC provides valuable information for policy purposes. Knowing MPC, one can predict the future course of income, consumption expenditure, and employment following a change in the government's fiscal policies.

[14]Data on PCE and GDP were available for 2006 but we purposely left them out to illustrate the topic discussed in this section. As we will discuss in subsequent chapters, it is a good idea to save a portion of the data to find out how well the fitted model predicts the out-of-sample observations.

8. Use of the Model for Control or Policy Purposes

Suppose we have the estimated consumption function given in Eq. (I.3.3). Suppose further the government believes that consumer expenditure of about 8750 (billions of 2000 dollars) will keep the unemployment rate at its current level of about 4.2 percent (early 2006). What level of income will guarantee the target amount of consumption expenditure?

If the regression results given in Eq. (I.3.3) seem reasonable, simple arithmetic will show that

$$8750 = -299.5913 + 0.7218(GDP_{2006}) \tag{I.3.6}$$

which gives $X = 12537$, approximately. That is, an income level of about 12537 (billion) dollars, given an MPC of about 0.72, will produce an expenditure of about 8750 billion dollars.

As these calculations suggest, an estimated model may be used for control, or policy, purposes. By appropriate fiscal and monetary policy mix, the government can manipulate the **control variable** X to produce the desired level of the **target variable** Y.

Figure I.4 summarizes the anatomy of classical econometric modeling.

Choosing among Competing Models

When a governmental agency (e.g., the U.S. Department of Commerce) collects economic data, such as that shown in Table I.1, it does not necessarily have any economic theory in mind. How then does one know that the data really support the Keynesian theory of consumption? Is it because the Keynesian consumption function (i.e., the regression line) shown in Figure I.3 is extremely close to the actual data points? Is it possible that another consumption model (theory) might equally fit the data as well? For example, Milton Friedman has developed a model of consumption, called the *permanent income*

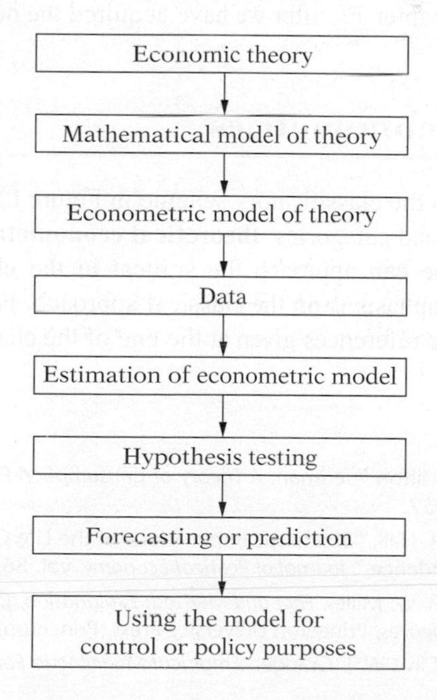

FIGURE I.4
Anatomy of econometric modeling.

hypothesis.[15] Robert Hall has also developed a model of consumption, called the *life-cycle permanent income hypothesis.*[16] Could one or both of these models also fit the data in Table I.1?

In short, the question facing a researcher in practice is how to choose among competing hypotheses or models of a given phenomenon, such as the consumption–income relationship. As Miller contends:

> No encounter with data is [a] step towards genuine confirmation unless the hypothesis does a better job of coping with the data than some natural rival. . . . What strengthens a hypothesis, here, is a victory that is, at the same time, a defeat for a plausible rival.[17]

How then does one choose among competing models or hypotheses? Here the advice given by Clive Granger is worth keeping in mind:[18]

> I would like to suggest that in the future, when you are presented with a new piece of theory or empirical model, you ask these questions:
>
> (i) What purpose does it have? What economic decisions does it help with?
>
> (ii) Is there any evidence being presented that allows me to evaluate its quality compared to alternative theories or models?
>
> I think attention to such questions will strengthen economic research and discussion.

As we progress through this book, we will come across several competing hypotheses trying to explain various economic phenomena. For example, students of economics are familiar with the concept of the production function, which is basically a relationship between output and inputs (say, capital and labor). In the literature, two of the best known are the *Cobb–Douglas* and the *constant elasticity of substitution* production functions. Given the data on output and inputs, we will have to find out which of the two production functions, if any, fits the data well.

The eight-step classical econometric methodology discussed above is neutral in the sense that it can be used to test any of these rival hypotheses.

Is it possible to develop a methodology that is comprehensive enough to include competing hypotheses? This is an involved and controversial topic. We will discuss it in Chapter 13, after we have acquired the necessary econometric theory.

I.4 Types of Econometrics

As the classificatory scheme in Figure I.5 suggests, econometrics may be divided into two broad categories: **theoretical econometrics** and **applied econometrics.** In each category, one can approach the subject in the **classical** or **Bayesian** tradition. In this book the emphasis is on the classical approach. For the Bayesian approach, the reader may consult the references given at the end of the chapter.

[15] Milton Friedman, *A Theory of Consumption Function,* Princeton University Press, Princeton, N.J., 1957.

[16] R. Hall, "Stochastic Implications of the Life Cycle Permanent Income Hypothesis: Theory and Evidence," *Journal of Political Economy,* vol. 86, 1978, pp. 971–987.

[17] R. W. Miller, *Fact and Method: Explanation, Confirmation, and Reality in the Natural and Social Sciences,* Princeton University Press, Princeton, N.J., 1978, p. 176.

[18] Clive W. J. Granger, *Empirical Modeling in Economics,* Cambridge University Press, U.K., 1999, p. 58.

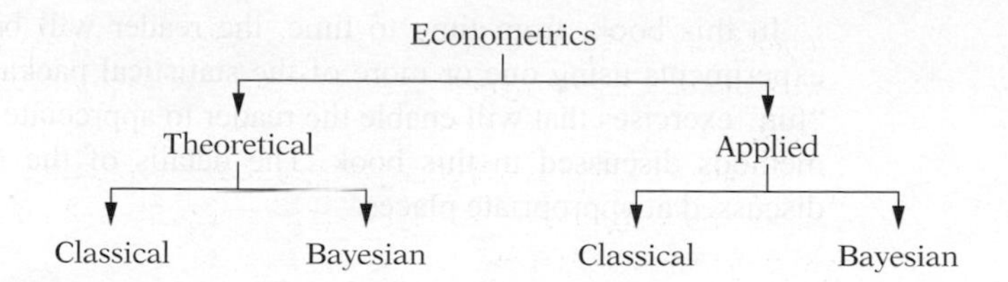

FIGURE I.5 Categories of econometrics.

Theoretical econometrics is concerned with the development of appropriate methods for measuring economic relationships specified by econometric models. In this aspect, econometrics leans heavily on mathematical statistics. For example, one of the methods used extensively in this book is **least squares.** Theoretical econometrics must spell out the assumptions of this method, its properties, and what happens to these properties when one or more of the assumptions of the method are not fulfilled.

In applied econometrics we use the tools of theoretical econometrics to study some special field(s) of economics and business, such as the production function, investment function, demand and supply functions, portfolio theory, etc.

This book is concerned largely with the development of econometric methods, their assumptions, their uses, and their limitations. These methods are illustrated with examples from various areas of economics and business. But this is *not* a book of applied econometrics in the sense that it delves deeply into any particular field of economic application. That job is best left to books written specifically for this purpose. References to some of these books are provided at the end of this book.

I.5 Mathematical and Statistical Prerequisites

Although this book is written at an elementary level, the author assumes that the reader is familiar with the basic concepts of statistical estimation and hypothesis testing. However, a broad but nontechnical overview of the basic statistical concepts used in this book is provided in **Appendix A** for the benefit of those who want to refresh their knowledge. Insofar as mathematics is concerned, a nodding acquaintance with the notions of differential calculus is desirable, although not essential. Although most graduate level books in econometrics make heavy use of matrix algebra, I want to make it clear that it is not needed to study this book. It is my strong belief that the fundamental ideas of econometrics can be conveyed without the use of matrix algebra. However, for the benefit of the mathematically inclined student, **Appendix C** gives the summary of basic regression theory in matrix notation. For these students, **Appendix B** provides a succinct summary of the main results from matrix algebra.

I.6 The Role of the Computer

Regression analysis, the bread-and-butter tool of econometrics, these days is unthinkable without the computer and some access to statistical software. (Believe me, I grew up in the generation of the slide rule!) Fortunately, several excellent regression packages are commercially available, both for the mainframe and the microcomputer, and the list is growing by the day. Regression software packages, such as **ET, LIMDEP, SHAZAM, MICRO TSP, MINITAB, EVIEWS, SAS, SPSS, STATA, Microfit, PcGive,** and **BMD** have most of the econometric techniques and tests discussed in this book.

In this book, from time to time, the reader will be asked to conduct **Monte Carlo** experiments using one or more of the statistical packages. Monte Carlo experiments are "fun" exercises that will enable the reader to appreciate the properties of several statistical methods discussed in this book. The details of the Monte Carlo experiments will be discussed at appropriate places.

I.7 Suggestions for Further Reading

The topic of econometric methodology is vast and controversial. For those interested in this topic, I suggest the following books:

Neil de Marchi and Christopher Gilbert, eds., *History and Methodology of Econometrics,* Oxford University Press, New York, 1989. This collection of readings discusses some early work on econometric methodology and has an extended discussion of the British approach to econometrics relating to time series data, that is, data collected over a period of time.

Wojciech W. Charemza and Derek F. Deadman, *New Directions in Econometric Practice: General to Specific Modelling, Cointegration and Vector Autogression, 2d* ed., Edward Elgar Publishing Ltd., Hants, England, 1997. The authors of this book critique the traditional approach to econometrics and give a detailed exposition of new approaches to econometric methodology.

Adrian C. Darnell and J. Lynne Evans, *The Limits of Econometrics,* Edward Elgar Publishing Ltd., Hants, England, 1990. The book provides a somewhat balanced discussion of the various methodological approaches to econometrics, with renewed allegiance to traditional econometric methodology.

Mary S. Morgan, *The History of Econometric Ideas,* Cambridge University Press, New York, 1990. The author provides an excellent historical perspective on the theory and practice of econometrics, with an in-depth discussion of the early contributions of Haavelmo (1990 Nobel Laureate in Economics) to econometrics. In the same spirit, David F. Hendry and Mary S. Morgan, *The Foundation of Econometric Analysis,* Cambridge University Press, U.K., 1995, have collected seminal writings in econometrics to show the evolution of econometric ideas over time.

David Colander and Reuven Brenner, eds., *Educating Economists,* University of Michigan Press, Ann Arbor, Michigan, 1992. This text presents a critical, at times agnostic, view of economic teaching and practice.

For Bayesian statistics and econometrics, the following books are very useful: John H. Dey, *Data in Doubt,* Basil Blackwell Ltd., Oxford University Press, England, 1985; Peter M. Lee, *Bayesian Statistics: An Introduction,* Oxford University Press, England, 1989; and Dale J. Porier, *Intermediate Statistics and Econometrics: A Comparative Approach,* MIT Press, Cambridge, Massachusetts, 1995. Arnold Zeller, *An Introduction to Bayesian Inference in Econometrics,* John Wiley & Sons, New York, 1971, is an advanced reference book. Another advanced reference book is the *Palgrave Handbook of Econometrics*: Volume 1: *Econometric Theory,* edited by Terence C. Mills and Kerry Patterson, Palgrave Macmillan, New York, 2007.

Part 1

Single-Equation Regression Models

Part 1 of this text introduces single-equation regression models. In these models, one variable, called the *dependent variable,* is expressed as a linear function of one or more other variables, called the *explanatory variables*. In such models it is assumed implicitly that causal relationships, if any, between the dependent and explanatory variables flow in one direction only, namely, from the explanatory variables to the dependent variable.

In Chapter 1, we discuss the historical as well as the modern interpretation of the term *regression* and illustrate the difference between the two interpretations with several examples drawn from economics and other fields.

In Chapter 2, we introduce some fundamental concepts of regression analysis with the aid of the two-variable linear regression model, a model in which the dependent variable is expressed as a linear function of only a single explanatory variable.

In Chapter 3, we continue to deal with the two-variable model and introduce what is known as the *classical linear regression model,* a model that makes several simplifying assumptions. With these assumptions, we introduce the method of *ordinary least squares* (OLS) to estimate the parameters of the two-variable regression model. The method of OLS is simple to apply, yet it has some very desirable statistical properties.

In Chapter 4, we introduce the (two-variable) classical *normal* linear regression model, a model that assumes that the random dependent variable follows the normal probability distribution. With this assumption, the OLS estimators obtained in Chapter 3 possess some stronger statistical properties than the nonnormal classical linear regression model—properties that enable us to engage in statistical inference, namely, hypothesis testing.

Chapter 5 is devoted to the topic of hypothesis testing. In this chapter, we try to find out whether the estimated regression coefficients are compatible with the hypothesized values of such coefficients, the hypothesized values being suggested by theory and/or prior empirical work.

Chapter 6 considers some extensions of the two-variable regression model. In particular, it discusses topics such as (1) regression through the origin, (2) scaling and units of measurement, and (3) functional forms of regression models such as double-log, semilog, and reciprocal models.

In Chapter 7, we consider the multiple regression model, a model in which there is more than one explanatory variable, and show how the method of OLS can be extended to estimate the parameters of such models.

In Chapter 8, we extend the concepts introduced in Chapter 5 to the multiple regression model and point out some of the complications arising from the introduction of several explanatory variables.

Chapter 9 on dummy, or qualitative, explanatory variables concludes Part 1 of the text. This chapter emphasizes that not all explanatory variables need to be quantitative (i.e., ratio scale). Variables, such as gender, race, religion, nationality, and region of residence, cannot be readily quantified, yet they play a valuable role in explaining many an economic phenomenon.

Chapter 1

The Nature of Regression Analysis

As mentioned in the Introduction, regression is a main tool of econometrics, and in this chapter we consider very briefly the nature of this tool.

1.1 Historical Origin of the Term *Regression*

The term *regression* was introduced by Francis Galton. In a famous paper, Galton found that, although there was a tendency for tall parents to have tall children and for short parents to have short children, the average height of children born of parents of a given height tended to move or "regress" toward the average height in the population as a whole.[1] In other words, the height of the children of unusually tall or unusually short parents tends to move toward the average height of the population. Galton's *law of universal regression* was confirmed by his friend Karl Pearson, who collected more than a thousand records of heights of members of family groups.[2] He found that the average height of sons of a group of tall fathers was less than their fathers' height and the average height of sons of a group of short fathers was greater than their fathers' height, thus "regressing" tall and short sons alike toward the average height of all men. In the words of Galton, this was "regression to mediocrity."

1.2 The Modern Interpretation of Regression

The modern interpretation of regression is, however, quite different. Broadly speaking, we may say

> Regression analysis is concerned with the study of the dependence of one variable, the *dependent variable,* on one or more other variables, the *explanatory variables,* with a view to estimating and/or predicting the (population) mean or average value of the former in terms of the known or fixed (in repeated sampling) values of the latter.

[1] Francis Galton, "Family Likeness in Stature," *Proceedings of Royal Society, London,* vol. 40, 1886, pp. 42–72.

[2] K. Pearson and A. Lee, "On the Laws of Inheritance," *Biometrika,* vol. 2, Nov. 1903, pp. 357–462.

The full import of this view of regression analysis will become clearer as we progress, but a few simple examples will make the basic concept quite clear.

Examples

1. Reconsider Galton's law of universal regression. Galton was interested in finding out why there was a stability in the distribution of heights in a population. But in the modern view our concern is not with this explanation but rather with finding out how the *average* height of sons changes, given the fathers' height. In other words, our concern is with predicting the average height of sons knowing the height of their fathers. To see how this can be done, consider Figure 1.1, which is a **scatter diagram,** or **scattergram.** This figure shows the distribution of heights of sons in a hypothetical population corresponding to the given or *fixed* values of the father's height. Notice that corresponding to any given height of a father is a *range* or distribution of the heights of the sons. However, notice that despite the variability of the height of sons for a given value of father's height, the average height of sons generally increases as the height of the father increases. To show this clearly, the circled crosses in the figure indicate the *average* height of sons corresponding to a given height of the father. Connecting these averages, we obtain the line shown in the figure. This line, as we shall see, is known as the **regression line.** It shows how the *average* height of sons increases with the father's height.[3]

2. Consider the scattergram in Figure 1.2, which gives the distribution in a hypothetical population of heights of boys measured at *fixed* ages. Corresponding to any given age, we have a range, or distribution, of heights. Obviously, not all boys of a given age are likely to have identical heights. But height *on the average* increases with age (of course, up to a

FIGURE 1.1 Hypothetical distribution of sons' heights corresponding to given heights of fathers.

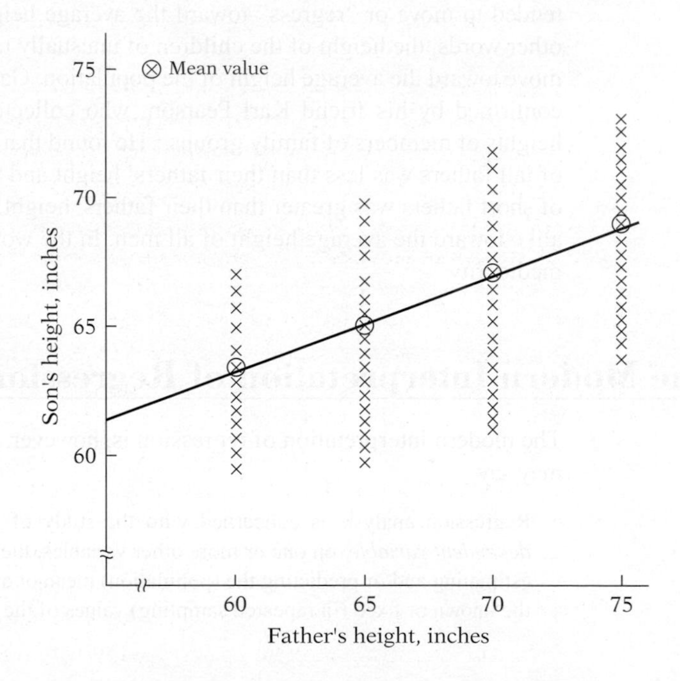

[3]At this stage of the development of the subject matter, we shall call this regression line simply the *line connecting the mean, or average, value of the dependent variable (son's height) corresponding to the given value of the explanatory variable (father's height)*. Note that this line has a positive slope but the slope is less than 1, which is in conformity with Galton's regression to mediocrity. (Why?)

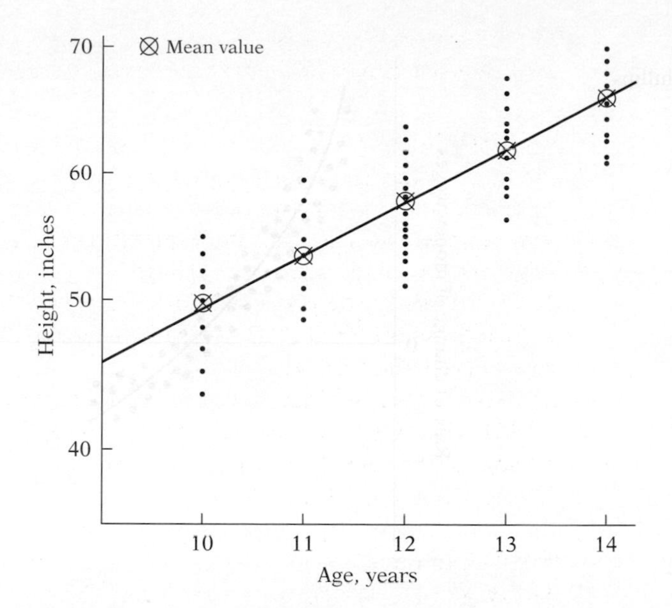

FIGURE 1.2 Hypothetical distribution of heights corresponding to selected ages.

certain age), which can be seen clearly if we draw a line (the regression line) through the circled points that represent the average height at the given ages. Thus, knowing the age, we may be able to predict from the regression line the average height corresponding to that age.

3. Turning to economic examples, an economist may be interested in studying the dependence of personal consumption expenditure on aftertax or disposable real personal income. Such an analysis may be helpful in estimating the marginal propensity to consume (MPC), that is, average change in consumption expenditure for, say, a dollar's worth of change in real income (see Figure 1.3).

4. A monopolist who can fix the price or output (but not both) may want to find out the response of the demand for a product to changes in price. Such an experiment may enable the estimation of the **price elasticity** (i.e., price responsiveness) of the demand for the product and may help determine the most profitable price.

5. A labor economist may want to study the rate of change of money wages in relation to the unemployment rate. The historical data are shown in the scattergram given in Figure 1.3. The curve in Figure 1.3 is an example of the celebrated *Phillips curve* relating changes in the money wages to the unemployment rate. Such a scattergram may enable the labor economist to predict the average change in money wages given a certain unemployment rate. Such knowledge may be helpful in stating something about the inflationary process in an economy, for increases in money wages are likely to be reflected in increased prices.

6. From monetary economics it is known that, other things remaining the same, the higher the rate of inflation π, the lower the proportion k of their income that people would want to hold in the form of money, as depicted in Figure 1.4. The slope of this line represents the change in k given a change in the inflation rate. A quantitative analysis of this relationship will enable the monetary economist to predict the amount of money, as a proportion of their income, that people would want to hold at various rates of inflation.

7. The marketing director of a company may want to know how the demand for the company's product is related to, say, advertising expenditure. Such a study will be of considerable help in finding out the **elasticity of demand** with respect to advertising expenditure, that is, the percent change in demand in response to, say, a 1 percent change in the advertising budget. This knowledge may be helpful in determining the "optimum" advertising budget.

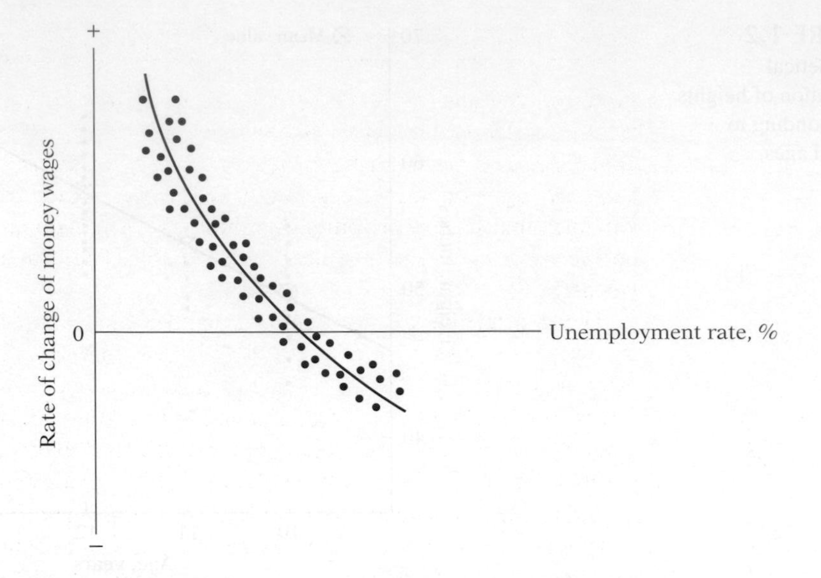

FIGURE 1.3
Hypothetical Phillips curve.

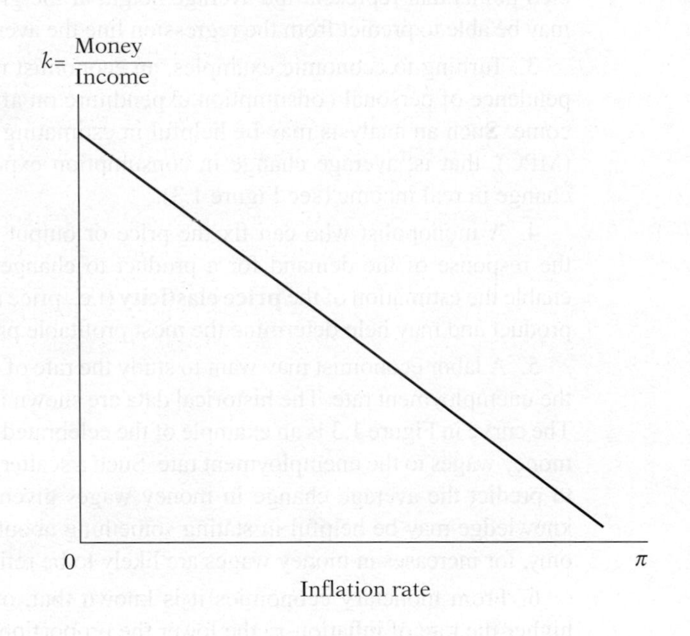

FIGURE 1.4
Money holding in relation to the inflation rate π.

8. Finally, an agronomist may be interested in studying the dependence of a particular crop yield, say, of wheat, on temperature, rainfall, amount of sunshine, and fertilizer. Such a dependence analysis may enable the prediction or forecasting of the average crop yield, given information about the explanatory variables.

The reader can supply scores of such examples of the dependence of one variable on one or more other variables. The techniques of regression analysis discussed in this text are specially designed to study such dependence among variables.

1.3 Statistical versus Deterministic Relationships

From the examples cited in Section 1.2, the reader will notice that in regression analysis we are concerned with what is known as the *statistical*, not *functional* or *deterministic*, dependence among variables, such as those of classical physics. In statistical relationships among variables we essentially deal with **random** or **stochastic**[4] variables, that is, variables that have probability distributions. In functional or deterministic dependency, on the other hand, we also deal with variables, but these variables are not random or stochastic.

The dependence of crop yield on temperature, rainfall, sunshine, and fertilizer, for example, is statistical in nature in the sense that the explanatory variables, although certainly important, will not enable the agronomist to predict crop yield exactly because of errors involved in measuring these variables as well as a host of other factors (variables) that collectively affect the yield but may be difficult to identify individually. Thus, there is bound to be some "intrinsic" or random variability in the dependent-variable crop yield that cannot be fully explained no matter how many explanatory variables we consider.

In deterministic phenomena, on the other hand, we deal with relationships of the type, say, exhibited by Newton's law of gravity, which states: Every particle in the universe attracts every other particle with a force directly proportional to the product of their masses and inversely proportional to the square of the distance between them. Symbolically, $F = k(m_1 m_2/r^2)$, where F = force, m_1 and m_2 are the masses of the two particles, r = distance, and k = constant of proportionality. Another example is Ohm's law, which states: For metallic conductors over a limited range of temperature the current C is proportional to the voltage V; that is, $C = (\frac{1}{k})V$ where $\frac{1}{k}$ is the constant of proportionality. Other examples of such deterministic relationships are Boyle's gas law, Kirchhoff's law of electricity, and Newton's law of motion.

In this text we are not concerned with such deterministic relationships. Of course, if there are errors of measurement, say, in the k of Newton's law of gravity, the otherwise deterministic relationship becomes a statistical relationship. In this situation, force can be predicted only approximately from the given value of k (and m_1, m_2, and r), which contains errors. The variable F in this case becomes a random variable.

1.4 Regression versus Causation

Although regression analysis deals with the dependence of one variable on other variables, it does not necessarily imply causation. In the words of Kendall and Stuart, "A statistical relationship, however strong and however suggestive, can never establish causal connection: our ideas of causation must come from outside statistics, ultimately from some theory or other."[5]

[4]The word *stochastic* comes from the Greek word *stokhos* meaning "a bull's eye." The outcome of throwing darts on a dart board is a stochastic process, that is, a process fraught with misses.

[5]M. G. Kendall and A. Stuart, *The Advanced Theory of Statistics,* Charles Griffin Publishers, New York, vol. 2, 1961, chap. 26, p. 279.

In the crop-yield example cited previously, there is no *statistical reason* to assume that rainfall does not depend on crop yield. The fact that we treat crop yield as dependent on rainfall (among other things) is due to nonstatistical considerations: Common sense suggests that the relationship cannot be reversed, for we cannot control rainfall by varying crop yield.

In all the examples cited in Section 1.2 the point to note is that **a statistical relationship in itself cannot logically imply causation.** To ascribe causality, one must appeal to a priori or theoretical considerations. Thus, in the third example cited, one can invoke economic theory in saying that consumption expenditure depends on real income.[6]

1.5 Regression versus Correlation

Closely related to but conceptually very much different from regression analysis is **correlation analysis,** where the primary objective is to measure the *strength* or *degree* of *linear association* between two variables. The **correlation coefficient,** which we shall study in detail in Chapter 3, measures this strength of (linear) association. For example, we may be interested in finding the correlation (coefficient) between smoking and lung cancer, between scores on statistics and mathematics examinations, between high school grades and college grades, and so on. In regression analysis, as already noted, we are not primarily interested in such a measure. Instead, we try to estimate or predict the average value of one variable on the basis of the fixed values of other variables. Thus, we may want to know whether we can predict the average score on a statistics examination by knowing a student's score on a mathematics examination.

Regression and correlation have some fundamental differences that are worth mentioning. In regression analysis there is an asymmetry in the way the dependent and explanatory variables are treated. The dependent variable is assumed to be statistical, random, or stochastic, that is, to have a probability distribution. The explanatory variables, on the other hand, are assumed to have fixed values (in repeated sampling),[7] which was made explicit in the definition of regression given in Section 1.2. Thus, in Figure 1.2 we assumed that the variable age was fixed at given levels and height measurements were obtained at these levels. In correlation analysis, on the other hand, we treat any (two) variables symmetrically; there is no distinction between the dependent and explanatory variables. After all, the correlation between scores on mathematics and statistics examinations is the same as that between scores on statistics and mathematics examinations. Moreover, both variables are assumed to be random. As we shall see, most of the correlation theory is based on the assumption of randomness of variables, whereas most of the regression theory to be expounded in this book is conditional upon the assumption that the dependent variable is stochastic but the explanatory variables are fixed or nonstochastic.[8]

[6]But as we shall see in Chapter 3, classical regression analysis is based on the assumption that the model used in the analysis is the correct model. Therefore, the direction of causality may be implicit in the model postulated.

[7]It is crucial to note that the explanatory variables may be intrinsically stochastic, but for the purpose of regression analysis we assume that their values are fixed in repeated sampling (that is, X assumes the same values in various samples), thus rendering them in effect nonrandom or nonstochastic. But more on this in Chapter 3, Sec. 3.2.

[8]In advanced treatment of econometrics, one can relax the assumption that the explanatory variables are nonstochastic (see introduction to Part 2).

1.6 Terminology and Notation

Before we proceed to a formal analysis of regression theory, let us dwell briefly on the matter of terminology and notation. In the literature the terms *dependent variable* and *explanatory variable* are described variously. A representative list is:

Dependent variable	**Explanatory variable**
⇕	⇕
Explained variable	Independent variable
⇕	⇕
Predictand	Predictor
⇕	⇕
Regressand	**Regressor**
⇕	⇕
Response	Stimulus
⇕	⇕
Endogenous	Exogenous
⇕	⇕
Outcome	Covariate
⇕	⇕
Controlled variable	Control variable

Although it is a matter of personal taste and tradition, in this text we will use the dependent variable/explanatory variable or the more neutral regressand and regressor terminology.

If we are studying the dependence of a variable on only a single explanatory variable, such as that of consumption expenditure on real income, such a study is known as *simple*, or **two-variable, regression analysis.** However, if we are studying the dependence of one variable on more than one explanatory variable, as in the crop-yield, rainfall, temperature, sunshine, and fertilizer example, it is known as **multiple regression analysis.** In other words, in two-variable regression there is only one explanatory variable, whereas in multiple regression there is more than one explanatory variable.

The term **random** is a synonym for the term **stochastic.** As noted earlier, a random or stochastic variable is a variable that can take on any set of values, positive or negative, with a given probability.[9]

Unless stated otherwise, the letter Y will denote the dependent variable and the X's ($X_1, X_2, \ldots, X_k$) will denote the explanatory variables, X_k being the kth explanatory variable. The subscript i or t will denote the ith or the tth observation or value. X_{ki} (or X_{kt}) will denote the ith (or tth) observation on variable X_k. N (or T) will denote the total number of observations or values in the population, and n (or t) the total number of observations in a sample. As a matter of convention, the observation subscript i will be used for **cross-sectional data** (i.e., data collected at one point in time) and the subscript t will be used for **time series data** (i.e., data collected over a period of time). The nature of cross-sectional and time series data, as well as the important topic of the nature and sources of data for empirical analysis, is discussed in the following section.

[9]See **Appendix A** for formal definition and further details.

1.7 The Nature and Sources of Data for Economic Analysis[10]

The success of any econometric analysis ultimately depends on the availability of the appropriate data. It is therefore essential that we spend some time discussing the nature, sources, and limitations of the data that one may encounter in empirical analysis.

Types of Data

Three types of data may be available for empirical analysis: **time series, cross-section,** and **pooled** (i.e., combination of time series and cross-section) data.

Time Series Data

The data shown in Table 1.1 of the Introduction are an example of time series data. A *time series* is a set of observations on the values that a variable takes at different times. Such data may be collected at regular time intervals, such as **daily** (e.g., stock prices, weather reports), **weekly** (e.g., money supply figures), **monthly** (e.g., the unemployment rate, the Consumer Price Index [CPI]), **quarterly** (e.g., GDP), **annually** (e.g., government budgets), **quinquennially,** that is, every 5 years (e.g., the census of manufactures), or **decennially,** that is, every 10 years (e.g., the census of population). Sometime data are available both quarterly as well as annually, as in the case of the data on GDP and consumer expenditure. With the advent of high-speed computers, data can now be collected over an extremely short interval of time, such as the data on stock prices, which can be obtained literally continuously (the so-called *real-time quote*).

Although time series data are used heavily in econometric studies, they present special problems for econometricians. As we will show in chapters on **time series econometrics** later on, most empirical work based on time series data assumes that the underlying time series is **stationary.** Although it is too early to introduce the precise technical meaning of stationarity at this juncture, *loosely speaking, a time series is stationary if its mean and variance do not vary systematically over time*. To see what this means, consider Figure 1.5, which depicts the behavior of the M1 money supply in the United States from January 1, 1959, to September, 1999. (The actual data are given in Exercise 1.4.) As you can see from this figure, the M1 money supply shows a steady upward **trend** as well as variability over the years, suggesting that the M1 time series is not stationary.[11] We will explore this topic fully in Chapter 21.

Cross-Section Data

Cross-section data are data on one or more variables collected *at the same point in time,* such as the census of population conducted by the Census Bureau every 10 years (the latest being in year 2000), the surveys of consumer expenditures conducted by the University of Michigan, and, of course, the opinion polls by Gallup and umpteen other organizations. A concrete example of cross-sectional data is given in Table 1.1. This table gives data on egg production and egg prices for the 50 states in the union for 1990 and 1991. For each

[10]For an informative account, see Michael D. Intriligator, *Econometric Models, Techniques, and Applications,* Prentice Hall, Englewood Cliffs, N.J., 1978, chap. 3.

[11]To see this more clearly, we divided the data into four time periods: 1951:01 to 1962:12; 1963:01 to 1974:12; 1975:01 to 1986:12, and 1987:01 to 1999:09: For these subperiods the mean values of the money supply (with corresponding standard deviations in parentheses) were, respectively, 165.88 (23.27), 323.20 (72.66), 788.12 (195.43), and 1099 (27.84), all figures in billions of dollars. This is a rough indication of the fact that the money supply over the entire period was not stationary.

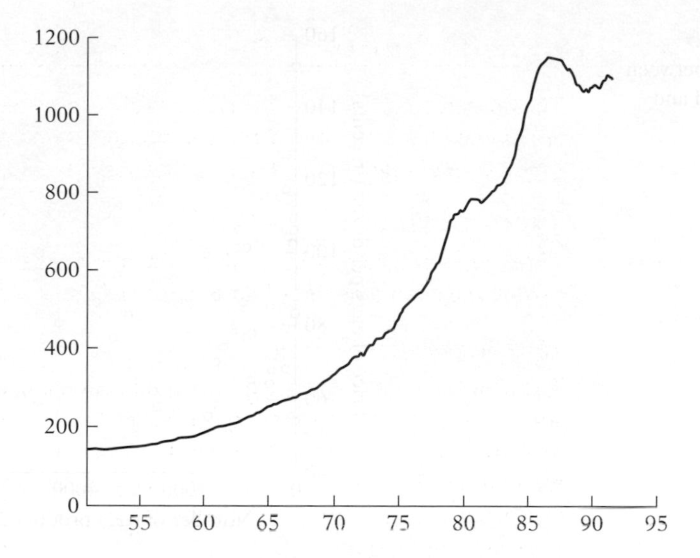

FIGURE 1.5
M1 money supply: United States, 1951:01–1999:09.

year the data on the 50 states are cross-sectional data. Thus, in Table 1.1 we have two cross-sectional samples.

Just as time series data create their own special problems (because of the stationarity issue), cross-sectional data too have their own problems, specifically the problem of *heterogeneity*. From the data given in Table 1.1 we see that we have some states that produce huge amounts of eggs (e.g., Pennsylvania) and some that produce very little (e.g., Alaska). When we include such heterogeneous units in a statistical analysis, the **size** or **scale effect** must be taken into account so as not to mix apples with oranges. To see this clearly, we plot in Figure 1.6 the data on eggs produced and their prices in 50 states for the year 1990. This figure shows how widely scattered the observations are. In Chapter 11 we will see how the scale effect can be an important factor in assessing relationships among economic variables.

Pooled Data

In pooled, or combined, data are elements of both time series and cross-section data. The data in Table 1.1 are an example of pooled data. For each year we have 50 cross-sectional observations and for each state we have two time series observations on prices and output of eggs, a total of 100 pooled (or combined) observations. Likewise, the data given in Exercise 1.1 are pooled data in that the Consumer Price Index (CPI) for each country for 1980–2005 is time series data, whereas the data on the CPI for the seven countries for a single year are cross-sectional data. In the pooled data we have 182 observations—26 annual observations for each of the seven countries.

Panel, Longitudinal, or Micropanel Data

This is a special type of pooled data in which the *same* cross-sectional unit (say, a family or a firm) is surveyed over time. For example, the U.S. Department of Commerce carries out a census of housing at periodic intervals. At each periodic survey the same household (or the people living at the same address) is interviewed to find out if there has been any change in the housing and financial conditions of that household since the last survey. By interviewing the same household periodically, the panel data provide very useful information on the dynamics of household behavior, as we shall see in Chapter 16.

FIGURE 1.6
Relationship between eggs produced and prices, 1990.

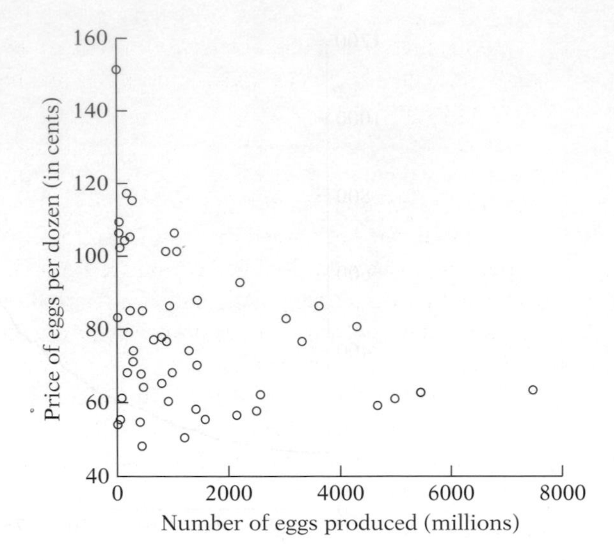

TABLE 1.1 **U.S. Egg Production**

State	Y_1	Y_2	X_1	X_2	State	Y_1	Y_2	X_1	X_2
AL	2,206	2,186	92.7	91.4	MT	172	164	68.0	66.0
AK	0.7	0.7	151.0	149.0	NE	1,202	1,400	50.3	48.9
AZ	73	74	61.0	56.0	NV	2.2	1.8	53.9	52.7
AR	3,620	3,737	86.3	91.8	NH	43	49	109.0	104.0
CA	7,472	7,444	63.4	58.4	NJ	442	491	85.0	83.0
CO	788	873	77.8	73.0	NM	283	302	74.0	70.0
CT	1,029	948	106.0	104.0	NY	975	987	68.1	64.0
DE	168	164	117.0	113.0	NC	3,033	3,045	82.8	78.7
FL	2,586	2,537	62.0	57.2	ND	51	45	55.2	48.0
GA	4,302	4,301	80.6	80.8	OH	4,667	4,637	59.1	54.7
HI	227.5	224.5	85.0	85.5	OK	869	830	101.0	100.0
ID	187	203	79.1	72.9	OR	652	686	77.0	74.6
IL	793	809	65.0	70.5	PA	4,976	5,130	61.0	52.0
IN	5,445	5,290	62.7	60.1	RI	53	50	102.0	99.0
IA	2,151	2,247	56.5	53.0	SC	1,422	1,420	70.1	65.9
KS	404	389	54.5	47.8	SD	435	602	48.0	45.8
KY	412	483	67.7	73.5	TN	277	279	71.0	80.7
LA	273	254	115.0	115.0	TX	3,317	3,356	76.7	72.6
ME	1,069	1,070	101.0	97.0	UT	456	486	64.0	59.0
MD	885	898	76.6	75.4	VT	31	30	106.0	102.0
MA	235	237	105.0	102.0	VA	943	988	86.3	81.2
MI	1,406	1,396	58.0	53.8	WA	1,287	1,313	74.1	71.5
MN	2,499	2,697	57.7	54.0	WV	136	174	104.0	109.0
MS	1,434	1,468	87.8	86.7	WI	910	873	60.1	54.0
MO	1,580	1,622	55.4	51.5	WY	1.7	1.7	83.0	83.0

Note: Y_1 = eggs produced in 1990 (millions).
Y_2 = eggs produced in 1991 (millions).
X_1 = price per dozen (cents) in 1990.
X_2 = price per dozen (cents) in 1991.

Source: *World Almanac,* 1993, p. 119. The data are from the Economic Research Service, U.S. Department of Agriculture.

As a concrete example, consider the data given in Table 1.2. The data in the table, originally collected by Y. Grunfeld, refer to the real investment, the real value of the firm, and the real capital stock of four U.S. companies, namely, General Electric (GM), U.S. Steel (US), General Motors (GM), and Westinghouse (WEST), for the period 1935–1954.[12] Since the data are for several companies collected over a number of years, this is a classic example of panel data. In this table, the number of observations for each company is the same, but this is not always the case. If all the companies have the same number of observations, we have what is called a **balanced panel.** If the number of observations is not the same for each company, it is called an **unbalanced panel.** In Chapter 16, Panel Data Regression Models, we will examine such data and show how to estimate such models.

Grunfeld's purpose in collecting these data was to find out how real gross investment (I) depends on the real value of the firm (F) a year earlier and real capital stock (C) a year earlier. Since the companies included in the sample operate in the same capital market, by studying them together, Grunfeld wanted to find out if they had similar investment functions.

The Sources of Data[13]

The data used in empirical analysis may be collected by a governmental agency (e.g., the Department of Commerce), an international agency (e.g., the International Monetary Fund [IMF] or the World Bank), a private organization (e.g., the Standard & Poor's Corporation), or an individual. Literally, there are thousands of such agencies collecting data for one purpose or another.

The Internet

The Internet has literally revolutionized data gathering. If you just "surf the net" with a keyword (e.g., exchange rates), you will be swamped with all kinds of data sources. In **Appendix E** we provide some of the frequently visited websites that provide economic and financial data of all sorts. Most of the data can be downloaded without much cost. You may want to bookmark the various websites that might provide you with useful economic data.

The data collected by various agencies may be **experimental** or **nonexperimental.** In experimental data, often collected in the natural sciences, the investigator may want to collect data while holding certain factors constant in order to assess the impact of some factors on a given phenomenon. For instance, in assessing the impact of obesity on blood pressure, the researcher would want to collect data while holding constant the eating, smoking, and drinking habits of the people in order to minimize the influence of these variables on blood pressure.

In the social sciences, the data that one generally encounters are nonexperimental in nature, that is, not subject to the control of the researcher.[14] For example, the data on GNP, unemployment, stock prices, etc., are not directly under the control of the investigator. As we shall see, this lack of control often creates special problems for the researcher in pinning down the exact cause or causes affecting a particular situation. For example, is it the money supply that determines the (nominal) GDP or is it the other way around?

[12] Y. Grunfeld, "The Determinants of Corporate Investment," unpublished PhD thesis, Department of Economics, University of Chicago, 1958. These data have become a workhorse for illustrating panel data regression models.

[13] For an illuminating account, see Albert T. Somers, *The U.S. Economy Demystified: What the Major Economic Statistics Mean and their Significance for Business,* D.C. Heath, Lexington, Mass., 1985.

[14] In the social sciences too sometimes one can have a controlled experiment. An example is given in Exercise 1.6.

TABLE 1.2 Investment Data for Four Companies, 1935–1954

Observation	I	F_{-1}	C_{-1}	Observation	I	F_{-1}	C_{-1}
	GE				US		
1935	33.1	1170.6	97.8	1935	209.9	1362.4	53.8
1936	45.0	2015.8	104.4	1936	355.3	1807.1	50.5
1937	77.2	2803.3	118.0	1937	469.9	2673.3	118.1
1938	44.6	2039.7	156.2	1938	262.3	1801.9	260.2
1939	48.1	2256.2	172.6	1939	230.4	1957.3	312.7
1940	74.4	2132.2	186.6	1940	361.6	2202.9	254.2
1941	113.0	1834.1	220.9	1941	472.8	2380.5	261.4
1942	91.9	1588.0	287.8	1942	445.6	2168.6	298.7
1943	61.3	1749.4	319.9	1943	361.6	1985.1	301.8
1944	56.8	1687.2	321.3	1944	288.2	1813.9	279.1
1945	93.6	2007.7	319.6	1945	258.7	1850.2	213.8
1946	159.9	2208.3	346.0	1946	420.3	2067.7	232.6
1947	147.2	1656.7	456.4	1947	420.5	1796.7	264.8
1948	146.3	1604.4	543.4	1948	494.5	1625.8	306.9
1949	98.3	1431.8	618.3	1949	405.1	1667.0	351.1
1950	93.5	1610.5	647.4	1950	418.8	1677.4	357.8
1951	135.2	1819.4	671.3	1951	588.2	2289.5	341.1
1952	157.3	2079.7	726.1	1952	645.2	2159.4	444.2
1953	179.5	2371.6	800.3	1953	641.0	2031.3	623.6
1954	189.6	2759.9	888.9	1954	459.3	2115.5	669.7
	GM				WEST		
1935	317.6	3078.5	2.8	1935	12.93	191.5	1.8
1936	391.8	4661.7	52.6	1936	25.90	516.0	0.8
1937	410.6	5387.1	156.9	1937	35.05	729.0	7.4
1938	257.7	2792.2	209.2	1938	22.89	560.4	18.1
1939	330.8	4313.2	203.4	1939	18.84	519.9	23.5
1940	461.2	4643.9	207.2	1940	28.57	628.5	26.5
1941	512.0	4551.2	255.2	1941	48.51	537.1	36.2
1942	448.0	3244.1	303.7	1942	43.34	561.2	60.8
1943	499.6	4053.7	264.1	1943	37.02	617.2	84.4
1944	547.5	4379.3	201.6	1944	37.81	626.7	91.2
1945	561.2	4840.9	265.0	1945	39.27	737.2	92.4
1946	688.1	4900.0	402.2	1946	53.46	760.5	86.0
1947	568.9	3526.5	761.5	1947	55.56	581.4	111.1
1948	529.2	3245.7	922.4	1948	49.56	662.3	130.6
1949	555.1	3700.2	1020.1	1949	32.04	583.8	141.8
1950	642.9	3755.6	1099.0	1950	32.24	635.2	136.7
1951	755.9	4833.0	1207.7	1951	54.38	732.8	129.7
1952	891.2	4924.9	1430.5	1952	71.78	864.1	145.5
1953	1304.4	6241.7	1777.3	1953	90.08	1193.5	174.8
1954	1486.7	5593.6	2226.3	1954	68.60	1188.9	213.5

Notes: $Y = I$ = gross investment = additions to plant and equipment plus maintenance and repairs, in millions of dollars deflated by P_1.
$X_2 = F$ = value of the firm = price of common and preferred shares at Dec. 31 (or average price of Dec. 31 and Jan. 31 of the following year) times number of common and preferred shares outstanding plus total book value of debt at Dec. 31, in millions of dollars deflated by P_2.
$X_3 = C$ = stock of plant and equipment = accumulated sum of net additions to plant and equipment deflated by P_1 minus depreciation allowance deflated by P_3 in these definitions.
P_1 = implicit price deflator of producers' durable equipment (1947 = 100).
P_2 = implicit price deflator of GNP (1947 = 100).
P_3 = depreciation expense deflator = 10-year moving average of wholesale price index of metals and metal products (1947 = 100).

Source: Reproduced from H. D. Vinod and Aman Ullah, *Recent Advances in Regression Methods,* Marcel Dekker, New York, 1981, pp. 259–261.

The Accuracy of Data[15]

Although plenty of data are available for economic research, the quality of the data is often not that good. There are several reasons for that.

1. As noted, most social science data are nonexperimental in nature. Therefore, there is the possibility of observational errors, either of omission or commission.
2. Even in experimentally collected data, errors of measurement arise from approximations and roundoffs.
3. In questionnaire-type surveys, the problem of nonresponse can be serious; a researcher is lucky to get a 40 percent response rate to a questionnaire. Analysis based on such a partial response rate may not truly reflect the behavior of the 60 percent who did not respond, thereby leading to what is known as (sample) selectivity bias. Then there is the further problem that those who do respond to the questionnaire may not answer all the questions, especially questions of a financially sensitive nature, thus leading to additional selectivity bias.
4. The sampling methods used in obtaining the data may vary so widely that it is often difficult to compare the results obtained from the various samples.
5. Economic data are generally available at a highly aggregate level. For example, most macrodata (e.g., GNP, employment, inflation, unemployment) are available for the economy as a whole or at the most for some broad geographical regions. Such highly aggregated data may not tell us much about the individuals or microunits that may be the ultimate object of study.
6. Because of confidentiality, certain data can be published only in highly aggregate form. The IRS, for example, is not allowed by law to disclose data on individual tax returns; it can only release some broad summary data. Therefore, if one wants to find out how much individuals with a certain level of income spent on health care, one cannot do so except at a very highly aggregate level. Such macroanalysis often fails to reveal the dynamics of the behavior of the microunits. Similarly, the Department of Commerce, which conducts the census of business every 5 years, is not allowed to disclose information on production, employment, energy consumption, research and development expenditure, etc., at the firm level. It is therefore difficult to study the interfirm differences on these items.

Because of all of these and many other problems, **the researcher should always keep in mind that the results of research are only as good as the quality of the data.** Therefore, if in given situations researchers find that the results of the research are "unsatisfactory," the cause may be not that they used the wrong model but that the quality of the data was poor. Unfortunately, because of the nonexperimental nature of the data used in most social science studies, researchers very often have no choice but to depend on the available data. But they should always keep in mind that the data used may not be the best and should try not to be too dogmatic about the results obtained from a given study, especially when the quality of the data is suspect.

A Note on the Measurement Scales of Variables[16]

The variables that we will generally encounter fall into four broad categories: *ratio scale, interval scale, ordinal scale,* and *nominal scale*. It is important that we understand each.

[15]For a critical review, see O. Morgenstern, *The Accuracy of Economic Observations,* 2d ed., Princeton University Press, Princeton, N.J., 1963.

[16]The following discussion relies heavily on Aris Spanos, *Probability Theory and Statistical Inference: Econometric Modeling with Observational Data,* Cambridge University Press, New York, 1999, p. 24.

Ratio Scale

For a variable X, taking two values, X_1 and X_2, the ratio X_1/X_2 and the distance $(X_2 - X_1)$ are meaningful quantities. Also, there is a natural ordering (ascending or descending) of the values along the scale. Therefore, comparisons such as $X_2 \leq X_1$ or $X_2 \geq X_1$ are meaningful. Most economic variables belong to this category. Thus, it is meaningful to ask how big this year's GDP is compared with the previous year's GDP. Personal income, measured in dollars, is a ratio variable; someone earning \$100,000 is making twice as much as another person earning \$50,000 (before taxes are assessed, of course!).

Interval Scale

An interval scale variable satisfies the last two properties of the ratio scale variable but not the first. Thus, the distance between two time periods, say (2000–1995) is meaningful, but not the ratio of two time periods (2000/1995). At 11:00 a.m. PST on August 11, 2007, Portland, Oregon, reported a temperature of 60 degrees Fahrenheit while Tallahassee, Florida, reached 90 degrees. Temperature is not measured on a ratio scale since it does not make sense to claim that Tallahassee was 50 percent warmer than Portland. This is mainly due to the fact that the Fahrenheit scale does not use 0 degrees as a natural base.

Ordinal Scale

A variable belongs to this category only if it satisfies the third property of the ratio scale (i.e., natural ordering). Examples are grading systems (A, B, C grades) or income class (upper, middle, lower). For these variables the ordering exists but the distances between the categories cannot be quantified. Students of economics will recall the *indifference curves* between two goods. Each higher indifference curve indicates a higher level of utility, but one cannot quantify by how much one indifference curve is higher than the others.

Nominal Scale

Variables in this category have none of the features of the ratio scale variables. Variables such as gender (male, female) and marital status (married, unmarried, divorced, separated) simply denote categories. *Question:* What is the reason why such variables cannot be expressed on the ratio, interval, or ordinal scales?

As we shall see, econometric techniques that may be suitable for ratio scale variables may not be suitable for nominal scale variables. Therefore, it is important to bear in mind the distinctions among the four types of measurement scales discussed above.

Summary and Conclusions

1. The key idea behind regression analysis is the statistical dependence of one variable, the dependent variable, on one or more other variables, the explanatory variables.
2. The objective of such analysis is to estimate and/or predict the mean or average value of the dependent variable on the basis of the known or fixed values of the explanatory variables.
3. In practice the success of regression analysis depends on the availability of the appropriate data. This chapter discussed the nature, sources, and limitations of the data that are generally available for research, especially in the social sciences.
4. In any research, the researcher should clearly state the sources of the data used in the analysis, their definitions, their methods of collection, and any gaps or omissions in the data as well as any revisions in the data. Keep in mind that the macroeconomic data published by the government are often revised.
5. Since the reader may not have the time, energy, or resources to track down the data, the reader has the right to presume that the data used by the researcher have been properly gathered and that the computations and analysis are correct.

EXERCISES

1.1. Table 1.3 gives data on the Consumer Price Index (CPI) for seven industrialized countries with 1982–1984 = 100 as the base of the index.

a. From the given data, compute the inflation rate for each country.[17]

b. Plot the inflation rate for each country against time (i.e., use the horizontal axis for time and the vertical axis for the inflation rate).

c. What broad conclusions can you draw about the inflation experience in the seven countries?

d. Which country's inflation rate seems to be most variable? Can you offer any explanation?

1.2. *a.* Using Table 1.3, plot the inflation rate of Canada, France, Germany, Italy, Japan, and the United Kingdom against the United States inflation rate.

b. Comment generally about the behavior of the inflation rate in the six countries vis-à-vis the U.S. inflation rate.

c. If you find that the six countries' inflation rates move in the same direction as the U.S. inflation rate, would that suggest that U.S. inflation "causes" inflation in the other countries? Why or why not?

TABLE 1.3
CPI in Seven Industrial Countries, 1980–2005 (1982–1984 = 100)

Source: *Economic Report of the President*, 2007, Table 108, p. 354.

Year	U.S.	Canada	Japan	France	Germany	Italy	U.K.
1980	82.4	76.1	91.0	72.2	86.7	63.9	78.5
1981	90.9	85.6	95.3	81.8	92.2	75.5	87.9
1982	96.5	94.9	98.1	91.7	97.0	87.8	95.4
1983	99.6	100.4	99.8	100.3	100.3	100.8	99.8
1984	103.9	104.7	102.1	108.0	102.7	111.4	104.8
1985	107.6	109.0	104.2	114.3	104.8	121.7	111.1
1986	109.6	113.5	104.9	117.2	104.6	128.9	114.9
1987	113.6	118.4	104.9	121.1	104.9	135.1	119.7
1988	118.3	123.2	105.6	124.3	106.3	141.9	125.6
1989	124.0	129.3	108.0	128.7	109.2	150.7	135.4
1990	130.7	135.5	111.4	132.9	112.2	160.4	148.2
1991	136.2	143.1	115.0	137.2	116.3	170.5	156.9
1992	140.3	145.3	117.0	140.4	122.2	179.5	162.7
1993	144.5	147.9	118.5	143.4	127.6	187.7	165.3
1994	148.2	148.2	119.3	145.8	131.1	195.3	169.3
1995	152.4	151.4	119.2	148.4	133.3	205.6	175.2
1996	156.9	153.8	119.3	151.4	135.3	213.8	179.4
1997	160.5	156.3	121.5	153.2	137.8	218.2	185.1
1998	163.0	157.8	122.2	154.2	139.1	222.5	191.4
1999	166.6	160.5	121.8	155.0	140.0	226.2	194.3
2000	172.2	164.9	121.0	157.6	142.0	231.9	200.1
2001	177.1	169.1	120.1	160.2	144.8	238.3	203.6
2002	179.9	172.9	119.0	163.3	146.7	244.3	207.0
2003	184.0	177.7	118.7	166.7	148.3	250.8	213.0
2004	188.9	181.0	118.7	170.3	150.8	256.3	219.4
2005	195.3	184.9	118.3	173.2	153.7	261.3	225.6

[17] Subtract from the current year's CPI the CPI from the previous year, divide the difference by the previous year's CPI, and multiply the result by 100. Thus, the inflation rate for Canada for 1981 is $[(85.6 - 76.1)/76.1] \times 100 = 12.48\%$ (approx.).

1.3. Table 1.4 gives the foreign exchange rates for nine industrialized countries for the years 1985–2006. Except for the United Kingdom, the exchange rate is defined as the units of foreign currency for one U.S. dollar; for the United Kingdom, it is defined as the number of U.S. dollars for one U.K. pound.

a. Plot these exchange rates against time and comment on the general behavior of the exchange rates over the given time period.

b. The dollar is said to *appreciate* if it can buy more units of a foreign currency. Contrarily, it is said to *depreciate* if it buys fewer units of a foreign currency. Over the time period 1985–2006, what has been the general behavior of the U.S. dollar? Incidentally, look up any textbook on macroeconomics or international economics to find out what factors determine the appreciation or depreciation of a currency.

1.4. The data behind the M1 money supply in Figure 1.5 are given in Table 1.5. Can you give reasons why the money supply has been increasing over the time period shown in the table?

1.5. Suppose you were to develop an economic model of criminal activities, say, the hours spent in criminal activities (e.g., selling illegal drugs). What variables would you consider in developing such a model? See if your model matches the one developed by the Nobel laureate economist Gary Becker.[18]

TABLE 1.4 Exchange Rates for Nine Countries: 1985–2006

Year	Australia	Canada	China P. R.	Japan	Mexico	South Korea	Sweden	Switzerland	United Kingdom
1985	0.7003	1.3659	2.9434	238.47	0.257	872.45	8.6032	2.4552	1.2974
1986	0.6709	1.3896	3.4616	168.35	0.612	884.60	7.1273	1.7979	1.4677
1987	0.7014	1.3259	3.7314	144.60	1.378	826.16	6.3469	1.4918	1.6398
1988	0.7841	1.2306	3.7314	128.17	2.273	734.52	6.1370	1.4643	1.7813
1989	0.7919	1.1842	3.7673	138.07	2.461	674.13	6.4559	1.6369	1.6382
1990	0.7807	1.1668	4.7921	145.00	2.813	710.64	5.9231	1.3901	1.7841
1991	0.7787	1.1460	5.3337	134.59	3.018	736.73	6.0521	1.4356	1.7674
1992	0.7352	1.2085	5.5206	126.78	3.095	784.66	5.8258	1.4064	1.7663
1993	0.6799	1.2902	5.7795	111.08	3.116	805.75	7.7956	1.4781	1.5016
1994	0.7316	1.3664	8.6397	102.18	3.385	806.93	7.7161	1.3667	1.5319
1995	0.7407	1.3725	8.3700	93.96	6.447	772.69	7.1406	1.1812	1.5785
1996	0.7828	1.3638	8.3389	108.78	7.600	805.00	6.7082	1.2361	1.5607
1997	0.7437	1.3849	8.3193	121.06	7.918	953.19	7.6446	1.4514	1.6376
1998	0.6291	1.4836	8.3008	130.99	9.152	1,400.40	7.9522	1.4506	1.6573
1999	0.6454	1.4858	8.2783	113.73	9.553	1,189.84	8.2740	1.5045	1.6172
2000	0.5815	1.4855	8.2784	107.80	9.459	1,130.90	9.1735	1.6904	1.5156
2001	0.5169	1.5487	8.2770	121.57	9.337	1,292.02	10.3425	1.6891	1.4396
2002	0.5437	1.5704	8.2771	125.22	9.663	1,250.31	9.7233	1.5567	1.5025
2003	0.6524	1.4008	8.2772	115.94	10.793	1,192.08	8.0787	1.3450	1.6347
2004	0.7365	1.3017	8.2768	108.15	11.290	1,145.24	7.3480	1.2428	1.8330
2005	0.7627	1.2115	8.1936	110.11	10.894	1,023.75	7.4710	1.2459	1.8204
2006	0.7535	1.1340	7.9723	116.31	10.906	954.32	7.3718	1.2532	1.8434

Source: *Economic Report of the President,* 2007, Table B–110, p. 356.

[18] G. S. Becker, "Crime and Punishment: An Economic Approach," *Journal of Political Economy,* vol. 76, 1968, pp. 169–217.

TABLE 1.5
Seasonally Adjusted M1 Supply: 1959:01–1999:07 (billions of dollars)

Source: Board of Governors, Federal Reserve Bank, USA.

1959:01	138.8900	139.3900	139.7400	139.6900	140.6800	141.1700
1959:07	141.7000	141.9000	141.0100	140.4700	140.3800	139.9500
1960:01	139.9800	139.8700	139.7500	139.5600	139.6100	139.5800
1960:07	140.1800	141.3100	141.1800	140.9200	140.8600	140.6900
1961:01	141.0600	141.6000	141.8700	142.1300	142.6600	142.8800
1961:07	142.9200	143.4900	143.7800	144.1400	144.7600	145.2000
1962:01	145.2400	145.6600	145.9600	146.4000	146.8400	146.5800
1962:07	146.4600	146.5700	146.3000	146.7100	147.2900	147.8200
1963:01	148.2600	148.9000	149.1700	149.7000	150.3900	150.4300
1963:07	151.3400	151.7800	151.9800	152.5500	153.6500	153.2900
1964:01	153.7400	154.3100	154.4800	154.7700	155.3300	155.6200
1964:07	156.8000	157.8200	158.7500	159.2400	159.9600	160.3000
1965:01	160.7100	160.9400	161.4700	162.0300	161.7000	162.1900
1965:07	163.0500	163.6800	164.8500	165.9700	166.7100	167.8500
1966:01	169.0800	169.6200	170.5100	171.8100	171.3300	171.5700
1966:07	170.3100	170.8100	171.9700	171.1600	171.3800	172.0300
1967:01	171.8600	172.9900	174.8100	174.1700	175.6800	177.0200
1967:07	178.1300	179.7100	180.6800	181.6400	182.3800	183.2600
1968:01	184.3300	184.7100	185.4700	186.6000	187.9900	189.4200
1968:07	190.4900	191.8400	192.7400	194.0200	196.0200	197.4100
1969:01	198.6900	199.3500	200.0200	200.7100	200.8100	201.2700
1969:07	201.6600	201.7300	202.1000	202.9000	203.5700	203.8800
1970:01	206.2200	205.0000	205.7500	206.7200	207.2200	207.5400
1970:07	207.9800	209.9300	211.8000	212.8800	213.6600	214.4100
1971:01	215.5400	217.4200	218.7700	220.0000	222.0200	223.4500
1971:07	224.8500	225.5800	226.4700	227.1600	227.7600	228.3200
1972:01	230.0900	232.3200	234.3000	235.5800	235.8900	236.6200
1972:07	238.7900	240.9300	243.1800	245.0200	246.4100	249.2500
1973:01	251.4700	252.1500	251.6700	252.7400	254.8900	256.6900
1973:07	257.5400	257.7600	257.8600	259.0400	260.9800	262.8800
1974:01	263.7600	265.3100	266.6800	267.2000	267.5600	268.4400
1974:07	269.2700	270.1200	271.0500	272.3500	273.7100	274.2000
1975:01	273.9000	275.0000	276.4200	276.1700	279.2000	282.4300
1975:07	283.6800	284.1500	285.6900	285.3900	286.8300	287.0700
1976:01	288.4200	290.7600	292.7000	294.6600	295.9300	296.1600
1976:07	297.2000	299.0500	299.6700	302.0400	303.5900	306.2500
1977:01	308.2600	311.5400	313.9400	316.0200	317.1900	318.7100
1977:07	320.1900	322.2700	324.4800	326.4000	328.6400	330.8700
1978:01	334.4000	335.3000	336.9600	339.9200	344.8600	346.8000
1978:07	347.6300	349.6600	352.2600	353.3500	355.4100	357.2800
1979:01	358.6000	359.9100	362.4500	368.0500	369.5900	373.3400
1979:07	377.2100	378.8200	379.2800	380.8700	380.8100	381.7700
1980:01	385.8500	389.7000	388.1300	383.4400	384.6000	389.4600
1980:07	394.9100	400.0600	405.3600	409.0600	410.3700	408.0600
1981:01	410.8300	414.3800	418.6900	427.0600	424.4300	425.5000
1981:07	427.9000	427.8500	427.4600	428.4500	430.8800	436.1700
1982:01	442.1300	441.4900	442.3700	446.7800	446.5300	447.8900
1982:07	449.0900	452.4900	457.5000	464.5700	471.1200	474.3000
1983:01	476.6800	483.8500	490.1800	492.7700	499.7800	504.3500
1983:07	508.9600	511.6000	513.4100	517.2100	518.5300	520.7900
1984:01	524.4000	526.9900	530.7800	534.0300	536.5900	540.5400
1984:07	542.1300	542.3900	543.8600	543.8700	547.3200	551.1900

(Continued)

TABLE 1.5
(Continued)

1985:01	555.6600	562.4800	565.7400	569.5500	575.0700	583.1700
1985:07	590.8200	598.0600	604.4700	607.9100	611.8300	619.3600
1986:01	620.4000	624.1400	632.8100	640.3500	652.0100	661.5200
1986:07	672.2000	680.7700	688.5100	695.2600	705.2400	724.2800
1987:01	729.3400	729.8400	733.0100	743.3900	746.0000	743.7200
1987:07	744.9600	746.9600	748.6600	756.5000	752.8300	749.6800
1988:01	755.5500	757.0700	761.1800	767.5700	771.6800	779.1000
1988:07	783.4000	785.0800	784.8200	783.6300	784.4600	786.2600
1989:01	784.9200	783.4000	782.7400	778.8200	774.7900	774.2200
1989:07	779.7100	781.1400	782.2000	787.0500	787.9500	792.5700
1990:01	794.9300	797.6500	801.2500	806.2400	804.3600	810.3300
1990:07	811.8000	817.8500	821.8300	820.3000	822.0600	824.5600
1991:01	826.7300	832.4000	838.6200	842.7300	848.9600	858.3300
1991:07	862.9500	868.6500	871.5600	878.4000	887.9500	896.7000
1992:01	910.4900	925.1300	936.0000	943.8900	950.7800	954.7100
1992:07	964.6000	975.7100	988.8400	1004.340	1016.040	1024.450
1993:01	1030.900	1033.150	1037.990	1047.470	1066.220	1075.610
1993:07	1085.880	1095.560	1105.430	1113.800	1123.900	1129.310
1994:01	1132.200	1136.130	1139.910	1141.420	1142.850	1145.650
1994:07	1151.490	1151.390	1152.440	1150.410	1150.440	1149.750
1995:01	1150.640	1146.740	1146.520	1149.480	1144.650	1144.240
1995:07	1146.500	1146.100	1142.270	1136.430	1133.550	1126.730
1996:01	1122.580	1117.530	1122.590	1124.520	1116.300	1115.470
1996:07	1112.340	1102.180	1095.610	1082.560	1080.490	1081.340
1997:01	1080.520	1076.200	1072.420	1067.450	1063.370	1065.990
1997:07	1067.570	1072.080	1064.820	1062.060	1067.530	1074.870
1998:01	1073.810	1076.020	1080.650	1082.090	1078.170	1077.780
1998:07	1075.370	1072.210	1074.650	1080.400	1088.960	1093.350
1999:01	1091.000	1092.650	1102.010	1108.400	1104.750	1101.110
1999:07	1099.530	1102.400	1093.460			

1.6. *Controlled experiments in economics:* On April 7, 2000, President Clinton signed into law a bill passed by both Houses of the U.S. Congress that lifted earnings limitations on Social Security recipients. Until then, recipients between the ages of 65 and 69 who earned more than $17,000 a year would lose $1 worth of Social Security benefit for every $3 of income earned in excess of $17,000. How would you devise a study to assess the impact of this change in the law? *Note:* There was no income limitation for recipients over the age of 70 under the old law.

1.7. The data presented in Table 1.6 were published in the March 1, 1984, issue of *The Wall Street Journal*. They relate to the advertising budget (in millions of dollars) of 21 firms for 1983 and millions of impressions retained per week by the viewers of the products of these firms. The data are based on a survey of 4000 adults in which users of the products were asked to cite a commercial they had seen for the product category in the past week.

a. Plot impressions on the vertical axis and advertising expenditure on the horizontal axis.

b. What can you say about the nature of the relationship between the two variables?

c. Looking at your graph, do you think it pays to advertise? Think about all those commercials shown on Super Bowl Sunday or during the World Series.

Note: We will explore further the data given in Table 1.6 in subsequent chapters.

TABLE 1.6
Impact of Advertising Expenditure

Source: http://lib.stat.cmu.edu/DASL/Datafiles/tvadsdat.html.

Firm	Impressions, millions	Expenditure, millions of 1983 dollars
1. Miller Lite	32.1	50.1
2. Pepsi	99.6	74.1
3. Stroh's	11.7	19.3
4. Fed'l Express	21.9	22.9
5. Burger King	60.8	82.4
6. Coca-Cola	78.6	40.1
7. McDonald's	92.4	185.9
8. MCl	50.7	26.9
9. Diet Cola	21.4	20.4
10. Ford	40.1	166.2
11. Levi's	40.8	27.0
12. Bud Lite	10.4	45.6
13. ATT/Bell	88.9	154.9
14. Calvin Klein	12.0	5.0
15. Wendy's	29.2	49.7
16. Polaroid	38.0	26.9
17. Shasta	10.0	5.7
18. Meow Mix	12.3	7.6
19. Oscar Meyer	23.4	9.2
20. Crest	71.1	32.4
21. Kibbles 'N Bits	4.4	6.1

Chapter 2

Two-Variable Regression Analysis: Some Basic Ideas

In Chapter 1 we discussed the concept of regression in broad terms. In this chapter we approach the subject somewhat formally. Specifically, this and the following three chapters introduce the reader to the theory underlying the simplest possible regression analysis, namely, the **bivariate,** or **two-variable,** regression in which the dependent variable (the regressand) is related to a single explanatory variable (the regressor). This case is considered first, not because of its practical adequacy, but because it presents the fundamental ideas of regression analysis as simply as possible and some of these ideas can be illustrated with the aid of two-dimensional graphs. Moreover, as we shall see, the more general **multiple** regression analysis in which the regressand is related to one or more regressors is in many ways a logical extension of the two-variable case.

2.1 A Hypothetical Example[1]

As noted in Section 1.2, regression analysis is largely concerned with estimating and/or predicting the (population) mean value of the dependent variable on the basis of the known or fixed values of the explanatory variable(s).[2] To understand this, consider the data given in Table 2.1. The data in the table refer to a total **population** of 60 families in a hypothetical community and their weekly income (X) and weekly consumption expenditure (Y), both in dollars. The 60 families are divided into 10 income groups (from \$80 to \$260) and the weekly expenditures of each family in the various groups are as shown in the table. Therefore, we have 10 *fixed* values of X and the corresponding Y values against each of the X values; so to speak, there are 10 Y subpopulations.

There is considerable variation in weekly consumption expenditure in each income group, which can be seen clearly from Figure 2.1. But the general picture that one gets is

[1] The reader whose statistical knowledge has become somewhat rusty may want to freshen it up by reading the statistical appendix, **Appendix A,** before reading this chapter.

[2] The expected value, or expectation, or population mean of a random variable Y is denoted by the symbol $E(Y)$. On the other hand, the mean value computed from a sample of values from the Y population is denoted as $\bar{Y}$, read as Y bar.

TABLE 2.1
Weekly Family Income X, $

$X\rightarrow$ / $Y\downarrow$	80	100	120	140	160	180	200	220	240	260
Weekly family consumption expenditure Y, $	55	65	79	80	102	110	120	135	137	150
	60	70	84	93	107	115	136	137	145	152
	65	74	90	95	110	120	140	140	155	175
	70	80	94	103	116	130	144	152	165	178
	75	85	98	108	118	135	145	157	175	180
	–	88	–	113	125	140	–	160	189	185
	–	–	–	115	–	–	–	162	–	191
Total	325	462	445	707	678	750	685	1043	966	1211
Conditional means of Y, $E(Y\mid X)$	65	77	89	101	113	125	137	149	161	173

that, despite the variability of weekly consumption expenditure within each income bracket, *on the average*, weekly consumption expenditure increases as income increases. To see this clearly, in Table 2.1 we have given the mean, or average, weekly consumption expenditure corresponding to each of the 10 levels of income. Thus, corresponding to the weekly income level of $80, the mean consumption expenditure is $65, while corresponding to the income level of $200, it is $137. In all we have 10 mean values for the 10 subpopulations of Y. We call these mean values **conditional expected values,** as they depend on the given values of the (conditioning) variable X. Symbolically, we denote them as $E(Y \mid X)$, which is read as the expected value of Y given the value of X (see also Table 2.2).

It is important to distinguish these conditional expected values from the **unconditional expected value** of weekly consumption expenditure, $E(Y)$. If we add the weekly consumption expenditures for all the 60 families in the *population* and divide this number by 60, we get the number $121.20 ($7272/60), which is the unconditional mean, or expected, value of weekly consumption expenditure, $E(Y)$; it is unconditional in the sense that in arriving at this number we have disregarded the income levels of the various families.[3] Obviously,

FIGURE 2.1
Conditional distribution of expenditure for various levels of income (data of Table 2.1).

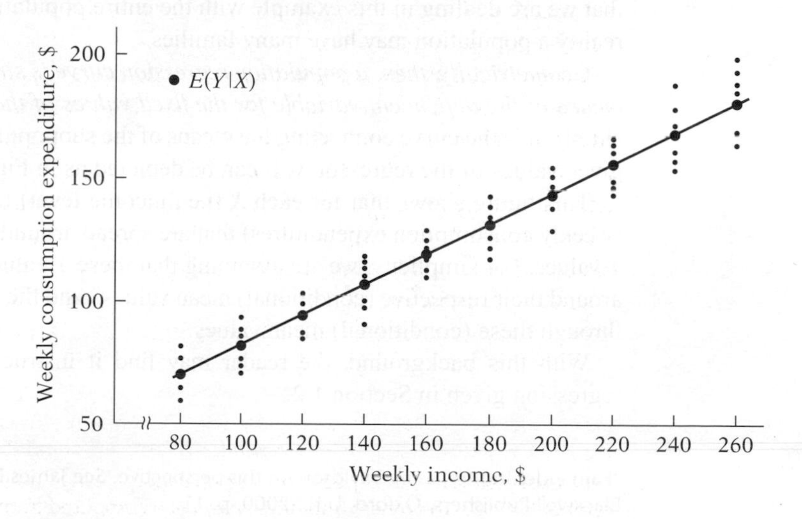

[3]As shown in **Appendix A,** in general the conditional and unconditional mean values are different.

TABLE 2.2
Conditional Probabilities $p(Y \mid X_i)$ for the Data of Table 2.1

$p(Y \mid X_i)$ ↓ / $X \rightarrow$	80	100	120	140	160	180	200	220	240	260
Conditional probabilities $p(Y \mid X_i)$	$\frac{1}{5}$	$\frac{1}{6}$	$\frac{1}{5}$	$\frac{1}{7}$	$\frac{1}{6}$	$\frac{1}{6}$	$\frac{1}{5}$	$\frac{1}{7}$	$\frac{1}{6}$	$\frac{1}{7}$
	$\frac{1}{5}$	$\frac{1}{6}$	$\frac{1}{5}$	$\frac{1}{7}$	$\frac{1}{6}$	$\frac{1}{6}$	$\frac{1}{5}$	$\frac{1}{7}$	$\frac{1}{6}$	$\frac{1}{7}$
	$\frac{1}{5}$	$\frac{1}{6}$	$\frac{1}{5}$	$\frac{1}{7}$	$\frac{1}{6}$	$\frac{1}{6}$	$\frac{1}{5}$	$\frac{1}{7}$	$\frac{1}{6}$	$\frac{1}{7}$
	$\frac{1}{5}$	$\frac{1}{6}$	$\frac{1}{5}$	$\frac{1}{7}$	$\frac{1}{6}$	$\frac{1}{6}$	$\frac{1}{5}$	$\frac{1}{7}$	$\frac{1}{6}$	$\frac{1}{7}$
	$\frac{1}{5}$	$\frac{1}{6}$	$\frac{1}{5}$	$\frac{1}{7}$	$\frac{1}{6}$	$\frac{1}{6}$	$\frac{1}{5}$	$\frac{1}{7}$	$\frac{1}{6}$	$\frac{1}{7}$
	—	$\frac{1}{6}$	—	$\frac{1}{7}$	$\frac{1}{6}$	$\frac{1}{6}$	—	$\frac{1}{7}$	$\frac{1}{6}$	$\frac{1}{7}$
	—	—	—	$\frac{1}{7}$	—	—	—	$\frac{1}{7}$	—	$\frac{1}{7}$
Conditional means of Y	65	77	89	101	113	125	137	149	161	173

the various conditional expected values of Y given in Table 2.1 are different from the unconditional expected value of Y of \$121.20. When we ask the question, "What is the *expected value* of weekly consumption expenditure of a family?" we get the answer \$121.20 (the unconditional mean). But if we ask the question, "What is the *expected value* of weekly consumption expenditure of a family whose monthly income is, say, \$140?" we get the answer \$101 (the conditional mean). To put it differently, if we ask the question, "What is the best (mean) prediction of weekly expenditure of families with a weekly income of \$140?" the answer would be \$101. Thus the knowledge of the income level may enable us to better predict the mean value of consumption expenditure than if we do not have that knowledge.[4] This probably is the essence of regression analysis, as we shall discover throughout this text.

The dark circled points in Figure 2.1 show the conditional mean values of Y against the various X values. If we join these conditional mean values, we obtain what is known as the **population regression line (PRL),** or more generally, the **population regression curve.**[5] More simply, it is the **regression of Y on X.** The adjective "population" comes from the fact that we are dealing in this example with the entire population of 60 families. Of course, in reality a population may have many families.

Geometrically, then, a population regression curve is simply the locus of the conditional means of the dependent variable for the fixed values of the explanatory variable(s). More simply, it is the curve connecting the means of the subpopulations of Y corresponding to the given values of the regressor X. It can be depicted as in Figure 2.2.

This figure shows that for each X (i.e., income level) there is a population of Y values (weekly consumption expenditures) that are spread around the (conditional) mean of those Y values. For simplicity, we are assuming that these Y values are distributed symmetrically around their respective (conditional) mean values. And the regression line (or curve) passes through these (conditional) mean values.

With this background, the reader may find it instructive to reread the definition of regression given in Section 1.2.

[4] I am indebted to James Davidson on this perspective. See James Davidson, *Econometric Theory,* Blackwell Publishers, Oxford, U.K., 2000, p. 11.

[5] In the present example the PRL is a straight line, but it could be a curve (see Figure 2.3).

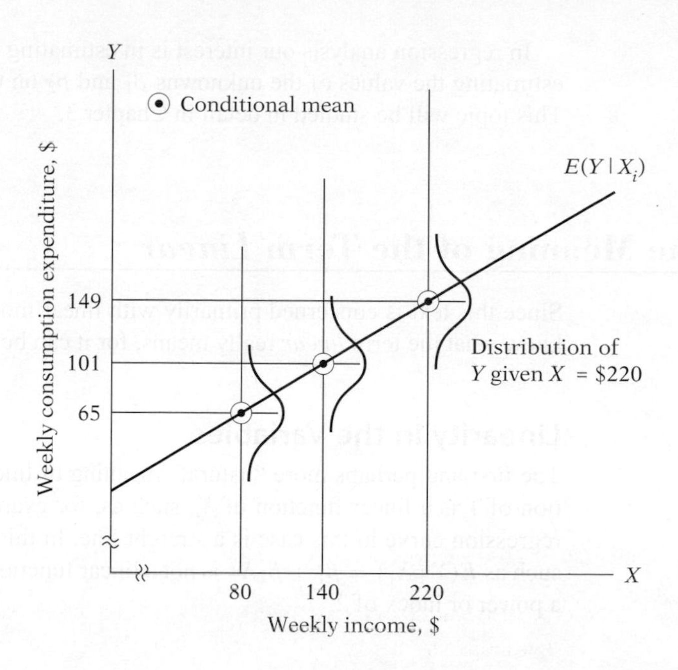

FIGURE 2.2
Population regression line (data of Table 2.1).

2.2 The Concept of Population Regression Function (PRF)

From the preceding discussion and Figures 2.1 and 2.2, it is clear that each conditional mean $E(Y \mid X_i)$ is a function of X_i, where X_i is a given value of X. Symbolically,

$$E(Y \mid X_i) = f(X_i) \tag{2.2.1}$$

where $f(X_i)$ denotes some function of the explanatory variable X. In our example, $E(Y \mid X_i)$ is a linear function of X_i. Equation 2.2.1 is known as the **conditional expectation function (CEF)** or **population regression function (PRF)** or **population regression (PR)** for short. It states merely that the *expected value* of the distribution of Y given X_i is functionally related to X_i. In simple terms, it tells how the mean or average response of Y varies with X.

What form does the function $f(X_i)$ assume? This is an important question because in real situations we do not have the entire population available for examination. The functional form of the PRF is therefore an empirical question, although in specific cases theory may have somthing to say. For example, an economist might posit that consumption expenditure is linearly related to income. Therefore, as a first approximation or a working hypothesis, we may assume that the PRF $E(Y \mid X_i)$ is a linear function of X_i, say, of the type

$$E(Y \mid X_i) = \beta_1 + \beta_2 X_i \tag{2.2.2}$$

where β_1 and β_2 are unknown but fixed parameters known as the **regression coefficients;** β_1 and β_2 are also known as **intercept** and **slope coefficients,** respectively. Equation 2.2.1 itself is known as the **linear population regression function.** Some alternative expressions used in the literature are *linear population regression model* or simply *linear population regression*. In the sequel, the terms **regression, regression equation,** and **regression model** will be used synonymously.

In regression analysis our interest is in estimating the PRFs like Equation 2.2.2, that is, estimating the values of the unknowns β_1 and β_2 on the basis of observations on Y and X. This topic will be studied in detail in Chapter 3.

2.3 The Meaning of the Term *Linear*

Since this text is concerned primarily with linear models like Eq. (2.2.2), it is essential to know what the term *linear* really means, for it can be interpreted in two different ways.

Linearity in the Variables

The first and perhaps more "natural" meaning of linearity is that the conditional expectation of Y is a linear function of X_i, such as, for example, Eq. (2.2.2).[6] Geometrically, the regression curve in this case is a straight line. In this interpretation, a regression function such as $E(Y \mid X_i) = \beta_1 + \beta_2 X_i^2$ is not a linear function because the variable X appears with a power or index of 2.

Linearity in the Parameters

The second interpretation of linearity is that the conditional expectation of Y, $E(Y \mid X_i)$, is a linear function of the parameters, the β's; it may or may not be linear in the variable X.[7] In this interpretation $E(Y \mid X_i) = \beta_1 + \beta_2 X_i^2$ is a linear (in the parameter) regression model. To see this, let us suppose X takes the value 3. Therefore, $E(Y \mid X = 3) = \beta_1 + 9\beta_2$, which is obviously linear in β_1 and β_2. All the models shown in Figure 2.3 are thus linear regression models, that is, models linear in the parameters.

Now consider the model $E(Y \mid X_i) = \beta_1 + \beta_2^2 X_i$. Now suppose $X = 3$; then we obtain $E(Y \mid X_i) = \beta_1 + 3\beta_2^2$, which is nonlinear in the parameter β_2. The preceding model is an example of a **nonlinear (in the parameter) regression model.** We will discuss such models in Chapter 14.

Of the two interpretations of linearity, linearity in the parameters is relevant for the development of the regression theory to be presented shortly. Therefore, *from now on, the term "linear" regression will always mean a regression that is linear in the parameters; the β's (that is, the parameters) are raised to the first power only. It may or may not be linear in the explanatory variables, the X's.* Schematically, we have Table 2.3. Thus, $E(Y \mid X_i) = \beta_1 + \beta_2 X_i$, which is linear both in the parameters and variable, is a LRM, and so is $E(Y \mid X_i) = \beta_1 + \beta_2 X_i^2$, which is linear in the parameters but nonlinear in variable X.

[6]A function $Y = f(X)$ is said to be linear in X if X appears with a power or index of 1 only (that is, terms such as X^2, $\sqrt{X}$, and so on, are excluded) and is not multiplied or divided by any other variable (for example, $X \cdot Z$ or X/Z, where Z is another variable). If Y depends on X alone, another way to state that Y is linearly related to X is that the rate of change of Y with respect to X (i.e., the slope, or derivative, of Y with respect to X, dY/dX) is independent of the value of X. Thus, if $Y = 4X$, $dY/dX = 4$, which is independent of the value of X. But if $Y = 4X^2$, $dY/dX = 8X$, which is not independent of the value taken by X. Hence this function is not linear in X.

[7]A function is said to be linear in the parameter, say, β_1, if β_1 appears with a power of 1 only and is not multiplied or divided by any other parameter (for example, $\beta_1\beta_2$, β_2/β_1, and so on).

FIGURE 2.3
Linear-in-parameter functions.

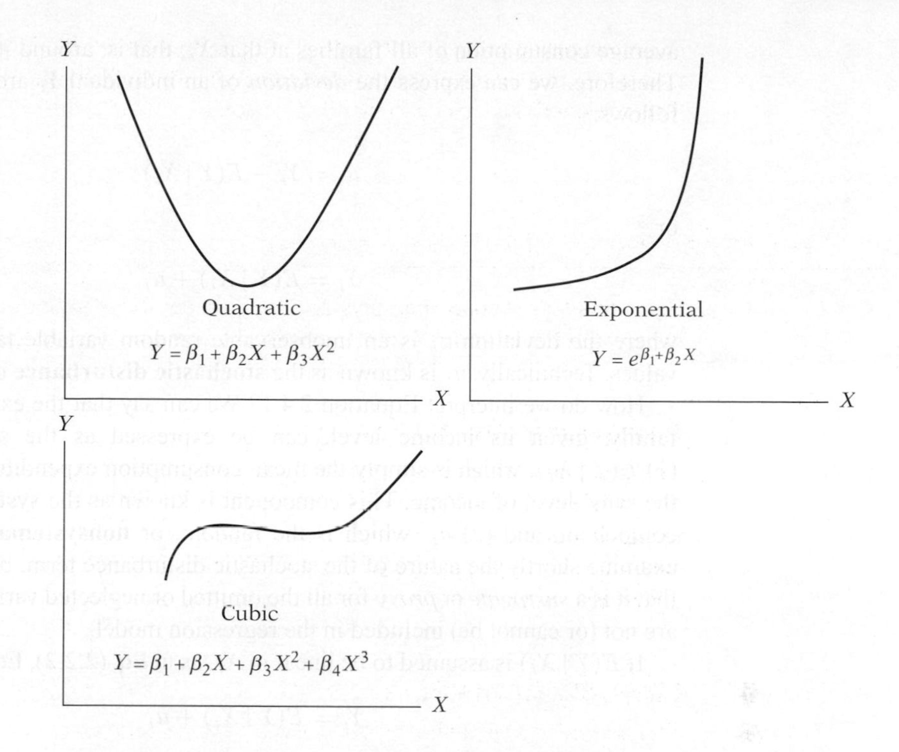

TABLE 2.3
Linear Regression Models

Model Linear in Parameters?	Model Linear in Variables?	
	Yes	No
Yes	LRM	LRM
No	NLRM	NLRM

Note: LRM = linear regression model
NLRM = nonlinear regression model

2.4 Stochastic Specification of PRF

It is clear from Figure 2.1 that, as family income increases, family consumption expenditure on the average increases, too. But what about the consumption expenditure of an individual family in relation to its (fixed) level of income? It is obvious from Table 2.1 and Figure 2.1 that an individual family's consumption expenditure does not necessarily increase as the income level increases. For example, from Table 2.1 we observe that corresponding to the income level of $100 there is one family whose consumption expenditure of $65 is less than the consumption expenditures of two families whose weekly income is only $80. But notice that the *average* consumption expenditure of families with a weekly income of $100 is greater than the average consumption expenditure of families with a weekly income of $80 ($77 versus $65).

What, then, can we say about the relationship between an individual family's consumption expenditure and a given level of income? We see from Figure 2.1 that, given the income level of X_i, an individual family's consumption expenditure is clustered around the average consumption of all families at that X_i, that is, around its conditional expectation. Therefore, we can express the *deviation* of an individual Y_i around its expected value as follows:

$$u_i = Y_i - E(Y \mid X_i)$$

or

$$Y_i = E(Y \mid X_i) + u_i \tag{2.4.1}$$

where the deviation u_i is an unobservable random variable taking positive or negative values. Technically, u_i is known as the **stochastic disturbance** or **stochastic error term.**

How do we interpret Equation 2.4.1? We can say that the expenditure of an individual family, given its income level, can be expressed as the sum of two components: (1) $E(Y \mid X_i)$, which is simply the mean consumption expenditure of all the families with the same level of income. This component is known as the **systematic,** or **deterministic,** component, and (2) u_i, which is the random, or **nonsystematic,** component. We shall examine shortly the nature of the stochastic disturbance term, but for the moment assume that it is a *surrogate* or *proxy* for all the omitted or neglected variables that may affect Y but are not (or cannot be) included in the regression model.

If $E(Y \mid X_i)$ is assumed to be linear in X_i, as in Eq. (2.2.2), Eq. (2.4.1) may be written as

$$\begin{aligned} Y_i &= E(Y \mid X_i) + u_i \\ &= \beta_1 + \beta_2 X_i + u_i \end{aligned} \tag{2.4.2}$$

Equation 2.4.2 posits that the consumption expenditure of a family is linearly related to its income plus the disturbance term. Thus, the individual consumption expenditures, given $X = \$80$ (see Table 2.1), can be expressed as

$$\begin{aligned} Y_1 &= 55 = \beta_1 + \beta_2(80) + u_1 \\ Y_2 &= 60 = \beta_1 + \beta_2(80) + u_2 \\ Y_3 &= 65 = \beta_1 + \beta_2(80) + u_3 \\ Y_4 &= 70 = \beta_1 + \beta_2(80) + u_4 \\ Y_5 &= 75 = \beta_1 + \beta_2(80) + u_5 \end{aligned} \tag{2.4.3}$$

Now if we take the expected value of Eq. (2.4.1) on both sides, we obtain

$$\begin{aligned} E(Y_i \mid X_i) &= E[E(Y \mid X_i)] + E(u_i \mid X_i) \\ &= E(Y \mid X_i) + E(u_i \mid X_i) \end{aligned} \tag{2.4.4}$$

where use is made of the fact that the expected value of a constant is that constant itself.[8] Notice carefully that in Equation 2.4.4 we have taken the conditional expectation, conditional upon the given X's.

Since $E(Y_i \mid X_i)$ is the same thing as $E(Y \mid X_i)$, Eq. (2.4.4) implies that

$$E(u_i \mid X_i) = 0 \tag{2.4.5}$$

[8]See **Appendix A** for a brief discussion of the properties of the expectation operator E. Note that $E(Y \mid X_i)$, once the value of X_i is fixed, is a constant.

Thus, the assumption that the regression line passes through the conditional means of Y (see Figure 2.2) implies that the conditional mean values of u_i (conditional upon the given X's) are zero.

From the previous discussion, it is clear Eq. (2.2.2) and Eq. (2.4.2) are equivalent forms if $E(u_i \mid X_i) = 0$.[9] But the stochastic specification in Eq. (2.4.2) has the advantage that it clearly shows that there are other variables besides income that affect consumption expenditure and that an individual family's consumption expenditure cannot be fully explained only by the variable(s) included in the regression model.

2.5 The Significance of the Stochastic Disturbance Term

As noted in Section 2.4, the disturbance term u_i is a surrogate for all those variables that are omitted from the model but that collectively affect Y. The obvious question is: Why not introduce these variables into the model explicitly? Stated otherwise, why not develop a multiple regression model with as many variables as possible? The reasons are many.

1. *Vagueness of theory:* The theory, if any, determining the behavior of Y may be, and often is, incomplete. We might know for certain that weekly income X influences weekly consumption expenditure Y, but we might be ignorant or unsure about the other variables affecting Y. Therefore, u_i may be used as a substitute for all the excluded or omitted variables from the model.

2. *Unavailability of data:* Even if we know what some of the excluded variables are and therefore consider a multiple regression rather than a simple regression, we may not have quantitative information about these variables. It is a common experience in empirical analysis that the data we would ideally like to have often are not available. For example, in principle we could introduce family wealth as an explanatory variable in addition to the income variable to explain family consumption expenditure. But unfortunately, information on family wealth generally is not available. Therefore, we may be forced to omit the wealth variable from our model despite its great theoretical relevance in explaining consumption expenditure.

3. *Core variables versus peripheral variables:* Assume in our consumption-income example that besides income X_1, the number of children per family X_2, sex X_3, religion X_4, education X_5, and geographical region X_6 also affect consumption expenditure. But it is quite possible that the joint influence of all or some of these variables may be so small and at best nonsystematic or random that as a practical matter and for cost considerations it does not pay to introduce them into the model explicitly. One hopes that their combined effect can be treated as a random variable u_i.[10]

4. *Intrinsic randomness in human behavior:* Even if we succeed in introducing all the relevant variables into the model, there is bound to be some "intrinsic" randomness in individual Y's that cannot be explained no matter how hard we try. The disturbances, the u's, may very well reflect this intrinsic randomness.

5. *Poor proxy variables:* Although the classical regression model (to be developed in Chapter 3) assumes that the variables Y and X are measured accurately, in practice the data

[9] As a matter of fact, in the method of least squares to be developed in Chapter 3, it is assumed explicitly that $E(u_i \mid X_i) = 0$. See Sec. 3.2.

[10] A further difficulty is that variables such as sex, education, and religion are difficult to quantify.

may be plagued by errors of measurement. Consider, for example, Milton Friedman's well-known theory of the consumption function.[11] He regards *permanent consumption* (Y^p) as a function of *permanent income* (X^p). But since data on these variables are not directly observable, in practice we use proxy variables, such as current consumption (Y) and current income (X), which can be observable. Since the observed Y and X may not equal Y^p and X^p, there is the problem of errors of measurement. The disturbance term u may in this case then also represent the errors of measurement. As we will see in a later chapter, if there are such errors of measurement, they can have serious implications for estimating the regression coefficients, the β's.

6. *Principle of parsimony:* Following Occam's razor,[12] we would like to keep our regression model as simple as possible. If we can explain the behavior of Y "substantially" with two or three explanatory variables and if our theory is not strong enough to suggest what other variables might be included, why introduce more variables? Let u_i represent all other variables. Of course, we should not exclude relevant and important variables just to keep the regression model simple.

7. *Wrong functional form:* Even if we have theoretically correct variables explaining a phenomenon and even if we can obtain data on these variables, very often we do not know the form of the functional relationship between the regressand and the regressors. Is consumption expenditure a linear (invariable) function of income or a nonlinear (invariable) function? If it is the former, $Y_i = \beta_1 + \beta_2 X_i + u_i$ is the proper functional relationship between Y and X, but if it is the latter, $Y_i = \beta_1 + \beta_2 X_i + \beta_3 X_i^2 + u_i$ may be the correct functional form. In two-variable models the functional form of the relationship can often be judged from the scattergram. But in a multiple regression model, it is not easy to determine the appropriate functional form, for graphically we cannot visualize scattergrams in multiple dimensions.

For all these reasons, the stochastic disturbances u_i assume an extremely critical role in regression analysis, which we will see as we progress.

2.6 The Sample Regression Function (SRF)

By confining our discussion so far to the population of Y values corresponding to the fixed X's, we have deliberately avoided sampling considerations (note that the data of Table 2.1 represent the population, not a sample). But it is about time to face up to the sampling problems, for in most practical situations what we have is but a sample of Y values corresponding to some fixed X's. Therefore, our task now is to estimate the PRF on the basis of the sample information.

As an illustration, pretend that the population of Table 2.1 was not known to us and the only information we had was a randomly selected sample of Y values for the fixed X's as given in Table 2.4. Unlike Table 2.1, we now have only one Y value corresponding to the given X's; each Y (given X_i) in Table 2.4 is chosen randomly from similar Y's corresponding to the same X_i from the population of Table 2.1.

[11]Milton Friedman, *A Theory of the Consumption Function,* Princeton University Press, Princeton, N.J., 1957.

[12]"That descriptions be kept as simple as possible until proved inadequate," *The World of Mathematics,* vol. 2, J. R. Newman (ed.), Simon & Schuster, New York, 1956, p. 1247, or, "Entities should not be multiplied beyond necessity," Donald F. Morrison, *Applied Linear Statistical Methods,* Prentice Hall, Englewood Cliffs, N.J., 1983, p. 58.

The question is: From the sample of Table 2.4 can we predict the average weekly consumption expenditure Y in the population as a whole corresponding to the chosen X's? In other words, can we estimate the PRF from the sample data? As the reader surely suspects, we may not be able to estimate the PRF "accurately" because of sampling fluctuations. To see this, suppose we draw another random sample from the population of Table 2.1, as presented in Table 2.5.

Plotting the data of Tables 2.4 and 2.5, we obtain the scattergram given in Figure 2.4. In the scattergram two sample regression lines are drawn so as to "fit" the scatters reasonably well: SRF_1 is based on the first sample, and SRF_2 is based on the second sample. Which of the two regression lines represents the "true" population regression line? If we avoid the temptation of looking at Figure 2.1, which purportedly represents the PR, there is no way we can be absolutely sure that either of the regression lines shown in Figure 2.4 represents the true population regression line (or curve). The regression lines in Figure 2.4 are known

TABLE 2.4
A Random Sample from the Population of Table 2.1

Y	X
70	80
65	100
90	120
95	140
110	160
115	180
120	200
140	220
155	240
150	260

TABLE 2.5
Another Random Sample from the Population of Table 2.1

Y	X
55	80
88	100
90	120
80	140
118	160
120	180
145	200
135	220
145	240
175	260

FIGURE 2.4
Regression lines based on two different samples.

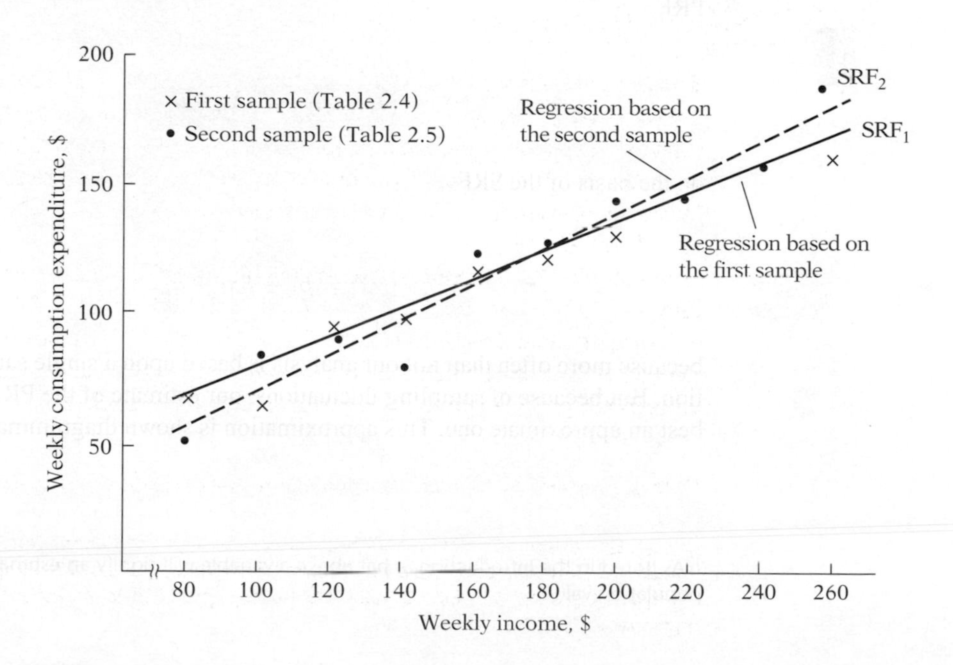

as the **sample regression lines.** Supposedly they represent the population regression line, but because of sampling fluctuations they are at best an approximation of the true PR. In general, we would get N different SRFs for N different samples, and these SRFs are not likely to be the same.

Now, analogously to the PRF that underlies the population regression line, we can develop the concept of the **sample regression function** (SRF) to represent the sample regression line. The sample counterpart of Eq. (2.2.2) may be written as

$$\hat{Y}_i = \hat{\beta}_1 + \hat{\beta}_2 X_i \tag{2.6.1}$$

where $\hat{Y}$ is read as "*Y*-hat" or "*Y*-cap"

$\hat{Y}_i$ = estimator of $E(Y \mid X_i)$
$\hat{\beta}_1$ = estimator of β_1
$\hat{\beta}_2$ = estimator of β_2

Note that an **estimator,** also known as a (sample) **statistic,** is simply a rule or formula or method that tells how to estimate the population parameter from the information provided by the sample at hand. A particular numerical value obtained by the estimator in an application is known as an **estimate.**[13] It should be noted that an estimator is random, but an estimate is nonrandom. (Why?)

Now just as we expressed the PRF in two equivalent forms, Eq. (2.2.2) and Eq. (2.4.2), we can express the SRF in Equation 2.6.1 in its stochastic form as follows:

$$Y_i = \hat{\beta}_1 + \hat{\beta}_2 X_i + \hat{u}_i \tag{2.6.2}$$

where, in addition to the symbols already defined, $\hat{u}_i$ denotes the (sample) **residual** term. Conceptually $\hat{u}_i$ is analogous to u_i and can be regarded as an *estimate* of u_i. It is introduced in the SRF for the same reasons as u_i was introduced in the PRF.

To sum up, then, we find our primary objective in regression analysis is to estimate the PRF

$$Y_i = \beta_1 + \beta_2 X_i + u_i \tag{2.4.2}$$

on the basis of the SRF

$$Y_i = \hat{\beta}_1 + \hat{\beta} x_i + \hat{u}_i \tag{2.6.2}$$

because more often than not our analysis is based upon a single sample from some population. But because of sampling fluctuations, our estimate of the PRF based on the SRF is at best an approximate one. This approximation is shown diagrammatically in Figure 2.5.

[13]As noted in the Introduction, a hat above a variable will signify an estimator of the relevant population value.

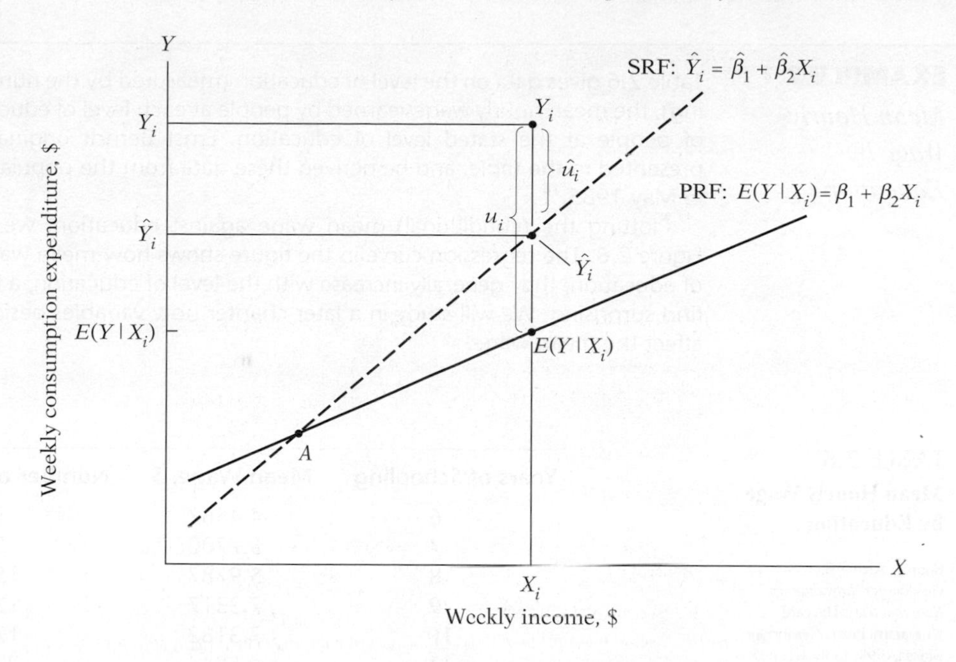

FIGURE 2.5
Sample and population regression lines.

For $X = X_i$, we have one (sample) observation, $Y = Y_i$. In terms of the SRF, the observed Y_i can be expressed as

$$Y_i = \hat{Y}_i + \hat{u}_i \tag{2.6.3}$$

and in terms of the PRF, it can be expressed as

$$Y_i = E(Y \mid X_i) + u_i \tag{2.6.4}$$

Now obviously in Figure 2.5 $\hat{Y}_i$ *overestimates* the true $E(Y \mid X_i)$ for the X_i shown therein. By the same token, for any X_i to the left of the point A, the SRF will *underestimate* the true PRF. But the reader can readily see that such over- and underestimation is inevitable because of sampling fluctuations.

The critical question now is: Granted that the SRF is but an approximation of the PRF, can we devise a rule or a method that will make this approximation as "close" as possible? In other words, how should the SRF be constructed so that $\hat{\beta}_1$ is as "close" as possible to the true β_1 and $\hat{\beta}_2$ is as "close" as possible to the true β_2 even though we will never know the true β_1 and β_2?

The answer to this question will occupy much of our attention in Chapter 3. We note here that we can develop procedures that tell us how to construct the SRF to mirror the PRF as faithfully as possible. It is fascinating to consider that this can be done even though we never actually determine the PRF itself.

2.7 Illustrative Examples

We conclude this chapter with two examples.

EXAMPLE 2.1

Mean Hourly Wage by Education

Table 2.6 gives data on the level of education (measured by the number of years of schooling), the mean hourly wages earned by people at each level of education, and the number of people at the stated level of education. Ernst Berndt originally obtained the data presented in the table, and he derived these data from the population survey conducted in May 1985.[14]

Plotting the (conditional) mean wage against education, we obtain the picture in Figure 2.6. The regression curve in the figure shows how mean wages vary with the level of education; they generally increase with the level of education, a finding one should not find surprising. We will study in a later chapter how variables besides education can also affect the mean wage.

TABLE 2.6
Mean Hourly Wage by Education

Years of Schooling	Mean Wage, $	Number of People
6	4.4567	3
7	5.7700	5
8	5.9787	15
9	7.3317	12
10	7.3182	17
11	6.5844	27
12	7.8182	218
13	7.8351	37
14	11.0223	56
15	10.6738	13
16	10.8361	70
17	13.6150	24
18	13.5310	31
	Total	528

Source: Arthur S. Goldberger, *Introductory Econometrics,* Harvard University Press, Cambridge, Mass., 1998, Table 1.1, p. 5 (adapted).

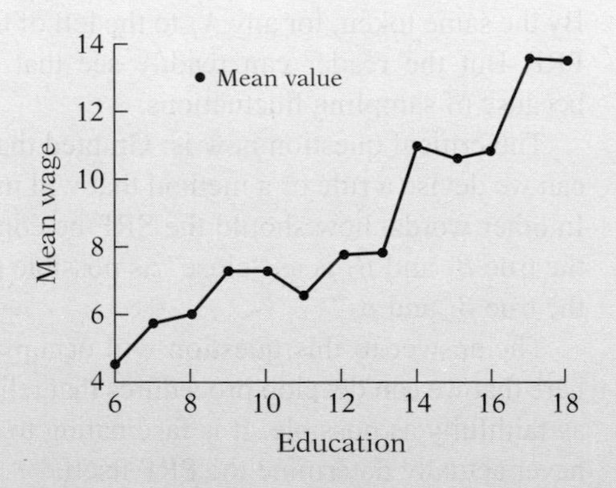

FIGURE 2.6
Relationship between mean wages and education.

[14]Ernst R. Berndt, *The Practice of Econometrics: Classic and Contemporary,* Addison Wesley, Reading, Mass., 1991. Incidentally, this is an excellent book that the reader may want to read to find out how econometricians go about doing research.

EXAMPLE 2.2
Mathematics SAT Scores by Family Income

Table 2.10 in Exercise 2.17 provides data on mean SAT (Scholastic Aptitude Test) scores on critical reading, mathematics, and writing for college-bound seniors based on 947,347 students taking the SAT examination in 2007. Plotting the mean mathematics scores on mean family income, we obtain the picture in Figure 2.7.

Note: Because of the open-ended income brackets for the first and last income categories shown in Table 2.10, the lowest average family income is assumed to be $5,000 and the highest average family income is assumed to be $150,000.

FIGURE 2.7
Relationship between mean mathematics SAT scores and mean family income.

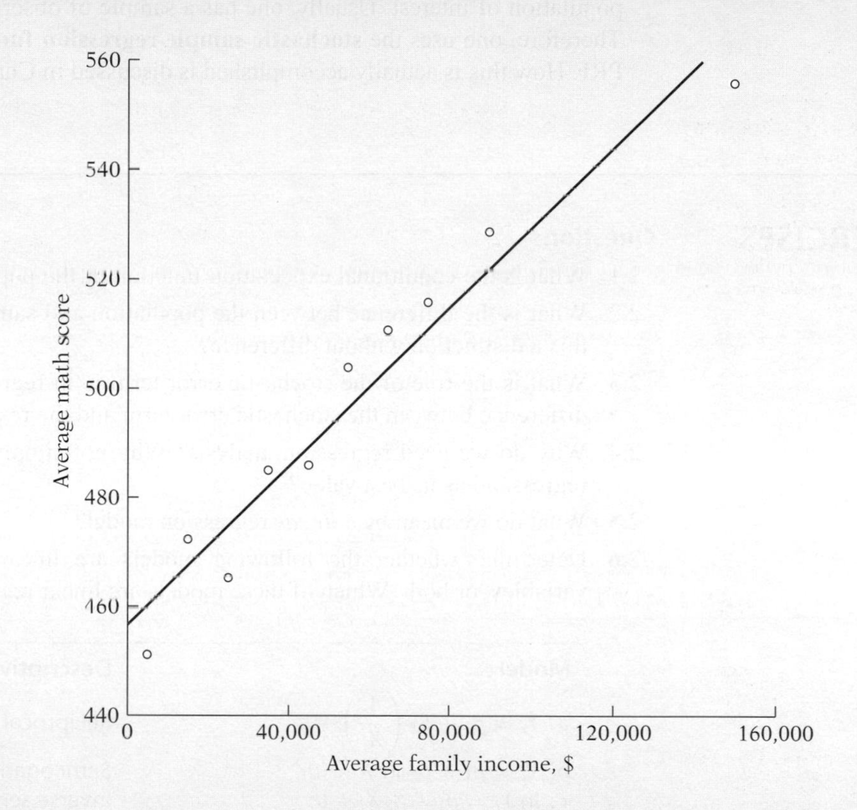

As Figure 2.7 shows, the average mathematics score increases as average family income increases. Since the number of students taking the SAT examination is quite large, it probably represents the entire population of seniors taking the examination. Therefore, the regression line sketched in Figure 2.7 probably represents the population regression line.

There may be several reasons for the observed positive relationship between the two variables. For example, one might argue that students with higher family income can better afford private tutoring for the SAT examinations. In addition, students with higher family income are more likely to have parents who are highly educated. It is also possible that students with higher mathematics scores come from better schools. The reader can provide other explanations for the observed positive relationship between the two variables.

Summary and Conclusions

1. The key concept underlying regression analysis is the concept of the **conditional expectation function (CEF),** or **population regression function (PRF).** Our objective in regression analysis is to find out how the average value of the dependent variable (or regressand) varies with the given value of the explanatory variable (or regressor).
2. This book largely deals with **linear PRFs,** that is, regressions that are linear in the parameters. They may or may not be linear in the regressand or the regressors.
3. For empirical purposes, it is the **stochastic PRF** that matters. The **stochastic disturbance term** u_i plays a critical role in estimating the PRF.
4. The PRF is an idealized concept, since in practice one rarely has access to the entire population of interest. Usually, one has a sample of observations from the population. Therefore, one uses the **stochastic sample regression function (SRF)** to estimate the PRF. How this is actually accomplished is discussed in Chapter 3.

EXERCISES

Questions

2.1. What is the conditional expectation function or the population regression function?

2.2. What is the difference between the population and sample regression functions? Is this a distinction without difference?

2.3. What is the role of the stochastic error term u_i in regression analysis? What is the difference between the stochastic error term and the residual, $\hat{u}_i$?

2.4. Why do we need regression analysis? Why not simply use the mean value of the regressand as its best value?

2.5. What do we mean by a *linear* regression model?

2.6. Determine whether the following models are linear in the parameters, or the variables, or both. Which of these models are linear regression models?

Model	Descriptive Title
a. $Y_i = \beta_1 + \beta_2 \left(\frac{1}{X_i}\right) + u_i$	Reciprocal
b. $Y_i = \beta_1 + \beta_2 \ln X_i + u_i$	Semilogarithmic
c. $\ln Y_i = \beta_1 + \beta_2 X_i + u_i$	Inverse semilogarithmic
d. $\ln Y_i = \ln \beta_1 + \beta_2 \ln X_i + u_i$	Logarithmic or double logarithmic
e. $\ln Y_i = \beta_1 - \beta_2 \left(\frac{1}{X_i}\right) + u_i$	Logarithmic reciprocal

Note: ln = natural log (i.e., log to the base *e*); u_i is the stochastic disturbance term. We will study these models in Chapter 6.

2.7. Are the following models linear regression models? Why or why not?

a. $Y_i = e^{\beta_1 + \beta_2 X_i + u_i}$

b. $Y_i = \dfrac{1}{1 + e^{\beta_1 + \beta_2 X_i + u_i}}$

c. $\ln Y_i = \beta_1 + \beta_2 \left(\dfrac{1}{X_i}\right) + u_i$

d. $Y_i = \beta_1 + (0.75 - \beta_1)e^{-\beta_2(X_i - 2)} + u_i$

e. $Y_i = \beta_1 + \beta_2^3 X_i + u_i$

2.8. What is meant by an *intrinsically linear* regression model? If β_2 in Exercise 2.7d were 0.8, would it be a linear or nonlinear regression model?

2.9. Consider the following nonstochastic models (i.e., models without the stochastic error term). Are they linear regression models? If not, is it possible, by suitable algebraic manipulations, to convert them into linear models?

a. $Y_i = \dfrac{1}{\beta_1 + \beta_2 X_i}$

b. $Y_i = \dfrac{X_i}{\beta_1 + \beta_2 X_i}$

c. $Y_i = \dfrac{1}{1 + \exp(-\beta_1 - \beta_2 X_i)}$

2.10. You are given the scattergram in Figure 2.8 along with the regression line. What general conclusion do you draw from this diagram? Is the regression line sketched in the diagram a population regression line or the sample regression line?

2.11. From the scattergram given in Figure 2.9, what general conclusions do you draw? What is the economic theory that underlies this scattergram? (*Hint:* Look up any international economics textbook and read up on the Heckscher–Ohlin model of trade.)

2.12. What does the scattergram in Figure 2.10 reveal? On the basis of this diagram, would you argue that minimum wage laws are good for economic well-being?

2.13. Is the regression line shown in Figure I.3 of the Introduction the PRF or the SRF? Why? How would you interpret the scatterpoints around the regression line? Besides GDP, what other factors, or variables, might determine personal consumption expenditure?

FIGURE 2.8
Growth rates of real manufacturing wages and exports. Data are for 50 developing countries during 1970–90.

Source: The World Bank, *World Development Report 1995,* p. 55. The original source is UNIDO data, World Bank data.

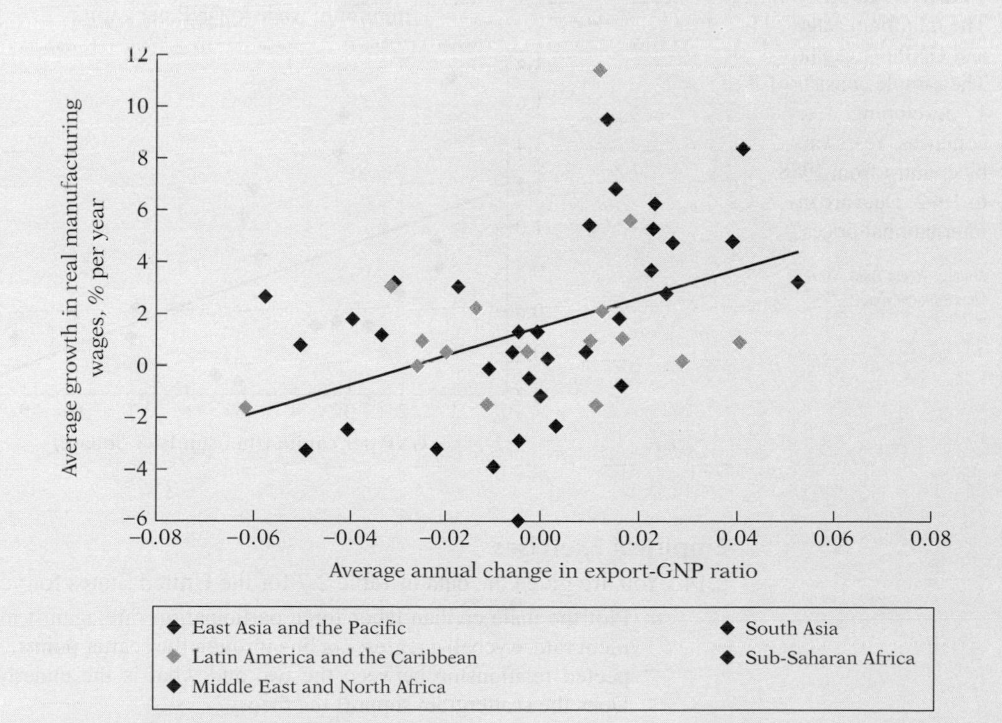

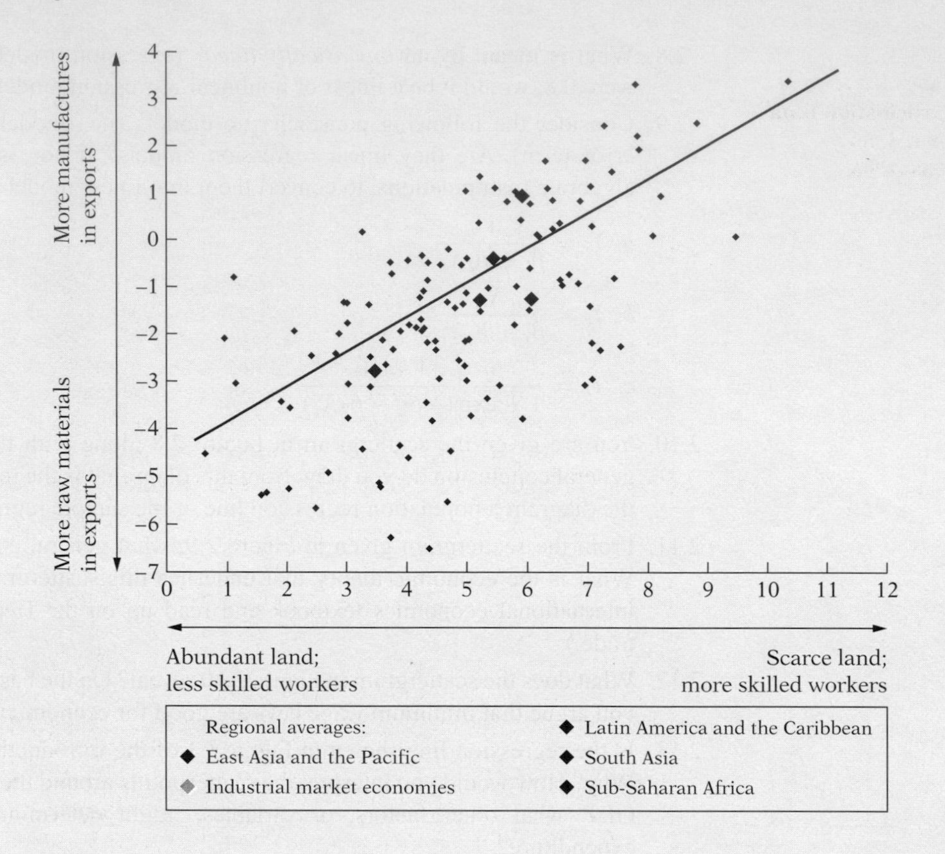

FIGURE 2.9 Skill intensity of exports and human capital endowment. Data are for 126 industrial and developing countries in 1985. Values along the horizontal axis are logarithms of the ratio of the country's average educational attainment to its land area; vertical axis values are logarithms of the ratio of manufactured to primary-products exports.

Source: World Bank, *World Development Report 1995*, p. 59. Original sources: Export data from United Nations Statistical Office COMTRADE database; education data from UNDP 1990; land data from the World Bank.

FIGURE 2.10 The minimum wage and GNP per capita. The sample consists of 17 developing countries. Years vary by country from 1988 to 1992. Data are in international prices.

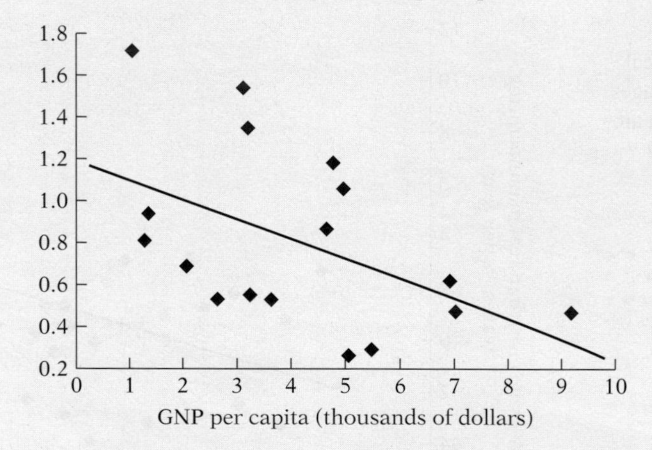

Source: World Bank, *World Development Report 1995*, p. 75.

Empirical Exercises

2.14. You are given the data in Table 2.7 for the United States for years 1980–2006.

a. Plot the male civilian labor force participation rate against male civilian unemployment rate. Eyeball a regression line through the scatter points. A priori, what is the expected relationship between the two and what is the underlying economic theory? Does the scattergram support the theory?

TABLE 2.7
Labor Force Participation Data for U.S. for 1980–2006

Source: *Economic Report of the President, 2007.*

Year	CLFPRM[1]	CLFPRF[2]	UNRM[3]	UNRF[4]	AHE82[5]	AHE[6]
1980	77.40000	51.50000	6.900000	7.400000	7.990000	6.840000
1981	77.00000	52.10000	7.400000	7.900000	7.880000	7.430000
1982	76.60000	52.60000	9.900000	9.400000	7.860000	7.860000
1983	76.40000	52.90000	9.900000	9.200000	7.950000	8.190000
1984	76.40000	53.60000	7.400000	7.600000	7.950000	8.480000
1985	76.30000	54.50000	7.000000	7.400000	7.910000	8.730000
1986	76.30000	55.30000	6.900000	7.100000	7.960000	8.920000
1987	76.20000	56.00000	6.200000	6.200000	7.860000	9.130000
1988	76.20000	56.60000	5.500000	5.600000	7.810000	9.430000
1989	76.40000	57.40000	5.200000	5.400000	7.750000	9.800000
1990	76.40000	57.50000	5.700000	5.500000	7.660000	10.190000
1991	75.80000	57.40000	7.200000	6.400000	7.580000	10.500000
1992	75.80000	57.80000	7.900000	7.000000	7.550000	10.760000
1993	75.40000	57.90000	7.200000	6.600000	7.520000	11.030000
1994	75.10000	58.80000	6.200000	6.000000	7.530000	11.320000
1995	75.00000	58.90000	5.600000	5.600000	7.530000	11.640000
1996	74.90000	59.30000	5.400000	5.400000	7.570000	12.030000
1997	75.00000	59.80000	4.900000	5.000000	7.680000	12.490000
1998	74.90000	59.80000	4.400000	4.600000	7.890000	13.000000
1999	74.70000	60.00000	4.100000	4.300000	8.000000	13.470000
2000	74.80000	59.90000	3.900000	4.100000	8.030000	14.000000
2001	74.40000	59.80000	4.800000	4.700000	8.110000	14.530000
2002	74.10000	59.60000	5.900000	5.600000	8.240000	14.950000
2003	73.50000	59.50000	6.300000	5.700000	8.270000	15.350000
2004	73.30000	59.20000	5.600000	5.400000	8.230000	15.670000
2005	73.30000	59.30000	5.100000	5.100000	8.170000	16.110000
2006	73.50000	59.40000	4.600000	4.600000	8.230000	16.730000

Table citations below refer to the source document.
[1]CLFPRM, Civilian labor force participation rate, male (%), Table B-39, p. 277.
[2]CLFPRF, Civilian labor force participation rate, female (%), Table B-39, p. 277.
[3]UNRM, Civilian unemployment rate, male (%) Table B-42, p. 280.
[4]UNRF, Civilian unemployment rate, female (%) Table B-42, p. 280.
[5]AHE82, Average hourly earnings (1982 dollars), Table B-47, p. 286.
[6]AHE, Average hourly earnings (current dollars), Table B-47, p. 286.

b. Repeat (a) for females.

c. Now plot both the male and female labor participation rates against average hourly earnings (in 1982 dollars). (You may use separate diagrams.) Now what do you find? And how would you rationalize your finding?

d. Can you plot the labor force participation rate against the unemployment rate and the average hourly earnings simultaneously? If not, how would you verbalize the relationship among the three variables?

2.15. Table 2.8 gives data on expenditure on food and total expenditure, measured in rupees, for a sample of 55 rural households from India. (In early 2000, a U.S. dollar was about 40 Indian rupees.)

a. Plot the data, using the vertical axis for expenditure on food and the horizontal axis for total expenditure, and sketch a regression line through the scatterpoints.

b. What broad conclusions can you draw from this example?

TABLE 2.8 Food and Total Expenditure (Rupees)

Observation	Food Expenditure	Total Expenditure	Observation	Food Expenditure	Total Expenditure
1	217.0000	382.0000	29	390.0000	655.0000
2	196.0000	388.0000	30	385.0000	662.0000
3	303.0000	391.0000	31	470.0000	663.0000
4	270.0000	415.0000	32	322.0000	677.0000
5	325.0000	456.0000	33	540.0000	680.0000
6	260.0000	460.0000	34	433.0000	690.0000
7	300.0000	472.0000	35	295.0000	695.0000
8	325.0000	478.0000	36	340.0000	695.0000
9	336.0000	494.0000	37	500.0000	695.0000
10	345.0000	516.0000	38	450.0000	720.0000
11	325.0000	525.0000	39	415.0000	721.0000
12	362.0000	554.0000	40	540.0000	730.0000
13	315.0000	575.0000	41	360.0000	731.0000
14	355.0000	579.0000	42	450.0000	733.0000
15	325.0000	585.0000	43	395.0000	745.0000
16	370.0000	586.0000	44	430.0000	751.0000
17	390.0000	590.0000	45	332.0000	752.0000
18	420.0000	608.0000	46	397.0000	752.0000
19	410.0000	610.0000	47	446.0000	769.0000
20	383.0000	616.0000	48	480.0000	773.0000
21	315.0000	618.0000	49	352.0000	773.0000
22	267.0000	623.0000	50	410.0000	775.0000
23	420.0000	627.0000	51	380.0000	785.0000
24	300.0000	630.0000	52	610.0000	788.0000
25	410.0000	635.0000	53	530.0000	790.0000
26	220.0000	640.0000	54	360.0000	795.0000
27	403.0000	648.0000	55	305.0000	801.0000
28	350.0000	650.0000			

Source: Chandan Mukherjee, Howard White, and Marc Wuyts, *Econometrics and Data Analysis for Developing Countries,* Routledge, New York, 1998, p. 457.

c. A priori, would you expect expenditure on food to increase linearly as total expenditure increases regardless of the level of total expenditure? Why or why not? You can use total expenditure as a proxy for total income.

2.16. Table 2.9 gives data on mean Scholastic Aptitude Test (SAT) scores for college-bound seniors for 1972–2007. These data represent the critical reading and mathematics test scores for both male and female students. The writing category was introduced in 2006. Therefore, these data are not included.

a. Use the horizontal axis for years and the vertical axis for SAT scores to plot the critical reading and math scores for males and females separately.

b. What general conclusions do you draw from these graphs?

c. Knowing the critical reading scores of males and females, how would you go about predicting their math scores?

d. Plot the female math scores against the male math scores. What do you observe?

TABLE 2.9
Total Group Mean SAT Reasoning Test Scores: College-Bound Seniors, 1972–2007

Source: College Board, 2007.

	Critical Reading			Mathematics		
Year	Male	Female	Total	Male	Female	Total
1972	531	529	530	527	489	509
1973	523	521	523	525	489	506
1974	524	520	521	524	488	505
1975	515	509	512	518	479	498
1976	511	508	509	520	475	497
1977	509	505	507	520	474	496
1978	511	503	507	517	474	494
1979	509	501	505	516	473	493
1980	506	498	502	515	473	492
1981	508	496	502	516	473	492
1982	509	499	504	516	473	493
1983	508	498	503	516	474	494
1984	511	498	504	518	478	497
1985	514	503	509	522	480	500
1986	515	504	509	523	479	500
1987	512	502	507	523	481	501
1988	512	499	505	521	483	501
1989	510	498	504	523	482	502
1990	505	496	500	521	483	501
1991	503	495	499	520	482	500
1992	504	496	500	521	484	501
1993	504	497	500	524	484	503
1994	501	497	499	523	487	504
1995	505	502	504	525	490	506
1996	507	503	505	527	492	508
1997	507	503	505	530	494	511
1998	509	502	505	531	496	512
1999	509	502	505	531	495	511
2000	507	504	505	533	498	514
2001	509	502	506	533	498	514
2002	507	502	504	534	500	516
2003	512	503	507	537	503	519
2004	512	504	508	537	501	518
2005	513	505	508	538	504	520
2006	505	502	503	536	502	518
2007	504	502	502	533	499	515

Note: For 1972–1986 a formula was applied to the original mean and standard deviation to convert the mean to the recentered scale. For 1987–1995 individual student scores were converted to the recentered scale and then the mean was recomputed. From 1996–1999, nearly all students received scores on the recentered scale. Any score on the original scale was converted to the recentered scale prior to computing the mean. From 2000–2007, all scores are reported on the recentered scale.

2.17. Table 2.10 presents data on mean SAT reasoning test scores classified by income for three kinds of tests: critical reading, mathematics, and writing. In Example 2.2, we presented Figure 2.7, which plotted mean math scores on mean family income.

a. Refer to Figure 2.7 and prepare a similar graph relating average critical reading scores to average family income. Compare your results with those shown in Figure 2.7.

TABLE 2.10
SAT Reasoning Test Classified by Family Income

Source: College Board, 2007 College-Bound Seniors, Table 11.

Family Income ($)	Number of Test Takers	Critical Reading		Mathematics		Writing	
		Mean	SD	Mean	SD	Mean	SD
<10,000	40610	427	107	451	122	423	104
10000–20000	72745	453	106	472	113	446	102
20000–30000	61244	454	102	465	107	444	97
30000–40000	83685	476	103	485	106	466	98
40000–50000	75836	489	103	486	105	477	99
50000–60000	80060	497	102	504	104	486	98
60000–70000	75763	504	102	511	103	493	98
70000–80000	81627	508	101	516	103	498	98
80000–100000	130752	520	102	529	104	510	100
>100000	245025	544	105	556	107	537	103

b. Repeat (a), relating average writing scores to average family income and compare your results with the other two graphs.

c. Looking at the three graphs, what general conclusion can you draw?

Chapter 3

Two-Variable Regression Model: The Problem of Estimation

As noted in Chapter 2, our first task is to estimate the population regression function (PRF) on the basis of the sample regression function (SRF) as accurately as possible. In **Appendix A** we have discussed two generally used methods of estimation: (1) **ordinary least squares (OLS)** and (2) **maximum likelihood (ML).** By and large, it is the method of OLS that is used extensively in regression analysis primarily because it is intuitively appealing and mathematically much simpler than the method of maximum likelihood. Besides, as we will show later, in the linear regression context the two methods generally give similar results.

3.1 The Method of Ordinary Least Squares

The method of ordinary least squares is attributed to Carl Friedrich Gauss, a German mathematician. Under certain assumptions (discussed in Section 3.2), the method of least squares has some very attractive statistical properties that have made it one of the most powerful and popular methods of regression analysis. To understand this method, we first explain the least-squares principle.

Recall the two-variable PRF:

$$Y_i = \beta_1 + \beta_2 X_i + u_i \tag{2.4.2}$$

However, as we noted in Chapter 2, the PRF is not directly observable. We estimate it from the SRF:

$$Y_i = \hat{\beta}_1 + \hat{\beta}_2 X_i + \hat{u}_i \tag{2.6.2}$$

$$= \hat{Y}_i + \hat{u}_i \tag{2.6.3}$$

where $\hat{Y}_i$ is the estimated (conditional mean) value of Y_i.

But how is the SRF itself determined? To see this, let us proceed as follows. First, express Equation 2.6.3 as

$$\begin{aligned} \hat{u}_i &= Y_i - \hat{Y}_i \\ &= Y_i - \hat{\beta}_1 - \hat{\beta}_2 X_i \end{aligned} \tag{3.1.1}$$

FIGURE 3.1 Least-squares criterion.

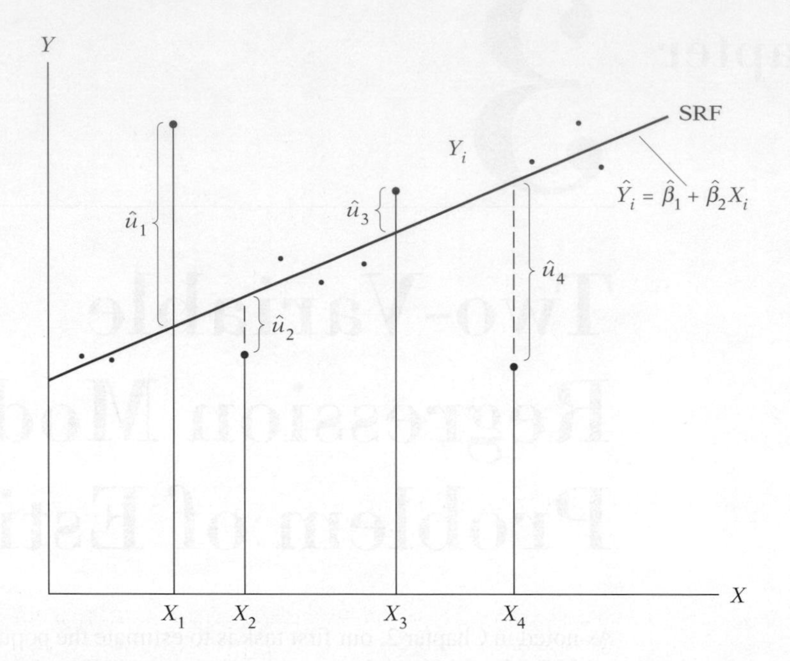

which shows that the $\hat{u}_i$ (the residuals) are simply the differences between the actual and estimated Y values.

Now given n pairs of observations on Y and X, we would like to determine the SRF in such a manner that it is as close as possible to the actual Y. To this end, we may adopt the following criterion: Choose the SRF in such a way that the sum of the residuals $\sum \hat{u}_i = \sum(Y_i - \hat{Y}_i)$ is as small as possible. Although intuitively appealing, this is not a very good criterion, as can be seen in the hypothetical scattergram shown in Figure 3.1.

If we adopt the criterion of minimizing $\sum \hat{u}_i$, Figure 3.1 shows that the residuals $\hat{u}_2$ and $\hat{u}_3$ as well as the residuals $\hat{u}_1$ and $\hat{u}_4$ receive the same weight in the sum $(\hat{u}_1 + \hat{u}_2 + \hat{u}_3 + \hat{u}_4)$, although the first two residuals are much closer to the SRF than the latter two. In other words, all the residuals receive equal importance no matter how close or how widely scattered the individual observations are from the SRF. A consequence of this is that it is quite possible that the algebraic sum of the $\hat{u}_i$ is small (even zero) although the $\hat{u}_i$ are widely scattered about the SRF. To see this, let $\hat{u}_1$, $\hat{u}_2$, $\hat{u}_3$, and $\hat{u}_4$ in Figure 3.1 assume the values of 10, −2, +2, and −10, respectively. The algebraic sum of these residuals is zero although $\hat{u}_1$ and $\hat{u}_4$ are scattered more widely around the SRF than $\hat{u}_2$ and $\hat{u}_3$. We can avoid this problem if we adopt the *least-squares criterion,* which states that the SRF can be fixed in such a way that

$$\begin{aligned}\sum \hat{u}_i^2 &= \sum(Y_i - \hat{Y}_i)^2 \\ &= \sum(Y_i - \hat{\beta}_1 - \hat{\beta}_2 X_i)^2\end{aligned} \tag{3.1.2}$$

is as small as possible, where $\hat{u}_i^2$ are the squared residuals. By squaring $\hat{u}_i$, this method gives more weight to residuals such as $\hat{u}_1$ and $\hat{u}_4$ in Figure 3.1 than the residuals $\hat{u}_2$ and $\hat{u}_3$. As noted previously, under the minimum $\sum \hat{u}_i$ criterion, the sum can be small even though the $\hat{u}_i$ are widely spread about the SRF. But this is not possible under the least-squares procedure, for the larger the $\hat{u}_i$ (in absolute value), the larger the $\sum \hat{u}_i^2$. A further justification for the least-squares method lies in the fact that the estimators obtained by it have some very desirable statistical properties, as we shall see shortly.

TABLE 3.1 Experimental Determination of the SRF

Y_i (1)	X_t (2)	$\hat{Y}_{1i}$ (3)	$\hat{u}_{1i}$ (4)	$\hat{u}_{1i}^2$ (5)	$\hat{Y}_{2i}$ (6)	$\hat{u}_{2i}$ (7)	$\hat{u}_{2i}^2$ (8)
4	1	2.929	1.071	1.147	4	0	0
5	4	7.000	−2.000	4.000	7	−2	4
7	5	8.357	−1.357	1.841	8	−1	1
12	6	9.714	2.286	5.226	9	3	9
Sum: 28	16		0.0	12.214		0	14

Notes: $\hat{Y}_{1i} = 1.572 + 1.357X_i$ (i.e., $\hat{\beta}_1 = 1.572$ and $\hat{\beta}_2 = 1.357$)
$\hat{Y}_{2i} = 3.0 + 1.0X_i$ (i.e., $\hat{\beta}_1 = 3$ and $\hat{\beta}_2 = 1.0$)
$\hat{u}_{1i} = (Y_i - \hat{Y}_{1i})$
$\hat{u}_{2i} = (Y_i - \hat{Y}_{2i})$

It is obvious from Equation 3.1.2 that

$$\sum \hat{u}_i^2 = f(\hat{\beta}_1, \hat{\beta}_2) \tag{3.1.3}$$

that is, the sum of the squared residuals is some function of the estimators $\hat{\beta}_1$ and $\hat{\beta}_2$. For any given set of data, choosing different values for $\hat{\beta}_1$ and $\hat{\beta}_2$ will give different $\hat{u}$'s and hence different values of $\sum \hat{u}_i^2$. To see this clearly, consider the hypothetical data on Y and X given in the first two columns of Table 3.1. Let us now conduct two experiments. In experiment 1, let $\hat{\beta}_1 = 1.572$ and $\hat{\beta}_2 = 1.357$ (let us not worry right now about how we got these values; say, it is just a guess).[1] Using these $\hat{\beta}$ values and the X values given in column (2) of Table 3.1, we can easily compute the estimated Y_i given in column (3) of the table as $\hat{Y}_{1i}$ (the subscript 1 is to denote the first experiment). Now let us conduct another experiment, but this time using the values of $\hat{\beta}_1 = 3$ and $\hat{\beta}_2 = 1$. The estimated values of Y_i from this experiment are given as $\hat{Y}_{2i}$ in column (6) of Table 3.1. Since the $\hat{\beta}$ values in the two experiments are different, we get different values for the estimated residuals, as shown in the table; $\hat{u}_{1i}$ are the residuals from the first experiment and $\hat{u}_{2i}$ from the second experiment. The squares of these residuals are given in columns (5) and (8). Obviously, as expected from Equation 3.1.3, these residual sums of squares are different since they are based on different sets of $\hat{\beta}$ values.

Now which sets of $\hat{\beta}$ values should we choose? Since the $\hat{\beta}$ values of the first experiment give us a lower $\sum \hat{u}_i^2$ (= 12.214) than that obtained from the $\hat{\beta}$ values of the second experiment (= 14), we might say that the $\hat{\beta}$'s of the first experiment are the "best" values. But how do we know? For, if we had infinite time and infinite patience, we could have conducted many more such experiments, choosing different sets of $\hat{\beta}$'s each time and comparing the resulting $\sum \hat{u}_i^2$ and then choosing that set of $\hat{\beta}$ values that gives us the least possible value of $\sum \hat{u}_i^2$ assuming of course that we have considered all the conceivable values of β_1 and β_2. But since time, and certainly patience, are generally in short supply, we need to consider some shortcuts to this trial-and-error process. Fortunately, the method of least squares provides us such a shortcut. The principle or the method of least squares chooses $\hat{\beta}_1$ and $\hat{\beta}_2$ in such a manner that, for a given sample or set of data, $\sum \hat{u}_i^2$ is as small as possible. In other words, for a given sample, the method of least squares provides us with unique estimates of β_1 and β_2 that give the smallest possible value of $\sum \hat{u}_i^2$. How is this accomplished? This is a

[1] For the curious, these values are obtained by the method of least squares, discussed shortly. See Eqs. (3.1.6) and (3.1.7).

straightforward exercise in differential calculus. As shown in Appendix 3A, Section 3A.1, the process of differentiation yields the following equations for estimating β_1 and β_2:

$$\sum Y_i = n\hat{\beta}_1 + \hat{\beta}_2 \sum X_i \tag{3.1.4}$$

$$\sum Y_i X_i = \hat{\beta}_1 \sum X_i + \hat{\beta}_2 \sum X_i^2 \tag{3.1.5}$$

where n is the sample size. These simultaneous equations are known as the **normal equations.**

Solving the normal equations simultaneously, we obtain

$$\begin{aligned}\hat{\beta}_2 &= \frac{n\sum X_i Y_i - \sum X_i \sum Y_i}{n\sum X_i^2 - \left(\sum X_i\right)^2} \\ &= \frac{\sum(X_i - \bar{X})(Y_i - \bar{Y})}{\sum(X_i - \bar{X})^2} \\ &= \frac{\sum x_i y_i}{\sum x_i^2}\end{aligned} \tag{3.1.6}$$

where $\bar{X}$ and $\bar{Y}$ are the sample means of X and Y and where we define $x_i = (X_i - \bar{X})$ and $y_i = (Y_i - \bar{Y})$. *Henceforth, we adopt the convention of letting the lowercase letters denote deviations from mean values.*

$$\begin{aligned}\hat{\beta}_1 &= \frac{\sum X_i^2 \sum Y_i - \sum X_i \sum X_i Y_i}{n\sum X_i^2 - \left(\sum X_i\right)^2} \\ &= \bar{Y} - \hat{\beta}_2 \bar{X}\end{aligned} \tag{3.1.7}$$

The last step in Equation 3.1.7 can be obtained directly from Eq. (3.1.4) by simple algebraic manipulations.

Incidentally, note that, by making use of simple algebraic identities, formula (3.1.6) for estimating β_2 can be alternatively expressed as

$$\begin{aligned}\hat{\beta}_2 &= \frac{\sum x_i y_i}{\sum x_i^2} \\ &= \frac{\sum x_i Y_i}{\sum X_i^2 - n\bar{X}^2} \\ &= \frac{\sum X_i y_i}{\sum X_i^2 - n\bar{X}^2}\end{aligned} \tag{3.1.8}$$[2]

[2] *Note 1:* $\sum x_i^2 = \sum(X_i - \bar{X})^2 = \sum X_i^2 - 2\sum X_i\bar{X} + \sum \bar{X}^2 = \sum X_i^2 - 2\bar{X}\sum X_i + \sum \bar{X}^2$, since $\bar{X}$ is a constant. Further noting that $\sum X_i = n\bar{X}$ and $\sum \bar{X}^2 = n\bar{X}^2$ since $\bar{X}$ is a constant, we finally get $\sum x_i^2 = \sum X_i^2 - n\bar{X}^2$.

Note 2: $\sum x_i y_i = \sum x_i(Y_i - \bar{Y}) = \sum x_i Y_i - \bar{Y}\sum x_i = \sum x_i Y_i - \bar{Y}\sum(X_i - \bar{X}) = \sum x_i Y_i$, since $\bar{Y}$ is a constant and since the sum of deviations of a variable from its mean value [e.g., $\sum(X_i - \bar{X})$] is always zero. Likewise, $\sum y_i = \sum(Y_i - \bar{Y}) = 0$.

The estimators obtained previously are known as the **least-squares estimators,** for they are derived from the least-squares principle. Note the following **numerical properties** of estimators obtained by the method of OLS: "Numerical properties are those that hold as a consequence of the use of ordinary least squares, regardless of how the data were generated."[3] Shortly, we will also consider the **statistical properties** of OLS estimators, that is, properties "that hold only under certain assumptions about the way the data were generated."[4] (See the classical linear regression model in Section 3.2.)

I. The OLS estimators are expressed solely in terms of the observable (i.e., sample) quantities (i.e., X and Y). Therefore, they can be easily computed.

II. They are **point estimators;** that is, given the sample, each estimator will provide only a single (point) value of the relevant population parameter. (In Chapter 5 we will consider the so-called **interval estimators,** which provide a range of possible values for the unknown population parameters.)

III. Once the OLS estimates are obtained from the sample data, the sample regression line (Figure 3.1) can be easily obtained. The regression line thus obtained has the following properties:

1. It passes through the sample means of Y and X. This fact is obvious from Eq. (3.1.7), for the latter can be written as $\bar{Y} = \hat{\beta}_1 + \hat{\beta}_2\bar{X}$, which is shown diagrammatically in Figure 3.2.

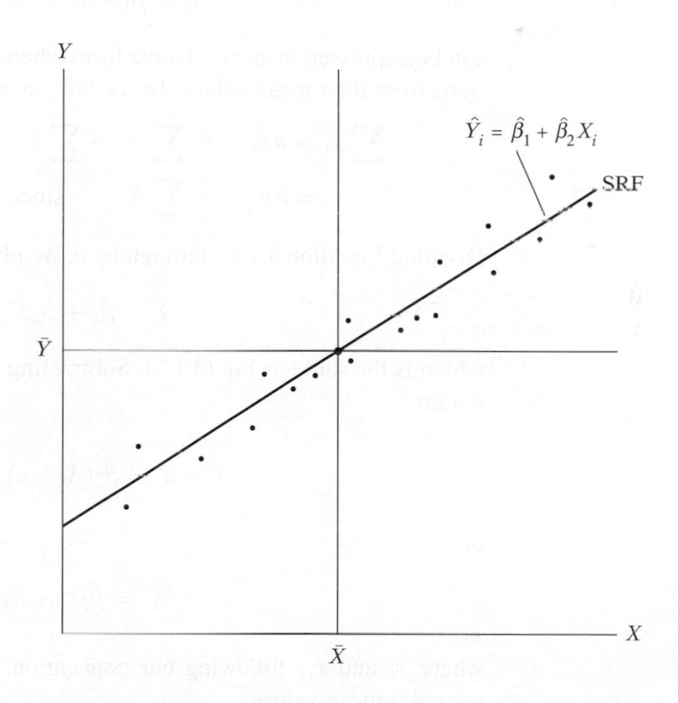

FIGURE 3.2
Diagram showing that the sample regression line passes through the sample mean values of Y and X.

[3] Russell Davidson and James G. MacKinnon, *Estimation and Inference in Econometrics,* Oxford University Press, New York, 1993, p. 3.

[4] *Ibid.*

2. The mean value of the estimated $Y = \hat{Y}_i$ is equal to the mean value of the actual Y for

$$\begin{aligned}\hat{Y}_i &= \hat{\beta}_1 + \hat{\beta}_2 X_i \\ &= (\bar{Y} - \hat{\beta}_2 \bar{X}) + \hat{\beta}_2 X_i \\ &= \bar{Y} + \hat{\beta}_2 (X_i - \bar{X})\end{aligned} \tag{3.1.9}$$

Summing both sides of this last equality over the sample values and dividing through by the sample size n gives

$$\bar{\hat{Y}} = \bar{Y} \tag{3.1.10}$$[5]

where use is made of the fact that $\sum (X_i - \bar{X}) = 0$. (Why?)

3. The mean value of the residuals $\hat{u}_i$ is zero. From Appendix 3A, Section 3A.1, the first equation is

$$-2 \sum (Y_i - \hat{\beta}_1 - \hat{\beta}_2 X_i) = 0$$

But since $\hat{u}_i = Y_i - \hat{\beta}_1 - \hat{\beta}_2 X_i$, the preceding equation reduces to $-2 \sum \hat{u}_i = 0$, whence $\bar{\hat{u}} = 0$.[6]

As a result of the preceding property, the sample regression

$$Y_i = \hat{\beta}_1 + \hat{\beta}_2 X_i + \hat{u}_i \tag{2.6.2}$$

can be expressed in an alternative form where both Y and X are expressed as deviations from their mean values. To see this, sum (2.6.2) on both sides to give

$$\begin{aligned}\sum Y_i &= n\hat{\beta}_1 + \hat{\beta}_2 \sum X_i + \sum \hat{u}_i \\ &= n\hat{\beta}_1 + \hat{\beta}_2 \sum X_i \qquad \text{since } \sum \hat{u}_i = 0\end{aligned} \tag{3.1.11}$$

Dividing Equation 3.1.11 through by n, we obtain

$$\bar{Y} = \hat{\beta}_1 + \hat{\beta}_2 \bar{X} \tag{3.1.12}$$

which is the same as Eq. (3.1.7). Subtracting Equation 3.1.12 from Eq. (2.6.2), we obtain

$$Y_i - \bar{Y} = \hat{\beta}_2 (X_i - \bar{X}) + \hat{u}_i$$

or

$$y_i = \hat{\beta}_2 x_i + \hat{u}_i \tag{3.1.13}$$

where y_i and x_i, following our convention, are deviations from their respective (sample) mean values.

[5]Note that this result is true only when the regression model has the intercept term β_1 in it. As **Appendix 6A, Sec. 6A.1** shows, this result need not hold when β_1 is absent from the model.

[6]This result also requires that the intercept term β_1 be present in the model (see **Appendix 6A, Sec. 6A.1**).

Equation 3.1.13 is known as the **deviation form.** Notice that the intercept term $\hat{\beta}_1$ is no longer present in it. But the intercept term can always be estimated by Eq. (3.1.7), that is, from the fact that the sample regression line passes through the sample means of Y and X. An advantage of the deviation form is that it often simplifies computing formulas.

In passing, note that in the deviation form, the SRF can be written as

$$\hat{y}_i = \hat{\beta}_2 x_i \tag{3.1.14}$$

whereas in the original units of measurement it was $\hat{Y}_i = \hat{\beta}_1 + \hat{\beta}_2 X_i$, as shown in Eq. (2.6.1).

4. The residuals $\hat{u}_i$ are uncorrelated with the predicted Y_i. This statement can be verified as follows: using the deviation form, we can write

$$\begin{aligned}
\sum \hat{y}_i \hat{u}_i &= \hat{\beta}_2 \sum x_i \hat{u}_i \\
&= \hat{\beta}_2 \sum x_i (y_i - \hat{\beta}_2 x_i) \\
&= \hat{\beta}_2 \sum x_i y_i - \hat{\beta}_2^2 \sum x_i^2 \\
&= \hat{\beta}_2^2 \sum x_i^2 - \hat{\beta}_2^2 \sum x_i^2 \\
&= 0
\end{aligned} \tag{3.1.15}$$

where use is made of the fact that $\hat{\beta}_2 = \sum x_i y_i / \sum x_i^2$.

5. The residuals $\hat{u}_i$ are uncorrelated with X_i; that is, $\sum \hat{u}_i X_i = 0$. This fact follows from Eq. (2) in Appendix 3A, Section 3A.1.

3.2 The Classical Linear Regression Model: The Assumptions Underlying the Method of Least Squares

If our objective is to estimate β_1 and β_2 only, the method of OLS discussed in the preceding section will suffice. But recall from Chapter 2 that in regression analysis our objective is not only to obtain $\hat{\beta}_1$ and $\hat{\beta}_2$ but also to draw inferences about the true β_1 and β_2. For example, we would like to know how close $\hat{\beta}_1$ and $\hat{\beta}_2$ are to their counterparts in the population or how close $\hat{Y}_i$ is to the true $E(Y \mid X_i)$. To that end, we must not only specify the functional form of the model, as in Eq. (2.4.2), but also make certain assumptions about the manner in which Y_i are generated. To see why this requirement is needed, look at the PRF: $Y_i = \beta_1 + \beta_2 X_i + u_i$. It shows that Y_i depends on both X_i and u_i. Therefore, unless we are specific about how X_i and u_i are created or generated, there is no way we can make any statistical inference about the Y_i and also, as we shall see, about β_1 and β_2. Thus, the assumptions made about the X_i variable(s) and the error term are extremely critical to the valid interpretation of the regression estimates.

The **Gaussian, standard,** or **classical linear regression model (CLRM),** which is the cornerstone of most econometric theory, makes 7 assumptions.[7] We first discuss these assumptions in the context of the two-variable regression model; and in Chapter 7 we extend them to multiple regression models, that is, models in which there is more than one regressor.

[7]It is classical in the sense that it was developed first by Gauss in 1821 and since then has served as a norm or a standard against which may be compared the regression models that do not satisfy the Gaussian assumptions.

ASSUMPTION 1 **Linear Regression Model:** The regression model is **linear in the parameters,** though it may or may not be linear in the variables. That is the regression model as shown in Eq. (2.4.2):

$$Y_i = \beta_1 + \beta_2 X_i + u_i \tag{2.4.2}$$

As will be discussed in Chapter 7, this model can be extended to include more explanatory variables.

We have already discussed model (2.4.2) in Chapter 2. Since linear-in-parameter regression models are the starting point of the CLRM, we will maintain this assumption for most of this book.[8] Keep in mind that the regressand Y and the regressor X may be nonlinear, as discussed in Chapter 2.

ASSUMPTION 2 **Fixed X Values or X Values Independent of the Error Term:** Values taken by the regressor X may be considered fixed in repeated samples (the case of fixed regressor) or they may be sampled along with the dependent variable Y (the case of stochastic regressor). In the latter case, it is assumed that the X variable(s) and the error term are independent, that is, cov $(X_i, u_i) = 0$.

This can be explained in terms of our example given in Table 2.1 (page 35). Consider the various Y populations corresponding to the levels of income shown in the table. Keeping the value of income X fixed, say, at level \$80, we draw at random a family and observe its weekly family consumption Y as, say, \$60. Still keeping X at \$80, we draw at random another family and observe its Y value at \$75. In each of these drawings (i.e., repeated sampling), the value of X is fixed at \$80. We can repeat this process for all the X values shown in Table 2.1. As a matter of fact, the sample data shown in Tables 2.4 and 2.5 were drawn in this fashion.

Why do we assume that the X values are nonstochastic? Given that, in most social sciences, data usually are collected randomly on both the Y and X variables, it seems natural to assume the opposite—that the X variable, like the Y variable, is also random or stochastic. But initially we assume that the X variable(s) is nonstochastic for the following reasons:

First, this is done initially to simplify the analysis and to introduce the reader to the complexities of regression analysis gradually. *Second,* in experimental situations it may not be unrealistic to assume that the X values are fixed. For example, a farmer may divide his land into several parcels and apply different amounts of fertilizer to these parcels to see its effect on crop yield. Likewise, a department store may decide to offer different rates of discount on a product to see its effect on consumers. Sometimes we may want to fix the X values for a specific purpose. Suppose we are trying to find out the average weekly earnings of workers (Y) with various levels of education (X), as in the case of the data given in Table 2.6. In this case, the X variable can be considered fixed or nonrandom. *Third,* as we show in Chapter 13, even if the X variables are stochastic, the statistical results of linear regression based

[8]However, a brief discussion of nonlinear-in-parameter regression models is given in Chapter 14 for the benefit of more advanced students.

on the case of fixed regressors are also valid when the X's are random, provided that some conditions are met. One condition is that regressor X and the error term u_i are independent. As James Davidson notes, ". . . this model [i.e., stochastic regressors] 'mimics' the fixed regressor model, and . . . many of the statistical properties of least squares in the fixed regressor model continue to hold."[9]

For all these reasons, we will first discuss the (fixed-regressor) CLRM in considerable detail. However, in Chapter 13 we will discuss the case of stochastic regressors in some detail and point out the occasions where we need to consider the stochastic regressor models. Incidentally, note that if the X variable(s) is stochastic, the resulting model is called the **neo-classical linear regression model (NLRM),**[10] in contrast to the CLRM, where the X's are treated as fixed or nonrandom. For discussion purposes, we will call the former the **stochastic regressor model** and the latter the **fixed regressor model.**

ASSUMPTION 3 **Zero Mean Value of Disturbance u_i:** Given the value of X_i, the mean, or expected, value of the random disturbance term u_i is zero. Symbolically, we have

$$E(u_i \mid X_i) = 0 \tag{3.2.1}$$

Or, if X is nonstochastic,

$$E(u_i) = 0$$

Assumption 3 states that the mean value of u_i conditional upon the given X_i is zero. Geometrically, this assumption can be pictured as in Figure 3.3, which shows a few values of the variable X and the Y populations associated with each of them. As shown, each Y

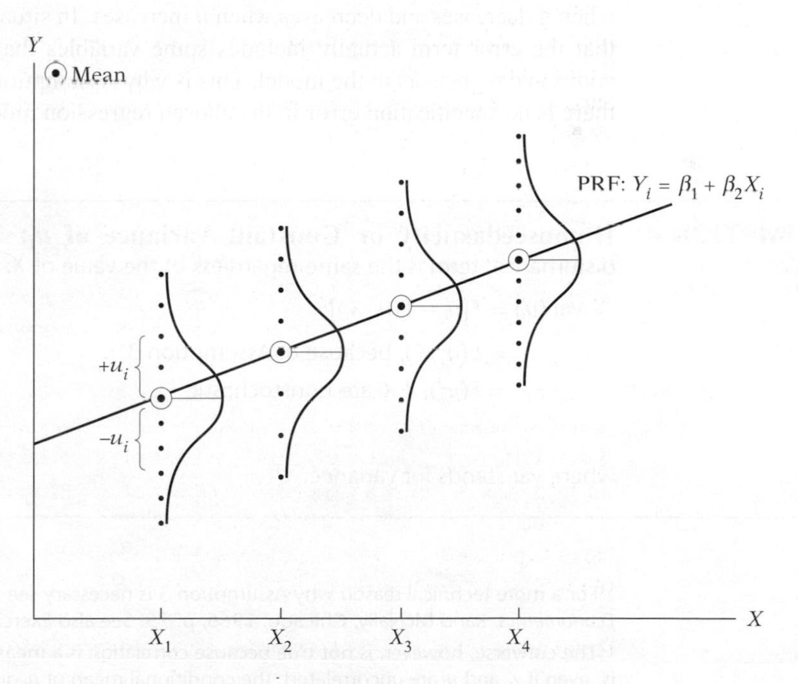

FIGURE 3.3 Conditional distribution of the disturbances u_i.

[9] James Davidson, *Econometric Theory,* Blackwell Publishers, U.K., 2000, p. 10.

[10] A term due to Arthur S. Goldberger, *A Course in Econometrics,* Harvard University Press, Cambridge, MA, 1991, p. 264.

population corresponding to a given X is distributed around its mean value (shown by the circled points on the PRF), with some Y values above the mean and some below it. The distances above and below the mean values are nothing but the u_i. Equation 3.2.1 requires that the average or mean value of these deviations corresponding to any given X should be zero.

This assumption should not be difficult to comprehend in view of the discussion in Section 2.4 (see Eq. [2.4.5]). Assumption 3 simply says that the factors not explicitly included in the model, and therefore subsumed in u_i, do not systematically affect the mean value of Y; in other words, the positive u_i values cancel out the negative u_i values so that their average or mean effect on Y is zero.[11]

In passing, note that the assumption $E(u_i | X_i) = 0$ implies that $E(Y_i | X_i) = \beta_1 + \beta_2 X_i$. (Why?) Therefore, the two assumption are equivalent.

It is important to point out that Assumption 3 implies that there is no **specification bias** or **specification error** in the model used in empirical analysis. In other words, the regression model is correctly specified. Leaving out important explanatory variables, including unnecessary variables, or choosing the wrong functional form of the relationship between the Y and X variables are some examples of specification error. We will discuss this topic in considerable detail in Chapter 13.

Note also that if the conditional mean of one random variable given another random variable is zero, the covariance between the two variables is zero and hence the two variables are uncorrelated. Assumption 3 therefore implies that X_i and u_i are uncorrelated.[12]

The reason for assuming that the disturbance term u and the explanatory variable(s) X are uncorrelated is simple. When we expressed the PRF as in Eq. (2.4.2), we assumed that X and u (which represent the influence of all omitted variables) have separate (and additive) influences on Y. But if X and u are correlated, it is not possible to assess their individual effects on Y. Thus, if X and u are positively correlated, X increases when u increases and decreases when u decreases. Similarly, if X and u are negatively correlated, X increases when u decreases and decreases when u increases. In situations like this it is quite possible that the error term actually includes some variables that should have been included as additional regressors in the model. This is why Assumption 3 is another way of stating that there is no specification error in the chosen regression model.

ASSUMPTION 4 **Homoscedasticity or Constant Variance of u_i:** The variance of the error, or disturbance, term is the same regardless of the value of X. Symbolically,

$$\begin{aligned} \text{var}(u_i) &= E[u_i - E(u_i | X_i)]^2 \\ &= E(u_i^2 | X_i), \text{ because of Assumption 3} \\ &= E(u_i^2), \text{ if } X_i \text{ are nonstochastic} \\ &= \sigma^2 \end{aligned} \tag{3.2.2}$$

where var stands for variance.

[11]For a more technical reason why Assumption 3 is necessary see E. Malinvaud, *Statistical Methods of Econometrics,* Rand McNally, Chicago, 1966, p. 75. See also Exercise 3.3.

[12]The converse, however, is not true because correlation is a measure of linear association only. That is, even if X_i and u_i are uncorrelated, the conditional mean of u_i given X_i may not be zero. However, if X_i and u_i are correlated, $E(u_i | X_i)$ must be nonzero, violating Assumption 3. We owe this point to Stock and Watson. See James H. Stock and Mark W. Watson, *Introduction to Econometrics,* Addison-Wesley, Boston, 2003, pp. 104–105.

Equation 3.2.2 states that the variance of u_i for each X_i (i.e., the conditional variance of u_i) is some positive constant number equal to σ^2. Technically, Eq. (3.2.2) represents the assumption of **homoscedasticity,** or *equal* (homo) *spread* (scedasticity) or *equal variance.* The word comes from the Greek verb *skedanime,* which mcans to disperse or scatter. Stated differently, Eq. (3.2.2) means that the Y populations corresponding to various X values have the same variance. Put simply, the variation around the regression line (which is the line of average relationship between Y and X) is the same across the X values; it neither increases nor decreases as X varies. Diagrammatically, the situation is as depicted in Figure 3.4.

In contrast, consider Figure 3.5, where the conditional variance of the Y population varies with X. This situation is known appropriately as **heteroscedasticity,** or *unequal spread,* or *variance*. Symbolically, in this situation, Eq. (3.2.2) can be written as

$$\operatorname{var}(u_i \mid X_i) = \sigma_i^2 \tag{3.2.3}$$

Notice the subscript on σ^2 in Equation (3.2.3), which indicates that the variance of the Y population is no longer constant.

FIGURE 3.4
Homoscedasticity.

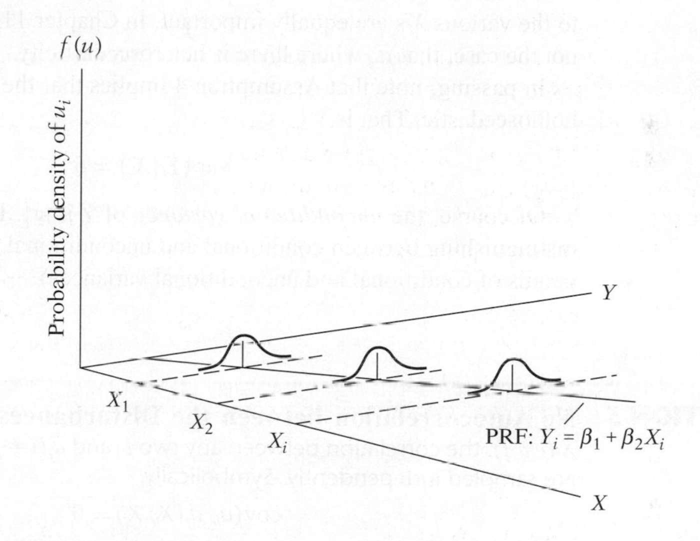

FIGURE 3.5
Heteroscedasticity.

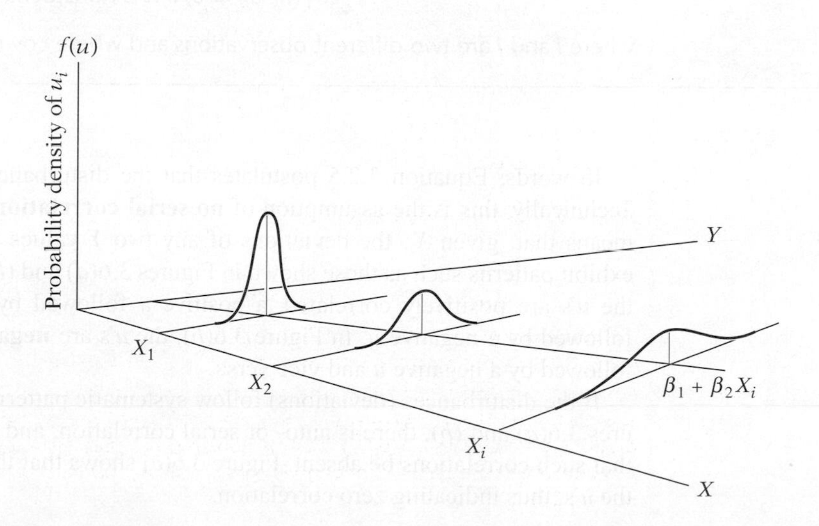

To make the difference between the two situations clear, let Y represent weekly consumption expenditure and X weekly income. Figures 3.4 and 3.5 show that as income increases, the average consumption expenditure also increases. But in Figure 3.4 the variance of consumption expenditure remains the same at all levels of income, whereas in Figure 3.5 it increases with increase in income. In other words, richer families on the average consume more than poorer families, but there is also more variability in the consumption expenditure of the former.

To understand the rationale behind this assumption, refer to Figure 3.5. As this figure shows, $\text{var}(u|X_1) < \text{var}(u|X_2), \ldots, < \text{var}(u|X_i)$. Therefore, the likelihood is that the Y observations coming from the population with $X = X_1$ would be closer to the PRF than those coming from populations corresponding to $X = X_2$, $X = X_3$, and so on. In short, not all Y values corresponding to the various X's will be equally reliable, reliability being judged by how closely or distantly the Y values are distributed around their means, that is, the points on the PRF. If this is in fact the case, would we not prefer to sample from those Y populations that are closer to their mean than those that are widely spread? But doing so might restrict the variation we obtain across X values.

By invoking Assumption 4, we are saying that at this stage, all Y values corresponding to the various X's are equally important. In Chapter 11 we shall see what happens if this is not the case, that is, where there is heteroscedasticity.

In passing, note that Assumption 4 implies that the conditional variances of Y_i are also homoscedastic. That is,

$$\text{var}(Y_i | X_i) = \sigma^2 \tag{3.2.4}$$

Of course, the *unconditional variance* of Y is σ_Y^2. Later we will see the importance of distinguishing between conditional and unconditional variances of Y (see **Appendix A** for details of conditional and unconditional variances).

ASSUMPTION 5 **No Autocorrelation between the Disturbances:** Given any two X values, X_i and $X_j (i \neq j)$, the correlation between any two u_i and $u_j (i \neq j)$ is zero. In short, the observations are sampled independently. Symbolically,

$$\text{cov}(u_i, u_j | X_i, X_j) = 0 \tag{3.2.5}$$

$$\text{cov}(u_i, u_j) = 0, \text{ if } X \text{ is nonstochastic}$$

where i and j are two different observations and where cov means covariance.

In words, Equation 3.2.5 postulates that the disturbances u_i and u_j are uncorrelated. Technically, this is the assumption of **no serial correlation,** or **no autocorrelation.** This means that, given X_i, the deviations of any two Y values from their mean value do not exhibit patterns such as those shown in Figures 3.6(*a*) and (*b*). In Figure 3.6(*a*), we see that the u's are positively correlated, a positive u followed by a positive u or a negative u followed by a negative u. In Figure 3.6(*b*), the u's are **negatively correlated,** a positive u followed by a negative u and vice versa.

If the disturbances (deviations) follow systematic patterns, such as those shown in Figures 3.6(*a*) and (*b*), there is auto- or serial correlation, and what Assumption 5 requires is that such correlations be absent. Figure 3.6(*c*) shows that there is no systematic pattern to the u's, thus indicating zero correlation.

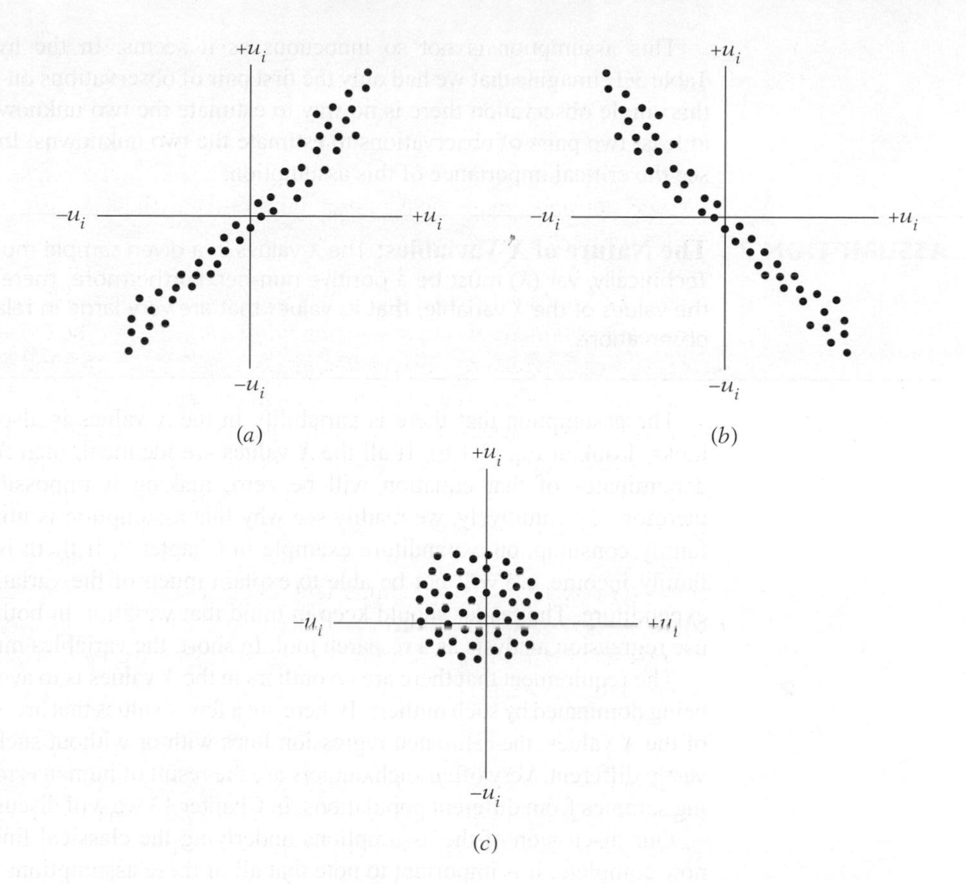

FIGURE 3.6 Patterns of correlation among the disturbances. (*a*) positive serial correlation; (*b*) negative serial correlation; (*c*) zero correlation.

The full import of this assumption will be explained thoroughly in Chapter 12. But intuitively one can explain this assumption as follows. Suppose in our PRF ($Y_t = \beta_1 + \beta_2 X_t + u_t$) that u_t and u_{t-1} are positively correlated. Then Y_t depends not only on X_t but also on u_{t-1}, for u_{t-1} to some extent determines u_t. At this stage of the development of the subject matter, by invoking Assumption 5, we are saying that we will consider the systematic effect, if any, of X_t on Y_t and not worry about the other influences that might act on Y as a result of the possible intercorrelations among the u's. But, as noted in Chapter 12, we will see how intercorrelations among the disturbances can be brought into the analysis and with what consequences.

But it should be added here that the justification of this assumption depends on the type of data used in the analysis. If the data are cross-sectional and are obtained as a random sample from the relevant population, this assumption can often be justified. However, if the data are time series, the assumption of independence is difficult to maintain, for successive observations of a time series, such as GDP, are highly correlated. But we will deal with this situation when we discuss time series econometrics later in the text.

ASSUMPTION 6 **The Number of Observations n Must Be Greater than the Number of Parameters to Be Estimated:** Alternatively, the number of observations must be greater than the number of explanatory variables.

This assumption is not so innocuous as it seems. In the hypothetical example of Table 3.1, imagine that we had only the first pair of observations on Y and X (4 and 1). From this single observation there is no way to estimate the two unknowns, β_1 and β_2. We need at least two pairs of observations to estimate the two unknowns. In a later chapter we will see the critical importance of this assumption.

ASSUMPTION 7 **The Nature of *X* Variables:** The X values in a given sample must not all be the same. Technically, var (X) must be a positive number. Furthermore, there can be no **outliers** in the values of the X variable, that is, values that are very large in relation to the rest of the observations.

The assumption that there is variability in the X values is also not as innocuous as it looks. Look at Eq. (3.1.6). If all the X values are identical, then $X_i = \bar{X}$ (Why?) and the denominator of that equation will be zero, making it impossible to estimate β_2 and therefore β_1. Intuitively, we readily see why this assumption is important. Looking at our family consumption expenditure example in Chapter 2, if there is very little variation in family income, we will not be able to explain much of the variation in the consumption expenditure. The reader should keep in mind that variation in both Y and X is essential to use regression analysis as a research tool. In short, the variables must vary!

The requirement that there are no outliers in the X values is to avoid the regression results being dominated by such outliers. If there are a few X values that are, say, 20 times the average of the X values, the estimated regression lines with or without such observations might be vastly different. Very often such outliers are the result of human errors of arithmetic or mixing samples from different populations. In Chapter 13 we will discuss this topic further.

Our discussion of the assumptions underlying the classical linear regression model is now complete. It is important to note that all of these assumptions pertain to the PRF only and not the SRF. But it is interesting to observe that the method of least squares discussed previously has some properties that are similar to the assumptions we have made about the PRF. For example, the finding that $\sum \hat{u}_i = 0$ and, therefore, $\bar{\hat{u}} = 0$, is akin to the assumption that $E(u_i \mid X_i) = 0$. Likewise, the finding that $\sum \hat{u}_i X_i = 0$ is similar to the assumption that $\text{cov}(u_i, X_i) = 0$. It is comforting to note that the method of least squares thus tries to "duplicate" some of the assumptions we have imposed on the PRF.

Of course, the SRF does not duplicate all the assumptions of the CLRM. As we will show later, although $\text{cov}(u_i, u_j) = 0$ $(i \neq j)$ by assumption, it is *not* true that the *sample* $\text{cov}(\hat{u}_i, \hat{u}_j) = 0$ $(i \neq j)$. As a matter of fact, we will show later that the residuals are not only autocorrelated but are also heteroscedastic (see Chapter 12).

A Word about These Assumptions

The million-dollar question is: How realistic are all these assumptions? The "reality of assumptions" is an age-old question in the philosophy of science. Some argue that it does not matter whether the assumptions are realistic. What matters are the predictions based on those assumptions. Notable among the "irrelevance-of-assumptions thesis" is Milton Friedman. To him, unreality of assumptions is a positive advantage: "to be important . . . a hypothesis must be descriptively false in its assumptions."[13]

One may not subscribe to this viewpoint fully, but recall that in any scientific study we make certain assumptions because they facilitate the development of the subject matter in gradual steps, not because they are necessarily realistic in the sense that they replicate

[13]Milton Friedman, *Essays in Positive Economics,* University of Chicago Press, Chicago, 1953, p. 14.

reality exactly. As one author notes, "... if simplicity is a desirable criterion of good theory, all good theories idealize and oversimplify outrageously."[14]

What we plan to do is first study the properties of the CLRM thoroughly, and then in later chapters examine in depth what happens if one or more of the assumptions of CLRM are not fulfilled. At the end of this chapter, we provide in Table 3.4 a guide to where one can find out what happens to the CLRM if a particular assumption is not satisfied.

As a colleague pointed out to us, when we review research done by others, we need to consider whether the assumptions made by the researcher are appropriate to the data and problem. All too often, published research is based on implicit assumptions about the problem and data that are likely not correct and that produce estimates based on these assumptions. Clearly, the knowledgeable reader should, realizing these problems, adopt a skeptical attitude toward the research. The assumptions listed in Table 3.4 therefore provide a checklist for guiding our research and for evaluating the research of others.

With this backdrop, we are now ready to study the CLRM. In particular, we want to find out the **statistical properties** of OLS compared with the purely **numerical properties** discussed earlier. The statistical properties of OLS are based on the assumptions of CLRM already discussed and are enshrined in the famous **Gauss–Markov theorem.** But before we turn to this theorem, which provides the theoretical justification for the popularity of OLS, we first need to consider the **precision** or **standard errors** of the least squares estimates.

3.3 Precision or Standard Errors of Least-Squares Estimates

From Eqs. (3.1.6) and (3.1.7), it is evident that least-squares estimates are a function of the sample data. But since the data are likely to change from sample to sample, the estimates will change ipso facto. Therefore, what is needed is some measure of "reliability" or **precision** of the estimators $\hat{\beta}_1$ and $\hat{\beta}_2$. In statistics the precision of an estimate is measured by its standard error (se).[15] Given the Gaussian assumptions, it is shown in Appendix 3A, Section 3A.3 that the standard errors of the OLS estimates can be obtained as follows:

$$\operatorname{var}(\hat{\beta}_2) = \frac{\sigma^2}{\sum x_i^2} \tag{3.3.1}$$

$$\operatorname{se}(\hat{\beta}_2) = \frac{\sigma}{\sqrt{\sum x_i^2}} \tag{3.3.2}$$

$$\operatorname{var}(\hat{\beta}_1) = \frac{\sum X_i^2}{n\sum x_i^2}\sigma^2 \tag{3.3.3}$$

$$\operatorname{se}(\hat{\beta}_1) = \sqrt{\frac{\sum X_i^2}{n\sum x_i^2}}\,\sigma \tag{3.3.4}$$

[14]Mark Blaug, *The Methodology of Economics: Or How Economists Explain,* 2d ed., Cambridge University Press, New York, 1992, p. 92.

[15]The **standard error** is nothing but the standard deviation of the sampling distribution of the estimator, and the sampling distribution of an estimator is simply a probability or frequency distribution of the estimator, that is, a distribution of the set of values of the estimator obtained from all possible samples of the same size from a given population. Sampling distributions are used to draw inferences about the values of the population parameters on the basis of the values of the estimators calculated from one or more samples. (For details, see **Appendix A.**)

where var = variance and se = standard error and where σ^2 is the constant or homoscedastic variance of u_i of Assumption 4.

All the quantities entering into the preceding equations except σ^2 can be estimated from the data. As shown in Appendix 3A, Section 3A.5, σ^2 itself is estimated by the following formula:

$$\hat{\sigma}^2 = \frac{\sum \hat{u}_i^2}{n-2} \tag{3.3.5}$$

where $\hat{\sigma}^2$ is the OLS estimator of the true but unknown σ^2 and where the expression $n-2$ is known as the **number of degrees of freedom (df),** $\sum \hat{u}_i^2$ being the sum of the residuals squared or the **residual sum of squares (RSS).**[16]

Once $\sum \hat{u}_i^2$ is known, $\hat{\sigma}^2$ can be easily computed. $\sum \hat{u}_i^2$ itself can be computed either from Eq. (3.1.2) or from the following expression (see Section 3.5 for the proof):

$$\sum \hat{u}_i^2 = \sum y_i^2 - \hat{\beta}_2^2 \sum x_i^2 \tag{3.3.6}$$

Compared with Eq. (3.1.2), Equation 3.3.6 is easy to use, for it does not require computing $\hat{u}_i$ for each observation although such a computation will be useful in its own right (as we shall see in Chapters 11 and 12).

Since

$$\hat{\beta}_2 = \frac{\sum x_i y_i}{\sum x_i^2}$$

an alternative expression for computing $\sum \hat{u}_i^2$ is

$$\sum \hat{u}_i^2 = \sum y_i^2 - \frac{\left(\sum x_i y_i\right)^2}{\sum x_i^2} \tag{3.3.7}$$

In passing, note that the positive square root of $\hat{\sigma}^2$

$$\hat{\sigma} = \sqrt{\frac{\sum \hat{u}_i^2}{n-2}} \tag{3.3.8}$$

is known as the **standard error of estimate** or the **standard error of the regression (se).** It is simply the standard deviation of the Y values about the estimated regression line and is often used as a summary measure of the "goodness of fit" of the estimated regression line, a topic discussed in Section 3.5.

Earlier we noted that, given X_i, σ^2 represents the (conditional) variance of both u_i and Y_i. Therefore, the standard error of the estimate can also be called the (conditional) standard deviation of u_i and Y_i. Of course, as usual, σ_Y^2 and σ_Y represent, respectively, the unconditional variance and unconditional standard deviation of Y.

[16]The term **number of degrees of freedom** means the total number of observations in the sample ($= n$) less the number of independent (linear) constraints or restrictions put on them. In other words, it is the number of independent observations out of a total of n observations. For example, before the RSS (3.1.2) can be computed, $\hat{\beta}_1$ and $\hat{\beta}_2$ must first be obtained. These two estimates therefore put two restrictions on the RSS. Therefore, there are $n-2$, not n, independent observations to compute the RSS. Following this logic, in the three-variable regression RSS will have $n-3$ df, and for the k-variable model it will have $n-k$ df. **The general rule is this:** df = (n – number of parameters estimated).

Note the following features of the variances (and therefore the standard errors) of $\hat{\beta}_1$ and $\hat{\beta}_2$.

1. The variance of $\hat{\beta}_2$ is directly proportional to σ^2 but inversely proportional to $\sum x_i^2$. That is, given σ^2, the larger the variation in the X values, the smaller the variance of $\hat{\beta}_2$ and hence the greater the precision with which β_2 can be estimated. In short, given σ^2, if there is substantial variation in the X values, β_2 can be measured more accurately than when the X_i do not vary substantially. Also, given $\sum x_i^2$, the larger the variance of σ^2, the larger the variance of β_2. Note that as the sample size n increases, the number of terms in the sum, $\sum x_i^2$, will increase. As n increases, the precision with which β_2 can be estimated also increases. (Why?)

2. The variance of $\hat{\beta}_1$ is directly proportional to σ^2 and $\sum X_i^2$ but inversely proportional to $\sum x_i^2$ and the sample size n.

3. Since $\hat{\beta}_1$ and $\hat{\beta}_2$ are estimators, they will not only vary from sample to sample but in a given sample they are likely to be dependent on each other, this dependence being measured by the covariance between them. It is shown in Appendix 3A, Section 3A.4 that

$$\begin{aligned} \operatorname{cov}(\hat{\beta}_1, \hat{\beta}_2) &= -\bar{X} \operatorname{var}(\hat{\beta}_2) \\ &= -\bar{X}\left(\frac{\sigma^2}{\sum x_i^2}\right) \end{aligned} \tag{3.3.9}$$

Since $\operatorname{var}(\hat{\beta}_2)$ is always positive, as is the variance of any variable, the nature of the covariance between $\hat{\beta}_1$ and $\hat{\beta}_2$ depends on the sign of $\bar{X}$. If $\bar{X}$ is positive, then as the formula shows, the covariance will be negative. Thus, if the slope coefficient β_2 is *overestimated* (i.e., the slope is too steep), the intercept coefficient β_1 will be *underestimated* (i.e., the intercept will be too small). Later on (especially in the chapter on multicollinearity, Chapter 10), we will see the utility of studying the covariances between the estimated regression coefficients.

How do the variances and standard errors of the estimated regression coefficients enable one to judge the reliability of these estimates? This is a problem in statistical inference, and it will be pursued in Chapters 4 and 5.

3.4 Properties of Least-Squares Estimators: The Gauss–Markov Theorem[17]

As noted earlier, given the assumptions of the classical linear regression model, the least-squares estimates possess some ideal or optimum properties. These properties are contained in the well-known **Gauss–Markov theorem.** To understand this theorem, we need to consider the **best linear unbiasedness property** of an estimator.[18] As explained in Appendix A, an estimator, say the OLS estimator $\hat{\beta}_2$, is said to be a best linear unbiased estimator (BLUE) of β_2 if the following hold:

1. It is **linear,** that is, a linear function of a random variable, such as the dependent variable Y in the regression model.

[17]Although known as the *Gauss–Markov theorem,* the least-squares approach of Gauss antedates (1821) the minimum-variance approach of Markov (1900).

[18]The reader should refer to **Appendix A** for the importance of linear estimators as well as for a general discussion of the desirable properties of statistical estimators.

2. It is **unbiased,** that is, its average or expected value, $E(\hat{\beta}_2)$, is equal to the true value, β_2.
3. It has minimum variance in the class of all such linear unbiased estimators; an unbiased estimator with the least variance is known as an **efficient estimator.**

In the regression context it can be proved that the OLS estimators are BLUE. This is the gist of the famous Gauss–Markov theorem, which can be stated as follows:

Gauss–Markov Theorem Given the assumptions of the classical linear regression model, the least-squares estimators, in the class of unbiased linear estimators, have minimum variance, that is, they are BLUE.

The proof of this theorem is sketched in **Appendix 3A, Section 3A.6**. The full import of the Gauss–Markov theorem will become clearer as we move along. It is sufficient to note here that the theorem has theoretical as well as practical importance.[19]

What all this means can be explained with the aid of Figure 3.7.

FIGURE 3.7
Sampling distribution of OLS estimator $\hat{\beta}_2$ and alternative estimator β_2^*.

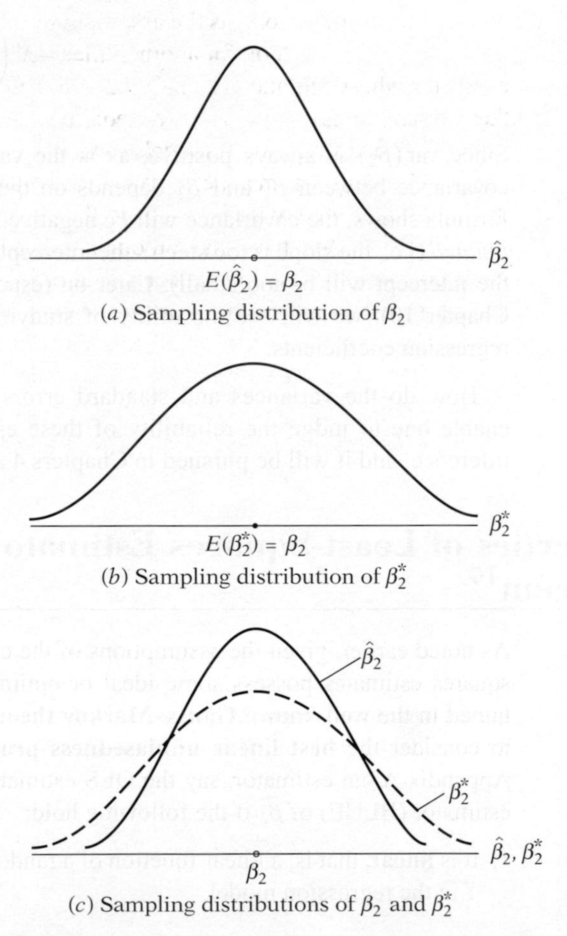

[19]For example, it can be proved that any linear combination of the β's, such as $(\beta_1 - 2\beta_2)$, can be estimated by $(\hat{\beta}_1 - 2\hat{\beta}_2)$, and this estimator is BLUE. For details, see Henri Theil, *Introduction to Econometrics,* Prentice-Hall, Englewood Cliffs, N.J., 1978, pp. 401–402. Note a technical point about the Gauss–Markov theorem: It provides only the sufficient (but not necessary) condition for OLS to be efficient. I am indebted to Michael McAleer of the University of Western Australia for bringing this point to my attention.

In Figure 3.7(*a*) we have shown the **sampling distribution** of the OLS estimator $\hat{\beta}_2$, that is, the distribution of the values taken by $\hat{\beta}_2$ in repeated sampling experiments (recall Table 3.1). For convenience we have assumed $\hat{\beta}_2$ to be distributed symmetrically (but more on this in Chapter 4). As the figure shows, the mean of the $\hat{\beta}_2$ values, $E(\hat{\beta}_2)$, is equal to the true β_2. In this situation we say that $\hat{\beta}_2$ is an *unbiased estimator* of β_2. In Figure 3.7(*b*) we have shown the sampling distribution of β_2^*, an alternative estimator of β_2 obtained by using another (i.e., other than OLS) method. For convenience, assume that β_2^*, like $\hat{\beta}_2$, is unbiased, that is, its average or expected value is equal to β_2. Assume further that both $\hat{\beta}_2$ and β_2^* are linear estimators, that is, they are linear functions of Y. Which estimator, $\hat{\beta}_2$ or β_2^*, would you choose?

To answer this question, superimpose the two figures, as in Figure 3.7(*c*). It is obvious that although both $\hat{\beta}_2$ and β_2^* are unbiased the distribution of β_2^* is more diffused or widespread around the mean value than the distribution of $\hat{\beta}_2$. In other words, the variance of β_2^* is larger than the variance of $\hat{\beta}_2$. Now given two estimators that are both linear and unbiased, one would choose the estimator with the smaller variance because it is more likely to be close to β_2 than the alternative estimator. In short, one would choose the BLUE estimator.

The Gauss–Markov theorem is remarkable in that it makes no assumptions about the probability distribution of the random variable u_i, and therefore of Y_i (in the next chapter we will take this up). As long as the assumptions of CLRM are satisfied, the theorem holds. As a result, we need not look for another linear unbiased estimator, for we will not find such an estimator whose variance is smaller than the OLS estimator. Of course, if one or more of these assumptions do not hold, the theorem is invalid. For example, if we consider nonlinear-in-the-parameter regression models (which are discussed in Chapter 14), we may be able to obtain estimators that may perform better than the OLS estimators. Also, as we will show in the chapter on heteroscedasticity, if the assumption of homoscedastic variance is not fulfilled, the OLS estimators, although unbiased and consistent, are no longer minimum variance estimators even in the class of linear estimators.

The statistical properties that we have just discussed are known as **finite sample properties:** These properties hold regardless of the sample size on which the estimators are based. Later we will have occasions to consider the **asymptotic properties,** that is, properties that hold only if the sample size is very large (technically, infinite). A general discussion of finite-sample and large-sample properties of estimators is given in **Appendix A.**

3.5 The Coefficient of Determination r^2: A Measure of "Goodness of Fit"

Thus far we were concerned with the problem of estimating regression coefficients, their standard errors, and some of their properties. We now consider the **goodness of fit** of the fitted regression line to a set of data; that is, we shall find out how "well" the sample regression line fits the data. From Figure 3.1 it is clear that if all the observations were to lie on the regression line, we would obtain a "perfect" fit, but this is rarely the case. Generally, there will be some positive $\hat{u}_i$ and some negative $\hat{u}_i$. What we hope for is that these residuals around the regression line are as small as possible. The **coefficient of determination** r^2 (two-variable case) or R^2 (multiple regression) is a summary measure that tells how well the sample regression line fits the data.

Before we show how r^2 is computed, let us consider a heuristic explanation of r^2 in terms of a graphical device, known as the **Venn diagram,** or the **Ballentine,** as shown in Figure 3.8.[20]

[20]See Peter Kennedy, "Ballentine: A Graphical Aid for Econometrics," *Australian Economics Papers,* vol. 20, 1981, pp. 414–416. The name Ballentine is derived from the emblem of the well-known Ballantine beer with its circles.

FIGURE 3.8
The Ballentine view of r^2: (*a*) $r^2 = 0$; (*f*) $r^2 = 1$.

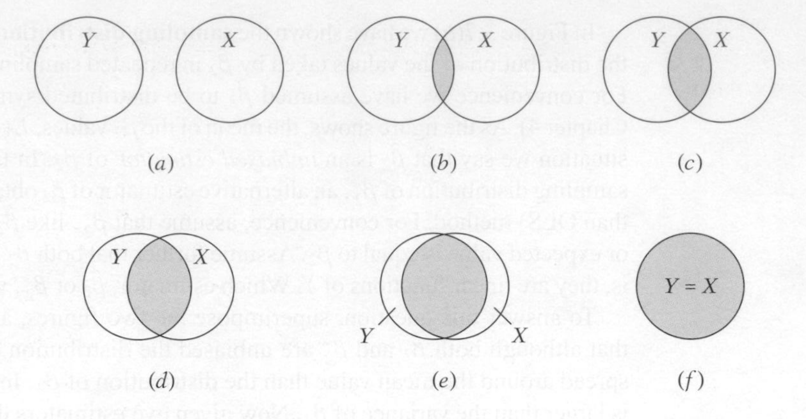

In this figure the circle Y represents variation in the dependent variable Y and the circle X represents variation in the explanatory variable X.[21] The overlap of the two circles (the shaded area) indicates the extent to which the variation in Y is explained by the variation in X (say, via an OLS regression). The greater the extent of the overlap, the greater the variation in Y is explained by X. The r^2 is simply a numerical measure of this overlap. In the figure, as we move from left to right, the area of the overlap increases, that is, successively a greater proportion of the variation in Y is explained by X. In short, r^2 increases. When there is no overlap, r^2 is obviously zero, but when the overlap is complete, r^2 is 1, since 100 percent of the variation in Y is explained by X. As we shall show shortly, r^2 lies between 0 and 1.

To compute this r^2, we proceed as follows: Recall that

$$Y_i = \hat{Y}_i + \hat{u}_i \tag{2.6.3}$$

or in the deviation form

$$y_i = \hat{y}_i + \hat{u}_i \tag{3.5.1}$$

where use is made of Eqs. (3.1.13) and (3.1.14). Squaring Equation 3.5.1 on both sides and summing over the sample, we obtain

$$\begin{aligned} \sum y_i^2 &= \sum \hat{y}_i^2 + \sum \hat{u}_i^2 + 2\sum \hat{y}_i \hat{u}_i \\ &= \sum \hat{y}_i^2 + \sum \hat{u}_i^2 \\ &= \hat{\beta}_2^2 \sum x_i^2 + \sum \hat{u}_i^2 \end{aligned} \tag{3.5.2}$$

since $\sum \hat{y}_i \hat{u}_i = 0$ (why?) and $\hat{y}_i = \hat{\beta}_2 x_i$.

The various sums of squares appearing in Equation 3.5.2 can be described as follows: $\sum y_i^2 = \sum (Y_i - \bar{Y})^2$ = total variation of the actual Y values about their sample mean, which may be called the **total sum of squares (TSS).** $\sum \hat{y}_i^2 = \sum (\hat{Y}_i - \bar{\hat{Y}})^2 = \sum (\hat{Y}_i - \bar{Y})^2 = \hat{\beta}_2^2 \sum x_i^2$ = variation of the estimated Y values about their mean ($\bar{\hat{Y}} = \bar{Y}$), which appropriately may be called the sum of squares due to regression [i.e., due to the explanatory variable(s)], or explained by regression, or simply the **explained sum of squares**

[21]The term *variation* and *variance* are different. Variation means the sum of squares of the deviations of a variable from its mean value. Variance is this sum of squares divided by the appropriate degrees of freedom. In short, variance = variation/df.

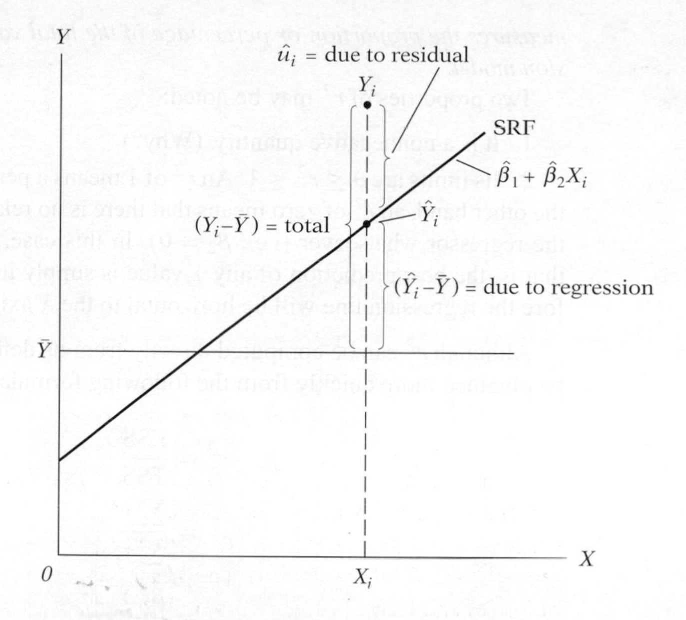

FIGURE 3.9 Breakdown of the variation of Y_i into two components.

(ESS). $\sum \hat{u}_i^2$ = residual or **unexplained** variation of the Y values about the regression line, or simply the **residual sum of squares (RSS).** Thus, Eq. (3.5.2) is

$$\text{TSS} = \text{ESS} + \text{RSS} \tag{3.5.3}$$

and shows that the total variation in the observed Y values about their mean value can be partitioned into two parts, one attributable to the regression line and the other to random forces because not all actual Y observations lie on the fitted line. Geometrically, we have Figure 3.9.

Now dividing Equation 3.5.3 by TSS on both sides, we obtain

$$\begin{aligned} 1 &= \frac{\text{ESS}}{\text{TSS}} + \frac{\text{RSS}}{\text{TSS}} \\ &= \frac{\sum(\hat{Y}_i - \bar{Y})^2}{\sum(Y_i - \bar{Y})^2} + \frac{\sum \hat{u}_i^2}{\sum(Y_i - \bar{Y})^2} \end{aligned} \tag{3.5.4}$$

We now define r^2 as

$$r^2 = \frac{\sum(\hat{Y}_i - \bar{Y})^2}{\sum(Y_i - \bar{Y})^2} = \frac{\text{ESS}}{\text{TSS}} \tag{3.5.5}$$

or, alternatively, as

$$\begin{aligned} r^2 &= 1 - \frac{\sum \hat{u}_i^2}{\sum(Y_i - \bar{Y})^2} \\ &= 1 - \frac{\text{RSS}}{\text{TSS}} \end{aligned} \tag{3.5.5a}$$

The quantity r^2 thus defined is known as the (sample) **coefficient of determination** and is the most commonly used measure of the goodness of fit of a regression line. Verbally, r^2

measures the proportion or percentage of the total variation in Y explained by the regression model.

Two properties of r^2 may be noted:

1. It is a nonnegative quantity. (Why?)
2. Its limits are $0 \le r^2 \le 1$. An r^2 of 1 means a perfect fit, that is, $\hat{Y}_i = Y_i$ for each i. On the other hand, an r^2 of zero means that there is no relationship between the regressand and the regressor whatsoever (i.e., $\hat{\beta}_2 = 0$). In this case, as Eq. (3.1.9) shows, $\hat{Y}_i = \hat{\beta}_1 = \bar{Y}$, that is, the best prediction of any Y value is simply its mean value. In this situation therefore the regression line will be horizontal to the X axis.

Although r^2 can be computed directly from its definition given in Equation 3.5.5, it can be obtained more quickly from the following formula:

$$\begin{aligned} r^2 &= \frac{\text{ESS}}{\text{TSS}} \\ &= \frac{\sum \hat{y}_i^2}{\sum y_i^2} \\ &= \frac{\hat{\beta}_2^2 \sum x_i^2}{\sum y_i^2} \\ &= \hat{\beta}_2^2 \left(\frac{\sum x_i^2}{\sum y_i^2} \right) \end{aligned} \tag{3.5.6}$$

If we divide the numerator and the denominator of Equation 3.5.6 by the sample size n (or $n - 1$ if the sample size is small), we obtain

$$r^2 = \hat{\beta}_2^2 \left(\frac{S_x^2}{S_y^2} \right) \tag{3.5.7}$$

where S_y^2 and S_x^2 are the sample variances of Y and X, respectively.

Since $\hat{\beta}_2 = \sum x_i y_i / \sum x_i^2$, Eq. (3.5.6) can also be expressed as

$$r^2 = \frac{\left(\sum x_i y_i\right)^2}{\sum x_i^2 \sum y_i^2} \tag{3.5.8}$$

an expression that may be computationally easy to obtain.

Given the definition of r^2, we can express ESS and RSS discussed earlier as follows:

$$\begin{aligned} \text{ESS} &= r^2 \cdot \text{TSS} \\ &= r^2 \sum y_i^2 \end{aligned} \tag{3.5.9}$$

$$\begin{aligned} \text{RSS} &= \text{TSS} - \text{ESS} \\ &= \text{TSS}(1 - \text{ESS/TSS}) \\ &= \sum y_i^2 \cdot (1 - r^2) \end{aligned} \tag{3.5.10}$$

Therefore, we can write

$$\begin{aligned} \text{TSS} &= \text{ESS} + \text{RSS} \\ \sum y_i^2 &= r^2 \sum y_i^2 + (1 - r^2) \sum y_i^2 \end{aligned} \tag{3.5.11}$$

an expression that we will find very useful later.

A quantity closely related to but conceptually very much different from r^2 is the **coefficient of correlation,** which, as noted in Chapter 1, is a measure of the degree of association between two variables. It can be computed either from

$$r = \pm\sqrt{r^2} \tag{3.5.12}$$

or from its definition

$$\begin{aligned} r &= \frac{\sum x_i y_i}{\sqrt{\left(\sum x_i^2\right)\left(\sum y_i^2\right)}} \\ &= \frac{n\sum X_i Y_i - \left(\sum X_i\right)\left(\sum Y_i\right)}{\sqrt{\left[n\sum X_i^2 - \left(\sum X_i\right)^2\right]\left[n\sum Y_i^2 - \left(\sum Y_i\right)^2\right]}} \end{aligned} \tag{3.5.13}$$

which is known as the **sample correlation coefficient.**[22]

Some of the properties of r are as follows (see Figure 3.10):

1. It can be positive or negative, the sign depending on the sign of the term in the numerator of Equation 3.5.13, which measures the sample *covariation* of two variables.
2. It lies between the limits of -1 and $+1$; that is, $-1 \le r \le 1$.
3. It is symmetrical in nature; that is, the coefficient of correlation between X and $Y(r_{XY})$ is the same as that between Y and $X(r_{YX})$.
4. It is independent of the origin and scale; that is, if we define $X_i^* = aX_i + C$ and $Y_i^* = bY_i + d$, where $a > 0$, $b > 0$, and c and d are constants, then r between X^* and Y^* is the same as that between the original variables X and Y.
5. If X and Y are statistically independent (see **Appendix A** for the definition), the correlation coefficient between them is zero; but if $r = 0$, it does not mean that two variables are independent. In other words, **zero correlation does not necessarily imply independence.** [See Figure 3.10(*h*).]
6. It is a measure of *linear association* or *linear dependence* only; it has no meaning for describing nonlinear relations. Thus in Figure 3.10(*h*), $Y = X^2$ is an exact relationship yet r is zero. (Why?)
7. Although it is a measure of linear association between two variables, it does not necessarily imply any cause-and-effect relationship, as noted in Chapter 1.

In the regression context, r^2 is a more meaningful measure than r, for the former tells us the proportion of variation in the dependent variable explained by the explanatory variable(s) and therefore provides an overall measure of the extent to which the variation in one variable determines the variation in the other. The latter does not have such value.[23] Moreover, as we shall see, the interpretation of $r\ (= R)$ in a multiple regression model is of dubious value. However, we will have more to say about r^2 in Chapter 7.

In passing, note that the r^2 defined previously *can also be computed as the squared coefficient of correlation between actual Y_i and the estimated Y_i*, namely, $\hat{Y}_i$. That is, using Eq. (3.5.13), we can write

$$r^2 = \frac{\left[\sum (Y_i - \bar{Y})(\hat{Y}_i - \bar{Y})\right]^2}{\sum (Y_i - \bar{Y})^2 \sum (\hat{Y}_i - \bar{Y})^2}$$

[22]The population correlation coefficient, denoted by ρ, is defined in **Appendix A**.

[23]In regression modeling the underlying theory will indicate the direction of causality between Y and X, which, in the context of single-equation models, is generally from X to Y.

FIGURE 3.10
Correlation patterns (adapted from Henri Theil, *Introduction to Econometrics,* Prentice-Hall, Englewood Cliffs, NJ, 1978, p. 86).

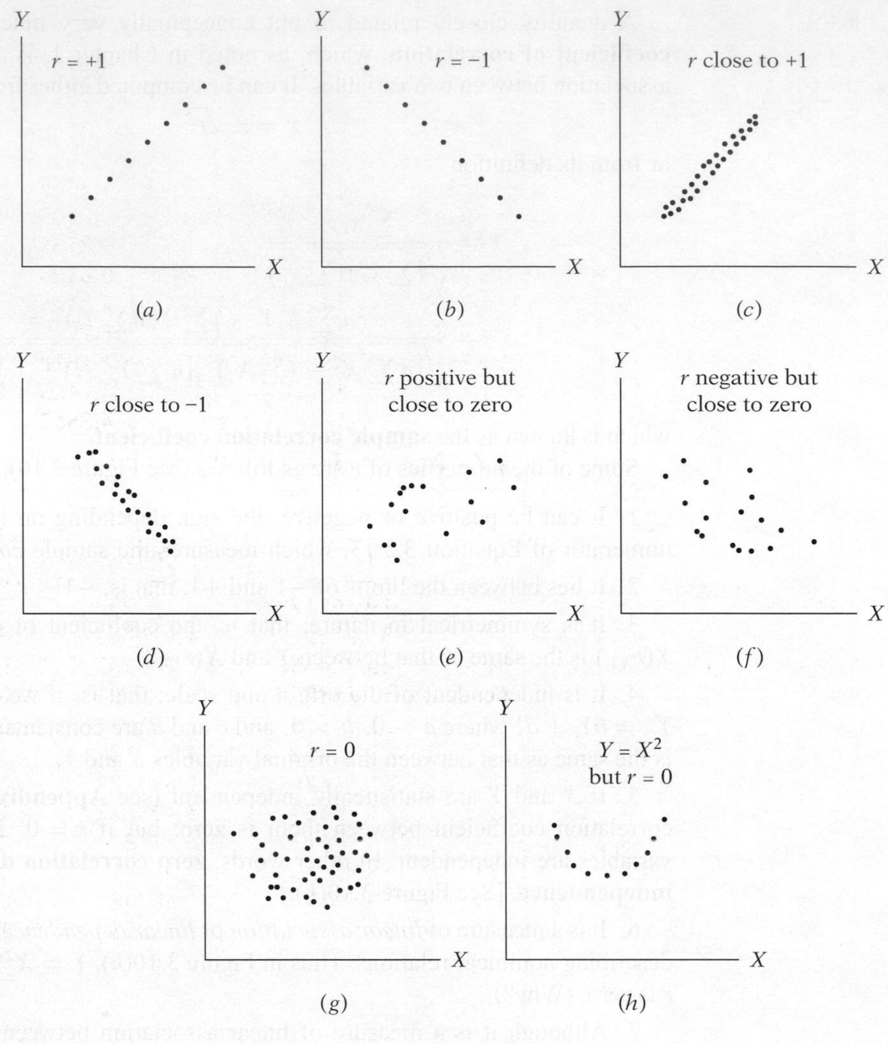

That is,

$$r^2 = \frac{\left(\sum y_i \hat{y}_i\right)^2}{\left(\sum y_i^2\right)\left(\sum \hat{y}_i^2\right)} \tag{3.5.14}$$

where Y_i = actual Y, $\hat{Y}_i$ = estimated Y, and $\bar{Y} = \bar{\hat{Y}}$ = the mean of Y. For proof, see Exercise 3.15. Expression 3.5.14 justifies the description of r^2 as a measure of goodness of fit, for it tells how close the estimated Y values are to their actual values.

3.6 A Numerical Example

We illustrate the econometric theory developed so far by considering the data given in Table 2.6, which relates mean hourly wage (Y) and years of schooling (X). Basic labor economics theory tells us, that among many variables, education is an important determinant of wages.

In Table 3.2 we provide the necessary raw data to estimate the quantitative impact of education on wages.

TABLE 3.2
Raw Data Based on Table 2.6

Obs	Y	X	x	y	x_i^2	$y_i x_i$
1	4.4567	6	−6	−4.218	36	25.308
2	5.77	7	−5	−2.9047	25	14.5235
3	5.9787	8	−4	−2.696	16	10.784
4	7.3317	9	−3	−1.343	9	4.029
5	7.3182	10	−2	−1.3565	4	2.713
6	6.5844	11	−1	−2.0903	1	2.0903
7	7.8182	12	0	−0.8565	0	0
8	7.8351	13	1	−0.8396	1	−0.8396
9	11.0223	14	2	2.3476	4	4.6952
10	10.6738	15	3	1.9991	9	5.9973
11	10.8361	16	4	2.1614	16	8.6456
12	13.615	17	5	4.9403	25	24.7015
13	13.531	18	6	4.8563	36	29.1378
Sum	112.7712	156	0	0	182	131.7856

Obs	X_i^2	Y_i^2	$\hat{Y}_i$	$\hat{u}_i = Y_i - \hat{Y}$	$\hat{u}_i^2$
1	36	19.86217	4.165294	0.291406	0.084917
2	49	33.2929	4.916863	0.853137	0.727843
3	64	35.74485	5.668432	0.310268	0.096266
4	81	53.75382	6.420001	0.911699	0.831195
5	100	53.55605	7.17157	0.14663	0.0215
6	121	43.35432	7.923139	−1.33874	1.792222
7	144	61.12425	8.674708	−0.85651	0.733606
8	169	61.38879	9.426277	−1.59118	2.531844
9	196	121.4911	10.17785	0.844454	0.713103
10	225	113.93	10.92941	−0.25562	0.065339
11	256	117.4211	11.68098	−0.84488	0.713829
12	289	185.3682	12.13255	1.182447	1.398181
13	324	183.088	13.18412	0.346878	0.120324
Sum	2054	1083.376	112.7712	≈0	9.83017

Note:

$$x_i = X_i - \bar{X};\ y_i = Y_i = \bar{Y}$$

$$\hat{\beta}_2 = \frac{\Sigma y_i x_i}{\Sigma x_i^2} = \frac{131.7856}{182.0} = 0.7240967$$

$$\hat{\beta}_1 = \bar{Y} - \hat{\beta}_2 \bar{X} = 8.674708 - 0.7240967x12 = -0.01445$$

$$\hat{\sigma}^2 = \frac{\Sigma \hat{u}_i^2}{n-2} = \frac{9.83017}{11} = 0.893652;\ \hat{\sigma} = 0.945332$$

$$\text{var}(\hat{\beta}_2) = \frac{\hat{\sigma}^2}{\Sigma x_i^2} = \frac{0.893652}{182.0} = 0.004910;\ \text{se}(\hat{\beta}_2) = \sqrt{0.00490} = 0.070072$$

$$r^2 = 1 - \frac{\Sigma \hat{u}_i^2}{\Sigma (Y_i - \bar{Y})^2} = 1 \frac{9.83017}{105.1188} = 0.9065$$

$$r = \sqrt{r^2} = 0.9521$$

$$\text{var}(\hat{\beta}_1) = \frac{\Sigma x_i^2}{n \Sigma x_i^2} = \frac{2054}{13(182)} = 0.868132;$$

$$\text{se}(\hat{\beta}_1) = \sqrt{0.868132} = 0.9317359$$

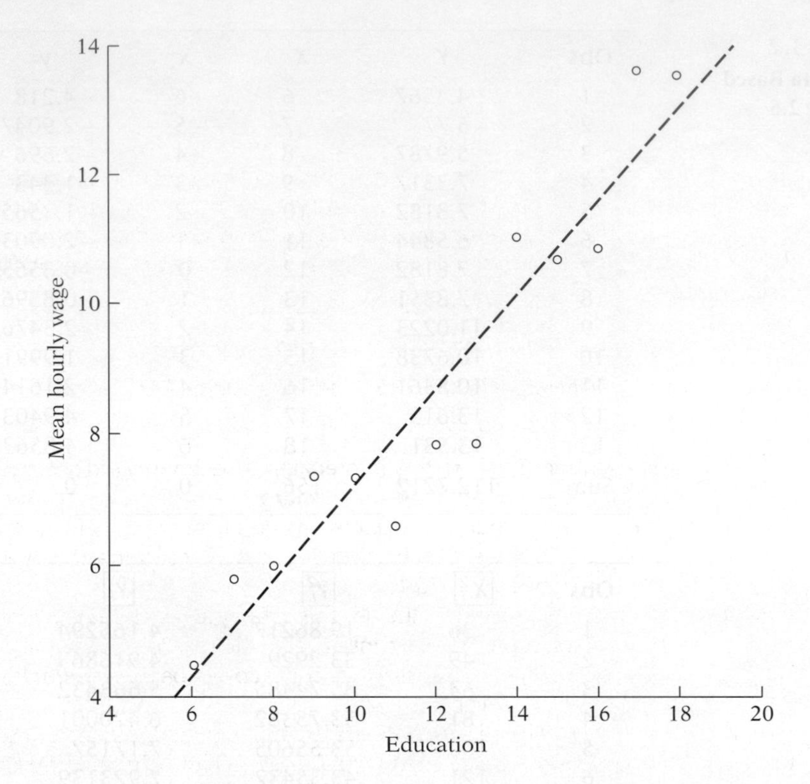

FIGURE 3.11 Estimated regression line for wage-education data from Table 2.6.

From the data given in this table, we obtain the estimated regression line as follows:

$$\hat{Y}_i = -0.0144 + 0.7240X_i \tag{3.6.1}$$

Geometrically, the estimated regression line is as shown in Figure 3.11.

As we know, each point on the regression line gives an estimate of the mean value of Y corresponding to the chosen X value, that is, $\hat{Y}_i$ is an estimate of $E(Y \mid X_i)$. The value of $\hat{\beta}_2 = 0.7240$, which measures the slope of the line, shows that, within the sample range of X between 6 and 18 years of education, as X increases by 1, the estimated increase in mean hourly wages is about 72 cents. That is, each additional year of schooling, on average, increases hourly wages by about 72 cents.

The value of $\hat{\beta}_1 = -0.0144$, which is the intercept of the line, indicates the average level of wages when the level of education is zero. Such literal interpretation of the intercept in the present case does not make any sense. How could there be negative wages? As we will see throughout this book, very often the intercept term has no viable practical meaning. Besides, zero level of education is not in the observed level of education in our sample. As we will see in Chapter 5, the observed value of the intercept is not statistically different from zero.

The r^2 value of about 0.90 suggests that education explains about 90 percent of the variation in hourly wage. Considering that r^2 can be at most 1, our regression line fits the data very well. The coefficient of correlation, $r = 0.9521$, shows that wages and education are highly positively correlated.

Before we leave our example, note that our model is extremely simple. Labor economics theory tells us that, besides education, variables such as gender, race, location, labor unions, and language are also important factors in the determination of hourly wages. After we study multiple regression in Chapters 7 and 8, we will consider a more extended model of wage determination.

3.7 Illustrative Examples

EXAMPLE 3.1

Consumption–Income Relationship in the United States, 1960–2005

Let us revisit the consumption income data given in Table I.1 of the Introduction. We have already shown the data in Figure I.3, along with the estimated regression line in Eq. (I.3.3). Now we provide the underlying OLS regression results, which were obtained from *EViews 6*. Note $Y =$ personal consumption expenditure (PCE) and $X =$ gross domestic product (GDP), both measured in 2000 billions of dollars. In this example the data are time series data.

$$\hat{Y}_t = -299.5913 + 0.7218X_t \tag{3.7.1}$$

$$\text{var}(\hat{\beta}_1) = 827.4195 \qquad \text{se}(\hat{\beta}_1) = 28.7649$$
$$\text{var}(\hat{\beta}_2) = 0.0000195 \qquad \text{se}(\hat{\beta}_2) = 0.004423$$
$$r^2 = 0.9983 \qquad \hat{\sigma}^2 = 73.56689$$

Equation 3.7.1 is the aggregate, or economywide, Keynesian consumption function. As this equation shows, the **marginal propensity to consume (MPC)** is about 0.72, suggesting that if (real income) goes up by a dollar, the average personal consumption expenditure goes up by about 72 cents. According to Keynesian theory, MPC is expected to lie between 0 and 1.

The intercept value in this example is negative, which has no viable economic interpretation. Literally interpreted, it means that if the value of GDP were zero, the average level of personal consumption expenditure would be a negative value of about 299 billion dollars.

The r^2 value of 0.9983 means approximately 99 percent of the variation in personal consumption expenditure is explained by variation in the GDP. This value is quite high, considering that r^2 can at most be 1. As we will see throughout this book, in regressions involving time series data one generally obtains high r^2 values. We will explore the reasons behind this in the chapter on autocorrelation and also in the chapter on time series econometrics.

EXAMPLE 3.2

Food Expenditure in India

Refer to the data given in Table 2.8 of Exercise 2.15. The data relate to a sample of 55 rural households in India. The regressand in this example is expenditure on food and the regressor is total expenditure, a proxy for income, both figures in rupees. The data in this example are thus *cross-sectional* data.

On the basis of the given data, we obtained the following regression:

$$\widehat{\text{FoodExp}}_i = 94.2087 + 0.4368 \text{ TotalExp}_i \tag{3.7.2}$$

$$\text{var}(\hat{\beta}_1) = 2560.9401 \qquad \text{se}(\hat{\beta}_1) = 50.8563$$
$$\text{var}(\hat{\beta}_2) = 0.0061 \qquad \text{se}(\hat{\beta}_2) = 0.0783$$
$$r^2 = 0.3698 \qquad \hat{\sigma}^2 = 4469.6913$$

From Equation 3.7.2 we see that if total expenditure increases by 1 rupee, on average, expenditure on food goes up by about 44 paise (1 rupee = 100 paise). If total expenditure were zero, the average expenditure on food would be about 94 rupees. Again, such a mechanical interpretation of the intercept may not be meaningful. However, in this example one could argue that even if total expenditure is zero (e.g., because of loss of a job), people may still maintain some minimum level of food expenditure by borrowing money or by dissaving.

The r^2 value of about 0.37 means that only 37 percent of the variation in food expenditure is explained by the total expenditure. This might seem a rather low value, but as we will see throughout this text, in cross-sectional data, typically one obtains low r^2 values, possibly because of the diversity of the units in the sample. We will discuss this topic further in the chapter on heteroscedasticity (see Chapter 11).

EXAMPLE 3.3 *Demand for Cellular Phones and Personal Computers in Relation to Per Capita Personal Income*

Table 3.3 gives data on the number of cell phone subscribers and the number of personal computers (PCs), both per 100 persons, and the purchasing-power adjusted per capita income in dollars for a sample of 34 countries. Thus we have cross-sectional data. These data are for the year 2003 and are obtained from the *Statistical Abstract of the United states, 2006*.

Although cell phones and personal computers are used extensively in the United States, that is not the case in many countries. To see if per capita income is a factor in the use of cell phones and PCs, we regressed each of these means of communication on per capita income using the sample of 34 countries. The results are as follows:

TABLE 3.3 Number of Cellular Phone Subscribers per Hundred Persons and Number of Personal Computers per 100 Persons and Per Capita Income in Selected Countries for 2003

Source: *Statistical Abstract of the United States*, 2006, Table 1364 for data on cell phones and computers and Table 1327 for purchasing-power adjusted per capita income.

Country	Cellphone	PCs	Per Capita Income ($)
Argentina	17.76	8.2	11410
Australia	71.95	60.18	28780
Belgium	79.28	31.81	28920
Brazil	26.36	7.48	7510
Bulgaria	46.64	5.19	75.4
Canada	41.9	48.7	30040
China	21.48	2.76	4980
Colombia	14.13	4.93	6410
Czech Republic	96.46	17.74	15600
Ecuador	18.92	3.24	3940
Egypt	8.45	2.91	3940
France	69.59	34.71	27640
Germany	78.52	48.47	27610
Greece	90.23	8.17	19900
Guatemala	13.15	1.44	4090
Hungary	76.88	10.84	13840
India	2.47	0.72	2880
Indonesia	8.74	1.19	3210
Italy	101.76	23.07	26,830
Japan	67.9	38.22	28450
Mexico	29.47	8.3	8980
Netherlands	76.76	46.66	28560
Pakistan	1.75	0.42	2040
Poland	45.09	14.2	11210
Russia	24.93	8.87	8950
Saudia Arabia	32.11	13.67	13230
South Africa	36.36	7.26	10130
Spain	91.61	19.6	22150
Sweden	98.05	62.13	26710
Switzerland	84.34	70.87	32220
Thailand	39.42	3.98	7450
U.K.	91.17	40.57	27690
U.S.	54.58	65.98	37750
Venezuela	27.3	6.09	4750

Note: The data on cell phones and personal computers are per 100 persons.

EXAMPLE 3.3
(Continued)

Demand for Cell Phones. Letting Y = number of cell phone subscribers and X = purchasing-power-adjusted per capita income, we obtained the following regression.

$$\hat{Y}_i = 14.4773 + 0.0022X_i \tag{3.7.3}$$

$$\text{se}(\hat{\beta}_1) = 6.1523; \quad \text{se}(\hat{\beta}_2) = 0.00032$$

$$r^2 = 0.6023$$

The slope coefficient suggests that if per capita income goes up by, say, \$1,000, on average, the number of cell phone subscribers goes up by about 2.2 per 100 persons. The intercept value of about 14.47 suggests that even if the per capita income is zero, the average number of cell phone subscribers is about 14 per 100 subscribers. Again, this interpretation may not have much meaning, for in our sample we do not have any country with zero per capita income. The r^2 value is moderately high. But notice that our sample includes a variety of countries with varying levels of income. In such a diverse sample we would not expect a very high r^2 value.

After we study Chapter 5, we will show how the estimated standard errors reported in Equation 3.7.3 can be used to assess the statistical significance of the estimated coefficients.

Demand for Personal Computers. Although the prices of personal computers have come down substantially over the years, PCs are still not ubiquitous. An important determinant of the demand for personal computers is personal income. Another determinant is price, but we do not have comparative data on PC prices for the countries in our sample.

Letting Y denote the number of PCs and X the per capita income, we have the following "partial" demand for the PCs (partial because we do not have comparative price data or data on other variables that might affect the demand for the PCs).

$$\hat{Y}_i = -6.5833 + 0.0018X_i \tag{3.7.4}$$

$$\text{se}(\hat{\beta}_1) = 2.7437; \quad \text{se}(\hat{\beta}_2) = 0.00014$$

$$r^2 = 0.8290$$

As these results suggest, per capita personal income has a positive relationship to the demand for PCs. After we study Chapter 5, you will see that, statistically, per capita personal income is an important determinant of the demand for PCs. The negative value of the intercept in the present instance has no practical significance. Despite the diversity of our sample, the estimated r^2 value is quite high. The interpretation of the slope coefficient is that if per capita income increases by, say, \$1,000, on average, the demand for personal computers goes up by about 2 units per 100 persons.

Even though the use of personal computers is spreading quickly, there are many countries which still use main-frame computers. Therefore, the total usage of computers in those countries may be much higher than that indicated by the sale of PCs.

3.8 A Note on Monte Carlo Experiments

In this chapter we showed that under the assumptions of CLRM the least-squares estimators have certain desirable statistical features summarized in the BLUE property. In the appendix to this chapter we prove this property more formally. But in practice how does one know that the BLUE property holds? For example, how does one find out if the OLS estimators are unbiased? The answer is provided by the so-called **Monte Carlo** experiments, which are essentially computer simulation, or sampling, experiments.

To introduce the basic ideas, consider our two-variable PRF:

$$Y_i = \beta_1 + \beta_2 X_i + u_i \tag{3.8.1}$$

A Monte Carlo experiment proceeds as follows:

1. Suppose the true values of the parameters are as follows: $\beta_1 = 20$ and $\beta_2 = 0.6$.
2. You choose the sample size, say $n = 25$.
3. You fix the values of X for each observation. In all you will have 25 X values.
4. Suppose you go to a random number table, choose 25 values, and call them u_i (these days most statistical packages have built-in random number generators).[24]
5. Since you *know* β_1, β_2, X_i, and u_i, using Equation 3.8.1 you obtain 25 Y_i values.
6. Now using the 25 Y_i values thus generated, you regress these on the 25 X values chosen in step 3, obtaining $\hat{\beta}_1$ and $\hat{\beta}_2$, the least-squares estimators.
7. Suppose you repeat this experiment 99 times, each time using the same β_1, β_2, and X values. Of course, the u_i values will vary from experiment to experiment. Therefore, in all you have 100 experiments, thus generating 100 values each of β_1 and β_2. (In practice, many such experiments are conducted, sometimes 1000 to 2000.)
8. You take the averages of these 100 estimates and call them $\bar{\hat{\beta}}_1$ and $\bar{\hat{\beta}}_2$.
9. If these average values are about the same as the true values of β_1 and β_2 assumed in step 1, this Monte Carlo experiment "establishes" that the least-squares estimators are indeed unbiased. Recall that under CLRM $E(\hat{\beta}_1) = \beta_1$ and $E(\hat{\beta}_2) = \beta_2$.

These steps characterize the general nature of the Monte Carlo experiments. Such experiments are often used to study the statistical properties of various methods of estimating population parameters. They are particularly useful to study the behavior of estimators in small, or finite, samples. These experiments are also an excellent means of driving home the concept of **repeated sampling** that is the basis of most of classical statistical inference, as we shall see in Chapter 5. We shall provide several examples of Monte Carlo experiments by way of exercises for classroom assignment. (See Exercise 3.27.)

Summary and Conclusions

The important topics and concepts developed in this chapter can be summarized as follows.

1. The basic framework of regression analysis is the **CLRM.**
2. The CLRM is based on a set of assumptions.
3. Based on these assumptions, the least-squares estimators take on certain properties summarized in the Gauss–Markov theorem, which states that in the class of linear unbiased estimators, the least-squares estimators have minimum variance. In short, they are BLUE.
4. The *precision* of OLS estimators is measured by their **standard errors.** In Chapters 4 and 5 we shall see how the standard errors enable one to draw inferences on the population parameters, the β coefficients.
5. The overall goodness of fit of the regression model is measured by the **coefficient of determination,** r^2. It tells what proportion of the variation in the dependent variable, or regressand, is explained by the explanatory variable, or regressor. This r^2 lies between 0 and 1; the closer it is to 1, the better is the fit.

[24]In practice it is assumed that u_i follows a certain probability distribution, say, normal, with certain parameters (e.g., the mean and variance). Once the values of the parameters are specified, one can easily generate the u_i using statistical packages.

6. A concept related to the coefficient of determination is the **coefficient of correlation,** r. It is a measure of *linear association* between two variables and it lies between -1 and $+1$.
7. The CLRM is a theoretical construct or abstraction because it is based on a set of assumptions that may be stringent or "unrealistic." But such abstraction is often necessary in the initial stages of studying any field of knowledge. Once the CLRM is mastered, one can find out what happens if one or more of its assumptions are not satisfied. The first part of this book is devoted to studying the CLRM. The other parts of the book consider the refinements of the CLRM. Table 3.4 gives the road map ahead.

TABLE 3.4
What Happens If the Assumptions of CLRM Are Violated?

Assumption Number	Type of Violation	Where to Study?
1	Nonlinearity in parameters	Chapter 14
2	Stochastic regressor(s)	Chapter 13
3	Nonzero mean of u_i	Introduction to Part II
4	Heteroscedasticity	Chapter 11
5	Autocorrelated disturbances	Chapter 12
6	Sample observations less than the number of regressors	Chapter 10
7	Insufficient variability in regressors	Chapter 10
8	Multicollinearity*	Chapter 10
9	Specification bias*	Chapters 13, 14
10**	Nonnormality of disturbances	Chapter 13

*These assumptions will be introduced in Chapter 7, when we discuss the multiple regression model.
**Note: The assumption that the disturbances u_i are normally distributed is not a part of the CLRM. But more on this in Chapter 4.

EXERCISES

Questions

3.1. Given the assumptions in column 1 of the table, show that the assumptions in column 2 are equivalent to them.

Assumptions of the Classical Model

(1)	(2)
$E(u_i \mid X_i) = 0$	$E(Y_i \mid X_i) = \beta_2 + \beta_2 X$
$\text{cov}\,(u_i, u_j) = 0 \; i \neq j$	$\text{cov}\,(Y_i, Y_j) = 0 \; i \neq j$
$\text{var}\,(u_i \mid X_i) = \sigma^2$	$\text{var}\,(Y_i \mid X_i) = \sigma^2$

3.2. Show that the estimates $\hat{\beta}_1 = 1.572$ and $\hat{\beta}_2 = 1.357$ used in the first experiment of Table 3.1 are in fact the OLS estimators.

3.3. According to Malinvaud (see footnote 11), the assumption that $E(u_i \mid X_i) = 0$ is quite important. To see this, consider the PRF: $Y = \beta_1 + \beta_2 X_i + u_i$. Now consider two situations: (i) $\beta_1 = 0$, $\beta_2 = 1$, and $E(u_i) = 0$; and (ii) $\beta_1 = 1$, $\beta_2 = 0$, and $E(u_i) = (X_i - 1)$. Now take the expectation of the PRF conditional upon X in the two preceding cases and see if you agree with Malinvaud about the significance of the assumption $E(u_i \mid X_i) = 0$.

3.4. Consider the sample regression

$$Y_i = \hat{\beta}_1 + \hat{\beta}_2 X_i + \hat{u}_i$$

Imposing the restrictions (i) $\sum \hat{u}_i = 0$ and (ii) $\sum \hat{u}_i X_i = 0$, obtain the estimators $\hat{\beta}_1$ and $\hat{\beta}_2$ and show that they are identical with the least-squares estimators given in Eqs. (3.1.6) and (3.1.7). This method of obtaining estimators is called the **analogy principle.** Give an intuitive justification for imposing restrictions (i) and (ii). (*Hint:* Recall the CLRM assumptions about u_i.) In passing, note that the analogy principle of estimating unknown parameters is also known as the **method of moments** in which sample moments (e.g., sample mean) are used to estimate population moments (e.g., the population mean). As noted in **Appendix A**, a **moment** is a summary statistic of a probability distribution, such as the expected value and variance.

3.5. Show that r^2 defined in (3.5.5) ranges between 0 and 1. You may use the Cauchy–Schwarz inequality, which states that for any random variables X and Y the following relationship holds true:

$$[E(XY)]^2 \leq E(X^2)E(Y^2)$$

3.6. Let $\hat{\beta}_{YX}$ and $\hat{\beta}_{XY}$ represent the slopes in the regression of Y on X and X on Y, respectively. Show that

$$\hat{\beta}_{YX}\hat{\beta}_{XY} = r^2$$

where r is the coefficient of correlation between X and Y.

3.7. Suppose in Exercise 3.6 that $\hat{\beta}_{YX}\hat{\beta}_{XY} = 1$. Does it matter then if we regress Y on X or X on Y? Explain carefully.

3.8. Spearman's rank correlation coefficient r_s is defined as follows:

$$r_s = 1 - \frac{6\sum d^2}{n(n^2 - 1)}$$

where d = difference in the ranks assigned to the same individual or phenomenon and n = number of individuals or phenomena ranked. Derive r_s from r defined in Eq. (3.5.13). *Hint:* Rank the X and Y values from 1 to n. Note that the sum of X and Y ranks is $n(n + 1)/2$ each and therefore their means are $(n + 1)/2$.

3.9. Consider the following formulations of the two-variable PRF:

$$\text{Model I:} \quad Y_i = \beta_1 + \beta_2 X_i + u_i$$

$$\text{Model II:} \quad Y_i = \alpha_1 + \alpha_2(X_i - \bar{X}) + u_i$$

a. Find the estimators of β_1 and α_1. Are they identical? Are their variances identical?

b. Find the estimators of β_2 and α_2. Are they identical? Are their variances identical?

c. What is the advantage, if any, of model II over model I?

3.10. Suppose you run the following regression:

$$y_i = \hat{\beta}_1 + \hat{\beta}_2 x_i + \hat{u}_i$$

where, as usual, y_i and x_i are deviations from their respective mean values. What will be the value of $\hat{\beta}_1$? Why? Will $\hat{\beta}_2$ be the same as that obtained from Eq. (3.1.6)? Why?

3.11. Let $r_1 =$ coefficient of correlation between n pairs of values (Y_i, X_i) and $r_2 =$ coefficient of correlation between n pairs of values $(aX_i + b,\ cY_i + d)$, where a, b, c, and d are constants. Show that $r_1 = r_2$ and hence *establish the principle that the coefficient of correlation is invariant with respect to the change of scale and the change of origin.*

Hint: Apply the definition of r given in Eq. (3.5.13).

Note: The operations aX_i, $X_i + b$, and $aX_i + b$ are known, respectively, as the *change of scale, change of origin,* and *change of both scale and origin.*

3.12. If r, the coefficient of correlation between n pairs of values (X_i, Y_i), is positive, then determine whether each of the following statements is true or false:

a. r between $(-X_i, -Y_i)$ is also positive.

b. r between $(-X_i, Y_i)$ and that between $(X_i, -Y_i)$ can be either positive or negative.

c. Both the slope coefficients β_{yx} and β_{xy} are positive, where $\beta_{yx} =$ slope coefficient in the regression of Y on X and $\beta_{xy} =$ slope coefficient in the regression of X on Y.

3.13. If X_1, X_2, and X_3 are uncorrelated variables each having the same standard deviation, show that the coefficient of correlation between $X_1 + X_2$ and $X_2 + X_3$ is equal to $\frac{1}{2}$. Why is the correlation coefficient not zero?

3.14. In the regression $Y_i = \beta_1 + \beta_2 X_i + u_i$ suppose we *multiply* each X value by a constant, say, 2. Will it change the residuals and fitted values of Y? Explain. What if we *add* a constant value, say, 2, to each X value?

3.15. Show that Eq. (3.5.14) in fact measures the coefficient of determination. *Hint:* Apply the definition of r given in Eq. (3.5.13) and recall that $\sum y_i \hat{y}_i = \sum(\hat{y}_i + \hat{u}_i)\hat{y}_i = \sum \hat{y}_i^2$, and remember Eq. (3.5.6).

3.16. Explain *with reason* whether the following statements are true, false, or uncertain:

a. Since the correlation between two variables, Y and X, can range from -1 to $+1$, this also means that cov (Y, X) also lies between these limits.

b. If the correlation between two variables is zero, it means that there is no relationship between the two variables whatsoever.

c. If you regress Y_i on $\hat{Y}_i$ (i.e., actual Y on estimated Y), the intercept and slope values will be 0 and 1, respectively.

3.17. *Regression without any regressor.* Suppose you are given the model: $Y_i = \beta_1 + u_i$. Use OLS to find the estimator of β_1. What is its variance and the RSS? Does the estimated β_1 make intuitive sense? Now consider the two-variable model $Y_i = \beta_1 + \beta_2 X_i + u_i$. Is it worth adding X_i to the model? If not, why bother with regression analysis?

Empirical Exercises

3.18. In Table 3.5, you are given the ranks of 10 students in midterm and final examinations in statistics. Compute Spearman's coefficient of rank correlation and interpret it.

TABLE 3.5

	Student									
Rank	A	B	C	D	E	F	G	H	I	J
Midterm	1	3	7	10	9	5	4	8	2	6
Final	3	2	8	7	9	6	5	10	1	4

3.19. *The relationship between nominal exchange rate and relative prices.* From annual observations from 1985 to 2005, the following regression results were obtained, where Y = exchange rate of the Canadian dollar to the U.S. dollar (CD/$) and X = ratio of the U.S. consumer price index to the Canadian consumer price index; that is, X represents the relative prices in the two countries:

$$\hat{Y}_t = -0.912 + 2.250X_t \qquad r^2 = 0.440$$
$$\text{se} = \qquad 0.096$$

a. Interpret this regression. How would you interpret r^2?

b. Does the positive value of X_t make economic sense? What is the underlying economic theory?

c. Suppose we were to redefine X as the ratio of the Canadian CPI to the U.S. CPI. Would that change the sign of X? Why?

3.20. Table 3.6 gives data on indexes of output per hour (X) and real compensation per hour (Y) for the business and nonfarm business sectors of the U.S. economy for 1960–2005. The base year of the indexes is 1992 = 100 and the indexes are seasonally adjusted.

a. Plot Y against X for the two sectors separately.

b. What is the economic theory behind the relationship between the two variables? Does the scattergram support the theory?

c. Estimate the OLS regression of Y on X. Save the results for a further look after we study Chapter 5.

3.21. From a sample of 10 observations, the following results were obtained:

$$\sum Y_i = 1{,}110 \quad \sum X_i = 1{,}700 \quad \sum X_i Y_i = 205{,}500$$
$$\sum X_i^2 = 322{,}000 \quad \sum Y_i^2 = 132{,}100$$

with coefficient of correlation $r = 0.9758$. But on rechecking these calculations it was found that two pairs of observations were recorded:

Y	X		Y	X
90	120	instead of	80	110
140	220		150	210

What will be the effect of this error on r? Obtain the correct r.

3.22. Table 3.7 gives data on gold prices, the Consumer Price Index (CPI), and the New York Stock Exchange (NYSE) Index for the United States for the period 1974–2006. The NYSE Index includes most of the stocks listed on the NYSE, some 1500-plus.

a. Plot in the same scattergram gold prices, CPI, and the NYSE Index.

b. An investment is supposed to be a hedge against inflation if its price and/or rate of return at least keeps pace with inflation. To test this hypothesis, suppose you decide to fit the following model, assuming the scatterplot in (a) suggests that this is appropriate:

$$\text{Gold price}_t = \beta_1 + \beta_2 \,\text{CPI}_t + u_t$$
$$\text{NYSE index}_t = \beta_1 + \beta_2 \,\text{CPI}_t + u_t$$

TABLE 3.6
Productivity and Related Data, Business Sector 1960–2005 (Index numbers, 1992 =100; quarterly data seasonally adjusted)

Source: *Economic Report of the President,* 2007, Table 49.

	Output per Hour of All Persons[1]		Real Compensation per Hour[2,3]	
Year	Business Sector	Nonfarm Business Sector	Business Sector	Nonfarm Business Sector
1960	48.9	51.9	60.8	63.3
1961	50.6	53.5	62.5	64.8
1962	52.9	55.9	64.6	66.7
1963	55.0	57.8	66.1	68.1
1964	56.8	59.6	67.7	69.3
1965	58.8	61.4	69.1	70.5
1966	61.2	63.6	71.7	72.6
1967	62.5	64.7	73.5	74.5
1968	64.7	66.9	76.2	77.1
1969	65.0	67.0	77.3	78.1
1970	66.3	68.0	78.8	79.2
1971	69.0	70.7	80.2	80.7
1972	71.2	73.1	82.6	83.2
1973	73.4	75.3	84.3	84.7
1974	72.3	74.2	83.3	83.8
1975	74.8	76.2	84.1	84.5
1976	77.1	78.7	86.4	86.6
1977	78.5	80.0	87.6	88.0
1978	79.3	81.0	89.1	89.6
1979	79.3	80.7	89.3	89.7
1980	79.2	80.6	89.1	89.6
1981	80.8	81.7	89.3	89.8
1982	80.1	80.8	90.4	90.8
1983	83.0	84.5	90.3	90.9
1984	85.2	86.1	90.7	91.1
1985	87.1	87.5	92.0	92.2
1986	89.7	90.2	94.9	95.2
1987	90.1	90.6	95.2	95.5
1988	91.5	92.1	96.5	96.7
1989	92.4	92.8	95.0	95.1
1990	94.4	94.5	96.2	96.1
1991	95.9	96.1	97.4	97.4
1992	100.0	100.0	100.0	100.0
1993	100.4	100.4	99.7	99.5
1994	101.3	101.5	99.0	99.1
1995	101.5	102.0	98.7	98.8
1996	104.5	104.7	99.4	99.4
1997	106.5	106.4	100.5	100.3
1998	109.5	109.4	105.2	104.9
1999	112.8	112.5	108.0	107.5
2000	116.1	115.7	112.0	111.5
2001	119.1	118.6	113.5	112.8
2002	124.0	123.5	115.7	115.1
2003	128.7	128.0	117.7	117.1
2004	132.7	131.8	119.0	118.2
2005	135.7	134.9	120.2	119.3

[1]Output refers to real gross domestic product in the sector.
[2]Wages and salaries of employees plus employers' contributions for social insurance and private benefit plans.
[3]Hourly compensation divided by the consumer price index for all urban consumers for recent quarters.

TABLE 3.7
Gold Prices, New York Stock Exchange Index, and Consumer Price Index for U.S. for 1974–2006

Year	Gold Price	NYSE	CPI
1974	159.2600	463.5400	49.30000
1975	161.0200	483.5500	53.80000
1976	124.8400	575.8500	56.90000
1977	157.7100	567.6600	60.60000
1978	193.2200	567.8100	65.20000
1979	306.6800	616.6800	72.60000
1980	612.5600	720.1500	82.40000
1981	460.0300	782.6200	90.90000
1982	375.6700	728.8400	96.50000
1983	424.3500	979.5200	99.60000
1984	360.4800	977.3300	103.9000
1985	317.2600	1142.970	107.6000
1986	367.6600	1438.020	109.6000
1987	446.4600	1709.790	113.6000
1988	436.9400	1585.140	118.3000
1989	381.4400	1903.360	124.0000
1990	383.5100	1939.470	130.7000
1991	362.1100	2181.720	136.2000
1992	343.8200	2421.510	140.3000
1993	359.7700	2638.960	144.5000
1994	384.0000	2687.020	148.2000
1995	384.1700	3078.560	152.4000
1996	387.7700	3787.200	156.9000
1997	331.0200	4827.350	160.5000
1998	294.2400	5818.260	163.0000
1999	278.8800	6546.810	166.6000
2000	279.1100	6805.890	172.2000
2001	274.0400	6397.850	177.1000
2002	309.7300	5578.890	179.9000
2003	363.3800	5447.460	184.0000
2004	409.7200	6612.620	188.9000
2005	444.7400	7349.000	195.3000
2006	603.4600	8357.990	201.6000

3.23. Table 3.8 gives data on gross domestic product (GDP) for the United States for the years 1959–2005.

a. Plot the GDP data in current and constant (i.e., 2000) dollars against time.

b. Letting Y denote GDP and X time (measured chronologically starting with 1 for 1959, 2 for 1960, through 47 for 2005), see if the following model fits the GDP data:

$$Y_t = \beta_1 + \beta_2 X_t + u_t$$

Estimate this model for both current and constant-dollar GDP.

c. How would you interpret β_2?

d. If there is a difference between β_2 estimated for current-dollar GDP and that estimated for constant-dollar GDP, what explains the difference?

e. From your results what can you say about the nature of inflation in the United States over the sample period?

TABLE 3.8
Nominal and Real Gross Domestic Product, 1959–2005 (billions of dollars, except as noted; quarterly data at seasonally adjusted annual rates; RGDP in billions of chained [2000] dollars)

Year	NGDP	RGDP	Year	NGDP	RGDP
1959	506.6	2,441.3	1983	3,536.7	5,423.8
1960	526.4	2,501.8	1984	3,933.2	5,813.6
1961	544.7	2,560.0	1985	4,220.3	6,053.7
1962	585.6	2,715.2	1986	4,462.8	6,263.6
1963	617.7	2,834.0	1987	4,739.5	6,475.1
1964	663.6	2,998.6	1988	5,103.8	6,742.7
1965	719.1	3,191.1	1989	5,484.4	6,981.4
1966	787.8	3,399.1	1990	5,803.1	7,112.5
1967	832.6	3,484.6	1991	5,995.9	7,100.5
1968	910.0	3,652.7	1992	6,337.7	7,336.6
1969	984.6	3,765.4	1993	6,657.4	7,532.7
1970	1,038.5	3,771.9	1994	7,072.2	7,835.5
1971	1,127.1	3,898.6	1995	7,397.7	8,031.7
1972	1,238.3	4,105.0	1996	7,816.9	8,328.9
1973	1,382.7	4,341.5	1997	8,304.3	8,703.5
1974	1,500.0	4,319.6	1998	8,747.0	9,066.9
1975	1,638.3	4,311.2	1999	9,268.4	9,470.3
1976	1,825.3	4,540.9	2000	9,817.0	9,817.0
1977	2,030.9	4,750.5	2001	10,128.0	9,890.7
1978	2,294.7	5,015.0	2002	10,469.6	10,048.8
1979	2,563.3	5,173.4	2003	10,960.8	10,301.0
1980	2,789.5	5,161.7	2004	11,712.5	10,703.5
1981	3,128.4	5,291.7	2005	12,455.8	11,048.6
1982	3,255.0	5,189.3			

Source: *Economic Report of the President,* 2007. Table B-1 and B-2.

3.24. Using the data given in Table I.1 of the Introduction, verify Eq. (3.7.1).

3.25. For the SAT example given in Exercise 2.16 do the following:

a. Plot the female reading score against the male reading score.

b. If the scatterplot suggests that a linear relationship between the two seems appropriate, obtain the regression of female reading score on male reading score.

c. If there is a relationship between the two reading scores, is the relationship *causal?*

3.26. Repeat Exercise 3.25, replacing math scores for reading scores.

3.27. Monte Carlo study *classroom assignment:* Refer to the 10 X values given in Table 2.4. Let $\beta_1 = 25$ and $\beta_2 = 0.5$. Assume $u_i \approx N(0, 9)$, that is, u_i are normally distributed with mean 0 and variance 9. Generate 100 samples using these values, obtaining 100 estimates of β_1 and β_2. Graph these estimates. What conclusions can you draw from the Monte Carlo study? *Note:* Most statistical packages now can generate random variables from most well-known probability distributions. Ask your instructor for help, in case you have difficulty generating such variables.

3.28. Using the data given in Table 3.3, plot the number of cell phone subscribers against the number of personal computers in use. Is there any discernible relationship between the two? If so, how do you rationalize the relationship?

Appendix 3A

3A.1 Derivation of Least-Squares Estimates

Differentiating Eq. (3.1.2) partially with respect to $\hat{\beta}_1$ and $\hat{\beta}_2$, we obtain

$$\frac{\partial\left(\sum \hat{u}_i^2\right)}{\partial \hat{\beta}_1} = -2\sum(Y_i - \hat{\beta}_1 - \hat{\beta}_2 X_i) = -2\sum \hat{u}_i \tag{1}$$

$$\frac{\partial\left(\sum \hat{u}_i^2\right)}{\partial \hat{\beta}_2} = -2\sum(Y_i - \hat{\beta}_1 - \hat{\beta}_2 X_i)X_i = -2\sum \hat{u}_i X_i \tag{2}$$

Setting these equations to zero, after algebraic simplification and manipulation, gives the estimators given in Eqs. (3.1.6) and (3.1.7).

3A.2 Linearity and Unbiasedness Properties of Least-Squares Estimators

From Eq. (3.1.8) we have

$$\hat{\beta}_2 = \frac{\sum x_i Y_i}{\sum x_i^2} = \sum k_i Y_i \tag{3}$$

where

$$k_i = \frac{x_i}{\left(\sum x_i^2\right)}$$

which shows that $\hat{\beta}_2$ is a **linear estimator** because it is a linear function of Y; actually it is a weighted average of Y_i with k_i serving as the weights. It can similarly be shown that $\hat{\beta}_1$ too is a linear estimator.

Incidentally, note these properties of the weights k_i:

1. Since the X_i are assumed to be nonstochastic, the k_i are nonstochastic too.
2. $\sum k_i = 0$.
3. $\sum k_i^2 = 1\big/\sum x_i^2$.
4. $\sum k_i x_i = \sum k_i X_i = 1$. These properties can be directly verified from the definition of k_i.

For example,

$$\sum k_i = \sum\left(\frac{x_i}{\sum x_i^2}\right) = \frac{1}{\sum x_i^2}\sum x_i, \quad \text{since for a given sample } \sum x_i^2 \text{ is known}$$

$$= 0, \quad \text{since } \sum x_i \text{, the sum of deviations from the mean value, is always zero}$$

Now substitute the PRF $Y_i = \beta_1 + \beta_2 X_i + u_i$ into Equation (3) to obtain

$$\begin{aligned}\hat{\beta}_2 &= \sum k_i(\beta_1 + \beta_2 X_i + u_i) \\ &= \beta_1 \sum k_i + \beta_2 \sum k_i X_i + \sum k_i u_i \\ &= \beta_2 + \sum k_i u_i\end{aligned} \tag{4}$$

where use is made of the properties of k_i noted earlier.

Now taking expectation of Equation (4) on both sides and noting that k_i, being nonstochastic, can be treated as constants, we obtain

$$\begin{aligned} E(\hat{\beta}_2) &= \beta_2 + \sum k_i E(u_i) \\ &= \beta_2 \end{aligned} \tag{5}$$

since $E(u_i) = 0$ by assumption. Therefore, $\hat{\beta}_2$ is an unbiased estimator of β_2. Likewise, it can be proved that $\hat{\beta}_1$ is also an unbiased estimator of β_1.

3A.3 Variances and Standard Errors of Least-Squares Estimators

Now by the definition of variance, we can write

$$\begin{aligned} \text{var}\,(\hat{\beta}_2) &= E[\hat{\beta}_2 - E(\hat{\beta}_2)]^2 \\ &= E(\hat{\beta}_2 - \beta_2)^2 \qquad \text{since } E(\hat{\beta}_2) = \beta_2 \\ &= E\left(\sum k_i u_i\right)^2 \qquad \text{using Eq. (4) above} \\ &= E\left(k_1^2 u_1^2 + k_2^2 u_2^2 + \cdots + k_n^2 u_n^2 + 2k_1 k_2 u_1 u_2 + \cdots + 2k_{n-1} k_n u_{n-1} u_n\right) \end{aligned} \tag{6}$$

Since by assumption, $E(u_i^2) = \sigma^2$ for each i and $E(u_i u_j) = 0,\ i \neq j$, it follows that

$$\begin{aligned} \text{var}\,(\hat{\beta}_2) &= \sigma^2 \sum k_i^2 \\ &= \frac{\sigma^2}{\sum x_i^2} \qquad \text{(using the definition of } k_i^2) \\ &= \text{Eq. (3.3.1)} \end{aligned} \tag{7}$$

The variance of $\hat{\beta}_1$ can be obtained following the same line of reasoning already given. Once the variances of $\hat{\beta}_1$ and $\hat{\beta}_2$ are obtained, their positive square roots give the corresponding standard errors.

3A.4 Covariance between $\hat{\beta}_1$ and $\hat{\beta}_2$

By definition,

$$\begin{aligned} \text{cov}\,(\hat{\beta}_1, \hat{\beta}_2) &= E\{[\hat{\beta}_1 - E(\hat{\beta}_1)][\hat{\beta}_2 - E(\hat{\beta}_2)]\} \\ &= E(\hat{\beta}_1 - \beta_1)(\hat{\beta}_2 - \beta_2) \qquad \text{(Why?)} \\ &= -\bar{X} E(\hat{\beta}_2 - \beta_2)^2 \\ &= -\bar{X}\,\text{var}\,(\hat{\beta}_2) \\ &= \text{Eq. (3.3.9)} \end{aligned} \tag{8}$$

where use is made of the fact that $\hat{\beta}_1 = \bar{Y} - \hat{\beta}_2 \bar{X}$ and $E(\hat{\beta}_1) = \bar{Y} - \beta_2 \bar{X}$, giving $\hat{\beta}_1 - E(\hat{\beta}_1) = -\bar{X}(\hat{\beta}_2 - \beta_2)$. *Note:* $\text{var}\,(\hat{\beta}_2)$ is given in Eq. (3.3.1).

3A.5 The Least-Squares Estimator of σ^2

Recall that

$$Y_i = \beta_1 + \beta_2 X_i + u_i \tag{9}$$

Therefore,

$$\bar{Y} = \beta_1 + \beta_2 \bar{X} + \bar{u} \tag{10}$$

Subtracting Equation (10) from Equation (9) gives

$$y_i = \beta_2 x_i + (u_i - \bar{u}) \tag{11}$$

Also recall that

$$\hat{u}_i = y_i - \hat{\beta}_2 x_i \tag{12}$$

Therefore, substituting Equation (11) into Equation (12) yields

$$\hat{u}_i = \beta_2 x_i + (u_i - \bar{u}) - \hat{\beta}_2 x_i \tag{13}$$

Collecting terms, squaring, and summing on both sides, we obtain

$$\sum \hat{u}_i^2 = (\hat{\beta}_2 - \beta_2)^2 \sum x_i^2 + \sum (u_i - \bar{u})^2 - 2(\hat{\beta}_2 - \beta_2) \sum x_i (u_i - \bar{u}) \tag{14}$$

Taking expectations on both sides gives

$$\begin{aligned}
E\left(\sum \hat{u}_i^2\right) &= \sum x_i^2 E(\hat{\beta}_2 - \beta_2)^2 + E\left[\sum (u_i - \bar{u})^2\right] - 2E\left[(\hat{\beta}_2 - \beta_2)\sum x_i(u_i - \bar{u})\right] \\
&= \sum x_i^2 \operatorname{var}(\hat{\beta}_2) + (n-1)\operatorname{var}(u_i) - 2E\left[\sum k_i u_i (x_i u_i)\right] \\
&= \sigma^2 + (n-1)\sigma^2 - 2E\left[\sum k_i x_i u_i^2\right] \qquad (15) \\
&= \sigma^2 + (n-1)\sigma^2 - 2\sigma^2 \\
&= (n-2)\sigma^2
\end{aligned}$$

where, in the last but one step, use is made of the definition of k_i given in Eq. (3) and the relation given in Eq. (4). Also note that

$$\begin{aligned}
E\sum (u_i - \bar{u})^2 &= E\left[\sum u_i^2 - n\bar{u}^2\right] \\
&= E\left[\sum u_i^2 - n\left(\frac{\sum u_i}{n}\right)^2\right] \\
&= E\left[\sum u_i^2 - \frac{1}{n}\sum\left(u_i^2\right)\right] \\
&= n\sigma^2 - \frac{n}{n}\sigma^2 = (n-1)\sigma^2
\end{aligned}$$

where use is made of the fact that the u_i are uncorrelated and the variance of each u_i is σ^2.

Thus, we obtain

$$E\left(\sum \hat{u}_i^2\right) = (n-2)\sigma^2 \tag{16}$$

Therefore, if we define

$$\hat{\sigma}^2 = \frac{\sum \hat{u}_i^2}{n-2} \tag{17}$$

its expected value is

$$E(\hat{\sigma}^2) = \frac{1}{n-2} E\left(\sum \hat{u}_i^2\right) = \sigma^2 \qquad \text{using Equation (16)} \tag{18}$$

which shows that $\hat{\sigma}^2$ is an unbiased estimator of true σ^2.

3A.6 Minimum-Variance Property of Least-Squares Estimators

It was shown in Appendix 3A, Section 3A.2, that the least-squares estimator $\hat{\beta}_2$ is linear as well as unbiased (this holds true of $\hat{\beta}_1$ too). To show that these estimators are also minimum variance in the class of all linear unbiased estimators, consider the least-squares estimator $\hat{\beta}_2$:

$$\hat{\beta}_2 = \sum k_i Y_i$$

where

$$k_i = \frac{X_i - \bar{X}}{\sum(X_i - \bar{X})^2} = \frac{x_i}{\sum x_i^2} \quad \text{(see Appendix 3A.2)} \tag{19}$$

which shows that $\hat{\beta}_2$ is a weighted average of the Y's, with k_i serving as the weights.

Let us define an alternative linear estimator of β_2 as follows:

$$\beta_2^* = \sum w_i Y_i \tag{20}$$

where w_i are also weights, not necessarily equal to k_i. Now

$$\begin{aligned} E(\beta_2^*) &= \sum w_i E(Y_i) \\ &= \sum w_i(\beta_1 + \beta_2 X_i) \\ &= \beta_1 \sum w_i + \beta_2 \sum w_i X_i \end{aligned} \tag{21}$$

Therefore, for β_2^* to be unbiased, we must have

$$\sum w_i = 0 \tag{22}$$

and

$$\sum w_i X_i = 1 \tag{23}$$

Also, we may write

$$\begin{aligned} \operatorname{var}(\beta_2^*) &= \operatorname{var} \sum w_i Y_i \\ &= \sum w_i^2 \operatorname{var} Y_i \qquad [\textit{Note:} \operatorname{var} Y_i = \operatorname{var} u_i = \sigma^2] \\ &= \sigma^2 \sum w_i^2 \qquad [\textit{Note:} \operatorname{cov}(Y_i, Y_j) = 0\ (i \neq j)] \\ &= \sigma^2 \sum \left(w_i - \frac{x_i}{\sum x_i^2} + \frac{x_i}{\sum x_i^2} \right)^2 \qquad \text{(Note the mathematical trick)} \\ &= \sigma^2 \sum \left(w_i - \frac{x_i}{\sum x_i^2} \right)^2 + \sigma^2 \frac{\sum x_i^2}{\left(\sum x_i^2\right)^2} + 2\sigma^2 \sum \left(w_i - \frac{x_i}{\sum x_i^2} \right)\left(\frac{x_i}{\sum x_i^2} \right) \\ &= \sigma^2 \sum \left(w_i - \frac{x_i}{\sum x_i^2} \right)^2 + \sigma^2 \left(\frac{1}{\sum x_i^2} \right) \end{aligned} \tag{24}$$

because the last term in the next to the last step drops out. (Why?)

Since the last term in Equation (24) is constant, the variance of (β_2^*) can be minimized only by manipulating the first term. If we let

$$w_i = \frac{x_i}{\sum x_i^2}$$

Eq. (24) reduces to

$$\begin{aligned} \operatorname{var}(\beta_2^*) &= \frac{\sigma^2}{\sum x_i^2} \\ &= \operatorname{var}(\hat{\beta}_2) \end{aligned} \tag{25}$$

In words, with weights $w_i = k_i$, which are the least-squares weights, the variance of the linear estimator β_2^* is equal to the variance of the least-squares estimator $\hat{\beta}_2$; otherwise $\text{var}(\beta_2^*) > \text{var}(\hat{\beta}_2)$. To put it differently, if there is a minimum-variance linear unbiased estimator of β_2, it must be the least-squares estimator. Similarly it can be shown that $\hat{\beta}_1$ is a minimum-variance linear unbiased estimator of β_1.

3A.7 Consistency of Least-Squares Estimators

We have shown that, in the framework of the classical linear regression model, the least-squares estimators are unbiased (and efficient) in any sample size, small or large. But sometimes, as discussed in **Appendix A,** an estimator may not satisfy one or more desirable statistical properties in small samples. But as the sample size increases indefinitely, the estimators possess several desirable statistical properties. These properties are known as the **large sample,** or **asymptotic, properties.** In this appendix, we will discuss one large sample property, namely, the property of **consistency,** which is discussed more fully in **Appendix A.** For the two-variable model we have already shown that the OLS estimator $\hat{\beta}_2$ is an unbiased estimator of the true β_2. Now we show that $\hat{\beta}_2$ is also a consistent estimator of β_2. As shown in **Appendix A,** a sufficient condition for consistency is that $\hat{\beta}_2$ is unbiased and that its variance tends to zero as the sample size n tends to infinity.

Since we have already proved the unbiasedness property, we need only show that the variance of $\hat{\beta}_2$ tends to zero as n increases indefinitely. We know that

$$\text{var}(\hat{\beta}_2) = \frac{\sigma^2}{\sum x_i^2} = \frac{\sigma^2/n}{\sum x_i^2/n} \tag{26}$$

By dividing the numerator and denominator by n, we do not change the equality.

Now

$$\underbrace{\lim \text{var}(\hat{\beta}_2)}_{n \to \infty} = \underbrace{\lim \left(\frac{\sigma^2/n}{\sum x_i^2/n} \right)}_{n \to \infty} = 0 \tag{27}$$

where use is made of the facts that (1) the limit of a ratio quantity is the limit of the quantity in the numerator to the limit of the quantity in the denominator (refer to any calculus book); (2) as n tends to infinity, σ^2/n tends to zero because σ^2 is a finite number; and $[(\sum x_i^2)/n] \neq 0$ because the variance of X has a finite limit because of Assumption 7 of CLRM.

The upshot of the preceding discussion is that the OLS estimator $\hat{\beta}_2$ is a consistent estimator of true β_2. In like fashion, we can establish that $\hat{\beta}_1$ is also a consistent estimator. Thus, in repeated (small) samples, the OLS estimators are unbiased and as the sample size increases indefinitely the OLS estimators are consistent. As we shall see later, even if some of the assumptions of CLRM are not satisfied, we may be able to obtain consistent estimators of the regression coefficients in several situations.

Chapter 4

Classical Normal Linear Regression Model (CNLRM)

What is known as the **classical theory of statistical inference** consists of two branches, namely, **estimation** and **hypothesis testing.** We have thus far covered the topic of estimation of the parameters of the (two-variable) linear regression model. Using the method of OLS we were able to estimate the parameters β_1, β_2, and σ^2. Under the assumptions of the *classical linear regression model* (CLRM), we were able to show that the estimators of these parameters, $\hat{\beta}_1$, $\hat{\beta}_2$, and $\hat{\sigma}^2$, satisfy several desirable statistical properties, such as unbiasedness, minimum variance, etc. (Recall the BLUE property.) Note that, since these are estimators, their values will change from sample to sample. Therefore, these estimators are *random variables.*

But estimation is half the battle. Hypothesis testing is the other half. Recall that in regression analysis our objective is not only to estimate the sample regression function (SRF), but also to use it to draw inferences about the population regression function (PRF), as emphasized in Chapter 2. Thus, we would like to find out how close $\hat{\beta}_1$ is to the true β_1 or how close $\hat{\sigma}^2$ is to the true σ^2. For instance, in Example 3.2, we estimated the SRF as shown in Eq. (3.7.2). But since this regression is based on a sample of 55 families, how do we know that the estimated MPC of 0.4368 represents the (true) MPC in the population as a whole?

Therefore, since $\hat{\beta}_1$, $\hat{\beta}_2$, and $\hat{\sigma}^2$ are random variables, we need to find out their probability distributions, for without that knowledge we will not be able to relate them to their true values.

4.1 The Probability Distribution of Disturbances u_i

To find out the probability distributions of the OLS estimators, we proceed as follows. Specifically, consider $\hat{\beta}_2$. As we showed in Appendix 3A.2,

$$\hat{\beta}_2 = \sum k_i Y_i \tag{4.1.1}$$

where $k_i = x_i / \sum x_i^2$. But since the X's are assumed fixed, or nonstochastic, because ours is conditional regression analysis, conditional on the fixed values of X_i, Equation 4.1.1 shows that $\hat{\beta}_2$ is a *linear* function of Y_i, which is random by assumption. But since $Y_i = \beta_1 + \beta_2 X_i + u_i$, we can write Eq. (4.1.1) as

$$\hat{\beta}_2 = \sum k_i(\beta_1 + \beta_2 X_i + u_i) \tag{4.1.2}$$

Because k_i, the betas, and X_i are all fixed, $\hat{\beta}_2$ is ultimately a *linear* function of the random variable u_i, which is random by assumption. Therefore, the probability distribution of $\hat{\beta}_2$ (and also of $\hat{\beta}_1$) will depend on the assumption made about the probability distribution of u_i. And since knowledge of the probability distributions of OLS estimators is necessary to draw inferences about their population values, the nature of the probability distribution of u_i assumes an extremely important role in hypothesis testing.

Since the method of OLS does not make any assumption about the probabilistic nature of u_i, it is of little help for the purpose of drawing inferences about the PRF from the SRF, the Gauss–Markov theorem notwithstanding. This void can be filled if we are willing to assume that the u's follow some probability distribution. For reasons to be explained shortly, in the regression context it is usually assumed that the u's follow the normal distribution. Adding the normality assumption for u_i to the assumptions of the classical linear regression model (CLRM) discussed in Chapter 3, we obtain what is known as the **classical normal linear regression model (CNLRM).**

4.2 The Normality Assumption for u_i

The classical *normal* linear regression model assumes that each u_i is distributed *normally* with

$$\text{Mean:} \quad E(u_i) = 0 \tag{4.2.1}$$

$$\text{Variance:} \quad E[u_i - E(u_i)]^2 = E(u_i^2) = \sigma^2 \tag{4.2.2}$$

$$\text{cov}(u_i, u_j): \quad E\{[(u_i - E(u_i)][u_j - E(u_j)]\} = E(u_i u_j) = 0 \quad i \neq j \tag{4.2.3}$$

The assumptions given above can be more compactly stated as

$$u_i \sim N(0, \sigma^2) \tag{4.2.4}$$

where the symbol $\sim$ means *distributed as* and N stands for the *normal distribution,* the terms in the parentheses representing the two parameters of the normal distribution, namely, the mean and the variance.

As noted in **Appendix A,** for **two normally distributed variables, zero covariance or correlation means independence of the two variables.** Therefore, with the normality assumption, Equation 4.2.4 means that u_i and u_j are not only uncorrelated but are also independently distributed.

Therefore, we can write Eq. (4.2.4) as

$$u_i \sim \text{NID}(0, \sigma^2) \tag{4.2.5}$$

where **NID** stands for *normally and independently distributed.*

Why the Normality Assumption?

Why do we employ the normality assumption? There are several reasons:

1. As pointed out in Section 2.5, u_i represent the combined influence (on the dependent variable) of a large number of independent variables that are not explicitly introduced in the regression model. As noted, we hope that the influence of these omitted or neglected variables is small and at best random. Now by the celebrated **central limit theorem (CLT)** of statistics (see **Appendix A** for details), it can be shown that if there are a large number of independent and identically distributed random variables, then, with a few exceptions, the distribution of their sum tends to a normal distribution as the number of such variables increases indefinitely.[1] It is the CLT that provides a theoretical justification for the assumption of normality of u_i.

2. A variant of the CLT states that, even if the number of variables is not very large or if these variables are not strictly independent, their sum may still be normally distributed.[2]

3. With the normality assumption, the probability distributions of OLS estimators can be easily derived because, as noted in **Appendix A,** one property of the normal distribution is that **any linear function of normally distributed variables is itself normally distributed.** As we discussed earlier, OLS estimators $\hat{\beta}_1$ and $\hat{\beta}_2$ are linear functions of u_i. Therefore, if u_i are normally distributed, so are $\hat{\beta}_1$ and $\hat{\beta}_2$, which makes our task of hypothesis testing very straightforward.

4. The normal distribution is a comparatively simple distribution involving only two parameters (mean and variance); it is very well known and its theoretical properties have been extensively studied in mathematical statistics. Besides, many phenomena seem to follow the normal distribution.

5. If we are dealing with a small, or finite, sample size, say data of less than 100 observations, the normality assumption assumes a critical role. It not only helps us to derive the exact probability distributions of OLS estimators but also enables us to use the *t*, *F*, and χ^2 statistical tests for regression models. The statistical properties of *t*, *F*, and χ^2 probability distributions are discussed in **Appendix A.** As we will show subsequently, if the sample size is reasonably large, we may be able to relax the normality assumption.

6. Finally, in *large samples, t* and *F* statistics have approximately the *t* and *F* probability distributions so that the *t* and *F* tests that are based on the assumption that the error term is normally distributed can still be applied validly.[3] These days there are many cross-section and time series data that have a fairly large number of observations. Therefore, the normality assumption may not be very crucial in large data sets.

A cautionary note: Since we are "imposing" the normality assumption, it behooves us to find out in practical applications involving small sample size data whether the normality

[1]For a relatively simple and straightforward discussion of this theorem, see Sheldon M. Ross, *Introduction to Probability and Statistics for Engineers and Scientists,* 2d ed., Harcourt Academic Press, New York, 2000, pp. 193–194. One exception to the theorem is the Cauchy distribution, which has no mean or higher moments. See M. G. Kendall and A. Stuart, *The Advanced Theory of Statistics,* Charles Griffin & Co., London, 1960, vol. 1, pp. 248–249.

[2]For the various forms of the CLT, see Harald Cramer, *Mathematical Methods of Statistics,* Princeton University Press, Princeton, NJ, 1946, Chap. 17.

[3]For a technical discussion on this point, see Christiaan Heij et al., *Econometric Methods with Applications in Business and Economics,* Oxford University Press, Oxford, 2004, p. 197.

assumption is appropriate. Later, we will develop some tests to do just that. Also, later we will come across situations where the normality assumption may be inappropriate. But until then we will continue with the normality assumption for the reasons discussed previously.

4.3 Properties of OLS Estimators under the Normality Assumption

With the assumption that u_i follow the normal distribution as in Equation 4.2.5, the OLS estimators have the following properties (**Appendix A** provides a general discussion of the desirable statistical properties of estimators):

1. They are unbiased.

2. They have minimum variance. Combined with 1, this means that they are **minimum-variance unbiased, or efficient estimators.**

3. They have **consistency;** that is, as the sample size increases indefinitely, the estimators converge to their true population values.

4. $\hat{\beta}_1$ (being a linear function of u_i) is *normally distributed* with

$$\text{Mean:} \quad E(\hat{\beta}_1) = \beta_1 \tag{4.3.1}$$

$$\text{var}(\hat{\beta}_1): \quad \sigma^2_{\hat{\beta}_1} = \frac{\sum X_i^2}{n \sum x_i^2}\sigma^2 \quad = (3.3.3) \tag{4.3.2}$$

Or more compactly,

$$\hat{\beta}_1 \sim N\left(\beta_1, \sigma^2_{\hat{\beta}_1}\right)$$

Then by the properties of the normal distribution, the variable Z, which is defined as

$$Z = \frac{\hat{\beta}_1 - \beta_1}{\sigma_{\hat{\beta}_1}} \tag{4.3.3}$$

follows the **standard normal distribution,** that is, a normal distribution with zero mean and unit (= 1) variance, or

$$Z \sim N(0, 1)$$

5. $\hat{\beta}_2$ (being a linear function of u_i) is *normally* distributed with

$$\text{Mean:} \quad E(\hat{\beta}_2) = \beta_2 \tag{4.3.4}$$

$$\text{var}(\hat{\beta}_2): \quad \sigma^2_{\hat{\beta}_2} = \frac{\sigma^2}{\sum x_i^2} \quad = (3.3.1) \tag{4.3.5}$$

Or, more compactly,

$$\hat{\beta}_2 \sim N\left(\beta_2, \sigma^2_{\hat{\beta}_2}\right)$$

Then, as in Equation 4.3.3,

$$Z = \frac{\hat{\beta}_2 - \beta_2}{\sigma_{\hat{\beta}_2}} \tag{4.3.6}$$

also follows the standard normal distribution.

Geometrically, the probability distributions of $\hat{\beta}_1$ and $\hat{\beta}_2$ are shown in Figure 4.1.

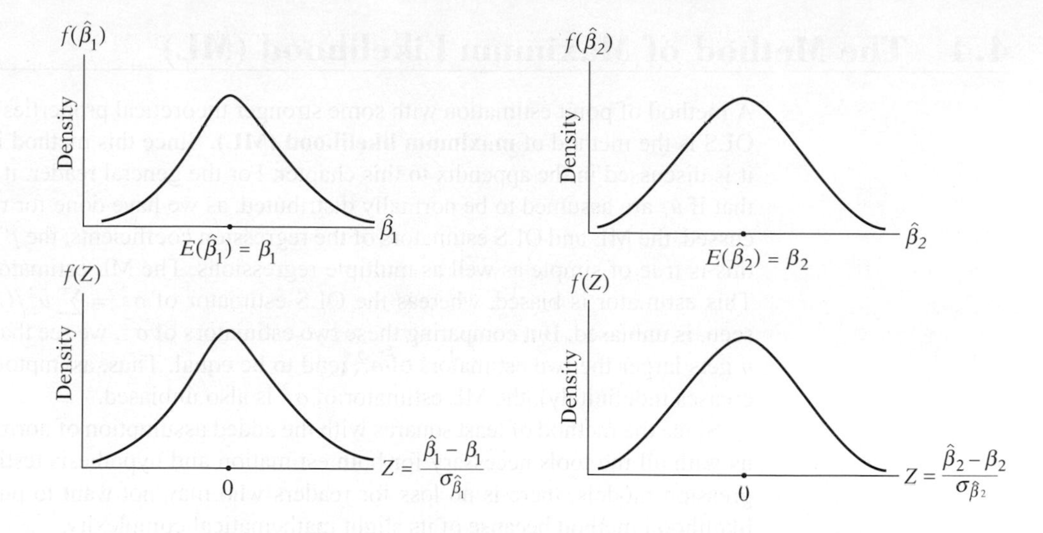

FIGURE 4.1 Probability distributions of $\hat{\beta}_1$ and $\hat{\beta}_2$.

6. $(n-2)(\hat{\sigma}^2/\sigma^2)$ is distributed as the χ^2 (chi-square) distribution with $(n-2)$df.[4] This knowledge will help us to draw inferences about the true σ^2 from the estimated σ^2, as we will show in Chapter 5. (The chi-square distribution and its properties are discussed in **Appendix A.**)

7. $(\hat{\beta}_1, \hat{\beta}_2)$ are distributed independently of $\hat{\sigma}^2$. The importance of this will be explained in the next chapter.

8. *$\hat{\beta}_1$ and $\hat{\beta}_2$ have minimum variance in the entire class of unbiased estimators, whether linear or not.* This result, due to Rao, is very powerful because, unlike the Gauss–Markov theorem, it is not restricted to the class of linear estimators only.[5] Therefore, we can say that the least-squares estimators are **best unbiased estimators (BUE);** that is, they have minimum variance in the entire class of unbiased estimators.

To sum up: The important point to note is that the normality assumption enables us to derive the probability, or sampling, distributions of $\hat{\beta}_1$ and $\hat{\beta}_2$ (both normal) and $\hat{\sigma}^2$ (related to the chi square). As we will see in the next chapter, this simplifies the task of establishing confidence intervals and testing (statistical) hypotheses.

In passing, note that, with the assumption that $u_i \sim N(0, \sigma^2)$, Y_i, being a linear function of u_i, is itself normally distributed with the mean and variance given by

$$E(Y_i) = \beta_1 + \beta_2 X_i \tag{4.3.7}$$

$$\operatorname{var}(Y_i) = \sigma^2 \tag{4.3.8}$$

More neatly, we can write

$$Y_i \sim N(\beta_1 + \beta_2 X_i, \sigma^2) \tag{4.3.9}$$

[4]The proof of this statement is slightly involved. An accessible source for the proof is Robert V. Hogg and Allen T. Craig, *Introduction to Mathematical Statistics*, 2d ed., Macmillan, New York, 1965, p. 144.

[5]C. R. Rao, *Linear Statistical Inference and Its Applications*, John Wiley & Sons, New York, 1965, p. 258.

4.4 The Method of Maximum Likelihood (ML)

A method of point estimation with some stronger theoretical properties than the method of OLS is the method of **maximum likelihood (ML).** Since this method is slightly involved, it is discussed in the appendix to this chapter. For the general reader, it will suffice to note that if u_i are assumed to be normally distributed, as we have done for reasons already discussed, the ML and OLS estimators of the regression coefficients, the β's, are identical, and this is true of simple as well as multiple regressions. The ML estimator of σ^2 is $\sum \hat{u}_i^2/n$. This estimator is biased, whereas the OLS estimator of $\sigma^2 = \sum \hat{u}_i^2/(n-2)$, as we have seen, is unbiased. But comparing these two estimators of σ^2, we see that as the sample size n gets larger the two estimators of σ^2 tend to be equal. Thus, asymptotically (i.e., as n increases indefinitely), the ML estimator of σ^2 is also unbiased.

Since the method of least squares with the added assumption of normality of u_i provides us with all the tools necessary for both estimation and hypothesis testing of the linear regression models, there is no loss for readers who may not want to pursue the maximum likelihood method because of its slight mathematical complexity.

Summary and Conclusions

1. This chapter discussed the classical *normal* linear regression model (CNLRM).
2. This model differs from the classical linear regression model (CLRM) in that it specifically assumes that the disturbance term u_i entering the regression model is normally distributed. The CLRM does not require any assumption about the probability distribution of u_i; it only requires that the mean value of u_i is zero and its variance is a finite constant.
3. The theoretical justification for the normality assumption is the **central limit theorem.**
4. Without the normality assumption, under the other assumptions discussed in Chapter 3, the Gauss–Markov theorem showed that the OLS estimators are BLUE.
5. With the additional assumption of normality, the OLS estimators are not only **best unbiased estimators (BUE)** but also follow well-known probability distributions. The OLS estimators of the intercept and slope are themselves normally distributed and the OLS estimator of the variance of u_i ($= \hat{\sigma}^2$) is related to the chi-square distribution.
6. In Chapters 5 and 8 we show how this knowledge is useful in drawing inferences about the values of the population parameters.
7. An alternative to the least-squares method is the method of **maximum likelihood (ML).** To use this method, however, one must make an assumption about the probability distribution of the disturbance term u_i. In the regression context, the assumption most popularly made is that u_i follows the normal distribution.
8. Under the normality assumption, the ML and OLS estimators of the intercept and slope parameters of the regression model are identical. However, the OLS and ML estimators of the variance of u_i are different. In large samples, however, these two estimators converge.
9. Thus the ML method is generally called a *large-sample method.* The ML method is of broader application in that it can also be applied to regression models that are nonlinear in the parameters. In the latter case, OLS is generally not used. For more on this, see Chapter 14.
10. In this text, we will largely rely on the OLS method for practical reasons: (*a*) Compared to ML, the OLS is easy to apply; (*b*) the ML and OLS estimators of β_1 and β_2 are identical (which is true of multiple regressions too); and (*c*) even in moderately large samples the OLS and ML estimators of σ^2 do not differ vastly.

However, for the benefit of the mathematically inclined reader, a brief introduction to ML is given in the appendix to this chapter and also in **Appendix A.**

Appendix 4A

4A.1 Maximum Likelihood Estimation of Two-Variable Regression Model

Assume that in the two-variable model $Y_i = \beta_1 + \beta_2 X_i + u_i$ the Y_i are normally and independently distributed with mean $= \beta_1 + \beta_2 X_i$ and variance $= \sigma^2$. (See Eq. [4.3.9].) As a result, the joint probability density function of $Y_1, Y_2, \ldots, Y_n$, given the preceding mean and variance, can be written as

$$f(Y_1, Y_2, \ldots, Y_n \mid \beta_1 + \beta_2 X_i, \sigma^2)$$

But in view of the independence of the Y's, this joint probability density function can be written as a product of n individual density functions as

$$\begin{aligned} &f(Y_1, Y_2, \ldots, Y_n \mid \beta_1 + \beta_2 X_i, \sigma^2) \\ &\quad = f(Y_1 \mid \beta_1 + \beta_2 X_i, \sigma^2) f(Y_2 \mid \beta_1 + \beta_2 X_i, \sigma^2) \cdots f(Y_n \mid \beta_1 + \beta_2 X_i, \sigma^2) \end{aligned} \tag{1}$$

where

$$f(Y_i) = \frac{1}{\sigma\sqrt{2\pi}} \exp\left\{-\frac{1}{2}\frac{(Y_i - \beta_1 - \beta_2 X_i)^2}{\sigma^2}\right\} \tag{2}$$

which is the density function of a normally distributed variable with the given mean and variance. (*Note:* exp means e to the power of the expression indicated by $\{\}$.)

Substituting Equation (2) for each Y_i into Equation (1) gives

$$f(Y_i, Y_2, \ldots, Y_n \mid \beta_1 + \beta_2 X_i, \sigma^2) = \frac{1}{\sigma^n \left(\sqrt{2\pi}\right)^n} \exp\left\{-\frac{1}{2}\sum \frac{(Y_i - \beta_1 - \beta_2 X_i)^2}{\sigma^2}\right\} \tag{3}$$

If $Y_1, Y_2, \ldots, Y_n$ are known or given, but β_1, β_2, and σ^2 are not known, the function in Equation (3) is called a **likelihood function,** denoted by LF$(\beta_1, \beta_2, \sigma^2)$, and written as[1]

$$\text{LF}(\beta_1, \beta_2, \sigma^2) = \frac{1}{\sigma^n \left(\sqrt{2\pi}\right)^n} \exp\left\{-\frac{1}{2}\sum \frac{(Y_i - \beta_1 - \beta_2 X_i)^2}{\sigma^2}\right\} \tag{4}$$

The **method of maximum likelihood,** as the name indicates, consists in estimating the unknown parameters in such a manner that the probability of observing the given Y's is as high (or maximum) as possible. Therefore, we have to find the maximum of the function in Equation (4). This is a straightforward exercise in differential calculus. For differentiation it is easier to express Equation (4) in the log term as follows.[2] (*Note:* ln = natural log.)

$$\begin{aligned} \ln \text{LF} &= -n \ln \sigma - \frac{n}{2}\ln(2\pi) - \frac{1}{2}\sum \frac{(Y_i - \beta_1 - \beta_2 X_i)^2}{\sigma^2} \\ &= -\frac{n}{2}\ln \sigma^2 - \frac{n}{2}\ln(2\pi) - \frac{1}{2}\sum \frac{(Y_i - \beta_1 - \beta_2 X_i)^2}{\sigma^2} \end{aligned} \tag{5}$$

[1] Of course, if β_1, β_2, and σ^2 are known but the Y_i are not known, Eq. (4) represents the joint probability density function—the probability of jointly observing the Y_i.

[2] Since a log function is a monotonic function, ln LF will attain its maximum value at the same point as LF.

Differentiating Equation (5) partially with respect to β_1, β_2, and σ^2, we obtain

$$\frac{\partial \ln \text{LF}}{\partial \beta_1} = -\frac{1}{\sigma^2} \sum (Y_i - \beta_1 - \beta_2 X_i)(-1) \tag{6}$$

$$\frac{\partial \ln \text{LF}}{\partial \beta_2} = -\frac{1}{\sigma^2} \sum (Y_i - \beta_1 - \beta_2 X_i)(-X_i) \tag{7}$$

$$\frac{\partial \ln \text{LF}}{\partial \sigma^2} = -\frac{n}{2\sigma^2} + \frac{1}{2\sigma^4} \sum (Y_i - \beta_1 - \beta_2 X_i)^2 \tag{8}$$

Setting these equations equal to zero (the first-order condition for optimization) and letting $\tilde{\beta}_1$, $\tilde{\beta}_2$, and $\tilde{\sigma}^2$ denote the ML estimators, we obtain[3]

$$\frac{1}{\tilde{\sigma}^2} \sum (Y_i - \tilde{\beta}_1 - \tilde{\beta}_2 X_i) = 0 \tag{9}$$

$$\frac{1}{\tilde{\sigma}^2} \sum (Y_i - \tilde{\beta}_1 - \tilde{\beta}_2 X_i) X_i = 0 \tag{10}$$

$$-\frac{n}{2\tilde{\sigma}^2} + \frac{1}{2\tilde{\sigma}^4} \sum (Y_i - \tilde{\beta}_1 - \tilde{\beta}_2 X_i)^2 = 0 \tag{11}$$

After simplifying, Eqs. (9) and (10) yield

$$\sum Y_i = n\tilde{\beta}_1 + \tilde{\beta}_2 \sum X_i \tag{12}$$

$$\sum Y_i X_i = \tilde{\beta}_1 \sum X_i + \tilde{\beta}_2 \sum X_i^2 \tag{13}$$

which are precisely the *normal equations* of the least-squares theory obtained in Eqs. (3.1.4) and (3.1.5). Therefore, the ML estimators, the $\tilde{\beta}$'s, are the same as the OLS estimators, the $\hat{\beta}$'s, given in Eqs. (3.1.6) and (3.1.7). This equality is not accidental. Examining the likelihood (5), we see that the last term enters with a negative sign. Therefore, maximizing Equation (5) amounts to minimizing this term, which is precisely the least-squares approach, as can be seen from Eq. (3.1.2).

Substituting the ML (= OLS) estimators into Equation (11) and simplifying, we obtain the ML estimator of $\tilde{\sigma}^2$ as

$$\begin{aligned} \tilde{\sigma}^2 &= \frac{1}{n} \sum (Y_i - \tilde{\beta}_1 - \tilde{\beta}_2 X_i)^2 \\ &= \frac{1}{n} \sum (Y_i - \hat{\beta}_1 - \hat{\beta}_2 X_i)^2 \\ &= \frac{1}{n} \sum \hat{u}_i^2 \end{aligned} \tag{14}$$

From Equation (14) it is obvious that the ML estimator $\tilde{\sigma}^2$ differs from the OLS estimator $\hat{\sigma}^2 = [1/(n-2)] \sum \hat{u}_i^2$, which was shown to be an unbiased estimator of σ^2 in Appendix 3A, Section 3A.5. Thus, the ML estimator of σ^2 is biased. The magnitude of this bias can be easily determined as follows.

[3]We use ˜ (tilde) for ML estimators and ˆ (cap or hat) for OLS estimators.

Taking the mathematical expectation of Equation (14) on both sides, we obtain

$$
\begin{aligned}
E(\tilde{\sigma}^2) &= \frac{1}{n} E\left(\sum \hat{u}_i^2\right) \\
&= \left(\frac{n-2}{n}\right)\sigma^2 \qquad \text{using Eq. (16) of Appendix 3A, Section 3A.5} \qquad (15) \\
&= \sigma^2 - \frac{2}{n}\sigma^2
\end{aligned}
$$

which shows that $\tilde{\sigma}^2$ is biased downward (i.e., it underestimates the true σ^2) in small samples. But notice that as n, the sample size, increases indefinitely, the second term in Equation (15), the bias factor, tends to be zero. Therefore, *asymptotically* (i.e., in a very large sample), $\tilde{\sigma}^2$ is *unbiased* too, that is, $\lim E(\tilde{\sigma}^2) = \sigma^2$ as $n \to \infty$. It can further be proved that $\tilde{\sigma}^2$ is also a **consistent** estimator[4]; that is, as n increases indefinitely, $\tilde{\sigma}^2$ converges to its true value σ^2.

4A.2 Maximum Likelihood Estimation of Food Expenditure in India

Return to Example 3.2 and Equation 3.7.2, which gives the regression of food expenditure on total expenditure for 55 rural households in India. Since under the normality assumption the OLS and ML estimators of the regression coefficients are the same, we obtain the ML estimators as $\tilde{\beta}_1 = \hat{\beta}_1 = 94.2087$ and $\tilde{\beta}_2 = \hat{\beta}_2 = 0.4368$. The OLS estimator of σ^2 is $\hat{\sigma}^2 = 4469.6913$, but the ML estimator is $\tilde{\sigma}^2 = 4407.1563$, which is smaller than the OLS estimator. As noted, in small samples the ML estimator is downward biased; that is, on average it underestimates the true variance σ^2. Of course, as you would expect, as the sample size gets bigger, the difference between the two estimators will narrow. Putting the values of the estimators in the log likelihood function, we obtain the value of -308.1625. If you want the maximum value of the LF, just take the antilog of -308.1625. No other values of the parameters will give you a higher probability of obtaining the sample that you have used in the analysis.

Appendix 4A Exercises

4.1. "If two random variables are statistically independent, the coefficient of correlation between the two is zero. But the converse is not necessarily true; that is, zero correlation does not imply statistical independence. However, if two variables are normally distributed, zero correlation necessarily implies statistical independence." Verify this statement for the following joint probability density function of two normally distributed variables Y_1 and Y_2 (this joint probability density function is known as the **bivariate normal probability density function**):

$$
f(Y_1, Y_2) = \frac{1}{2\pi\sigma_1\sigma_2\sqrt{1-\rho^2}} \exp\left\{-\frac{1}{2(1-\rho^2)} \times \left[\left(\frac{Y_1-\mu_1}{\sigma_1}\right)^2 - 2\rho\frac{(Y_1-\mu_1)(Y_2-\mu_2)}{\sigma_1\sigma_2} + \left(\frac{Y_2-\mu_2}{\sigma^2}\right)^2\right]\right\}
$$

[4]See **Appendix A** for a general discussion of the properties of the maximum likelihood estimators as well as for the distinction between asymptotic unbiasedness and consistency. Roughly speaking, in asymptotic unbiasedness we try to find out the lim $E(\tilde{\sigma}_n^2)$ as n tends to infinity, where n is the sample size on which the estimator is based, whereas in consistency we try to find out how $\tilde{\sigma}_n^2$ behaves as n increases indefinitely. Notice that the unbiasedness property is a repeated sampling property of an estimator based on a sample of given size, whereas in consistency we are concerned with the behavior of an estimator as the sample size increases indefinitely.

where μ_1 = mean of Y_1
μ_2 = mean of Y_2
σ_1 = standard deviation of Y_1
σ_2 = standard deviation of Y_2
ρ = coefficient of correlation between Y_1 and Y_2

4.2. By applying the second-order conditions for optimization (i.e., second-derivative test), show that the ML estimators of β_1, β_2, and σ^2 obtained by solving Eqs. (9), (10), and (11) do in fact maximize the likelihood function in Eq. (4).

4.3. A random variable X follows the **exponential distribution** if it has the following probability density function (PDF):

$$f(X) = (1/\theta)e^{-X/\theta} \quad \text{for } X > 0$$
$$= 0 \quad \text{elsewhere}$$

where $\theta > 0$ is the parameter of the distribution. Using the ML method, show that the ML estimator of θ is $\hat{\theta} = \sum X_i/n$, where n is the sample size. That is, show that the ML estimator of θ is the sample mean $\bar{X}$.

4.4. Suppose that the outcome of an experiment is classified as either a success or a failure. Letting $X = 1$ when the outcome is a success and $X = 0$ when it is a failure, the probability density, or mass, function of X is given by

$$p(X = 0) = 1 - p$$
$$p(X = 1) = p, 0 \leq p \leq 1$$

What is the maximum likelihood estimator of p, the probability of success?

Chapter 5

Two-Variable Regression: Interval Estimation and Hypothesis Testing

Beware of testing too many hypotheses; the more you torture the data, the more likely they are to confess, but confession obtained under duress may not be admissible in the court of scientific opinion.[1]

As pointed out in Chapter 4, estimation and hypothesis testing constitute the two major branches of classical statistics. The theory of estimation consists of two parts: point estimation and interval estimation. We have discussed point estimation thoroughly in the previous two chapters where we introduced the OLS and ML methods of point estimation. In this chapter we first consider interval estimation and then take up the topic of hypothesis testing, a topic intimately related to interval estimation.

5.1 Statistical Prerequisites

Before we demonstrate the actual mechanics of establishing confidence intervals and testing statistical hypotheses, it is assumed that the reader is familiar with the fundamental concepts of probability and statistics. Although not a substitute for a basic course in statistics, **Appendix A** provides the essentials of statistics with which the reader should be totally familiar. Key concepts such as **probability, probability distributions, Type I and Type II errors, level of significance, power of a statistical test,** and **confidence interval** are crucial for understanding the material covered in this and the following chapters.

[1] Stephen M. Stigler, "Testing Hypothesis or Fitting Models? Another Look at Mass Extinctions," in Matthew H. Nitecki and Antoni Hoffman, eds., *Neutral Models in Biology,* Oxford University Press, Oxford, 1987, p. 148.

5.2 Interval Estimation: Some Basic Ideas

To fix the ideas, consider the wages-education example of Chapter 3. Equation (3.6.1) shows that the estimated average increase in mean hourly wage related to a one-year increase in schooling ($\hat{\beta}_2$) is 0.7240, which is a one number (point) estimate of the unknown population value β_2. How reliable is this estimate? As noted in Chapter 3, because of sampling fluctuations, a single estimate is likely to differ from the true value, although in repeated sampling its mean value is expected to be equal to the true value. [*Note:* $E(\hat{\beta}_2) = \beta_2$.] Now in statistics, the reliability of a point estimator is measured by its standard error. Therefore, instead of relying on the point estimate alone, we may construct an interval around the point estimator, say within two or three standard errors on either side of the point estimator, such that this interval has, say, 95 percent probability of including the true parameter value. This is roughly the idea behind **interval estimation.**

To be more specific, assume that we want to find out how "close," say, $\hat{\beta}_2$ is to β_2. For this purpose we try to find out two positive numbers δ and α, the latter lying between 0 and 1, such that the probability that the **random interval** $(\hat{\beta}_2 - \delta, \hat{\beta}_2 + \delta)$ contains the true β_2 is $1 - \alpha$. Symbolically,

$$\Pr\,(\hat{\beta}_2 - \delta \leq \beta_2 \leq \hat{\beta}_2 + \delta) = 1 - \alpha \tag{5.2.1}$$

Such an interval, if it exists, is known as a **confidence interval;** $1 - \alpha$ is known as the **confidence coefficient;** and α $(0 < \alpha < 1)$ is known as the **level of significance.**[2] The end-points of the confidence interval are known as the **confidence limits** (also known as *critical values*), $\hat{\beta}_2 - \delta$ being the **lower confidence** *limit* and $\hat{\beta}_2 + \delta$ the **upper confidence** *limit.* In passing, note that in practice α and $1 - \alpha$ are often expressed in percentage forms as 100α and $100(1 - \alpha)$ percent.

Equation 5.2.1 shows that an **interval estimator,** in contrast to a point estimator, is an interval constructed in such a manner that it has a specified probability $1 - \alpha$ of including within its limits the true value of the parameter. For example, if $\alpha = 0.05$, or 5 percent, Eq. (5.2.1) would read: The probability that the (random) interval shown there includes the true β_2 is 0.95, or 95 percent. The interval estimator thus gives a range of values within which the true β_2 may lie.

It is very important to know the following aspects of interval estimation:

1. Eq. (5.2.1) does not say that the probability of β_2 lying between the given limits is $1 - \alpha$. Since β_2, although an unknown, is assumed to be some fixed number, either it lies in the interval or it does not. What Eq. (5.2.1) states is that, for the method described in this chapter, the probability of constructing an interval that contains β_2 is $1 - \alpha$.

2. The interval in Eq. (5.2.1) is a **random interval;** that is, it will vary from one sample to the next because it is based on $\hat{\beta}_2$, which is random. (Why?)

3. Since the confidence interval is random, the probability statements attached to it should be understood in the long-run sense, that is, repeated sampling. More specifically, Eq. (5.2.1) means: If in repeated sampling confidence intervals like it are constructed a

[2]Also known as the **probability of committing a Type I error.** A Type I error consists in rejecting a true hypothesis, whereas a Type II error consists in accepting a false hypothesis. (This topic is discussed more fully in **Appendix A.**) The symbol α is also known as the **size of the (statistical) test.**

great many times on the $1 - \alpha$ probability basis, then, in the long run, on the average, such intervals will enclose in $1 - \alpha$ of the cases the true value of the parameter.

4. As noted in (2), the interval in Eq. (5.2.1) is random so long as $\hat{\beta}_2$ is not known. But once we have a specific sample and once we obtain a specific numerical value of $\hat{\beta}_2$, the interval in Eq. (5.2.1) is no longer random; it is fixed. In this case, we **cannot** make the probabilistic statement in Eq. (5.2.1); that is, we cannot say that the probability is $1 - \alpha$ that a given *fixed* interval includes the true β_2. In this situation, β_2 is either in the fixed interval or outside it. Therefore, the probability is either 1 or 0. Thus, for our wages-education example, if the 95 percent confidence interval were obtained as $(0.5700 \leq \beta_2 \leq 0.8780)$, as we do shortly in Eq. (5.3.9), we **cannot** say the probability is 95 percent that this interval includes the true β_2. That probability is either 1 or 0.

How are the confidence intervals constructed? From the preceding discussion one may expect that if the **sampling or probability distributions** of the estimators are known, one can make confidence interval statements such as Eq. (5.2.1). In Chapter 4 we saw that under the assumption of normality of the disturbances u_i the OLS estimators $\hat{\beta}_1$ and $\hat{\beta}_2$ are themselves normally distributed and that the OLS estimator $\hat{\sigma}^2$ is related to the χ^2 (chi-square) distribution. It would then seem that the task of constructing confidence intervals is a simple one. And it is!

5.3 Confidence Intervals for Regression Coefficients β_1 and β_2

Confidence Interval for β_2

It was shown in Chapter 4, Section 4.3, that, with the normality assumption for u_i, the OLS estimators $\hat{\beta}_1$ and $\hat{\beta}_2$ are themselves normally distributed with means and variances given therein. Therefore, for example, the variable

$$
\begin{aligned}
Z &= \frac{\hat{\beta}_2 - \beta_2}{\operatorname{se}(\hat{\beta}_2)} \\
&= \frac{(\hat{\beta}_2 - \beta_2)\sqrt{\sum x_i^2}}{\sigma}
\end{aligned}
\tag{5.3.1}
$$

as noted in Eq. (4.3.6), is a standardized normal variable. It therefore seems that we can use the normal distribution to make probabilistic statements about β_2 provided the truc population variance σ^2 is known. If σ^2 is known, an important property of a normally distributed variable with mean μ and variance σ^2 is that the area under the normal curve between $\mu \pm \sigma$ is about 68 percent, that between the limits $\mu \pm 2\sigma$ is about 95 percent, and that between $\mu \pm 3\sigma$ is about 99.7 percent.

But σ^2 is rarely known, and in practice it is determined by the unbiased estimator $\hat{\sigma}^2$. If we replace σ by $\hat{\sigma}$, Equation 5.3.1 may be written as

$$
\begin{aligned}
t &= \frac{\hat{\beta}_2 - \beta_2}{\operatorname{se}(\hat{\beta}_2)} = \frac{\text{Estimator} - \text{Parameter}}{\text{Estimated standard error of estimator}} \\
&= \frac{(\hat{\beta}_2 - \beta_2)\sqrt{\sum x_i^2}}{\hat{\sigma}}
\end{aligned}
\tag{5.3.2}
$$

where the se $(\hat{\beta}_2)$ now refers to the estimated standard error. It can be shown (see Appendix 5A, Section 5A.2) that the t variable thus defined follows the t distribution with $n - 2$ df. [Note the difference between Eqs. (5.3.1) and (5.3.2).] Therefore, instead of using the normal distribution, we can use the t distribution to establish a confidence interval for β_2 as follows:

$$\Pr(-t_{\alpha/2} \le t \le t_{\alpha/2}) = 1 - \alpha \tag{5.3.3}$$

where the t value in the middle of this double inequality is the t value given by Equation 5.3.2 and where $t_{\alpha/2}$ is the value of the t variable obtained from the t distribution for $\alpha/2$ level of significance and $n - 2$ df; it is often called the **critical** t value at $\alpha/2$ level of significance. Substitution of Eq. (5.3.2) into Equation 5.3.3 yields

$$\Pr\left[-t_{\alpha/2} \le \frac{\hat{\beta}_2 - \beta_2}{\text{se}\,(\hat{\beta}_2)} \le t_{\alpha/2}\right] = 1 - \alpha \tag{5.3.4}$$

Rearranging Equation 5.3.4, we obtain

$$\Pr\,[\hat{\beta}_2 - t_{\alpha/2}\,\text{se}\,(\hat{\beta}_2) \le \beta_2 \le \hat{\beta}_2 + t_{\alpha/2}\,\text{se}\,(\hat{\beta}_2)] = 1 - \alpha \qquad (5.3.5)^3$$

Equation 5.3.5 provides a $100(1 - \alpha)$ percent **confidence interval** for β_2, which can be written more compactly as

$100(1 - \alpha)\%$ confidence interval for β_2:

$$\hat{\beta}_2 \pm t_{\alpha/2}\,\text{se}\,(\hat{\beta}_2) \tag{5.3.6}$$

Arguing analogously, and using Eqs. (4.3.1) and (4.3.2), we can then write:

$$\Pr\,[\hat{\beta}_1 - t_{\alpha/2}\,\text{se}\,(\hat{\beta}_1) \le \beta_1 \le \hat{\beta}_1 + t_{\alpha/2}\,\text{se}\,(\hat{\beta}_1)] = 1 - \alpha \tag{5.3.7}$$

or, more compactly,

$100(1 - \alpha)\%$ confidence interval for β_1:

$$\hat{\beta}_1 \pm t_{\alpha/2}\,\text{se}\,(\hat{\beta}_1) \tag{5.3.8}$$

Notice an important feature of the confidence intervals given in Equations 5.3.6 and 5.3.8: In both cases *the width of the confidence interval is proportional to the standard error of the estimator*. That is, the larger the standard error, the larger is the width of the confidence interval. Put differently, the larger the standard error of the estimator, the greater is the uncertainty of estimating the true value of the unknown parameter. Thus, the standard error of an estimator is often described as a measure of the **precision** of the estimator (i.e., how precisely the estimator measures the true population value).

[3]Some authors prefer to write Eq. (5.3.5) with the df explicitly indicated. Thus, they would write

$$\Pr\,[\hat{\beta}_2 - t_{(n-2),\alpha/2}\,\text{se}\,(\hat{\beta}_2) \le \beta_2 \le \hat{\beta}_2 + t_{(n-2)\alpha/2}\,\text{se}\,(\hat{\beta}_2)] = 1 - \alpha$$

But for simplicity we will stick to our notation; the context clarifies the appropriate df involved.

Returning to our regression example in Chapter 3 (Section 3.6) of mean hourly wages (Y) on education (X), recall that we found in Table 3.2 that $\hat{\beta}_2 = 0.7240$; $\text{se}(\hat{\beta}_2) = 0.0700$. Since there are 13 observations, the degrees of freedom (df) are 11. If we assume $\alpha = 5\%$, that is, a 95% confidence coefficient, then the t table shows that for 11 df the **critical** $t_{\alpha/2} = 2.201$. Substituting these values in Eq. (5.3.5), the reader should verify that the 95 percent confidence interval for β_2 is as follows:[4]

$$0.5700 \le \beta_2 \le 0.8780 \tag{5.3.9}$$

Or, using Eq. (5.3.6), it is

$$0.7240 \pm 2.201(0.0700)$$

that is,

$$0.7240 \pm 0.1540 \tag{5.3.10}$$

The interpretation of this confidence interval is: Given the confidence coefficient of 95 percent, in 95 out of 100 cases intervals like Equation 5.3.9 will contain the true β_2. But, as warned earlier, we cannot say that the probability is 95 percent that the specific interval in Eq. (5.3.9) contains the true β_2 because this interval is now fixed and no longer random; therefore β_2 either lies in it or it does not: The probability that the specified fixed interval includes the true β_2 is therefore 1 or 0.

Following Eq. (5.3.7), and the data in Table 3.2, the reader can easily verify that the 95 percent confidence interval for β_1 for our example is

$$-1.8871 \le \beta_1 \le 1.8583 \tag{5.3.11}$$

Again you should be careful in interpreting this confidence interval. In 95 out of 100 cases, intervals like Equation 5.3.11 will contain the true β_1; the probability that this particular fixed interval includes the true β_1 is either 1 or 0.

Confidence Interval for β_1 and β_2 Simultaneously

There are occasions when one needs to construct a *joint confidence interval* for β_1 and β_2 such that with a confidence coefficient $(1 - \alpha)$, say, 95 percent, that interval includes β_1 and β_2 simultaneously. Since this topic is involved, the interested reader may want to consult appropriate references.[5] We will touch on this topic briefly in Chapters 8 and 10.

5.4 Confidence Interval for σ^2

As pointed out in Chapter 4, Section 4.3, under the normality assumption, the variable

$$\chi^2 = (n-2)\frac{\hat{\sigma}^2}{\sigma^2} \tag{5.4.1}$$

[4]Because of rounding errors in Table 3.2, the answers given below may not exactly match the answers obtained from a statistical package.

[5]For an accessible discussion, see John Neter, William Wasserman, and Michael H. Kutner, *Applied Linear Regression Models,* Richard D. Irwin, Homewood, Ill., 1983, Chap. 5.

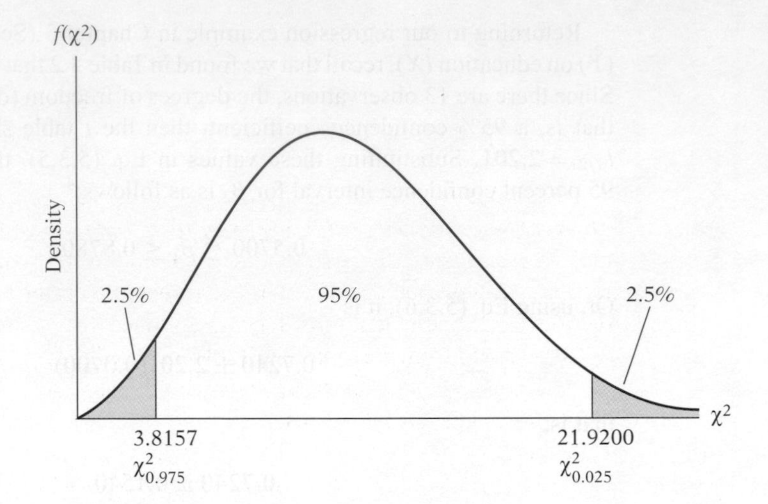

FIGURE 5.1 The 95% confidence interval for χ^2 (11 df).

follows the χ^2 distribution with $n - 2$ df.[6] Therefore, we can use the χ^2 distribution to establish a confidence interval for σ^2

$$\Pr\left(\chi^2_{1-\alpha/2} \leq \chi^2 \leq \chi^2_{\alpha/2}\right) = 1 - \alpha \tag{5.4.2}$$

where the χ^2 value in the middle of this double inequality is as given by Equation 5.4.1 and where $\chi^2_{1-\alpha/2}$ and $\chi^2_{\alpha/2}$ are two values of χ^2 (the **critical** χ^2 values) obtained from the chi-square table for $n - 2$ df in such a manner that they cut off $100(\alpha/2)$ percent tail areas of the χ^2 distribution, as shown in Figure 5.1.

Substituting χ^2 from Eq. (5.4.1) into Equation 5.4.2 and rearranging the terms, we obtain

$$\Pr\left[(n-2)\frac{\hat{\sigma}^2}{\chi^2_{\alpha/2}} \leq \sigma^2 \leq (n-2)\frac{\hat{\sigma}^2}{\chi^2_{1-\alpha/2}}\right] = 1 - \alpha \tag{5.4.3}$$

which gives the $100(1 - \alpha)\%$ confidence interval for σ^2.

Continuing with our wages-education example, we found in Table 3.2 that for our data we have $\hat{\sigma}^2 = 0.8936$. If we choose α of 5%, the chi-square table for 11 df gives the following critical values: $\chi^2_{0.025} = 21.9200$, and $\chi^2_{0.975} = 3.8157$. These values show that the probability of a chi-square value exceeding 21.9200 is 2.5 percent and that of 3.8157 is 97.5 percent. Therefore, the interval between these two values is the 95 percent confidence interval for χ^2, as shown in Figure 5.1. (Note the skewed characteristic of the chi-square distribution.)

Substituting the data of our example into Eq. (5.4.3), the reader can verify that the 95 percent confidence interval for σ^2 is as follows:

$$0.4484 \leq \sigma^2 \leq 2.5760 \tag{5.4.4}$$

The interpretation of this interval is: If we establish 95 percent confidence limits on σ^2 and if we maintain a priori that these limits will include the true σ^2, we will be right in the long run 95 percent of the time.

[6]For proof, see Robert V. Hogg and Allen T. Craig, *Introduction to Mathematical Statistics*, 2d ed., Macmillan, New York, 1965, p. 144.

5.5 Hypothesis Testing: General Comments

Having discussed the problem of point and interval estimation, we shall now consider the topic of hypothesis testing. In this section we discuss briefly some general aspects of this topic; **Appendix A** gives some additional details.

The problem of statistical hypothesis testing may be stated simply as follows: *Is a given observation or finding compatible with some stated hypothesis or not?* The word "compatible," as used here, means "sufficiently" close to the hypothesized value so that we do not reject the stated hypothesis. Thus, if some theory or prior experience leads us to believe that the true slope coefficient β_2 of the wages-education example is unity, is the observed $\hat{\beta}_2 = 0.724$ obtained from the sample of Table 3.2 consistent with the stated hypothesis? If it is, we do not reject the hypothesis; otherwise, we may reject it.

In the language of statistics, the stated hypothesis is known as the **null hypothesis** and is denoted by the symbol H_0. The null hypothesis is usually tested against an **alternative hypothesis** (also known as **maintained hypothesis**) denoted by H_1, which may state, for example, that true β_2 is different from unity. The alternative hypothesis may be **simple** or **composite.**[7] For example, $H_1: \beta_2 = 1.5$ is a simple hypothesis, but $H_1: \beta_2 \neq 1.5$ is a composite hypothesis.

The theory of hypothesis testing is concerned with developing rules or procedures for deciding whether to reject or not reject the null hypothesis. There are two *mutually complementary* approaches for devising such rules, namely, **confidence interval** and **test of significance.** Both these approaches predicate that the variable (statistic or estimator) under consideration has some probability distribution and that hypothesis testing involves making statements or assertions about the value(s) of the parameter(s) of such distribution. For example, we know that with the normality assumption $\hat{\beta}_2$ is normally distributed with mean equal to β_2 and variance given by Eq. (4.3.5). If we hypothesize that $\beta_2 = 1$, we are making an assertion about one of the parameters of the normal distribution, namely, the mean. Most of the statistical hypotheses encountered in this text will be of this type—making assertions about one or more values of the parameters of some assumed probability distribution such as the normal, *F*, *t*, or χ^2. How this is accomplished is discussed in the following two sections.

5.6 Hypothesis Testing: The Confidence-Interval Approach

Two-Sided or Two-Tail Test

To illustrate the confidence interval approach, once again we revert to our wages-education example. From the regression results given in Eq. (3.6.1), we know that the slope coefficient is 0.7240. Suppose we postulate that

$$H_0: \beta_2 = 0.5$$
$$H_1: \beta_2 \neq 0.5$$

that is, the true slope coefficient is 0.5 under the null hypothesis but less than or greater than 0.5 under the alternative hypothesis. The null hypothesis is a simple hypothesis, whereas

[7]A statistical hypothesis is called a **simple hypothesis** if it specifies the precise value(s) of the parameter(s) of a probability density function; otherwise, it is called a **composite hypothesis.** For example, in the normal pdf $(1/\sigma\sqrt{2\pi}) \exp\{-\frac{1}{2}[(X-\mu)/\sigma]^2\}$, if we assert that $H_1: \mu = 15$ and $\sigma = 2$, it is a simple hypothesis; but if $H_1: \mu = 15$ and $\sigma > 15$, it is a composite hypothesis, because the standard deviation does not have a specific value.

FIGURE 5.2
A $100(1-\alpha)\%$ confidence interval for β_2.

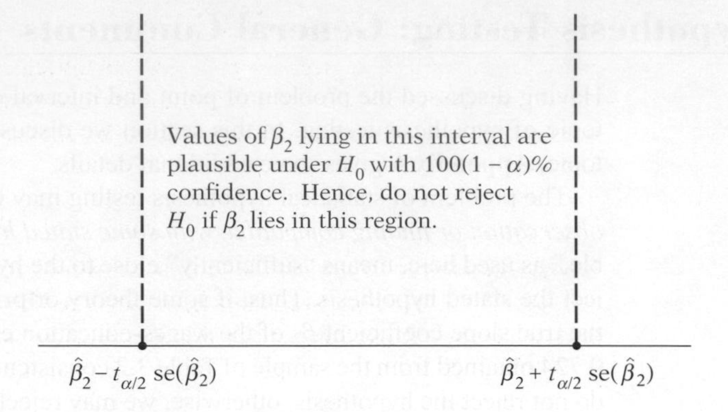

the alternative hypothesis is composite; actually it is what is known as a **two-sided hypothesis.** Very often such a two-sided alternative hypothesis reflects the fact that we do not have a strong a priori or theoretical expectation about the direction in which the alternative hypothesis should move from the null hypothesis.

Is the observed $\hat{\beta}_2$ compatible with H_0? To answer this question, let us refer to the confidence interval in Eq. (5.3.9). We know that in the long run intervals like (0.5700, 0.8780) will contain the true β_2 with 95 percent probability. Consequently, in the long run (i.e., repeated sampling) such intervals provide a range or limits within which the true β_2 may lie with a confidence coefficient of, say, 95 percent. Thus, the confidence interval provides a set of plausible null hypotheses. Therefore, if β_2 under H_0 falls within the $100(1-\alpha)\%$ confidence interval, we do not reject the null hypothesis; if it lies outside the interval, we may reject it.[8] This range is illustrated schematically in Figure 5.2.

Decision Rule Construct a $100(1-\alpha)\%$ confidence interval for β_2. If the β_2 under H_0 falls within this confidence interval, do not reject H_0, but if it falls outside this interval, reject H_0.

Following this rule, for our hypothetical example, H_0: $\beta_2 = 0.5$ clearly lies outside the 95 percent confidence interval given in Eq. (5.3.9). Therefore, we can reject the hypothesis that the true slope is 0.5, with 95 percent confidence. If the null hypothesis were true, the probability of our obtaining a value of slope of as much as 0.7240 by sheer chance or fluke is at the most about 5 percent, a small probability.

In statistics, when we reject the null hypothesis, we say that our finding is **statistically significant.** On the other hand, when we do not reject the null hypothesis, we say that our finding is **not statistically significant.**

Some authors use a phrase such as "highly statistically significant." By this they usually mean that when they reject the null hypothesis, the probability of committing a Type I error (i.e., α) is a small number, usually 1 percent. But as our discussion of the **p value** in Section 5.8 will show, it is better to leave it to the researcher to decide whether a statistical finding is "significant," "moderately significant," or "highly significant."

[8]Always bear in mind that there is a 100α percent chance that the confidence interval does not contain β_2 under H_0 even though the hypothesis is correct. In short, there is a 100α percent chance of committing a **Type I error.** Thus, if $\alpha = 0.05$, there is a 5 percent chance that we could reject the null hypothesis even though it is true.

One-Sided or One-Tail Test

Sometimes we have a strong a priori or theoretical expectation (or expectations based on some previous empirical work) that the alternative hypothesis is one-sided or unidirectional rather than two-sided, as just discussed. Thus, for our wages-education example, one could postulate that

$$H_0: \beta_2 \leq 0.5 \quad \text{and} \quad H_1: \beta_2 > 0.5$$

Perhaps economic theory or prior empirical work suggests that the slope is greater than 0.5. Although the procedure to test this hypothesis can be easily derived from Eq. (5.3.5), the actual mechanics are better explained in terms of the test-of-significance approach discussed next.[9]

5.7 Hypothesis Testing: The Test-of-Significance Approach

Testing the Significance of Regression Coefficients: The *t* Test

An *alternative but complementary approach* to the confidence-interval method of testing statistical hypotheses is the **test-of-significance approach** developed along independent lines by R. A. Fisher and jointly by Neyman and Pearson.[10] **Broadly speaking, a test of significance is a procedure by which sample results are used to verify the truth or falsity of a null hypothesis.** The key idea behind tests of significance is that of a **test statistic** (estimator) and the sampling distribution of such a statistic under the null hypothesis. The decision to accept or reject H_0 is made on the basis of the value of the test statistic obtained from the data at hand.

As an illustration, recall that under the normality assumption the variable

$$t = \frac{\hat{\beta}_2 - \beta_2}{\text{se}\,(\hat{\beta}_2)} = \frac{(\hat{\beta}_2 - \beta_2)\sqrt{\sum x_i^2}}{\hat{\sigma}} \tag{5.3.2}$$

follows the t distribution with $n - 2$ df. If the value of true β_2 is specified under the null hypothesis, the t value of Eq. (5.3.2) can readily be computed from the available sample, and therefore it can serve as a test statistic. And since this test statistic follows the t distribution, confidence-interval statements such as the following can be made:

$$\Pr\left[-t_{\alpha/2} \leq \frac{\hat{\beta}_2 - \beta_2^*}{\text{se}\,(\hat{\beta}_2)} \leq t_{\alpha/2}\right] = 1 - \alpha \tag{5.7.1}$$

where β_2^* is the value of β_2 under H_0 and where $-t_{\alpha/2}$ and $t_{\alpha/2}$ are the values of t (the **critical** t values) obtained from the t table for $(\alpha/2)$ level of significance and $n - 2$ df [cf. Eq. (5.3.4)]. The t table is given in **Appendix D.**

[9] If you want to use the confidence interval approach, construct a $(100 - \alpha)\%$ *one-sided* or *one-tail* confidence interval for β_2. Why?

[10] Details may be found in E. L. Lehman, *Testing Statistical Hypotheses*, John Wiley & Sons, New York, 1959.

Rearranging Equation 5.7.1, we obtain

$$\Pr\,[\beta_2^* - t_{\alpha/2}\,\text{se}\,(\hat{\beta}_2) \le \hat{\beta}_2 \le \beta_2^* + t_{\alpha/2}\,\text{se}\,(\hat{\beta}_2)] = 1 - \alpha \tag{5.7.2}$$

which gives the interval in which $\hat{\beta}_2$ will fall with $1 - \alpha$ probability, given $\beta_2 = \beta_2^*$. In the language of hypothesis testing, the $100(1 - \alpha)\%$ confidence interval established in Equation 5.7.2 is known as the **region of acceptance** (of the null hypothesis) and the *region(s)* outside the confidence interval is (are) called the **region(s) of rejection** (of H_0) or the **critical region(s).** As noted previously, the confidence limits, the endpoints of the confidence interval, are also called **critical values.**

The intimate connection between the confidence-interval and test-of-significance approaches to hypothesis testing can now be seen by comparing Eq. (5.3.5) with Eq. (5.7.2). In the confidence-interval procedure we try to establish a range or an interval that has a certain probability of including the true but unknown β_2, whereas in the test-of-significance approach we hypothesize some value for β_2 and try to see whether the computed $\hat{\beta}_2$ lies within reasonable (confidence) limits around the hypothesized value.

Once again let us return to our wages-education example. We know that $\hat{\beta}_2 = 0.7240$, $\text{se}\,(\hat{\beta}_2) = 0.0700$, and df = 11. If we assume $\alpha = 5\%$, $t_{\alpha/2} = 2.201$.

If we assume H_0: $\beta_2 = \beta_2^* = 0.5$ *and* H_1: $\beta_2 \neq 0.5$, Eq. (5.7.2) becomes

$$\Pr\,(0.3460 \le \hat{\beta}_2 \le 0.6540) \tag{5.7.3}$$ [11]

as shown diagrammatically in Figure 5.3.

In practice, there is no need to estimate Eq. (5.7.2) explicitly. One can compute the t value in the middle of the double inequality given by Eq. (5.7.1) and see whether it lies between the critical t values or outside them. For our example,

$$t = \frac{0.7240 - 0.5}{0.0700} = 3.2 \tag{5.7.4}$$

which clearly lies in the critical region of Figure 5.4. The conclusion remains the same; namely, we reject H_0.

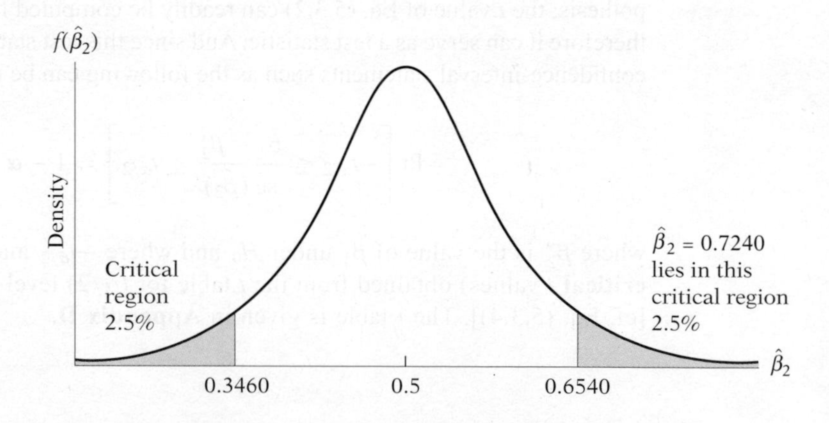

FIGURE 5.3
The 95% confidence interval for $\hat{\beta}_2$ under the hypothesis that $\beta_2 = 0.5$.

[11] In Sec. 5.2, point 4, it was stated that we *cannot* say that the probability is 95 percent that the fixed interval (0.5700, 0.8780) includes the true β_2. But we can make the probabilistic statement given in Eq. (5.7.3) because $\hat{\beta}_2$, being an estimator, is a random variable.

FIGURE 5.4
The 95% confidence interval for t(11 df).

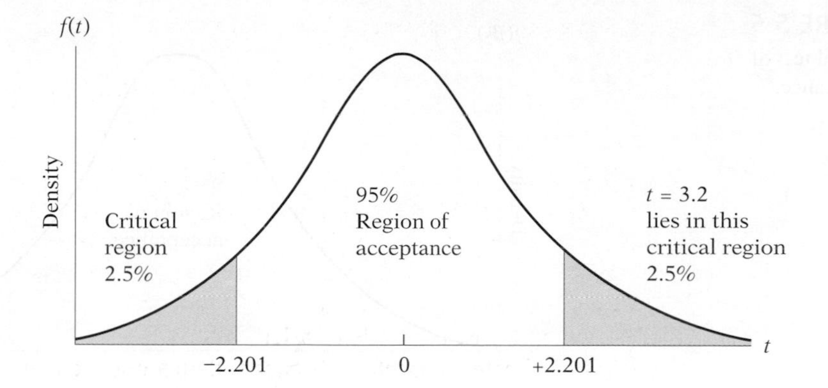

Notice that if the estimated β_2 ($= \hat{\beta}_2$) is equal to the hypothesized β_2, the t value in Equation 5.7.4 will be zero. However, as the estimated β_2 value departs from the hypothesized β_2 value, $|t|$ (that is, the absolute t value; *note:* t can be positive as well as negative) will be increasingly large. *Therefore, a "large" $|t|$ value will be evidence against the null hypothesis.* Of course, we can always use the t table to determine whether a particular t value is large or small; the answer, as we know, depends on the degrees of freedom as well as on the probability of Type I error that we are willing to accept. If you take a look at the t table given in **Appendix D** (Table D.2), you will observe that for any given value of df the probability of obtaining an increasingly large $|t|$ value becomes progressively smaller. Thus, for 20 df the probability of obtaining a $|t|$ value of 1.725 or greater is 0.10 or 10 percent, but for the same df the probability of obtaining a $|t|$ value of 3.552 or greater is only 0.002 or 0.2 percent.

Since we use the t distribution, the preceding testing procedure is called appropriately the ***t* test. In the language of significance tests, a statistic is said to be statistically significant if the value of the test statistic lies in the critical region. In this case the null hypothesis is rejected. By the same token, a test is said to be statistically insignificant if the value of the test statistic lies in the acceptance region.** In this situation, the null hypothesis is not rejected. In our example, the t test is significant and hence we reject the null hypothesis.

Before concluding our discussion of hypothesis testing, note that the testing procedure just outlined is known as a **two-sided,** or **two-tail,** test-of-significance procedure in that we consider the two extreme tails of the relevant probability distribution, the rejection regions, and reject the null hypothesis if it lies in either tail. But this happens because our H_1 was a two-sided composite hypothesis; $\beta_2 \neq 0.5$ means β_2 is either greater than or less than 0.5. But suppose prior experience suggests to us that the slope is expected to be greater than 0.5. In this case we have: H_0: $\beta_2 \leq 0.5$ and H_1: $\beta_2 > 0.5$. Although H_1 is still a composite hypothesis, it is now one-sided. To test this hypothesis, we use the **one-tail test** (the right tail), as shown in Figure 5.5. (See also the discussion in Section 5.6.)

The test procedure is the same as before except that the upper confidence limit or critical value now corresponds to $t_\alpha = t_{.05}$, that is, the 5 percent level. As Figure 5.5 shows, we need not consider the lower tail of the t distribution in this case. Whether one uses a two- or one-tail test of significance will depend upon how the alternative hypothesis is formulated, which, in turn, may depend upon some a priori considerations or prior empirical experience. (But more on this in Section 5.8.)

We can summarize the t test of significance approach to hypothesis testing as shown in Table 5.1.

FIGURE 5.5
One-tail test of significance.

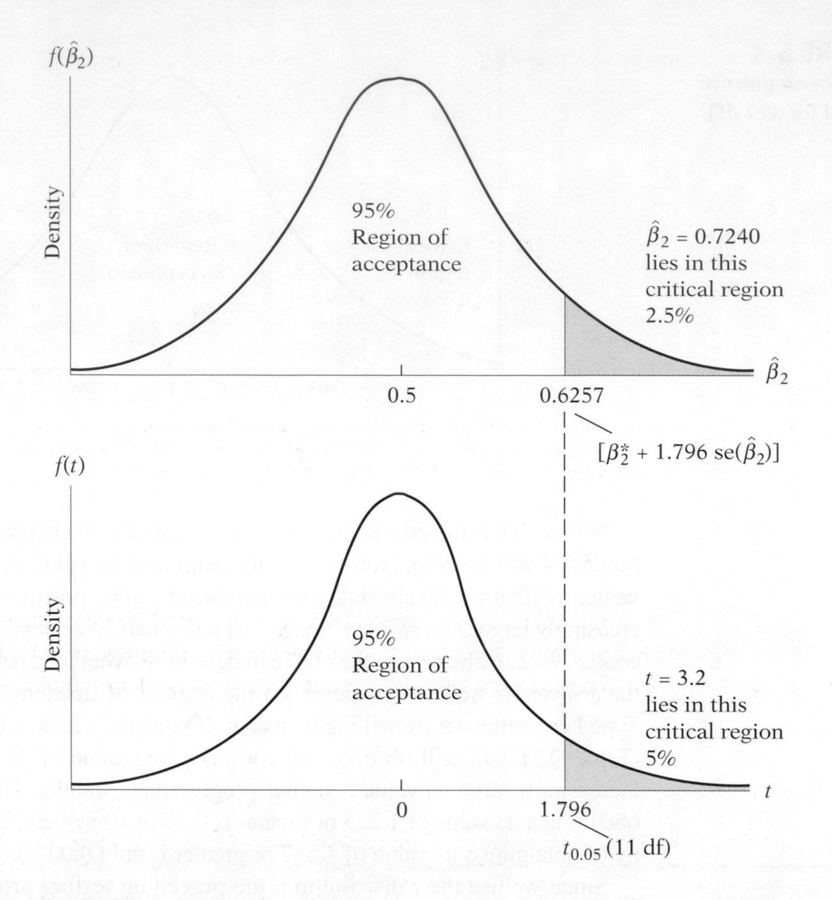

TABLE 5.1
The *t* Test of Significance: Decision Rules

Type of Hypothesis	H_0: The Null Hypothesis	H_1: The Alternative Hypothesis	Decision Rule: Reject H_0 If
Two-tail	$\beta_2 = \beta_2^*$	$\beta_2 \neq \beta_2^*$	$\|t\| > t_{\alpha/2,\text{df}}$
Right-tail	$\beta_2 \leq \beta_2^*$	$\beta_2 > \beta_2^*$	$t > t_{\alpha,\text{df}}$
Left-tail	$\beta_2 \geq \beta_2^*$	$\beta_2 < \beta_2^*$	$t < -t_{\alpha,\text{df}}$

Notes: β_2^* is the hypothesized numerical value of β_2.
$|t|$ means the absolute value of t.
t_α or $t_{\alpha/2}$ means the critical t value at the α or $\alpha/2$ level of significance.
df: degrees of freedom, $(n - 2)$ for the two-variable model, $(n - 3)$ for the three-variable model, and so on.
The same procedure holds to test hypotheses about β_1.

Testing the Significance of σ^2: The χ^2 Test

As another illustration of the test-of-significance methodology, consider the following variable:

$$\chi^2 = (n-2)\frac{\hat{\sigma}^2}{\sigma^2} \tag{5.4.1}$$

which, as noted previously, follows the χ^2 distribution with $n - 2$ df. For our example, $\hat{\sigma}^2 = 0.8937$ and df $= 11$. If we postulate that $H_0\colon \sigma^2 = 0.6$ versus $H_1\colon \sigma^2 \neq 0.6$, Equation 5.4.1 provides the test statistic for H_0. Substituting the appropriate values in Eq. (5.4.1), it can be found that under H_0, $\chi^2 = 16.3845$. If we assume $\alpha = 5\%$, the critical χ^2 values

TABLE 5.2
A Summary of the χ^2 Test

H_0: The Null Hypothesis	H_1: The Alternative Hypothesis	Critical Region: Reject H_0 If
$\sigma^2 = \sigma_0^2$	$\sigma^2 > \sigma_0^2$	$\frac{\text{df}(\hat{\sigma}^2)}{\sigma_0^2} > \chi^2_{\alpha,\text{df}}$
$\sigma^2 = \sigma_0^2$	$\sigma^2 < \sigma_0^2$	$\frac{\text{df}(\hat{\sigma}^2)}{\sigma_0^2} < \chi^2_{(1-\alpha),\text{df}}$
$\sigma^2 = \sigma_0^2$	$\sigma^2 \neq \sigma_0^2$	$\frac{\text{df}(\hat{\sigma}^2)}{\sigma_0^2} > \chi^2_{\alpha/2,\text{df}}$ or $< \chi^2_{(1-\alpha/2),\text{df}}$

Note: σ_0^2 is the value of σ^2 under the null hypothesis. The first subscript on χ^2 in the last column is the level of significance, and the second subscript is the degrees of freedom. These are critical chi-square values. Note that df is $(n - 2)$ for the two-variable regression model, $(n - 3)$ for the three-variable regression model, and so on.

are 3.81575 and 21.9200. Since the computed χ^2 lies between these limits, the data support the null hypothesis and we do not reject it. (See Figure 5.1.) This test procedure is called the **chi-square test of significance.** The χ^2 test of significance approach to hypothesis testing is summarized in Table 5.2.

5.8 Hypothesis Testing: Some Practical Aspects

The Meaning of "Accepting" or "Rejecting" a Hypothesis

If, on the basis of a test of significance, say, the t test, we decide to "accept" the null hypothesis, all we are saying is that on the basis of the sample evidence we have no reason to reject it; we are not saying that the null hypothesis is true beyond any doubt. Why? To answer this, let us return to our wages-education example and assume that H_0: $\beta_2 = 0.70$. Now the estimated value of the slope is $\hat{\beta}_2 = 0.7241$ with a se $(\hat{\beta}_2) = 0.0701$. Then on the basis of the t test we find that $t = \frac{(0.7241 - 0.7)}{0.0701} = 0.3438$, which is insignificant, say, at $\alpha = 5\%$. Therefore, we say "accept" H_0. But now let us assume H_0: $\beta_2 = 0.6$. Applying the t test again, we obtain $t = \frac{(0.7241 - 0.6)}{0.0701} = 1.7703$, which is also statistically insignificant. So now we say "accept" this H_0. Which of these two null hypotheses is the "truth"? We do not know. Therefore, in "accepting" a null hypothesis we should always be aware that another null hypothesis may be equally compatible with the data. It is therefore preferable to say that we *may* accept the null hypothesis rather than we (do) accept it. Better still,

> . . . just as a court pronounces a verdict as "not guilty" rather than "innocent," so the conclusion of a statistical test is "do not reject" rather than "accept."[12]

[12]Jan Kmenta, *Elements of Econometrics,* Macmillan, New York, 1971, p. 114.

The "Zero" Null Hypothesis and the "2-t" Rule of Thumb

A null hypothesis that is commonly tested in empirical work is $H_0: \beta_2 = 0$, that is, the slope coefficient is zero. This "zero" null hypothesis is a kind of straw man, the objective being to find out whether Y is related at all to X, the explanatory variable. If there is no relationship between Y and X to begin with, then testing a hypothesis such as $\beta_2 = 0.3$ or any other value is meaningless.

This null hypothesis can be easily tested by the confidence interval or the t-test approach discussed in the preceding sections. But very often such formal testing can be shortcut by adopting the "2-t" rule of significance, which may be stated as

"2-t" Rule of Thumb

If the number of degrees of freedom is 20 or more and if α, the level of significance, is set at 0.05, then the null hypothesis $\beta_2 = 0$ can be rejected if the t value $[= \hat{\beta}_2/\text{se}\,(\hat{\beta}_2)]$ computed from Eq. (5.3.2) exceeds 2 in absolute value.

The rationale for this rule is not too difficult to grasp. From Eq. (5.7.1) we know that we will reject $H_0: \beta_2 = 0$ if

$$t = \hat{\beta}_2/\text{se}\,(\hat{\beta}_2) > t_{\alpha/2} \qquad \text{when } \hat{\beta}_2 > 0$$

or

$$t = \hat{\beta}_2/\text{se}\,(\hat{\beta}_2) < -t_{\alpha/2} \qquad \text{when } \hat{\beta}_2 < 0$$

or when

$$|t| = \left| \frac{\hat{\beta}_2}{\text{se}\,(\hat{\beta}_2)} \right| > t_{\alpha/2} \tag{5.8.1}$$

for the appropriate degrees of freedom.

Now if we examine the t table given in **Appendix D,** we see that for df of about 20 or more a computed t value in excess of 2 (in absolute terms), say, 2.1, is statistically significant at the 5 percent level, implying rejection of the null hypothesis. Therefore, if we find that for 20 or more df the computed t value is, say, 2.5 or 3, we do not even have to refer to the t table to assess the significance of the estimated slope coefficient. Of course, one can always refer to the t table to obtain the precise level of significance, and one should always do so when the df are fewer than, say, 20.

In passing, note that if we are testing the one-sided hypothesis $\beta_2 = 0$ versus $\beta_2 > 0$ or $\beta_2 < 0$, then we should reject the null hypothesis if

$$|t| = \left| \frac{\hat{\beta}_2}{\text{se}\,(\hat{\beta}_2)} \right| > t_{\alpha} \tag{5.8.2}$$

If we fix α at 0.05, then from the t table we observe that for 20 or more df a t value in excess of 1.73 is statistically significant at the 5 percent level of significance (one-tail). Hence, whenever a t value exceeds, say, 1.8 (in absolute terms) and the df are 20 or more, one need not consult the t table for the statistical significance of the observed coefficient. Of course, if we choose α at 0.01 or any other level, we will have to decide on the appropriate t value as the benchmark value. But by now the reader should be able to do that.

Forming the Null and Alternative Hypotheses[13]

Given the null and the alternative hypotheses, testing them for statistical significance should no longer be a mystery. But how does one formulate these hypotheses? There are no hard-and-fast rules. Very often the phenomenon under study will suggest the nature of the null and alternative hypotheses. For example, consider the capital market line (CML) of portfolio theory, which postulates that $E_i = \beta_1 + \beta_2 \sigma_i$, where $E =$ expected return on portfolio and $\sigma =$ the standard deviation of return, a measure of risk. Since return and risk are expected to be positively related—the higher the risk, the higher the return—the natural alternative hypothesis to the null hypothesis that $\beta_2 = 0$ would be $\beta_2 > 0$. That is, one would not choose to consider values of β_2 less than zero.

But consider the case of the demand for money. As we shall show later, one of the important determinants of the demand for money is income. Prior studies of the money demand functions have shown that the income elasticity of demand for money (the percent change in the demand for money for a 1 percent change in income) has typically ranged between 0.7 and 1.3. Therefore, in a new study of demand for money, if one postulates that the income-elasticity coefficient β_2 is 1, the alternative hypothesis could be that $\beta_2 \neq 1$, a two-sided alternative hypothesis.

Thus, theoretical expectations or prior empirical work or both can be relied upon to formulate hypotheses. But no matter how the hypotheses are formed, *it is extremely important that the researcher establish these hypotheses before carrying out the empirical investigation*. Otherwise, he or she will be guilty of circular reasoning or self-fulfilling prophesies. That is, if one were to formulate hypotheses after examining the empirical results, there may be the temptation to form hypotheses that justify one's results. Such a practice should be avoided at all costs, at least for the sake of scientific objectivity. Keep in mind the Stigler quotation given at the beginning of this chapter!

Choosing α, the Level of Significance

It should be clear from the discussion so far that whether we reject or do not reject the null hypothesis depends critically on α, the level of significance or the *probability of committing a* ***Type I*** *error*—the probability of rejecting the true hypothesis. In **Appendix A** we discuss fully the nature of a Type I error, its relationship to a ***Type II*** *error* (the probability of accepting the false hypothesis) and why classical statistics generally concentrates on a Type I error. But even then, why is α commonly fixed at the 1, 5, or, at the most, 10 percent levels? As a matter of fact, there is nothing sacrosanct about these values; any other values will do just as well.

In an introductory book like this it is not possible to discuss in depth why one chooses the 1, 5, or 10 percent levels of significance, for that will take us into the field of statistical decision making, a discipline unto itself. A brief summary, however, can be offered. As we discuss in **Appendix A,** for a given sample size, if we try to reduce a *Type I error*, a *Type II error* increases, and vice versa. That is, given the sample size, if we try to reduce the probability of rejecting the true hypothesis, we at the same time increase the probability of accepting the false hypothesis. So there is a trade-off involved between these two types of errors,

[13]For an interesting discussion about formulating hypotheses, see J. Bradford De Long and Kevin Lang, "Are All Economic Hypotheses False?" *Journal of Political Economy*, vol. 100, no. 6, 1992, pp. 1257–1272.

given the sample size. Now the only way we can decide about the trade-off is to find out the relative costs of the two types of errors. Then,

> If the error of rejecting the null hypothesis which is in fact true (Error Type I) is costly relative to the error of not rejecting the null hypothesis which is in fact false (Error Type II), it will be rational to set the probability of the first kind of error low. If, on the other hand, the cost of making Error Type I is low relative to the cost of making Error Type II, it will pay to make the probability of the first kind of error high (thus making the probability of the second type of error low).[14]

Of course, the rub is that we rarely know the costs of making the two types of errors. Thus, applied econometricians generally follow the practice of setting the value of α at a 1 or a 5 or at most a 10 percent level and choose a test statistic that would make the probability of committing a Type II error as small as possible. Since one minus the probability of committing a Type II error is known as the **power of the test,** this procedure amounts to maximizing the power of the test. (See **Appendix A** for a discussion of the power of a test.)

Fortunately, the dilemma of choosing the appropriate value of α can be avoided by using what is known as the ***p value*** of the test statistic, which is discussed next.

The Exact Level of Significance: The *p* Value

As just noted, the Achilles heel of the classical approach to hypothesis testing is its arbitrariness in selecting α. Once a test statistic (e.g., the t statistic) is obtained in a given example, why not simply go to the appropriate statistical table and find out the actual probability of obtaining a value of the test statistic as much as or greater than that obtained in the example? This probability is called the ***p* value** (i.e., **probability value**), also known as the **observed** or **exact level of significance** or the **exact probability of committing a Type I error.** More technically, the p value is defined as **the lowest significance level at which a null hypothesis can be rejected.**

To illustrate, let us return to our wages-education example. Given the null hypothesis that the true coefficient of education is 0.5, we obtained a t value of 3.2 in Eq. (5.7.4). What is the p value of obtaining a t value of as much as or greater than 3.2? Looking up the t table given in **Appendix D,** we observe that for 11 df the probability of obtaining such a t value must be smaller than 0.005 (one-tail) or 0.010 (two-tail).

If you use Stata or EViews statistical packages, you will find that the p value of obtaining a t value of 3.2 or greater is about 0.00001, that is, extremely small. This is the p value of the observed t statistic. This exact level of significance of the t statistic is much smaller than the conventionally, and arbitrarily, fixed level of significance, such as 1, 5, or 10 percent. As a matter of fact, if we were to use the p value just computed, and reject the null hypothesis that the true coefficient of education is 0.5, the probability of our committing a Type I error would be only about 1 in 100,000!

As we noted earlier, if the data do not support the null hypothesis, $|t|$ obtained under the null hypothesis will be "large" and therefore the p value of obtaining such a $|t|$ value will be "small." In other words, for a given sample size, as $|t|$ increases, the p value decreases, and one can therefore reject the null hypothesis with increasing confidence.

What is the relationship of the p value to the level of significance α? If we make the habit of fixing α equal to the p value of a test statistic (e.g., the t statistic), then there is no conflict between the two values. To put it differently, **it is better to give up fixing α arbitrarily at**

[14]Jan Kmenta, *Elements of Econometrics,* Macmillan, New York, 1971, pp. 126–127.

some level and simply choose the p value of the test statistic. It is preferable to leave it to the reader to decide whether to reject the null hypothesis at the given p value. If in an application the p value of a test statistic happens to be, say, 0.145, or 14.5 percent, and if the reader wants to reject the null hypothesis at this (exact) level of significance, so be it. Nothing is wrong with taking a chance of being wrong 14.5 percent of the time if you reject the true null hypothesis. Similarly, as in our wages-education example, there is nothing wrong if the researcher wants to choose a p value of about 0.02 percent and not take a chance of being wrong more than 2 out of 10,000 times. After all, some investigators may be risk-lovers and some risk-averters!

In the rest of this text, we will generally quote the p value of a given test statistic. Some readers may want to fix α at some level and reject the null hypothesis if the p value is less than α. That is their choice.

Statistical Significance versus Practical Significance

Look back at Example 3.1 and the regression results given in Equation (3.7.1). This regression relates personal consumption expenditure (PCE) to gross domestic product (GDP) in the U.S. for the period 1960–2005, both variables being measured in 2000 billions of dollars.

From this regression we see that the marginal propensity to consume (MPC), that is, the additional consumption as a result of an additional dollar of income (as measured by GDP) is about 0.72 or about 72 cents. Using the data in Eq. (3.7.1), the reader can verify that the 95 percent confidence interval for the MPC is (0.7129, 0.7306). (*Note:* Since there are 44 df in this problem, we do not have a precise critical t value for these df. Hence, you can use the 2-t rule of thumb to compute the 95 percent confidence interval.)

Suppose someone maintains that the true MPC is 0.74. Is this number different from 0.72? It is, if we strictly adhere to the confidence interval established above.

But what is the practical or substantive significance of our finding? That is, what difference does it make if we take the MPC to be 0.74 rather than 0.72? Is this difference of 0.02 between the two MPCs that important practically?

The answer to this question depends on what we plan to do with these estimates. For example, from macroeconomics we know that the income multiplier is $1/(1 - \text{MPC})$. Thus, if the MPC is 0.72, the multiplier is 3.57, but it is 3.84 if the MPC is 0.74. If the government were to increase its expenditure by \$1 to lift the economy out of a recession, income would eventually increase by \$3.57 if the MPC were 0.72, but it would increase by \$3.84 if the MPC were 0.74. And that difference may or may not be crucial to resuscitating the economy.

The point of all this discussion is that one should not confuse statistical significance with practical, or economic, significance. As Goldberger notes:

> When a null, say, $\beta_j = 1$, is specified, the likely intent is that β_j is *close* to 1, so close that for all practical purposes it may be treated *as if it were* 1. But whether 1.1 is "practically the same as" 1.0 is a matter of economics, not of statistics. One cannot resolve the matter by relying on a hypothesis test, because the test statistic $[t =](b_j - 1)/\hat{\sigma}_{bj}$ measures the estimated coefficient in standard error units, which are not meaningful units in which to measure the economic parameter $\beta_j - 1$. It may be a good idea to reserve the term "significance" for the statistical concept, adopting "substantial" for the economic concept.[15]

[15]Arthur S. Goldberger, *A Course in Econometrics,* Harvard University Press, Cambridge, Massachusetts, 1991, p. 240. Note b_j is the OLS estimator of β_j and $\hat{\sigma}_{bj}$ is its standard error. For a corroborating view, see D. N. McCloskey, "The Loss Function Has Been Mislaid: The Rhetoric of Significance Tests," *American Economic Review,* vol. 75, 1985, pp. 201–205. See also D. N. McCloskey and S. T. Ziliak, "The Standard Error of Regression," *Journal of Economic Literature,* vol. 37, 1996, pp. 97–114.

The point made by Goldberger is important. As sample size becomes very large, issues of statistical significance become much less important but issues of economic significance become critical. Indeed, since with very large samples almost any null hypothesis will be rejected, there may be studies in which the magnitude of the point estimates may be the only issue.

The Choice between Confidence-Interval and Test-of-Significance Approaches to Hypothesis Testing

In most applied economic analyses, the null hypothesis is set up as a straw man and the objective of the empirical work is to knock it down, that is, reject the null hypothesis. Thus, in our consumption–income example, the null hypothesis that the MPC $\beta_2 = 0$ is patently absurd, but we often use it to dramatize the empirical results. Apparently editors of reputed journals do not find it exciting to publish an empirical piece that does not reject the null hypothesis. Somehow the finding that the MPC is statistically different from zero is more newsworthy than the finding that it is equal to, say, 0.7!

Thus, J. Bradford De Long and Kevin Lang argue that it is better for economists

> . . . to concentrate on the magnitudes of coefficients and to report confidence levels and not significance tests. If all or almost all null hypotheses are false, there is little point in concentrating on whether or not an estimate is indistinguishable from its predicted value under the null. Instead, we wish to cast light on what models are good approximations, which requires that we know ranges of parameter values that are excluded by empirical estimates.[16]

In short, these authors prefer the confidence-interval approach to the test-of-significance approach. The reader may want to keep this advice in mind.[17]

5.9 Regression Analysis and Analysis of Variance

In this section we study regression analysis from the point of view of the analysis of variance and introduce the reader to an illuminating and complementary way of looking at the statistical inference problem.

In Chapter 3, Section 3.5, we developed the following identity:

$$\sum y_i^2 = \sum \hat{y}_i^2 + \sum \hat{u}_i^2 = \hat{\beta}_2^2 \sum x_i^2 + \sum \hat{u}_i^2 \tag{3.5.2}$$

that is, TSS = ESS + RSS, which decomposed the total sum of squares (TSS) into two components: explained sum of squares (ESS) and residual sum of squares (RSS). A study of these components of TSS is known as the **analysis of variance** (ANOVA) from the regression viewpoint.

Associated with any sum of squares is its df, the number of independent observations on which it is based. TSS has $n - 1$ df because we lose 1 df in computing the sample mean $\bar{Y}$. RSS has $n - 2$ df. (Why?) (*Note:* This is true only for the two-variable regression model with the intercept β_1 present.) ESS has 1 df (again true of the two-variable case only), which follows from the fact that ESS $= \hat{\beta}_2^2 \sum x_i^2$ is a function of $\hat{\beta}_2$ only, since $\sum x_i^2$ is known.

[16]See their article cited in footnote 13, p. 1271.

[17]For a somewhat different perspective, see Carter Hill, William Griffiths, and George Judge, *Undergraduate Econometrics,* Wiley & Sons, New York, 2001, p. 108.

TABLE 5.3
ANOVA Table for the Two-Variable Regression Model

Source of Variation	SS*	df	MSS†
Due to regression (ESS)	$\sum \hat{y}_i^2 = \hat{\beta}_2^2 \sum x_i^2$	1	$\hat{\beta}_2^2 \sum x_i^2$
Due to residuals (RSS)	$\sum \hat{u}_i^2$	$n-2$	$\dfrac{\sum \hat{u}_i^2}{n-2} = \hat{\sigma}^2$
TSS	$\sum y_i^2$	$n-1$	

*SS means sum of squares.
†Mean sum of squares, which is obtained by dividing SS by their df.

Let us arrange the various sums of squares and their associated df in Table 5.3, which is the standard form of the AOV table, sometimes called the **ANOVA table.** Given the entries of Table 5.3, we now consider the following variable:

$$
\begin{aligned}
F &= \frac{\text{MSS of ESS}}{\text{MSS of RSS}} \\
&= \frac{\hat{\beta}_2^2 \sum x_i^2}{\sum \hat{u}_i^2/(n-2)} \\
&= \frac{\hat{\beta}_2^2 \sum x_i^2}{\hat{\sigma}^2}
\end{aligned}
\tag{5.9.1}
$$

If we assume that the disturbances u_i are normally distributed, which we do under the CNLRM, and if the null hypothesis (H_0) is that $\beta_2 = 0$, then it can be shown that the F variable of Equation 5.9.1 follows the F distribution with 1 df in the numerator and $(n-2)$ df in the denominator. (See Appendix 5A, Section 5A.3, for the proof. The general properties of the F distribution are discussed in **Appendix A.**)

What use can be made of the preceding F ratio? It can be shown[18] that

$$E\left(\hat{\beta}_2^2 \sum x_i^2\right) = \sigma^2 + \beta_2^2 \sum x_i^2 \tag{5.9.2}$$

and

$$E\frac{\sum \hat{u}_i^2}{n-2} = E(\hat{\sigma}^2) = \sigma^2 \tag{5.9.3}$$

(Note that β_2 and σ^2 appearing on the right sides of these equations are the true parameters.) Therefore, if β_2 is in fact zero, Equations 5.9.2 and 5.9.3 both provide us with identical estimates of true σ^2. In this situation, the explanatory variable X has no linear influence on Y whatsoever and the entire variation in Y is explained by the random disturbances u_i. If, on the other hand, β_2 is not zero, Eqs. (5.9.2) and (5.9.3) will be different and part of the variation in Y will be ascribable to X. Therefore, the F ratio of Eq. (5.9.1) provides a test of the null hypothesis H_0: $\beta_2 = 0$. Since all the quantities entering into this equation can be obtained from the available sample, this F ratio provides a test statistic to test the null hypothesis that true β_2 is zero. All that needs to be done is to compute the F ratio and compare it with the critical F value obtained from the F tables at the chosen level of significance, or obtain the ***p* value** of the computed F statistic.

[18]For proof, see K. A. Brownlee, *Statistical Theory and Methodology in Science and Engineering,* John Wiley & Sons, New York, 1960, pp. 278–280.

TABLE 5.4
ANOVA Table for the Wages-Education Example

Source of Variation	SS	df	MSS	
Due to regression (ESS)	95.4255	1	95.4255	$F = \frac{95.4255}{0.8811}$
Due to residuals (RSS)	9.6928	11	0.8811	$= 108.3026$
TSS	105.1183	12		

To illustrate, let us continue with our illustrative example. The ANOVA table for this example is as shown in Table 5.4. The computed F value is seen to be 108.3026. The p value of this F statistic corresponding to 1 and 11 df cannot be obtained from the F table given in **Appendix D,** but by using electronic statistical tables it can be shown that the p value is 0.0000001, an extremely small probability indeed. If you decide to choose the level-of-significance approach to hypothesis testing and fix α at 0.01, or a 1 percent level, you can see that the computed F of 108.3026 is obviously significant at this level. Therefore, if we reject the null hypothesis that $\beta_2 = 0$, the probability of committing a Type I error is very small. For all practical purposes, our sample could not have come from a population with zero β_2 value and we can conclude with great confidence that X, education, does affect Y, average wages.

Refer to Theorem 5.7 of Appendix 5A.1, which states that the square of the t value with k df is an F value with 1 df in the numerator and k df in the denominator. For our example, if we assume H_0: $\beta_2 = 0$, then from Eq. (5.3.2) it can be easily verified that the estimated t value is 10.41. This t value has 11 df. Under the same null hypothesis, the F value was 108.3026 with 1 and 11 df. Hence $(10.3428)^2 = F$ value, except for the rounding errors.

Thus, the t and the F tests provide us with two alternative but complementary ways of testing the null hypothesis that $\beta_2 = 0$. If this is the case, why not just rely on the t test and not worry about the F test and the accompanying analysis of variance? For the two-variable model there really is no need to resort to the F test. But when we consider the topic of multiple regression we will see that the F test has several interesting applications that make it a very useful and powerful method of testing statistical hypotheses.

5.10 Application of Regression Analysis: The Problem of Prediction

On the basis of the sample data of Table 3.2 we obtained the following sample regression:

$$\hat{Y}_i = -0.0144 + 0.7240X_i \tag{3.6.1}$$

where $\hat{Y}_i$ is the estimator of true $E(Y_i)$ corresponding to given X. What use can be made of this **historical regression?** One use is to "predict" or "forecast" the future mean wages Y corresponding to some given level of education X. Now there are two kinds of predictions: (1) prediction of the conditional mean value of Y corresponding to a chosen X, say, X_0, that is the point on the population regression line itself (see Figure 2.2), and (2) prediction of an individual Y value corresponding to X_0. We shall call these two predictions the **mean prediction** and **individual prediction.**

Mean Prediction[19]

To fix the ideas, assume that $X_0 = 20$ and we want to predict $E(Y \mid X_0 = 20)$. Now it can be shown that the historical regression in Eq. (3.6.1) provides the point estimate of this mean prediction as follows:

$$\begin{aligned}\hat{Y}_0 &= \hat{\beta}_1 + \hat{\beta}_2 X_0 \\ &= -0.0144 + 0.7240(20) \\ &= 14.4656\end{aligned} \tag{5.10.1}$$

where $\hat{Y}_0$ = estimator of $E(Y \mid X_0)$. It can be proved that this point predictor is a best linear unbiased estimator (BLUE).

Since $\hat{Y}_0$ is an estimator, it is likely to be different from its true value. The difference between the two values will give some idea about the prediction or forecast error. To assess this error, we need to find out the sampling distribution of $\hat{Y}_0$. It is shown in Appendix 5A, Section 5A.4, that $\hat{Y}_0$ in Equation 5.10.1 is normally distributed with mean $(\beta_1 + \beta_2 X_0)$ and the variance is given by the following formula:

$$\operatorname{var}(\hat{Y}_0) = \sigma^2 \left[\frac{1}{n} + \frac{(X_0 - \bar{X})^2}{\sum x_i^2} \right] \tag{5.10.2}$$

By replacing the unknown σ^2 by its unbiased estimator $\hat{\sigma}^2$, we see that the variable

$$t = \frac{\hat{Y}_0 - (\beta_1 + \beta_2 X_0)}{\operatorname{se}(\hat{Y}_0)} \tag{5.10.3}$$

follows the t distribution with $n - 2$ df. The t distribution can therefore be used to derive confidence intervals for the true $E(Y_0 \mid X_0)$ and test hypotheses about it in the usual manner, namely,

$$\Pr[\hat{\beta}_1 + \hat{\beta}_2 X_0 - t_{\alpha/2} \operatorname{se}(\hat{Y}_0) \le \beta_1 + \beta_2 X_0 \le \hat{\beta}_1 + \hat{\beta}_2 X_0 + t_{\alpha/2} \operatorname{se}(\hat{Y}_0)] = 1 - \alpha \tag{5.10.4}$$

where $\operatorname{se}(\hat{Y}_0)$ is obtained from Eq. (5.10.2).

For our data (see Table 3.2),

$$\begin{aligned}\operatorname{var}(\hat{Y}_0) &= 0.8936 \left[\frac{1}{13} + \frac{(20 - 12)^2}{182} \right] \\ &= 0.3826\end{aligned}$$

and

$$\operatorname{se}(\hat{Y}_0) = 0.6185$$

Therefore, the 95 percent confidence interval for true $E(Y \mid X_0) = \beta_1 + \beta_2 X_0$ is given by

$$14.4656 - 2.201(.6185) \le E(Y_0 \mid X = 20) \le 14.4656 + 2.20(0.6185)$$

[19]For the proofs of the various statements made, see App. 5A, Sec. 5A.4.

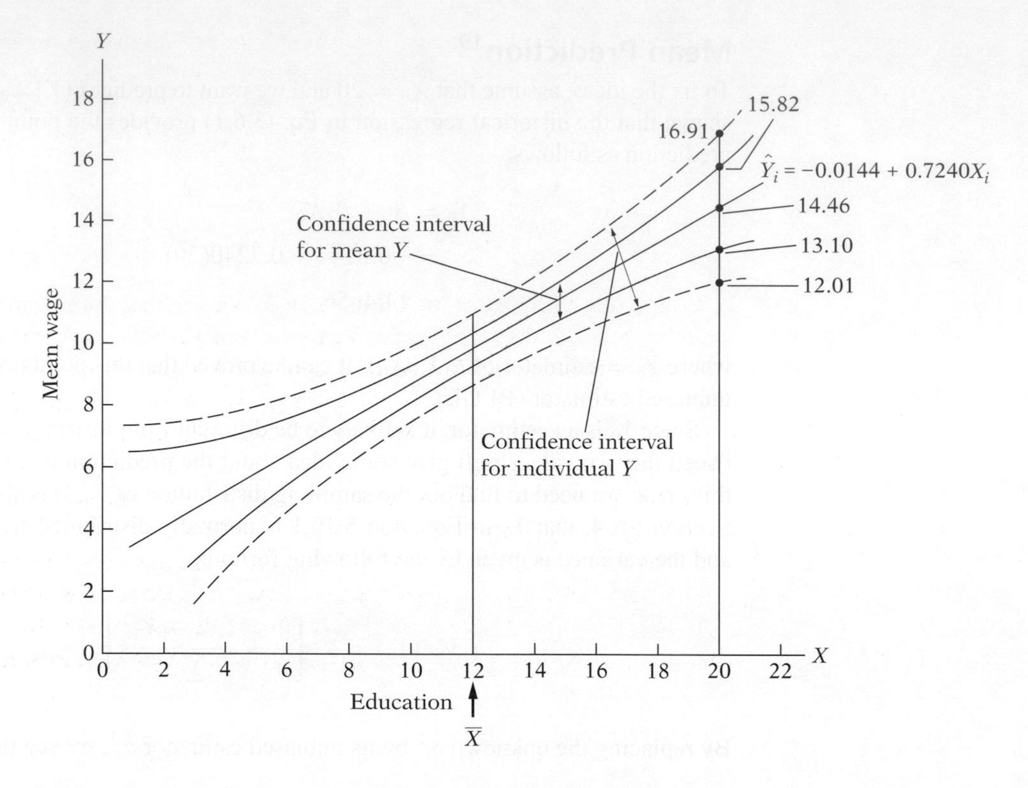

FIGURE 5.6 Confidence intervals (bands) for mean Y and individual Y values.

that is,

$$13.1043 \leq E(Y \mid X = 20) \leq 15.8260 \tag{5.10.5}$$

Thus, given $X_0 = 100$, in repeated sampling, 95 out of 100 intervals like Equation 5.10.5 will include the true mean value; the single best estimate of the true mean value is of course the point estimate 14.4656.

If we obtain 95 percent confidence intervals like Eq. (5.10.5) for each of the X values given in Table 3.2, we obtain what is known as the **confidence interval,** or **confidence band,** for the population regression function, which is shown in Figure 5.6.

Individual Prediction

If our interest lies in predicting an individual Y value, Y_0, corresponding to a given X value, say, X_0, then, as shown in Appendix 5, Section 5A.4, a best linear unbiased estimator of Y_0 is also given by Eq. (5.10.1), but its variance is as follows:

$$\operatorname{var}(Y_0 - \hat{Y}_0) = E[Y_0 - \hat{Y}_0]^2 = \sigma^2\left[1 + \frac{1}{n} + \frac{(X_0 - \bar{X})^2}{\sum x_i^2}\right] \tag{5.10.6}$$

It can be shown further that Y_0 also follows the normal distribution with mean and variance given by Eqs. (5.10.1) and (5.10.6), respectively. Substituting $\hat{\sigma}^2$ for the unknown σ^2, it follows that

$$t = \frac{Y_0 - \hat{Y}_0}{\operatorname{se}(Y_0 - \hat{Y}_0)}$$

also follows the t distribution. Therefore, the t distribution can be used to draw inferences about the true Y_0. Continuing with our example, we see that the point prediction of Y_0 is 14.4656, the same as that of $\hat{Y}_0$, and its variance is 1.2357 (the reader should verify this calculation). Therefore, the 95 percent confidence interval for Y_0 corresponding to $X_0 = 100$ is seen to be

$$(12.0190 \le Y_0 \mid X_0 = 20 \le 16.9122) \qquad (5.10.7)$$

Comparing this interval with Eq. (5.10.5), we see that the confidence interval for individual Y_0 is wider than that for the mean value of Y_0. (Why?) Computing confidence intervals like Equation 5.10.7 conditional upon the X values given in Table 3.2, we obtain the 95 percent confidence band for the individual Y values corresponding to these X values. This confidence band along with the confidence band for $\hat{Y}_0$ associated with the same X's is shown in Figure 5.6.

Notice an important feature of the confidence bands shown in Figure 5.6. The width of these bands is smallest when $X_0 = \bar{X}$. (Why?) However, the width widens sharply as X_0 moves away from $\bar{X}$. (Why?) This change would suggest that the predictive ability of the *historical* sample regression line falls markedly as X_0 departs progressively from $\bar{X}$. **Therefore, one should exercise great caution in "extrapolating" the historical regression line to predict $E(Y \mid X_0)$ or Y_0 associated with a given X_0 that is far removed from the sample mean $\bar{X}$.**

5.11 Reporting the Results of Regression Analysis

There are various ways of reporting the results of regression analysis, but in this text we shall use the following format, employing the wages education example of Chapter 3 as an illustration:

$$\begin{aligned}
\hat{Y}_i &= -0.0144 \quad + \quad 0.7240X_i \\
\text{se} &= (0.9317) \qquad (0.0700) \qquad r^2 = 0.9065 \\
t &= (-0.0154) \qquad (10.3428) \qquad \text{df} = 11 \\
p &= (0.987) \qquad (0.000) \qquad F_{1,11} = 108.30
\end{aligned} \qquad (5.11.1)$$

In Equation 5.11.1 the figures in the first set of parentheses are the estimated standard errors of the regression coefficients, the figures in the second set are estimated t values computed from Eq. (5.3.2) under the null hypothesis that the true population value of each regression coefficient individually is zero (e.g., $10.3428 = \frac{0.7240}{0.0700}$), and the figures in the third set are the estimated p values. Thus, for 11 df the probability of obtaining a t value of 10.3428 or greater is 0.00009, which is practically zero.

By presenting the p values of the estimated t coefficients, we can see at once the exact level of significance of each estimated t value. Thus, under the null hypothesis that the true population slope value is zero (i.e., that is, education has no effect on mean wages), the exact probability of obtaining a t value of 10.3428 or greater is practically zero. Recall that the smaller the p value, the smaller the probability of making a mistake if we reject the null hypothesis.

Earlier we showed the intimate connection between the F and t statistics, namely, $F_{1,k} = t_k^2$. Under the null hypothesis that the true $\beta_2 = 0$, Eq. (5.11.1) shows that the F value is 108.30 (for 1 numerator and 11 denominator df) and the t value is about 10.34 (11 df); as expected, the former value is the square of the latter value, except for the round-off errors. The ANOVA table for this problem has already been discussed.

5.12 Evaluating the Results of Regression Analysis

In Figure I.4 of the Introduction we sketched the anatomy of econometric modeling. Now that we have presented the results of regression analysis of our wages-education example in Eq. (5.11.1), we would like to question the adequacy of the fitted model. How "good" is the fitted model? We need some criteria with which to answer this question.

First, are the signs of the estimated coefficients in accordance with theoretical or prior expectations? A priori, β_2 in the wages-education example should be positive. In the present example it is. Second, if theory says that the relationship should be not only positive but also statistically significant, is this the case in the present application? As we discussed in Section 5.11, the education coefficient is not only positive but also statistically significantly different from zero; the p value of the estimated t value is extremely small. The comment about significance applies about the intercept coefficient. Third, how well does the regression model explain variation in our example? One can use r^2 to answer this question. In the present example r^2 is about 0.90, which is a very high value considering that r^2 can be at most 1.

Thus, the model we have chosen for explaining mean wages seems quite good. But before we sign off, we would like to find out whether our model satisfies the assumptions of CNLRM. We will not look at the various assumptions now because the model is patently so simple. But there is one assumption that we would like to check, namely, the normality of the disturbance term, u_i. Recall that the t and F tests used before require that the error term follow the normal distribution. Otherwise, the testing procedure will not be valid in small, or finite, samples.

Normality Tests

Although several tests of normality are discussed in the literature, we will consider just three: (1) histogram of residuals; (2) normal probability plot (NPP), a graphical device; and (3) the **Jarque–Bera** test.

Histogram of Residuals

A histogram of residuals is a simple graphic device that is used to learn something about the shape of the probability density function (PDF) of a random variable. On the horizontal axis, we divide the values of the variable of interest (e.g., OLS residuals) into suitable intervals, and in each class interval we erect rectangles equal in height to the number of observations (i.e., frequency) in that class interval. If you mentally superimpose the bell-shaped normal distribution curve on the histogram, you will get some idea as to whether normal (PDF) approximation may be appropriate. For the wages-education regression, the histogram of the residuals is as shown in Figure 5.7.

This diagram shows that the residuals are not perfectly normally distributed; for a normally distributed variable the skewness (a measure of symmetry) should be zero and kurtosis (which measures how tall or squatty the normal distribution is) should be 3.

But it is always a good practice to plot the histogram of residuals from any regression as a rough and ready method of testing for the normality assumption.

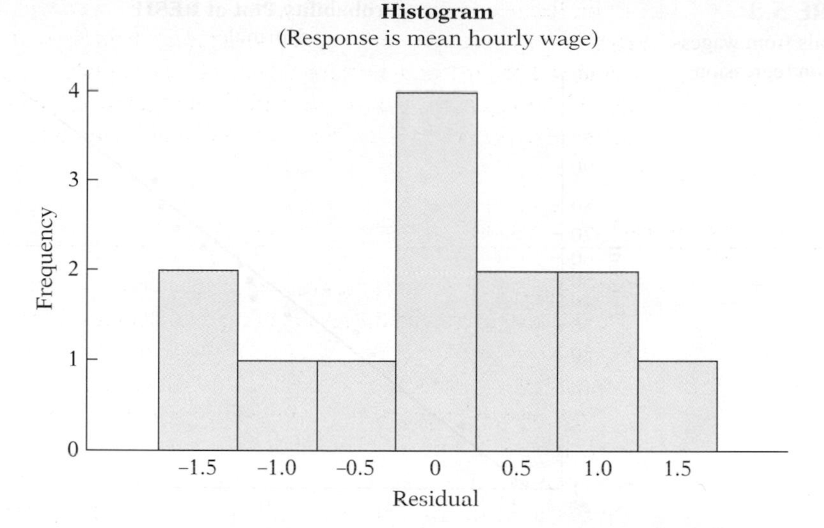

FIGURE 5.7 Histogram of residuals for wages—education data.

Normal Probability Plot

A comparatively simple graphical device to study the shape of the probability density function (PDF) of a random variable is the **normal probability plot (NPP),** which makes use of *normal probability paper,* a specially designed graph paper. On the horizontal, or X, axis, we plot values of the variable of interest (say, OLS residuals, $\hat{u}_i$), and on the vertical, or Y, axis, we show the expected value of this variable if it were normally distributed. Therefore, if the variable is in fact from the normal population, the NPP will be approximately a straight line. The NPP of the residuals from our wages-education regression is shown in Figure 5.8, which is obtained from the MINITAB software package, version 15. As noted earlier, if the fitted line in the NPP is approximately a straight line, one can conclude that the variable of interest is normally distributed. In Figure 5.8, we see that residuals from our illustrative example are approximately normally distributed, because a straight line seems to fit the data reasonably well.

MINITAB also produces the **Anderson–Darling normality test,** known as the A^2 **statistic.** The underlying null hypothesis is that the variable under consideration is normally distributed. As Figure 5.8 shows, for our example, the computed A^2 statistic is 0.289. The *p value* of obtaining such a value of A^2 is 0.558, which is reasonably high. Therefore, we do not reject the hypothesis that the residuals from our illustrative example are normally distributed. Incidentally, Figure 5.8 shows the parameters of the (normal) distribution, the mean is approximately 0, and the standard deviation is about 0.8987.

Jarque–Bera (JB) Test of Normality[20]

The JB test of normality is an *asymptotic,* or large-sample, test. It is also based on the OLS residuals. This test first computes the **skewness** and **kurtosis** (discussed in **Appendix A**) measures of the OLS residuals and uses the following test statistic:

$$\mathrm{JB} = n\left[\frac{S^2}{6} + \frac{(K-3)^2}{24}\right] \tag{5.12.1}$$

[20]See C. M. Jarque and A. K. Bera, "A Test for Normality of Observations and Regression Residuals," *International Statistical Review,* vol. 55, 1987, pp. 163–172.

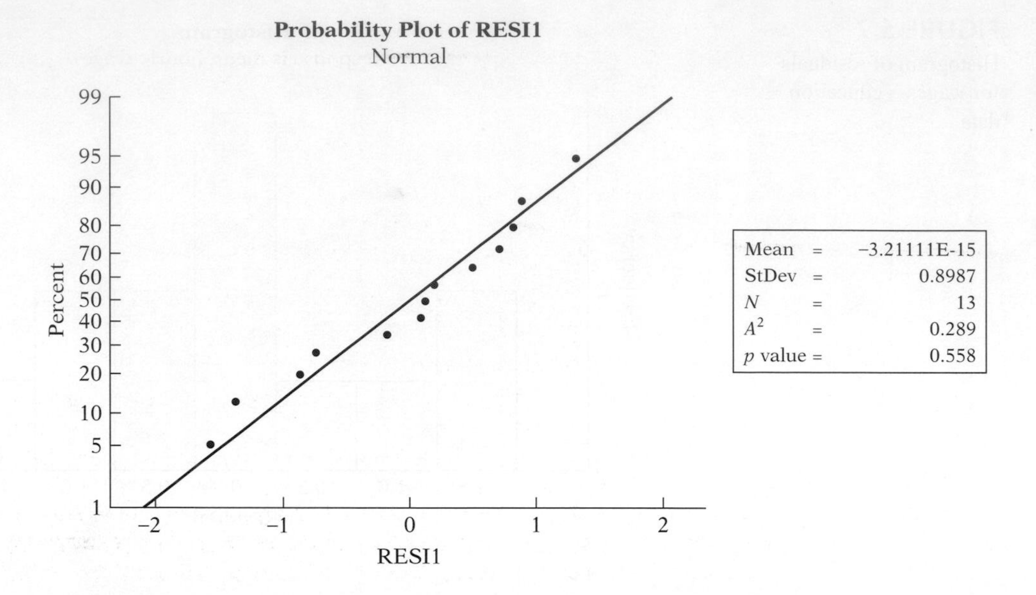

FIGURE 5.8 Residuals from wages-education regression.

where $n =$ sample size, $S =$ skewness coefficient, and $K =$ kurtosis coefficient. For a normally distributed variable, $S = 0$ and $K = 3$. Therefore, the JB test of normality is a test of the joint hypothesis that S and K are 0 and 3, respectively. In that case the value of the JB statistic is expected to be 0.

Under the null hypothesis that the residuals are normally distributed, Jarque and Bera showed that *asymptotically (i.e., in large samples) the JB statistic given in Equation (5.12.1) follows the chi-square distribution with 2 df.* If the computed p value of the JB statistic in an application is sufficiently low, which will happen if the value of the statistic is very different from 0, one can reject the hypothesis that the residuals are normally distributed. But if the p value is reasonably high, which will happen if the value of the statistic is close to zero, we do not reject the normality assumption.

For our example, the estimated JB statistic for our wages-education example is 0.8286. The null hypothesis that the residuals in the present example are normally distributed cannot be rejected, for the p value of obtaining a JB statistic as much as 0.8286 or greater is about 0.66 or 66 percent. This probability is quite high. Note that although our regression has 13 observations, these observations were obtained from a sample of 528 observations, which seems reasonably high.

Other Tests of Model Adequacy

Remember that the CNLRM makes many more assumptions than the normality of the error term. As we examine econometric theory further, we will consider several tests of model adequacy (see Chapter 13). Until then, keep in mind that our regression modeling is based on several simplifying assumptions that may not hold in each and every case.

A Concluding Example

Let us return to Example 3.2 about food expenditure in India. Using the data given in Equation (3.7.2) and adopting the format of Equation (5.11.1), we obtain the following expenditure equation:

$$
\begin{aligned}
\widehat{\text{FoodExp}}_i &= 94.2087 + 0.4368\ \text{TotalExp}_i \\
\text{se} &= (50.8563) \quad (0.0783) \\
t &= (1.8524) \quad (5.5770) \\
p &= (0.0695) \quad (0.0000)^* \\
r^2 &= 0.3698; \quad \text{df} = 53 \\
F_{1,53} &= 31.1034 \quad (p\ \text{value} = 0.0000)^*
\end{aligned}
\tag{5.12.2}
$$

where* denotes extremely small.

First, let us interpret this regression. As expected, there is a positive relationship between expenditure on food and total expenditure. If total expenditure went up by a rupee, on average, expenditure on food increased by about 44 paise. If total expenditure were zero, the average expenditure on food would be about 94 rupees. Of course, this mechanical interpretation of the intercept may not make much economic sense. The r^2 value of about 0.37 means that 37 percent of the variation in food expenditure is explained by total expenditure, a proxy for income.

Suppose we want to test the null hypothesis that there is no relationship between food expenditure and total expenditure, that is, the true slope coefficient $\beta_2 = 0$. The estimated value of β_2 is 0.4368. If the null hypothesis were true, what is the probability of obtaining a value of 0.4368? Under the null hypothesis, we observe from Eq. (5.12.2) that the t value is 5.5770 and the p value of obtaining such a t value is practically zero. In other words, we can reject the null hypothesis resoundingly. But suppose the null hypothesis were that $\beta_2 = 0.5$. Now what? Using the t test we obtain:

$$t = \frac{0.4368 - 0.5}{0.0783} = -0.8071$$

The probability of obtaining a $|t|$ of 0.8071 is greater than 20 percent. Hence we do not reject the hypothesis that the true β_2 is 0.5.

Notice that, under the null hypothesis, the true slope coefficient is zero, the F value is 31.1034, as shown in Eq. (5.12.2). Under the same null hypothesis, we obtained a t value of 5.5770. If we square this value, we obtain 31.1029, which is about the same as the F value, again showing the close relationship between the t and the F statistic. (*Note:* The numerator df for the F statistic must be 1, which is the case here.)

Using the estimated residuals from the regression, what can we say about the probability distribution of the error term? The information is given in Figure 5.9. As the figure shows,

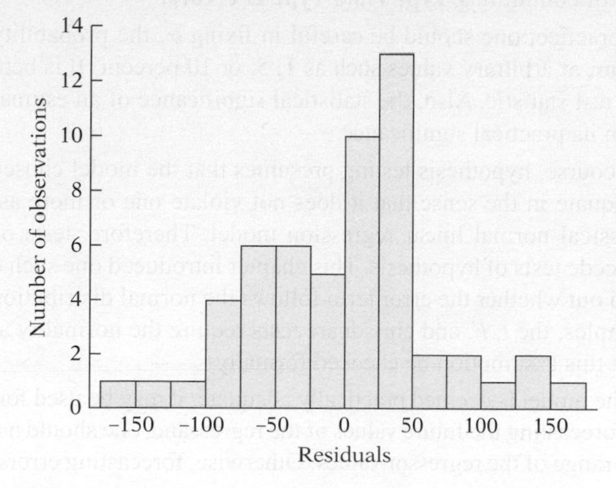

FIGURE 5.9 Residuals from the food expenditure regression.

(Continued)

A Concluding Example (Continued)

the residuals from the food expenditure regression seem to be symmetrically distributed. Application of the Jarque–Bera test shows that the JB statistic is about 0.2576, and the probability of obtaining such a statistic under the normality assumption is about 88 percent. Therefore, we do not reject the hypothesis that the error terms are normally distributed. But keep in mind that the sample size of 55 observations may not be large enough.

We leave it to the reader to establish confidence intervals for the two regression coefficients as well as to obtain the normal probability plot and do mean and individual predictions.

Summary and Conclusions

1. Estimation and hypothesis testing constitute the two main branches of classical statistics. Having discussed the problem of estimation in Chapters 3 and 4, we have taken up the problem of hypothesis testing in this chapter.
2. Hypothesis testing answers this question: Is a given finding compatible with a stated hypothesis or not?
3. There are two mutually complementary approaches to answering the preceding question: **confidence interval** and **test of significance.**
4. Underlying the confidence-interval approach is the concept of **interval estimation.** An interval estimator is an interval or range constructed in such a manner that it has a specified probability of including within its limits the true value of the unknown parameter. The interval thus constructed is known as a **confidence interval,** which is often stated in percent form, such as 90 or 95 percent. The confidence interval provides a set of plausible hypotheses about the value of the unknown parameter. If the null-hypothesized value lies in the confidence interval, the hypothesis is not rejected, whereas if it lies outside this interval, the null hypothesis can be rejected.
5. In the **significance test** procedure, one develops a **test statistic** and examines its sampling distribution under the null hypothesis. The test statistic usually follows a well-defined probability distribution such as the normal, t, F, or chi-square. Once a test statistic (e.g., the t statistic) is computed from the data at hand, its p value can be easily obtained. The p value gives the exact probability of obtaining the estimated test statistic under the null hypothesis. If this p value is small, one can reject the null hypothesis, but if it is large one may not reject it. What constitutes a small or large p value is up to the investigator. In choosing the p value the investigator has to bear in mind the probabilities of committing **Type I** and **Type II errors.**
6. In practice, one should be careful in fixing α, the probability of committing a **Type I error,** at arbitrary values such as 1, 5, or 10 percent. It is better to quote the ***p* value** of the test statistic. Also, the statistical significance of an estimate should not be confused with its practical significance.
7. Of course, hypothesis testing presumes that the model chosen for empirical analysis is adequate in the sense that it does not violate one or more assumptions underlying the classical normal linear regression model. Therefore, tests of model adequacy should precede tests of hypothesis. This chapter introduced one such test, the **normality test,** to find out whether the error term follows the normal distribution. Since in small, or finite, samples, the t, F, and chi-square tests require the normality assumption, it is important that this assumption be checked formally.
8. If the model is deemed practically adequate, it may be used for forecasting purposes. But in forecasting the future values of the regressand, one should not go too far out of the sample range of the regressor values. Otherwise, forecasting errors can increase dramatically.

EXERCISES

Questions

5.1. State with reason whether the following statements are true, false, or uncertain. Be precise.

a. The t test of significance discussed in this chapter requires that the sampling distributions of estimators $\hat{\beta}_1$ and $\hat{\beta}_2$ follow the normal distribution.

b. Even though the disturbance term in the CLRM is not normally distributed, the OLS estimators are still unbiased.

c. If there is no intercept in the regression model, the estimated $u_i (= \hat{u}_i)$ will not sum to zero.

d. The p value and the size of a test statistic mean the same thing.

e. In a regression model that contains the intercept, the sum of the residuals is always zero.

f. If a null hypothesis is not rejected, it is true.

g. The higher the value of σ^2, the larger is the variance of $\hat{\beta}_2$ given in Eq. (3.3.1).

h. The conditional and unconditional means of a random variable are the same things.

i. In the two-variable PRF, if the slope coefficient β_2 is zero, the intercept β_1 is estimated by the sample mean $\bar{Y}$.

j. The conditional variance, $\text{var}(Y_i \mid X_i) = \sigma^2$, and the unconditional variance of Y, $\text{var}(Y) = \sigma_Y^2$, will be the same if X had no influence on Y.

5.2. Set up the ANOVA table in the manner of Table 5.4 for the regression model given in Eq. (3.7.2) and test the hypothesis that there is no relationship between food expenditure and total expenditure in India.

5.3. Refer to the demand for cell phones regression given in Eq. (3.7.3).

a. Is the estimated intercept coefficient significant at the 5 percent level of significance? What is the null hypothesis you are testing?

b. Is the estimated slope coefficient significant at the 5 percent level? What is the underlying null hypothesis?

c. Establish a 95 percent confidence for the true slope coefficient.

d. What is the mean forecast value of cell phones demanded if the per capita income is \$9,000? What is the 95 percent confidence interval for the forecast value?

5.4. Let ρ^2 represent the true population coefficient of determination. Suppose you want to test the hypothesis that $\rho^2 = 0$. Verbally explain how you would test this hypothesis. *Hint:* Use Eq. (3.5.11). See also Exercise 5.7.

5.5. What is known as the **characteristic line** of modern investment analysis is simply the regression line obtained from the following model:

$$r_{it} = \alpha_i + \beta_i r_{mt} + u_t$$

where r_{it} = the rate of return on the ith security in time t
r_{mt} = the rate of return on the market portfolio in time t
u_t = stochastic disturbance term

In this model β_i is known as the **beta coefficient** of the ith security, a measure of market (or systematic) risk of a security.*

*See Haim Levy and Marshall Sarnat, *Portfolio and Investment Selection: Theory and Practice,* Prentice Hall International, Englewood Cliffs, NJ, 1984, Chap. 12.

On the basis of 240 monthly rates of return for the period 1956–1976, Fogler and Ganapathy obtained the following characteristic line for IBM stock in relation to the market portfolio index developed at the University of Chicago:*

$$\hat{r}_{it} = 0.7264 + 1.0598 r_{mt} \qquad r^2 = 0.4710$$
$$\text{se} = (0.3001)\,(0.0728) \qquad \text{df} = 238$$
$$F_{1,238} = 211.896$$

a. A security whose beta coefficient is greater than one is said to be a volatile or aggressive security. Was IBM a volatile security in the time period under study?

b. Is the intercept coefficient significantly different from zero? If it is, what is its practical meaning?

5.6. Equation (5.3.5) can also be written as

$$\Pr\,[\hat{\beta}_2 - t_{\alpha/2}\text{se}\,(\hat{\beta}_2) < \beta_2 < \hat{\beta}_2 + t_{\alpha/2}\text{se}\,(\hat{\beta}_2)] = 1 - \alpha$$

That is, the weak inequality ($\leq$) can be replaced by the strong inequality ($<$). Why?

5.7. R. A. Fisher has derived the sampling distribution of the correlation coefficient defined in Eq. (3.5.13). If it is assumed that the variables X and Y are jointly normally distributed, that is, if they come from a bivariate normal distribution (see Appendix 4A, Exercise 4.1), then under the assumption that the population correlation coefficient ρ is zero, it can be shown that $t = r\sqrt{n-2}/\sqrt{1-r^2}$ follows Student's t distribution with $n - 2$ df.** Show that this t value is identical with the t value given in Eq. (5.3.2) under the null hypothesis that $\beta_2 = 0$. Hence establish that under the same null hypothesis $F = t^2$. (See Section 5.9.)

5.8. Consider the following regression output:†

$$\hat{Y}_i = 0.2033 + 0.6560 X_t$$
$$\text{se} = (0.0976) \quad (0.1961)$$
$$r^2 = 0.397 \qquad \text{RSS} = 0.0544 \qquad \text{ESS} = 0.0358$$

where Y = labor force participation rate (LFPR) of women in 1972 and X = LFPR of women in 1968. The regression results were obtained from a sample of 19 cities in the United States.

a. How do you interpret this regression?

b. Test the hypothesis: H_0: $\beta_2 = 1$ against H_1: $\beta_2 > 1$. Which test do you use? And why? What are the underlying assumptions of the test(s) you use?

c. Suppose that the LFPR in 1968 was 0.58 (or 58 percent). On the basis of the regression results given above, what is the mean LFPR in 1972? Establish a 95 percent confidence interval for the mean prediction.

d. How would you test the hypothesis that the error term in the population regression is normally distributed? Show the necessary calculations.

*H. Russell Fogler and Sundaram Ganapathy, *Financial Econometrics,* Prentice Hall, Englewood Cliffs, NJ, 1982, p. 13.

**If ρ is in fact zero, Fisher has shown that r follows the same t distribution provided either X or Y is normally distributed. But if ρ is not equal to zero, both variables must be normally distributed. See R. L. Anderson and T. A. Bancroft, *Statistical Theory in Research,* McGraw-Hill, New York, 1952, pp. 87–88.

†Adapted from Samprit Chatterjee, Ali S. Hadi, and Bertram Price, *Regression Analysis by Example,* 3d ed., Wiley Interscience, New York, 2000, pp. 46–47.

TABLE 5.5
Average Salary and Per Pupil Spending (dollars), 1985

Source: National Education Association, as reported by *Albuquerque Tribune,* Nov. 7, 1986.

Observation	Salary	Spending	Observation	Salary	Spending
1	19,583	3346	27	22,795	3366
2	20,263	3114	28	21,570	2920
3	20,325	3554	29	22,080	2980
4	26,800	4642	30	22,250	3731
5	29,470	4669	31	20,940	2853
6	26,610	4888	32	21,800	2533
7	30,678	5710	33	22,934	2729
8	27,170	5536	34	18,443	2305
9	25,853	4168	35	19,538	2642
10	24,500	3547	36	20,460	3124
11	24,274	3159	37	21,419	2752
12	27,170	3621	38	25,160	3429
13	30,168	3782	39	22,482	3947
14	26,525	4247	40	20,969	2509
15	27,360	3982	41	27,224	5440
16	21,690	3568	42	25,892	4042
17	21,974	3155	43	22,644	3402
18	20,816	3059	44	24,640	2829
19	18,095	2967	45	22,341	2297
20	20,939	3285	46	25,610	2932
21	22,644	3914	47	26,015	3705
22	24,624	4517	48	25,788	4123
23	27,186	4349	49	29,132	3608
24	33,990	5020	50	41,480	8349
25	23,382	3594	51	25,845	3766
26	20,627	2821			

Empirical Exercises

5.9. Table 5.5 gives data on average public teacher pay (annual salary in dollars) and spending on public schools per pupil (dollars) in 1985 for 50 states and the District of Columbia.

To find out if there is any relationship between teacher's pay and per pupil expenditure in public schools, the following model was suggested: $\text{Pay}_i = \beta_1 + \beta_2 \text{Spend}_i + u_i$, where Pay stands for teacher's salary and Spend stands for per pupil expenditure.

a. Plot the data and eyeball a regression line.

b. Suppose on the basis of (*a*) you decide to estimate the above regression model. Obtain the estimates of the parameters, their standard errors, r^2, RSS, and ESS.

c. Interpret the regression. Does it make economic sense?

d. Establish a 95 percent confidence interval for β_2. Would you reject the hypothesis that the true slope coefficient is 3.0?

e. Obtain the mean and individual forecast value of Pay if per pupil spending is $5,000. Also establish 95 percent confidence intervals for the true mean and individual values of Pay for the given spending figure.

f. How would you test the assumption of the normality of the error term? Show the test(s) you use.

5.10. Refer to Exercise 3.20 and set up the ANOVA tables and test the hypothesis that there is no relationship between productivity and real wage compensation. Do this for both the business and nonfarm business sectors.

5.11. Refer to Exercise 1.7.

a. Plot the data with impressions on the vertical axis and advertising expenditure on the horizontal axis. What kind of relationship do you observe?

b. Would it be appropriate to fit a bivariate linear regression model to the data? Why or why not? If not, what type of regression model will you fit the data to? Do we have the necessary tools to fit such a model?

c. Suppose you do not plot the data and simply fit the bivariate regression model to the data. Obtain the usual regression output. Save the results for a later look at this problem.

5.12. Refer to Exercise 1.1.

a. Plot the U.S. Consumer Price Index (CPI) against the Canadian CPI. What does the plot show?

b. Suppose you want to predict the U.S. CPI on the basis of the Canadian CPI. Develop a suitable model.

c. Test the hypothesis that there is no relationship between the two CPIs. Use $\alpha = 5\%$. If you reject the null hypothesis, does that mean the Canadian CPI "causes" the U.S. CPI? Why or why not?

5.13. Refer to Problem 3.22.

a. Estimate the two regressions given there, obtaining standard errors and the other usual output.

b. Test the hypothesis that the disturbances in the two regression models are normally distributed.

c. In the gold price regression, test the hypothesis that $\beta_2 = 1$, that is, there is a one-to-one relationship between gold prices and CPI (i.e., gold is a perfect hedge). What is the p value of the estimated test statistic?

d. Repeat step (*c*) for the NYSE Index regression. Is investment in the stock market a perfect hedge against inflation? What is the null hypothesis you are testing? What is its p value?

e. Between gold and stock, which investment would you choose? What is the basis of your decision?

5.14. Table 5.6 gives data on GNP and four definitions of the money stock for the United States for 1970–1983. Regressing GNP on the various definitions of money, we obtain the results shown in Table 5.7.

The monetarists or quantity theorists maintain that nominal income (i.e., nominal GNP) is largely determined by changes in the quantity or the stock of money, although there is no consensus as to the "right" definition of money. Given the results in the preceding table, consider these questions:

a. Which definition of money seems to be closely related to nominal GNP?

b. Since the r^2 terms are uniformly high, does this fact mean that our choice for definition of money does not matter?

c. If the Fed wants to control the money supply, which one of these money measures is a better target for that purpose? Can you tell from the regression results?

5.15. Suppose the equation of an **indifference curve** between two goods is

$$X_i Y_i = \beta_1 + \beta_2 X_i$$

How would you estimate the parameters of this model? Apply the preceding model to the data in Table 5.8 and comment on your results.

TABLE 5.6
GNP and Four Measures of Money Stock

Source: *Economic Report of the President,* 1985, GNP data from Table B-1, p. 232; money stock data from Table B-61, p. 303.

Year	GNP $ billion	Money Stock Measure, $ billion M_1	M_2	M_3	L
1970	992.70	216.6	628.2	677.5	816.3
1971	1,077.6	230.8	712.8	776.2	903.1
1972	1,185.9	252.0	805.2	886.0	1,023.0
1973	1,326.4	265.9	861.0	985.0	1,141.7
1974	1,434.2	277.6	908.5	1,070.5	1,249.3
1975	1,549.2	291.2	1,023.3	1,174.2	1,367.9
1976	1,718.0	310.4	1,163.6	1,311.9	1,516.6
1977	1,918.3	335.4	1,286.7	1,472.9	1,704.7
1978	2,163.9	363.1	1,389.1	1,647.1	1,910.6
1979	2,417.8	389.1	1,498.5	1,804.8	2,117.1
1980	2,631.7	414.9	1,632.6	1,990.0	2,326.2
1981	2,957.8	441.9	1,796.6	2,238.2	2,599.8
1982	3,069.3	480.5	1,965.4	2,462.5	2,870.8
1983	3,304.8	525.4	2,196.3	2,710.4	3,183.1

Definitions:
M_1 = Currency + Demand deposits + Travelers checks and other checkable deposits (OCDs).
M_2 = M_1 + Overnight RPs and Eurodollars + MMMF (Money market mutual fund) balances + MMDAs (Money market deposit accounts) + Savings and small deposits.
M_3 = M_2 + Large time deposits + Term RPs + Institutional MMMF.
L = M_3 + Other liquid assets.

TABLE 5.7
GNP–Money Stock Regressions, 1970–1983

1) $\widehat{\text{GNP}}_t = -787.4723 + 8.0863\, M_{1t}$ $\quad r^2 = 0.9912$
$\quad (77.9664) \quad (0.2197)$

2) $\widehat{\text{GNP}}_t = -44.0626 + 1.5875\, M_{2t}$ $\quad r^2 = 0.9905$
$\quad (61.0134) \quad (0.0448)$

3) $\widehat{\text{GNP}}_t = 159.1366 + 1.2034\, M_{3t}$ $\quad r^2 = 0.9943$
$\quad (42.9882) \quad (0.0262)$

4) $\widehat{\text{GNP}}_t = 164.2071 + 1.0290\, L_t$ $\quad r^2 = 0.9938$
$\quad (44.7658) \quad (0.0234)$

Note: The figures in parentheses are the estimated standard errors.

TABLE 5.8

Consumption of good X:	1	2	3	4	5
Consumption of good Y:	4	3.5	2.8	1.9	0.8

5.16. Since 1986 the *Economist* has been publishing the Big Mac Index as a crude, and hilarious, measure of whether international currencies are at their "correct" exchange rate, as judged by the theory of **purchasing power parity (PPP).** The PPP holds that a unit of currency should be able to buy the same bundle of goods in all countries. The proponents of PPP argue that, in the long run, currencies tend to move toward their PPP. The *Economist* uses McDonald's Big Mac as a representative bundle and gives the information in Table 5.9.

Consider the following regression model:

$$Y_i = \beta_1 + \beta_2 X_i + u_i$$

where Y = actual exchange rate and X = implied PPP of the dollar.

a. If the PPP holds, what values of β_1 and β_2 would you expect a priori?

TABLE 5.9
The Hamburger Standard

Source: McDonald's; *The Economist,* February 1, 2007.

	Big Mac Prices				
	In Local Currency	In Dollars	Implied PPP* of the Dollar	Actual Dollar Exchange Rate, Jan 31st	Under (−)/ Over (+) Valuation against the Dollar, %
United States†	$3.22	3.22			
Argentina	Peso 8.25	2.65	2.56	3.11	−18
Australia	A$3.45	2.67	1.07	1.29	−17
Brazil	Real 6.4	3.01	1.99	2.13	−6
Britain	£1.99	3.90	1.62‡	1.96‡	+21
Canada	C$3.63	3.08	1.13	1.18	−4
Chile	Peso 1,670	3.07	519	544	−5
China	Yuan 11.0	1.41	3.42	7.77	−56
Colombia	Peso 6,900	3.06	2,143	2,254	−5
Costa Rica	Colones 1,130	2.18	351	519	−32
Czech Republic	Koruna 52.1	2.41	16.2	21.6	−25
Denmark	DKr27.75	4.84	8.62	5.74	+50
Egypt	Pound 9.09	1.60	2.82	5.70	−50
Estonia	Kroon 30	2.49	9.32	12.0	−23
Euro area§	€2.94	3.82	1.10**	1.30**	+19
Hong Kong	HK$12.0	1.54	3.73	7.81	−52
Hungary	Forint 590	3.00	183	197	−7
Iceland	Kronur 509	7.44	158	68.4	+131
Indonesia	Rupiah 15,900	1.75	4,938	9,100	−46
Japan	¥280	2.31	87.0	121	−28
Latvia	Lats 1.35	2.52	0.42	0.54	−22
Lithuania	Litas 6.50	2.45	2.02	2.66	−24
Malaysia	Ringgit 5.50	1.57	1.71	3.50	−51
Mexico	Peso 29.0	2.66	9.01	10.9	−17
New Zealand	NZ$4.60	3.16	1.43	1.45	−2
Norway	Kroner 41.5	6.63	12.9	6.26	+106
Pakistan	Rupee 140	2.31	43.5	60.7	−28
Paraguay	Guarani 10,000	1.90	3,106	5,250	−41
Peru	New Sol 9.50	2.97	2.95	3.20	−8
Philippines	Peso 85.0	1.74	26.4	48.9	−46
Poland	Zloty 6.90	2.29	2.14	3.01	−29
Russia	Rouble 49.0	1.85	15.2	26.5	−43
Saudi Arabia	Riyal 9.00	2.40	2.80	3.75	−25
Singapore	S$3.60	2.34	1.12	1.54	−27
Slovakia	Crown 57.98	2.13	18.0	27.2	−34
South Africa	Rand 15.5	2.14	4.81	7.25	−34
South Korea	Won 2,900	3.08	901	942	−4
Sri Lanka	Rupee 190	1.75	59.0	109	−46
Sweden	SKr32.0	4.59	9.94	6.97	+43
Switzerland	SFr6.30	5.05	1.96	1.25	+57
Taiwan	NT$75.0	2.28	23.3	32.9	−29
Thailand	Baht 62.0	1.78	19.3	34.7	−45
Turkey	Lire 4.55	3.22	1.41	1.41	nil
UAE	Dirhams 10.0	2.72	3.11	3.67	−15
Ukraine	Hryvnia 9.00	1.71	2.80	5.27	−47
Uruguay	Peso 55.0	2.17	17.1	25.3	−33
Venezuela	Bolivar 6,800	1.58	2,112	4,307	−51

*Purchasing power parity: local price divided by price in the United States.
**Dollars per euro.
†Average of New York, Chicago, San Francisco, and Atlanta.
‡Dollars per pound.
§Weighted average of prices in euro area.

b. Do the regression results support your expectation? What formal test do you use to test your hypothesis?

c. Should the *Economist* continue to publish the Big Mac Index? Why or why not?

5.17. Refer to the SAT data given in Exercise 2.16. Suppose you want to predict the male math (Y) scores on the basis of the female math scores (X) by running the following regression:

$$Y_t = \beta_1 + \beta_2 X_t + u_t$$

a. Estimate the preceding model.

b. From the estimated residuals, find out if the normality assumption can be sustained.

c. Now test the hypothesis that $\beta_2 = 1$, that is, there is a one-to-one correspondence between male and female math scores.

d. Set up the ANOVA table for this problem.

5.18. Repeat the exercise in the preceding problem but let Y and X denote the male and female critical reading scores, respectively.

5.19. Table 5.10 gives annual data on the Consumer Price Index (CPI) and the Wholesale Price Index (WPI), also called Producer Price Index (PPI), for the U.S. economy for the period 1980–2006.

TABLE 5.10
CPI and PPI, USA, 1980–2006

Source: *Economic Report of the President*, 2007, Tables B-62 and B-65.

	CPI Total	PPI (Total Finished Goods)
1980	82.4	88.0
1981	90.9	96.1
1982	96.5	100.0
1983	99.6	101.6
1984	103.9	103.7
1985	107.6	104.7
1986	109.6	103.2
1987	113.6	105.4
1988	118.3	108.0
1989	124.0	113.6
1990	130.7	119.2
1991	136.2	121.7
1992	140.3	123.2
1993	144.5	124.7
1994	148.2	125.5
1995	152.4	127.9
1996	156.9	131.3
1997	160.5	131.8
1998	163.0	130.7
1999	166.6	133.0
2000	172.2	138.0
2001	177.1	140.7
2002	179.9	138.9
2003	184.0	143.3
2004	188.9	148.5
2005	195.3	155.7
2006	201.6	160.3

a. Plot the CPI on the vertical axis and the WPI on the horizontal axis. A priori, what kind of relationship do you expect between the two indexes? Why?

b. Suppose you want to predict one of these indexes on the basis of the other index. Which will you use as the regressand and which as the regressor? Why?

c. Run the regression you have decided in (*b*). Show the standard output. Test the hypothesis that there is a one-to-one relationship between the two indexes.

d. From the residuals obtained from the regression in (*c*), can you entertain the hypothesis that the true error term is normally distributed? Show the tests you use.

5.20. Table 5.11 provides data on the lung cancer mortality index (100 = average) and the smoking index (100 = average) for 25 occupational groups.

a. Plot the cancer mortality index against the smoking index. What general pattern do you observe?

b. Letting $Y =$ cancer mortality index and $X =$ smoking index, estimate a linear regression model and obtain the usual regression statistics.

c. Test the hypothesis that smoking has no influence on lung cancer at $\alpha = 5\%$.

d. Which are the risky occupations in terms of lung cancer mortality? Can you give some reasons why this might be so?

e. Is there any way to bring occupation category explicitly into the regression analysis?

TABLE 5.11
Smoking and Lung Cancer

Source: http://lib.stat.cmu.edu/ DASL/Datafiles/SmokingandCancer.html.

Occupation	Smoking	Cancer
Farmers, foresters, fishermen	77	84
Miners and quarrymen	137	116
Gas, coke, and chemical makers	117	123
Glass and ceramic makers	94	128
Furnace forge foundry workers	116	155
Electrical and electronic workers	102	101
Engineering and allied trades	111	118
Wood workers	93	113
Leather workers	88	104
Textile workers	102	88
Clothing workers	91	104
Food, drink, and tobacco workers	104	129
Paper and printing workers	107	86
Makers of other products	112	96
Construction workers	113	144
Painters and decorators	110	139
Drivers of engines, cranes, etc.	125	113
Laborers not included elsewhere	113	146
Transportation, and communication workers	115	128
Warehousemen, store keepers, etc.	105	115
Clerical workers	87	79
Sales workers	91	85
Service, sports, recreation workers	100	120
Administrators and managers	76	60
Artists and professional and technical workers	66	51

Appendix 5A

5A.1 Probability Distributions Related to the Normal Distribution

The ***t***, **chi-square** (χ^2), and ***F*** probability distributions, whose salient features are discussed in **Appendix A,** are intimately related to the normal distribution. Since we will make heavy use of these probability distributions in the following chapters, we summarize their relationship with the normal distribution in the following theorem; the proofs, which are beyond the scope of this book, can be found in the references.[1]

Theorem 5.1. If $Z_1, Z_2, \ldots, Z_n$ are normally and independently distributed random variables such that $Z_i \sim N(\mu_i, \sigma_i^2)$, then the sum $Z = \sum k_i Z_i$, where k_i are constants not all zero, is also distributed normally with mean $\sum k_i \mu_i$ and variance $\sum k_i^2 \sigma_i^2$; that is, $Z \sim N(\sum k_i \mu_i, \sum k_i^2 \sigma_i^2)$. *Note:* μ denotes the mean value.

In short, linear combinations of normal variables are themselves normally distributed. For example, if Z_1 and Z_2 are normally and independently distributed as $Z_1 \sim N(10, 2)$ and $Z_2 \sim N(8, 1.5)$, then the linear combination $Z = 0.8Z_1 + 0.2Z_2$ is also normally distributed with mean $= 0.8(10) + 0.2(8) = 9.6$ and variance $= 0.64(2) + 0.04(1.5) = 1.34$, that is, $Z \sim (9.6, 1.34)$.

Theorem 5.2. If $Z_1, Z_2, \ldots, Z_n$ are normally distributed but are not independent, the sum $Z = \sum k_i Z_i$, where k_i are constants not all zero, is also normally distributed with mean $\sum k_i \mu_i$ and variance $[\sum k_i^2 \sigma_i^2 + 2 \sum k_i k_j \operatorname{cov}(Z_i, Z_j), i \neq j]$.

Thus, if $Z_1 \sim N(6, 2)$ and $Z_2 \sim N(7, 3)$ and $\operatorname{cov}(Z_1, Z_2) = 0.8$, then the linear combination $0.6Z_1 + 0.4Z_2$ is also normally distributed with mean $= 0.6(6) + 0.4(7) = 6.4$ and variance $= [0.36(2) + 0.16(3) + 2(0.6)(0.4)(0.8)] = 1.584$.

Theorem 5.3. If $Z_1, Z_2, \ldots, Z_n$ are normally and independently distributed random variables such that each $Z_i \sim N(0, 1)$, that is, a standardized normal variable, then $\sum Z_i^2 = Z_1^2 + Z_2^2 + \cdots + Z_n^2$ follows the chi-square distribution with n df. Symbolically, $\sum Z_i^2 \sim \chi_n^2$, where n denotes the degrees of freedom, df.

In short, "the sum of the squares of independent standard normal variables has a chi-square distribution with degrees of freedom equal to the number of terms in the sum."[2]

Theorem 5.4. If $Z_1, Z_2, \ldots, Z_n$ are independently distributed random variables each following chi-square distribution with k_i df, then the sum $\sum Z_i = Z_1 + Z_2 + \cdots + Z_n$ also follows a chi-square distribution with $k = \sum k_i$ df.

Thus, if Z_1 and Z_2 are independent χ^2 variables with df of k_1 and k_2, respectively, then $Z = Z_1 + Z_2$ is also a χ^2 variable with $(k_1 + k_2)$ degrees of freedom. This is called the **reproductive property** of the χ^2 distribution.

[1]For proofs of the various theorems, see Alexander M. Mood, Franklin A. Graybill, and Duane C. Bose, *Introduction to the Theory of Statistics,* 3d ed., McGraw-Hill, New York, 1974, pp. 239–249.

[2]Ibid., p. 243.

Theorem 5.5. If Z_1 is a standardized normal variable $[Z_1 \sim N(0, 1)]$ and another variable Z_2 follows the chi-square distribution with k df and is independent of Z_1, then the variable defined as

$$t = \frac{Z_1}{\sqrt{Z_2}/\sqrt{k}} = \frac{Z_1\sqrt{k}}{\sqrt{Z_2}} = \frac{\text{Standard normal variable}}{\sqrt{\text{Independent chi-square variable/df}}} \sim t_k$$

follows Student's t distribution with k df. *Note:* This distribution is discussed in **Appendix A** and is illustrated in Chapter 5.

Incidentally, note that as k, the df, increases indefinitely (i.e., as $k \to \infty$), the Student's t distribution approaches the standardized normal distribution.[3] As a matter of convention, the notation t_k means Student's t distribution or variable with k df.

Theorem 5.6. If Z_1 and Z_2 are independently distributed chi-square variables with k_1 and k_2 df, respectively, then the variable

$$F = \frac{Z_1/k_1}{Z_2/k_2} \sim F_{k_1,k_2}$$

has the F distribution with k_1 and k_2 degrees of freedom, where k_1 is known as the **numerator degrees of freedom** and k_2 the **denominator degrees of freedom.**

Again as a matter of convention, the notation F_{k_1,k_2} means an F variable with k_1 and k_2 degrees of freedom, the df in the numerator being quoted first.

In other words, Theorem 5.6 states that the F variable is simply the ratio of two independently distributed chi-square variables divided by their respective degrees of freedom.

Theorem 5.7. The square of (Student's) t variable with k df has an F distribution with $k_1 = 1$ df in the numerator and $k_2 = k$ df in the denominator.[4] That is,

$$F_{1,k} = t_k^2$$

Note that for this equality to hold, the numerator df of the F variable must be 1. Thus, $F_{1,4} = t_4^2$ or $F_{1,23} = t_{23}^2$ and so on.

As noted, we will see the practical utility of the preceding theorems as we progress.

Theorem 5.8. For large denominator df, the numerator df times the F value is approximately equal to the chi-square value with the numerator df. Thus,

$$m\ F_{m,n} = \chi_m^2 \qquad \text{as } n \to \infty$$

Theorem 5.9. For sufficiently large df, the chi-square distribution can be approximated by the standard normal distribution as follows:

$$Z = \sqrt{2\chi^2} - \sqrt{2k - 1} \sim N(0, 1)$$

where k denotes df.

[3]For proof, see Henri Theil, *Introduction to Econometrics,* Prentice Hall, Englewood Cliffs, NJ, 1978, pp. 237–245.

[4]For proof, see Eqs. (5.3.2) and (5.9.1).

5A.2 Derivation of Equation (5.3.2)

Let

$$Z_1 = \frac{\hat{\beta}_2 - \beta_2}{\text{se}(\hat{\beta}_2)} = \frac{(\hat{\beta}_2 - \beta_2)\sqrt{x_i^2}}{\sigma} \tag{1}$$

and

$$Z_2 = (n-2)\frac{\hat{\sigma}^2}{\sigma^2} \tag{2}$$

Provided σ is known, Z_1 follows the standardized normal distribution; that is, $Z_1 \sim N(0, 1)$. (Why?) Z_2 follows the χ^2 distribution with $(n - 2)$ df.[5] Furthermore, it can be shown that Z_2 is distributed independently of Z_1.[6] Therefore, by virtue of Theorem 5.5, the variable

$$t = \frac{Z_1\sqrt{n-2}}{\sqrt{Z_2}} \tag{3}$$

follows the t distribution with $n - 2$ df. Substitution of Eqs. (1) and (2) into Eq. (3) gives Eq. (5.3.2).

5A.3 Derivation of Equation (5.9.1)

Equation (1) shows that $Z_1 \sim N(0, 1)$. Therefore, by Theorem 5.3, the preceding quantity

$$Z_1^2 = \frac{(\hat{\beta}_2 - \beta_2)^2 \sum x_i^2}{\sigma^2}$$

follows the χ^2 distribution with 1 df. As noted in Section 5A.1,

$$Z_2 = (n-2)\frac{\hat{\sigma}^2}{\sigma^2} = \frac{\sum \hat{u}_i^2}{\sigma^2}$$

also follows the χ^2 distribution with $n - 2$ df. Moreover, as noted in Section 4.3, Z_2 is distributed independently of Z_1. Then from Theorem 5.6, it follows that

$$F = \frac{Z_1^2/1}{Z_2/(n-2)} = \frac{(\hat{\beta}_2 - \beta_2)^2\left(\sum x_i^2\right)}{\sum \hat{u}_i^2/(n-2)}$$

follows the F distribution with 1 and $n - 2$ df, respectively. Under the null hypothesis H_0: $\beta_2 = 0$, the preceding F ratio reduces to Eq. (5.9.1).

5A.4 Derivations of Equations (5.10.2) and (5.10.6)

Variance of Mean Prediction

Given $X_i = X_0$, the true mean prediction $E(Y_0 \mid X_0)$ is given by

$$E(Y_0 \mid X_0) = \beta_1 + \beta_2 X_0 \tag{1}$$

[5]For proof, see Robert V. Hogg and Allen T. Craig, *Introduction to Mathematical Statistics,* 2d ed., Macmillan, New York, 1965, p. 144.

[6]For proof, see J. Johnston, *Econometric Methods,* 3d ed., McGraw-Hill, New York, 1984, pp. 181–182. (Knowledge of matrix algebra is required to follow the proof.)

We estimate Eq. (1) from

$$\hat{Y}_0 = \hat{\beta}_1 + \hat{\beta}_2 X_0 \tag{2}$$

Taking the expectation of Eq. (2), given X_0, we get

$$\begin{aligned} E(\hat{Y}_0) &= E(\hat{\beta}_1) + E(\hat{\beta}_2)X_0 \\ &= \beta_1 + \beta_2 X_0 \end{aligned}$$

because $\hat{\beta}_1$ and $\hat{\beta}_2$ are unbiased estimators. Therefore,

$$E(\hat{Y}_0) = E(Y_0 \mid X_0) = \beta_1 + \beta_2 X_0 \tag{3}$$

That is, $\hat{Y}_0$ is an unbiased predictor of $E(Y_0 \mid X_0)$.

Now using the property that $\operatorname{var}(a+b) = \operatorname{var}(a) + \operatorname{var}(b) + 2\operatorname{cov}(a,b)$, we obtain

$$\operatorname{var}(\hat{Y}_0) = \operatorname{var}(\hat{\beta}_1) + \operatorname{var}(\hat{\beta}_2)X_0^2 + 2\operatorname{cov}(\hat{\beta}_1\hat{\beta}_2)X_0 \tag{4}$$

Using the formulas for variances and covariance of $\hat{\beta}_1$ and $\hat{\beta}_2$ given in Eqs. (3.3.1), (3.3.3), and (3.3.9) and manipulating terms, we obtain

$$\operatorname{var}(\hat{Y}_0) = \sigma^2\left[\frac{1}{n} + \frac{(X_0 - \bar{X})^2}{\sum x_i^2}\right] \quad = (5.10.2)$$

Variance of Individual Prediction

We want to predict an individual Y corresponding to $X = X_0$; that is, we want to obtain

$$Y_0 = \beta_1 + \beta_2 X_0 + u_0 \tag{5}$$

We predict this as

$$\hat{Y}_0 = \hat{\beta}_1 + \hat{\beta}_2 X_0 \tag{6}$$

The prediction error, $Y_0 - \hat{Y}_0$, is

$$\begin{aligned} Y_0 - \hat{Y}_0 &= \beta_1 + \beta_2 X_0 + u_0 - (\hat{\beta}_1 + \hat{\beta}_2 X_0) \\ &= (\beta_1 - \hat{\beta}_1) + (\beta_2 - \hat{\beta}_2)X_0 + u_0 \end{aligned} \tag{7}$$

Therefore,

$$\begin{aligned} E(Y_0 - \hat{Y}_0) &= E(\beta_1 - \hat{\beta}_1) + E(\beta_2 - \hat{\beta}_2)X_0 - E(u_0) \\ &= 0 \end{aligned}$$

because $\hat{\beta}_1$, $\hat{\beta}_2$ are unbiased, X_0 is a fixed number, and $E(u_0)$ is zero by assumption.

Squaring Eq. (7) on both sides and taking expectations, we get $\operatorname{var}(Y_0 - \hat{Y}_0) = \operatorname{var}(\hat{\beta}_1) + X_0^2 \operatorname{var}(\hat{\beta}_2) + 2X_0 \operatorname{cov}(\beta_1, \beta_2) + \operatorname{var}(u_0)$. Using the variance and covariance formulas for $\hat{\beta}_1$ and $\hat{\beta}_2$ given earlier, and noting that $\operatorname{var}(u_0) = \sigma^2$, we obtain

$$\operatorname{var}(Y_0 - \hat{Y}_0) = \sigma^2\left[1 + \frac{1}{n} + \frac{(X_0 - \bar{X})^2}{\sum x_i^2}\right] \quad = (5.10.6)$$

Chapter 6

Extensions of the Two-Variable Linear Regression Model

Some aspects of linear regression analysis can be easily introduced within the framework of the two-variable linear regression model that we have been discussing so far. First we consider the case of **regression through the origin,** that is, a situation where the intercept term, β_1, is absent from the model. Then we consider the question of the **units of measurement,** that is, how the Y and X variables are measured and whether a change in the units of measurement affects the regression results. Finally, we consider the question of the **functional form** of the linear regression model. So far we have considered models that are linear in the parameters as well as in the variables. But recall that the regression theory developed in the previous chapters requires only that the parameters be linear; the variables may or may not enter linearly in the model. By considering models that are linear in the parameters but not necessarily in the variables, we show in this chapter how the two-variable models can deal with some interesting practical problems.

Once the ideas introduced in this chapter are grasped, their extension to multiple regression models is quite straightforward, as we shall show in Chapters 7 and 8.

6.1 Regression through the Origin

There are occasions when the two-variable population regression function (PRF) assumes the following form:

$$Y_i = \beta_2 X_i + u_i \tag{6.1.1}$$

In this model the intercept term is absent or zero, hence the name **regression through the origin.**

As an illustration, consider the capital asset pricing model (CAPM) of modern portfolio theory, which, in its risk-premium form, may be expressed as[1]

$$(\text{ER}_i - r_f) = \beta_i(\text{ER}_m - r_f) \tag{6.1.2}$$

[1]See Haim Levy and Marshall Sarnat, *Portfolio and Investment Selection: Theory and Practice*, Prentice-Hall International, Englewood Cliffs, NJ, 1984, Chap. 14.

where ER_i = expected rate of return on security i
ER_m = expected rate of return on the market portfolio as represented by, say, the S&P 500 composite stock index
r_f = risk-free rate of return, say, the return on 90-day Treasury bills
β_i = the Beta coefficient, a measure of systematic risk, i.e., risk that cannot be eliminated through diversification. Also, a measure of the extent to which the ith security's rate of return moves with the market. A $\beta_i > 1$ implies a volatile or aggressive security, whereas a $\beta_i < 1$ suggests a defensive security. (*Note:* Do not confuse this β_i with the slope coefficient of the two-variable regression, β_2.)

If capital markets work efficiently, then CAPM postulates that security i's expected risk premium ($= ER_i - r_f$) is equal to that security's β coefficient times the expected market risk premium ($= ER_m - r_f$). If the CAPM holds, we have the situation depicted in Figure 6.1. The line shown in the figure is known as the **security market line** (SML).

For empirical purposes, Equation 6.1.2 is often expressed as

$$R_i - r_f = \beta_i(R_m - r_f) + u_i \tag{6.1.3}$$

or

$$R_i - r_f = \alpha_i + \beta_i(R_m - r_f) + u_i \tag{6.1.4}$$

The latter model is known as the **Market Model.**[2] If CAPM holds, α_i is expected to be zero. (See Figure 6.2.)

In passing, note that in Equation 6.1.4 the dependent variable, Y, is $(R_i - r_f)$ and the explanatory variable, X, is β_i, the volatility coefficient, and *not* $(R_m - r_f)$. Therefore, to run regression Eq. (6.1.4), one must first estimate β_i, which is usually derived from the **characteristic line,** as described in Exercise 5.5. (For further details, see Exercise 8.28.)

As this example shows, sometimes the underlying theory dictates that the intercept term be absent from the model. Other instances where the zero-intercept model may be appropriate are Milton Friedman's permanent income hypothesis, which states that permanent consumption is proportional to permanent income; cost analysis theory, where it is

FIGURE 6.1
Systematic risk.

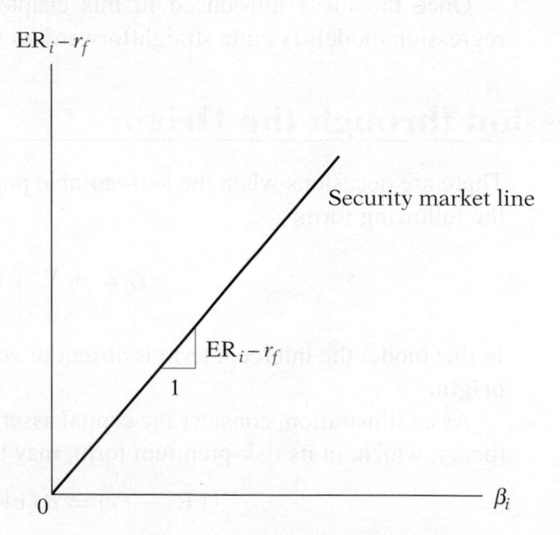

[2]See, for instance, Diana R. Harrington, *Modern Portfolio Theory and the Capital Asset Pricing Model: A User's Guide*, Prentice Hall, Englewood Cliffs, NJ, 1983, p. 71.

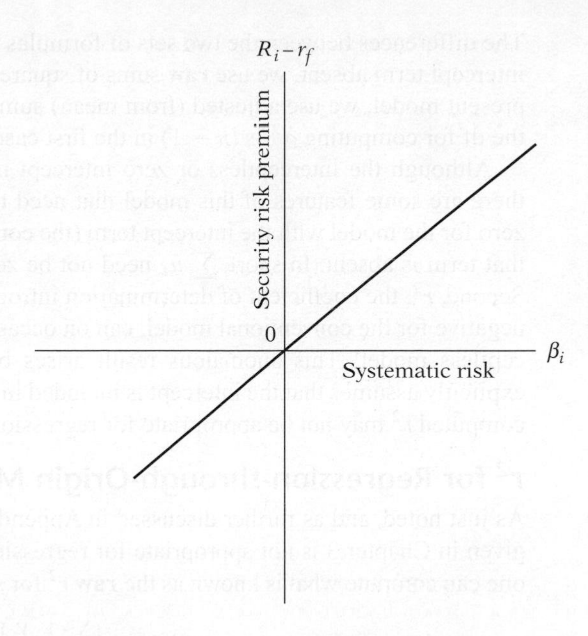

FIGURE 6.2
The Market Model of Portfolio Theory (assuming $\alpha_i = 0$).

postulated that the variable cost of production is proportional to output; and some versions of monetarist theory that state that the rate of change of prices (i.e., the rate of inflation) is proportional to the rate of change of the money supply.

How do we estimate models like Eq. (6.1.1), and what special problems do they pose? To answer these questions, let us first write the sample regression function (SRF) of Eq. (6.1.1), namely,

$$Y_i = \hat{\beta}_2 X_i + \hat{u}_i \tag{6.1.5}$$

Now applying the ordinary least squares (OLS) method to Eq. (6.1.5), we obtain the following formulas for $\hat{\beta}_2$ and its variance (proofs are given in Appendix 6A, Section 6A.1):

$$\hat{\beta}_2 = \frac{\sum X_i Y_i}{\sum X_i^2} \tag{6.1.6}$$

$$\text{var}(\hat{\beta}_2) = \frac{\sigma^2}{\sum X_i^2} \tag{6.1.7}$$

where σ^2 is estimated by

$$\hat{\sigma}^2 = \frac{\sum \hat{u}_i^2}{n-1} \tag{6.1.8}$$

It is interesting to compare these formulas with those obtained when the intercept term is included in the model:

$$\hat{\beta}_2 = \frac{\sum x_i y_i}{\sum x_i^2} \tag{3.1.6}$$

$$\text{var}(\hat{\beta}_2) = \frac{\sigma^2}{\sum x_i^2} \tag{3.3.1}$$

$$\hat{\sigma}^2 = \frac{\sum \hat{u}_i^2}{n-2} \tag{3.3.5}$$

The differences between the two sets of formulas should be obvious: In the model with the intercept term absent, we use **raw** sums of squares and cross products but in the intercept-present model, we use adjusted (from mean) sums of squares and cross products. Second, the df for computing $\hat{\sigma}^2$ is $(n - 1)$ in the first case and $(n - 2)$ in the second case. (Why?)

Although the interceptless or zero intercept model may be appropriate on occasions, there are some features of this model that need to be noted. First, $\sum \hat{u}_i$, which is always zero for the model with the intercept term (the conventional model), need not be zero when that term is absent. In short, $\sum \hat{u}_i$ need not be zero for the regression through the origin. Second, r^2, the coefficient of determination introduced in Chapter 3, which is always nonnegative for the conventional model, can on occasions turn out to be *negative* for the interceptless model! This anomalous result arises because the r^2 introduced in Chapter 3 explicitly assumes that the intercept is included in the model. Therefore, the conventionally computed r^2 may not be appropriate for regression-through-the-origin models.[3]

r^2 for Regression-through-Origin Model

As just noted, and as further discussed in Appendix 6A, Section 6A.1, the conventional r^2 given in Chapter 3 is not appropriate for regressions that do not contain the intercept. But one can compute what is known as the **raw r^2** for such models, which is defined as

$$\text{raw } r^2 = \frac{\left(\sum X_i Y_i\right)^2}{\sum X_i^2 \sum Y_i^2} \tag{6.1.9}$$

Note: These are raw (i.e., not mean-corrected) sums of squares and cross products.

Although this raw r^2 satisfies the relation $0 < r^2 < 1$, it is not directly comparable to the conventional r^2 value. For this reason some authors do not report the r^2 value for zero intercept regression models.

Because of these special features of this model, one needs to exercise great caution in using the zero intercept regression model. *Unless there is very strong a priori expectation,* one would be well advised to stick to the conventional, intercept-present model. This has a dual advantage. First, if the intercept term is included in the model but it turns out to be statistically insignificant (i.e., statistically equal to zero), for all practical purposes we have a regression through the origin.[4] Second, and more important, if in fact there is an intercept in the model but we insist on fitting a regression through the origin, we would be committing a **specification error.** We will discuss this more in Chapter 7.

EXAMPLE 6.1

Table 6.1 gives data on excess returns Y_t (%) on an index of 104 stocks in the sector of cyclical consumer goods and excess returns X_t (%) on the overall stock market index for the U.K. for the monthly data for the period 1980–1999, for a total of 240 observations.[5] Excess return refers to return in excess of return on a riskless asset (see the CAPM model).

[3]For additional discussion, see Dennis J. Aigner, *Basic Econometrics,* Prentice Hall, Englewood Cliffs, NJ, 1971, pp. 85–88.

[4]Henri Theil points out that if the intercept is in fact absent, the slope coefficient may be estimated with far greater precision than with the intercept term left in. See his *Introduction to Econometrics,* Prentice Hall, Englewood Cliffs, NJ, 1978, p. 76. See also the numerical example given next.

[5]These data, originally obtained from *DataStream* databank, are reproduced from Christiaan Heij et al., *Econometrics Methods with Applications in Business and Economics,* Oxford University Press, Oxford, U.K., 2004.

TABLE 6.1

OBS	Y	X
1980:01	6.08022852	7.263448404
1980:02	−0.924185461	6.339895504
1980:03	−3.286174252	−9.285216834
1980:04	5.211976571	0.793290771
1980:05	−16.16421111	−2.902420985
1980:06	−1.054703649	8.613150875
1980:07	11.17237699	3.982062848
1980:08	−11.06327551	−1.150170907
1980:09	−16.77699609	3.486125868
1980:10	−7.021834032	4.329850278
1980:11	−9.71684668	0.936875279
1980:12	5.215705717	−5.202455846
1981:01	−6.612000956	−2.082757509
1981:02	4.264498443	2.728522893
1981:03	4.916710821	0.653397106
1981:04	22.20495946	6.436071962
1981:05	−11.29868524	−4.259197932
1981:06	−5.770507783	0.543909707
1981:07	−5.217764717	−0.486845933
1981:08	16.19620175	2.843999508
1981:09	−17.16995395	−16.4572142
1981:10	1.105334728	4.468938171
1981:11	11.6853367	5.885519658
1981:12	−2.301451728	−0.390698164
1982:01	8.643728679	2.499567896
1982:02	−11.12907503	−4.033607075
1982:03	1.724627956	3.042525777
1982:04	0.157879967	0.734564665
1982:05	−1.875202616	2.779732288
1982:06	−10.62481767	−5.900116576
1982:07	−5.761135416	3.005344385
1982:08	5.481432596	3.954990619
1982:09	−17.02207459	2.547127067
1982:10	7.625420708	4.329008106
1982:11	−6.575721646	0.191940594
1982:12	−2.372829861	−0.92167555
1983:01	17.52374936	3.394682577
1983:02	1.354655809	0.758714353
1983:03	16.26861049	1.862073664
1983:04	−6.074547158	6.797751341
1983:05	−0.826650702	−1.699253628
1983:06	3.807881996	4.092592402
1983:07	0.57570091	−2.926299262
1983:08	3.755563441	1.773424306
1983:09	−5.365927271	−2.800815667
1983:10	−3.750302815	−1.505394995
1983:11	4.898751703	4.18696284
1983:12	4.379256151	1.201416981
1984:01	16.56016188	6.769320788
1984:02	1.523127464	−1.686027417
1984:03	1.0206078	5.245806105
1984:04	−3.899307684	1.728710264
1984:05	−14.32501615	−7.279075595
1984:06	3.056627177	−0.77947067
1984:07	−0.02153592	−2.439634487
1984:08	3.355102212	8.445977813
1984:09	0.100006778	1.221080129
1984:10	1.691250318	2.733386772
1984:11	8.20075301	5.12753329
1984:12	3.52786616	3.191554763
1985:01	4.554587707	3.907838688
1985:02	5.365478677	−1.708567484
1985:03	4.525231564	0.435218492
1985:04	2.944654344	0.958067845
1985:05	−0.268599528	1.095477375
1985:06	−3.661040481	−6.816108909
1985:07	−4.540505062	2.785054354
1985:08	9.195292816	3.900209023
1985:09	−1.894817019	−4.203004414
1985:10	12.00661274	5.60179802
1985:11	1.233987382	1.570093976
1985:12	−1.446329607	−1.084427121
1986:01	6.023618851	0.778669473
1986:02	10.51235756	6.470651262
1986:03	13.40071024	8.953781192
1986:04	−7.796262998	−2.387761685
1986:05	0.211540446	−2.873838588
1986:06	6.471111064	3.440269098
1986:07	−9.037475168	−5.891053375
1986:08	−5.47838091	6.375582004
1986:09	−6.756881852	−5.734839396
1986:10	−2.564960223	3.63088408
1986:11	2.456599468	−1.31606687
1986:12	1.476421303	3.521601216
1987:01	17.0694004	8.673412896
1987:02	7.565726727	6.914361923
1987:03	−3.239325817	−0.460660854
1987:04	3.662578335	4.295976077
1987:05	7.157455113	7.719692529
1987:06	4.774901623	3.039887622
1987:07	4.23770166	2.510223804
1987:08	−0.881352219	−3.039443563
1987:09	11.49688416	3.787092018
1987:10	−35.56617624	−27.86969311
1987:11	−14.59137369	−9.956367094
1987:12	14.87271664	7.975865948
1988:01	1.748599294	3.936938398
1988:02	−0.606016446	−0.32797064
1988:03	−6.078095523	−2.161544202
1988:04	3.976153828	2.721787842
1988:05	−1.050910058	−0.514825422
1988:06	3.317856956	3.128796482
1988:07	0.407100105	0.181502075
1988:08	−11.87932524	−7.892363786
1988:09	−8.801026046	3.347081899
1988:10	6.784211277	3.158592144
1988:11	−10.20578119	−4.816470363
1988:12	−6.73805381	−0.008549997
1989:01	12.83903643	13.46098219
1989:02	3.302860922	−0.764474692
1989:03	−0.155918301	2.298491097
1989:04	3.623090767	0.762074588
1989:05	−1.167680873	−0.495796117
1989:06	−1.221603303	1.206636013
1989:07	5.262902744	4.637026116
1989:08	4.845013219	2.680874116
1989:09	−5.069564838	−5.303858035
1989:10	−13.57963526	−7.210655599

(*Continued*)

OBS	*Y*	*X*	OBS	*Y*	*X*
1989:11	1.100607603	5.350185944	1994:12	−4.225370964	0.264280259
1989:12	4.925083189	4.106245855	1995:01	−6.302392617	−2.420388431
1990:01	−2.532068851	−3.629547374	1995:02	1.27867637	0.138795213
1990:02	−6.601872876	−5.205804299	1995:03	10.90890516	3.231656585
1990:03	−1.023768943	−2.183244863	1995:04	2.497849434	2.215804682
1990:04	−7.097917266	−5.408563794	1995:05	2.891526594	3.856813589
1990:05	6.376626925	10.57599169	1995:06	−3.773000069	−0.952204306
1990:06	1.861974711	−0.338612099	1995:07	8.776288715	4.020036363
1990:07	−5.591527585	−2.21316202	1995:08	2.88256097	1.423600345
1990:08	−15.31758975	−8.476177427	1995:09	2.14691333	−0.037912571
1990:09	−10.17227358	−7.45941471	1995:10	−4.590104662	−1.17655329
1990:10	−2.217396045	−0.085887763	1995:11	−1.293255187	3.760277356
1990:11	5.974205798	5.034770534	1995:12	−4.244101531	0.434626357
1990:12	−0.857289036	−1.767714908	1996:01	6.647088904	1.906345103
1991:01	−3.780184589	0.189108456	1996:02	1.635900742	0.301898961
1991:02	20.64721437	10.38741504	1996:03	7.8581899	−0.314132324
1991:03	10.94068018	2.921913827	1996:04	0.789544896	3.034331741
1991:04	−3.145639589	0.971720188	1996:05	−0.907725397	−1.497346299
1991:05	−3.142887645	−0.4317819	1996:06	−0.392246948	−0.894676854
1991:06	−1.960866141	−3.342924986	1996:07	−1.035896351	−0.532816274
1991:07	7.330964031	5.242811509	1996:08	2.556816005	3.863737088
1991:08	7.854387926	2.880654691	1996:09	3.131830038	2.118254897
1991:09	2.539177843	−1.121472224	1996:10	−0.020947358	−0.853553262
1991:10	−1.233244642	−3.969577956	1996:11	−5.312287782	1.770340939
1991:11	−11.7460404	−5.707995062	1996:12	−5.196176326	1.702551635
1991:12	1.078226286	1.502567049	1997:01	−0.753247124	3.465753348
1992:01	5.937904622	2.599565094	1997:02	−2.474343938	1.115253221
1992:02	4.113184542	0.135881087	1997:03	2.47647802	−2.057818461
1992:03	−0.655199392	−6.146138064	1997:04	−1.119104196	3.57089955
1992:04	15.28430278	10.45736831	1997:05	3.352076269	1.953480438
1992:05	3.994517585	1.415987046	1997:06	−1.910172239	2.458700404
1992:06	−11.94450998	−8.261109424	1997:07	0.142814607	2.992341297
1992:07	−2.530701327	−3.778812167	1997:08	10.50199263	−0.457968038
1992:08	−9.842366221	−5.386818488	1997:09	12.98501943	8.111278967
1992:09	18.11573724	11.19436372	1997:10	−4.134761655	−6.967124504
1992:10	0.200950206	3.999870038	1997:11	−4.148579856	−0.155924791
1992:11	1.125853097	3.620674752	1997:12	−1.752478236	3.853283433
1992:12	7.639180786	2.887222251	1998:01	−3.349121498	7.379466014
1993:01	2.919569408	1.336746091	1998:02	14.07471304	4.299097886
1993:02	−1.062404105	1.240273846	1998:03	7.791650968	3.410780517
1993:03	1.292641409	0.407144312	1998:04	5.154679109	−0.081494993
1993:04	0.420241384	−1.734930047	1998:05	3.293686179	−1.613131159
1993:05	−2.514080553	1.111533687	1998:06	−13.25461802	−0.397288954
1993:06	0.419362276	1.354127742	1998:07	−7.714205916	−2.237365283
1993:07	4.374024535	1.943061568	1998:08	−15.26340483	−12.4631993
1993:08	1.733528075	4.961979827	1998:09	−15.22865141	−5.170734985
1993:09	−3.659808969	−1.618729936	1998:10	15.96218038	11.70544788
1993:10	5.85690764	4.215408608	1998:11	−8.684089113	−0.380200223
1993:11	−1.365550294	1.880360165	1998:12	17.13842369	4.986705187
1993:12	−1.346979017	5.826352413	1999:01	−1.468448611	2.493727994
1994:01	12.89578758	2.973540693	1999:02	8.5036	0.937105259
1994:02	−5.346700561	−5.479858563	1999:03	10.8943073	4.280082506
1994:03	−7.614726564	−5.784547088	1999:04	13.03497394	3.960824402
1994:04	10.22042923	1.157083438	1999:05	−5.654671597	−4.499198079
1994:05	−6.928422261	−6.356199493	1999:06	8.321969316	3.656745699
1994:06	−5.065919037	−0.843583888	1999:07	0.507652273	−2.503971473
1994:07	7.483498556	5.779953224	1999:08	−5.022980561	−0.121901923
1994:08	1.828762662	3.298130184	1999:09	−2.305448839	−5.388032432
1994:09	−5.69293279	−7.110010085	1999:10	−1.876879466	4.010989716
1994:10	−2.426962489	2.968005597	1999:11	1.348824769	6.265312975
1994:11	2.125100668	−1.531245158	1999:12	−2.64164938	4.045658427

EXAMPLE 6.1 (*Continued*)

First we fit model (6.1.3) to these data. Using *EViews6* we obtained the following regression results, which are given in the standard *EViews* format.

Dependent Variable: *Y*
Method: Least Squares
Sample: 1980M01 1999M12
Included observations: 240

	Coefficient	Std. Error	*t*-Statistic	Prob.
X	1.155512	0.074396	15.53200	0.0000

R-squared	0.500309	Mean dependent var.	0.499826
Adjusted *R*-squared†	0.500309	S.D. dependent var.	7.849594
S.E. of regression	5.548786	Durbin-Watson stat.*	1.972853
Sum squared resid.	7358.578		

*We will discuss this statistic in Chapter 12.
†See Chapter 7.

As these results show, the slope coefficient, which is the Beta coefficient, is highly significant, for its *p* value is extremely small. The interpretation here is that if the excess market rate goes up by 1 percentage point, the excess return on the index of consumer goods sector goes up by about 1.15 percentage points. Not only is the slope coefficient statistically significant, but it is significantly greater than 1 (can you verify this?). If a Beta coefficient is greater than 1, such a security (here a portfolio of 104 stocks) is said to be volatile; it moves more than proportionately with the overall stock market index. But this finding should not be surprising, for in this example we are considering stocks from the sector of cyclical consumer goods such as houshold durables, automobiles, textiles, and sports equipment.

If we fit model (6.1.4), we obtain the following results:

Dependent Variable: *Y*
Method: Least Squares
Sample: 1980M01 1999M12
Included observations: 240

	Coefficient	Std. Error	*t*-Statistic	Prob.
C	−0.447481	0.362943	−1.232924	0.2188
X	1.171128	0.075386	15.53500	0.0000

R-squared	0.503480	Mean dependent var.	0.499826
Adjusted *R*-squared	0.501394	S.D. dependent var.	7.849594
S.E. of regression	5.542759	Durbin-Watson stat.	1.984746
Sum squared resid.	7311.877	Prob. (*F*-statistic)	0.000000
F-statistic	241.3363		

From these results we see that the intercept is not statistically different from zero, although the slope coefficient (the Beta coefficient) is highly statistically significant. This suggests that the regression-through-the-origin model fits the data well. Besides, statistically there is no difference in the value of the slope coefficient in the two models. Note that the standard error of the slope coefficient in the regression-through-the-origin model is slightly lower than the one in the intercept-present model, thus supporting Theil's argument given in footnote 4. Even then, the slope coefficient is statistically greater than 1, once again confirming that returns on the stocks in the cyclical consumer goods sector are volatile.

By the way, note that the r^2 value given for the regression-through-the-origin model should be taken with a grain of salt, for the traditional formula of r^2 is not applicable for such models. *EViews,* however, routinely presents the standard r^2 value even for such models.

6.2 Scaling and Units of Measurement

To grasp the ideas developed in this section, consider the data given in Table 6.2, which refers to U.S. gross private domestic investment (GPDI) and gross domestic product (GDP), in billions as well as millions of (chained) 2000 dollars.

Suppose in the regression of GPDI on GDP one researcher uses data in billions of dollars but another expresses data in millions of dollars. Will the regression results be the same in both cases? If not, which results should one use? In short, do the units in which the regressand and regressor(s) are measured make any difference in the regression results? If so, what is the sensible course to follow in choosing units of measurement for regression analysis? To answer these questions, let us proceed systematically. Let

$$Y_i = \hat{\beta}_1 + \hat{\beta}_2 X_i + \hat{u}_i \tag{6.2.1}$$

where $Y =$ GPDI and $X =$ GDP. Define

$$Y_i^* = w_1 Y_i \tag{6.2.2}$$

$$X_i^* = w_2 X_i \tag{6.2.3}$$

where w_1 and w_2 are constants, called the **scale factors;** w_1 may equal w_2 or be different.

From Equations 6.2.2 and 6.2.3 it is clear that Y_i^* and X_i^* are *rescaled* Y_i and X_i. Thus, if Y_i and X_i are measured in billions of dollars and one wants to express them in millions of dollars, we will have $Y_i^* = 1000\ Y_i$ and $X_i^* = 1000\ X_i$; here $w_1 = w_2 = 1000$.

Now consider the regression using Y_i^* and X_i^* variables:

$$Y_i^* = \hat{\beta}_1^* + \hat{\beta}_2^* X_i^* + \hat{u}_i^* \tag{6.2.4}$$

where $Y_i^* = w_1 Y_i$, $X_i^* = w_2 X_i$, and $\hat{u}_i^* = w_1 \hat{u}_i$. (Why?)

TABLE 6.2 **Gross Private Domestic Investment and GDP, United States, 1990–2005 (Billions of chained [2000] dollars, except as noted; quarterly data at seasonally adjusted annual rates)**

Source: *Economic Report of the President,* 2007, Table B-2, p. 328.

Year	GPDIBL	GPDIM	GDPB	GDPM
1990	886.6	886,600.0	7,112.5	7,112,500.0
1991	829.1	829,100.0	7,100.5	7,100,500.0
1992	878.3	878,300.0	7,336.6	7,336,600.0
1993	953.5	953,500.0	7,532.7	7,532,700.0
1994	1,042.3	1,042,300.0	7,835.5	7,835,500.0
1995	1,109.6	1,109,600.0	8,031.7	8,031,700.0
1996	1,209.2	1,209,200.0	8,328.9	8,328,900.0
1997	1,320.6	1,320,600.0	8,703.5	8,703,500.0
1998	1,455.0	1,455,000.0	9,066.9	9,066,900.0
1999	1,576.3	1,576,300.0	9,470.3	9,470,300.0
2000	1,679.0	1,679,000.0	9,817.0	9,817,000.0
2001	1,629.4	1,629,400.0	9,890.7	9,890,700.0
2002	1,544.6	1,544,600.0	10,048.8	10,048,800.0
2003	1,596.9	1,596,900.0	10,301.0	10,301,000.0
2004	1,713.9	1,713,900.0	10,703.5	10,703,500.0
2005	1,842.0	1,842,000.0	11,048.6	11,048,600.0

Note: GPDIBL = gross private domestic investment, billions of 2000 dollars.
GPDIM = gross private domestic investments, millions of 2000 dollars.
GDPB = gross domestic product, billions of 2000 dollars.
GDPM = gross domestic product, millions of 2000 dollars.

We want to find out the relationships between the following pairs:

1. $\hat{\beta}_1$ and $\hat{\beta}_1^*$
2. $\hat{\beta}_2$ and $\hat{\beta}_2^*$
3. $\text{var}(\hat{\beta}_1)$ and $\text{var}(\hat{\beta}_1^*)$
4. $\text{var}(\hat{\beta}_2)$ and $\text{var}(\hat{\beta}_2^*)$
5. $\hat{\sigma}^2$ and $\hat{\sigma}^{*2}$
6. r_{xy}^2 and $r_{x^*y^*}^2$

From least-squares theory we know (see Chapter 3) that

$$\hat{\beta}_1 = \bar{Y} - \hat{\beta}_2 \bar{X} \tag{6.2.5}$$

$$\hat{\beta}_2 = \frac{\sum x_i y_i}{\sum x_i^2} \tag{6.2.6}$$

$$\text{var}(\hat{\beta}_1) = \frac{\sum X_i^2}{n \sum x_i^2} \cdot \sigma^2 \tag{6.2.7}$$

$$\text{var}(\hat{\beta}_2) = \frac{\sigma^2}{\sum x_i^2} \tag{6.2.8}$$

$$\hat{\sigma}^2 = \frac{\sum \hat{u}_i^2}{n-2} \tag{6.2.9}$$

Applying the OLS method to Equation 6.2.4, we obtain similarly

$$\hat{\beta}_1^* = \bar{Y}^* - \hat{\beta}_2^* \bar{X}^* \tag{6.2.10}$$

$$\hat{\beta}_2^* = \frac{\sum x_i^* y_i^*}{\sum x_i^{*2}} \tag{6.2.11}$$

$$\text{var}(\hat{\beta}_1^*) = \frac{\sum X_i^{*2}}{n \sum x_i^{*2}} \cdot \sigma^{*2} \tag{6.2.12}$$

$$\text{var}(\hat{\beta}_2^*) = \frac{\sigma^{*2}}{\sum x_i^{*2}} \tag{6.2.13}$$

$$\hat{\sigma}^{*2} = \frac{\sum \hat{u}_i^{*2}}{(n-2)} \tag{6.2.14}$$

From these results it is easy to establish relationships between the two sets of parameter estimates. All that one has to do is recall these definitional relationships: $Y_i^* = w_1 Y_i$ (or $y_i^* = w_1 y_i$); $X_i^* = w_2 X_i$ (or $x_i^* = w_2 x_i$); $\hat{u}_i^* = w_1 \hat{u}_i$; $\bar{Y}^* = w_1 \bar{Y}$; and $\bar{X}^* = w_2 \bar{X}$. Making use of these definitions, the reader can easily verify that

$$\hat{\beta}_2^* = \left(\frac{w_1}{w_2}\right) \hat{\beta}_2 \tag{6.2.15}$$

$$\hat{\beta}_1^* = w_1 \hat{\beta}_1 \tag{6.2.16}$$

$$\hat{\sigma}^{*2} = w_1^2 \hat{\sigma}^2 \tag{6.2.17}$$

$$\text{var}(\hat{\beta}_1^*) = w_1^2 \,\text{var}(\hat{\beta}_1) \tag{6.2.18}$$

$$\operatorname{var}(\hat{\beta}_2^*) = \left(\frac{w_1}{w_2}\right)^2 \operatorname{var}(\hat{\beta}_2) \tag{6.2.19}$$

$$r_{xy}^2 = r_{x^*y^*}^2 \tag{6.2.20}$$

From the preceding results it should be clear that, given the regression results based on one scale of measurement, one can derive the results based on another scale of measurement once the scaling factors, the w's, are known. In practice, though, one should choose the units of measurement sensibly; there is little point in carrying all those zeros in expressing numbers in millions or billions of dollars.

From the results given in (6.2.15) through (6.2.20) one can easily derive some special cases. For instance, if $w_1 = w_2$, that is, the scaling factors are identical, the slope coefficient and its standard error remain unaffected in going from the (Y_i, X_i) to the (Y_i^*, X_i^*) scale, which should be intuitively clear. However, the intercept and its standard error are both multiplied by w_1. But if the X scale is not changed (i.e., $w_2 = 1$) and the Y scale is changed by the factor w_1, the slope as well as the intercept coefficients and their respective standard errors are all multiplied by the same w_1 factor. Finally, if the Y scale remains unchanged (i.e., $w_1 = 1$) but the X scale is changed by the factor w_2, the slope coefficient and its standard error are multiplied by the factor $(1/w_2)$ but the intercept coefficient and its standard error remain unaffected.

It should, however, be noted that the transformation from the (Y, X) to the (Y^*, X^*) scale does not affect the properties of the OLS estimators discussed in the preceding chapters.

EXAMPLE 6.2

The Relationship between the GDPI and GDP, United States, 1990–2005

To substantiate the preceding theoretical results, let us return to the data given in Table 6.2 and examine the following results (numbers in parentheses are the estimated standard errors).

Both GPDI and GDP in billions of dollars:

$$\begin{aligned}\widehat{\text{GPDI}}_t &= -926.090 + 0.2535\ \text{GDP}_t \\ \text{se} &= \quad (116.358) \quad (0.0129) \qquad r^2 = 0.9648\end{aligned} \tag{6.2.21}$$

Both GPDI and GDP in millions of dollars:

$$\begin{aligned}\widehat{\text{GPDI}}_t &= -926{,}090 + 0.2535\ \text{GDP}_t \\ \text{se} &= \quad (116{,}358) \quad (0.0129) \qquad r^2 = 0.9648\end{aligned} \tag{6.2.22}$$

Notice that the intercept as well as its standard error is 1000 times the corresponding values in the regression (6.2.21) (note that $w_1 = 1000$ in going from billions to millions of dollars), but the slope coefficient as well as its standard error is unchanged, in accordance with the theory.

GPDI in billions of dollars and GDP in millions of dollars:

$$\begin{aligned}\widehat{\text{GPDI}}_t &= -926.090 + 0.0002535\ \text{GDP}_t \\ \text{se} &= \quad (116.358) \quad (0.0000129) \qquad r^2 = 0.9648\end{aligned} \tag{6.2.23}$$

As expected, the slope coefficient as well as its standard error is 1/1000 its value in Eq. (6.2.21), since only the X, or GDP, scale is changed.

GPDI in millions of dollars and GDP in billions of dollars:

$$\begin{aligned}\widehat{\text{GPDI}}_t &= -926{,}090 + 253.524\ \text{GDP}_t \\ \text{se} &= \quad (116{,}358.7) \quad (12.9465) \qquad r^2 = 0.9648\end{aligned} \tag{6.2.24}$$

EXAMPLE 6.2 (*Continued*)

Again notice that both the intercept and the slope coefficients as well as their respective standard errors are 1000 times their values in Eq. (6.2.21), in accordance with our theoretical results.

Notice that in all the regressions presented above, the r^2 value remains the same, which is not surprising because the r^2 value is *invariant* to changes in the unit of measurement, as it is a pure, or dimensionless, number.

A Word about Interpretation

Since the slope coefficient β_2 is simply the rate of change, it is measured in the units of the ratio

$$\frac{\text{Units of the dependent variable}}{\text{Units of the explanatory variable}}$$

Thus in regression (6.2.21) the interpretation of the slope coefficient 0.2535 is that if GDP changes by a unit, which is 1 billion dollars, GPDI on the average changes by 0.2535 billion dollars. In regression (6.2.23) a unit change in GDP, which is 1 million dollars, leads on average to a 0.0002535 billion dollar change in GPDI. The two results are of course identical in the effects of GDP on GPDI; they are simply expressed in different units of measurement.

6.3 Regression on Standardized Variables

We saw in the previous section that the units in which the regressand and regressor(s) are expressed affect the interpretation of the regression coefficients. This can be avoided if we are willing to express the regressand and regressor(s) as *standardized variables*. A variable is said to be standardized if we subtract the mean value of the variable from its individual values and divide the difference by the standard deviation of that variable.

Thus, in the regression of Y and X, if we redefine these variables as

$$Y_i^* = \frac{Y_i - \bar{Y}}{S_Y} \tag{6.3.1}$$

$$X_i^* = \frac{X_i - \bar{X}}{S_X} \tag{6.3.2}$$

where $\bar{Y}$ = sample mean of Y, S_Y = sample standard deviation of Y, $\bar{X}$ = sample mean of X, and S_X is the sample standard deviation of X; the variables Y_i^* and X_i^* are called **standardized variables.**

An interesting property of a standardized variable is that its mean value is always zero and its standard deviation is always 1. (For proof, see Appendix 6A, Section 6A.2.)

As a result, it does not matter in what unit the regressand and regressor(s) are measured. Therefore, instead of running the standard (bivariate) regression:

$$Y_i = \beta_1 + \beta_2 X_i + u_i \tag{6.3.3}$$

we could run regression on the standardized variables as

$$Y_i^* = \beta_1^* + \beta_2^* X_i^* + u_i^* \tag{6.3.4}$$

$$= \beta_2^* X_i^* + u_i^* \tag{6.3.5}$$

since it is easy to show that, in the regression involving standardized regressand and regressor(s), the intercept term is always zero.[6] The regression coefficients of the standardized variables, denoted by β_1^* and β_2^*, are known in the literature as the **beta coefficients.**[7] Incidentally, notice that (6.3.5) is a regression through the origin.

How do we interpret the beta coefficients? The interpretation is that if the (standardized) regressor increases by one standard deviation, on average, the (standardized) regressand increases by β_2^* standard deviation units. Thus, unlike the traditional model in Eq. (6.3.3), we measure the effect not in terms of the original units in which Y and X are expressed, but in standard deviation units.

To show the difference between Eqs. (6.3.3) and (6.3.5), let us return to the GPDI and GDP example discussed in the preceding section. The results of (6.2.21) discussed previously are reproduced here for convenience.

$$\begin{aligned} \widehat{\text{GPDI}}_t &= -926.090 + 0.2535\ \text{GDP}_t \\ \text{se} &= (116.358) \quad (0.0129) \qquad r^2 = 0.9648 \end{aligned} \tag{6.3.6}$$

where GPDI and GDP are measured in billions of dollars.

The results corresponding to Eq. (6.3.5) are as follows, where the starred variables are standardized variables:

$$\begin{aligned} \widehat{\text{GPDI}}_t^* &= 0.9822\ \text{GDP}_t^* \\ \text{se} &= (0.0485) \end{aligned} \tag{6.3.7}$$

We know how to interpret Eq. (6.3.6): If GDP goes up by a dollar, on average GPDI goes up by about 25 cents. How about Eq. (6.3.7)? Here the interpretation is that if the (standardized) GDP increases by one standard deviation, on average, the (standardized) GPDI increases by about 0.98 standard deviations.

What is the advantage of the standardized regression model over the traditional model? The advantage becomes more apparent if there is more than one regressor, a topic we will take up in Chapter 7. By standardizing all regressors, we put them on an equal basis and therefore can compare them directly. If the coefficient of a standardized regressor is larger than that of another standardized regressor appearing in that model, then the latter contributes more relatively to the explanation of the regressand than the former. In other words, we can use the beta coefficients as a measure of relative strength of the various regressors. But more on this in the next two chapters.

Before we leave this topic, two points may be noted. First, for the standardized regression in Eq. (6.3.7) we have not given the r^2 value because this is a regression through the origin for which the usual r^2 is not applicable, as pointed out in Section 6.1. Second, there is an interesting relationship between the β coefficients of the conventional model and the beta coefficients. For the bivariate case, the relationship is as follows:

$$\hat{\beta}_2^* = \hat{\beta}_2 \left(\frac{S_x}{S_y} \right) \tag{6.3.8}$$

where $S_x =$ the sample standard deviation of the X regressor and $S_y =$ the sample standard deviation of the regressand. Therefore, we can crisscross between the β and beta coefficients

[6]Recall from Eq. (3.1.7) that Intercept = Mean value of the dependent variable − Slope × Mean value of the regressor. But for the standardized variables the mean values of the dependent variable and the regressor are zero. Hence the intercept value is zero.

[7]Do not confuse these beta coefficients with the beta coefficients of finance theory.

if we know the (sample) standard deviation of the regressor and regressand. We will see in the next chapter that this relationship holds true in the multiple regression also. It is left as an exercise for the reader to verify Eq. (6.3.8) for our illustrative example.

6.4 Functional Forms of Regression Models

As noted in Chapter 2, this text is concerned primarily with models that are linear in the parameters; they may or may not be linear in the variables. In the sections that follow we consider some commonly used regression models that may be nonlinear in the variables but are linear in the parameters or that can be made so by suitable transformations of the variables. In particular, we discuss the following regression models:

1. The log-linear model
2. Semilog models
3. Reciprocal models
4. The logarithmic reciprocal model

We discuss the special features of each model, when they are appropriate, and how they are estimated. Each model is illustrated with suitable examples.

6.5 How to Measure Elasticity: The Log-Linear Model

Consider the following model, known as the **exponential regression model:**

$$Y_i = \beta_1 X_i^{\beta_2} e^{u_i} \tag{6.5.1}$$

which may be expressed alternatively as[8]

$$\ln Y_i = \ln \beta_1 + \beta_2 \ln X_i + u_i \tag{6.5.2}$$

where ln = natural log (i.e., log to the base e, and where $e = 2.718$).[9]

If we write Eq. (6.5.2) as

$$\ln Y_i = \alpha + \beta_2 \ln X_i + u_i \tag{6.5.3}$$

where $\alpha = \ln \beta_1$, this model is linear in the parameters α and β_2, linear in the logarithms of the variables Y and X, and can be estimated by OLS regression. Because of this linearity, such models are called **log-log, double-log,** or **log-linear** models. See Appendix 6A.3 for the properties of logarithms.

If the assumptions of the classical linear regression model are fulfilled, the parameters of Eq. (6.5.3) can be estimated by the OLS method by letting

$$Y_i^* = \alpha + \beta_2 X_i^* + u_i \tag{6.5.4}$$

where $Y_i^* = \ln Y_i$ and $X_i^* = \ln X_i$. The OLS estimators $\hat{\alpha}$ and $\hat{\beta}_2$ obtained will be best linear unbiased estimators of α and β_2, respectively.

[8]Note these properties of the logarithms: (1) $\ln(AB) = \ln A + \ln B$, (2) $\ln(A/B) = \ln A - \ln B$, and (3) $\ln(A^k) = k \ln A$, assuming that A and B are positive, and where k is some constant.

[9]In practice one may use common logarithms, that is, log to the base 10. The relationship between the natural log and common log is: $\ln_e X = 2.3026 \log_{10} X$. By convention, ln means natural logarithm, and log means logarithm to the base 10; hence there is no need to write the subscripts e and 10 explicitly.

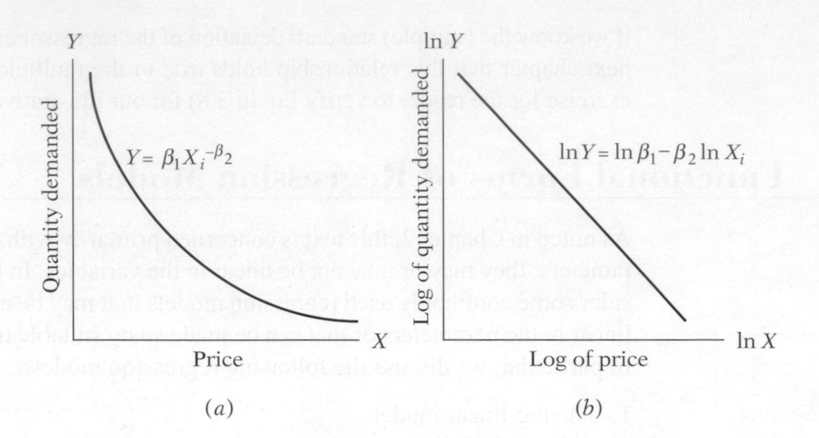

FIGURE 6.3 Constant elasticity model.

One attractive feature of the log-log model, which has made it popular in applied work, is that the slope coefficient β_2 measures the **elasticity** of Y with respect to X, that is, the percentage change in Y for a given (small) percentage change in X.[10] Thus, if Y represents the quantity of a commodity demanded and X its unit price, β_2 measures the price elasticity of demand, a parameter of considerable economic interest. If the relationship between quantity demanded and price is as shown in Figure 6.3*a*, the double-log transformation as shown in Figure 6.3*b* will then give the estimate of the price elasticity $(-\beta_2)$.

Two special features of the log-linear model may be noted: The model assumes that the elasticity coefficient between Y and X, β_2, remains constant throughout (why?), hence the alternative name **constant elasticity model.**[11] In other words, as Figure 6.3*b* shows, the change in $\ln Y$ per unit change in $\ln X$ (i.e., the elasticity, β_2) remains the same no matter at which $\ln X$ we measure the elasticity. Another feature of the model is that although $\hat{\alpha}$ and $\hat{\beta}_2$ are unbiased estimates of α and β_2, β_1 (the parameter entering the original model) when estimated as $\hat{\beta}_1 = \text{antilog}\,(\hat{\alpha})$ is itself a biased estimator. In most practical problems, however, the intercept term is of secondary importance, and one need not worry about obtaining its unbiased estimate.[12]

[10]The elasticity coefficient, in calculus notation, is defined as $(dY/Y)/(dX/X) = [(dY/dX)(X/Y)]$. Readers familiar with differential calculus will readily see that β_2 is in fact the elasticity coefficient.

A technical note: The calculus-minded reader will note that $d(\ln X)/dX = 1/X$ or $d(\ln X) = dX/X$, that is, for infinitesimally small changes (note the differential operator d) the change in $\ln X$ is equal to the relative or proportional change in X. In practice, though, if the change in X is small, this relationship can be written as: change in $\ln X \doteq$ relative change in X, where $\doteq$ means approximately. Thus, for small changes,

$$(\ln X_t - \ln X_{t-1}) \doteq (X_t - X_{t-1})/X_{t-1} = \text{relative change in } X$$

Incidentally, the reader should note these terms, which will occur frequently: (1) **absolute change,** (2) **relative** or **proportional change,** and (3) **percentage change,** or **percent growth rate.** Thus, $(X_t - X_{t-1})$ represents absolute change, $(X_t - X_{t-1})/X_{t-1} = (X_t/X_{t-1} - 1)$ is relative or proportional change, and $[(X_t - X_{t-1})/X_{t-1}]100$ is the percentage change, or the growth rate. X_t and X_{t-1} are, respectively, the current and previous values of the variable X.

[11]A constant elasticity model will give a constant total revenue change for a given percentage change in price regardless of the absolute level of price. Readers should contrast this result with the elasticity conditions implied by a simple linear demand function, $Y_i = \beta_1 + \beta_2 X_i + u_i$. However, a simple linear function gives a constant quantity change per unit change in price. Contrast this with what the log-linear model implies for a given dollar change in price.

[12]Concerning the nature of the bias and what can be done about it, see Arthur S. Goldberger, *Topics in Regression Analysis*, Macmillan, New York, 1978, p. 120.

In the two-variable model, the simplest way to decide whether the log-linear model fits the data is to plot the scattergram of $\ln Y_i$ against $\ln X_i$ and see if the scatter points lie approximately on a straight line, as in Figure 6.3*b*.

A cautionary note: The reader should be aware of the distinction between a percent change and a percentage point change. For example, the unemployment rate is often expressed in percent form, say, the unemployment rate of 6%. If this rate goes to 8%, we say that the percentage point change in the unemployment rate is 2, whereas the percent change in the unemployment rate is (8 – 6)/6, or about 33%. So be careful when you deal with percent and percentage point changes, for the two are very different concepts.

EXAMPLE 6.3
Expenditure on Durable Goods in Relation to Total Personal Consumption Expenditure

Table 6.3 presents data on total personal consumption expenditure (PCEXP), expenditure on durable goods (EXPDUR), expenditure on nondurable goods (EXPNONDUR), and expenditure on services (EXPSERVICES), all measured in 2000 billions of dollars.[13]

Suppose we wish to find the elasticity of expenditure on durable goods with respect to total personal consumption expenditure. Plotting the log of expenditure on durable goods against the log of total personal consumption expenditure, you will see that the relationship between the two variables is linear. Hence, the double-log model may be appropriate. The regression results are as follows:

$$\begin{aligned} \widehat{\ln \text{EXDUR}_t} &= -7.5417 + 1.6266 \ln \text{PCEX}_t \\ \text{se} &= \quad (0.7161) \qquad (0.0800) \\ t &= (-10.5309)^* \quad (20.3152)^* \qquad r^2 = 0.9695 \end{aligned} \tag{6.5.5}$$

where * indicates that the *p* value is extremely small.

TABLE 6.3
Total Personal Expenditure and Categories (Billions of chained [2000] dollars; quarterly data at seasonally adjusted annual rates)

Sources: Department of Commerce, Bureau of Economic Analysis. *Economic Report of the President*, 2007, Table B-17, p. 347.

Year or quarter	EXPSERVICES	EXPDUR	EXPNONDUR	PCEXP
2003-I	4,143.3	971.4	2,072.5	7,184.9
2003-II	4,161.3	1,009.8	2,084.2	7,249.3
2003-III	4,190.7	1,049.6	2,123.0	7,352.9
2003-IV	4,220.2	1,051.4	2,132.5	7,394.3
2004-I	4,268.2	1,067.0	2,155.3	7,479.8
2004-II	4,308.4	1,071.4	2,164.3	7,534.4
2004-III	4,341.5	1,093.9	2,184.0	7,607.1
2004-IV	4,377.4	1,110.3	2,213.1	7,687.1
2005-I	4,395.3	1,116.8	2,241.5	7,739.4
2005-II	4,420.0	1,150.8	2,268.4	7,819.8
2005-III	4,454.5	1,175.9	2,287.6	7,895.3
2005-IV	4,476.7	1,137.9	2,309.6	7,910.2
2006-I	4,494.5	1,190.5	2,342.8	8,003.8
2006-II	4,535.4	1,190.3	2,351.1	8,055.0
2006-III	4,566.6	1,208.8	2,360.1	8,111.2

Note: See Table B-2 for data for total personal consumption expenditures for 1959–1989.
EXPSERVICES = expenditure on services, billions of 2000 dollars.
EXPDUR = expenditure on durable goods, billions of 2000 dollars.
EXPNONDUR = expenditure on nondurable goods, billions of 2000 dollars.
PCEXP = total personal consumption expenditure, billions of 2000 dollars.

(Continued)

[13]Durable goods include motor vehicles and parts, furniture, and household equipment; nondurable goods include food, clothing, gasoline and oil, fuel oil and coal; and services include housing, electricity and gas, transportation, and medical care.

EXAMPLE 6.3 *(Continued)*

As these results show, the elasticity of EXPDUR with respect to PCEX is about 1.63, suggesting that if total personal expenditure goes up by 1 percent, on average, the expenditure on durable goods goes up by about 1.63 percent. Thus, expenditure on durable goods is very responsive to changes in personal consumption expenditure. This is one reason why producers of durable goods keep a keen eye on changes in personal income and personal consumption expenditure. In Exercise 6.18, the reader is asked to carry out a similar exercise for nondurable goods expenditure.

6.6 Semilog Models: Log–Lin and Lin–Log Models

How to Measure the Growth Rate: The Log–Lin Model

Economists, businesspeople, and governments are often interested in finding out the rate of growth of certain economic variables, such as population, GNP, money supply, employment, productivity, and trade deficit.

Suppose we want to find out the growth rate of personal consumption expenditure on services for the data given in Table 6.3. Let Y_t denote real expenditure on services at time t and Y_0 the initial value of the expenditure on services (i.e., the value at the end of 2002-IV). You may recall the following well-known compound interest formula from your introductory course in economics.

$$Y_t = Y_0(1 + r)^t \tag{6.6.1}$$

where r is the compound (i.e., over time) rate of growth of Y. Taking the natural logarithm of Equation 6.6.1, we can write

$$\ln Y_t = \ln Y_0 + t \ln(1 + r) \tag{6.6.2}$$

Now letting

$$\beta_1 = \ln Y_0 \tag{6.6.3}$$

$$\beta_2 = \ln(1 + r) \tag{6.6.4}$$

we can write Equation 6.6.2 as

$$\ln Y_t = \beta_1 + \beta_2 t \tag{6.6.5}$$

Adding the disturbance term to Equation 6.6.5, we obtain[14]

$$\ln Y_t = \beta_1 + \beta_2 t + u_t \tag{6.6.6}$$

This model is like any other linear regression model in that the parameters β_1 and β_2 are linear. The only difference is that the regressand is the logarithm of Y and the regressor is "time," which will take values of 1, 2, 3, etc.

Models like Eq. (6.6.6) are called **semilog models** because only one variable (in this case the regressand) appears in the logarithmic form. For descriptive purposes a model in which the regressand is logarithmic will be called a **log–lin model.** Later we will consider a model in which the regressand is linear but the regressor(s) is logarithmic and call it a **lin–log model.**

[14]We add the error term because the compound interest formula will not hold exactly. Why we add the error after the logarithmic transformation is explained in Sec. 6.8.

Before we present the regression results, let us examine the properties of model (6.6.5). In this model *the slope coefficient measures the constant proportional or relative change in Y for a given absolute change in the value of the regressor* (in this case the variable *t*), that is,[15]

$$\beta_2 = \frac{\text{relative change in regressand}}{\text{absolute change in regressor}} \tag{6.6.7}$$

If we multiply the relative change in *Y* by 100, Equation 6.6.7 will then give the percentage change, or the *growth rate,* in *Y* for an absolute change in *X*, the regressor. That is, 100 times β_2 gives the growth rate in *Y*; 100 times β_2 is known in the literature as the **semielasticity** of *Y* with respect to *X*. (Question: To get the elasticity, what will we have to do?)[16]

EXAMPLE 6.4

The Rate of Growth Expenditure on Services

To illustrate the growth model (6.6.6), consider the data on expenditure on services given in Table 6.3. The regression results over time (*t*) are as follows:

$$\begin{aligned}\widehat{\ln \text{EXS}_t} &= \quad 8.3226 \quad + \quad 0.00705t \\ \text{se} &= \quad (0.0016) \qquad (0.00018) \qquad r^2 = 0.9919 \\ t &= (5201.625)^* \quad (39.1667)^*\end{aligned} \tag{6.6.8}$$

Note: EXS stands for expenditure on services and * denotes that the *p* value is extremely small.

The interpretation of Equation 6.6.8 is that over the quarterly period 2003-I to 2006-III, expenditures on services increased at the (quarterly) rate of 0.705 percent. Roughly, this is equal to an annual growth rate of 2.82 percent. Since 8.3226 = log of EXS at the beginning of the study period, by taking its antilog we obtain 4115.96 (billion dollars) as the beginning value of EXS (i.e., the value at the beginning of 2003). The regression line obtained in Eq. (6.6.8) is sketched in Figure 6.4.

FIGURE 6.4

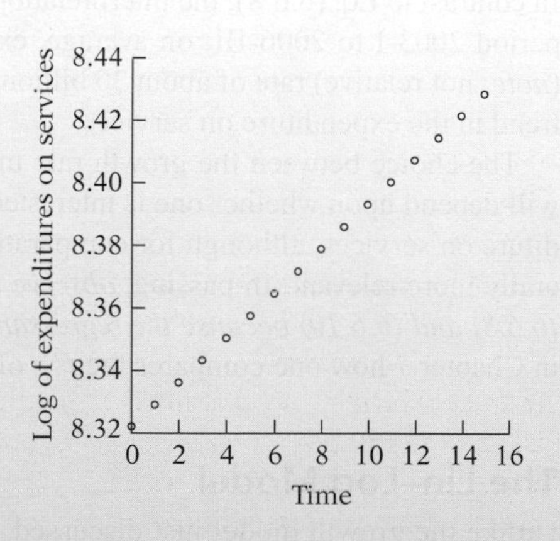

[15]Using differential calculus one can show that $\beta_2 = d(\ln Y)/dX = (1/Y)(dY/dX) = (dY/Y)/dX$, which is nothing but Eq. (6.6.7). For small changes in *Y* and *X* this relation may be approximated by

$$\frac{(Y_t - Y_{t-1})/Y_{t-1}}{(X_t - X_{t-1})}$$

Note: Here, $X = t$.

[16]See Appendix 6A.4 for various growth formulas.

Instantaneous versus Compound Rate of Growth

The coefficient of the trend variable in the growth model (6.6.6), β_2, gives the **instantaneous** (at a point in time) rate of growth and not the **compound** (over a period of time) rate of growth. But the latter can be easily found from Eq. (6.6.4) by taking the antilog of the estimated β_2 and subtracting 1 from it and multiplying the difference by 100. Thus, for our illustrative example, the estimated slope coefficient is 0.00705. Therefore, [antilog(0.00705) − 1] = 0.00708 or 0.708 percent. Thus, in the illustrative example, the *compound rate of growth* on expenditure on services was about 0.708 percent per quarter, which is slightly higher than the instantaneous growth rate of 0.705 percent. This is of course due to the compounding effect.

Linear Trend Model

Instead of estimating model (6.6.6), researchers sometimes estimate the following model:

$$Y_t = \beta_1 + \beta_2 t + u_t \tag{6.6.9}$$

That is, instead of regressing the log of Y on time, they regress Y on time, where Y is the regressand under consideration. Such a model is called a **linear trend model** and the time variable t is known as the *trend variable.* If the slope coefficient in Equation 6.6.9 is positive, there is an **upward trend** in Y, whereas if it is negative, there is a **downward trend** in Y.

For the expenditure on services data that we considered earlier, the results of fitting the linear trend model (6.6.9) are as follows:

$$\begin{aligned} \widehat{\text{EXS}}_t &= 4111.545 \quad + \quad 30.674t \\ t &= (655.5628) \quad (44.4671) \qquad r^2 = 0.9935 \end{aligned} \tag{6.6.10}$$

In contrast to Eq. (6.6.8), the interpretation of Eq. (6.6.10) is as follows: Over the quarterly period 2003-I to 2006-III, on average, expenditure on services increased at the absolute (*note:* not relative) rate of about 30 billion dollars per quarter. That is, there was an upward trend in the expenditure on services.

The choice between the growth rate model (6.6.8) and the linear trend model (6.6.10) will depend upon whether one is interested in the relative or absolute change in the expenditure on services, although for comparative purposes it is the relative change that is generally more relevant. In passing, *observe that we cannot compare the r^2 values of models (6.6.8) and (6.6.10) because the regressands in the two models are different.* We will show in Chapter 7 how one compares the r^2's of models like (6.6.8) and (6.6.10).

The Lin–Log Model

Unlike the growth model just discussed, in which we were interested in finding the percent growth in Y for an absolute change in X, suppose we now want to find the absolute change in Y for a percent change in X. A model that can accomplish this purpose can be written as:

$$Y_i = \beta_1 + \beta_2 \ln X_i + u_i \tag{6.6.11}$$

For descriptive purposes we call such a model a **lin–log model.**

Let us interpret the slope coefficient β_2.[17] As usual,

$$\beta_2 = \frac{\text{Change in } Y}{\text{Change in } \ln X} = \frac{\text{Change in } Y}{\text{relative change in } X}$$

The second step follows from the fact that *a change in the log of a number is a relative change.*

Symbolically, we have

$$\beta_2 = \frac{\Delta Y}{\Delta X / X} \tag{6.6.12}$$

where, as usual, Δ denotes a small change. Equation 6.6.12 can be written, equivalently, as

$$\Delta Y = \beta_2(\Delta X / X) \tag{6.6.13}$$

This equation states that the absolute change in $Y (= \Delta Y)$ is equal to slope times the relative change in X. If the latter is multiplied by 100, then Eq. (6.6.13) gives the absolute change in Y for a percentage change in X. Thus, if $(\Delta X/X)$ changes by 0.01 unit (or 1 percent), the absolute change in Y is $0.01(\beta_2)$; if in an application one finds that $\beta_2 = 500$, the absolute change in Y is $(0.01)(500) = 5.0$. Therefore, when regression (6.6.11) is estimated by OLS, do not forget to multiply the value of the estimated slope coefficient by 0.01, or, what amounts to the same thing, divide it by 100. *If you do not keep this in mind, your interpretation in an application will be highly misleading.*

The practical question is: When is a lin–log model like Eq. (6.6.11) useful? An interesting application has been found in the so-called **Engel expenditure** models, named after the German statistician Ernst Engel, 1821–1896. (See Exercise 6.10.) Engel postulated that "the total expenditure that is devoted to food tends to increase in arithmetic progression as total expenditure increases in geometric progression."[18]

EXAMPLE 6.5

As an illustration of the lin–log model, let us revisit our example on food expenditure in India, Example 3.2. There we fitted a linear-in-variables model as a first approximation. But if we plot the data we obtain the plot in Figure 6.5. As this figure suggests, food expenditure increases more slowly as total expenditure increases, perhaps giving credence to Engel's law. The results of fitting the lin–log model to the data are as follows:

$$\begin{aligned} \widehat{\text{FoodExp}_i} &= -1283.912 \quad + 257.2700 \ln \text{TotalExp}_i \\ t &= \quad (-4.3848)^* \qquad (5.6625)^* \qquad r^2 = 0.3769 \end{aligned} \tag{6.6.14}$$

Note: * denotes an extremely small *p value.*

(*Continued*)

[17]Again, using differential calculus, we have

$$\frac{dY}{dX} = \beta_2\left(\frac{1}{X}\right)$$

Therefore,

$$\beta_2 = \frac{dY}{\frac{dX}{X}} = (6.6.12)$$

[18]See Chandan Mukherjee, Howard White, and Marc Wuyts, *Econometrics and Data Analysis for Developing Countries,* Routledge, London, 1998, p. 158. This quote is attributed to H. Working, "Statistical Laws of Family Expenditure," *Journal of the American Statistical Association,* vol. 38, 1943, pp. 43–56.

EXAMPLE 6.5
(Continued)

FIGURE 6.5

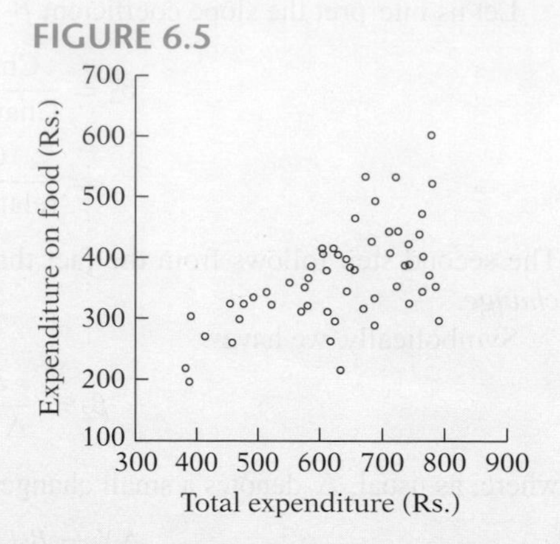

Interpreted in the manner described earlier, the slope coefficient of about 257 means that an increase in the total food expenditure of 1 percent, on average, leads to about 2.57 rupees increase in the expenditure on food of the 55 families included in the sample. (*Note:* We have divided the estimated slope coefficient by 100.)

Before proceeding further, note that if you want to compute the elasticity coefficient for the log–lin or lin–log models, you can do so from the definition of the elasticity coefficient given before, namely,

$$\text{Elasticity} = \frac{dY}{dX}\frac{X}{Y}$$

As a matter of fact, once the functional form of a model is known, one can compute elasticities by applying the preceding definition. (Table 6.6, given later, summarizes the elasticity coefficients for the various models.)

It may be noted that sometimes logarithmic transformation is used to reduce heteroscedasticity as well as skewness. (See Chapter 11.) A common feature of many economic variables, is that they are positively skewed (e.g., size distribution of firms or distribution of income or wealth) and they are heteroscedastic. A logarithmic transformation of such variables reduces both skewness and heteroscedasticity. That is why labor economists often use the logarithms of wages in the regression of wages on, say, schooling, as measured by years of education.

6.7 Reciprocal Models

Models of the following type are known as **reciprocal** models.

$$Y_i = \beta_1 + \beta_2\left(\frac{1}{X_i}\right) + u_i \tag{6.7.1}$$

Although this model is nonlinear in the variable X because it enters inversely or reciprocally, the model is linear in β_1 and β_2 and is therefore a linear regression model.[19]

This model has these features: As X increases indefinitely, the term $\beta_2(1/X)$ approaches zero (*note:* β_2 is a constant) and Y approaches the limiting or *asymptotic* value β_1.

[19]If we let $X_i^* = (1/X_i)$, then Eq. (6.7.1) is linear in the parameters as well as the variables Y_i and X_i^*.

FIGURE 6.6
The reciprocal model:
$Y = \beta_1 + \beta_2\left(\frac{1}{X}\right)$.

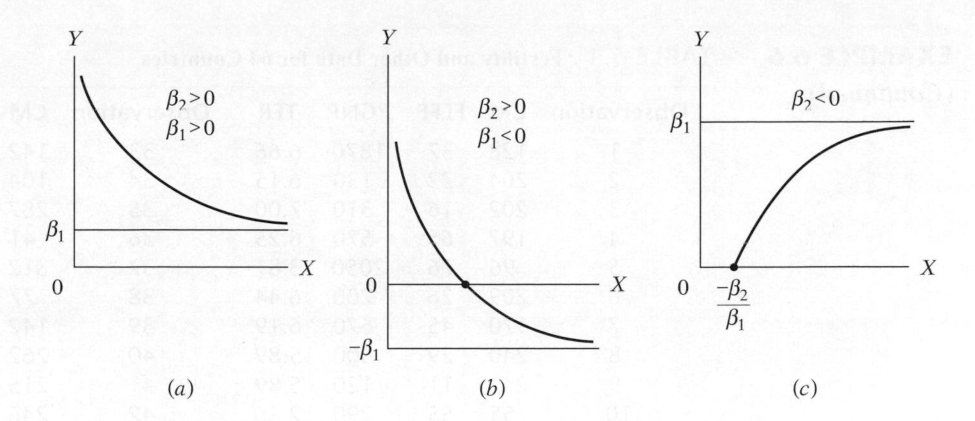

Therefore, models like (6.7.1) have built in them an **asymptote** or limit value that the dependent variable will take when the value of the X variable increases indefinitely.[20] Some likely shapes of the curve corresponding to Eq. (6.7.1) are shown in Figure 6.6.

EXAMPLE 6.6

As an illustration of Figure 6.6*a*, consider the data given in Table 6.4. These are cross-sectional data for 64 countries on child mortality and a few other variables. For now, concentrate on the variables child mortality (CM) and per capita GNP, which are plotted in Figure 6.7.

As you can see, this figure resembles Figure 6.6*a*: As per capita GNP increases, one would expect child mortality to decrease because people can afford to spend more on health care, assuming all other factors remain constant. But the relationship is not a straight line one: As per capita GNP increases, initially there is a dramatic drop in CM but the drop tapers off as per capita GNP continues to increase.

FIGURE 6.7
Relationship between child mortality and per capita GNP in 66 countries.

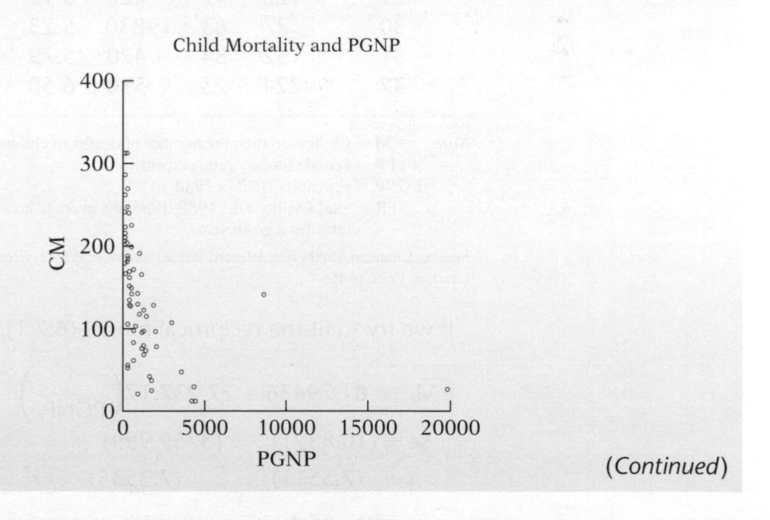

(Continued)

[20]The slope of Eq. (6.7.1) is: $dY/dX = -\beta_2(1/X^2)$, implying that if β_2 is positive, the slope is negative throughout, and if β_2 is negative, the slope is positive throughout. See Figures 6.6*a* and 6.6*c*, respectively.

EXAMPLE 6.6 *(Continued)*

TABLE 6.4 Fertility and Other Data for 64 Countries

Observation	CM	FLFP	PGNP	TFR	Observation	CM	FLFP	PGNP	TFR
1	128	37	1870	6.66	33	142	50	8640	7.17
2	204	22	130	6.15	34	104	62	350	6.60
3	202	16	310	7.00	35	287	31	230	7.00
4	197	65	570	6.25	36	41	66	1620	3.91
5	96	76	2050	3.81	37	312	11	190	6.70
6	209	26	200	6.44	38	77	88	2090	4.20
7	170	45	670	6.19	39	142	22	900	5.43
8	240	29	300	5.89	40	262	22	230	6.50
9	241	11	120	5.89	41	215	12	140	6.25
10	55	55	290	2.36	42	246	9	330	7.10
11	75	87	1180	3.93	43	191	31	1010	7.10
12	129	55	900	5.99	44	182	19	300	7.00
13	24	93	1730	3.50	45	37	88	1730	3.46
14	165	31	1150	7.41	46	103	35	780	5.66
15	94	77	1160	4.21	47	67	85	1300	4.82
16	96	80	1270	5.00	48	143	78	930	5.00
17	148	30	580	5.27	49	83	85	690	4.74
18	98	69	660	5.21	50	223	33	200	8.49
19	161	43	420	6.50	51	240	19	450	6.50
20	118	47	1080	6.12	52	312	21	280	6.50
21	269	17	290	6.19	53	12	79	4430	1.69
22	189	35	270	5.05	54	52	83	270	3.25
23	126	58	560	6.16	55	79	43	1340	7.17
24	12	81	4240	1.80	56	61	88	670	3.52
25	167	29	240	4.75	57	168	28	410	6.09
26	135	65	430	4.10	58	28	95	4370	2.86
27	107	87	3020	6.66	59	121	41	1310	4.88
28	72	63	1420	7.28	60	115	62	1470	3.89
29	128	49	420	8.12	61	186	45	300	6.90
30	27	63	19830	5.23	62	47	85	3630	4.10
31	152	84	420	5.79	63	178	45	220	6.09
32	224	23	530	6.50	64	142	67	560	7.20

Note: CM = Child mortality, the number of deaths of children under age 5 in a year per 1000 live births.
FLFP = Female literacy rate, percent.
PGNP = per capita GNP in 1980.
TFR = total fertility rate, 1980–1985, the average number of children born to a woman, using age-specific fertility rates for a given year.

Source: Chandan Mukherjee, Howard White, and Marc Whyte, *Econometrics and Data Analysis for Developing Countries,* Routledge, London, 1998, p. 456.

If we try to fit the reciprocal model (6.7.1), we obtain the following regression results:

$$\begin{aligned} \widehat{\text{CM}}_i &= 81.79436 + 27{,}237.17\left(\frac{1}{\text{PGNP}_i}\right) \\ \text{se} &= (10.8321) \qquad (3759.999) \\ t &= (7.5511) \qquad (7.2535) \qquad r^2 = 0.4590 \end{aligned} \tag{6.7.2}$$

As per capita GNP increases indefinitely, child mortality approaches its asymptotic value of about 82 deaths per thousand. As explained in footnote 20, the positive value of the coefficient of $(1/\text{PGNP}_t)$ implies that the rate of change of CM with respect to PGNP is negative.

EXAMPLE 6.6
(Continued)

FIGURE 6.8 The Phillips curve.

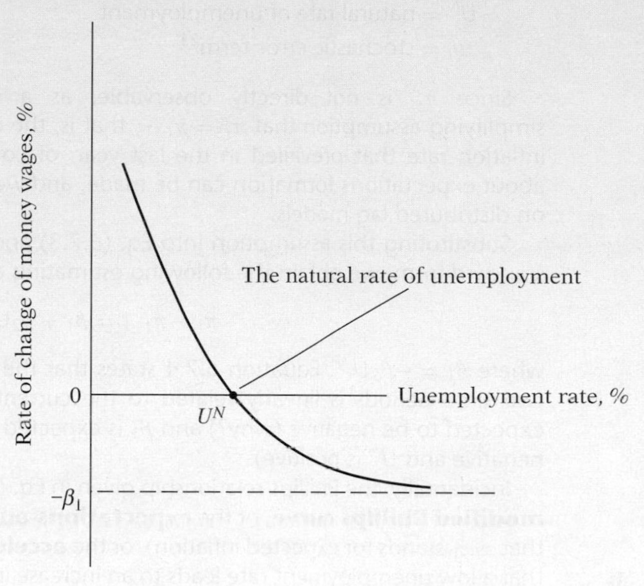

One of the important applications of Figure 6.6*b* is the celebrated Phillips curve of macroeconomics. Using the data on percent rate of change of money wages (*Y*) and the unemployment rate (*X*) for the United Kingdom for the period 1861–1957, Phillips obtained a curve whose general shape resembles Figure 6.6*b* (Figure 6.8).[21]

As Figure 6.8 shows, there is an asymmetry in the response of wage changes to the level of the unemployment rate: Wages rise faster for a unit change in unemployment if the unemployment rate is below U^N, which is called the *natural rate of unemployment* by economists (defined as the rate of unemployment required to keep [wage] inflation constant), and then they fall slowly for an equivalent change when the unemployment rate is above the natural rate, U^N, indicating the asymptotic floor, or $-\beta_1$, for wage change. This particular feature of the Phillips curve may be due to institutional factors, such as union bargaining power, minimum wages, unemployment compensation, etc.

Since the publication of Phillips's article, there has been very extensive research on the Phillips curve at the theoretical as well as empirical levels. Space does not permit us to go into the details of the controversy surrounding the Phillips curve. The Phillips curve itself has gone through several incarnations. A comparatively recent formulation is provided by Olivier Blanchard.[22] If we let π_t denote the inflation rate at time *t*, which is defined as the percentage change in the price level as measured by a representative price index, such as the Consumer Price Index (CPI), and UN_t denote the unemployment rate at time *t*, then a modern version of the Phillips curve can be expressed in the following format:

$$\pi_t - \pi_t^e = \beta_2(\text{UN}_t - U^N) + u_t \tag{6.7.3}$$

where π_t = actual inflation rate at time *t*

π_t^e = expected inflation rate at time *t*, the expectation being formed in year $(t-1)$

(Continued)

[21] A. W. Phillips, "The Relationship between Unemployment and the Rate of Change of Money Wages in the United Kingdom, 1861–1957," *Economica,* November 1958, vol. 15, pp. 283–299. Note that the original curve did not cross the unemployment rate axis, but Fig. 6.8 represents a later version of the curve.

[22] See Olivier Blanchard, *Macroeconomics,* Prentice Hall, Englewood Cliffs, NJ, 1997, Chap. 17.

EXAMPLE 6.6
(Continued)

UN_t = actual unemployment rate prevailing at time t
U^N = natural rate of unemployment
u_t = stochastic error term[23]

Since π_t^e is not directly observable, as a starting point one can make the simplifying assumption that $\pi_t^e = \pi_{t-1}$; that is, the inflation rate expected this year is the inflation rate that prevailed in the last year; of course, more complicated assumptions about expectations formation can be made, and we will discuss this topic in Chapter 17, on distributed lag models.

Substituting this assumption into Eq. (6.7.3) and writing the regression model in the standard form, we obtain the following estimating equation:

$$\pi_t - \pi_{t-1} = \beta_1 + \beta_2 \text{UN}_t + u_t \tag{6.7.4}$$

where $\beta_1 = -\beta_2 U^N$. Equation 6.7.4 states that the change in the inflation rate between two time periods is linearly related to the current unemployment rate. A priori, β_2 is expected to be negative (why?) and β_1 is expected to be positive (this figures, since β_2 is negative and U^N is positive).

Incidentally, the Phillips relationship given in Eq. (6.7.3) is known in the literature as the **modified Phillips curve,** or the **expectations-augmented Phillips curve** (to indicate that π_{t-1} stands for expected inflation), or the **accelerationist Phillips curve** (to suggest that a low unemployment rate leads to an increase in the inflation rate and hence an *acceleration* of the price level).

EXAMPLE 6.7

As an illustration of the modified Phillips curve, we present in Table 6.5 data on inflation as measured by year-to-year percentage in the Consumer Price Index (CPIflation) and the unemployment rate for the period 1960–2006. The unemployment rate represents the civilian unemployment rate. From these data we obtained the change in the inflation rate $(\pi_t - \pi_{t-1})$ and plotted it against the civilian unemployment rate; we are using the CPI as a measure of inflation. The resulting graph appears in Figure 6.9.

As expected, the relation between the change in inflation rate and the unemployment rate is negative—a low unemployment rate leads to an increase in the inflation rate and therefore an acceleration of the price level, hence the name accelerationist Phillips curve.

Looking at Figure 6.9, it is not obvious whether a linear (straight line) regression model or a reciprocal model fits the data; there may be a curvilinear relationship between the two variables. We present below regressions based on both the models. However, keep in mind that for the reciprocal model the intercept term is expected to be negative and the slope positive, as noted in footnote 20.

Linear model:
$$\widehat{(\pi_t - \pi_{t-1})} = 3.7844 - 0.6385\,\text{UN}_t$$
$$t = (4.1912) \quad (-4.2756) \qquad r^2 = 0.2935 \tag{6.7.5}$$

Reciprocal model:
$$\widehat{(\pi_t - \pi_{t-1})} = -3.0684 + 17.2077\left(\frac{1}{\text{UN}_t}\right)$$
$$t = (-3.1635) \quad (3.2886) \qquad r^2 = 0.1973 \tag{6.7.6}$$

All the estimated coefficients in both the models are *individually* statistically significant, all the p values being lower than the 0.005 level.

[23]Economists believe this error term represents some kind of supply shock, such as the OPEC oil embargoes of 1973 and 1979.

TABLE 6.5
Inflation Rate and Unemployment Rate, United States, 1960–2006 (For all urban consumers; 1982–1984 = 100, except as noted)

Source: *Economic Report of the President,* 2007, Table B-60, p. 399, for CPI changes and Table B-42, p. 376, for the unemployment rate.

Year	INFLRATE	UNRATE	Year	INFLRATE	UNRATE
1960	1.718	5.5	1984	4.317	7.5
1961	1.014	6.7	1985	3.561	7.2
1962	1.003	5.5	1986	1.859	7.0
1963	1.325	5.7	1987	3.650	6.2
1964	1.307	5.2	1988	4.137	5.5
1965	1.613	4.5	1989	4.818	5.3
1966	2.857	3.8	1990	5.403	5.6
1967	3.086	3.8	1991	4.208	6.8
1968	4.192	3.6	1992	3.010	7.5
1969	5.460	3.5	1993	2.994	6.9
1970	5.722	4.9	1994	2.561	6.1
1971	4.381	5.9	1995	2.834	5.6
1972	3.210	5.6	1996	2.953	5.4
1973	6.220	4.9	1997	2.294	4.9
1974	11.036	5.6	1998	1.558	4.5
1975	9.128	8.5	1999	2.209	4.2
1976	5.762	7.7	2000	3.361	4.0
1977	6.503	7.1	2001	2.846	4.7
1978	7.591	6.1	2002	1.581	5.8
1979	11.350	5.8	2003	2.279	6.0
1980	13.499	7.1	2004	2.663	5.5
1981	10.316	7.6	2005	3.388	5.1
1982	6.161	9.7	2006	3.226	4.6
1983	3.212	9.6			

Note: The inflation rate is the percent year-to-year change in CPI. The unemployment rate is the civilian unemployment rate.

FIGURE 6.9
The modified Phillips curve.

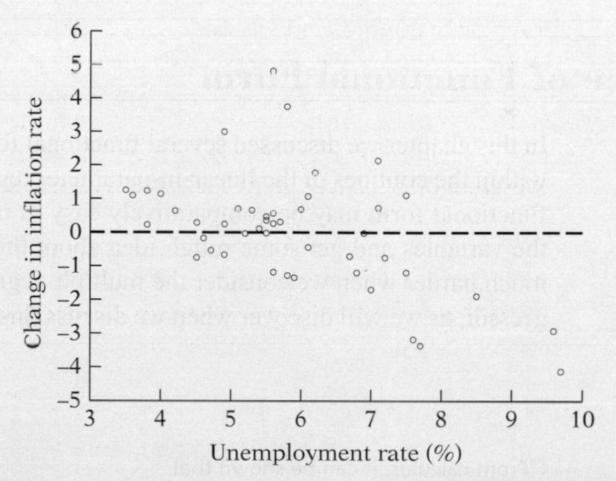

Model (6.7.5) shows that if the unemployment rate goes down by 1 percentage point, on average, the change in the inflation rate goes up by about 0.64 percentage points, and vice versa. Model (6.7.6) shows that even if the unemployment rate increases indefinitely, the most the change in the inflation rate will go down will be about 3.07 percentage points. Incidentally, from Eq. (6.7.5), we can compute the underlying natural rate of unemployment as:

$$U^N = \frac{\hat{\beta}_1}{-\hat{\beta}_2} = \frac{3.7844}{0.6385} = 5.9270 \tag{6.7.7}$$

That is, the natural rate of unemployment is about 5.93%. Economists put the natural rate between 5 and 6%, although in the recent past in the United States the actual rate has been much below this rate.

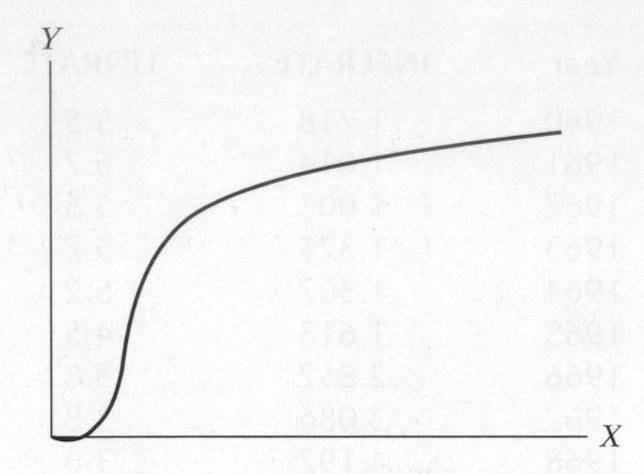

FIGURE 6.10
The log reciprocal model.

Log Hyperbola or Logarithmic Reciprocal Model

We conclude our discussion of reciprocal models by considering the logarithmic reciprocal model, which takes the following form:

$$\ln Y_i = \beta_1 - \beta_2 \left(\frac{1}{X_i} \right) + u_i \tag{6.7.8}$$

Its shape is as depicted in Figure 6.10. As this figure shows, initially Y increases at an increasing rate (i.e., the curve is initially convex) and then it increases at a decreasing rate (i.e., the curve becomes concave).[24] Such a model may therefore be appropriate to model a short-run production function. Recall from microeconomics that if labor and capital are the inputs in a production function and if we keep the capital input constant but increase the labor input, the short-run output–labor relationship will resemble Figure 6.10. (See Example 7.3, Chapter 7.)

6.8 Choice of Functional Form

In this chapter we discussed several functional forms an empirical model can assume, even within the confines of the linear-in-parameter regression models. The choice of a particular functional form may be comparatively easy in the two-variable case, because we can plot the variables and get some rough idea about the appropriate model. The choice becomes much harder when we consider the multiple regression model involving more than one regressor, as we will discover when we discuss this topic in the next two chapters. There is no

[24]From calculus, it can be shown that

$$\frac{d}{dX}(\ln Y) = -\beta_2 \left(-\frac{1}{X^2} \right) = \beta_2 \left(\frac{1}{X^2} \right)$$

But

$$\frac{d}{dX}(\ln Y) = \frac{1}{Y}\frac{dY}{dX}$$

Making this substitution, we obtain

$$\frac{dY}{dX} = \beta_2 \frac{Y}{X^2}$$

which is the slope of Y with respect to X.

TABLE 6.6

Model	Equation	Slope $\left(=\frac{dY}{dX}\right)$	Elasticity $\left(=\frac{dY}{dX}\frac{X}{Y}\right)$
Linear	$Y=\beta_1+\beta_2 X$	β_2	$\beta_2\left(\frac{X}{Y}\right)^*$
Log–linear	$\ln Y=\beta_1+\beta_2 \ln X$	$\beta_2\left(\frac{Y}{X}\right)$	β_2
Log–lin	$\ln Y=\beta_1+\beta_2 X$	$\beta_2\,(Y)$	$\beta_2\,(X)^*$
Lin–log	$Y=\beta_1+\beta_2 \ln X$	$\beta_2\left(\frac{1}{X}\right)$	$\beta_2\left(\frac{1}{Y}\right)^*$
Reciprocal	$Y=\beta_1+\beta_2\left(\frac{1}{X}\right)$	$-\beta_2\left(\frac{1}{X^2}\right)$	$-\beta_2\left(\frac{1}{XY}\right)^*$
Log reciprocal	$\ln Y=\beta_1-\beta_2\left(\frac{1}{X}\right)$	$\beta_2\left(\frac{Y}{X^2}\right)$	$\beta_2\left(\frac{1}{X}\right)^*$

Note: * indicates that the elasticity is variable, depending on the value taken by X or Y or both. When no X and Y values are specified, in practice, very often these elasticities are measured at the mean values of these variables, namely, $\bar{X}$ and $\bar{Y}$.

denying that a great deal of skill and experience are required in choosing an appropriate model for empirical estimation. But some guidelines can be offered:

1. The underlying theory (e.g., the Phillips curve) may suggest a particular functional form.

2. It is good practice to find out the rate of change (i.e., the slope) of the regressand with respect to the regressor as well as to find out the elasticity of the regressand with respect to the regressor. For the various models considered in this chapter, we provide the necessary formulas for the slope and elasticity coefficients of the various models in Table 6.6. The knowledge of these formulas will help us to compare the various models.

3. The coefficients of the model chosen should satisfy certain a priori expectations. For example, if we are considering the demand for automobiles as a function of price and some other variables, we should expect a negative coefficient for the price variable.

4. Sometimes more than one model may fit a given set of data reasonably well. In the modified Phillips curve, we fitted both a linear and a reciprocal model to the same data. In both cases the coefficients were in line with prior expectations and they were all statistically significant. One major difference was that the r^2 value of the linear model was larger than that of the reciprocal model. One may therefore give a slight edge to the linear model over the reciprocal model. *But make sure that in comparing two r^2 values the dependent variable, or the regressand, of the two models is the same; the regressor(s) can take any form.* We will explain the reason for this in the next chapter.

5. In general *one should not overemphasize* the r^2 measure in the sense that the higher the r^2 the better the model. As we will discuss in the next chapter, r^2 increases as we add more regressors to the model. What is of greater importance is the theoretical underpinning of the chosen model, the signs of the estimated coefficients and their statistical significance. If a model is good on these criteria, a model with a lower r^2 may be quite acceptable. We will revisit this important topic in greater depth in Chapter 13.

6. In some situations it may not be easy to settle on a particular functional form, in which case we may use the so-called Box-Cox transformations. Since this topic is rather technical, we discuss the Box-Cox procedure in Appendix 6A.5.

*6.9 A Note on the Nature of the Stochastic Error Term: Additive versus Multiplicative Stochastic Error Term

Consider the following regression model, which is the same as Eq. (6.5.1) but without the error term:

$$Y_i = \beta_1 X_i^{\beta_2} \tag{6.9.1}$$

For estimation purposes, we can express this model in three different forms:

$$Y_i = \beta_1 X_i^{\beta_2} u_i \tag{6.9.2}$$

$$Y_i = \beta_1 X_i^{\beta_2} e^{u_i} \tag{6.9.3}$$

$$Y_i = \beta_1 X_i^{\beta_2} + u_i \tag{6.9.4}$$

Taking the logarithms on both sides of these equations, we obtain

$$\ln Y_i = \alpha + \beta_2 \ln X_i + \ln u_i \tag{6.9.2a}$$

$$\ln Y_i = \alpha + \beta_2 \ln X_i + u_i \tag{6.9.3a}$$

$$\ln Y_i = \ln\left(\beta_1 X_i^{\beta_2} + u_i\right) \tag{6.9.4a}$$

where $\alpha = \ln \beta_1$.

Models like Eq. (6.9.2) are *intrinsically linear (in-parameter)* regression models in the sense that by suitable (log) transformation the models can be made linear in the parameters α and β_2. (*Note:* These models are nonlinear in β_1.) But model (6.9.4) is *intrinsically nonlinear-in-parameter.* There is no simple way to take the log of Eq. (6.9.4) because $\ln(A + B) \neq \ln A + \ln B$.

Although Eqs. (6.9.2) and (6.9.3) are linear regression models and can be estimated by ordinary least squares (OLS) or maximum likelihood (ML), we have to be careful about the properties of the stochastic error term that enters these models. Remember that the BLUE property of OLS (best linear unbiased estimator) requires that u_i has zero mean value, constant variance, and zero autocorrelation. For hypothesis testing, we further assume that u_i follows the normal distribution with mean and variance values just discussed. In short, we have assumed that $u_i \sim N(0, \sigma^2)$.

Now consider model (6.9.2). Its statistical counterpart is given in (6.9.2*a*). To use the classical normal linear regression model (CNLRM), we have to assume that

$$\ln u_i \sim N(0, \sigma^2) \tag{6.9.5}$$

Therefore, when we run the regression (6.9.2*a*), we will have to apply the normality tests discussed in Chapter 5 to the residuals obtained from this regression. Incidentally, note that if $\ln u_i$ follows the normal distribution with zero mean and constant variance, then statistical theory shows that u_i in Eq. (6.9.2) must follow the **log-normal distribution** with mean $e^{\sigma^2/2}$ and variance $e^{\sigma^2}(e^{\sigma^2} - 1)$.

As the preceding analysis shows, one has to pay very careful attention to the error term in transforming a model for regression analysis. As for Eq. (6.9.4), this model is a *nonlinear-in-parameter* regression model and will have to be solved by some iterative computer routine. Model (6.9.3) should not pose any problems for estimation.

*Optional

To sum up, pay very careful attention to the disturbance term when you transform a model for regression analysis. Otherwise, a blind application of OLS to the transformed model will not produce a model with desirable statistical properties.

Summary and Conclusions

This chapter introduced several of the finer points of the classical linear regression model (CLRM).

1. Sometimes a regression model may not contain an explicit intercept term. Such models are known as **regression through the origin.** Although the algebra of estimating such models is simple, one should use such models with caution. In such models the sum of the residuals $\sum \hat{u}_i$ is nonzero; additionally, the conventionally computed r^2 may not be meaningful. Unless there is a strong theoretical reason, it is better to introduce the intercept in the model explicitly.
2. The units and scale in which the regressand and the regressor(s) are expressed are very important because the interpretation of regression coefficients critically depends on them. In empirical research the researcher should not only quote the sources of data but also state explicitly how the variables are measured.
3. Just as important is the functional form of the relationship between the regressand and the regressor(s). Some of the important functional forms discussed in this chapter are (*a*) the log–linear or constant elasticity model, (*b*) semilog regression models, and (*c*) reciprocal models.
4. In the log–linear model both the regressand and the regressor(s) are expressed in the logarithmic form. The regression coefficient attached to the log of a regressor is interpreted as the elasticity of the regressand with respect to the regressor.
5. In the semilog model either the regressand or the regressor(s) are in the log form. In the semilog model where the regressand is logarithmic and the regressor X is time, the estimated slope coefficient (multiplied by 100) measures the (instantaneous) rate of growth of the regressand. Such models are often used to measure the growth rate of many economic phenomena. In the semilog model if the regressor is logarithmic, its coefficient measures the absolute rate of change in the regressand for a given percent change in the value of the regressor.
6. In the reciprocal models, either the regressand or the regressor is expressed in reciprocal, or inverse, form to capture nonlinear relationships between economic variables, as in the celebrated Phillips curve.
7. In choosing the various functional forms, great attention should be paid to the stochastic disturbance term u_i. As noted in Chapter 5, the CLRM explicitly assumes that the disturbance term has zero mean value and constant (homoscedastic) variance and that it is uncorrelated with the regressor(s). It is under these assumptions that the OLS estimators are BLUE. Further, under the CNLRM, the OLS estimators are also normally distributed. One should therefore find out if these assumptions hold in the functional form chosen for empirical analysis. After the regression is run, the researcher should apply diagnostic tests, such as the normality test, discussed in Chapter 5. This point cannot be overemphasized, for the classical tests of hypothesis, such as the t, F, and χ^2, rest on the assumption that the disturbances are normally distributed. This is especially critical if the sample size is small.
8. Although the discussion so far has been confined to two-variable regression models, the subsequent chapters will show that in many cases the extension to multiple regression models simply involves more algebra without necessarily introducing more fundamental concepts. That is why it is so very important that the reader have a firm grasp of the two-variable regression model.

EXERCISES

Questions

6.1. Consider the regression model

$$y_i = \beta_1 + \beta_2 x_i + u_i$$

where $y_i = (Y_i - \bar{Y})$ and $x_i = (X_i - \bar{X})$. In this case, the regression line must pass through the origin. True or false? Show your calculations.

6.2. The following regression results were based on monthly data over the period January 1978 to December 1987:

$$\begin{aligned}\hat{Y}_t &= 0.00681 \quad + 0.75815X_t \\ \text{se} &= (0.02596) \quad (0.27009) \\ t &= (0.26229) \quad (2.80700) \\ p \text{ value} &= (0.7984) \quad (0.0186) \qquad r^2 = 0.4406 \\ \hat{Y}_t &= 0.76214X_t \\ \text{se} &= (0.265799) \\ t &= (2.95408) \\ p \text{ value} &= (0.0131) \qquad r^2 = 0.43684\end{aligned}$$

where Y = monthly rate of return on Texaco common stock, %, and X = monthly market rate of return,%.*

a. What is the difference between the two regression models?

b. Given the preceding results, would you retain the intercept term in the first model? Why or why not?

c. How would you interpret the slope coefficients in the two models?

d. What is the theory underlying the two models?

e. Can you compare the r^2 terms of the two models? Why or why not?

f. The Jarque–Bera normality statistic for the first model in this problem is 1.1167 and for the second model it is 1.1170. What conclusions can you draw from these statistics?

g. The t value of the slope coefficient in the zero intercept model is about 2.95, whereas that with the intercept present is about 2.81. Can you rationalize this result?

6.3. Consider the following regression model:

$$\frac{1}{Y_i} = \beta_1 + \beta_2\left(\frac{1}{X_i}\right) + u_i$$

Note: Neither Y nor X assumes zero value.

a. Is this a linear regression model?

b. How would you estimate this model?

c. What is the behavior of Y as X tends to infinity?

d. Can you give an example where such a model may be appropriate?

*The underlying data were obtained from the data diskette included in Ernst R. Berndt, *The Practice of Econometrics: Classic and Contemporary,* Addison-Wesley, Reading, Mass., 1991.

6.4. Consider the log–linear model:

$$\ln Y_i = \beta_1 + \beta_2 \ln X_i + u_i$$

Plot Y on the vertical axis and X on the horizontal axis. Draw the curves showing the relationship between Y and X when $\beta_2 = 1$, and when $\beta_2 > 1$, and when $\beta_2 < 1$.

6.5. Consider the following models:

$$\text{Model I:} \quad Y_i = \beta_1 + \beta_2 X_i + u_i$$

$$\text{Model II:} \quad Y_i^* = \alpha_1 + \alpha_2 X_i^* + u_i$$

where Y^* and X^* are standardized variables. Show that $\hat{\alpha}_2 = \hat{\beta}_2(S_x/S_y)$ and hence *establish that although the regression slope coefficients are independent of the change of origin they are not independent of the change of scale.*

6.6. Consider the following models:

$$\ln Y_i^* = \alpha_1 + \alpha_2 \ln X_i^* + u_i^*$$

$$\ln Y_i = \beta_1 + \beta_2 \ln X_i + u_i$$

where $Y_i^* = w_1 Y_i$ and $X_i^* = w_2 X_i$, the w's being constants.

a. Establish the relationships between the two sets of regression coefficients and their standard errors.

b. Is the r^2 different between the two models?

6.7. Between regressions (6.6.8) and (6.6.10), which model do you prefer? Why?

6.8. For the regression (6.6.8), test the hypothesis that the slope coefficient is not significantly different from 0.005.

6.9. From the Phillips curve given in Eq. (6.7.3), is it possible to estimate the natural rate of unemployment? How?

6.10. The Engel expenditure curve relates a consumer's expenditure on a commodity to his or her total income. Letting Y = consumption expenditure on a commodity and X = consumer income, consider the following models:

$$Y_i = \beta_1 + \beta_2 X_i + u_i$$

$$Y_i = \beta_1 + \beta_2(1/X_i) + u_i$$

$$\ln Y_i = \ln \beta_1 + \beta_2 \ln X_i + u_i$$

$$\ln Y_i = \ln \beta_1 + \beta_2(1/X_i) + u_i$$

$$Y_i = \beta_1 + \beta_2 \ln X_i + u_i$$

Which of these model(s) would you choose for the Engel expenditure curve and why? (*Hint:* Interpret the various slope coefficients, find out the expressions for elasticity of expenditure with respect to income, etc.)

6.11. Consider the following model:

$$Y_i = \frac{e^{\beta_1 + \beta_2 X_i}}{1 + e^{\beta_1 + \beta_2 X_i}}$$

As it stands, is this a linear regression model? If not, what "trick," if any, can you use to make it a linear regression model? How would you interpret the resulting model? Under what circumstances might such a model be appropriate?

6.12. Graph the following models (for ease of exposition, we have omitted the observation subscript, i):

a. $Y = \beta_1 X^{\beta_2}$, for $\beta_2 > 1$, $\beta_2 = 1$, $0 < \beta_2 < 1$, ...

b. $Y = \beta_1 e^{\beta_2 X}$, for $\beta_2 > 0$ and $\beta_2 < 0$.

Discuss where such models might be appropriate.

6.13. Consider the following regression:*

$$\text{SPI}_i = -17.8 + 33.2\ \text{Gini}_i$$
$$\text{se} = \quad (4.9) \quad (11.8) \qquad r^2 = 0.16$$

Where SPI = index of sociopolitical instability, average for 1960–1985, and Gini = Gini coefficient for 1975 or the closest available year within the range of 1970–1980. The sample consist of 40 countries.

The Gini coefficient is a measure of income inequality and it lies between 0 and 1. The closer it is to 0, the greater the income equality, and the closer it is to 1, the greater the income inequality.

a. How do you interpret this regression?

b. Suppose the Gini coefficient increases from 0.25 to 0.55. By how much does SPI go up? What does that mean in practice?

c. Is the estimated slope coefficient statistically significant at the 5% level? Show the necessary calculations.

d. Based on the preceding regression, can you argue that countries with greater income inequality are politically unstable?

Empirical Exercises

6.14. You are given the data in Table 6.7.** Fit the following model to these data and obtain the usual regression statistics and interpret the results:

$$\frac{100}{100 - Y_i} = \beta_1 + \beta_2\left(\frac{1}{X_i}\right)$$

TABLE 6.7

Y_i	86	79	76	69	65	62	52	51	51	48
X_i	3	7	12	17	25	35	45	55	70	120

6.15. To study the relationship between investment rate (investment expenditure as a ratio of the GDP) and savings rate (savings as a ratio of GDP), Martin Feldstein and Charles Horioka obtained data for a sample of 21 countries. (See Table 6.8.) The investment rate for each country is the average rate for the period 1960–1974 and the savings rate is the average savings rate for the period 1960–1974. The variable Invrate represents the investment rate and the variable Savrate represents the savings rate.†

a. Plot the investment rate against the savings rate.

*See David N. Weil, *Economic Growth,* Addison Wesley, Boston, 2005, p. 392.

**Adapted from J. Johnston, *Econometric Methods,* 3d ed., McGraw-Hill, New York, 1984, p. 87. Actually this is taken from an econometric examination of Oxford University in 1975.

†Martin Feldstein and Charles Horioka, "Domestic Saving and International Capital Flows," *Economic Journal,* vol. 90, June 1980, pp. 314–329. Data reproduced from Michael P. Murray, *Econometrics: A Modern Introduction*, Addison-Wesley, Boston, 2006.

TABLE 6.8

	SAVRATE	INVRATE
Australia	0.250	0.270
Austria	0.285	0.282
Belgium	0.235	0.224
Canada	0.219	0.231
Denmark	0.202	0.224
Finland	0.288	0.305
France	0.254	0.260
Germany	0.271	0.264
Greece	0.219	0.248
Ireland	0.190	0.218
Italy	0.235	0.224
Japan	0.372	0.368
Luxembourg	0.313	0.277
Netherlands	0.273	0.266
New Zealand	0.232	0.249
Norway	0.278	0.299
Spain	0.235	0.241
Sweden	0.241	0.242
Switzerland	0.297	0.297
U.K.	0.184	0.192
U.S.	0.186	0.186

Note: SAVRATE = Savings as a ratio of GDP.
INVRATE = Investment expenditure as a ratio of GDP.

b. Based on this plot, do you think the following models might fit the data equally well?

$$\text{Invrate}_i = \beta_1 + \beta_2 \text{Savrate}_i + u_i$$
$$\ln \text{Invrate}_i = \alpha_1 + \alpha_2 \ln \text{Savrate}_i + u_i$$

c. Estimate both of these models and obtain the usual statistics.

d. How would you interpret the slope coefficient in the linear model? In the log–linear model? Is there a difference in the interpretation of these coefficients?

e. How would you interpret the intercepts in the two models? Is there a difference in your interpretation?

f. Would you compare the two r^2 coefficients? Why or why not?

g. Suppose you want to compute the elasticity of the investment rate with respect to the savings rate. How would you obtain this elasticity for the linear model? For the log–linear model? Note that this elasticity is defined as the percentage change in the investment rate for a percentage change in the savings rate.

h. Given the results of the two regression models, which model would you prefer? Why?

6.16. Table 6.9* gives the variable definitions for various kinds of expenditures, total expenditure, income, age of household, and the number of children for a sample of 1,519 households drawn from the 1980–1982 British Family Expenditure Surveys.

*The data are from Richard Blundell and Krishna Pendakur, "Semiparametric Estimation and Consumer Demand," *Journal of Applied Econometrics*, vol. 13, no. 5, 1998, pp. 435–462. Data reproduced from R. Carter Hill, William E. Griffiths, and George G. Judge, *Undergraduate Econometrics*, 2d ed., John Wiley & Sons, New York, 2001.

TABLE 6.9

List of Variables:

wfood = budget share for food expenditure
wfuel = budget share for fuel expenditure
wcloth = budget share for clothing expenditure
walc = budget share for alcohol expenditure
wtrans = budget share for transportation expenditure
wother = budget share for other expenditures

totexp = total household expenditure (rounded to the nearest 10 U.K. pounds sterling)
income = total net household income (rounded to the nearest 10 U.K. pounds sterling)
age = age of household head
nk = number of children

The budget share of a commodity, say food, is defined as:

$$wfood = \frac{\text{expenditure on food}}{\text{total expenditure}}$$

The actual dataset can be found on this text's website. The data include only households with one or two children living in Greater London. The sample does not include self-employed or retired households.

a. Using the data on food expenditure in relation to total expenditure, determine which of the models summarized in Table 6.6 fits the data.

b. Based on the regression results obtained in (*a*), which model seems appropriate in the present instance?

Note: Save these data for further analysis in the next chapter on multiple regression.

6.17. Refer to Table 6.3. Find out the rate of growth of expenditure on durable goods. What is the estimated *semielasticity?* Interpret your results. Would it make sense to run a double-log regression with expenditure on durable goods as the regressand and time as the regressor? How would you interpret the slope coefficient in this case?

6.18. From the data given in Table 6.3, find out the growth rate of expenditure on nondurable goods and compare your results with those obtained from Exercise 6.17.

6.19. Table 6.10 gives data for the U.K. on total consumer expenditure (in £ millions) and advertising expenditure (in £ millions) for 29 product categories.*

a. Considering the various functional forms we have discussed in the chapter, which functional form might fit the data given in Table 6.10?

b. Estimate the parameters of the chosen regression model and interpret your results.

c. If you take the ratio of advertising expenditure to total consumer expenditure, what do you observe? Are there any product categories for which this ratio seems unusually high? Is there anything special about these product categories that might explain the relatively high expenditure on advertising?

6.20. Refer to Example 3.3 in Chapter 3 to complete the following:

a. Plot cell phone demand against purchasing power (PP) adjusted per capita income.

b. Plot the log of cell phone demand against the log of PP-adjusted per capita income.

c. What is the difference between the two graphs?

d. From these two graphs, do you think that a double-log model might provide a better fit to the data than the linear model? Estimate the double-log model.

e. How do you interpret the slope coefficient in the double-log model?

f. Is the estimated slope coefficient in the double-log model statistically significant at the 5% level?

*These data are from *Advertising Statistics Year Book,* 1996, and are reproduced from http://www.Economicswebinstitute.org/ecdata.htm.

TABLE 6.10
Advertising Expenditure and Total Expenditure (in £ millions) for 29 Product Categories in the U.K.

Source: http://www.Economicswebinstitute.org/ecdata.htm.

obs	ADEXP	CONEXP	RATIO
1	87957.00	13599.00	0.006468
2	23578.00	4699.000	0.005018
3	16345.00	5473.000	0.002986
4	6550.000	6119.000	0.001070
5	10230.00	8811.000	0.001161
6	9127.000	1142.000	0.007992
7	1675.000	143.0000	0.011713
8	1110.000	138.0000	0.008043
9	3351.000	85.00000	0.039424
10	1140.000	108.0000	0.010556
11	6376.000	307.0000	0.020769
12	4500.000	1545.000	0.002913
13	1899.000	943.0000	0.002014
14	10101.00	369.0000	0.027374
15	3831.000	285.0000	0.013442
16	99528.00	1052.000	0.094608
17	15855.00	862.0000	0.018393
18	8827.000	84.00000	0.105083
19	54517.00	1174.000	0.046437
20	49593.00	2531.000	0.019594
21	39664.00	408.0000	0.097216
22	327.0000	295.0000	0.001108
23	22549.00	488.0000	0.046207
24	416422.0	19200.00	0.021689
25	14212.00	94.00000	0.151191
26	54174.00	5320.000	0.010183
27	20218.00	357.0000	0.056633
28	11041.00	159.0000	0.069440
29	22542.00	244.0000	0.092385

Note: ADEXP = Advertising expenditure (£, millions)
CONEXP = Total consumer expenditure (£, millions)

g. How would you estimate the elasticity of cell phone demand with respect to PP-adjusted income for the linear model given in Eq. (3.7.3)? What additional information, if any, do you need? Call the estimated elasticity the *income elasticity*.

h. Is there a difference between the income elasticity estimated from the double-log model and that estimated from the linear model? If so, which model would you choose?

6.21. Repeat Exercise 6.20 but refer to the demand for personal computers given in Eq. (3.7.4). Is there a difference between the estimated income elasticities for cell phones and personal computers? If so, what factors might account for the difference?

6.22. Refer to the data in Table 3.3. To find out if people who own PCs also own cell phones, run the following regression:

$$\text{CellPhone}_i = \beta_1 + \beta_2 \text{PCs}_i + u_i$$

a. Estimate the parameters of this regression.

b. Is the estimated slope coefficient statistically significant?

c. Does it matter if you run the following regression?

$$\text{PCs}_i = \alpha_1 + \alpha_2 \text{Cellphone}_i + u_i$$

d. Estimate the preceding regression and test the statistical significance of the estimated slope coefficient.

e. How would you decide between the first and the second regression?

Appendix 6A

6A.1 Derivation of Least-Squares Estimators for Regression through the Origin

We want to minimize

$$\sum \hat{u}_i^2 = \sum (Y_i - \hat{\beta}_2 X_i)^2 \tag{1}$$

with respect to $\hat{\beta}_2$.

Differentiating (1) with respect to $\hat{\beta}_2$, we obtain

$$\frac{d \sum \hat{u}_i^2}{d\hat{\beta}_2} = 2\sum (Y_i - \hat{\beta}_2 X_i)(-X_i) \tag{2}$$

Setting Eq. (2) equal to zero and simplifying, we get

$$\hat{\beta}_2 = \frac{\sum X_i Y_i}{\sum X_i^2} \qquad (6.1.6) = (3)$$

Now substituting the PRF: $Y_i = \beta_2 X_i + u_i$ into this equation, we obtain

$$\begin{aligned} \hat{\beta}_2 &= \frac{\sum X_i(\beta_2 X_i + u_i)}{\sum X_i^2} \\ &= \beta_2 + \frac{\sum X_i u_i}{\sum X_i^2} \end{aligned} \tag{4}$$

[*Note:* $E(\hat{\beta}_2) = \beta_2$.] Therefore,

$$E(\hat{\beta}_2 - \beta_2)^2 = E\left[\frac{\sum X_i u_i}{\sum X_i^2}\right]^2 \tag{5}$$

Expanding the right-hand side of Eq. (5) and noting that the X_i are nonstochastic and the u_i are homoscedastic and uncorrelated, we obtain

$$\text{var}(\hat{\beta}_2) = E(\hat{\beta}_2 - \beta_2)^2 = \frac{\sigma^2}{\sum X_i^2} \qquad (6.1.7) = (6)$$

Incidentally, note that from Eq. (2) we get, after equating it to zero,

$$\sum \hat{u}_i X_i = 0 \tag{7}$$

From Appendix 3A, Section 3A.1, we see that when the intercept term is present in the model, we get in addition to Eq. (7) the condition $\sum \hat{u}_i = 0$. From the mathematics just given it should be clear why the regression through the origin model may not have the error sum, $\sum \hat{u}_i$, equal to zero.

Suppose we want to impose the condition that $\sum \hat{u}_i = 0$. In that case we have

$$\begin{aligned} \sum Y_i &= \hat{\beta}_2 \sum X_i + \sum \hat{u}_i \\ &= \hat{\beta}_2 \sum X_i, \qquad \text{since } \sum \hat{u}_i = 0 \text{ by construction} \end{aligned} \tag{8}$$

This expression then gives

$$\begin{aligned} \hat{\beta}_2 &= \frac{\sum Y_i}{\sum X_i} \\ &= \frac{\bar{Y}}{\bar{X}} = \frac{\text{mean value of } Y}{\text{mean value of } X} \end{aligned} \tag{9}$$

But this estimator is not the same as Eq. (3) above or Eq. (6.1.6). And since the $\hat{\beta}_2$ of Eq. (3) is unbiased (why?), the $\hat{\beta}_2$ of Eq. (9) cannot be unbiased.

The upshot is that, in regression through the origin, we cannot have both $\sum \hat{u}_i X_i$ and $\sum \hat{u}_i$ equal to zero, as in the conventional model. The only condition that is satisfied is that $\sum \hat{u}_i X_i$ is zero.

Recall that

$$Y_i = \hat{Y}_i + \hat{u}_i \tag{2.6.3}$$

Summing this equation on both sides and dividing by N, the sample size, we obtain

$$\bar{Y} = \bar{\hat{Y}} + \bar{\hat{u}} \tag{10}$$

Since for the zero intercept model $\sum \hat{u}_i$ and, therefore $\bar{\hat{u}}$, need not be zero, it then follows that

$$\bar{Y} \neq \bar{\hat{Y}} \tag{11}$$

that is, the mean of actual Y values need not be equal to the mean of the estimated Y values; the two mean values are identical for the intercept-present model, as can be seen from Eq. (3.1.10).

It was noted that, for the zero-intercept model, r^2 can be negative, whereas for the conventional model it can never be negative. This condition can be shown as follows.

Using Eq. (3.5.5*a*), we can write

$$r^2 = 1 - \frac{\text{RSS}}{\text{TSS}} = 1 - \frac{\sum \hat{u}_i^2}{\sum y_i^2} \tag{12}$$

Now for the conventional, or intercept-present, model, Eq. (3.3.6) shows that

$$\text{RSS} = \sum \hat{u}_i^2 = \sum y_i^2 - \hat{\beta}_2^2 \sum x_i^2 \leq \sum y_i^2 \tag{13}$$

unless $\hat{\beta}_2$ is zero (i.e., X has no influence on Y whatsoever). That is, for the conventional model, RSS $\leq$ TSS, or, r^2 can never be negative.

For the zero-intercept model it can be shown analogously that

$$\text{RSS} = \sum \hat{u}_i^2 = \sum Y_i^2 - \hat{\beta}_2^2 \sum X_i^2 \tag{14}$$

(*Note:* The sums of squares of Y and X are not mean-adjusted.) Now there is no guarantee that this RSS will always be less than $\sum y_i^2 = \sum Y_i^2 - N\bar{Y}^2$ (the TSS), which suggests that RSS can be greater than TSS, implying that r^2, as conventionally defined, can be negative. Incidentally, notice that in this case RSS will be greater than TSS if $\hat{\beta}_2^2 \sum X_i^2 < N\bar{Y}^2$.

6A.2 Proof that a Standardized Variable Has Zero Mean and Unit Variance

Consider the random variable (r.v.) Y with the (sample) mean value of $\bar{Y}$ and (sample) standard deviation of S_y. Define

$$Y_i^* = \frac{Y_i - \bar{Y}}{S_y} \tag{15}$$

Hence Y_i^* is a standardized variable. Notice that standardization involves a dual operation: (1) change of the origin, which is the numerator of Eq. (15), and (2) change of scale, which is the denominator. Thus, standardization involves both a change of the origin and change of scale.

Now

$$\bar{Y}_i^* = \frac{1}{S_y} \frac{\sum (Y_i - \bar{Y})}{n} = 0 \tag{16}$$

since the sum of deviation of a variable from its mean value is always zero. Hence the mean value of the standardized value is zero. (*Note:* We could pull out the S_y term from the summation sign because its value is known.)

Now

$$\begin{aligned} S_{y^*}^2 &= \sum \frac{(Y_i - \bar{Y})^2/(n-1)}{S_y^2} \\ &= \frac{1}{(n-1)S_y^2} \sum (Y_i - \bar{Y})^2 \\ &= \frac{(n-1)S_y^2}{(n-1)S_y^2} = 1 \end{aligned} \tag{17}$$

Note that

$$S_y^2 = \frac{\sum(Y_i - \bar{Y})^2}{n-1}$$

which is the sample variance of Y.

6A.3 Logarithms

Consider the numbers 5 and 25. We know that

$$25 = 5^2 \tag{18}$$

We say that the *exponent* 2 is the *logarithm* of 25 to the *base* 5. More formally, the logarithm of a number (e.g., 25) to a given base (e.g., 5) is the power (2) to which the base (5) must be raised to obtain the given number (25).

More generally, if

$$Y = b^X \; (b > 0) \tag{19}$$

then

$$\log_b Y = X \tag{20}$$

In mathematics the function (19) is called an *exponential function* and the function (20) is called the *logarithmic function*. As is clear from Eqs. (19) and (20), one function is the inverse of the other function.

Although any (positive) base can be used, in practice, the two commonly used bases are 10 and the mathematical number $e = 2.71828\ldots$.

Logarithms to base 10 are called *common logarithms*. Thus,

$$\log_{10} 100 = 2 \quad \log_{10} 30 \approx 1.48$$

That is, in the first case, $100 = 10^2$ and in the latter case, $30 \approx 10^{1.48}$.

Logarithms to the base e are called *natural logarithms*. Thus,

$$\log_e 100 \approx 4.6051 \quad \text{and} \quad \log_e 30 \approx 3.4012$$

All these calculations can be done routinely on a hand calculator.

By convention, the logarithm to base 10 is denoted by the letters log and to the base e by ln. Thus, in the preceding example, we can write log 100 or log 30 or ln 100 or ln 30.

There is a fixed relationship between the common log and natural log, which is

$$\ln X = 2.3026 \log X \tag{21}$$

That is, the natural log of the number X is equal to 2.3026 times the log of X to the base 10. Thus,

$$\ln 30 = 2.3026 \log 30 = 2.3026(1.48) = 3.4012 \text{ (approx.)}$$

as before. Therefore, it does not matter whether one uses common or natural logs. But in mathematics the base that is usually preferred is e, that is, the natural logarithm. Hence, in this book all logs are natural logs, unless stated explicitly. Of course, we can convert the log of a number from one basis to the other using Eq. (21).

Keep in mind that logarithms of negative numbers are not defined. Thus, the log of (-5) or the ln (-5) is not defined.

Some properties of logarithms are as follows: If A and B are any positive numbers, then it can be shown that:

1. $$\ln (A \times B) = \ln A + \ln B \tag{22}$$

That is, the log of the product of two (positive) numbers A and B is equal to the sum of their logs.

2. $$\ln (A/B) = \ln A - \ln B \tag{23}$$

That is, the log of the ratio of A to B is the difference in the logs of A and B.

3. $$\ln(A \pm B) \neq \ln A \pm \ln B \tag{24}$$

That is,the log of the sum or difference of A and B is not equal to the sum or difference of their logs.

4. $$\ln(A^k) = k \ln A \tag{25}$$

That is, the log of A raised to power k is k times the log of A.

5. $$\ln e = 1 \tag{26}$$

That is, the log of e to itself as a base is 1 (as is the log of 10 to the base 10).

6. $$\ln 1 = 0 \tag{27}$$

That is, the natural log of the number 1 is zero (as is the common log of number 1).

7. If $Y = \ln X$,

$$\frac{dY}{dX} = \frac{1}{X} \tag{28}$$

That is, the rate of change (i.e., the derivative) of Y with respect to X is 1 over X. The exponential and (natural) logarithmic functions are depicted in Figure 6A.1.

Although the number whose log is taken is always positive, the logarithm of that number can be positive as well as negative. It can be easily verified that if

$$0 < Y < 1 \quad \text{then} \quad \ln Y < 0$$
$$Y = 1 \quad \text{then} \quad \ln Y = 0$$
$$Y > 1 \quad \text{then} \quad \ln Y > 0$$

Also note that although the logarithmic curve shown in Figure 6A.1(*b*) is positively sloping, implying that the larger the number is, the larger its logarithmic value will be, the curve is increasing at a decreasing rate (mathematically, the second derivative of the function is negative). Thus, $\ln(10) = 2.3026$ (approx.) and $\ln(20) = 2.9957$ (approx.). That is, if a number is doubled, its logarithm does not double.

This is why the logarithm transformation is called a nonlinear transformation. This can also be seen from Equation (28), which notes that if $Y = \ln X$, $dY/dX = 1/X$. This means that the slope of the logarithmic function depends on the value of X; that is, it is not constant (recall the definition of linearity in the variable).

Logarithms and percentages: Since $\frac{d(\ln X)}{dX} = \frac{1}{X}$, or $d(\ln X) = \frac{dX}{X}$, for very small changes the change in $\ln X$ is equal to the relative or proportional change in X. In practice, if the change in X is reasonably small, the preceding relationship can be written as the change in $\ln X \approx$ to the relative change in X, where $\approx$ means approximately.

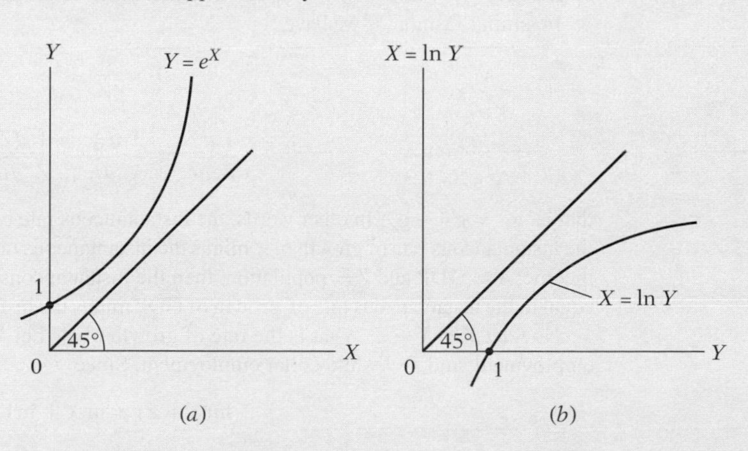

FIGURE 6A.1 Exponential and logarithmic functions: (*a*) Exponential function; (*b*) logarithmic function.

Thus, for small changes,

$$(\ln X_t - \ln X_{t-1}) \approx \frac{(X_t - X_{t-1})}{X_{t-1}} = \text{relative change in } X$$

6A.4 Growth Rate Formulas

Let the variable Y be a function of time, $Y = f(t)$, where t denotes time. The instantaneous (i.e., a point in time) rate of growth of Y, g_Y is defined as

$$g_Y = \frac{dY/dt}{Y} = \frac{1}{Y}\frac{dY}{dt} \tag{29}$$

Note that if we multiply g_Y by 100, we get the percent rate of growth, where $\frac{dY}{dt}$ is the rate of change of Y with respect to time.

Now if we let $\ln Y = \ln f(t)$, where ln stands for the natural logarithm, then

$$\frac{d \ln Y}{dt} = \frac{1}{Y}\frac{dY}{dt} \tag{30}$$

This is the same as Eq. (29).

Therefore, logarithmic transformations are very useful in computing growth rates, especially if Y is a function of some other time-dependent variables, as the following example will show. Let

$$Y = X \cdot Z \tag{31}$$

where Y is nominal GDP, X is real GDP, and Z is the (GDP) price deflator. In words, the nominal GDP is real GDP multiplied by the (GDP) price deflator. All these variables are functions of time, as they vary over time.

Now taking logs on both sides of Eq. (31), we obtain:

$$\ln Y = \ln X + \ln Z \tag{32}$$

Differentiating Eq. (32) with respect to time, we get

$$\frac{1}{Y}\frac{dY}{dt} = \frac{1}{X}\frac{dX}{dt} + \frac{1}{Z}\frac{dZ}{dt} \tag{33}$$

that is, $g_Y = g_X + g_Z$, where g denotes growth rate.

In words, the instantaneous rate of growth of Y is equal to the sum of the instantaneous rate of growth of X plus the instantaneous rate of growth of Z. In the present example, the instantaneous rate of growth of nominal GDP is equal to the sum of the instantaneous rate of growth of real GDP and the instantaneous rate of growth of the GDP price deflator.

More generally, the instantaneous rate of growth of a product is the sum of the instantaneous rates of growth of its components. This can be generalized to the product of more than two variables.

In similar fashion, if we have

$$Y = \frac{X}{Z} \tag{34}$$

$$\frac{1}{Y}\frac{dY}{dt} = \frac{1}{X}\frac{dX}{dt} - \frac{1}{Z}\frac{dZ}{dt} \tag{35}$$

that is, $g_Y = g_X - g_Z$. In other words, the instantaneous rate of growth of Y is the difference between the instantaneous rate of growth of X minus the instantaneous rate of growth of Z. Thus if Y = per capita income, X = GDP and Z = population, then the instantaneous rate of growth of per capita income is equal to the instantaneous rate of growth of GDP minus the instantaneous rate of growth of population.

Now let $Y = X + Z$. What is the rate of growth of Y? Let Y = total employment, X = blue collar employment, and Z = white collar employment. Since

$$\ln(X + Z) \neq \ln X + \ln Y,$$

it is not easy to compute the rate of growth of Y, but with some algebra, it can be shown that

$$g_Y = \frac{X}{X+Z} g_X + \frac{Z}{X+Z} g_Z \tag{36}$$

That is, the rate of growth of a sum is a weighted average of the rates of growth of its components. For our example, the rate of growth of total employment is a weighted average of the rates of growth of white collar employment and blue collar employment, the weights being the share of each component in total employment.

6A.5 Box-Cox Regression Model

Consider the following regression model

$$Y_i^{\lambda} = \beta_1 + \beta_2 X_i + u_i \quad Y > 0 \tag{37}$$

where λ (Greek lamda) is a parameter, which may be negative, zero, or positive. Since Y is raised to the power λ, we will get several transformations of Y, depending on the value of λ.

Equation (37) is known as the Box-Cox regression model, named after the statisticians Box and Cox.[1] Depending on the value of λ, we have the following regression models, which are shown in tabular form:

Value of λ	Regression Model
1	$Y_i = \beta_1 + \beta_2 X_i + u_i$
2	$Y_i^2 = \beta_1 + \beta_2 X_i + u_i$
0.5	$\sqrt{Y_i} = \beta_1 + \beta_2 X_i + u_i$
0	$\ln Y_i = \beta_1 + \beta_2 X_i + u_i$
−0.5	$\frac{1}{\sqrt{Y_i}} = \beta_1 + \beta_2 X_i + u_i$
−1.0	$\frac{1}{Y_i} = \beta_1 + \beta_2 X_i + u_i$

As you can see, linear and log-linear models are special cases of the Box-Cox family of transformations.

Of course, we can apply such transformations to the X variable(s) also. It is interesting to note that when λ is zero, we get the log-transformation of Y. The proof of this is slightly involved and is best left for the references. (Calculus-minded readers will have to recall the l'Hopital Rule.)

But how do we actually determine the appropriate value of λ in a given situation? We cannot estimate Eq. (37) directly, for it involves not only the regression parameters β_1 and β_2 but also λ, which enters nonlinearly. But it can be shown that we can use the method of maximum likelihood to estimate all these parameters. Regression packages exist to do just that.

We will not pursue this topic here because the procedure is somewhat involved.

However, we can proceed by trial and error. Choose several values of λ, transform Y accordingly, run regression (37), and obtain the residual sum of squares (RSS) for each transformed regression. Choose the value of λ that gives the minimum RSS.[2]

[1] G.E.P. Box and D.R. Cox, "An Analysis of Transformations," *Journal of the Royal Statistical Society,* B26, 1964, pp. 211–243.

[2] For an accessible discussion, refer to John Neter, Michael Kutner, Christopher Nachtsheim, and William Wasserman, *Applied Linear Regression Models,* 3rd ed., Richard D. Irwin, Chicago, 1996.

Chapter 

Multiple Regression Analysis: The Problem of Estimation

The two-variable model studied extensively in the previous chapters is often inadequate in practice. In our consumption–income example (Example 3.1), for instance, it was assumed implicitly that only income X is related to consumption Y. But economic theory is seldom so simple for, besides income, a number of other variables are also likely to affect consumption expenditure. An obvious example is wealth of the consumer. As another example, the demand for a commodity is likely to depend not only on its own price but also on the prices of other competing or complementary goods, income of the consumer, social status, etc. Therefore, we need to extend our simple two-variable regression model to cover models involving more than two variables. Adding more variables leads us to the discussion of multiple regression models, that is, models in which the dependent variable, or regressand, Y depends on two or more explanatory variables, or regressors.

The simplest possible multiple regression model is three-variable regression, with one dependent variable and two explanatory variables. In this and the next chapter we shall study this model. Throughout, we are concerned with multiple linear regression models, that is, models linear in the parameters; they may or may not be linear in the variables.

7.1 The Three-Variable Model: Notation and Assumptions

Generalizing the two-variable population regression function (PRF) Eq. (2.4.2), we may write the three-variable PRF as

$$Y_i = \beta_1 + \beta_2 X_{2i} + \beta_3 X_{3i} + u_i \tag{7.1.1}$$

where Y is the dependent variable, X_2 and X_3 the explanatory variables (or regressors), u the stochastic disturbance term, and i the ith observation; in case the data are time series, the subscript t will denote the tth observation.[1]

[1]For notational symmetry, Eq. (7.1.1) can also be written as

$$Y_i = \beta_1 X_{1i} + \beta_2 X_{2i} + \beta_3 X_{3i} + u_i$$

with the provision that $X_{1i} = 1$ for all i.

In Eq. (7.1.1) β_1 is the intercept term. As usual, it gives the mean or average effect on Y of all the variables excluded from the model, although its mechanical interpretation is the average value of Y when X_2 and X_3 are set equal to zero. The coefficients β_2 and β_3 are called the **partial regression coefficients,** and their meaning will be explained shortly.

We continue to operate within the framework of the classical linear regression model (CLRM) first introduced in Chapter 3. As a reminder, we assume the following:

ASSUMPTIONS

1. Linear regression model, or *linear in the parameters.* **(7.1.2)**
2. Fixed X values or X values independent of the error term. Here, this means we require zero covariance between u_i and each X variables.

$$\text{cov}\,(u_i, X_{2i}) = \text{cov}\,(u_i, X_{3i}) = 0 \qquad \textbf{(7.1.3)}^2$$

3. Zero mean value of disturbance u_i.

$$E(u_i \mid X_{2i}, X_{3i}) = 0 \qquad \text{for each } i \qquad \textbf{(7.1.4)}$$

4. Homoscedasticity or constant variance of u_i.

$$\text{var}\,(u_i) = \sigma^2 \qquad \textbf{(7.1.5)}$$

5. No autocorrelation, or serial correlation, between the disturbances.

$$\text{cov}\,(u_i, u_j) = 0 \qquad i \neq j \qquad \textbf{(7.1.6)}$$

6. The number of observations n must be greater than the number of parameters to be estimated, which is 3 in our current case. **(7.1.7)**
7. There must be variation in the values of the X variables. **(7.1.8)**

We will also address two other requirements.

8. No exact collinearity between the X variables.

No **exact linear relationship** between X_2 and X_3 **(7.1.9)**

In Section 7.7, we will spend more time discussing the final assumption.

9. There is no *specification bias.*

The model is correctly specified. **(7.1.10)**

The rationale for assumptions (7.1.2) through (7.1.10) is the same as that discussed in Section 3.2. Assumption (7.1.9), that there is no exact linear relationship between X_2 and X_3, is technically known as the assumption of *no collinearity* or **no multicollinearity** if more than one exact linear relationship is involved.

Informally, no collinearity means none of the regressors can be written as *exact* linear combinations of the remaining regressors in the model.

Formally, no collinearity means that there exists no set of numbers, λ_2 and λ_3, not both zero such that

$$\lambda_2 X_{2i} + \lambda_3 X_{3i} = 0 \qquad \textbf{(7.1.11)}$$

[2]This assumption is automatically fulfilled if X_2 and X_3 are nonstochastic and Eq. (7.1.4) holds.

If such an exact linear relationship exists, then X_2 and X_3 are said to be **collinear** or linearly dependent. On the other hand, if Eq. (7.1.11) holds true only when $\lambda_2 = \lambda_3 = 0$, then X_2 and X_3 are said to be *linearly independent.*

Thus, if

$$X_{2i} = -4X_{3i} \quad \text{or} \quad X_{2i} + 4X_{3i} = 0 \tag{7.1.12}$$

the two variables are linearly dependent, and if both are included in a regression model, we will have perfect collinearity or an exact linear relationship between the two regressors.

Although we shall consider the problem of multicollinearity in depth in Chapter 10, intuitively the logic behind the assumption of no multicollinearity is not too difficult to grasp. Suppose that in Eq. (7.1.1) Y, X_2, and X_3 represent consumption expenditure, income, and wealth of the consumer, respectively. In postulating that consumption expenditure is linearly related to income and wealth, economic theory presumes that wealth and income may have some independent influence on consumption. If not, there is no sense in including both income and wealth variables in the model. In the extreme, if there is an exact linear relationship between income and wealth, we have only one independent variable, not two, and there is no way to assess the *separate* influence of income and wealth on consumption. To see this clearly, let $X_{3i} = 2X_{2i}$ in the consumption–income–wealth regression. Then the regression (7.1.1) becomes

$$\begin{aligned} Y_i &= \beta_1 + \beta_2 X_{2i} + \beta_3(2X_{2i}) + u_i \\ &= \beta_1 + (\beta_2 + 2\beta_3)X_{2i} + u_i \\ &= \beta_1 + \alpha X_{2i} + u_i \end{aligned} \tag{7.1.13}$$

where $\alpha = (\beta_2 + 2\beta_3)$. That is, we in fact have a two-variable and not a three-variable regression. Moreover, if we run the regression (7.1.13) and obtain α, there is no way to estimate the separate influence of X_2 $(= \beta_2)$ and X_3 $(= \beta_3)$ on Y, for α gives the *combined influence* of X_2 and X_3 on Y.[3]

In short, the assumption of no multicollinearity requires that in the PRF we include only those variables that are not exact linear functions of one or more variables in the model. Although we will discuss this topic more fully in Chapter 10, a couple of points may be noted here.

First, the assumption of no multicollinearity pertains to our theoretical (i.e., PRF) model. In practice, when we collect data for empirical analysis there is no guarantee that there will not be correlations among the regressors. As a matter of fact, in most applied work it is almost impossible to find two or more (economic) variables that may not be correlated to some extent, as we will show in our illustrative examples later in the chapter. What we require is that there be no exact linear relationships among the regressors, as in Eq. (7.1.12).

Second, keep in mind that we are talking only about perfect *linear* relationships between two or more variables. Multicollinearity does not rule out *nonlinear* relationships between variables. Suppose $X_{3i} = X_{2i}^2$. This does not violate the assumption of no perfect collinearity, as the relationship between the variables here is nonlinear.

[3]Mathematically speaking, $\alpha = (\beta_2 + 2\beta_3)$ is one equation in two unknowns and there is no *unique* way of estimating β_2 and β_3 from the estimated α.

7.2 Interpretation of Multiple Regression Equation

Given the assumptions of the classical regression model, it follows that, on taking the conditional expectation of Y on both sides of Eq. (7.1.1), we obtain

$$E(Y_i \mid X_{2i}, X_{3i}) = \beta_1 + \beta_2 X_{2i} + \beta_{3i} X_{3i} \tag{7.2.1}$$

In words, Eq. (7.2.1) gives the **conditional mean or expected value of Y conditional upon the given or fixed values of** X_2 and X_3. Therefore, as in the two-variable case, multiple regression analysis is regression analysis conditional upon the fixed values of the regressors, and what we obtain is the average or mean value of Y or the mean response of Y for the given values of the regressors.

7.3 The Meaning of Partial Regression Coefficients

As mentioned earlier, the regression coefficients β_2 and β_3 are known as **partial regression** or **partial slope coefficients.** The meaning of partial regression coefficient is as follows: β_2 measures the *change* in the mean value of Y, $E(Y)$, per unit change in X_2, holding the value of X_3 constant. Put differently, it gives the "direct" or the "net" effect of a unit change in X_2 on the mean value of Y, net of any effect that X_3 may have on mean Y. Likewise, β_3 measures the change in the mean value of Y per unit change in X_3, holding the value of X_2 constant.[4] That is, it gives the "direct" or "net" effect of a unit change in X_3 on the mean value of Y, net of any effect that X_2 may have on mean Y.[5]

How do we actually go about holding the influence of a regressor constant? To explain this, let us revert to our child mortality example (Example 6.6). Recall that in that example, Y = child mortality (CM), X_2 = per capita GNP (PGNP), and X_3 = female literacy rate (FLR). Let us suppose we want to hold the influence of FLR constant. Since FLR may have some effect on CM as well as PGNP in any given concrete data, what we can do is remove the (linear) influence of FLR from both CM and PGNP by running the regression of CM on FLR and of PGNP on FLR separately and then looking at the residuals obtained from these regressions. Using the data given in Table 6.4, we obtain the following regressions:

$$\begin{aligned} \widehat{\text{CM}}_i &= 263.8635 - 2.3905\ \text{FLR}_i + \hat{u}_{1i} \\ \text{se} &= (12.2249) \quad (0.2133) \qquad r^2 = 0.6695 \end{aligned} \tag{7.3.1}$$

where $\hat{u}_{1i}$ represents the residual term of this regression.

$$\begin{aligned} \widehat{\text{PGNP}}_i &= -39.3033 + 28.1427\ \text{FLR}_i + \hat{u}_{2i} \\ \text{se} &= (734.9526) \quad (12.8211) \qquad r^2 = 0.0721 \end{aligned} \tag{7.3.2}$$

where $\hat{u}_{2i}$ represents the residual term of this regression.

[4]The calculus-minded reader will notice at once that β_2 and β_3 are the partial derivatives of $E(Y \mid X_2, X_3)$ with respect to X_2 and X_3.

[5]Incidentally, the terms *holding constant, controlling for, allowing or accounting for the influence of, correcting the influence of,* and *sweeping out the influence of* are synonymous and will be used interchangeably in this text.

Now

$$\hat{u}_{1i} = (\text{CM}_i - 263.8635 + 2.3905\ \text{FLR}_i) \tag{7.3.3}$$

represents that part of CM left after removing from it the (linear) influence of FLR. Likewise,

$$\hat{u}_{2i} = (\text{PGNP}_i + 39.3033 - 28.1427\ \text{FLR}_i) \tag{7.3.4}$$

represents that part of PGNP left after removing from it the (linear) influence of FLR.

Therefore, if we now regress $\hat{u}_{1i}$ on $\hat{u}_{2i}$, which are "purified" of the (linear) influence of FLR, wouldn't we obtain the net effect of PGNP on CM? That is indeed the case (see Appendix 7A, Section 7A.2). The regression results are as follows:

$$\begin{aligned} \hat{\hat{u}}_{1i} &= -0.0056\hat{u}_{2i} \\ \text{se} &= \ (0.0019) \qquad r^2 = 0.1152 \end{aligned} \tag{7.3.5}$$

Note: This regression has no intercept term because the mean value of the OLS residuals $\hat{u}_{1i}$ and $\hat{u}_{2i}$ is zero. (Why?)

The slope coefficient of −0.0056 now gives the "true" or net effect of a unit change in PGNP on CM or the true slope of CM with respect to PGNP. That is, it gives the partial regression coefficient of CM with respect to PGNP, β_2.

Readers who want to get the partial regression coefficient of CM with respect to FLR can replicate the above procedure by first regressing CM on PGNP and getting the residuals from this regression ($\hat{u}_{1i}$), then regressing FLR on PGNP and obtaining the residuals from this regression ($\hat{u}_{2i}$), and then regressing $\hat{u}_{1i}$ on $\hat{u}_{2i}$. I am sure readers get the idea.

Do we have to go through this multistep procedure every time we want to find out the true partial regression coefficient? Fortunately, we do not have to do that, for the same job can be accomplished fairly quickly and routinely by the OLS procedure discussed in the next section. The multistep procedure just outlined is merely for pedagogic purposes to drive home the meaning of "partial" regression coefficient.

7.4 OLS and ML Estimation of the Partial Regression Coefficients

To estimate the parameters of the three-variable regression model (7.1.1), we first consider the method of ordinary least squares (OLS) introduced in Chapter 3 and then consider briefly the method of maximum likelihood (ML) discussed in Chapter 4.

OLS Estimators

To find the OLS estimators, let us first write the sample regression function (SRF) corresponding to the PRF of Eq. (7.1.1) as follows:

$$Y_i = \hat{\beta}_1 + \hat{\beta}_2 X_{2i} + \hat{\beta}_3 X_{3i} + \hat{u}_i \tag{7.4.1}$$

where $\hat{u}_i$ is the residual term, the sample counterpart of the stochastic disturbance term u_i.

As noted in Chapter 3, the OLS procedure consists of choosing the values of the unknown parameters so that the residual sum of squares (RSS) $\sum \hat{u}_i^2$ is as small as possible. Symbolically,

$$\min \sum \hat{u}_i^2 = \sum (Y_i - \hat{\beta}_1 - \hat{\beta}_2 X_{2i} - \hat{\beta}_3 X_{3i})^2 \tag{7.4.2}$$

where the expression for the RSS is obtained by simple algebraic manipulations of Eq. (7.4.1).

The most straightforward procedure to obtain the estimators that will minimize Eq. (7.4.2) is to differentiate it with respect to the unknowns, set the resulting expressions to zero, and solve them simultaneously. As shown in Appendix 7A, Section 7A.1, this procedure gives the following *normal equations* [cf. Eqs. (3.1.4) and (3.1.5)]:

$$\bar{Y} = \hat{\beta}_1 + \hat{\beta}_2 \bar{X}_2 + \hat{\beta}_3 \bar{X}_3 \tag{7.4.3}$$

$$\sum Y_i X_{2i} = \hat{\beta}_1 \sum X_{2i} + \hat{\beta}_2 \sum X_{2i}^2 + \hat{\beta}_3 \sum X_{2i} X_{3i} \tag{7.4.4}$$

$$\sum Y_i X_{3i} = \hat{\beta}_1 \sum X_{3i} + \hat{\beta}_2 \sum X_{2i} X_{3i} + \hat{\beta}_3 \sum X_{3i}^2 \tag{7.4.5}$$

From Eq. (7.4.3) we see at once that

$$\hat{\beta}_1 = \bar{Y} - \hat{\beta}_2 \bar{X}_2 - \hat{\beta}_3 \bar{X}_3 \tag{7.4.6}$$

which is the OLS estimator of the population intercept β_1.

Following the convention of letting the lowercase letters denote deviations from sample mean values, one can derive the following formulas from the normal equations (7.4.3) to (7.4.5):

$$\hat{\beta}_2 = \frac{\left(\sum y_i x_{2i}\right)\left(\sum x_{3i}^2\right) - \left(\sum y_i x_{3i}\right)\left(\sum x_{2i} x_{3i}\right)}{\left(\sum x_{2i}^2\right)\left(\sum x_{3i}^2\right) - \left(\sum x_{2i} x_{3i}\right)^2} \tag{7.4.7}$$ [6]

$$\hat{\beta}_3 = \frac{\left(\sum y_i x_{3i}\right)\left(\sum x_{2i}^2\right) - \left(\sum y_i x_{2i}\right)\left(\sum x_{2i} x_{3i}\right)}{\left(\sum x_{2i}^2\right)\left(\sum x_{3i}^2\right) - \left(\sum x_{2i} x_{3i}\right)^2} \tag{7.4.8}$$

which give the OLS estimators of the population partial regression coefficients β_2 and β_3, respectively.

In passing, note the following: (1) Equations (7.4.7) and (7.4.8) are symmetrical in nature because one can be obtained from the other by interchanging the roles of X_2 and X_3; (2) the denominators of these two equations are identical; and (3) the three-variable case is a natural extension of the two-variable case.

[6] This estimator is equal to that of Eq. (7.3.5), as shown in App. 7A, Sec. 7A.2.

Variances and Standard Errors of OLS Estimators

Having obtained the OLS estimators of the partial regression coefficients, we can derive the variances and standard errors of these estimators in the manner indicated in Appendix 3A.3. As in the two-variable case, we need the standard errors for two main purposes: to establish confidence intervals and to test statistical hypotheses. The relevant formulas are as follows:[7]

$$\operatorname{var}(\hat{\beta}_1) = \left[\frac{1}{n} + \frac{\bar{X}_2^2 \sum x_{3i}^2 + \bar{X}_3^2 \sum x_{2i}^2 - 2\bar{X}_2\bar{X}_3 \sum x_{2i}x_{3i}}{\sum x_{2i}^2 \sum x_{3i}^2 - \left(\sum x_{2i}x_{3i}\right)^2}\right] \cdot \sigma^2 \tag{7.4.9}$$

$$\operatorname{se}(\hat{\beta}_1) = +\sqrt{\operatorname{var}(\hat{\beta}_1)} \tag{7.4.10}$$

$$\operatorname{var}(\hat{\beta}_2) = \frac{\sum x_{3i}^2}{\left(\sum x_{2i}^2\right)\left(\sum x_{3i}^2\right) - \left(\sum x_{2i}x_{3i}\right)^2}\sigma^2 \tag{7.4.11}$$

or, equivalently,

$$\operatorname{var}(\hat{\beta}_2) = \frac{\sigma^2}{\sum x_{2i}^2\left(1 - r_{23}^2\right)} \tag{7.4.12}$$

where r_{23} is the sample coefficient of correlation between X_2 and X_3 as defined in Chapter 3.[8]

$$\operatorname{se}(\hat{\beta}_2) = +\sqrt{\operatorname{var}(\hat{\beta}_2)} \tag{7.4.13}$$

$$\operatorname{var}(\hat{\beta}_3) = \frac{\sum x_{2i}^2}{\left(\sum x_{2i}^2\right)\left(\sum x_{3i}^2\right) - \left(\sum x_{2i}x_{3i}\right)^2}\sigma^2 \tag{7.4.14}$$

or, equivalently,

$$\operatorname{var}(\hat{\beta}_3) = \frac{\sigma^2}{\sum x_{3i}^2\left(1 - r_{23}^2\right)} \tag{7.4.15}$$

$$\operatorname{se}(\hat{\beta}_3) = +\sqrt{\operatorname{var}(\hat{\beta}_3)} \tag{7.4.16}$$

$$\operatorname{cov}(\hat{\beta}_2, \hat{\beta}_3) = \frac{-r_{23}\sigma^2}{\left(1 - r_{23}^2\right)\sqrt{\sum x_{2i}^2}\sqrt{\sum x_{3i}^2}} \tag{7.4.17}$$

In all these formulas σ^2 is the (homoscedastic) variance of the population disturbances u_i.

Following the argument of Appendix 3A, Section 3A.5, the reader can verify that an unbiased estimator of σ^2 is given by

$$\hat{\sigma}^2 = \frac{\sum \hat{u}_i^2}{n - 3} \tag{7.4.18}$$

[7]The derivations of these formulas are easier using matrix notation. Advanced readers may refer to **Appendix C.**

[8]Using the definition of r given in Chapter 3, we have

$$r_{23}^2 = \frac{\left(\sum x_{2i}x_{3i}\right)^2}{\sum x_{2i}^2 \sum x_{3i}^2}$$

Note the similarity between this estimator of σ^2 and its two-variable counterpart $[\hat{\sigma}^2 = (\sum \hat{u}_i^2)/(n-2)]$. The degrees of freedom are now $(n-3)$ because in estimating $\sum \hat{u}_i^2$ we must first estimate β_1, β_2, and β_3, which consume 3 df. (The argument is quite general. Thus, in the four-variable case the df will be $n-4$.)

The estimator $\hat{\sigma}^2$ can be computed from Eq. (7.4.18) once the residuals are available, but it can also be obtained more readily by using the following relation (for proof, see Appendix 7A, Section 7A.3):

$$\sum \hat{u}_i^2 = \sum y_i^2 - \hat{\beta}_2 \sum y_i x_{2i} - \hat{\beta}_3 \sum y_i x_{3i} \tag{7.4.19}$$

which is the three-variable counterpart of the relation given in Eq. (3.3.6).

Properties of OLS Estimators

The properties of OLS estimators of the multiple regression model parallel those of the two-variable model. Specifically:

1. The three-variable regression line (surface) passes through the means $\bar{Y}$, $\bar{X}_2$, and $\bar{X}_3$, which is evident from Eq. (7.4.3) (cf. Eq. [3.1.7] of the two-variable model). This property holds generally. Thus in the k-variable linear regression model (a regressand and $[k-1]$ regressors)

$$Y_i = \beta_1 + \beta_2 X_{2i} + \beta_3 X_{3i} + \cdots + \beta_k X_{ki} + u_i \tag{7.4.20}$$

we have

$$\hat{\beta}_1 = \bar{Y} - \beta_2 \bar{X}_2 - \beta_3 \bar{X}_3 - \cdots - \beta_k \bar{X}_k \tag{7.4.21}$$

2. The mean value of the estimated Y_i $(= \hat{Y}_i)$ is equal to the mean value of the actual Y_i, which is easy to prove:

$$\begin{aligned} \hat{Y}_i &= \hat{\beta}_1 + \hat{\beta}_2 X_{2i} + \hat{\beta}_3 X_{3i} \\ &= (\bar{Y} - \hat{\beta}_2 \bar{X}_2 - \hat{\beta}_3 \bar{X}_3) + \hat{\beta}_2 X_{2i} + \hat{\beta}_3 X_{3i} \qquad \text{(Why?)} \\ &= \bar{Y} + \hat{\beta}_2 (X_{2i} - \bar{X}_2) + \hat{\beta}_3 (X_{3i} - \bar{X}_3) \\ &= \bar{Y} + \hat{\beta}_2 x_{2i} + \hat{\beta}_3 x_{3i} \end{aligned} \tag{7.4.22}$$

where as usual small letters indicate values of the variables as deviations from their respective means.

Summing both sides of Eq. (7.4.22) over the sample values and dividing through by the sample size n gives $\bar{\hat{Y}} = \bar{Y}$. (*Note:* $\sum x_{2i} = \sum x_{3i} = 0$. Why?) Notice that by virtue of Eq. (7.4.22) we can write

$$\hat{y}_i = \hat{\beta}_2 x_{2i} + \hat{\beta}_3 x_{3i} \tag{7.4.23}$$

where $\hat{y}_i = (\hat{Y}_i - \bar{Y})$.

Therefore, the SRF (7.4.1) can be expressed in the *deviation form* as

$$y_i = \hat{y}_i + \hat{u}_i = \hat{\beta}_2 x_{2i} + \hat{\beta}_3 x_{3i} + \hat{u}_i \tag{7.4.24}$$

3. $\sum \hat{u}_i = \bar{\hat{u}} = 0$, which can be verified from Eq. (7.4.24). (*Hint:* Sum both sides of Eq. [7.4.24] over the sample values.)

4. The residuals $\hat{u}_i$ are uncorrelated with X_{2i} and X_{3i}, that is, $\sum \hat{u}_i X_{2i} = \sum \hat{u}_i X_{3i} = 0$ (see Appendix 7A.1 for proof).

5. The residuals $\hat{u}_i$ are uncorrelated with $\hat{Y}_i$; that is, $\sum \hat{u}_i \hat{Y}_i = 0$. Why? (*Hint:* Multiply Eq. [7.4.23] on both sides by $\hat{u}_i$ and sum over the sample values.)

6. From Eqs. (7.4.12) and (7.4.15) it is evident that as r_{23}, the correlation coefficient between X_2 and X_3, increases toward 1, the variances of $\hat{\beta}_2$ and $\hat{\beta}_3$ increase for given values of σ^2 and $\sum x_{2i}^2$ or $\sum x_{3i}^2$. In the limit, when $r_{23} = 1$ (i.e., perfect collinearity), these variances become infinite. The implications of this will be explored fully in Chapter 10, but intuitively the reader can see that as r_{23} increases it is going to be increasingly difficult to know what the true values of β_2 and β_3 are. (More on this in the next chapter, but refer to Eq. [7.1.13].)

7. It is also clear from Eqs. (7.4.12) and (7.4.15) that for given values of r_{23} and $\sum x_{2i}^2$ or $\sum x_{3i}^2$, the variances of the OLS estimators are directly proportional to σ^2; that is, they increase as σ^2 increases. Similarly, for given values of σ^2 and r_{23}, the variance of $\hat{\beta}_2$ is inversely proportional to $\sum x_{2i}^2$; that is, the greater the variation in the sample values of X_2, the smaller the variance of $\hat{\beta}_2$ and therefore β_2 can be estimated more precisely. A similar statement can be made about the variance of $\hat{\beta}_3$.

8. Given the assumptions of the classical linear regression model, which are spelled out in Section 7.1, one can prove that the OLS estimators of the partial regression coefficients not only are linear and unbiased but also have minimum variance in the class of all linear unbiased estimators. In short, *they are BLUE.* Put differently, they satisfy the Gauss–Markov theorem. (The proof parallels the two-variable case proved in Appendix 3A, Section 3A.6 and will be presented more compactly using matrix notation in **Appendix C.**)

Maximum Likelihood Estimators

We noted in Chapter 4 that under the assumption that u_i, the population disturbances, are normally distributed with zero mean and constant variance σ^2, the maximum likelihood (ML) estimators and the OLS estimators of the regression coefficients of the two-variable model are identical. This equality extends to models containing any number of variables. (For proof, see Appendix 7A, Section 7A.4.) However, this is not true of the estimator of σ^2. It can be shown that the ML estimator of σ^2 is $\sum \hat{u}_i^2/n$ regardless of the number of variables in the model, whereas the OLS estimator of σ^2 is $\sum \hat{u}_i^2/(n-2)$ in the two-variable case, $\sum \hat{u}_i^2/(n-3)$ in the three-variable case, and $\sum \hat{u}_i^2/(n-k)$ in the case of the k-variable model (7.4.20). In short, the OLS estimator of σ^2 takes into account the number of degrees of freedom, whereas the ML estimator does not. Of course, if n is very large, the ML and OLS estimators of σ^2 will tend to be close to each other. (Why?)

7.5 The Multiple Coefficient of Determination R^2 and the Multiple Coefficient of Correlation R

In the two-variable case we saw that r^2 as defined in Eq. (3.5.5) measures the goodness of fit of the regression equation; that is, it gives the proportion or percentage of the total variation in the dependent variable Y explained by the (single) explanatory variable X. This notation of r^2 can be easily extended to regression models containing more than two variables. Thus, in the three-variable model we would like to know the proportion of the variation in Y explained by the variables X_2 and X_3 jointly. The quantity that gives this information is known as the **multiple coefficient of determination** and is denoted by R^2; conceptually it is akin to r^2.

To derive R^2, we may follow the derivation of r^2 given in Section 3.5. Recall that

$$\begin{aligned} Y_i &= \hat{\beta}_1 + \hat{\beta}_2 X_{2i} + \hat{\beta}_3 X_{3i} + \hat{u}_i \\ &= \hat{Y}_i + \hat{u}_i \end{aligned} \tag{7.5.1}$$

where $\hat{Y}_i$ is the estimated value of Y_i from the fitted regression line and is an estimator of true $E(Y_i \mid X_{2i}, X_{3i})$. Upon shifting to lowercase letters to indicate deviations from the mean values, Eq. (7.5.1) may be written as

$$\begin{aligned} y_i &= \hat{\beta}_2 x_{2i} + \hat{\beta}_3 x_{3i} + \hat{u}_i \\ &= \hat{y}_i + \hat{u}_i \end{aligned} \tag{7.5.2}$$

Squaring Eq. (7.5.2) on both sides and summing over the sample values, we obtain

$$\begin{aligned} \sum y_i^2 &= \sum \hat{y}_i^2 + \sum \hat{u}_i^2 + 2 \sum \hat{y}_i \hat{u}_i \\ &= \sum \hat{y}_i^2 + \sum \hat{u}_i^2 \qquad \text{(Why?)} \end{aligned} \tag{7.5.3}$$

Verbally, Eq. (7.5.3) states that the total sum of squares (TSS) equals the explained sum of squares (ESS) plus the residual sum of squares (RSS). Now substituting for $\sum \hat{u}_i^2$ from Eq. (7.4.19), we obtain

$$\sum y_i^2 = \sum \hat{y}_i^2 + \sum y_i^2 - \hat{\beta}_2 \sum y_i x_{2i} - \hat{\beta}_3 \sum y_i x_{3i}$$

which, on rearranging, gives

$$\text{ESS} = \sum \hat{y}_i^2 = \hat{\beta}_2 \sum y_i x_{2i} + \hat{\beta}_3 \sum y_i x_{3i} \tag{7.5.4}$$

Now, by definition

$$\begin{aligned} R^2 &= \frac{\text{ESS}}{\text{TSS}} \\ &= \frac{\hat{\beta}_2 \sum y_i x_{2i} + \hat{\beta}_3 \sum y_i x_{3i}}{\sum y_i^2} \end{aligned} \tag{7.5.5}$$[9]

(cf. Eq. [7.5.5] with Eq. [3.5.6]).

Since the quantities entering Eq. (7.5.5) are generally computed routinely, R^2 can be computed easily. Note that R^2, like r^2, lies between 0 and 1. If it is 1, the fitted regression line explains 100 percent of the variation in Y. On the other hand, if it is 0, the model does not explain any of the variation in Y. Typically, however, R^2 lies between these extreme values. The fit of the model is said to be "better" the closer R^2 is to 1.

[9]Note that R^2 can also be computed as follows:

$$R^2 = 1 - \frac{\text{RSS}}{\text{TSS}} = 1 - \frac{\sum \hat{u}_i^2}{\sum y_i^2} = 1 - \frac{(n-3)\hat{\sigma}^2}{(n-1)S_y^2}$$

Recall that in the two-variable case we defined the quantity r as the coefficient of correlation and indicated that it measures the degree of (linear) association between two variables. The three-or-more-variable analogue of r is the coefficient of **multiple correlation,** denoted by R, and it is a measure of the degree of association between Y and all the explanatory variables jointly. Although r can be positive or negative, R is always taken to be positive. In practice, however, R is of little importance. The more meaningful quantity is R^2.

Before proceeding further, let us note the following relationship between R^2 and the variance of a partial regression coefficient in the k-variable multiple regression model given in Eq. (7.4.20):

$$\operatorname{var}(\hat{\beta}_j) = \frac{\sigma^2}{\sum x_j^2}\left(\frac{1}{1 - R_j^2}\right) \tag{7.5.6}$$

where $\hat{\beta}_j$ is the partial regression coefficient of regressor X_j and R_j^2 is the R^2 in the regression of X_j on the remaining $(k - 2)$ regressors. (*Note:* There are $[k - 1]$ regressors in the k-variable regression model.) Although the utility of Eq. (7.5.6) will become apparent in Chapter 10 on multicollinearity, observe that this equation is simply an extension of the formula given in Eq. (7.4.12) or Eq. (7.4.15) for the three-variable regression model, one regressand and two regressors.

7.6 An Illustrative Example

EXAMPLE 7.1

Child Mortality in Relation to per Capita GNP and Female Literacy Rate

In Chapter 6 we considered the behavior of child mortality (CM) in relation to per capita GNP (PGNP). There we found that PGNP has a negative impact on CM, as one would expect. Now let us bring in female literacy as measured by the female literacy rate (FLR). A priori, we expect that FLR too will have a negative impact on CM. Now when we introduce both the variables in our model, we need to net out the influence of each of the regressors. That is, we need to estimate the (partial) regression coefficients of each regressor. Thus our model is:

$$\text{CM}_i = \beta_1 + \beta_2\text{PGNP}_i + \beta_3\text{FLR}_i + u_i \tag{7.6.1}$$

The necessary data are given in Table 6.4. Keep in mind that CM is the number of deaths of children under five per 1000 live births, PGNP is per capita GNP in 1980, and FLR is measured in percent. Our sample consists of 64 countries.

Using the *EViews6* statistical package, we obtained the following results:

$$\begin{aligned}\widehat{\text{CM}}_i &= 263.6416 \quad - \quad 0.0056\ \text{PGNP}_i - \quad 2.2316\ \text{FLR}_i \\ \text{se} &= (11.5932) \quad (0.0019) \qquad\quad (0.2099) \qquad R^2 = 0.7077 \\ &\qquad\qquad\qquad\qquad\qquad\qquad\qquad\qquad\quad \bar{R}^2 = 0.6981^*\end{aligned} \tag{7.6.2}$$

where figures in parentheses are the estimated standard errors. Before we interpret this regression, observe the partial slope coefficient of PGNP, namely, −0.0056. Is it not precisely the same as that obtained from the three-step procedure discussed in the previous section (see Eq. [7.3.5])? But should that surprise you? Not only that, but the two standard errors are precisely the same, which is again unsurprising. But we did so without the three-step cumbersome procedure.

*On this, see Section 7.8.

EXAMPLE 7.1 *(Continued)*

Let us now interpret these regression coefficients: −0.0056 is the partial regression coefficient of PGNP and tells us that with the influence of FLR held constant, as PGNP increases, say, by a dollar, on average, child mortality goes down by 0.0056 units. To make it more economically interpretable, if the per capita GNP goes up by a thousand dollars, on average, the number of deaths of children under age 5 goes down by about 5.6 per thousand live births. The coefficient −2.2316 tells us that holding the influence of PGNP constant, on average, the number of deaths of children under age 5 goes down by about 2.23 per thousand live births as the female literacy rate increases by one percentage point. The intercept value of about 263, mechanically interpreted, means that if the values of PGNP and FLR rate were fixed at zero, the mean child mortality rate would be about 263 deaths per thousand live births. Of course, such an interpretation should be taken with a grain of salt. All one could infer is that if the two regressors were fixed at zero, child mortality will be quite high, which makes practical sense. The R^2 value of about 0.71 means that about 71 percent of the variation in child mortality is explained by PGNP and FLR, a fairly high value considering that the maximum value of R^2 can at most be 1. All told, the regression results make sense.

What about the statistical significance of the estimated coefficients? We will take this topic up in Chapter 8. As we will see there, in many ways this chapter will be an extension of Chapter 5, which dealt with the two-variable model. As we will also show, there are some important differences in statistical inference (i.e., hypothesis testing) between the two-variable and multivariable regression models.

Regression on Standardized Variables

In the preceding chapter we introduced the topic of regression on standardized variables and stated that the analysis can be extended to multivariable regressions. Recall that a variable is said to be standardized or in standard deviation units if it is expressed in terms of deviation from its mean and divided by its standard deviation.

For our child mortality example, the results are as follows:

$$\begin{aligned} \widehat{\text{CM}}^* &= -\ 0.2026\ \text{PGNP}_i^* - 0.7639\ \text{FLR}_i^* \\ \text{se} &= \quad (0.0713) \qquad\qquad (0.0713) \qquad r^2 = 0.7077 \end{aligned} \tag{7.6.3}$$

Note: The starred variables are standardized variables. Also note that there is no intercept in the model for reasons already discussed in the previous chapter.

As you can see from this regression, with FLR held constant, a standard deviation increase in PGNP leads, on average, to a 0.2026 standard deviation decrease in CM. Similarly, holding PGNP constant, a standard deviation increase in FLR, on average, leads to a 0.7639 standard deviation decrease in CM. Relatively speaking, female literacy has more impact on child mortality than per capita GNP. Here you will see the advantage of using standardized variables, for standardization puts all variables on equal footing because all standardized variables have zero means and unit variances.

Impact on the Dependent Variable of a Unit Change in More than One Regressor

Before proceeding further, suppose we want to find out what would happen to the child mortality rate if we were to increase PGNP and FLR simultaneously. Suppose per capita GNP were to increase by a dollar and at the same time the female literacy rate were to go up by one percentage point. What would be the impact of this simultaneous change on the child mortality rate? To find out, all we have to do is multiply the coefficients of PGNP and FLR by the proposed changes and add the resulting terms. In our example this gives us:

$$-0.0056(1) - 2.2316(1) = 2.2372$$

That is, as a result of this simultaneous change in PGNP and FLR, the number of deaths of children under age 5 would go down by about 2.24 deaths.

More generally, if we want to find out the total impact on the dependent variable of a unit change in more than one regressor, all we have to do is multiply the coefficients of those regressors by the proposed changes and add up the products. Note that the intercept term does not enter into these calculations. (Why?)

7.7 Simple Regression in the Context of Multiple Regression: Introduction to Specification Bias

Recall that assumption (7.1.10) of the classical linear regression model states that the regression model used in the analysis is "correctly" specified; that is, there is no **specification bias or specification error** (see Chapter 3 for some introductory remarks). Although the topic of specification error will be discussed more fully in Chapter 13, the illustrative example given in the preceding section provides a splendid opportunity not only to drive home the importance of assumption (7.1.10) but also to shed additional light on the meaning of partial regression coefficient and provide a somewhat informal introduction to the topic of specification bias.

Assume that Eq. (7.6.1) is the "true" model explaining the behavior of child mortality in relation to per capita GNP and female literacy rate (FLR). But suppose we disregard FLR and estimate the following simple regression:

$$Y_i = \alpha_1 + \alpha_2 X_{2i} + u_{1i} \tag{7.7.1}$$

where $Y =$ CM and $X_2 =$ PGNP.

Since Eq. (7.6.1) is the true model, estimating Eq. (7.7.1) would constitute a specification error; the error here consists in *omitting* the variable X_3, the female literacy rate. Notice that we are using different parameter symbols (the alphas) in Eq. (7.7.1) to distinguish them from the true parameters (the betas) given in Eq. (7.6.1).

Now will α_2 provide an unbiased estimate of the true impact of PGNP, which is given by β_2 in model (7.6.1)? Will $E(\hat{\alpha}_2) = \beta_2$, where $\hat{\alpha}_2$ is the estimated value of α_2? In other words, will the coefficient of PGNP in Eq. (7.7.1) provide an unbiased estimate of the true impact of PGNP on CM, knowing that we have omitted the variable X_3 (FLR) from the model? As you would suspect, *in general,* $\hat{\alpha}_2$ will not be an unbiased estimator of the true β_2. To give a glimpse of the bias, let us run the regression (7.7.1), which gave the following results.

$$\begin{aligned} \widehat{\text{CM}}_i &= 157.4244 \quad - \quad 0.0114\ \text{PGNP}_i \\ \text{se} &= \quad (9.8455) \qquad\quad (0.0032) \qquad r^2 = 0.1662 \end{aligned} \tag{7.7.2}$$

Observe several things about this regression compared to the "true" multiple regression (7.6.1):

1. In absolute terms (i.e., disregarding the sign), the PGNP coefficient has increased from 0.0056 to 0.0114, almost a two-fold increase.

2. The standard errors are different.
3. The intercept values are different.
4. The r^2 values are dramatically different, although it is generally the case that, as the number of regressors in the model increases, the r^2 value increases.

Now suppose that you regress child mortality on female literacy rate, disregarding the influence of PGNP. You will obtain the following results:

$$\begin{aligned} \widehat{\text{CM}}_i &= 263.8635 \quad - \quad 2.3905\ \text{FLR}_i \\ \text{se} &= (21.2249) \quad (0.2133) \qquad\qquad r^2 = 0.6696 \end{aligned} \tag{7.7.3}$$

Again if you compare the results of this (misspecified) regression with the "true" multiple regression, you will see that the results are different, although the difference here is not as noticeable as in the case of regression (7.7.2).

The important point to note is that serious consequences can ensue if you misfit a model. We will look into this topic more thoroughly in Chapter 13, on specification errors.

7.8 R^2 and the Adjusted R^2

An important property of R^2 is that it is a nondecreasing function of the number of explanatory variables or regressors present in the model, unless the added variable is perfectly collinear with the other regressors; as the number of regressors increases, R^2 almost invariably increases and never decreases. Stated differently, an additional X variable will not decrease R^2. Compare, for instance, regression (7.7.2) or (7.7.3) with (7.6.2). To see this, recall the definition of the coefficient of determination:

$$\begin{aligned} R^2 &= \frac{\text{ESS}}{\text{TSS}} \\ &= 1 - \frac{\text{RSS}}{\text{TSS}} \\ &= 1 - \frac{\sum \hat{u}_i^2}{\sum y_i^2} \end{aligned} \tag{7.8.1}$$

Now $\sum y_i^2$ is independent of the number of X variables in the model because it is simply $\sum (Y_i - \bar{Y})^2$. The RSS, $\sum \hat{u}_i^2$, however, depends on the number of regressors present in the model. Intuitively, it is clear that as the number of X variables increases, $\sum \hat{u}_i^2$ is likely to decrease (at least it will not increase); hence R^2 as defined in Eq. (7.8.1) will increase. In view of this, in comparing two regression models with the *same dependent variable* but differing number of X variables, one should be very wary of choosing the model with the highest R^2.

To compare two R^2 terms, one must take into account the number of X variables present in the model. This can be done readily if we consider an alternative coefficient of determination, which is as follows:

$$\bar{R}^2 = 1 - \frac{\sum \hat{u}_i^2/(n-k)}{\sum y_i^2/(n-1)} \tag{7.8.2}$$

where $k =$ the number of parameters in the model *including the intercept term*. (In the three-variable regression, $k = 3$. Why?) The R^2 thus defined is known as the **adjusted R^2**, denoted by $\bar{R}^2$. The term *adjusted* means adjusted for the df associated with the sums of squares entering into Eq. (7.8.1): $\sum \hat{u}_i^2$ has $n - k$ df in a model involving k parameters, which include the intercept term, and $\sum y_i^2$ has $n - 1$ df. (Why?) For the three-variable case, we know that $\sum \hat{u}_i^2$ has $n - 3$ df.

Equation (7.8.2) can also be written as

$$\bar{R}^2 = 1 - \frac{\hat{\sigma}^2}{S_Y^2} \tag{7.8.3}$$

where $\hat{\sigma}^2$ is the residual variance, an unbiased estimator of true σ^2, and S_Y^2 is the sample variance of Y.

It is easy to see that $\bar{R}^2$ and R^2 are related because, substituting Eq. (7.8.1) into Eq. (7.8.2), we obtain

$$\bar{R}^2 = 1 - (1 - R^2)\frac{n-1}{n-k} \tag{7.8.4}$$

It is immediately apparent from Eq. (7.8.4) that (1) for $k > 1$, $\bar{R}^2 < R^2$ which implies that as the number of X variables increases, the adjusted R^2 increases less than the unadjusted R^2; and (2) $\bar{R}^2$ can be negative, although R^2 is necessarily nonnegative.[10] In case $\bar{R}^2$ turns out to be negative in an application, its value is taken as zero.

Which R^2 should one use in practice? As Theil notes:

> . . . it is good practice to use $\bar{R}^2$ rather than R^2 because R^2 tends to give an overly optimistic picture of the fit of the regression, particularly when the number of explanatory variables is not very small compared with the number of observations.[11]

But Theil's view is not uniformly shared, for he has offered no general theoretical justification for the "superiority" of $\bar{R}^2$. For example, Goldberger argues that the following R^2, call it **modified** R^2, will do just as well:[12]

$$\text{Modified } R^2 = (1 - k/n)R^2 \tag{7.8.5}$$

His advice is to report R^2, n, and k and let the reader decide how to adjust R^2 by allowing for n and k.

[10] Note, however, that if $R^2 = 1$, $\bar{R}^2 = R^2 = 1$. When $R^2 = 0$, $\bar{R}^2 = (1 - k)/(n - k)$, in which case $\bar{R}^2$ can be negative if $k > 1$.

[11] Henri Theil, *Introduction to Econometrics*, Prentice Hall, Englewood Cliffs, NJ, 1978, p. 135.

[12] Arthur S. Goldberger, *A Course in Econometrics*, Harvard University Press, Cambridge, Mass., 1991, p. 178. For a more critical view of R^2, see S. Cameron, "Why Is the R Squared Adjusted Reported?" *Journal of Quantitative Economics*, vol. 9, no. 1, January 1993, pp. 183–186. He argues that "It [R^2] is NOT a test statistic and there seems to be no clear intuitive justification for its use as a descriptive statistic. Finally, we should be clear that it is not an effective tool for the prevention of data mining" (p. 186).

Despite this advice, it is the adjusted R^2, as given in Eq. (7.8.4), that is reported by most statistical packages along with the conventional R^2. The reader is well advised to treat $\bar{R}^2$ as just another summary statistic.

Incidentally, for the child mortality regression (7.6.2), the reader should verify that $\bar{R}^2$ is 0.6981, keeping in mind that in this example $(n - 1) = 63$ and $(n - k) = 60$. As expected, $\bar{R}^2$ of 0.6981 is less than R^2 of 0.7077.

Besides R^2 and adjusted R^2 as goodness of fit measures, other criteria are often used to judge the adequacy of a regression model. Two of these are **Akaike's Information criterion** and **Amemiya's Prediction criteria,** which are used to select between competing models. We will discuss these criteria when we consider the problem of model selection in greater detail in a later chapter (see Chapter 13).

Comparing Two R^2 Values

It is crucial to note that in comparing two models on the basis of the coefficient of determination, whether adjusted or not, *the sample size n and the dependent variable must be the same;* the explanatory variables may take any form. Thus for the models

$$\ln Y_i = \beta_1 + \beta_2 X_{2i} + \beta_3 X_{3i} + u_i \tag{7.8.6}$$

$$Y_i = \alpha_1 + \alpha_2 X_{2i} + \alpha_3 X_{3i} + u_i \tag{7.8.7}$$

the computed R^2 terms cannot be compared. The reason is as follows: By definition, R^2 measures the proportion of the variation in the dependent variable accounted for by the explanatory variable(s). Therefore, in Eq. (7.8.6) R^2 measures the proportion of the *variation in* $\ln Y$ explained by X_2 and X_3, whereas in Eq. (7.8.7) it measures the proportion of the *variation in* Y, and the two are not the same thing: As noted in Chapter 6, a change in $\ln Y$ gives a relative or proportional change in Y, whereas a change in Y gives an absolute change. Therefore, $\text{var}\,\hat{Y}_i/\text{var}\,Y_i$ is not equal to $\text{var}\,(\widehat{\ln Y_i})/\text{var}\,(\ln Y_i)$; that is, the two coefficients of determination are not the same.[13]

How then does one compare the R^2's of two models when the regressand is not in the same form? To answer this question, let us first consider a numerical example.

[13]From the definition of R^2, we know that

$$1 - R^2 = \frac{\text{RSS}}{\text{TSS}} = \frac{\sum \hat{u}_i^2}{\sum (Y_i - \bar{Y})^2}$$

for the linear model and

$$1 - R^2 = \frac{\sum \hat{u}_i^2}{\sum (\ln Y_i - \overline{\ln Y})^2}$$

for the log model. Since the denominators on the right-hand sides of these expressions are different, we cannot compare the two R^2 terms directly.

As shown in Example 7.2, for the linear specification, the RSS = 0.1491 (the residual sum of squares of coffee consumption), and for the log–linear specification, the RSS = 0.0226 (the residual sum of squares of log of coffee consumption). These residuals are of different orders of magnitude and hence are not directly comparable.

EXAMPLE 7.2
Coffee Consumption in the United States, 1970–1980

Consider the data in Table 7.1. The data pertain to consumption of cups of coffee per day (Y) and real retail price of coffee (X) in the United States for years 1970–1980. Applying OLS to the data, we obtain the following regression results:

$$\hat{Y}_t = 2.6911 - 0.4795X_t$$
$$\text{se} = (0.1216) \quad (0.1140) \qquad \text{RSS} = 0.1491;\ r^2 = 0.6628 \tag{7.8.8}$$

The results make economic sense: As the price of coffee increases, on average, coffee consumption goes down by about half a cup per day. The r^2 value of about 0.66 means that the price of coffee explains about 66 percent of the variation in coffee consumption. The reader can readily verify that the slope coefficient is statistically significant.

From the same data, the following double-log, or constant elasticity, model can be estimated:

$$\widehat{\ln Y_t} = 0.7774 - 0.2530 \ln X_t$$
$$\text{se} = (0.0152) \quad (0.0494) \qquad \text{RSS} = 0.0226;\ r^2 = 0.7448 \tag{7.8.9}$$

Since this is a double-log model, the slope coefficient gives a direct estimate of the price elasticity coefficient. In the present instance, it tells us that if the price of coffee per pound goes up by 1 percent, on average, per day coffee consumption goes down by about 0.25 percent. Remember that in the linear model (7.8.8) the slope coefficient only gives the rate of change of coffee consumption with respect to price. (How will you estimate the price elasticity for the linear model?) The r^2 value of about 0.74 means that about 74 percent of the variation in the log of coffee demand is explained by the variation in the log of coffee price.

Since the r^2 value of the linear model of 0.6628 is smaller than the r^2 value of 0.7448 of the log–linear model, you might be tempted to choose the latter model because of its

TABLE 7.1
U.S. Coffee Consumption (Y) in Relation to Average Real Retail Price (X),* 1970–1980

Year	Y, Cups per Person per Day	X, \$ per lb
1970	2.57	0.77
1971	2.50	0.74
1972	2.35	0.72
1973	2.30	0.73
1974	2.25	0.76
1975	2.20	0.75
1976	2.11	1.08
1977	1.94	1.81
1978	1.97	1.39
1979	2.06	1.20
1980	2.02	1.17

*Note: The nominal price was divided by the Consumer Price Index (CPI) for food and beverages, 1967 = 100.

Source: The data for Y are from *Summary of National Coffee Drinking Study*, Data Group, Elkins Park, Penn., 1981; and the data on nominal X (i.e., X in current prices) are from *Nielsen Food Index*, A. C. Nielsen, New York, 1981.

I am indebted to Scott E. Sandberg for collecting the data.

EXAMPLE 7.2 *(Continued)*

high r^2 value. But for reasons already noted, we cannot do so. But if you do want to compare the two r^2 values, you may proceed as follows:

1. Obtain $\widehat{\ln Y_t}$ from Eq. (7.8.9) for each observation; that is, obtain the estimated log value of each observation from this model. Take the antilog of these values and then compute r^2 between these antilog values and actual Y_t in the manner indicated by Eq. (3.5.14). This r^2 value is comparable to the r^2 value of the linear model (7.8.8).
2. *Alternatively,* assuming all Y values are positive, take logarithms of the Y values, ln Y. Obtain the estimated Y values, $\hat{Y}_t$, from the linear model (7.8.8), take the logarithms of these estimated Y values (i.e., ln $\hat{Y}_t$), and compute the r^2 between (ln Y_t) and (ln $\hat{Y}_t$) in the manner indicated in Eq. (3.5.14). This r^2 value is comparable to the r^2 value obtained from Eq. (7.8.9).

For our coffee example, we present the necessary raw data to compute the comparable r^2's in Table 7.2. To compare the r^2 value of the linear model (7.8.8) with that of (7.8.9), we first obtain log of ($\hat{Y}_t$) (given in column [6] of Table 7.2), then we obtain the log of actual Y values (given in column [5] of the table), and then compute r^2 between these two sets of values using Eq. (3.5.14). The result is an r^2 value of 0.6779, which is now comparable with the r^2 value of the log–linear model of 0.7448. The difference between the two r^2 values is about 0.07.

On the other hand, if we want to compare the r^2 value of the log–linear model with the linear model, we obtain $\widehat{\ln Y_t}$ for each observation from Eq. (7.8.9) (given in column [3] of the table), obtain their antilog values (given in column [4] of the table), and finally compute r^2 between these antilog values and the actual Y values, using formula (3.5.14). This will give an r^2 value of 0.7187, which is slightly higher than that obtained from the linear model (7.8.8), namely, 0.6628.

Using either method, it seems that the log–linear model gives a slightly better fit.

TABLE 7.2
Raw Data for Comparing Two R^2 Values

Year	Y_t (1)	$\hat{Y}_t$ (2)	$\widehat{\ln Y_t}$ (3)	Antilog of $\widehat{\ln Y_t}$ (4)	ln Y_t (5)	ln ($\hat{Y}_t$) (6)
1970	2.57	2.321887	0.843555	2.324616	0.943906	0.842380
1971	2.50	2.336272	0.853611	2.348111	0.916291	0.848557
1972	2.35	2.345863	0.860544	2.364447	0.854415	0.852653
1973	2.30	2.341068	0.857054	2.356209	0.832909	0.850607
1974	2.25	2.326682	0.846863	2.332318	0.810930	0.844443
1975	2.20	2.331477	0.850214	2.340149	0.788457	0.846502
1976	2.11	2.173233	0.757943	2.133882	0.746688	0.776216
1977	1.94	1.823176	0.627279	1.872508	0.662688	0.600580
1978	1.97	2.024579	0.694089	2.001884	0.678034	0.705362
1979	2.06	2.115689	0.731282	2.077742	0.722706	0.749381
1980	2.02	2.130075	0.737688	2.091096	0.703098	0.756157

Notes: Column (1): Actual Y values from Table 7.1.
Column (2): Estimated Y values from the linear model (7.8.8).
Column (3): Estimated log Y values from the double-log model (7.8.9).
Column (4): Antilog of values in column (3).
Column (5): Log values of Y in column (1).
Column (6): Log values of $\hat{Y}_t$ in column (2).

Allocating R^2 among Regressors

Let us return to our child mortality example. We saw in Eq. (7.6.2) that the two regressors PGNP and FLR explain 0.7077 or 70.77 percent of the variation in child mortality. But now consider the regression (7.7.2) where we dropped the FLR variable and as a result the r^2 value dropped to 0.1662. Does that mean the difference in the r^2 value of 0.5415 (0.7077 − 0.1662) is attributable to the dropped variable FLR? On the other hand, if you consider regression (7.7.3), where we dropped the PGNP variable, the r^2 value drops to 0.6696. Does that mean the difference in the r^2 value of 0.0381 (0.7077 − 0.6696) is due to the omitted variable PGNP?

The question then is: Can we allocate the multiple R^2 of 0.7077 between the two regressors, PGNP and FLR, in this manner? Unfortunately, we cannot do so, for the allocation depends on the order in which the regressors are introduced, as we just illustrated. Part of the problem here is that the two regressors are correlated, the correlation coefficient between the two being 0.2685 (verify it from the data given in Table 6.4). In most applied work with several regressors, correlation among them is a common problem. Of course, the problem will be very serious if there is perfect collinearity among the regressors.

The best practical advice is that there is little point in trying to allocate the R^2 value to its constituent regressors.

The "Game" of Maximizing $\bar{R}^2$

In concluding this section, a warning is in order: Sometimes researchers play the game of maximizing $\bar{R}^2$, that is, choosing the model that gives the highest $\bar{R}^2$. But this may be dangerous, for in regression analysis our objective is not to obtain a high $\bar{R}^2$ per se but rather to obtain dependable estimates of the true population regression coefficients and draw statistical inferences about them. In empirical analysis it is not unusual to obtain a very high $\bar{R}^2$ but find that some of the regression coefficients either are statistically insignificant or have signs that are contrary to a priori expectations. Therefore, the researcher should be more concerned about the logical or theoretical relevance of the explanatory variables to the dependent variable and their statistical significance. If in this process we obtain a high $\bar{R}^2$, well and good; on the other hand, if $\bar{R}^2$ is low, it does not mean the model is necessarily bad.[14]

As a matter of fact, Goldberger is very critical about the role of R^2. He has said:

> From our perspective, R^2 has a very modest role in regression analysis, being a measure of the goodness of fit of a sample LS [least-squares] linear regression in a body of data. Nothing in the CR [CLRM] model requires that R^2 be high. Hence a high R^2 is not evidence in favor of the model and a low R^2 is not evidence against it.
>
> In fact the most important thing about R^2 is that it is not important in the CR model. The CR model is concerned with parameters in a population, not with goodness of fit in the

[14]Some authors would like to deemphasize the use of R^2 as a measure of goodness of fit as well as its use for comparing two or more R^2 values. See Christopher H. Achen, *Interpreting and Using Regression,* Sage Publications, Beverly Hills, Calif., 1982, pp. 58–67, and C. Granger and P. Newbold, "R^2 and the Transformation of Regression Variables," *Journal of Econometrics,* vol. 4, 1976, pp. 205–210. Incidentally, the practice of choosing a model on the basis of highest R^2, a kind of data mining, introduces what is known as **pretest bias,** which might destroy some of the properties of OLS estimators of the classical linear regression model. On this topic, the reader may want to consult George G. Judge, Carter R. Hill, William E. Griffiths, Helmut Lütkepohl, and Tsoung-Chao Lee, *Introduction to the Theory and Practice of Econometrics,* John Wiley, New York, 1982, Chapter 21.

sample. . . . If one insists on a measure of predictive success (or rather failure), then σ^2 might suffice: after all, the parameter σ^2 is the expected squared forecast error that would result if the population CEF [PRF] were used as the predictor. Alternatively, the squared standard error of forecast . . . at relevant values of x [regressors] may be informative.[15]

7.9 The Cobb–Douglas Production Function: More on Functional Form

In Section 6.4 we showed how with appropriate transformations we can convert nonlinear relationships into linear ones so that we can work within the framework of the classical linear regression model. The various transformations discussed there in the context of the two-variable case can be easily extended to multiple regression models. We demonstrate transformations in this section by taking up the multivariable extension of the two-variable log–linear model; others can be found in the exercises and in the illustrative examples discussed throughout the rest of this book. The specific example we discuss is the celebrated **Cobb–Douglas production function** of production theory.

The Cobb–Douglas production function, in its stochastic form, may be expressed as

$$Y_i = \beta_1 X_{2i}^{\beta_2} X_{3i}^{\beta_3} e^{u_i} \tag{7.9.1}$$

where $Y =$ output
$X_2 =$ labor input
$X_3 =$ capital input
$u =$ stochastic disturbance term
$e =$ base of natural logarithm

From Eq. (7.9.1) it is clear that the relationship between output and the two inputs is nonlinear. However, if we log-transform this model, we obtain:

$$\begin{aligned} \ln Y_i &= \ln \beta_1 + \beta_2 \ln X_{2i} + \beta_3 \ln X_{3i} + u_i \\ &= \beta_0 + \beta_2 \ln X_{2i} + \beta_3 \ln X_{3i} + u_i \end{aligned} \tag{7.9.2}$$

where $\beta_0 = \ln \beta_1$.

Thus written, the model is linear in the parameters β_0, β_2, and β_3 and is therefore a linear regression model. Notice, though, it is nonlinear in the variables Y and X but linear in the logs of these variables. In short, Eq. (7.9.2) is a *log-log, double-log,* or *log–linear model,* the multiple regression counterpart of the two-variable log–linear model (6.5.3).

The properties of the Cobb–Douglas production function are quite well known:

1. β_2 is the (partial) elasticity of output with respect to the labor input, that is, it measures the percentage change in output for, say, a 1 percent change in the labor input, holding the capital input constant (see Exercise 7.9).

2. Likewise, β_3 is the (partial) elasticity of output with respect to the capital input, holding the labor input constant.

3. The sum $(\beta_2 + \beta_3)$ gives information about the *returns to scale,* that is, the response of output to a proportionate change in the inputs. If this sum is 1, then there are *constant returns to scale,* that is, doubling the inputs will double the output, tripling the inputs will

[15]Arther S. Goldberger, op. cit., pp. 177–178.

triple the output, and so on. If the sum is less than 1, there are *decreasing returns to scale*—doubling the inputs will less than double the output. Finally, if the sum is greater than 1, there are *increasing returns to scale*—doubling the inputs will more than double the output.

Before proceeding further, note that whenever you have a log–linear regression model involving any number of variables the coefficient of each of the X variables measures the (partial) elasticity of the dependent variable Y with respect to that variable. Thus, if you have a k-variable log–linear model:

$$\ln Y_i = \beta_0 + \beta_2 \ln X_{2i} + \beta_3 \ln X_{3i} + \cdots + \beta_k \ln X_{ki} + u_i \tag{7.9.3}$$

each of the (partial) regression coefficients, β_2 through β_k, is the (partial) elasticity of Y with respect to variables X_2 through X_k.[16]

EXAMPLE 7.3

Value Added, Labor Hours, and Capital Input in the Manufacturing Sector

To illustrate the Cobb–Douglas production function, we obtained the data shown in Table 7.3; these data are for the manufacturing sector of all 50 states and Washington, DC, for 2005.

Assuming that the model (7.9.2) satisfies the assumptions of the classical linear regression model,[17] we obtained the following regression by the OLS method (see Appendix 7A, Section 7A.5 for the computer printout):

TABLE 7.3
Value Added, Labor Hours, and Capital Input in the Manufacturing Sector of the U.S., 2005

Source: *2005 Annual Survey of Manufacturers*, Sector 31: Supplemental Statistics for U.S.

Area	Output Value Added (thousands of $) Y	Labor Input Worker Hrs (thousands) X2	Capital Input Capital Expenditure (thousands of $) X3
Alabama	38,372,840	424,471	2,689,076
Alaska	1,805,427	19,895	57,997
Arizona	23,736,129	206,893	2,308,272
Arkansas	26,981,983	304,055	1,376,235
California	217,546,032	1,809,756	13,554,116
Colorado	19,462,751	180,366	1,790,751
Connecticut	28,972,772	224,267	1,210,229
Delaware	14,313,157	54,455	421,064
District of Columbia	159,921	2,029	7,188
Florida	47,289,846	471,211	2,761,281
Georgia	63,015,125	659,379	3,540,475
Hawaii	1,809,052	17,528	146,371
Idaho	10,511,786	75,414	848,220
Illinois	105,324,866	963,156	5,870,409
Indiana	90,120,459	835,083	5,832,503
Iowa	39,079,550	336,159	1,795,976
Kansas	22,826,760	246,144	1,595,118
Kentucky	38,686,340	384,484	2,503,693
Louisiana	69,910,555	216,149	4,726,625

[16]To see this, differentiate Eq. (7.9.3) partially with respect to the log of each X variable. Therefore, $\partial \ln Y/\partial \ln X_2 = (\partial Y/\partial X_2)(X_2/Y) = \beta_2$, which, by definition, is the elasticity of Y with respect to X_2 and $\partial \ln Y/\partial \ln X_3 = (\partial Y/\partial X_3)(X_3/Y) = \beta_3$, which is the elasticity of Y with respect to X_3, and so on.

[17]Notice that in the Cobb–Douglas production function (7.9.1) we have introduced the stochastic error term in a special way so that in the resulting logarithmic transformation it enters in the usual linear form. On this, see Section 6.9.

EXAMPLE 7.3
(Continued)

Maine	7,856,947	82,021	415,131
Maryland	21,352,966	174,855	1,729,116
Massachusetts	46,044,292	355,701	2,706,065
Michigan	92,335,528	943,298	5,294,356
Minnesota	48,304,274	456,553	2,833,525
Mississippi	17,207,903	267,806	1,212,281
Missouri	47,340,157	439,427	2,404,122
Montana	2,644,567	24,167	334,008
Nebraska	14,650,080	163,637	627,806
Nevada	7,290,360	59,737	522,335
New Hampshire	9,188,322	96,106	507,488
New Jersey	51,298,516	407,076	3,295,056
New Mexico	20,401,410	43,079	404,749
New York	87,756,129	727,177	4,260,353
North Carolina	101,268,432	820,013	4,086,558
North Dakota	3,556,025	34,723	184,700
Ohio	124,986,166	1,174,540	6,301,421
Oklahoma	20,451,196	201,284	1,327,353
Oregon	34,808,109	257,820	1,456,683
Pennsylvania	104,858,322	944,998	5,896,392
Rhode Island	6,541,356	68,987	297,618
South Carolina	37,668,126	400,317	2,500,071
South Dakota	4,988,905	56,524	311,251
Tennessee	62,828,100	582,241	4,126,465
Texas	172,960,157	1,120,382	11,588,283
Utah	15,702,637	150,030	762,671
Vermont	5,418,786	48,134	276,293
Virginia	49,166,991	425,346	2,731,669
Washington	46,164,427	313,279	1,945,860
West Virginia	9,185,967	89,639	685,587
Wisconsin	66,964,978	694,628	3,902,823
Wyoming	2,979,475	15,221	361,536

$$\begin{aligned}\widehat{\ln Y_i} &= \underset{(0.3962)}{3.8876} + \underset{(0.0989)}{0.4683}\ln X_{2i} + \underset{(0.0969)}{0.5213}\ln X_{3i} \\ t &= (9.8115) \quad (4.7342) \quad (5.3803) \\ R^2 &= 0.9642 \qquad \text{df} = 48 \\ \bar{R}^2 &= 0.9627\end{aligned} \tag{7.9.4}$$

From Eq. (7.9.4) we see that in the U.S. manufacturing sector for 2005, the output elasticities of labor and capital were 0.4683 and 0.5213, respectively. In other words, over the 50 U.S. states and the District of Columbia, holding the capital input constant, a 1 percent increase in the labor input led on the average to about a 0.47 percent increase in the output. Similarly, holding the labor input constant, a 1 percent increase in the capital input led on the average to about a 0.52 percent increase in the output. Adding the two output elasticities, we obtain 0.99, which gives the value of the returns to scale parameter. As is evident, the manufacturing sector for the 50 United States and the District of Columbia was characterized by constant returns to scale.

From a purely statistics viewpoint, the estimated regression line fits the data quite well. The R^2 value of 0.9642 means that about 96 percent of the variation in the (log of) output is explained by the (logs of) labor and capital. In Chapter 8, we shall see how the estimated standard errors can be used to test hypotheses about the "true" values of the parameters of the Cobb–Douglas production function for the U.S. manufacturing sector of the economy.

7.10 Polynomial Regression Models

We now consider a class of multiple regression models, the **polynomial regression models,** that have found extensive use in econometric research relating to cost and production functions. In introducing these models, we further extend the range of models to which the classical linear regression model can easily be applied.

To fix the ideas, consider Figure 7.1, which relates the short-run marginal cost (MC) of production (Y) of a commodity to the level of its output (X). The visually-drawn MC curve in the figure, the textbook U-shaped curve, shows that the relationship between MC and output is nonlinear. If we were to quantify this relationship from the given scatterpoints, how would we go about it? In other words, what type of econometric model would capture first the declining and then the increasing nature of marginal cost?

Geometrically, the MC curve depicted in Figure 7.1 represents a *parabola*. Mathematically, the parabola is represented by the following equation:

$$Y = \beta_0 + \beta_1 X + \beta_2 X^2 \tag{7.10.1}$$

which is called a *quadratic function,* or more generally, a *second-degree polynomial* in the variable X—the highest power of X represents the degree of the polynomial (if X^3 were added to the preceding function, it would be a third-degree polynomial, and so on).

The stochastic version of Eq. (7.10.1) may be written as

$$Y_i = \beta_0 + \beta_1 X_i + \beta_2 X_i^2 + u_i \tag{7.10.2}$$

which is called a *second-degree polynomial* regression.

The general *kth degree polynomial regression* may be written as

$$Y_i = \beta_0 + \beta_1 X_i + \beta_2 X_i^2 + \cdots + \beta_k X_i^k + u_i \tag{7.10.3}$$

Notice that in these types of polynomial regressions there is only one explanatory variable on the right-hand side but it appears with various powers, thus making them multiple regression models. Incidentally, note that if X_i is assumed to be fixed or nonstochastic, the powered terms of X_i also become fixed or nonstochastic.

Do these models present any special estimation problems? Since the second-degree polynomial (7.10.2) or the kth degree polynomial (7.10.13) is linear in the parameters, the β's, they can be estimated by the usual OLS or ML methodology. But what about the

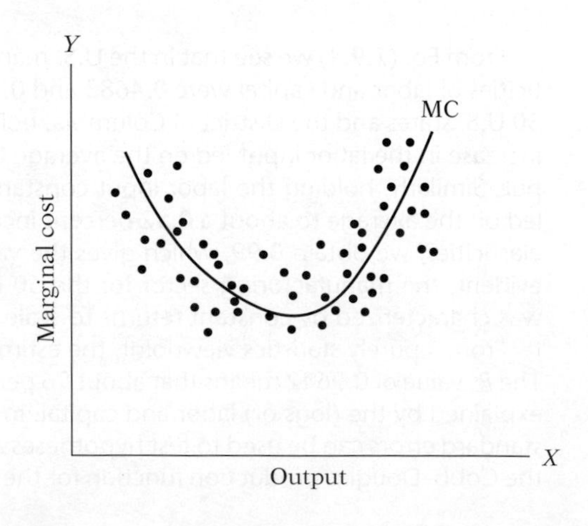

FIGURE 7.1
The U-shaped marginal cost curve.

collinearity problem? Aren't the various X's highly correlated since they are all powers of X? Yes, but remember that terms like X^2, X^3, X^4, etc., are all nonlinear functions of X and hence, strictly speaking, do not violate the no multicollinearity assumption. In short, polynomial regression models can be estimated by the techniques presented in this chapter and present no new estimation problems.

EXAMPLE 7.4
Estimating the Total Cost Function

As an example of the polynomial regression, consider the data on output and total cost of production of a commodity in the short run given in Table 7.4. What type of regression model will fit these data? For this purpose, let us first draw the scattergram, which is shown in Figure 7.2.

From this figure it is clear that the relationship between total cost and output resembles the elongated S curve; notice how the total cost curve first increases gradually and then rapidly, as predicted by the celebrated law of *diminishing returns.* This S shape of the total cost curve can be captured by the following cubic or *third-degree polynomial:*

$$Y_i = \beta_0 + \beta_1 X_i + \beta_2 X_i^2 + \beta_3 X_i^3 + u_i \tag{7.10.4}$$

where Y = total cost and X = output.

Given the data of Table 7.4, we can apply the OLS method to estimate the parameters of Eq. (7.10.4). But before we do that, let us find out what economic theory has to say about the short-run cubic cost function (7.10.4). Elementary price theory shows that in the short run the marginal cost (MC) and average cost (AC) curves of production are typically U-shaped—initially, as output increases both MC and AC decline, but after a certain level of output they both turn upward, again the consequence of the law of diminishing return. This can be seen in Figure 7.3 (see also Figure 7.1). And since the MC and AC curves are derived from the total cost curve, the U-shaped nature of these curves puts some restrictions on the parameters of the total cost curve (7.10.4). As a matter of

TABLE 7.4
Total Cost (Y) and Output (X)

Output	Total Cost, $
1	193
2	226
3	240
4	244
5	257
6	260
7	274
8	297
9	350
10	420

FIGURE 7.2 The total cost curve.

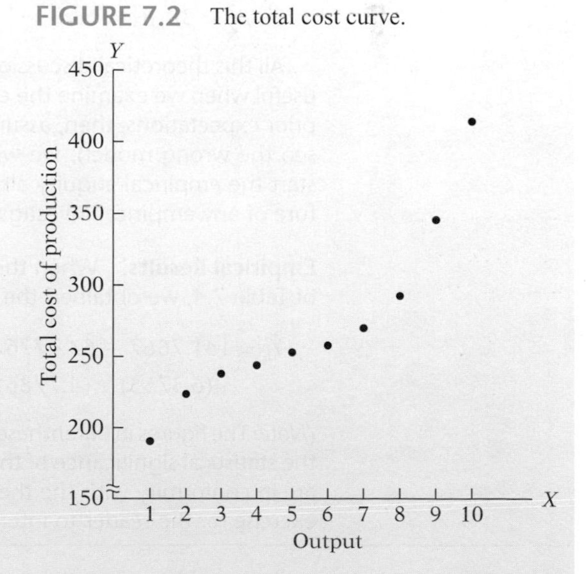

(Continued)

EXAMPLE 7.4 *(Continued)*

FIGURE 7.3 Short-run cost functions.

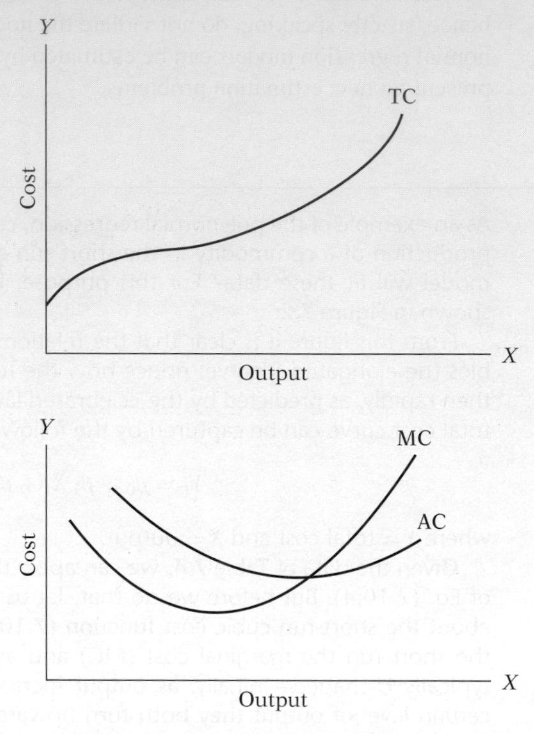

fact, it can be shown that the parameters of Eq. (7.10.4) must satisfy the following restrictions if one is to observe the typical U-shaped short-run marginal and average cost curves:[18]

$$\begin{aligned} &1.\ \beta_0, \beta_1, \text{and } \beta_3 > 0 \\ &2.\ \beta_2 < 0 \\ &3.\ \beta_2^2 < 3\beta_1\beta_3 \end{aligned} \tag{7.10.5}$$

All this theoretical discussion might seem a bit tedious. But this knowledge is extremely useful when we examine the empirical results, for if the empirical results do not agree with prior expectations, then, assuming we have not committed a specification error (i.e., chosen the wrong model), we will have to modify our theory or look for a new theory and start the empirical enquiry all over again. But as noted in the Introduction, this is the nature of any empirical investigation.

Empirical Results. When the third-degree polynomial regression was fitted to the data of Table 7.4, we obtained the following results:

$$\hat{Y}_i = 141.7667 + 63.4776X_i - 12.9615X_i^2 + 0.9396X_i^3$$
$$(6.3753) \quad (4.7786) \quad (0.9857) \quad (0.0591) \qquad R^2 = 0.9983 \tag{7.10.6}$$

(*Note:* The figures in parentheses are the estimated standard errors.) Although we will examine the statistical significance of these results in the next chapter, the reader can verify that they are in conformity with the theoretical expectations listed in Eq. (7.10.5). We leave it as an exercise for the reader to interpret the regression (7.10.6).

[18]See Alpha C. Chiang, *Fundamental Methods of Mathematical Economics,* 3d ed., McGraw-Hill, New York, 1984, pp. 250–252.

EXAMPLE 7.5

GDP Growth Rate and Relative per Capita GDP for 2007 in 190 Countries (in billions of 2000 dollars)

Source: World Bank World Development Indicators, adjusted to 2000 base and estimated and projected values developed by the Economic Research Service.

As an additional economic example of the polynomial regression model, consider the following regression results:

$$\begin{aligned}\widehat{GDPG}_i &= 5.5347 - 5.5788\ RGDP + 2.8378\ RGDP^2 \\ se &= (0.2435)\quad (1.5995) \qquad\qquad (1.4391) \\ R^2 &= 0.1092 \qquad adj\ R^2 = 0.0996\end{aligned} \tag{7.10.7}$$

Where GDPG = GDP growth rate, percent in 2007, and RGDP = relative per capita GDP in 2007 (percentage of U.S. GDP per capita, 2007). The adjusted R^2 (adj R^2) tells us that after taking into account the number of regressors, the model explains only about 9.96 percent of the variation in GDPG. Even the unadjusted R^2 of 0.1092 seems low. This might seem to be a disappointing value, but as we shall show in the next chapter, such low R^2 values are frequently encountered in cross-sectional data with a large number of observations. Besides, even an apparently low R^2 value can be statistically significant (i.e., different from zero), as we will show in the next chapter.

*7.11 Partial Correlation Coefficients

Explanation of Simple and Partial Correlation Coefficients

In Chapter 3 we introduced the coefficient of correlation r as a measure of the degree of linear association between two variables. For the three-variable regression model we can compute three correlation coefficients: r_{12} (correlation between Y and X_2), r_{13} (correlation coefficient between Y and X_3), and r_{23} (correlation coefficient between X_2 and X_3); notice that we are letting the subscript 1 represent Y for notational convenience. These correlation coefficients are called **gross** or **simple correlation coefficients,** or **correlation coefficients of zero order.** These coefficients can be computed by the definition of correlation coefficient given in Eq. (3.5.13).

But now consider this question: Does, say, r_{12} in fact measure the "true" degree of (linear) association between Y and X_2 when a third variable X_3 may be associated with both of them? This question is analogous to the following question: Suppose the true regression model is (7.1.1) but we omit from the model the variable X_3 and simply regress Y on X_2, obtaining the slope coefficient of, say, b_{12}. Will this coefficient be equal to the true coefficient β_2 if the model (7.1.1) were estimated to begin with? The answer should be apparent from our discussion in Section 7.7. In general, r_{12} is not likely to reflect the true degree of association between Y and X_2 in the presence of X_3. As a matter of fact, it is likely to give a false impression of the nature of association between Y and X_2, as will be shown shortly. Therefore, what we need is a correlation coefficient that is independent of the influence, if any, of X_3 on X_2 and Y. Such a correlation coefficient can be obtained and is known appropriately as the **partial correlation coefficient.** Conceptually, it is similar to the partial regression coefficient. We define

$r_{12.3}$ = partial correlation coefficient between Y and X_2, holding X_3 constant

$r_{13.2}$ = partial correlation coefficient between Y and X_3, holding X_2 constant

$r_{23.1}$ = partial correlation coefficient between X_2 and X_3, holding Y constant

*Optional.

These partial correlations can be easily obtained from the simple or zero-order, correlation coefficients as follows (for proofs, see the exercises):[19]

$$r_{12.3} = \frac{r_{12} - r_{13}r_{23}}{\sqrt{\left(1 - r_{13}^2\right)\left(1 - r_{23}^2\right)}} \tag{7.11.1}$$

$$r_{13.2} = \frac{r_{13} - r_{12}r_{23}}{\sqrt{\left(1 - r_{12}^2\right)\left(1 - r_{23}^2\right)}} \tag{7.11.2}$$

$$r_{23.1} = \frac{r_{23} - r_{12}r_{13}}{\sqrt{\left(1 - r_{12}^2\right)\left(1 - r_{13}^2\right)}} \tag{7.11.3}$$

The partial correlations given in Eqs. (7.11.1) to (7.11.3) are called **first-order correlation coefficients.** By *order* we mean the number of secondary subscripts. Thus $r_{12.34}$ would be the correlation coefficient of order two, $r_{12.345}$ would be the correlation coefficient of order three, and so on. As noted previously, r_{12}, r_{13}, and so on are called *simple* or *zero-order correlations.* The interpretation of, say, $r_{12.34}$ is that it gives the coefficient of correlation between Y and X_2, holding X_3 and X_4 constant.

Interpretation of Simple and Partial Correlation Coefficients

In the two-variable case, the simple r had a straightforward meaning: It measured the degree of (linear) association (and not causation) between the dependent variable Y and the single explanatory variable X. But once we go beyond the two-variable case, we need to pay careful attention to the interpretation of the simple correlation coefficient. From Eq. (7.11.1), for example, we observe the following:

1. Even if $r_{12} = 0$, $r_{12.3}$ will not be zero unless r_{13} or r_{23} or both are zero.
2. If $r_{12} = 0$ and r_{13} and r_{23} are nonzero and are of the same sign, $r_{12.3}$ will be negative, whereas if they are of the opposite signs, it will be positive. An example will make this point clear. Let Y = crop yield, X_2 = rainfall, and X_3 = temperature. Assume $r_{12} = 0$, that is, no association between crop yield and rainfall. Assume further that r_{13} is positive and r_{23} is negative. Then, as Eq. (7.11.1) shows, $r_{12.3}$ will be positive; that is, holding temperature constant, there is a positive association between yield and rainfall. This seemingly paradoxical result, however, is not surprising. Since temperature X_3 affects both yield Y and rainfall X_2, in order to find out the net relationship between crop yield and rainfall, we need to remove the influence of the "nuisance" variable temperature. This example shows how one might be misled by the simple coefficient of correlation.
3. The terms $r_{12.3}$ and r_{12} (and similar comparisons) need not have the same sign.
4. In the two-variable case we have seen that r^2 lies between 0 and 1. The same property holds true of the squared partial correlation coefficients. Using this fact, the reader should verify that one can obtain the following expression from Eq. (7.11.1):

$$0 \le r_{12}^2 + r_{13}^2 + r_{23}^2 - 2r_{12}r_{13}r_{23} \le 1 \tag{7.11.4}$$

[19]Most computer programs for multiple regression analysis routinely compute the simple correlation coefficients; hence the partial correlation coefficients can be readily computed.

which gives the interrelationships among the three zero-order correlation coefficients. Similar expressions can be derived from Eqs. (7.11.2) and (7.11.3).

5. Suppose that $r_{13} = r_{23} = 0$. Does this mean that r_{12} is also zero? The answer is obvious from Eq. (7.11.4). The fact that Y and X_3 and X_2 and X_3 are uncorrelated does not mean that Y and X_2 are uncorrelated.

In passing, note that the expression $r^2_{12.3}$ may be called the **coefficient of partial determination** and may be interpreted as the proportion of the variation in Y not explained by the variable X_3 that has been explained by the inclusion of X_2 into the model (see Exercise 7.5). Conceptually it is similar to R^2.

Before moving on, note the following relationships between R^2, simple correlation coefficients, and partial correlation coefficients:

$$R^2 = \frac{r^2_{12} + r^2_{13} - 2r_{12}r_{13}r_{23}}{1 - r^2_{23}} \tag{7.11.5}$$

$$R^2 = r^2_{12} + \left(1 - r^2_{12}\right) r^2_{13.2} \tag{7.11.6}$$

$$R^2 = r^2_{13} + \left(1 - r^2_{13}\right) r^2_{12.3} \tag{7.11.7}$$

In concluding this section, consider the following: It was stated previously that R^2 will not decrease if an additional explanatory variable is introduced into the model, which can be seen clearly from Eq. (7.11.6). This equation states that the proportion of the variation in Y explained by X_2 and X_3 jointly is the sum of two parts: the part explained by X_2 alone $(= r^2_{12})$ and the part not explained by X_2 $(= 1 - r^2_{12})$ times the proportion that is explained by X_3 after holding the influence of X_2 constant. Now $R^2 > r^2_{12}$ so long as $r^2_{13.2} > 0$. At worst, $r^2_{13.2}$ will be zero, in which case $R^2 = r^2_{12}$.

Summary and Conclusions

1. This chapter introduced the simplest possible multiple linear regression model, namely, the three-variable regression model. It is understood that the term *linear* refers to linearity in the parameters and not necessarily in the variables.
2. Although a three-variable regression model is in many ways an extension of the two-variable model, there are some new concepts involved, such as *partial regression coefficients, partial correlation coefficients, multiple correlation coefficient, adjusted and unadjusted (for degrees of freedom)* R^2, *multicollinearity,* and *specification bias.*
3. This chapter also considered the functional form of the multiple regression model, such as the *Cobb–Douglas production function* and the *polynomial regression model.*
4. Although R^2 and adjusted R^2 are overall measures of how the chosen model fits a given set of data, their importance should not be overplayed. What is critical is the underlying theoretical expectations about the model in terms of a priori signs of the coefficients of the variables entering the model and, as it is shown in the following chapter, their statistical significance.
5. The results presented in this chapter can be easily generalized to a multiple linear regression model involving any number of regressors. But the algebra becomes very tedious. This tedium can be avoided by resorting to matrix algebra. For the interested reader, the extension to the k-variable regression model using matrix algebra is presented in **Appendix C,** which is optional. But the general reader can read the remainder of the text without knowing much of matrix algebra.

EXERCISES

Questions

7.1. Consider the data in Table 7.5.

TABLE 7.5

Y	X_2	X_3
1	1	2
3	2	1
8	3	−3

Based on these data, estimate the following regressions:

$$Y_i = \alpha_1 + \alpha_2 X_{2i} + u_{1i} \quad (1)$$

$$Y_i = \lambda_1 + \lambda_3 X_{3i} + u_{2i} \quad (2)$$

$$Y_i = \beta_1 + \beta_2 X_{2i} + \beta_3 X_{3i} + u_i \quad (3)$$

Note: Estimate only the coefficients and not the standard errors.

a. Is $\alpha_2 = \beta_2$? Why or why not?

b. Is $\lambda_3 = \beta_3$? Why or why not?

What important conclusion do you draw from this exercise?

7.2. From the following data estimate the partial regression coefficients, their standard errors, and the adjusted and unadjusted R^2 values:

$$\bar{Y} = 367.693 \qquad \bar{X}_2 = 402.760 \qquad \bar{X}_3 = 8.0$$

$$\sum (Y_i - \bar{Y})^2 = 66042.269 \qquad \sum (X_{2i} - \bar{X}_2)^2 = 84855.096$$

$$\sum (X_{3i} - \bar{X}_3)^2 = 280.000 \qquad \sum (Y_i - \bar{Y})(X_{2i} - \bar{X}_2) = 74778.346$$

$$\sum (Y_i - \bar{Y})(X_{3i} - \bar{X}_3) = 4250.900 \qquad \sum (X_{2i} - \bar{X}_2)(X_{3i} - \bar{X}_3) = 4796.000$$

$$n = 15$$

7.3. Show that Eq. (7.4.7) can also be expressed as

$$\hat{\beta}_2 = \frac{\sum y_i (x_{2i} - b_{23} x_{3i})}{\sum (x_{2i} - b_{23} x_{3i})^2}$$

$$= \frac{\text{net (of } x_3\text{) covariation between } y \text{ and } x_2}{\text{net (of } x_3\text{) variation in } x_2}$$

where b_{23} is the slope coefficient in the regression of X_2 on X_3. (*Hint:* Recall that $b_{23} = \sum x_{2i} x_{3i} / \sum x_{3i}^2$.)

7.4. In a multiple regression model you are told that the error term u_i has the following probability distribution, namely, $u_i \sim N(0, 4)$. How would you set up a *Monte Carlo* experiment to verify that the true variance is in fact 4?

7.5. Show that $r_{12.3}^2 = (R^2 - r_{13}^2)/(1 - r_{13}^2)$ and interpret the equation.

7.6. If the relation $\alpha_1 X_1 + \alpha_2 X_2 + \alpha_3 X_3 = 0$ holds true for all values of X_1, X_2, and X_3, find the values of the three partial correlation coefficients.

7.7. Is it possible to obtain the following from a set of data?

a. $r_{23} = 0.9, r_{13} = -0.2, r_{12} = 0.8$

b. $r_{12} = 0.6, r_{23} = -0.9, r_{31} = -0.5$

c. $r_{21} = 0.01, r_{13} = 0.66, r_{23} = -0.7$

7.8. Consider the following model:

$$Y_i = \beta_1 + \beta_2 \text{ Education}_i + \beta_2 \text{ Years of experience} + u_i$$

Suppose you leave out the years of experience variable. What kinds of problems or biases would you expect? Explain verbally.

7.9. Show that β_2 and β_3 in Eq. (7.9.2) do, in fact, give output elasticities of labor and capital. (This question can be answered without using calculus; just recall the definition of the elasticity coefficient and remember that a change in the logarithm of a variable is a relative change, assuming the changes are rather small.)

7.10. Consider the three-variable linear regression model discussed in this chapter.

a. Suppose you multiply all the X_2 values by 2. What will be the effect of this rescaling, if any, on the estimates of the parameters and their standard errors?

b. Now instead of (*a*), suppose you multiply all the Y values by 2. What will be the effect of this, if any, on the estimated parameters and their standard errors?

7.11. In general $R^2 \neq r_{12}^2 + r_{13}^2$, but it is so only if $r_{23} = 0$. Comment and point out the significance of this finding. (*Hint:* See Eq. [7.11.5].)

7.12. Consider the following models.*

$$\text{Model A:} \quad Y_t = \alpha_1 + \alpha_2 X_{2t} + \alpha_3 X_{3t} + u_{1t}$$
$$\text{Model B:} \quad (Y_t - X_{2t}) = \beta_1 + \beta_2 X_{2t} + \beta_3 X_{3t} + u_{2t}$$

a. Will OLS estimates of α_1 and β_1 be the same? Why?

b. Will OLS estimates of α_3 and β_3 be the same? Why?

c. What is the relationship between α_2 and β_2?

d. Can you compare the R^2 terms of the two models? Why or why not?

7.13. Suppose you estimate the consumption function†

$$Y_i = \alpha_1 + \alpha_2 X_i + u_{1i}$$

and the savings function

$$Z_i = \beta_1 + \beta_2 X_i + u_{2i}$$

where $Y =$ consumption, $Z =$ savings, $X =$ income, and $X = Y + Z$, that is, income is equal to consumption plus savings.

a. What is the relationship, if any, between α_2 and β_2? Show your calculations.

b. Will the residual sum of squares, RSS, be the same for the two models? Explain.

c. Can you compare the R^2 terms of the two models? Why or why not?

7.14. Suppose you express the Cobb–Douglas model given in Eq. (7.9.1) as follows:

$$Y_i = \beta_1 X_{2i}^{\beta_2} X_{3i}^{\beta_3} u_i$$

If you take the log-transform of this model, you will have $\ln u_i$ as the disturbance term on the right-hand side.

a. What probabilistic assumptions do you have to make about $\ln u_i$ to be able to apply the classical normal linear regression model (CNLRM)? How would you test this with the data given in Table 7.3?

b. Do the same assumptions apply to u_i? Why or why not?

*Adapted from Wojciech W. Charemza and Derek F. Deadman, *Econometric Practice: General to Specific Modelling, Cointegration and Vector Autogression*, Edward Elgar, Brookfield, Vermont, 1992, p. 18.

†Adapted from Peter Kennedy, *A Guide to Econometrics*, 3d ed., The MIT Press, Cambridge, Massachusetts, 1992, p. 308, Question #9.

7.15. *Regression through the origin.* Consider the following regression through the origin:

$$Y_i = \hat{\beta}_2 X_{2i} + \hat{\beta}_3 X_{3i} + \hat{u}_i$$

a. How would you go about estimating the unknowns?
b. Will $\sum \hat{u}_i$ be zero for this model? Why or why not?
c. Will $\sum \hat{u}_i X_{2i} = \sum \hat{u}_i X_{3i} = 0$ for this model?
d. When would you use such a model?
e. Can you generalize your results to the *k*-variable model?
(*Hint:* Follow the discussion for the two-variable case given in Chapter 6.)

Empirical Exercises

7.16. *The demand for roses.*[*] Table 7.6 gives quarterly data on these variables:

Y = quantity of roses sold, dozens
X_2 = average wholesale price of roses, \$/dozen
X_3 = average wholesale price of carnations, \$/dozen
X_4 = average weekly family disposable income, \$/week
X_5 = the trend variable taking values of 1, 2, and so on, for the period 1971–III to 1975–II in the Detroit metropolitan area

You are asked to consider the following demand functions:

$$Y_t = \alpha_1 + \alpha_2 X_{2t} + \alpha_3 X_{3t} + \alpha_4 X_{4t} + \alpha_5 X_{5t} + u_t$$

$$\ln Y_t = \beta_1 + \beta_2 \ln X_{2t} + \beta_3 \ln X_{3t} + \beta_4 \ln X_{4t} + \beta_5 X_{5t} + u_t$$

a. Estimate the parameters of the linear model and interpret the results.
b. Estimate the parameters of the log–linear model and interpret the results.

TABLE 7.6
Quarterly Demand for Roses in Metro Detroit Area, from 1971-III to 1975-II

Year and Quarter	Y	X_2	X_3	X_4	X_5
1971–III	11,484	2.26	3.49	158.11	1
–IV	9,348	2.54	2.85	173.36	2
1972–I	8,429	3.07	4.06	165.26	3
–II	10,079	2.91	3.64	172.92	4
–III	9,240	2.73	3.21	178.46	5
–IV	8,862	2.77	3.66	198.62	6
1973–I	6,216	3.59	3.76	186.28	7
–II	8,253	3.23	3.49	188.98	8
–III	8,038	2.60	3.13	180.49	9
–IV	7,476	2.89	3.20	183.33	10
1974–I	5,911	3.77	3.65	181.87	11
–II	7,950	3.64	3.60	185.00	12
–III	6,134	2.82	2.94	184.00	13
–IV	5,868	2.96	3.12	188.20	14
1975–I	3,160	4.24	3.58	175.67	15
–II	5,872	3.69	3.53	188.00	16

[*] I am indebted to Joe Walsh for collecting these data from a major wholesaler in the Detroit metropolitan area and subsequently processing them.

c. β_2, β_3, and β_4 give, respectively, the *own-price, cross-price,* and *income elasticities* of demand. What are their a priori signs? Do the results concur with the a priori expectations?

d. How would you compute the own-price, cross-price, and income elasticities for the linear model?

e. On the basis of your analysis, which model, if either, would you choose and why?

7.17. *Wildcat activity.* Wildcats are wells drilled to find and produce oil and/or gas in an improved area or to find a new reservoir in a field previously found to be productive of oil or gas or to extend the limit of a known oil or gas reservoir. Table 7.7 gives data on these variables:*

Y = the number of wildcats drilled

X_2 = price at the wellhead in the previous period (in constant dollars, 1972 = 100)

X_3 = domestic output

X_4 = GNP constant dollars (1972 = 100)

X_5 = trend variable, 1948 = 1, 1949 = 2, . . . , 1978 = 31

See if the following model fits the data:

$$Y_t = \beta_1 + \beta_2 X_{2t} + \beta_3 \ln X_{3t} + \beta_4 X_{4t} + \beta_5 X_{5t} + u_t$$

a. Can you offer an a priori rationale to this model?

b. Assuming the model is acceptable, estimate the parameters of the model and their standard errors, and obtain R^2 and $\bar{R}^2$.

c. Comment on your results in view of your prior expectations.

d. What other specification would you suggest to explain wildcat activity? Why?

7.18. *U.S. defense budget outlays, 1962–1981.* In order to explain the U.S. defense budget, you are asked to consider the following model:

$$Y_t = \beta_1 + \beta_2 X_{2t} + \beta_3 X_{3t} + \beta_4 X_{4t} + \beta_5 X_{5t} + u_t$$

where Y_t = defense budget-outlay for year t, \$ billions

X_{2t} = GNP for year t, \$ billions

X_{3t} = U.S. military sales/assistance in year t, \$ billions

X_{4t} = aerospace industry sales, \$ billions

X_{5t} = military conflicts involving more than 100,000 troops. This variable takes a value of 1 when 100,000 or more troops are involved but is equal to zero when that number is under 100,000.

To test this model, you are given the data in Table 7.8.

a. Estimate the parameters of this model and their standard errors and obtain R^2, modified R^2, and $\bar{R}^2$.

b. Comment on the results, taking into account any prior expectations you have about the relationship between Y and the various X variables.

c. What other variable(s) might you want to include in the model and why?

*I am indebted to Raymond Savino for collecting and processing these data.

TABLE 7.7
Wildcat Activity

Source: Energy Information Administration, 1978 Report to Congress.

Thousands of Wildcats, (Y)	Per Barrel Price, Constant $ (X_2)	Domestic Output (millions of barrels per day) (X_3)	GNP, Constant $ Billions (X_4)	Time (X_5)
8.01	4.89	5.52	487.67	1948 = 1
9.06	4.83	5.05	490.59	1949 = 2
10.31	4.68	5.41	533.55	1950 = 3
11.76	4.42	6.16	576.57	1951 = 4
12.43	4.36	6.26	598.62	1952 = 5
13.31	4.55	6.34	621.77	1953 = 6
13.10	4.66	6.81	613.67	1954 = 7
14.94	4.54	7.15	654.80	1955 = 8
16.17	4.44	7.17	668.84	1956 = 9
14.71	4.75	6.71	681.02	1957 = 10
13.20	4.56	7.05	679.53	1958 = 11
13.19	4.29	7.04	720.53	1959 = 12
11.70	4.19	7.18	736.86	1960 = 13
10.99	4.17	7.33	755.34	1961 = 14
10.80	4.11	7.54	799.15	1962 = 15
10.66	4.04	7.61	830.70	1963 = 16
10.75	3.96	7.80	874.29	1964 = 17
9.47	3.85	8.30	925.86	1965 = 18
10.31	3.75	8.81	980.98	1966 = 19
8.88	3.69	8.66	1,007.72	1967 = 20
8.88	3.56	8.78	1,051.83	1968 = 21
9.70	3.56	9.18	1,078.76	1969 = 22
7.69	3.48	9.03	1,075.31	1970 = 23
6.92	3.53	9.00	1,107.48	1971 = 24
7.54	3.39	8.78	1,171.10	1972 = 25
7.47	3.68	8.38	1,234.97	1973 = 26
8.63	5.92	8.01	1,217.81	1974 = 27
9.21	6.03	7.78	1,202.36	1975 = 28
9.23	6.12	7.88	1,271.01	1976 = 29
9.96	6.05	7.88	1,332.67	1977 = 30
10.78	5.89	8.67	1,385.10	1978 = 31

7.19. *The demand for chicken in the United States, 1960–1982.* To study the per capita consumption of chicken in the United States, you are given the data in Table 7.9,

where Y = per capita consumption of chickens, lb

X_2 = real disposable income per capita, $

X_3 = real retail price of chicken per lb, ¢

X_4 = real retail price of pork per lb, ¢

X_5 = real retail price of beef per lb, ¢

X_6 = composite real price of chicken substitutes per lb, ¢, which is a weighted average of the real retail prices per lb of pork and beef, the weights being the relative consumptions of beef and pork in total beef and pork consumption

TABLE 7.8
U.S. Defense Budget Outlays, 1962–1981

Source: These data were collected by Albert Lucchino from various government publications.

Year	Defense Budget Outlays (Y)	GNP (X_2)	U.S. Military Sales/ Assistance (X_3)	Aerospace Industry Sales (X_4)	Conflicts 100,000+ (X_5)
1962	51.1	560.3	0.6	16.0	0
1963	52.3	590.5	0.9	16.4	0
1964	53.6	632.4	1.1	16.7	0
1965	49.6	684.9	1.4	17.0	1
1966	56.8	749.9	1.6	20.2	1
1967	70.1	793.9	1.0	23.4	1
1968	80.5	865.0	0.8	25.6	1
1969	81.2	931.4	1.5	24.6	1
1970	80.3	992.7	1.0	24.8	1
1971	77.7	1,077.6	1.5	21.7	1
1972	78.3	1,185.9	2.95	21.5	1
1973	74.5	1,326.4	4.8	24.3	0
1974	77.8	1,434.2	10.3	26.8	0
1975	85.6	1,549.2	16.0	29.5	0
1976	89.4	1,718.0	14.7	30.4	0
1977	97.5	1,918.3	8.3	33.3	0
1978	105.2	2,163.9	11.0	38.0	0
1979	117.7	2,417.8	13.0	46.2	0
1980	135.9	2,633.1	15.3	57.6	0
1981	162.1	2,937.7	18.0	68.9	0

TABLE 7.9
Demand for Chicken in the U.S., 1960–1982

Source: Data on Y are from *Citibase* and on X_2 through X_6 are from the U.S. Department of Agriculture. I am indebted to Robert J. Fisher for collecting the data and for the statistical analysis.

Year	Y	X_2	X_3	X_4	X_5	X_6
1960	27.8	397.5	42.2	50.7	78.3	65.8
1961	29.9	413.3	38.1	52.0	79.2	66.9
1962	29.8	439.2	40.3	54.0	79.2	67.8
1963	30.8	459.7	39.5	55.3	79.2	69.6
1964	31.2	492.9	37.3	54.7	77.4	68.7
1965	33.3	528.6	38.1	63.7	80.2	73.6
1966	35.6	560.3	39.3	69.8	80.4	76.3
1967	36.4	624.6	37.8	65.9	83.9	77.2
1968	36.7	666.4	38.4	64.5	85.5	78.1
1969	38.4	717.8	40.1	70.0	93.7	84.7
1970	40.4	768.2	38.6	73.2	106.1	93.3
1971	40.3	843.3	39.8	67.8	104.8	89.7
1972	41.8	911.6	39.7	79.1	114.0	100.7
1973	40.4	931.1	52.1	95.4	124.1	113.5
1974	40.7	1,021.5	48.9	94.2	127.6	115.3
1975	40.1	1,165.9	58.3	123.5	142.9	136.7
1976	42.7	1,349.6	57.9	129.9	143.6	139.2
1977	44.1	1,449.4	56.5	117.6	139.2	132.0
1978	46.7	1,575.5	63.7	130.9	165.5	132.1
1979	50.6	1,759.1	61.6	129.8	203.3	154.4
1980	50.1	1,994.2	58.9	128.0	219.6	174.9
1981	51.7	2,258.1	66.4	141.0	221.6	180.8
1982	52.9	2,478.7	70.4	168.2	232.6	189.4

Note: The real prices were obtained by dividing the nominal prices by the Consumer Price Index for food

Now consider the following demand functions:

$$\ln Y_t = \alpha_1 + \alpha_2 \ln X_{2t} + \alpha_3 \ln X_{3t} + u_t \quad (1)$$
$$\ln Y_t = \gamma_1 + \gamma_2 \ln X_{2t} + \gamma_3 \ln X_{3t} + \gamma_4 \ln X_{4t} + u_t \quad (2)$$
$$\ln Y_t = \lambda_1 + \lambda_2 \ln X_{2t} + \lambda_3 \ln X_{3t} + \lambda_4 \ln X_{5t} + u_t \quad (3)$$
$$\ln Y_t = \theta_1 + \theta_2 \ln X_{2t} + \theta_3 \ln X_{3t} + \theta_4 \ln X_{4t} + \theta_5 \ln X_{5t} + u_t \quad (4)$$
$$\ln Y_t = \beta_1 + \beta_2 \ln X_{2t} + \beta_3 \ln X_{3t} + \beta_4 \ln X_{6t} + u_t \quad (5)$$

From microeconomic theory it is known that the demand for a commodity generally depends on the real income of the consumer, the real price of the commodity, and the real prices of competing or complementary commodities. In view of these considerations, answer the following questions.

a. Which demand function among the ones given here would you choose, and why?

b. How would you interpret the coefficients of $\ln X_{2t}$ and $\ln X_{3t}$ in these models?

c. What is the difference between specifications (2) and (4)?

d. What problems do you foresee if you adopt specification (4)? (*Hint:* Prices of both pork and beef are included along with the price of chicken.)

e. Since specification (5) includes the composite price of beef and pork, would you prefer the demand function (5) to the function (4)? Why?

f. Are pork and/or beef competing or substitute products to chicken? How do you know?

g. Assume function (5) is the "correct" demand function. Estimate the parameters of this model, obtain their standard errors, and R^2, $\bar{R}^2$, and modified R^2. Interpret your results.

h. Now suppose you run the "incorrect" model (2). Assess the consequences of this mis-specification by considering the values of γ_2 and γ_3 in relation to β_2 and β_3, respectively. (*Hint:* Pay attention to the discussion in Section 7.7.)

7.20. In a study of turnover in the labor market, James F. Ragan, Jr., obtained the following results for the U.S. economy for the period of 1950–I to 1979–IV.* (Figures in the parentheses are the estimated t statistics.)

$$\widehat{\ln Y_t} = \underset{(4.28)}{4.47} - \underset{(-5.31)}{0.34} \ln X_{2t} + \underset{(3.64)}{1.22} \ln X_{3t} + \underset{(3.10)}{1.22} \ln X_{4t}$$
$$+ \underset{(1.10)}{0.80} \ln X_{5t} - \underset{(-3.09)}{0.0055} X_{6t} \qquad \bar{R}^2 = 0.5370$$

Note: We will discuss the t statistics in the next chapter.

where Y = quit rate in manufacturing, defined as number of people leaving jobs voluntarily per 100 employees
X_2 = an instrumental or proxy variable for adult male unemployment rate
X_3 = percentage of employees younger than 25
$X_4 = N_{t-1}/N_{t-4}$ = ratio of manufacturing employment in quarter $(t-1)$ to that in quarter $(t-4)$
X_5 = percentage of women employees
X_6 = time trend (1950–I = 1)

*Source: See Ragan's article, "Turnover in the Labor Market: A Study of Quit and Layoff Rates," *Economic Review,* Federal Reserve Bank of Kansas City, May 1981, pp. 13–22.

a. Interpret the foregoing results.

b. Is the observed negative relationship between the logs of Y and X_2 justifiable a priori?

c. Why is the coefficient of $\ln X_3$ positive?

d. Since the trend coefficient is negative, there is a secular decline of what percent in the quit rate and why is there such a decline?

e. Is the $\bar{R}^2$ "too" low?

f. Can you estimate the standard errors of the regression coefficients from the given data? Why or why not?

7.21. Consider the following demand function for money in the United States for the period 1980–1998:

$$M_t = \beta_1 Y_t^{\beta_2} r_t^{\beta_3} e^{u_t}$$

where M = real money demand, using the M2 definition of money
Y = real GDP
r = interest rate

To estimate the above demand for money function, you are given the data in Table 7.10.

Note: To convert nominal quantities into real quantities, divide M and GDP by CPI. There is no need to divide the interest rate variable by CPI. Also, note that we have given two interest rates, a short-term rate as measured by the 3-month treasury bill rate and the long-term rate as measured by the yield on the 30-year treasury bond, as prior empirical studies have used both types of interest rates.

TABLE 7.10
Demand for Money in the United States, 1980–1998

Source: *Economic Report of the President,* 2000, Tables B-1, B-58, B-67, B-71.

Observation	GDP	M2	CPI	LTRATE	TBRATE
1980	2795.6	1600.4	82.4	11.27	11.506
1981	3131.3	1756.1	90.9	13.45	14.029
1982	3259.2	1911.2	96.5	12.76	10.686
1983	3534.9	2127.8	99.6	11.18	8.630
1984	3932.7	2311.7	103.9	12.41	9.580
1985	4213.0	2497.4	107.6	10.79	7.480
1986	4452.9	2734.0	109.6	7.78	5.980
1987	4742.5	2832.8	113.6	8.59	5.820
1988	5108.3	2995.8	118.3	8.96	6.690
1989	5489.1	3159.9	124.0	8.45	8.120
1990	5803.2	3279.1	130.7	8.61	7.510
1991	5986.2	3379.8	136.2	8.14	5.420
1992	6318.9	3434.1	140.3	7.67	3.450
1993	6642.3	3487.5	144.5	6.59	3.020
1994	7054.3	3502.2	148.2	7.37	4.290
1995	7400.5	3649.3	152.4	6.88	5.510
1996	7813.2	3824.2	156.9	6.71	5.020
1997	8300.8	4046.7	160.5	6.61	5.070
1998	8759.9	4401.4	163.0	5.58	4.810

Notes: GDP: gross domestic product ($ billions).
M_2: M_2 money supply.
CPI: Consumer Price Index (1982–1984 = 100).
LTRATE: long-term interest rate (30-year Treasury bond).
TBRATE: three-month Treasury bill rate (% per annum).

a. Given the data, estimate the above demand function. What are the income and interest rate elasticities of demand for money?

b. Instead of estimating the above demand function, suppose you were to fit the function $(M/Y)_t = \alpha_1 r_t^{\alpha_2} e^{u_t}$. How would you interpret the results? Show the necessary calculations.

c. How will you decide which is a better specification? (*Note:* A formal statistical test will be given in Chapter 8.)

7.22. Table 7.11 gives data for the manufacturing sector of the Greek economy for the period 1961–1987.

a. See if the Cobb–Douglas production function fits the data given in the table and interpret the results. What general conclusion do you draw?

b. Now consider the following model:

$$\text{Output/labor} = A(K/L)^{\beta} e^{u}$$

where the regressand represents labor productivity and the regressor represents the capital labor ratio. What is the economic significance of such a relationship, if any? Estimate the parameters of this model and interpret your results.

TABLE 7.11
Greek Industrial Sector

Source: I am indebted to George K. Zestos of Christopher Newport University, Virginia, for these data.

Observation	Output*	Capital	Labor†	Capital-to-Labor Ratio
1961	35.858	59.600	637.0	0.0936
1962	37.504	64.200	643.2	0.0998
1963	40.378	68.800	651.0	0.1057
1964	46.147	75.500	685.7	0.1101
1965	51.047	84.400	710.7	0.1188
1966	53.871	91.800	724.3	0.1267
1967	56.834	99.900	735.2	0.1359
1968	65.439	109.100	760.3	0.1435
1969	74.939	120.700	777.6	0.1552
1970	80.976	132.000	780.8	0.1691
1971	90.802	146.600	825.8	0.1775
1972	101.955	162.700	864.1	0.1883
1973	114.367	180.600	894.2	0.2020
1974	101.823	197.100	891.2	0.2212
1975	107.572	209.600	887.5	0.2362
1976	117.600	221.900	892.3	0.2487
1977	123.224	232.500	930.1	0.2500
1978	130.971	243.500	969.9	0.2511
1979	138.842	257.700	1006.9	0.2559
1980	135.486	274.400	1020.9	0.2688
1981	133.441	289.500	1017.1	0.2846
1982	130.388	301.900	1016.1	0.2971
1983	130.615	314.900	1008.1	0.3124
1984	132.244	327.700	985.1	0.3327
1985	137.318	339.400	977.1	0.3474
1986	137.468	349.492	1007.2	0.3470
1987	135.750	358.231	1000.0	0.3582

*Billions of Drachmas at constant 1970 prices.
†Thousands of workers per year.

7.23. *Monte Carlo experiment:* Consider the following model:

$$Y_i = \beta_1 + \beta_2 X_{2i} + \beta_3 X_{3i} + u_i$$

You are told that $\beta_1 = 262$, $\beta_2 = -0.006$, $\beta_3 = -2.4$, $\sigma^2 = 42$, and $u_i \sim N(0, 42)$. Generate 10 sets of 64 observations on u_i from the given normal distribution and use the 64 observations given in Table 6.4, where $Y = \text{CM}$, $X_2 = \text{PGNP}$, and $X_3 = \text{FLR}$ to generate 10 sets of the estimated β coefficients (each set will have the three estimated parameters). Take the averages of each of the estimated β coefficients and relate them to the true values of these coefficients given above. What overall conclusion do you draw?

7.24. Table 7.12 gives data for real consumption expenditure, real income, real wealth, and real interest rates for the U.S. for the years 1947–2000. These data will be used again for Exercise 8.35.

a. Given the data in the table, estimate the linear consumption function using income, wealth, and interest rate. What is the fitted equation?

b. What do the estimated coefficients indicate about the variables' relationships to consumption expenditure?

TABLE 7.12
Real Consumption Expenditure, Real Income, Real Wealth, and Real Interest Rates for the U.S., 1947–2000

Sources: *C*, Yd, and quarterly and annual chain-type price indexes (1996 = 100): Bureau of Economic Analysis, U.S. Department of Commerce (http://www.bea.doc.gov/bea/dn1.htm).
Nominal annual yield on 3-month Treasury securities: Economic Report of the President, 2002.
Nominal wealth = end-of-year nominal net worth of households and nonprofits (from Federal Reserve flow of funds data: http://www.federalreserve.gov).

Year	C	Yd	Wealth	Interest Rate
1947	976.4	1035.2	5166.8	−10.351
1948	998.1	1090.0	5280.8	−4.720
1949	1025.3	1095.6	5607.4	1.044
1950	1090.9	1192.7	5759.5	0.407
1951	1107.1	1227.0	6086.1	−5.283
1952	1142.4	1266.8	6243.9	−0.277
1953	1197.2	1327.5	6355.6	0.561
1954	1221.9	1344.0	6797.0	−0.138
1955	1310.4	1433.8	7172.2	0.262
1956	1348.8	1502.3	7375.2	−0.736
1957	1381.8	1539.5	7315.3	−0.261
1958	1393.0	1553.7	7870.0	−0.575
1959	1470.7	1623.8	8188.1	2.296
1960	1510.8	1664.8	8351.8	1.511
1961	1541.2	1720.0	8971.9	1.296
1962	1617.3	1803.5	9091.5	1.396
1963	1684.0	1871.5	9436.1	2.058
1964	1784.8	2006.9	10003.4	2.027
1965	1897.6	2131.0	10562.8	2.112
1966	2006.1	2244.6	10522.0	2.020
1967	2066.2	2340.5	11312.1	1.213
1968	2184.2	2448.2	12145.4	1.055
1969	2264.8	2524.3	11672.3	1.732
1970	2314.5	2630.0	11650.0	1.166
1971	2405.2	2745.3	12312.9	−0.712
1972	2550.5	2874.3	13499.9	−0.156
1973	2675.9	3072.3	13081.0	1.414
1974	2653.7	3051.9	11868.8	−1.043
1975	2710.9	3108.5	12634.4	−3.534
1976	2868.9	3243.5	13456.8	−0.657

Continued

TABLE 7.12
(Continued)

Year	C	Yd	Wealth	Interest Rate
1977	2992.1	3360.7	13786.3	−1.190
1978	3124.7	3527.5	14450.5	0.113
1979	3203.2	3628.6	15340.0	1.704
1980	3193.0	3658.0	15965.0	2.298
1981	3236.0	3741.1	15965.0	4.704
1982	3275.5	3791.7	16312.5	4.449
1983	3454.3	3906.9	16944.8	4.691
1984	3640.6	4207.6	17526.7	5.848
1985	3820.9	4347.8	19068.3	4.331
1986	3981.2	4486.6	20530.0	3.768
1987	4113.4	4582.5	21235.7	2.819
1988	4279.5	4784.1	22332.0	3.287
1989	4393.7	4906.5	23659.8	4.318
1990	4474.5	5014.2	23105.1	3.595
1991	4466.6	5033.0	24050.2	1.803
1992	4594.5	5189.3	24418.2	1.007
1993	4748.9	5261.3	25092.3	0.625
1994	4928.1	5397.2	25218.6	2.206
1995	5075.6	5539.1	27439.7	3.333
1996	5237.5	5677.7	29448.2	3.083
1997	5423.9	5854.5	32664.1	3.120
1998	5683.7	6168.6	35587.0	3.584
1999	5968.4	6320.0	39591.3	3.245
2000	6257.8	6539.2	38167.7	3.576

Notes: Year = calendar year.
C = real consumption expenditures in billions of chained 1996 dollars.
Yd = real personal disposable income in billions of chained 1996 dollars.
Wealth = real wealth in billions of chained 1996 dollars.
Interest = nominal annual yield on 3-month Treasury securities–inflation rate (measured by the annual % change in annual chained price index).

The nominal real wealth variable was created using data from the Federal Reserve Board's measure of end-of-year net worth for households and nonprofits in the flow of funds accounts. The price index used to convert this nominal wealth variable to a real wealth variable was the average of the chained price index from the 4th quarter of the current year and the 1st quarter of the subsequent year.

7.25. *Estimating Qualcomm stock prices*. As an example of the polynomial regression, consider data on the weekly stock prices of Qualcomm, Inc., a digital wireless telecommunications designer and manufacturer over the time period of 1995 to 2000. The full data can be found on the textbook's website in Table 7.13. During the late 1990, technological stocks were particularly profitable, but what type of regression model will best fit these data? Figure 7.4 shows a basic plot of the data for those years.

This plot does seem to resemble an elongated S curve; there seems to be a slight increase in the average stock price, but then the rate increases dramatically toward the far right side of the graph. As the demand for more specialized phones dramatically increased and the technology boom got under way, the stock price followed suit and increased at a much faster rate.

a. Estimate a linear model to predict the *closing stock price* based on *time*. Does this model seem to fit the data well?

b. Now estimate a squared model by using both *time* and *time-squared*. Is this a better fit than in (*a*)?

FIGURE 7.4
Qualcomm stock prices over time.

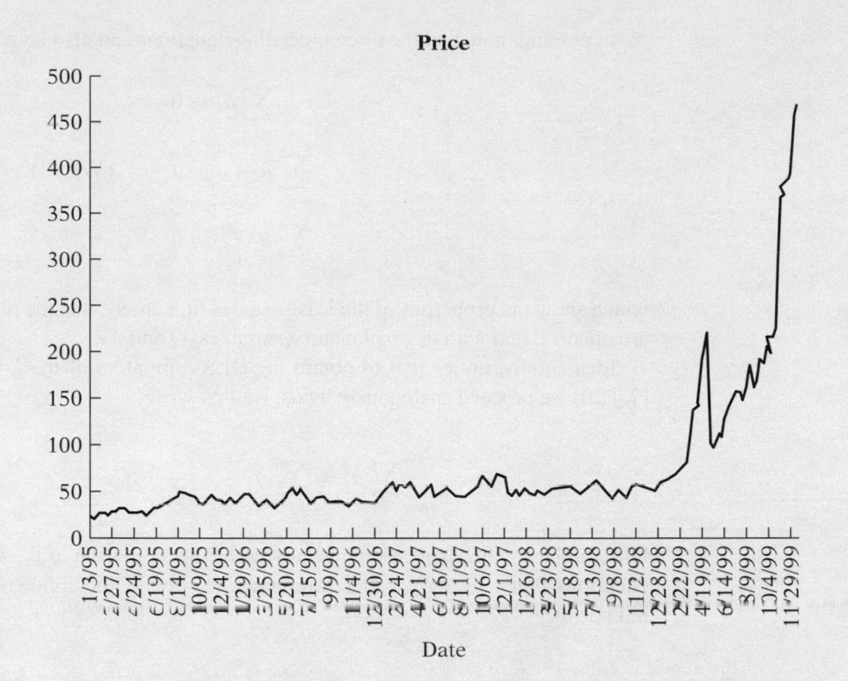

c. Finally, fit the following cubic or *third-degree polynomial:*

$$Y_i = \beta_0 + \beta_1 X_i + \beta_2 X_i^2 + \beta_3 X_i^3 + u_i$$

where $Y =$ stock price and $X =$ time. Which model seems to be the best estimator for the stock prices?

Appendix 7A

7A.1 Derivation of OLS Estimators Given in Equations (7.4.3) to (7.4.5)

Differentiating the equation

$$\sum \hat{u}_i^2 = \sum (Y_i - \hat{\beta}_1 - \hat{\beta}_2 X_{2i} - \hat{\beta}_3 X_{3i})^2 \tag{7.4.2}$$

partially with respect to the three unknowns and setting the resulting equations to zero, we obtain

$$\frac{\partial \sum \hat{u}_i^2}{\partial \hat{\beta}_1} = 2 \sum (Y_i - \hat{\beta}_1 - \hat{\beta}_2 X_{2i} - \hat{\beta}_3 X_{3i})(-1) = 0$$

$$\frac{\partial \sum \hat{u}_i^2}{\partial \hat{\beta}_2} = 2 \sum (Y_i - \hat{\beta}_1 - \hat{\beta}_2 X_{2i} - \hat{\beta}_3 X_{3i})(-X_{2i}) = 0$$

$$\frac{\partial \sum \hat{u}_i^2}{\partial \hat{\beta}_3} = 2 \sum (Y_i - \hat{\beta}_1 - \hat{\beta}_2 X_{2i} - \hat{\beta}_3 X_{3i})(-X_{3i}) = 0$$

Simplifying these, we obtain Eqs. (7.4.3) to (7.4.5).

In passing, note that the three preceding equations can also be written as

$$\sum \hat{u}_i = 0$$

$$\sum \hat{u}_i X_{2i} = 0 \qquad \text{(Why?)}$$

$$\sum \hat{u}_i X_{3i} = 0$$

which show the properties of the least-squares fit, namely, that the residuals sum to zero and that they are uncorrelated with the explanatory variables X_2 and X_3.

Incidentally, notice that to obtain the OLS estimators of the k-variable linear regression model (7.4.20) we proceed analogously. Thus, we first write

$$\sum \hat{u}_i^2 = \sum (Y_i - \hat{\beta}_1 - \hat{\beta}_2 X_{2i} - \cdots - \hat{\beta}_k X_{ki})^2$$

Differentiating this expression partially with respect to each of the k unknowns, setting the resulting equations equal to zero, and rearranging, we obtain the following k normal equations in the k unknowns:

$$\sum Y_i = n\hat{\beta}_1 + \hat{\beta}_2 \sum X_{2i} + \hat{\beta}_3 \sum X_{3i} + \cdots + \hat{\beta}_k \sum X_{ki}$$

$$\sum Y_i X_{2i} = \hat{\beta}_1 \sum X_{2i} + \hat{\beta}_2 \sum X_{2i}^2 + \hat{\beta}_3 \sum X_{2i} X_{3i} + \cdots + \hat{\beta}_k \sum X_{2i} X_{ki}$$

$$\sum Y_i X_{3i} = \hat{\beta}_1 \sum X_{3i} + \hat{\beta}_2 \sum X_{2i} X_{3i} + \hat{\beta}_3 \sum X_{3i}^2 + \cdots + \hat{\beta}_k \sum X_{3i} X_{ki}$$

$$\cdots\cdots\cdots\cdots\cdots\cdots\cdots\cdots\cdots\cdots\cdots\cdots\cdots\cdots\cdots\cdots$$

$$\sum Y_i X_{ki} = \hat{\beta}_1 \sum X_{ki} + \hat{\beta}_2 \sum X_{2i} X_{ki} + \hat{\beta}_3 \sum X_{3i} X_{ki} + \cdots + \hat{\beta}_k \sum X_{ki}^2$$

Or, switching to small letters, these equations can be expressed as

$$\sum y_i x_{2i} = \hat{\beta}_2 \sum x_{2i}^2 + \hat{\beta}_3 \sum x_{2i} x_{3i} + \cdots + \hat{\beta}_k \sum x_{2i} x_{ki}$$

$$\sum y_i x_{3i} = \hat{\beta}_2 \sum x_{2i} x_{3i} + \hat{\beta}_3 \sum x_{3i}^2 + \cdots + \hat{\beta}_k \sum x_{3i} x_{ki}$$

$$\cdots\cdots\cdots\cdots\cdots\cdots\cdots\cdots\cdots\cdots\cdots\cdots\cdots\cdots\cdots\cdots$$

$$\sum y_i x_{ki} = \hat{\beta}_2 \sum x_{2i} x_{ki} + \hat{\beta}_3 \sum x_{3i} x_{ki} + \cdots + \hat{\beta}_k \sum x_{ki}^2$$

It should further be noted that the k-variable model also satisfies these equations:

$$\sum \hat{u}_i = 0$$

$$\sum \hat{u}_i X_{2i} = \sum \hat{u}_i X_{3i} = \cdots = \sum \hat{u}_i X_{ki} = 0$$

7A.2 Equality between the Coefficients of PGNP in Equations (7.3.5) and (7.6.2)

Letting $Y = \text{CM}$, $X_2 = \text{PGNP}$, and $X_3 = \text{FLR}$ and using the deviation form, write

$$y_i = b_{13}x_{3i} + \hat{u}_{1i} \tag{1}$$

$$x_{2i} = b_{23}x_{3i} + \hat{u}_{2i} \tag{2}$$

Now regress $\hat{u}_1$ on $\hat{u}_2$ to obtain:

$$a_1 = \frac{\sum \hat{u}_{1i}\hat{u}_{2i}}{\hat{u}_{2i}^2} = -0.0056 \qquad \text{(for our example)} \tag{3}$$

Note that because the $\hat{u}$'s are residuals, their mean values are zero. Using (1) and (2), we can write (3) as

$$a_1 = \frac{\sum(y_i - b_{13}x_{3i})(x_{2i} - b_{23}x_{3i})}{\sum(x_{2i} - b_{23}x_{3i})^2} \tag{4}$$

Expand the preceding expression, and note that

$$b_{23} = \frac{\sum x_{2i}x_{3i}}{\sum x_{3i}^2} \tag{5}$$

and

$$b_{13} = \frac{\sum y_i x_{3i}}{\sum x_{3i}^2} \tag{6}$$

Making these substitutions into (4), we get

$$\hat{\beta}_2 = \frac{\left(\sum y_i x_{2i}\right)\left(\sum x_{3i}^2\right) - \left(\sum y_i x_{3i}\right)\left(\sum x_{2i}x_{3i}\right)}{\left(\sum x_{2i}^2\right)\left(\sum x_{3i}^2\right) - \left(\sum x_{2i}x_{3i}\right)^2} \tag{7.4.7}$$

$$= -0.0056 \qquad \text{(for our example)}$$

7A.3 Derivation of Equation (7.4.19)

Recall that

$$\hat{u}_i = Y_i - \hat{\beta}_1 - \hat{\beta}_2 X_{2i} - \hat{\beta}_3 X_{3i}$$

which can also be written as

$$\hat{u}_i = y_i - \hat{\beta}_2 x_{2i} - \hat{\beta}_3 x_{3i}$$

where small letters, as usual, indicate deviations from mean values.

Now

$$\begin{aligned}\sum \hat{u}_i^2 &= \sum(\hat{u}_i\hat{u}_i) \\ &= \sum \hat{u}_i(y_i - \hat{\beta}_2 x_{2i} - \hat{\beta}_3 x_{3i}) \\ &= \sum \hat{u}_i y_i\end{aligned}$$

where use is made of the fact that $\sum \hat{u}_i x_{2i} = \sum \hat{u}_i x_{3i} = 0$. (Why?) Also

$$\sum \hat{u}_i y_i = \sum y_i \hat{u}_i = \sum y_i (y_i - \hat{\beta}_2 x_{2i} - \hat{\beta}_3 x_{3i})$$

that is,

$$\sum \hat{u}_i^2 = \sum y_i^2 - \hat{\beta}_2 \sum y_i x_{2i} - \hat{\beta}_3 \sum y_i x_{3i} \tag{7.4.19}$$

which is the required result.

7A.4 Maximum Likelihood Estimation of the Multiple Regression Model

Extending the ideas introduced in Chapter 4, Appendix 4A, we can write the log-likelihood function for the k-variable linear regression model (7.4.20) as

$$\ln L = -\frac{n}{2} \ln \sigma^2 - \frac{n}{2} \ln(2\pi) - \frac{1}{2} \sum \frac{(Y_i - \beta_1 - \beta_2 X_{2i} - \cdots - \beta_k X_{ki})^2}{\sigma^2}$$

Differentiating this function partially with respect to $\beta_1, \beta_2, \ldots, \beta_k$ and σ^2, we obtain the following $(K + 1)$ equations:

$$\frac{\partial \ln L}{\partial \beta_1} = -\frac{1}{\sigma^2} \sum (Y_i - \beta_1 - \beta_2 X_{2i} - \cdots - \beta_k X_{ki})(-1) \tag{1}$$

$$\frac{\partial \ln L}{\partial \beta_2} = -\frac{1}{\sigma^2} \sum (Y_i - \beta_1 - \beta_2 X_{2i} - \cdots - \beta_k X_{ki})(-X_{2i}) \tag{2}$$

$$\cdots\cdots\cdots\cdots\cdots\cdots\cdots\cdots\cdots\cdots\cdots$$

$$\frac{\partial \ln L}{\partial \beta_k} = -\frac{1}{\sigma^2} \sum (Y_i - \beta_1 - \beta_2 X_{2i} - \cdots - \beta_k X_{ki})(-X_{ki}) \tag{K}$$

$$\frac{\partial \ln L}{\partial \sigma^2} = -\frac{n}{2\sigma^2} + \frac{1}{2\sigma^4} \sum (Y_i - \beta_1 - \beta_2 X_{2i} - \cdots - \beta_k X_{ki})^2 \tag{K+1}$$

Setting these equations equal to zero (the first-order condition for optimization) and letting $\tilde{\beta}_1, \tilde{\beta}_2, \ldots, \tilde{\beta}_k$ and $\tilde{\sigma}^2$ denote the ML estimators, we obtain, after simple algebraic manipulations,

$$\sum Y_i = n\tilde{\beta}_1 + \tilde{\beta}_2 \sum X_{2i} + \cdots + \tilde{\beta}_k \sum X_{ki}$$

$$\sum Y_i X_{2i} = \tilde{\beta}_1 \sum X_{2i} + \tilde{\beta}_2 \sum X_{2i}^2 + \cdots + \tilde{\beta}_k \sum X_{2i} X_{ki}$$

$$\cdots\cdots\cdots\cdots\cdots\cdots\cdots\cdots\cdots\cdots\cdots$$

$$\sum Y_i X_{ki} = \tilde{\beta}_1 \sum X_{ki} + \tilde{\beta}_2 \sum X_{2i} X_{ki} + \cdots + \tilde{\beta}_k \sum X_{ki}^2$$

which are precisely the normal equations of the least-squares theory, as can be seen from Appendix 7A, Section 7A.1. Therefore, the ML estimators, the $\tilde{\beta}$'s, are the same as the OLS estimators, the $\hat{\beta}$'s, given previously. But as noted in Chapter 4, Appendix 4A, this equality is not accidental.

Substituting the ML (= OLS) estimators into the $(K + 1)$st equation just given, we obtain, after simplification, the ML estimator of σ^2 as

$$\begin{aligned}
\tilde{\sigma}^2 &= \frac{1}{n} \sum (Y_i - \tilde{\beta}_1 - \tilde{\beta}_2 X_{2i} - \cdots - \tilde{\beta}_k X_{ki})^2 \\
&= \frac{1}{n} \sum \hat{u}_i^2
\end{aligned}$$

As noted in the text, this estimator differs from the OLS estimator $\hat{\sigma}^2 = \sum \hat{u}_i^2/(n-k)$. And since the latter is an unbiased estimator of σ^2, this conclusion implies that the ML estimator $\tilde{\sigma}^2$ is a biased estimator. But, as can be readily verified, asymptotically, $\tilde{\sigma}^2$ is unbiased too.

7A.5 EViews Output of the Cobb–Douglas Production Function in Equation (7.9.4)

Dependent Variable: Y1
Method: Least Squares
Included observations: 51

	Coefficient	Std. Error	*t*-Statistic	Prob.
C	3.887600	0.396228	9.811514	0.0000
Y2	0.468332	0.098926	4.734170	0.0000
Y3	0.521279	0.096887	5.380274	0.0000

R-squared	0.964175	Mean dependent var.	16.94139
Adjusted R-squared	0.962683	S.D. dependent var.	1.380870
S.E. of regression	0.266752	Akaike info criterion	0.252028
Sum squared resid.	3.415520	Schwarz criterion	0.365665
Log likelihood	−3.426721	Hannan-Quinn criterion	0.295452
F-statistic	645.9311	Durbin-Watson stat.	1.946387
Prob. (*F*-statistic)	0.000000		

Covariance of Estimates

	C	Y2	Y3
C	0.156997	0.010364	−0.020014
Y2	0.010364	0.009786	−0.009205
Y3	−0.020014	−0.009205	0.009387

Y	X2	X3	Y1	Y2	Y3	Y1HAT	Y1RESID
38,372,840	424,471	2,689,076	17.4629	12.9586	14.8047	17.6739	0.2110
1,805,427	19,895	57,997	14.4063	9.8982	10.9681	14.2407	0.1656
23,736,129	206,893	2,308,272	16.9825	12.2400	14.6520	17.2577	−0.2752
26,981,983	304,055	1,376,235	17.1107	12.6250	14.1349	17.1685	−0.0578
217,546,032	1,809,756	13,554,116	19.1979	14.4087	16.4222	19.1962	0.0017
19,462,751	180,366	1,790,751	16.7840	12.1027	14.3981	17.0612	−0.2771
28,972,772	224,267	1,210,229	17.1819	12.3206	14.0063	16.9589	0.2229
14,313,157	54,455	421,064	16.4767	10.9051	12.9505	15.7457	0.7310
159,921	2,029	7,188	11.9824	7.6153	8.8802	12.0831	−0.1007
47,289,846	471,211	2,761,281	17.6718	13.0631	14.8312	17.7366	−0.0648
63,015,125	659,379	3,540,475	17.9589	13.3991	15.0798	18.0236	−0.0647
1,809,052	17,528	146,371	14.4083	9.7716	11.8939	14.6640	−0.2557
10,511,786	75,414	848,220	16.1680	11.2307	13.6509	16.2632	−0.0952
105,324,866	963,156	5,870,409	18.4726	13.7780	15.5854	18.4646	0.0079
90,120,459	835,083	5,832,503	18.3167	13.6353	15.5790	18.3944	−0.0778
39,079,550	336,159	1,795,976	17.4811	12.7253	14.4011	17.3543	0.1269
22,826,760	246,144	1,595,118	16.9434	12.4137	14.2825	17.1465	−0.2030
38,686,340	384,484	2,503,693	17.4710	12.8597	14.7333	17.5903	−0.1193
69,910,555	216,149	4,726,625	18.0627	12.2837	15.3687	17.6519	0.4109
7,856,947	82,021	415,131	15.8769	11.3147	12.9363	15.9301	−0.0532
21,352,966	174,855	1,729,116	16.8767	12.0717	14.3631	17.0284	−0.1517
46,044,292	355,701	2,706,065	17.6451	12.7818	14.8110	17.5944	0.0507

(*Continued*)

Y	X2	X3	Y1	Y2	Y3	Y1HAT	Y1RESID
92,335,528	943,298	5,294,356	18.3409	13.7571	15.4822	18.4010	−0.0601
48,304,274	456,553	2,833,525	17.6930	13.0315	14.8570	17.7353	−0.0423
17,207,903	267,806	1,212,281	16.6609	12.4980	14.0080	17.0429	−0.3820
47,340,157	439,427	2,404,122	17.6729	12.9932	14.6927	17.6317	0.0411
2,644,567	24,167	334,008	14.7880	10.0927	12.7189	15.2445	−0.4564
14,650,080	163,637	627,806	16.5000	12.0054	13.3500	16.4692	0.0308
7,290,360	59,737	522,335	15.8021	10.9977	13.1661	15.9014	−0.0993
9,188,322	96,106	507,488	16.0334	11.4732	13.1372	16.1090	−0.0756
51,298,516	407,076	3,295,056	17.7532	12.9168	15.0079	17.7603	−0.0071
20,401,410	43,079	404,749	16.8311	10.6708	12.9110	15.6153	1.2158
87,756,129	727,177	4,260,353	18.2901	13.4969	15.2649	18.1659	0.1242
101,268,432	820,013	4,086,558	18.4333	13.6171	15.2232	18.2005	0.2328
3,556,025	34,723	184,700	15.0842	10.4552	12.1265	15.1054	−0.0212
124,986,166	1,174,540	6,301,421	18.6437	13.9764	15.6563	18.5945	0.0492
20,451,196	201,284	1,327,353	16.8336	12.2125	14.0987	16.9564	−0.1229
34,808,109	257,820	1,456,683	17.3654	12.4600	14.1917	17.1208	0.2445
104,858,322	944,998	5,896,392	18.4681	13.7589	15.5899	18.4580	0.0101
6,541,356	68,987	297,618	15.6937	11.1417	12.6036	15.6756	0.0181
37,668,126	400,317	2,500,071	17.4443	12.9000	14.7318	17.6085	−0.1642
4,988,905	56,524	311,251	15.4227	10.9424	12.6484	15.6056	−0.1829
62,828,100	582,241	4,126,465	17.9559	13.2746	15.2329	18.0451	−0.0892
172,960,157	1,120,382	11,588,283	18.9686	13.9292	16.2655	18.8899	0.0786
15,702,637	150,030	762,671	16.5693	11.9186	13.5446	16.5300	0.0394
5,418,786	48,134	276,293	15.5054	10.7817	12.5292	15.4683	0.0371
49,166,991	425,346	2,731,669	17.7107	12.9607	14.8204	17.6831	0.0277
46,164,427	313,279	1,945,860	17.6477	12.6548	14.4812	17.3630	0.2847
9,185,967	89,639	685,587	16.0332	11.4035	13.4380	16.2332	−0.2000
66,964,978	694,628	3,902,823	18.0197	13.4511	15.1772	18.0988	−0.0791
2,979,475	15,221	361,536	14.9073	9.6304	12.7981	15.0692	−0.1620

Notes: Y1 = ln Y; Y2 = ln X2; Y3 = ln X3.
The eigenvalues are 3.7861 and 187,5269, which will be used in Chapter 10.

Chapter 8

Multiple Regression Analysis: The Problem of Inference

This chapter, a continuation of Chapter 5, extends the ideas of interval estimation and hypothesis testing developed there to models involving three or more variables. Although in many ways the concepts developed in Chapter 5 can be applied straightforwardly to the multiple regression model, a few additional features are unique to such models, and it is these features that will receive more attention in this chapter.

8.1 The Normality Assumption Once Again

We know by now that if our sole objective is point estimation of the parameters of the regression models, the method of ordinary least squares (OLS), which does not make any assumption about the probability distribution of the disturbances u_i, will suffice. But if our objective is estimation as well as inference, then, as argued in Chapters 4 and 5, we need to assume that the u_i follow some probability distribution.

For reasons already clearly spelled out, we assumed that the u_i follow the normal distribution with zero mean and constant variance σ^2. We continue to make the same assumption for multiple regression models. With the normality assumption and following the discussion of Chapters 4 and 7, we find that the OLS estimators of the partial regression coefficients, which are identical with the maximum likelihood (ML) estimators, are best linear unbiased estimators (BLUE).[1] Moreover, the estimators $\hat{\beta}_2$, $\hat{\beta}_3$, and $\hat{\beta}_1$ are themselves normally distributed with means equal to true β_2, β_3, and β_1 and the variances given in Chapter 7. Furthermore, $(n-3)\hat{\sigma}^2/\sigma^2$ follows the χ^2 distribution with $n-3$ df, and the three OLS estimators are distributed independently of $\hat{\sigma}^2$. The proofs follow the two-variable case discussed in Appendix 3A, Section 3A. As a result and following Chapter 5,

[1] With the normality assumption, the OLS estimators $\hat{\beta}_2$, $\hat{\beta}_3$, and $\hat{\beta}_1$ are minimum-variance estimators in the entire class of unbiased estimators, whether linear or not. In short, they are BUE (best unbiased estimators). See C. R. Rao, *Linear Statistical Inference and Its Applications*, John Wiley & Sons, New York, 1965, p. 258.

one can show that, upon replacing σ^2 by its unbiased estimator $\hat{\sigma}^2$ in the computation of the standard errors, each of the following variables

$$t = \frac{\hat{\beta}_1 - \beta_1}{\text{se}(\hat{\beta}_1)} \tag{8.1.1}$$

$$t = \frac{\hat{\beta}_2 - \beta_2}{\text{se}(\hat{\beta}_2)} \tag{8.1.2}$$

$$t = \frac{\hat{\beta}_3 - \beta_3}{\text{se}(\hat{\beta}_3)} \tag{8.1.3}$$

follows the t distribution with $n - 3$ df.

Note that the df are now $n - 3$ because in computing $\sum \hat{u}_i^2$ and hence $\hat{\sigma}^2$ we first need to estimate the three partial regression coefficients, which therefore put three restrictions on the residual sum of squares (RSS) (following this logic in the four-variable case there will be $n - 4$ df, and so on). Therefore, the t distribution can be used to establish confidence intervals as well as test statistical hypotheses about the true population partial regression coefficients. Similarly, the χ^2 distribution can be used to test hypotheses about the true σ^2. To demonstrate the actual mechanics, we use the following illustrative example.

EXAMPLE 8.1 *Child Mortality Example Revisited*

In Chapter 7 we regressed child mortality (CM) on per capita GNP (PGNP) and the female literacy rate (FLR) for a sample of 64 countries. The regression results given in Eq. (7.6.2) are reproduced below with some additional information:

$$\begin{aligned}
\widehat{\text{CM}}_i &= 263.6416 \quad - \quad 0.0056\ \text{PGNP}_i \quad - \quad 2.2316\ \text{FLR}_i \\
\text{se} &= (11.5932) \qquad (0.0019) \qquad (0.2099) \\
t &= (22.7411) \qquad (-2.8187) \qquad (-10.6293) \\
p\ \text{value} &= (0.0000)^* \qquad (0.0065) \qquad (0.0000)^* \\
& \qquad R^2 = 0.7077 \qquad \bar{R}^2 = 0.6981
\end{aligned} \tag{8.1.4}$$

where * denotes extremely low value.

In Eq. (8.1.4) we have followed the format first introduced in Eq. (5.11.1), where the figures in the first set of parentheses are the estimated standard errors, those in the second set are the t values under the null hypothesis that the relevant population coefficient has a value of zero, and those in the third are the estimated p values. Also given are R^2 and adjusted R^2 values. We have already interpreted this regression in Example 7.1.

What about the statistical significance of the observed results? Consider, for example, the coefficient of PGNP of −0.0056. Is this coefficient statistically significant, that is, statistically different from zero? Likewise, is the coefficient of FLR of −2.2316 statistically significant? Are both coefficients statistically significant? To answer this and related questions, let us first consider the kinds of hypothesis testing that one may encounter in the context of a multiple regression model.

8.2 Hypothesis Testing in Multiple Regression: General Comments

Once we go beyond the simple world of the two-variable linear regression model, hypothesis testing assumes several interesting forms, such as the following:

1. Testing hypotheses about an individual partial regression coefficient (Section 8.3).
2. Testing the overall significance of the estimated multiple regression model, that is, finding out if all the partial slope coefficients are simultaneously equal to zero (Section 8.4).

3. Testing that two or more coefficients are equal to one another (Section 8.5).
4. Testing that the partial regression coefficients satisfy certain restrictions (Section 8.6).
5. Testing the stability of the estimated regression model over time or in different cross-sectional units (Section 8.7).
6. Testing the functional form of regression models (Section 8.8).

Since testing of one or more of these types occurs so commonly in empirical analysis, we devote a section to each type.

8.3 Hypothesis Testing about Individual Regression Coefficients

If we invoke the assumption that $u_i \sim N(0, \sigma^2)$, then, as noted in Section 8.1, we can use the t test to test a hypothesis about any *individual* partial regression coefficient. To illustrate the mechanics, consider the child mortality regression, Eq. (8.1.4). Let us postulate that

$$H_0: \beta_2 = 0 \qquad \text{and} \qquad H_1: \beta_2 \neq 0$$

The null hypothesis states that, with X_3 (female literacy rate) held constant, X_2 (PGNP) has no (linear) influence on Y (child mortality).[2] To test the null hypothesis, we use the t test given in Eq. (8.1.2). Following Chapter 5 (see Table 5.1), if the computed t value exceeds the critical t value at the chosen level of significance, we may reject the null hypothesis; otherwise, we may not reject it. For our illustrative example, using Eq. (8.1.2) and noting that $\beta_2 = 0$ under the null hypothesis, we obtain

$$t = \frac{-0.0056}{0.0020} = -2.8187 \tag{8.3.1}$$

as shown in Eq. (8.1.4).

Notice that we have 64 observations. Therefore, the degrees of freedom in this example are 61 (why?). If you refer to the t table given in **Appendix D,** we do not have data corresponding to 61 df. The closest we have are for 60 df. If we use these df, and assume α, the level of significance (i.e., the probability of committing a Type I error) of 5 percent, the critical t value is 2.0 for a two-tail test (look up $t_{\alpha/2}$ for 60 df) or 1.671 for a one-tail test (look up t_α for 60 df).

For our example, the alternative hypothesis is two-sided. Therefore, we use the two-tail t value. Since the computed t value of 2.8187 (in absolute terms) exceeds the critical t value of 2, we can reject the null hypothesis that PGNP has no effect on child mortality. To put it more positively, with the female literacy rate held constant, per capita GNP has a significant (negative) effect on child mortality, as one would expect a priori. Graphically, the situation is as shown in Figure 8.1.

In practice, one does not have to assume a particular value of α to conduct hypothesis testing. One can simply use the p value given in Eq. (8.1.4), which in the present case is 0.0065. The interpretation of this p value (i.e., the exact level of significance) is that if the null hypothesis were true, the probability of obtaining a t value of as much as 2.8187 or greater (in absolute terms) is only 0.0065 or 0.65 percent, which is indeed a small probability, much smaller than the artificially adopted value of $\alpha = 5\%$.

[2]In most empirical investigations the null hypothesis is stated in this form, that is, taking the extreme position (a kind of straw man) that there is no relationship between the dependent variable and the explanatory variable under consideration. The idea here is to find out whether the relationship between the two is a trivial one to begin with.

FIGURE 8.1 The 95% confidence interval for t (60 df).

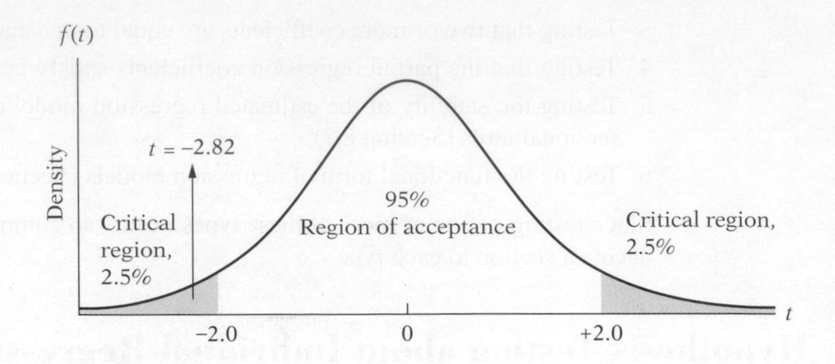

This example provides us an opportunity to decide whether we want to use a one-tail or a two-tail t test. Since a priori child mortality and per capita GNP are expected to be negatively related (why?), we should use the one-tail test. That is, our null and alternative hypothesis should be:

$$H_0\colon \beta_2 < 0 \quad \text{and} \quad H_1\colon \beta_2 \geq 0$$

As the reader knows by now, we can reject the null hypothesis on the basis of the one-tail t test in the present instance. If we can reject the null hypothesis in a two-sided test, we will have enough evidence to reject in the one-sided scenario as long as the statistic is in the same direction as the test.

In Chapter 5 we saw the intimate connection between hypothesis testing and confidence interval estimation. For our example, the 95 percent confidence interval for β_2 is:

$$\hat{\beta}_2 - t_{\alpha/2}\,\text{se}\,(\hat{\beta}_2) \leq \beta_2 \leq \hat{\beta}_2 + t_{\alpha/2}\,\text{se}\,(\hat{\beta}_2)$$

which in our example becomes

$$-0.0056 - 2(0.0020) \leq \beta_2 \leq -0.0056 + 2(0.0020)$$

that is,

$$-0.0096 \leq \beta_2 \leq -0.0016 \tag{8.3.2}$$

that is, the interval, −0.0096 to −0.0016 includes the true β_2 coefficient with 95 percent confidence coefficient. Thus, if 100 samples of size 64 are selected and 100 confidence intervals like Eq. (8.3.2) are constructed, we expect 95 of them to contain the true population parameter β_2. Since the interval (8.3.2) does not include the null-hypothesized value of zero, we can reject the null hypothesis that the true β_2 is zero with 95 percent confidence.

Thus, whether we use the t test of significance as in (8.3.1) or the confidence interval estimation as in (8.3.2), we reach the same conclusion. However, this should not be surprising in view of the close connection between confidence interval estimation and hypothesis testing.

Following the procedure just described, we can test hypotheses about the other parameters of our child mortality regression model. The necessary data are already provided in Eq. (8.1.4). For example, suppose we want to test the hypothesis that, with the influence of PGNP held constant, the female literacy rate has no effect whatsoever on child mortality. We can confidently reject this hypothesis, for under this null hypothesis the p value of obtaining an absolute t value of as much as 10.6 or greater is practically zero.

Before moving on, remember that the t-testing procedure is based on the assumption that the error term u_i follows the normal distribution. Although we cannot directly observe

FIGURE 8.2
Histogram of residuals from regression (8.1.4).

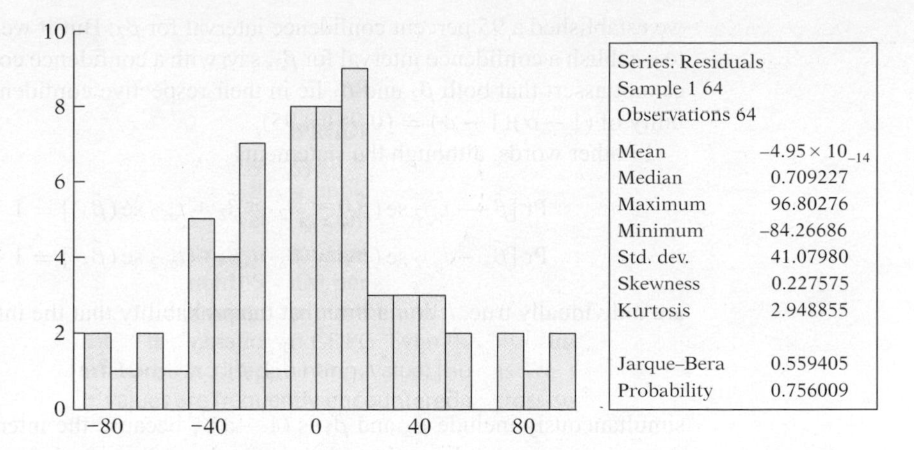

u_i, we can observe their proxy, the $\hat{u}_i$, that is, the residuals. For our mortality regression, the histogram of the residuals is as shown in Figure 8.2.

From the histogram it seems that the residuals are normally distributed. We can also compute the **Jarque–Bera** (JB) test of normality, as shown in Eq. (5.12.1). In our case the JB value is 0.5594 with a p value 0.76.[3] Therefore, it seems that the error term in our example follows the normal distribution. Of course, keep in mind that the JB test is a large-sample test and our sample of 64 observations may not be necessarily large.

8.4 Testing the Overall Significance of the Sample Regression

Throughout the previous section we were concerned with testing the significance of the estimated partial regression coefficients individually, that is, under the separate hypothesis that each true population partial regression coefficient was zero. But now consider the following hypothesis:

$$H_0: \beta_2 = \beta_3 = 0 \tag{8.4.1}$$

This null hypothesis is a joint hypothesis that β_2 and β_3 are jointly or simultaneously equal to zero. A test of such a hypothesis is called a test of the **overall significance** of the observed or estimated regression line, that is, whether Y is linearly related to both X_2 and X_3.

Can the joint hypothesis in Eq. (8.4.1) be tested by testing the significance of $\hat{\beta}_2$ and $\hat{\beta}_3$ individually as in Section 8.3? The answer is no, and the reasoning is as follows.

In testing the individual significance of an observed partial regression coefficient in Section 8.3, we assumed implicitly that each test of significance was based on a different (i.e., independent) sample. Thus, in testing the significance of $\hat{\beta}_2$ under the hypothesis that $\beta_2 = 0$, it was assumed tacitly that the testing was based on a different sample from the one used in testing the significance of $\hat{\beta}_3$ under the null hypothesis that $\beta_3 = 0$. But to test the joint hypothesis of Eq. (8.4.1), if we use the same sample data, we shall be violating the assumption underlying the test procedure.[4] The matter can be put differently: In Eq. (8.3.2)

[3]For our example, the skewness value is 0.2276 and the kurtosis value is 2.9488. Recall that for a normally distributed variable the skewness and kurtosis values are, respectively, 0 and 3.

[4]In any given sample the cov $(\hat{\beta}_2, \hat{\beta}_3)$ may not be zero; that is, $\hat{\beta}_2$ and $\hat{\beta}_3$ may be correlated. See Eq. (7.4.17).

we established a 95 percent confidence interval for β_2. But if we use the same sample data to establish a confidence interval for β_3, say, with a confidence coefficient of 95 percent, we cannot assert that both β_2 and β_3 lie in their respective confidence intervals with a probability of $(1-\alpha)(1-\alpha) = (0.95)(0.95)$.

In other words, although the statements

$$\Pr[\hat{\beta}_2 - t_{\alpha/2}\,\text{se}(\hat{\beta}_2) \le \beta_2 \le \hat{\beta}_2 + t_{\alpha/2}\,\text{se}(\hat{\beta}_2)] = 1-\alpha$$

$$\Pr[\hat{\beta}_3 - t_{\alpha/2}\,\text{se}(\hat{\beta}_3) \le \beta_3 \le \hat{\beta}_3 + t_{\alpha/2}\,\text{se}(\hat{\beta}_3)] = 1-\alpha$$

are individually true, *it is not true* that the probability that the intervals

$$[\hat{\beta}_2 \pm t_{\alpha/2}\,\text{se}(\hat{\beta}_2),\ \hat{\beta}_3 \pm t_{\alpha/2}\,\text{se}(\hat{\beta}_3)]$$

simultaneously include β_2 and β_3 is $(1-\alpha)^2$, because the intervals may not be independent when the same data are used to derive them. To state the matter differently,

> . . . testing a series of single [individual] hypotheses is *not* equivalent to testing those same hypotheses jointly. The intuitive reason for this is that in a joint test of several hypotheses any single hypothesis is "affected" by the information in the other hypotheses.[5]

The upshot of the preceding argument is that for a given example (sample) only one confidence interval or only one test of significance can be obtained. How, then, does one test the simultaneous null hypothesis that $\beta_2 = \beta_3 = 0$? The answer follows.

The Analysis of Variance Approach to Testing the Overall Significance of an Observed Multiple Regression: The *F* Test

For reasons just explained, we cannot use the usual *t* test to test the joint hypothesis that the true partial slope coefficients are zero simultaneously. However, this joint hypothesis can be tested by the **analysis of variance** (ANOVA) technique first introduced in Section 5.9, which can be demonstrated as follows.

Recall the identity

$$\underset{\text{TSS}}{\sum y_i^2} = \underset{\text{ESS}}{\hat{\beta}_2 \sum y_i x_{2i} + \hat{\beta}_3 \sum y_i x_{3i}} + \underset{\text{RSS}}{\sum \hat{u}_i^2} \tag{8.4.2}$$

TSS has, as usual, $n-1$ df and RSS has $n-3$ df for reasons already discussed. ESS has 2 df since it is a function of $\hat{\beta}_2$ and $\hat{\beta}_3$. Therefore, following the ANOVA procedure discussed in Section 5.9, we can set up Table 8.1.

Now it can be shown[6] that, under the assumption of normal distribution for u_i and the null hypothesis $\beta_2 = \beta_3 = 0$, the variable

$$F = \frac{\left(\hat{\beta}_2 \sum y_i x_{2i} + \hat{\beta}_3 \sum y_i x_{3i}\right)/2}{\sum \hat{u}_i^2/(n-3)} = \frac{\text{ESS/df}}{\text{RSS/df}} \tag{8.4.3}$$

is distributed as the *F* distribution with 2 and $n-3$ df.

[5]Thomas B. Fomby, R. Carter Hill, and Stanley R. Johnson, *Advanced Econometric Methods*, Springer-Verlag, New York, 1984, p. 37.

[6]See K. A. Brownlee, *Statistical Theory and Methodology in Science and Engineering*, John Wiley & Sons, New York, 1960, pp. 278–280.

TABLE 8.1
ANOVA Table for the Three-Variable Regression

Source of Variation	SS	df	MSS
Due to regression (ESS)	$\hat{\beta}_2 \sum y_i x_{2i} + \hat{\beta}_3 \sum y_i x_{3i}$	2	$\dfrac{\hat{\beta}_2 \sum y_i x_{2i} + \hat{\beta}_3 \sum y_i x_{3i}}{2}$
Due to residual (RSS)	$\sum \hat{u}_i^2$	$n - 3$	$\hat{\sigma}^2 = \dfrac{\sum \hat{u}_i^2}{n-3}$
Total	$\sum y_i^2$	$n - 1$	

What use can be made of the preceding F ratio? It can be proved[7] that under the assumption that the $u_i \sim N(0, \sigma^2)$,

$$E \frac{\sum \hat{u}_i^2}{n-3} = E(\hat{\sigma}^2) = \sigma^2 \tag{8.4.4}$$

With the additional assumption that $\beta_2 = \beta_3 = 0$, it can be shown that

$$\frac{E\left(\hat{\beta}_2 \sum y_i x_{2i} + \hat{\beta}_3 \sum y_i x_{3i}\right)}{2} = \sigma^2 \tag{8.4.5}$$

Therefore, if the null hypothesis is true, both Eqs. (8.4.4) and (8.4.5) give identical estimates of true σ^2. This statement should not be surprising because if there is a trivial relationship between Y and X_2 and X_3, the sole source of variation in Y is due to the random forces represented by u_i. If, however, the null hypothesis is false, that is, X_2 and X_3 definitely influence Y, the equality between Eqs. (8.4.4) and (8.4.5) will not hold. In this case, the ESS will be relatively larger than the RSS, taking due account of their respective df. Therefore, the F value of Eq. (8.4.3) provides a test of the null hypothesis that the true slope coefficients are simultaneously zero. If the F value computed from Eq. (8.4.3) exceeds the critical F value from the F table at the α percent level of significance, we reject H_0; otherwise we do not reject it. Alternatively, if the p value of the observed F is sufficiently low, we can reject H_0.

Table 8.2 summarizes the F test. Turning to our illustrative example, we obtain the ANOVA table, as shown in Table 8.3.

TABLE 8.2
A Summary of the F Statistic

Null Hypothesis H_0	Alternative Hypothesis H_1	Critical Region-Reject H_0 If
$\sigma_1^2 = \sigma_2^2$	$\sigma_1^2 > \sigma_2^2$	$\dfrac{S_1^2}{S_2^2} > F_{\alpha,\text{ndf},\text{ddf}}$
$\sigma_1^2 = \sigma_2^2$	$\sigma_1^2 \neq \sigma_2^2$	$\dfrac{S_1^2}{S_2^2} > F_{\alpha/2,\text{ndf},\text{ddf}}$ or $< F_{(1-\alpha/2),\text{ndf},\text{ddf}}$

Notes:

1. σ_1^2 and σ_2^2 are the two population variances.
2. S_1^2 and S_2^2 are the two sample variances.
3. $n$df and $d$df denote, respectively, the numerator and denominator df.
4. In computing the F ratio, put the larger S^2 value in the numerator.
5. The critical F values are given in the last column. The first subscript of F is the level of significance and the second subscript is the numerator and denominator df.
6. Note that $F_{(1-\alpha/2),n\text{df},d\text{df}} = 1/F_{\alpha/2,d\text{df},n\text{df}}$.

[7] See K. A. Brownlee, *Statistical Theory and Methodology in Science and Engineering,* John Wiley & Sons, New York, 1960, pp. 278–280.

TABLE 8.3
ANOVA Table for the Child Mortality Example

Source of Variation	SS	df	MSS
Due to regression	257,362.4	2	128,681.2
Due to residuals	106,315.6	61	1742.88
Total	363,678	63	

Using Eq. (8.4.3), we obtain

$$F = \frac{128{,}681.2}{1742.88} = 73.8325 \tag{8.4.6}$$

The p value of obtaining an F value of as much as 73.8325 or greater is almost zero, leading to the rejection of the hypothesis that together PGNP and FLR have no effect on child mortality. If you were to use the conventional 5 percent level-of-significance value, the critical F value for 2 df in the numerator and 60 df in the denominator (the actual df, however, are 61) is about 3.15, or about 4.98 if you were to use the 1 percent level of significance. Obviously, the observed F of about 74 far exceeds any of these critical F values.

We can generalize the preceding F-testing procedure as follows.

Testing the Overall Significance of a Multiple Regression: The F Test

Decision Rule

Given the k-variable regression model:

$$Y_i = \beta_1 + \beta_2 X_{2i} + \beta_3 X_{3i} + \cdots + \beta_k X_{ki} + u_i$$

To test the hypothesis

$$H_0\colon \beta_2 = \beta_3 = \cdots = \beta_k = 0$$

(i.e., all slope coefficients are simultaneously zero) versus

$$H_1\colon \text{Not all slope coefficients are simultaneously zero}$$

compute

$$F = \frac{\text{ESS/df}}{\text{RSS/df}} = \frac{\text{ESS}/(k-1)}{\text{RSS}/(n-k)} \tag{8.4.7}$$

If $F > F_\alpha(k-1, n-k)$, reject H_0; otherwise you do not reject it, where $F_\alpha(k-1, n-k)$ is the *critical* F value at the α level of significance and $(k-1)$ numerator df and $(n-k)$ denominator df. Alternatively, if the p value of F obtained from Eq. (8.4.7) is sufficiently low, one can reject H_0.

Needless to say, in the three-variable case (Y and X_2, X_3) k is 3, in the four-variable case k is 4, and so on.

In passing, note that most regression packages routinely calculate the F value (given in the analysis of variance table) along with the usual regression output, such as the estimated coefficients, their standard errors, t values, etc. The null hypothesis for the t computation is usually assumed to be $\beta_i = 0$.

Individual versus Joint Testing of Hypotheses

In Section 8.3 we discussed the test of significance of a single regression coefficient and in Section 8.4 we have discussed the joint or overall test of significance of the estimated regression (i.e., all slope coefficients are simultaneously equal to zero). **We reiterate that these tests are different.** Thus, on the basis of the t test or confidence interval (of Section 8.3) it is possible to accept the hypothesis that a particular slope coefficient, β_k, is zero, and yet reject the joint hypothesis that all slope coefficients are zero.

> The lesson to be learned is that the joint "message" of individual confidence intervals is no substitute for a joint confidence region [implied by the F test] in performing joint tests of hypotheses and making joint confidence statements.[8]

An Important Relationship between R^2 and F

There is an intimate relationship between the coefficient of determination R^2 and the F test used in the analysis of variance. Assuming the normal distribution for the disturbances u_i and the null hypothesis that $\beta_2 = \beta_3 = 0$, we have seen that

$$F = \frac{\text{ESS}/2}{\text{RSS}/(n-3)} \tag{8.4.8}$$

is distributed as the F distribution with 2 and $n-3$ df.

More generally, in the k-variable case (including intercept), if we assume that the disturbances are normally distributed and that the null hypothesis is

$$H_0\colon \beta_2 = \beta_3 = \cdots = \beta_k = 0 \tag{8.4.9}$$

then it follows that

$$F = \frac{\text{ESS}/(k-1)}{\text{RSS}/(n-k)} \qquad (8.4.7) = (8.4.10)$$

follows the F distribution with $k-1$ and $n-k$ df. (*Note:* The total number of parameters to be estimated is k, of which 1 is the intercept term.)

Let us manipulate Eq. (8.4.10) as follows:

$$\begin{aligned} F &= \frac{n-k}{k-1}\frac{\text{ESS}}{\text{RSS}} \\ &= \frac{n-k}{k-1}\frac{\text{ESS}}{\text{TSS}-\text{ESS}} \\ &= \frac{n-k}{k-1}\frac{\text{ESS}/\text{TSS}}{1-(\text{ESS}/\text{TSS})} \\ &= \frac{n-k}{k-1}\frac{R^2}{1-R^2} \\ &= \frac{R^2/(k-1)}{(1-R^2)/(n-k)} \end{aligned} \tag{8.4.11}$$

[8]Fomby et al., op. cit., p. 42.

TABLE 8.4
ANOVA Table in Terms of R^2

Source of Variation	SS	df	MSS*
Due to regression	$R^2(\sum y_i^2)$	2	$R^2(\sum y_i^2)/2$
Due to residuals	$(1 - R^2)(\sum y_i^2)$	$n - 3$	$(1 - R^2)(\sum y_i^2)/(n - 3)$
Total	$\sum y_i^2$	$n - 1$	

*Note that in computing the F value there is no need to multiply R^2 and $(1 - R^2)$ by $\sum y_i^2$ because it drops out, as shown in Eq. (8.4.12).

where use is made of the definition $R^2 = \text{ESS/TSS}$. Equation (8.4.11) shows how F and R^2 are related. These two vary directly. When $R^2 = 0$, F is zero ipso facto. The larger the R^2, the greater the F value. In the limit, when $R^2 = 1$, F is infinite. *Thus the F test, which is a measure of the overall significance of the estimated regression, is also a test of significance of R^2.* In other words, testing the null hypothesis in Eq. (8.4.9) is equivalent to testing the null hypothesis that (the population) R^2 is zero.

For the three-variable case, Eq. (8.4.11) becomes

$$F = \frac{R^2/2}{(1 - R^2)/(n - 3)} \tag{8.4.12}$$

By virtue of the close connection between F and R^2, the ANOVA Table (Table 8.1) can be recast as Table 8.4.

For our illustrative example, using Eq. (8.4.12) we obtain:

$$F = \frac{0.7077/2}{(1 - 0.7077)/61} = 73.8726$$

which is about the same as obtained before, except for the rounding errors.

One advantage of the F test expressed in terms of R^2 is its ease of computation: All that one needs to know is the R^2 value. Therefore, the overall F test of significance given in Eq. (8.4.7) can be recast in terms of R^2 as shown in Table 8.4.

Testing the Overall Significance of a Multiple Regression in Terms of R^2

Decision Rule

Testing the overall significance of a regression in terms of R^2: Alternative but equivalent test to Eq. (8.4.7).

Given the k-variable regression model:

$$Y_i = \beta_i + \beta_2 X_{2i} + \beta_3 X_{3i} + \cdots + \beta_x X_{ki} + u_i$$

To test the hypothesis

$$H_0\colon \beta_2 = \beta_3 = \cdots = \beta_k = 0$$

versus

H_1: Not all slope coefficients are simultaneously zero

compute

$$F = \frac{R^2/(k - 1)}{(1 - R^2)/(n - k)} \tag{8.4.13}$$

If $F > F_{\alpha(k-1,n-k)}$, reject H_0; otherwise you may accept H_0 where $F_{\alpha(k-1,n-k)}$ is the critical F value at the α level of significance and $(k - 1)$ numerator df and $(n - k)$ denominator df. Alternatively, if the p value of F obtained from Eq. (8.4.13) is sufficiently low, reject H_0.

Before moving on, return to Example 7.5 in Chapter 7. From regression (7.10.7) we observe that RGDP (relative per capita GDP) and RGDP squared explain only about 10.92 percent of the variation in GDPG (GDP growth rate) in a sample of 190 countries. This R^2 of 0.1092 seems a "low" value. Is it really statistically different from zero? How do we find that out?

Recall our earlier discussion in "An Important Relationship between R^2 and F" about the relationship between R^2 and the F value as given in Eq. (8.4.11) or Eq. (8.4.12) for the specific case of two regressors. As noted, if R^2 is zero, then F is zero ipso facto, which will be the case if the regressors have no impact whatsoever on the regressand. Therefore, if we insert $R^2 = 0.1092$ into formula (8.4.12), we obtain

$$F = \frac{0.1092/2}{(1 - 0.1092)/187} = 11.4618 \tag{8.4.13}$$

Under the null hypothesis that $R^2 = 0$, the preceding F value follows the F distribution with 2 and 187 df in the numerator, respectively. (*Note:* There are 190 observations and two regressors.) From the F table we see that this F value is significant at about the 5 percent level; the p value is actually 0.00002. Therefore, we can reject the null hypothesis that the two regressors have no impact on the regressand, notwithstanding the fact that the R^2 is only 0.1092.

This example brings out an important empirical observation that in cross-sectional data involving several observations, one generally obtains low R^2 because of the diversity of the cross-sectional units. Therefore, one should not be surprised or worried about finding low R^2's in cross-sectional regressions. What is relevant is that the model is correctly specified, that the regressors have the correct (i.e., theoretically expected) signs, and that (hopefully) the regression coefficients are statistically significant. The reader should check that *individually* both of the regressors in Eq. (7.10.7) are statistically significant at the 5 percent or better level (i.e., lower than 5 percent).

The "Incremental" or "Marginal" Contribution of an Explanatory Variable

In Chapter 7 we stated that generally we cannot allocate the R^2 value among the various regressors. In our child mortality example we found that the R^2 was 0.7077 but we cannot say what part of this value is due to the regressor PGNP and what part is due to female literacy rate (FLR) because of possible correlation between the two regressors in the sample at hand. We can shed more light on this using the analysis of variance technique.

For our illustrative example we found that *individually* X_2 (PGNP) and X_3 (FLR) were statistically significant on the basis of (*separate*) t tests. We have also found that on the basis of the F test *collectively* both the regressors have a significant effect on the regressand Y (child mortality).

Now suppose we introduce PGNP and FLR *sequentially;* that is, we first regress child mortality on PGNP and assess its significance and then add FLR to the model to find out whether it contributes anything (of course, the order in which PGNP and FLR enter can be reversed). By contribution we mean whether the addition of the variable to the model increases ESS (and hence R^2) "significantly" in relation to the RSS. This contribution may appropriately be called the **incremental,** or **marginal,** contribution of an explanatory variable.

The topic of incremental contribution is an important one in practice. In most empirical investigations the researcher may not be completely sure whether it is worth adding an X variable to the model knowing that several other X variables are already present in the model. One does not wish to include a variable(s) that contributes very little toward ESS. By the same token, one does not want to exclude a variable(s) that substantially increases

TABLE 8.5
ANOVA Table for Regression Equation (8.4.14)

Source of Variation	SS	df	MSS
ESS (due to PGNP)	60,449.5	1	60,449.5
RSS	303,228.5	62	4890.7822
Total	363,678	63	

ESS. But how does one decide whether an X variable significantly reduces RSS? The analysis of variance technique can be easily extended to answer this question.

Suppose we first regress child mortality on PGNP and obtain the following regression:

$$\begin{aligned} \widehat{\text{CM}}_i &= 157.4244 \quad - \quad 0.0114\ \text{PGNP} \\ t &= (15.9894) \quad (-3.5156) \qquad r^2 = 0.1662 \\ p \text{ value} &= (0.0000) \quad (0.0008) \qquad \text{adj } r^2 = 0.1528 \end{aligned} \tag{8.4.14}$$

As these results show, PGNP has a significant effect on CM. The ANOVA table corresponding to the preceding regression is given in Table 8.5.

Assuming the disturbances u_i are normally distributed and the hypothesis that PGNP has no effect on CM, we obtain the F value of

$$F = \frac{60{,}449.5}{4890.7822} = 12.3598 \tag{8.4.15}$$

which follows the F distribution with 1 and 62 df. This F value is highly significant, as the computed p value is 0.0008. Thus, as before, we reject the hypothesis that PGNP has no effect on CM. Incidentally, note that $t^2 = (-3.5156)^2 = 12.3594$, which is approximately the same as the F value of Eq. (8.4.15), where the t value is obtained from Eq. (8.4.14). But this should not be surprising in view of the fact that the square of the t statistic with n df is equal to the F value with 1 df in the numerator and n df in the denominator, a relationship first established in Chapter 5. Note that in the present example, $n = 64$.

Having run the regression (8.4.14), let us suppose we decide to add FLR to the model and obtain the multiple regression (8.1.4). The questions we want to answer are:

1. What is the marginal, or incremental, contribution of FLR, knowing that PGNP is already in the model and that it is significantly related to CM?
2. Is the incremental contribution of FLR statistically significant?
3. What is the criterion for adding variables to the model?

The preceding questions can be answered by the ANOVA technique. To see this, let us construct Table 8.6. In this table X_2 refers to PGNP and X_3 refers to FLR.

To assess the *incremental* contribution of X_3 after allowing for the contribution of X_2, we form

$$\begin{aligned} F &= \frac{Q_2/\text{df}}{Q_4/\text{df}} \\ &= \frac{(\text{ESS}_{\text{new}} - \text{ESS}_{\text{old}})/\text{number of new regressors}}{\text{RSS}_{\text{new}}/\text{df}(= n - \text{number of parameters in the new model})} \\ &= \frac{Q_2/1}{Q_4/61} \quad \text{for our example} \end{aligned} \tag{8.4.16}$$

TABLE 8.6
ANOVA Table to Assess Incremental Contribution of a Variable(s)

Source of Variation	SS	df	MSS
ESS due to X_2 alone	$Q_1 = \hat{\beta}_{12}^2 \sum x_2^2$	1	$\frac{Q_1}{1}$
ESS due to the addition of X_3	$Q_2 = Q_3 - Q_1$	1	$\frac{Q_2}{1}$
ESS due to both X_2, X_3	$Q_3 = \hat{\beta}_2 \sum y_i x_{2i} + \hat{\beta}_3 \sum y_i x_{3i}$	2	$\frac{Q_3}{2}$
RSS	$Q_4 = Q_5 - Q_3$	$n - 3$	$\frac{Q_4}{n-3}$
Total	$Q_5 = \sum y_i^2$	$n - 1$	

where ESS_{new} = ESS under the new model (i.e., after adding the new regressors $= Q_3$), ESS_{old} = ESS under the old model ($= Q_1$), and RSS_{new} = RSS under the new model (i.e., after taking into account all the regressors $= Q_4$). For our illustrative example the results are as shown in Table 8.7.

Now applying Eq. (8.4.16), we obtain:

$$F = \frac{196{,}912.9}{1742.8786} = 112.9814 \tag{8.4.17}$$

Under the usual assumptions, this F value follows the F distribution with 1 and 62 df. The reader should check that this F value is highly significant, suggesting that the addition of FLR to the model significantly increases ESS and hence the R^2 value. Therefore, FLR should be added to the model. Again, note that if you square the t-statistic value of the FLR coefficient in the multiple regression (8.1.4), which is $(-10.6293)^2$, you will obtain the F value of Eq. (8.4.17), save for the rounding errors.

Incidentally, the F ratio of Eq. (8.4.16) can be recast by using the R^2 values only, as we did in Eq. (8.4.13). As Exercise 8.2 shows, the F ratio of Eq. (8.4.16) is *equivalent* to the following F ratio:[9]

$$\begin{aligned} F &= \frac{(R_{\text{new}}^2 - R_{\text{old}}^2)/\text{df}}{(1 - R_{\text{new}}^2)/\text{df}} \\ &= \frac{(R_{\text{new}}^2 - R_{\text{old}}^2)/\text{number of new regressors}}{(1 - R_{\text{new}}^2)/\text{df}(= n - \text{number of parameters in the new model})} \end{aligned} \tag{8.4.18}$$

TABLE 8.7
ANOVA Table for the Illustrative Example: Incremental Analysis

Source of Variation	SS	df	MSS
ESS due to PGNP	60,449.5	1	60,449.5
ESS due to the addition of FLR	196,912.9	1	196,912.9
ESS due to PGNP and FLR	257,362.4	2	128,681.2
RSS	106,315.6	61	1742.8786
Total	363,678	63	

[9] The following F test is a special case of the more general F test given in Eq. (8.6.9) or Eq. (8.6.10) in Section 8.6.

This F ratio follows the F distribution with the appropriate numerator and denominator df, 1 and 61 in our illustrative example.

For our example, $R^2_{\text{new}} = 0.7077$ (from Eq. [8.1.4]) and $R^2_{\text{old}} = 0.1662$ (from Eq. [8.4.14]). Therefore,

$$F = \frac{(0.7077 - 0.1662)/1}{(1 - 0.7077)/61} = 113.05 \tag{8.4.19}$$

which is about the same as that obtained from Eq. (8.4.17), except for the rounding errors. This F is highly significant, reinforcing our earlier finding that the variable FLR belongs in the model.

A cautionary note: If you use the R^2 version of the F test given in Eq. (8.4.11), make sure that the dependent variable in the new and the old models is the same. If they are different, use the F test given in Eq. (8.4.16).

When to Add a New Variable

The F-test procedure just outlined provides a formal method of deciding whether a variable should be added to a regression model. Often researchers are faced with the task of choosing from several competing models **involving the same dependent variable** but with different explanatory variables. As a matter of ad hoc choice (because very often the theoretical foundation of the analysis is weak), these researchers frequently choose the model that gives the highest adjusted R^2. Therefore, if the inclusion of a variable increases $\bar{R}^2$, it is retained in the model although it does not reduce RSS significantly in the statistical sense. The question then becomes: When does the adjusted R^2 increase? It can be shown that *$\bar{R}^2$ will increase if the t value of the coefficient of the newly added variable is larger than 1 in absolute value*, where the t value is computed under the hypothesis that the population value of the said coefficient is zero (i.e., the t value computed from Eq. [5.3.2] under the hypothesis that the true β value is zero).[10] The preceding criterion can also be stated differently: *$\bar{R}^2$ will increase with the addition of an extra explanatory variable only if the $F(= t^2)$ value of that variable exceeds 1.*

Applying either criterion, the FLR variable in our child mortality example with a t value of -10.6293 or an F value of 112.9814 should increase $\bar{R}^2$, which indeed it does—when FLR is added to the model, $\bar{R}^2$ increases from 0.1528 to 0.6981.

When to Add a Group of Variables

Can we develop a similar rule for deciding whether it is worth adding (or dropping) a group of variables from a model? The answer should be apparent from Eq. (8.4.18): *If adding (dropping) a group of variables to the model gives an F value greater (less) than 1, R^2 will increase (decrease).* Of course, from Eq. (8.4.18) one can easily find out whether the addition (subtraction) of a group of variables significantly increases (decreases) the explanatory power of a regression model.

8.5 Testing the Equality of Two Regression Coefficients

Suppose in the multiple regression

$$Y_i = \beta_1 + \beta_2 X_{2i} + \beta_3 X_{3i} + \beta_4 X_{4i} + u_i \tag{8.5.1}$$

[10]For proof, see Dennis J. Aigner, *Basic Econometrics*, Prentice Hall, Englewood Cliffs, NJ, 1971, pp. 91–92.

we want to test the hypotheses

$$\begin{aligned} H_0&: \beta_3 = \beta_4 \quad \text{or} \quad (\beta_3 - \beta_4) = 0 \\ H_1&: \beta_3 \neq \beta_4 \quad \text{or} \quad (\beta_3 - \beta_4) \neq 0 \end{aligned} \tag{8.5.2}$$

that is, the two slope coefficients β_3 and β_4 are equal.

Such a null hypothesis is of practical importance. For example, let Eq. (8.5.1) represent the demand function for a commodity where Y = amount of a commodity demanded, X_2 = price of the commodity, X_3 = income of the consumer, and X_4 = wealth of the consumer. The null hypothesis in this case means that the income and wealth coefficients are the same. Or, if Y_i and the X's are expressed in logarithmic form, the null hypothesis in Eq. (8.5.2) implies that the income and wealth elasticities of consumption are the same. (Why?)

How do we test such a null hypothesis? Under the classical assumptions, it can be shown that

$$t = \frac{(\hat{\beta}_3 - \hat{\beta}_4) - (\beta_3 - \beta_4)}{\text{se}\,(\hat{\beta}_3 - \hat{\beta}_4)} \tag{8.5.3}$$

follows the t distribution with $(n - 4)$ df because Eq. (8.5.1) is a four-variable model or, more generally, with $(n - k)$ df, where k is the total number of parameters estimated, including the constant term. The $\text{se}\,(\hat{\beta}_3 - \hat{\beta}_4)$ is obtained from the following well-known formula (see **Appendix A** for details):

$$\text{se}\,(\hat{\beta}_3 - \hat{\beta}_4) = \sqrt{\text{var}\,(\hat{\beta}_3) + \text{var}\,(\hat{\beta}_4) - 2\,\text{cov}\,(\hat{\beta}_3, \hat{\beta}_4)} \tag{8.5.4}$$

If we substitute the null hypothesis and the expression for the $\text{se}\,(\hat{\beta}_3 - \hat{\beta}_4)$ into Eq. (8.5.3), our test statistic becomes

$$t = \frac{\hat{\beta}_3 - \hat{\beta}_4}{\sqrt{\text{var}\,(\hat{\beta}_3) + \text{var}\,(\hat{\beta}_4) - 2\,\text{cov}\,(\hat{\beta}_3, \hat{\beta}_4)}} \tag{8.5.5}$$

Now the testing procedure involves the following steps:

1. Estimate $\hat{\beta}_3$ and $\hat{\beta}_4$. Any standard computer package can do that.
2. Most standard computer packages routinely compute the variances and covariances of the estimated parameters.[11] From these estimates the standard error in the denominator of Eq. (8.5.5) can be easily obtained.
3. Obtain the t ratio from Eq. (8.5.5). Note the null hypothesis in the present case is $(\beta_3 - \beta_4) = 0$.
4. If the t variable computed from Eq. (8.5.5) exceeds the critical t value at the designated level of significance for given df, then you can reject the null hypothesis; otherwise, you do not reject it. Alternatively, if the p value of the t statistic from Eq. (8.5.5) is reasonably low, one can reject the null hypothesis. Note that the lower the p value, the greater the evidence against the null hypothesis. Therefore, when we say that a p value is low or reasonably low, we mean that it is less than the significance level, such as 10, 5, or 1 percent. Some personal judgment is involved in this decision.

[11]The algebraic expression for the covariance formula is rather involved. **Appendix C** provides a compact expression for it, however, using matrix notation.

EXAMPLE 8.2
The Cubic Cost Function Revisited

Recall the cubic total cost function estimated in Example 7.4, Section 7.10, which for convenience is reproduced below:

$$\begin{aligned} \hat{Y}_i &= 141.7667 \quad + 63.4777X_i - 12.9615X_i^2 + 0.9396X_i^3 \\ \text{se} &= \quad (6.3753) \quad (4.7786) \quad (0.9857) \quad (0.0591) \\ &\text{cov}(\hat{\beta}_3, \hat{\beta}_4) = -0.0576; \quad R^2 = 0.9983 \end{aligned} \tag{7.10.6}$$

where Y is total cost and X is output, and where the figures in parentheses are the estimated standard errors.

Suppose we want to test the hypothesis that the coefficients of the X^2 and X^3 terms in the cubic cost function are the same, that is, $\beta_3 = \beta_4$ or $(\beta_3 - \beta_4) = 0$. In the regression (7.10.6) we have all the necessary output to conduct the t test of Eq. (8.5.5). The actual mechanics are as follows:

$$\begin{aligned} t &= \frac{\hat{\beta}_3 - \hat{\beta}_4}{\sqrt{\text{var}(\hat{\beta}_3) + \text{var}(\hat{\beta}_4) - 2\,\text{cov}(\hat{\beta}_3, \hat{\beta}_4)}} \\ &= \frac{-12.9615 - 0.9396}{\sqrt{(0.9867)^2 + (0.0591)^2 - 2(-0.0576)}} \\ &= \frac{-13.9011}{1.0442} = -13.3130 \end{aligned} \tag{8.5.6}$$

The reader can verify that for 6 df (why?) the observed t value exceeds the critical t value even at the 0.002 (or 0.2 percent) level of significance (two-tail test); the p value is extremely small, 0.000006. Hence we can reject the hypothesis that the coefficients of X^2 and X^3 in the cubic cost function are identical.

8.6 Restricted Least Squares: Testing Linear Equality Restrictions

There are occasions where economic theory may suggest that the coefficients in a regression model satisfy some linear equality restrictions. For instance, consider the Cobb–Douglas production function:

$$Y_i = \beta_1 X_{2i}^{\beta_2} X_{3i}^{\beta_3} e^{u_i} \tag{7.9.1) = (8.6.1}$$

where Y = output, X_2 = labor input, and X_3 = capital input. Written in log form, the equation becomes

$$\ln Y_i = \beta_0 + \beta_2 \ln X_{2i} + \beta_3 \ln X_{3i} + u_i \tag{8.6.2}$$

where $\beta_0 = \ln \beta_1$.

Now if there are constant returns to scale (equiproportional change in output for an equiproportional change in the inputs), economic theory would suggest that

$$\beta_2 + \beta_3 = 1 \tag{8.6.3}$$

which is an example of a linear equality restriction.[12]

How does one find out if there are constant returns to scale, that is, if the restriction (8.6.3) is valid? There are two approaches.

[12]If we had $\beta_2 + \beta_3 < 1$, this relation would be an example of a linear inequality restriction. To handle such restrictions, one needs to use mathematical programming techniques.

The *t*-Test Approach

The simplest procedure is to estimate Eq. (8.6.2) in the usual manner without taking into account the restriction (8.6.3) explicitly. This is called the **unrestricted** or **unconstrained regression.** Having estimated β_2 and β_3 (say, by the OLS method), a test of the hypothesis or restriction (8.6.3) can be conducted by the t test of Eq. (8.5.3), namely,

$$\begin{aligned} t &= \frac{(\hat{\beta}_2 + \hat{\beta}_3) - (\beta_2 + \beta_3)}{\text{se}\,(\hat{\beta}_2 + \hat{\beta}_3)} \\ &= \frac{(\hat{\beta}_2 + \hat{\beta}_3) - 1}{\sqrt{\text{var}\,(\hat{\beta}_2) + \text{var}\,(\hat{\beta}_3) + 2\,\text{cov}\,(\hat{\beta}_2, \hat{\beta}_3)}} \end{aligned} \tag{8.6.4}$$

where $(\beta_2 + \beta_3) = 1$ under the null hypothesis and where the denominator is the standard error of $(\hat{\beta}_2 + \hat{\beta}_3)$. Then following Section 8.5, if the t value computed from Eq. (8.6.4) exceeds the critical t value at the chosen level of significance, we reject the hypothesis of constant returns to scale; otherwise we do not reject it.

The *F*-Test Approach: Restricted Least Squares

The preceding t test is a kind of postmortem examination because we try to find out whether the linear restriction is satisfied after estimating the "unrestricted" regression. A direct approach would be to incorporate the restriction (8.6.3) into the estimating procedure at the outset. In the present example, this procedure can be done easily. From (8.6.3) we see that

$$\beta_2 = 1 - \beta_3 \tag{8.6.5}$$

or

$$\beta_3 = 1 - \beta_2 \tag{8.6.6}$$

Therefore, using either of these equalities, we can eliminate one of the β coefficients in Eq. (8.6.2) and estimate the resulting equation. Thus, if we use Eq. (8.6.5), we can write the Cobb–Douglas production function as

$$\begin{aligned} \ln Y_i &= \beta_0 + (1 - \beta_3) \ln X_{2i} + \beta_3 \ln X_{3i} + u_i \\ &= \beta_0 + \ln X_{2i} + \beta_3(\ln X_{3i} - \ln X_{2i}) + u_i \end{aligned}$$

or

$$(\ln Y_i - \ln X_{2i}) = \beta_0 + \beta_3(\ln X_{3i} - \ln X_{2i}) + u_i \tag{8.6.7}$$

or

$$\ln\,(Y_i/X_{2i}) = \beta_0 + \beta_3 \ln\,(X_{3i}/X_{2i}) + u_i \tag{8.6.8}$$

where (Y_i/X_{2i}) = output/labor ratio and (X_{3i}/X_{2i}) = capital labor ratio, quantities of great economic importance.

Notice how the original equation (8.6.2) is transformed. Once we estimate β_3 from Eq. (8.6.7) or Eq. (8.6.8), β_2 can be easily estimated from the relation (8.6.5). Needless to say, this procedure will guarantee that the sum of the estimated coefficients of the two inputs will equal 1. The procedure outlined in Eq. (8.6.7) or Eq. (8.6.8) is known as **restricted least squares (RLS).** This procedure can be generalized to models containing any number of explanatory variables and more than one linear equality restriction. The generalization can be found in Theil.[13] (See also general F testing below.)

[13]Henri Theil, *Principles of Econometrics,* John Wiley & Sons, New York, 1971, pp. 43–45.

How do we compare the unrestricted and restricted least-squares regressions? In other words, how do we know that, say, the restriction (8.6.3) is valid? This question can be answered by applying the F test as follows. Let

$\sum \hat{u}_{\text{UR}}^2$ = RSS of the unrestricted regression (8.6.2)

$\sum \hat{u}_{\text{R}}^2$ = RSS of the restricted regression (8.6.7)

m = number of linear restrictions (1 in the present example)

k = number of parameters in the unrestricted regression

n = number of observations

Then,

$$F = \frac{(\text{RSS}_{\text{R}} - \text{RSS}_{\text{UR}})/m}{\text{RSS}_{\text{UR}}/(n-k)} = \frac{\left(\sum \hat{u}_{\text{R}}^2 - \sum \hat{u}_{\text{UR}}^2\right)/m}{\sum \hat{u}_{\text{UR}}^2/(n-k)} \tag{8.6.9}$$

follows the F distribution with m, $(n-k)$ df. (*Note:* UR and R stand for unrestricted and restricted, respectively.)

The F test above can also be expressed in terms of R^2 as follows:

$$F = \frac{\left(R_{\text{UR}}^2 - R_{\text{R}}^2\right)/m}{\left(1 - R_{\text{UR}}^2\right)/(n-k)} \tag{8.6.10}$$

where R_{UR}^2 and R_{R}^2 are, respectively, the R^2 values obtained from the unrestricted and restricted regressions, that is, from the regressions (8.6.2) and (8.6.7). It should be noted that

$$R_{\text{UR}}^2 \geq R_{\text{R}}^2 \tag{8.6.11}$$

and

$$\sum \hat{u}_{\text{UR}}^2 \leq \sum \hat{u}_{\text{R}}^2 \tag{8.6.12}$$

In Exercise 8.4 you are asked to justify these statements.

A cautionary note: In using Eq. (8.6.10) keep in mind that if the dependent variable in the restricted and unrestricted models is not the same, R_{UR}^2 and R_{R}^2 are not directly comparable. In that case, use the procedure described in Chapter 7 to render the two R^2 values comparable (see Example 8.3 below) or use the F test given in Eq. (8.6.9).

EXAMPLE 8.3
The Cobb–Douglas Production Function for the Mexican Economy, 1955–1974

By way of illustrating the preceding discussion, consider the data given in Table 8.8. Attempting to fit the Cobb–Douglas production function to these data yielded the following results:

$$\begin{aligned} \widehat{\ln \text{GDP}}_t &= -1.6524 + 0.3397 \ln \text{Labor}_t + 0.8460 \ln \text{Capital}_t \\ t &= (-2.7259) \quad (1.8295) \quad (9.0625) \\ p \text{ value} &= (0.0144) \quad (0.0849) \quad (0.0000) \\ & R^2 = 0.9951 \qquad \text{RSS}_{\text{UR}} = 0.0136 \end{aligned} \tag{8.6.13}$$

TABLE 8.8
Real GDP, Employment, and Real Fixed Capital—Mexico

Source: Victor J. Elias, *Sources of Growth: A Study of Seven Latin American Economies,* International Center for Economic Growth, ICS Press, San Francisco, 1992. Data from Tables E5, E12, and E14.

Year	GDP*	Employment†	Fixed Capital‡
1955	114043	8310	182113
1956	120410	8529	193749
1957	129187	8738	205192
1958	134705	8952	215130
1959	139960	9171	225021
1960	150511	9569	237026
1961	157897	9527	248897
1962	165286	9662	260661
1963	178491	10334	275466
1964	199457	10981	295378
1965	212323	11746	315715
1966	226977	11521	337642
1967	241194	11540	363599
1968	260881	12066	391847
1969	277498	12297	422382
1970	296530	12955	455049
1971	306712	13338	484677
1972	329030	13738	520553
1973	354057	15924	561531
1974	374977	14154	609825

*Millions of 1960 pesos.
†Thousands of people.
‡Millions of 1960 pesos.

where RSS_{UR} is the unrestricted RSS, as we have put no restrictions on estimating Eq. (8.6.13).

We have already seen in Chapter 7 how to interpret the coefficients of the Cobb–Douglas production function. As you can see, the output/labor elasticity is about 0.34 and the output/capital elasticity is about 0.85. If we add these coefficients, we obtain 1.19, suggesting that perhaps the Mexican economy during the stated time period was experiencing increasing returns to scale. Of course, we do not know if 1.19 is statistically different from 1.

To see if that is the case, let us impose the restriction of constant returns to scale, which gives the following regression:

$$\begin{aligned} \widehat{\ln(\text{GDP/Labor})_t} &= -0.4947 + 1.0153 \ln(\text{Capital/Labor})_t \\ t &= (-4.0612) \quad (28.1056) \\ p \text{ value} &= (0.0007) \quad (0.0000) \\ R_R^2 &= 0.9777 \qquad RSS_R = 0.0166 \end{aligned} \tag{8.6.14}$$

where RSS_R is the restricted RSS, for we have imposed the restriction that there are constant returns to scale.

(Continued)

EXAMPLE 8.3 *(Continued)*

Since the dependent variable in the preceding two regressions is different, we have to use the F test given in Eq. (8.6.9). We have the necessary data to obtain the F value.

$$F = \frac{(\text{RSS}_R - \text{RSS}_{UR})/m}{\text{RSS}_{UR}/(n-k)}$$

$$= \frac{(0.0166 - 0.0136)/1}{(0.0136)/(20-3)}$$

$$= 3.75$$

Note in the present case $m = 1$, as we have imposed only one restriction and $(n - k)$ is 17, since we have 20 observations and three parameters in the unrestricted regression.

This F value follows the F distribution with 1 df in the numerator and 17 df in the denominator. The reader can easily check that this F value is not significant at the 5% level. (See **Appendix D,** Table D.3.)

The conclusion then is that the Mexican economy was probably characterized by constant returns to scale over the sample period and therefore there may be no harm in using the restricted regression given in Eq. (8.6.14). As this regression shows, if capital/labor ratio increased by 1 percent, on average, labor productivity went up by about 1 percent.

General F Testing[14]

The F test given in Eq. (8.6.10) or its equivalent in Eq. (8.6.9) provides a general method of testing hypotheses about one or more parameters of the k-variable regression model:

$$Y_i = \beta_1 + \beta_2 X_{2i} + \beta_3 X_{3i} + \cdots + \beta_k X_{ki} + u_i \tag{8.6.15}$$

The F test of Eq. (8.4.16) or the t test of Eq. (8.5.3) is but a specific application of Eq. (8.6.10). Thus, hypotheses such as

$$H_0\colon \beta_2 = \beta_3 \tag{8.6.16}$$

$$H_0\colon \beta_3 + \beta_4 + \beta_5 = 3 \tag{8.6.17}$$

which involve some linear restrictions on the parameters of the k-variable model, or hypotheses such as

$$H_0\colon \beta_3 = \beta_4 = \beta_5 = \beta_6 = 0 \tag{8.6.18}$$

which imply that some regressors are absent from the model, can all be tested by the F test of Eq. (8.6.10).

From the discussion in Sections 8.4 and 8.6, the reader will have noticed that the general strategy of F testing is this: There is a larger model, the *unconstrained model* (8.6.15), and then there is a smaller model, the *constrained* or *restricted model*, which is obtained from the larger model by deleting some variables from it, e.g., Eq. (8.6.18), or by putting some linear restrictions on one or more coefficients of the larger model, e.g., Eq. (8.6.16) or Eq. (8.6.17).

[14]If one is using the maximum likelihood approach to estimation, then a test similar to the one discussed shortly is the **likelihood ratio test,** which is slightly involved and is therefore discussed in the appendix to the chapter. For further discussion, see Theil, op. cit., pp. 179–184.

We then fit the unconstrained and constrained models to the data and obtain the respective coefficients of determination, namely, R^2_{UR} and R^2_{R}. We note the df in the unconstrained model ($= n - k$) and also note the df in the constrained model ($= m$), m being the number of linear restriction (e.g., 1 in Eq. [8.6.16] or Eq. [8.6.18]) or the number of regressors omitted from the model (e.g., $m = 4$ if Eq. [8.6.18] holds, since four regressors are assumed to be absent from the model). We then compute the F ratio as indicated in Eq. (8.6.9) or Eq. (8.6.10) and use this *Decision Rule: If the computed F exceeds $F_\alpha(m, n-k)$, where $F_\alpha(m, n-k)$ is the critical F at the α level of significance, we reject the null hypothesis: otherwise we do not reject it.*

Let us illustrate:

EXAMPLE 8.4

The Demand for Chicken in the United States, 1960–1982

In Exercise 7.19, among other things, you were asked to consider the following demand function for chicken:

$$\ln Y_t = \beta_1 + \beta_2 \ln X_{2t} + \beta_3 \ln X_{3t} + \beta_4 \ln X_{4t} + \beta_5 \ln X_{5t} + u_i \tag{8.6.19}$$

where Y = per capita consumption of chicken, lb, X_2 = real disposable per capita income, \$, X_3 = real retail price of chicken per lb, ¢, X_4 = real retail price of pork per lb, ¢, and X_5 = real retail price of beef per lb, ¢.

In this model β_2, β_3, β_4, and β_5 are, respectively, the income, own-price, cross-price (pork), and cross-price (beef) elasticities. (Why?) According to economic theory,

$$\begin{aligned}
&\beta_2 > 0\\
&\beta_3 < 0\\
&\beta_4 > 0, && \text{if chicken and pork are competing products}\\
&\quad\;\; < 0, && \text{if chicken and pork are complementary products}\\
&\quad\;\; = 0, && \text{if chicken and pork are unrelated products}\\
&\beta_5 > 0, && \text{if chicken and beef are competing products}\\
&\quad\;\; < 0, && \text{if chicken and pork are complementary products}\\
&\quad\;\; = 0, && \text{if chicken and pork are unrelated products}
\end{aligned} \tag{8.6.20}$$

Suppose someone maintains that chicken and pork and beef are unrelated products in the sense that chicken consumption is not affected by the prices of pork and beef. In short,

$$H_0\colon \beta_4 = \beta_5 = 0 \tag{8.6.21}$$

Therefore, the constrained regression becomes

$$\ln Y_t = \beta_1 + \beta_2 \ln X_{2t} + \beta_3 \ln X_{3t} + u_t \tag{8.6.22}$$

Equation (8.6.19) is of course the unconstrained regression.

Using the data given in Exercise 7.19, we obtain the following:

Unconstrained regression:

$$\begin{aligned}
\widehat{\ln Y_t} = {} & 2.1898 + 0.3425 \ln X_{2t} - 0.5046 \ln X_{3t} + 0.1485 \ln X_{4t} + 0.0911 \ln X_{5t}\\
& (0.1557) \quad (0.0833) \qquad\quad (0.1109) \qquad\quad (0.0997) \qquad\quad (0.1007)\\
& R^2_{\text{UR}} = 0.9823
\end{aligned} \tag{8.6.23}$$

Constrained regression:

$$\begin{aligned}
\widehat{\ln Y_t} = {} & 2.0328 + 0.4515 \ln X_{2t} - 0.3772 \ln X_{3t}\\
& (0.1162) \quad (0.0247) \qquad\quad (0.0635)\\
& R^2_{\text{R}} = 0.9801
\end{aligned} \tag{8.6.24}$$

(*Continued*)

EXAMPLE 8.4
(Continued)

where the figures in parentheses are the estimated standard errors. *Note:* The R^2 values of Eqs. (8.6.23) and (8.6.24) are comparable since the dependent variable in the two models is the same.

Now the F ratio to test the hypothesis of Eq. (8.6.21) is

$$F = \frac{(R^2_{\text{UR}} - R^2_{\text{R}})/m}{(1 - R^2_{\text{UR}})/(n-k)} \tag{8.6.10}$$

The value of m in the present case is 2, since there are two restrictions involved: $\beta_4 = 0$ and $\beta_5 = 0$. The denominator df, $(n-k)$, is 18, since $n = 23$ and $k = 5$ (5 β coefficients).

Therefore, the F ratio is

$$F = \frac{(0.9823 - 0.9801)/2}{(1 - 0.9823)/18} = 1.1224 \tag{8.6.25}$$

which has the F distribution with 2 and 18 df.

At 5 percent, clearly this F value is not statistically significant $[F_{0.5}(2,18) = 3.55]$. The p value is 0.3472. Therefore, there is no reason to reject the null hypothesis—the demand for chicken does not depend on pork and beef prices. In short, we can accept the constrained regression (8.6.24) as representing the demand function for chicken.

Notice that the demand function satisfies a priori economic expectations in that the own-price elasticity is negative and that the income elasticity is positive. However, the estimated price elasticity, in absolute value, is statistically less than unity, implying that the demand for chicken is price inelastic. (Why?) Also, the income elasticity, although positive, is also statistically less than unity, suggesting that chicken is not a luxury item; by convention, an item is said to be a luxury item if its income elasticity is greater than 1.

8.7 Testing for Structural or Parameter Stability of Regression Models: The Chow Test

When we use a regression model involving time series data, it may happen that there is a **structural change** in the relationship between the regressand Y and the regressors. By structural change, we mean that the values of the parameters of the model do not remain the same through the entire time period. Sometimes the structural change may be due to external forces (e.g., the oil embargoes imposed by the OPEC oil cartel in 1973 and 1979 or the Gulf War of 1990–1991), policy changes (such as the switch from a fixed exchange-rate system to a flexible exchange-rate system around 1973), actions taken by Congress (e.g., the tax changes initiated by President Reagan in his two terms in office or changes in the minimum wage rate), or a variety of other causes.

How do we find out that a structural change has in fact occurred? To be specific, consider the data given in Table 8.9. This table gives data on disposable personal income and personal savings, in billions of dollars, for the United States for the period 1970–1995. Suppose we want to estimate a simple savings function that relates savings (Y) to disposable personal income DPI (X). Since we have the data, we can obtain an OLS regression of Y on X. But if we do that, we are maintaining that the relationship between savings and DPI has not changed much over the span of 26 years. That may be a tall assumption. For example, it is well known that in 1982 the United States suffered its worst peacetime recession. The civilian unemployment rate that year reached 9.7 percent, the highest since 1948. An

TABLE 8.9
Savings and Personal Disposable Income (billions of dollars), United States, 1970–1995

Source: *Economic Report of the President,* 1997, Table B-28, p. 332.

Observation	Savings	Income	Observation	Savings	Income
1970	61.0	727.1	1983	167.0	2522.4
1971	68.6	790.2	1984	235.7	2810.0
1972	63.6	855.3	1985	206.2	3002.0
1973	89.6	965.0	1986	196.5	3187.6
1974	97.6	1054.2	1987	168.4	3363.1
1975	104.4	1159.2	1988	189.1	3640.8
1976	96.4	1273.0	1989	187.8	3894.5
1977	92.5	1401.4	1990	208.7	4166.8
1978	112.6	1580.1	1991	246.4	4343.7
1979	130.1	1769.5	1992	272.6	4613.7
1980	161.8	1973.3	1993	214.4	4790.2
1981	199.1	2200.2	1994	189.4	5021.7
1982	205.5	2347.3	1995	249.3	5320.8

event such as this might disturb the relationship between savings and DPI. To see if this happened, let us divide our sample data into two time periods: 1970–1981 and 1982–1995, the pre- and post-1982 recession periods.

Now we have three possible regressions:

$$\text{Time period 1970–1981:}\quad Y_t = \lambda_1 + \lambda_2 X_t + u_{1t} \qquad n_1 = 12 \tag{8.7.1}$$

$$\text{Time period 1982–1995:}\quad Y_t = \gamma_1 + \gamma_2 X_t + u_{2t} \qquad n_2 = 14 \tag{8.7.2}$$

$$\text{Time period 1970–1995:}\quad Y_t = \alpha_1 + \alpha_2 X_t + u_t \qquad n = (n_1 + n_2) = 26 \tag{8.7.3}$$

Regression (8.7.3) assumes that there is no difference between the two time periods and therefore estimates the relationship between savings and DPI for the entire time period consisting of 26 observations. In other words, this regression assumes that the intercept as well as the slope coefficient remains the same over the entire period; that is, there is no structural change. If this is in fact the situation, then $\alpha_1 = \lambda_1 = \gamma_1$ and $\alpha_2 = \lambda_2 = \gamma_2$.

Regressions (8.7.1) and (8.7.2) assume that the regressions in the two time periods are different; that is, the intercept and the slope coefficients are different, as indicated by the subscripted parameters. In the preceding regressions, the u's represent the error terms and the n's represent the number of observations.

For the data given in Table 8.9, the empirical counterparts of the preceding three regressions are as follows:

$$\begin{aligned} \hat{Y}_t &= 1.0161 + 0.0803\,X_t \\ t &= (0.0873) \quad (9.6015) \\ R^2 = 0.9021 \quad & \text{RSS}_1 = 1785.032 \quad \text{df} = 10 \end{aligned} \tag{8.7.1a}$$

$$\begin{aligned} \hat{Y}_t &= 153.4947 + 0.0148X_t \\ t &= (4.6922) \quad (1.7707) \\ R^2 = 0.2971 \quad & \text{RSS}_2 = 10{,}005.22 \quad \text{df} = 12 \end{aligned} \tag{8.7.2a}$$

$$\begin{aligned} \hat{Y}_t &= 62.4226 + 0.0376\,X_t + \cdots \\ t &= (4.8917) \quad (8.8937) + \cdots \\ R^2 = 0.7672 \quad & \text{RSS}_3 = 23{,}248.30 \quad \text{df} = 24 \end{aligned} \tag{8.7.3a}$$

FIGURE 8.3

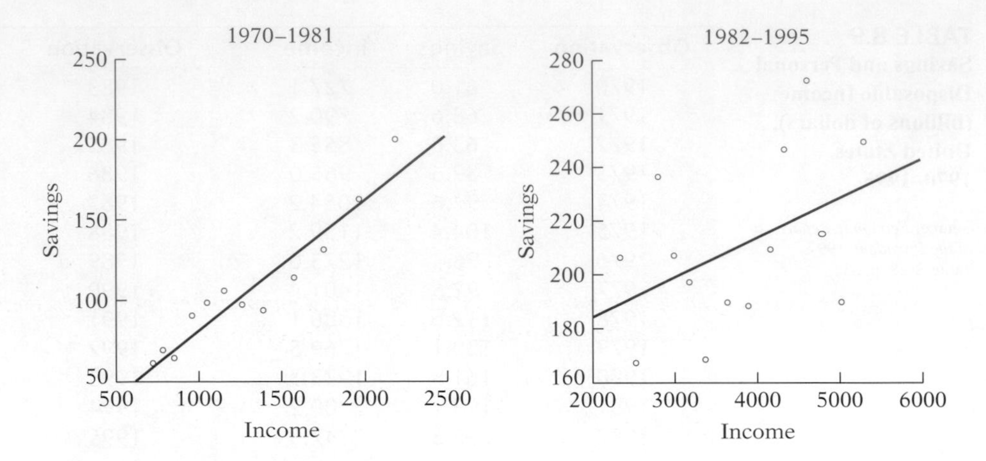

In the preceding regressions, RSS denotes the residual sum of squares, and the figures in parentheses are the estimated t values.

A look at the estimated regressions suggests that the relationship between savings and DPI is not the same in the two subperiods. The slope in the preceding savings-income regressions represents the **marginal propensity to save (MPS),** that is, the (mean) change in savings as a result of a dollar's increase in disposable personal income. In the period 1970–1981 the MPS was about 0.08, whereas in the period 1982–1995 it was about 0.02. Whether this change was due to the economic policies pursued by President Reagan is hard to say. This further suggests that the **pooled regression** (8.7.3a)—that is, the one that pools all the 26 observations and runs a common regression, disregarding possible differences in the two subperiods—may not be appropriate. Of course, the preceding statements need to be supported by an appropriate statistical test(s). Incidentally, the scattergrams and the estimated regression lines are as shown in Figure 8.3.

Now the possible differences, that is, structural changes, may be caused by differences in the intercept or the slope coefficient or both. How do we find that out? A visual feeling about this can be obtained as shown in Figure 8.3. But it would be useful to have a formal test.

This is where the **Chow test** comes in handy.[15] This test assumes that:

1. $u_{1t} \sim N(0, \sigma^2)$ and $u_{2t} \sim N(0, \sigma^2)$. That is, the error terms in the subperiod regressions are normally distributed with the same (homoscedastic) variance σ^2.
2. The two error terms u_{1t} and u_{2t} are independently distributed.

The mechanics of the Chow test are as follows:

1. Estimate regression (8.7.3), which is appropriate if there is no parameter instability, and obtain RSS_3 with df $= (n_1 + n_2 - k)$, where k is the number of parameters estimated, 2 in the present case. For our example $\text{RSS}_3 = 23{,}248.30$. We call RSS_3 the **restricted residual sum of squares (RSS_R)** because it is obtained by imposing the restrictions that $\lambda_1 = \gamma_1$ and $\lambda_2 = \gamma_2$, that is, the subperiod regressions are not different.

2. Estimate Eq. (8.7.1) and obtain its residual sum of squares, RSS_1, with df $= (n_1 - k)$. In our example, $\text{RSS}_1 = 1785.032$ and df $= 10$.

3. Estimate Eq. (8.7.2) and obtain its residual sum of squares, RSS_2, with df $= (n_2 - k)$. In our example, $\text{RSS}_2 = 10{,}005.22$ with df $= 12$.

[15]Gregory C. Chow, "Tests of Equality Between Sets of Coefficients in Two Linear Regressions," *Econometrica,* vol. 28, no. 3, 1960, pp. 591–605.

4. Since the two sets of samples are deemed independent, we can add RSS_1 and RSS_2 to obtain what may be called the **unrestricted residual sum of squares (RSS_{UR})**, that is,

$$RSS_{UR} = RSS_1 + RSS_2 \qquad \text{with df} = (n_1 + n_2 - 2k)$$

In the present case,

$$RSS_{UR} = (1785.032 + 10{,}005.22) = 11{,}790.252$$

5. Now the idea behind the Chow test is that if in fact there is no structural change (i.e., regressions [8.7.1] and [8.7.2] are essentially the same), then the RSS_R and RSS_{UR} should not be statistically different. Therefore, if we form the following ratio:

$$F = \frac{(RSS_R - RSS_{UR})/k}{(RSS_{UR})/(n_1 + n_2 - 2k)} \sim F_{[k,(n_1+n_2-2k)]} \tag{8.7.4}$$

then Chow has shown that under the null hypothesis the regressions (8.7.1) and (8.7.2) are (statistically) the same (i.e., no structural change or break) and the F ratio given above follows the F distribution with k and $(n_1 + n_2 - 2k)$ df in the numerator and denominator, respectively.

6. Therefore, we do not reject the null hypothesis of *parameter stability* (i.e., no structural change) if the computed F value in an application does not exceed the critical F value obtained from the F table at the chosen level of significance (or the p value). In this case we may be justified in using the pooled (restricted?) regression (8.7.3). Contrarily, if the computed F value exceeds the critical F value, we reject the hypothesis of parameter stability and conclude that the regressions (8.7.1) and (8.7.2) are different, in which case the pooled regression (8.7.3) is of dubious value, to say the least.

Returning to our example, we find that

$$\begin{aligned} F &= \frac{(23{,}248.30 - 11{,}790.252)/2}{(11{,}790.252)/22} \\ &= 10.69 \end{aligned} \tag{8.7.5}$$

From the F tables, we find that for 2 and 22 df the 1 percent critical F value is 5.72. Therefore, the probability of obtaining an F value of as much as or greater than 10.69 is much smaller than 1 percent; actually the p value is only 0.00057.

The Chow test therefore seems to support our earlier hunch that the savings–income relation has undergone a structural change in the United States over the period 1970–1995, assuming that the assumptions underlying the test are fulfilled. We will have more to say about this shortly.

Incidentally, note that the Chow test can be easily generalized to handle cases of more than one structural break. For example, if we believe that the savings–income relation changed after President Clinton took office in January 1992, we could divide our sample into three periods: 1970–1981, 1982–1991, 1992–1995, and carry out the Chow test. Of course, we will have four RSS terms, one for each subperiod and one for the pooled data. But the logic of the test remains the same. Data through 2007 are now available to extend the last period to 2007.

There are some caveats about the Chow test that must be kept in mind:

1. The assumptions underlying the test must be fulfilled. For example, one should find out if the error variances in the regressions (8.7.1) and (8.7.2) are the same. We will discuss this point shortly.

2. The Chow test will tell us only if the two regressions (8.7.1) and (8.7.2) are different, without telling us whether the difference is on account of the intercepts, or the slopes, or both. But in Chapter 9, on dummy variables, we will see how we can answer this question.

3. The Chow test assumes that we know the point(s) of structural break. In our example, we assumed it to be in 1982. However, if it is not possible to determine when the structural change actually took place, we may have to use other methods.[16]

Before we leave the Chow test and our savings–income regression, let us examine one of the assumptions underlying the Chow test, namely, that the error variances in the two periods are the same. Since we cannot observe the true error variances, we can obtain their estimates from the RSS given in the regressions (8.7.1a) and (8.7.2a), namely,

$$\hat{\sigma}_1^2 = \frac{\text{RSS}_1}{n_1 - 2} = \frac{1785.032}{10} = 178.5032 \tag{8.7.6}$$

$$\hat{\sigma}_2^2 = \frac{\text{RSS}_2}{n_2 - 2} = \frac{10{,}005.22}{14 - 2} = 833.7683 \tag{8.7.7}$$

Notice that, since there are two parameters estimated in each equation, we deduct 2 from the number of observations to obtain the df. Given the assumptions underlying the Chow test, $\hat{\sigma}_1^2$ and $\hat{\sigma}_2^2$ are unbiased estimators of the true variances in the two subperiods. As a result, if $\sigma_1^2 = \sigma_2^2$, that is, the variances in the two subpopulations are the same (as assumed by the Chow test), then it can be shown that

$$\frac{(\hat{\sigma}_1^2/\sigma_1^2)}{(\hat{\sigma}_2^2/\sigma_2^2)} \sim F_{(n_1-k),(n_2-k)} \tag{8.7.8}$$

follows the F distribution with $(n_1 - k)$ and $(n_2 - k)$ df in the numerator and the denominator, respectively, in our example $k = 2$, since there are only two parameters in each subregression.

Of course, if $\sigma_1^2 = \sigma_2^2$, the preceding F test reduces to computing

$$F = \frac{\hat{\sigma}_1^2}{\hat{\sigma}_2^2} \tag{8.7.9}$$

Note: By convention we put the larger of the two estimated variances in the numerator. (See **Appendix A** for the details of the F and other probability distributions.)

Computing this F in an application and comparing it with the critical F value with the appropriate df, one can decide to reject or not reject the null hypothesis that the variances in the two subpopulations are the same. If the null hypothesis is not rejected, then one can use the Chow test.

Returning to our savings–income regression, we obtain the following result:

$$F = \frac{833.7683}{178.5032} = 4.6701 \tag{8.7.10}$$

Under the null hypothesis of equality of variances in the two subpopulations, this F value follows the F distribution with 12 and 10 df, in the numerator and denominator, respectively. (*Note:* We have put the larger of the two estimated variances in the numerator.) From the F tables in **Appendix D**, we see that the 5 and 1 percent critical F values for 12 and

[16]For a detailed discussion, see William H. Greene, *Econometric Analysis,* 4th ed., Prentice Hall, Englewood Cliffs, NJ, 2000, pp. 293–297.

10 df are 2.91 and 4.71, respectively. The computed F value is significant at the 5 percent level and is almost significant at the 1 percent level. Thus, our conclusion would be that the two subpopulation variances are not the same and, therefore, strictly speaking we should not use the Chow test.

Our purpose here has been to demonstrate the mechanics of the Chow test, which is used popularly in applied work. If the error variances in the two subpopulations are heteroscedastic, the Chow test can be modified. But the procedure is beyond the scope of this book.[17]

Another point we made earlier was that the Chow test is sensitive to the choice of the time at which the regression parameters might have changed. In our example, we assumed that the change probably took place in the recession year of 1982. If we had assumed it to be 1981, when Ronald Reagan began his presidency, we might have found the computed F value to be different. As a matter of fact, in Exercise 8.34 the reader is asked to check this out.

If we do not want to choose the point at which the break in the underlying relationship might have occurred, we could choose alternative methods, such as the **recursive residual test.** We will take this topic up in Chapter 13, the chapter on model specification analysis.

8.8 Prediction with Multiple Regression

In Section 5.10 we showed how the estimated two-variable regression model can be used for (1) *mean prediction,* that is, predicting the point on the population regression function (PRF), as well as for (2) *individual prediction,* that is, predicting an individual value of Y given the value of the regressor $X = X_0$, where X_0 is the specified numerical value of X.

The estimated multiple regression too can be used for similar purposes, and the procedure for doing that is a straightforward extension of the two-variable case, except the formulas for estimating the variances and standard errors of the forecast value (comparable to Eqs. [5.10.2] and [5.10.6] of the two-variable model) are rather involved and are better handled by the matrix methods discussed in **Appendix C.** Of course, most standard regression packages can do this routinely, so there is no need to look up the matrix formulation. It is given in **Appendix C** for the benefit of the mathematically inclined students. This appendix also gives a fully worked out example.

*8.9 The Troika of Hypothesis Tests: The Likelihood Ratio (LR), Wald (W), and Lagrange Multiplier (LM) Tests[18]

In this and the previous chapters we have, by and large, used the t, F, and chi-square tests to test a variety of hypotheses in the context of linear (in-parameter) regression models. But once we go beyond the somewhat comfortable world of linear regression models, we need a method(s) to test hypotheses that can handle regression models, linear or not.

The well-known trinity of **likelihood, Wald, and Lagrange multiplier tests** can accomplish this purpose. The interesting thing to note is that *asymptotically* (i.e., in large

*Optional.

[17]For a discussion of the Chow test under heteroscedasticity, see William H. Greene, *Econometric Analysis,* 4th ed., Prentice Hall, Englewood Cliffs, NJ, 2000, pp. 292–293, and Adrian C. Darnell, *A Dictionary of Econometrics,* Edward Elgar, U.K., 1994, p. 51.

[18]For an accessible discussion, see A. Buse, "The Likelihood Ratio, Wald and Lagrange Multiplier Tests: An Expository Note," *American Statistician,* vol. 36, 1982, pp. 153–157.

samples) all three tests are equivalent in that the test statistic associated with each of these tests follows the chi-square distribution.

Although we will discuss the **likelihood ratio test** in the appendix to this chapter, in general we will not use these tests in this textbook for the pragmatic reason that in small, or finite, samples, which is unfortunately what most researchers deal with, the F test that we have used so far will suffice. As Davidson and MacKinnon note:

> For linear regression models, with or without normal errors, there is of course no need to look at LM, W and LR at all, since no information is gained from doing so over and above what is already contained in F.[19]

*8.10 Testing the Functional Form of Regression: Choosing between Linear and Log–Linear Regression Models

The choice between a linear regression model (the regressand is a linear function of the regressors) or a log–linear regression model (the log of the regressand is a function of the logs of the regressors) is a perennial question in empirical analysis. We can use a test proposed by MacKinnon, White, and Davidson, which for brevity we call the **MWD test,** to choose between the two models.[20]

To illustrate this test, assume the following

H_0: *Linear Model:* Y is a linear function of regressors, the X's.

H_1: *Log–Linear Model:* $\ln Y$ is a linear function of logs of regressors, the logs of X's.

where, as usual, H_0 and H_1 denote the null and alternative hypotheses.

The MWD test involves the following steps:[21]

Step I: Estimate the linear model and obtain the estimated Y values. Call them Yf (i.e., $\hat{Y}$).

Step: II: Estimate the log–linear model and obtain the estimated $\ln Y$ values; call them $\ln f$ (i.e., $\widehat{\ln Y}$).

Step III: Obtain $Z_1 = (\ln Yf - \ln f)$.

Step IV: Regress Y on X's and Z_1 obtained in Step III. Reject H_0 if the coefficient of Z_1 is statistically significant by the usual t test.

Step V: Obtain $Z_2 = (\text{antilog of } \ln f - Yf)$.

Step VI: Regress log of Y on the logs of X's and Z_2. Reject H_1 if the coefficient of Z_2 is statistically significant by the usual t test.

Although the MWD test seems involved, the logic of the test is quite simple. If the linear model is in fact the correct model, the constructed variable Z_1 should not be statistically significant in Step IV, for in that case the estimated Y values from the linear model and those estimated from the log–linear model (after taking their antilog values for comparative purposes) should not be different. The same comment applies to the alternative hypothesis H_1.

*Optional.

[19]Russell Davidson and James G. MacKinnon, *Estimation and Inference in Econometrics,* Oxford University Press, New York, 1993, p. 456.

[20]J. MacKinnon, H. White, and R. Davidson, "Tests for Model Specification in the Presence of Alternative Hypothesis; Some Further Results," *Journal of Econometrics,* vol. 21, 1983, pp. 53–70. A similar test is proposed in A. K. Bera and C. M. Jarque, "Model Specification Tests: A Simultaneous Approach," *Journal of Econometrics,* vol. 20, 1982, pp. 59–82.

[21]This discussion is based on William H. Greene, *ET. The Econometrics Toolkit Version 3,* Econometric Software, Bellport, New York, 1992, pp. 245–246.

EXAMPLE 8.5

The Demand for Roses

Refer to Exercise 7.16 where we have presented data on the demand for roses in the Detroit metropolitan area for the period 1971–III to 1975–II. For illustrative purposes, we will consider the demand for roses as a function only of the prices of roses and carnations, leaving out the income variable for the time being. Now we consider the following models:

$$\text{Linear model:} \quad Y_t = \alpha_1 + \alpha_2 X_{2t} + \alpha_3 X_{3t} + u_t \tag{8.10.1}$$

$$\text{Log–linear model:} \quad \ln Y_t = \beta_1 + \beta_2 \ln X_{2t} + \beta_3 \ln X_{3t} + u_t \tag{8.10.2}$$

where Y is the quantity of roses in dozens, X_2 is the average wholesale price of roses ($/dozen), and X_3 is the average wholesale price of carnations ($/dozen). A priori, α_2 and β_2 are expected to be negative (why?), and α_3 and β_3 are expected to be positive (why?). As we know, the slope coefficients in the log–linear model are elasticity coefficients.

The regression results are as follows:

$$\begin{aligned} \hat{Y}_t &= 9734.2176 \;-\; 3782.1956X_{2t} + 2815.2515X_{3t} \\ t &= \quad (3.3705) \qquad (-6.6069) \qquad (2.9712) \\ & \qquad\qquad F = 21.84 \qquad R^2 = 0.77096 \end{aligned} \tag{8.10.3}$$

$$\begin{aligned} \widehat{\ln Y_t} &= \quad 9.2278 \;-\; 1.7607 \ln X_{2t} + 1.3398 \ln X_{3t} \\ t &= (16.2349) \quad (-5.9044) \qquad (2.5407) \\ & \qquad F = 17.50 \qquad R^2 = 0.7292 \end{aligned} \tag{8.10.4}$$

As these results show, both the linear and the log–linear models seem to fit the data reasonably well: The parameters have the expected signs and the t and R^2 values are statistically significant.

To decide between these models on the basis of the **MWD test**, we first test the hypothesis that the true model is linear. Then, following Step IV of the test, we obtain the following regression:

$$\begin{aligned} \hat{Y}_t &= 9727.5685 \;-\; 3783.0623X_{2t} + 2817.7157X_{3t} + 85.2319Z_{1t} \\ t &= \quad (3.2178) \qquad (-6.3337) \qquad (2.8366) \qquad (0.0207) \\ & \qquad F = 13.44 \qquad R^2 = 0.7707 \end{aligned} \tag{8.10.5}$$

Since the coefficient of Z_1 is not statistically significant (the p value of the estimated t is 0.98), we do not reject the hypothesis that the true model is linear.

Suppose we switch gears and assume that the true model is log–linear. Following step VI of the MWD test, we obtain the following regression results:

$$\begin{aligned} \widehat{\ln Y_t} &= \quad 9.1486 \;-\; 1.9699 \ln X_t + 1.5891 \ln X_{2t} \;-\; 0.0013Z_{2t} \\ t &= (17.0825) \quad (-6.4189) \qquad (3.0728) \qquad (-1.6612) \\ & \qquad F = 14.17 \qquad R^2 = 0.7798 \end{aligned} \tag{8.10.6}$$

The coefficient of Z_2 is statistically significant at about the 12 percent level (p value is 0.1225). Therefore, we can reject the hypothesis that the true model is log–linear at this level of significance. Of course, if one sticks to the conventional 1 or 5 percent significance levels, then one cannot reject the hypothesis that the true model is log–linear. As this example shows, it is quite possible that in a given situation we cannot reject either of the specifications.

Summary and Conclusions

1. This chapter extended and refined the ideas of interval estimation and hypothesis testing first introduced in Chapter 5 in the context of the two-variable linear regression model.
2. In a multiple regression, testing the *individual significance* of a partial regression coefficient (using the t test) and testing the *overall significance* of the regression (i.e., H_0: all partial slope coefficients are zero or $R^2 = 0$) are not the same thing.
3. In particular, the finding that one or more partial regression coefficients are statistically insignificant on the basis of the *individual* t test does not mean that all partial regression coefficients are also (collectively) statistically insignificant. The latter hypothesis can be tested only by the F test.
4. The ***F* test** is versatile in that it can test a variety of hypotheses, such as whether (1) an individual regression coefficient is statistically significant, (2) all partial slope coefficients are zero, (3) two or more coefficients are statistically equal, (4) the coefficients satisfy some linear restrictions, and (5) there is structural stability of the regression model.
5. As in the two-variable case, the multiple regression model can be used for the purpose of mean and/or individual prediction.

EXERCISES

Questions

8.1. Suppose you want to study the behavior of sales of a product, say, automobiles over a number of years and suppose someone suggests you try the following models:

$$Y_t = \beta_0 + \beta_1 t$$
$$Y_t = \alpha_0 + \alpha_1 t + \alpha_2 t^2$$

where Y_t = sales at time t and t = time, measured in years. The first model postulates that sales is a linear function of time, whereas the second model states that it is a quadratic function of time.

a. Discuss the properties of these models.

b. How would you decide between the two models?

c. In what situations will the quadratic model be useful?

d. Try to obtain data on automobile sales in the United States over the past 20 years and see which of the models fits the data better.

8.2. Show that the F ratio of Eq. (8.4.16) is equal to the F ratio of Eq. (8.4.18). (*Hint:* ESS/TSS $= R^2$.)

8.3. Show that F tests of Eq. (8.4.18) and Eq. (8.6.10) are equivalent.

8.4. Establish statements (8.6.11) and (8.6.12).

8.5. Consider the Cobb–Douglas production function

$$Y = \beta_1 L^{\beta_2} K^{\beta_3} \tag{1}$$

where Y = output, L = labor input, and K = capital input. Dividing (1) through by K, we get

$$(Y/K) = \beta_1 (L/K)^{\beta_2} K^{\beta_2+\beta_3-1} \tag{2}$$

Taking the natural log of (2) and adding the error term, we obtain

$$\ln(Y/K) = \beta_0 + \beta_2 \ln(L/K) + (\beta_2 + \beta_3 - 1) \ln K + u_i \tag{3}$$

where $\beta_0 = \ln \beta_1$.

a. Suppose you had data to run the regression (3). How would you test the hypothesis that there are constant returns to scale, i.e., $(\beta_2 + \beta_3) = 1$?

b. If there are constant returns to scale, how would you interpret regression (3)?

c. Does it make any difference whether we divide (1) by L rather than by K?

8.6. **Critical values of R^2 when true $R^2 = 0$.** Equation (8.4.11) gave the relationship between F and R^2 under the hypothesis that all partial slope coefficients are simultaneously equal to zero (i.e., $R^2 = 0$). Just as we can find the critical F value at the α level of significance from the F table, we can find the critical R^2 value from the following relation:

$$R^2 = \frac{(k-1)F}{(k-1)F + (n-k)}$$

where k is the number of parameters in the regression model including the intercept and where F is the critical F value at the α level of significance. If the observed R^2 exceeds the critical R^2 obtained from the preceding formula, we can reject the hypothesis that the true R^2 is zero.

Establish the preceding formula and find out the critical R^2 value (at $\alpha = 5$ percent) for the regression (8.1.4).

8.7. From annual data for the years 1968–1987, the following regression results were obtained:

$$\hat{Y}_t = -859.92 + 0.6470X_{2t} - 23.195X_{3t} \qquad R^2 = 0.9776 \qquad (1)$$

$$\hat{Y}_t = -261.09 + 0.2452X_{2t} \qquad R^2 = 0.9388 \qquad (2)$$

where Y = U.S. expenditure on imported goods, billions of 1982 dollars, X_2 = personal disposable income, billions of 1982 dollars, and X_3 = trend variable. *True or false:* The standard error of X_3 in (1) is 4.2750. Show your calculations. (*Hint:* Use the relationship between R^2, F, and t.)

8.8. Suppose in the regression

$$\ln(Y_i/X_{2i}) = \alpha_1 + \alpha_2 \ln X_{2i} + \alpha_3 \ln X_{3i} + u_i$$

the values of the regression coefficients and their standard errors are known.* From this knowledge, how would you estimate the parameters and standard errors of the following regression model?

$$\ln Y_i = \beta_1 + \beta_2 \ln X_{2i} + \beta_3 \ln X_{3i} + u_i$$

8.9. Assume the following:

$$Y_i = \beta_1 + \beta_2 X_{2i} + \beta_3 X_{3i} + \beta_4 X_{2i} X_{3i} + u_i$$

where Y is personal consumption expenditure, X_2 is personal income, and X_3 is personal wealth.† The term $(X_{2i}X_{3i})$ is known as the **interaction term.** What is meant by this expression? How would you test the hypothesis that the marginal propensity to consume (MPC) (i.e., β_2) is independent of the wealth of the consumer?

*Adapted from Peter Kennedy, *A Guide to Econometrics*, the MIT Press, 3d ed., Cambridge, Mass., 1992, p. 310.

†Ibid., p. 327.

8.10. You are given the following regression results:

$$\hat{Y}_t = 16{,}899 - 2978.5X_{2t} \qquad R^2 = 0.6149$$
$$t = (8.5152) \quad (-4.7280)$$
$$\hat{Y}_t = 9734.2 - 3782.2X_{2t} + 2815X_{3t} \qquad R^2 = 0.7706$$
$$t = (3.3705) \quad (-6.6070) \quad (2.9712)$$

Can you find out the sample size underlying these results? (*Hint:* Recall the relationship between R^2, F, and t values.)

8.11. Based on our discussion of *individual* and *joint* tests of hypothesis based, respectively, on the t and F tests, which of the following situations are likely?

1. Reject the joint null on the basis of the F statistic, but do not reject each separate null on the basis of the individual t tests.
2. Reject the joint null on the basis of the F statistic, reject one individual hypothesis on the basis of the t test, and do not reject the other individual hypotheses on the basis of the t test.
3. Reject the joint null hypothesis on the basis of the F statistic, and reject each separate null hypothesis on the basis of the individual t tests.
4. Do not reject the joint null on the basis of the F statistic, and do not reject each separate null on the basis of individual t tests.
5. Do not reject the joint null on the basis of the F statistic, reject one individual hypothesis on the basis of a t test, and do not reject the other individual hypotheses on the basis of the t test.
6. Do not reject the joint null on the basis of the F statistic, but reject each separate null on the basis of individual t tests.*

Empirical Exercises

8.12. Refer to Exercise 7.21.

a. What are the real income and interest rate elasticities of real cash balances?

b. Are the preceding elasticities statistically significant individually?

c. Test the overall significance of the estimated regression.

d. Is the income elasticity of demand for real cash balances significantly different from unity?

e. Should the interest rate variable be retained in the model? Why?

8.13. From the data for 46 states in the United States for 1992, Baltagi obtained the following regression results:†

$$\widehat{\log C} = 4.30 - 1.34 \log P + 0.17 \log Y \qquad \bar{R}^2 = 0.27$$
$$\text{se} = (0.91) \quad (0.32) \quad (0.20)$$

where C = cigarette consumption, packs per year
P = real price per pack
Y = real disposable income per capita

*Quoted from Ernst R. Berndt, *The Practice of Econometrics: Classic and Contemporary,* Addison-Wesley, Reading, Mass., 1991, p. 79.

†See Badi H. Baltagi, *Econometrics,* Springer-Verlag, New York, 1998, p. 111.

a. What is the elasticity of demand for cigarettes with respect to price? Is it statistically significant? If so, is it statistically different from 1?

b. What is the income elasticity of demand for cigarettes? Is it statistically significant? If not, what might be the reasons for it?

c. How would you retrieve R^2 from the *adjusted* R^2 given above?

8.14. From a sample of 209 firms, Wooldridge obtained the following regression results:*

$$\widehat{\log(\text{salary})} = 4.32 + 0.280 \log(\text{sales}) + 0.0174 \text{ roe} + 0.00024 \text{ ros}$$

$$\text{se} = (0.32) \quad (0.035) \quad (0.0041) \quad (0.00054)$$

$$R^2 = 0.283$$

where salary = salary of CEO
sales = annual firm sales
roe = return on equity in percent
ros = return on firm's stock

and where figures in the parentheses are the estimated standard errors.

a. Interpret the preceding regression taking into account any prior expectations that you may have about the signs of the various coefficients.

b. Which of the coefficients are *individually* statistically significant at the 5 percent level?

c. What is the overall significance of the regression? Which test do you use? And why?

d. Can you interpret the coefficients of roe and ros as elasticity coefficients? Why or why not?

8.15. Assuming that Y and $X_2, X_3, \ldots, X_k$ are jointly normally distributed and assuming that the null hypothesis is that the population partial correlations are individually equal to zero, R. A. Fisher has shown that

$$t = \frac{r_{12.34\ldots k}\sqrt{n-k-2}}{\sqrt{1-r^2_{12.34\ldots k}}}$$

follows the t distribution with $n-k-2$ df, where k is the kth-order partial correlation coefficient and where n is the total number of observations. (*Note:* $r_{12.3}$ is a first-order partial correlation coefficient, $r_{12.34}$ is a second-order partial correlation coefficient, and so on.) Refer to Exercise 7.2. Assuming Y and X_2 and X_3 to be jointly normally distributed, compute the three partial correlations $r_{12.3}$, $r_{13.2}$, and $r_{23.1}$ and test their significance under the hypothesis that the corresponding population correlations are individually equal to zero.

8.16. In studying the demand for farm tractors in the United States for the periods 1921–1941 and 1948–1957, Griliches† obtained the following results:

$$\widehat{\log Y_t} = \text{constant} - 0.519 \log X_{2t} - 4.933 \log X_{3t} \qquad R^2 = 0.793$$

$$(0.231) \qquad (0.477)$$

*See Jeffrey M. Wooldridge, *Introductory Econometrics,* South-Western Publishing Co., 2000, pp. 154–155.

†Z. Griliches, "The Demand for a Durable Input: Farm Tractors in the United States, 1921–1957," in *The Demand for Durable Goods,* Arnold C. Harberger (ed.), The University of Chicago Press, Chicago, 1960, Table 1, p. 192.

where Y_t = value of stock of tractors on farms as of January 1, in 1935–1939 dollars, X_2 = index of prices paid for tractors divided by an index of prices received for all crops at time $t-1$, and X_3 = interest rate prevailing in year $t-1$. The estimated standard errors are given in the parentheses.

a. Interpret the preceding regression.

b. Are the estimated slope coefficients individually statistically significant? Are they significantly different from unity?

c. Use the analysis of variance technique to test the significance of the overall regression. *Hint:* Use the R^2 variant of the ANOVA technique.

d. How would you compute the interest-rate elasticity of demand for farm tractors?

e. How would you test the significance of estimated R^2?

8.17. Consider the following wage-determination equation for the British economy* for the period 1950–1969:

$$\begin{aligned}\hat{W}_t = {} & \underset{(1.129)}{8.582} + \underset{(0.080)}{0.364}(\mathrm{PF})_t + \underset{(0.072)}{0.004}(\mathrm{PF})_{t-1} - \underset{(0.658)}{2.560}U_t\\ & R^2 = 0.873 \qquad \mathrm{df} = 15\end{aligned}$$

where W = wages and salaries per employee
PF = prices of final output at factor cost
U = unemployment in Great Britain as a percentage of the total number of employees in Great Britain
t = time

(The figures in the parentheses are the estimated standard errors.)

a. Interpret the preceding equation.

b. Are the estimated coefficients individually significant?

c. What is the rationale for the introduction of $(\mathrm{PF})_{t-1}$?

d. Should the variable $(\mathrm{PF})_{t-1}$ be dropped from the model? Why?

e. How would you compute the elasticity of wages and salaries per employee with respect to the unemployment rate U?

8.18. A variation of the wage-determination equation given in Exercise 8.17 is as follows:†

$$\begin{aligned}\hat{W}_t = {} & \underset{(0.797)}{1.073} + \underset{(0.812)}{5.288}V_t - \underset{(0.111)}{0.116}X_t + \underset{(0.022)}{0.054}M_t + \underset{(0.019)}{0.046}M_{t-1}\\ & R^2 = 0.934 \quad \mathrm{df} = 14\end{aligned}$$

where W = wages and salaries per employee
V = unfilled job vacancies in Great Britain as a percentage of the total number of employees in Great Britain
X = gross domestic product per person employed
M = import prices
M_{t-1} = import prices in the previous (or lagged) year

(The estimated standard errors are given in the parentheses.)

*Taken from *Prices and Earnings in 1951–1969: An Econometric Assessment,* Dept. of Employment, HMSO, 1971, Eq. (19), p. 35.

†Ibid., Eq. (67), p. 37.

a. Interpret the preceding equation.

b. Which of the estimated coefficients are individually statistically significant?

c. What is the rationale for the introduction of the X variable? A priori, is the sign of X expected to be negative?

d. What is the purpose of introducing both M_t and M_{t-1} in the model?

e. Which of the variables may be dropped from the model? Why?

f. Test the overall significance of the observed regression.

8.19. For the demand for chicken function estimated in Eq. (8.6.24), is the estimated income elasticity equal to 1? Is the price elasticity equal to -1?

8.20. For the demand function in Eq. (8.6.24) how would you test the hypothesis that the income elasticity is equal in value but opposite in sign to the price elasticity of demand? Show the necessary calculations. (*Note:* cov $[\hat{\beta}_2, \hat{\beta}_3] = -0.00142$.)

8.21. Refer to the demand for roses function of Exercise 7.16. Confining your considerations to the logarithmic specification,

a. What is the estimated own-price elasticity of demand (i.e., elasticity with respect to the price of roses)?

b. Is it statistically significant?

c. If so, is it significantly different from unity?

d. A priori, what are the expected signs of X_3 (price of carnations) and X_4 (income)? Are the empirical results in accord with these expectations?

e. If the coefficients of X_3 and X_4 are statistically insignificant, what may be the reasons?

8.22. Refer to Exercise 7.17 relating to wildcat activity.

a. Is each of the estimated slope coefficients individually statistically significant at the 5 percent level?

b. Would you reject the hypothesis that $R^2 = 0$?

c. What is the instantaneous rate of growth of wildcat activity over the period 1948–1978? The corresponding compound rate of growth?

8.23. Refer to the U.S. defense budget outlay regression estimated in Exercise 7.18.

a. Comment generally on the estimated regression results.

b. Set up the ANOVA table and test the hypothesis that all the partial slope coefficients are zero.

8.24. The following is known as the **transcendental production function** (TPF), a generalization of the well-known Cobb–Douglas production function:

$$Y_i = \beta_1 L^{\beta_2} k^{\beta_3} e^{\beta_4 L + \beta_5 K}$$

where Y = output, L = labor input, and K = capital input.

After taking logarithms and adding the stochastic disturbance term, we obtain the stochastic TPF as

$$\ln Y_i = \beta_0 + \beta_2 \ln L_i + \beta_3 \ln K_i + \beta_4 L_i + \beta_5 K_i + u_i$$

where $\beta_0 = \ln \beta_1$.

a. What are the properties of this function?

b. For the TPF to reduce to the Cobb–Douglas production function, what must be the values of β_4 and β_5?

c. If you had the data, how would you go about finding out whether the TPF reduces to the Cobb–Douglas production function? What testing procedure would you use?

d. See if the TPF fits the data given in Table 8.8. Show your calculations.

8.25. *Energy prices and capital formation: United States, 1948–1978.* To test the hypothesis that a rise in the price of energy relative to output leads to a decline in the productivity of *existing* capital and labor resources, John A. Tatom estimated the following production function for the United States for the quarterly period 1948–I to 1978–II:*

$$\widehat{\ln(y/k)} = \underset{(16.33)}{1.5492} + \underset{(21.69)}{0.7135}\ln(h/k) - \underset{(-6.42)}{0.1081}\ln(P_e/P) + \underset{(15.86)}{0.0045}t \qquad R^2 = 0.98$$

where y = real output in the private business sector
k = a measure of the flow of capital services
h = person hours in the private business sector
P_e = producer price index for fuel and related products
P = private business sector price deflator
t = time

The numbers in parentheses are t statistics.

a. Do the results support the author's hypothesis?

b. Between 1972 and 1977 the relative price of energy, (P_e/P), increased by 60 percent. From the estimated regression, what is the loss in productivity?

c. After allowing for the changes in (h/k) and (P_e/P), what has been the trend rate of growth of productivity over the sample period?

d. How would you interpret the coefficient value of 0.7135?

e. Does the fact that each estimated partial slope coefficient is individually statistically significant (why?) mean we can reject the hypothesis that $R^2 = 0$? Why or why not?

8.26. *The demand for cable.* Table 8.10 gives data used by a telephone cable manufacturer to predict sales to a major customer for the period 1968–1983.†

The variables in the table are defined as follows:

Y = annual sales in MPF, million paired feet
X_2 = gross national product (GNP), $, billions
X_3 = housing starts, thousands of units
X_4 = unemployment rate, %
X_5 = prime rate lagged 6 months
X_6 = Customer line gains, %

*See his "Energy Prices and Capital Formation: 1972–1977," *Review,* Federal Reserve Bank of St. Louis, vol. 61, no. 5, May 1979, p. 4.

†I am indebted to Daniel J. Reardon for collecting and processing the data.

TABLE 8.10 Regression Variables

Year	X_2, GNP	X_3, Housing Starts	X_4, Unemployment, %	X_5, Prime Rate Lag, 6 mos.	X_6, Customer Line Gains, %	Y, Annual Sales (MPF)
1968	1051.8	1503.6	3.6	5.8	5.9	5873
1969	1078.8	1486.7	3.5	6.7	4.5	7852
1970	1075.3	1434.8	5.0	8.4	4.2	8189
1971	1107.5	2035.6	6.0	6.2	4.2	7497
1972	1171.1	2360.8	5.6	5.4	4.9	8534
1973	1235.0	2043.9	4.9	5.9	5.0	8688
1974	1217.8	1331.9	5.6	9.4	4.1	7270
1975	1202.3	1160.0	8.5	9.4	3.4	5020
1976	1271.0	1535.0	7.7	7.2	4.2	6035
1977	1332.7	1961.8	7.0	6.6	4.5	7425
1978	1399.2	2009.3	6.0	7.6	3.9	9400
1979	1431.6	1721.9	6.0	10.6	4.4	9350
1980	1480.7	1298.0	7.2	14.9	3.9	6540
1981	1510.3	1100.0	7.6	16.6	3.1	7675
1982	1492.2	1039.0	9.2	17.5	0.6	7419
1983	1535.4	1200.0	8.8	16.0	1.5	7923

You are to consider the following model:

$$Y_i = \beta_1 + \beta_2 X_{2t} + \beta_3 X_{3t} + \beta_4 X_{4t} + \beta_5 X_{5t} + \beta_6 X_{6t} + u_t$$

a. Estimate the preceding regression.

b. What are the expected signs of the coefficients of this model?

c. Are the empirical results in accordance with prior expectations?

d. Are the estimated partial regression coefficients individually statistically significant at the 5 percent level of significance?

e. Suppose you first regress Y on X_2, X_3, and X_4 only and then decide to add the variables X_5 and X_6. How would you find out if it is worth adding the variables X_5 and X_6? Which test do you use? Show the necessary calculations.

8.27. Marc Nerlove has estimated the following cost function for electricity generation:*

$$Y = AX^{\beta} P^{\alpha_1} P^{\alpha_2} P^{\alpha_3} u \qquad (1)$$

where Y = total cost of production
X = output in kilowatt hours
P_1 = price of labor input
P_2 = price of capital input
P_3 = price of fuel
u = disturbance term

*Marc Nerlove, "Returns to Scale in Electric Supply," in Carl Christ, ed., *Measurement in Economics*, Stanford University Press, Palo Alto, Calif., 1963. The notation has been changed.

Theoretically, the sum of the price elasticities is expected to be unity, i.e., $(\alpha_1 + \alpha_2 + \alpha_3) = 1$. By imposing this restriction, the preceding cost function can be written as

$$(Y/P_3) = AX^{\beta}(P_1/P_3)^{\alpha_1}(P_2/P_3)^{\alpha_2}u \tag{2}$$

In other words, (1) is an unrestricted and (2) is the restricted cost function.

On the basis of a sample of 29 medium-sized firms, and after logarithmic transformation, Nerlove obtained the following regression results:

$$\begin{aligned} \widehat{\ln Y_i} &= -4.93 \quad + 0.94 \ln X_i + 0.31 \ln P_1 \\ \text{se} &= \quad (1.96) \qquad (0.11) \qquad (0.23) \\ &\quad -0.26 \ln P_2 + 0.44 \ln P_3 \\ &\quad (0.29) \qquad (0.07) \qquad \text{RSS} = 0.336 \end{aligned} \tag{3}$$

$$\begin{aligned} \widehat{\ln (Y/P_3)} &= -6.55 + 0.91 \ln X + 0.51 \ln (P_1/P_3) + 0.09 \ln (P_2/P_3) \\ \text{se} &= \quad (0.16) \quad (0.11) \qquad (0.19) \qquad (0.16) \qquad \text{RSS} = 0.364 \end{aligned} \tag{4}$$

a. Interpret Eqs. (3) and (4).

b. How would you find out if the restriction $(\alpha_1 + \alpha_2 + \alpha_3) = 1$ is valid? Show your calculations.

8.28. *Estimating the capital asset pricing model (CAPM).* In Section 6.1 we considered briefly the well-known capital asset pricing model of modern portfolio theory. In empirical analysis, the CAPM is estimated in two stages.

Stage I (Time-series regression). For each of the N securities included in the sample, we run the following regression over time:

$$R_{it} = \hat{\alpha}_i + \hat{\beta}_i R_{mt} + e_{it} \tag{1}$$

where R_{it} and R_{mt} are the rates of return on the ith security and on the market portfolio (say, the S&P 500) in year t; β_i, as noted elsewhere, is the Beta or market volatility coefficient of the ith security, and e_{it} are the residuals. In all there are N such regressions, one for each security, giving therefore N estimates of β_i.

Stage II (Cross-section regression). In this stage we run the following regression over the N securities:

$$\bar{R}_i = \hat{\gamma}_1 + \hat{\gamma}_2 \hat{\beta}_i + u_i \tag{2}$$

where $\bar{R}_i$ is the average or mean rate of return for security i computed over the sample period covered by Stage I, $\hat{\beta}_i$ is the estimated beta coefficient from the first-stage regression, and u_i is the residual term.

Comparing the second-stage regression (2) with the CAPM Eq. (6.1.2), written as

$$\text{ER}_i = r_f + \beta_i(\text{ER}_m - r_f) \tag{3}$$

where r_f is the risk-free rate of return, we see that $\hat{\gamma}_1$ is an estimate of r_f and $\hat{\gamma}_2$ is an estimate of $(\text{ER}_m - r_f)$, the market risk premium.

Thus, in the empirical testing of CAPM, $\bar{R}_i$ and $\hat{\beta}_i$ are used as estimators of ER_i and β_i, respectively. Now if CAPM holds, statistically,

$$\hat{\gamma}_1 = r_f$$

$$\hat{\gamma}_2 = R_m - r_f, \text{ the estimator of } (\text{ER}_m - r_f)$$

Next consider an alternative model:

$$\bar{R}_i = \hat{\gamma}_1 + \hat{\gamma}_2\hat{\beta}_i + \hat{\gamma}_3 s_{e_i}^2 + u_i \tag{4}$$

where $s_{e_i}^2$ is the residual variance of the ith security from the first-stage regression. Then, if CAPM is valid, $\hat{\gamma}_3$ should not be significantly different from zero.

To test the CAPM, Levy ran regressions (2) and (4) on a sample of 101 stocks for the period 1948–1968 and obtained the following results:*

$$\begin{aligned} \hat{\bar{R}}_i &= \underset{(0.009)}{0.109} + \underset{(0.008)}{0.037}\beta_i \\ t &= (12.0) \quad\quad (5.1) \qquad R^2 = 0.21 \end{aligned} \tag{2)'$$

$$\begin{aligned} \hat{\bar{R}}_i &= \underset{(0.008)}{0.106} + \underset{(0.007)}{0.0024}\hat{\beta}_i + \underset{(0.038)}{0.201}s_{ei}^2 \\ t &= (13.2) \quad\quad (3.3) \quad\quad (5.3) \qquad R^2 = 0.39 \end{aligned} \tag{4)'$$

a. Are these results supportive of the CAPM?

b. Is it worth adding the variable $s_{e_i}^2$ to the model? How do you know?

c. If the CAPM holds, $\hat{\gamma}_1$ in (2)′ should approximate the average value of the risk free rate, r_f. The estimated value is 10.9 percent. Does this seem a reasonable estimate of the risk-free rate of return during the observation period, 1948–1968? (You may consider the rate of return on Treasury bills or a similar comparatively risk-free asset.)

d. If the CAPM holds, the market risk premium $(\bar{R}_m - r_f)$ from (2)′ is about 3.7 percent. If r_f is assumed to be 10.9 percent, this implies $\bar{R}_m$ for the sample period was about 14.6 percent. Does this sound like a reasonable estimate?

e. What can you say about the CAPM generally?

8.29. Refer to Exercise 7.21c. Now that you have the necessary tools, which test(s) would you use to choose between the two models? Show the necessary computations. Note that the dependent variables in the two models are different.

8.30. Refer to Example 8.3. Use the t test as shown in Eq. (8.6.4) to find out if there were constant returns to scale in the Mexican economy for the period of the study.

8.31. Return to the child mortality example that we have discussed several times. In regression (7.6.2) we regressed child mortality (CM) on per capita GNP (PGNP) and female literacy rate (FLR). Now we extend this model by including total

*H. Levy, "Equilibrium in an Imperfect Market: A Constraint on the Number of Securities in the Portfolio," *American Economic Review,* vol. 68, no. 4, September 1978, pp. 643–658.

fertility rate (TFR). The data on all these variables are already given in Table 6.4. We reproduce regression (7.6.2) and give results of the extended regression model below:

$$1.\ \widehat{CM}_i = 263.6416 - 0.0056\ \text{PGNP}_i - 2.2316\ \text{FLR}_i \tag{7.6.2}$$
$$\text{se} = (11.5932)\quad (0.0019)\quad (0.2099)\qquad R^2 = 0.7077$$

$$2.\ \widehat{CM}_i = 168.3067 - 0.0055\ \text{PGNP}_i - 1.7680\ \text{FLR}_i + 12.8686\text{TFR}_i$$
$$\text{se} = (32.8916)\quad (0.0018)\quad (0.2480)\quad (?)$$
$$R^2 = 0.7474$$

a. How would you interpret the coefficient of TFR? A priori, would you expect a positive or negative relationship between CM and TFR? Justify your answer.

b. Have the coefficient values of PGNP and FR changed between the two equations? If so, what may be the reason(s) for such a change? Is the observed difference statistically significant? Which test do you use and why?

c. How would you choose between models 1 and 2? Which statistical test would you use to answer this question? Show the necessary calculations.

d. We have not given the standard error of the coefficient of TFR. Can you find it out? (*Hint:* Recall the relationship between the t and F distributions.)

8.32. Return to Exercise 1.7, which gave data on advertising impressions retained and advertising expenditure for a sample of 21 firms. In Exercise 5.11 you were asked to plot these data and decide on an appropriate model about the relationship between impressions and advertising expenditure. Letting Y represent impressions retained and X the advertising expenditure, the following regressions were obtained:

$$\text{Model I:}\quad \hat{Y}_i = 22.163 + 0.3631X_i$$
$$\text{se} = (7.089)\quad (0.0971)\qquad r^2 = 0.424$$

$$\text{Model II:}\quad \hat{Y}_i = 7.059 + 1.0847X_i - 0.0040X_i^2$$
$$\text{se} = (9.986)\quad (0.3699)\quad (0.0019)\qquad R^2 = 0.53$$

a. Interpret both models.

b. Which is a better model? Why?

c. Which statistical test(s) would you use to choose between the two models?

d. Are there "diminishing returns" to advertising expenditure, that is, after a certain level of advertising expenditure (the saturation level), does it not pay to advertise? Can you find out what that level of expenditure might be? Show the necessary calculations.

8.33. In regression (7.9.4), we presented the results of the Cobb–Douglas production function fitted to the manufacturing sector of all 50 states and Washington, DC, for 2005. On the basis of that regression, find out if there are constant returns to scale in that sector, using

a. The t test given in Eq. (8.6.4). You are told that the covariance between the two slope estimators is −0.03843.

b. The F test given in Eq. (8.6.9).

c. Is there a difference in the two test results? And what is your conclusion regarding the returns to scale in the manufacturing sector of the 50 states and Washington, DC, over the sample period?

8.34. Reconsider the savings–income regression in Section 8.7. Suppose we divide the sample into two periods as 1970–1982 and 1983–1995. Using the Chow test, decide if there is a structural change in the savings–income regression in the two periods. Comparing your results with those given in Section 8.7, what overall conclusion do you draw about the sensitivity of the Chow test to the choice of the break point that divides the sample into two (or more) periods?

8.35. Refer to Exercise 7.24 and the data in Table 7.12 concerning four economic variables in the U.S. from 1947–2000.

a. Based on the regression of consumption expenditure on real income, real wealth and real interest rate, find out which of the regression coefficients are individually statistically significant at the 5 percent level of significance. Are the signs of the estimated coefficients in accord with economic theory?

b. Based on the results in (*a*), how would you estimate the income, wealth, and interest rate elasticities? What additional information, if any, do you need to compute the elasticities?

c. How would you test the hypothesis that the income and wealth elasticities are the same? Show the necessary calculations.

d. Suppose instead of the linear consumption function estimated in (*a*), you regress the logarithm of consumption expenditure on the logarithms of income and wealth and the interest rate. Show the regression results. How would you interpret the results?

e. What are the income and wealth elasticities estimated in (*d*)? How would you interpret the coefficient of the interest rate estimated in (*d*)?

f. In the regression in (*d*) could you have used the logarithm of the interest rate instead of the interest rate? Why or why not?

g. How would you compare the elasticities estimated in (*b*) and in (*d*)?

h. Between the regression models estimated in (*a*) and (*d*), which would you prefer? Why?

i. Suppose instead of estimating the model given in (*d*), you only regress the logarithm of consumption expenditure on the logarithm of income. How would you decide if it is worth adding the logarithm of wealth in the model? And how would you decide if it is worth adding both the logarithm of wealth and interest rate variables in the model? Show the necessary calculations.

8.36. Refer to Section 8.8 and the data in Table 8.9 concerning disposable personal income and personal savings for the period 1970–1995. In that section, the Chow test was introduced to see if a structural change occurred within the data between two time periods. Table 8.11 includes updated data containing the values from 1970–2005. According to the National Bureau of Economic Research, the most recent U.S. business contraction cycle ended in late 2001. Split the data into three sections: (1) 1970–1981, (2) 1982–2001, and (3) 2002–2005.

a. Estimate both the model for the full dataset (years 1970–2005) and the third section (post-2002). Using the Chow test, determine if there is a significant break between the third period and the full dataset.

b. With this new data in Table 8.11, determine if there is still a significant difference between the first set of years (1970–1981) and the full dataset, now that there are more observations available.

c. Perform the Chow test on the middle period (1982–2001) versus the full dataset to see if the data in this period behave significantly differently than the rest of the data.

TABLE 8.11
Savings and Personal Disposable Income (billions of dollars), United States, 1970–2005 (billions of dollars, except as noted; quarterly data at seasonally adjusted annual rates)

Source: Department of Commerce, Bureau of Economic Analysis.

Year	Savings	Income
1970	69.5	735.7
1971	80.6	801.8
1972	77.2	869.1
1973	102.7	978.3
1974	113.6	1,071.6
1975	125.6	1,187.4
1976	122.3	1,302.5
1977	125.3	1,435.7
1978	142.5	1,608.3
1979	159.1	1,793.5
1980	201.4	2,009.0
1981	244.3	2,246.1
1982	270.8	2,421.2
1983	233.6	2,608.4
1984	314.8	2,912.0
1985	280.0	3,109.3
1986	268.4	3,285.1
1987	241.4	3,458.3
1988	272.9	3,748.7
1989	287.1	4,021.7
1990	299.4	4,285.8
1991	324.2	4,464.3
1992	366.0	4,751.4
1993	284.0	4,911.9
1994	249.5	5,151.8
1995	250.9	5,408.2
1996	228.4	5,688.5
1997	218.3	5,988.8
1998	276.8	6,395.9
1999	158.6	6,695.0
2000	168.5	7,194.0
2001	132.3	7,486.8
2002	184.7	7,830.1
2003	174.9	8,162.5
2004	174.3	8,681.6
2005	34.8	9,036.1

*Appendix 8A2

Likelihood Ratio (LR) Test

The **LR test** is based on the maximum likelihood (ML) principle discussed in Appendix 4A, where we showed how one obtains the ML estimators of the two-variable regression model. The principle can be straightforwardly extended to the multiple regression model. Under the assumption that the disturbances u_i are normally distributed, we showed that, for the two-variable regression model, the OLS and ML estimators of the regression coefficients are identical, but the estimated error

*Optional.

variances are different. The OLS estimator of σ^2 is $\sum \hat{u}_i^2/(n-2)$ but the ML estimator is $\sum \hat{u}_i^2/n$, the former being unbiased and the latter biased, although in large samples the bias tends to disappear.

The same is true in the multiple regression case. To illustrate, consider the three-variable regression model:

$$Y_i = \beta_1 + \beta_2 X_{2i} + \beta_3 X_{3i} + u_i \tag{1}$$

Corresponding to Eq. (5) of Appendix 4A, the log-likelihood function for the model (1) can be written as:

$$\ln \text{LF} = -\frac{n}{2}\ln(\sigma^2) - \frac{n}{2}\ln(2\pi) - \frac{1}{2\sigma^2}\sum(Y_i - \beta_1 - \beta_2 X_{2i} - \beta_3 X_{3i})^2 \tag{2}$$

As shown in Appendix 4A, differentiating this function with respect to β_1, β_2, β_3, and σ^2, setting the resulting expressions to zero, and solving, we obtain the ML estimators of these estimators. The ML estimators of β_1, β_2, and β_3 will be identical to OLS estimators, which are already given in Eqs. (7.4.6) to (7.4.8), but the error variance will be different in that the residual sum of squares (RSS) will be divided by n rather than by $(n-3)$, as in the case of OLS.

Now let us suppose that our null hypothesis H_0 is that β_3, the coefficient of X_3, is zero. In this case, log LF given in (2) will become

$$\ln \text{LF} = -\frac{n}{2}\ln(\sigma^2) - \frac{n}{2}\ln(2\pi) - \frac{1}{2\sigma^2}\sum(Y_i - \beta_1 - \beta_2 X_{2i})^2 \tag{3}$$

Equation (3) is known as the **restricted log-likelihood function (RLLF)** because it is estimated with the restriction that a priori β_3 is zero, whereas Eq. (1) is known as the **unrestricted log LF (ULLF)** because a priori there are no restrictions put on the parameters. To test the validity of the a priori restriction that β_3 is zero, the LR test obtains the following test statistic:

$$\lambda = 2(\text{ULLF} - \text{RLLF}) \tag{4}^*$$

where ULLF and RLLF are, respectively, the unrestricted log-likelihood function (Eq. [2]) and the restricted log-likelihood function (Eq. [3]). If the sample size is large, it can be shown that the test statistic λ given in Eq. (4) follows the chi-square (χ^2) distribution with df equal to the number of restrictions imposed by the null hypothesis, 1 in the present case.

The basic idea behind the LR test is simple: If the a priori restriction(s) is valid, the restricted and unrestricted (log) LF should not be different, in which case λ in Eq. (4) will be zero. But if that is not the case, the two LFs will diverge. And since in a large sample we know that λ follows the chi-square distribution, we can find out if the divergence is statistically significant, say, at a 1 or 5 percent level of significance. Or else, we can find out the p value of the estimated λ.

Let us illustrate the LR test with our child mortality example. If we regress child mortality (CM) on per capita GNP (PGNP) and female literacy rate (FLR) as we did in Eq. (8.1.4), we obtain ULLF of −328.1012, but if we regress CM on PGNP only, we obtain the RLLF of −361.6396. In absolute value (i.e., disregarding the sign), the former is smaller than the latter, which makes sense since we have an additional variable in the former model.

The question now is whether it is worth adding the FLR variable. If it is not, the restricted and unrestricted LLF should not differ much, but if it is, the LLFs will be different. To see if this difference is statistically significant, we now use the LR test given in Eq. (4), which gives:

$$\lambda = 2[-328.1012 - (-361.6396)] = 67.0768$$

*This expression can also be expressed as −2(RLLF − ULLF) or as −2 ln (RLF/ULF).

Asymptotically, this is distributed as the chi-square distribution with 1 df (because we have only one restriction imposed when we omitted the FLR variable from the full model). The p value of obtaining such a chi-square value for 1 df is almost zero, leading to the conclusion that the FLR variable should *not* be excluded from the model. In other words, the restricted regression in the present instance is not valid.

Letting RRSS and URSS denote the restricted and unrestricted residual sums of squares, Eq. (4) can also be expressed as:

$$-2 \ln \lambda = n(\ln \text{RRSS} - \ln \text{URSS}) \tag{5}$$

which is distributed as χ^2 with r degrees of freedom, where r is the number of restrictions imposed on the model (i.e., the number of r coefficients omitted from the original model).

Although we will not go into the details of the Wald and LM tests, these tests can be implemented as follows:

$$\text{Wald Statistic (W)} = \frac{(n-k)(\text{RRSS} - \text{URSS})}{\text{URSS}} \sim \chi_r^2 \tag{6}$$

$$\text{Lagrange Multiplier Statistic (LM)} = \frac{(n-k+r)(\text{RRSS} - \text{URSS})}{\text{RRSS}} \sim \chi_r^2 \tag{7}$$

Where k is the number of regressors in the unrestricted model and r is the number of restrictions.

As you can see from the preceding equations, all three tests are asymptotically (i.e., in large samples) equivalent, that is, they give similar answers. However, in small samples the answers can differ. There is an interesting relationship among these statistics in that it can be shown that:

$$\text{W} \geq \text{LR} \geq \text{LM}$$

Therefore, in small samples, a hypothesis can be rejected by the Wald statistic but *not* rejected by the LM statistic.*

As noted in the text, for most of our purposes the t and F tests will suffice. But the three tests discussed above are of general applicability in that they can be applied to testing nonlinear hypotheses in linear models, or testing restrictions on variance-covariance matrices. They also can be applied in situations where the assumption that the errors are normally distributed is not tenable.

Because of the mathematical complexity of the Wald and LM tests, we will not go into more detail here. But as noted, asymptotically, the LR, Wald, and LM tests give identical answers, the choice of the test depending on computational convenience.

*For an explanation, see G. S. Maddala, *Introduction to Econometrics,* 3d ed., John Wiley & Sons, New York, 2001, p. 177.

Chapter 

Dummy Variable Regression Models

In Chapter 1 we discussed briefly the four types of variables that one generally encounters in empirical analysis: These are: **ratio scale, interval scale, ordinal scale,** and **nominal scale.** The types of variables that we have encountered in the preceding chapters were essentially *ratio scale.* But this should not give the impression that regression models can deal only with ratio scale variables. Regression models can also handle other types of variables mentioned previously. In this chapter, we consider models that may involve not only ratio scale variables but also **nominal scale** variables. Such variables are also known as **indicator variables, categorical variables, qualitative variables,** or **dummy variables.**[1]

9.1 The Nature of Dummy Variables

In regression analysis the dependent variable, or regressand, is frequently influenced not only by ratio scale variables (e.g., income, output, prices, costs, height, temperature) but also by variables that are essentially qualitative, or nominal scale, in nature, such as sex, race, color, religion, nationality, geographical region, political upheavals, and party affiliation. For example, holding all other factors constant, female workers are found to earn less than their male counterparts or nonwhite workers are found to earn less than whites.[2] This pattern may result from sex or racial discrimination, but whatever the reason, qualitative variables such as sex and race seem to influence the regressand and clearly should be included among the explanatory variables, or the regressors.

Since such variables usually indicate the presence or absence of a "quality" or an attribute, such as male or female, black or white, Catholic or non-Catholic, Democrat or Republican, they are essentially *nominal scale* variables. One way we could "quantify" such attributes is by constructing artificial variables that take on values of 1 or 0, 1 indicating the presence (or possession) of that attribute and 0 indicating the absence of that attribute. For example, 1 may indicate that a person is a female and 0 may designate a male; or 1 may indicate that a person is a college graduate, and 0 that the person is not, and so on.

[1]We will discuss ordinal scale variables in Chapter 15.

[2]For a review of the evidence on this subject, see Bruce E. Kaufman and Julie L. Hotchkiss, *The Economics of Labor Markets,* 5th ed., Dryden Press, New York, 2000.

Variables that assume such 0 and 1 values are called **dummy variables.**[3] *Such variables are thus essentially a device to classify data into mutually exclusive categories such as male or female.*

Dummy variables can be incorporated in regression models just as easily as quantitative variables. As a matter of fact, a regression model may contain regressors that are all exclusively dummy, or qualitative, in nature. Such models are called **Analysis of Variance (ANOVA) models.**[4]

9.2 ANOVA Models

To illustrate the ANOVA models, consider the following example.

EXAMPLE 9.1

Public School Teachers' Salaries by Geographical Region

Table 9.1 gives data on average salary (in dollars) of public school teachers in 50 states and the District of Columbia for the academic year 2005–2006. These 51 areas are classified into three geographical regions: (1) Northeast and North Central (21 states in all), (2) South (17 states in all), and (3) West (13 states in all). For the time being, do not worry about the format of the table and the other data given in the table.

Suppose we want to find out if the average annual salary of public school teachers differs among the three geographical regions of the country. If you take the simple arithmetic average of the average salaries of the teachers in the three regions, you will find that these averages for the three regions are as follows: \$49,538.71 (Northeast and North Central), \$46,293.59 (South), and \$48,104.62 (West). These numbers look different, but are they statistically different from one another? There are various statistical techniques to compare two or more mean values, which generally go by the name of **analysis of variance.**[5] But the same objective can be accomplished within the framework of regression analysis.

To see this, consider the following model:

$$Y_i = \beta_1 + \beta_2 D_{2i} + \beta_{3i} D_{3i} + u_i \tag{9.2.1}$$

where
Y_i = (average) salary of public school teacher in state i
D_{2i} = 1 if the state is in the Northeast or North Central
= 0 otherwise (i.e., in other regions of the country)
D_{3i} = 1 if the state is in the South
= 0 otherwise (i.e., in other regions of the country)

Note that Eq. (9.2.1) is like any multiple regression model considered previously, except that, instead of quantitative regressors, we have only qualitative, or dummy, regressors,

[3]It is not absolutely essential that dummy variables take the values of 0 and 1. The pair (0,1) can be transformed into any other pair by a linear function such that $Z = a + bD$ $(b \neq 0)$, where a and b are constants and where $D = 1$ or 0. When $D = 1$, we have $Z = a + b$, and when $D = 0$, we have $Z = a$. Thus the pair (0, 1) becomes $(a, a + b)$. For example, if $a = 1$ and $b = 2$, the dummy variables will be (1, 3). *This expression shows that qualitative, or dummy, variables do not have a natural scale of measurement.* That is why they are described as nominal scale variables.

[4]ANOVA models are used to assess the statistical significance of the relationship between a quantitative regressand and qualitative or dummy regressors. They are often used to compare the differences in the mean values of two or more groups or categories, and are therefore more general than the t test, which can be used to compare the means of two groups or categories only.

[5]For an applied treatment, see John Fox, *Applied Regression Analysis, Linear Models, and Related Methods*, Sage Publications, 1997, Chapter 8.

TABLE 9.1 Average Salary of Public School Teachers by State, 2005–2006

	Salary	Spending	D_2	D_3		Salary	Spending	D_2	D_3
Connecticut	60,822	12,436	1	0	Georgia	49,905	8,534	0	1
Illinois	58,246	9,275	1	0	Kentucky	43,646	8,300	0	1
Indiana	47,831	8,935	1	0	Louisiana	42,816	8,519	0	1
Iowa	43,130	7,807	1	0	Maryland	56,927	9,771	0	1
Kansas	43,334	8,373	1	0	Mississippi	40,182	7,215	0	1
Maine	41,596	11,285	1	0	North Carolina	46,410	7,675	0	1
Massachusetts	58,624	12,596	1	0	Oklahoma	42,379	6,944	0	1
Michigan	54,895	9,880	1	0	South Carolina	44,133	8,377	0	1
Minnesota	49,634	9,675	1	0	Tennessee	43,816	6,979	0	1
Missouri	41,839	7,840	1	0	Texas	44,897	7,547	0	1
Nebraska	42,044	7,900	1	0	Virginia	44,727	9,275	0	1
New Hampshire	46,527	10,206	1	0	West Virginia	40,531	9,886	0	1
New Jersey	59,920	13,781	1	0	Alaska	54,658	10,171	0	0
New York	58,537	13,551	1	0	Arizona	45,941	5,585	0	0
North Dakota	38,822	7,807	1	0	California	63,640	8,486	0	0
Ohio	51,937	10,034	1	0	Colorado	45,833	8,861	0	0
Pennsylvania	54,970	10,711	1	0	Hawaii	51,922	9,879	0	0
Rhode Island	55,956	11,089	1	0	Idaho	42,798	7,042	0	0
South Dakota	35,378	7,911	1	0	Montana	41,225	8,361	0	0
Vermont	48,370	12,475	1	0	Nevada	45,342	6,755	0	0
Wisconsin	47,901	9,965	1	0	New Mexico	42,780	8,622	0	0
Alabama	43,389	7,706	0	1	Oregon	50,911	8,649	0	0
Arkansas	44,245	8,402	0	1	Utah	40,566	5,347	0	0
Delaware	54,680	12,036	0	1	Washington, D.C.	47,882	7,958	0	0
District of Columbia	59,000	15,508	0	1	Wyoming	50,692	11,596	0	0
Florida	45,308	7,762	0	1					

Note: $D_2 = 1$ for states in the Northeast and North Central; 0 otherwise.
$D_3 = 1$ for states in the South; 0 otherwise.

Source: National Educational Association, as reported in 2007.

taking the value of 1 if the observation belongs to a particular category and 0 if it does not belong to that category or group. *Hereafter, we shall designate all dummy variables by the letter D.* Table 9.1 shows the dummy variables thus constructed.

What does the model (9.2.1) tell us? Assuming that the error term satisfies the usual OLS assumptions, on taking expectation of Eq. (9.2.1) on both sides, we obtain:

Mean salary of public school teachers in the Northeast and North Central:

$$E(Y_i \mid D_{2i} = 1, D_{3i} = 0) = \beta_1 + \beta_2 \tag{9.2.2}$$

Mean salary of public school teachers in the South:

$$E(Y_i \mid D_{2i} = 0, D_{3i} = 1) = \beta_1 + \beta_3 \tag{9.2.3}$$

You might wonder how we find out the mean salary of teachers in the West. If you guessed that this is equal to β_1, you would be absolutely right, for

Mean salary of public school teachers in the West:

$$E(Y_i \mid D_{2i} = 0, D_{3i} = 0) = \beta_1 \tag{9.2.4}$$

(Continued)

EXAMPLE 9.1 *(Continued)*

In other words, the mean salary of public school teachers in the West is given by the intercept, β_1, in the multiple regression (9.2.1), and the "slope" coefficients β_2 and β_3 tell by how much the mean salaries of teachers in the Northeast and North Central and in the South differ from the mean salary of teachers in the West. But how do we know if these differences are statistically significant? Before we answer this question, let us present the results based on the regression (9.2.1). Using the data given in Table 9.1, we obtain the following results:

$$
\begin{aligned}
\hat{Y}_i &= 48{,}014.615 \quad + 1{,}524.099D_{2i} - 1{,}721.027D_{3i} \\
\text{se} &= \quad (1857.204) \qquad (2363.139) \qquad (2467.151) \\
t &= \quad (25.853) \qquad (0.645) \qquad (-0.698) \\
& \quad (0.0000)^* \qquad (0.5220)^* \qquad (0.4888)^* \qquad R^2 = 0.0440
\end{aligned}
\tag{9.2.5}
$$

where * indicates the p values.

As these regression results show, the mean salary of teachers in the West is about \$48,015, that of teachers in the Northeast and North Central is higher by about \$1,524, and that of teachers in the South is lower by about \$1,721. The actual mean salaries in the last two regions can be easily obtained by adding these differential salaries to the mean salary of teachers in the West, as shown in Eqs. (9.2.3) and (9.2.4). Doing this, we will find that the mean salaries in the latter two regions are about \$49,539 and \$46,294.

But how do we know that these mean salaries are statistically different from the mean salary of teachers in the West, the comparison category? That is easy enough. All we have to do is to find out if each of the "slope" coefficients in Eq. (9.2.5) is statistically significant. As can be seen from this regression, the estimated slope coefficient for Northeast and North Central is not statistically significant, as its p value is 52 percent, and that of the South is also not statistically significant, as the p value is about 49 percent. Therefore, the overall conclusion is that statistically the mean salaries of public school teachers in the West, the Northeast and North Central, and the South are about the same. Diagrammatically, the situation is shown in Figure 9.1.

A caution is in order in interpreting these differences. The dummy variables will simply point out the differences, if they exist, but they do not suggest the reasons for the differences. Differences in educational levels, cost of living indexes, gender, and race may all have some effect on the observed differences. Therefore, unless we take into account all the other variables that may affect a teacher's salary, we will not be able to pin down the cause(s) of the differences.

From the preceding discussion, it is clear that all one has to do is see if the coefficients attached to the various dummy variables are individually statistically significant. This example also shows how easy it is to incorporate qualitative, or dummy, regressors in the regression models.

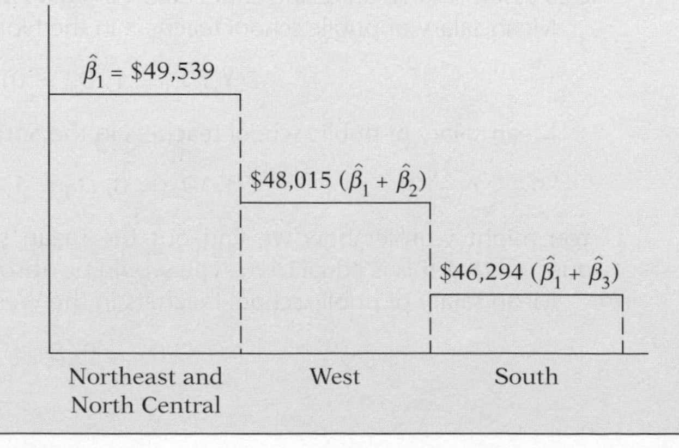

FIGURE 9.1 Average salary (in dollars) of public school teachers in three regions.

Caution in the Use of Dummy Variables

Although they are easy to incorporate in the regression models, one must use the dummy variables carefully. In particular, consider the following aspects:

1. In Example 9.1, to distinguish the three regions, we used only two dummy variables, D_2 and D_3. Why did we not use three dummies to distinguish the three regions? Suppose we do that and write the model (9.2.1) as:

$$Y_i = \alpha + \beta_1 D_{1i} + \beta_2 D_{2i} + \beta_3 D_{3i} + u_i \tag{9.2.6}$$

where D_{1i} takes a value of 1 for states in the West and 0 otherwise. Thus, we now have a dummy variable for each of the three geographical regions. Using the data in Table 9.1, if you were to run the regression (9.2.6), the computer would "refuse" to run the regression (try it).[6] Why? The reason is that in the setup of Eq. (9.2.6) where you have a dummy variable for each category or group and also an intercept, you have a case of **perfect collinearity,** that is, exact linear relationships among the variables. Why? Refer to Table 9.1. Imagine that now we add the D_1 column, taking the value of 1 whenever a state is in the West and 0 otherwise. Now if you add the three D columns horizontally, you will obtain a column that has 51 ones in it. But since the value of the intercept α is (implicitly) 1 for each observation, you will have a column that also contains 51 ones. In other words, the sum of the three D columns will simply reproduce the intercept column, thus leading to perfect collinearity. In this case, estimation of the model (9.2.6) is impossible.

The message here is: **If a qualitative variable has *m* categories, introduce only ($m - 1$) dummy variables.** In our example, since the qualitative variable "region" has three categories, we introduced only two dummies. If you do not follow this rule, you will fall into what is called the **dummy variable trap,** that is, the situation of perfect collinearity or perfect multicollinearity, if there is more than one exact relationship among the variables. This rule also applies if we have more than one qualitative variable in the model, an example of which is presented later. Thus we should restate the preceding rule as: **For each qualitative regressor, the number of dummy variables introduced must be one less than the categories of that variable.** Thus, if in Example 9.1 we had information about the gender of the teacher, we would use an additional dummy variable (but not two) taking a value of 1 for female and 0 for male or vice versa.

2. The category for which no dummy variable is assigned is known as the **base, benchmark, control, comparison, reference,** or **omitted category.** And all comparisons are made in relation to the benchmark category.

3. The intercept value (β_1) represents the *mean value* of the benchmark category. In Example 9.1, the benchmark category is the Western region. Hence, in the regression (9.2.5) the intercept value of about 48,015 represents the mean salary of teachers in the Western states.

4. The coefficients attached to the dummy variables in Eq. (9.2.1) are known as the **differential intercept coefficients** because they tell by how much the value of the category that receives the value of 1 differs from the intercept coefficient of the benchmark category. For example, in Eq. (9.2.5), the value of about 1,524 tells us that the mean salary of teachers in the Northeast or North Central is larger by about $1,524 than the mean salary of about $48,015 for the benchmark category, the West.

[6] Actually you will get a message saying that the data matrix is singular.

5. If a qualitative variable has more than one category, as in our illustrative example, the choice of the benchmark category is strictly up to the researcher. Sometimes the choice of the benchmark is dictated by the particular problem at hand. In our illustrative example, we could have chosen the South as the benchmark category. In that case the regression results given in Eq. (9.2.5) will change, because now all comparisons are made in relation to the South. Of course, this will not change the overall conclusion of our example (why?). In this case, the intercept value will be about \$46,294, which is the mean salary of teachers in the South.

6. We warned above about the dummy variable trap. There is a way to circumvent this trap by introducing as many dummy variables as the number of categories of that variable, *provided we do not introduce the intercept in such a model.* Thus, if we drop the intercept term from Eq. (9.2.6), and consider the following model,

$$Y_i = \beta_1 D_{1i} + \beta_2 D_{2i} + \beta_3 D_{3i} + u_i \tag{9.2.7}$$

we do not fall into the dummy variable trap, as there is no longer perfect collinearity. *But make sure that when you run this regression, you use the no-intercept option in your regression package.*

How do we interpret regression (9.2.7)? If you take the expectation of Eq. (9.2.7), you will find that:

$\beta_1 =$ mean salary of teachers in the West

$\beta_2 =$ mean salary of teachers in the Northeast and North Central

$\beta_3 =$ mean salary of teachers in the South

In other words, *with the intercept suppressed, and allowing a dummy variable for each category, we obtain directly the mean values of the various categories.* The results of Eq. (9.2.7) for our illustrative example are as follows:

$$\begin{aligned} \hat{Y}_i &= 48{,}014.62D_{1i} + 49{,}538.71D_{2i} + 46{,}293.59D_{3i} \\ \text{se} &= \quad (1857.204) \qquad (1461.240) \qquad (1624.077) \\ t &= \quad (25.853)^* \qquad (33.902)^* \qquad (28.505)^* \\ & \qquad\qquad\qquad\qquad\qquad\qquad R^2 = 0.044 \end{aligned} \tag{9.2.8}$$

where * indicates that the p values of these t ratios are very small.

As you can see, the dummy coefficients give directly the mean (salary) values in the three regions? West, Northeast and North Central, and South.

7. Which is a better method of introducing a dummy variable: (1) introduce a dummy for each category and omit the intercept term or (2) include the intercept term and introduce only $(m - 1)$ dummies, where m is the number of categories of the dummy variable? As Kennedy notes:

> Most researchers find the equation with an intercept more convenient because it allows them to address more easily the questions in which they usually have the most interest, namely, whether or not the categorization makes a difference, and if so, by how much. If the categorization does make a difference, by how much is measured directly by the dummy variable coefficient estimates. Testing whether or not the categorization is relevant can be done by running a t test of a dummy variable coefficient against zero (or, to be more general, an F test on the appropriate set of dummy variable coefficient estimates).[7]

[7]Peter Kennedy, A *Guide to Econometrics,* 4th ed., MIT Press, Cambridge, Mass., 1998, p. 223.

9.3 ANOVA Models with Two Qualitative Variables

In the previous section we considered an ANOVA model with one qualitative variable with three categories. In this section we consider another ANOVA model, but with two qualitative variables, and bring out some additional points about dummy variables.

EXAMPLE 9.2
Hourly Wages in Relation to Marital Status and Region of Residence

From a sample of 528 persons in May 1985, the following regression results were obtained.[8]

$$\begin{aligned} \hat{Y}_i &= 8.8148 + 1.0997D_{2i} - 1.6729D_{3i} \\ \text{se} &= (0.4015) \quad (0.4642) \quad (0.4854) \\ t &= (21.9528) \quad (2.3688) \quad (-3.4462) \\ & \quad\; (0.0000)^* \quad (0.0182)^* \quad (0.0006)^* \\ & \qquad\qquad R^2 = 0.0322 \end{aligned} \tag{9.3.1}$$

where Y = hourly wage ($)
D_2 = married status; 1 = married, 0 = otherwise
D_3 = region of residence; 1 = South, 0 = otherwise

and * denotes the p values.

In this example we have two qualitative regressors, each with two categories. Hence we have assigned a single dummy variable for each category.

Which is the benchmark category here? Obviously, it is unmarried, non-South residence. In other words, unmarried persons who do not live in the South are the omitted category. Therefore, all comparisons are made in relation to this group. The mean hourly wage in this benchmark is about $8.81. Compared with this, the average hourly wage of those who are married is higher by about $1.10, for an actual average wage of $9.91 (= 8.81 + 1.10). By contrast, for those who live in the South, the average hourly wage is lower by about $1.67, for an actual average hourly wage of $7.14.

Are the preceding average hourly wages statistically different compared to the base category? They are, for all the differential intercepts are statistically significant, as their p values are quite low.

The point to note about this example is this: *Once you go beyond one qualitative variable, you have to pay close attention to the category that is treated as the base category, since all comparisons are made in relation to that category. This is especially important when you have several qualitative regressors, each with several categories.* But the mechanics of introducing several qualitative variables should be clear by now.

9.4 Regression with a Mixture of Quantitative and Qualitative Regressors: The ANCOVA Models

ANOVA models of the type discussed in the preceding two sections, although common in fields such as sociology, psychology, education, and market research, are not that common in economics. Typically, in most economic research a regression model contains

[8] The data are obtained from the data disk in Arthur S. Goldberger, *Introductory Econometrics,* Harvard University Press, Cambridge, Mass., 1998. We have already considered these data in Chapter 2.

some explanatory variables that are quantitative and some that are qualitative. Regression models containing an admixture of quantitative and qualitative variables are called **analysis of covariance (ANCOVA) models.** ANCOVA models are an extension of the ANOVA models in that they provide a method of statistically controlling the effects of quantitative regressors, called **covariates** or **control variables,** in a model that includes both quantitative and qualitative, or dummy, regressors. We now illustrate the ANCOVA models.

EXAMPLE 9.3 *Teachers' Salary in Relation to Region and Spending on Public School per Pupil*

To motivate the analysis, let us reconsider Example 9.1 by maintaining that the average salary of public school teachers may not be different in the three regions if we take into account any variables that cannot be standardized across the regions. Consider, for example, the variable *expenditure on public schools by local authorities,* as public education is primarily a local and state question. To see if this is the case, we develop the following model:

$$Y_i = \beta_1 + \beta_2 D_{2i} + \beta_3 D_{3i} + \beta_4 X_i + u_i \tag{9.4.1}$$

where Y_i = average annual salary of public school teachers in state ($)
X_i = spending on public school per pupil ($)
D_{2i} = 1, if the state is in the Northeast or North Central
= 0, otherwise
D_{3i} = 1, if the state is in the South
= 0, otherwise

The data on X are given in Table 9.1. Keep in mind that we are treating the West as the benchmark category. Also, note that besides the two qualitative regressors, we have a quantitative variable, X, which in the context of the ANCOVA models is known as a **covariate**, as noted earlier.

From the data in Table 9.1, the results of the model (9.4.1) are as follows:

$$\begin{aligned}
\hat{Y}_i &= 28{,}694.918 \quad - 2{,}954.127 D_{2i} - 3{,}112.194 D_{3i} + 2.3404 X_i \\
\text{se} &= \quad (3262.521) \qquad (1862.576) \qquad (1819.873) \qquad (0.3592) \\
t &= \quad (8.795)^{*} \qquad (-1.586)^{**} \qquad (-1.710)^{**} \qquad (6.515)^{*} \\
& \qquad\qquad\qquad\qquad\qquad\qquad\qquad\qquad R^2 = 0.4977
\end{aligned} \tag{9.4.2}$$

where * indicates p values less than 5 percent, and ** indicates p values greater than 5 percent.

As these results suggest, *ceteris paribus:* as public expenditure goes up by a dollar, on average, a public school teacher's salary goes up by about $2.34. Controlling for spending on education, we now see that the differential intercept coefficient is not significant for either the Northeast and North Central region or for the South. These results are different from those of Eq. (9.2.5). But this should not be surprising, for in Eq. (9.2.5) we did not account for the covariate, differences in per pupil public spending on education. Diagrammatically, we have the situation shown in Figure 9.2.

Note that although we have shown three regression lines for the three regions, statistically the regression lines are the same for all three regions. Also note that the three regression lines are drawn parallel. (Why?)

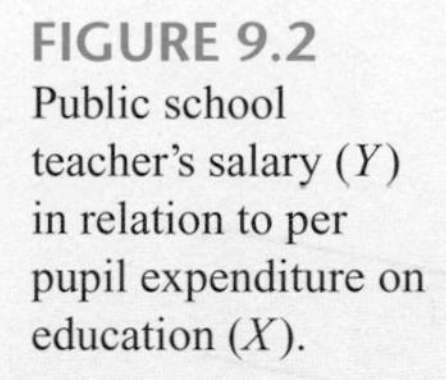

FIGURE 9.2
Public school teacher's salary (Y) in relation to per pupil expenditure on education (X).

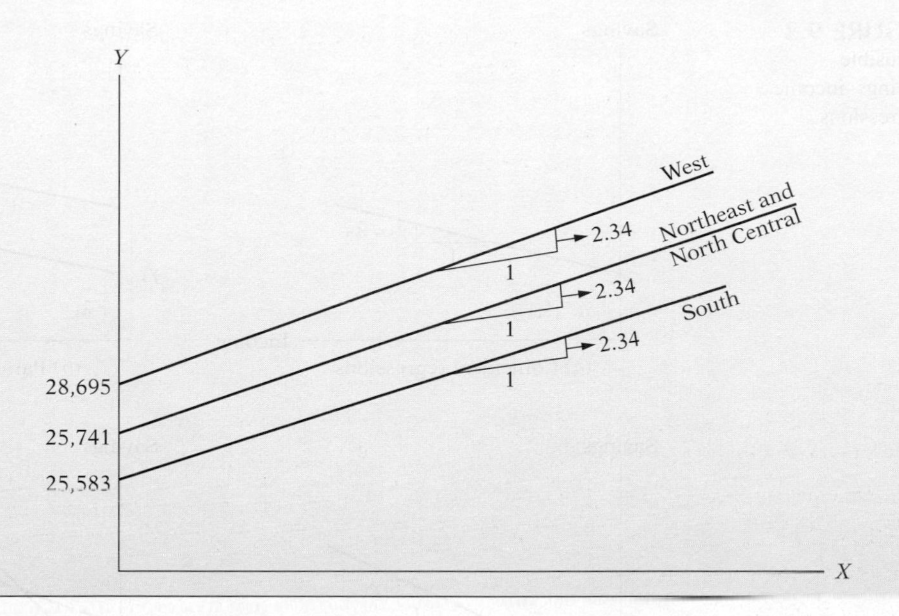

9.5 The Dummy Variable Alternative to the Chow Test[9]

In Section 8.7 we discussed the Chow test to examine the structural stability of a regression model. The example we discussed there related to the relationship between savings and income in the United States over the period 1970–1995. We divided the sample period into two, 1970–1981 and 1982–1995, and showed on the basis of the Chow test that there was a difference in the regression of savings on income between the two periods.

However, we could not tell whether the difference in the two regressions was because of differences in the intercept terms or the slope coefficients or both. Very often this knowledge itself is very useful.

Referring to Eqs. (8.7.1) and (8.7.2), we see that there are four possibilities, which we illustrate in Figure 9.3.

1. Both the intercept and the slope coefficients are the same in the two regressions. This, the case of **coincident regressions,** is shown in Figure 9.3*a*.
2. Only the intercepts in the two regressions are different but the slopes are the same. This is the case of **parallel regressions,** which is shown in Figure 9.3*b*.
3. The intercepts in the two regressions are the same, but the slopes are different. This is the situation of **concurrent regressions** (Figure 9.3*c*).
4. Both the intercepts and slopes in the two regressions are different. This is the case of **dissimilar regressions,** which is shown in Figure 9.3*d*.

The multistep Chow test procedure discussed in Section 8.7, as noted earlier, tells us only if two (or more) regressions are different without telling us what the source of the difference is.

[9]The material in this section draws on the author's articles, "Use of Dummy Variables in Testing for Equality between Sets of Coefficients in Two Linear Regressions: A Note," and "Use of Dummy Variables . . . A Generalization," both published in the *American Statistician,* vol. 24, nos. 1 and 5, 1970, pp. 50–52 and 18–21.

FIGURE 9.3 Plausible savings–income regressions.

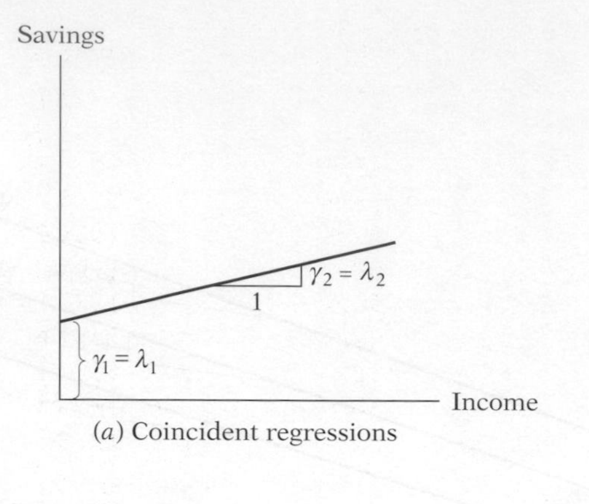

(*a*) Coincident regressions

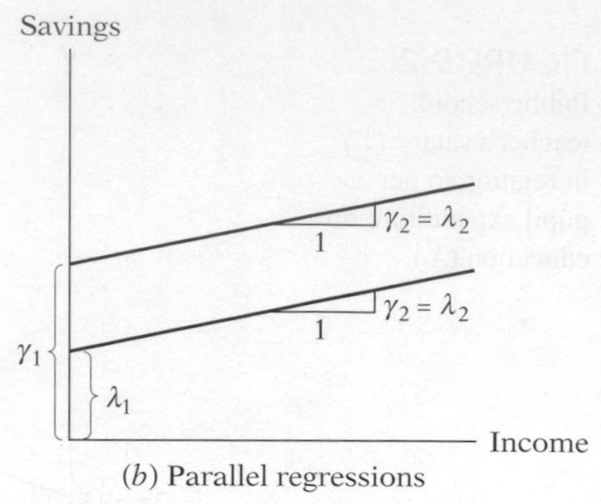

(*b*) Parallel regressions

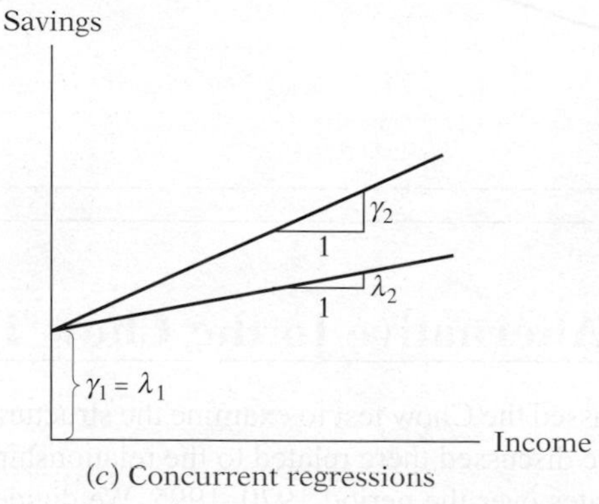

(*c*) Concurrent regressions

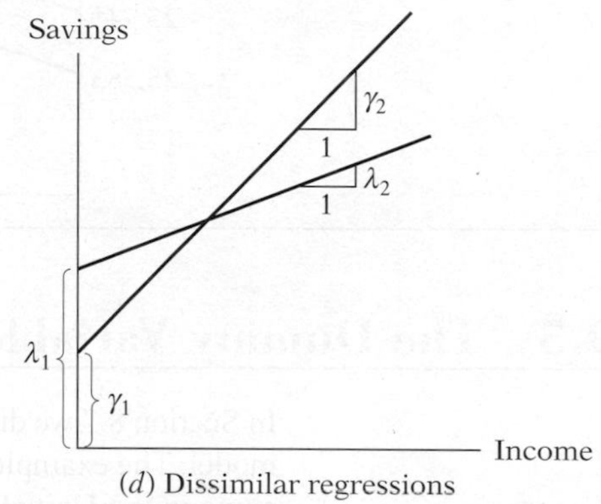

(*d*) Dissimilar regressions

The source of difference, if any, can be pinned down by pooling all the observations (26 in all) and running just one multiple regression as shown below:[10]

$$Y_t = \alpha_1 + \alpha_2 D_t + \beta_1 X_t + \beta_2 (D_t X_t) + u_t \tag{9.5.1}$$

where Y = savings
X = income
t = time
D = 1 for observations in 1982–1995
= 0, otherwise (i.e., for observations in 1970–1981)

Table 9.2 shows the structure of the data matrix.

To see the implications of Eq. (9.5.1), and, assuming, as usual, that $E(u_i) = 0$, we obtain:

Mean savings function for 1970–1981:

$$E(Y_t \mid D_t = 0, X_t) = \alpha_1 + \beta_1 X_t \tag{9.5.2}$$

Mean savings function for 1982–1995:

$$E(Y_t \mid D_t = 1, X_t) = (\alpha_1 + \alpha_2) + (\beta_1 + \beta_2) X_t \tag{9.5.3}$$

The reader will notice that these are the same functions as Eqs. (8.7.1) and (8.7.2), with $\lambda_1 = \alpha_1$, $\lambda_2 = \beta_1$, $\gamma_1 = (\alpha_1 + \alpha_2)$, and $\gamma_2 = (\beta_1 + \beta_2)$. Therefore, estimating Eq. (9.5.1) is equivalent to estimating the two individual savings functions in Eqs. (8.7.1) and (8.7.2).

[10]As in the Chow test, the pooling technique assumes homoscedasticity, that is, $\sigma_1^2 = \sigma_2^2 = \sigma^2$.

TABLE 9.2
Savings and Income Data, United States, 1970–1995

Source: *Economic Report of the President,* 1997, Table B-28, p. 332.

Observation	Savings	Income	Dum
1970	61	727.1	0
1971	68.6	790.2	0
1972	63.6	855.3	0
1973	89.6	965	0
1974	97.6	1054.2	0
1975	104.4	1159.2	0
1976	96.4	1273	0
1977	92.5	1401.4	0
1978	112.6	1580.1	0
1979	130.1	1769.5	0
1980	161.8	1973.3	0
1981	199.1	2200.2	0
1982	205.5	2347.3	1
1983	167	2522.4	1
1984	235.7	2810	1
1985	206.2	3002	1
1986	196.5	3187.6	1
1987	168.4	3363.1	1
1988	189.1	3640.8	1
1989	187.8	3894.5	1
1990	208.7	4166.8	1
1991	246.4	4343.7	1
1992	272.6	4613.7	1
1993	214.4	4790.2	1
1994	189.4	5021.7	1
1995	249.3	5320.8	1

Note: Dum = 1 for observations beginning in 1982; 0 otherwise.
Savings and income figures are in billions of dollars.

In Eq. (9.5.1), α_2 is the **differential intercept,** as previously, and β_2 is the **differential slope coefficient** (also called the **slope drifter**), indicating by how much the slope coefficient of the second period's savings function (the category that receives the dummy value of 1) differs from that of the first period. Notice how the introduction of the dummy variable D in the **interactive,** or **multiplicative, form** (D multiplied by X) enables us to differentiate between slope coefficients of the two periods, just as the introduction of the dummy variable in the **additive form** enabled us to distinguish between the intercepts of the two periods.

EXAMPLE 9.4
Structural Differences in the U.S. Savings–Income Regression, the Dummy Variable Approach

Before we proceed further, let us first present the regression results of model (9.5.1) applied to the U.S. savings–income data.

$$\begin{aligned}\hat{Y}_t &= 1.0161 \quad + 152.4786D_t + 0.0803X_t - 0.0655(D_tX_t)\\ \text{se} &= (20.1648) \quad (33.0824) \quad (0.0144) \quad (0.0159)\\ t &= (0.0504)^{**} \quad (4.6090)^{*} \quad (5.5413)^{*} \quad (-4.0963)^{*}\\ &\qquad\qquad R^2 = 0.8819\end{aligned} \tag{9.5.4}$$

where * indicates p values less than 5 percent and ** indicates p values greater than 5 percent.

(Continued)

EXAMPLE 9.4 *(Continued)*

As these regression results show, both the differential intercept and slope coefficients are statistically significant, strongly suggesting that the savings–income regressions for the two time periods are different, as in Figure 9.3*d*.

From Eq. (9.5.4), we can derive equations (9.5.2) and (9.5.3), which are:

Savings–income regression, 1970–1981:

$$\hat{Y}_t = 1.0161 + 0.0803X_t \tag{9.5.5}$$

Savings–income regression, 1982–1995:

$$\begin{aligned} \hat{Y}_t &= (1.0161 + 152.4786) + (0.0803 - 0.0655)X_t \\ &= 153.4947 + 0.0148X_t \end{aligned} \tag{9.5.6}$$

These are precisely the results we obtained in Eqs. (8.7.1a) and (8.7.2a), which should not be surprising. These regressions are already shown in Figure 8.3.

The advantages of the dummy variable technique (i.e., estimating Eq. [9.5.1]) over the Chow test (i.e., estimating the three regressions [8.7.1], [8.7.2], and [8.7.3]) can now be seen readily:

1. We need to run only a single regression because the individual regressions can easily be derived from it in the manner indicated by equations (9.5.2) and (9.5.3).
2. The single regression (9.5.1) can be used to test a variety of hypotheses. Thus if the *differential intercept* coefficient α_2 is statistically insignificant, we may accept the hypothesis that the two regressions have the same intercept, that is, the two regressions are concurrent (see Figure 9.3*c*). Similarly, if the *differential slope* coefficient β_2 is statistically insignificant but α_2 is significant, we may not reject the hypothesis that the two regressions have the same slope, that is, the two regression lines are parallel (cf. Figure 9.3*b*). The test of the stability of the entire regression (i.e., $\alpha_2 = \beta_2 = 0$, simultaneously) can be made by the usual *F* test (recall the restricted least-squares *F* test). If this hypothesis is not rejected, the regression lines will be coincident, as shown in Figure 9.3*a*.
3. The Chow test does not explicitly tell us *which* coefficient, intercept, or slope is different, or whether (as in this example) both are different in the two periods. That is, one can obtain a significant Chow test because the *slope* only is different or the *intercept* only is different, or both are different. In other words, we cannot tell, via the Chow test, which one of the four possibilities depicted in Figure 9.3 exists in a given instance. In this respect, the dummy variable approach has a distinct advantage, for it not only tells if the two are different but also pinpoints the source(s) of the difference—whether it is due to the intercept or the slope or both. In practice, the knowledge that two regressions differ in this or that coefficient is as important as, if not more than, the plain knowledge that they are different.
4. Finally, since pooling (i.e., including all the observations in one regression) increases the degrees of freedom, it may improve the relative precision of the estimated parameters. Of course, keep in mind that every addition of a dummy variable will consume one degree of freedom.

9.6 Interaction Effects Using Dummy Variables

Dummy variables are a flexible tool that can handle a variety of interesting problems. To see this, consider the following model:

$$Y_i = \alpha_1 + \alpha_2 D_{2i} + \alpha_3 D_{3i} + \beta X_i + u_i \tag{9.6.1}$$

where Y = hourly wage in dollars
X = education (years of schooling)
D_2 = 1 if female, 0 otherwise
D_3 = 1 if nonwhite and non-Hispanic, 0 otherwise

In this model gender and race are qualitative regressors and education is a quantitative regressor.[11] Implicit in this model is the assumption that the differential effect of the gender dummy D_2 is constant across the two categories of race and the differential effect of the race dummy D_3 is also constant across the two sexes. That is to say, if the mean salary is higher for males than for females, this is so whether they are nonwhite/non-Hispanic or not. Likewise, if, say, nonwhite/non-Hispanics have lower mean wages, this is so whether they are females or males.

In many applications such an assumption may be untenable. A female nonwhite/non-Hispanic may earn lower wages than a male nonwhite/non-Hispanic. In other words, there may be **interaction** between the two qualitative variables D_2 and D_3. Therefore their effect on mean Y may not be simply **additive** as in Eq. (9.6.1) but **multiplicative** as well, as in the following model.

$$Y_i = \alpha_1 + \alpha_2 D_{2i} + \alpha_3 D_{3i} + \alpha_4 (D_{2i} D_{3i}) + \beta X_i + u_i \tag{9.6.2}$$

where the variables are as defined for model (9.6.1).

From Eq. (9.6.2), we obtain:

$$E(Y_i \mid D_{2i} = 1, D_{3i} = 1, X_i) = (\alpha_1 + \alpha_2 + \alpha_3 + \alpha_4) + \beta X_i \tag{9.6.3}$$

which is the mean hourly wage function for female nonwhite/non-Hispanic workers. Observe that

α_2 = differential effect of being a female
α_3 = differential effect of being a nonwhite/non-Hispanic
α_4 = differential effect of being a female nonwhite/non-Hispanic

which shows that the mean hourly wages of female nonwhite/non-Hispanics is different (by α_4) from the mean hourly wages of females or nonwhite/non-Hispanics. If, for instance, all the three differential dummy coefficients are negative, this would imply that female nonwhite/non-Hispanic workers earn much lower mean hourly wages than female or nonwhite/non-Hispanic workers as compared with the base category, which in the present example is male white or Hispanic.

Now the reader can see how the **interaction dummy** (i.e., the product of two qualitative or dummy variables) modifies the effect of the two attributes considered individually (i.e., additively).

EXAMPLE 9.5
Average Hourly Earnings in Relation to Education, Gender, and Race

Let us first present the regression results based on model (9.6.1). Using the data that were used to estimate regression (9.3.1), we obtained the following results:

$$\begin{aligned}\hat{Y}_i &= -0.2610 \quad 2.3606D_{2i} - \quad 1.7327D_{3i} + \quad 0.8028X_i \\ t &= (-0.2357)^{**} \quad (-5.4873)^{*} \quad (-2.1803)^{*} \quad (9.9094)^{*} \\ & \qquad R^2 = 0.2032 \qquad n = 528\end{aligned} \tag{9.6.4}$$

where * indicates p values less than 5 percent and ** indicates p values greater than 5 percent.

(Continued)

[11]If we were to define education as less than high school, high school, and more than high school, we could then use two dummies to represent the three classes.

EXAMPLE 9.5
(Continued)

The reader can check that the differential intercept coefficients are statistically significant, that they have the expected signs (why?), and that education has a strong positive effect on hourly wage, an unsurprising finding.

As Eq. (9.6.4) shows, *ceteris paribus*, the average hourly earnings of females are lower by about \$2.36, and the average hourly earnings of nonwhite non-Hispanic workers are also lower by about \$1.73.

We now consider the results of model (9.6.2), which includes the interaction dummy.

$$\begin{aligned} \hat{Y}_i = &-0.26100 - 2.3606D_{2i} - 1.7327D_{3i} + 2.1289D_{2i}D_{3i} + 0.8028X_i \\ t = &(-0.2357)^{**} \quad (-5.4873)^{*} \quad (-2.1803)^{*} \quad (1.7420)^{**} \quad (9.9095)^{**} \\ &R^2 = 0.2032 \qquad n = 528 \end{aligned} \tag{9.6.5}$$

where * indicates p values less than 5 percent and ** indicates p values greater than 5 percent.

As you can see, the two additive dummies are still statistically significant, but the interactive dummy is not at the conventional 5 percent level; the actual p value of the interaction dummy is about the 8 percent level. If you think this is a low enough probability, then the results of Eq. (9.6.5) can be interpreted as follows: Holding the level of education constant, if you add the three dummy coefficients you will obtain: $-1.964\ (= -2.3605 - 1.7327 + 2.1289)$, which means that mean hourly wages of nonwhite/non-Hispanic female workers is lower by about \$1.96, which is between the value of -2.3605 (gender difference alone) and -1.7327 (race difference alone).

The preceding example clearly reveals the role of interaction dummies when two or more qualitative regressors are included in the model. It is important to note that in the model (9.6.5) we are assuming that the rate of increase of hourly earnings with respect to education (of about 80 cents per additional year of schooling) remains constant across gender and race. But this may not be the case. If you want to test for this, you will have to introduce differential slope coefficients (see Exercise 9.25).

9.7 The Use of Dummy Variables in Seasonal Analysis

Many economic time series based on monthly or quarterly data exhibit seasonal patterns (regular oscillatory movements). Examples are sales of department stores at Christmas and other major holiday times, demand for money (or cash balances) by households at holiday times, demand for ice cream and soft drinks during summer, prices of crops right after harvesting season, demand for air travel, etc. Often it is desirable to remove the seasonal factor, or *component,* from a time series so that one can concentrate on the other components, such as the trend.[12] The process of removing the seasonal component from a time series is known as **deseasonalization** or **seasonal adjustment,** and the time series thus obtained is called the **deseasonalized,** or **seasonally adjusted,** time series. Important economic time series, such as the unemployment rate, the consumer price index (CPI), the producer's price index (PPI), and the index of industrial production, are usually published in seasonally adjusted form.

[12]A time series may contain four components: (1) **seasonal,** (2) **cyclical,** (3) **trend,** and (4) strictly random.

TABLE 9.3
Quarterly Data on Appliance Sales (in thousands) and Expenditure on Durable Goods (1978–I to 1985–IV)

Source: *Business Statistics and Survey of Current Business*, Department of Commerce (various issues).

DISH	DISP	FRIG	WASH	DUR	DISH	DISP	FRIG	WASH	DUR
841	798	1317	1271	252.6	480	706	943	1036	247.7
957	837	1615	1295	272.4	530	582	1175	1019	249.1
999	821	1662	1313	270.9	557	659	1269	1047	251.8
960	858	1295	1150	273.9	602	837	973	918	262
894	837	1271	1289	268.9	658	867	1102	1137	263.3
851	838	1555	1245	262.9	749	860	1344	1167	280
863	832	1639	1270	270.9	827	918	1641	1230	288.5
878	818	1238	1103	263.4	858	1017	1225	1081	300.5
792	868	1277	1273	260.6	808	1063	1429	1326	312.6
589	623	1258	1031	231.9	840	955	1699	1228	322.5
657	662	1417	1143	242.7	893	973	1749	1297	324.3
699	822	1185	1101	248.6	950	1096	1117	1198	333.1
675	871	1196	1181	258.7	838	1086	1242	1292	344.8
652	791	1410	1116	248.4	884	990	1684	1342	350.3
628	759	1417	1190	255.5	905	1028	1764	1323	369.1
529	734	919	1125	240.4	909	1003	1328	1274	356.4

Note: DISH = dishwashers; DISP = garbage disposers; FRIG = refrigerators; WASH = washing machines; DUR = durable goods expenditure, billions of 1982 dollars.

There are several methods of deseasonalizing a time series, but we will consider only one of these methods, namely, the *method of dummy variables.*[13] To illustrate how the dummy variables can be used to deseasonalize economic time series, consider the data given in Table 9.3. This table gives quarterly data for the years 1978–1995 on the sale of four major appliances, dishwashers, garbage disposers, refrigerators, and washing machines, all data in thousands of units. The table also gives data on durable goods expenditure in 1982 billions of dollars.

To illustrate the dummy technique, we will consider only the sales of refrigerators over the sample period. But first let us look at the data, which is shown in Figure 9.4. This figure suggests that perhaps there is a seasonal pattern in the data associated with the various quarters. To see if this is the case, consider the following model:

$$Y_t = \alpha_1 D_{1t} + \alpha_2 D_{2t} + \alpha_{3t} D_{3t} + \alpha_4 D_{4t} + u_t \tag{9.7.1}$$

where Y_t = sales of refrigerators (in thousands) and the D's are the dummies, taking a value of 1 in the relevant quarter and 0 otherwise. *Note that to avoid the dummy variable trap, we are assigning a dummy to each quarter of the year, but omitting the intercept term.* If there is any seasonal effect in a given quarter, that will be indicated by a statistically significant t value of the dummy coefficient for that quarter.[14]

Notice that in Eq. (9.7.1) we are regressing Y effectively on an intercept, except that we allow for a different intercept in each season (i.e., quarter). As a result, the dummy coefficient of each quarter will give us the mean refrigerator sales in each quarter or season (why?).

[13]For the various methods of seasonal adjustment, see, for instance, Francis X. Diebold, *Elements of Forecasting,* 2d ed., South-Western Publishing, 2001, Chapter 5.

[14]Note a technical point. This method of assigning a dummy to each quarter assumes that the seasonal factor, if present, is deterministic and not stochastic. We will revisit this topic when we discuss time series econometrics in Part V of this book.

FIGURE 9.4
Sales of refrigerators 1978–1985 (quarterly).

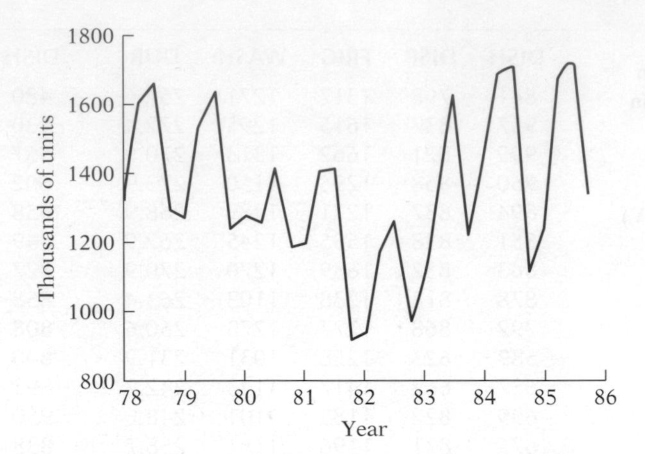

EXAMPLE 9.6
Seasonality in Refrigerator Sales

From the data on refrigerator sales given in Table 9.4, we obtain the following regression results:

$$\hat{Y}_t = 1{,}222.125D_{1t} + 1{,}467.500D_{2t} + 1{,}569.750D_{3t} + 1{,}160.000D_{4t}$$
$$t = \quad (20.3720) \qquad (24.4622) \qquad (26.1666) \qquad (19.3364) \tag{9.7.2}$$
$$R^2 = 0.5317$$

Note: We have not given the standard errors of the estimated coefficients, as each standard error is equal to 59.9904, because all the dummies take only a value of 1 or zero.

The estimated α coefficients in Eq. (9.7.2) represent the average, or *mean,* sales of refrigerators (in thousands of units) in each season (i.e., quarter). Thus, the average sale of refrigerators in the first quarter, in thousands of units, is about 1,222, that in the second quarter about 1,468, that in the third quarter about 1,570, and that in the fourth quarter about 1,160.

TABLE 9.4
U.S. Refrigerator Sales (thousands), 1978–1985 (quarterly)

Source: *Business Statistics and Survey of Current Business,* Department of Commerce (various issues).

FRIG	DUR	D_2	D_3	D_4	FRIG	DUR	D_2	D_3	D_4
1317	252.6	0	0	0	943	247.7	0	0	0
1615	272.4	1	0	0	1175	249.1	1	0	0
1662	270.9	0	1	0	1269	251.8	0	1	0
1295	273.9	0	0	1	973	262.0	0	0	1
1271	268.9	0	0	0	1102	263.3	0	0	0
1555	262.9	1	0	0	1344	280.0	1	0	0
1639	270.9	0	1	0	1641	288.5	0	1	0
1238	263.4	0	0	1	1225	300.5	0	0	1
1277	260.6	0	0	0	1429	312.6	0	0	0
1258	231.9	1	0	0	1699	322.5	1	0	0
1417	242.7	0	1	0	1749	324.3	0	1	0
1185	248.6	0	0	1	1117	333.1	0	0	1
1196	258.7	0	0	0	1242	344.8	0	0	0
1410	248.4	1	0	0	1684	350.3	1	0	0
1417	255.5	0	1	0	1764	369.1	0	1	0
919	240.4	0	0	1	1328	356.4	0	0	1

Note: FRIG = refrigerator sales, thousands.
DUR = durable goods expenditure, billions of 1982 dollars.
D_2 = 1 in the second quarter, 0 otherwise.
D_3 = 1 in the third quarter, 0 otherwise.
D_4 = 1 in the fourth quarter, 0 otherwise.

EXAMPLE 9.6
(Continued)

Incidentally, instead of assigning a dummy for each quarter and suppressing the intercept term to avoid the dummy variable trap, we could assign only three dummies and include the intercept term. Suppose we treat the first quarter as the reference quarter and assign dummies to the second, third, and fourth quarters. This produces the following regression results (see Table 9.4 for the data setup):

$$\begin{aligned} \hat{Y}_t &= 1{,}222.1250 \quad + 245.3750D_{2t} + 347.6250D_{3t} - \quad 62.1250D_{4t} \\ t &= \quad (20.3720)^* \qquad (2.8922)^* \qquad (4.0974)^* \qquad (-0.7322)^{**} \\ & \qquad\qquad\qquad\qquad\qquad\qquad\qquad\qquad R^2 = 0.5318 \end{aligned} \tag{9.7.3}$$

where * indicates *p* values less than 5 percent and ** indicates *p* values greater than 5 percent.

Since we are treating the first quarter as the benchmark, the coefficients attached to the various dummies are now *differential intercepts,* showing by how much the *average value* of Y in the quarter that receives a dummy value of 1 differs from that of the benchmark quarter. Put differently, the coefficients on the seasonal dummies will give the seasonal increase or decrease in the average value of Y relative to the base season. If you add the various differential intercept values to the benchmark average value of 1,222.125, you will get the average value for the various quarters. Doing so, you will reproduce exactly Eq. (9.7.2), except for the rounding errors.

But now you will see the value of treating one quarter as the benchmark quarter, for Eq. (9.7.3) shows that the average value of Y for the fourth quarter is not statistically different from the average value for the first quarter, as the dummy coefficient for the fourth quarter is not statistically significant. Of course, your answer will change, depending on which quarter you treat as the benchmark quarter, but the overall conclusion will not change.

How do we obtain the deseasonalized time series of refrigerator sales? This can be done easily. You estimate the values of Y from model (9.7.2) (or [9.7.3]) for each observation and subtract them from the actual values of Y, that is, you obtain $(Y_t - \hat{Y}_t)$ which are simply the residuals from the regression (9.7.2). We show them in Table 9.5.[15] To these residuals, we have to add the mean of the Y series to get the forecasted values.

What do these residuals represent? They represent the remaining components of the refrigerator time series, namely, the trend, cycle, and random components (but see the caution given in footnote 15).

Since models (9.7.2) and (9.7.3) do not contain any covariates, will the picture change if we bring in a quantitative regressor in the model? Since expenditure on durable goods has an important factor influence on the demand for refrigerators, let us expand our model (9.7.3) by bringing in this variable. The data for durable goods expenditure in billions of 1982 dollars are already given in Table 9.3. This is our (quantitative) X variable in the model. The regression results are as follows

$$\begin{aligned} \hat{Y}_t &= 456.2440 \quad + 242.4976D_{2t} + 325.2643D_{3t} - \quad 86.0804D_{4t} + \; 2.7734X_t \\ t &= \quad (2.5593)^* \qquad (3.6951)^* \qquad (4.9421)^* \qquad (-1.3073)^{**} \qquad (4.4496)^* \\ & \qquad\qquad\qquad\qquad\qquad\qquad\qquad\qquad\qquad\qquad R^2 = 0.7298 \end{aligned} \tag{9.7.4}$$

where * indicates *p* values less than 5 percent and ** indicates *p* values greater than 5 percent.

(Continued)

[15]Of course, this assumes that the dummy variables technique is an appropriate method of deseasonalizing a time series and that a time series (TS) can be represented as: TS $= s + c + t + u$, where s represents the seasonal, t the trend, c the cyclical, and u the random component. However, if the time series is of the form, TS $= (s)(c)(t)(u)$, where the four components enter multiplicatively, the preceding method of deseasonalization is inappropriate, for that method assumes that the four components of a time series are additive. But we will have more to say about this topic in the chapters on time series econometrics.

EXAMPLE 9.6
(Continued)

TABLE 9.5 **Refrigerator Sales Regression: Actual, Fitted, and Residual Values (Eq. 9.7.3)**

	Actual	Fitted	Residuals	Residuals Graph 0
1978–I	1317	1222.12	94.875	. | *
1978–II	1615	1467.50	147.500	. | *
1978–III	1662	1569.75	92.250	. | *.
1978–IV	1295	1160.00	135.000	. | *
1979–I	1271	1222.12	48.875	. | * .
1979–II	1555	1467.50	87.500	. | *.
1979–III	1639	1569.75	69.250	. | *.
1979–IV	1238	1160.00	78.000	. | *.
1980–I	1277	1222.12	54.875	. | * .
1980–II	1258	1467.50	−209.500	*. | .
1980–III	1417	1569.75	−152.750	* | .
1980–IV	1185	1160.00	25.000	. | * .
1981–I	1196	1222.12	−26.125	. *| .
1981–II	1410	1467.50	−57.500	. * | .
1981–III	1417	1569.75	−152.750	.* | .
1981–IV	919	1160.00	−241.000	*. | .
1982–I	943	1222.12	−279.125	* . | .
1982–II	1175	1467.50	−292.500	* . | .
1982–III	1269	1569.75	−300.750	* . | .
1982–IV	973	1160.00	−187.000	*. | .
1983–I	1102	1222.12	−120.125	. * | .
1983–II	1344	1467.50	−123.500	.* | .
1983–III	1641	1569.75	71.250	. | * .
1983–IV	1225	1160.00	65.000	. | * .
1984–I	1429	1222.12	206.875	. | .*
1984–II	1699	1467.50	231.500	. | . *
1984–III	1749	1569.75	179.250	. | .*
1984–IV	1117	1160.00	−43.000	. * | .
1985–I	1242	1222.12	19.875	. | * .
1985–II	1684	1467.50	216.500	. | . *
1985–III	1764	1569.75	194.250	. | .*
1985–IV	1328	1160.00	168.000	. | *
				− 0 +

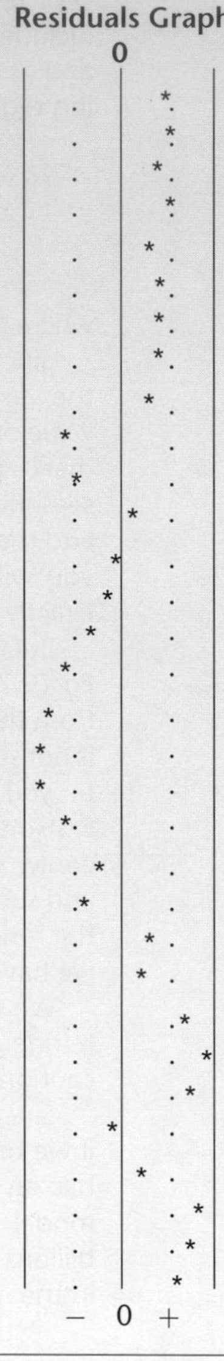

Again, keep in mind that we are treating the first quarter as our base. As in Eq. (9.7.3), we see that the differential intercept coefficients for the second and third quarters are statistically different from that of the first quarter, but the intercepts of the fourth quarter and the first quarter are statistically about the same. The coefficient of X (durable goods expenditure) of about 2.77 tells us that, allowing for seasonal effects, if expenditure on durable goods goes up by a dollar, on average, sales of refrigerators go up by about 2.77 units, that is, approximately 3 units; bear in mind that refrigerators are in thousands of units and X is in (1982) billions of dollars.

An interesting question here is: Just as sales of refrigerators exhibit seasonal patterns, would not expenditure on durable goods also exhibit seasonal patterns? How then do we take into account seasonality in X? The interesting thing about Eq. (9.7.4) is that the dummy variables in that model not only remove the seasonality in Y but also the seasonality, if any, in X. (This follows from a well-known theorem in statistics, known as the

EXAMPLE 9.6
(Continued)

Frisch–Waugh theorem.[16]) So to speak, we kill (deseasonalize) two birds (two series) with one stone (the dummy technique).

If you want an informal proof of the preceding statement, just follow these steps: (1) Run the regression of Y on the dummies as in Eq. (9.7.2) or Eq. (9.7.3) and save the residuals, say, S_1; these residuals represent deseasonalized Y. (2) Run a similar regression for X and obtain the residuals from this regression, say, S_2; these residuals represent deseasonalized X. (3) Regress S_1 on S_2. You will find that the slope coefficient in this regression is precisely the coefficient of X in the regression (9.7.4).

9.8 Piecewise Linear Regression

To illustrate yet another use of dummy variables, consider Figure 9.5, which shows how a hypothetical company remunerates its sales representatives. It pays commissions based on sales in such a manner that up to a certain level, the *target,* or *threshold,* level X^*, there is one (stochastic) commission structure and beyond that level another. (*Note:* Besides sales, other factors affect sales commission. Assume that these other factors are represented by the stochastic disturbance term.) More specifically, it is assumed that sales commission increases linearly with sales until the threshold level X^*, after which it continues to increase linearly with sales but at a much steeper rate. Thus, we have a **piecewise linear regression** consisting of two linear pieces or segments, which are labeled I and II in Figure 9.5, and the commission function changes its slope at the threshold value. Given the data on commission, sales, and the value of the threshold level X^*, the technique of dummy variables can be used to estimate the (differing) slopes of the two segments of the piecewise linear regression shown in Figure 9.5. We proceed as follows:

$$Y_i = \alpha_1 + \beta_1 X_i + \beta_2 (X_i - X^*) D_i + u_i \tag{9.8.1}$$

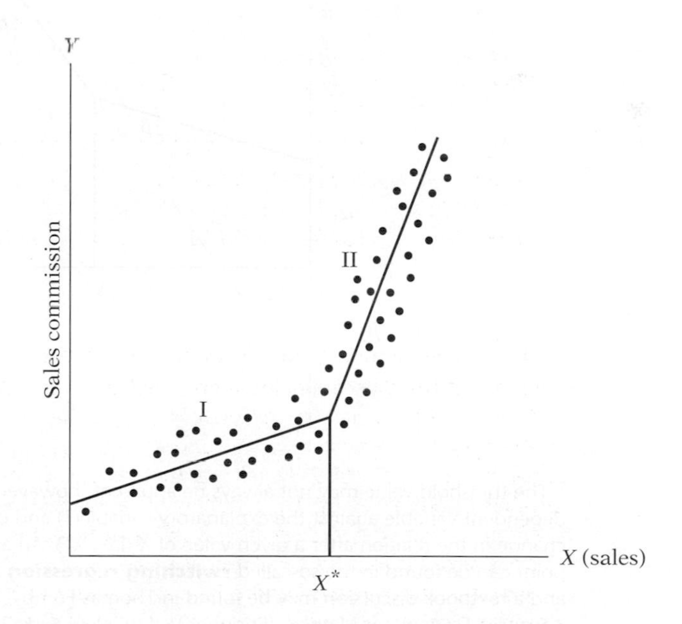

FIGURE 9.5 Hypothetical relationship between sales commission and sales volume. (*Note:* The intercept on the Y axis denotes minimum guaranteed commission.)

[16]For proof, see Adrian C. Darnell, *A Dictionary of Econometrics,* Edward Elgar, Lyme, U.K., 1995, pp. 150–152.

where Y_i = sales commission
X_i = volume of sales generated by the sales person
X^* = threshold value of sales also known as a **knot** (known in advance)[17]
$D = 1 \quad \text{if } X_i > X^*$
$\;\;\; = 0 \quad \text{if } X_i < X^*$

Assuming $E(u_i) = 0$, we see at once that

$$E(Y_i \mid D_i = 0, X_i, X^*) = \alpha_1 + \beta_1 X_i \qquad \textbf{(9.8.2)}$$

which gives the mean sales commission up to the target level X^* and

$$E(Y_i \mid D_i = 1, X_i, X^*) = \alpha_1 - \beta_2 X^* + (\beta_1 + \beta_2) X_i \qquad \textbf{(9.8.3)}$$

which gives the mean sales commission beyond the target level X^*.

Thus, β_1 gives the slope of the regression line in segment I, and $\beta_1 + \beta_2$ gives the slope of the regression line in segment II of the piecewise linear regression shown in Figure 9.5. A test of the hypothesis that there is no break in the regression at the threshold value X^* can be conducted easily by noting the statistical significance of the estimated differential slope coefficient $\hat{\beta}_2$ (see Figure 9.6).

Incidentally, the piecewise linear regression we have just discussed is an example of a more general class of functions known as **spline functions.**[18]

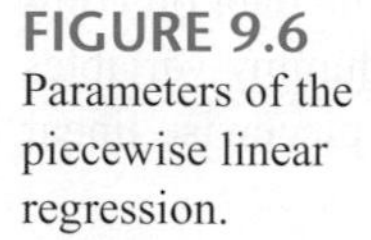

FIGURE 9.6 Parameters of the piecewise linear regression.

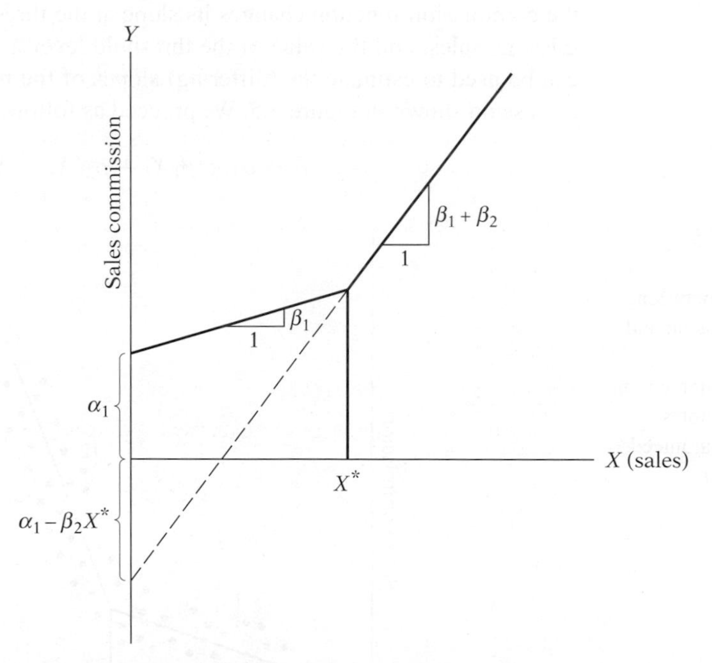

[17]The threshold value may not always be apparent, however. An ad hoc approach is to plot the dependent variable against the explanatory variable(s) and observe if there seems to be a sharp change in the relation after a given value of X (i.e., X^*). An analytical approach to finding the break point can be found in the so-called **switching regression models.** But this is an advanced topic and a textbook discussion may be found in Thomas Fomby, R. Carter Hill, and Stanley Johnson, *Advanced Econometric Methods,* Springer-Verlag, New York, 1984, Chapter 14.

[18]For an accessible discussion on splines (i.e., piecewise polynomials of order k), see Douglas C. Montgomery, Elizabeth A. Peck, and G. Geoffrey Vining, *Introduction to Linear Regression Analysis,* John Wiley & Sons, 3d ed., New York, 2001, pp. 228–230.

EXAMPLE 9.7

Total Cost in Relation to Output

As an example of the application of the piecewise linear regression, consider the hypothetical total cost–total output data given in Table 9.6. We are told that the total cost may change its slope at the output level of 5,500 units.

Letting Y in Eq. (9.8.4) represent total cost and X total output, we obtain the following results:

$$
\begin{aligned}
\hat{Y}_i &= -145.72 \quad + 0.2791X_i + 0.0945(X_i - X_i^*)D_i \\
t &= \;\;(-0.8245) \quad (6.0669) \quad (1.1447) \\
& \qquad R^2 = 0.9737 \qquad X^* = 5{,}500
\end{aligned}
\tag{9.8.4}
$$

As these results show, the marginal cost of production is about 28 cents per unit and although it is about 37 cents (28 + 9) for output over 5,500 units, the difference between the two is not statistically significant because the dummy variable is not significant at, say, the 5 percent level. For all practical purposes, then, one can regress total cost on total output, dropping the dummy variable.

TABLE 9.6
Hypothetical Data on Output and Total Cost

Total Cost, Dollars	Output, Units
256	1,000
414	2,000
634	3,000
778	4,000
1,003	5,000
1,839	6,000
2,081	7,000
2,423	8,000
2,734	9,000
2,914	10,000

9.9 Panel Data Regression Models

Recall that in Chapter 1 we discussed a variety of data that are available for empirical analysis, such as *cross-section, time series, pooled* (combination of time series and cross-section data), and *panel data.* The technique of dummy variable can be easily extended to pooled and panel data. Since the use of panel data is becoming increasingly common in applied work, we will consider this topic in some detail in Chapter 16.

9.10 Some Technical Aspects of the Dummy Variable Technique

The Interpretation of Dummy Variables in Semilogarithmic Regressions

In Chapter 6 we discussed the log–lin models, where the regressand is logarithmic and the regressors are linear. In such a model, the slope coefficients of the regressors give the *semi*elasticity, that is, the percentage change in the regressand for a unit change in the regressor. *This is only so if the regressor is quantitative.* What happens if a regressor is a dummy variable? To be specific, consider the following model:

$$\ln Y_i = \beta_1 + \beta_2 D_i + u_i \tag{9.10.1}$$

where Y = hourly wage rate ($) and $D = 1$ for female and 0 for male.

How do we interpret such a model? Assuming $E(u_i) = 0$, we obtain:

Wage function for male workers:

$$E(\ln Y_i \mid D_i = 0) = \beta_1 \tag{9.10.2}$$

Wage function for female workers:

$$E(\ln Y_i \mid D_i = 1) = \beta_1 + \beta_2 \tag{9.10.3}$$

Therefore, the intercept β_1 gives the *mean log hourly earnings* and the "slope" coefficient gives the difference in the mean log hourly earnings of male and females. This is a rather awkward way of stating things. But if we take the antilog of β_1, what we obtain is *not* the mean hourly wages of male workers, but their **median** wages. As you know, *mean, median,* and *mode* are the three measures of central tendency of a random variable. And if we take the antilog of $(\beta_1 + \beta_2)$, we obtain the median hourly wages of female workers.

EXAMPLE 9.8

Logarithm of Hourly Wages in Relation to Gender

To illustrate Eq. (9.10.1), we use the data that underlie Example 9.2. The regression results based on 528 observations are as follows:

$$\begin{aligned} \widehat{\ln Y_i} &= \quad 2.1763 \quad - \quad 0.2437 D_i \\ t &= (72.2943)^* \quad (-5.5048)^* \\ &\qquad R^2 = 0.0544 \end{aligned} \tag{9.10.4}$$

where * indicates p values are practically zero.

Taking the antilog of 2.1763, we find 8.8136 ($), which is the median hourly earnings of male workers, and taking the antilog of [(2.1763 − 0.2437) = 1.92857], we obtain 6.8796 ($), which is the median hourly earnings of female workers. Thus, the female workers' median hourly earnings are lower by about 21.94 percent compared to their male counterparts [(8.8136 − 6.8796)/8.8136].

Interestingly, we can obtain semielasticity for a dummy regressor directly by the device suggested by Halvorsen and Palmquist.[19] *Take the antilog (to base e) of the estimated dummy coefficient and subtract 1 from it and multiply the difference by 100.* (For the underlying logic, see Appendix 9.A.1.) Therefore, if you take the antilog of −0.2437, you will obtain 0.78366. Subtracting 1 from this gives −0.2163. After multiplying this by 100, we get −21.63 percent, suggesting that a female worker's ($D = 1$) median salary is lower than that of her male counterpart by about 21.63 percent, the same as we obtained previously, save the rounding errors.

Dummy Variables and Heteroscedasticity

Let us revisit our savings–income regression for the United States for the periods 1970–1981 and 1982–1995 and for the entire period 1970–1995. In testing for structural stability using the dummy technique, we assumed that the error var (u_{1i}) = var $(u_{2i}) = \sigma^2$,

[19]Robert Halvorsen and Raymond Palmquist, "The Interpretation of Dummy Variables in Semilogarithmic Equations," *American Economic Review,* vol. 70, no. 3, pp. 474–475.

that is, the error variances in the two periods, were the same. This was also the assumption underlying the Chow test. If this assumption is not valid—that is, the error variances in the two subperiods are different—it is quite possible to draw misleading conclusions. Therefore, one must first check on the equality of variances in the subperiod, using suitable statistical techniques. Although we will discuss this topic more thoroughly in the chapter on heteroscedasticity, in Chapter 8 we showed how the F test can be used for this purpose.[20] (See our discussion of the Chow test in that chapter.) As we showed there, it seems the error variances in the two periods are not the same. Hence, the results of both the Chow test and the dummy variable technique presented before may not be entirely reliable. Of course, our purpose here is to illustrate the various techniques that one can use to handle a problem (e.g., the problem of structural stability). In any particular application, these techniques may not be valid. But that is par for most statistical techniques. Of course, one can take appropriate remedial actions to resolve the problem, as we will do in the chapter on heteroscedasticity later (however, see Exercise 9.28).

Dummy Variables and Autocorrelation

Besides homoscedasticity, the classical linear regression model assumes that the error term in the regression models is uncorrelated. But what happens if that is not the case, especially in models involving dummy regressors? Since we will discuss the topic of autocorrelation in depth in the chapter on autocorrelation, we will defer the answer to this question until then.

What Happens If the Dependent Variable Is a Dummy Variable?

So far we have considered models in which the regressand is quantitative and the regressors are quantitative or qualitative or both. But there are occasions where the regressand can also be qualitative or dummy. Consider, for example, the decision of a worker to participate in the labor force. The decision to participate is of the yes or no type, yes if the person decides to participate and no otherwise. Thus, the labor force participation variable is a dummy variable. Of course, the decision to participate in the labor force depends on several factors, such as the starting wage rate, education, and conditions in the labor market (as measured by the unemployment rate).

Can we still use ordinary least squares (OLS) to estimate regression models where the regressand is dummy? Yes, mechanically, we can do so. But there are several statistical problems that one faces in such models. And since there are alternatives to OLS estimation that do not face these problems, we will discuss this topic in a later chapter (see Chapter 15 on logit and probit models). In that chapter we will also discuss models in which the regressand has more than two categories; for example, the decision to travel to work by car, bus, or train, or the decision to work part-time, full time, or not work at all. Such models are called **polytomous dependent variable** models in contrast to **dichotomous dependent variable models** in which the dependent variable has only two categories.

[20]The Chow test procedure can be performed even in the presence of heteroscedasticity, but then one will have to use the **Wald test.** The mathematics involved behind the test are somewhat involved. But in the chapter on heteroscedasticity, we will revisit this topic.

9.11 Topics for Further Study

Several topics related to dummy variables are discussed in the literature that are rather advanced, including (1) **random, or varying, parameters models,** (2) **switching regression models,** and (3) **disequilibrium models.**

In the regression models considered in this text it is assumed that the parameters, the β's, are unknown but fixed entities. The random coefficient models—and there are several versions of them—assume the β's can be random too. A major reference work in this area is by Swamy.[21]

In the dummy variable model using both differential intercepts and slopes, it is implicitly assumed that we know the point of break. Thus, in our savings–income example for 1970–1995, we divided the period into 1970–1981 and 1982–1995, the pre- and postrecession periods, under the belief that the recession in 1982 changed the relation between savings and income. Sometimes it is not easy to pinpoint when the break has taken place. The technique of **switching regression models (SRM)** has been developed for such situations. SRM treats the breakpoint as a random variable and through an iterative process determines when the break might have actually taken place. The seminal work in this area is by Goldfeld and Quandt.[22]

Special estimation techniques are required to deal with what are known as **disequilibrium situations,** that is, situations where markets do not clear (i.e., demand is not equal to supply). The classic example is that of demand for and supply of a commodity. The demand for a commodity is a function of its price and other variables, and the supply of the commodity is a function of its price and other variables, some of which are different from those entering the demand function. Now the quantity actually bought and sold of the commodity may not necessarily be equal to the one obtained by equating the demand to supply, thus leading to disequilibrium. For a thorough discussion of **disequilibrium models,** the reader may refer to Quandt.[23]

9.12 A Concluding Example

We end this chapter with an example that illustrates some of the points made in this chapter. Table 9.7 provides data on a sample of 261 workers in an industrial town in southern India in 1990.

The variables are defined as follows:

WI = weekly wage income in rupees
Age = age in years
D_{sex} = 1 for male workers and 0 for female workers
DE_2 = a dummy variable taking a value of 1 for workers with an education level up to primary
DE_3 = a dummy variable taking a value of 1 for workers up to a secondary level of education
DE_4 = a dummy variable taking a value of 1 for workers with higher than secondary education
DPT = a dummy variable taking a value of 1 for workers with permanent jobs and a value of 0 for temporary workers

[21]P. A.V. B. Swamy, *Statistical Inference in Random Coefficient Regression Models,* Springer-Verlag, Berlin, 1971.

[22]S. Goldfeld and R. Quandt, *Nonlinear Methods in Econometrics,* North Holland, Amsterdam, 1972.

[23]Richard E. Quandt, *The Econometrics of Disequilibrium,* Basil Blackwell, New York, 1988.

TABLE 9.7 **Indian Wage Earners, 1990**

WI	AGE	DE_2	DE_3	DE_4	DPT	D_{SEX}	WI	AGE	DE_2	DE_3	DE_4	DPT	D_{SEX}
120	57	0	0	0	0	0	120	21	0	0	0	0	0
224	48	0	0	1	1	0	25	18	0	0	0	0	1
132	38	0	0	0	0	0	25	11	0	0	0	0	1
75	27	0	1	0	0	0	30	38	0	0	0	1	1
111	23	0	1	0	0	1	30	17	0	0	0	1	1
127	22	0	1	0	0	0	122	20	0	0	0	0	0
30	18	0	0	0	0	0	288	50	0	1	0	1	0
24	12	0	0	0	0	0	75	45	0	0	0	0	1
119	38	0	0	0	1	0	79	60	0	0	0	0	0
75	55	0	0	0	0	0	85.3	26	0	0	0	0	1
324	26	0	1	0	0	0	350	42	0	1	0	1	0
42	18	0	0	0	0	0	54	62	0	0	0	1	0
100	32	0	0	0	0	0	110	23	0	0	0	0	0
136	41	0	0	0	0	0	342	56	0	0	0	1	0
107	48	0	0	0	0	0	77.5	19	0	0	0	1	0
50	16	1	0	0	0	1	370	46	0	0	0	0	0
90	45	0	0	0	0	0	156	26	0	0	0	1	0
377	46	0	0	0	1	0	261	23	0	0	0	0	0
150	30	0	1	0	0	0	54	16	0	1	0	0	0
162	40	0	0	0	0	0	130	33	0	0	0	0	0
18	19	1	0	0	0	0	112	27	1	0	0	0	0
128	25	1	0	0	0	0	82	22	1	0	0	0	0
47.5	46	0	0	0	0	1	385	30	0	1	0	1	0
135	25	0	1	0	0	0	94.3	22	0	0	1	1	1
400	57	0	0	0	1	0	350	57	0	0	0	1	0
91.8	35	0	0	1	1	0	108	26	0	0	0	0	0
140	44	0	0	0	1	0	20	14	0	0	0	0	0
49.2	22	0	0	0	0	0	53.8	14	0	0	0	0	1
30	19	1	0	0	0	0	427	55	0	0	0	1	0
40.5	37	0	0	0	0	1	18	12	0	0	0	0	0
81	20	0	0	0	0	0	120	38	0	0	0	0	0
105	40	0	0	0	0	0	40.5	17	0	0	0	0	0
200	30	0	0	0	0	0	375	42	1	0	0	1	0
140	30	0	0	0	1	0	120	34	0	0	0	0	0
80	26	0	0	0	0	0	175	33	1	0	0	1	0
47	41	0	0	0	0	1	50	26	0	0	0	0	1
125	22	0	0	0	0	0	100	33	1	0	0	1	0
500	21	0	0	0	0	0	25	22	0	0	0	1	1
100	19	0	0	0	0	0	40	15	0	0	0	1	0
105	35	0	0	0	0	0	65	14	0	0	0	1	0
300	35	0	1	0	1	0	47.5	25	0	0	0	1	1
115	33	0	1	0	1	1	163	25	0	0	0	1	0
103	27	0	0	1	1	1	175	50	0	0	0	1	1
190	62	1	0	0	0	0	150	24	0	0	0	1	1
62.5	18	0	1	0	0	0	163	28	0	0	0	1	0
50	25	1	0	0	0	0	163	30	1	0	0	1	0
273	43	0	0	1	1	1	50	25	0	0	0	1	1
175	40	0	1	0	1	0	395	45	0	1	0	1	0
117	26	1	0	0	1	0	175	40	0	0	0	1	1
950	47	0	0	1	0	0	87.5	25	1	0	0	0	0
100	30	0	0	0	0	0	75	18	0	0	0	0	0
140	30	0	0	0	0	0	163	24	0	0	0	1	0
97	25	0	1	0	0	0	325	55	0	0	0	1	0
150	36	0	0	0	0	0	121	27	0	1	0	0	0
25	28	0	0	0	0	1	600	35	1	0	0	0	0
15	13	0	0	0	0	1	52	19	0	0	0	0	0
131	55	0	0	0	0	0	117	28	1	0	0	0	0

The reference category is male workers with no primary education and temporary jobs. Our interest is in finding out how weekly wages relate to age, sex, level of education, and job tenure. For this purpose, we estimate the following regression model:

$$\ln \mathrm{WI}_i = \beta_1 + \beta_2 \mathrm{AGE}_i + \beta_3 D_{\mathrm{SEX}} + \beta_4 DE_2 + \beta_5 DE_3 + \beta_6 DE_4 + \beta_7 DPT + u_i$$

Following the literature in Labor Economics, we are expressing the (natural) log of wages as a function of the explanatory variables. As noted in Chapter 6, the size distribution of variables such as wages tends to be skewed; logarithmic transformations of such variables reduce both skewness and heteroscedasticity.

Using *EViews6,* we obtain the following regression results.

Dependent Variable: Ln(WI)
Method: Least Squares
Sample: 1 261
Included observations: 261

	Coefficient	Std. Error	*t*-Statistic	Prob.
C	3.706872	0.113845	32.56055	0.0000
AGE	0.026549	0.003117	8.516848	0.0000
D_{SEX}	-0.656338	0.088796	-7.391529	0.0000
DE_2	0.113862	0.098542	1.155473	0.2490
DE_3	0.412589	0.096383	4.280732	0.0000
DE_4	0.554129	0.155224	3.569862	0.0004
DPT	0.558348	0.079990	6.980248	0.0000

R-squared	0.534969	Mean dependent var.	4.793390
Adjusted R-squared	0.523984	S.D. dependent var.	0.834277
S.E. of regression	0.575600	Akaike info criterion	1.759648
Sum squared resid.	84.15421	Schwarz criterion	1.855248
Log likelihood	-222.6340	Hannan-Quinn criter.	1.798076
F-statistic	48.70008	Durbin-Watson stat.	1.853361
Prob(*F*-statistic)	0.000000		

These results show that the logarithm of wages is positively related to age, education, and job permanency but negatively related to gender, an unsurprising finding. Although there seems to be no practical difference in the weekly wages of workers with primary or less-than-primary education, the weekly wages are higher for workers with secondary education and much more so for workers with higher education.

The coefficients of the dummy variables are to be interpreted as differential values from the reference category. Thus, the coefficient of the *DPT* variable suggests that those workers who have permanent jobs on average make more money than those workers whose jobs are temporary.

As we know from Chapter 6, in a log–lin model (dependent variable in the logarithm form and the explanatory variables in the linear form), the slope coefficient of an explanatory variable represents semielasticity, that is, it gives the relative or percentage change in the dependent variable for a unit change in the value of the explanatory variable. But as noted in the text, when the explanatory variable is a dummy variable, we have to be very careful. Here we have to take the anti-log of the estimated dummy coefficient, subtract 1 from it, and multiply the result by 100. Thus, to find out the percentage change in weekly wages for those workers who have permanent jobs versus those who have temporary jobs, we take the anti-log of the *DPT* coefficient of 0.558348, subtract 1, and then multiply the difference by 100. For our example, this turns out to be $(e^{0.558348}-1) = (1.74778-1) = 0.74778$, or about 75%. The reader is advised to calculate such percentage changes for the other dummy variables included in the model.

Our results show that gender and education have differential effects on weekly earnings. Is it possible that there is an interaction between gender and the level of education? Do male workers with higher education earn higher weekly wages than female workers with higher education? To examine this possibility, we can extend the above wage regression by interacting gender with education. The regression results are as follows:

```
Dependent Variable: Ln(WI)
Method: Least Squares
Sample: 1 261
Included observations: 261
```

	Coefficient	Std. Error	*t*-Statistic	Prob.
C	3.717540	0.114536	32.45734	0.0000
AGE	0.027051	0.003133	8.634553	0.0000
D_{SEX}	-0.758975	0.110410	-6.874148	0.0000
DE_2	0.088923	0.106827	0.832402	0.4060
DE_3	0.350574	0.104309	3.360913	0.0009
DE_4	0.438673	0.186996	2.345898	0.0198
$D_{SEX}*DE_2$	0.114908	0.275039	0.417788	0.6765
$D_{SEX}*DE_3$	0.391052	0.259261	1.508337	0.1327
$D_{SEX}*DE_4$	0.369520	0.313503	1.178681	0.2396
DPT	0.551658	0.080076	6.889198	0.0000

R-squared	0.540810	Mean dependent var.	4.793390
Adjusted R-squared	0.524345	S.D. dependent var.	0.834277
S.E. of regression	0.575382	Akaike info criterion	1.769997
Sum squared resid.	83.09731	Schwarz criterion	1.906569
Log likelihood	-220.9847	Hannan-Quinn criter.	1.824895
F-statistic	32.84603	Durbin-Watson stat.	1.856488
Prob (*F*-statistic)	0.000000		

Although the interaction dummies show that there is some interaction between gender and the level of education, the effect is not statistically significant, for all the interaction coefficients are not individually statistically significant.

Interestingly, if we drop the education dummies but retain the interaction dummies, we obtain the following results:

Dependent Variable: LOG(WI)
Method: Least Squares
Sample: 1 261
Included observations: 261

	Coefficient	Std. Error	*t*-Statistic	Prob.
C	3.836483	0.106785	35.92725	0.0000
AGE	0.025990	0.003170	8.197991	0.0000
D_{SEX}	-0.868617	0.106429	-8.161508	0.0000
$D_{SEX}*DE_2$	0.200823	0.259511	0.773851	0.4397
$D_{SEX}*DE_3$	0.716722	0.245021	2.925140	0.0038
$D_{SEX}*DE_4$	0.752652	0.265975	2.829789	0.0050
DPT	0.627272	0.078869	7.953332	0.0000

R-squared	0.514449	Mean dependent var.	4.793390
Adjusted R-squared	0.502979	S.D. dependent var.	0.834277
S.E. of regression	0.588163	Akaike info criterion	1.802828
Sum squared resid.	87.86766	Schwarz criterion	1.898429
Log likelihood	-228.2691	Hannan-Quinn criter.	1.841257
F-statistic	44.85284	Durbin-Watson stat.	1.873421
Prob (*F*-statistic)	0.000000		

It now seems that education dummies by themselves have no effect on weekly wages, but introduced in an interactive format they seem to. As this exercise shows, one must be careful in the use of dummy variables. It is left as an exercise for the reader to find out if the education dummies interact with DPT.

Summary and Conclusions

1. Dummy variables, taking values of 1 and zero (or their linear transforms), are a means of introducing qualitative regressors in regression models.
2. Dummy variables are a data-classifying device in that they divide a sample into various subgroups based on qualities or attributes (gender, marital status, race, religion, etc.) and *implicitly* allow one to run individual regressions for each subgroup. If there are differences in the response of the regressand to the variation in the qualitative variables in the various subgroups, they will be reflected in the differences in the intercepts or slope coefficients, or both, of the various subgroup regressions.
3. Although a versatile tool, the dummy variable technique needs to be handled carefully. *First,* if the regression contains a constant term, the number of dummy variables must be one less than the number of classifications of each qualitative variable. *Second,* the coefficient attached to the dummy variables must *always* be interpreted in relation to the base, or reference, group—that is, the group that receives the value of zero. The base chosen will depend on the purpose of research at hand. *Finally,* if a model has several qualitative variables with several classes, introduction of dummy variables can consume a large number of degrees of freedom. Therefore, one should always weigh the number of dummy variables to be introduced against the total number of observations available for analysis.

4. Among its various applications, this chapter considered but a few. These included (1) comparing two (or more) regressions, (2) deseasonalizing time series data, (3) interactive dummies, (4) interpretation of dummies in semilog models, and (4) piecewise linear regression models.
5. We also sounded cautionary notes in the use of dummy variables in situations of heteroscedasticity and autocorrelation. But since we will cover these topics fully in subsequent chapters, we will revisit these topics then.

EXERCISES

Questions

9.1. If you have monthly data over a number of years, how many dummy variables will you introduce to test the following hypotheses:

a. All the 12 months of the year exhibit seasonal patterns.

b. Only February, April, June, August, October, and December exhibit seasonal patterns.

9.2. Consider the following regression results (t ratios are in parentheses):*

$$\begin{aligned} \hat{Y}_i = 1286 \quad &+ 104.97X_{2i} - 0.026X_{3i} + 1.20X_{4i} + 0.69X_{5i} \\ t = (4.67) \quad &\quad (3.70) \qquad (-3.80) \qquad (0.24) \qquad (0.08) \\ -19.47X_{6i} + &\ 266.06X_{7i} \qquad - 118.64X_{8i} - 110.61X_{9i} \\ (-0.40) \quad &\quad (6.94) \qquad\qquad (-3.04) \qquad (-6.14) \\ & R^2 = 0.383 \qquad n = 1543 \end{aligned}$$

where Y = wife's annual desired hours of work, calculated as usual hours of work per year plus weeks looking for work

X_2 = after-tax real average hourly earnings of wife

X_3 = husband's previous year after-tax real annual earnings

X_4 = wife's age in years

X_5 = years of schooling completed by wife

X_6 = attitude variable, 1 = if respondent felt that it was all right for a woman to work if she desired and her husband agrees, 0 = otherwise

X_7 = attitude variable, 1 = if the respondent's husband favored his wife's working, 0 = otherwise

X_8 = number of children less than 6 years of age

X_9 = number of children in age groups 6 to 13

a. Do the signs of the coefficients of the various nondummy regressors make economic sense? Justify your answer.

b. How would you interpret the dummy variables, X_6 and X_7? Are these dummies statistically significant? Since the sample is quite large, you may use the "2-t" rule of thumb to answer the question.

c. Why do you think that age and education variables are not significant factors in a woman's labor force participation decision in this study?

*Jane Leuthold, "The Effect of Taxation on the Hours Worked by Married Women," *Industrial and Labor Relations Review,* no. 4, July 1978, pp. 520–526 (notation changed to suit our format).

TABLE 9.8
Data Matrix for Regression, in Exercise 9.3

Source: Damodar Gujarati, "The Behaviour of Unemployment and Unfilled Vacancies: Great Britain, 1958–1971," *The Economic Journal*, vol. 82, March 1972, p. 202.

Year and Quarter	Unemployment Rate UN, %	Job Vacancy Rate V, %	D	DV	Year and Quarter	Unemployment Rate UN, %	Job Vacancy Rate V, %	D	DV
1958–IV	1.915	0.510	0	0	1965–I	1.201	0.997	0	0
1959–I	1.876	0.541	0	0	–II	1.192	1.035	0	0
–II	1.842	0.541	0	0	–III	1.259	1.040	0	0
–III	1.750	0.690	0	0	–IV	1.192	1.086	0	0
–IV	1.648	0.771	0	0	1966–I	1.089	1.101	0	0
1960–I	1.450	0.836	0	0	–II	1.101	1.058	0	0
–II	1.393	0.908	0	0	–III	1.243	0.987	0	0
–III	1.322	0.968	0	0	–IV	1.623	0.819	1	0.819
–IV	1.260	0.998	0	0	1967–I	1.821	0.740	1	0.740
1961–I	1.171	0.968	0	0	–II	1.990	0.661	1	0.661
–II	1.182	0.964	0	0	–III	2.114	0.660	1	0.660
–III	1.221	0.952	0	0	–IV	2.115	0.698	1	0.698
–IV	1.340	0.849	0	0	1968–I	2.150	0.695	1	0.695
1962–I	1.411	0.748	0	0	–II	2.141	0.732	1	0.732
–II	1.600	0.658	0	0	–III	2.167	0.749	1	0.749
–III	1.780	0.562	0	0	–IV	2.107	0.800	1	0.800
–IV	1.941	0.510	0	0	1969–I	2.104	0.783	1	0.783
1963–I	2.178	0.510	0	0	–II	2.056	0.800	1	0.800
–II	2.067	0.544	0	0	–III	2.170	0.794	1	0.794
–III	1.942	0.568	0	0	–IV	2.161	0.790	1	0.790
–IV	1.764	0.677	0	0	1970–I	2.225	0.757	1	0.757
1964–I	1.532	0.794	0	0	–II	2.241	0.746	1	0.746
–II	1.455	0.838	0	0	–III	2.366	0.739	1	0.739
–III	1.409	0.885	0	0	–IV	2.324	0.707	1	0.707
–IV	1.296	0.978	0	0	1971–I	2.516*	0.583*	1	0.583*
					–II	2.909*	0.524*	1	0.524*

*Preliminary estimates.

9.3. Consider the following regression results.* (The actual data are in Table 9.8.)

$$\widehat{\text{UN}}_t = 2.7491 + 1.1507D_t - 1.5294V_t - 0.8511(D_tV_t)$$
$$t = (26.896) \quad (3.6288) \quad (-12.5552) \quad (-1.9819)$$
$$R^2 = 0.9128$$

where UN = unemployment rate, %
V = job vacancy rate, %
D = 1, for period beginning in 1966–IV
= 0, for period before 1966–IV
t = time, measured in quarters

Note: In the fourth quarter of 1966, the (then) Labor government liberalized the National Insurance Act by replacing the flat-rate system of short-term unemployment benefits by a mixed system of flat-rate and (previous) earnings-related benefits, which increased the level of unemployment benefits.

*Damodar Gujarati, "The Behaviour of Unemployment and Unfilled Vacancies: Great Britain, 1958–1971," *The Economic Journal,* vol. 82, March 1972, pp. 195–202.

a. What are your prior expectations about the relationship between the unemployment and vacancy rates?

b. Holding the job vacancy rate constant, what is the average unemployment rate in the period beginning in the fourth quarter of 1966? Is it statistically different from the period before 1966 fourth quarter? How do you know?

c. Are the slopes in the pre- and post-1966 fourth quarter statistically different? How do you know?

d. Is it safe to conclude from this study that generous unemployment benefits lead to higher unemployment rates? Does this make economic sense?

9.4. From annual data for 1972–1979, William Nordhaus estimated the following model to explain the OPEC's oil price behavior (standard errors in parentheses).*

$$\hat{y}_t = \underset{(0.03)}{0.3x_{1t}} + \underset{(0.50)}{5.22x_{2t}}$$

$$\text{se} = (0.03) \quad (0.50)$$

where y = difference between current and previous year's price (dollars per barrel)
x_1 = difference between current year's spot price and OPEC's price in the previous year
x_2 = 1 for 1974 and 0 otherwise

Interpret this result and show the results graphically. What do these results suggest about OPEC's monopoly power?

9.5. Consider the following model

$$Y_i = \alpha_1 + \alpha_2 D_i + \beta X_i + u_i$$

where Y = annual salary of a college professor
X = years of teaching experience
D = dummy for gender

Consider three ways of defining the dummy variable.

a. $D = 1$ for male, 0 for female.

b. $D = 1$ for female, 2 for male.

c. $D = 1$ for female, -1 for male.

Interpret the preceding regression model for each dummy assignment. Is one method preferable to another? Justify your answer.

9.6. Refer to regression (9.7.3). How would you test the hypothesis that the coefficients of D_2 and D_3 are the same? And that the coefficients of D_2 and D_4 are the same? If the coefficient of D_3 is statistically different from that of D_2 and the coefficient of D_4 is different from that of D_2, does that mean that the coefficients D_3 and D_4 are also different?

Hint: $\text{var}(A \pm B) = \text{var}(A) + \text{var}(B) \pm 2\,\text{cov}(A, B)$

9.7. Refer to the U.S. savings–income example discussed in Section 9.5.

a. How would you obtain the standard errors of the regression coefficients given in Eqs. (9.5.5) and (9.5.6), which were obtained from the pooled regression (9.5.4)?

b. To obtain numerical answers, what additional information, if any, is required?

*"Oil and Economic Performance in Industrial Countries," *Brookings Papers on Economic Activity,* 1980, pp. 341–388.

9.8. In his study on the labor hours spent by the FDIC (Federal Deposit Insurance Corporation) on 91 bank examinations, R. J. Miller estimated the following function:[*]

$$\widehat{\ln Y} = \underset{}{2.41} + \underset{(0.0477)}{0.3674 \ln X_1} + \underset{(0.0628)}{0.2217 \ln X_2} + \underset{(0.0287)}{0.0803 \ln X_3}$$

$$-\underset{(0.2905)}{0.1755 D_1} + \underset{(0.1044)}{0.2799 D_2} + \underset{(0.1657)}{0.5634 D_3} - \underset{(0.0787)}{0.2572 D_4}$$

$$R^2 = 0.766$$

where Y = FDIC examiner labor hours
X_1 = total assets of bank
X_2 = total number of offices in bank
X_3 = ratio of classified loans to total loans for bank
D_1 = 1 if management rating was "good"
D_2 = 1 if management rating was "fair"
D_3 = 1 if management rating was "satisfactory"
D_4 = 1 if examination was conducted jointly with the state

The figures in parentheses are the estimated standard errors.

a. Interpret these results.

b. Is there any problem in interpreting the dummy variables in this model since Y is in the log form?

c. How would you interpret the dummy coefficients?

9.9. To assess the effect of the Fed's policy of deregulating interest rates beginning in July 1979, Sidney Langer, a student of mine, estimated the following model for the quarterly period of 1975–III to 1983–II.[†]

$$\begin{aligned} \hat{Y}_t &= \underset{(1.9563)}{8.5871} - \underset{(0.0992)}{0.1328 P_t} - \underset{(0.1909)}{0.7102 \text{Un}_t} - \underset{(0.0727)}{0.2389 M_t} \\ &\quad + \underset{(0.1036)}{0.6592 Y_{t-1}} + \underset{(0.7549)}{2.5831 \text{Dum}_t} \qquad R^2 = 0.9156 \end{aligned}$$

(se = standard errors in parentheses)

where Y = 3-month Treasury bill rate
P = expected rate of inflation
Un = seasonally adjusted unemployment rate
M = changes in the monetary base
Dum = dummy, taking value of 1 for observations beginning July 1, 1979

a. Interpret these results.

b. What has been the effect of interest rate deregulation? Do the results make economic sense?

c. The coefficients of P_t, Un_t, and M_t are negative. Can you offer an economic rationale?

9.10. Refer to the piecewise regression discussed in the text. Suppose there not only is a change in the slope coefficient at X^* but also the regression line jumps, as shown in Figure 9.7. How would you modify Eq. (9.8.1) to take into account the jump in the regression line at X^*?

[*]"Examination of Man-Hour Cost for Independent, Joint, and Divided Examination Programs," *Journal of Bank Research,* vol. 11, 1980, pp. 28–35. *Note:* The notations have been altered to conform with our notations.

[†]Sidney Langer, "Interest Rate Deregulation and Short-Term Interest Rates," unpublished term paper.

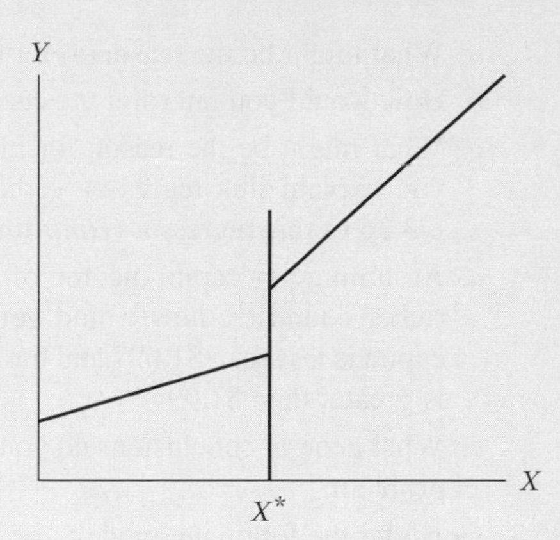

FIGURE 9.7 Discontinuous piecewise linear regression.

9.11. *Determinants of price per ounce of cola.* Cathy Schaefer, a student of mine, estimated the following regression from cross-sectional data of 77 observations:*

$$P_i = \beta_0 + \beta_1 D_{1i} + \beta_2 D_{2i} + \beta_3 D_{3i} + \mu_i$$

where P_i = price per ounce of cola
D_{1i} = 001 if discount store
= 010 if chain store
= 100 if convenience store
D_{2i} = 10 if branded good
= 01 if unbranded good
D_{3l} = 0001 if 67.6 ounce (2 liter) bottle
= 0010 if 28–33.8 ounce bottles (*Note:* 33.8 oz = 1 liter)
= 0100 if 16-ounce bottle
= 1000 if 12-ounce can

The results were as follows:

$$\begin{aligned} \hat{P}_i &= 0.0143 - 0.000004D_{1i} + 0.0090D_{2i} + 0.00001D_{3i} \\ \text{se} &= \qquad\qquad (0.00001) \qquad (0.00011) \qquad (0.00000) \\ t &= \qquad\qquad (-0.3837) \qquad (8.3927) \qquad (5.8125) \\ & \qquad\qquad\qquad\qquad\qquad\qquad\qquad R^2 = 0.6033 \end{aligned}$$

Note: The standard errors are shown only to five decimal places.

a. Comment on the way the dummies have been introduced in the model.

b. Assuming the dummy setup is acceptable, how would you interpret the results?

c. The coefficient of D_3 is positive and statistically significant. How do you rationalize this result?

9.12. From data for 101 countries on per capita income in dollars (X) and life expectancy in years (Y) in the early 1970s, Sen and Srivastava obtained the following regression results:†

$$\begin{aligned} \hat{Y}_i &= -2.40 + 9.39 \ln X_i - 3.36 [D_i(\ln X_i - 7)] \\ \text{se} &= (4.73) \quad (0.859) \qquad (2.42) \qquad\qquad R^2 = 0.752 \end{aligned}$$

where $D_i = 1$ if $\ln X_i > 7$, and $D_i = 0$ otherwise. *Note:* When $\ln X_i = 7$, $X =$ \$1,097 (approximately).

*Cathy Schaefer, "Price Per Ounce of Cola Beverage as a Function of Place of Purchase, Size of Container, and Branded or Unbranded Product," unpublished term project.

†Ashish Sen and Muni Srivastava, *Regression Analysis: Theory, Methods, and Applications*, Springer-Verlag, New York, 1990, p. 92. Notation changed.

a. What might be the reason(s) for introducing the income variable in the log form?

b. How would you interpret the coefficient 9.39 of $\ln X_i$?

c. What might be the reason for introducing the regressor $D_i(\ln X_i - 7)$? How do you explain this regressor verbally? And how do you interpret the coefficient -3.36 of this regressor (*Hint:* linear piecewise regression)?

d. Assuming per capita income of \$1,097 as the dividing line between poorer and richer countries, how would you derive the regression for countries whose per capita is less than \$1,097 and the regression for countries whose per capita income is greater than \$1,097?

e. What general conclusions do you draw from the regression result presented in this problem?

9.13. Consider the following model:

$$Y_i = \beta_1 + \beta_2 D_i + u_i$$

where $D_i = 0$ for the first 20 observations and $D_i = 1$ for the remaining 30 observations. You are also told that $\text{var}(u_i^2) = 300$.

a. How would you interpret β_1 and β_2?

b. What are the mean values of the two groups?

c. How would you compute the variance of $(\hat{\beta}_1 + \hat{\beta}_2)$? *Note:* You are given that the $\text{cov}(\hat{\beta}_1, \hat{\beta}_2) = -15$.

9.14. To assess the effect of state right-to-work laws (which do not require membership in the union as a precondition of employment) on union membership, the following regression results were obtained, from the data for 50 states in the United States for 1982:*

$$\widehat{\text{PVT}}_i = 19.8066 - 9.3917\,\text{RTW}_i$$
$$t = (17.0352) \quad (-5.1086)$$
$$r^2 = 0.3522$$

where PVT = percentage of private sector employees in unions, 1982, and RTW = 1 if right-to-work law exists, 0 otherwise. *Note:* In 1982, twenty states had right-to-work laws.

a. A priori, what is the expected relationship between PVT and RTW?

b. Do the regression results support the prior expectations?

c. Interpret the regression results.

d. What was the average percent of private sector employees in unions in the states that did not have the right-to-work laws?

9.15. In the following regression model:

$$Y_i = \beta_1 + \beta_2 D_i + u_i$$

Y represents hourly wage in dollars and *D* is the dummy variable, taking a value of 1 for a college graduate and a value of 0 for a high-school graduate. Using the OLS formulas given in Chapter 3, show that $\hat{\beta}_1 = \bar{Y}_{\text{hg}}$ and $\hat{\beta}_2 = \bar{Y}_{\text{cg}} - \bar{Y}_{\text{hg}}$, where the subscripts have the following meanings: hg = high-school graduate, cg = college graduate. In all, there are n_1 high-school graduates and n_2 college graduates, for a total sample of $n = n_1 + n_2$.

*The data used in the regression results were obtained from N. M. Meltz, "Interstate and Interprovincial Differences in Union Density," *Industrial Relations,* vol. 28, no. 2, 1989, pp. 142–158.

9.16. To study the rate of growth of population in Belize over the period 1970–1992, Mukherjee et al. estimated the following models:*

Model I: $\widehat{\ln(\text{Pop})_t} = 4.73 + 0.024t$
$t = (781.25) \quad (54.71)$

Model II: $\widehat{\ln(\text{Pop})_t} = 4.77 + 0.015t - 0.075D_t + 0.011(D_t t)$
$t = (2477.92) \quad (34.01) \quad (-17.03) \quad (25.54)$

where Pop = population in millions, t = trend variable, $D_t = 1$ for observations beginning in 1978 and 0 before 1978, and ln stands for natural logarithm.

a. In Model I, what is the rate of growth of Belize's population over the sample period?

b. Are the population growth rates statistically different pre- and post-1978? How do you know? If they are different, what are the growth rates for 1972–1977 and 1978–1992?

Empirical Exercises

9.17. Using the data given in Table 9.8, test the hypothesis that the error variances in the two subperiods 1958–IV to 1966–III and 1966–IV to 1971–II are the same.

9.18. Using the methodology discussed in Chapter 8, compare the unrestricted and restricted regressions (9.7.3) and (9.7.4); that is, test for the validity of the imposed restrictions.

9.19. In the U.S. savings–income regression (9.5.4) discussed in the chapter, suppose that instead of using 1 and 0 values for the dummy variable you use $Z_i = a + bD_i$, where $D_i = 1$ and 0, $a = 2$, and $b = 3$. Compare your results.

9.20. Continuing with the savings–income regression (9.5.4), suppose you were to assign $D_i = 0$ to observations in the second period and $D_i = 1$ to observations in the first period. How would the results shown in Eq. (9.5.4) change?

9.21. Use the data given in Table 9.2 and consider the following model:

$$\ln \text{Savings}_i = \beta_1 + \beta_2 \ln \text{Income}_i + \beta_3 \ln D_i + u_i$$

where ln stands for natural log and where $D_i = 1$ for 1970–1981 and 10 for 1982–1995.

a. What is the rationale behind assigning dummy values as suggested?

b. Estimate the preceding model and interpret your results.

c. What are the intercept values of the savings function in the two subperiods and how do you interpret them?

9.22. Refer to the quarterly appliance sales data given in Table 9.3. Consider the following model:

$$\text{Sales}_i = \alpha_1 + \alpha_2 D_{2i} + \alpha_3 D_{3i} + \alpha_4 D_{4i} + u_i$$

where the D's are dummies taking 1 and 0 values for quarters II through IV.

a. Estimate the preceding model for dishwashers, disposers, and washing machines individually.

b. How would you interpret the estimated slope coefficients?

c. How would you use the estimated α's to deseasonalize the sales data for individual appliances?

*Chandan Mukherjee, Howard White, and Marc Wuyts, *Econometrics and Data Analysis for Developing Countries,* Routledge, London, 1998, pp. 372–375. Notations adapted.

TABLE 9.9
U.S. Presidential Elections, 1916–2004

Obs.	Year	*V*	*W*	*D*	*G*	*I*	*N*	*P*
1	1916	0.5168	0	1	2.229	1	3	4.252
2	1920	0.3612	1	0	−11.46	1	5	16.535
3	1924	0.4176	0	−1	−3.872	−1	10	5.161
4	1928	0.4118	0	0	4.623	−1	7	0.183
5	1932	0.5916	0	−1	−14.9	−1	4	7.069
6	1936	0.6246	0	1	11.921	1	9	2.362
7	1940	0.55	0	1	3.708	1	8	0.028
8	1944	0.5377	1	1	4.119	1	14	5.678
9	1948	0.5237	1	1	1.849	1	5	8.722
10	1952	0.446	0	0	0.627	1	6	2.288
11	1956	0.4224	0	−1	−1.527	−1	5	1.936
12	1960	0.5009	0	0	0.114	−1	5	1.932
13	1964	0.6134	0	1	5.054	1	10	1.247
14	1968	0.496	0	0	4.836	1	7	3.215
15	1972	0.3821	0	−1	6.278	−1	4	4.766
16	1976	0.5105	0	0	3.663	−1	4	7.657
17	1980	0.447	0	1	−3.789	1	5	8.093
18	1984	0.4083	0	−1	5.387	−1	7	5.403
19	1988	0.461	0	0	2.068	−1	6	3.272
20	1992	0.5345	0	−1	2.293	−1	1	3.692
21	1996	0.5474	0	1	2.918	1	3	2.268
22	2000	0.50265	0	0	1.219	1	8	1.605
23	2004	0.51233	0	1	2.69	−1	1	2.325

Notes:
Year Election year
V Incumbent share of the two-party presidential vote.
W Indicator variable (1 for the elections of 1920, 1944, and 1948, and 0 otherwise).
D Indicator variable (1 if a Democratic incumbent is running for election, −1 if a Republican incumbent is running for election, and 0 otherwise).
G Growth rate of real per capita GDP in the first three quarters of the election year.
I Indicator variable (1 if there is a Democratic incumbent at the time of the election and −1 if there is a Republican incumbent).
N Number of quarters in the first 15 quarters of the administration in which the growth rate of real per capita GDP is greater than 3.2%.
P Absolute value of the growth rate of the GDP deflator in the first 15 quarters of the administration.

9.23. Reestimate the model in Exercise 9.22 by adding the regressor, expenditure on durable goods.

a. Is there a difference in the regression results you obtained in Exercise 9.22 and in this exercise? If so, what explains the difference?

b. If there is seasonality in the durable goods expenditure data, how would you account for it?

9.24. Table 9.9 gives data on quadrennial presidential elections in the United States from 1916 to 2004.[*]

a. Using the data given in Table 9.9, develop a suitable model to predict the Democratic share of the two-party presidential vote.

b. How would you use this model to predict the outcome of a presidential election?

[*]These data were originally compiled by Ray Fair of Yale University, who has been predicting the outcome of presidential elections for several years. The data are reproduced from Samprit Chatterjee, Ali S. Hadi, and Bertram Price, *Regression Analysis by Example,* 3d ed., John Wiley & Sons, New York, 2000, pp. 150–151 and updated from http://fairmodel.econ.yale.edu/rayfair/pdf/2006CHTM.HTM.

c. Chatterjee et al. suggested considering the following model as a trial model to predict presidential elections:

$$V = \beta_0 + \beta_1 I + \beta_2 D + \beta_3 W + \beta_4 (GI) + \beta_5 P + \beta_6 N + u$$

Estimate this model and comment on the results in relation to the results of the model you have chosen.

9.25. Refer to regression (9.6.4). Test the hypothesis that the rate of increase of average hourly earnings with respect to education differs by gender and race. (*Hint:* Use multiplicative dummies.)

9.26. Refer to the regression (9.3.1). How would you modify the model to find out if there is any interaction between the gender and the region of residence dummies? Present the results based on this model and compare them with those given in Eq. (9.3.1).

9.27. In the model $Y_i = \beta_1 + \beta_2 D_i + u_i$, let $D_i = 0$ for the first 40 observations and $D_i = 1$ for the remaining 60 observations. You are told that u_i has zero mean and a variance of 100. What are the mean values and variances of the two sets of observations?*

9.28. Refer to the U.S. savings–income regression discussed in the chapter. As an alternative to Eq. (9.5.1), consider the following model:

$$\ln Y_t = \beta_1 + \beta_2 D_t + \beta_3 X_t + \beta_4 (D_t X_t) + u_t$$

where Y is savings and X is income.

a. Estimate the preceding model and compare the results with those given in Eq. (9.5.4). Which is a better model?

b. How would you interpret the dummy coefficient in this model?

c. As we will see in the chapter on heteroscedasticity, very often a log transformation of the dependent variable reduces heteroscedasticity in the data. See if this is the case in the present example by running the regression of log of Y on X for the two periods and see if the estimated error variances in the two periods are statistically the same. If they are, the Chow test can be used to pool the data in the manner indicated in the chapter.

9.29. Refer to the Indian wage earners example (Section 9.12) and the data in Table 9.7.† As a reminder, the variables are defined as follows:

WI = weekly wage income in rupees
Age = age in years
D_{sex} = 1 for male workers and 0 for female workers
DE_2 = a dummy variable taking a value of 1 for workers with up to a primary education
DE_3 = a dummy variable taking a value of 1 for workers with up to a secondary education
DE_4 = a dummy variable taking a value of 1 for workers with higher education
DPT = a dummy variable taking a value of 1 for workers with permanent jobs and a value of 0 for temporary workers

The reference category is male workers with no primary education and temporary jobs.

*This example is adapted from Peter Kennedy, *A Guide to Econometrics,* 4th ed., MIT Press, Cambridge, Mass., 1998, p. 347.

†The data come from *Econometrics and Data Analysis for Developing Countries,* by Chandan Mukherjee, Howard White, and Marc Wuyts, Routledge Press, London, 1998, in the Appendix.

In Section 9.12, interaction terms were created between the education variables (DE_2, DE_3, and DE_4) and the gender variable (D_{sex}). What happens if we create interaction terms between the education dummies and the permanent worker dummy variable (DPT)?

a. Estimate the model predicting ln WI containing age, gender, the education dummy variables, and three new interaction terms: $DE_2 \times DPT$, $DE_3 \times DPT$, and $DE_4 \times DPT$. Does there appear to be a significant interaction effect among the new terms?

b. Is there a significant difference between workers with an education level up to primary and those without a primary education? Assess this with respect to both the education dummy variable and the interaction term and explain the results. What about the difference between workers with a secondary level of education and those without a primary level of education? What about the difference between those with an education level beyond secondary, compared to those without a primary level of education?

c. Now assess the results of deleting the education dummies from the model. Do the interaction terms change in significance?

Appendix 9A

Semilogarithmic Regression with Dummy Regressor

In Section 9.10 we noted that in models of the type

$$\ln Y_i = \beta_1 + \beta_2 D_i \tag{1}$$

the relative change in Y (i.e., semielasticity), with respect to the dummy regressor taking values of 1 or 0, can be obtained as (antilog of estimated β_2) − 1 times 100, that is, as

$$(e^{\hat{\beta}_2} - 1) \times 100 \tag{2}$$

The proof is as follows: Since ln and exp (= e) are inverse functions, we can write Eq. (1) as:

$$\ln Y_i = \beta_1 + \ln(e^{\beta_2 D_i}) \tag{3}$$

Now when $D = 0$, $e^{\beta_2 D_i} = 1$ and when $D = 1$, $e^{\beta_2 D_i} = e^{\beta_2}$. Therefore, in going from state 0 to state 1, $\ln Y_i$ changes by $(e^{\beta_2} - 1)$. But a change in the log of a variable is a relative change, which after multiplication by 100 becomes a percentage change. Hence the percentage change is $(e^{\beta_2} - 1) \times 100$, as claimed. (*Note:* $\ln_e e = 1$, that is, the log of e to base e is 1, just as the log of 10 to base 10 is 1. Recall that log to base e is called the *natural* log and that log to base 10 is called the *common* log.)

Relaxing the Assumptions of the Classical Model

Part 2

In Part 1 we considered at length the classical normal linear regression model and showed how it can be used to handle the twin problems of statistical inference, namely, estimation and hypothesis testing, as well as the problem of prediction. But recall that this model is based on several simplifying assumptions, which are as follows.

Assumption 1. The regression model is linear in the parameters.

Assumption 2. The values of the regressors, the X's, are fixed, or X values are independent of the error term. Here, this means we require zero covariance between u_i and each X variable.

Assumption 3. For given X's, the mean value of disturbance u_i is zero.

Assumption 4. For given X's, the variance of u_i is constant or homoscedastic.

Assumption 5. For given X's, there is no autocorrelation, or serial correlation, between the disturbances.

Assumption 6. The number of observations n must be greater than the number of parameters to be estimated.

Assumption 7. There must be sufficient variation in the values of the X variables.

We are also including the following 3 assumptions in this part of the text:

Assumption 8. There is no exact collinearity between the X variables.

Assumption 9. The model is correctly specified, so there is no specification bias.

Assumption 10. The stochastic (disturbance) term u_i is normally distributed.

Before proceeding further, let us note that most textbooks list fewer than 10 assumptions. For example, assumptions 6 and 7 are taken for granted rather than spelled out explicitly. We decided to state them explicitly because distinguishing between the assumptions required for ordinary least squares (OLS) to have desirable statistical properties (such as BLUE) and the conditions required for OLS to be useful seems sensible. For example, OLS estimators are BLUE (best linear unbiased estimators) even if assumption 7 is not satisfied. But in that case the standard errors of the OLS estimators will be large relative to their coefficients (i.e., the t ratios will be small), thereby making it difficult to assess the contribution of one or more regressors to the explained sum of squares.

As Wetherill notes, in practice two major types of problems arise in applying the classical linear regression model: (1) those due to assumptions about the specification of the model and about the disturbances u_i and (2) those due to assumptions about the data.[1] In the first category are Assumptions 1, 2, 3, 4, 5, 9, and 10. Those in the second category include Assumptions 6, 7, and 8. In addition, data problems, such as outliers (unusual or untypical observations) and errors of measurement in the data, also fall into the second category.

With respect to problems arising from the assumptions about disturbances and model specifications, three major questions arise: (1) How severe must the departure be from a particular assumption before it really matters? For example, if u_i are not exactly normally distributed, what level of departure from this assumption can one accept before the BLUE property of the OLS estimators is destroyed? (2) How do we find out whether a particular assumption is in fact violated in a concrete case? Thus, how does one find out if the disturbances are normally distributed in a given application? We have already discussed the **Anderson–Darling A^2 statistic** and **Jarque–Bera** tests of normality. (3) What remedial measures can we take if one or more of the assumptions are false? For example, if the assumption of homoscedasticity is found to be false in an application, what do we do then?

With regard to problems attributable to assumptions about the data, we also face similar questions. (1) How serious is a particular problem? For example, is multicollinearity so severe that it makes estimation and inference very difficult? (2) How do we find out the severity of the data problem? For example, how do we decide whether the inclusion or exclusion of an observation or observations that may represent outliers will make a tremendous difference in the analysis? (3) Can some of the data problems be easily remedied? For example, can one have access to the original data to find out the sources of errors of measurement in the data?

Unfortunately, satisfactory answers cannot be given to all these questions. In the rest of Part 2 we will look at some of the assumptions more critically, but not all will receive full scrutiny. In particular, we will not discuss in depth the following: Assumptions 2, 3, and 10. The reasons are as follows:

Assumption 2: Fixed versus Stochastic Regressors

Remember that our regression analysis is based on the assumption that the regressors are nonstochastic and assume fixed values in repeated sampling. There is a good reason for this strategy. Unlike scientists in the physical sciences, as noted in Chapter 1, economists generally have no control over the data they use. More often than not, economists depend on secondary data, that is, data collected by someone else, such as the government and private organizations. Therefore, the practical strategy to follow is to assume that for the problem at hand the values of the explanatory variables are given even though the variables themselves may be intrinsically stochastic or random. Hence, the results of the regression analysis are conditional upon these given values.

But suppose that we cannot regard the X's as truly nonstochastic or fixed. This is the case of **random** or **stochastic regressors.** Now the situation is rather involved. The u_i, by

[1] G. Barrie Wetherill, *Regression Analysis with Applications*, Chapman and Hall, New York, 1986, pp. 14–15.

assumption, are stochastic. If the X's too are stochastic, then we must specify how the X's and u_i are distributed. If we are willing to make Assumption 2 (i.e., the X's, although random, are distributed independently of, or at least uncorrelated with, u_i), then for all practical purposes we can continue to operate as if the X's were nonstochastic. As Kmenta notes:

> Thus, *relaxing the assumption that X is nonstochastic and replacing it by the assumption that X is stochastic but independent of* [*u*] *does not change the desirable properties and feasibility of least squares estimation.*[2]

Therefore, we will retain Assumption 2 until we come to deal with simultaneous equations models in Part 4.[3] Also, a brief discussion of nonstochastic regressors will be given in Chapter 13.

Assumption 3: Zero Mean Value of u_i

Recall the k-variable linear regression model:

$$Y_i = \beta_1 + \beta_2 X_{2i} + \beta_3 X_{3i} + \cdots + \beta_k X_{ki} + u_i \tag{1}$$

Let us now assume that

$$E(u_i | X_{2i}, X_{3i}, \ldots, X_{ki}) = w \tag{2}$$

where w is a constant; note in the standard model $w = 0$, but now we let it be any constant.

Taking the conditional expectation of Eq.(1), we obtain

$$\begin{aligned} E(Y_i | X_{2i}, X_{3i}, \ldots, X_{ki}) &= \beta_1 + \beta_2 X_{2i} + \beta_3 X_{3i} + \cdots + \beta_k X_{ki} + w \\ &= (\beta_1 + w) + \beta_2 X_{2i} + \beta_3 X_{3i} + \cdots + \beta_k X_{ki} \\ &= \alpha + \beta_2 X_{2i} + \beta_3 X_{3i} + \cdots + \beta_k X_{ki} \end{aligned} \tag{3}$$

where $\alpha = (\beta_1 + w)$ and where in taking the expectations one should note that the X's are treated as constants. (Why?)

Therefore, if Assumption 3 is not fulfilled, we see that we cannot estimate the original intercept β_1; what we obtain is α, which contains β_1 and $E(u_i) = w$. In short, we obtain a *biased* estimate of β_1.

But as we have noted on many occasions, in many practical situations the intercept term, β_1, is of little importance; the more meaningful quantities are the slope coefficients, which remain unaffected even if Assumption 3 is violated.[4] Besides, in many applications the intercept term has no physical interpretation.

[2]Jan Kmenta, *Elements of Econometrics,* 2d ed., Macmillan, New York, 1986, p. 338. (Emphasis in the original.)

[3]A technical point may be noted here. Instead of the strong assumption that the X's and u are independent, we may use the weaker assumption that the values of X variables and u are uncorrelated contemporaneously (i.e., at the same point in time). In this case OLS estimators may be biased but they are **consistent,** that is, as the sample size increases indefinitely, the estimators converge on their true values. If, however, the X's and u are contemporaneously correlated, the OLS estimators are biased as well as inconsistent. In Chapter 17 we will show how the method of **instrumental variables** can sometimes be used to obtain consistent estimators in this situation.

[4]It is very important to note that this statement is true only if $E(u_i) = w$ for each i. However, if $E(u_i) = w_i$, that is, a different constant for each i, the partial slope coefficients may be biased as well as inconsistent. In this case violation of Assumption 3 will be critical. For proof and further details, see Peter Schmidt, *Econometrics,* Marcel Dekker, New York, 1976, pp. 36–39.

Assumption 10: Normality of u

This assumption is not essential if our objective is estimation only. As noted in Chapter 3, the OLS estimators are BLUE regardless of whether the u_i are normally distributed or not. With the normality assumption, however, we were able to establish that the OLS estimators of the regression coefficients follow the normal distribution, that $(n - k)\hat{\sigma}^2/\sigma^2$ has the χ^2 distribution, and that one could use the t and F tests to test various statistical hypotheses regardless of the sample size.

But what happens if the u_i are not normally distributed? We then rely on the following extension of the central limit theorem; recall that it was the central limit theorem we invoked to justify the normality assumption in the first place:

> If the disturbances [u_i] are independently and identically distributed with zero mean and [constant] variance σ^2 and if the explanatory variables are constant in repeated samples, the [O]LS coefficient estimators are asymptotically normally distributed with means equal to the corresponding β's.[5]

Therefore, the usual test procedures—the t and F tests—are still valid *asymptotically,* that is, in the large sample, but not in the finite or small samples.

The fact that if the disturbances are not normally distributed the OLS estimators are still normally distributed asymptotically (under the assumption of homoscedastic variance and fixed X's) is of little comfort to practicing economists, who often do not have the luxury of large-sample data. Therefore, the normality assumption becomes extremely important for the purposes of hypothesis testing and prediction. Hence, with the twin problems of estimation and hypothesis testing in mind, and given the fact that small samples are the rule rather than the exception in most economic analyses, we shall continue to use the normality assumption.[6] (But see Chapter 13, Section 13.12.)

Of course, this means that when we deal with a finite sample, we must explicitly test for the normality assumption. We have already considered the **Anderson–Darling** and the **Jarque–Bera tests** of normality. The reader is strongly urged to apply these or other tests of normality to regression residuals. Keep in mind that in finite samples without the normality assumption the usual t and F statistics may not follow the t and F distributions.

We are left with Assumptions 1, 4, 5, 6, 7, 8, and 9. Assumptions 6, 7, and 8 are closely related and are discussed in the chapter on multicollinearity (Chapter 10). Assumption 4 is discussed in the chapter on heteroscedasticity (Chapter 11). Assumption 5 is discussed in the chapter on autocorrelation (Chapter 12). Assumption 9 is discussed in the chapter on model specification and diagnostic testing (Chapter 13). Because of its specialized nature and mathematical demands, Assumption 1 is discussed as a special topic in Part 3 (Chapter 14).

For pedagogical reasons, in each of these chapters we follow a common format, namely, (1) identify the nature of the problem, (2) examine its consequences, (3) suggest methods of detecting it, and (4) consider remedial measures so that they may lead to estimators that possess the desirable statistical properties discussed in Part 1.

[5]Henri Theil, *Introduction to Econometrics,* Prentice-Hall, Englewood Cliffs, NJ, 1978, p. 240. It must be noted the assumptions of fixed X's and constant σ^2 are crucial for this result.

[6]In passing, note that the effects of departure from normality and related topics are often discussed under the topic of **robust estimation** in the literature, a topic beyond the scope of this book.

A cautionary note is in order: As noted earlier, satisfactory answers to all the problems arising out of the violation of the assumptions of the classical linear regression model (CLRM) do not exist. Moreover, there may be more than one solution to a particular problem, and often it is not clear which method is best. Besides, in a particular application more than one violation of the CLRM may be involved. Thus, specification bias, multicollinearity, and heteroscedasticity may coexist in an application, and there is no single omnipotent test that will solve all the problems simultaneously.[7] Furthermore, a particular test that was popular at one time may not be in vogue later because somebody found a flaw in the earlier test. But this is how science progresses. Econometrics is no exception.

[7]This is not for lack of trying. See A. K. Bera and C. M. Jarque, "Efficient Tests for Normality, Homoscedasticity and Serial Independence of Regression Residuals: Monte Carlo Evidence," *Economic Letters,* vol. 7, 1981, pp. 313–318.

Chapter 10

Multicollinearity: What Happens If the Regressors Are Correlated?

There is no pair of words that is more misused both in econometrics texts and in the applied literature than the pair "multi-collinearity problem." That many of our explanatory variables are highly collinear is a fact of life. And it is completely clear that there are experimental designs **X′X** [i.e., data matrix] which would be much preferred to the designs the natural experiment has provided us [i.e., the sample at hand]. But a complaint about the apparent malevolence of nature is not at all constructive, and the *ad hoc* cures for a bad design, such as stepwise regression or ridge regression, can be disastrously inappropriate. Better that we should rightly accept the fact that our non-experiments [i.e., data not collected by designed experiments] are sometimes not very informative about parameters of interest.[1]

Assumption 8 of the *classical linear regression model* (CLRM) is that there is no **multicollinearity** among the regressors included in the regression model. In this chapter we take a critical look at this assumption by seeking answers to the following questions:

1. What is the nature of multicollinearity?
2. Is multicollinearity really a problem?
3. What are its practical consequences?
4. How does one detect it?
5. What remedial measures can be taken to alleviate the problem of multicollinearity?

In this chapter we also discuss Assumption 6 of the CLRM, namely, that the number of observations in the sample must be greater than the number of regressors, and Assumption 7, which requires that there be sufficient variability in the values of the regressors, for they are

[1]Edward E. Leamer, "Model Choice and Specification Analysis," in Zvi Griliches and Michael D. Intriligator, eds., *Handbook of Econometrics*, vol. I, North Holland Publishing Company, Amsterdam, 1983, pp. 300–301.

intimately related to the assumption of no multicollinearity. Arthur Goldberger has christened Assumption 6 as the problem of **micronumerosity,**[2] which simply means small sample size.

10.1 The Nature of Multicollinearity

The term *multicollinearity* is due to Ragnar Frisch.[3] Originally it meant the existence of a "perfect," or exact, linear relationship among some or all explanatory variables of a regression model.[4] For the k-variable regression involving explanatory variables $X_1, X_2, \ldots, X_k$ (where $X_1 = 1$ for all observations to allow for the intercept term), an exact linear relationship is said to exist if the following condition is satisfied:

$$\lambda_1 X_1 + \lambda_2 X_2 + \cdots + \lambda_k X_k = 0 \qquad (10.1.1)$$

where $\lambda_1, \lambda_2, \ldots, \lambda_k$ are constants such that not all of them are zero simultaneously.[5]

Today, however, the term multicollinearity is used in a broader sense to include the case of perfect multicollinearity, as shown by Eq. (10.1.1), as well as the case where the X variables are intercorrelated but not perfectly so, as follows:[6]

$$\lambda_1 X_1 + \lambda_2 X_2 + \cdots + \lambda_2 X_k + v_i = 0 \qquad (10.1.2)$$

where v_i is a stochastic error term.

To see the difference between *perfect* and *less than perfect* multicollinearity, assume, for example, that $\lambda_2 \neq 0$. Then, Eq. (10.1.1) can be written as

$$X_{2i} = -\frac{\lambda_1}{\lambda_2} X_{1i} - \frac{\lambda_3}{\lambda_2} X_{3i} - \cdots - \frac{\lambda_k}{\lambda_2} X_{ki} \qquad (10.1.3)$$

which shows how X_2 is exactly linearly related to other variables or how it can be derived from a linear combination of other X variables. In this situation, the coefficient of correlation between the variable X_2 and the linear combination on the right side of Eq. (10.1.3) is bound to be unity.

Similarly, if $\lambda_2 \neq 0$, Eq. (10.1.2) can be written as

$$X_{2i} = -\frac{\lambda_1}{\lambda_2} X_{1i} - \frac{\lambda_3}{\lambda_2} X_{3i} - \cdots - \frac{\lambda_k}{\lambda_2} X_{ki} - \frac{1}{\lambda_2} v_i \qquad (10.1.4)$$

which shows that X_2 is not an exact linear combination of other X's because it is also determined by the stochastic error term v_i.

[2]See his *A Course in Econometrics,* Harvard University Press, Cambridge, Mass., 1991, p. 249.

[3]Ragnar Frisch, *Statistical Confluence Analysis by Means of Complete Regression Systems,* Institute of Economics, Oslo University, publ. no. 5, 1934.

[4]Strictly speaking, *multicollinearity* refers to the existence of more than one exact linear relationship, and *collinearity* refers to the existence of a single linear relationship. But this distinction is rarely maintained in practice, and multicollinearity refers to both cases.

[5]The chances of one's obtaining a sample of values where the regressors are related in this fashion are indeed very small in practice except by design when, for example, the number of observations is smaller than the number of regressors or if one falls into the "dummy variable trap" as discussed in Chapter 9. See Exercise 10.2.

[6]If there are only two explanatory variables, *intercorrelation* can be measured by the zero-order or simple correlation coefficient. But if there are more than two X variables, intercorrelation can be measured by the partial correlation coefficients or by the multiple correlation coefficient R of one X variable with all other X variables taken together.

As a numerical example, consider the following hypothetical data:

X_2	X_3	X_3^*
10	50	52
15	75	75
18	90	97
24	120	129
30	150	152

It is apparent that $X_{3i} = 5X_{2i}$. Therefore, there is perfect collinearity between X_2 and X_3 since the coefficient of correlation r_{23} is unity. The variable X_3^* was created from X_3 by simply adding to it the following numbers, which were taken from a table of random numbers: 2, 0, 7, 9, 2. Now there is no longer perfect collinearity between X_2 and X_3^*. However, the two variables are highly correlated because calculations will show that the coefficient of correlation between them is 0.9959.

The preceding algebraic approach to multicollinearity can be portrayed succinctly by the Ballentine (recall Figure 3.8, reproduced in Figure 10.1). In this figure the circles Y, X_2, and X_3 represent, respectively, the variations in Y (the dependent variable) and X_2 and X_3 (the explanatory variables). The degree of collinearity can be measured by the extent of the overlap (shaded area) of the X_2 and X_3 circles. In Figure 10.1*a* there is no overlap between X_2 and X_3, and hence no collinearity. In Figure 10.1*b* through 10.1*e* there is a "low" to "high" degree of collinearity—the greater the overlap between X_2 and X_3 (i.e., the larger the

FIGURE 10.1
The Ballentine view of multicollinearity.

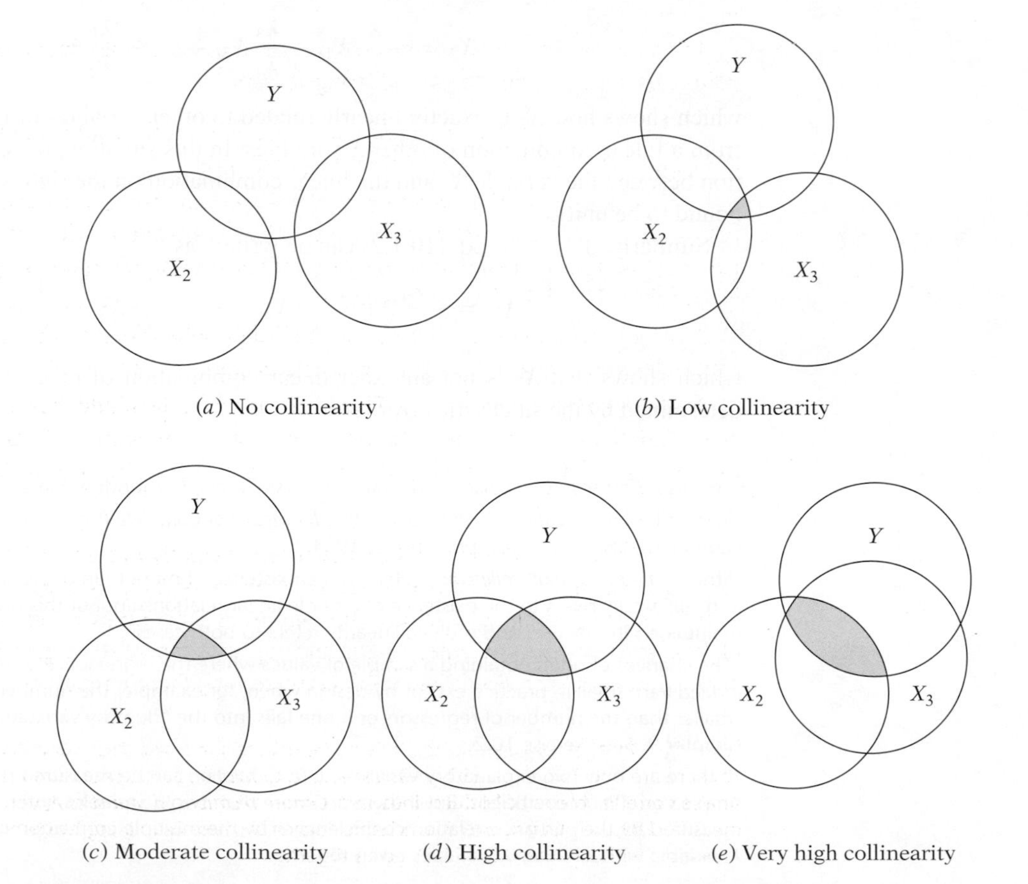

shaded area), the higher the degree of collinearity. In the extreme, if X_2 and X_3 were to overlap completely (or if X_2 were completely inside X_3, or vice versa), collinearity would be perfect.

In passing, note that multicollinearity, as we have defined it, refers only to linear relationships among the X variables. It does not rule out nonlinear relationships among them. For example, consider the following regression model:

$$Y_i = \beta_0 + \beta_1 X_i + \beta_2 X_i^2 + \beta_3 X_i^3 + u_i \tag{10.1.5}$$

where, say, $Y =$ total cost of production and $X =$ output. The variables X_i^2 (output squared) and X_i^3 (output cubed) are obviously functionally related to X_i, but the relationship is nonlinear. Strictly, therefore, models such as Eq. (10.1.5) do not violate the assumption of no multicollinearity. However, in concrete applications, the conventionally measured correlation coefficient will show X_i, X_i^2, and X_i^3 to be highly correlated, which, as we shall show, will make it difficult to estimate the parameters of Eq. (10.1.5) with greater precision (i.e., with smaller standard errors).

Why does the classical linear regression model assume that there is no multicollinearity among the X's? The reasoning is this: **If multicollinearity is perfect in the sense of Eq. (10.1.1), the regression coefficients of the X variables are indeterminate and their standard errors are infinite. If multicollinearity is less than perfect, as in Eq. (10.1.2), the regression coefficients, although determinate, possess large standard errors (in relation to the coefficients themselves), which means the coefficients cannot be estimated with great precision or accuracy.** The proofs of these statements are given in the following sections.

There are several sources of multicollinearity. As Montgomery and Peck note, multicollinearity may be due to the following factors:[7]

1. *The data collection method employed.* For example, sampling over a limited range of the values taken by the regressors in the population.
2. *Constraints on the model or in the population being sampled.* For example, in the regression of electricity consumption on income (X_2) and house size (X_3) there is a physical constraint in the population in that families with higher incomes generally have larger homes than families with lower incomes.
3. *Model specification.* For example, adding polynomial terms to a regression model, especially when the range of the X variable is small.
4. *An overdetermined model.* This happens when the model has more explanatory variables than the number of observations. This could happen in medical research where there may be a small number of patients about whom information is collected on a large number of variables.

An additional reason for multicollinearity, especially in time series data, may be that the regressors included in the model share a *common trend,* that is, they all increase or decrease over time. Thus, in the regression of consumption expenditure on income, wealth, and population, the regressors income, wealth, and population may all be growing over time at more or less the same rate, leading to collinearity among these variables.

[7]Douglas Montgomery and Elizabeth Peck, *Introduction to Linear Regression Analysis*, John Wiley & Sons, New York, 1982, pp. 289–290. See also R. L. Mason, R. F. Gunst, and J. T. Webster, "Regression Analysis and Problems of Multicollinearity," *Communications in Statistics A*, vol. 4, no. 3, 1975, pp. 277–292; R. F. Gunst, and R. L. Mason, "Advantages of Examining Multicollinearities in Regression Analysis," *Biometrics*, vol. 33, 1977, pp. 249–260.

10.2 Estimation in the Presence of Perfect Multicollinearity

It was stated previously that in the case of perfect multicollinearity the regression coefficients remain indeterminate and their standard errors are infinite. This fact can be demonstrated readily in terms of the three-variable regression model. Using the deviation form, where all the variables are expressed as deviations from their sample means, we can write the three-variable regression model as

$$y_i = \hat{\beta}_2 x_{2i} + \hat{\beta}_3 x_{3i} + \hat{u}_i \tag{10.2.1}$$

Now from Chapter 7 we obtain

$$\hat{\beta}_2 = \frac{\left(\sum y_i x_{2i}\right)\left(\sum x_{3i}^2\right) - \left(\sum y_i x_{3i}\right)\left(\sum x_{2i} x_{3i}\right)}{\left(\sum x_{2i}^2\right)\left(\sum x_{3i}^2\right) - \left(\sum x_{2i} x_{3i}\right)^2} \tag{7.4.7}$$

$$\hat{\beta}_3 = \frac{\left(\sum y_i x_{3i}\right)\left(\sum x_{2i}^2\right) - \left(\sum y_i x_{2i}\right)\left(\sum x_{2i} x_{3i}\right)}{\left(\sum x_{2i}^2\right)\left(\sum x_{3i}^2\right) - \left(\sum x_{2i} x_{3i}\right)^2} \tag{7.4.8}$$

Assume that $X_{3i} = \lambda X_{2i}$, where λ is a nonzero constant (e.g., 2, 4, 1.8, etc.). Substituting this into Eq. (7.4.7), we obtain

$$\begin{aligned} \hat{\beta}_2 &= \frac{\left(\sum y_i x_{2i}\right)\left(\lambda^2 \sum x_{2i}^2\right) - \left(\lambda \sum y_i x_{2i}\right)\left(\lambda \sum x_{2i}^2\right)}{\left(\sum x_{2i}^2\right)\left(\lambda^2 \sum x_{2i}^2\right) - \lambda^2 \left(\sum x_{2i}^2\right)^2} \\ &= \frac{0}{0} \end{aligned} \tag{10.2.2}$$

which is an indeterminate expression. The reader can verify that $\hat{\beta}_3$ is also indeterminate.[8]

Why do we obtain the result shown in Eq. (10.2.2)? Recall the meaning of $\hat{\beta}_2$: It gives the rate of change in the average value of Y as X_2 changes by a unit, holding X_3 constant. But if X_3 and X_2 are perfectly collinear, there is no way X_3 can be kept constant: As X_2 changes, so does X_3 by the factor λ. What it means, then, is that there is no way of disentangling the separate influences of X_2 and X_3 from the given sample: For practical purposes X_2 and X_3 are indistinguishable. In applied econometrics this problem is most damaging since the entire intent is to separate the partial effects of each X upon the dependent variable.

To see this differently, let us substitute $X_{3i} = \lambda X_{2i}$ into Eq. (10.2.1) and obtain the following [see also Eq. (7.1.12)]:

$$\begin{aligned} y_i &= \hat{\beta}_2 x_{2i} + \hat{\beta}_3(\lambda x_{2i}) + \hat{u}_i \\ &= (\hat{\beta}_2 + \lambda \hat{\beta}_3) x_{2i} + \hat{u}_i \\ &= \hat{\alpha} x_{2i} + \hat{u}_i \end{aligned} \tag{10.2.3}$$

where

$$\hat{\alpha} = (\hat{\beta}_2 + \lambda \hat{\beta}_3) \tag{10.2.4}$$

[8]Another way of seeing this is as follows: By definition, the coefficient of correlation between X_2 and X_3, r_{23}, is $\sum x_{2i} x_{3i} / \sqrt{\sum x_{2i}^2 \sum x_{3i}^2}$. If $r_{23}^2 = 1$, i.e., perfect collinearity between X_2 and X_3, the denominator of Eq. (7.4.7) will be zero, making estimation of β_2 (or of β_3) impossible.

Applying the usual OLS formula to Eq. (10.2.3), we get

$$\hat{\alpha} = (\hat{\beta}_2 + \lambda\hat{\beta}_3) = \frac{\sum x_{2i} y_i}{\sum x_{2i}^2} \tag{10.2.5}$$

Therefore, although we can estimate α uniquely, there is no way to estimate β_2 and β_3 uniquely; mathematically

$$\hat{\alpha} = \hat{\beta}_2 + \lambda\hat{\beta}_3 \tag{10.2.6}$$

gives us only one equation in two unknowns (note λ is given) and there is an infinity of solutions to Eq. (10.2.6) for given values of $\hat{\alpha}$ and λ. To put this idea in concrete terms, let $\hat{\alpha} = 0.8$ and $\lambda = 2$. Then we have

$$0.8 = \hat{\beta}_2 + 2\hat{\beta}_3 \tag{10.2.7}$$

or

$$\hat{\beta}_2 = 0.8 - 2\hat{\beta}_3 \tag{10.2.8}$$

Now choose a value of $\hat{\beta}_3$ arbitrarily, and we will have a solution for $\hat{\beta}_2$. Choose another value for $\hat{\beta}_3$, and we will have another solution for $\hat{\beta}_2$. No matter how hard we try, there is no unique value for $\hat{\beta}_2$.

The upshot of the preceding discussion is that in the case of perfect multicollinearity one cannot get a unique solution for the individual regression coefficients. But notice that one can get a unique solution for linear combinations of these coefficients. The linear combination $(\beta_2 + \lambda\beta_3)$ is uniquely estimated by α, given the value of λ.[9]

In passing, note that in the case of perfect multicollinearity the variances and standard errors of $\hat{\beta}_2$ and $\hat{\beta}_3$ individually are infinite. (See Exercise 10.21.)

10.3 Estimation in the Presence of "High" but "Imperfect" Multicollinearity

The perfect multicollinearity situation is a pathological extreme. Generally, there is no exact linear relationship among the *X* variables, especially in data involving economic time series. Thus, turning to the three-variable model in the deviation form given in Eq. (10.2.1), instead of exact multicollinearity, we may have

$$x_{3i} = \lambda x_{2i} + v_i \tag{10.3.1}$$

where $\lambda \neq 0$ and where v_i is a stochastic error term such that $\sum x_{2i} v_i = 0$. (Why?)

Incidentally, the Ballentines shown in Figure 10.1*b* to 10.1*e* represent cases of imperfect collinearity.

In this case, estimation of regression coefficients β_2 and β_3 may be possible. For example, substituting Eq. (10.3.1) into Eq. (7.4.7), we obtain

$$\hat{\beta}_2 = \frac{\sum(y_i x_{2i})\left(\lambda^2 \sum x_{2i}^2 + \sum v_i^2\right) - \left(\lambda \sum y_i x_{2i} + \sum y_i v_i\right)\left(\lambda \sum x_{2i}^2\right)}{\sum x_{2i}^2 \left(\lambda^2 \sum x_{2i}^2 + \sum v_i^2\right) - \left(\lambda \sum x_{2i}^2\right)^2} \tag{10.3.2}$$

where use is made of $\sum x_{2i} v_i = 0$. A similar expression can be derived for $\hat{\beta}_3$.

[9]In econometric literature, a function such as $(\beta_2 + \lambda\beta_3)$ is known as an **estimable function.**

Now, unlike Eq. (10.2.2), there is no reason to believe a priori that Eq. (10.3.2) cannot be estimated. Of course, if v_i is sufficiently small, say, very close to zero, Eq. (10.3.1) will indicate almost perfect collinearity and we shall be back to the indeterminate case of Eq. (10.2.2).

10.4 Multicollinearity: Much Ado about Nothing? Theoretical Consequences of Multicollinearity

Recall that if the assumptions of the classical model are satisfied, the OLS estimators of the regression estimators are BLUE (or BUE, if the normality assumption is added). Now it can be shown that even if multicollinearity is very high, as in the case of *near multicollinearity,* the OLS estimators still retain the property of BLUE.[10] Then what is the multicollinearity fuss all about? As Christopher Achen remarks (note also the Leamer quote at the beginning of this chapter):

> Beginning students of methodology occasionally worry that their independent variables are correlated—the so-called multicollinearity problem. But multicollinearity violates no regression assumptions. Unbiased, consistent estimates will occur, and their standard errors will be correctly estimated. The only effect of multicollinearity is to make it hard to get coefficient estimates with small standard error. But having a small number of observations also has that effect, as does having independent variables with small variances. (In fact, at a theoretical level, multicollinearity, few observations and small variances on the independent variables are essentially all the same problem.) Thus "What should I do about multicollinearity?" is a question like "What should I do if I don't have many observations?" No statistical answer can be given.[11]

To drive home the importance of sample size, Goldberger coined the term **micronumerosity,** to counter the exotic polysyllabic name *multicollinearity*. According to Goldberger, **exact micronumerosity** (the counterpart of exact multicollinearity) arises when n, the sample size, is zero, in which case any kind of estimation is impossible. *Near micronumerosity,* like near multicollinearity, arises when the number of observations barely exceeds the number of parameters to be estimated.

Leamer, Achen, and Goldberger are right in bemoaning the lack of attention given to the sample size problem and the undue attention to the multicollinearity problem. Unfortunately, in applied work involving secondary data (i.e., data collected by some agency, such as the GNP data collected by the government), an individual researcher may not be able to do much about the size of the sample data and may have to face "estimating problems important enough to warrant our treating it [i.e., multicollinearity] as a violation of the CLR [classical linear regression] model."[12]

First, it is true that even in the case of near multicollinearity the OLS estimators are unbiased. But unbiasedness is a multisample or repeated sampling property. What it means is that, keeping the values of the X variables fixed, if one obtains repeated samples and computes the OLS estimators for each of these samples, the average of the sample values will converge to the true population values of the estimators as the number of samples increases. But this says nothing about the properties of estimators in any given sample.

[10]Since near multicollinearity per se does not violate the other assumptions listed in Chapter 7, the OLS estimators are BLUE as indicated there.

[11]Christopher H. Achen, *Interpreting and Using Regression*, Sage Publications, Beverly Hills, Calif., 1982, pp. 82–83.

[12]Peter Kennedy, *A Guide to Econometrics*, 3d ed., The MIT Press, Cambridge, Mass., 1992, p. 177.

Second, it is also true that collinearity does not destroy the property of minimum variance: In the class of all linear unbiased estimators, the OLS estimators have minimum variance; that is, they are efficient. But this does not mean that the variance of an OLS estimator will necessarily be small (in relation to the value of the estimator) in any given sample, as we shall demonstrate shortly.

Third, *multicollinearity is essentially a sample (regression) phenomenon* in the sense that, even if the X variables are not linearly related in the population, they may be so related in the particular sample at hand: When we postulate the theoretical or population regression function (PRF), we believe that all the X variables included in the model have a separate or independent influence on the dependent variable Y. But it may happen that in any given sample that is used to test the PRF some or all of the X variables are so highly collinear that we cannot isolate their individual influence on Y. So to speak, our sample lets us down, although the theory says that all the X's are important. In short, our sample may not be "rich" enough to accommodate all X variables in the analysis.

As an illustration, reconsider the consumption–income example of Chapter 3 (Example 3.1). Economists theorize that, besides income, the wealth of the consumer is also an important determinant of consumption expenditure. Thus, we may write

$$\text{Consumption}_i = \beta_1 + \beta_2 \text{ Income}_i + \beta_3 \text{ Wealth}_i + u_i$$

Now it may happen that when we obtain data on income and wealth, the two variables may be highly, if not perfectly, correlated: Wealthier people generally tend to have higher incomes. Thus, although in theory income and wealth are logical candidates to explain the behavior of consumption expenditure, in practice (i.e., in the sample) it may be difficult to disentangle the separate influences of income and wealth on consumption expenditure.

Ideally, to assess the individual effects of wealth and income on consumption expenditure we need a sufficient number of sample observations of wealthy individuals with low income, and high-income individuals with low wealth (recall Assumption 7). Although this may be possible in cross-sectional studies (by increasing the sample size), it is very difficult to achieve in aggregate time series work.

For all these reasons, the fact that the OLS estimators are BLUE despite multicollinearity is of little consolation in practice. We must see what happens or is likely to happen in any given sample, a topic discussed in the following section.

10.5 Practical Consequences of Multicollinearity

In cases of near or high multicollinearity, one is likely to encounter the following consequences:

1. Although BLUE, the OLS estimators have large variances and covariances, making precise estimation difficult.
2. Because of consequence 1, the confidence intervals tend to be much wider, leading to the acceptance of the "zero null hypothesis" (i.e., the true population coefficient is zero) more readily.
3. Also because of consequence 1, the t ratio of one or more coefficients tends to be statistically insignificant.
4. Although the t ratio of one or more coefficients is statistically insignificant, R^2, the overall measure of goodness of fit, can be very high.
5. The OLS estimators and their standard errors can be sensitive to small changes in the data.

The preceding consequences can be demonstrated as follows.

Large Variances and Covariances of OLS Estimators

To see large variances and covariances, recall that for the model (10.2.1) the variances and covariances of $\hat{\beta}_2$ and $\hat{\beta}_3$ are given by

$$\operatorname{var}(\hat{\beta}_2) = \frac{\sigma^2}{\sum x_{2i}^2 (1 - r_{23}^2)} \tag{7.4.12}$$

$$\operatorname{var}(\hat{\beta}_3) = \frac{\sigma^2}{\sum x_{3i}^2 (1 - r_{23}^2)} \tag{7.4.15}$$

$$\operatorname{cov}(\hat{\beta}_2, \hat{\beta}_3) = \frac{-r_{23}\sigma^2}{(1 - r_{23}^2)\sqrt{\sum x_{2i}^2 \sum x_{3i}^2}} \tag{7.4.17}$$

where r_{23} is the coefficient of correlation between X_2 and X_3.

It is apparent from Eqs. (7.4.12) and (7.4.15) that as r_{23} tends toward 1, that is, as collinearity increases, the variances of the two estimators increase and in the limit when $r_{23} = 1$, they are infinite. It is equally clear from Eq. (7.4.17) that as r_{23} increases toward 1, the covariance of the two estimators also increases in absolute value. [*Note:* $\operatorname{cov}(\hat{\beta}_2, \hat{\beta}_3) \equiv \operatorname{cov}(\hat{\beta}_3, \hat{\beta}_2)$.]

The speed with which variances and covariances increase can be seen with the **variance-inflating factor (VIF),** which is defined as

$$\text{VIF} = \frac{1}{(1 - r_{23}^2)} \tag{10.5.1}$$

VIF shows how the variance of an estimator is *inflated* by the presence of multicollinearity. As r_{23}^2 approaches 1, the VIF approaches infinity. That is, as the extent of collinearity increases, the variance of an estimator increases, and in the limit it can become infinite. As can be readily seen, if there is no collinearity between X_2 and X_3, VIF will be 1.

Using this definition, we can express Eqs. (7.4.12) and (7.4.15) as

$$\operatorname{var}(\hat{\beta}_2) = \frac{\sigma^2}{\sum x_{2i}^2}\text{VIF} \tag{10.5.2}$$

$$\operatorname{var}(\hat{\beta}_3) = \frac{\sigma^2}{\sum x_{3i}^2}\text{VIF} \tag{10.5.3}$$

which show that the variances of $\hat{\beta}_2$ and $\hat{\beta}_3$ are directly proportional to the VIF.

To give some idea about how fast the variances and covariances increase as r_{23} increases, consider Table 10.1, which gives these variances and covariances for selected values of r_{23}. As this table shows, increases in r_{23} have a dramatic effect on the estimated variances and covariances of the OLS estimators. When $r_{23} = 0.50$, the var $(\hat{\beta}_2)$ is 1.33 times the variance when r_{23} is zero, but by the time r_{23} reaches 0.95 it is about 10 times as high as when there is no collinearity. And lo and behold, an increase of r_{23} from 0.95 to 0.995 makes the estimated variance 100 times that when collinearity is zero. The same dramatic effect is seen on the estimated covariance. All this can be seen in Figure 10.2.

The results just discussed can be easily extended to the k-variable model. In such a model, the variance of the kth coefficient, as noted in Eq. (7.5.6), can be expressed as:

$$\operatorname{var}(\hat{\beta}_j) = \frac{\sigma^2}{\sum x_j^2}\left(\frac{1}{1 - R_j^2}\right) \tag{7.5.6}$$

TABLE 10.1
The Effect of Increasing r_{23} on var ($\hat{\beta}_2$) and cov ($\hat{\beta}_2, \hat{\beta}_3$)

Value of r_{23} (1)	VIF (2)	var ($\hat{\beta}_2$) (3)*	$\frac{\text{var}(\hat{\beta}_2)(r_{23} \neq 0)}{\text{var}(\hat{\beta}_2)(r_{23} = 0)}$ (4)	cov ($\hat{\beta}_2, \hat{\beta}_3$) (5)
0.00	1.00	$\frac{\sigma^2}{\sum x_{2i}^2} = A$	—	0
0.50	1.33	1.33 × A	1.33	0.67 × B
0.70	1.96	1.96 × A	1.96	1.37 × B
0.80	2.78	2.78 × A	2.78	2.22 × B
0.90	5.76	5.26 × A	5.26	4.73 × B
0.95	10.26	10.26 × A	10.26	9.74 × B
0.97	16.92	16.92 × A	16.92	16.41 × B
0.99	50.25	50.25 × A	50.25	49.75 × B
0.995	100.00	100.00 × A	100.00	99.50 × B
0.999	500.00	500.00 × A	500.00	499.50 × B

Note: $A = \frac{\sigma^2}{\sum x_{2i}^2}$

$B = \frac{-\sigma^2}{\sqrt{\sum x_{2i}^2 \sum x_{3i}^2}}$

× = times

*To find out the effect of increasing r_{23} on var ($\hat{\beta}_3$), note that $A = \sigma^2 / \sum x_{3i}^2$ when $r_{23} = 0$, but the variance and covariance magnifying factors remain the same.

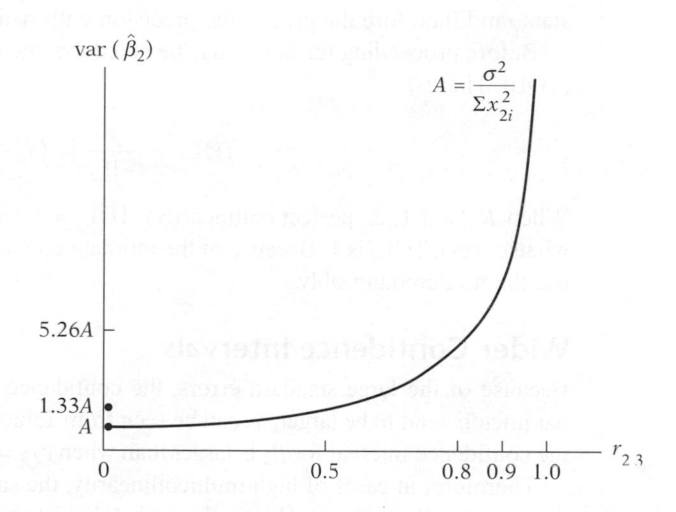

FIGURE 10.2 The behavior of var ($\hat{\beta}_2$) as a function of r_{23}.

where $\hat{\beta}_j$ = (estimated) partial regression coefficient of regressor X_j
$R_j^2 = R^2$ in the regression of X_j on the remaining $(k - 2)$ regressions (*Note:* There are $[k - 1]$ regressors in the k-variable regression model.)
$\sum x_j^2 = \sum (X_j - \bar{X}_j)^2$

We can also write Eq. (7.5.6) as

$$\text{var}(\hat{\beta}_j) = \frac{\sigma^2}{\sum x_j^2} \text{VIF}_j \tag{10.5.4}$$

As you can see from this expression, var ($\hat{\beta}_j$) is proportional to σ^2 and VIF but inversely proportional to $\sum x_j^2$. Thus, whether var ($\hat{\beta}_j$) is large or small will depend on the three

TABLE 10.2
The Effect of Increasing Collinearity on the 95% Confidence Interval for β_2: $\hat{\beta}_2 \pm 1.96\ \text{se}(\hat{\beta}_2)$

Value of r_{23}	95% Confidence Interval for β_2
0.00	$\hat{\beta}_2 \pm 1.96\sqrt{\dfrac{\sigma^2}{\sum x_{2i}^2}}$
0.50	$\hat{\beta}_2 \pm 1.96\sqrt{(1.33)}\sqrt{\dfrac{\sigma^2}{\sum x_{2i}^2}}$
0.95	$\hat{\beta}_2 \pm 1.96\sqrt{(10.26)}\sqrt{\dfrac{\sigma^2}{\sum x_{2i}^2}}$
0.995	$\hat{\beta}_2 \pm 1.96\sqrt{(100)}\sqrt{\dfrac{\sigma^2}{\sum x_{2i}^2}}$
0.999	$\hat{\beta}_2 \pm 1.96\sqrt{(500)}\sqrt{\dfrac{\sigma^2}{\sum x_{2i}^2}}$

Note: We are using the normal distribution because σ^2 is assumed for convenience to be known. Hence the use of 1.96, the 95% confidence factor for the normal distribution.

The standard errors corresponding to the various r_{23} values are obtained from Table 10.1.

ingredients: (1) σ^2, (2) VIF, and (3) $\sum x_j^2$. The last one, which ties in with Assumption 8 of the classical model, states that the larger the variability in a regressor, the smaller the variance of the coefficient of that regressor, assuming the other two ingredients are constant, and therefore the greater the precision with which that coefficient can be estimated.

Before proceeding further, it may be noted that the inverse of the VIF is called **tolerance** (TOL). That is,

$$\text{TOL}_j = \frac{1}{\text{VIF}_j} = \left(1 - R_j^2\right) \tag{10.5.5}$$

When $R_j^2 = 1$ (i.e., perfect collinearity), $\text{TOL}_j = 0$ and when $R_j^2 = 0$ (i.e., no collinearity whatsoever), TOL_j is 1. Because of the intimate connection between VIF and TOL, one can use them interchangeably.

Wider Confidence Intervals

Because of the large standard errors, the confidence intervals for the relevant population parameters tend to be larger, as can be seen from Table 10.2. For example, when $r_{23} = 0.95$, the confidence interval for β_2 is larger than when $r_{23} = 0$ by a factor of $\sqrt{10.26}$, or about 3.

Therefore, in cases of high multicollinearity, the sample data may be compatible with a diverse set of hypotheses. Hence, the probability of accepting a false hypothesis (i.e., type II error) increases.

"Insignificant" *t* Ratios

Recall that to test the null hypothesis that, say, $\beta_2 = 0$, we use the *t* ratio, that is, $\hat{\beta}_2/\text{se}(\hat{\beta}_2)$, and compare the estimated *t* value with the critical *t* value from the *t* table. But as we have seen, in cases of high collinearity the estimated standard errors increase dramatically, thereby making the *t* values smaller. Therefore, in such cases, one will increasingly accept the null hypothesis that the relevant true population value is zero.[13]

[13]In terms of the confidence intervals, $\beta_2 = 0$ value will lie increasingly in the acceptance region as the degree of collinearity increases.

A High R^2 but Few Significant t Ratios

Consider the k-variable linear regression model:

$$Y_i = \beta_1 + \beta_2 X_{2i} + \beta_3 X_{3i} + \cdots + \beta_k X_{ki} + u_i$$

In cases of high collinearity, it is possible to find, as we have just noted, that one or more of the partial slope coefficients are individually statistically insignificant on the basis of the t test. Yet the R^2 in such situations may be so high, say, in excess of 0.9, that on the basis of the F test one can convincingly reject the hypothesis that $\beta_2 = \beta_3 = \cdots = \beta_k = 0$. Indeed, this is one of the signals of multicollinearity—insignificant t values but a high overall R^2 (and a significant F value)!

We shall demonstrate this signal in the next section, but this outcome should not be surprising in view of our discussion on individual versus joint testing in Chapter 8. As you may recall, the real problem here is the covariances between the estimators, which, as formula (7.4.17) indicates, are related to the correlations between the regressors.

Sensitivity of OLS Estimators and Their Standard Errors to Small Changes in Data

As long as multicollinearity is not perfect, estimation of the regression coefficients is possible but the estimates and their standard errors become very sensitive to even the slightest change in the data.

To see this, consider Table 10.3. Based on these data, we obtain the following multiple regression:

$$\begin{aligned} \hat{Y}_i &= 1.1939 + 0.4463X_{2i} + 0.0030X_{3i} \\ &\quad (0.7737) \quad (0.1848) \quad (0.0851) \\ t &= (1.5431) \quad (2.4151) \quad (0.0358) \\ &R^2 = 0.8101 \qquad r_{23} = 0.5523 \\ &\operatorname{cov}(\hat{\beta}_2, \hat{\beta}_3) = -0.00868 \qquad \text{df} = 2 \end{aligned} \tag{10.5.6}$$

Regression (10.5.6) shows that none of the regression coefficients is individually significant at the conventional 1 or 5 percent levels of significance, although $\hat{\beta}_2$ is significant at the 10 percent level on the basis of a one-tail t test.

Now consider Table 10.4. The only difference between Tables 10.3 and 10.4 is that the third and fourth values of X_3 are interchanged. Using the data of Table 10.4, we now obtain

$$\begin{aligned} \hat{Y}_i &= 1.2108 + 0.4014X_{2i} + 0.0270X_{3i} \\ &\quad (0.7480) \quad (0.2721) \quad (0.1252) \\ t &= (1.6187) \quad (1.4752) \quad (0.2158) \\ &R^2 = 0.8143 \qquad r_{23} = 0.8285 \\ &\operatorname{cov}(\hat{\beta}_2, \hat{\beta}_3) = -0.0282 \qquad \text{df} = 2 \end{aligned} \tag{10.5.7}$$

As a result of a slight change in the data, we see that $\hat{\beta}_2$, which was statistically significant before at the 10 percent level of significance, is no longer significant even at that level. Also note that in Eq. (10.5.6) $\operatorname{cov}(\hat{\beta}_2, \hat{\beta}_3) = -0.00868$ whereas in Eq. (10.5.7) it is -0.0282, a more than threefold increase. All these changes may be attributable to increased multicollinearity: In Eq. (10.5.6) $r_{23} = 0.5523$, whereas in Eq. (10.5.7) it is 0.8285. Similarly, the

TABLE 10.3 Hypothetical Data on Y, X_2, and X_3

Y	X_2	X_3
1	2	4
2	0	2
3	4	12
4	6	0
5	8	16

TABLE 10.4 Hypothetical Data on Y, X_2, and X_3

Y	X_2	X_3
1	2	4
2	0	2
3	4	0
4	6	12
5	8	16

standard errors of $\hat{\beta}_2$ and $\hat{\beta}_3$ increase between the two regressions, a usual symptom of collinearity.

We noted earlier that in the presence of high collinearity one cannot estimate the individual regression coefficients precisely but that linear combinations of these coefficients may be estimated more precisely. This fact can be substantiated from the regressions (10.5.6) and (10.5.7). In the first regression the sum of the two partial slope coefficients is 0.4493 and in the second it is 0.4284, practically the same. Not only that, their standard errors are practically the same, 0.1550 vs. 0.1823.[14] Note, however, the coefficient of X_3 has changed dramatically, from 0.003 to 0.027.

Consequences of Micronumerosity

In a parody of the consequences of multicollinearity, and in a tongue-in-cheek manner, Goldberger cites exactly similar consequences of micronumerosity, that is, analysis based on small sample size.[15] The reader is advised to read Goldberger's analysis to see why he regards micronumerosity as being as important as multicollinearity.

10.6 An Illustrative Example

EXAMPLE 10.1

Consumption Expenditure in Relation to Income and Wealth

To illustrate the various points made thus far, let us consider the consumption–income example from the introduction. Table 10.5 contains hypothetical data on consumption, income, and wealth. If we assume that consumption expenditure is linearly related to income and wealth, then, from Table 10.5 we obtain the following regression:

$$\begin{aligned}
\hat{Y}_i &= 24.7747 + 0.9415X_{2i} - 0.0424X_{3i} \\
&\quad\ (6.7525) \quad (0.8229) \quad\ (0.0807) \\
t &= (3.6690) \quad (1.1442) \quad (-0.5261) \\
R^2 &= 0.9635 \quad \bar{R}^2 = 0.9531 \quad \text{df} = 7
\end{aligned} \tag{10.6.1}$$

[14]These standard errors are obtained from the formula

$$\text{se}(\hat{\beta}_2 + \hat{\beta}_3) = \sqrt{\text{var}(\hat{\beta}_2) + \text{var}(\hat{\beta}_3) + 2\,\text{cov}(\hat{\beta}_2, \hat{\beta}_3)}$$

Note that increasing collinearity increases the variances of $\hat{\beta}_2$ and $\hat{\beta}_3$, but these variances may be offset if there is high negative covariance between the two, as our results clearly point out.

[15]Goldberger, op. cit., pp. 248–250.

EXAMPLE 10.1 *(Continued)*

TABLE 10.5 **Hypothetical Data on Consumption Expenditure Y, Income X_2, and Wealth X_3**

Y, $	X_2, $	X_3, $
70	80	810
65	100	1009
90	120	1273
95	140	1425
110	160	1633
115	180	1876
120	200	2052
140	220	2201
155	240	2435
150	260	2686

TABLE 10.6 **ANOVA Table for the Consumption–Income–Wealth Example**

Source of Variation	SS	df	MSS
Due to regression	8,565.5541	2	4,282.7770
Due to residual	324.4459	7	46.3494

Regression (10.6.1) shows that income and wealth together explain about 96 percent of the variation in consumption expenditure, and yet neither of the slope coefficients is individually statistically significant. Moreover, not only is the wealth variable statistically insignificant but also it has the wrong sign. A priori, one would expect a positive relationship between consumption and wealth. Although $\hat{\beta}_2$ and $\hat{\beta}_3$ are individually statistically insignificant, if we test the hypothesis that $\beta_2 = \beta_3 = 0$ simultaneously, this hypothesis can be rejected, as Table 10.6 shows. Under the usual assumption we obtain

$$F = \frac{4282.7770}{46.3494} = 92.4019 \tag{10.6.2}$$

This F value is obviously highly significant.

It is interesting to look at this result geometrically. (See Figure 10.3.) Based on the regression (10.6.1), we have established the individual 95 percent confidence intervals for β_2 and β_3 following the usual procedure discussed in Chapter 8. As these intervals show, individually each of them includes the value of zero. Therefore, *individually* we can accept the hypothesis that the two partial slopes are zero. But, when we establish the joint confidence interval to test the hypothesis that $\beta_2 = \beta_3 = 0$, that hypothesis cannot be accepted since the joint confidence interval, actually an ellipse, does not include the origin.[16] As already pointed out, when collinearity is high, tests on individual regressors are not reliable; in such cases it is the overall F test that will show if Y is related to the various regressors.

Our example shows dramatically what multicollinearity does. The fact that the F test is significant but the t values of X_2 and X_3 are individually insignificant means that the two variables are so highly correlated that it is impossible to isolate the individual impact of

(Continued)

[16]As noted in Section 5.3, the topic of joint confidence interval is rather involved. The interested reader may consult the reference cited there.

EXAMPLE 10.1 (*Continued*)

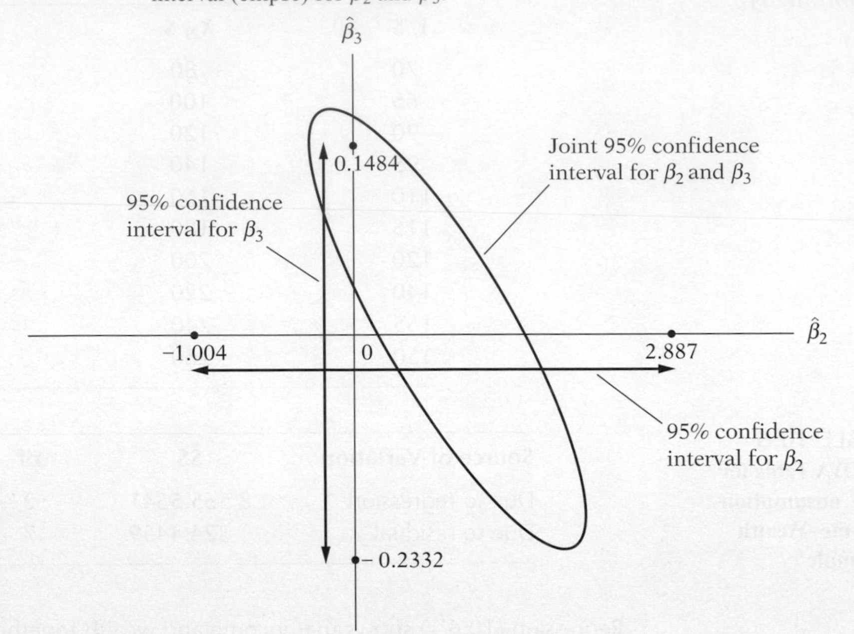

FIGURE 10.3 Individual confidence intervals for β_2 and β_3 and joint confidence interval (ellipse) for β_2 and β_3.

either income or wealth on consumption. As a matter of fact, if we regress X_3 on X_2, we obtain

$$\begin{aligned} \hat{X}_{3i} &= 7.5454 + 10.1909X_{2i} \\ &\quad\;(29.4758) \quad (0.1643) \\ t &= (0.2560) \quad (62.0405) \qquad R^2 = 0.9979 \end{aligned} \tag{10.6.3}$$

which shows that there is almost perfect collinearity between X_3 and X_2.

Now let us see what happens if we regress Y on X_2 only:

$$\begin{aligned} \hat{Y}_i &= 24.4545 + 0.5091X_{2i} \\ &\quad\;(6.4138) \quad (0.0357) \\ t &= (3.8128) \quad (14.2432) \qquad R^2 = 0.9621 \end{aligned} \tag{10.6.4}$$

In Eq. (10.6.1) the income variable was statistically insignificant, whereas now it is highly significant. If instead of regressing Y on X_2, we regress it on X_3, we obtain

$$\begin{aligned} \hat{Y}_i &= 24.411 + 0.0498X_{3i} \\ &\quad\;(6.874) \quad (0.0037) \\ t &= (3.551) \quad (13.29) \qquad R^2 = 0.9567 \end{aligned} \tag{10.6.5}$$

We see that wealth has now a significant impact on consumption expenditure, whereas in Eq. (10.6.1) it had no effect on consumption expenditure.

Regressions (10.6.4) and (10.6.5) show very clearly that in situations of extreme multicollinearity dropping the highly collinear variable will often make the other X variable statistically significant. This result would suggest that a way out of extreme collinearity is to drop the collinear variable, but we shall have more to say about it in Section 10.8.

EXAMPLE 10.2
Consumption Function for United States, 1947–2000

Source: See Table 7.12.

We now consider a concrete set of data on real consumption expenditure (C), real disposable personal income (Yd), real wealth (W), and real interest rate (I) for the United States for the period 1947–2000. The raw data are given in Table 10.7.

TABLE 10.7 U.S. Consumption Expenditure for the Period 1947–2000

Year	C	Yd	W	I
1947	976.4	1035.2	5166.815	−10.35094
1948	998.1	1090	5280.757	−4.719804
1949	1025.3	1095.6	5607.351	1.044063
1950	1090.9	1192.7	5759.515	0.407346
1951	1107.1	1227	6086.056	−5.283152
1952	1142.4	1266.8	6243.864	−0.277011
1953	1197.2	1327.5	6355.613	0.561137
1954	1221.9	1344	6797.027	−0.138476
1955	1310.4	1433.8	7172.242	0.261997
1956	1348.8	1502.3	7375.18	−0.736124
1957	1381.8	1539.5	7315.286	−0.260683
1958	1393	1553.7	7869.975	−0.57463
1959	1470.7	1623.8	8188.054	2.295943
1960	1510.8	1664.8	8351.757	1.511181
1961	1541.2	1720	8971.872	1.296432
1962	1617.3	1803.5	9091.545	1.395922
1963	1684	1871.5	9436.097	2.057616
1964	1784.8	2006.9	10003.4	2.026599
1965	1897.6	2131	10562.81	2.111669
1966	2006.1	2244.6	10522.04	2.020251
1967	2066.2	2340.5	11312.07	1.212616
1968	2184.2	2448.2	12145.41	1.054986
1969	2264.8	2524.3	11672.25	1.732154
1970	2317.5	2630	11650.04	1.166228
1971	2405.2	2745.3	12312.92	−0.712241
1972	2550.5	2874.3	13499.92	−0.155737
1973	2675.9	3072.3	13080.96	1.413839
1974	2653.7	3051.9	11868.79	−1.042571
1975	2710.9	3108.5	12634.36	−3.533585
1976	2868.9	3243.5	13456.78	−0.656766
1977	2992.1	3360.7	13786.31	−1.190427
1978	3124.7	3527.5	14450.5	0.113048
1979	3203.2	3628.6	15340	1.70421
1980	3193	3658	15964.95	2.298496
1981	3236	3741.1	15964.99	4.703847
1982	3275.5	3791.7	16312.51	4.449027
1983	3454.3	3906.9	16944.85	4.690972
1984	3640.6	4207.6	17526.75	5.848332
1985	3820.9	4347.8	19068.35	4.330504
1986	3981.2	4486.6	20530.04	3.768031
1987	4113.4	4582.5	21235.69	2.819469
1988	4279.5	4784.1	22331.99	3.287061

(Continued)

EXAMPLE 10.2 *(Continued)*

TABLE 10.7 *Continued*

Year	C	Yd	W	I
1989	4393.7	4906.5	23659.8	4.317956
1990	4474.5	5014.2	23105.13	3.595025
1991	4466.6	5033	24050.21	1.802757
1992	4594.5	5189.3	24418.2	1.007439
1993	4748.9	5261.3	25092.33	0.62479
1994	4928.1	5397.2	25218.6	2.206002
1995	5075.6	5539.1	27439.73	3.333143
1996	5237.5	5677.7	29448.19	3.083201
1997	5423.9	5854.5	32664.07	3.12
1998	5683.7	6168.6	35587.02	3.583909
1999	5968.4	6320	39591.26	3.245271
2000	6257.8	6539.2	38167.72	3.57597

We use the following for analysis

$$\ln C_t = \beta_1 + \beta_2 \ln Yd_t + \beta_3 \ln W_t + \beta_4 I_t + u_t \quad \textbf{(10.6.6)}$$

where ln stands for logarithm.

In this model the coefficients β_2 *and* β_3 give income and wealth elasticities, respectively (why?) and β_4 gives semielasticity (why?). The results of regression (10.6.6) are given in the following table.

```
Dependent Variable: LOG (C)
Method: Least Squares
Sample: 1947-2000
Included observations: 54
```

	Coefficient	Std. Error	t-Statistic	Prob.
C	-0.467711	0.042778	-10.93343	0.0000
LOG (YD)	0.804873	0.017498	45.99836	0.0000
LOG (WEALTH)	0.201270	0.017593	11.44060	0.0000
INTEREST	-0.002689	0.000762	-3.529265	0.0009

R-squared	0.999560	Mean dependent var.	7.826093
Adjusted *R*-squared	0.999533	S.D. dependent var.	0.552368
S.E. of regression	0.011934	Akaike info criterion	-5.947703
Sum squared resid.	0.007121	Schwarz criterion	-5.800371
Log likelihood	164.5880	Hannan-Quinn cariter.	-5.890883
F-statistic	37832.59	Durbin-Watson stat.	1.289219
Prob(*F*-statistic)	0.000000		

Note: LOG stands for natural log.

The results show that all the estimated coefficients are highly statistically significant, for their *p* values are extremely small. The estimated coefficients are interpreted as follows. The income elasticity is ≈ 0.80, suggesting that, holding other variables constant, if income goes up by 1 percent, the mean consumption expenditure goes up by about

EXAMPLE 10.2 *(Continued)*

0.8 percent. The wealth coefficient is ≈ 0.20, meaning that if wealth goes up by 1 percent, mean consumption goes up by only 0.2 percent, again holding other variables constant. The coefficient of the interest rate variable tells us that as the interest rate goes up by *one percentage point*, consumption expenditure goes *down* by 0.26 percent, ceteris paribus.

All the regressors have signs that accord with prior expectations, that is, income and wealth both have a positive impact on consumption but interest rate has a negative impact.

Do we have to worry about the problem of multicollinearity in the present case? Apparently not, because all the coefficients have the right signs, each coefficient is individually statistically significant, and the F value is also statistically highly significant, suggesting that, collectively, all the variables have a significant impact on consumption expenditure. The R^2 value is also quite high.

Of course, there is usually some degree of collinearity among economic variables. As long as it is not exact, we can still estimate the parameters of the model. For now, all we can say is that, in the present example, collinearity, if any, does not seem to be very severe. But in Section 10.7 we provide some diagnostic tests to detect collinearity and reexamine the U.S. consumption function to determine whether it is plagued by the collinearity problem.

10.7 Detection of Multicollinearity

Having studied the nature and consequences of multicollinearity, the natural question is: How does one know that collinearity is present in any given situation, especially in models involving more than two explanatory variables? Here it is useful to bear in mind Kmenta's warning:

> **1.** Multicollinearity is a question of degree and not of kind. The meaningful distinction is not between the presence and the absence of multicollinearity, but between its various degrees.
>
> **2.** Since multicollinearity refers to the condition of the explanatory variables that are assumed to be nonstochastic, it is a feature of the sample and not of the population.
>
> Therefore, we do not "test for multicollinearity" but can, if we wish, measure its degree in any particular sample.[17]

Since multicollinearity is essentially a sample phenomenon, arising out of the largely nonexperimental data collected in most social sciences, we do not have one unique method of detecting it or measuring its strength. What we have are some rules of thumb, some informal and some formal, but rules of thumb all the same. We now consider some of these rules.

1. **High R^2 but few significant t ratios.** As noted, this is the "classic" symptom of multicollinearity. If R^2 is high, say, in excess of 0.8, the F test in most cases will reject the hypothesis that the partial slope coefficients are simultaneously equal to zero, but the individual t tests will show that none or very few of the partial slope coefficients are statistically different from zero. This fact was clearly demonstrated by our consumption–income–wealth example.

Although this diagnostic is sensible, its disadvantage is that "it is too strong in the sense that multicollinearity is considered as harmful only when all of the influences of the explanatory variables on Y cannot be disentangled."[18]

[17] Jan Kmenta, *Elements of Econometrics*, 2d ed., Macmillan, New York, 1986, p. 431.

[18] Ibid., p. 439.

2. **High pair-wise correlations among regressors.** Another suggested rule of thumb is that if the pair-wise or zero-order correlation coefficient between two regressors is high, say, in excess of 0.8, then multicollinearity is a serious problem. The problem with this criterion is that, although high zero-order correlations may suggest collinearity, it is not necessary that they be high to have collinearity in any specific case. To put the matter somewhat technically, *high zero-order correlations are a sufficient but not a necessary condition for the existence of multicollinearity because it can exist even though the zero-order or simple correlations are comparatively low* (say, less than 0.50). To see this relationship, suppose we have a four-variable model:

$$Y_i = \beta_1 + \beta_2 X_{2i} + \beta_3 X_{3i} + \beta_4 X_{4i} + u_i$$

and suppose that

$$X_{4i} = \lambda_2 X_{2i} + \lambda_3 X_{3i}$$

where λ_2 and λ_3 are constants, not both zero. Obviously, X_4 is an exact linear combination of X_2 and X_3, giving $R^2_{4.23} = 1$, the coefficient of determination in the regression of X_4 on X_2 and X_3.

Now recalling the formula (7.11.5) from Chapter 7, we can write

$$R^2_{4.23} = \frac{r^2_{42} + r^2_{43} - 2r_{42}r_{43}r_{23}}{1 - r^2_{23}} \tag{10.7.1}$$

But since $R^2_{4.23} = 1$ because of perfect collinearity, we obtain

$$1 = \frac{r^2_{42} + r^2_{43} - 2r_{42}r_{43}r_{23}}{1 - r^2_{23}} \tag{10.7.2}$$

It is not difficult to see that Eq. (10.7.2) is satisfied by $r_{42} = 0.5, r_{43} = 0.5$, and $r_{23} = -0.5$, which are not very high values.

Therefore, in models involving more than two explanatory variables, the simple or zero-order correlation will not provide an infallible guide to the presence of multicollinearity. Of course, if there are only two explanatory variables, the zero-order correlations will suffice.

3. **Examination of partial correlations.** Because of the problem just mentioned in relying on zero-order correlations, Farrar and Glauber have suggested that one should look at the partial correlation coefficients.[19] Thus, in the regression of Y on X_2, X_3, and X_4, a finding that $R^2_{1.234}$ is very high but $r^2_{12.34}$, $r^2_{13.24}$, and $r^2_{14.23}$ are comparatively low may suggest that the variables X_2, X_3, and X_4 are highly intercorrelated and that at least one of these variables is superfluous.

Although a study of the partial correlations may be useful, there is no guarantee that they will provide an infallible guide to multicollinearity, for it may happen that both R^2 and all the partial correlations are sufficiently high. But more importantly, C. Robert Wichers has shown[20] that the Farrar–Glauber partial correlation test is ineffective in that a given partial correlation may be compatible with different multicollinearity patterns. The

[19]D. E. Farrar and R. R. Glauber, "Multicollinearity in Regression Analysis: The Problem Revisited," *Review of Economics and Statistics,* vol. 49, 1967, pp. 92–107.

[20]"The Detection of Multicollinearity: A Comment," *Review of Economics and Statistics,* vol. 57, 1975, pp. 365–366.

Farrar–Glauber test has also been severely criticized by T. Krishna Kumar[21] and John O'Hagan and Brendan McCabe.[22]

4. **Auxiliary regressions.** Since multicollinearity arises because one or more of the regressors are exact or approximately linear combinations of the other regressors, one way of finding out which X variable is related to other X variables is to regress each X_i on the remaining X variables and compute the corresponding R^2, which we designate as R_i^2; each one of these regressions is called an **auxiliary regression,** auxiliary to the main regression of Y on the X's. Then, following the relationship between F and R^2 established in Eq. (8.4.11), the variable

$$F_i = \frac{R^2_{x_i \cdot x_2 x_3 \cdots x_k} \big/ (k-2)}{\left(1 - R^2_{x_i \cdot x_2 x_3 \cdots x_k}\right) \big/ (n-k+1)} \tag{10.7.3}$$

follows the F distribution with $k-2$ and $n-k+1$ df. In Eq. (10.7.3) n stands for the sample size, k stands for the number of explanatory variables including the intercept term, and $R^2_{x_i \cdot x_2 x_3 \cdots x_k}$ is the coefficient of determination in the regression of variable X_i on the remaining X variables.[23]

If the computed F exceeds the critical F_i at the chosen level of significance, it is taken to mean that the particular X_i is collinear with other X's; if it does not exceed the critical F_i, we say that it is not collinear with other X's, in which case we may retain that variable in the model. If F_i is statistically significant, we will still have to decide whether the particular X_i should be dropped from the model. This question will be taken up in Section 10.8.

But this method is not without its drawbacks, for

> . . . if the multicollinearity involves only a few variables so that the auxiliary regressions do not suffer from extensive multicollinearity, the estimated coefficients may reveal the nature of the linear dependence among the regressors. Unfortunately, if there are several complex linear associations, this curve fitting exercise may not prove to be of much value as it will be difficult to identify the separate interrelationships.[24]

Instead of formally testing all auxiliary R^2 values, one may adopt **Klein' rule of thumb,** which suggests that multicollinearity may be a troublesome problem only if the R^2 obtained from an auxiliary regression is greater than the overall R^2, that is, that obtained from the regression of Y on all the regressors.[25] Of course, like all other rules of thumb, this one should be used judiciously.

5. **Eigenvalues and condition index.** From *EViews* and *Stata*, we can find the *eigenvalues* and the *condition index,* to diagnose multicollinearity. We will not discuss eigenvalues here, for that would take us into topics in matrix algebra that are beyond the scope of this

[21]"Multicollinearity in Regression Analysis," *Review of Economics and Statistics,* vol. 57, 1975, pp. 366–368.

[22]"Tests for the Severity of Multicollinearity in Regression Analysis: A Comment," *Review of Economics and Statistics,* vol. 57, 1975, pp. 368–370.

[23]For example, $R^2_{x_2}$ can be obtained by regressing X_{2i} as follows: $X_{2i} = a_1 + a_3 X_{3i} + a_4 X_{4i} + \cdots + a_k X_{ki} + \hat{u}_i$.

[24]George G. Judge, R. Carter Hill, William E. Griffiths, Helmut Lütkepohl, and Tsoung-Chao Lee, *Introduction to the Theory and Practice of Econometrics,* John Wiley & Sons, New York, 1982, p. 621.

[25]Lawrence R. Klein, *An Introduction to Econometrics,* Prentice-Hall, Englewood Cliffs, NJ, 1962, p. 101.

book. From these eigenvalues, however, we can derive what is known as the **condition number *k*** defined as

$$k = \frac{\text{Maximum eigenvalue}}{\text{Minimum eigenvalue}}$$

and the **condition index (CI)** defined as

$$\text{CI} = \sqrt{\frac{\text{Maximum eigenvalue}}{\text{Minimum eigenvalue}}} = \sqrt{k}$$

Then we have this rule of thumb: If k is between 100 and 1000 there is moderate to strong multicollinearity and if it exceeds 1000 there is severe multicollinearity. Alternatively, if the CI $(= \sqrt{k})$ is between 10 and 30, there is moderate to strong multicollinearity and if it exceeds 30 there is severe multicollinearity.

For the illustrative example in App. 7A.5, the smallest eigenvalue is 3.786 and the largest eigenvalue is 187.5269 giving $k = 187.5269/3.786$ or about 49.53. Therefore $\text{CI} = \sqrt{49.53} = 7.0377$. Both k and CI suggest that we do not have a serious collinearity problem. Incidentally, note that a low eigenvalue (in relation to the maximum eigenvalue) is generally an indication of near-linear dependencies in the data.

Some authors believe that the condition index is the best available multicollinearity diagnostic. But this opinion is not shared widely. For us, then, the CI is just a rule of thumb, a bit more sophisticated perhaps. But for further details, the reader may consult the references.[26]

6. **Tolerance and variance inflation factor.** We have already introduced TOL and VIF. As R_j^2, the coefficient of determination in the regression of regressor X_j on the remaining regressors in the model, increases toward unity, that is, as the collinearity of X_j with the other regressors increases, VIF also increases and in the limit it can be infinite.

Some authors therefore use the VIF as an indicator of multicollinearity. The larger the value of VIF_j, the more "troublesome" or collinear the variable X_j. **As a rule of thumb,** if the VIF of a variable exceeds 10, which will happen if R_j^2 exceeds 0.90, that variable is said be highly collinear.[27]

Of course, one could use TOL_j as a measure of multicollinearity in view of its intimate connection with VIF_j. The closer TOL_j is to zero, the greater the degree of collinearity of that variable with the other regressors. On the other hand, the closer TOL_j is to 1, the greater the evidence that X_j is not collinear with the other regressors.

VIF (or tolerance) as a measure of collinearity is not free of criticism. As Eq. (10.5.4) shows, var $(\hat{\beta}_j)$ depends on three factors: σ^2, $\sum x_j^2$, and VIF_j. A high VIF can be counterbalanced by a low σ^2 or a high $\sum x_j^2$. To put it differently, a high VIF is neither necessary nor sufficient to get high variances and high standard errors. Therefore, high multicollinearity, as measured by a high VIF, may not necessarily cause high standard errors. In all this discussion, the terms *high* and *low* are used in a relative sense.

7. **Scatterplot.** It is a good practice to use a scatterplot to see how the various variables in a regression model are related. Figure 10.4 presents the scatterplot for the U.S.

[26]See especially D. A. Belsley, E. Kuh, and R. E. Welsch, *Regression Diagnostics: Identifying Influential Data and Sources of Collinearity,* John Wiley & Sons, New York, 1980, Chapter 3. However, this book is not for the beginner.

[27]See David G. Kleinbaum, Lawrence L. Kupper, and Keith E. Muller, *Applied Regression Analysis and Other Multivariate Methods,* 2d ed., PWS-Kent, Boston, Mass., 1988, p. 210.

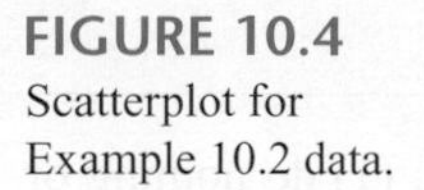

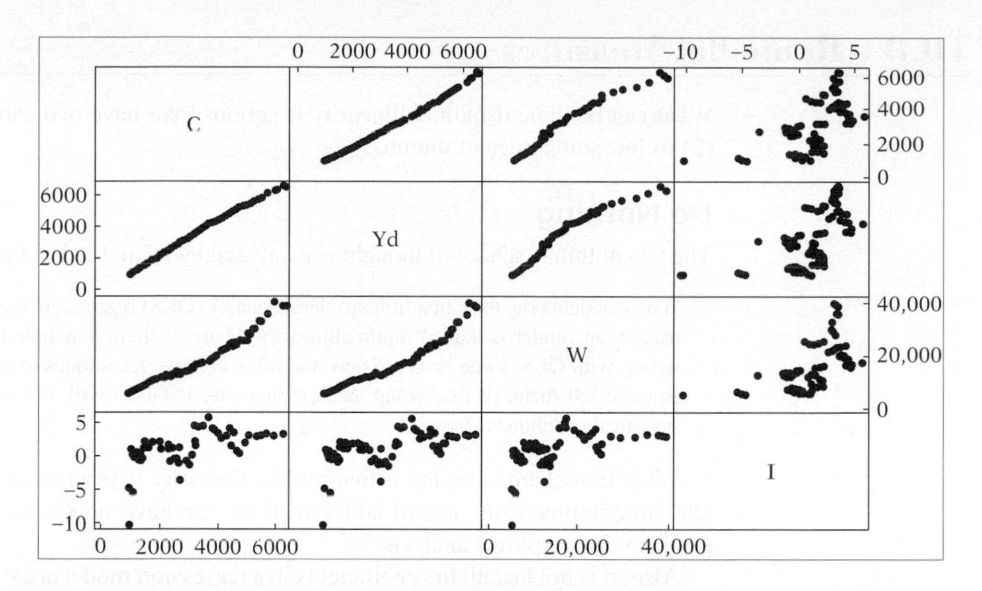

FIGURE 10.4 Scatterplot for Example 10.2 data.

consumption example discussed in the previous section (Example 10.2). This is a four-by-four box diagram because we have four variables in the model, a dependent variable (C) and three explanatory variables: real disposable personal income (Yd), real wealth (W), and real interest rate (I).

First consider the main diagonal, going from the upper left-hand corner to the lower right-hand corner. There are no scatterpoints in these boxes that lie on the main diagonal. If there were, they would have a correlation coefficient of 1, for the plots would be of a given variable against itself. The off-diagonal boxes show intercorrelations among the variables. Take, for instance, the wealth box (W). It shows that wealth and income are highly correlated (the correlation coefficient between the two is 0.97), but not perfectly so. If they were perfectly correlated (i.e., if they had a correlation coefficient of 1), we would not have been able to estimate the regression (10.6.6) because we would have an exact linear relationship between wealth and income. The scatterplot also shows that the interest rate is not highly correlated with the other three variables.

Since the scatterplot function is now included in several statistical packages, this diagnostic should be considered along with the ones discussed earlier. But keep in mind that simple correlations between pairs of variables may not be a definitive indicator of collinearity, as pointed out earlier.

To conclude our discussion of detecting multicollinearity, we stress that the various methods we have discussed are essentially in the nature of "fishing expeditions," for we cannot tell which of these methods will work in any particular application. Alas, not much can be done about it, for multicollinearity is specific to a given sample over which the researcher may not have much control, especially if the data are nonexperimental in nature—the usual fate of researchers in the social sciences.

Again as a parody of multicollinearity, Goldberger cites numerous ways of detecting micronumerosity, such as developing critical values of the sample size, n^*, such that micronumerosity is a problem only if the actual sample size, n, is smaller than n^*. The point of Goldberger's parody is to emphasize that small sample size and lack of variability in the explanatory variables may cause problems that are at least as serious as those due to multicollinearity.

10.8 Remedial Measures

What can be done if multicollinearity is serious? We have two choices: (1) do nothing or (2) follow some rules of thumb.

Do Nothing

The "do nothing" school of thought is expressed by Blanchard as follows:[28]

> When students run their first ordinary least squares (OLS) regression, the first problem that they usually encounter is that of multicollinearity. Many of them conclude that there is something wrong with OLS; some resort to new and often creative techniques to get around the problem. But, we tell them, this is wrong. Multicollinearity is God's will, not a problem with OLS or statistical technique in general.

What Blanchard is saying is that multicollinearity is essentially a data deficiency problem (micronumerosity, again) and sometimes we have no choice over the data we have available for empirical analysis.

Also, it is not that all the coefficients in a regression model are statistically insignificant. Moreover, even if we cannot estimate one or more regression coefficients with greater precision, a linear combination of them (i.e., estimable function) can be estimated relatively efficiently. As we saw in Eq. (10.2.3), we can estimate α uniquely, even if we cannot estimate its two components given there individually. Sometimes this is the best we can do with a given set of data.[29]

Rule-of-Thumb Procedures

One can try the following rules of thumb to address the problem of multicollinearity; their success will depend on the severity of the collinearity problem.

1. **A priori information.** Suppose we consider the model

$$Y_i = \beta_1 + \beta_2 X_{2i} + \beta_3 X_{3i} + u_i$$

where Y = consumption, X_2 = income, and X_3 = wealth. As noted before, income and wealth variables tend to be highly collinear. But suppose a priori we believe that $\beta_3 = 0.10\beta_2$; that is, the rate of change of consumption with respect to wealth is one-tenth the corresponding rate with respect to income. We can then run the following regression:

$$\begin{aligned} Y_i &= \beta_1 + \beta_2 X_{2i} + 0.10\,\beta_2 X_{3i} + u_i \\ &= \beta_1 + \beta_2 X_i + u_i \end{aligned}$$

where $X_i = X_{2i} + 0.1X_{3i}$. Once we obtain $\hat{\beta}_2$, we can estimate $\hat{\beta}_3$ from the postulated relationship between β_2 and β_3.

How does one obtain a priori information? It could come from previous empirical work in which the collinearity problem happens to be less serious or from the relevant theory

[28] O. J. Blanchard, Comment, *Journal of Business and Economic Statistics,* vol. 5, 1967, pp. 449–451. The quote is reproduced from Peter Kennedy, *A Guide to Econometrics,* 4th ed., MIT Press, Cambridge, Mass., 1998, p. 190.

[29] For an interesting discussion on this, see J. Conlisk, "When Collinearity Is Desirable," *Western Economic Journal,* vol. 9, 1971, pp. 393–407.

underlying the field of study. For example, in the Cobb–Douglas–type production function (7.9.1), if one expects constant returns to scale to prevail, then $(\beta_2 + \beta_3) = 1$, in which case we could run the regression (8.6.14), regressing the output-labor ratio on the capital-labor ratio. If there is collinearity between labor and capital, as generally is the case in most sample data, such a transformation may reduce or eliminate the collinearity problem. But a warning is in order here regarding imposing such a priori restrictions, ". . . since in general we will want to test economic theory's a priori predictions rather than simply impose them on data for which they may not be true."[30] However, we know from Section 8.6 how to test for the validity of such restrictions explicitly.

2. **Combining cross-sectional and time series data.** A variant of the extraneous or a priori information technique is the combination of cross-sectional and time series data, known as *pooling the data.* Suppose we want to study the demand for automobiles in the United States and assume we have time series data on the number of cars sold, average price of the car, and consumer income. Suppose also that

$$\ln Y_t = \beta_1 + \beta_2 \ln P_t + \beta_3 \ln I_t + u_t$$

where $Y =$ number of cars sold, $P =$ average price, $I =$ income, and $t =$ time. Our objective is to estimate the price elasticity, β_2, and income elasticity, β_3.

In time series data the price and income variables generally tend to be highly collinear. Therefore, if we run the preceding regression, we shall be faced with the usual multicollinearity problem. A way out of this has been suggested by Tobin.[31] He says that if we have cross-sectional data (for example, data generated by consumer panels, or budget studies conducted by various private and governmental agencies), we can obtain a fairly reliable estimate of the income elasticity β_3 because in such data, which are at a point in time, the prices do not vary much. Let the cross-sectionally estimated income elasticity be $\hat{\beta}_3$. Using this estimate, we may write the preceding time series regression as

$$Y_t^* = \beta_1 + \beta_2 \ln P_t + u_t$$

where $Y^* = \ln Y - \hat{\beta}_3 \ln I$, that is, Y^* represents that value of Y after removing from it the effect of income. We can now obtain an estimate of the price elasticity β_2 from the preceding regression.

Although it is an appealing technique, pooling the time series and cross-sectional data in the manner just suggested may create problems of interpretation, because we are assuming implicitly that the cross-sectionally estimated income elasticity is the same thing as that which would be obtained from a pure time series analysis.[32] Nonetheless, the technique has been used in many applications and is worthy of consideration in situations where the cross-sectional estimates do not vary substantially from one cross section to another. An example of this technique is provided in Exercise 10.26.

3. **Dropping a variable(s) and specification bias.** When faced with severe multicollinearity, one of the "simplest" things to do is to drop one of the collinear variables.

[30]Mark B. Stewart and Kenneth F. Wallis, *Introductory Econometrics,* 2d ed., John Wiley & Sons, A Halstead Press Book, New York, 1981, p. 154.

[31]J. Tobin, "A Statistical Demand Function for Food in the U.S.A.," *Journal of the Royal Statistical Society,* Ser. A, 1950, pp. 113–141.

[32]For a thorough discussion and application of the pooling technique, see Edwin Kuh, *Capital Stock Growth: A Micro-Econometric Approach*, North-Holland Publishing Company, Amsterdam, 1963, Chapters 5 and 6.

Thus, in our consumption–income–wealth illustration, when we drop the wealth variable, we obtain regression (10.6.4), which shows that, whereas in the original model the income variable was statistically insignificant, it is now "highly" significant.

But in dropping a variable from the model we may be committing a **specification bias** or **specification error.** Specification bias arises from incorrect specification of the model used in the analysis. Thus, if economic theory says that income and wealth should both be included in the model explaining the consumption expenditure, dropping the wealth variable would constitute specification bias.

Although we will discuss the topic of specification bias in Chapter 13, we caught a glimpse of it in Section 7.7. If, for example, the true model is

$$Y_i = \beta_1 + \beta_2 X_{2i} + \beta_3 X_{3i} + u_i$$

but we mistakenly fit the model

$$Y_i = b_1 + b_{12} X_{2i} + \hat{u}_i \tag{10.8.1}$$

then it can be shown that (see Appendix 13A.1)

$$E(b_{12}) = \beta_2 + \beta_3 b_{32} \tag{10.8.2}$$

where b_{32} = slope coefficient in the regression of X_3 on X_2. Therefore, it is obvious from Eq. (10.8.2) that b_{12} will be a biased estimate of β_2 as long as b_{32} is different from zero (it is assumed that β_3 is different from zero; otherwise there is no sense in including X_3 in the original model).[33] Of course, if b_{32} is zero, we have no multicollinearity problem to begin with. It is also clear from Eq. (10.8.2) that if both b_{32} and β_3 are positive (or both are negative), $E(b_{12})$ will be greater than β_2; hence, on the average b_{12} will overestimate β_2, leading to a positive bias. Similarly, if the product $b_{32}\beta_3$ is negative, on the average b_{12} will underestimate β_2, leading to a negative bias.

From the preceding discussion it is clear that dropping a variable from the model to alleviate the problem of multicollinearity may lead to the specification bias. Hence the remedy may be worse than the disease in some situations because, whereas multicollinearity may prevent precise estimation of the parameters of the model, omitting a variable may seriously mislead us as to the true values of the parameters. Recall that OLS estimators are BLUE despite near collinearity.

4. **Transformation of variables.** Suppose we have time series data on consumption expenditure, income, and wealth. One reason for high multicollinearity between income and wealth in such data is that over time both the variables tend to move in the same direction. One way of minimizing this dependence is to proceed as follows.

If the relation

$$Y_t = \beta_1 + \beta_2 X_{2t} + \beta_3 X_{3t} + u_t \tag{10.8.3}$$

holds at time t, it must also hold at time $t - 1$ because the origin of time is arbitrary anyway. Therefore, we have

$$Y_{t-1} = \beta_1 + \beta_2 X_{2,t-1} + \beta_3 X_{3,t-1} + u_{t-1} \tag{10.8.4}$$

If we subtract Eq. (10.8.4) from Eq. (10.8.3), we obtain

$$Y_t - Y_{t-1} = \beta_2(X_{2t} - X_{2,t-1}) + \beta_3(X_{3t} - X_{3,t-1}) + v_t \tag{10.8.5}$$

[33]Note further that if b_{32} does not approach zero as the sample size is increased indefinitely, then b_{12} will be not only biased but also inconsistent.

where $v_t = u_t - u_{t-1}$. Equation (10.8.5) is known as the **first difference form** because we run the regression not on the original variables but on the differences of successive values of the variables.

The first difference regression model often reduces the severity of multicollinearity because, although the levels of X_2 and X_3 may be highly correlated, there is no a priori reason to believe that their differences will also be highly correlated.

As we shall see in the chapters on **time series econometrics,** an incidental advantage of the first difference transformation is that it may make a nonstationary time series stationary. In those chapters we will see the importance of stationary time series. As noted in Chapter 1, loosely speaking, a time series, say, Y_t, is stationary if its mean and variance do not change systematically over time.

Another commonly used transformation in practice is the **ratio transformation.** Consider the model:

$$Y_t = \beta_1 + \beta_2 X_{2t} + \beta_3 X_{3t} + u_t \tag{10.8.6}$$

where Y is consumption expenditure in real dollars, X_2 is GDP, and X_3 is total population. Since GDP and population grow over time, they are likely to be correlated. One "solution" to this problem is to express the model on a per capita basis, that is, by dividing Eq. (10.8.4) by X_3, to obtain:

$$\frac{Y_t}{X_{3t}} = \beta_1\left(\frac{1}{X_{3t}}\right) + \beta_2\left(\frac{X_{2t}}{X_{3t}}\right) + \beta_3 + \left(\frac{u_t}{X_{3t}}\right) \tag{10.8.7}$$

Such a transformation may reduce collinearity in the original variables.

But the first difference or ratio transformations are not without problems. For instance, the error term v_t in Eq. (10.8.5) may not satisfy one of the assumptions of the classical linear regression model, namely, that the disturbances are serially uncorrelated. As we will see in Chapter 12, if the original disturbance term u_t is serially uncorrelated, the error term v_t obtained previously will in most cases be serially correlated. Therefore, the remedy may be worse than the disease. Moreover, there is a loss of one observation due to the differencing procedure, and therefore the degrees of freedom are reduced by one. In a small sample, this could be a factor one would wish at least to take into consideration. Furthermore, the first-differencing procedure may not be appropriate in cross-sectional data where there is no logical ordering of the observations.

Similarly, in the ratio model (10.8.7), the error term

$$\left(\frac{u_t}{X_{3t}}\right)$$

will be heteroscedastic, if the original error term u_t is homoscedastic, as we shall see in Chapter 11. Again, the remedy may be worse than the disease of collinearity.

In short, one should be careful in using the first difference or ratio method of transforming the data to resolve the problem of multicollinearity.

5. **Additional or new data.** Since multicollinearity is a sample feature, it is possible that in another sample involving the same variables collinearity may not be so serious as in the first sample. Sometimes simply increasing the size of the sample (if possible) may attenuate the collinearity problem. For example, in the three-variable model we saw that

$$\operatorname{var}(\hat{\beta}_2) = \frac{\sigma^2}{\sum x_{2i}^2 (1 - r_{23}^2)}$$

Now as the sample size increases, $\sum x_{2i}^2$ will generally increase. (Why?) Therefore, for any given r_{23}, the variance of $\hat{\beta}_2$ will decrease, thus decreasing the standard error, which will enable us to estimate β_2 more precisely.

As an illustration, consider the following regression of consumption expenditure Y on income X_2 and wealth X_3 based on 10 observations:[34]

$$\begin{aligned} \hat{Y}_i &= 24.377 + 0.8716X_{2i} - 0.0349X_{3i} \\ t &= (3.875) \quad (2.7726) \quad (-1.1595) \qquad R^2 = 0.9682 \end{aligned} \tag{10.8.8}$$

The wealth coefficient in this regression not only has the wrong sign but is also statistically insignificant at the 5 percent level. But when the sample size was increased to 40 observations (micronumerosity?), the following results were obtained:

$$\begin{aligned} \hat{Y}_i &= 2.0907 + 0.7299X_{2i} + 0.0605X_{3i} \\ t &= (0.8713) \quad (6.0014) \quad (2.0014) \qquad R^2 = 0.9672 \end{aligned} \tag{10.8.9}$$

Now the wealth coefficient not only has the correct sign but also is statistically significant at the 5 percent level.

Obtaining additional or "better" data is not always that easy, for as Judge et al. note:

> Unfortunately, economists seldom can obtain additional data without bearing large costs, much less choose the values of the explanatory variables they desire. In addition, when adding new variables in situations that are not controlled, we must be aware of adding observations that were generated by a process other than that associated with the original data set; that is, we must be sure that the economic structure associated with the new observations is the same as the original structure.[35]

6. **Reducing collinearity in polynomial regressions.** In Section 7.10 we discussed polynomial regression models. A special feature of these models is that the explanatory variable(s) appears with various powers. Thus, in the total cubic cost function involving the regression of total cost on output, (output)^2, and (output)^3, as in Eq. (7.10.4), the various output terms are going to be correlated, making it difficult to estimate the various slope coefficients precisely.[36] In practice though, it has been found that if the explanatory variable(s) is expressed in the deviation form (i.e., deviation from the mean value), multicollinearity is substantially reduced. But even then the problem may persist,[37] in which case one may want to consider techniques such as **orthogonal polynomials.**[38]

7. **Other methods of remedying multicollinearity.** Multivariate statistical techniques such as **factor analysis** and **principal components** or techniques such as **ridge regression** are often employed to "solve" the problem of multicollinearity. Unfortunately, these techniques are beyond the scope of this book, for they cannot be discussed competently without resorting to matrix algebra.[39]

[34] I am indebted to the late Albert Zucker for providing the results given in the following regressions.

[35] Judge et al., op. cit., p. 625. See also Section 10.9.

[36] As noted, since the relationship between X, X^2, and X^3 is nonlinear, polynomial regressions do not violate the assumption of no multicollinearity of the classical model, strictly speaking.

[37] See R. A. Bradley and S. S. Srivastava, "Correlation and Polynomial Regression," *American Statistician,* vol. 33, 1979, pp. 11–14.

[38] See Norman Draper and Harry Smith, *Applied Regression Analysis,* 2d ed., John Wiley & Sons, New York, 1981, pp. 266–274.

[39] A readable account of these techniques from an applied viewpoint can be found in Samprit Chatterjee and Bertram Price, *Regression Analysis by Example,* John Wiley & Sons, New York, 1977, Chapters 7 and 8. See also H. D. Vinod, "A Survey of Ridge Regression and Related Techniques for Improvements over Ordinary Least Squares," *Review of Economics and Statistics,* vol. 60, February 1978, pp. 121–131.

10.9 Is Multicollinearity Necessarily Bad? Maybe Not, If the Objective Is Prediction Only

It has been said that if the sole purpose of regression analysis is prediction or forecasting, then multicollinearity is not a serious problem because the higher the R^2, the better the prediction.[40] But this may be so "... as long as the values of the explanatory variables for which predictions are desired obey the same near-exact linear dependencies as the original design [data] matrix X."[41] Thus, if in an estimated regression it was found that $X_2 = 2X_3$ approximately, then in a future sample used to forecast Y, X_2 should also be approximately equal to $2X_3$, a condition difficult to meet in practice (see footnote 35), in which case prediction will become increasingly uncertain.[42] Moreover, if the objective of the analysis is not only prediction but also reliable estimation of the parameters, serious multicollinearity will be a problem because we have seen that it leads to large standard errors of the estimators.

In one situation, however, multicollinearity may not pose a serious problem. This is the case when R^2 is high and the regression coefficients are individually significant as revealed by the higher t values. Yet, multicollinearity diagnostics, say, the condition index, indicate that there is serious collinearity in the data. When can such a situation arise? As Johnston notes:

> This can arise if individual coefficients happen to be numerically well in excess of the true value, so that the effect still shows up in spite of the inflated standard error and/or because the true value itself is so large that even an estimate on the downside still shows up as significant.[43]

10.10 An Extended Example: The Longley Data

We conclude this chapter by analyzing the data collected by Longley.[44] Although originally collected to assess the computational accuracy of least-squares estimates in several computer programs, the Longley data have become the workhorse to illustrate several econometric problems, including multicollinearity. The data are reproduced in Table 10.8. The data are time series for the years 1947–1962 and pertain to Y = number of people employed, in thousands; X_1 = GNP implicit price deflator; X_2 = GNP, millions of dollars; X_3 = number of people unemployed in thousands, X_4 = number of people in the armed forces, X_5 = noninstitutionalized population over 14 years of age; and X_6 = year, equal to 1 in 1947, 2 in 1948, and 16 in 1962.

[40]See R. C. Geary, "Some Results about Relations between Stochastic Variables: A Discussion Document," *Review of International Statistical Institute*, vol. 31, 1963, pp. 163–181.

[41]Judge et al., op. cit., p. 619. You will also find on this page proof of why, despite collinearity, one can obtain better mean predictions if the existing collinearity structure also continues in the future samples.

[42]For an excellent discussion, see E. Malinvaud, *Statistical Methods of Econometrics*, 2d ed., North-Holland Publishing Company, Amsterdam, 1970, pp. 220–221.

[43]J. Johnston, *Econometric Methods*, 3d ed., McGraw-Hill, New York, 1984, p. 249.

[44]J. Longley, "An Appraisal of Least-Squares Programs from the Point of the User," *Journal of the American Statistical Association*, vol. 62, 1967, pp. 819–841.

TABLE 10.8
Longley Data

Source: J. Longley, "An Appraisal of Least-Squares Programs from the Point of the User," *Journal of the American Statistical Association*, vol. 62, 1967, pp. 819–841.

Observation	Y	X_1	X_2	X_3	X_4	X_5	Time
1947	60,323	830	234,289	2,356	1,590	107,608	1
1948	61,122	885	259,426	2,325	1,456	108,632	2
1949	60,171	882	258,054	3,682	1,616	109,773	3
1950	61,187	895	284,599	3,351	1,650	110,929	4
1951	63,221	962	328,975	2,099	3,099	112,075	5
1952	63,639	981	346,999	1,932	3,594	113,270	6
1953	64,989	990	365,385	1,870	3,547	115,094	7
1954	63,761	1,000	363,112	3,578	3,350	116,219	8
1955	66,019	1,012	397,469	2,904	3,048	117,388	9
1956	67,857	1,046	419,180	2,822	2,857	118,734	10
1957	68,169	1,084	442,769	2,936	2,798	120,445	11
1958	66,513	1,108	444,546	4,681	2,637	121,950	12
1959	68,655	1,126	482,704	3,813	2,552	123,366	13
1960	69,564	1,142	502,601	3,931	2,514	125,368	14
1961	69,331	1,157	518,173	4,806	2,572	127,852	15
1962	70,551	1,169	554,894	4,007	2,827	130,081	16

Assume that our objective is to predict Y on the basis of the six X variables. Using *EViews6*, we obtain the following regression results:

Dependent Variable: Y
Sample: 1947–1962

Variable	Coefficient	Std. Error	*t*-Statistic	Prob.
C	-3482259.	890420.4	-3.910803	0.0036
X_1	15.06187	84.91493	0.177376	0.8631
X_2	-0.035819	0.033491	-1.069516	0.3127
X_3	-2.020230	0.488400	-4.136427	0.0025
X_4	-1.033227	0.214274	-4.821985	0.0009
X_5	-0.051104	0.226073	-0.226051	0.8262
X_6	1829.151	455.4785	4.015890	0.0030

R-squared	0.995479	Mean dependent var.	65317.00
Adjusted *R*-squared	0.992465	S.D. dependent var.	3511.968
S.E. of regression	304.8541	Akaike info criterion	14.57718
Sum squared resid.	836424.1	Schwarz criterion	14.91519
Log likelihood	-109.6174	*F*-statistic	330.2853
Durbin-Watson stat.	2.559488	Prob(*F*-statistic)	0.000000

A glance at these results would suggest that we have the collinearity problem, for the R^2 value is very high, but quite a few variables are statistically insignificant (X_1, X_2, and X_5), a classic symptom of multicollinearity. To shed more light on this, we show in Table 10.9 the intercorrelations among the six regressors.

This table gives what is called the **correlation matrix.** In this table the entries on the main diagonal (those running from the upper left-hand corner to the lower right-hand corner) give the correlation of one variable with itself, which is always 1 by definition, and the entries off the main diagonal are the pair-wise correlations among the X variables. If you take the first row of this table, this gives the correlation of X_1 with the other X variables.

TABLE 10.9
Intercorrelations

	X_1	X_2	X_3	X_4	X_5	X_6
X_1	1.000000	0.991589	0.620633	0.464744	0.979163	0.991149
X_2	0.991589	1.000000	0.604261	0.446437	0.991090	0.995273
X_3	0.620633	0.604261	1.000000	−0.177421	0.686552	0.668257
X_4	0.464744	0.446437	−0.177421	1.000000	0.364416	0.417245
X_5	0.979163	0.991090	0.686552	0.364416	1.000000	0.993953
X_6	0.991149	0.995273	0.668257	0.417245	0.993953	1.000000

For example, 0.991589 is the correlation between X_1 and X_2, 0.620633 is the correlation between X_1 and X_3, and so on.

As you can see, several of these pair-wise correlations are quite high, suggesting that there may be a severe collinearity problem. Of course, remember the warning given earlier that such pair-wise correlations may be a sufficient but not a necessary condition for the existence of multicollinearity.

To shed further light on the nature of the multicollinearity problem, let us run the auxiliary regressions, that is the regression of each X variable on the remaining X variables. To save space, we will present only the R^2 values obtained from these regressions, which are given in Table 10.10. Since the R^2 values in the auxiliary regressions are very high (with the possible exception of the regression of X_4) on the remaining X variables, it seems that we do have a serious collinearity problem. The same information is obtained from the tolerance factors. As noted previously, the closer the tolerance factor is to zero, the greater is the evidence of collinearity.

Applying Klein's rule of thumb, we see that the R^2 values obtained from the auxiliary regressions exceed the overall R^2 value (that is, the one obtained from the regression of Y on all the X variables) of 0.9954 in 3 out of 6 auxiliary regressions, again suggesting that indeed the Longley data are plagued by the multicollinearity problem. Incidentally, applying the F test given in Eq. (10.7.3) the reader should verify that the R^2 values given in the preceding tables are all statistically significantly different from zero.

We noted earlier that the OLS estimators and their standard errors are sensitive to small changes in the data. In Exercise 10.32 the reader is asked to rerun the regression of Y on all the six X variables but drop the last data observations, that is, run the regression for the period 1947–1961. You will see how the regression results change by dropping just a single year's observations.

Now that we have established that we have the multicollinearity problem, what "remedial" actions can we take? Let us reconsider our original model. First of all, we could express GNP not in nominal terms, but in real terms, which we can do by dividing nominal GNP by the implicit price deflator. Second, since noninstitutional population over 14 years of age grows over time because of natural population growth, it will be highly correlated with time, the variable X_6 in our model. Therefore, instead of keeping both these variables, we will keep the variable X_5 and drop X_6. Third, there is no compelling reason to include X_3,

TABLE 10.10
R^2 Values from the Auxiliary Regressions

Dependent Variable	R^2 Value	Tolerance (TOL) = 1 − R^2
X_1	0.9926	0.0074
X_2	0.9994	0.0006
X_3	0.9702	0.0298
X_4	0.7213	0.2787
X_5	0.9970	0.0030
X_6	0.9986	0.0014

the number of people unemployed; perhaps the unemployment rate would have been a better measure of labor market conditions. But we have no data on the latter. So, we will drop the variable X_3. Making these changes, we obtain the following regression results (RGNP = real GNP):[45]

Dependent Variable: Y
Sample: 1947–1962

Variable	Coefficient	Std. Error	*t*-Statistic	Prob.
C	65720.37	10624.81	6.185558	0.0000
RGNP	9.736496	1.791552	5.434671	0.0002
X_4	-0.687966	0.322238	-2.134965	0.0541
X_5	-0.299537	0.141761	-2.112965	0.0562

R-squared	0.981404	Mean dependent var.	65317.00
Adjusted *R*-squared	0.976755	S.D. dependent var.	3511.968
S.E. of regression	535.4492	Akaike info criterion	15.61641
Sum squared resid.	3440470.	Schwarz criterion	15.80955
Log likelihood	-120.9313	*F*-statistic	211.0972
Durbin-Watson stat.	1.654069	Prob(*F*-statistic)	0.000000

Although the R^2 value has declined slightly compared with the original R^2, it is still very high. Now all the estimated coefficients are significant and the signs of the coefficients make economic sense.

We leave it for the reader to devise alternative models and see how the results change. Also keep in mind the warning sounded earlier about using the ratio method of transforming the data to alleviate the problem of collinearity. We will revisit this question in Chapter 11.

Summary and Conclusions

1. One of the assumptions of the classical linear regression model is that there is no multicollinearity among the explanatory variables, the *X*'s. Broadly interpreted, multicollinearity refers to the situation where there is either an exact or approximately exact linear relationship among the *X* variables.
2. The consequences of multicollinearity are as follows: If there is perfect collinearity among the *X*'s, their regression coefficients are indeterminate and their standard errors are not defined. If collinearity is high but not perfect, estimation of regression coefficients is possible but their standard errors tend to be large. As a result, the population values of the coefficients cannot be estimated precisely. However, if the objective is to estimate linear combinations of these coefficients, *the estimable functions,* this can be done even in the presence of perfect multicollinearity.
3. Although there are no sure methods of detecting collinearity, there are several indicators of it, which are as follows:
   (*a*) The clearest sign of multicollinearity is when R^2 is very high but none of the regression coefficients is statistically significant on the basis of the conventional *t* test. This case is, of course, extreme.

[45]The coefficient of correlation between X_5 and X_6 is about 0.9939, a very high correlation indeed.

(*b*) In models involving just two explanatory variables, a fairly good idea of collinearity can be obtained by examining the zero-order, or simple, correlation coefficient between the two variables. If this correlation is high, multicollinearity is generally the culprit.

(*c*) However, the zero-order correlation coefficients can be misleading in models involving more than two X variables since it is possible to have low zero-order correlations and yet find high multicollinearity. In situations like these, one may need to examine the partial correlation coefficients.

(*d*) If R^2 is high but the partial correlations are low, multicollinearity is a possibility. Here one or more variables may be superfluous. But if R^2 is high and the partial correlations are also high, multicollinearity may not be readily detectable. Also, as pointed out by C. Robert Wichers, Krishna Kumar, John O'Hagan, and Brendan McCabe, there are some statistical problems with the partial correlation test suggested by Farrar and Glauber.

(*e*) Therefore, one may regress each of the X_i variables on the remaining X variables in the model and find out the corresponding coefficients of determination R_i^2. A high R_i^2 would suggest that X_i is highly correlated with the rest of the X's. Thus, one may drop that X_i from the model, provided it does not lead to serious specification bias.

4. Detection of multicollinearity is half the battle. The other half is concerned with how to get rid of the problem. Again there are no sure methods, only a few rules of thumb. Some of these rules are as follows: (1) using extraneous or prior information, (2) combining cross-sectional and time series data, (3) omitting a highly collinear variable, (4) transforming data, and (5) obtaining additional or new data. Of course, which of these rules will work in practice will depend on the nature of the data and severity of the collinearity problem.
5. We noted the role of multicollinearity in prediction and pointed out that unless the collinearity structure continues in the future sample it is hazardous to use the estimated regression that has been plagued by multicollinearity for the purpose of forecasting.
6. Although multicollinearity has received extensive (some would say excessive) attention in the literature, an equally important problem encountered in empirical research is that of micronumerosity, smallness of sample size. According to Goldberger, "When a research article complains about multicollinearity, readers ought to see whether the complaints would be convincing if "micronumerosity" were substituted for "multicollinearity."[46] He suggests that the reader ought to decide how small n, the number of observations, is before deciding that one has a small-sample problem, just as one decides how high an R^2 value is in an auxiliary regression before declaring that the collinearity problem is very severe.

EXERCISES

Questions

10.1. In the k-variable linear regression model there are k normal equations to estimate the k unknowns. These normal equations are given in **Appendix C.** Assume that X_k is a perfect linear combination of the remaining X variables. How would you show that in this case it is impossible to estimate the k regression coefficients?

[46] Goldberger, op. cit., p. 250.

TABLE 10.11

Y	X_2	X_3
−10	1	1
−8	2	3
−6	3	5
−4	4	7
−2	5	9
0	6	11
2	7	13
4	8	15
6	9	17
8	10	19
10	11	21

10.2. Consider the set of hypothetical data in Table 10.11. Suppose you want to fit the model

$$Y_i = \beta_1 + \beta_2 X_{2i} + \beta_3 X_{3i} + u_i$$

to the data.

a. Can you estimate the three unknowns? Why or why not?

b. If not, what linear functions of these parameters, the estimable functions, can you estimate? Show the necessary calculations.

10.3. Refer to the child mortality example discussed in Chapter 8 (Example 8.1). The example there involved the regression of the child mortality (CM) rate on per capita GNP (PGNP) and female literacy rate (FLR). Now suppose we add the variable, total fertility rate (TFR). This gives the following regression results.

Dependent Variable: CM

Variable	Coefficient	Std. Error	*t*-Statistic	Prob.
C	168.3067	32.89165	5.117003	0.0000
PGNP	-0.005511	0.001878	-2.934275	0.0047
FLR	-1.768029	0.248017	-7.128663	0.0000
TFR	12.86864	4.190533	3.070883	0.0032

R-squared	0.747372	Mean dependent var.	141.5000
Adjusted *R*-squared	0.734740	S.D. dependent var.	75.97807
S.E. of regression	39.13127	Akaike info criterion	10.23218
Sum squared resid.	91875.38	Schwarz criterion	10.36711
Log likelihood	-323.4298	*F*-statistic	59.16767
Durbin-Watson stat.	2.170318	Prob(*F*-statistic)	0.000000

a. Compare these regression results with those given in Eq. (8.1.4). What changes do you see? How do you account for them?

b. Is it worth adding the variable TFR to the model? Why?

c. Since all the individual t coefficients are statistically significant, can we say that we do not have a collinearity problem in the present case?

10.4. If the relation $\lambda_1 X_{1i} + \lambda_2 X_{2i} + \lambda_3 X_{3i} = 0$ holds true for all values of λ_1, λ_2, and λ_3, estimate $r_{12.3}$, $r_{13.2}$, and $r_{23.1}$. Also find $R^2_{1.23}$, $R^2_{2.13}$, and $R^2_{3.12}$. What is the degree of multicollinearity in this situation? *Note:* $R^2_{1.23}$ is the coefficient of determination in the regression of Y on X_2 and X_3. Other R^2 values are to be interpreted similarly.

10.5. Consider the following model:

$$Y_t = \beta_1 + \beta_2 X_t + \beta_3 X_{t-1} + \beta_4 X_{t-2} + \beta_5 X_{t-3} + \beta_6 X_{t-4} + u_t$$

where Y = consumption, X = income, and t = time. The preceding model postulates that consumption expenditure at time t is a function not only of income at time t but also of income through previous periods. Thus, consumption expenditure in the first quarter of 2000 is a function of income in that quarter and the four quarters of 1999. Such models are called **distributed lag models,** and we shall discuss them in a later chapter.

a. Would you expect multicollinearity in such models and why?

b. If collinearity is expected, how would you resolve the problem?

10.6. Consider the illustrative example of Section 10.6 (Example 10.1). How would you reconcile the difference in the marginal propensity to consume obtained from Eqs. (10.6.1) and (10.6.4)?

10.7. In data involving economic time series such as GNP, money supply, prices, income, unemployment, etc., multicollinearity is usually suspected. Why?

10.8. Suppose in the model

$$Y_i = \beta_1 + \beta_2 X_{2i} + \beta_3 X_{3i} + u_i$$

that r_{23}, the coefficient of correlation between X_2 and X_3, is zero. Therefore, someone suggests that you run the following regressions:

$$Y_i = \alpha_1 + \alpha_2 X_{2i} + u_{1i}$$

$$Y_i = \gamma_1 + \gamma_3 X_{3i} + u_{2i}$$

a. Will $\hat{\alpha}_2 = \hat{\beta}_2$ and $\hat{\gamma}_3 = \hat{\beta}_3$? Why?

b. Will $\hat{\beta}_1$ equal $\hat{\alpha}_1$ or $\hat{\gamma}_1$ or some combination thereof?

c. Will $\text{var}(\hat{\beta}_2) = \text{var}(\hat{\alpha}_2)$ and $\text{var}(\hat{\beta}_3) = \text{var}(\hat{\gamma}_3)$?

10.9. Refer to the illustrative example of Chapter 7 where we fitted the Cobb–Douglas production function to the manufacturing sector of all 50 states and the District of Columbia for 2005. The results of the regression given in Eq. (7.9.4) show that both the labor and capital coefficients are individually statistically significant.

a. Find out whether the variables labor and capital are highly correlated.

b. If your answer to (*a*) is affirmative, would you drop, say, the labor variable from the model and regress the output variable on capital input only?

c. If you do so, what kind of specification bias is committed? Find out the nature of this bias.

10.10. Refer to Example 7.4. For this problem the correlation matrix is as follows:

	X_i	X_i^2	X_i^3
X_i	1	0.9742	0.9284
X_i^2		1.0	0.9872
X_i^3			1.0

a. "Since the zero-order correlations are very high, there must be serious multicollinearity." Comment.

b. Would you drop variables X_i^2 and X_i^3 from the model?

c. If you drop them, what will happen to the value of the coefficient of X_i?

10.11. *Stepwise regression.* In deciding on the "best" set of explanatory variables for a regression model, researchers often follow the method of stepwise regression. In this method one proceeds either by introducing the X variables one at a time (**stepwise forward regression**) or by including all the possible X variables in one multiple regression and rejecting them one at a time (**stepwise backward regression**). The decision to add or drop a variable is usually made on the basis of the contribution of that variable to the ESS, as judged by the F test. Knowing what you do now about multicollinearity, would you recommend either procedure? Why or why not?*

10.12. State *with reason* whether the following statements are true, false, or uncertain:

a. Despite perfect multicollinearity, OLS estimators are BLUE.

b. In cases of high multicollinearity, it is not possible to assess the individual significance of one or more partial regression coefficients.

c. If an auxiliary regression shows that a particular R_i^2 is high, there is definite evidence of high collinearity.

d. High pair-wise correlations do not suggest that there is high multicollinearity.

e. Multicollinearity is harmless if the objective of the analysis is prediction only.

f. Ceteris paribus, the higher the VIF is, the larger the variances of OLS estimators.

g. The tolerance (TOL) is a better measure of multicollinearity than the VIF.

h. You will not obtain a high R^2 value in a multiple regression if all the partial slope coefficients are *individually* statistically insignificant on the basis of the usual t test.

i. In the regression of Y on X_2 and X_3, suppose there is little variability in the values of X_3. This would increase $\operatorname{var}(\hat{\beta}_3)$. In the extreme, if all X_3 are identical, $\operatorname{var}(\hat{\beta}_3)$ is infinite.

10.13. *a.* Show that if $r_{1i} = 0$ for $i = 2, 3, \ldots, k$ then

$$R_{1.23\ldots k} = 0$$

b. What is the importance of this finding for the regression of variable $X_1 (= Y)$ on $X_2, X_3, \ldots, X_k$?

10.14. Suppose all the zero-order correlation coefficients of $X_1 (= Y), X_2, \ldots, X_k$ are equal to r.

a. What is the value of $R^2_{1.23\ldots k}$?

b. What are the values of the first-order correlation coefficients?

10.15. In matrix notation it can be shown (see **Appendix C) that

$$\hat{\boldsymbol{\beta}} = (\mathbf{X}'\mathbf{X})^{-1}\mathbf{X}'\mathbf{y}$$

a. What happens to $\hat{\boldsymbol{\beta}}$ when there is perfect collinearity among the X's?

b. How would you know if perfect collinearity exists?

*See if your reasoning agrees with that of Arthur S. Goldberger and D. B. Jochems, "Note on Stepwise Least-Squares," *Journal of the American Statistical Association*, vol. 56, March 1961, pp. 105–110.

**Optional.

*10.16. Using matrix notation, it can be shown

$$\text{var–cov}\,(\hat{\boldsymbol{\beta}}) = \sigma^2(\mathbf{X}'\mathbf{X})^{-1}$$

What happens to this var–cov matrix:

a. When there is perfect multicollinearity?

b. When collinearity is high but not perfect?

*10.17. Consider the following **correlation matrix:**

$$\mathbf{R} = \begin{array}{c} \\ X_2 \\ X_3 \\ \\ X_k \end{array} \begin{array}{c} \begin{array}{cccc} X_2 & X_3 & \cdots & X_k \end{array} \\ \begin{bmatrix} 1 & r_{23} & \cdots & r_{2k} \\ r_{32} & 1 & \cdots & r_{3k} \\ \cdots & \cdots & & \cdots \\ r_{k2} & r_{k3} & \cdots & 1 \end{bmatrix} \end{array}$$

Describe how you would find out from the correlation matrix whether (*a*) there is perfect collinearity, (*b*) there is less than perfect collinearity, and (*c*) the *X*'s are uncorrelated.

Hint: You may use $|\mathbf{R}|$ to answer these questions, where $|\mathbf{R}|$ denotes the determinant of **R**.

*10.18. *Orthogonal explanatory variables.* Suppose in the model

$$Y_i = \beta_1 + \beta_2 X_{2i} + \beta_3 X_{3i} + \cdots + \beta_k X_{ki} + u_i$$

X_2 to X_k are all uncorrelated. Such variables are called **orthogonal variables.** If this is the case:

a. What will be the structure of the $(\mathbf{X}'\mathbf{X})$ matrix?

b. How would you obtain $\hat{\boldsymbol{\beta}} = (\mathbf{X}'\mathbf{X})^{-1}\mathbf{X}'\mathbf{y}$?

c. What will be the nature of the var–cov matrix of $\hat{\boldsymbol{\beta}}$?

d. Suppose you have run the regression and afterward you want to introduce another orthogonal variable, say, X_{k+1} into the model. Do you have to recompute all the previous coefficients $\hat{\beta}_1$ to $\hat{\beta}_k$? Why or why not?

10.19. Consider the following model:

$$\text{GNP}_t = \beta_1 + \beta_2 \text{M}_t + \beta_3 \text{M}_{t-1} + \beta_4(\text{M}_t - \text{M}_{t-1}) + u_t$$

where GNP_t = GNP at time *t*, M_t = money supply at time *t*, M_{t-1} = money supply at time $(t-1)$, and $(\text{M}_t - \text{M}_{t-1})$ = change in the money supply between time *t* and time $(t-1)$. This model thus postulates that the level of GNP at time *t* is a function of the money supply at time *t* and time $(t-1)$ as well as the change in the money supply between these time periods.

a. Assuming you have the data to estimate the preceding model, would you succeed in estimating all the coefficients of this model? Why or why not?

b. If not, what coefficients can be estimated?

c. Suppose that the $\beta_3 \text{M}_{t-1}$ terms were absent from the model. Would your answer to (*a*) be the same?

d. Repeat (*c*), assuming that the terms $\beta_2 \text{M}_t$ were absent from the model.

*Optional.

10.20. Show that Eqs. (7.4.7) and (7.4.8) can also be expressed as

$$\hat{\beta}_2 = \frac{\left(\sum y_i x_{2i}\right)\left(\sum x_{3i}^2\right) - \left(\sum y_i x_{3i}\right)\left(\sum x_{2i} x_{3i}\right)}{\left(\sum x_{2i}^2\right)\left(\sum x_{3i}^2\right)\left(1 - r_{23}^2\right)}$$

$$\hat{\beta}_3 = \frac{\left(\sum y_i x_{3i}\right)\left(\sum x_{2i}^2\right) - \left(\sum y_i x_{2i}\right)\left(\sum x_{2i} x_{3i}\right)}{\left(\sum x_{2i}^2\right)\left(\sum x_{3i}^2\right)\left(1 - r_{23}^2\right)}$$

where r_{23} is the coefficient of correlation between X_2 and X_3.

10.21. Using Eqs. (7.4.12) and (7.4.15), show that when there is perfect collinearity, the variances of $\hat{\beta}_2$ and $\hat{\beta}_3$ are infinite.

10.22. Verify that the standard errors of the sums of the slope coefficients estimated from Eqs. (10.5.6) and (10.5.7) are, respectively, 0.1549 and 0.1825. (See Section 10.5.)

10.23. For the k-variable regression model, it can be shown that the variance of the kth $(k = 2, 3, \ldots, K)$ partial regression coefficient given in Eq. (7.5.6) can also be expressed as*

$$\operatorname{var}(\hat{\beta}_k) = \frac{1}{n-k}\frac{\sigma_y^2}{\sigma_k^2}\left(\frac{1-R^2}{1-R_k^2}\right)$$

where σ_y^2 = variance of Y, σ_k^2 = variance of the kth explanatory variable, $R_k^2 = R^2$ from the regression of X_k on the remaining X variables, and R^2 = coefficient of determination from the multiple regression, that is, regression of Y on all the X variables.

a. Other things the same, if σ_k^2 increases, what happens to $\operatorname{var}(\hat{\beta}_k)$? What are the implications for the multicollinearity problem?

b. What happens to the preceding formula when collinearity is perfect?

c. True or false: "The variance of $\hat{\beta}_k$ decreases as R^2 rises, so that the effect of a high R_k^2 can be offset by a high R^2."

10.24. From the annual data for the U.S. manufacturing sector for 1899–1922, Dougherty obtained the following regression results:†

$$\widehat{\log Y} = 2.81 - 0.53 \log K + 0.91 \log L + 0.047t$$
$$\text{se} = (1.38) \quad (0.34) \quad (0.14) \quad (0.021) \qquad (1)$$
$$R^2 = 0.97 \qquad F = 189.8$$

where Y = index of real output, K = index of real capital input, L = index of real labor input, t = time or trend.

Using the same data, he also obtained the following regression:

$$\widehat{\log (Y/L)} = -0.11 + 0.11 \log (K/L) + 0.006t$$
$$\text{se} = (0.03) \quad (0.15) \quad (0.006) \qquad (2)$$
$$R^2 = 0.65 \qquad F = 19.5$$

*This formula is given by R. Stone, "The Analysis of Market Demand," *Journal of the Royal Statistical Society*, vol. B7, 1945, p. 297. Also recall Eq. (7.5.6). For further discussion, see Peter Kennedy, *A Guide to Econometrics*, 2d ed., The MIT Press, Cambridge, Mass., 1985, p. 156.

†Christopher Dougherty, *Introduction to Econometrics*, Oxford University Press, New York, 1992, pp. 159–160.

a. Is there multicollinearity in regression (1)? How do you know?

b. In regression (1), what is the a priori sign of log K? Do the results conform to this expectation? Why or why not?

c. How would you justify the functional form of regression (1)? (*Hint:* Cobb–Douglas production function.)

d. Interpret regression (1). What is the role of the trend variable in this regression?

e. What is the logic behind estimating regression (2)?

f. If there was multicollinearity in regression (1), has that been reduced by regression (2)? How do you know?

g. If regression (2) is a restricted version of regression (1), what restriction is imposed by the author? (*Hint:* returns to scale.) How do you know if this restriction is valid? Which test do you use? Show all your calculations.

h. Are the R^2 values of the two regressions comparable? Why or why not? How would you make them comparable, if they are not comparable in the present form?

10.25. Critically evaluate the following statements:

a. "In fact, multicollinearity is not a modeling error. It is a condition of deficient data."*

b. "If it is not feasible to obtain more data, then one must accept the fact that the data one has contain a limited amount of information and must simplify the model accordingly. Trying to estimate models that are too complicated is one of the most common mistakes among inexperienced applied econometricians."**

c. "It is common for researchers to claim that multicollinearity is at work whenever their hypothesized signs are not found in the regression results, when variables that they know *a priori* to be important have insignificant t values, or when various regression results are changed substantively whenever an explanatory variable is deleted. Unfortunately, none of these conditions is either necessary or sufficient for the existence of collinearity, and furthermore none provides any useful suggestions as to what kind of extra information might be required to solve the estimation problem they present."†

d. ". . . any time series regression containing more than four independent variables results in garbage."‡

Empirical Exercises

10.26. Klein and Goldberger attempted to fit the following regression model to the U.S. economy:

$$Y_i = \beta_1 + \beta_2 X_{2i} + \beta_3 X_{3i} + \beta_4 X_{4i} + u_i$$

where Y = consumption, X_2 = wage income, X_3 = nonwage, nonfarm income, and X_4 = farm income. But since X_2, X_3, and X_4 are expected to be highly collinear, they obtained estimates of β_3 and β_4 from cross-sectional analysis as follows:

*Samprit Chatterjee, Ali S. Hadi, and Bertram Price, *Regression Analysis by Example,* 3d ed., John Wiley & Sons, New York, 2000, p. 226.

**Russel Davidson and James G. MacKinnon, *Estimation and Inference in Econometrics,* Oxford University Press, New York, 1993, p. 186.

†Peter Kennedy, *A Guide to Econometrics,* 4th ed., MIT Press, Cambridge, Mass., 1998, p. 187.

‡This quote attributed to the late econometrician Zvi Griliches, is obtained from Ernst R. Berndt, *The Practice of Econometrics: Classic and Contemporary,* Addison Wesley, Reading, Mass., 1991, p. 224.

TABLE 10.12

Source: L. R. Klein and A. S. Goldberger, *An Economic Model of the United States, 1929–1952*, North Holland Publishing Company, Amsterdam, 1964, p. 131.

Year	Y	X_2	X_3	X_4	Year	Y	X_2	X_3	X_4
1936	62.8	43.41	17.10	3.96	1946	95.7	76.73	28.26	9.76
1937	65.0	46.44	18.65	5.48	1947	98.3	75.91	27.91	9.31
1938	63.9	44.35	17.09	4.37	1948	100.3	77.62	32.30	9.85
1939	67.5	47.82	19.28	4.51	1949	103.2	78.01	31.39	7.21
1940	71.3	51.02	23.24	4.88	1950	108.9	83.57	35.61	7.39
1941	76.6	58.71	28.11	6.37	1951	108.5	90.59	37.58	7.98
1945*	86.3	87.69	30.29	8.96	1952	111.4	95.47	35.17	7.42

*The data for the war years 1942–1944 are missing. The data for other years are billions of 1939 dollars.

$\beta_3 = 0.75\beta_2$ and $\beta_4 = 0.625\beta_2$. Using these estimates, they reformulated their consumption function as follows:

$$Y_i = \beta_1 + \beta_2(X_{2i} + 0.75X_{3i} + 0.625X_{4i}) + u_i = \beta_1 + \beta_2 Z_i + u_i$$

where $Z_i = X_{2i} + 0.75X_{3i} + 0.625X_{4i}$.

a. Fit the modified model to the data in Table 10.12 and obtain estimates of β_1 to β_4.

b. How would you interpret the variable Z?

10.27. Table 10.13 gives data on imports, GDP, and the Consumer Price Index (CPI) for the United States over the period 1975–2005. You are asked to consider the following model:

$$\ln \text{Imports}_t = \beta_1 + \beta_2 \ln \text{GDP}_t + \beta_3 \ln \text{CPI}_t + u_t$$

a. Estimate the parameters of this model using the data given in the table.

b. Do you suspect that there is multicollinearity in the data?

c. Regress: (1) $\ln \text{Imports}_t = A_1 + A_2 \ln \text{GDP}_t$

(2) $\ln \text{Imports}_t = B_1 + B_2 \ln \text{CPI}_t$

(3) $\ln \text{GDP}_t = C_1 + C_2 \ln \text{CPI}_t$

On the basis of these regressions, what can you say about the nature of multicollinearity in the data?

TABLE 10.13

U.S. Imports, GDP, and CPI, 1975–2005 (For all urban consumers; 1982–84 = 100, except as noted)

Source: Department of Labor, Bureau of Labor Statistics.

Year	CPI	GDP	Imports	Year	CPI	GDP	Imports
1975	53.8	1,638.3	98185	1991	136.2	5,995.9	491020
1976	56.9	1,825.3	124228	1992	140.3	6,337.7	536528
1977	60.6	2,030.9	151907	1993	144.5	6,657.4	589394
1978	65.2	2,294.7	176002	1994	148.2	7,072.2	668690
1979	72.6	2,563.3	212007	1995	152.4	7,397.7	749374
1980	82.4	2,789.5	249750	1996	156.9	7,816.9	803113
1981	90.9	3,128.4	265067	1997	160.5	8,304.3	876470
1982	96.5	3,225.0	247642	1998	163.0	8,747.0	917103
1983	99.6	3,536.7	268901	1999	166.6	9,268.4	1029980
1984	103.9	3,933.2	332418	2000	172.2	9,817.0	1224408
1985	107.6	4,220.3	338088	2001	177.1	10,128.0	1145900
1986	109.6	4,462.8	368425	2002	179.9	10,469.6	1164720
1987	113.6	4,739.5	409765	2003	184.0	10,960.8	1260717
1988	118.3	5,103.8	447189	2004	188.9	11,712.5	1472926
1989	124.0	5,484.4	477665	2005	195.3	12,455.8	1677371
1990	130.7	5,803.1	498438				

d. Suppose there is multicollinearity in the data but $\hat{\beta}_2$ and $\hat{\beta}_3$ are individually significant at the 5 percent level and the overall F test is also significant. In this case should we worry about the collinearity problem?

10.28. Refer to Exercise 7.19 about the demand function for chicken in the United States.

a. Using the log–linear, or double-log, model, estimate the various auxiliary regressions. How many are there?

b. From these auxiliary regressions, how do you decide which regressor(s) is highly collinear? Which test do you use? Show the details of your calculations.

c. If there is significant collinearity in the data, which variable(s) would you drop to reduce the severity of the collinearity problem? If you do that, what econometric problems do you face?

d. Do you have any suggestions, other than dropping variables, to ameliorate the collinearity problem? Explain.

10.29. Table 10.14 gives data on new passenger cars sold in the United States as a function of several variables.

a. Develop a suitable linear or log–linear model to estimate a demand function for automobiles in the United States.

b. If you decide to include all the regressors given in the table as explanatory variables, do you expect to face the multicollinearity problem? Why?

c. If you do expect to face the multicollinearity problem, how will you go about resolving the problem? State your assumptions clearly and show all the calculations explicitly.

10.30. To assess the feasibility of a guaranteed annual wage (negative income tax), the Rand Corporation conducted a study to assess the response of labor supply (average

TABLE 10.14
Passenger Car Data

Source: *Business Statistics, 1986,* A Supplement to the *Current Survey of Business,* U.S. Department of Commerce.

Year	Y	X_2	X_3	X_4	X_5	X_6
1971	10,227	112.0	121.3	776.8	4.89	79,367
1972	10,872	111.0	125.3	839.6	4.55	82,153
1973	11,350	111.1	133.1	949.8	7.38	85,064
1974	8,775	117.5	147.7	1,038.4	8.61	86,794
1975	8,539	127.6	161.2	1,142.8	6.16	85,846
1976	9,994	135.7	170.5	1,252.6	5.22	88,752
1977	11,046	142.9	181.5	1,379.3	5.50	92,017
1978	11,164	153.8	195.3	1,551.2	7.78	96,048
1979	10,559	166.0	217.7	1,729.3	10.25	98,824
1980	8,979	179.3	247.0	1,918.0	11.28	99,303
1981	8,535	190.2	272.3	2,127.6	13.73	100,397
1982	7,980	197.6	286.6	2,261.4	11.20	99,526
1983	9,179	202.6	297.4	2,428.1	8.69	100,834
1984	10,394	208.5	307.6	2,670.6	9.65	105,005
1985	11,039	215.2	318.5	2,841.1	7.75	107,150
1986	11,450	224.4	323.4	3,022.1	6.31	109,597

Y = new passenger cars sold (thousands), seasonally unadjusted.
X_2 = new cars, Consumer Price Index, 1967 = 100, seasonally unadjusted.
X_3 = Consumer Price Index, all items, all urban consumers, 1967 = 100, seasonally unadjusted.
X_4 = the personal disposable income (PDI), billions of dollars, unadjusted for seasonal variation.
X_5 = the interest rate, percent, finance company paper placed directly.
X_6 = the employed civilian labor force (thousands), unadjusted for seasonal variation.

hours of work) to increasing hourly wages.* The data for this study were drawn from a national sample of 6,000 households with a male head earning less than $15,000 annually. The data were divided into 39 demographic groups for analysis. These data are given in Table 10.15. Because data for four demographic groups were missing for some variables, the data given in the table refer to only 35 demographic groups. The definitions of the various variables used in the analysis are given at the end of the table.

TABLE 10.15
Hours of Work and Other Data for 35 Groups

Source: D. H. Greenberg and M. Kosters, *Income Guarantees and the Working Poor,* Rand Corporation, R-579-OEO, December 1970.

Observation	Hours	Rate	ERSP	ERNO	NEIN	Assets	Age	DEP	School
1	2157	2.905	1121	291	380	7250	38.5	2.340	10.5
2	2174	2.970	1128	301	398	7744	39.3	2.335	10.5
3	2062	2.350	1214	326	185	3068	40.1	2.851	8.9
4	2111	2.511	1203	49	117	1632	22.4	1.159	11.5
5	2134	2.791	1013	594	730	12710	57.7	1.229	8.8
6	2185	3.040	1135	287	382	7706	38.6	2.602	10.7
7	2210	3.222	1100	295	474	9338	39.0	2.187	11.2
8	2105	2.493	1180	310	255	4730	39.9	2.616	9.3
9	2267	2.838	1298	252	431	8317	38.9	2.024	11.1
10	2205	2.356	885	264	373	6789	38.8	2.662	9.5
11	2121	2.922	1251	328	312	5907	39.8	2.287	10.3
12	2109	2.499	1207	347	271	5069	39.7	3.193	8.9
13	2108	2.796	1036	300	259	4614	38.2	2.040	9.2
14	2047	2.453	1213	297	139	1987	40.3	2.545	9.1
15	2174	3.582	1141	414	498	10239	40.0	2.064	11.7
16	2067	2.909	1805	290	239	4439	39.1	2.301	10.5
17	2159	2.511	1075	289	308	5621	39.3	2.486	9.5
18	2257	2.516	1093	176	392	7293	37.9	2.042	10.1
19	1985	1.423	553	381	146	1866	40.6	3.833	6.6
20	2184	3.636	1091	291	560	11240	39.1	2.328	11.6
21	2084	2.983	1327	331	296	5653	39.8	2.208	10.2
22	2051	2.573	1194	279	172	2806	40.0	2.362	9.1
23	2127	3.262	1226	314	408	8042	39.5	2.259	10.8
24	2102	3.234	1188	414	352	7557	39.8	2.019	10.7
25	2098	2.280	973	364	272	4400	40.6	2.661	8.4
26	2042	2.304	1085	328	140	1739	41.8	2.444	8.2
27	2181	2.912	1072	304	383	7340	39.0	2.337	10.2
28	2186	3.015	1122	30	352	7292	37.2	2.046	10.9
29	2188	3.010	990	366	374	7325	38.4	2.847	10.6
30	2077	1.901	350	209	95	1370	37.4	4.158	8.2
31	2196	3.009	947	294	342	6888	37.5	3.047	10.6
32	2093	1.899	342	311	120	1425	37.5	4.512	8.1
33	2173	2.959	1116	296	387	7625	39.2	2.342	10.5
34	2179	2.971	1128	312	397	7779	39.4	2.341	10.5
35	2200	2.980	1126	204	393	7885	39.2	2.341	10.6

Notes: Hours = average hours worked during the year.
Rate = average hourly wage (dollars).
ERSP = average yearly earnings of spouse (dollars).
ERNO = average yearly earnings of other family members (dollars).
NEIN = average yearly nonearned income.
Assets = average family asset holdings (bank account, etc.) (dollars).
Age = average age of respondent.
Dep = average number of dependents.
School = average highest grade of school completed.

*D. H. Greenberg and M. Kosters, *Income Guarantees and the Working Poor,* Rand Corporation, R-579-OEO, December 1970.

a. Regress average hours worked during the year on the variables given in the table and interpret your regression.

b. Is there evidence of multicollinearity in the data? How do you know?

c. Compute the variance inflation factors (VIF) and TOL measures for the various regressors.

d. If there is the multicollinearity problem, what remedial action, if any, would you take?

e. What does this study tell about the feasibility of a negative income tax?

10.31. Table 10.16 gives data on the crime rate in 47 states in the United States for 1960. Try to develop a suitable model to explain the crime rate in relation to the 14 socioeconomic variables given in the table. Pay particular attention to the collinearity problem in developing your model.

10.32. Refer to the Longley data given in Section 10.10. Repeat the regression given in the table there by omitting the data for 1962; that is, run the regression for the period 1947–1961. Compare the two regressions. What general conclusion can you draw from this exercise?

10.33. *Updated Longley data.* We have extended the data given in Section 10.10 to include observations from 1959–2005. The new data are in Table 10.17. The data pertain to $Y =$ number of people employed, in thousands; $X_1 =$ GNP implicit price deflator; $X_2 =$ GNP, millions of dollars; $X_3 =$ number of people unemployed in thousands; $X_4 =$ number of people in the armed forces in thousands; $X_5 =$ noninstitutionalized population over 16 years of age; and $X_6 =$ year, equal to 1 in 1959, 2 in 1960, and 47 in 2005.

a. Create scatterplots as suggested in the chapter to assess the relationships between the independent variables. Are there any strong relationships? Do they seem linear?

b. Create a correlation matrix. Which variables seem to be the most related to each other, not including the dependent variable?

c. Run a standard OLS regression to predict the number of people employed in thousands. Do the coefficients on the independent variables behave as you would expect?

d. Based on the above results, do you believe these data suffer from multicollinearity?

*10.34. As cheese ages, several chemical processes take place that determine the taste of the final product. The data given in Table 10.18 pertain to concentrations of various chemicals in a sample of 30 mature cheddar cheeses and subjective measures of taste for each sample. The variables acetic and H_2S are the natural logarithm of concentration of acetic acid and hydrogen sulfide, respectively. The variable lactic has not been log-transformed.

a. Draw a scatterplot of the four variables.

b. Perform a bivariate regression of taste on acetic and H_2S and interpret your results.

c. Perform a bivariate regression of taste on lactic and H_2S, and interpret the results.

d. Perform a multiple regression of taste on acetic, H_2S, and lactic. Interpret your results.

e. Knowing what you know about multicollinearity, how would you decide among these regressions?

f. What overall conclusions can you draw from your analysis?

*Optional.

TABLE 10.16 U.S. Crime Data for 47 States in 1960

Observation	R	Age	S	ED	EX_0	EX_1	LF	M	N	NW	U_1	U_2	W	X
1	79.1	151	1	91	58	56	510	950	33	301	108	41	394	261
2	163.5	143	0	113	103	95	583	1012	13	102	96	36	557	194
3	57.8	142	1	89	45	44	533	969	18	219	94	33	318	250
4	196.9	136	0	121	149	141	577	994	157	80	102	39	673	167
5	123.4	141	0	121	109	101	591	985	18	30	91	20	578	174
6	68.2	121	0	110	118	115	547	964	25	44	84	29	689	126
7	96.3	127	1	111	82	79	519	982	4	139	97	38	620	168
8	155.5	131	1	109	115	109	542	969	50	179	79	35	472	206
9	85.6	157	1	90	65	62	553	955	39	286	81	28	421	239
10	70.5	140	0	118	71	68	632	1029	7	15	100	24	526	174
11	167.4	124	0	105	121	116	580	966	101	106	77	35	657	170
12	84.9	134	0	108	75	71	595	972	47	59	83	31	580	172
13	51.1	128	0	113	67	60	624	972	28	10	77	25	507	206
14	66.4	135	0	117	62	61	595	986	22	46	77	27	529	190
15	79.8	152	1	87	57	53	530	986	30	72	92	43	405	264
16	94.6	142	1	88	81	77	497	956	33	321	116	47	427	247
17	53.9	143	0	110	66	63	537	977	10	6	114	35	487	166
18	92.9	135	1	104	123	115	537	978	31	170	89	34	631	165
19	75.0	130	0	116	128	128	536	934	51	24	78	34	627	135
20	122.5	125	0	108	113	105	567	985	78	94	130	58	626	166
21	74.2	126	0	108	74	67	602	984	34	12	102	33	557	195
22	43.9	157	1	89	47	44	512	962	22	423	97	34	288	276
23	121.6	132	0	96	87	83	564	953	43	92	83	32	513	227
24	96.8	131	0	116	78	73	574	1038	7	36	142	42	540	176
25	52.3	130	0	116	63	57	641	984	14	26	70	21	486	196
26	199.3	131	0	121	160	143	631	1071	3	77	102	41	674	152
27	34.2	135	0	109	69	71	540	965	6	4	80	22	564	139
28	121.6	152	0	112	82	76	571	1018	10	79	103	28	537	215
29	104.3	119	0	107	166	157	521	938	168	89	92	36	637	154
30	69.6	166	1	89	58	54	521	973	46	254	72	26	396	237
31	37.3	140	0	93	55	54	535	1045	6	20	135	40	453	200
32	75.4	125	0	109	90	81	586	964	97	82	105	43	617	163
33	107.2	147	1	104	63	64	560	972	23	95	76	24	462	233
34	92.3	126	0	118	97	97	542	990	18	21	102	35	589	166
35	65.3	123	0	102	97	87	526	948	113	76	124	50	572	158
36	127.2	150	0	100	109	98	531	964	9	24	87	38	559	153
37	83.1	177	1	87	58	56	638	974	24	349	76	28	382	254
38	56.6	133	0	104	51	47	599	1024	7	40	99	27	425	225
39	82.6	149	1	88	61	54	515	953	36	165	86	35	395	251
40	115.1	145	1	104	82	74	560	981	96	126	88	31	488	228
41	88.0	148	0	122	72	66	601	998	9	19	84	20	590	144
42	54.2	141	0	109	56	54	523	968	4	2	107	37	489	170
43	82.3	162	1	99	75	70	522	996	40	208	73	27	496	224
44	103.0	136	0	121	95	96	574	1012	29	36	111	37	622	162
45	45.5	139	1	88	46	41	480	968	19	49	135	53	457	249
46	50.8	126	0	104	106	97	599	989	40	24	78	25	593	171
47	84.9	130	0	121	90	91	623	1049	3	22	113	40	588	160

Source: W. Vandaele, "Participation in Illegitimate Activities: Erlich Revisted," in A. Blumstein, J. Cohen, and D. Nagin, eds., *Deterrence and Incapacitation,* National Academy of Sciences, 1978, pp. 270–335.

Definitions of variables:

R = crime rate, number of offenses reported to police per million population.
Age = number of males of age 14–24 per 1,000 population.
S = indicator variable for southern states (0 = no, 1 = yes).
ED = mean number of years of schooling times 10 for persons age 25 or older.
EX_0 = 1960 per capita expenditure on police by state and local government.
EX_1 = 1959 per capita expenditure on police by state and local government.
LF = labor force participation rate per 1,000 civilian urban males age 14–24.
M = number of males per 1,000 females.
N = state population size in hundred thousands.
NW = number of nonwhites per 1,000 population.
U_1 = unemployment rate of urban males per 1,000 of age 14–24.
U_2 = unemployment rate of urban males per 1,000 of age 35–39.
W = median value of transferable goods and assets or family income in tens of dollars.
X = the number of families per 1,000 earnings ½ the median income.
Observation = state (47 states for the year 1960).

TABLE 10.17
Updated Longley Data, 1959–2005

Source: Department of Labor, Bureau of Labor Statistics and http://siadapp.dmdc.osd.mil/personnel/MILITARY/Miltop.htm.

Observation	Y	X_1	X_2	X_3	X_4	X_5	X_6
1959	64,630	82.908	509,300	3,740	2552	120,287	1
1960	65,778	84.074	529,500	3,852	2514	121,836	2
1961	65,746	85.015	548,200	4,714	2573	123,404	3
1962	66,702	86.186	589,700	3,911	2827	124,864	4
1963	67,762	87.103	622,200	4,070	2737	127,274	5
1964	69,305	88.438	668,500	3,786	2738	129,427	6
1965	71,088	90.055	724,400	3,366	2722	131,541	7
1966	72,895	92.624	792,900	2,875	3123	133,650	8
1967	74,372	95.491	838,000	2,975	3446	135,905	9
1968	75,920	99.56	916,100	2,817	3535	138,171	10
1969	77,902	104.504	990,700	2,832	3506	140,461	11
1970	78,678	110.046	1,044,900	4,093	3188	143,070	12
1971	79,367	115.549	1,134,700	5,016	2816	145,826	13
1972	82,153	120.556	1,246,800	4,882	2449	148,592	14
1973	85,064	127.307	1,395,300	4,365	2327	151,476	15
1974	86,794	138.82	1,515,500	5,156	2229	154,378	16
1975	85,846	151.857	1,651,300	7,929	2180	157,344	17
1976	88,752	160.68	1,842,100	7,406	2144	160,319	18
1977	92,017	170.884	2,051,200	6,991	2133	163,377	19
1978	96,048	182.863	2,316,300	6,202	2117	166,422	20
1979	98,824	198.077	2,595,300	6,137	2088	169,440	21
1980	99,303	216.073	2,823,700	7,637	2102	172,437	22
1981	100,397	236.385	3,161,400	8,273	2142	174,929	23
1982	99,526	250.798	3,291,500	10,678	2179	177,176	24
1983	100,834	260.68	3,573,800	10,717	2199	179,234	25
1984	105,005	270.496	3,969,500	8,539	2219	181,192	26
1985	107,150	278.759	4,246,800	8,312	2234	183,174	27
1986	109,597	284.895	4,480,600	8,237	2244	185,284	28
1987	112,440	292.691	4,757,400	7,425	2257	187,419	29
1988	114,968	302.68	5,127,400	6,701	2224	189,233	30
1989	117,342	314.179	5,510,600	6,528	2208	190,862	31
1990	118,793	326.357	5,837,900	7,047	2167	192,644	32
1991	117,718	337.747	6,026,300	8,628	2118	194,936	33
1992	118,492	345.477	6,367,400	9,613	1966	197,205	34
1993	120,259	353.516	6,689,300	8,940	1760	199,622	35
1994	123,060	361.026	7,098,400	7,996	1673	201,970	36
1995	124,900	368.444	7,433,400	7,404	1579	204,420	37
1996	126,708	375.429	7,851,900	7,236	1502	207,087	38
1997	129,558	381.663	8,337,300	6,739	1457	209,846	39
1998	131,463	385.881	8,768,300	6,210	1423	212,638	40
1999	133,488	391.452	9,302,200	5,880	1380	215,404	41
2000	136,891	399.986	9,855,900	5,692	1405	218,061	42
2001	136,933	409.582	10,171,600	6,801	1412	220,800	43
2002	136,485	416.704	10,500,200	8,378	1425	223,532	44
2003	137,736	425.553	11,017,600	8,774	1423	226,223	45
2004	139,252	437.795	11,762,100	8,149	1411	228,892	46
2005	141,730	451.946	12,502,400	7,591	1378	231,552	47

TABLE 10.18
Chemicals in Cheeses

Source: http://lib.stat.cmu.edu/DASL/Datafiles/Cheese.html.

Obs.	Taste	Acetic	H_2S	Lactic
1	12.30000	4.543000	3.135000	0.860000
2	20.90000	5.159000	5.043000	1.530000
3	39.00000	5.366000	5.438000	1.570000
4	47.90000	5.759000	7.496000	1.810000
5	5.600000	4.663000	3.807000	0.990000
6	25.90000	5.697000	7.601000	1.090000
7	37.30000	5.892000	8.726000	1.290000
8	21.90000	6.078000	7.966000	1.780000
9	18.10000	4.898000	3.850000	1.290000
10	21.00000	5.242000	4.174000	1.580000
11	34.90000	5.740000	6.142000	1.680000
12	57.20000	6.446000	7.908000	1.900000
13	0.700000	4.477000	2.996000	1.060000
14	25.90000	5.236000	4.942000	1.300000
15	54.90000	6.151000	6.752000	1.520000
16	40.90000	3.365000	9.588000	1.740000
17	15.90000	4.787000	3.912000	1.160000
18	6.400000	5.142000	4.700000	1.490000
19	18.00000	5.247000	6.174000	1.630000
20	38.90000	5.438000	9.064000	1.990000
21	14.00000	4.564000	4.949000	1.150000
22	15.20000	5.298000	5.220000	1.330000
23	32.00000	5.455000	9.242000	1.440000
24	56.70000	5.855000	10.19900	2.010000
25	16.80000	5.366000	3.664000	1.310000
26	11.60000	6.043000	3.219000	1.460000
27	26.50000	6.458000	6.962000	1.720000
28	0.700000	5.328000	3.912000	1.250000
29	13.40000	5.802000	6.685000	1.080000
30	5.500000	6.176000	4.787000	1.250000

Chapter 11

Heteroscedasticity: What Happens If the Error Variance Is Nonconstant?

An important assumption of the classical linear regression model (Assumption 4) is that the disturbances u_i appearing in the population regression function are homoscedastic; that is, they all have the same variance. In this chapter we examine the validity of this assumption and find out what happens if this assumption is not fulfilled. As in Chapter 10, we seek answers to the following questions:

1. What is the nature of heteroscedasticity?
2. What are its consequences?
3. How does one detect it?
4. What are the remedial measures?

11.1 The Nature of Heteroscedasticity

As noted in Chapter 3, one of the important assumptions of the classical linear regression model is that the variance of each disturbance term u_i, conditional on the chosen values of the explanatory variables, is some constant number equal to σ^2. This is the assumption of **homoscedasticity,** or *equal* (homo) *spread* (scedasticity), that is, *equal variance.* Symbolically,

$$E(u_i^2) = \sigma^2 \quad i = 1, 2, \ldots, n \tag{11.1.1}$$

Diagrammatically, in the two-variable regression model homoscedasticity can be shown as in Figure 3.4, which, for convenience, is reproduced as Figure 11.1. As Figure 11.1 shows, the conditional variance of Y_i (which is equal to that of u_i), conditional upon the given X_i, remains the same regardless of the values taken by the variable X.

In contrast, consider Figure 11.2, which shows that the conditional variance of Y_i increases as X increases. Here, the variances of Y_i are not the same. Hence, there is heteroscedasticity. Symbolically,

$$E(u_i^2) = \sigma_i^2 \tag{11.1.2}$$

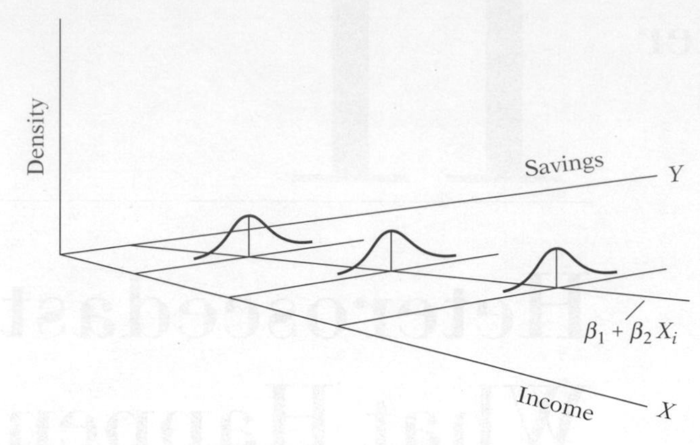

FIGURE 11.1 Homoscedastic disturbances.

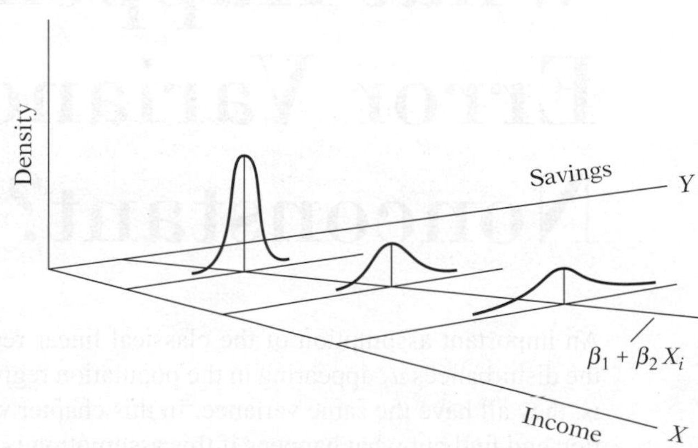

FIGURE 11.2 Heteroscedastic disturbances.

Notice the subscript of σ^2, which reminds us that the conditional variances of u_i ($=$ conditional variances of Y_i) are no longer constant.

To make the difference between homoscedasticity and heteroscedasticity clear, assume that in the two-variable model $Y_i = \beta_1 + \beta_2 X_i + u_i$, Y represents savings and X represents income. Figures 11.1 and 11.2 show that as income increases, savings on the average also increase. But in Figure 11.1 the variance of savings remains the same at all levels of income, whereas in Figure 11.2 it increases with income. It seems that in Figure 11.2 the higher-income families on the average save more than the lower-income families, but there is also more variability in their savings.

There are several reasons why the variances of u_i may be variable, some of which are as follows.[1]

1. Following the *error-learning models,* as people learn, their errors of behavior become smaller over time or the number of errors becomes more consistent. In this case, σ_i^2 is expected to decrease. As an example, consider Figure 11.3, which relates the number of typing errors made in a given time period on a test to the hours put in typing practice. As Figure 11.3 shows, as the number of hours of typing practice increases, the average number of typing errors as well as their variances decreases.

2. As incomes grow, people have more *discretionary income*[2] and hence more scope for choice about the disposition of their income. Hence, σ_i^2 is likely to increase with

[1] See Stefan Valavanis, *Econometrics*, McGraw-Hill, New York, 1959, p. 48.

[2] As Valavanis puts it, "Income grows, and people now barely discern dollars whereas previously they discerned dimes," ibid., p. 48.

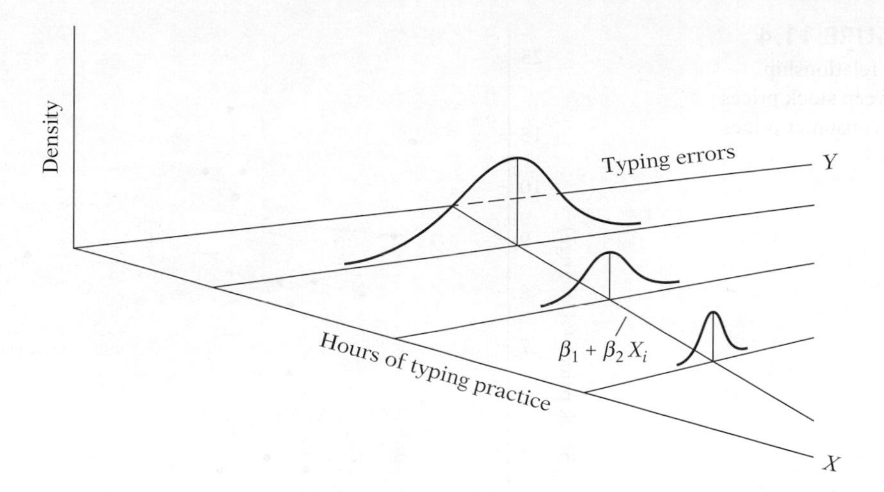

FIGURE 11.3 Illustration of heteroscedasticity.

income. Thus in the regression of savings on income one is likely to find σ_i^2 increasing with income (as in Figure 11.2) because people have more choices about their savings behavior. Similarly, companies with larger profits are generally expected to show greater variability in their dividend policies than companies with lower profits. Also, *growth-oriented* companies are likely to show more variability in their dividend payout ratio than established companies.

3. As data collecting techniques improve, σ_i^2 is likely to decrease. Thus, banks that have sophisticated data processing equipment are likely to commit fewer errors in the monthly or quarterly statements of their customers than banks without such facilities.

4. Heteroscedasticity can also arise as a result of the presence of **outliers.** An outlying observation, or outlier, is an observation that is much different (either very small or very large) in relation to the observations in the sample. More precisely, an outlier is an observation from a different population to that generating the remaining sample observations.[3] The inclusion or exclusion of such an observation, especially if the sample size is small, can substantially alter the results of regression analysis.

As an example, consider the scattergram given in Figure 11.4. Based on the data given in Table 11.9 in Exercise 11.22, this figure plots percent rate of change of stock prices (Y) and consumer prices (X) for the post–World War II period through 1969 for 20 countries. In this figure the observation on Y and X for Chile can be regarded as an outlier because the given Y and X values are much larger than for the rest of the countries. In situations such as this, it would be hard to maintain the assumption of homoscedasticity. In Exercise 11.22, you are asked to find out what happens to the regression results if the observations for Chile are dropped from the analysis.

5. Another source of heteroscedasticity arises from violating Assumption 9 of the classical linear regression model (CLRM), namely, that the regression model is correctly specified. Although we will discuss the topic of specification errors more fully in Chapter 13, very often what looks like heteroscedasticity may be due to the fact that some important variables are omitted from the model. Thus, in the demand function for a commodity, if we do not include the prices of commodities complementary to or competing with the commodity in question (the omitted variable bias), the residuals obtained from the regression may give the distinct impression that the error variance may not be constant. But if the omitted variables are included in the model, that impression may disappear.

[3] I am indebted to Michael McAleer for pointing this out to me.

FIGURE 11.4
The relationship between stock prices and consumer prices.

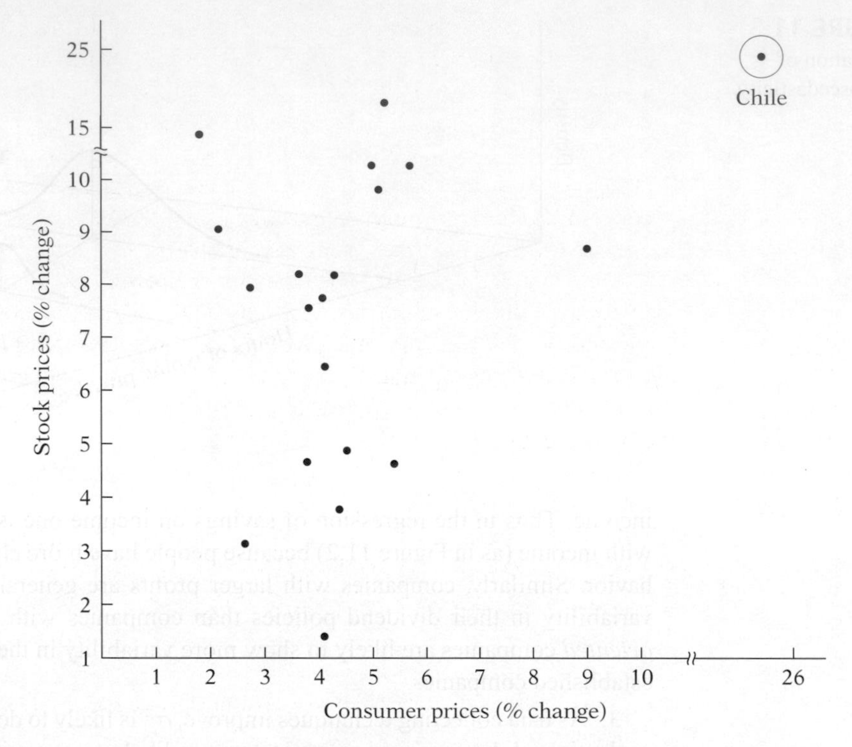

As a concrete example, recall our study of advertising impressions retained (Y) in relation to advertising expenditure (X). (See Exercise 8.32.) If you regress Y on X only and observe the residuals from this regression, you will see one pattern, but if you regress Y on X and X^2, you will see another pattern, which can be seen clearly from Figure 11.5. We have already seen that X^2 belongs in the model. (See Exercise 8.32.)

6. Another source of heteroscedasticity is **skewness** in the distribution of one or more regressors included in the model. Examples are economic variables such as income, wealth, and education. It is well known that the distribution of income and wealth in most societies is uneven, with the bulk of the income and wealth being owned by a few at the top.

7. Other sources of heteroscedasticity: As David Hendry notes, heteroscedasticity can also arise because of (1) incorrect data transformation (e.g., ratio or first difference transformations) and (2) incorrect functional form (e.g., linear versus log–linear models).[4]

FIGURE 11.5
Residuals from the regression of (*a*) impressions of advertising expenditure and (*b*) impression on Adexp and Adexp^2.

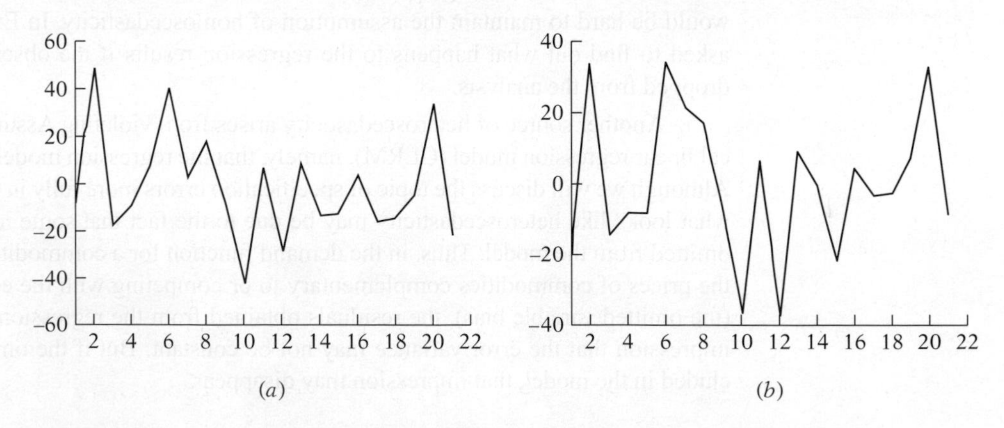

[4]David F. Hendry, *Dynamic Econometrics*, Oxford University Press, 1995, p. 45.

Note that the problem of heteroscedasticity is likely to be more common in cross-sectional than in time series data. In cross-sectional data, one usually deals with members of a population at a given point in time, such as individual consumers or their families, firms, industries, or geographical subdivisions such as state, country, city, etc. Moreover, these members may be of different sizes, such as small, medium, or large firms or low, medium, or high income. In time series data, on the other hand, the variables tend to be of similar orders of magnitude because one generally collects the data for the same entity over a period of time. Examples are gross national product (GNP), consumption expenditure, savings, or employment in the United States, say, for the period 1955–2005.

As an illustration of heteroscedasticity likely to be encountered in cross-sectional analysis, consider Table 11.1. This table gives data on compensation per employee in 10 nondurable goods manufacturing industries, classified by the employment size of the firm or the establishment for the year 1958. Also given in the table are average productivity figures for nine employment classes.

Although the industries differ in their output composition, Table 11.1 shows clearly that on the average large firms pay more than small firms. As an example, firms employing one to four employees paid on the average about $3,396, whereas those employing 1,000 to 2,499 employees on the average paid about $4,843. But notice that there is considerable variability in earnings among various employment classes as indicated by the estimated

TABLE 11.1 Compensation per Employee ($) in Nondurable Manufacturing Industries According to Employment Size of Establishment, 1958

	Employment Size (average number of employees)								
Industry	1–4	5–9	10–19	20–49	50–99	100–249	250–499	500–999	1,000–2,499
Food and kindred products	2,994	3,295	3,565	3,907	4,189	4,486	4,676	4,968	5,342
Tobacco products	1,721	2,057	3,336	3,320	2,980	2,848	3,072	2,969	3,822
Textile mill products	3,600	3,657	3,674	3,437	3,340	3,334	3,225	3,163	3,168
Apparel and related products	3,494	3,787	3,533	3,215	3,030	2,834	2,750	2,967	3,453
Paper and allied products	3,498	3,847	3,913	4,135	4,445	4,885	5,132	5,342	5,326
Printing and publishing	3,611	4,206	4,695	5,083	5,301	5,269	5,182	5,395	5,552
Chemicals and allied products	3,875	4,660	4,930	5,005	5,114	5,248	5,630	5,870	5,876
Petroleum and coal products	4,616	5,181	5,317	5,337	5,421	5,710	6,316	6,455	6,347
Rubber and plastic products	3,538	3,984	4,014	4,287	4,221	4,539	4,721	4,905	5,481
Leather and leather products	3,016	3,196	3,149	3,317	3,414	3,254	3,177	3,346	4,067
Average compensation	3,396	3,787	4,013	4,104	4,146	4,241	4,388	4,538	4,843
Standard deviation	742.2	851.4	727.8	805.06	929.9	1,080.6	1,241.2	1,307.7	1,110.7
Average productivity	9,355	8,584	7,962	8,275	8,389	9,418	9,795	10,281	11,750

Source: *The Census of Manufacturers*, U.S. Department of Commerce, 1958 (computed by author).

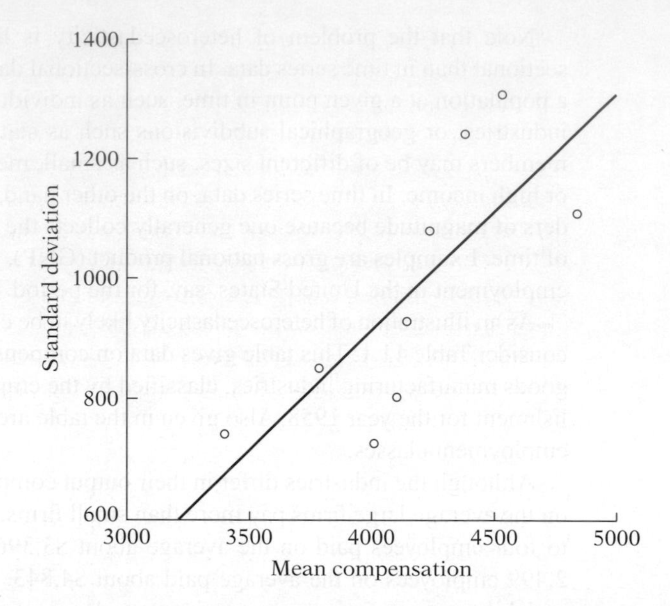

FIGURE 11.6 Standard deviation of compensation and mean compensation.

standard deviations of earnings. This can be seen also from Figure 11.6, which plots the standard deviation of compensation and average compensation in each employment class. As can be seen clearly, on average, the standard deviation of compensation increases with the average value of compensation.

11.2 OLS Estimation in the Presence of Heteroscedasticity

What happens to ordinary least squares (OLS) estimators and their variances if we introduce heteroscedasticity by letting $E(u_i^2) = \sigma_i^2$ but retain all other assumptions of the classical model? To answer this question, let us revert to the two-variable model:

$$Y_i = \beta_1 + \beta_2 X_i + u_i$$

Applying the usual formula, the OLS estimator of β_2 is

$$\hat{\beta}_2 = \frac{\sum x_i y_i}{\sum x_i^2}$$

$$= \frac{n \sum X_i Y_i - \sum X_i \sum Y_i}{n \sum X_i^2 - (\sum X_i)^2} \tag{11.2.1}$$

but its variance is now given by the following expression (see Appendix 11A, Section 11A.1):

$$\operatorname{var}(\hat{\beta}_2) = \frac{\sum x_i^2 \sigma_i^2}{\left(\sum x_i^2\right)^2} \tag{11.2.2}$$

which is obviously different from the usual variance formula obtained under the assumption of homoscedasticity, namely,

$$\operatorname{var}(\hat{\beta}_2) = \frac{\sigma^2}{\sum x_i^2} \tag{11.2.3}$$

Of course, if $\sigma_i^2 = \sigma^2$ for each i, the two formulas will be identical. (Why?)

Recall that $\hat{\beta}_2$ is best linear unbiased estimator (BLUE) if the assumptions of the classical model, including homoscedasticity, hold. Is it still BLUE when we drop only the homoscedasticity assumption and replace it with the assumption of heteroscedasticity? It is easy to prove that $\hat{\beta}_2$ is still linear and unbiased. As a matter of fact, as shown in Appendix 3A, Section 3A.2, to establish the unbiasedness of $\hat{\beta}_2$ it is not necessary that the disturbances (u_i) be homoscedastic. In fact, the variance of u_i, homoscedastic or heteroscedastic, plays no part in the determination of the unbiasedness property. Recall that in Appendix 3A, Section 3A.7, we showed that $\hat{\beta}_2$ is a consistent estimator under the assumptions of the classical linear regression model. Although we will not prove it, it can be shown that $\hat{\beta}_2$ is a consistent estimator despite heteroscedasticity; that is, as the sample size increases indefinitely, the estimated β_2 converges to its true value. Furthermore, it can also be shown that under certain conditions (called regularity conditions), $\hat{\beta}_2$ is *asymptotically normally distributed.* Of course, what we have said about $\hat{\beta}_2$ also holds true of other parameters of a multiple regression model.

Granted that $\hat{\beta}_2$ is still linear unbiased and consistent, is it "efficient" or "best"? That is, does it have minimum variance in the class of unbiased estimators? And is that minimum variance given by Eq. (11.2.2)? The answer is *no* to both the questions: $\hat{\beta}_2$ is no longer best and the minimum variance is not given by Eq. (11.2.2). Then what is BLUE in the presence of heteroscedasticity? The answer is given in the following section.

11.3 The Method of Generalized Least Squares (GLS)

Why is the usual OLS estimator of β_2 given in Eq. (11.2.1) not best, although it is still unbiased? Intuitively, we can see the reason from Table 11.1. As the table shows, there is considerable variability in the earnings between employment classes. If we were to regress per-employee compensation on the size of employment, we would like to make use of the knowledge that there is considerable interclass variability in earnings. Ideally, we would like to devise the estimating scheme in such a manner that observations coming from populations with greater variability are given less weight than those coming from populations with smaller variability. Examining Table 11.1, we would like to weight observations coming from employment classes 10–19 and 20–49 more heavily than those coming from employment classes like 5–9 and 250–499, for the former are more closely clustered around their mean values than the latter, thereby enabling us to estimate the population regression function (PRF) more accurately.

Unfortunately, the usual OLS method does not follow this strategy and therefore does not make use of the "information" contained in the unequal variability of the dependent variable Y, say, employee compensation of Table 11.1: It assigns equal weight or importance to each observation. But a method of estimation, known as **generalized least squares (GLS),** takes such information into account explicitly and is therefore capable of producing estimators that are BLUE. To see how this is accomplished, let us continue with the now-familiar two-variable model:

$$Y_i = \beta_1 + \beta_2 X_i + u_i \tag{11.3.1}$$

which for ease of algebraic manipulation we write as

$$Y_i = \beta_1 X_{0i} + \beta_2 X_i + u_i \tag{11.3.2}$$

where $X_{0i} = 1$ for each i. The reader can see that these two formulations are identical.

Now assume that the heteroscedastic variances σ_i^2 are *known*. Divide Eq. (11.3.2) through by σ_i to obtain

$$\frac{Y_i}{\sigma_i} = \beta_1\left(\frac{X_{0i}}{\sigma_i}\right) + \beta_2\left(\frac{X_i}{\sigma_i}\right) + \left(\frac{u_i}{\sigma_i}\right) \tag{11.3.3}$$

which for ease of exposition we write as

$$Y_i^* = \beta_1^* X_{0i}^* + \beta_2^* X_i^* + u_i^* \tag{11.3.4}$$

where the starred, or transformed, variables are the original variables divided by (the known) σ_i. We use the notation β_1^* and β_2^*, the parameters of the transformed model, to distinguish them from the usual OLS parameters β_1 and β_2.

What is the purpose of transforming the original model? To see this, notice the following feature of the transformed error term u_i^*:

$$\begin{aligned} \operatorname{var}(u_i^*) = E(u_i^*)^2 &= E\left(\frac{u_i}{\sigma_i}\right)^2 && \text{since } E(u_i^*) = 0 \\ &= \frac{1}{\sigma_i^2}E\left(u_i^2\right) && \text{since } \sigma_i^2 \text{ is known} \\ &= \frac{1}{\sigma_i^2}\left(\sigma_i^2\right) && \text{since } E\left(u_i^2\right) = \sigma_i^2 \\ &= 1 \end{aligned} \tag{11.3.5}$$

which is a constant. That is, the variance of the transformed disturbance term u_i^* is now homoscedastic. Since we are still retaining the other assumptions of the classical model, the finding that it is u^* that is homoscedastic suggests that if we apply OLS to the transformed model (11.3.3) it will produce estimators that are BLUE. In short, the estimated β_1^* and β_2^* are now BLUE and not the OLS estimators $\hat{\beta}_1$ and $\hat{\beta}_2$.

This procedure of transforming the original variables in such a way that the transformed variables satisfy the assumptions of the classical model and then applying OLS to them is known as the method of generalized least squares (GLS). *In short, GLS is OLS on the transformed variables that satisfy the standard least-squares assumptions.* The estimators thus obtained are known as **GLS estimators,** and it is these estimators that are BLUE.

The actual mechanics of estimating β_1^* and β_2^* are as follows. First, we write down the sample regression function (SRF) of Eq. (11.3.3)

$$\frac{Y_i}{\sigma_i} = \hat{\beta}_1^*\left(\frac{X_{0i}}{\sigma_i}\right) + \hat{\beta}_2^*\left(\frac{X_i}{\sigma_i}\right) + \left(\frac{\hat{u}_i}{\sigma_i}\right)$$

or

$$Y_i^* = \hat{\beta}_1^* X_{0i}^* + \hat{\beta}_2^* X_i^* + \hat{u}_i^* \tag{11.3.6}$$

Now, to obtain the GLS estimators, we minimize

$$\sum \hat{u}_i^{2*} = \sum (Y_i^* - \hat{\beta}_1^* X_{0i}^* - \hat{\beta}_2^* X_i^*)^2$$

that is,

$$\sum \left(\frac{\hat{u}_i}{\sigma_i}\right)^2 = \sum \left[\left(\frac{Y_i}{\sigma_i}\right) - \hat{\beta}_1^*\left(\frac{X_{0i}}{\sigma_i}\right) - \hat{\beta}_2^*\left(\frac{X_i}{\sigma_i}\right)\right]^2 \tag{11.3.7}$$

The actual mechanics of minimizing Eq. (11.3.7) follow the standard calculus techniques and are given in Appendix 11A, Section 11A.2. As shown there, the GLS estimator of β_2^* is

$$\hat{\beta}_2^* = \frac{\left(\sum w_i\right)\left(\sum w_i X_i Y_i\right) - \left(\sum w_i X_i\right)\left(\sum w_i Y_i\right)}{\left(\sum w_i\right)\left(\sum w_i X_i^2\right) - \left(\sum w_i X_i\right)^2} \tag{11.3.8}$$

and its variance is given by

$$\operatorname{var}(\hat{\beta}_2^*) = \frac{\sum w_i}{\left(\sum w_i\right)\left(\sum w_i X_i^2\right) - \left(\sum w_i X_i\right)^2} \tag{11.3.9}$$

where $w_i = 1/\sigma_i^2$.

Difference between OLS and GLS

Recall from Chapter 3 that in OLS we minimize

$$\sum \hat{u}_i^2 = \sum (Y_i - \hat{\beta}_1 - \hat{\beta}_2 X_i)^2 \tag{11.3.10}$$

but in GLS we minimize the expression (11.3.7), which can also be written as

$$\sum w_i \hat{u}_i^2 = \sum w_i (Y_i - \hat{\beta}_1^* X_{0i} - \hat{\beta}_2^* X_i)^2 \tag{11.3.11}$$

where $w_i = 1/\sigma_i^2$ (verify that Eq. [11.3.11] and Eq. [11.3.7] are identical).

Thus, in GLS we minimize a *weighted sum of residual squares* with $w_i = 1/\sigma_i^2$ acting as the weights, but in OLS we minimize an unweighted or (what amounts to the same thing) equally weighted residual sum of squares (RSS). As Eq. (11.3.7) shows, in GLS the weight assigned to each observation is inversely proportional to its σ_i, that is, observations coming from a population with larger σ_i will get relatively smaller weight and those from a population with smaller σ_i will get proportionately larger weight in minimizing the RSS (11.3.11). To see the difference between OLS and GLS clearly, consider the hypothetical scattergram given in Figure 11.7.

In the (unweighted) OLS, each $\hat{u}_i^2$ associated with points A, B, and C will receive the same weight in minimizing the RSS. Obviously, in this case the $\hat{u}_i^2$ associated with point C will dominate the RSS. But in GLS the extreme observation C will get relatively smaller weight than the other two observations. As noted earlier, this is the right strategy, for in estimating the population regression function (PRF) more reliably we would like to give more weight to observations that are closely clustered around their (population) mean than to those that are widely scattered about.

Since Eq. (11.3.11) minimizes a weighted RSS, it is appropriately known as **weighted least squares (WLS),** and the estimators thus obtained and given in Eqs. (11.3.8) and (11.3.9) are known as **WLS estimators.** But WLS is just a special case of the more general estimating technique, GLS. In the context of heteroscedasticity, one can treat the two terms WLS and GLS interchangeably. In later chapters we will come across other special cases of GLS.

In passing, note that if $w_i = w$, a constant for all i, $\hat{\beta}_2^*$ is identical with $\hat{\beta}_2$ and $\operatorname{var}(\hat{\beta}_2^*)$ is identical with the usual (i.e., homoscedastic) $\operatorname{var}(\hat{\beta}_2)$ given in Eq. (11.2.3), which should not be surprising. (Why?) (See Exercise 11.8.)

FIGURE 11.7 Hypothetical scattergram.

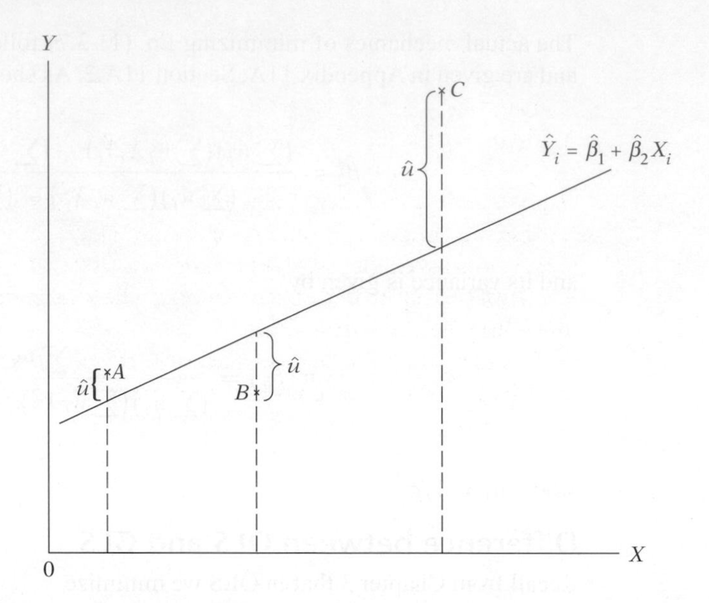

11.4 Consequences of Using OLS in the Presence of Heteroscedasticity

As we have seen, both $\hat{\beta}_2^*$ and $\hat{\beta}_2$ are (linear) unbiased estimators: In repeated sampling, on the average, $\hat{\beta}_2^*$ and $\hat{\beta}_2$ will equal the true β_2; that is, they are both unbiased estimators. But we know that it is $\hat{\beta}_2^*$ that is efficient, that is, has the smallest variance. What happens to our confidence interval, hypotheses testing, and other procedures if we continue to use the OLS estimator $\hat{\beta}_2$? We distinguish two cases.

OLS Estimation Allowing for Heteroscedasticity

Suppose we use $\hat{\beta}_2$ and use the variance formula given in Eq. (11.2.2), which takes into account heteroscedasticity explicitly. Using this variance, and assuming σ_i^2 are known, can we establish confidence intervals and test hypotheses with the usual t and F tests? The answer generally is no because it can be shown that $\text{var}(\hat{\beta}_2^*) \leq \text{var}(\hat{\beta}_2)$,[5] which means that confidence intervals based on the latter will be unnecessarily larger. As a result, the t and F tests are likely to give us inaccurate results in that $\text{var}(\hat{\beta}_2)$ is overly large and what appears to be a statistically insignificant coefficient (because the t value is smaller than what is appropriate) may in fact be significant if the correct confidence intervals were established on the basis of the GLS procedure.

OLS Estimation Disregarding Heteroscedasticity

The situation can become serious if we not only use $\hat{\beta}_2$ but also continue to use the usual (homoscedastic) variance formula given in Eq. (11.2.3) even if heteroscedasticity is present or suspected: Note that this is the more likely case of the two we discuss here, because running a standard OLS regression package and ignoring (or being ignorant of) heteroscedasticity will yield variance of $\hat{\beta}_2$ as given in Eq. (11.2.3). First of all, $\text{var}(\hat{\beta}_2)$ given in Eq. (11.2.3) is a *biased* estimator of $\text{var}(\hat{\beta}_2)$ given in Eq. (11.2.2), that is, on the

[5]A formal proof can be found in Phoebus J. Dhrymes, *Introductory Econometrics*, Springer-Verlag, New York, 1978, pp. 110–111. In passing, note that the loss of efficiency of $\hat{\beta}_2$ (i.e., by how much $\text{var}[\hat{\beta}_2]$ exceeds $\text{var}[\hat{\beta}_2^*]$) depends on the sample values of the X variables and the value of σ_i^2.

average it overestimates or underestimates the latter, and *in general* we cannot tell whether the bias is positive (overestimation) or negative (underestimation) because it depends on the nature of the relationship between σ_i^2 and the values taken by the explanatory variable X, as can be seen clearly from Eq. (11.2.2) (see Exercise 11.9). The bias arises from the fact that $\hat{\sigma}^2$, the conventional estimator of σ^2, namely, $\sum \hat{u}_i^2/(n-2)$ is no longer an unbiased estimator of the latter when heteroscedasticity is present (see Appendix 11A.3). As a result, we can no longer rely on the conventionally computed confidence intervals and the conventionally employed t and F tests.[6] **In short, if we persist in using the usual testing procedures despite heteroscedasticity, whatever conclusions we draw or inferences we make may be very misleading.**

To throw more light on this topic, we refer to a **Monte Carlo** study conducted by Davidson and MacKinnon.[7] They consider the following simple model, which in our notation is

$$Y_i = \beta_1 + \beta_2 X_i + u_i \tag{11.4.1}$$

They assume that $\beta_1 = 1$, $\beta_2 = 1$, and $u_i \sim N(0, X_i^\alpha)$. As the last expression shows, they assume that the error variance is heteroscedastic and is related to the value of the regressor X with power α. If, for example, $\alpha = 1$, the error variance is proportional to the value of X; if $\alpha = 2$, the error variance is proportional to the square of the value of X, and so on. In Section 11.6 we will consider the logic behind such a procedure. Based on 20,000 replications and allowing for various values for α, they obtain the standard errors of the two regression coefficients using OLS (see Eq. [11.2.3]), OLS allowing for heteroscedasticity (see Eq. [11.2.2]), and GLS (see Eq. [11.3.9]). We quote their results for selected values of α:

	Standard error of $\hat{\beta}_1$			Standard error of $\hat{\beta}_2$		
Value of α	OLS	OLS_{het}	GLS	OLS	OLS_{het}	GLS
0.5	0.164	0.134	0.110	0.285	0.277	0.243
1.0	0.142	0.101	0.048	0.246	0.247	0.173
2.0	0.116	0.074	0.0073	0.200	0.220	0.109
3.0	0.100	0.064	0.0013	0.173	0.206	0.056
4.0	0.089	0.059	0.0003	0.154	0.195	0.017

Note: OLS_{het} means OLS allowing for heteroscedasticity.

The most striking feature of these results is that OLS, with or without correction for heteroscedasticity, consistently overestimates the true standard error obtained by the (correct) GLS procedure, especially for large values of α, thus establishing the superiority of GLS. These results also show that if we do not use GLS and rely on OLS—allowing for or not allowing for heteroscedasticity—the picture is mixed. The usual OLS standard errors are either too large (for the intercept) or *generally* too small (for the slope coefficient) in relation to those obtained by OLS allowing for heteroscedasticity. The message is clear: In the presence of heteroscedasticity, use GLS. However, for reasons explained later in the chapter, in practice it is not always easy to apply GLS. Also, as we discuss later, unless heteroscedasticity is very severe, one may not abandon OLS in favor of GLS or WLS.

From the preceding discussion it is clear that heteroscedasticity is potentially a serious problem and the researcher needs to know whether it is present in a given situation. If its

[6]From Eq. (5.3.6) we know that the $100(1-\alpha)\%$ confidence interval for β_2 is $[\hat{\beta}_2 \pm t_{\alpha/2}\,\text{se}(\hat{\beta}_2)]$. But if $\text{se}(\hat{\beta}_2)$ cannot be estimated unbiasedly, what trust can we put in the conventionally computed confidence interval?

[7]Russell Davidson and James G. MacKinnon, *Estimation and Inference in Econometrics*, Oxford University Press, New York, 1993, pp. 549–550.

presence is detected, then one can take corrective action, such as using the weighted least-squares regression or some other technique. Before we turn to examining the various corrective procedures, however, we must first find out whether heteroscedasticity is present or likely to be present in a given case. This topic is discussed in the following section.

A Technical Note

Although we have stated that, in cases of heteroscedasticity, it is the GLS, not the OLS, that is BLUE, there are examples where OLS can be BLUE, despite heteroscedasticity.[8] But such examples are infrequent in practice.

11.5 Detection of Heteroscedasticity

As with multicollinearity, the important practical question is: How does one know that heteroscedasticity is present in a specific situation? Again, as in the case of multicollinearity, there are no hard-and-fast rules for detecting heteroscedasticity, only a few rules of thumb. But this situation is inevitable because σ_i^2 can be known only if we have the entire Y population corresponding to the chosen X's, such as the population shown in Table 2.1 or Table 11.1. But such data are an exception rather than the rule in most economic investigations. In this respect the econometrician differs from scientists in fields such as agriculture and biology, where researchers have a good deal of control over their subjects. More often than not, in economic studies there is only one sample Y value corresponding to a particular value of X. And there is no way one can know σ_i^2 from just one Y observation. Therefore, in most cases involving econometric investigations, heteroscedasticity may be a matter of intuition, educated guesswork, prior empirical experience, or sheer speculation.

With the preceding caveat in mind, let us examine some of the informal and formal methods of detecting heteroscedasticity. As the following discussion will reveal, most of these methods are based on the examination of the OLS residuals $\hat{u}_i$ since they are the ones we observe, and not the disturbances u_i. One hopes that they are good estimates of u_i, a hope that may be fulfilled if the sample size is fairly large.

Informal Methods

Nature of the Problem

Very often the nature of the problem under consideration suggests whether heteroscedasticity is likely to be encountered. For example, following the pioneering work of Prais and Houthakker on family budget studies, where they found that the residual variance around the regression of consumption on income increased with income, one now generally assumes that in similar surveys one can expect unequal variances among the disturbances.[9] As a matter of fact, in cross-sectional data involving heterogeneous units, heteroscedasticity may be the rule rather than the exception. Thus, in a cross-sectional analysis involving the investment expenditure in relation to sales, rate of interest, etc., heteroscedasticity is generally expected if small-, medium-, and large-size firms are sampled together.

[8]The reason for this is that the Gauss–Markov theorem provides the sufficient (but not necessary) condition for OLS to be efficient. The necessary and sufficient condition for OLS to be BLUE is given by **Kruskal's theorem.** But this topic is beyond the scope of this book. I am indebted to Michael McAleer for bringing this to my attention. For further details, see Denzil G. Fiebig, Michael McAleer, and Robert Bartels, "Properties of Ordinary Least Squares Estimators in Regression Models with Nonspherical Disturbances," *Journal of Econometrics*, vol. 54, No. 1–3, Oct.–Dec., 1992, pp. 321–334. For the mathematically inclined student, I discuss this topic further in **Appendix C,** using matrix algebra.

[9]S. J. Prais and H. S. Houthakker, *The Analysis of Family Budgets*, Cambridge University Press, New York, 1955.

As a matter of fact, we have already come across examples of this. In Chapter 2 we discussed the relationship between mean, or average, hourly wages in relation to years of schooling in the United States. In that chapter we also discussed the relationship between expenditure on food and total expenditure for 55 families in India (see Exercise 11.16).

Graphical Method

If there is no a priori or empirical information about the nature of heteroscedasticity, in practice one can do the regression analysis on the assumption that there is no heteroscedasticity and then do a postmortem examination of the residual squared $\hat{u}_i^2$ to see if they exhibit any systematic pattern. Although $\hat{u}_i^2$ are not the same thing as u_i^2, they can be used as proxies especially if the sample size is sufficiently large.[10] An examination of the $\hat{u}_i^2$ may reveal patterns such as those shown in Figure 11.8.

In Figure 11.8, $\hat{u}_i^2$ are plotted against $\hat{Y}_i$, the estimated Y_i from the regression line, the idea being to find out whether the estimated mean value of Y is systematically related to the squared residual. In Figure 11.8*a* we see that there is no systematic pattern between the two variables, suggesting that perhaps no heteroscedasticity is present in the data. Figures 11.8*b* to *e*, however, exhibit definite patterns. For instance, Figure 11.8*c* suggests a linear relationship, whereas Figures 11.8*d* and *e* indicate a quadratic relationship between $\hat{u}_i^2$ and $\hat{Y}_i$. Using such knowledge, albeit informal, one may transform the data in such a manner that the transformed data do not exhibit heteroscedasticity. In Section 11.6 we shall examine several such transformations.

Instead of plotting $\hat{u}_i^2$ against $\hat{Y}_i$, one may plot them against one of the explanatory variables, especially if plotting $\hat{u}_i^2$ against $\hat{Y}_i$ results in the pattern shown in Figure 11.8*a*. Such a plot, which is shown in Figure 11.9, may reveal patterns similar to those given in Figure 11.8. (In the case of the two-variable model, plotting $\hat{u}_i^2$ against $\hat{Y}_i$ is equivalent to

FIGURE 11.8 Hypothetical patterns of estimated squared residuals.

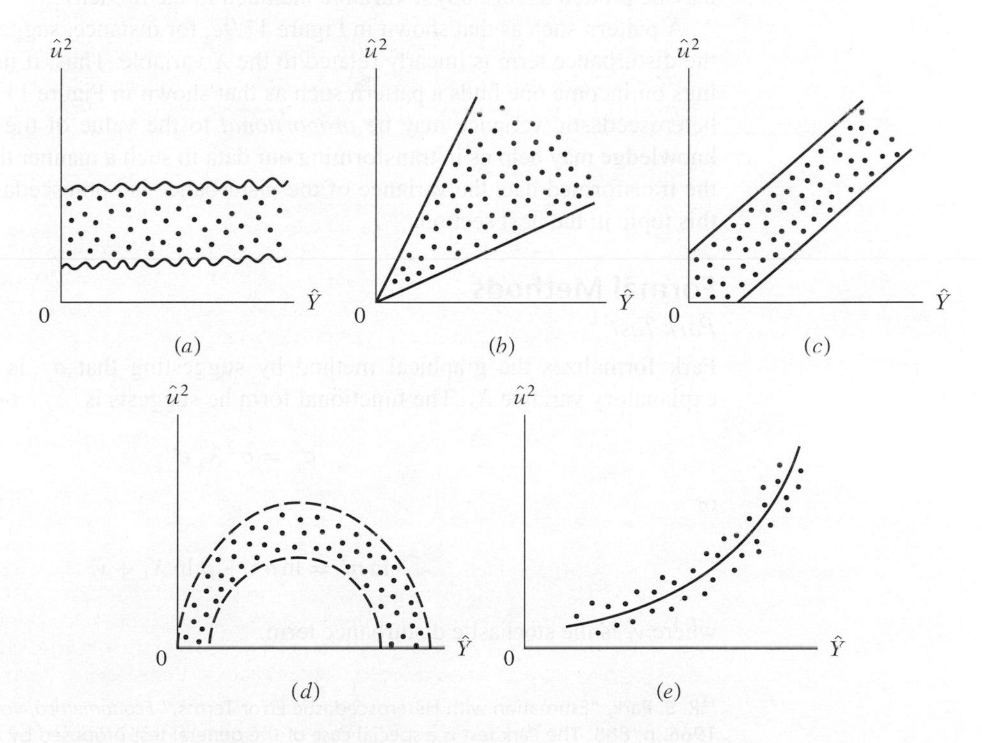

[10]For the relationship between $\hat{u}_i$ and u_i, see E. Malinvaud, *Statistical Methods of Econometrics*, North Holland Publishing Company, Amsterdam, 1970, pp. 88–89.

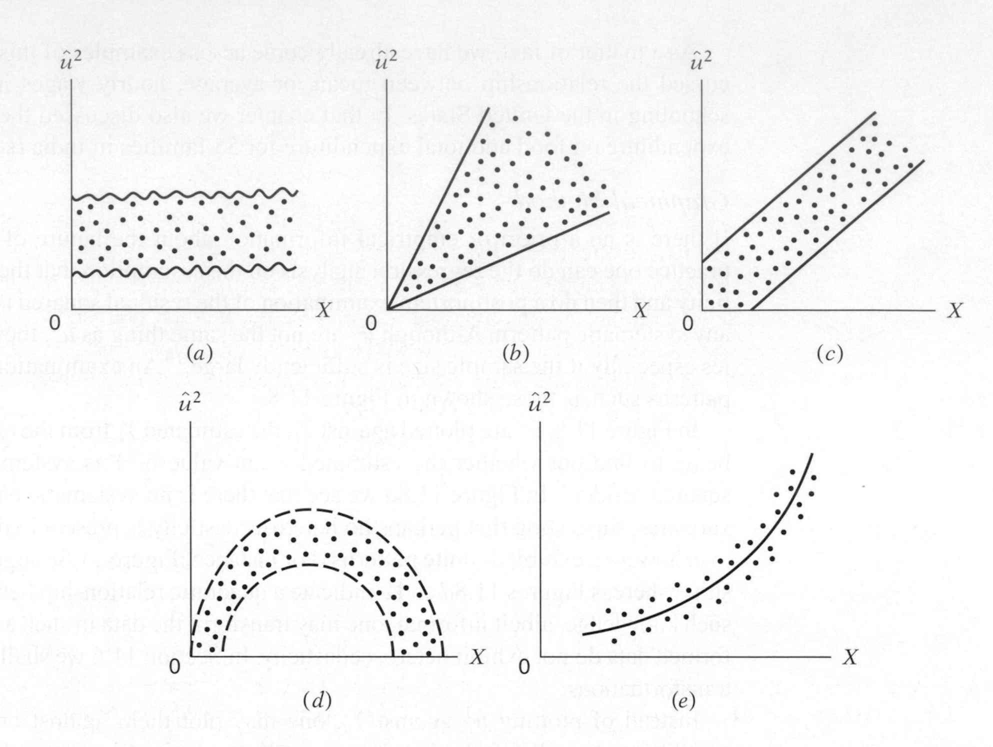

FIGURE 11.9 Scattergram of estimated squared residuals against *X*.

plotting it against X_i, and therefore Figure 11.9 is similar to Figure 11.8. But this is not the situation when we consider a model involving two or more *X* variables; in this instance, $\hat{u}_i^2$ may be plotted against any *X* variable included in the model.)

A pattern such as that shown in Figure 11.9*c*, for instance, suggests that the variance of the disturbance term is linearly related to the *X* variable. Thus, if in the regression of savings on income one finds a pattern such as that shown in Figure 11.9*c*, it suggests that the heteroscedastic variance may be *proportional* to the value of the income variable. This knowledge may help us in transforming our data in such a manner that in the regression on the transformed data the variance of the disturbance is homoscedastic. We shall return to this topic in the next section.

Formal Methods

Park Test[11]

Park formalizes the graphical method by suggesting that σ_i^2 is some function of the explanatory variable X_i. The functional form he suggests is

$$\sigma_i^2 = \sigma^2 X_i^\beta e^{vi}$$

or

$$\ln \sigma_i^2 = \ln \sigma^2 + \beta \ln X_i + v_i \tag{11.5.1}$$

where v_i is the stochastic disturbance term.

[11]R. E. Park, "Estimation with Heteroscedastic Error Terms," *Econometrica*, vol. 34, no. 4, October 1966, p. 888. The Park test is a special case of the general test proposed by A. C. Harvey in "Estimating Regression Models with Multiplicative Heteroscedasticity," *Econometrica*, vol. 44, no. 3, 1976, pp. 461–465.

Since σ_i^2 is generally not known, Park suggests using $\hat{u}_i^2$ as a proxy and running the following regression:

$$\begin{aligned} \ln \hat{u}_i^2 &= \ln \sigma^2 + \beta \ln X_i + v_i \\ &= \alpha + \beta \ln X_i + v_i \end{aligned} \tag{11.5.2}$$

If β turns out to be statistically significant, it would suggest that heteroscedasticity is present in the data. If it turns out to be insignificant, we may accept the assumption of homoscedasticity. The Park test is thus a two-stage procedure. In the first stage we run the OLS regression disregarding the heteroscedasticity question. We obtain $\hat{u}_i$ from this regression, and then in the second stage we run the regression (11.5.2).

Although empirically appealing, the Park test has some problems. Goldfeld and Quandt have argued that the error term v_i entering into Eq. (11.5.2) may not satisfy the OLS assumptions and may itself be heteroscedastic.[12] Nonetheless, as a strictly exploratory method, one may use the Park test.

EXAMPLE 11.1 *Relationship between Compensation and Productivity*

To illustrate the Park approach, we use the data given in Table 11.1 to run the following regression:

$$Y_i = \beta_1 + \beta_2 X_i + u_i$$

where Y = average compensation in thousands of dollars, X = average productivity in thousands of dollars, and i = ith employment size of the establishment. The results of the regression are as follows:

$$\begin{aligned} \hat{Y}_i &= 1992.3452 + 0.2329X_i \\ \text{se} &= (936.4791) \quad (0.0998) \\ t &= (2.1275) \quad (2.333) \qquad R^2 = 0.4375 \end{aligned} \tag{11.5.3}$$

The results reveal that the estimated slope coefficient is significant at the 5 percent level on the basis of a one-tail t test. The equation shows that as labor productivity increases by, say, a dollar, labor compensation on the average increases by about 23 cents.

The residuals obtained from regression (11.5.3) are then regressed on X_i as suggested in Eq. (11.5.2), giving the following results:

$$\begin{aligned} \widehat{\ln \hat{u}_i^2} &= 35.817 - 2.8099 \ln X_i \\ \text{se} &= (38.319) \quad (4.216) \\ t &= (0.934) \quad (-0.667) \qquad R^2 = 0.0595 \end{aligned} \tag{11.5.4}$$

Obviously, there is no statistically significant relationship between the two variables. Following the Park test, one may conclude that there is no heteroscedasticity in the error variance.[13]

Glejser Test[14]

The Glejser test is similar in spirit to the Park test. After obtaining the residuals $\hat{u}_i$ from the OLS regression, Glejser suggests regressing the absolute values of $\hat{u}_i$ on the X variable that

[12]Stephen M. Goldfeld and Richard E. Quandt, *Nonlinear Methods in Econometrics*, North Holland Publishing Company, Amsterdam, 1972, pp. 93–94.

[13]The particular functional form chosen by Park is only suggestive. A different functional form may reveal significant relationships. For example, one may use $\hat{u}_i^2$ instead of $\ln \hat{u}_i^2$ as the dependent variable.

[14]H. Glejser, "A New Test for Heteroscedasticity," *Journal of the American Statistical Association*, vol. 64, 1969, pp. 316–323.

is thought to be closely associated with σ_i^2. In his experiments, Glejser uses the following functional forms:

$$|\hat{u}_i| = \beta_1 + \beta_2 X_i + v_i$$

$$|\hat{u}_i| = \beta_1 + \beta_2 \sqrt{X_i} + v_i$$

$$|\hat{u}_i| = \beta_1 + \beta_2 \frac{1}{X_i} + v_i$$

$$|\hat{u}_i| = \beta_1 + \beta_2 \frac{1}{\sqrt{X_i}} + v_i$$

$$|\hat{u}_i| = \sqrt{\beta_1 + \beta_2 X_i} + v_i$$

$$|\hat{u}_i| = \sqrt{\beta_1 + \beta_2 X_i^2} + v_i$$

where v_i is the error term.

Again as an empirical or practical matter, one may use the Glejser approach. But Goldfeld and Quandt point out that the error term v_i has some problems in that its expected value is nonzero, it is serially correlated (see Chapter 12), and, ironically, it is heteroscedastic.[15] An additional difficulty with the Glejser method is that models such as

$$|\hat{u}_i| = \sqrt{\beta_1 + \beta_2 X_i} + v_i$$

and

$$|\hat{u}_i| = \sqrt{\beta_1 + \beta_2 X_i^2} + v_i$$

are nonlinear in the parameters and therefore cannot be estimated with the usual OLS procedure.

Glejser has found that for large samples the first four of the preceding models give generally satisfactory results in detecting heteroscedasticity. As a practical matter, therefore, the Glejser technique may be used for large samples and may be used in the small samples strictly as a qualitative device to learn something about heteroscedasticity.

EXAMPLE 11.2

Relationship between Compensation and Productivity: The Glejser Test

Continuing with Example 11.1, the absolute value of the residuals obtained from regression (11.5.3) were regressed on average productivity (X), giving the following results:

$$\begin{aligned} \widehat{|\hat{u}_i|} &= 407.2783 - 0.0203X_i \\ \text{se} &= (633.1621) \quad (0.0675) \quad r^2 = 0.0127 \\ t &= (0.6432) \quad (-0.3012) \end{aligned} \tag{11.5.5}$$

As you can see from this regression, there is no relationship between the absolute value of the residuals and the regressor, average productivity. This reinforces the conclusion based on the Park test.

Spearman's Rank Correlation Test

In Exercise 3.8 we defined the Spearman's rank correlation coefficient as

$$r_s = 1 - 6\left[\frac{\sum d_i^2}{n(n^2 - 1)}\right] \tag{11.5.6}$$

[15]For details, see Goldfeld and Quandt, op. cit., Chapter 3.

where d_i = difference in the ranks assigned to two different characteristics of the ith individual or phenomenon and n = number of individuals or phenomena ranked. The preceding rank correlation coefficient can be used to detect heteroscedasticity as follows: Assume $Y_i = \beta_0 + \beta_1 X_i + u_i$.

Step 1. Fit the regression to the data on Y and X and obtain the residuals $\hat{u}_i$.

Step 2. Ignoring the sign of $\hat{u}_i$, that is, taking their absolute value $|\hat{u}_i|$, rank both $|\hat{u}_i|$ and X_i (or $\hat{Y}_i$) according to an ascending or descending order and compute the Spearman's rank correlation coefficient given previously.

Step 3. Assuming that the population rank correlation coefficient ρ_s is zero and $n > 8$, the significance of the sample r_s can be tested by the t test as follows:[16]

$$t = \frac{r_s\sqrt{n-2}}{\sqrt{1-r_s^2}} \tag{11.5.7}$$

with df $= n - 2$.

If the computed t value exceeds the critical t value, we may accept the hypothesis of heteroscedasticity; otherwise we may reject it. If the regression model involves more than one X variable, r_s can be computed between $|\hat{u}_i|$ and each of the X variables separately and can be tested for statistical significance by the t test given in Eq. (11.5.7).

EXAMPLE 11.3 *Illustration of the Rank Correlation Test*

To illustrate the rank correlation test, consider the data given in Table 11.2. The data pertain to the average annual return (E, %) and the standard deviation of annual return (σ_i, %) of 10 mutual funds.

TABLE 11.2 Rank Correlation Test of Heteroscedasticity

Name of Mutual Fund	E_i, Average Annual Return, %	σ_i, Standard Deviation of Annual Return, %	$\hat{E}_i$†	$\lvert\hat{u}_i\rvert$‡ Residuals, $\lvert(E_i - \hat{E}_i)\rvert$	Rank of $\lvert\hat{u}_i\rvert$	Rank of σ_i	d, Difference between Two Rankings	d^2
Boston Fund	12.4	12.1	11.37	1.03	9	4	5	25
Delaware Fund	14.4	21.4	15.64	1.24	10	9	1	1
Equity Fund	14.6	18.7	14.40	0.20	4	7	−3	9
Fundamental Investors	16.0	21.7	15.78	0.22	5	10	−5	25
Investors Mutual	11.3	12.5	11.56	0.26	6	5	1	1
Loomis-Sales Mutual Fund	10.0	10.4	10.59	0.59	7	2	5	25
Massachusetts Investors Trust	16.2	20.8	15.37	0.83	8	8	0	0
New England Fund	10.4	10.2	10.50	0.10	3	1	2	4
Putnam Fund of Boston	13.1	16.0	13.16	0.06	2	6	−4	16
Wellington Fund	11.3	12.0	11.33	0.03	1	3	−2	4
Total							0	110

†Obtained from the regression: $\hat{E}_i = 5.8194 + 0.4590\,\sigma_i$.
‡Absolute value of the residuals.
Note: The ranking is in ascending order of values.

(Continued)

[16]See G. Udny Yule and M. G. Kendall, *An Introduction to the Theory of Statistics*, Charles Griffin & Company, London, 1953, p. 455.

EXAMPLE 11.3 (*Continued*)

The capital market line (CML) of portfolio theory postulates a linear relationship between expected return (E_i) and risk (as measured by the standard deviation, σ) of a portfolio as follows:

$$E_i = \beta_i + \beta_2 \sigma_i$$

Using the data in Table 11.2, the preceding model was estimated and the residuals from this model were computed. Since the data relate to 10 mutual funds of differing sizes and investment goals, a priori one might expect heteroscedasticity. To test this hypothesis, we apply the rank correlation test. The necessary calculations are given in Table 11.2.

Applying formula (11.5.6), we obtain

$$\begin{aligned} r_s &= 1 - 6\frac{110}{10(100-1)} \\ &= 0.3333 \end{aligned} \tag{11.5.8}$$

Applying the t test given in Eq. (11.5.7), we obtain

$$\begin{aligned} t &= \frac{(0.3333)(\sqrt{8})}{\sqrt{1-0.1110}} \\ &= 0.9998 \end{aligned} \tag{11.5.9}$$

For 8 df this t value is not significant even at the 10 percent level of significance; the p value is 0.17. Thus, there is no evidence of a systematic relationship between the explanatory variable and the absolute values of the residuals, which might suggest that there is no heteroscedasticity.

Goldfeld–Quandt Test[17]

This popular method is applicable if one assumes that the heteroscedastic variance, σ_i^2, is positively related to *one* of the explanatory variables in the regression model. For simplicity, consider the usual two-variable model:

$$Y_i = \beta_1 + \beta_2 X_i + u_i$$

Suppose σ_i^2 is positively related to X_i as

$$\sigma_i^2 = \sigma^2 X_i^2 \tag{11.5.10}$$

where σ^2 is a constant.[18]

Assumption (11.5.10) postulates that σ_i^2 is proportional to the square of the X variable. Such an assumption has been found quite useful by Prais and Houthakker in their study of family budgets. (See Section 11.5, informal methods.)

If Eq. (11.5.10) is appropriate, it would mean σ_i^2 would be larger, the larger the values of X_i. If that turns out to be the case, heteroscedasticity is most likely to be present in the model. To test this explicitly, Goldfeld and Quandt suggest the following steps:

Step 1. Order or rank the observations according to the values of X_i, beginning with the lowest X value.

Step 2. Omit c central observations, where c is specified a priori, and divide the remaining $(n - c)$ observations into two groups each of $(n - c)/2$ observations.

Step 3. Fit separate OLS regressions to the first $(n - c)/2$ observations and the last $(n - c)/2$ observations, and obtain the respective residual sums of squares RSS_1 and

[17] Goldfeld and Quandt, op. cit., Chapter 3.

[18] This is only one plausible assumption. Actually, what is required is that σ_i^2 be monotonically related to X_i.

RSS_2, RSS_1 representing the RSS from the regression corresponding to the smaller X_i values (the small variance group) and RSS_2 that from the larger X_i values (the large variance group). These RSS each have

$$\frac{(n-c)}{2} - k \quad \text{or} \quad \left(\frac{n-c-2k}{2}\right) \text{df}$$

where k is the number of parameters to be estimated, including the intercept. (Why?) For the two-variable case k is of course 2.

Step 4. Compute the ratio

$$\lambda = \frac{RSS_2/\text{df}}{RSS_1/\text{df}} \tag{11.5.11}$$

If we assume u_i are normally distributed (which we usually do), and *if the assumption of homoscedasticity is valid,* then it can be shown that λ of Eq. (11.5.10) follows the F distribution with numerator and denominator df each of $(n-c-2k)/2$.

If in an application the computed $\lambda\,(=F)$ is greater than the critical F at the chosen level of significance, we can reject the hypothesis of homoscedasticity, that is, we can say that heteroscedasticity is very likely.

Before illustrating the test, a word about omitting the c central observations is in order. These observations are omitted to sharpen or accentuate the difference between the small variance group (i.e., RSS_1) and the large variance group (i.e., RSS_2). But the ability of the Goldfeld Quandt test to do this successfully depends on how c is chosen.[19] For the two-variable model the Monte Carlo experiments done by Goldfeld and Quandt suggest that c is about 8 if the sample size is about 30, and it is about 16 if the sample size is about 60. But Judge et al. note that $c = 4$ if $n = 30$ and $c = 10$ if n is about 60 have been found satisfactory in practice.[20]

Before moving on, it may be noted that in case there is more than one X variable in the model, the ranking of observations, the first step in the test, can be done according to any one of them. Thus in the model: $Y_i = \beta_1 + \beta_2 X_{2i} + \beta_3 X_{3i} + \beta_4 X_{4i} + u_i$, we can rank-order the data according to any one of these X's. If a priori we are not sure which X variable is appropriate, we can conduct the test on each of the X variables, or via a Park test, in turn, on each X.

EXAMPLE 11.4 *The Goldfeld–Quandt Test*

To illustrate the Goldfeld–Quandt test, we present in Table 11.3 data on consumption expenditure in relation to income for a cross section of 30 families. Suppose we postulate that consumption expenditure is linearly related to income but that heteroscedasticity is present in the data. We further postulate that the nature of heteroscedasticity is as given in Eq. (11.5.10). The necessary reordering of the data for the application of the test is also presented in Table 11.3.

Dropping the middle 4 observations, the OLS regressions based on the first 13 and the last 13 observations and their associated residual sums of squares are as shown next (standard errors in the parentheses).

(Continued)

[19]Technically, the **power** of the test depends on how c is chosen. In statistics, the *power of a test* is measured by the probability of rejecting the null hypothesis when it is false (i.e., by 1 − Prob [type II error]). Here the null hypothesis is that the variances of the two groups are the same, i.e., homoscedasticity. For further discussion, see M. M. Ali and C. Giaccotto, "A Study of Several New and Existing Tests for Heteroscedasticity in the General Linear Model," *Journal of Econometrics*, vol. 26, 1984, pp. 355–373.

[20]George G. Judge, R. Carter Hill, William E. Griffiths, Helmut Lütkepohl, and Tsoung-Chao Lee, *Introduction to the Theory and Practice of Econometrics*, John Wiley & Sons, New York, 1982, p. 422.

EXAMPLE 11.4 *(Continued)*

TABLE 11.3 **Hypothetical Data on Consumption Expenditure Y($) and Income X($) to Illustrate the Goldfeld–Quandt Test**

Y	X	Data Ranked by X Values: Y	Data Ranked by X Values: X	
55	80	55	80	
65	100	70	85	
70	85	75	90	
80	110	65	100	
79	120	74	105	
84	115	80	110	
98	130	84	115	
95	140	79	120	
90	125	90	125	
75	90	98	130	
74	105	95	140	
110	160	108	145	
113	150	113	150	
125	165	110	160	Middle 4 observations
108	145	125	165	Middle 4 observations
115	180	115	180	Middle 4 observations
140	225	130	185	Middle 4 observations
120	200	135	190	
145	240	120	200	
130	185	140	205	
152	220	144	210	
144	210	152	220	
175	245	140	225	
180	260	137	230	
135	190	145	240	
140	205	175	245	
178	265	189	250	
191	270	180	260	
137	230	178	265	
189	250	191	270	

Regression based on the first 13 observations:

$$\hat{Y}_i = 3.4094 + 0.6968X_i$$
$$(8.7049) \quad (0.0744) \quad r^2 = 0.8887 \quad RSS_1 = 377.17 \quad df = 11$$

Regression based on the last 13 observations:

$$\hat{Y}_i = -28.0272 + 0.7941X_i$$
$$(30.6421) \quad (0.1319) \quad r^2 = 0.7681 \quad RSS_2 = 1536.8 \quad df = 11$$

From these results we obtain

$$\lambda = \frac{RSS_2/df}{RSS_1/df} = \frac{1536.8/11}{377.17/11}$$
$$\lambda = 4.07$$

The critical F value for 11 numerator and 11 denominator df at the 5 percent level is 2.82. Since the estimated $F (= \lambda)$ value exceeds the critical value, we may conclude that there is heteroscedasticity in the error variance. However, if the level of significance is fixed at 1 percent, we may not reject the assumption of homoscedasticity. (Why?) Note that the p value of the observed λ is 0.014.

Breusch–Pagan–Godfrey Test[21]

The success of the Goldfeld–Quandt test depends not only on the value of c (the number of central observations to be omitted) but also on identifying the correct X variable with which to order the observations. This limitation of this test can be avoided if we consider the Breusch–Pagan–Godfrey (BPG) test.

To illustrate this test, consider the k-variable linear regression model

$$Y_i = \beta_1 + \beta_2 X_{2i} + \cdots + \beta_k X_{ki} + u_i \tag{11.5.12}$$

Assume that the error variance σ_i^2 is described as

$$\sigma_i^2 = f(\alpha_1 + \alpha_2 Z_{2i} + \cdots + \alpha_m Z_{mi}) \tag{11.5.13}$$

that is, σ_i^2 is some function of the nonstochastic Z variables; some or all of the X's can serve as Z's. Specifically, assume that

$$\sigma_i^2 = \alpha_1 + \alpha_2 Z_{2i} + \cdots + \alpha_m Z_{mi} \tag{11.5.14}$$

that is, σ_i^2 is a linear function of the Z's. If $\alpha_2 = \alpha_3 = \cdots = \alpha_m = 0$, $\sigma_i^2 = \alpha_1$, which is a constant. Therefore, to test whether σ_i^2 is homoscedastic, one can test the hypothesis that $\alpha_2 = \alpha_3 = \cdots = \alpha_m = 0$. This is the basic idea behind the Breusch–Pagan–Godfrey test. The actual test procedure is as follows.

Step 1. Estimate Eq. (11.5.12) by OLS and obtain the residuals $\hat{u}_1, \hat{u}_2, \ldots, \hat{u}_n$.

Step 2. Obtain $\tilde{\sigma}^2 = \sum \hat{u}_i^2/n$. Recall from Chapter 4 that this is the maximum likelihood (ML) estimator of σ^2. (*Note:* The OLS estimator is $\sum \hat{u}_i^2/[n-k]$.)

Step 3. Construct variables p_i defined as

$$p_i = \hat{u}_i^2/\tilde{\sigma}^2$$

which is simply each residual squared divided by $\tilde{\sigma}^2$.

Step 4. Regress p_i thus constructed on the Z's as

$$p_i = \alpha_1 + \alpha_2 Z_{2i} + \cdots + \alpha_m Z_{mi} + v_i \tag{11.5.15}$$

where v_i is the residual term of this regression.

Step 5. Obtain the ESS (explained sum of squares) from Eq. (11.5.15) and define

$$\Theta = \frac{1}{2}(\text{ESS}) \tag{11.5.16}$$

Assuming u_i are normally distributed, one can show that if there is homoscedasticity and if the sample size n increases indefinitely, then

$$\Theta \underset{\text{asy}}{\sim} \chi^2_{m-1} \tag{11.5.17}$$

that is, Θ follows the chi-square distribution with $(m-1)$ degrees of freedom. (*Note:* asy means asymptotically.)

[21] T. Breusch and A. Pagan, "A Simple Test for Heteroscedasticity and Random Coefficient Variation," *Econometrica*, vol. 47, 1979, pp. 1287–1294. See also L. Godfrey, "Testing for Multiplicative Heteroscedasticity," *Journal of Econometrics*, vol. 8, 1978, pp. 227–236. Because of similarity, these tests are known as Breusch–Pagan–Godfrey tests of heteroscedasticity.

Therefore, if in an application the computed Θ ($= \chi^2$) exceeds the critical χ^2 value at the chosen level of significance, one can reject the hypothesis of homoscedasticity; otherwise one does not reject it.

The reader may wonder why BPG chose $\frac{1}{2}$ESS as the test statistic. The reasoning is slightly involved and is left for the references.[22]

EXAMPLE 11.5

The Breusch–Pagan–Godfrey (BPG) Test

As an example, let us revisit the data (Table 11.3) that were used to illustrate the Goldfeld–Quandt heteroscedasticity test. Regressing Y on X, we obtain the following:

Step 1.

$$\hat{Y}_i = 9.2903 + 0.6378X_i$$
$$\text{se} = (5.2314) \quad (0.0286) \qquad \text{RSS} = 2361.153 \qquad R^2 = 0.9466 \tag{11.5.18}$$

Step 2.

$$\tilde{\sigma}^2 = \sum \hat{u}_i^2/30 = 2361.153/30 = 78.7051$$

Step 3. Divide the squared residuals $\hat{u}_i$ obtained from regression (11.5.18) by 78.7051 to construct the variable p_i.

Step 4. Assuming that p_i are linearly related to $X_i(= Z_i)$ as per Eq. (11.5.14), we obtain the regression

$$\hat{p}_i = -0.7426 + 0.0101X_i$$
$$\text{se} = (0.7529) \quad (0.0041) \qquad \text{ESS} = 10.4280 \qquad R^2 = 0.18 \tag{11.5.19}$$

Step 5.

$$\Theta = \frac{1}{2}(\text{ESS}) = 5.2140 \tag{11.5.20}$$

Under the assumptions of the BPG test Θ in Eq. (11.5.20) asymptotically follows the chi-square distribution with 1 df. (*Note:* There is only one regressor in Eq. [11.5.19].) Now from the chi-square table we find that for 1 df the 5 percent critical chi-square value is 3.8414 and the 1 percent critical χ^2 value is 6.6349. Thus, the observed chi-square value of 5.2140 is significant at the 5 percent but not the 1 percent level of significance. Therefore, we reach the same conclusion as the Goldfeld–Quandt test. But keep in mind that, strictly speaking, the BPG test is an asymptotic, or large-sample, test and in the present example 30 observations may not constitute a large sample. It should also be pointed out that in small samples the test is sensitive to the assumption that the disturbances u_i are normally distributed. Of course, we can test the normality assumption by the tests discussed in Chapter 5.[23]

White's General Heteroscedasticity Test

Unlike the Goldfeld–Quandt test, which requires reordering the observations with respect to the X variable that supposedly caused heteroscedasticity, or the BPG test, which is sensitive to the normality assumption, the general test of heteroscedasticity proposed by White

[22] See Adrian C. Darnell, *A Dictionary of Econometrics,* Edward Elgar, Cheltenham, U.K., 1994, pp. 178–179.

[23] On this, see R. Koenker, "A Note on Studentizing a Test for Heteroscedasticity," *Journal of Econometrics*, vol. 17, 1981, pp. 1180–1200.

does not rely on the normality assumption and is easy to implement.[24] As an illustration of the basic idea, consider the following three-variable regression model (the generalization to the *k*-variable model is straightforward):

$$Y_i = \beta_1 + \beta_2 X_{2i} + \beta_3 X_{3i} + u_i \tag{11.5.21}$$

The White test proceeds as follows:

Step 1. Given the data, we estimate Eq. (11.5.21) and obtain the residuals, $\hat{u}_i$.

Step 2. We then run the following (*auxiliary*) regression:

$$\hat{u}_i^2 = \alpha_1 + \alpha_2 X_{2i} + \alpha_3 X_{3i} + \alpha_4 X_{2i}^2 + \alpha_5 X_{3i}^2 + \alpha_6 X_{2i} X_{3i} + v_i \qquad (11.5.22)^{25}$$

That is, the squared residuals from the original regression are regressed on the original *X* variables or regressors, their squared values, and the cross product(s) of the regressors. Higher powers of regressors can also be introduced. Note that there is a constant term in this equation even though the original regression may or may not contain it. Obtain the R^2 from this (auxiliary) regression.

Step 3. Under the null hypothesis that there is no heteroscedasticity, it can be shown that sample size (n) times the R^2 obtained from the auxiliary regression *asymptotically* follows the chi-square distribution with df equal to the number of regressors (excluding the constant term) in the auxiliary regression. That is,

$$n \cdot R^2 \underset{\text{asy}}{\sim} \chi^2_{\text{df}} \tag{11.5.23}$$

where df is as defined previously. In our example, there are 5 df since there are 5 regressors in the auxiliary regression.

Step 4. If the chi-square value obtained in Eq. (11.5.23) exceeds the critical chi-square value at the chosen level of significance, the conclusion is that there is heteroscedasticity. If it does not exceed the critical chi-square value, there is no heteroscedasticity, which is to say that in the auxiliary regression (11.5.22), $\alpha_2 = \alpha_3 = \alpha_4 = \alpha_5 = \alpha_6 = 0$ (see footnote 25).

EXAMPLE 11.6
White's Heteroscedasticity Test

From cross-sectional data on 41 countries, Stephen Lewis estimated the following regression model:[26]

$$\ln Y_i = \beta_1 + \beta_2 \ln X_{2i} + \beta_3 \ln X_{3i} + u_i \tag{11.5.24}$$

where Y = ratio of trade taxes (import and export taxes) to total government revenue, X_2 = ratio of the sum of exports plus imports to GNP, and X_3 = GNP per capita; and ln stands for natural log. His hypotheses were that Y and X_2 would be positively related (the higher the trade volume, the higher the trade tax revenue) and that Y and X_3 would be

(*Continued*)

[24] H. White, "A Heteroscedasticity Consistent Covariance Matrix Estimator and a Direct Test of Heteroscedasticity," *Econometrica*, vol. 48, 1980, pp. 817–818.

[25] Implied in this procedure is the assumption that the error variance of u_i, σ_i^2, is functionally related to the regressors, their squares, and their cross products. If all the partial slope coefficients in this regression are simultaneously equal to zero, then the error variance is the homoscedastic constant equal to α_1.

[26] Stephen R. Lewis, "Government Revenue from Foreign Trade," *Manchester School of Economics and Social Studies*, vol. 31, 1963, pp. 39–47.

EXAMPLE 11.6 *(Continued)*

negatively related (as income increases, government finds it is easier to collect direct taxes—e.g., income tax—than it is to rely on trade taxes).

The empirical results supported the hypotheses. For our purpose, the important point is whether there is heteroscedasticity in the data. Since the data are cross-sectional involving a heterogeneity of countries, a priori one would expect heteroscedasticity in the error variance. By applying White's heteroscedasticity test to the residuals obtained from regression (11.5.24), the following results were obtained:[27]

$$\begin{aligned}\widehat{\hat{u}_i^2} &= -5.8417 + 2.5629 \ln \text{Trade}_i + 0.6918 \ln \text{GNP}_i \\ &\quad -0.4081(\ln \text{Trade}_i)^2 - 0.0491(\ln \text{GNP}_i)^2 \\ &\quad +0.0015(\ln \text{Trade}_i)(\ln \text{GNP}_i) \qquad R^2 = 0.1148\end{aligned} \tag{11.5.25}$$

Note: The standard errors are not given, as they are not pertinent for our purpose here.

Now $n \cdot R^2 = 41(0.1148) = 4.7068$, which has, asymptotically, a chi-square distribution with 5 df (why?). The 5 percent critical chi-square value for 5 df is 11.0705, the 10 percent critical value is 9.2363, and the 25 percent critical value is 6.62568. For all practical purposes, one can conclude, on the basis of the White test, that there is no heteroscedasticity.

A comment is in order regarding the White test. If a model has several regressors, then introducing all the regressors, their squared (or higher-powered) terms, and their cross products can quickly consume degrees of freedom. Therefore, one must use caution in using the test.[28]

In cases where the White test statistic given in Eq. (11.5.25) is statistically significant, heteroscedasticity may not necessarily be the cause, but specification errors, about which more will be said in Chapter 13 (recall point 5 of Section 11.1). In other words, **the White test can be a test of (pure) heteroscedasticity or specification error or both.** It has been argued that if no cross-product terms are present in the White test procedure, then it is a test of pure heteroscedasticity. If cross-product terms are present, then it is a test of both heteroscedasticity and specification bias.[29]

Other Tests of Heteroscedasticity

There are several other tests of heteroscedasticity, each based on certain assumptions. The interested reader may want to consult the references.[30] We mention but one of these tests because of its simplicity. This is the **Koenker–Bassett (KB) test.** Like the Park, Breusch–Pagan–Godfrey, and White's tests of heteroscedasticity, the KB test is based on the squared residuals, $\hat{u}_i^2$, but instead of being regressed on one or more regressors, the squared residuals are regressed on the squared estimated values of the regressand. Specifically, if the original model is:

$$Y_i = \beta_1 + \beta_2 X_{2i} + \beta_3 X_{3i} + \cdots + \beta_k X_{ki} + u_i \tag{11.5.26}$$

[27]These results, with change in notation, are reproduced from William F. Lott and Subhash C. Ray, *Applied Econometrics: Problems with Data Sets*, Instructor's Manual, Chapter 22, pp. 137–140.

[28]Sometimes the test can be modified to conserve degrees of freedom. See Exercise 11.18.

[29]See Richard Harris, *Using Cointegration Analysis in Econometrics Modelling*, Prentice Hall & Harvester Wheatsheaf, U.K., 1995, p. 68.

[30]See M. J. Harrison and B. P. McCabe, "A Test for Heteroscedasticity Based on Ordinary Least Squares Residuals," *Journal of the American Statistical Association*, vol. 74, 1979, pp. 494–499; J. Szroeter, "A Class of Parametric Tests for Heteroscedasticity in Linear Econometric Models," *Econometrica*, vol. 46, 1978, pp. 1311–1327; M. A. Evans and M. L. King, "A Further Class of Tests for Heteroscedasticity," *Journal of Econometrics*, vol. 37, 1988, pp. 265–276; and R. Koenker and G. Bassett, "Robust Tests for Heteroscedasticity Based on Regression Quantiles," *Econometrica*, vol. 50, 1982, pp. 43–61.

you estimate this model, obtain $\hat{u}_i$ from this model, and then estimate

$$\hat{u}_i^2 = \alpha_1 + \alpha_2(\hat{Y}_i)^2 + v_i \tag{11.5.27}$$

where $\hat{Y}_i$ are the estimated values from the model (11.5.26). The null hypothesis is that $\alpha_2 = 0$. If this is not rejected, then one could conclude that there is no heteroscedasticity. The null hypothesis can be tested by the usual t test or the F test. (Note that $F_{1,k} = t_k{}^2$.) If the model (11.5.26) is double log, then the squared residuals are regressed on $(\log \hat{Y}_i)^2$. One other advantage of the KB test is that it is applicable even if the error term in the original model (11.5.26) is not normally distributed. If you apply the KB test to Example 11.1, you will find that the slope coefficient in the regression of the squared residuals obtained from Eq. (11.5.3) on the estimated $\hat{Y}_i^2$ from Eq. (11.5.3) is statistically not different from zero, thus reinforcing the Park test. This result should not be surprising since in the present instance we only have a single regressor. But the KB test is applicable if there is one regressor or many.

A Note Regarding the Tests of Heteroscedasticity

We have discussed several tests of heteroscedasticity in this section. So how do we decide which is the best test? This is not an easy question to answer, for these tests are based on various assumptions. In comparing the tests, we need to pay attention to their size (or level of significance), power (the probability of rejecting a false hypothesis), and sensitivity to outliers.

We have already pointed out some of the limitations of the popular and easy-to-apply White's test of heteroscedasticity. As a result of these limitations, it may have low power against the alternatives. Besides, the test is of little help in identifying the factors or variables that cause heteroscedasticity.

Similarly, the Breusch–Pagan–Godfrey test is sensitive to the assumption of normality. In contrast, the test of Koenker–Bassett does not rely on the normality assumption and may therefore be more powerful.[31] In the Goldfeld–Quandt test if we omit too many observations, we may diminish the power of the test.

It is beyond the scope of this text to provide a comparative analysis of the various heteroscedasticity tests. But the interested reader may refer to the article by John Lyon and Chin-Ling Tsai to get some idea about the strengths and weaknesses of the various tests of heteroscedasticity.[32]

11.6 Remedial Measures

As we have seen, heteroscedasticity does not destroy the unbiasedness and consistency properties of the OLS estimators, but they are no longer efficient, not even asymptotically (i.e., large sample size). This lack of efficiency makes the usual hypothesis-testing procedure of dubious value. Therefore, remedial measures may be called for. There are two approaches to remediation: when σ_i^2 is known and when σ_i^2 is not known.

When σ_i^2 Is Known: The Method of Weighted Least Squares

As we have seen in Section 11.3, if σ_i^2 is known, the most straightforward method of correcting heteroscedasticity is by means of weighted least squares, for the estimators thus obtained are BLUE.

[31]For details, see William H. Green, *Econometric Analysis,* 6th ed., Pearson/Prentice-Hall, New Jersey, 2008, pp. 165–167.

[32]See their article, "A Comparison of Tests of Heteroscedasticity," *The Statistician,* vol. 45, no. 3, 1996, pp. 337–349.

EXAMPLE 11.7

Illustration of the Method of Weighted Least Squares

To illustrate the method, suppose we want to study the relationship between compensation and employment size for the data presented in Table 11.1. For simplicity, we measure employment size by 1 (1–4 employees), 2 (5–9 employees), . . . , 9 (1,000–2499 employees), although we could also measure it by the midpoint of the various employment classes given in the table.

Now letting Y represent average compensation per employee ($) and X the employment size, we run the following regression (see Eq. [11.3.6]):

$$Y_i/\sigma_i = \hat{\beta}_1^*(1/\sigma_i) + \hat{\beta}_2^*(X_i/\sigma_i) + (\hat{u}_i/\sigma_i) \tag{11.6.1}$$

where σ_i are the standard deviations of wages as reported in Table 11.1. The necessary raw data to run this regression are given in Table 11.4.

TABLE 11.4

Illustration of Weighted Least-Squares Regression

Source: Data on Y and σ_i (standard deviation of compensation) are from Table 11.1. Employment size: 1 = 1–4 employees, 2 = 5–9 employees, etc. The latter data are also from Table 11.1.

Compensation, Y	**Employment Size,** X	σ_i	Y_i/σ_i	X_i/σ_i
3,396	1	742.2	4.5664	0.0013
3,787	2	851.4	4.4480	0.0023
4,013	3	727.8	5.5139	0.0041
4,104	4	805.06	5.0978	0.0050
4,146	5	929.9	4.4585	0.0054
4,241	6	1,080.6	3.9247	0.0055
4,387	7	1,241.2	3.5288	0.0056
4,538	8	1,307.7	3.4702	0.0061
4,843	9	1,110.7	4.3532	0.0081

Note: In regression (11.6.2), the dependent variable is (Y_i/σ_i) and the independent variables are $(1/\sigma_i)$ and (X_i/σ_i).

Before going on to the regression results, note that Eq. (11.6.1) has no intercept term. (Why?) Therefore, one will have to use the regression-through-the-origin model to estimate β_1^* and β_2^*, a topic discussed in Chapter 6. But most computer packages these days have an option to suppress the intercept term (see *Minitab* or *EViews*, for example). Also note another interesting feature of Eq. (11.6.1): It has two explanatory variables, $(1/\sigma_i)$ and (X_i/σ_i), whereas if we were to use OLS, regressing compensation on employment size, that regression would have a single explanatory variable, X_i. (Why?)

The regression results of WLS are as follows:

$$\begin{aligned} \widehat{(Y_i/\sigma_i)} &= 3406.639(1/\sigma_i) + 154.153(X_i/\sigma_i) \\ &\qquad (80.983) \qquad\quad (16.959) \\ t &= \quad (42.066) \qquad\quad (9.090) \\ R^2 &= 0.9993^{33} \end{aligned} \tag{11.6.2}$$

For comparison, we give the usual or unweighted OLS regression results:

$$\begin{aligned} \hat{Y}_i &= 3417.833 + 148.767 X_i \\ &\quad (81.136) \quad (14.418) \\ t &= (42.125) \quad (10.318) \qquad R^2 = 0.9383 \end{aligned} \tag{11.6.3}$$

In Exercise 11.7 you are asked to compare these two regressions.

[33] As noted in footnote 3 of Chapter 6, the R^2 of the regression through the origin is not directly comparable with the R^2 of the intercept-present model. The reported R^2 of 0.9993 takes this difference into account. (See the various packages for further details about how the R^2 is corrected to take into account the absence of the intercept term. See also Appendix 6A, Sec. 6A1.)

When σ_i^2 Is Not Known

As noted earlier, if true σ_i^2 are known, we can use the WLS method to obtain BLUE estimators. Since the true σ_i^2 are rarely known, is there a way of obtaining *consistent* (in the statistical sense) estimates of the variances and covariances of OLS estimators even if there is heteroscedasticity? The answer is yes.

White's Heteroscedasticity-Consistent Variances and Standard Errors

White has shown that this estimate can be performed so that *asymptotically* valid (i.e., large-sample) statistical inferences can be made about the true parameter values.[34] We will not present the mathematical details, for they are beyond the scope of this book. However, Appendix 11A.4 outlines White's procedure. Nowadays, several computer packages present White's heteroscedasticity-corrected variances and standard errors along with the usual OLS variances and standard errors.[35] Incidentally, White's heteroscedasticity-corrected standard errors are also known as **robust standard errors.**

EXAMPLE 11.8
Illustration of White's Procedure

As an example, we quote the following results due to Greene:[36]

$$
\begin{aligned}
\hat{Y}_i &= 832.91 \quad - 1834.2\,(\text{Income}) + 1587.04\,(\text{Income})^2 \\
\text{OLS se} &= (327.3) \qquad (829.0) \qquad\qquad (519.1) \\
t &= \ (2.54) \qquad\ \ (2.21) \qquad\qquad\ (3.06) \\
\text{White se} &= (460.9) \qquad (1243.0) \qquad\quad\ (830.0) \\
t &= \ (1.81) \qquad (-1.48) \qquad\qquad (1.91)
\end{aligned}
\tag{11.6.4}
$$

where Y = per capita expenditure on public schools by state in 1979 and Income = per capita income by state in 1979. The sample consisted of 50 states plus Washington, DC.

As the preceding results show, (White's) heteroscedasticity-corrected standard errors are considerably larger than the OLS standard errors and therefore the estimated t values are much smaller than those obtained by OLS. On the basis of the latter, both the regressors are statistically significant at the 5 percent level, whereas on the basis of White estimators they are not. However, it should be pointed out that White's heteroscedasticity-corrected standard errors can be larger or smaller than the uncorrected standard errors.

Since White's heteroscedasticity-consistent estimators of the variances are now available in established regression packages, it is recommended that the reader report them. As Wallace and Silver note:

> Generally speaking, it is probably a good idea to use the WHITE option [available in regression programs] routinely, perhaps comparing the output with regular OLS output as a check to see whether heteroscedasticity is a serious problem in a particular set of data.[37]

Plausible Assumptions about Heteroscedasticity Pattern

Apart from being a large-sample procedure, one drawback of the White procedure is that the estimators thus obtained may not be so efficient as those obtained by methods that

[34] See H. White, op. cit.

[35] More technically, they are known as **heteroscedasticity-consistent covariance matrix estimators.**

[36] William H. Greene, *Econometric Analysis,* 2d ed., Macmillan, New York, 1993, p. 385.

[37] T. Dudley Wallace and J. Lew Silver, *Econometrics: An Introduction,* Addison-Wesley, Reading, Mass., 1988, p. 265.

transform data to reflect specific types of heteroscedasticity. To illustrate this, let us revert to the two-variable regression model:

$$Y_i = \beta_1 + \beta_2 X_i + u_i$$

We now consider several assumptions about the pattern of heteroscedasticity.

ASSUMPTION 1 The error variance is proportional to X_i^2:

$$E(u_i^2) = \sigma^2 X_i^2 \qquad \textbf{(11.6.5)}^{38}$$

If, as a matter of "speculation," graphical methods, or Park and Glejser approaches, it is believed that the variance of u_i is proportional to the square of the explanatory variable X (see Figure 11.10), one may transform the original model as follows. Divide the original model through by X_i:

$$\begin{aligned}\frac{Y_i}{X_i} &= \frac{\beta_1}{X_i} + \beta_2 + \frac{u_i}{X_i} \\ &= \beta_1 \frac{1}{X_i} + \beta_2 + v_i\end{aligned} \qquad \textbf{(11.6.6)}$$

where v_i is the transformed disturbance term, equal to u_i/X_i. Now it is easy to verify that

$$\begin{aligned}E(v_i^2) = E\left(\frac{u_i}{X_i}\right)^2 &= \frac{1}{X_i^2} E(u_i^2) \\ &= \sigma^2 \quad \text{using (11.6.5)}\end{aligned}$$

Hence the variance of v_i is now homoscedastic, and one may proceed to apply OLS to the transformed equation (11.6.6), regressing Y_i/X_i on $1/X_i$.

FIGURE 11.10 Error variance proportional to X^2.

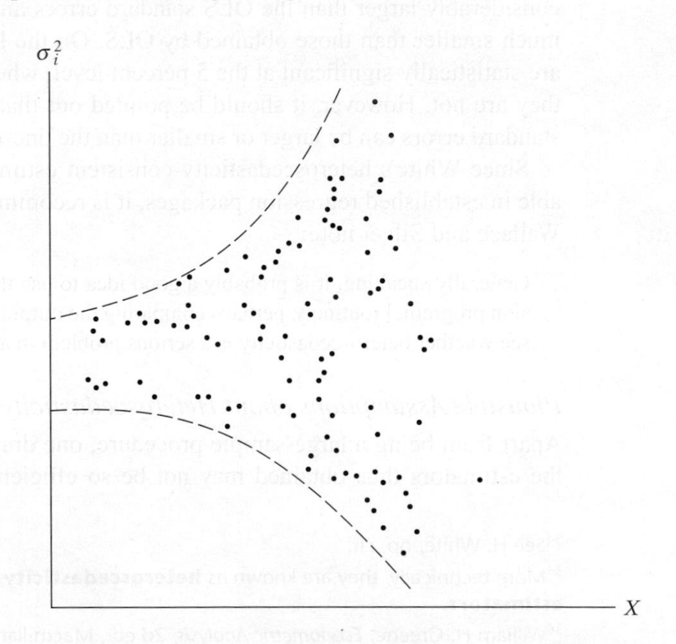

[38]Recall that we have already encountered this assumption in our discussion of the Goldfeld–Quandt test.

Notice that in the transformed regression the intercept term β_2 is the slope coefficient in the original equation and the slope coefficient β_1 is the intercept term in the original model. Therefore, to get back to the original model we shall have to multiply the estimated Eq. (11.6.6) by X_i. An application of this transformation is given in Exercise 11.20.

ASSUMPTION 2 The error variance is proportional to X_i. The **square root transformation:**

$$E\left(u_i^2\right) = \sigma^2 X_i \tag{11.6.7}$$

If it is believed that the variance of u_i, instead of being proportional to the squared X_i, is proportional to X_i itself, then the original model can be transformed as follows (see Figure 11.11):

$$\begin{aligned}\frac{Y_i}{\sqrt{X_i}} &= \frac{\beta_1}{\sqrt{X_i}} + \beta_2\sqrt{X_i} + \frac{u_i}{\sqrt{X_i}} \\ &= \beta_1\frac{1}{\sqrt{X_i}} + \beta_2\sqrt{X_i} + v_i\end{aligned} \tag{11.6.8}$$

where $v_i = u_i/\sqrt{X_i}$ and where $X_i > 0$.

Given assumption 2, one can readily verify that $E(v_i^2) = \sigma^2$, a homoscedastic situation. Therefore, one may proceed to apply OLS to Eq. (11.6.8), regressing $Y_i/\sqrt{X_i}$ on $1/\sqrt{X_i}$ and $\sqrt{X_i}$.

Note an important feature of the transformed model: It has no intercept term. Therefore, one will have to use the regression-through-the-origin model to estimate β_1 and β_2. Having run Eq. (11.6.8), one can get back to the original model simply by multiplying Eq. (11.6.8) by $\sqrt{X_i}$.

An interesting case is the zero intercept model, namely, $Y_i = \beta_2 X_i + u_i$. In this case, Eq. (11.6.8) becomes:

$$\frac{Y_i}{\sqrt{X_i}} = \beta_2\sqrt{X_i} + \frac{u_i}{\sqrt{X_i}} \tag{11.6.8a}$$

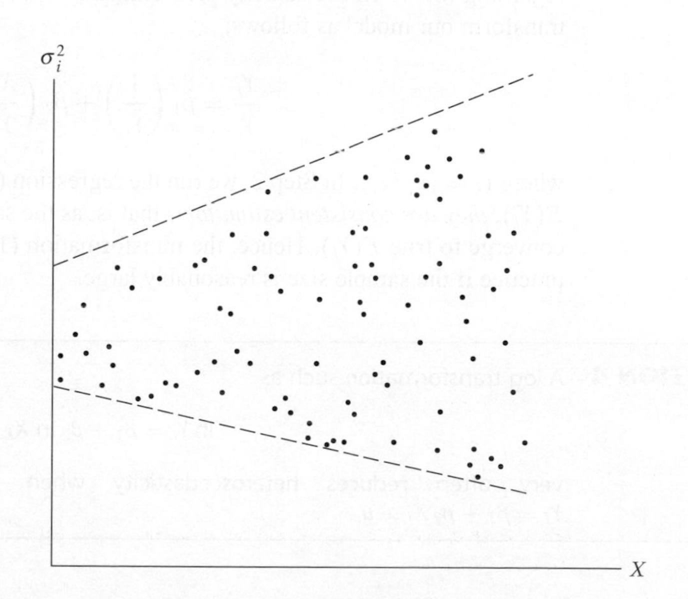

FIGURE 11.11
Error variance proportional to *X*.

And it can be shown that

$$\hat{\beta}_2 = \frac{\bar{Y}}{\bar{X}} \tag{11.6.8b}$$

That is, the weighted least-squares estimator is simply the ratio of the means of the dependent and explanatory variables. (To prove Eq. [11.6.8b], just apply the regression-through-the-origin formula given in Eq. [6.1.6].)

ASSUMPTION 3 The error variance is proportional to the square of the mean value of Y.

$$E\left(u_i^2\right) = \sigma^2[E(Y_i)]^2 \tag{11.6.9}$$

Equation (11.6.9) postulates that the variance of u_i is proportional to the square of the expected value of Y (see Figure 11.8*e*). Now

$$E(Y_i) = \beta_1 + \beta_2 X_i$$

Therefore, if we transform the original equation as follows,

$$\begin{aligned}\frac{Y_i}{E(Y_i)} &= \frac{\beta_1}{E(Y_i)} + \beta_2 \frac{X_i}{E(Y_i)} + \frac{u_i}{E(Y_i)} \\ &= \beta_1 \left(\frac{1}{E(Y_i)}\right) + \beta_2 \frac{X_i}{E(Y_i)} + v_i\end{aligned} \tag{11.6.10}$$

where $v_i = u_i/E(Y_i)$, it can be seen that $E(v_i^2) = \sigma^2$; that is, the disturbances v_i are homoscedastic. Hence, it is regression (11.6.10) that will satisfy the homoscedasticity assumption of the classical linear regression model.

The transformation (11.6.10) is, however, inoperational because $E(Y_i)$ depends on β_1 and β_2, which are unknown. Of course, we know $\hat{Y}_i = \hat{\beta}_1 + \hat{\beta}_2 X_i$, which is an estimator of $E(Y_i)$. Therefore, we may proceed in two steps: First, we run the usual OLS regression, disregarding the heteroscedasticity problem, and obtain $\hat{Y}_i$. Then, using the estimated $\hat{Y}_i$, we transform our model as follows:

$$\frac{Y_i}{\hat{Y}_i} = \beta_1 \left(\frac{1}{\hat{Y}_i}\right) + \beta_2 \left(\frac{X_i}{\hat{Y}_i}\right) + v_i \tag{11.6.11}$$

where $v_i = (u_i/\hat{Y}_i)$. In Step 2, we run the regression (11.6.11). Although $\hat{Y}_i$ are not exactly $E(Y_i)$, *they are consistent estimators;* that is, as the sample size increases indefinitely, they converge to true $E(Y_i)$. Hence, the transformation (11.6.11) will perform satisfactorily in practice if the sample size is reasonably large.

ASSUMPTION 4 A log transformation such as

$$\ln Y_i = \beta_1 + \beta_2 \ln X_i + u_i \tag{11.6.12}$$

very often reduces heteroscedasticity when compared with the regression $Y_i = \beta_1 + \beta_2 X_i + u_i$.

This result arises because log transformation compresses the scales in which the variables are measured, thereby reducing a tenfold difference between two values to a twofold difference. Thus, the number 80 is 10 times the number 8, but ln 80 (= 4.3280) is about twice as large as ln 8 (= 2.0794).

An additional advantage of the log transformation is that the slope coefficient β_2 measures the elasticity of Y with respect to X, that is, the percentage change in Y for a percentage change in X. For example, if Y is consumption and X is income, β_2 in Eq. (11.6.12) will measure income elasticity, whereas in the original model β_2 measures only the rate of change of mean consumption for a unit change in income. It is one reason why the log models are quite popular in empirical econometrics. (For some of the problems associated with log transformation, see Exercise 11.4.)

To conclude our discussion of the remedial measures, we reemphasize that all the transformations discussed previously are ad hoc; we are essentially speculating about the nature of σ_i^2. Which of the transformations discussed previously will work will depend on the nature of the problem and the severity of heteroscedasticity. There are some additional problems with the transformations we have considered that should be borne in mind:

1. When we go beyond the two-variable model, we may not know a priori which of the X variables should be chosen for transforming the data.[39]

2. Log transformation as discussed in Assumption 4 is not applicable if some of the Y and X values are zero or negative.[40]

3. Then there is the problem of **spurious correlation.** This term, due to Karl Pearson, refers to the situation where correlation is found to be present between the ratios of variables even though the original variables are uncorrelated or random.[41] Thus, in the model $Y_i = \beta_1 + \beta_2 X_i + u_i$, Y and X may not be correlated but in the transformed model $Y_i/X_i = \beta_1(1/X_i) + \beta_2$, Y_i/X_i and $1/X_i$ are often found to be correlated.

4. When σ_i^2 are not directly known and are estimated from one or more of the transformations that we have discussed earlier, all our testing procedures using the t tests, F tests, etc., are, *strictly speaking, valid only in large samples.* Therefore, one has to be careful in interpreting the results based on the various transformations in small or finite samples.[42]

11.7 Concluding Examples

In concluding our discussion of heteroscedasticity we present three examples illustrating the main points made in this chapter.

[39]However, as a practical matter, one may plot $\hat{u}_i^2$ against each variable and decide which X variable may be used for transforming the data. (See Fig. 11.9.)

[40]Sometimes we can use $\ln(Y_i + k)$ or $\ln(X_i + k)$, where k is a positive number chosen in such a way that all the values of Y and X become positive.

[41]For example, if X_1, X_2, and X_3 are mutually uncorrelated $r_{12} = r_{13} = r_{23} = 0$ and we find that the (values of the) ratios X_1/X_3 and X_2/X_3 are correlated, then there is spurious correlation. "More generally, correlation may be described as spurious if it is induced by the method of handling the data and is not present in the original material." M. G. Kendall and W. R. Buckland, *A Dictionary of Statistical Terms,* Hafner Publishing, New York, 1972, p. 143.

[42]For further details, see George G. Judge et al., op. cit., Section 14.4, pp. 415–420.

EXAMPLE 11.9

Child Mortality Revisited

Let us return to the child mortality example we have considered on several occasions. From data for 64 countries, we obtained the regression results shown in Eq. (8.1.4). Since the data are cross-sectional, involving diverse countries with different child mortality experiences, it is likely that we might encounter heteroscedasticity. To find this out, let us first consider the residuals obtained from Eq. (8.1.4). These residuals are plotted in Figure 11.12. From this figure it seems that the residuals do not show any distinct pattern that might suggest heteroscedasticity. Nonetheless, appearances can be deceptive. So, let us apply the Park, Glejser, and White tests to see if there is any evidence of heteroscedasticity.

Park Test. Since there are two regressors, GNP and FLR, we can regress the squared residuals from regression (8.1.4) on either of these variables. Or, we can regress them on the estimated CM values ($= \widehat{CM}$) from regression (8.1.4). Using the latter, we obtained the following results.

$$
\begin{aligned}
\widehat{\hat{u}_i^2} &= 854.4006 + 5.7016\,\widehat{CM}_i \\
t &= (1.2010) \quad (1.2428) \qquad r^2 = 0.024
\end{aligned}
\tag{11.7.1}
$$

Note: $\hat{u}_i$ are the residuals obtained from regression (8.1.4) and $\widehat{CM}$ are the estimated values of CM from regression (8.1.4).

As this regression shows, there is no systematic relation between the squared residuals and the estimated CM values (why?), suggesting that the assumption of homoscedasticity may be valid. Incidentally, regressing the log of the squared residual values on the log of $\widehat{CM}$ did not change the conclusion.

Glejser Test. The absolute values of the residual obtained from Eq. (8.1.4), when regressed on the estimated CM value from the same regression, gave the following results:

$$
\begin{aligned}
\widehat{|\hat{u}_i|} &= 22.3127 + 0.0646\,\widehat{CM}_i \\
t &= (2.8086) \quad (1.2622) \qquad r^2 = 0.0250
\end{aligned}
\tag{11.7.2}
$$

Again, there is not much systematic relationship between the absolute values of the residuals and the estimated CM values, as the *t* value of the slope coefficient is not statistically significant.

White Test. Applying White's heteroscedasticity test with and without cross-product terms, we did not find any evidence of heteroscedasticity. We also reestimated Eq. (8.1.4) to obtain White's heteroscedasticity-consistent standard errors and *t* values, but the results were quite similar to those given in Eq. (8.1.4), which should not be surprising in view of the various heteroscedasticity tests we conducted earlier.

In sum, it seems that our child mortality regression (8.1.4) does not suffer from heteroscedasticity.

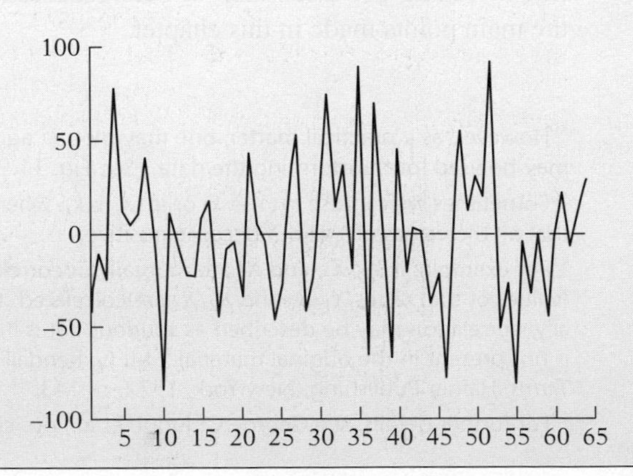

FIGURE 11.12 Residuals from regression (8.1.4).

EXAMPLE 11.10

R&D Expenditure, Sales, and Profits in 14 Industry Groupings in the United States, 2005

Table 11.5 gives data on research and development (R&D) expenditure, sales, and profits for 14 industry groupings in the United States (all figures in millions of dollars). Since the cross-sectional data presented in this table are quite heterogeneous, in a regression of R&D on sales, heteroscedasticity is likely. The regression results are as follows:

$$\begin{aligned}\widehat{\text{R\&D}}_i &= 1338 \quad + \quad 0.0437\ \text{Sales}_i \\ \text{se} &= (5015) \qquad (0.0277) \\ t &= (0.27) \qquad (1.58) \qquad r^2 = 0.172\end{aligned} \tag{11.7.3}$$

Not surprisingly, there is a positive relationship between R&D and sales, although it is not statistically significant at the traditional levels.

TABLE 11.5
Sales and Employment for Companies Performing Industrial R&D in the United States, by Industry, 2005 (values are in millions of dollars)

Source: National Science Foundation, Division of Science Resources Statistics, Survey of Industrial Research and Development: 2005 and the U.S. Census Bureau Annual Survey of Manufacturers, 2005.

	Industry	Sales	R&D	Profits
1	Food	374,342	2,716	234,662
2	Textiles, apparel, and leather	51,639	816	53,510
3	Basic chemicals	109,899	2,277	75,168
4	Resin, synthetic rubber, fibers, and filament	132,934	2,294	34,645
5	Pharmaceuticals and medicines	273,377	34,839	127,639
6	Plastics and rubber products	90,176	1,760	96,162
7	Fabricated metal products	174,165	1,375	155,801
8	Machinery	230,941	8,531	143,472
9	Computers and peripheral equipment	91,010	4,955	34,004
10	Semiconductor and other electronic components	176,054	18,724	81,317
11	Navigational, measuring, electromedical, and control instruments	118,648	15,204	73,258
12	Electrical equipment, appliances, and components	101,398	2,424	54,742
13	Aerospace products and parts	227,271	15,005	72,090
14	Medical equipment and supplies	56,661	4,374	52,443

To see if the regression (11.7.3) suffers from heteroscedasticity, we obtained the residuals, $\hat{u}_i$, and the squared residuals, $\hat{u}_i^2$, from the model and plotted them against sales, as shown in Figure 11.13. It seems from this figure that there is a systematic pattern between the residuals and squared residuals and sales, perhaps suggesting that there is heteroscedasticity. To test this formally, we used the Park, Glejser, and White tests, which gave the following results:

Park Test

$$\begin{aligned}\widehat{\hat{u}_i^2} &= -72{,}493{,}719 \;+\; 916.1\ \text{Sales}_i \\ \text{se} &= (54{,}940{,}238) \quad (303.9) \\ t &= \quad (-1.32) \qquad (3.01) \qquad r^2 = 0.431\end{aligned} \tag{11.7.4}$$

The Park test suggests that there is a statistically significant positive relationship between squared residuals and sales.

(Continued)

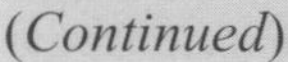

EXAMPLE 11.10 (*Continued*)

FIGURE 11.13 Residuals (*a*) and squared residuals (*b*) on sales.

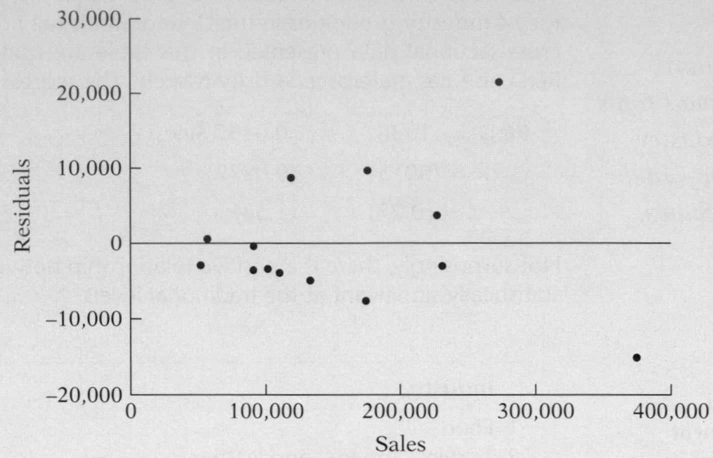

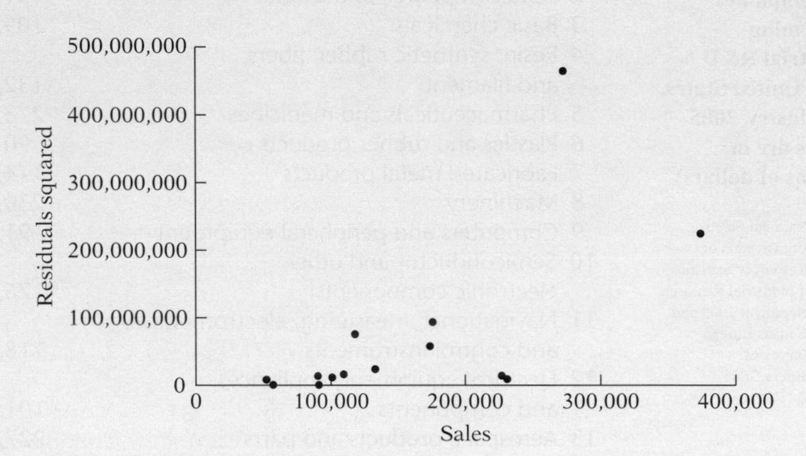

Glejser Test

$$\begin{aligned} \widehat{|\hat{u}_i|} &= -1003 \ + \ 0.04639 \ \text{Sales}_i \\ \text{se} &= \quad (2316) \qquad (0.0128) \\ t &= (-0.43) \qquad (3.62) \qquad r^2 = 0.522 \end{aligned} \tag{11.7.5}$$

The Glejser test also suggests that there is a systematic relationship between the absolute values of the residuals and sales, raising the possibility that the regression (11.7.3) suffers from heteroscedasticity.

White Test

$$\begin{aligned} \widehat{\hat{u}_i^2} &= -46{,}746{,}325 \ + \ 578 \ \text{Sales}_i \ + \ 0.000846 \ \text{Sales}_i^2 \\ \text{se} &= (112{,}224{,}348) \qquad (1308) \qquad (0.003171) \\ t &= \qquad (-0.42) \qquad (0.44) \qquad (0.27) \\ & \qquad\qquad\qquad\qquad\qquad\qquad R^2 = 0.435 \end{aligned} \tag{11.7.6}$$

Using the R^2 value and $n = 14$, we obtain $nR^2 = 6.090$. Under the null hypothesis of no heteroscedasticity, this should follow a chi-square distribution with 2 df (because there are two regressors in Eq. [11.7.6]). The p value of obtaining a chi-square value of as much as 6.090 or greater is about 0.0476. Since this is a low value, the White test also suggests that there is heteroscedasticity.

EXAMPLE 11.10 (*Continued*)

In sum, then, on the basis of the residual graphs and the Park, Glejser, and White tests, it seems that our R&D regression (11.7.3) suffers from heteroscedasticity. Since the true error variance is unknown, we cannot use the method of weighted least squares to obtain heteroscedasticity-corrected standard errors and t values. Therefore, we would have to make some educated guesses about the nature of the error variance.

To conclude our example, we present below White's heteroscedasticity-consistent standard errors, as discussed in Section 11.6.

$$\begin{aligned} \widehat{R\ \&\ D}_i &= 1337.87 \quad + 0.0437\ \text{Sales}_i \\ \text{se} &= (4892.447) \quad (0.0411) \\ t &= \quad (0.27) \qquad (1.06) \qquad\qquad r^2 = 0.172 \end{aligned} \tag{11.7.7}$$

Comparing Eq. (11.7.7) with Eq. (11.7.3) (the latter not having been corrected for heteroscedasticity), we see that the parameter estimates have not changed (as we would expect), the standard error of the intercept coefficient has decreased slightly, and the standard error of the slope coefficient has increased slightly. But remember that the White procedure is strictly a large-sample procedure, whereas we have only 14 observations.

EXAMPLE 11.11

Table 11.6 on the textbook website provides salary and related data on 94 school districts in Northwest Ohio. Initially, the following regression was estimated from these data:

$$\ln(\text{Salary})_i = \beta_1 + \beta_2 \ln(\text{Famincome}) + \beta_3 \ln(\text{Propvalue}) + u_i$$

Where Salary = mean salary of classroom teachers ($), famincome = mean family income in the district ($), and propvalue = mean property value in the district ($).

Since this is a double-log model, all the slope coefficients are elasticities. Based on the various heteroscedasticity tests discussed in the text, it was found that the preceding model suffered from heteroscedasticity. We, therefore, obtained (White's) robust standard errors. The following table gives the results of the preceding regression with and without robust standard errors.

Variable	Coefficient	OLS se	Robust se
Intercept	7.0198	0.8053	0.7721
		(8.7171)	(9.0908)
ln(famincome)	0.2575	0.0799	0.1009
		(3.2230)	(2.5516)
ln(propvalue)	0.0704	0.0207	0.0460
		(3.3976)	(1.5311)
R^2	0.2198		

Note: Figures in parentheses are the estimated t ratios.

Although the coefficient values and R^2 remain the same whether we use OLS or White's method, the standard errors have changed; the most dramatic change is in the standard error of the ln(propvalue) coefficient. The usual OLS would suggest that the estimated coefficient of this variable is highly statistically significant, whereas White's robust standard error suggests that this coefficient is not significant even at the 10 percent level. The point of this example is that if there is heteroscedasticity, we should take it into account in estimating a model.

11.8 A Caution about Overreacting to Heteroscedasticity

Reverting to the R&D example discussed in the previous section, we saw that when we used the square root transformation to correct for heteroscedasticity in the original model (11.7.3), the standard error of the slope coefficient decreased and its t value increased. Is this change so significant that one should worry about it in practice? To put the matter differently, when should we really worry about the heteroscedasticity problem? As one author contends, "heteroscedasticity has never been a reason to throw out an otherwise good model."[43]

Here it may be useful to bear in mind the caution sounded by John Fox:

> . . . unequal error variance is worth correcting only when the problem is severe.
>
> The impact of nonconstant error variance on the efficiency of ordinary least-squares estimator and on the validity of least-squares inference depends on several factors, including the sample size, the degree of variation in the σ_i^2, the configuration of the X [i.e., regressor] values, and the relationship between the error variance and the X's. It is therefore not possible to develop wholly general conclusions concerning the harm produced by heteroscedasticity.[44]

Returning to the model (11.3.1), we saw earlier that variance of the slope estimator, var $(\hat{\beta}_2)$, is given by the usual formula shown in (11.2.3). Under GLS the variance of the slope estimator, var $(\hat{\beta}_2^*)$, is given by (11.3.9). We know that the latter is more efficient than the former. But how large does the former (i.e., OLS) variance have to be in relation to the GLS variance before one should really worry about it? As a rule of thumb, Fox suggests that we worry about this problem ". . . when the largest error variance is more than about 10 times the smallest."[45] Thus, returning to the Monte Carlo simulations results of Davidson and MacKinnon presented in Section 11.4, consider the value of $\alpha = 2$. The variance of the estimated β_2 is 0.04 under OLS and 0.012 under GLS, the ratio of the former to the latter thus being about 3.33.[46] According to the Fox rule, the severity of heteroscedasticity in this case may not be large enough to worry about.

Also remember that, despite heteroscedasticity, OLS estimators are linear unbiased and are (under general conditions) asymptotically (i.e., in large samples) normally distributed.

As we will see when we discuss other violations of the assumptions of the classical linear regression model, the caution sounded in this section is appropriate as a general rule. Otherwise, one can go overboard.

Summary and Conclusions

1. A critical assumption of the classical linear regression model is that the disturbances u_i have all the same variance, σ^2. If this assumption is not satisfied, there is heteroscedasticity.
2. Heteroscedasticity does not destroy the unbiasedness and consistency properties of OLS estimators.
3. But these estimators are no longer minimum variance or efficient. That is, they are not BLUE.

[43]N. Gregory Mankiw, "A Quick Refresher Course in Macroeconomics," *Journal of Economic Literature*, vol. XXVIII, December 1990, p. 1648.

[44]John Fox, *Applied Regression Analysis, Linear Models, and Related Methods,* Sage Publications, California, 1997, p. 306.

[45]Ibid., p. 307.

[46]Note that we have squared the standard errors to obtain the variances.

4. The BLUE estimators are provided by the method of weighted least squares, provided the heteroscedastic error variances, σ_i^2, are known.
5. In the presence of heteroscedasticity, the variances of OLS estimators are not provided by the usual OLS formulas. But if we persist in using the usual OLS formulas, the t and F tests based on them can be highly misleading, resulting in erroneous conclusions.
6. Documenting the consequences of heteroscedasticity is easier than detecting it. There are several diagnostic tests available, but one cannot tell for sure which will work in a given situation.
7. Even if heteroscedasticity is suspected and detected, it is not easy to correct the problem. If the sample is large, one can obtain White's heteroscedasticity-corrected standard errors of OLS estimators and conduct statistical inference based on these standard errors.
8. Otherwise, on the basis of OLS residuals, one can make educated guesses of the likely pattern of heteroscedasticity and transform the original data in such a way that in the transformed data there is no heteroscedasticity.

EXERCISES

Questions

11.1. State *with brief reason* whether the following statements are true, false, or uncertain:

a. In the presence of heteroscedasticity OLS estimators are biased as well as inefficient.

b. If heteroscedasticity is present, the conventional t and F tests are invalid.

c. In the presence of heteroscedasticity the usual OLS method always overestimates the standard errors of estimators.

d. If residuals estimated from an OLS regression exhibit a systematic pattern, it means heteroscedasticity is present in the data.

e. There is no general test of heteroscedasticity that is free of any assumption about which variable the error term is correlated with.

f. If a regression model is mis-specified (e.g., an important variable is omitted), the OLS residuals will show a distinct pattern.

g. If a regressor that has nonconstant variance is (incorrectly) omitted from a model, the (OLS) residuals will be heteroscedastic.

11.2. In a regression of average wages (W, \$) on the number of employees (N) for a random sample of 30 firms, the following regression results were obtained:*

$$\widehat{W} = 7.5 + 0.009N$$
$$t = \text{n.a.} \quad (16.10) \qquad R^2 = 0.90 \tag{1}$$

$$\widehat{W}/N = 0.008 + 7.8(1/N)$$
$$t = (14.43) \quad (76.58) \qquad R^2 = 0.99 \tag{2}$$

a. How do you interpret the two regressions?

b. What is the author assuming in going from Eq. (1) to Eq. (2)? Was he worried about heteroscedasticity? How do you know?

c. Can you relate the slopes and intercepts of the two models?

d. Can you compare the R^2 values of the two models? Why or why not?

*See Dominick Salvatore, *Managerial Economics*, McGraw-Hill, New York, 1989, p. 157.

11.3. *a.* Can you estimate the parameters of the models

$$|\hat{u}_i| = \sqrt{\beta_1 + \beta_2 X_i} + v_i$$

$$|\hat{u}_i| = \sqrt{\beta_1 + \beta_2 X_i^2} + v_i$$

by the method of ordinary least squares? Why or why not?

b. If not, can you suggest a method, informal or formal, of estimating the parameters of such models? (See Chapter 14.)

11.4. Although log models as shown in Eq. (11.6.12) often reduce heteroscedasticity, one has to pay careful attention to the properties of the disturbance term of such models. For example, the model

$$Y_i = \beta_1 X_i^{\beta_2} u_i \tag{1}$$

can be written as

$$\ln Y_i = \ln \beta_1 + \beta_2 \ln X_i + \ln u_i \tag{2}$$

a. If $\ln u_i$ is to have zero expectation, what must be the distribution of u_i?

b. If $E(u_i) = 1$, will $E(\ln u_i) = 0$? Why or why not?

c. If $E(\ln u_i)$ is not zero, what can be done to make it zero?

11.5. Show that β_2^* of Eq. (11.3.8) can also be expressed as

$$\beta_2^* = \frac{\sum w_i y_i^* x_i^*}{\sum w_i x_i^{2*}}$$

and var (β_2^*) given in Eq. (11.3.9) can also be expressed as

$$\text{var}\,(\beta_2^*) = \frac{1}{\sum w_i x_i^{2*}}$$

where $y_i^* = Y_i - \bar{Y}^*$ and $x_i^* = X_i - \bar{X}^*$ represent deviations from the weighted means $\bar{Y}^*$ and $\bar{X}^*$ defined as

$$\bar{Y}^* = \sum w_i Y_i \Big/ \sum w_i$$

$$\bar{X}^* = \sum w_i X_i \Big/ \sum w_i$$

11.6. For pedagogic purposes Hanushek and Jackson estimate the following model:

$$C_t = \beta_1 + \beta_2 \text{GNP}_t + \beta_3 D_t + u_i \tag{1}$$

where C_t = aggregate private consumption expenditure in year t, GNP_t = gross national product in year t, and D = national defense expenditures in year t, the objective of the analysis being to study the effect of defense expenditures on other expenditures in the economy.

Postulating that $\sigma_t^2 = \sigma^2(\text{GNP}_t)^2$, they transform (1) and estimate

$$C_t/\text{GNP}_t = \beta_1\,(1/\text{GNP}_t) + \beta_2 + \beta_3\,(D_t/\text{GNP}_t) + u_t/\text{GNP}_t \tag{2}$$

The empirical results based on the data for 1946–1975 were as follows (standard errors in the parentheses):*

$$\begin{aligned}
\hat{C}_t &= 26.19 + 0.6248\ \text{GNP}_t - 0.4398\ D_t \\
&\quad\ (2.73) \qquad (0.0060) \qquad\quad (0.0736) \qquad R^2 = 0.999
\end{aligned}$$

$$\begin{aligned}
\widehat{C_t/\text{GNP}_t} &= 25.92\,(1/\text{GNP}_t) + 0.6246 - 0.4315\,(D_t/\text{GNP}_t) \\
&\quad\ (2.22) \qquad\qquad\quad (0.0068) \qquad (0.0597) \qquad R^2 = 0.875
\end{aligned}$$

a. What assumption is made by the authors about the nature of heteroscedasticity? Can you justify it?

b. Compare the results of the two regressions. Has the transformation of the original model improved the results, that is, reduced the estimated standard errors? Why or why not?

c. Can you compare the two R^2 values? Why or why not? (*Hint:* Examine the dependent variables.)

11.7. Refer to the estimated regression in Eqs. (11.6.2) and (11.6.3). The regression results are quite similar. What could account for this outcome?

11.8. Prove that if $w_i = w$, a constant, for each i, β_2^* and $\hat{\beta}_2$ as well as their variance are identical.

11.9. Refer to formulas (11.2.2) and (11.2.3). Assume

$$\sigma_i^2 = \sigma^2 k_i$$

where σ^2 is a constant and where k_i are *known* weights, not necessarily all equal.

Using this assumption, show that the variance given in Eq. (11.2.2) can be expressed as

$$\operatorname{var}(\hat{\beta}_2) = \frac{\sigma^2}{\sum x_i^2} \cdot \frac{\sum x_i^2 k_i}{\sum x_i^2}$$

The first term on the right side is the variance formula given in Eq. (11.2.3), that is, $\operatorname{var}(\hat{\beta}_2)$ under homoscedasticity. What can you say about the nature of the relationship between $\operatorname{var}(\hat{\beta}_2)$ under heteroscedasticity and under homoscedasticity? (*Hint:* Examine the second term on the right side of the preceding formula.) Can you draw any general conclusions about the relationships between Eqs. (11.2.2) and (11.2.3)?

11.10. In the model

$$Y_i = \beta_2 X_i + u_i \quad (\textit{Note:} \text{ there is no intercept})$$

you are told that $\operatorname{var}(u_i) = \sigma^2 X_i^2$. Show that

$$\operatorname{var}(\hat{\beta}_2) = \frac{\sigma^2 \sum X_i^4}{\left(\sum X_i^2\right)^2}$$

*Eric A. Hanushek and John E. Jackson, *Statistical Methods for Social Scientists*, Academic, New York, 1977, p. 160.

Empirical Exercises

11.11. For the data given in Table 11.1, regress average compensation Y on average productivity X, treating employment size as the unit of observation. Interpret your results, and see if your results agree with those given in Eq. (11.5.3).

a. From the preceding regression obtain the residuals $\hat{u}_i$.

b. Following the Park test, regress $\ln \hat{u}_i^2$ on $\ln X_i$ and verify the regression Eq. (11.5.4).

c. Following the Glejser approach, regress $|\hat{u}_i|$ on X_i and then regress $|\hat{u}_i|$ on $\sqrt{X_i}$ and comment on your results.

d. Find the rank correlation between $|\hat{u}_i|$ and X_i and comment on the nature of heteroscedasticity, if any, present in the data.

11.12. Table 11.6 gives data on the sales/cash ratio in U.S. manufacturing industries classified by the asset size of the establishment for the period 1971–I to 1973–IV. (The data are on a quarterly basis.) The sales/cash ratio may be regarded as a measure of income velocity in the corporate sector, that is, the number of times a dollar turns over.

a. For each asset size compute the mean and standard deviation of the sales/cash ratio.

b. Plot the mean value against the standard deviation as computed in (*a*), using asset size as the unit of observation.

c. By means of a suitable regression model decide whether standard deviation of the ratio increases with the mean value. If not, how would you rationalize the result?

d. If there is a statistically significant relationship between the two, how would you transform the data so that there is no heteroscedasticity?

11.13. *Bartlett's homogeneity-of-variance test.** Suppose there are k independent sample variances $s_1^2, s_2^2, \ldots, s_k^2$ with $f_1, f_2, \ldots, f_k$ df, each from populations which are normally distributed with mean μ and variance σ_i^2. Suppose further that we want to test the null hypothesis H_0: $\sigma_1^2 = \sigma_2^2 = \cdots = \sigma_k^2 = \sigma^2$; that is, each sample variance is an estimate of the same population variance σ^2.

If the null hypothesis is true, then

$$s^2 = \frac{\sum_{i=1}^{k} f_i s_i^2}{\sum f_i} = \frac{\sum f_i s_i^2}{f}$$

TABLE 11.6
Asset Size (millions of dollars)

Source: *Quarterly Financial Report for Manufacturing Corporations,* Federal Trade Commission and the Securities and Exchange Commission, U.S. government, various issues (computed).

Year and Quarter	1–10	10–25	25–50	50–100	100–250	250–1,000	1,000 +
1971–I	6.696	6.929	6.858	6.966	7.819	7.557	7.860
–II	6.826	7.311	7.299	7.081	7.907	7.685	7.351
–III	6.338	7.035	7.082	7.145	7.691	7.309	7.088
–IV	6.272	6.265	6.874	6.485	6.778	7.120	6.765
1972–I	6.692	6.236	7.101	7.060	7.104	7.584	6.717
–II	6.818	7.010	7.719	7.009	8.064	7.457	7.280
–III	6.783	6.934	7.182	6.923	7.784	7.142	6.619
–IV	6.779	6.988	6.531	7.146	7.279	6.928	6.919
1973–I	7.291	7.428	7.272	7.571	7.583	7.053	6.630
–II	7.766	9.071	7.818	8.692	8.608	7.571	6.805
–III	7.733	8.357	8.090	8.357	7.680	7.654	6.772
–IV	8.316	7.621	7.766	7.867	7.666	7.380	7.072

*See "Properties of Sufficiency and Statistical Tests," *Proceedings of the Royal Society of London A,* vol. 160, 1937, p. 268.

provides an estimate of the common (pooled) estimate of the population variance σ^2, where $f_i = (n_i - 1)$, n_i being the number of observations in the ith group and where $f = \sum_{i=1}^{k} f_i$.

Bartlett has shown that the null hypothesis can be tested by the ratio A/B, which is approximately distributed as the χ^2 distribution with $k - 1$ df, where

$$A = f \ln s^2 - \sum (f_i \ln s_i^2)$$

and

$$B = 1 + \frac{1}{3(k-1)}\left[\sum\left(\frac{1}{f_i}\right) - \frac{1}{f}\right]$$

Apply Bartlett's test to the data of Table 11.1 and verify that the hypothesis that population variances of employee compensation are the same in each employment size of the establishment cannot be rejected at the 5 percent level of significance.

Note: f_i, the df for each sample variance, is 9, since n_i for each sample (i.e., employment class) is 10.

11.14. Consider the following regression-through-the origin model:

$$Y_i = \beta X_i + u_i, \quad \text{for } i = 1, 2$$

You are told that $u_1 \sim N(0, \sigma^2)$ and $u_2 \sim N(0, 2\sigma^2)$ and that they are statistically independent. If $X_1 = +1$ and $X_2 = -1$, obtain the *weighted* least-squares (WLS) estimate of β and its variance. If in this situation you had assumed incorrectly that the two error variances were the same (say, equal to σ^2), what would be the OLS estimator of β? And its variance? Compare these estimates with the estimates obtained by the method of WLS. What general conclusion do you draw?*

11.15. Table 11.7 gives data on 81 cars about MPG (average miles per gallons), HP (engine horsepower), VOL (cubic feet of cab space), SP (top speed, miles per hour), and WT (vehicle weight in 100 lbs.).

a. Consider the following model:

$$\text{MPG}_i = \beta_1 + \beta_2\text{SP}_i + \beta_3\text{HP}_i + \beta_4\text{WT}_i + u_i$$

Estimate the parameters of this model and interpret the results. Do they make economic sense?

b. Would you expect the error variance in the preceding model to be heteroscedastic? Why?

c. Use the White test to find out if the error variance is heteroscedastic.

d. Obtain White's heteroscedasticity-consistent standard errors and t values and compare your results with those obtained from OLS.

e. If heteroscedasticity is established, how would you transform the data so that in the transformed data the error variance is homoscedastic? Show the necessary calculations.

11.16. *Food expenditure in India.* In Table 2.8 we have given data on expenditure on food and total expenditure for 55 families in India.

a. Regress expenditure on food on total expenditure, and examine the residuals obtained from this regression.

b. Plot the residuals obtained in (*a*) against total expenditure and see if you observe any systematic pattern.

*Adapted from F. A. F. Seber, *Linear Regression Analysis,* John Wiley & Sons, New York, 1977, p. 64.

TABLE 11.7 Passenger Car Mileage Data

Observation	MPG	SP	HP	VOL	WT	Observation	MPG	SP	HP	VOL	WT
1	65.4	96	49	89	17.5	42	32.2	106	95	106	30.0
2	56.0	97	55	92	20.0	43	32.2	109	102	92	30.0
3	55.9	97	55	92	20.0	44	32.2	106	95	88	30.0
4	49.0	105	70	92	20.0	45	31.5	105	93	102	30.0
5	46.5	96	53	92	20.0	46	31.5	108	100	99	30.0
6	46.2	105	70	89	20.0	47	31.4	108	100	111	30.0
7	45.4	97	55	92	20.0	48	31.4	107	98	103	30.0
8	59.2	98	62	50	22.5	49	31.2	120	130	86	30.0
9	53.3	98	62	50	22.5	50	33.7	109	115	101	35.0
10	43.4	107	80	94	22.5	51	32.6	109	115	101	35.0
11	41.1	103	73	89	22.5	52	31.3	109	115	101	35.0
12	40.9	113	92	50	22.5	53	31.3	109	115	124	35.0
13	40.9	113	92	99	22.5	54	30.4	133	180	113	35.0
14	40.4	103	73	89	22.5	55	28.9	125	160	113	35.0
15	39.6	100	66	89	22.5	56	28.0	115	130	124	35.0
16	39.3	103	73	89	22.5	57	28.0	102	96	92	35.0
17	38.9	106	78	91	22.5	58	28.0	109	115	101	35.0
18	38.8	113	92	50	22.5	59	28.0	104	100	94	35.0
19	38.2	106	78	91	22.5	60	28.0	105	100	115	35.0
20	42.2	109	90	103	25.0	61	27.7	120	145	111	35.0
21	40.9	110	92	99	25.0	62	25.6	107	120	116	40.0
22	40.7	101	74	107	25.0	63	25.3	114	140	131	40.0
23	40.0	111	95	101	25.0	64	23.9	114	140	123	40.0
24	39.3	105	81	96	25.0	65	23.6	117	150	121	40.0
25	38.8	111	95	89	25.0	66	23.6	122	165	50	40.0
26	38.4	110	92	50	25.0	67	23.6	122	165	114	40.0
27	38.4	110	92	117	25.0	68	23.6	122	165	127	40.0
28	38.4	110	92	99	25.0	69	23.6	122	165	123	40.0
29	46.9	90	52	104	27.5	70	23.5	148	245	112	40.0
30	36.3	112	103	107	27.5	71	23.4	160	280	50	40.0
31	36.1	103	84	114	27.5	72	23.4	121	162	135	40.0
32	36.1	103	84	101	27.5	73	23.1	121	162	132	40.0
33	35.4	111	102	97	27.5	74	22.9	110	140	160	45.0
34	35.3	111	102	113	27.5	75	22.9	110	140	129	45.0
35	35.1	102	81	101	27.5	76	19.5	121	175	129	45.0
36	35.1	106	90	98	27.5	77	18.1	165	322	50	45.0
37	35.0	106	90	88	27.5	78	17.2	140	238	115	45.0
38	33.2	109	102	86	30.0	79	17.0	147	263	50	45.0
39	32.9	109	102	86	30.0	80	16.7	157	295	119	45.0
40	32.3	120	130	92	30.0	81	13.2	130	236	107	55.0
41	32.2	106	95	113	30.0						

Note:

VOL = cubic feet of cab space.
HP = engine horsepower.
MPG = average miles per gallon.
SP = top speed, miles per hour.
WT = vehicle weight, hundreds of pounds.
Observation = car observation number (Names of cars not disclosed).

Source: U.S. Environmental Protection Agency, 1991, Report EPA/AA/CTAB/91-02.

c. If the plot in (*b*) suggests that there is heteroscedasticity, apply the Park, Glejser, and White tests to find out if the impression of heteroscedasticity observed in (*b*) is supported by these tests.

d. Obtain White's heteroscedasticity-consistent standard errors and compare those with the OLS standard errors. Decide if it is worth correcting for heteroscedasticity in this example.

11.17. Repeat Exercise 11.16, but this time regress the logarithm of expenditure on food on the logarithm of total expenditure. If you observe heteroscedasticity in the linear model of Exercise 11.16 but not in the log–linear model, what conclusion do you draw? Show all the necessary calculations.

11.18. *A shortcut to White's test.* As noted in the text, the White test can consume degrees of freedom if there are several regressors and if we introduce all the regressors, their squared terms, and their cross products. Therefore, instead of estimating regressions like Eq. (11.5.22), why not simply run the following regression:

$$\hat{u}_i^2 = \alpha_1 + \alpha_2 \hat{Y}_i + \alpha_2 \hat{Y}_i^2 + \nu_i$$

where $\hat{Y}_i$ are the estimated Y (i.e., regressand) values from whatever model you are estimating? After all, $\hat{Y}_i$ is simply the weighted average of the regressors, with the estimated regression coefficients serving as the weights.

Obtain the R^2 value from the preceding regression and use Eq. (11.5.22) to test the hypothesis that there is no heteroscedasticity.

Apply the preceding test to the food expenditure example of Exercise 11.16.

11.19. Return to the R&D example discussed in Section 11.7 (Exercise 11.10). Repeat the example using profits as the regressor. A priori, would you expect your results to be different from those using sales as the regressor? Why or why not?

11.20. Table 11.8 gives data on median salaries of full professors in statistics in research universities in the United States for the academic year 2007.

a. Plot median salaries against years in rank (as a measure of years of experience). For the plotting purposes, assume that the median salaries refer to the midpoint of years in rank. Thus, the salary $124,578 in the range 4–5 refers to 4.5 years in the rank, and so on. For the last group, assume that the range is 31–33.

b. Consider the following regression models:

$$Y_i = \alpha_1 + \alpha_2 X_i + u_i \quad (1)$$

$$Y_i = \beta_1 + \beta_2 X_i + \beta_3 X_i^2 + \nu_i \quad (2)$$

TABLE 11.8
Median Salaries of Full Professors in Statistics, 2007

Source: American Statistical Association, "2007 Salary Report."

Years in Rank	Count	Median
0 to 1	40	$101,478
2 to 3	24	102,400
4 to 5	35	124,578
6 to 7	34	122,850
8 to 9	33	116,900
10 to 14	73	119,465
15 to 19	69	114,900
20 to 24	54	129,072
25 to 30	44	131,704
31 or more	25	143,000

where Y = median salary, X = years in rank (measured at midpoint of the range), and u and v are the error terms. Can you argue why model (2) might be preferable to model (1)? From the data given, estimate both the models.

c. If you observe heteroscedasticity in model (1) but not in model (2), what conclusion would you draw? Show the necessary computations.

d. If heteroscedasticity is observed in model (2), how would you transform the data so that in the transformed model there is no heteroscedasticity?

11.21. You are given the following data:

$$\text{RSS}_1 \text{ based on the first 30 observations} = 55, \text{ df} = 25$$

$$\text{RSS}_2 \text{ based on the last 30 observations} = 140, \text{ df} = 25$$

Carry out the Goldfeld–Quandt test of heteroscedasticity at the 5 percent level of significance.

11.22. Table 11.9 gives data on percent change per year for stock prices (Y) and consumer prices (X) for a cross section of 20 countries.

a. Plot the data in a scattergram.

b. Regress Y on X and examine the residuals from this regression. What do you observe?

c. Since the data for Chile seem atypical (outlier?), repeat the regression in (*b*), dropping the data on Chile. Now examine the residuals from this regression. What do you observe?

d. If on the basis of the results in (*b*) you conclude that there was heteroscedasticity in error variance but on the basis of the results in (*c*) you reverse your conclusion, what general conclusions do you draw?

TABLE 11.9
Stock and Consumer Prices, Post–World War II Period (through 1969)

Source: Phillip Cagan, *Common Stock Values and Inflation: The Historical Record of Many Countries,* National Bureau of Economic Research, Suppl., March 1974, Table 1, p. 4.

	Rate of Change, % per Year	
Country	Stock Prices, Y	Consumer Prices, X
1. Australia	5.0	4.3
2. Austria	11.1	4.6
3. Belgium	3.2	2.4
4. Canada	7.9	2.4
5. Chile	25.5	26.4
6. Denmark	3.8	4.2
7. Finland	11.1	5.5
8. France	9.9	4.7
9. Germany	13.3	2.2
10. India	1.5	4.0
11. Ireland	6.4	4.0
12. Israel	8.9	8.4
13. Italy	8.1	3.3
14. Japan	13.5	4.7
15. Mexico	4.7	5.2
16. Netherlands	7.5	3.6
17. New Zealand	4.7	3.6
18. Sweden	8.0	4.0
19. United Kingdom	7.5	3.9
20. United States	9.0	2.1

11.23. Table 11.10 from the website gives salary and related data on 447 executives of Fortune 500 companies. Data include salary = 1999 salary and bonuses; totcomp = 1999 CEO total compensation; tenure = number of years as CEO (0 if less than 6 months); age = age of CEO; sales = total 1998 sales revenue of the firm; profits = 1998 profits for the firm; and assets = total assets of the firm in 1998.

a. Estimate the following regression from these data and obtain the Breusch–Pagan–Godfrey statistic to check for heteroscedasticity:

$$\text{salary}_i = \beta_1 + \beta_2 \text{tenure}_i + \beta_3 \text{age}_i + \beta_4 \text{sales}_i + \beta_5 \text{profits}_i + \beta_6 \text{assets}_i + u_i$$

Does there seem to be a problem with heteroscedasticity?

b. Now create a second model using ln(Salary) as the dependent variable. Is there any improvement in the heteroscedasticity?

c. Create scattergrams of salary vs. each of the independent variables. Can you discern which variable(s) is (are) contributing to the issue? What suggestions would you make now to address this? What is your final model?

Appendix 11A

11A.1 Proof of Equation (11.2.2)

From Appendix 3A, Section 3A.3, we have

$$\begin{aligned}\text{var}(\hat{\beta}_2) &= E\left(k_1^2 u_1^2 + k_2^2 u_2^2 + \cdots + k_n^2 u_n^2 + 2 \text{ cross-product terms}\right)\\ &= E\left(k_1^2 u_1^2 + k_2^2 u_2^2 + \cdots + k_n^2 u_n^2\right)\end{aligned}$$

since the expectations of the cross-product terms are zero because of the assumption of no serial correlation,

$$\text{var}(\hat{\beta}_2) = k_1^2 E\left(u_1^2\right) + k_2^2 E\left(u_2^2\right) + \cdots + k_n^2 E\left(u_n^2\right)$$

since the k_i are known. (Why?)

$$\text{var}(\hat{\beta}_2) = k_1^2 \sigma_1^2 + k_2^2 \sigma_2^2 + \cdots + k_n^2 \sigma_n^2$$

since $E(u_i^2) = \sigma_i^2$.

$$\begin{aligned}\text{var}(\hat{\beta}_2) &= \sum k_i^2 \sigma_i^2\\ &= \sum \left[\left(\frac{x_i}{\sum x_i^2}\right)^2 \sigma_i^2\right] \qquad \text{since } k_i = \frac{x_i}{\sum x_i^2} \qquad (11.2.2)\\ &= \frac{\sum x_i^2 \sigma_i^2}{\left(\sum x_i^2\right)^2}\end{aligned}$$

11A.2 The Method of Weighted Least Squares

To illustrate the method, we use the two-variable model $Y_i = \beta_1 + \beta_2 X_i + u_i$. The unweighted least-squares method minimizes

$$\sum \hat{u}_i^2 = \sum (Y_i - \hat{\beta}_1 - \hat{\beta}_2 X_i)^2 \qquad (1)$$

to obtain the estimates, whereas the weighted least-squares method minimizes the weighted residual sum of squares:

$$\sum w_i \hat{u}_i^2 = \sum w_i (Y_i - \hat{\beta}_1^* - \hat{\beta}_2^* X_i)^2 \tag{2}$$

where β_1^* and β_2^* are the weighted least-squares estimators and where the weights w_i are such that

$$w_i = \frac{1}{\sigma_i^2} \tag{3}$$

that is, the weights are inversely proportional to the variance of u_i or Y_i conditional upon the given X_i, it being understood that $\text{var}(u_i \mid X_i) = \text{var}(Y_i \mid X_i) = \sigma_i^2$.

Differentiating Eq. (2) with respect to $\hat{\beta}_1^*$ and $\hat{\beta}_2^*$, we obtain

$$\frac{\partial \sum w_i \hat{u}_i^2}{\partial \beta_1^*} = 2 \sum w_i (Y_i - \hat{\beta}_1^* - \hat{\beta}_2^* X_i)(-1)$$

$$\frac{\partial \sum w_i \hat{u}_i^2}{\partial \beta_2^*} = 2 \sum w_i (Y_i - \hat{\beta}_1^* - \hat{\beta}_2^* X_i)(-X_i)$$

Setting the preceding expressions equal to zero, we obtain the following two normal equations:

$$\sum w_i Y_i = \hat{\beta}_1^* \sum w_i + \hat{\beta}_2^* \sum w_i X_i \tag{4}$$

$$\sum w_i X_i Y_i = \hat{\beta}_1^* \sum w_i X_i + \hat{\beta}_2^* \sum w_i X_i^2 \tag{5}$$

Notice the similarity between these normal equations and the normal equations of the unweighted least squares.

Solving these equations simultaneously, we obtain

$$\hat{\beta}_1^* = \bar{Y}^* - \hat{\beta}_2^* \bar{X}^* \tag{6}$$

and

$$\hat{\beta}_2^* = \frac{\left(\sum w_i\right)\left(\sum w_i X_i Y_i\right) - \left(\sum w_i X_i\right)\left(\sum w_i Y_i\right)}{\left(\sum w_i\right)\left(\sum w_i X_i^2\right) - \left(\sum w_i X_i\right)^2} \tag{(11.3.8) = (7)}$$

The variance of $\hat{\beta}_2^*$ shown in Eq. (11.3.9) can be obtained in the manner of the variance of $\hat{\beta}_2$ shown in Appendix 3A, Section 3A.3.

Note: $\bar{Y}^* = \sum w_i Y_i / \sum w_i$ and $\bar{X}^* = \sum w_i X_i / \sum w_i$. As can be readily verified, these weighted means coincide with the usual or unweighted means $\bar{Y}$ and $\bar{X}$ when $w_i = w$, a constant, for all i.

11A.3 Proof that $E(\hat{\sigma}^2) \neq \sigma^2$ in the Presence of Heteroscedasticity

Consider the two-variable model:

$$Y_i = \beta_1 + \beta_2 X_i + u_i \tag{1}$$

where $\text{var}(u_i) = \sigma_i^2$

Now

$$\begin{aligned}\hat{\sigma}^2 = \frac{\sum \hat{u}_i^2}{n-2} = \frac{\sum (Y_i - \hat{Y}_i)^2}{n-2} &= \frac{\sum [\beta_1 + \beta_2 X_i + u_i - \hat{\beta}_1 - \hat{\beta}_2 X_i]^2}{n-2} \\ &= \frac{\sum [-(\hat{\beta}_1 - \beta_1) - (\hat{\beta}_2 - \beta_2) X_i + u_i]^2}{n-2}\end{aligned} \tag{2}$$

Noting that $(\hat{\beta}_1 - \beta_1) = -(\hat{\beta}_2 - \beta_2)\bar{X} + \bar{u}$, and substituting this into Eq. (2) and taking expectations on both sides, we get:

$$E(\hat{\sigma}^2) = \frac{1}{n-2}\left\{-\sum x_i^2 \operatorname{var}(\hat{\beta}_2) + E\left[\sum (u_i - \bar{u})^2\right]\right\}$$
$$= \frac{1}{n-2}\left[-\frac{\sum x_i^2 \sigma_i^2}{\sum x_i^2} + \frac{(n-1)\sum \sigma_i^2}{n}\right] \tag{3}$$

where use is made of Eq. (11.2.2).

As you can see from Eq. (3), if there is homoscedasticity, that is, $\sigma_i^2 = \sigma^2$ for each i, $E(\hat{\sigma}^2) = \sigma^2$. Therefore, the expected value of the conventionally computed $\hat{\sigma}^2 = \sum \hat{u}^2/(n-2)$ will not be equal to the true σ^2 in the presence of heteroscedasticity.[1]

11A.4 White's Robust Standard Errors

To give you some idea about White's heteroscedasticity-corrected standard errors, consider the two-variable regression model:

$$Y_i = \beta_1 + \beta_2 X_i + u_i \qquad \operatorname{var}(u_i) = \sigma_i^2 \tag{1}$$

As shown in Eq. (11.2.2),

$$\operatorname{var}(\hat{\beta}_2) = \frac{\sum x_i^2 \sigma_i^2}{\left(\sum x_i^2\right)^2} \tag{2}$$

Since σ_i^2 are not directly observable, White suggests using $\hat{u}_i^2$, the squared residual for each i, in place of σ_i^2 and estimating the var $(\hat{\beta}_2)$ as follows:

$$\operatorname{var}(\hat{\beta}_2) = \frac{\sum x_i^2 \hat{u}_i^2}{\left(\sum x_i^2\right)^2} \tag{3}$$

White has shown that Eq. (3) is a consistent estimator of Eq. (2), that is, as the sample size increases indefinitely, Eq. (3) converges to Eq. (2).[2]

Incidentally, note that if your software package does not contain White's robust standard error procedure, you can do it as shown in Eq. (3) by first running the usual OLS regression, obtaining the residuals from this regression, and then using formula (3).

White's procedure can be generalized to the k-variable regression model

$$Y_i = \beta_1 + \beta_2 X_{2i} + \beta_3 X_{3i} + \cdots + \beta_k X_{ki} + u_i \tag{4}$$

The variance of any partial regression coefficient, say $\hat{\beta}_j$, is obtained as follows:

$$\operatorname{var}(\hat{\beta}_j) = \frac{\sum \hat{w}_{ji}^2 \hat{u}_i^2}{\left(\sum \hat{w}_{ji}^2\right)^2} \tag{5}$$

where $\hat{u}_i$ are the residuals obtained from the (original) regression (4) and $\hat{w}_j$ are the residuals obtained from the (auxiliary) regression of the regressor X_j on the remaining regressors in Eq. (4).

Obviously, this is a time-consuming procedure, for you will have to estimate Eq. (5) for each X variable. Of course, all this labor can be avoided if you have a statistical package that does this routinely. Packages such as PC-GIVE, *EViews*, MICROFIT, SHAZAM, STATA, and LIMDEP now obtain White's heteroscedasticity-robust standard errors very easily.

[1]Further details can be obtained from Jan Kmenta, *Elements of Econometrics,* 2d. ed., Macmillan, New York, 1986, pp. 276–278.

[2]To be more precise, n times Eq. (3) converges in probability to $E[(X_i - \mu_X)^2 u_i^2]/(\sigma_X^2)^2$, which is the probability limit of n times Eq. (2), where n is the sample size, μ_x is the expected value of X, and σ_X^2 is the (population) variance of X. For more details, see Jeffrey M. Wooldridge, *Introductory Econometrics: A Modern Approach,* South-Western Publishing, 2000, p. 250.

Chapter 12

Autocorrelation: What Happens If the Error Terms Are Correlated?

The reader may recall that there are generally three types of data that are available for empirical analysis: (1) cross section, (2) time series, and (3) combination of cross section and time series, also known as pooled data. In developing the classical linear regression model (CLRM) in **Part 1** we made several assumptions, which were discussed in Section 7.1. However, we noted that not *all* of these assumptions would hold in every type of data. As a matter of fact, we saw in the previous chapter that the assumption of homoscedasticity, or equal error variance, may not always be tenable in cross-sectional data. In other words, cross-sectional data are often plagued by the problem of heteroscedasticity.

However, in cross-section studies, data are often collected on the basis of a random sample of cross-sectional units, such as households (in a consumption function analysis) or firms (in an investment study analysis) so that there is no prior reason to believe that the error term pertaining to one household or firm is correlated with the error term of another household or firm. If by chance such a correlation is observed in cross-sectional units, it is called **spatial autocorrelation,** that is, correlation in space rather than over time. However, it is important to remember that, in cross-sectional analysis, the ordering of the data must have some logic, or economic interest, to make sense of any determination of whether (spatial) autocorrelation is present or not.

The situation, however, is likely to be very different if we are dealing with time series data, for the observations in such data follow a natural ordering over time so that successive observations are likely to exhibit intercorrelations, especially if the time interval between successive observations is short, such as a day, a week, or a month rather than a year. If you observe stock price indexes, such as the Dow Jones or S&P 500, over successive days, it is not unusual to find that these indexes move up or down for several days in succession. Obviously, in situations like this, the assumption of **no auto-**, or **serial, correlation** in the error terms that underlies the CLRM will be violated.

In this chapter we take a critical look at this assumption with a view to answering the following questions:

1. What is the nature of autocorrelation?
2. What are the theoretical and practical consequences of autocorrelation?

3. Since the assumption of no autocorrelation relates to the unobservable disturbances u_t, how does one know that there is autocorrelation in any given situation? Notice that we now use the subscript t to emphasize that we are dealing with time series data.
4. How does one remedy the problem of autocorrelation?

The reader will find this chapter in many ways similar to the preceding chapter on heteroscedasticity in that **under both heteroscedasticity and autocorrelation the usual OLS estimators, although linear, unbiased, and asymptotically (i.e., in large samples) normally distributed,[1] are no longer minimum variance among all linear unbiased estimators. In short, they are not efficient relative to other linear and unbiased estimators. Put differently, they may not be best linear unbiased estimators (BLUE). As a result, the usual, *t*, *F*, and χ^2 may not be valid.**

12.1 The Nature of the Problem

The term **autocorrelation** may be defined as "correlation between members of series of observations ordered in time [as in time series data] or space [as in cross-sectional data]."[2] In the regression context, the classical linear regression model assumes that such autocorrelation does not exist in the disturbances u_i. Symbolically,

$$\operatorname{cov}(u_i, u_j | x_i, x_j) = E(u_i u_j) = 0 \qquad i \neq j \tag{3.2.5}$$

Put simply, the classical model assumes that the disturbance term relating to any observation is not influenced by the disturbance term relating to any other observation. For example, if we are dealing with quarterly time series data involving the regression of output on labor and capital inputs and if, say, there is a labor strike affecting output in one quarter, there is no reason to believe that this disruption will be carried over to the next quarter. That is, if output is lower this quarter, there is no reason to expect it to be lower next quarter. Similarly, if we are dealing with cross-sectional data involving the regression of family consumption expenditure on family income, the effect of an increase of one family's income on its consumption expenditure is not expected to affect the consumption expenditure of another family.

However, if there is such a dependence, we have autocorrelation. Symbolically,

$$E(u_i u_j) \neq 0 \qquad i \neq j \tag{12.1.1}$$

In this situation, the disruption caused by a strike this quarter may very well affect output next quarter, or the increases in the consumption expenditure of one family may very well prompt another family to increase its consumption expenditure if it wants to keep up with the Joneses.

Before we find out why autocorrelation exists, it is essential to clear up some terminological questions. Although it is now a common practice to treat the terms **autocorrelation** and **serial correlation** synonymously, some authors prefer to distinguish the two terms. For example, Tintner defines autocorrelation as "lag correlation of a given series with itself, lagged by a number of time units," whereas he reserves the term serial correlation to define

[1]On this, see William H. Greene, *Econometric Analysis,* 4th ed., Prentice Hall, NJ, 2000, Chapter 11, and Paul A. Rudd, *An Introduction to Classical Econometric Theory,* Oxford University Press, 2000, Chapter 19.

[2]Maurice G. Kendall and William R. Buckland, *A Dictionary of Statistical Terms,* Hafner Publishing Company, New York, 1971, p. 8.

"lag correlation between two different series."[3] Thus, correlation between two time series such as $u_1, u_2, \ldots, u_{10}$ and $u_2, u_3, \ldots, u_{11}$, where the former is the latter series lagged by one time period, is *autocorrelation,* whereas correlation between time series such as $u_1, u_2, \ldots, u_{10}$ and $v_2, v_3, \ldots, v_{11}$, where u and v are two different time series, is called *serial correlation*. Although the distinction between the two terms may be useful, in this book we shall treat them synonymously.

Let us visualize some of the plausible patterns of auto- and nonautocorrelation, which are given in Figure 12.1. Figures 12.1*a* to *d* show that there is a discernible pattern among the u's. Figure 12.1*a* shows a cyclical pattern; Figures 12.1*b* and *c* suggest an upward or downward linear trend in the disturbances; whereas Figure 12.1*d* indicates that both linear and quadratic trend terms are present in the disturbances. Only Figure 12.1*e* indicates no systematic pattern, supporting the nonautocorrelation assumption of the classical linear regression model.

The natural question is: Why does serial correlation occur? There are several reasons, some of which are as follows:

Inertia

A salient feature of most economic time series is inertia, or sluggishness. As is well known, time series such as GNP, price indexes, production, employment, and unemployment exhibit (business) cycles. Starting at the bottom of the recession, when economic recovery starts, most of these series start moving upward. In this upswing, the value of a series at one point in time is greater than its previous value. Thus there is a "momentum" built into them, and it continues until something happens (e.g., increase in interest rate or taxes or both) to slow them down. Therefore, in regressions involving time series data, successive observations are likely to be interdependent.

Specification Bias: Excluded Variables Case

In empirical analysis the researcher often starts with a plausible regression model that may not be the most "perfect" one. After the regression analysis, the researcher does the post-mortem to find out whether the results accord with a priori expectations. If not, surgery is begun. For example, the researcher may plot the residuals $\hat{u}_i$ obtained from the fitted regression and may observe patterns such as those shown in Figure 12.1*a* to *d*. These residuals (which are proxies for u_i) may suggest that some variables that were originally candidates but were not included in the model for a variety of reasons should be included. This is the case of **excluded variable** specification bias. Often the inclusion of such variables removes the correlation pattern observed among the residuals. For example, suppose we have the following demand model:

$$Y_t = \beta_1 + \beta_2 X_{2t} + \beta_3 X_{3t} + \beta_4 X_{4t} + u_t \tag{12.1.2}$$

where Y = quantity of beef demanded, X_2 = price of beef, X_3 = consumer income, X_4 = price of pork, and t = time.[4] However, for some reason we run the following regression:

$$Y_t = \beta_1 + \beta_2 X_{2t} + \beta_3 X_{3t} + v_t \tag{12.1.3}$$

Now if Eq. (12.1.2) is the "correct" model or the "truth" or true relation, running Eq. (12.1.3) is tantamount to letting $v_t = \beta_4 X_{4t} + u_t$. And to the extent the price of pork affects the consumption of beef, the error or disturbance term v will reflect a systematic

[3] Gerhard Tintner, *Econometrics*, John Wiley & Sons, New York, 1965.

[4] As a matter of convention, we shall use the subscript t to denote time series data and the usual subscript i for cross-sectional data.

FIGURE 12.1
Patterns of autocorrelation and nonautocorrelation.

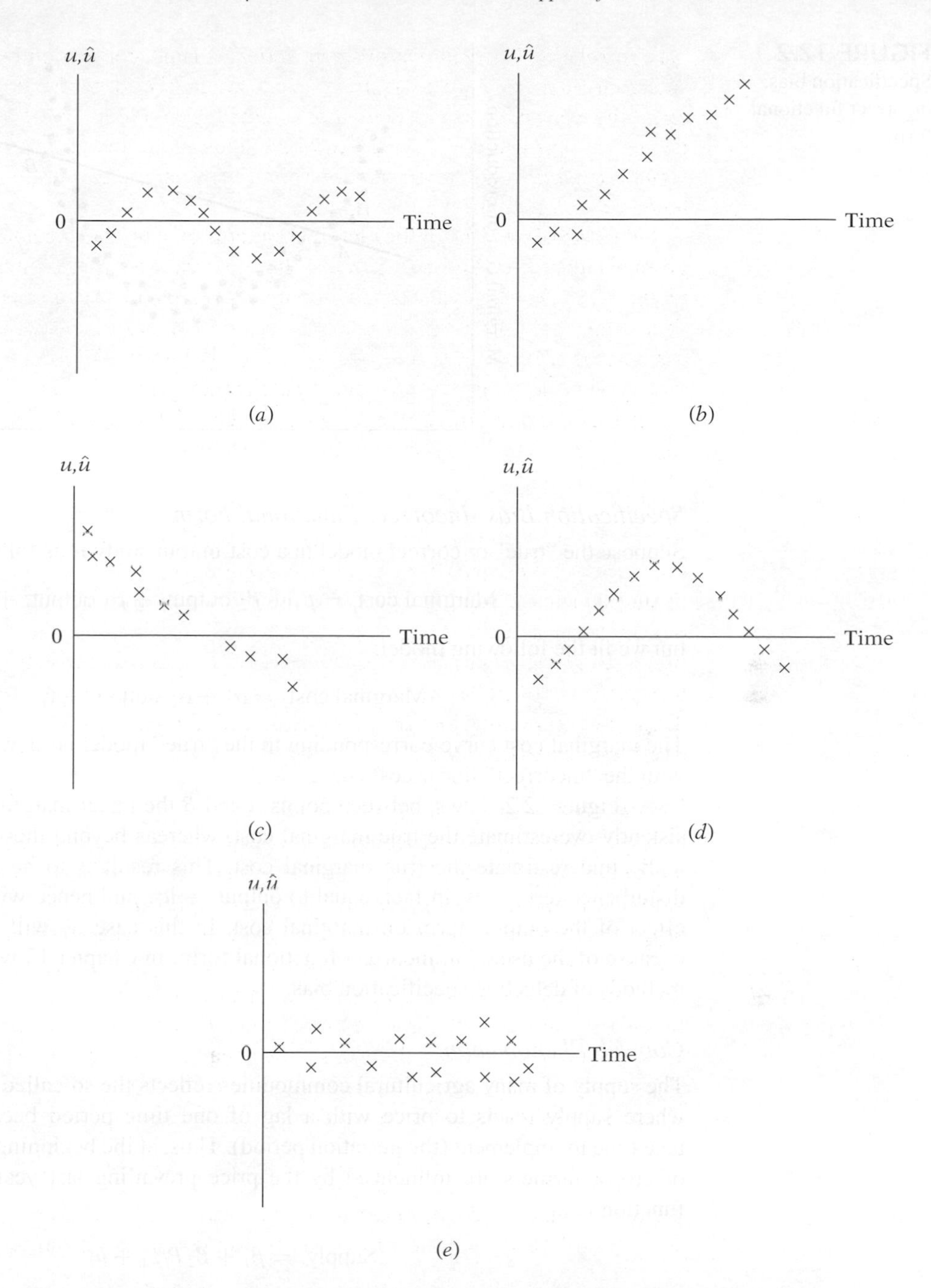

pattern, thus creating (false) autocorrelation. A simple test of this would be to run both Eqs. (12.1.2) and (12.1.3) and see whether autocorrelation, if any, observed in model (12.1.3) disappears when model (12.1.2) is run.[5] The actual mechanics of detecting autocorrelation will be discussed in Section 12.6 where we will show that a plot of the residuals from regressions (12.1.2) and (12.1.3) will often shed considerable light on serial correlation.

[5]If it is found that the real problem is one of specification bias, not autocorrelation, then as will be shown in Chapter 13, the OLS estimators of the parameters in Eq. (12.1.3) may be biased as well as inconsistent.

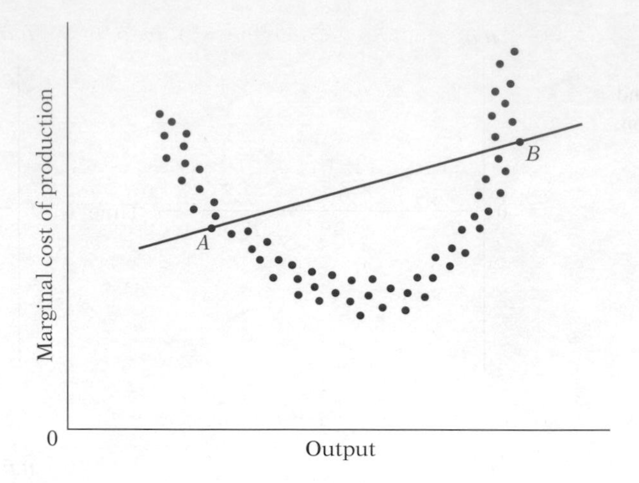

FIGURE 12.2 Specification bias: incorrect functional form.

Specification Bias: Incorrect Functional Form

Suppose the "true" or correct model in a cost-output study is as follows:

$$\text{Marginal cost}_i = \beta_1 + \beta_2 \text{ output}_i + \beta_3 \text{ output}_i^2 + u_i \tag{12.1.4}$$

but we fit the following model:

$$\text{Marginal cost}_i = \alpha_1 + \alpha_2 \text{ output}_i + v_i \tag{12.1.5}$$

The marginal cost curve corresponding to the "true" model is shown in Figure 12.2 along with the "incorrect" linear cost curve.

As Figure 12.2 shows, between points A and B the linear marginal cost curve will consistently overestimate the true marginal cost, whereas beyond these points it will consistently underestimate the true marginal cost. This result is to be expected, because the disturbance term v_i is, in fact, equal to output$^2 + u_i$, and hence will catch the systematic effect of the output^2 term on marginal cost. In this case, v_i will reflect autocorrelation because of the use of an incorrect functional form. In Chapter 13 we will consider several methods of detecting specification bias.

Cobweb Phenomenon

The supply of many agricultural commodities reflects the so-called cobweb phenomenon, where supply reacts to price with a lag of one time period because supply decisions take time to implement (the gestation period). Thus, at the beginning of this year's planting of crops, farmers are influenced by the price prevailing last year, so that their supply function is

$$\text{Supply}_t = \beta_1 + \beta_2 P_{t-1} + u_t \tag{12.1.6}$$

Suppose at the end of period t, price P_t turns out to be lower than P_{t-1}. Therefore, in period $t+1$ farmers may very well decide to produce less than they did in period t. Obviously, in this situation the disturbances u_t are not expected to be random because if the farmers overproduce in year t, they are likely to reduce their production in $t+1$, and so on, leading to a cobweb pattern.

Lags

In a time series regression of consumption expenditure on income, it is not uncommon to find that the consumption expenditure in the current period depends, among other things, on the consumption expenditure of the previous period. That is,

$$\text{Consumption}_t = \beta_1 + \beta_2 \text{ income}_t + \beta_3 \text{ consumption}_{t-1} + u_t \qquad (12.1.7)$$

A regression such as Eq. (12.1.7) is known as **autoregression** because one of the explanatory variables is the lagged value of the dependent variable. (We shall study such models in Chapter 17.) The rationale for a model such as Eq. (12.1.7) is simple. Consumers do not change their consumption habits readily for psychological, technological, or institutional reasons. Now if we neglect the lagged term in Eq. (12.1.7), the resulting error term will reflect a systematic pattern due to the influence of lagged consumption on current consumption.

"Manipulation" of Data

In empirical analysis, the raw data are often "manipulated." For example, in time series regressions involving quarterly data, such data are usually derived from the monthly data by simply adding three monthly observations and dividing the sum by 3. This averaging introduces smoothness into the data by dampening the fluctuations in the monthly data. Therefore, the graph plotting the quarterly data looks much smoother than the monthly data, and this smoothness may itself lend to a systematic pattern in the disturbances, thereby introducing autocorrelation. Another source of manipulation is **interpolation** or **extrapolation** of data. For example, the Census of Population is conducted every 10 years in this country, the last being in 2000 and the one before that in 1990. Now if there is a need to obtain data for some year within the intercensus period 1990–2000, the common practice is to interpolate on the basis of some ad hoc assumptions. All such data "massaging" techniques might impose upon the data a systematic pattern that might not exist in the original data.[6]

Data Transformation

As an example of this, consider the following model:

$$Y_t = \beta_1 + \beta_2 X_t + u_t \qquad (12.1.8)$$

where, say, Y = consumption expenditure and X = income. Since Eq. (12.1.8) holds true at every time period, it holds true also in the previous time period, $(t-1)$. So, we can write Eq. (12.1.8) as

$$Y_{t-1} = \beta_1 + \beta_2 X_{t-1} + u_{t-1} \qquad (12.1.9)$$

Y_{t-1}, X_{t-1}, and u_{t-1} are known as the **lagged values** of Y, X, and u, respectively, here lagged by one period. We will see the importance of the lagged values later in the chapter as well in several places in the text.

Now if we subtract Eq. (12.1.9) from Eq. (12.1.8), we obtain

$$\Delta Y_t = \beta_2 \Delta X_t + \Delta u_t \qquad (12.1.10)$$

where Δ, known as the **first difference operator,** tells us to take successive differences of the variables in question. Thus, $\Delta Y_t = (Y_t - Y_{t-1})$, $\Delta X_t = (X_t - X_{t-1})$, and $\Delta u_t = (u_t - u_{t-1})$. For empirical purposes, we write Eq. (12.1.10) as

$$\Delta Y_t = \beta_2 \Delta X_t + v_t \qquad (12.1.11)$$

where $v_t = \Delta u_t = (u_t - u_{t-1})$.

[6]On this, see William H. Greene, op. cit., p. 526.

Equation (12.1.9) is known as the **level form** and Eq. (12.1.10) is known as the **(first) difference form.** Both forms are often used in empirical analysis. For example, if in Eq. (12.1.9) Y and X represent the logarithms of consumption expenditure and income, then in Eq. (12.1.10) ΔY and ΔX will represent changes in the logs of consumption expenditure and income. But as we know, a change in the log of a variable is a relative change, or a percentage change, if the former is multiplied by 100. So, instead of studying relationships between variables in the level form, we may be interested in their relationships in the growth form.

Now if the error term in Eq. (12.1.8) satisfies the standard OLS assumptions, particularly the assumption of no autocorrelation, it can be shown that the error term v_t in Eq. (12.1.11) is autocorrelated. (The proof is given in Appendix 12A, Section 12A.1.) It may be noted here that models like Eq. (12.1.11) are known as **dynamic regression models,** that is, models involving lagged regressands. We will study such models in depth in Chapter 17.

The point of the preceding example is that sometimes autocorrelation may be induced as a result of transforming the original model.

Nonstationarity

We mentioned in Chapter 1 that, while dealing with time series data, we may have to find out if a given time series is stationary. Although we will discuss the topic of nonstationary time series more thoroughly in the chapters on time series econometrics in **Part 5** of the text, loosely speaking, a time series is stationary if its characteristics (e.g., mean, variance, and covariance) are *time invariant;* that is, they do not change over time. If that is not the case, we have a nonstationary time series.

As we will discuss in **Part 5,** in a regression model such as Eq. (12.1.8), it is quite possible that both Y and X are nonstationary and therefore the error u is also nonstationary.[7] In that case, the error term will exhibit autocorrelation.

In summary, then, there are a variety of reasons why the error term in a regression model may be autocorrelated. In the rest of the chapter we investigate in some detail the problems posed by autocorrelation and what can be done about it.

It should be noted also that autocorrelation can be positive (Figure 12.3*a*) as well as negative, although most economic time series generally exhibit positive autocorrelation because most of them ether move upward or downward over extended time periods and do not exhibit a constant up-and-down movement such as that shown in Figure 12.3*b*.

12.2 OLS Estimation in the Presence of Autocorrelation

What happens to the OLS estimators and their variances if we introduce autocorrelation in the disturbances by assuming that $E(u_t u_{t+s}) \neq 0$ $(s \neq 0)$ but retain all the other assumptions of the classical model?[8] Note again that we are now using the subscript t on the disturbances to emphasize that we are dealing with time series data.

We revert once again to the two-variable regression model to explain the basic ideas involved, namely, $Y_t = \beta_1 + \beta_2 X_t + u_t$. To make any headway, we must assume the mechanism that generates u_t, for $E(u_t u_{t+s}) \neq 0$ $(s \neq 0)$ is too general an assumption to be of

[7]As we will also see in **Part 5,** even though Y and X are nonstationary, it is possible to find u to be stationary. We will explore the implication of that later on.

[8]If $s = 0$, we obtain $E(u_t^2)$. Since $E(u_t) = 0$ by assumption, $E(u_t^2)$ will represent the variance of the error term, which obviously is nonzero (why?).

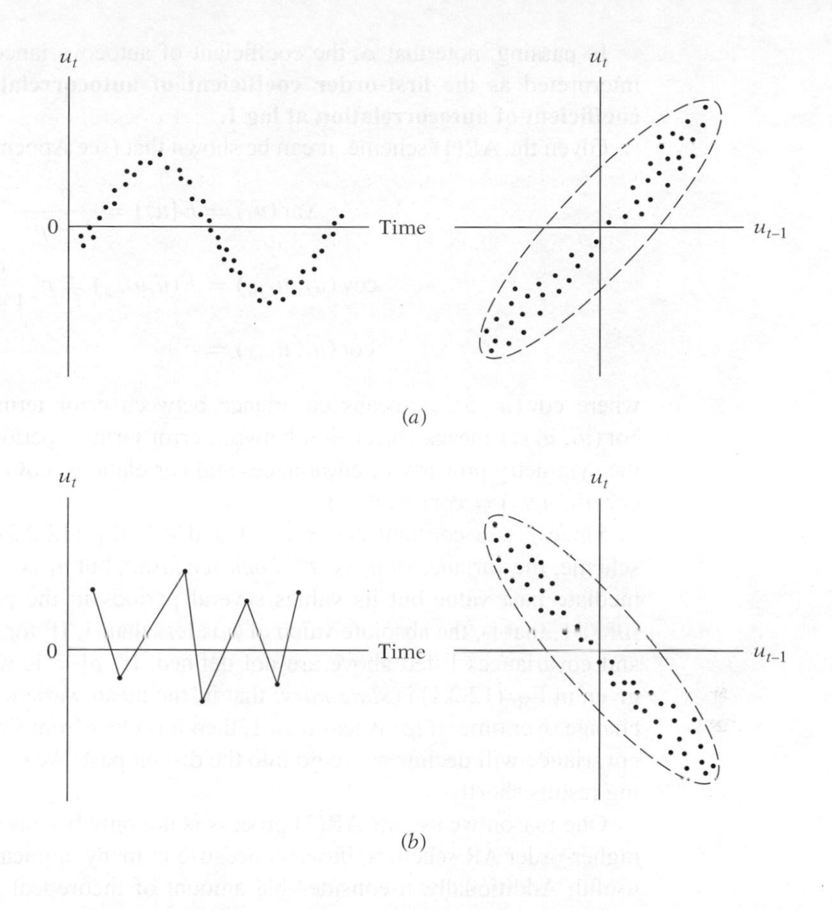

FIGURE 12.3 (*a*) Positive and (*b*) negative autocorrelation.

any practical use. As a starting point, or first approximation, one can assume that the disturbance, or error, terms are generated by the following mechanism.

$$u_t = \rho u_{t-1} + \varepsilon_t \qquad -1 < \rho < 1 \tag{12.2.1}$$

where ρ (= rho) is known as the **coefficient of autocovariance** and where ε_t is the stochastic disturbance term such that it satisfies the standard OLS assumptions, namely,

$$\begin{aligned} E(\varepsilon_t) &= 0 \\ \operatorname{var}(\varepsilon_t) &= \sigma_\varepsilon^2 \\ \operatorname{cov}(\varepsilon_t, \varepsilon_{t+s}) &= 0 \qquad s \neq 0 \end{aligned} \tag{12.2.2}$$

In the engineering literature, an error term with the preceding properties is often called a **white noise error term.** What Eq. (12.2.1) postulates is that the value of the disturbance term in period t is equal to ρ times its value in the previous period plus a purely random error term.

The scheme (12.2.1) is known as a **Markov first-order autoregressive scheme,** or simply a **first-order autoregressive scheme,** usually denoted as **AR(1).** The name *autoregressive* is appropriate because Eq. (12.2.1) can be interpreted as the regression of u_t on itself lagged one period. It is first order because u_t and its immediate past value are involved; that is, the maximum lag is 1. If the model were $u_t = \rho_1 u_{t-1} + \rho_2 u_{t-2} + \varepsilon_t$, it would be an AR(2), or second-order, autoregressive scheme, and so on. We will examine such higher-order schemes in the chapters on time series econometrics in **Part 5.**

In passing, note that ρ, the coefficient of autocovariance in Eq. (12.2.1), can also be interpreted as the **first-order coefficient of autocorrelation,** or more accurately, the **coefficient of autocorrelation at lag 1.**[9]

Given the AR(1) scheme, it can be shown that (see Appendix 12A, Section 12A.2):

$$\operatorname{var}(u_t) = E(u_t^2) = \frac{\sigma_\varepsilon^2}{1-\rho^2} \tag{12.2.3}$$

$$\operatorname{cov}(u_t, u_{t+s}) = E(u_t u_{t-s}) = \rho^s \frac{\sigma_\varepsilon^2}{1-\rho^2} \tag{12.2.4}$$

$$\operatorname{cor}(u_t, u_{t+s}) = \rho^s \tag{12.2.5}$$

where $\operatorname{cov}(u_t, u_{t+s})$ means covariance between error terms s periods apart and where $\operatorname{cor}(u_t, u_{t+s})$ means correlation between error terms s periods apart. Note that because of the symmetry property of covariances and correlations, $\operatorname{cov}(u_t, u_{t+s}) = \operatorname{cov}(u_t, u_{t-s})$ and $\operatorname{cor}(u_t, u_{t+s}) = \operatorname{cor}(u_t, u_{t-s})$.

Since ρ is a constant between -1 and $+1$, Eq. (12.2.3) shows that under the AR(1) scheme, the variance of u_t is *still homoscedastic*, but u_t is correlated not only with its immediate past value but its values several periods in the past. It is *critical* to note that $|\rho| < 1$, that is, the absolute value of ρ is less than 1. If, for example, ρ is 1, the variances and covariances listed above are not defined. If $|\rho| < 1$, we say that the AR(1) process given in Eq. (12.2.1) is *stationary;* that is, the mean, variance, and covariance of u_t do not change over time. If $|\rho|$ is less than 1, then it is clear from Eq. (12.2.4) that the value of the covariance will decline as we go into the distant past. We will see the utility of the preceding results shortly.

One reason we use the AR(1) process is not only because of its simplicity compared to higher-order AR schemes, but also because in many applications it has proved to be quite useful. Additionally, a considerable amount of theoretical and empirical work has been done on the AR(1) scheme.

Now return to our two-variable regression model: $Y_t = \beta_1 + \beta_2 X_t + u_t$. We know from Chapter 3 that the OLS estimator of the slope coefficient is

$$\hat{\beta}_2 = \frac{\sum x_t y_t}{\sum x_t^2} \tag{12.2.6}$$

and its variance is given by

$$\operatorname{var}(\hat{\beta}_2) = \frac{\sigma^2}{\sum x_i^2} \tag{12.2.7}$$

where the small letters as usual denote deviation from the mean values.

[9] This name can be easily justified. By definition, the (population) coefficient of correlation between u_t and u_{t-1} is

$$\rho = \frac{E\{[u_t - E(u_t)][u_{t-1} - E(u_{t-1})]\}}{\sqrt{\operatorname{var}(u_t)}\sqrt{\operatorname{var}(u_{t-1})}}$$

$$= \frac{E(u_t u_{t-1})}{\operatorname{var}(u_{t-1})}$$

since $E(u_t) = 0$ for each t and $\operatorname{var}(u_t) = \operatorname{var}(u_{t-1})$ because we are retaining the assumption of homoscedasticity. The reader can see that ρ is also the slope coefficient in the regression of u_t on u_{t-1}.

Now under the AR(1) scheme, it can be shown that the variance of this estimator is:

$$\operatorname{var}(\hat{\beta}_2)_{\text{AR1}} = \frac{\sigma^2}{\sum x_t^2}\left[1 + 2\rho\frac{\sum x_t x_{t-1}}{\sum x_t^2} + 2\rho^2\frac{\sum x_t x_{t-2}}{\sum x_t^2} + \cdots + 2\rho^{n-1}\frac{x_1 x_n}{\sum x_t^2}\right] \tag{12.2.8}$$

where $\operatorname{var}(\hat{\beta}_2)_{\text{AR1}}$ means the variance of $\hat{\beta}_2$ under a first-order autoregressive scheme.

A comparison of Eq. (12.2.8) with Eq. (12.2.7) shows the former is equal to the latter times a term that depends on ρ as well as the sample autocorrelations between the values taken by the regressor X at various lags.[10] And in general we cannot foretell whether $\operatorname{var}(\hat{\beta}_2)$ is less than or greater than $\operatorname{var}(\hat{\beta}_2)_{\text{AR1}}$ (but see Eq. [12.4.1] below). Of course, if ρ is zero, the two formulas will coincide, as they should (why?). Also, if the correlations among the successive values of the regressor are very small, the usual OLS variance of the slope estimator will not be seriously biased. But, as a general principle, the two variances will not be the same.

To give some idea about the difference between the variances given in Eqs. (12.2.7) and (12.2.8), assume that the regressor X also follows the first-order autoregressive scheme with a coefficient of autocorrelation of r. Then it can be shown that Eq. (12.2.8) reduces to:

$$\operatorname{var}(\hat{\beta}_2)_{\text{AR(1)}} = \frac{\sigma^2}{\sum x_t^2}\left(\frac{1 + r\rho}{1 - r\rho}\right) = \operatorname{var}(\hat{\beta}_2)_{\text{OLS}}\left(\frac{1 + r\rho}{1 - r\rho}\right) \tag{12.2.9}$$

If, for example, $r = 0.6$ and $\rho = 0.8$, using Eq. (12.2.9) we can check that $\operatorname{var}(\hat{\beta}_2)_{\text{AR1}} = 2.8461 \operatorname{var}(\hat{\beta}_2)_{\text{OLS}}$. To put it another way, $\operatorname{var}(\hat{\beta}_2)_{\text{OLS}} = \frac{1}{2.8461}\operatorname{var}(\hat{\beta}_2)_{\text{AR1}} = 0.3513 \operatorname{var}(\hat{\beta}_2)_{\text{AR1}}$. That is, the usual OLS formula (i.e., Eq. [12.2.7]) will underestimate the variance of $(\hat{\beta}_2)_{\text{AR1}}$ by about 65 percent. As you will realize, this answer is specific for the given values of r and ρ. But the point of this exercise is to warn you that a blind application of the usual OLS formulas to compute the variances and standard errors of the OLS estimators could give seriously misleading results.

Suppose we continue to use the OLS estimator $\hat{\beta}_2$ and adjust the usual variance formula by taking into account the AR(1) scheme. That is, we use $\hat{\beta}_2$ given by Eq. (12.2.6) but use the variance formula given by Eq. (12.2.8). What now are the properties of $\hat{\beta}_2$? It is easy to prove that $\hat{\beta}_2$ is still linear and unbiased. As a matter of fact, as shown in Appendix 3A, Section 3A.2, the assumption of no serial correlation, like the assumption of no heteroscedasticity, is not required to prove that $\hat{\beta}_2$ is unbiased. Is $\hat{\beta}_2$ still BLUE? Unfortunately, it is not; in the class of linear unbiased estimators, it does not have minimum variance. In short, $\hat{\beta}_2$, although linear-unbiased, is not efficient (relatively speaking, of course). The reader will notice that this finding is quite similar to the finding that $\hat{\beta}_2$ is less efficient in the presence of heteroscedasticity. There we saw that it was the weighted least-square estimator $\hat{\beta}_2^*$ given in Eq. (11.3.8), a special case of the generalized least-squares (GLS) estimator, that was efficient. In the case of autocorrelation can we find an estimator that is BLUE? The answer is yes, as can be seen from the discussion in the following section.

[10]Note that the term $r = \sum x_t x_{t+1} / \sum x_t^2$ is the correlation between X_t and X_{t+1} (or X_{t-1}, since the correlation coefficient is symmetric); $r^2 = \sum x_t x_{t+2} / \sum x_t^2$ is the correlation between the X's lagged two periods; and so on.

12.3 The BLUE Estimator in the Presence of Autocorrelation

Continuing with the two-variable model and assuming the AR(1) process, we can show that the BLUE estimator of β_2 is given by the following expression:[11]

$$\hat{\beta}_2^{\text{GLS}} = \frac{\sum_{t=2}^{n}(x_t - \rho x_{t-1})(y_t - \rho y_{t-1})}{\sum_{t=2}^{n}(x_t - \rho x_{t-1})^2} + C \tag{12.3.1}$$

where C is a correction factor that may be disregarded in practice. Note that the subscript t now runs from $t = 2$ to $t = n$. And its variance is given by

$$\operatorname{var} \hat{\beta}_2^{\text{GLS}} = \frac{\sigma^2}{\sum_{t=2}^{n}(x_t - \rho x_{t-1})^2} + D \tag{12.3.2}$$

where D too is a correction factor that may also be disregarded in practice. (See Exercise 12.18.)

The estimator $\hat{\beta}_2^{\text{GLS}}$, as the superscript suggests, is obtained by the method of GLS. As noted in Chapter 11, in GLS we incorporate any additional information we have (e.g., the nature of the heteroscedasticity or of the autocorrelation) directly into the estimating procedure by transforming the variables, whereas in OLS such side information is not directly taken into consideration. As the reader can see, the GLS estimator of β_2 given in Eq. (12.3.1) incorporates the autocorrelation parameter ρ in the estimating formula, whereas the OLS formula given in Eq. (12.2.6) simply neglects it. Intuitively, this is the reason why the GLS estimator is BLUE and not the OLS estimator—the GLS estimator makes the most use of the available information.[12] It hardly needs to be added that if $\rho = 0$, there is no additional information to be considered and hence both the GLS and OLS estimators are identical.

In short, under autocorrelation, it is the GLS estimator given in Eq. (12.3.1) that is BLUE, and the minimum variance is now given by Eq. (12.3.2) and not by Eq. (12.2.8) and obviously not by Eq. (12.2.7).

A Technical Note

As we noted in the previous chapter, the Gauss–Markov theorem provides only the sufficient condition for OLS to be BLUE. The necessary and sufficient conditions for OLS to be BLUE are given by **Kruskal's theorem,** mentioned in the previous chapter. Therefore, in some cases it can happen that OLS is BLUE despite autocorrelation. But such cases are infrequent in practice.

What happens if we blithely continue to work with the usual OLS procedure despite autocorrelation? The answer is provided in the following section.

[11]For proofs, see Jan Kmenta, *Elements of Econometrics,* Macmillan, New York, 1971, pp. 274–275. The correction factor C pertains to the first observation, (Y_1, X_1). On this point see Exercise 12.18.

[12]The formal proof that $\hat{\beta}_2^{\text{GLS}}$ is BLUE can be found in Kmenta, ibid. But the tedious algebraic proof can be simplified considerably using matrix notation. See J. Johnston, *Econometric Methods,* 3d ed., McGraw-Hill, New York, 1984, pp. 291–293.

12.4 Consequences of Using OLS in the Presence of Autocorrelation

As in the case of heteroscedasticity, in the presence of autocorrelation the OLS estimators are still linear unbiased as well as consistent and asymptotically normally distributed, but they are no longer efficient (i.e., minimum variance). What then happens to our usual hypothesis testing procedures if we continue to use the OLS estimators? Again, as in the case of heteroscedasticity, we distinguish two cases. For pedagogical purposes we still continue to work with the two-variable model, although the following discussion can be extended to multiple regressions without much trouble.[13]

OLS Estimation Allowing for Autocorrelation

As noted, $\hat{\beta}_2$ is not BLUE, and even if we use $\text{var}(\hat{\beta}_2)_{\text{AR1}}$, the confidence intervals derived from there are likely to be wider than those based on the GLS procedure. As Kmenta shows, this result is likely to be the case even if the sample size increases indefinitely.[14] That is, *$\hat{\beta}_2$ is not asymptotically efficient*. The implication of this finding for hypothesis testing is clear: We are likely to declare a coefficient statistically insignificant (i.e., not different from zero) even though in fact (i.e., based on the correct GLS procedure) it may be. This difference can be seen clearly from Figure 12.4. In this figure we show the 95% OLS [AR(1)] and GLS confidence intervals assuming that true $\beta_2 = 0$. Consider a particular estimate of β_2, say, b_2. Since b_2 lies in the OLS confidence interval, we could accept the hypothesis that true β_2 is zero with 95 percent confidence. But if we were to use the (correct) GLS confidence interval, we could reject the null hypothesis that true β_2 is zero, for b_2 lies in the region of rejection.

The message is: To establish confidence intervals and to test hypotheses, one should use GLS and not OLS even though the estimators derived from the latter are unbiased and consistent. (However, see Section 12.11 later.)

FIGURE 12.4
GLS and OLS 95% confidence intervals.

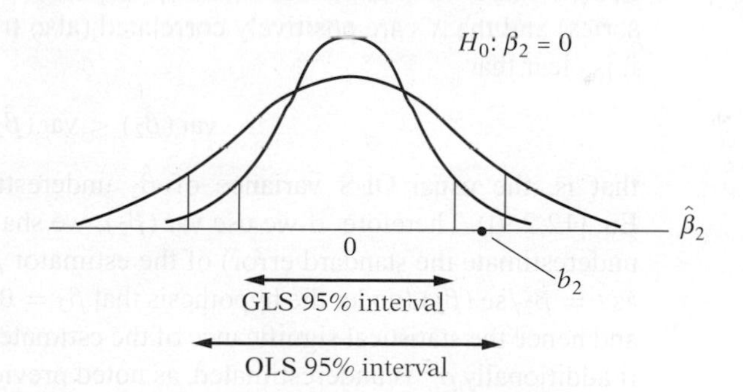

OLS Estimation Disregarding Autocorrelation

The situation is potentially very serious if we not only use $\hat{\beta}_2$ but also continue to use $\text{var}(\hat{\beta}_2) = \sigma^2/\sum x_t^2$, which completely disregards the problem of autocorrelation, that is, we mistakenly believe that the usual assumptions of the classical model hold true. Errors will arise for the following reasons:

1. The residual variance $\hat{\sigma}^2 = \sum \hat{u}_t^2/(n-2)$ is likely to underestimate the true σ^2.
2. As a result, we are likely to overestimate R^2.

[13]But matrix algebra becomes almost a necessity to avoid tedious algebraic manipulations.

[14]See Kmenta, op. cit., pp. 277–278.

3. Even if σ^2 is not underestimated, var $(\hat{\beta}_2)$ may underestimate var $(\hat{\beta}_2)_{\text{AR1}}$ (Eq. [12.2.8]), its variance under (first-order) autocorrelation, even though the latter is inefficient compared to var $(\hat{\beta}_2)^{\text{GLS}}$.
4. Therefore, the usual t and F tests of significance are no longer valid, and if applied, are likely to give seriously misleading conclusions about the statistical significance of the estimated regression coefficients.

To establish some of these propositions, let us revert to the two-variable model. We know from Chapter 3 that under the classical assumption

$$\hat{\sigma}^2 = \frac{\sum \hat{u}_i^2}{(n-2)}$$

provides an unbiased estimator of σ^2, that is, $E(\hat{\sigma}^2) = \sigma^2$. But if there is autocorrelation, given by AR(1), it can be shown that

$$E(\hat{\sigma}^2) = \frac{\sigma^2\{n - [2/(1-\rho)] - 2\rho r\}}{n-2} \tag{12.4.1}$$

where $r = \sum_{t=1}^{n-1} x_t x_{t-1} / \sum_{t=1}^{n} x_t^2$, which can be interpreted as the (sample) correlation coefficient between successive values of the X's.[15] If ρ and r are both positive (not an unlikely assumption for most economic time series), it is apparent from Eq. (12.4.1) that $E(\hat{\sigma}^2) < \sigma^2$; that is, the usual residual variance formula, on average, will underestimate the true σ^2. In other words, $\hat{\sigma}^2$ will be biased downward. Needless to say, this bias in $\hat{\sigma}^2$ will be transmitted to var $(\hat{\beta}_2)$ because in practice we estimate the latter by the formula $\hat{\sigma}^2 / \sum x_t^2$.

But even if σ^2 is not underestimated, var $(\hat{\beta}_2)$ is a *biased* estimator of var $(\hat{\beta}_2)_{\text{AR1}}$, which can be readily seen by comparing Eq. (12.2.7) with Eq. (12.2.8),[16] for the two formulas are not the same. As a matter of fact, if ρ is positive (which is true of most economic time series) and the X's are positively correlated (also true of most economic time series), then it is clear that

$$\text{var}(\hat{\beta}_2) < \text{var}(\hat{\beta}_2)_{\text{AR1}} \tag{12.4.2}$$

that is, the usual OLS variance of $\hat{\beta}_2$ underestimates its variance under AR(1) (see Eq. [12.2.9]). Therefore, if we use var $(\hat{\beta}_2)$, we shall inflate the precision or accuracy (i.e., underestimate the standard error) of the estimator $\hat{\beta}_2$. As a result, in computing the t ratio as $t = \hat{\beta}_2 / \text{se}(\hat{\beta}_2)$ (under the hypothesis that $\beta_2 = 0$), we shall be overestimating the t value and hence the statistical significance of the estimated β_2. The situation is likely to get worse if additionally σ^2 is underestimated, as noted previously.

To see how OLS is likely to underestimate σ^2 and the variance of $\hat{\beta}_2$, let us conduct the following **Monte Carlo experiment.** Suppose in the two-variable model we "know" that the true $\beta_1 = 1$ and $\beta_2 = 0.8$. Therefore, the stochastic PRF is

$$Y_t = 1.0 + 0.8X_t + u_t \tag{12.4.3}$$

[15]See S. M. Goldfeld and R. E. Quandt, *Nonlinear Methods in Econometrics*, North Holland Publishing Company, Amsterdam, 1972, p. 183. In passing, note that if the errors are positively autocorrelated, the R^2 value tends to have an upward bias, that is, it tends to be larger than the R^2 in the absence of such correlation.

[16]For a formal proof, see Kmenta, op. cit., p. 281.

TABLE 12.1
A Hypothetical Example of Positively Autocorrelated Error Terms

	ε_t	$u_t = 0.7u_{t-1} + \varepsilon_t$
0	0	$u_0 = 5$ (assumed)
1	0.464	$u_1 = 0.7(5) + 0.464 = 3.964$
2	2.026	$u_2 = 0.7(3.964) + 2.0262 = 4.8008$
3	2.455	$u_3 = 0.7(4.8010) + 2.455 = 5.8157$
4	−0.323	$u_4 = 0.7(5.8157) - 0.323 = 3.7480$
5	−0.068	$u_5 = 0.7(3.7480) - 0.068 = 2.5556$
6	0.296	$u_6 = 0.7(2.5556) + 0.296 = 2.0849$
7	−0.288	$u_7 = 0.7(2.0849) - 0.288 = 1.1714$
8	1.298	$u_8 = 0.7(1.1714) + 1.298 = 2.1180$
9	0.241	$u_9 = 0.7(2.1180) + 0.241 = 1.7236$
10	−0.957	$u_{10} = 0.7(1.7236) - 0.957 = 0.2495$

Note: ε_t data obtained from *A Million Random Digits and One Hundred Thousand Deviates,* Rand Corporation, Santa Monica, Calif., 1950.

Hence,

$$E(Y_t \mid X_t) = 1.0 + 0.8X_t \tag{12.4.4}$$

which gives the true population regression line. Let us assume that u_t are generated by the first-order autoregressive scheme as follows:

$$u_t = 0.7u_{t-1} + \varepsilon_t \tag{12.4.5}$$

where ε_t satisfy all the OLS assumptions. We assume further for convenience that the ε_t are normally distributed with zero mean and unit (= 1) variance. Equation (12.4.5) postulates that the successive disturbances are positively correlated, with a coefficient of autocorrelation of +0.7, a rather high degree of dependence.

Now, using a table of random normal numbers with zero mean and unit variance, we generated 10 random numbers shown in Table 12.1 and then by the scheme (12.4.5) we generated u_t. To start off the scheme, we need to specify the initial value of u, say, $u_0 = 5$.

Plotting the u_t generated in Table 12.1, we obtain Figure 12.5, which shows that initially each successive u_t is higher than its previous value and subsequently it is generally smaller than its previous value showing, in general, a positive autocorrelation.

Now suppose the values of X are fixed at 1, 2, 3, . . . , 10. Then, given these X's, we can generate a sample of 10 Y values from Eq. (12.4.3) and the values of u_t given in Table 12.1. The details are given in Table 12.2. Using the data of Table 12.2, if we regress Y on X, we obtain the following (sample) regression:

$$\begin{aligned} \hat{Y}_t = &\ 6.5452 + 0.3051X_t \\ &(0.6153) \quad (0.0992) \\ t = &\ (10.6366) \quad (3.0763) \\ & r^2 = 0.5419 \qquad \hat{\sigma}^2 = 0.8114 \end{aligned} \tag{12.4.6}$$

whereas the true regression line is as given by Eq. (12.4.4). Both the regression lines are given in Figure 12.6, which shows clearly how much the fitted regression line distorts the true regression line; it seriously underestimates the true slope coefficient but overestimates the true intercept. (But note that the OLS estimators are still unbiased.)

Figure 12.6 also shows why the true variance of u_i is likely to be underestimated by the estimator $\hat{\sigma}^2$, which is computed from the $\hat{u}_i$. The $\hat{u}_i$ are generally close to the fitted line

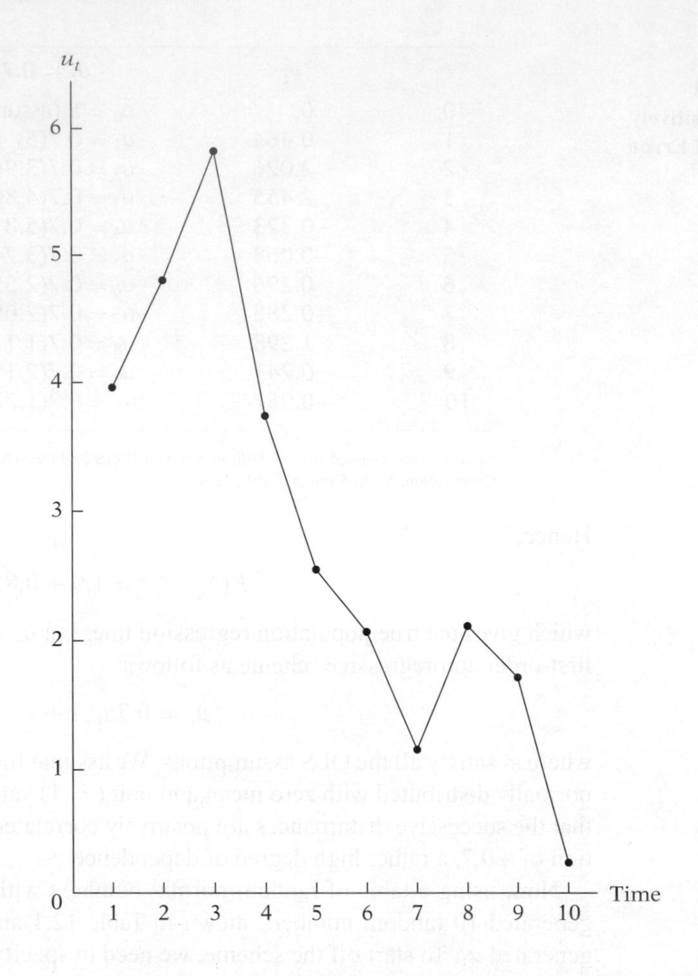

FIGURE 12.5 Correlation generated by the scheme $u_t = 0.7u_{t-1} + \varepsilon_t$ (Table 12.1).

TABLE 12.2 Generation of Y Sample Values

X_t	u_t	$Y_t = 1.0 + 0.8X_t + u_t$
1	3.9640	$Y_1 = 1.0 + 0.8(1) + 3.9640 = 5.7640$
2	4.8010	$Y_2 = 1.0 + 0.8(2) + 4.8008 = 7.4008$
3	5.8157	$Y_3 = 1.0 + 0.8(3) + 5.8157 = 9.2157$
4	3.7480	$Y_4 = 1.0 + 0.8(4) + 3.7480 = 7.9480$
5	2.5556	$Y_5 = 1.0 + 0.8(5) + 2.5556 = 7.5556$
6	2.0849	$Y_6 = 1.0 + 0.8(6) + 2.0849 = 7.8849$
7	1.1714	$Y_7 = 1.0 + 0.8(7) + 1.1714 = 7.7714$
8	2.1180	$Y_8 = 1.0 + 0.8(8) + 2.1180 = 9.5180$
9	1.7236	$Y_9 = 1.0 + 0.8(9) + 1.7236 = 9.9236$
10	0.2495	$Y_{10} = 1.0 + 0.8(10) + 0.2495 = 9.2495$

Note: u_t data obtained from Table 12.1.

(which is due to the OLS procedure) but deviate substantially from the true PRF. Hence, they do not give a correct picture of u_i. To gain some insight into the extent of underestimation of true σ^2, suppose we conduct another sampling experiment. Keeping the X_t and ε_t given in Tables 12.1 and 12.2, let us assume $\rho = 0$, that is, no autocorrelation. The new sample of Y values thus generated is given in Table 12.3.

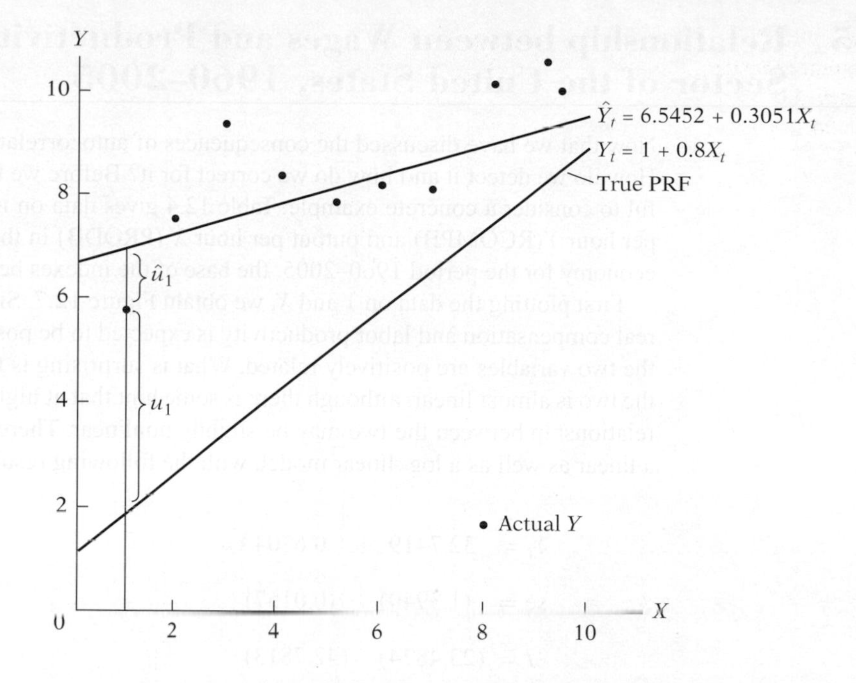

FIGURE 12.6 True PRF and the estimated regression line for the data of Table 12.2.

TABLE 12.3 **Sample of Y Values with Zero Serial Correlation**

X_t	$\varepsilon_t = u_t$	$Y_t = 1.0 + 0.8X_t + \varepsilon_t$
1	0.464	2.264
2	2.026	4.626
3	2.455	5.855
4	−0.323	3.877
5	0.068	4.932
6	0.296	6.096
7	−0.288	6.312
8	1.298	8.698
9	0.241	8.441
10	−0.957	8.043

Note: Since there is no autocorrelation, the u_t and ε_t are identical. The ε_t are from Table 12.1.

The regression based on Table 12.3 is as follows:

$$\begin{aligned} \hat{Y}_t &= 2.5345 + 0.6145X_t \\ &\quad\ (0.6796) \quad (0.1087) \\ t &= (3.7910) \quad (5.6541) \\ &\qquad r^2 = 0.7997 \qquad \hat{\sigma}^2 = 0.9752 \end{aligned} \tag{12.4.7}$$

This regression is much closer to the "truth" because the Y's are now essentially random. Notice that $\hat{\sigma}^2$ has increased from 0.8114 ($\rho = 0.7$) to 0.9752 ($\rho = 0$). Also notice that the standard errors of $\hat{\beta}_1$ and $\hat{\beta}_2$ have increased. This result is in accord with the theoretical results considered previously.

12.5 Relationship between Wages and Productivity in the Business Sector of the United States, 1960–2005

Now that we have discussed the consequences of autocorrelation, the obvious question is, How do we detect it and how do we correct for it? Before we turn to these topics, it is useful to consider a concrete example. Table 12.4 gives data on indexes of real compensation per hour Y(RCOMPB) and output per hour X (PRODB) in the business sector of the U.S. economy for the period 1960–2005, the base of the indexes being 1992 = 100.

First plotting the data on Y and X, we obtain Figure 12.7. Since the relationship between real compensation and labor productivity is expected to be positive, it is not surprising that the two variables are positively related. What is surprising is that the relationship between the two is almost linear, although there is some hint that at higher values of productivity the relationship between the two may be slightly nonlinear. Therefore, we decided to estimate a linear as well as a log–linear model, with the following results:

$$
\begin{aligned}
\hat{Y}_t &= 32.7419 + 0.6704X_t \\
\text{se} &= (1.3940) \quad (0.0157) \\
t &= (23.4874) \quad (42.7813) \\
& r^2 = 0.9765 \quad d = 0.1739 \quad \hat{\sigma} = 2.3845
\end{aligned}
\tag{12.5.1}
$$

TABLE 12.4
Indexes of Real Compensation and Productivity, U.S., 1960–2005 (Index numbers, 1992 = 100; quarterly data seasonally adjusted)

Source: Economic Report of the President, 2007, Table B-49.

Year	Y	X	Year	Y	X
1960	60.8	48.9	1983	90.3	83.0
1961	62.5	50.6	1984	90.7	85.2
1962	64.6	52.9	1985	92.0	87.1
1963	66.1	55.0	1986	94.9	89.7
1964	67.7	56.8	1987	95.2	90.1
1965	69.1	58.8	1988	96.5	91.5
1966	71.7	61.2	1989	95.0	92.4
1967	73.5	62.5	1990	96.2	94.4
1968	76.2	64.7	1991	97.4	95.9
1969	77.3	65.0	1992	100.0	100.0
1970	78.8	66.3	1993	99.7	100.4
1971	80.2	69.0	1994	99.0	101.3
1972	82.6	71.2	1995	98.7	101.5
1973	84.3	73.4	1996	99.4	104.5
1974	83.3	72.3	1997	100.5	106.5
1975	84.1	74.8	1998	105.2	109.5
1976	86.4	77.1	1999	108.0	112.8
1977	87.6	78.5	2000	112.0	116.1
1978	89.1	79.3	2001	113.5	119.1
1979	89.3	79.3	2002	115.7	124.0
1980	89.1	79.2	2003	117.7	128.7
1981	89.3	80.8	2004	119.0	132.7
1982	90.4	80.1	2005	120.2	135.7

Notes: Y = index of real compensation per hour, business sector (1992 = 100).
X = index of output, business sector (1992 = 100).

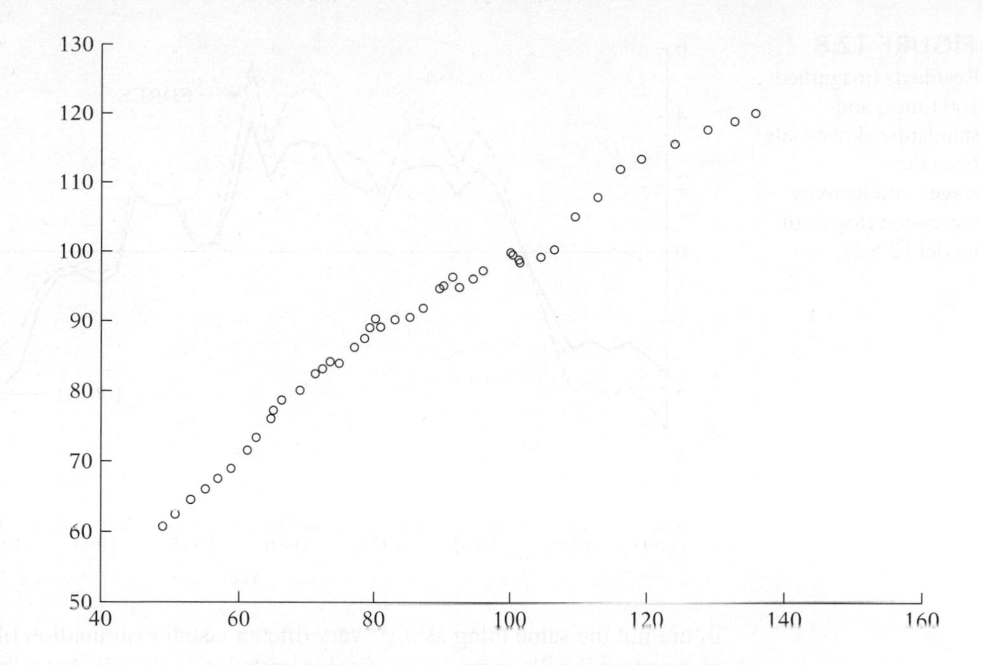

FIGURE 12.7 Index of compensation (Y) and index of productivity (X), United States, 1960–2005.

where d is the Durbin–Watson statistic, which will be discussed shortly.

$$\begin{aligned} \widehat{\ln Y_t} &= \quad 1.6067 + \quad 0.6522 \ln X_t \\ \text{se} &= \quad (0.0547) \qquad (0.0124) \\ t &= (29.3680) \qquad (52.7996) \\ & \qquad r^2 = 0.9845 \qquad d = 0.2176 \qquad \hat{\sigma} = 0.0221 \end{aligned} \tag{12.5.2}$$

Since the above model is double-log, the slope coefficient represents elasticity. In the present case, we see that if labor productivity goes up by 1 percent, the average compensation goes up by about 0.65 percent.

Qualitatively, both the models give similar results. In both cases the estimated coefficients are "highly" significant, as indicated by the high t values. In the linear model, if the index of productivity goes up by a unit, on average, the index of compensation goes up by about 0.67 units. In the log–linear model, the slope coefficient being elasticity (why?), we find that if the index of productivity goes up by 1 percent, on average, the index of real compensation goes up by about 0.65 percent.

How reliable are the results given in Eqs. (12.5.1) and (12.5.2) if there is autocorrelation? As stated previously, if there is autocorrelation, the estimated standard errors are biased, as a result of which the estimated t ratios are unreliable. We obviously need to find out if our data suffer from autocorrelation. In the following section we discuss several methods of detecting autocorrelation. We will illustrate these methods with the log–linear model (12.5.2).

12.6 Detecting Autocorrelation

I. Graphical Method

Recall that the assumption of nonautocorrelation of the classical model relates to the population disturbances u_t, which are not directly observable. What we have instead are their proxies, the residuals $\hat{u}_t$, which can be obtained by the usual OLS procedure. Although the

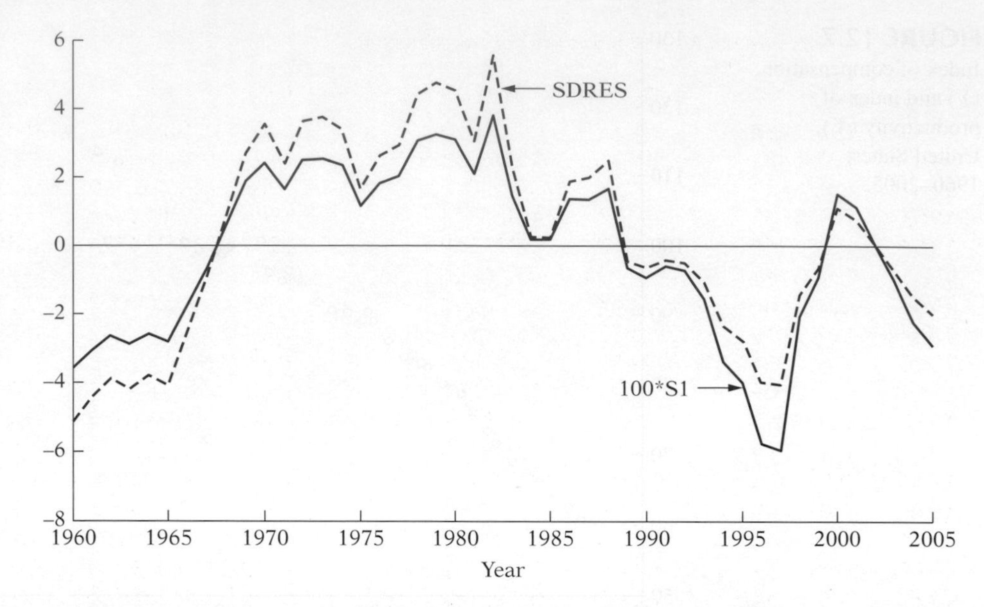

FIGURE 12.8
Residuals (magnified 100 times) and standardized residuals from the wages–productivity regression (log form: model 12.5.2).

$\hat{u}_t$ are not the same thing as u_t,[17] very often a visual examination of the $\hat{u}$'s gives us some clues about the likely presence of autocorrelation in the u's. Actually, a visual examination of $\hat{u}_t$ or $(\hat{u}_t^2)$ can provide useful information not only about autocorrelation but also about heteroscedasticity (as we saw in the preceding chapter), model inadequacy, or specification bias, as we shall see in the next chapter. As one author notes:

> The importance of producing and analyzing plots [of residuals] as a standard part of statistical analysis cannot be overemphasized. Besides occasionally providing an easy to understand summary of a complex problem, they allow the simultaneous examination of the data as an aggregate while clearly displaying the behavior of individual cases.[18]

There are various ways of examining the residuals. We can simply plot them against time, the **time sequence plot,** as we have done in Figure 12.8, which shows the residuals obtained from the log wages–productivity regression (12.5.2). The values of these residuals are given in Table 12.5 along with some other data.

Alternatively, we can plot the **standardized residuals** against time, which are also shown in Figure 12.8 and Table 12.5. The standardized residuals are simply the residuals $(\hat{u}_t)$ divided by the standard error of the regression $(\sqrt{\hat{\sigma}^2})$, that is, they are $(\hat{u}_t/\hat{\sigma})$. Notice that $\hat{u}_t$ and $\hat{\sigma}$ are measured in the units in which the regressand Y is measured. The values of the standardized residuals will therefore be pure numbers (devoid of units of measurement) and can be compared with the standardized residuals of other regressions. Moreover, the standardized residuals, like $\hat{u}_t$, have zero mean (why?) and *approximately* unit variance.[19]

[17]Even if the disturbances u_t are homoscedastic and uncorrelated, their estimators, the residuals, $\hat{u}_t$, are heteroscedastic and autocorrelated. On this, see G. S. Maddala, *Introduction to Econometrics,* 2d ed., Macmillan, New York, 1992, pp. 480–481. However, it can be shown that as the sample size increases indefinitely, the residuals tend to converge to their true values, the u_t's. On this see, E. Malinvaud, *Statistical Methods of Econometrics,* 2d ed., North-Holland Publishers, Amsterdam, 1970, p. 88.

[18]Stanford Weisberg, *Applied Linear Regression,* John Wiley & Sons, New York, 1980, p. 120.

[19]Actually, it is the so-called **Studentized** residuals that have a unit variance. But in practice the standardized residuals will give the same picture, and hence we may rely on them. On this, see Norman Draper and Harry Smith, *Applied Regression Analysis,* 3d ed., John Wiley & Sons, New York, 1998, pp. 207–208.

TABLE 12.5 Residuals: Actual, Standardized, and Lagged

Obs.	S1	SDRES	S1(−1)	Obs.	S1	SDRES	S1(−1)
1960	−0.036068	−1.639433	NA	1983	0.014416	0.655291	0.038719
1961	−0.030780	−1.399078	−0.036068	1984	0.001774	0.080626	0.014416
1962	−0.026724	−1.214729	−0.030780	1985	0.001620	0.073640	0.001774
1963	−0.029160	−1.325472	−0.026724	1986	0.013471	0.612317	0.001620
1964	−0.026246	−1.193017	−0.029160	1987	0.013725	0.623875	0.013471
1965	−0.028348	−1.288551	−0.026246	1988	0.017232	0.783269	0.013725
1966	−0.017504	−0.795647	−0.028348	1989	−0.004818	−0.219005	0.017232
1967	−0.006419	−0.291762	−0.017504	1990	−0.006232	−0.283285	−0.004818
1968	0.007094	0.322459	−0.006419	1991	−0.004118	−0.187161	−0.006232
1969	0.018409	0.836791	0.007094	1992	−0.005078	−0.230822	−0.004118
1970	0.024713	1.123311	0.018409	1993	−0.010686	−0.485739	−0.005078
1971	0.016289	0.740413	0.024713	1994	−0.023553	−1.070573	−0.010686
1972	0.025305	1.150208	0.016289	1995	−0.027874	−1.266997	−0.023553
1973	0.025829	1.174049	0.025305	1996	−0.039805	−1.809304	−0.027874
1974	0.023744	1.079278	0.025829	1997	−0.041164	−1.871079	−0.039805
1975	0.011131	0.505948	0.023744	1998	−0.013576	−0.617112	−0.041164
1976	0.018359	0.834515	0.011131	1999	−0.006674	−0.303364	−0.013576
1977	0.020416	0.927990	0.018359	2000	0.010887	0.494846	−0.006674
1978	0.030781	1.399135	0.020416	2001	0.007551	0.343250	0.010887
1979	0.033023	1.501051	0.030781	2002	0.000453	0.020599	0.007551
1980	0.031604	1.436543	0.033023	2003	−0.006673	−0.303298	0.000453
1981	0.020801	0.945516	0.031604	2004	−0.015650	−0.711380	−0.006673
1982	0.038719	1.759960	0.020801	2005	−0.020198	−0.918070	−0.015650

Notes: S1 = residuals from the wages–productivity regression (log form).
S1 (−1) = residuals lagged one period.
SDRES = standardized residuals = residuals/standard error of estimate.

In large samples $(\hat{u}_t/\hat{\sigma})$ is approximately normally distributed with zero mean and unit variance. For our example, $\hat{\sigma} = 2.6755$.

Examining the time sequence plot given in Figure 12.8, we observe that both $\hat{u}_t$ and the standardized $\hat{u}_t$ exhibit a pattern observed in Figure 12.1*d*, suggesting that perhaps u_t are not random.

To see this differently, we can plot $\hat{u}_t$ against $\hat{u}_{t-1}$, that is, plot the residuals at time t against their value at time $(t-1)$, a kind of empirical test of the AR(1) scheme. If the residuals are nonrandom, we should obtain pictures similar to those shown in Figure 12.3. This plot for our log wages–productivity regression is as shown in Figure 12.9; the underlying data are given in Table 12.5. As this figure reveals, most of the residuals are bunched in the second (northeast) and the fourth (southwest) quadrants, suggesting a strong positive correlation in the residuals.

The graphical method we have just discussed, although powerful and suggestive, is subjective or qualitative in nature. But there are several quantitative tests that one can use to supplement the purely qualitative approach. We now consider some of these tests.

II. The Runs Test

If we carefully examine Figure 12.8, we notice a peculiar feature: Initially, we have several residuals that are negative, then there is a series of positive residuals, and then there are several residuals that are negative. If these residuals were purely random, could we observe

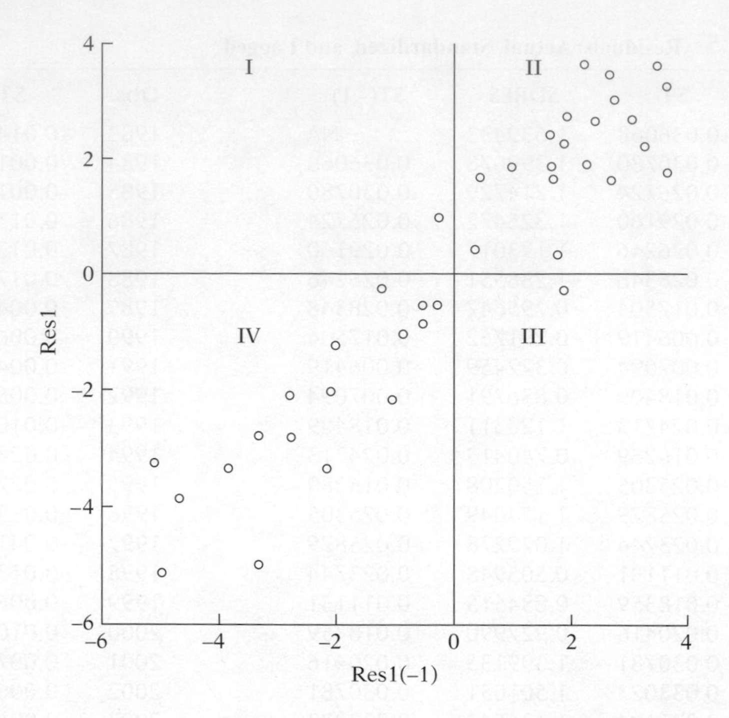

FIGURE 12.9 Current residuals versus lagged residuals.

such a pattern? Intuitively, it seems unlikely. This intuition can be checked by the so-called **runs test,** sometimes also known as the **Geary test,** a nonparametric test.[20]

To explain the runs test, let us simply note down the signs (+ or −) of the residuals obtained from the wages–productivity regression, which are given in the first column of Table 12.5.

$$(--------)(+++++++++++++++++++++)(-----------)(+++)(---) \tag{12.6.1}$$

Thus there are 8 negative residuals, followed by 21 positive residuals, followed by 11 negative residuals, followed by 3 positive residuals, followed by 3 negative residuals, for a total of 46 observations.

We now define a **run** as an uninterrupted sequence of one symbol or attribute, such as + or −. We further define the **length of a run** as the number of elements in it. In the sequence shown in Eq. (12.6.1), there are 5 runs: a run of 8 minuses (i.e., of length 8), a run of 21 pluses (i.e., of length 21), a run of 11 minuses (i.e., of length 11), a run of 3 pluses (i.e., of length 3), and a run of 3 minuses (i.e., of length 3). For a better visual effect, we have presented the various runs in parentheses.

By examining how runs behave in a strictly random sequence of observations, one can derive a test of randomness of runs. We ask this question: Are the 5 runs observed in our illustrative example consisting of 46 observations too many or too few compared with the number of runs expected in a strictly random sequence of 46 observations? If there are too

[20]In **nonparametric** tests we make no assumptions about the (probability) distribution from which the observations are drawn. On the Geary test, see R. C. Geary, "Relative Efficiency of Count Sign Changes for Assessing Residual Autoregression in Least Squares Regression," *Biometrika,* vol. 57, 1970, pp. 123–127.

many runs, it would mean that in our example the residuals change sign frequently, thus indicating negative serial correlation (cf. Figure 12.3*b*). Similarly, if there are too few runs, they may suggest positive autocorrelation, as in Figure 12.3*a*. A priori, then, Figure 12.8 would indicate positive correlation in the residuals.

Now let

N = total number of observations = $N_1 + N_2$

N_1 = number of + symbols (i.e., + residuals)

N_2 = number of − symbols (i.e., − residuals)

R = number of runs

Then under the null hypothesis that the successive outcomes (here, residuals) are independent, and assuming that $N_1 > 10$ and $N_2 > 10$, the number of runs is (*asymptotically*) *normally distributed* with

$$\text{Mean:} \quad E(R) = \frac{2N_1N_2}{N} + 1$$
$$\text{Variance:} \quad \sigma_R^2 = \frac{2N_1N_2(2N_1N_2 - N)}{(N)^2(N-1)} \tag{12.6.2}$$

Note: $N = N_1 + N_2$.

If the null hypothesis of randomness is sustainable, following the properties of the normal distribution, we should expect that

$$\text{Prob}\,[E(R) - 1.96\sigma_R \le R \le E(R) + 1.96\sigma_R] = 0.95 \tag{12.6.3}$$

That is, the probability is 95 percent that the preceding interval will include R. Therefore we have this rule:

Decision Rule Do not reject the null hypothesis of randomness with 95% confidence if R, the number of runs, lies in the preceding confidence interval; reject the null hypothesis if the estimated R lies outside these limits. (*Note:* You can choose any level of confidence you want.)

Returning to our example, we know that N_1, the number of pluses, is 24 and N_2, the number of minuses, is 22 and $R = 5$. Using the formulas given in Eq. (12.6.2), we obtain:

$$E(R) = 24$$
$$\sigma_R^2 = 11 \tag{12.6.4}$$
$$\sigma_R = 3.32$$

The 95% confidence interval for R in our example is thus:

$$[24 \pm 1.96(3.32)] = (17.5, 30.5)$$

Obviously, this interval does not include 5. Hence, we can *reject* the hypothesis that the residuals in our wages–productivity regression are random with 95% confidence. In other words, the residuals exhibit autocorrelation. As a general rule, if there is positive autocorrelation, the number of runs will be few, whereas if there is negative autocorrelation, the number of runs will be many. Of course, from Eq. (12.6.2) we can find out whether we have too many runs or too few runs.

Swed and Eisenhart have developed special tables that give critical values of the runs expected in a random sequence of N observations if N_1 or N_2 is smaller than 20. These tables are given in **Appendix D,** Table D.6. Using these tables, the reader can verify that the residuals in our wages–productivity regression are indeed nonrandom; actually they are positively correlated.

III. Durbin–Watson *d* Test[21]

The most celebrated test for detecting serial correlation is that developed by statisticians Durbin and Watson. It is popularly known as the **Durbin–Watson *d* statistic,** which is defined as

$$d = \frac{\sum_{t=2}^{t=n}(\hat{u}_t - \hat{u}_{t-1})^2}{\sum_{t=1}^{t=n}\hat{u}_t^2} \tag{12.6.5}$$

which is simply the ratio of the sum of squared differences in successive residuals to the RSS. Note that in the numerator of the d statistic the number of observations is $n - 1$ because one observation is lost in taking successive differences.

A great advantage of the d statistic is that it is based on the estimated residuals, which are routinely computed in regression analysis. Because of this advantage, it is now a common practice to report the Durbin–Watson d along with summary measures, such as R^2, adjusted R^2, t, and F. Although it is now routinely used, it is **important to note the assumptions underlying the *d* statistic.**

1. The regression model includes the intercept term. If it is not present, as in the case of the regression through the origin, it is essential to rerun the regression including the intercept term to obtain the RSS.[22]
2. The explanatory variables, the X's, are nonstochastic, or fixed in repeated sampling.
3. The disturbances u_t are generated by the first-order autoregressive scheme: $u_t = \rho u_{t-1} + \varepsilon_t$. Therefore, it cannot be used to detect higher-order autoregressive schemes.
4. The error term u_t is assumed to be normally distributed.
5. The regression model does not include the lagged value(s) of the dependent variable as one of the explanatory variables. Thus, the test is inapplicable in models of the following type:

$$Y_t = \beta_1 + \beta_2 X_{2t} + \beta_3 X_{3t} + \cdots + \beta_k X_{kt} + \gamma Y_{t-1} + u_t \tag{12.6.6}$$

where Y_{t-1} is the one period lagged value of Y. Such models are known as **autoregressive models,** which we will study in Chapter 17.

6. There are no missing observations in the data. Thus, in our wages–productivity regression for the period 1960–2005, if observations for, say, 1978 and 1982 were missing for some reason, the d statistic would make no allowance for such missing observations.[23]

[21] J. Durbin and G. S. Watson, "Testing for Serial Correlation in Least-Squares Regression," *Biometrika,* vol. 38, 1951, pp. 159–171.

[22] However, R. W. Farebrother has calculated d values when the intercept term is absent from the model. See his "The Durbin–Watson Test for Serial Correlation When There Is No Intercept in the Regression," *Econometrica,* vol. 48, 1980, pp. 1553–1563.

[23] For further details, see Gabor Korosi, Laszlo Matyas, and Istvan P. Szekey, *Practical Econometrics,* Avebury Press, England, 1992, pp. 88–89.

FIGURE 12.10
Durbin–Watson d statistic.

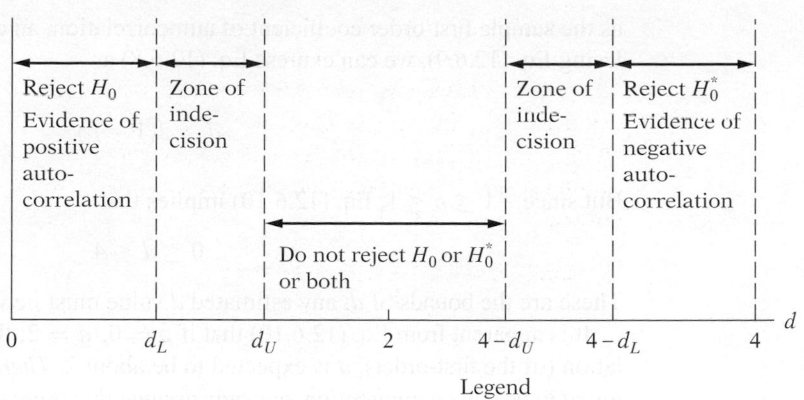

The exact sampling or probability distribution of the d statistic given in Eq. (12.6.5) is difficult to derive because, as Durbin and Watson have shown, it depends in a complicated way on the X values present in a given sample.[24] This difficulty should be understandable because d is computed from $\hat{u}_t$, which are, of course, dependent on the given X's. Therefore, unlike the t, F, or χ^2 tests, there is no unique critical value that will lead to the rejection or the acceptance of the null hypothesis that there is no first-order serial correlation in the disturbances u_i. However, Durbin and Watson were successful in deriving a lower bound d_L and an upper bound d_U such that if the computed d from Eq. (12.6.5) lies outside these critical values, a decision can be made regarding the presence of positive or negative serial correlation. Moreover, these limits depend only on the number of observations n and the number of explanatory variables and do not depend on the values taken by these explanatory variables. These limits, for n going from 6 to 200 and up to 20 explanatory variables, have been tabulated by Durbin and Watson and are reproduced in **Appendix D, Table D.5** (up to 20 explanatory variables).

The actual test procedure can be explained better with the aid of Figure 12.10, which shows that the limits of d are 0 and 4. These can be established as follows. Expand Eq. (12.6.5) to obtain

$$d = \frac{\sum \hat{u}_t^2 + \sum \hat{u}_{t-1}^2 - 2\sum \hat{u}_t \hat{u}_{t-1}}{\sum \hat{u}_t^2} \tag{12.6.7}$$

Since $\sum \hat{u}_t^2$ and $\sum \hat{u}_{t-1}^2$ differ in only one observation, they are approximately equal. Therefore, setting $\sum \hat{u}_{t-1}^2 \approx \sum \hat{u}_t^2$, Eq. (12.6.7) may be written as

$$d \approx 2\left(1 - \frac{\sum \hat{u}_t \hat{u}_{t-1}}{\sum \hat{u}_t^2}\right) \tag{12.6.8}$$

where $\approx$ means approximately.

Now let us define

$$\hat{\rho} = \frac{\sum \hat{u}_t \hat{u}_{t-1}}{\sum \hat{u}_t^2} \tag{12.6.9}$$

[24]But see the discussion on the "exact" Durbin–Watson test given later in the section.

as the sample first-order coefficient of autocorrelation, an estimator of ρ. (See footnote 9.) Using Eq. (12.6.9), we can express Eq. (12.6.8) as

$$d \approx 2(1 - \hat{\rho}) \tag{12.6.10}$$

But since $-1 \leq \rho \leq 1$, Eq. (12.6.10) implies that

$$0 \leq d \leq 4 \tag{12.6.11}$$

These are the bounds of d; any estimated d value must lie within these limits.

It is apparent from Eq. (12.6.10) that if $\hat{\rho} = 0$, $d = 2$; that is, if there is no serial correlation (of the first-order), d is expected to be about 2. *Therefore, as a rule of thumb, if d is found to be 2 in an application, one may assume that there is no first-order autocorrelation, either positive or negative.* If $\hat{\rho} = +1$, indicating perfect positive correlation in the residuals, $d \approx 0$. Therefore, the closer d is to 0, the greater the evidence of positive serial correlation. This relationship should be evident from Eq. (12.6.5) because if there is positive autocorrelation, the $\hat{u}_t$'s will be bunched together and their differences will therefore tend to be small. As a result, the numerator sum of squares will be smaller in comparison with the denominator sum of squares, which remains a unique value for any given regression.

If $\hat{\rho} = -1$, that is, there is perfect negative correlation among successive residuals, $d \approx 4$. Hence, the closer d is to 4, the greater the evidence of negative serial correlation. Again, looking at Eq. (12.6.5), this is understandable. For if there is negative autocorrelation, a positive $\hat{u}_t$ will tend to be followed by a negative $\hat{u}_t$ and vice versa so that $|\hat{u}_t - \hat{u}_{t-1}|$ will usually be greater than $|\hat{u}_t|$. Therefore, the numerator of d will be comparatively larger than the denominator.

The mechanics of the Durbin–Watson test are as follows, assuming that the assumptions underlying the test are fulfilled:

1. Run the OLS regression and obtain the residuals.
2. Compute d from Eq. (12.6.5). (Most computer programs now do this routinely.)
3. For the given sample size and given number of explanatory variables, find out the critical d_L and d_U values.
4. Now follow the decision rules given in Table 12.6. For ease of reference, these decision rules are also depicted in Figure 12.10.

To illustrate the mechanics, let us return to our wages–productivity regression. From the data given in Table 12.5 the estimated d value can be shown to be 0.2175, suggesting that there is positive serial correlation in the residuals. From the Durbin–Watson tables, we find that for 46 observations and one explanatory variable, $d_L = 1.475$ and $d_U = 1.566$ at the 5 percent level. Since the computed d of 0.2175 lies below d_L, we cannot reject the hypothesis that there is positive serial correlation in the residuals.

Although extremely popular, the d test has one great drawback in that, if it falls in the **indecisive zone,** one cannot conclude that (first-order) autocorrelation does or does not

TABLE 12.6
Durbin–Watson *d* Test: Decision Rules

Null Hypothesis	Decision	If
No positive autocorrelation	Reject	$0 < d < d_L$
No positive autocorrelation	No decision	$d_L \leq d \leq d_U$
No negative correlation	Reject	$4 - d_L < d < 4$
No negative correlation	No decision	$4 - d_U \leq d \leq 4 - d_L$
No autocorrelation, positive or negative	Do not reject	$d_U < d < 4 - d_U$

exist. To solve this problem, several authors have proposed modifications of the d test but they are rather involved and beyond the scope of this book.[25] In many situations, however, it has been found that the upper limit d_U is approximately the true significance limit and therefore in case d lies in the indecisive zone, one can use the following **modified *d* test:** Given the level of significance α,

1. H_0: $\rho = 0$ versus H_1: $\rho > 0$. Reject H_0 at α level if $d < d_U$. That is, there is statistically significant positive autocorrelation.
2. H_0: $\rho = 0$ versus H_1: $\rho < 0$. Reject H_0 at α level if the estimated $(4 - d) < d_U$, that is, there is statistically significant evidence of negative autocorrelation.
3. H_0: $\rho = 0$ versus H_1: $\rho \neq 0$. Reject H_0 at 2α level if $d < d_U$ or $(4 - d) < d_U$, that is, there is statistically significant evidence of autocorrelation, positive or negative.

It may be pointed out that the indecisive zone narrows as the sample size increases, which can be seen clearly from the Durbin–Watson tables. For example, with 4 regressors and 20 observations, the 5 percent lower and upper d values are 0.894 and 1.828, respectively, but these values are 1.515 and 1.739 if the sample size is 75.

The computer program SHAZAM performs an *exact d test,* that is, it gives the p value, the exact probability of the computed d value. With modern computing facilities, it is no longer difficult to find the p value of the computed d statistic. Using SHAZAM (version 9) for our wages–productivity regression, we find the p value of the computed d of 0.2176 is practically zero, thereby reconfirming our earlier conclusion based on the Durbin–Watson tables.

The Durbin–Watson d test has become so venerable that practitioners often forget the assumptions underlying the test. In particular, the assumptions that (1) the explanatory variables, or regressors, are nonstochastic; (2) the error term follows the normal distribution; (3) the regression models do not include the lagged value(s) of the regressand; and (4) only the first-order serial correlation is taken into account are very important for the application of the d test. It should also be added that a significant d statistic may not necessarily indicate autocorrelation. Rather, it may be an indication of omission of relevant variables from the model.

If a regression model contains lagged value(s) of the regressand, the d value in such cases is often around 2, which would suggest that there is no (first-order) autocorrelation in such models. Thus, there is a built-in bias against discovering (first-order) autocorrelation in such models. This does not mean that autoregressive models do not suffer from the autocorrelation problem. As a matter of fact, Durbin has developed the so-called ***h* test** to test serial correlation in such models. But this test is not as powerful, in a statistical sense, as the **Breusch–Godfrey test** to be discussed shortly, so there is no need to use the ***h* test.** However, because of its historical importance, it is discussed in Exercise 12.36.

Also, if the error term u_t are not NIID, the routinely used d test may not be reliable.[26] In this respect the **runs test** discussed earlier has an advantage in that it does not make any (probability) distributional assumption about the error term. However, if the sample is large (technically infinite), we can use the Durbin–Watson d, for it can be shown that[27]

$$\sqrt{n}\left(1 - \frac{1}{2}d\right) \approx N(0, 1) \tag{12.6.12}$$

[25]For details, see Thomas B. Fomby, R. Carter Hill, and Stanley R. Johnson, *Advanced Econometric Methods,* Springer Verlag, New York, 1984, pp. 225–228.

[26]For an advanced discussion, see Ron C. Mittelhammer, George G. Judge, and Douglas J. Miller, *Econometric Foundations,* Cambridge University Press, New York, 2000, p. 550.

[27]See James Davidson, *Econometric Theory,* Blackwell Publishers, New York, 2000, p. 161.

That is, in large samples the d statistic as transformed in Eq. (12.6.12) follows the standard normal distribution. Incidentally, in view of the relationship between d and $\hat{\rho}$, the estimated first-order autocorrelation coefficient, shown in Eq. (12.6.10), it follows that

$$\sqrt{n}\hat{\rho} \approx N(0, 1) \tag{12.6.13}$$

that is, in large samples, the square root of the sample size times the estimated first-order autocorrelation coefficient also follows the standard normal distribution.

As an illustration of the test, for our wages–productivity example, we found that $d = 0.2176$ with $n = 46$. Therefore, from Eq. (12.6.12) we find that

$$\sqrt{46}\left(1 - \frac{0.2176}{2}\right) \approx 6.0447$$

Asymptotically, if the null hypothesis of zero (first-order) autocorrelation were true, the probability of obtaining a Z value (i.e., a standardized normal variable) of as much as 6.0447 or greater is extremely small. Recall that for a standard normal distribution, the (two-tail) critical 5 percent Z value is only 1.96 and the 1 percent critical Z value is about 2.58. Although our sample size is only 46, for practical purposes it may be large enough to use the normal approximation. The conclusion remains the same, namely, that the residuals from the wages–productivity regression suffer from autocorrelation.

But the most serious problem with the d test is the assumption that the regressors are nonstochastic, that is, their values are fixed in repeated sampling. If this is not the case, then the d test is not valid either in finite, or small, samples or in large samples.[28] And since this assumption is usually difficult to maintain in economic models involving time series data, one author contends that the Durbin–Watson statistic may not be useful in econometrics involving time series data.[29] In his view, more useful tests of autocorrelation are available, but they are all based on large samples. We discuss one such test below, the **Breusch–Godfrey test.**

IV. A General Test of Autocorrelation: The Breusch–Godfrey (BG) Test[30]

To avoid some of the pitfalls of the Durbin–Watson d test of autocorrelation, statisticians Breusch and Godfrey have developed a test of autocorrelation that is general in the sense that it allows for (1) nonstochastic regressors, such as the lagged values of the regressand; (2) higher-order autoregressive schemes, such as AR(1), AR(2), etc.; and (3) simple or higher-order **moving averages** of white noise error terms, such as ε_t in Eq. (12.2.1).[31]

Without going into the mathematical details, which can be obtained from the references, the **BG test,** which is also known as the **LM test,**[32] proceeds as follows: We use the

[28]Ibid., p. 161.

[29]Fumio Hayashi, *Econometrics,* Princeton University Press, Princeton, NJ, 2000, p. 45.

[30]See, L. G. Godfrey, "Testing Against General Autoregressive and Moving Average Error Models When the Regressor Includes Lagged Dependent Variables," *Econometrica,* vol. 46, 1978, pp. 1293–1302, and T. S. Breusch, "Testing for Autocorrelation in Dynamic Linear Models," *Australian Economic Papers,* vol. 17, 1978, pp. 334–355.

[31]For example, in the regression $Y_t = \beta_1 + \beta_2 X_t + u_t$ the error term can be represented as $u_t = \varepsilon_t + \lambda_1\varepsilon_{t-1} + \lambda_2\varepsilon_{t-2}$, which represents a three-period moving average of the white noise error term ε_t.

[32]The test is based on the **Lagrange multiplier principle** briefly mentioned in Chapter 8.

two-variable regression model to illustrate the test, although many regressors can be added to the model. Also, lagged values of the regressand can be added to the model. Let

$$Y_t = \beta_1 + \beta_2 X_t + u_t \tag{12.6.14}$$

Assume that the error term u_t follows the pth-order autoregressive, AR(p), scheme as follows:

$$u_t = \rho_1 u_{t-1} + \rho_2 u_{t-2} + \cdots + \rho_p u_{t-p} + \varepsilon_t \tag{12.6.15}$$

where ε_t is a white noise error term as discussed previously. As you will recognize, this is simply the extension of the AR(1) scheme.

The null hypothesis H_0 to be tested is that

$$H_0: \rho_1 = \rho_2 = \cdots = \rho_p = 0 \tag{12.6.16}$$

That is, there is no serial correlation of any order. The BG test involves the following steps:

1. Estimate Eq. (12.6.14) by OLS and obtain the residuals, $\hat{u}_t$.
2. Regress $\hat{u}_t$ on the original X_t (if there is more than one X variable in the original model, include them also) and $\hat{u}_{t-1}, \hat{u}_{t-2}, \ldots, \hat{u}_{t-p}$, where the latter are the lagged values of the estimated residuals in step 1. Thus, if $p = 4$, we will introduce four lagged values of the residuals as additional regressors in the model. Note that to run this regression we will have only $(n - p)$ observations (why?). In short, run the following regression:

$$\hat{u}_t = \alpha_1 + \alpha_2 X_t + \hat{\rho}_1 \hat{u}_{t-1} + \hat{\rho}_2 \hat{u}_{t-2} + \cdots + \hat{\rho}_p \hat{u}_{t-p} + \varepsilon_t \tag{12.6.17}$$

and obtain R^2 from this (auxiliary) regression.[33]

3. If the sample size is large (technically, infinite), Breusch and Godfrey have shown that

$$(n - p)R^2 \sim \chi^2_p \tag{12.6.18}$$

That is, asymptotically, $n - p$ times the R^2 value obtained from the auxiliary regression (12.6.17) follows the chi-square distribution with p df. If in an application, $(n - p)R^2$ exceeds the critical chi-square value at the chosen level of significance, we reject the null hypothesis, in which case at least one ρ in Eq. (12.6.15) is statistically significantly different from zero.

The following *practical points* about the BG test may be noted:

1. The regressors included in the regression model may contain lagged values of the regressand Y, that is, Y_{t-1}, Y_{t-2}, etc., may appear as explanatory variables. Contrast this model with the Durbin–Watson test restriction that there may be no lagged values of the regressand among the regressors.
2. As noted earlier, the BG test is applicable even if the disturbances follow a pth-order **moving average (MA)** process, that is, the u_t are generated as follows:

$$u_t = \varepsilon_t + \lambda_1 \varepsilon_{t-1} + \lambda_2 \varepsilon_{t-2} + \cdots + \lambda_p \varepsilon_{t-p} \tag{12.6.19}$$

where ε_t is a white noise error term, that is, the error term that satisfies all the classical assumptions.

[33]The reason that the original regressor X is included in the model is to allow for the fact that X may not be strictly nonstochastic. But if it is strictly nonstochastic, it may be omitted from the model. On this, see Jeffrey M. Wooldridge, *Introductory Econometrics: A Modern Approach,* South-Western Publishing Co., 2003, p. 386.

In the chapters on time series econometrics, we will study in some detail the pth-order autoregressive and moving average processes.

3. If in Eq. (12.6.15) $p = 1$, meaning first-order autoregression, then the BG test is known as **Durbin's M test.**

4. A drawback of the BG test is that the value of p, the length of the lag, cannot be specified a priori. Some experimentation with the p value is inevitable. Sometimes one can use the so-called **Akaike** and **Schwarz** information criteria to select the lag length. We will discuss these criteria in Chapter 13 and later in the chapters on time series econometrics.

5. Given the values of the X variable(s) and the lagged values of u, the test assumes that the variance of u in Eq. (12.6.15) is homoscedastic.

Illustration of the BG Test: The Wages–Productivity Relation

To illustrate the test, we will apply it to our illustrative example. Using an AR(6) scheme, we obtained the results shown in Exercise 12.25. From the regression results given there, it can be seen that $(n - p) = 40$ and $R^2 = 0.7498$. Therefore, multiplying these two, we obtain a chi-square value of 29.992. For 6 df (why?), the probability of obtaining a chi-square value of as much as 29.992 or greater is extremely small; the chi-square table in Appendix D.4 shows that the probability of obtaining a chi-square value of as much as 18.5476 or greater is only 0.005. Therefore, for the same df, the probability of obtaining a chi-square value of about 30 must be extremely small. As a matter of fact, the actual p value is almost zero.

Therefore, the conclusion is that, for our example, at least one of the six autocorrelations must be nonzero.

Trying varying lag lengths from 1 to 6, we find that only the AR(1) coefficient is significant, suggesting that there is no need to consider more than one lag. In essence the BG test in this case turns out to be **Durbin's m test.**

Why So Many Tests of Autocorrelation?

The answer to this question is that ". . . no particular test has yet been judged to be unequivocally best [i.e., more powerful in the statistical sense], and thus the analyst is still in the unenviable position of considering a varied collection of test procedures for detecting the presence or structure, or both, of autocorrelation."[34] Of course, a similar argument can be made about the various tests of heteroscedasticity discussed in the previous chapter.

12.7 What to Do When You Find Autocorrelation: Remedial Measures

If after applying one or more of the diagnostic tests of autocorrelation discussed in the previous section, we find that there is autocorrelation, what then? We have four options:

1. Try to find out if the autocorrelation is **pure autocorrelation** and not the result of mis-specification of the model. As we discussed in Section 12.1, sometimes we observe patterns in residuals because the model is mis-specified—that is, it has excluded some important variables—or because its functional form is incorrect.

[34] Ron C. Mittelhammer et al., op. cit., p. 547. Recall that the **power of a statistical test** is 1 minus the probability of committing a Type II error, that is, 1 minus the probability of accepting a false hypothesis. The maximum power of a test is 1 and the minimum is 0. The closer the power of a test is to zero, the worse is that test, and the closer it is to 1, the more powerful is that test. What these authors are essentially saying is that there is no single most powerful test of autocorrelation.

2. If it is pure autocorrelation, one can use appropriate transformation of the original model so that in the transformed model we do not have the problem of (pure) autocorrelation. As in the case of heteroscedasticity, we will have to use some type of **generalized least-square (GLS) method.**

3. In large samples, we can use the **Newey–West** method to obtain standard errors of OLS estimators that are corrected for autocorrelation. This method is actually an extension of White's heteroscedasticity-consistent standard errors method that we discussed in the previous chapter.

4. In some situations we can continue to use the OLS method.

Because of the importance of each of these topics, we devote a section to each one.

12.8 Model Mis-Specification versus Pure Autocorrelation

Let us return to our wages–productivity regression given in Eq. (12.5.2). There we saw that the d value was 0.2176 and based on the Durbin–Watson d test we concluded that there was positive correlation in the error term. Could this correlation have arisen because our model was not correctly specified? Since the data underlying regression (12.5.1) is time series data, it is quite possible that both wages and productivity exhibit trends. If that is the case, then we need to include the time or trend, t, variable in the model to see the relationship between wages and productivity net of the trends in the two variables.

To test this, we included the trend variable in Eq. (12.5.2) and obtained the following results

$$\begin{aligned} \hat{Y}_t &= 0.1209 + 1.0283X_t - 0.0075t \\ \text{se} &= (0.3070) \quad (0.0776) \quad (0.0015) \\ t &= (0.3939) \quad (13.2594) \quad (-4.8903) \\ & R^2 = 0.9900; \quad d = 0.4497 \end{aligned} \tag{12.8.1}$$

The interpretation of this model is straightforward: Over time, the index of real wages has been decreasing by about 0.75 units per year. After allowing for this, if the productivity index went up by one unit, on average, the real compensation went up by about one unit. What is interesting to note is that even allowing for the trend variable, the d value is still very low, suggesting that Eq. (12.8.1) suffers from pure autocorrelation and not necessarily specification error.

How do we know that Eq. (12.8.1) is the correct specification? To test this, we regress Y on X and X^2 to test for the possibility that the real wage index may be nonlinearly related to the productivity index. The results of this regression are as follows:

$$\begin{aligned} \hat{Y}_t &= -1.7843 + 2.1963X_t - 0.1752X_t^2 \\ t &= (-2.7713) \quad (7.5040) \quad (-5.2785) \\ & R^2 = 0.9906 \quad d = 0.3561 \end{aligned} \tag{12.8.2}$$

We leave it to the reader to interpret these results. For the present purposes, look at the Durbin–Watson, which is still quite low, suggesting that we still have positive serial correlation in the residuals.

It may be safe to conclude from the preceding analysis that our wages–productivity regression probably suffers from pure autocorrelation and not necessarily from specification bias. Knowing the consequences of autocorrelation, we may therefore want to take some corrective action. We will do so shortly.

Incidentally, for all the wages–productivity regressions that we have presented above, we applied the **Jarque–Bera test of normality** and found that the residuals were normally distributed, which is comforting because the d test assumes normality of the error term.

12.9 Correcting for (Pure) Autocorrelation: The Method of Generalized Least Squares (GLS)

Knowing the consequences of autocorrelation, especially the lack of efficiency of OLS estimators, we may need to remedy the problem. The remedy depends on the knowledge one has about the nature of interdependence among the disturbances, that is, knowledge about the structure of autocorrelation.

As a starter, consider the two-variable regression model:

$$Y_t = \beta_1 + \beta_2 X_t + u_t \tag{12.9.1}$$

and assume that the error term follows the AR(1) scheme, namely,

$$u_t = \rho u_{t-1} + \varepsilon_t \qquad -1 < \rho < 1 \tag{12.9.2}$$

Now we consider two cases: (1) ρ is known and (2) ρ is not known but has to be estimated.

When ρ Is Known

If the coefficient of first-order autocorrelation is known, the problem of autocorrelation can be easily solved. If Eq. (12.9.1) holds true at time t, it also holds true at time $(t-1)$. Hence,

$$Y_{t-1} = \beta_1 + \beta_2 X_{t-1} + u_{t-1} \tag{12.9.3}$$

Multiplying Eq. (12.9.3) by ρ on both sides, we obtain

$$\rho Y_{t-1} = \rho\beta_1 + \rho\beta_2 X_{t-1} + \rho u_{t-1} \tag{12.9.4}$$

Subtracting Eq. (12.9.4) from Eq. (12.9.1) gives

$$(Y_t - \rho Y_{t-1}) = \beta_1(1-\rho) + \beta_2(X_t - \rho X_{t-1}) + \varepsilon_t \tag{12.9.5}$$

where $\varepsilon_t = (u_t - \rho u_{t-1})$

We can express Eq. (12.9.5) as

$$Y_t^* = \beta_1^* + \beta_2^* X_t^* + \varepsilon_t \tag{12.9.6}$$

where $\beta_1^* = \beta_1(1-\rho)$, $Y_t^* = (Y_t - \rho Y_{t-1})$, $X_t^* = (X_t - \rho X_{t-1})$, and $\beta_2^* = \beta_2$.

Since the error term in Eq. (12.9.6) satisfies the usual OLS assumptions, we can apply OLS to the transformed variables Y^* and X^* and obtain estimators with all the optimum properties, namely, BLUE. In effect, running Eq. (12.9.6) is tantamount to using generalized least squares (GLS) discussed in the previous chapter—recall that GLS is nothing but OLS applied to the transformed model that satisfies the classical assumptions.

Regression (12.9.5) is known as the **generalized, or quasi, difference equation.** It involves regressing Y on X, not in the original form, but in the **difference form,** which is obtained by subtracting a proportion ($=\rho$) of the value of a variable in the previous time period from its value in the current time period. In this differencing procedure we lose one observation because the first observation has no antecedent. To avoid this loss of one observation, the first observation on Y and X is transformed as follows:[35] $Y_1\sqrt{1-\rho^2}$ and $X_1\sqrt{1-\rho^2}$. This transformation is known as the **Prais–Winsten transformation.**

When ρ Is Not Known

Although conceptually straightforward to apply, the method of generalized difference given in Eq. (12.9.5) is difficult to implement because ρ is rarely known in practice. Therefore, we need to find ways of estimating ρ. We have several possibilities.

The First-Difference Method

Since ρ lies between 0 and ±1, one could start from two extreme positions. At one extreme, one could assume that $\rho = 0$, that is, no (first-order) serial correlation, and at the other extreme we could let $\rho = \pm1$, that is, perfect positive or negative correlation. As a matter of fact, when a regression is run, one generally assumes that there is no autocorrelation and then lets the Durbin–Watson or other test show whether this assumption is justified. If, however, $\rho = +1$, the generalized difference equation (12.9.5) reduces to the **first-difference equation:**

$$Y_t - Y_{t-1} = \beta_2(X_t - X_{t-1}) + (u_t - u_{t-1})$$

or

$$\Delta Y_t = \beta_2 \Delta X_t + \varepsilon_t \tag{12.9.7}$$

where Δ is the first-difference operator introduced in Eq. (12.1.10).

Since the error term in Eq. (12.9.7) is free from (first-order) serial correlation (why?), to run the regression (12.9.7) all one has to do is form the first differences of both the regressand and regressor(s) and run the regression on these first differences.

The first-difference transformation may be appropriate if the coefficient of autocorrelation is very high, say in excess of 0.8, or the Durbin–Watson d is quite low. Maddala has proposed this rough rule of thumb: *Use the first-difference form whenever* $d < R^2$.[36] This is the case in our wages–productivity regression (12.5.2), where we found that $d = 0.2176$ and $r^2 = 0.9845$. The first-difference regression for our illustrative example will be presented shortly.

An interesting feature of the first-difference model (12.9.7) is that **there is no intercept in it.** Hence, to estimate Eq. (12.9.7), you have to use the **regression through the origin** routine (that is, suppress the intercept term), which is now available in most software packages. If, however, you forget to drop the intercept term in the model and estimate the following model that includes the intercept term

$$\Delta Y_t = \beta_1 + \beta_2 \Delta X_t + \varepsilon_t \tag{12.9.8}$$

[35]The loss of one observation may not be very serious in large samples but can make a substantial difference in the results in small samples. Without transforming the first observation as indicated, the error variance will not be homoscedastic. On this, see Jeffrey Wooldridge, op. cit., p. 388. For some Monte Carlo results on the importance of the first observation, see Russell Davidson and James G. MacKinnon, *Estimation and Inference in Econometrics,* Oxford University Press, New York, 1993, Table 10.1, p. 349.

[36]Maddala, op. cit., p. 232.

then the original model must have a *trend* in it and β_1 represents the coefficient of the trend variable.[37] Therefore, one "accidental" benefit of introducing the intercept term in the first-difference model is to test for the presence of a trend variable in the original model.

Returning to our wages–productivity regression (12.5.2), and given the AR(1) scheme and a low d value in relation to r^2, we rerun Eq. (12.5.2) in the first-difference form without the intercept term; remember that Eq. (12.5.2) is in the *level form*. The results are as follows:[38]

$$\widehat{\Delta Y_t} = 0.6539 \Delta X_t$$
$$t = (11.4042) \qquad r^2 = 0.4264 \qquad d = 1.7442 \tag{12.9.9}$$

Compared with the level form regression (12.5.2), we see that the slope coefficient has not changed much, but the r^2 value has dropped considerably. This is generally the case because by taking the first differences we are essentially studying the behavior of variables around their (linear) trend values. Of course, we cannot compare the r^2 of Eq. (12.9.9) directly with that of the r^2 of Eq. (12.5.2) because the dependent variables in the two models are different.[39] Also, notice that compared with the original regression, the d value has increased dramatically, perhaps indicating that there is little autocorrelation in the first-difference regression.[40]

Another interesting aspect of the first-difference transformation relates to the *stationarity* properties of the underlying time series. Return to Eq. (12.2.1), which describes the AR(1) scheme. Now if in fact $\rho = 1$, then it is clear from Eqs. (12.2.3) and (12.2.4) that the series u_t is *nonstationary*, for the variances and covariances become infinite. That is why, when we discussed this topic, we put the restriction that $|\rho| < 1$. But it is clear from Eq. (12.2.1) that if the autocorrelation coefficient is in fact 1, then Eq. (12.2.1) becomes

$$u_t = u_{t-1} + \varepsilon_t$$

or

$$(u_t - u_{t-1}) = \Delta u_t = \varepsilon_t \tag{12.9.10}$$

That is, it is the first-differenced u_t that becomes stationary, for it is equal to ε_t, which is a white noise error term.

The point of the preceding discussion is that if the original time series are nonstationary, very often their first differences become stationary. And, therefore, first-difference transformation serves a dual purpose in that it might get rid of (first-order) autocorrelation and also render the time series stationary. We will revisit this topic in **Part 5**, where we discuss the econometrics of time series analysis in some depth.

We mentioned that the first-difference transformation may be appropriate if ρ is high or d is low. Strictly speaking, the first-difference transformation is valid only if $\rho = 1$. As a

[37]This is easy to show. Let $Y_t = \alpha_1 + \beta_1 t + \beta_2 X_t + u_t$. Therefore, $Y_{t-1} = \alpha + \beta_1(t-1) + \beta_2 X_{t-1} + u_{t-1}$. Subtracting the latter from the former, you will obtain: $\Delta Y_t = \beta_1 + \beta_2 \Delta X_t + \varepsilon_t$, which shows that the intercept term in this equation is indeed the coefficient of the trend variable in the original model. Remember that we are assuming that $\rho = 1$.

[38]In Exercise 12.38 you are asked to run this model, including the constant term.

[39]The comparison of r^2 in the level and first-difference form is slightly involved. For an extended discussion on this, see Maddala, op. cit., Chapter 6.

[40]It is not clear whether the computed d in the first-difference regression can be interpreted in the same way as it was in the original, level form regression. However, applying the runs test, it can be seen that there is no evidence of autocorrelation in the residuals of the first-difference regression.

matter of fact, there is a test, called the **Berenblutt–Webb test,**[41] to test the hypothesis that $\rho = 1$. The test statistic they use is called the ***g* statistic,** which is defined as follows:

$$g = \frac{\sum_2^n \hat{e}_t^2}{\sum_1^n \hat{u}_t^2} \tag{12.9.11}$$

where $\hat{u}_t$ are the OLS residuals from the original (i.e., level form) regression and e_t are the OLS residuals from the first-difference regression. Keep in mind that in the first-difference form there is no intercept.

To test the significance of the g statistic, assuming that the level form regression contains the intercept term, we can use the Durbin–Watson tables except that now the null hypothesis is that $\rho = 1$ rather than the Durbin–Watson hypothesis that $\rho = 0$.

Revisiting our wages–productivity regression, for the original regression (12.5.2) we obtain $\sum \hat{u}_t^2 = 0.0214$ and $\sum \hat{e}_t^2 = 0.0046$. Putting these values into the g statistic given in Eq. (12.9.11), we obtain

$$g = \frac{0.0046}{0.0214} = 0.2149 \tag{12.9.12}$$

Consulting the Durbin–Watson table for 45 observations (the number closest to 45 observations) and 1 explanatory variable (Appendix D, Table D.5), we find that $d_L = 1.288$ and $d_U = 1.376$ (5 percent level). Since the observed g lies below the lower limit of d, we do not reject the hypothesis that true $\rho = 1$. *Keep in mind that although we use the same Durbin–Watson tables, now the null hypothesis is that* $\rho = 1$ *and not that* $\rho = 0$. In view of this finding, the results given in Eq. (12.9.9) may be acceptable.

ρ Based on Durbin–Watson d Statistic

If we cannot use the first-difference transformation because ρ is not sufficiently close to unity, we have an easy method of estimating it from the relationship between d and ρ established previously in Eq. (12.6.10), from which we can estimate ρ as follows:

$$\hat{\rho} \approx 1 - \frac{d}{2} \tag{12.9.13}$$

Thus, in reasonably large samples one can obtain ρ from Eq. (12.9.13) and use it to transform the data as shown in the generalized difference equation (12.9.5). Keep in mind that the relationship between ρ and d given in Eq. (12.9.13) may not hold true in small samples, for which Theil and Nagar have proposed a modification, which is given in Exercise 12.6.

In our wages–productivity regression (12.5.2), we obtain a d value of 0.2176. Using this value in Eq. (12.9.13), we obtain $\hat{\rho} \approx 0.8912$. Using this estimated ρ value, we can estimate regression (12.9.5). All we have to do is subtract 0.8912 times the previous value of Y from its current value and similarly subtract 0.8912 times the previous value of X from its current value and run the OLS regression on the variables thus transformed as in Eq. (12.9.6), where $Y_t^* = (Y_t - 0.8912Y_{t-1})$ and $X_t^* = (X_t - 0.8912X_{t-1})$.

ρ Estimated from the Residuals

If the AR(1) scheme $u_t = \rho u_{t-1} + \varepsilon_t$ is valid, a simple way to estimate ρ is to regress the residuals $\hat{u}_t$ on $\hat{u}_{t-1}$, for the $\hat{u}_t$ are consistent estimators of the true u_t, as noted previously. That is, we run the following regression:

$$\hat{u}_t = \rho \, . \, \hat{u}_{t-1} + v_t \tag{12.9.14}$$

[41] I. I. Berenblutt and G. I. Webb, "A New Test for Autocorrelated Errors in the Linear Regression Model," *Journal of the Royal Statistical Society,* Series B, vol. 35, no.1, 1973, pp. 33–50.

where $\hat{u}_t$ are the residuals obtained from the original (level form) regression and where v_t are the error term of this regression. Note that there is no need to introduce the intercept term in Eq. (12.9.14), for we know the OLS residuals sum to zero.

The residuals from our wages–productivity regression given in Eq. (12.5.1) are already shown in Table 12.5. Using these residuals, the following regression results were obtained:

$$\widehat{\hat{u}_t} = 0.8678\hat{u}_{t-1}$$
$$t = (12.7359) \qquad r^2 = 0.7863 \tag{12.9.15}$$

As this regression shows, $\hat{\rho} = 0.8678$. Using this estimate, one can transform the original model as per Eq. (12.9.6). Since the ρ estimated by this procedure is about the same as that obtained from the Durbin–Watson *d*, the regression results using the ρ of Eq. (12.9.15) should not be very different from those obtained from the ρ estimated from the Durbin–Watson *d*. We leave it to the reader to verify this.

Iterative Methods of Estimating ρ

All the methods of estimating ρ discussed previously provide us with only a single estimate of ρ. But there are the so-called **iterative methods** that estimate ρ iteratively, that is, by successive approximation, starting with some initial value of ρ. Among these methods the following may be mentioned: the **Cochrane–Orcutt iterative procedure,** the **Cochrane–Orcutt two-step procedure,** the **Durbin two-step procedure,** and the **Hildreth–Lu scanning or search procedure.** Of these, the most popular is the Cochran–Orcutt iterative method. To save space, the iterative methods are discussed by way of exercises. Remember that the ultimate objective of these methods is to provide an estimate of ρ that may be used to obtain GLS estimates of the parameters. One advantage of the Cochrane–Orcutt iterative method is that it can be used to estimate not only an AR(1) scheme, but also higher-order autoregressive schemes, such as $\hat{u}_t = \hat{\rho}_1\hat{u}_{t-1} + \hat{\rho}_2\hat{u}_{t-2} + v_t$, which is AR(2). Having obtained the two ρs, one can easily extend the generalized difference equation (12.9.6). Of course, the computer can now do all this.

Returning to our wages–productivity regression, and assuming an AR(1) scheme, we use the Cochrane–Orcutt iterative method, which gives the following estimates of ρ: 0.8876, 0.9944, and 0.8827. The last value of 0.8827 can now be used to transform the original model as in Eq. (12.9.6) and estimate it by OLS. Of course, OLS on the transformed model is simply the GLS. The results are as follows:

Stata can estimate the coefficients of the model along with ρ. For example, if we assume the AR(1), Stata produces the following results:

$$\hat{Y}_t^* = 43.1042 + 0.5712X_t$$
$$\text{se} = (4.3722) \quad (0.0415) \tag{12.9.16}$$
$$t = (9.8586) \quad (13.7638) \qquad r^2 = 0.8146$$

From these results, we can see that the estimated rho ($\hat{\rho}$) is $\approx$0.8827, which is not very much different from the $\hat{\rho}$ in Eq. (12.9.15).

As noted before, in the generalized difference equation (12.9.6) we lose one observation because the first observation has no antecedent. To avoid losing the first observation, we can use the *Prais–Winsten transformation.* Using this transformation, and using STATA (version #10), we obtain the following results for our wages–productivity regression:

$$\text{Rcompb}_t = 32.0434 + 0.6628\ \text{Prodb}_t$$
$$\text{se} = (3.7182) \quad (0.0386) \qquad r^2 = 0.8799 \tag{12.9.17}$$

In this transformation, the ρ value was 0.9193, which was obtained after 13 iterations. *It should be pointed out that if we do not transform the first observation à la Prais–Winsten and drop that observation, the results sometimes are substantially different, especially in small samples.* Notice that the ρ obtained here is not much different from the one obtained in Eq. (12.9.15).

General Comments

There are several points about correcting for autocorrelation using the various methods discussed above.

First, since the OLS estimators are consistent despite autocorrelation, in large samples, it makes little difference whether we estimate ρ from the Durbin–Watson d, or from the regression of the residuals in the current period on the residuals in the previous period, or from the Cochrane–Orcutt iterative procedure because they all provide consistent estimates of the true ρ. *Second,* the various methods discussed above are basically two-step methods. In step 1 we obtain an estimate of the unknown ρ and in step 2 we use that estimate to transform the variables to estimate the generalized difference equation, which is basically GLS. But since we use $\hat{\rho}$ instead of the true ρ, all these methods of estimation are known in the literature as **feasible GLS (FGLS)** or **estimated GLS (EGLS)** methods.

Third, it is important to note that whenever we use an **FGLS** or **EGLS** method to estimate the parameters of the transformed model, the estimated coefficients will not necessarily have the usual optimum properties of the classical model, such as BLUE, especially in small samples. Without going into complex technicalities, it may be stated *as a general principle that whenever we use an estimator in place of its true value, the estimated OLS coefficients may have the usual optimum properties asymptotically, that is, in large samples. Also, the conventional hypothesis testing procedures are, strictly speaking, valid asymptotically. In small samples, therefore, one has to be careful in interpreting the estimated results.*

Fourth, in using EGLS, if we do not include the first observation (as was originally the case with the Cochrane–Orcutt procedure), not only the numerical values but also the efficiency of the estimators can be adversely affected, especially if the sample size is small and if the regressors are not strictly speaking nonstochastic.[42] Therefore, in small samples it is important to keep the first observation *à la* Prais–Winsten. Of course, if the sample size is reasonably large, EGLS, with or without the first observation, gives similar results. Incidentally, in the literature EGLS with Prais–Winsten transformation is known as the **full EGLS,** or **FEGLS,** for short.

12.10 The Newey–West Method of Correcting the OLS Standard Errors

Instead of using the FGLS methods discussed in the previous section, we can still use OLS but correct the standard errors for autocorrelation by a procedure developed by Newey and West.[43] This is an extension of White's heteroscedasticity-consistent standard errors that we discussed in the previous chapter. The corrected standard errors are known as **HAC (heteroscedasticity- and autocorrelation-consistent) standard errors** or simply **Newey–West standard errors.** We will not present the mathematics behind the

[42]This is especially so if the regressors exhibit a trend, which is quite common in economic data.

[43]W. K. Newey and K. West, "A Simple Positive Semi-Definite Heteroscedasticity and Autocorrelation Consistent Covariance Matrix, *Econometrica,* vol. 55, 1987, pp. 703–708.

Newey–West procedure, for it is involved.[44] But most modern computer packages now calculate the Newey–West standard errors. It is important to point out that the Newey–West procedure is *strictly speaking valid in large samples* and may not be appropriate in small samples. But in large samples we now have a method that produces autocorrelation-corrected standard errors so that we do not have to worry about the EGLS transformations discussed in the previous section. Therefore, if a sample is reasonably large, one should use the Newey–West procedure to correct OLS standard errors not only in situations of autocorrelation only but also in cases of heteroscedasticity, for the HAC method can handle both, unlike the White method, which was designed specifically for heteroscedasticity.

Once again let us return to our wages–productivity regression (12.5.1). We know that this regression suffers from autocorrelation. Our sample of 46 observations is reasonably large, so we can use the HAC procedure. Using *EViews 4,* we obtain the following regression results:

$$\begin{aligned} \hat{Y}_t &= 32.7419 + 0.6704X_t \\ \text{se} &= (2.9162)^{*} \quad (0.0302)^{*} \\ & r^2 = 0.9765 \qquad d = 0.1719 \end{aligned} \tag{12.10.1}$$

where * denotes HAC standard errors.

Comparing this regression with Eq. (12.5.1), we find that in both the equations the estimated coefficients and the r^2 value are the same. But, importantly, note that the HAC standard errors are much greater than the OLS standard errors and therefore the HAC t ratios are much smaller than the OLS t ratios. This shows that OLS had in fact underestimated the true standard errors. Curiously, the d statistics in both Eqs. (12.5.1) and (12.10.1) are the same. But don't worry, for the HAC procedure has already taken this into account in correcting the OLS standard errors.

12.11 OLS versus FGLS and HAC

The practical problem facing the researcher is this: In the presence of autocorrelation, OLS estimators, although unbiased, consistent, and asymptotically normally distributed, are not efficient. Therefore, the usual inference procedure based on the t, F, and χ^2 tests is no longer appropriate. On the other hand, FGLS and HAC produce estimators that are efficient, but the finite, or small-sample, properties of these estimators are not well documented. This means in small samples the FGLS and HAC might actually do worse than OLS. As a matter of fact, in a Monte Carlo study Griliches and Rao[45] found that if the sample is relatively small and the coefficient of autocorrelation, ρ, is less than 0.3, OLS is as good or better than FGLS. As a practical matter, then, one may use OLS in small samples in which the estimated ρ is, say, less than 0.3. Of course, what is a large and what is a small sample are relative questions, and one has to use some practical judgment. If you have only 15 to 20 observations, the sample may be small, but if you have, say, 50 or more observations, the sample may be reasonably large.

[44] If you can handle matrix algebra, the method is discussed in Greene, op. cit, 4th ed., pp. 462–463.

[45] Z. Griliches, and P. Rao, "Small Sample Properties of Several Two-stage Regression Methods in the Context of Autocorrelated Errors," *Journal of the American Statistical Association,* vol. 64, 1969, pp. 253–272.

12.12 Additional Aspects of Autocorrelation

Dummy Variables and Autocorrelation

In Chapter 9 we considered dummy variable regression models. In particular, recall the U.S. savings–income regression model for 1970–1995 that we presented in Eq. (9.5.1), which for convenience is reproduced below:

$$Y_t = \alpha_1 + \alpha_2 D_t + \beta_1 X_t + \beta_2 (D_t X_t) + u_t \qquad (12.12.1)$$

where Y = savings
X = income
$D = 1$ for observations in period 1982–1995
$D = 0$ for observations in period 1970–1981

The regression results based on this model are given in Eq. (9.5.4). Of course, this model was estimated with the usual OLS assumptions.

But now suppose that u_t follows a first-order autoregressive, AR(1), scheme. That is, $u_t = \rho u_{t-1} + \varepsilon_t$. Ordinarily, if ρ is known or can be estimated by one of the methods discussed above, we can use the generalized difference method to estimate the parameters of the model that is free from (first-order) autocorrelation. However, the presence of the dummy variable D poses a special problem: Note that the dummy variable simply classifies an observation as belonging to the first or second period. How do we transform it? One can follow the following procedure.[46]

1. In Eq. (12.12.1), values of D are zero for all observations in the first period; in period 2 the value of D for the **first** observation is $1/(1 - \rho)$ instead of 1, and 1 for all other observations.

2. The variable X_t is transformed as $(X_t - \rho X_{t-1})$. Note that we lose one observation in this transformation, unless one resorts to **Prais–Winsten transformation** for the first observation, as noted earlier.

3. The value of $D_t X_t$ is zero for all observations in the first period (*note:* D_t is zero in the first period); in the second period the first observation takes the value of $D_t X_t = X_t$ and the remaining observations in the second period are set to $(D_t X_t - D_t \rho X_{t-1}) = (X_t - \rho X_{t-1})$. (*Note:* the value of D_t in the second period is 1.)

As the preceding discussion points out, the *critical observation* is the first observation in the second period. If this is taken care of in the manner just suggested, there should be no problem in estimating regressions like Eq. (12.12.1) subject to AR(1) autocorrelation. In Exercise 12.37, the reader is asked to carry such a transformation for the data on U.S. savings and income given in Chapter 9.

ARCH and GARCH Models

Just as the error term u at time t can be correlated with the error term at time $(t - 1)$ in an AR(1) scheme or with various lagged error terms in a general AR(p) scheme, can there be autocorrelation in the variance σ^2 at time t with its values lagged one or more periods? Such an autocorrelation has been observed by researchers engaged in forecasting financial time series, such as stock prices, inflation rates, and foreign exchange rates. Such autocorrelation is given the rather daunting names **autoregressive conditional heteroscedasticity (ARCH)** if the error variance is related to the squared error term in the previous term and **generalized autoregressive conditional heteroscedasticity (GARCH)** if the error variance is related to

[46]See Maddala, op. cit., pp. 321–322.

squared error terms several periods in the past. Since this topic belongs in the general area of time series econometrics, we will discuss it in some depth in the chapters on time series econometrics. Our objective here is to point out that autocorrelation is not confined to relationships between current and past error terms but also with current and past error variances.

Coexistence of Autocorrelation and Heteroscedasticity

What happens if a regression model suffers from both heteroscedasticity and autocorrelation? Can we solve the problem sequentially, that is, take care of heteroscedasticity first and then autocorrelation? As a matter of fact, one author contends that, "Autoregression can only be detected after the heteroscedasticity is controlled for."[47] But can we develop an omnipotent test that can solve these and other problems (e.g., model specification) simultaneously? Yes, such tests exist, but their discussion will take us far afield. It is better to leave them for references.[48] However, as noted earlier, we can use the HAC standard errors, for they take into account both autocorrelation and heteroscedasticity, provided the sample is reasonably large.

12.13 A Concluding Example

In Example 10.2, we presented data on consumption, income, wealth, and interest rates for the U.S., all in real terms. Based on these data, we estimated the following consumption function for the U.S. for the period 1947–2000, regressing the log of consumption on the logs of income and wealth. We did not express the interest rate in the log form because some of the real interest rate figures were negative.

```
Dependent Variable: ln(CONSUMPTION)
Method: Least Squares
Sample: 1947-2000
Included observations: 54
```

	Coefficient	Std. Error	*t*-Statistic	Prob.
C	-0.467711	0.042778	-10.93343	0.0000
ln(INCOME)	0.804873	0.017498	45.99836	0.0000
ln(WEALTH)	0.201270	0.017593	11.44060	0.0000
INTEREST	-0.002689	0.000762	-3.529265	0.0009

R-squared	0.999560	Mean dependent var.	7.826093
Adjusted R-squared	0.999533	S.D. dependent var.	0.552368
S.E. of regression	0.011934	*F*-statistic	37832.59
Sum squared resid.	0.007121	Prob. (*F*-statistic)	0.000000
Log likelihood	164.5880	Durbin-Watson stat.	1.289219

As expected, the income and wealth elasticities are positive and the interest rate semielasticity is negative. Although the estimated coefficients seem to be individually highly statistically significant, we need to check for possible autocorrelation in the error term. As we know, in the presence of autocorrelation, the estimated standard errors may be underestimated. Examing

[47]Lois W. Sayrs, *Pooled Time Series Analysis*, Sage Publications, California, 1989, p. 19.

[48]See Jeffrey M. Wooldridge, op. cit., pp. 402–403, and A. K. Bera and C. M. Jarque, "Efficient Tests for Normality, Homoscedasticity and Serial Independence of Regression Residuals: Monte Carlo Evidence," *Economic Letters*, vol. 7, 1981, pp. 313–318.

the Durbin–Watson *d* statistic, it seems the error terms in the consumption function suffer from (first-degree) autocorrelation (check this out).

To confirm this, we estimated the consumption function, allowing for AR(1) autocorrelation. The results are as follows:

Dependent Variable: lnCONSUMPTION
Method: Least Squares
Sample (adjusted): 1948–2000
Included observations: 53 after adjustments
Convergence achieved after 11 iterations

	Coefficient	Std. Error	*t*-Statistic	Prob.
C	-0.399833	0.070954	-5.635112	0.0000
lnINCOME	0.845854	0.029275	28.89313	0.0000
lnWEALTH	0.159131	0.027462	5.794501	0.0000
INTEREST	0.001214	0.000925	1.312986	0.1954
AR(1)	0.612443	0.100591	6.088462	0.0000

R-squared	0.999688	Mean dependent var.	7.843871
Adjusted R-squared	0.999662	S.D. dependent var.	0.541833
S.E. of regression	0.009954	*F*-statistic	38503.91
Sum squared resid.	0.004756	Prob. (*F*-statistic)	0.00000
Log likelihood	171.7381	Durbin-Watson stat.	1.874724

These results clearly show that our regression suffers from autocorrelation. We leave it to the reader to remove autocorrelation using some of the transformations discussed in this chapter. You may use the estimated ρ of 0.6124 for the transformations. Below, we present the results based on Newey–West (HAC) standard errors that take into account autocorrelation.

Dependent Variable: LCONSUMPTION
Method: Least Squares
Sample: 1947–2000
Included observations: 54
Newey-West HAC Standard Errors & Convariance (lag truncation = 3)

	Coefficient	Std. Error	*t*-Statistic	Prob.
C	-0.467714	0.043937	-10.64516	0.0000
LINCOME	0.804871	0.017117	47.02132	0.0000
LWEALTH	0.201272	0.015447	13.02988	0.0000
INTEREST	-0.002689	0.000880	-3.056306	0.0036

R-squared	0.999560	Mean dependent var.	7.826093
Adjusted R-squared	0.999533	S.D. dependent var.	0.552368
S.E. of regression	0.011934	*F*-statistic	37832.71
Sum squared resid.	0.007121	Prob. (*F*-statistic)	0.000000
		Durbin-Watson stat.	1.289237

The major difference between the first and the last of the above regressions is that the standard errors of the estimated coefficients have changed substantially. Despite this, the estimated slope coefficients are still highly statistically significant. However, there is no guarantee that this will always be the case.

Summary and Conclusions

1. If the assumption of the classical linear regression model—that the errors or disturbances u_t entering into the population regression function (PRF) are random or uncorrelated—is violated, the problem of serial or autocorrelation arises.
2. Autocorrelation can arise for several reasons, such as inertia or sluggishness of economic time series, specification bias resulting from excluding important variables from the model or using incorrect functional form, the cobweb phenomenon, data massaging, and data transformation. As a result, it is useful to distinguish between pure autocorrelation and "induced" autocorrelation because of one or more factors just discussed.
3. Although in the presence of autocorrelation the OLS estimators remain unbiased, consistent, and asymptotically normally distributed, they are no longer efficient. As a consequence, the usual t, F, and χ^2 tests cannot be legitimately applied. Hence, remedial results may be called for.
4. The remedy depends on the nature of the interdependence among the disturbances u_t. But since the disturbances are unobservable, the common practice is to assume that they are generated by some mechanism.
5. The mechanism that is commonly assumed is the Markov first-order autoregressive scheme, which assumes that the disturbance in the current time period is linearly related to the disturbance term in the previous time period, the coefficient of autocorrelation ρ providing the extent of the interdependence. This mechanism is known as the AR(1) scheme.
6. If the AR(1) scheme is valid and the coefficient of autocorrelation is known, the serial correlation problem can be easily attacked by transforming the data following the generalized difference procedure. The AR(1) scheme can be easily generalized to an AR(p). One can also assume a moving average (MA) mechanism or a mixture of AR and MA schemes, known as ARMA. This topic will be discussed in the chapters on time series econometrics.
7. Even if we use an AR(1) scheme, the coefficient of autocorrelation is not known a priori. We considered several methods of estimating ρ, such as the Durbin–Watson d, Theil–Nagar modified d, Cochrane–Orcutt (C–O) iterative procedure, C–O two-step method, and the Durbin two-step procedure. In large samples, these methods generally yield similar estimates of ρ, although in small samples they perform differently. In practice, the C–O iterative method has become quite popular.
8. Using any of the methods just discussed, we can use the generalized difference method to estimate the parameters of the transformed model by OLS, which essentially amounts to GLS. But since we estimate $\rho\ (= \hat{\rho})$, we call the method of estimation feasible, or estimated, GLS, or FGLS or EGLS for short.
9. In using EGLS, one has to be careful in dropping the first observation, for in small samples the inclusion or exclusion of the first observation can make a dramatic difference in the results. Therefore, in small samples it is advisable to transform the first observation according to the Prais–Winsten procedure. In large samples, however, it makes little difference if the first observation is included or not.
10. It is very important to note that the method of EGLS has the usual optimum statistical properties only in large samples. In small samples, OLS may actually do better that EGLS, especially if $\rho < 0.3$.
11. Instead of using EGLS, we can still use OLS but correct the standard errors for autocorrelation by the Newey–West HAC procedure. Strictly speaking, this procedure is

valid in large samples. One advantage of the HAC procedure is that it not only corrects for autocorrelation but also for heteroscedasticity, if it is present.

12. Of course, before remediation comes detection of autocorrelation. There are formal and informal methods of detection. Among the informal methods, one can simply plot the actual or standardized residuals, or plot current residuals against past residuals. Among formal methods, one can use the runs test, the Durbin–Watson d test, the asymptotic normality test, the Berenblutt–Webb test, and the Breusch–Godfrey (BG) test. Of these, the most popular and routinely used is the Durbin–Watson d test. Despite its hoary past, this test has severe limitations. It is better to use the BG test, for it is much more general in that it allows for both AR and MA error structures as well as the presence of lagged regressand as an explanatory variable. But keep in mind that it is a large sample test.
13. In this chapter we also discussed very briefly the detection of autocorrelation in the presence of dummy regressors.

EXERCISES

Questions

12.1. State whether the following statements are true or false. Briefly justify your answer.

a. When autocorrelation is present, OLS estimators are biased as well as inefficient.

b. The Durbin–Watson d test assumes that the variance of the error term u_t is homoscedastic.

c. The first-difference transformation to eliminate autocorrelation assumes that the coefficient of autocorrelation ρ is -1.

d. The R^2 values of two models, one involving regression in the first-difference form and another in the level form, are not directly comparable.

e. A significant Durbin–Watson d does not necessarily mean there is autocorrelation of the first order.

f. In the presence of autocorrelation, the conventionally computed variances and standard errors of forecast values are inefficient.

g. The exclusion of an important variable(s) from a regression model may give a significant d value.

h. In the AR(1) scheme, a test of the hypothesis that $\rho = 1$ can be made by the Berenblutt–Webb g statistic as well as the Durbin–Watson d statistic.

i. In the regression of the first difference of Y on the first differences of X, if there is a constant term and a linear trend term, it means in the original model there is a linear as well as a quadratic trend term.

12.2. Given a sample of 50 observations and 4 explanatory variables, what can you say about autocorrelation if (*a*) $d = 1.05$? (*b*) $d = 1.40$? (*c*) $d = 2.50$? (*d*) $d = 3.97$?

12.3. In studying the movement in the production workers' share in the value added (i.e., labor's share), the following models were considered by Gujarati:*

$$\text{Model A:} \quad Y_t = \beta_0 + \beta_1 t + u_t$$

$$\text{Model B:} \quad Y_t = \alpha_0 + \alpha_1 t + \alpha_2 t^2 + u_t$$

*Damodar Gujarati, "Labor's Share in Manufacturing Industries," *Industrial and Labor Relations Review*, vol. 23, no. 1, October 1969, pp. 65–75.

where Y = labor's share and t = time. Based on annual data for 1949–1964, the following results were obtained for the primary metal industry:

$$\text{Model A:} \quad \hat{Y}_t = 0.4529 - \underset{(-3.9608)}{0.0041t} \qquad R^2 = 0.5284 \qquad d = 0.8252$$

$$\text{Model B:} \quad \hat{Y}_t = 0.4786 - \underset{(-3.2724)}{0.0127t} + \underset{(2.7777)}{0.0005t^2}$$

$$R^2 = 0.6629 \qquad d = 1.82$$

where the figures in the parentheses are t ratios.

a. Is there serial correlation in model A? In model B?

b. What accounts for the serial correlation?

c. How would you distinguish between "pure" autocorrelation and specification bias?

12.4. *Detecting autocorrelation: von Neumann ratio test.** Assuming that the residual $\hat{u}_t$ are random drawings from normal distribution, von Neumann has shown that for *large n*, the ratio

$$\frac{\delta^2}{s^2} = \frac{\sum(\hat{u}_i - \hat{u}_{i-1})^2/(n-1)}{\sum(\hat{u}_i - \bar{\hat{u}})^2/n} \qquad \textit{Note}: \bar{\hat{u}} = 0 \text{ in OLS}$$

called the **von Neumann ratio,** is approximately normally distributed with mean

$$E\frac{\delta^2}{s^2} = \frac{2n}{n-1}$$

and variance

$$\text{var}\,\frac{\delta^2}{s^2} = 4n^2\frac{n-2}{(n+1)(n-1)^3}$$

a. If n is sufficiently large, how would you use the von Neumann ratio to test for autocorrelation?

b. What is the relationship between the Durbin–Watson d and the von Neumann ratio?

c. The d statistic lies between 0 and 4. What are the corresponding limits for the von Neumann ratio?

d. Since the ratio depends on the assumption that the $\hat{u}$'s are random drawings from normal distribution, how valid is this assumption for the OLS residuals?

e. Suppose in an application the ratio was found to be 2.88 with 100 observations. Test the hypothesis that there is no serial correlation in the data.

Note: B. I. Hart has tabulated the critical values of the von Neumann ratio for sample sizes of up to 60 observations.†

12.5. In a sequence of 17 residuals, 11 positive and 6 negative, the number of runs was 3. Is there evidence of autocorrelation? Would the answer change if there were 14 runs?

*J. von Neumann, "Distribution of the Ratio of the Mean Square Successive Difference to the Variance," *Annals of Mathematical Statistics,* vol. 12, 1941, pp. 367–395.

†The table may be found in Johnston, op. cit., 3d ed., p. 559.

12.6. *Theil–Nagar ρ estimate based on d statistic.* Theil and Nagar have suggested that, in small samples, instead of estimating ρ as $(1 - d/2)$, it should be estimated as

$$\hat{\rho} = \frac{n^2(1 - d/2) + k^2}{n^2 - k^2}$$

where n = total number of observations, d = Durbin–Watson d, and k = number of coefficients (including the intercept) to be estimated.

Show that for large n, this estimate of ρ is equal to the one obtained by the simpler formula $(1 - d/2)$.

12.7. *Estimating ρ: The Hildreth–Lu scanning or search procedure.*[*] Since in the first-order autoregressive scheme

$$u_t = \rho u_{t-1} + \varepsilon_t$$

ρ is expected to lie between -1 and $+1$, Hildreth and Lu suggest a systematic "scanning" or search procedure to locate it. They recommend selecting ρ between -1 and $+1$ using, say, 0.1 unit intervals and transforming the data by the generalized difference equation (12.6.5). Thus, one may choose ρ from $-0.9, -0.8, \ldots, 0.8, 0.9$. For each chosen ρ we run the generalized difference equation and obtain the associated RSS: $\sum \hat{u}_t^2$. Hildreth and Lu suggest choosing that ρ which minimizes the RSS (hence maximizing the R^2). If further refinement is needed, they suggest using smaller unit intervals, say, 0.01 units such as $-0.99, -0.98, \ldots, 0.90, 0.91$, and so on.

a. What are the advantages of the Hildreth–Lu procedure?

b. How does one know that the ρ value ultimately chosen to transform the data will, in fact, guarantee minimum $\sum \hat{u}_t^2$?

12.8. *Estimating ρ: The Cochrane–Orcutt (C–O) iterative procedure.*[†] As an illustration of this procedure, consider the two-variable model:

$$Y_t = \beta_1 + \beta_2 X_t + u_t \tag{1}$$

and the AR(1) scheme

$$u_t = \rho u_{t-1} + \varepsilon_t, \quad -1 < \rho < 1 \tag{2}$$

Cochrane and Orcutt then recommend the following steps to estimate ρ.

1. Estimate Eq. (1) by the usual OLS routine and obtain the residuals, $\hat{u}_t$. Incidentally, note that you can have more than one X variable in the model.
2. Using the residuals obtained in step 1, run the following regression:

$$\hat{u}_t = \hat{\rho}\hat{u}_{t-1} + v_t \tag{3}$$

which is the empirical counterpart of Eq. (2).[‡]

3. Using $\hat{\rho}$ obtained in Eq. (3), estimate the generalized difference equation (12.9.6).

[*] G. Hildreth and J. Y. Lu, "Demand Relations with Autocorrelated Disturbances," Michigan State University, *Agricultural Experiment Station,* Tech. Bull. 276, November 1960.

[†] D. Cochrane and G. H. Orcutt, "Applications of Least-Squares Regressions to Relationships Containing Autocorrelated Error Terms," *Journal of the American Statistical Association,* vol. 44, 1949, pp 32–61.

[‡] Note that $\hat{\rho} = \sum \hat{u}_t \hat{u}_{t-1} / \sum \hat{u}_t^2$ (why?). Although biased, $\hat{\rho}$ is a consistent estimator of the true ρ.

4. Since a priori it is not known if the $\hat{\rho}$ obtained from Eq. (3) is the best estimate of ρ, substitute the values of $\hat{\beta}_1^*$ and $\hat{\beta}_2^*$ obtained in step (3) in the original regression Eq. (1) and obtain the new residuals, say, $\hat{u}_t^*$ as

$$\hat{u}_t^* = Y_t - \hat{\beta}_1^* - \hat{\beta}_2^* X_t \tag{4}$$

which can be easily computed since Y_t, X_t, $\hat{\beta}_1^*$, and $\hat{\beta}_2^*$ are all known.

5. Now estimate the following regression:

$$\hat{u}_t^* = \hat{\rho}^* \hat{u}_{t-1}^* + w_t \tag{5}$$

which is similar to Eq. (3) and thus provides the second-round estimate of ρ.

Since we do not know whether this second-round estimate of ρ is the best estimate of the true ρ, we go into the third-round estimate, and so on. That is why the C–O procedure is called an iterative procedure. But how long should we go on this (merry-) go-round? The general recommendation is to stop carrying out iterations when the successive estimates of ρ differ by a small amount, say, by less than 0.01 or 0.005. In our wages–productivity example, it took about three iterations before we stopped.

a. Use the Cochrane–Orcutt iterative procedure to estimate ρ for the wages–productivity regression, Eq. (12.5.2). How many iterations were involved before you obtained the "final" estimate of ρ?

b. Using the final estimate of ρ obtained in (*a*), estimate the wages–productivity regression, dropping the first observation as well as retaining the first observation. What difference you see in the results?

c. Do you think that it is important to keep the first observation in transforming the data to solve the autocorrelation problem?

12.9. *Estimating ρ: The Cochrane–Orcutt two-step procedure.* This is a shortened version of the C–O iterative procedure. In step 1, we estimate ρ from the first iteration, that is from Eq. (3) in the preceding exercise, and in step 2 we use that estimate of ρ to run the generalized difference equation, as in Eq. (4) in the preceding exercise. Sometimes in practice, this two-step method gives results quite similar to those obtained from the more elaborate C–O iterative procedure.

Apply the C–O two-step method to the illustrative wages–productivity regression (12.5.1) given in this chapter and compare your results with those obtained from the iterative method. Pay special attention to the first observation in the transformation.

12.10. *Estimating ρ: Durbin's two-step method.*[*] To explain this method, we can write the generalized difference equation (12.9.5) equivalently as follows:

$$Y_t = \beta_1(1-\rho) + \beta_2 X_t - \beta_2 \rho X_{t-1} + \rho Y_{t-1} + \varepsilon_t \tag{1}$$

Durbin suggests the following two-step procedure to estimate ρ. *First,* treat Eq. (1) as a multiple regression model, regressing Y_t on X_t, X_{t-1}, and Y_{t-1} and treat the estimated value of the regression coefficient of Y_{t-1} ($= \hat{\rho}$) as an estimate of ρ. *Second,* having obtained $\hat{\rho}$, use it to estimate the parameters of generalized difference equation (12.9.5) or its equivalent, Eq. (12.9.6).

[*] J. Durbin, "Estimation of Parameters in Time-Series Regression Models," *Journal of the Royal Statistical Society,* series B, vol. 22, 1960, p. 139–153.

a. Apply the Durbin two-step method to the wages–productivity example discussed in this chapter and compare your results with those obtained from the Cochrane–Orcutt iterative procedure and the C–O two-step method. Comment on the "quality" of your results.

b. If you examine Eq. (1) above, you will observe that the coefficient of $X_{t-1}\ (= -\rho\beta_2)$ is equal to minus 1 times the product of the coefficient of $X_t\ (= \beta_2)$ and the coefficient of $Y_{t-1}\ (= \rho)$. How would you test that coefficients obey the preceding restriction?

12.11. In measuring returns to scale in electricity supply, Nerlove used cross-sectional data of 145 privately owned utilities in the United States for the period 1955 and regressed the log of total cost on the logs of output, wage rate, price of capital, and price of fuel. He found that the residuals estimated from this regression exhibited "serial" correlation, as judged by the Durbin–Watson *d*. To seek a remedy, he plotted the estimated residuals on the log of output and obtained Figure 12.11.

a. What does Figure 12.11 show?

b. How can you get rid of "serial" correlation in the preceding situation?

12.12. The residuals from a regression when plotted against time gave the scattergram in Figure 12.12. The encircled "extreme" residual is called an *outlier*. An outlier is an observation whose value exceeds the values of other observations in the sample by a

FIGURE 12.11 Regression residuals from the Nerlove study. (Adapted from Marc Nerlove, "Return to Scale in Electric Supply," in Carl F. Christ et al., *Measurement in Economics,* Stanford University Press, Stanford, Calif., 1963.)

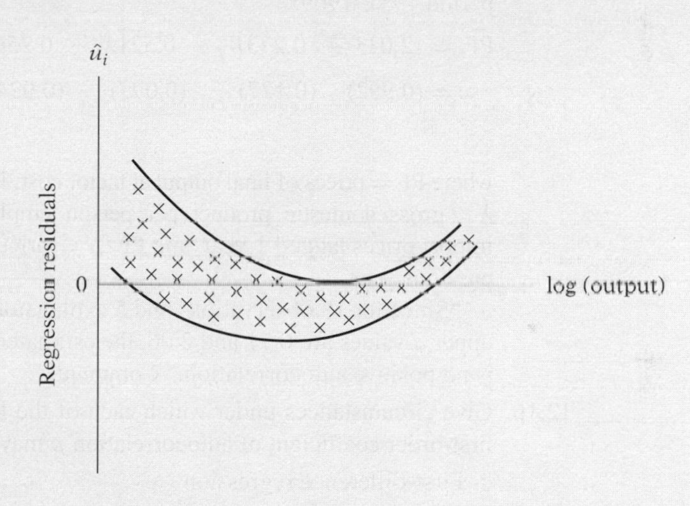

FIGURE 12.12 Hypothetical regression residuals plotted against time.

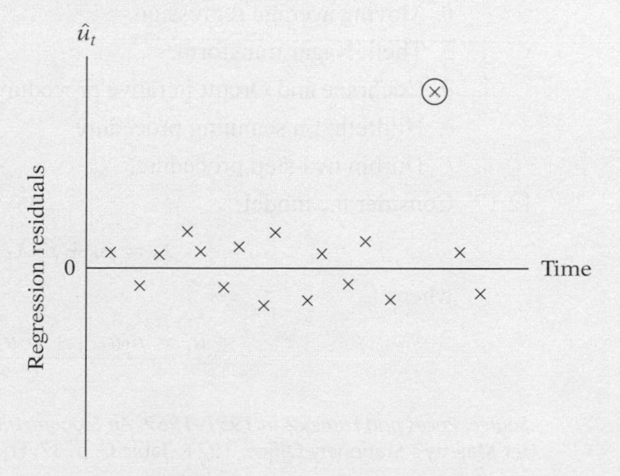

large amount, perhaps three or four standard deviations away from the mean value of all the observations.

a. What are the reasons for the existence of the outlier(s)?

b. If there is an outlier(s), should that observation(s) be discarded and the regression run on the remaining observations?

c. Is the Durbin–Watson d applicable in the presence of the outlier(s)?

12.13. Based on the Durbin–Watson d statistic, how would you distinguish "pure" autocorrelation from specification bias?

12.14. Suppose in the model

$$Y_t = \beta_1 + \beta_2 X_t + u_t$$

the u's are in fact serially independent. What would happen in this situation if, assuming that $u_t = \rho u_{t-1} + \varepsilon_t$, we were to use the following generalized difference regression?

$$Y_t - \rho Y_{t-1} = \beta_1(1 - \rho) + \beta_2 X_t - \rho\beta_2 X_{t-1} + \varepsilon_t$$

Discuss in particular the properties of the disturbance term ε_t.

12.15. In a study of the determination of prices of final output at factor cost in the United Kingdom, the following results were obtained on the basis of annual data for the period 1951–1969:

$$\widehat{\text{PF}}_t = 2.033 + 0.273W_t - 0.521X_t + 0.256M_t + 0.028M_{t-1} + 0.121PF_{t-1}$$
$$\text{se} = (0.992) \quad (0.127) \quad (0.099) \quad (0.024) \quad (0.039) \quad (0.119)$$
$$R^2 = 0.984 \qquad d = 2.54$$

where PF = prices of final output at factor cost, W = wages and salaries per employee, X = gross domestic product per person employed, M = import prices, M_{t-1} = import prices lagged 1 year, and PF_{t-1} = prices of final output at factor cost in the previous year.*

"Since for 18 observations and 5 explanatory variables, the 5 percent lower and upper d values are 0.71 and 2.06, the estimated d value of 2.54 indicates that there is no positive autocorrelation." Comment.

12.16. Give circumstances under which each of the following methods of estimating the first-order coefficient of autocorrelation ρ may be appropriate:

a. First-difference regression.

b. Moving average regression.

c. Theil–Nagar transform.

d. Cochrane and Orcutt iterative procedure.

e. Hildreth–Lu scanning procedure.

f. Durbin two-step procedure.

12.17. Consider the model:

$$Y_t = \beta_1 + \beta_2 X_t + u_t$$

where

$$u_t = \rho_1 u_{t-1} + \rho_2 u_{t-2} + \varepsilon_t$$

*Source: *Prices and Earnings in 1951–1969: An Econometric Assessment,* Department of Employment, Her Majesty's Stationery Office, 1971, Table C, p. 37, Eq. 63.

that is, the error term follows an AR(2) scheme and ε_t is a white noise error term. Outline the steps you would take to estimate the model taking into account the second-order autoregression.

12.18. Including the correction factor C, the formula for $\hat{\beta}_2^{\text{GLS}}$ given in Eq. (12.3.1) is

$$\hat{\beta}_2^{\text{GLS}} = \frac{(1-\rho^2)x_1 y_1 + \sum_{t=2}^{n}(x_t - \rho x_{t-1})(y_t - \rho y_{t-1})}{(1-\rho^2)x_1^2 + \sum_{t=2}^{n}(x_t - \rho x_{t-1})^2}$$

Given this formula and Eq. (12.3.1), find the expression for the correction factor C.

12.19. Show that estimating Eq. (12.9.5) is equivalent to estimating the GLS discussed in Section 12.3, excluding the first observation on Y and X.

12.20. For regression (12.9.9), the estimated residuals have the following signs, which for ease of exposition are bracketed.

(++++)(−)(+++++++)(−)(++++)(−−)(+)(−−)(+)(−−)(++)(−)
(+)(−−−−−−−−−)(+)

On the basis of the runs test, do you reject the null hypothesis that there is no autocorrelation in the residuals?

*12.21. *Testing for higher-order serial correlation.* Suppose we have time series data on a quarterly basis. In regression models involving quarterly data, instead of using the AR(1) scheme given in Eq. (12.2.1), it may be more appropriate to assume an AR(4) scheme as follows:

$$u_t = \rho_4 u_{t-4} + \varepsilon_t$$

that is, to assume that the current disturbance term is correlated with that of the same quarter in the previous year rather than that of the preceding quarter.

To test the hypothesis that $\rho_4 = 0$, Wallis[†] suggests the following modified Durbin–Watson d test:

$$d_4 = \frac{\sum_{t=5}^{n}(\hat{u}_t - \hat{u}_{t-4})^2}{\sum_{t=1}^{n}\hat{u}_t^2}$$

The testing procedure follows the usual d test routine discussed in the text. Wallis has prepared d_4 tables, which may be found in his original article.

Suppose now we have monthly data. Could the Durbin–Watson test be generalized to take into account such data? If so, write down the appropriate d_{12} formula.

12.22. Suppose you estimate the following regression:

$$\Delta \ln \text{output}_t = \beta_1 + \beta_2 \Delta \ln L_t + \beta_3 \Delta \ln K_t + u_t$$

where Y is output, L is labor input, K is capital input, and Δ is the first-difference operator. How would you interpret β_1 in this model? Could it be regarded as an estimate of technological change? Justify your answer.

*Optional.

[†]Kenneth Wallis, "Testing for Fourth Order Autocorrelation in Quarterly Regression Equations," *Econometrica,* vol. 40, 1972, pp. 617–636. Tables of d_4 can also be found in J. Johnston, op. cit., 3d ed., p. 558.

12.23. As noted in the text, Maddala has suggested that if the Durbin–Watson d is smaller than R^2, one may run the regression in the first-difference form. What is the logic behind this suggestion?

12.24. Refer to Eq. (12.4.1). Assume $r = 0$ but $\rho \neq 0$. What is the effect on $E(\hat{\sigma}^2)$ if (*a*) $0 < \rho < 1$ and (*b*) $-1 < \rho < 0$? When will the bias in $\hat{\sigma}^2$ be reasonably small?

12.25. The residuals from the wages–productivity regression given in Eq. (12.5.2) were regressed on lagged residuals going back six periods (i.e., AR[6]), yielding the following results:

```
Dependent Variable: S1
Method: Least Squares
Sample (adjusted): 1966-2005
Included observations: 40 after adjustments
```

	Coefficient	Std. Error	*t*-Statistic	Prob.
S1(-1)	1.019716	0.170999	5.963275	0.0000
S1(-2)	-0.029679	0.244152	-0.121560	0.9040
S1(-3)	-0.286782	0.241975	-1.185171	0.2442
S1(-4)	0.149212	0.242076	0.616386	0.5417
S1(-5)	-0.071371	0.243386	-0.293240	0.7711
S1(-6)	0.034362	0.167077	0.205663	0.8383

R-squared	0.749857	Mean dependent var.	0.004433
Adjusted R-squared	0.713071	S.D. dependent var.	0.019843
S.E. of regression	0.010629	Durbin-Waston stat.	1.956818
Sum squared resid.	0.003841		

a. From the preceding results, what can you say about the nature of autocorrelation in the logarithmic wages–productivity data?

b. If you think that an AR(1) mechanism characterizes autocorrelation in our data, would you use the first-difference transformation to get rid of autocorrelation? Justify your answer.

Empirical Exercises

12.26. Refer to the data on the copper industry given in Table 12.7.

a. From these data estimate the following regression model:

$$\ln C_t = \beta_1 + \beta_2 \ln I_t + \beta_3 \ln L_t + \beta_4 \ln H_t + \beta_5 \ln A_t + u_t$$

Interpret the results.

b. Obtain the residuals and standardized residuals from the preceding regression and plot them. What can you surmise about the presence of autocorrelation in these residuals?

c. Estimate the Durbin–Watson d statistic and comment on the nature of autocorrelation present in the data.

d. Carry out the runs test and see if your answer differs from that just given in (*c*).

e. How would you find out if an AR(p) process better describes autocorrelation than an AR(1) process?

Note: Save the data for further analysis. (See Exercise 12.28.)

TABLE 12.7
Determinants of U.S. Domestic Price of Copper, 1951–1980

Year	C	G	I	L	H	A
1951	21.89	330.2	45.1	220.4	1,491.0	19.00
52	22.29	347.2	50.9	259.5	1,504.0	19.41
53	19.63	366.1	53.3	256.3	1,438.0	20.93
54	22.85	366.3	53.6	249.3	1,551.0	21.78
55	33.77	399.3	54.6	352.3	1,646.0	23.68
56	39.18	420.7	61.1	329.1	1,349.0	26.01
57	30.58	442.0	61.9	219.6	1,224.0	27.52
58	26.30	447.0	57.9	234.8	1,382.0	26.89
59	30.70	483.0	64.8	237.4	1,553.7	26.85
60	32.10	506.0	66.2	245.8	1,296.1	27.23
61	30.00	523.3	66.7	229.2	1,365.0	25.46
62	30.80	563.8	72.2	233.9	1,492.5	23.88
63	30.80	594.7	76.5	234.2	1,634.9	22.62
64	32.60	635.7	81.7	347.0	1,561.0	23.72
65	35.40	688.1	89.8	468.1	1,509.7	24.50
66	36.60	753.0	97.8	555.0	1,195.8	24.50
67	38.60	796.3	100.0	418.0	1,321.9	24.98
68	42.20	868.5	106.3	525.2	1,545.4	25.58
69	47.90	935.5	111.1	620.7	1,499.5	27.18
70	58.20	982.4	107.8	588.6	1,469.0	28.72
71	52.00	1,063.4	109.6	444.4	2,084.5	29.00
72	51.20	1,171.1	119.7	427.8	2,378.5	26.67
73	59.50	1,306.6	129.8	727.1	2,057.5	25.33
74	77.30	1,412.9	129.3	877.6	1,352.5	34.06
75	64.20	1,528.8	117.8	556.6	1,171.4	39.79
76	69.60	1,700.1	129.8	780.6	1,547.6	44.49
77	66.80	1,887.2	137.1	750.7	1,989.8	51.23
78	66.50	2,127.6	145.2	709.8	2,023.3	54.42
79	98.30	2,628.8	152.5	935.7	1,749.2	61.01
80	101.40	2,633.1	147.1	940.9	1,298.5	70.87

Note: The data were collected by Gary R. Smith from sources such as *American Metal Market, Metals Week,* and U.S. Department of Commerce publications.
$C =$ 12-month average U.S. domestic price of copper (cents per pound).
$G =$ annual gross national product ($, billions).
$I =$ 12-month average index of industrial production.
$L =$ 12-month average London Metal Exchange price of copper (pounds sterling).
$H =$ number of housing starts per year (thousands of units).
$A =$ 12-month average price of aluminum (cents per pound).

12.27. You are given the data in Table 12.8.

a. Verify that Durbin–Watson $d = 0.4148$.

b. Is there positive serial correlation in the disturbances?

c. If so, estimate ρ by the
 i. Theil–Nagar method.
 ii. Durbin two-step procedure.
 iii. Cochrane–Orcutt method.

d. Use the Theil–Nagar method to transform the data and run the regression on the transformed data.

e. Does the regression estimated in (*d*) exhibit autocorrelation? If so, how would you get rid of it?

TABLE 12.8

Y, Personal Consumption Expenditure, Billions of 1958 Dollars	X, Time	$\hat{Y}$, Estimated Y	$\hat{u}$, Residuals
281.4	1 (= 1956)	261.4208	19.9791
288.1	2	276.6026	11.4973
290.0	3	291.7844	−1.7844
307.3	4	306.9661	0.3338
316.1	5	322.1479	−6.0479
322.5	6	337.3297	−14.8297
338.4	7	352.5115	−14.1115
353.3	8	367.6933	−14.3933
373.7	9	382.8751	−9.1751
397.7	10	398.0569	−0.3569
418.1	11	413.2386	4.8613
430.1	12	428.4206	1.6795
452.7	13	443.6022	9.0977
469.1	14	458.7840	10.3159
476.9	15 (= 1970)	473.9658	2.9341

Note: Data for $\hat{Y}$ obtained from the regression $Y_t = \beta_0 + \beta_1 X_t + u_t$.

12.28. Refer to Exercise 12.26 and the data given in Table 12.7. If the results of this exercise show serial correlation,

a. Use the Cochrane–Orcutt two-stage procedure and obtain the estimates of the feasible GLS or the generalized difference regression and compare your results.

b. If the ρ estimated from the Cochrane–Orcutt method in (*a*) differs substantially from that estimated from the *d* statistic, which method of estimating ρ would you choose and why?

12.29. Refer to Example 7.4. Omitting the variables X^2 and X^3, run the regression and examine the residuals for "serial" correlation. If serial correlation is found, how would you rationalize it? What remedial measures would you suggest?

12.30. Refer to Exercise 7.21. A priori autocorrelation is expected in such data. Therefore, it is suggested that you regress the log of real money supply on the logs of real national income and long-term interest rate in the first-difference form. Run this regression, and then rerun the regression in the original form. Is the assumption underlying the first-difference transformation satisfied? If not, what kinds of biases are likely to result from such a transformation? Illustrate with the data at hand.

12.31. *The use of Durbin–Watson d for testing nonlinearity.* Continue with Exercise 12.29. Arrange the residuals obtained in that regression according to increasing values of *X*. Using the formula given in Eq. (12.6.5), estimate *d* from the rearranged residuals. If the computed *d* value indicates autocorrelation, this would imply that the linear model was incorrect and that the full model should include X_i^2 and X_i^3 terms. Can you give an intuitive justification for such a procedure? See if your answer agrees with that given by Henri Theil.*

12.32. Refer to Exercise 11.22. Obtain the residuals and find out if there is autocorrelation in the residuals. How would you transform the data in case serial correlation is detected? What is the meaning of serial correlation in the present instance?

*Henri Theil, *Introduction to Econometrics,* Prentice Hall, Englewood Cliffs, NJ, 1978, pp. 307–308.

12.33. *Monte Carlo experiment.* Refer to Tables 12.1 and 12.2. Using ε_t and X_t data given there, generate a sample of 10 Y values from the model

$$Y_t = 3.0 + 0.5X_t + u_t$$

where $u_t = 0.9u_{t-1} + \varepsilon_t$. Assume $u_0 = 10$.

a. Estimate the equation and comment on your results.

b. Now assume $u_0 = 17$. Repeat this exercise 10 times and comment on the results.

c. Keep the preceding setup intact except now let $\rho = 0.3$ instead of $\rho = 0.9$ and compare your results with those given in (*b*).

12.34. Using the data given in Table 12.9, estimate the model

$$Y_t = \beta_1 + \beta_2 X_t + u_t$$

where Y = inventories and X = sales, both measured in billions of dollars.

a. Estimate the preceding regression.

b. From the estimated residuals find out if there is positive autocorrelation using (*i*) the Durbin–Watson test and (*ii*) the large-sample normality test given in Eq. (12.6.13).

c. If ρ is positive, apply the Berenblutt–Webb test to test the hypothesis that $\rho = 1$.

d. If you suspect that the autoregressive error structure is of order p, use the Breusch–Godfrey test to verify this. How would you choose the order of p?

e. On the basis of the results of this test, how would you transform the data to remove autocorrelation? Show all your calculations.

TABLE 12.9 Inventories and Sales in U.S. Manufacturing, 1950–1991 (millions of dollars)

Year	Sales*	Inventories†	Ratio	Year	Sales*	Inventories†	Ratio
1950	46,486	84,646	1.82	1971	224,619	369,374	1.57
1951	50,229	90,560	1.80	1972	236,698	391,212	1.63
1952	53,501	98,145	1.83	1973	242,686	405,073	1.65
1953	52,805	101,599	1.92	1974	239,847	390,950	1.65
1954	55,906	102,567	1.83	1975	250,394	382,510	1.54
1955	63,027	108,121	1.72	1976	242,002	378,762	1.57
1956	72,931	124,499	1.71	1977	251,708	379,706	1.50
1957	84,790	157,625	1.86	1978	269,843	399,970	1.44
1958	86,589	159,708	1.84	1979	289,973	424,843	1.44
1959	98,797	174,636	1.77	1980	299,766	430,518	1.43
1960	113,201	188,378	1.66	1981	319,558	443,622	1.37
1961	126,905	211,691	1.67	1982	324,984	449,083	1.38
1962	143,936	242,157	1.68	1983	335,991	463,563	1.35
1963	154,391	265,215	1.72	1984	350,715	481,633	1.35
1964	168,129	283,413	1.69	1985	330,875	428,108	1.38
1965	163,351	311,852	1.95	1986	326,227	423,082	1.29
1966	172,547	312,379	1.78	1987	334,616	408,226	1.24
1967	190,682	339,516	1.73	1988	359,081	439,821	1.18
1968	194,538	334,749	1.73	1989	394,615	479,106	1.17
1969	194,657	322,654	1.68	1990	411,663	509,902	1.21
1970	206,326	338,109	1.59				

*Annual data are averages of monthly, not seasonally adjusted, figures.

†Seasonally adjusted, end of period figures beginning 1982 are not comparable with earlier period.

Source: *Economic Report of the President,* 1993, Table B-53, p. 408.

f. Repeat the preceding steps using the following model:

$$\ln Y_t = \beta_1 + \beta_2 \ln X_t + u_t$$

g. How would you decide between the linear and log–linear specifications? Show explicitly the test(s) you use.

12.35. Table 12.10 gives data on real rate of return on common stocks at time (RR_t), output growth in period $(t+1)$, (OG_{t+1}), and inflation in period t(Inf_t), all in percent form, for the U.S. economy for the period 1954–1981.

a. Regress RR_t on inflation.

b. Regress RR_t on OG_{t+1} and Inf_t

c. Comment on the two regression results in view of Eugene Fama's observation that "the negative simple correlation between real stock returns and inflation is spurious because it is the result of two structural relationships: a positive relation between current real stock returns and expected output growth [measured by OG_{t+1}], and a negative relationship between expected output growth and current inflation."

d. Would you expect autocorrelation in either of the regressions in (*a*) and (*b*)? Why or why not? If you do, take the appropriate corrective action and present the revised results.

TABLE 12.10
Rate of Return, Output Growth and Inflation, United States, 1954–1981

Observation	RR	Growth	Inflation
1954	53.0	6.7	−0.4
1955	31.2	2.1	0.4
1956	3.7	1.8	2.9
1957	−13.8	−0.4	3.0
1958	41.7	6.0	1.7
1959	10.5	2.1	1.5
1960	−1.3	2.6	1.8
1961	26.1	5.8	0.8
1962	−10.5	4.0	1.8
1963	21.2	5.3	1.6
1964	15.5	6.0	1.0
1965	10.2	6.0	2.3
1966	−13.3	2.7	3.2
1967	21.3	4.6	2.7
1968	6.8	2.8	4.3
1969	−13.5	−0.2	5.0
1970	−0.4	3.4	4.4
1971	10.5	5.7	3.8
1972	15.4	5.8	3.6
1973	−22.6	−0.6	7.9
1974	−37.3	−1.2	10.8
1975	31.2	5.4	6.0
1976	19.1	5.5	4.7
1977	−13.1	5.0	5.9
1978	−1.3	2.8	7.9
1979	8.6	−0.3	9.8
1980	−22.2	2.6	10.2
1981	−12.2	−1.9	7.3

12.36. *The Durbin h statistic.* Consider the following model of wage determination:

$$Y_t = \beta_1 + \beta_2 X_t + \beta_3 Y_{t-1} + u_t$$

where Y = wages = index of real compensation per hour
X = productivity = index of output per hour.

a. Using the data in Table 12.4, estimate the above model and interpret your results.

b. Since the model contains lagged regressand as a regressor, the Durbin–Watson d is not appropriate to find out if there is serial correlation in the data. For such models, called autoregressive models, Durbin has developed the so-called ***h* statistic** to test for first-order autocorrelation, which is defined as:*

$$h = \hat{\rho}\sqrt{\frac{n}{1 - n[\text{var}(\hat{\beta}_3)]}}$$

where n = sample size, var $(\hat{\beta}_3)$ = variance of the coefficient of the lagged Y_{t-1}, and $\hat{\rho}$ = estimate of the first-order serial correlation.

For large sample size (technically, asymptotic), Durbin has shown that, under the null hypothesis that $\rho = 0$,

$$h \sim N(0, 1)$$

that is, the h statistic follows the standard normal distribution. From the properties of the normal distribution we know that the probability of $|h| > 1.96$ is about 5 percent. Therefore, if in an application $|h| > 1.96$, we can reject the null hypothesis that $\rho = 0$, that is, there is evidence of first-order autocorrelation in the autoregressive model given above.

To apply the test, we proceed as follows: *First,* estimate the above model by OLS (don't worry about any estimation problems at this stage). *Second,* note var $(\hat{\beta}_3)$ in this model as well as the routinely computed d statistic. *Third,* using the d value, obtain $\hat{\rho} \approx (1 - d/2)$. It is interesting to note that although we cannot use the d value to test for serial correlation in this model, we can use it to obtain an estimate of ρ. *Fourth,* now compute the h statistic. *Fifth,* if the sample size is reasonably large and if the computed $|h|$ exceeds 1.96, we can conclude that there is evidence of first-order autocorrelation. Of course, you can use any level of significance you want.

Apply the h test to the autoregressive wage determination model given earlier and draw appropriate conclusions and compare your results with those given in regression (12.5.1).

12.37. *Dummy variables and autocorrelation.* Refer to the savings–income regression discussed in Chapter 9. Using the data given in Table 9.2, and assuming an AR(1) scheme, reestimate the savings–income regression, taking into account autocorrelation. Pay close attention to the transformation of the dummy variable. Compare your results with those presented in Chapter 9.

12.38. Using the wages–productivity data given in Table 12.4, estimate model (12.9.8) and compare your results with those given in regression (12.9.9). What conclusion(s) do you draw?

*J. Durbin, "Testing for Serial Correlation in Least-squares Regression When Some of the Regressors Are Lagged Dependent Variables," *Econometrica,* vol. 38, pp. 410–421.

Appendix 12A

12A.1 Proof that the Error Term v_t in Equation (12.1.11) Is Autocorrelated

Since $v_t = u_t - u_{t-1}$, it is easy to show that $E(v_t) = E(u_t - u_{t-1}) = E(u_t) - E(u_{t-1}) = 0$, since $E(u) = 0$, for each t. Now, $\text{var}(v_t) = \text{var}(u_t - u_{t-1}) = \text{var}(u_t) + \text{var}(u_{t-1}) = 2\sigma^2$, since the variance of each u_t is σ^2 and the u's are independently distributed. Hence, v_t is homoscedastic. But

$$\begin{aligned}\text{cov}(v_t, v_{t-1}) &= E(v_t v_{t-1}) = E[(u_t - u_{t-1})(u_{t-1} - u_{t-2})] \\ &= -\sigma^2\end{aligned}$$

which is obviously nonzero. Therefore, although the u's are not autocorrelated, the v's are.

12A.2 Proof of Equations (12.2.3), (12.2.4), and (12.2.5)

Under AR(1),

$$u_t = \rho u_{t-1} + \varepsilon_t \tag{1}$$

Therefore,

$$E(u_t) = \rho E(u_{t-1}) + E(\varepsilon_t) = 0 \tag{2}$$

So,

$$\text{var}(u_t) = \rho^2\,\text{var}(u_{t-1}) + \text{var}(\varepsilon_t) \tag{3}$$

because the u's and ε's are uncorrelated.

Since $\text{var}(u_t) = \text{var}(u_{t-1}) = \sigma^2$ and $\text{var}(\varepsilon_t) = \sigma_\varepsilon^2$, we get

$$\text{var}(u_t) = \frac{\sigma_\varepsilon^2}{1-\rho^2} \tag{4}$$

Now multiply Eq. (1) by u_{t-1} and take expectations on both sides to obtain:

$$\text{cov}(u_t, u_{t-1}) = E(u_t u_{t-1}) = E\left[\rho u_{t-1}^2 + u_{t-1}\varepsilon_t\right] = \rho E\left(u_{t-1}^2\right)$$

Noting that the covariance between u_{t-1} and ε_t is zero (why?) and that $\text{var}(u_t) = \text{var}(u_{t-1}) = \sigma_\varepsilon^2/(1-\rho^2)$, we obtain

$$\text{cov}(u_t, u_{t-1}) = \rho\frac{\sigma_\varepsilon^2}{(1-\rho^2)} \tag{5}$$

Continuing in this fashion,

$$\text{cov}(u_t, u_{t-2}) = \rho^2\frac{\sigma_\varepsilon^2}{(1-\rho^2)}$$

$$\text{cov}(u_t, u_{t-3}) = \rho^3\frac{\sigma_\varepsilon^2}{(1-\rho^2)}$$

and so on. Now the correlation coefficient is the ratio of covariance to variance. Hence,

$$\text{cor}(u_t, u_{t-1}) = \rho \qquad \text{cov}(u_t, u_{t-2}) = \rho^2$$

and so on.

Chapter 13

Econometric Modeling: Model Specification and Diagnostic Testing

Applied econometrics cannot be done mechanically; it needs understanding, intuition and skill.[1]

. . . we generally drive across bridges without worrying about the soundness of their construction because we are reasonably sure that someone rigorously checked their engineering principles and practice. Economists must do likewise with models or else attach the warning "not responsible if attempted use leads to collapse."[2]

Economists' search for "truth" has over the years given rise to the view that economists are people searching in a dark room for a non-existent black cat; econometricians are regularly accused of finding one.[3]

One of the assumptions of the classical linear regression model (CLRM), Assumption 9, is that the regression model used in the analysis is "correctly" specified: If the model is not "correctly" specified, we encounter the problem of **model specification error** or **model specification bias.** In this chapter we take a close and critical look at this assumption, because searching for the correct model is like searching for the Holy Grail. In particular we examine the following questions:

1. How does one go about finding the "correct" model? In other words, what are the criteria in choosing a model for empirical analysis?
2. What types of model specification errors is one likely to encounter in practice?
3. What are the consequences of specification errors?
4. How does one detect specification errors? In other words, what are some of the diagnostic tools that one can use?
5. Having detected specification errors, what remedies can one adopt and with what benefits?
6. How does one evaluate the performance of competing models?

[1]Keith Cuthbertson, Stephen G. Hall, and Mark P. Taylor, *Applied Econometrics Techniques,* Michigan University Press, 1992, p. X.

[2]David F. Hendry, *Dynamic Econometrics,* Oxford University Press, U.K., 1995, p. 68.

[3]Peter Kennedy, *A Guide to Econometrics,* 3d ed., The MIT Press, Cambridge, Mass., 1992, p. 82.

The topic of model specification and evaluation is vast, and very extensive empirical work has been done in this area. Not only that, but there are philosophical differences on this topic. Although we cannot do full justice to this topic in one chapter, we hope to bring out some of the essential issues involved in model specification and model evaluation.

13.1 Model Selection Criteria

According to Hendry and Richard, a model chosen for empirical analysis should satisfy the following criteria:[4]

1. *Be data admissible;* that is, predictions made from the model must be logically possible.
2. *Be consistent with theory;* that is, it must make good economic sense. For example, if Milton Friedman's **permanent income hypothesis** holds, the intercept value in the regression of permanent consumption on permanent income is expected to be zero.
3. *Have weakly exogenous regressors;* that is, the explanatory variables, or regressors, must be uncorrelated with the error term. It may be added that in some situations the exogenous regressors may be **strictly exogenous.** A strictly exogenous variable is independent of current, future, and past values of the error term.
4. *Exhibit parameter constancy;* that is, the values of the parameters should be stable. Otherwise, forecasting will be difficult. As Friedman notes, "The only relevant test of the validity of a hypothesis [model] is comparison of its predictions with experience."[5] In the absence of parameter constancy, such predictions will not be reliable.
5. *Exhibit data coherency;* that is, the residuals estimated from the model must be purely random (technically, white noise). In other words, if the regression model is adequate, the residuals from this model must be white noise. If that is not the case, there is some specification error in the model. Shortly, we will explore the nature of specification error(s).
6. *Be encompassing;* that is, the model should *encompass* or include all the rival models in the sense that it is capable of explaining their results. In short, other models cannot be an improvement over the chosen model.

It is one thing to list criteria of a "good" model and quite another to actually develop it, for in practice one is likely to commit various model specification errors, which we discuss in the next section.

13.2 Types of Specification Errors

Assume that on the basis of the criteria just listed we arrive at a model that we accept as a good model. To be concrete, let this model be

$$Y_i = \beta_1 + \beta_2 X_i + \beta_3 X_i^2 + \beta_4 X_i^3 + u_{1i} \tag{13.2.1}$$

where $Y =$ total cost of production and $X =$ output. Equation (13.2.1) is the familiar textbook example of the cubic total cost function.

[4] D. F. Hendry and J. F. Richard, "The Econometric Analysis of Economic Time Series," *International Statistical Review,* vol. 51, 1983, pp. 3–33.

[5] Milton Friedman, "The Methodology of Positive Economics," in *Essays in Positive Economics,* University of Chicago Press, Chicago, 1953, p. 7.

But suppose for some reason (say, laziness in plotting the scattergram) a researcher decides to use the following model:

$$Y_i = \alpha_1 + \alpha_2 X_i + \alpha_3 X_i^2 + u_{2i} \tag{13.2.2}$$

Note that we have changed the notation to distinguish this model from the true model.

Since Eq. (13.2.1) is assumed true, adopting Eq. (13.2.2) would constitute a specification error, the error consisting in **omitting a relevant variable** (X_i^3). Therefore, the error term u_{2i} in Eq. (13.2.2) is in fact

$$u_{2i} = u_{1i} + \beta_4 X_i^3 \tag{13.2.3}$$

We shall see shortly the importance of this relationship.

Now suppose that another researcher uses the following model:

$$Y_i = \lambda_1 + \lambda_2 X_i + \lambda_3 X_i^2 + \lambda_4 X_i^3 + \lambda_5 X_i^4 + u_{3i} \tag{13.2.4}$$

If Eq. (13.2.1) is the "truth," Eq. (13.2.4) also constitutes a specification error, the error here consisting in **including an unnecessary or irrelevant variable** in the sense that the true model assumes λ_5 to be zero. The new error term is in fact

$$\begin{aligned} u_{3i} &= u_{1i} - \lambda_5 X_i^4 \\ &= u_{1i} \qquad \text{since } \lambda_5 = 0 \text{ in the true model} \qquad \text{(Why?)} \end{aligned} \tag{13.2.5}$$

Now assume that yet another researcher postulates the following model:

$$\ln Y_i = \gamma_1 + \gamma_2 X_i + \gamma_3 X_i^2 + \gamma_4 X_i^3 + u_{4i} \tag{13.2.6}$$

In relation to the true model, Eq. (13.2.6) would also constitute a specification bias, the bias here being the use of the **wrong functional form:** In Eq. (13.2.1) Y appears linearly, whereas in Eq. (13.2.6) it appears log-linearly.

Finally, consider the researcher who uses the following model:

$$Y_i^* = \beta_1^* + \beta_2^* X_i^* + \beta_3^* X_i^{*2} + \beta_4^* X_i^{*3} + u_i^* \tag{13.2.7}$$

where $Y_i^* = Y_i + \varepsilon_i$ and $X_i^* = X_i + w_i$, ε_i and w_i being the errors of measurement. What Eq. (13.2.7) states is that instead of using the true Y_i and X_i we use their proxies, Y_i^* and X_i^*, which may contain errors of measurement. Therefore, in Eq. (13.2.7) we commit the **errors of measurement bias.** In applied work data are plagued by errors of approximations or errors of incomplete coverage or simply errors of omitting some observations. In the social sciences we often depend on secondary data and usually have no way of knowing the types of errors, if any, made by the primary data-collecting agency.

Another type of specification error relates to the way the stochastic error u_i (or u_t) enters the regression model. Consider for instance, the following bivariate regression model without the intercept term:

$$Y_i = \beta X_i u_i \tag{13.2.8}$$

where the stochastic error term enters multiplicatively with the property that $\ln u_i$ satisfies the assumptions of the CLRM, against the following model

$$Y_i = \alpha X_i + u_i \tag{13.2.9}$$

where the error term enters additively. Although the variables are the same in the two models, we have denoted the slope coefficient in Eq. (13.2.8) by β and the slope coefficient in Eq. (13.2.9) by α. Now if Eq. (13.2.8) is the "correct" or "true" model, would the estimated α provide an unbiased estimate of the true β? That is, will $E(\hat{\alpha}) = \beta$? If that is not the case, improper stochastic specification of the error term will constitute another source of specification error.

A specification error that is sometimes overlooked is the **interaction among the regressors,** that is, the **multiplicative effect of one or more regressors on the regressand.** To illustrate, consider the following simplified wage function:

$$\begin{aligned} \ln W_i = \beta_1 + \beta_2 \text{ Education}_i + \beta_3 \text{ Gender}_i \\ + \beta_4 \text{ (Education) (Gender)} + u \end{aligned} \tag{13.2.10}$$

In this model, the change in the relative wages with respect to education depends not only on education but also on the gender $\left(\frac{\partial \ln W}{\partial \text{Education}} = \beta_2 + \beta_4 \text{Gender}\right)$. Likewise, the change in relative wages with respect to gender depends not only on gender but also on education.

To sum up, in developing an empirical model, one is likely to commit one or more of the following specification errors:

1. Omission of a relevant variable(s).
2. Inclusion of an unnecessary variable(s).
3. Adoption of the wrong functional form.
4. Errors of measurement.
5. Incorrect specification of the stochastic error term.
6. Assumption that the error term is normally distributed.

Before turning to an examination of these specification errors in some detail, it may be fruitful to distinguish between **model specification errors** and **model mis-specification errors.** The first four types of error discussed above are essentially in the nature of model specification errors in that we have in mind a "true" model but somehow we do not estimate the correct model. In model mis-specification errors, we do not know what the true model is to begin with. In this context one may recall the controversy between the Keynesians and the monetarists. The monetarists give primacy to money in explaining changes in GDP, whereas the Keynesians emphasize the role of government expenditure to explain changes in GDP. So to speak, these are two competing models.

In what follows, we will first consider model specification errors and then examine model mis-specification errors.

13.3 Consequences of Model Specification Errors

Whatever the sources of specification errors, what are the consequences? To keep the discussion simple, we will answer this question in the context of the three-variable model and consider in this section the first two types of specification errors discussed earlier, namely, (1) **underfitting a model,** that is, omitting relevant variables, and (2) **overfitting a model,** that is, including unnecessary variables. Our discussion here can be easily generalized to more than two regressors, but with tedious algebra;[6] matrix algebra becomes almost a necessity once we go beyond the three-variable case.

[6]But see Exercise 13.32.

Underfitting a Model (Omitting a Relevant Variable)

Suppose the true model is:

$$Y_i = \beta_1 + \beta_2 X_{2i} + \beta_3 X_{3i} + u_i \tag{13.3.1}$$

but for some reason we fit the following model:

$$Y_i = \alpha_1 + \alpha_2 X_{2i} + v_i \tag{13.3.2}$$

The consequences of omitting variable X_3 are as follows:

1. If the left-out, or omitted, variable X_3 is correlated with the included variable X_2, that is, r_{23}, the correlation coefficient between the two variables is *nonzero* and $\hat{\alpha}_1$ and $\hat{\alpha}_2$ are *biased as well as inconsistent.* That is, $E(\hat{\alpha}_1) \neq \beta_1$ and $E(\hat{\alpha}_2) \neq \beta_2$, and the bias does not disappear as the sample size gets larger.
2. Even if X_2 and X_3 are not correlated, $\hat{\alpha}_1$ is biased, although $\hat{\alpha}_2$ is now unbiased.
3. The disturbance variance σ^2 is incorrectly estimated.
4. The conventionally measured variance of $\hat{\alpha}_2$ $(= \sigma^2/\sum x_{2i}^2)$ is a *biased* estimator of the variance of the true estimator $\hat{\beta}_2$.
5. In consequence, the usual confidence interval and hypothesis-testing procedures are likely to give misleading conclusions about the statistical significance of the estimated parameters.
6. As another consequence, the forecasts based on the incorrect model and the forecast (confidence) intervals will be unreliable.

Although proofs of each of the above statements will take us far afield,[7] it is shown in Appendix 13A, Section 13A.1, that

$$E(\hat{\alpha}_2) = \beta_2 + \beta_3 b_{32} \tag{13.3.3}$$

where b_{32} is the slope in the regression of the excluded variable X_3 on the included variable X_2 $(b_{32} = \sum x_{3i}x_{2i}/\sum x_{2i}^2)$. As Eq. (13.3.3) shows, $\hat{\alpha}_2$ is biased, unless β_3 or b_{32} or both are zero. We rule out β_3 being zero, because in that case we do not have specification error to begin with. The coefficient b_{32} will be zero if X_2 and X_3 are uncorrelated, which is unlikely in most economic data.

Generally, however, the extent of the bias will depend on the *bias term* $\beta_3 b_{32}$. If, for instance, β_3 is positive (i.e., X_3 has a positive effect on Y) and b_{32} is positive (i.e., X_2 and X_3 are positively correlated), $\hat{\alpha}_2$, on average, will overestimate the true β_2 (i.e., positive bias). But this result should not be surprising, for X_2 represents not only its *direct effect* on Y but also its *indirect effect* (via X_3) on Y. In short, X_2 gets credit for the influence that is rightly attributable to X_3, the latter being prevented from showing its effect explicitly because it is not "allowed" to enter the model. As a concrete example, consider the example discussed in Chapter 7 (Example 7.1).

[7]For an algebraic treatment, see Jan Kmenta, *Elements of Econometrics,* Macmillan, New York, 1971, pp. 391–399. Those with a matrix algebra background may want to consult J. Johnston, *Econometrics Methods,* 4th ed., McGraw-Hill, New York, 1997, pp. 119–112.

EXAMPLE 13.1

Illustrative Example: Child Mortality Revisited

Regressing child mortality (CM) on per capita GNP (PGNP) and the female literacy rate (FLR), we obtained the regression results shown in Eq. (7.6.2), giving the partial slope coefficient values of the two variables as −0.0056 and −2.2316, respectively. But if we now drop the FLR variable, we obtain the results shown in Eq. (7.7.2). If we regard Eq. (7.6.2) as the correct model, then Eq. (7.7.2) is a mis-specified model in that it omits the relevant variable FLR. Now you can see that in the correct model the coefficient of the PGNP variable was −0.0056, whereas in the "incorrect" model (7.7.2) it is now −0.0114.

In absolute terms, now PGNP has a greater impact on CM as compared with the true model. But if we regress FLR on PGNP (regression of the excluded variable on the included variable), the slope coefficient in this regression (b_{32} in terms of Eq. [13.3.3]) is 0.00256.[8] This suggests that as PGNP increases by a unit, on average, FLR goes up by 0.00256 units. But if FLR goes up by these units, its effect on CM will be (−2.2316) (0.00256) $= \hat{\beta}_3 b_{32} = -0.00543$.

Therefore, from Eq. (13.3.3) we finally have $(\hat{\beta}_2 + \hat{\beta}_3 b_{32}) = [-0.0056 + (-2.2316)(0.00256)] \approx -0.0111$, which is about the value of the PGNP coefficient obtained in the incorrect model (7.7.2).[9] As this example illustrates, the true impact of PGNP on CM is much less (−0.0056) than that suggested by the incorrect model (7.7.2), namely, (−0.0114).

Now let us examine the variances of $\hat{\alpha}_2$ and $\hat{\beta}_2$

$$\operatorname{var}(\hat{\alpha}_2) = \frac{\sigma^2}{\sum x_{2i}^2} \tag{13.3.4}$$

$$\operatorname{var}(\hat{\beta}_2) = \frac{\sigma^2}{\sum x_{2i}^2 (1 - r_{23}^2)} = \frac{\sigma^2}{\sum x_{2i}^2}\text{VIF} \tag{13.3.5}$$

where VIF (a measure of collinearity) is the variance inflation factor $[= 1/(1 - r_{23}^2)]$ discussed in Chapter 10 and r_{23} is the correlation coefficient between variables X_2 and X_3; Eqs. (13.3.4) and (13.3.5) are familiar to us from Chapters 3 and 7.

As formulas (13.3.4) and (13.3.5) are not the same, in general, $\operatorname{var}(\hat{\alpha}_2)$ will be different from $\operatorname{var}(\hat{\beta}_2)$. But we know that $\operatorname{var}(\hat{\beta}_2)$ is unbiased (why?). Therefore, $\operatorname{var}(\hat{\alpha}_2)$ is biased, thus substantiating the statement made in point 4 earlier. Since $0 < r_{23}^2 < 1$, it would *seem* that in the present case $\operatorname{var}(\hat{\alpha}_2) < \operatorname{var}(\hat{\beta}_2)$. Now we face a dilemma: Although $\hat{\alpha}_2$ is biased, its variance is smaller than the variance of the unbiased estimator $\hat{\beta}_2$ (of course, we are ruling out the case where $r_{23} = 0$, since in practice there is some correlation between regressors). So, there is a trade-off involved here.[10]

The story is not complete yet, however, for the σ^2 estimated from model (13.3.2) and that estimated from the true model (13.3.1) are not the same because the residual sum of squares (RSS) of the two models as well as their degrees of freedom (df) are different. You may recall that we obtain an estimate of σ^2 as $\hat{\sigma}^2 = \text{RSS/df}$, which depends on the number of regressors included in the model as well as the df ($= n$, number of parameters

[8]The regression results are:

$$\widehat{\text{FLR}} = 47.5971 + 0.00256\text{PGNP}$$
$$\text{se} = (3.5553) \quad (0.0011) \qquad r^2 = 0.0721$$

[9]Note that in the true model $\hat{\beta}_2$ and $\hat{\beta}_3$ are unbiased estimates of their true values.

[10]To bypass the trade-off between bias and efficiency, one could choose to minimize the mean square error (MSE), since it accounts for both bias and efficiency. On MSE, see the statistical appendix, **Appendix A.** See also Exercise 13.6.

estimated). Now if we add variables to the model, the RSS generally decreases (recall that as more variables are added to the model, the R^2 increases), but the degrees of freedom also decrease because more parameters are estimated. The net outcome depends on whether the RSS decreases sufficiently to offset the loss of degrees of freedom due to the addition of regressors. It is quite possible that if a regressor has a strong impact on the regressand—for example, it may reduce RSS more than the loss in degrees of freedom as a result of its addition to the model—inclusion of such variables will not only reduce the bias but will also increase the precision (i.e., reduce the standard errors) of the estimators.

On the other hand, if the relevant variables have only a marginal impact on the regressand, and if they are highly correlated (i.e., VIF is larger), we may reduce the bias in the coefficients of the variables already included in the model, but increase their standard errors (i.e., make them less efficient). Indeed, the trade-off in this situation between bias and precision can be substantial. As you can see from this discussion, the trade-off will depend on the relative importance of the various regressors.

To conclude this discussion, let us consider the special case where $r_{23} = 0$, that is, X_2 and X_3 are uncorrelated. This will result in b_{32} being zero (why?). Therefore, it can be seen from Eq. (13.3.3) that $\hat{\alpha}_2$ is now unbiased.[11] Also, it seems from Eqs. (13.3.4) and (13.3.5) that the variances of $\hat{\alpha}_2$ and $\hat{\beta}_2$ are the same. Is there no harm in dropping the variable X_3 from the model even though it may be relevant theoretically? The answer generally is no, for in this case, as noted earlier, var $(\hat{\alpha}_2)$ estimated from Eq. (13.3.4) is still biased and therefore our hypothesis-testing procedures are likely to remain suspect.[12] Besides, in most economic research X_2 and X_3 will be correlated, thus creating the problems discussed previously. **The point is clear: Once a model is formulated on the basis of the relevant theory, one is ill-advised to drop a variable from such a model.**

Inclusion of an Irrelevant Variable (Overfitting a Model)

Now let us assume that

$$Y_i = \beta_1 + \beta_2 X_{2i} + u_i \tag{13.3.6}$$

is the truth, but we fit the following model:

$$Y_i = \alpha_1 + \alpha_2 X_{2i} + \alpha_3 X_{3i} + v_i \tag{13.3.7}$$

and thus commit the specification error of including an unnecessary variable in the model.

The consequences of this specification error are as follows:

1. The OLS estimators of the parameters of the "incorrect" model are all *unbiased and consistent*, that is, $E(\alpha_1) = \beta_1$, $E(\hat{\alpha}_2) = \beta_2$, and $E(\hat{\alpha}_3) = \beta_3 = 0$.
2. The error variance σ^2 is correctly estimated.
3. The usual confidence interval and hypothesis-testing procedures remain valid.
4. However, the estimated α's will be generally inefficient, that is, their variances will be generally larger than those of the $\hat{\beta}$'s of the true model. The proofs of some of these statements can be found in Appendix 13A, Section 13A.2. The point of interest here is the relative inefficiency of the $\hat{\alpha}$'s. This can be shown easily.

[11]Note, though, $\hat{\alpha}_1$ is still biased, which can be seen intuitively as follows: We know that $\hat{\beta}_1 = \bar{Y} - \hat{\beta}_2\bar{X}_2 - \hat{\beta}_3\bar{X}_3$, whereas $\hat{\alpha}_1 = \bar{Y} - \hat{\alpha}_2\bar{X}_2$, and even if $\hat{\alpha}_2 = \hat{\beta}_2$, the two intercept estimators will not be the same.

[12]For details, see Adrian C. Darnell, *A Dictionary of Econometrics,* Edward Elgar Publisher, 1994, pp. 371–372.

From the usual OLS formula we know that

$$\operatorname{var}(\hat{\beta}_2) = \frac{\sigma^2}{\sum x_{2i}^2} \tag{13.3.8}$$

and

$$\operatorname{var}(\hat{\alpha}_2) = \frac{\sigma^2}{\sum x_{2i}^2 (1 - r_{23}^2)} \tag{13.3.9}$$

Therefore,

$$\frac{\operatorname{var}(\hat{\alpha}_2)}{\operatorname{var}(\hat{\beta}_2)} = \frac{1}{1 - r_{23}^2} \tag{13.3.10}$$

Since $0 \le r_{23}^2 \le 1$, it follows that $\operatorname{var}(\hat{\alpha}_2) \ge \operatorname{var}(\hat{\beta}_2)$; that is, the variance of $\hat{\alpha}_2$ is generally greater than the variance of $\hat{\beta}_2$ even though, on average, $\hat{\alpha}_2 = \beta_2$ [i.e., $E(\hat{\alpha}_2) = \beta_2$].

The implication of this finding is that the inclusion of the unnecessary variable X_3 makes the variance of $\hat{\alpha}_2$ larger than necessary, thereby making $\hat{\alpha}_2$ less precise. This is also true of $\hat{\alpha}_1$.

Notice the **asymmetry** in the two types of specification biases we have considered. If we exclude a relevant variable, the coefficients of the variables retained in the model are generally biased as well as inconsistent, the error variance is incorrectly estimated, and the usual hypothesis-testing procedures become invalid. On the other hand, including an irrelevant variable in the model still gives us unbiased and consistent estimates of the coefficients in the true model, the error variance is correctly estimated, and the conventional hypothesis-testing methods are still valid; the only penalty we pay for the inclusion of the superfluous variable is that the estimated variances of the coefficients are larger, and as a result our probability inferences about the parameters are less precise. An unwanted conclusion here would be that it is better to include irrelevant variables than to omit the relevant ones. But this philosophy is not to be espoused because the addition of unnecessary variables will lead to a loss in the efficiency of the estimators and may also lead to the problem of multicollinearity (why?), not to mention the loss of degrees of freedom. Therefore,

> In general, the best approach is to include only explanatory variables that, on theoretical grounds, *directly* influence the dependent variable and that are not accounted for by other included variables.[13]

13.4 Tests of Specification Errors

Knowing the consequences of specification errors is one thing but finding out whether one has committed such errors is quite another, for we do not deliberately set out to commit such errors. Very often specification biases arise inadvertently, perhaps from our inability to formulate the model as precisely as possible because the underlying theory is weak or because we do not have the right kind of data to test the model. As Davidson notes, "Because of the non-experimental nature of economics, we are never sure how the observed data were generated. The test of any hypothesis in economics always turns out to depend on additional assumptions necessary to specify a reasonably parsimonious model, which may or may not be justified."[14]

[13]Michael D. Intriligator, *Econometric Models, Techniques and Applications,* Prentice Hall, Englewood Cliffs, NJ, 1978, p. 189. Recall the Occam's razor principle.

[14]James Davidson, *Econometric Theory,* Blackwell Publishers, Oxford, U.K., 2000, p. 153.

The practical question then is not why specification errors are made, for they generally are, but how to detect them. Once it is found that specification errors have been made, the remedies often suggest themselves. If, for example, it can be shown that a variable is inappropriately omitted from a model, the obvious remedy is to include that variable in the analysis, assuming, of course, the data on that variable are available.

In this section we discuss some tests that one may use to detect specification errors.

Detecting the Presence of Unnecessary Variables (Overfitting a Model)

Suppose we develop a k-variable model to explain a phenomenon:

$$Y_i = \beta_1 + \beta_2 X_{2i} + \cdots + \beta_k X_{ki} + u_i \tag{13.4.1}$$

However, we are not totally sure that, say, the variable X_k really belongs in the model. One simple way to find this out is to test the significance of the estimated β_k with the usual t test: $t = \hat{\beta}_k/\mathrm{se}(\hat{\beta}_k)$. But suppose that we are not sure whether, say, X_3 and X_4 legitimately belong in the model. This can be easily ascertained by the F test discussed in Chapter 8. Thus, detecting the presence of an irrelevant variable (or variables) is not a difficult task.

It is, however, very important to remember that in carrying out these tests of significance we have a specific model in mind. We accept that model as the **maintained hypothesis** or the "truth," however tentative it may be. Given that model, then, we can find out whether one or more regressors are really relevant by the usual t and F tests. But note carefully that we should not use the t and F tests to build a model *iteratively,* that is, we should not say that initially Y is related to X_2 only because $\hat{\beta}_2$ is statistically significant and then expand the model to include X_3 and decide to keep that variable in the model if $\hat{\beta}_3$ turns out to be statistically significant, and so on. This strategy of building a model is called the **bottom-up approach** (starting with a smaller model and expanding it as one goes along) or by the somewhat pejorative term, **data mining** (other names are **regression fishing, data grubbing, data snooping,** and **number crunching**).

The primary objective of data mining is to develop the "best" model after several diagnostic tests so that the model finally chosen is a "good" model in the sense that all the estimated coefficients have the "right" signs, they are statistically significant on the basis of the t and F tests, the R^2 value is reasonably high, and the Durbin–Watson d has acceptable value (around 2), etc. The purists in the profession look down on the practice of data mining. In the words of William Pool, ". . . making an empirical regularity the foundation, rather than an implication of economic theory, is always dangerous."[15] One reason for "condemning" data mining is as follows.

Nominal versus True Level of Significance in the Presence of Data Mining

A danger of data mining that the unwary researcher faces is that the conventional levels of significance (α) such as 1, 5, or 10 percent are *not the true levels of significance*. Lovell has suggested that if there are c candidate regressors out of which k are finally selected ($k \le c$) on the basis of data mining, then the true level of significance (α^*) is related to the nominal level of significance (α) as follows:[16]

$$\alpha^* = 1 - (1 - \alpha)^{c/k} \tag{13.4.2}$$

[15] William Pool, "Is Inflation Too Low?" the *Cato Journal*, vol. 18, no. 3, Winter 1999, p. 456.

[16] M. Lovell, "Data Mining," *Review of Economics and Statistics*, vol. 65, 1983, pp. 1–12.

or approximately as

$$\alpha^* \approx (c/k)\alpha \tag{13.4.3}$$

For example, if $c = 15$, $k = 5$, and $\alpha = 5$ percent, from Eq. (13.4.3) the true level of significance is $(15/5)(5) = 15$ percent. Therefore, if a researcher data-mines and selects 5 out of 15 regressors and reports only the results of the condensed model at the nominal 5 percent level of significance and declares that the results are statistically significant, one should take this conclusion with a big grain of salt, for we know the (true) level of significance is in fact 15 percent. It should be noted that if $c = k$, that is, there is no data mining, the true and nominal levels of significance are the same. Of course, in practice most researchers report only the results of their "final" regression without necessarily telling about all the data mining, or **pretesting,** that has gone before.[17]

Despite some of its obvious drawbacks, there is increasing recognition, especially among applied econometricians, that the purist (i.e., non–data mining) approach to model building is not tenable. As Zaman notes:

> Unfortunately, experience with real data sets shows that such a [purist approach] is neither feasible nor desirable. It is not feasible because it is a rare economic theory which leads to a unique model. It is not desirable because a crucial aspect of learning from the data is learning what types of models are and are not supported by data. Even if, by rare luck, the initial model shows a good fit, it is frequently important to explore and learn the types of the models the data does or does not agree with.[18]

A similar view is expressed by Kerry Patterson, who maintains that:

> This [data mining] approach suggests that economic theory and empirical specification [should] interact rather than be kept in separate compartments.[19]

Instead of getting caught in the data mining versus the purist approach to model-building controversy, one can endorse the view expressed by Peter Kennedy:

> [that model specification] needs to be a well-thought-out combination of theory and data, and that testing procedures used in specification searches should be designed to minimize the costs of data mining. Examples of such procedures are setting aside data for out-of-sample prediction tests, adjusting significance levels [a la Lovell], and avoiding questionable criteria such as maximizing R^2.[20]

If we look at data mining in a broader perspective as a process of discovering empirical regularities that might suggest errors and/or omissions in (existing) theoretical models, it has a very useful role to play. To quote Kennedy again, "The art of the applied econometrician is to allow for data-driven theory while avoiding the considerable dangers in data mining."[21]

[17]For a detailed discussion of pretesting and the biases it can lead to, see T. D. Wallace, "Pretest Estimation in Regression: A Survey," *American Journal of Agricultural Economics,* vol. 59, 1977, pp. 431–443.

[18]Asad Zaman, *Statistical Foundations for Econometric Techniques,* Academic Press, New York, 1996, p. 226.

[19]Kerry Patterson, *An Introduction to Applied Econometrics,* St. Martin's Press, New York, 2000, p. 10.

[20]Peter Kennedy, "Sinning in the Basement: What Are the Rules? The Ten Commandments of Applied Econometrics," unpublished manuscript.

[21]Kennedy, op. cit., p. 13.

Tests for Omitted Variables and Incorrect Functional Form

In practice we are never sure that the model adopted for empirical testing is "the truth, the whole truth and nothing but the truth." On the basis of theory or introspection and prior empirical work, we develop a model that we believe captures the essence of the subject under study. We then subject the model to empirical testing. After we obtain the results, we begin the post-mortem, keeping in mind the criteria of a good model discussed earlier. It is at this stage that we come to know if the chosen model is adequate. In determining model adequacy, we look at some broad features of the results, such as the $\bar{R}^2$ value, the estimated t ratios, the signs of the estimated coefficients in relation to their prior expectations, the Durbin–Watson statistic, and the like. If these diagnostics are reasonably good, we proclaim that the chosen model is a fair representation of reality. By the same token, if the results do not look encouraging because the $\bar{R}^2$ value is too low or because very few coefficients are statistically significant or have the correct signs or because the Durbin–Watson d is too low, then we begin to worry about model adequacy and look for remedies: Maybe we have omitted an important variable, or have used the wrong functional form, or have not first-differenced the time series (to remove serial correlation), and so on. To aid us in determining whether model inadequacy is on account of one or more of these problems, we can use some of the following methods.

Examination of Residuals

As noted in Chapter 12, examination of the residuals is a good visual diagnostic to detect autocorrelation or heteroscedasticity. But these residuals can also be examined, especially in cross-sectional data, for model specification errors, such as omission of an important variable or incorrect functional form. If in fact there are such errors, a plot of the residuals will exhibit distinct patterns.

To illustrate, let us reconsider the cubic total cost of production function first considered in Chapter 7. Assume that the true total cost function is described as follows, where $Y =$ total cost and $X =$ output:

$$Y_i = \beta_1 + \beta_2 X_i + \beta_3 X_i^2 + \beta_4 X_i^3 + u_i \qquad (13.4.4)$$

but a researcher fits the following quadratic function:

$$Y_i = \alpha_1 + \alpha_2 X_i + \alpha_3 X_i^2 + u_{2i} \qquad (13.4.5)$$

and another researcher fits the following linear function:

$$Y_i = \lambda_1 + \lambda_2 X_i + u_{3i} \qquad (13.4.6)$$

Although we know that both researchers have made specification errors, for pedagogical purposes let us see how the estimated residuals look in the three models. (The cost-output data are given in Table 7.4.) Figure 13.1 speaks for itself: As we move from left to right, that is, as we approach the truth, not only are the residuals smaller (in absolute value) but also they do not exhibit the pronounced cyclical swings associated with the misfitted models.

The utility of examining the residual plot is thus clear: If there are specification errors, the residuals will exhibit noticeable patterns.

The Durbin–Watson d Statistic Once Again

If we examine the routinely calculated Durbin–Watson d in Table 13.1, we see that for the linear cost function the estimated d is 0.716, suggesting that there is positive "correlation" in the estimated residuals: for $n = 10$ and $k' = 1$, the 5 percent critical d values are

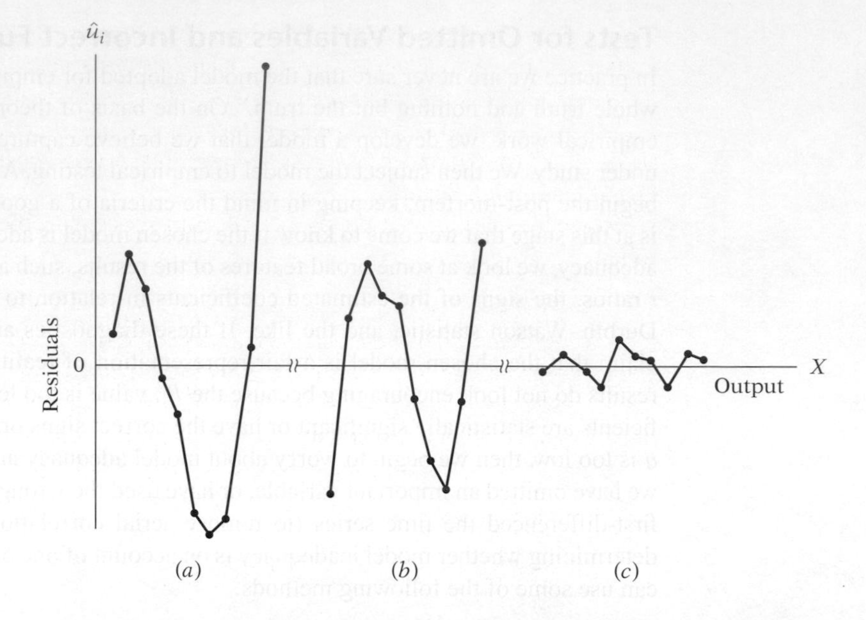

FIGURE 13.1 Residuals $\hat{u}_i$ from (*a*) linear, (*b*) quadratic, and (*c*) cubic total cost functions.

TABLE 13.1 Estimated Residuals from the Linear, Quadratic, and Cubic Total Cost Functions

Observation Number	$\hat{u}_i$, Linear Model*	$\hat{u}_i$, Quadratic Model†	$\hat{u}_i$, Cubic Model**
1	6.600	−23.900	−0.222
2	19.667	9.500	1.607
3	13.733	18.817	−0.915
4	−2.200	13.050	−4.426
5	−9.133	11.200	4.435
6	−26.067	−5.733	1.032
7	−32.000	−16.750	0.726
8	−28.933	−23.850	−4.119
9	4.133	−6.033	1.859
10	54.200	23.700	0.022

$$*\hat{Y}_i = \underset{(19.021)\ (8.752)}{166.467} + \underset{(3.066)\ (6.502)}{19.933X_i} \qquad R^2 = 0.8409 \quad \bar{R}^2 = 0.8210 \quad d = 0.716$$

$$^{\dagger}\hat{Y}_i = \underset{(23.488)\ (9.468)}{222.383} - \underset{(9.809)\ (-0.818)}{8.0250X_i} + \underset{(0.869)\ (2.925)}{2.542X_i^2} \qquad R^2 = 0.9284 \quad \bar{R}^2 = 0.9079 \quad d = 1.038$$

$$^{**}\hat{Y}_i = \underset{(6.375)\ (22.238)}{141.767} + \underset{(4.778)\ (13.285)}{63.478X_i} - \underset{(0.9856)\ (-13.151)}{12.962X_i^2} + \underset{(0.0592)\ (15.861)}{0.939X_i^3} \qquad R^2 = 0.9983 \quad \bar{R}^2 = 0.9975 \quad d = 2.70$$

$d_L = 0.879$ and $d_U = 1.320$. Likewise, the computed d value for the quadratic cost function is 1.038, whereas the 5 percent critical values are $d_L = 0.697$ and $d_U = 1.641$, indicating indecision. But if we use the modified d test (see Chapter 12), we can say that there is positive "correlation" in the residuals, for the computed d is less than d_U. For the cubic cost function, the true specification, the estimated d value does not indicate any positive "correlation" in the residuals.[22]

The observed positive "correlation" in the residuals when we fit the linear or quadratic model is not a measure of (first-order) serial correlation but of (model) specification

[22]In the present context, a value of $d = 2$ will mean no specification error. (Why?)

error(s). The observed correlation simply reflects the fact that some variable(s) that belongs in the model is included in the error term and needs to be culled out from it and introduced in its own right as an explanatory variable: If we exclude the X_i^3 from the cost function, then as Eq. (13.2.3) shows, the error term in the mis-specified model (13.2.2) is in fact $(u_{1i} + \beta_4 X_i^3)$ and it will exhibit a systematic pattern (e.g., positive autocorrelation) if X_i^3 in fact affects Y significantly.

To use the Durbin–Watson test for detecting model specification error(s), we proceed as follows:

1. From the assumed model, obtain the ordinary least squares (OLS) residuals.

2. If it is believed that the assumed model is mis-specified because it excludes a relevant explanatory variable, say, Z from the model, order the residuals obtained in Step 1 according to increasing values of Z. *Note:* The Z variable could be one of the X variables included in the assumed model or it could be some function of that variable, such as X^2 or X^3.

3. Compute the d statistic from the residuals thus ordered by the usual d formula, namely,

$$d = \frac{\sum_{t=2}^{n} (\hat{u}_t - \hat{u}_{t-1})^2}{\sum_{t=1}^{n} \hat{u}_t^2}$$

Note: The subscript t is the index of observation here and does not necessarily mean that the data are time series.

4. From the Durbin–Watson tables, if the estimated d value is significant, then one can accept the hypothesis of model mis-specification. If that turns out to be the case, the remedial measures will naturally suggest themselves.

In our cost example, the $Z (= X)$ variable (output) was already ordered.[23] Therefore, we do not have to compute the d statistic afresh. As we have seen, the d statistic for both the linear and quadratic cost functions suggests specification errors. The remedies are clear: Introduce the quadratic and cubic terms in the linear cost function and the cubic term in the quadratic cost function. In short, run the cubic cost model.

Ramsey's RESET Test

Ramsey has proposed a general test of specification error called RESET (regression specification error test).[24] Here we will illustrate only the simplest version of the test. To fix ideas, let us continue with our cost-output example and assume that the cost function is linear in output as

$$Y_i = \lambda_1 + \lambda_2 X_i + u_{3i} \quad \textbf{(13.4.6)}$$

where Y = total cost and X = output. Now if we plot the residuals $\hat{u}_i$ obtained from this regression against $\hat{Y}_i$, the estimated Y_i from this model, we get the picture shown in Figure 13.2. Although $\sum \hat{u}_i$ and $\sum \hat{u}_i \hat{Y}_i$ are necessarily zero (why? see Chapter 3), the residuals in this figure show a pattern in which their mean changes systematically with $\hat{Y}_i$. This would suggest that if we introduce $\hat{Y}_i$ in some form as a regressor(s) in Eq. (13.4.6), it should increase R^2. And if the increase in R^2 is statistically significant (on the basis of the F test discussed in Chapter 8), it would suggest that the linear cost function (13.4.6) was

[23]It does not matter if we order $\hat{u}_i$ according to X_i^2 or X_i^3 since these are functions of X_i, which is already ordered.

[24]J. B. Ramsey, "Tests for Specification Errors in Classical Linear Least Squares Regression Analysis," *Journal of the Royal Statistical Society*, series B, vol. 31, 1969, pp. 350–371.

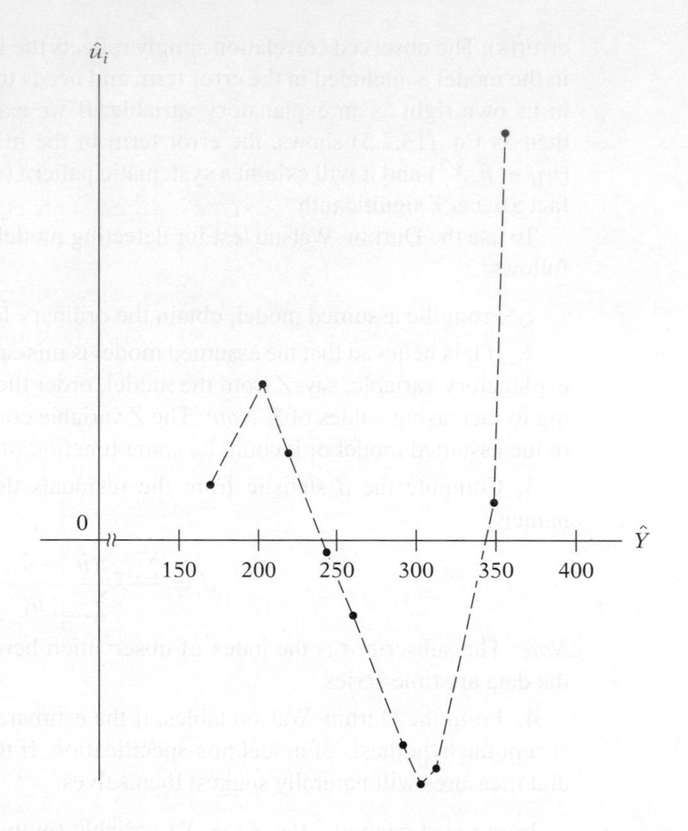

FIGURE 13.2 Residuals $\hat{u}_i$ and estimated Y from the linear cost function: $Y_i = \lambda_1 + \lambda_2 X_i + u_i$.

mis-specified. This is essentially the idea behind RESET. The steps involved in RESET are as follows:

1. From the chosen model, e.g., Eq. (13.4.6), obtain the estimated Y_i, that is, $\hat{Y}_i$.
2. Rerun Eq. (13.4.6) introducing $\hat{Y}_i$ in some form as an additional regressor(s). From Figure 13.2, we observe that there is a curvilinear relationship between $\hat{u}_i$ and $\hat{Y}_i$, suggesting that one can introduce $\hat{Y}_i^2$ and $\hat{Y}_i^3$ as additional regressors. Thus, we run

$$Y_i = \beta_1 + \beta_2 X_i + \beta_3 \hat{Y}_i^2 + \beta_4 \hat{Y}_i^3 + u_i \tag{13.4.7}$$

3. Let the R^2 obtained from Eq. (13.4.7) be R^2_{new} and that obtained from Eq. (13.4.6) be R^2_{old}. Then we can use the F test first introduced in Eq. (8.4.18), namely,

$$F = \frac{\left(R^2_{\text{new}} - R^2_{\text{old}}\right)/\text{number of new regressors}}{\left(1 - R^2_{\text{new}}\right)/(n - \text{number of parameters in the new model})} \tag{8.4.18}$$

to find out if the increase in R^2 from using Eq. (13.4.7) is statistically significant.

4. If the computed F value is significant, say, at the 5 percent level, one can accept the hypothesis that the model (13.4.6) is mis-specified.

Returning to our illustrative example, we have the following results (standard errors in parentheses):

$$\begin{aligned} \hat{Y}_i &= 166.467 \;\; + 19.933X_i \\ &\quad\; (19.021) \quad\; (3.066) \qquad R^2 = 0.8409 \end{aligned} \tag{13.4.8}$$

$$\hat{Y}_i = 2140.7223 + 476.6557X_i - 0.09187\hat{Y}_i^2 + 0.000119\hat{Y}_i^3$$
$$(132.0044) \quad (33.3951) \quad (0.00620) \quad (0.0000074) \qquad (13.4.9)$$
$$R^2 = 0.9983$$

Note: $\hat{Y}_i^2$ and $\hat{Y}_i^3$ in Eq. (13.4.9) are obtained from Eq. (13.4.8).

Now applying the F test we find

$$F = \frac{(0.9983 - 0.8409)/2}{(1 - 0.9983)/(10 - 4)} = 284.4035 \qquad (13.4.10)$$

The reader can easily verify that this F value is highly significant, indicating that the model (13.4.8) is mis-specified. Of course, we have reached the same conclusion on the basis of the visual examination of the residuals as well as the Durbin–Watson d value. It should be added that, since $\hat{Y}_i$ is estimated, it is a random variable and, therefore, the usual tests of significance apply if the sample is reasonably large.

One advantage of RESET is that it is easy to apply, for it does not require one to specify what the alternative model is. But that is also its disadvantage because knowing that a model is mis-specified does not help us necessarily in choosing a better alternative.

As one author notes:

> In practice, the RESET test may not be particularly good at detecting any specific alternative to a proposed model, and its usefulness lies in acting as a general indicator that something is wrong. For this reason, a test such as RESET is sometimes described as a test of *misspecification,* as opposed to a test of specification. This distinction is rather subtle, but the basic idea is that a specification test looks at some particular aspect of a given equation, with clear null and alternative hypotheses in mind. A *misspecification* test, on the other hand, can detect a range of alternatives and indicate that something is wrong under the null, without necessarily giving clear guidance as to what alternative hypothesis is appropriate.[25]

Lagrange Multiplier (LM) Test for Adding Variables

This is an alternative to Ramsey's RESET test. To illustrate this test, we will continue with the preceding illustrative example.

If we compare the linear cost function (13.4.6) with the cubic cost function (13.4.4), the former is a *restricted version* of the latter (recall our discussion of **restricted least squares** from Chapter 8). The restricted regression (13.4.6) assumes that the coefficients of the squared and cubed output terms are equal to zero. To test this, the LM test proceeds as follows:

1. Estimate the restricted regression (13.4.6) by OLS and obtain the residuals, $\hat{u}_i$.
2. If in fact the unrestricted regression (13.4.4) is the true regression, the residuals obtained in Eq. (13.4.6) should be related to the squared and cubed output terms, that is, X_i^2 and X_i^3.
3. This suggests that we regress the $\hat{u}_i$ obtained in Step 1 on all the regressors (including those in the restricted regression), which in the present case means

$$\hat{u}_i = \alpha_1 + \alpha_2 X_i + \alpha_3 X_i^2 + \alpha_4 X_i^3 + v_i \qquad (13.4.11)$$

where v is an error term with the usual properties.

[25] Jon Stewart and Len Gill, *Econometrics,* 2d ed., Prentice-Hall Europe, 1998, p. 69.

4. For large-sample size, Engle has shown that n (the sample size) times the R^2 estimated from the (auxiliary) regression (13.4.11) follows the chi-square distribution with df equal to the number of restrictions imposed by the restricted regression, two in the present example since the terms X_i^2 and X_i^3 are dropped from the model.[26] Symbolically, we write

$$nR^2 \underset{\text{asy}}{\sim} \chi^2_{(\text{number of restrictions})} \tag{13.4.12}$$

where asy means asymptotically, that is, in large samples.

5. If the chi-square value obtained from Eq. (13.4.12) exceeds the critical chi-square value at the chosen level of significance, we reject the restricted regression. Otherwise, we do not reject it.

For our example, the regression results are as follows:

$$\hat{Y}_i = 166.467 + 19.333X_i \tag{13.4.13}$$

where Y is total cost and X is output. The standard errors for this regression are already given in Table 13.1.

When the residuals from Eq. (13.4.13) are regressed as just suggested in Step 3, we obtain the following results:

$$\begin{aligned}\hat{u}_i &= -24.7 \quad + 43.5443X_i - 12.9615X_i^2 + 0.9396X_i^3 \\ \text{se} &= \quad (6.375) \quad (4.779) \qquad (0.986) \qquad (0.059) \\ &\qquad\qquad\qquad\qquad R^2 = 0.9896\end{aligned} \tag{13.4.14}$$

Although our sample size of 10 is by no means large, just to illustrate the LM mechanism, we obtain $nR^2 = (10)(0.9896) = 9.896$. From the chi-square table we observe that for 2 df the 1 percent critical chi-square value is about 9.21. Therefore, the observed value of 9.896 is significant at the 1 percent level, and our conclusion would be to reject the restricted regression (i.e., the linear cost function). We reached a similar conclusion on the basis of Ramsey's RESET test.

13.5 Errors of Measurement

All along we have assumed implicitly that the dependent variable Y and the explanatory variables, the X's, are measured without any errors. Thus, in the regression of consumption expenditure on income and wealth of households, we assume that the data on these variables are "accurate"; they are not *guess estimates,* extrapolated, interpolated, or rounded off in any systematic manner, such as to the nearest hundredth dollar, and so on. Unfortunately, this ideal is not met in practice for a variety of reasons, such as nonresponse errors, reporting errors, and computing errors. Whatever the reasons, error of measurement is a potentially troublesome problem, for it constitutes yet another example of specification bias with the consequences noted below.

Errors of Measurement in the Dependent Variable *Y*

Consider the following model:

$$Y_i^* = \alpha + \beta X_i + u_i \tag{13.5.1}$$

[26]R. F. Engle, "A General Approach to Lagrangian Multiplier Model Diagnostics," *Journal of Econometrics,* vol. 20, 1982, pp. 83–104.

where $Y_i^* =$ permanent consumption expenditure[27]
$X_i =$ current income
$u_i =$ stochastic disturbance term

Since Y_i^* is not directly measurable, we may use an observable expenditure variable Y_i such that

$$Y_i = Y_i^* + \varepsilon_i \tag{13.5.2}$$

where ε_i denote errors of measurement in Y_i^*. Therefore, instead of estimating Eq. (13.5.1), we estimate

$$\begin{aligned} Y_i &= (\alpha + \beta X_i + u_i) + \varepsilon_i \\ &= \alpha + \beta X_i + (u_i + \varepsilon_i) \\ &= \alpha + \beta X_i + v_i \end{aligned} \tag{13.5.3}$$

where $v_i = u_i + \varepsilon_i$ is a composite error term, containing the population disturbance term (which may be called the *equation error term*) and the measurement error term.

For simplicity assume that $E(u_i) = E(\varepsilon_i) = 0$, cov $(X_i, u_i) = 0$ (which is the assumption of the classical linear regression), and cov $(X_i, \varepsilon_i) = 0$; that is, the errors of measurement in Y_i^* are uncorrelated with X_i, and cov $(u_i, \varepsilon_i) = 0$; that is, the equation error and the measurement error are uncorrelated. With these assumptions, it can be seen that β estimated from either Eq. (13.5.1) or Eq. (13.5.3) will be an unbiased estimator of the true β (see Exercise 13.7); that is, the errors of measurement in the dependent variable Y do not destroy the unbiasedness property of the OLS estimators. However, the variances and standard errors of β estimated from Eqs. (13.5.1) and (13.5.3) will be different because, employing the usual formulas (see Chapter 3), we obtain

$$\text{Model (13.5.1):} \qquad \operatorname{var}(\hat{\beta}) = \frac{\sigma_u^2}{\sum x_i^2} \tag{13.5.4}$$

$$\begin{aligned} \text{Model (13.5.3):} \qquad \operatorname{var}(\hat{\beta}) &= \frac{\sigma_v^2}{\sum x_i^2} \\ &= \frac{\sigma_u^2 + \sigma_\varepsilon^2}{\sum x_i^2} \end{aligned} \tag{13.5.5}$$

Obviously, the latter variance is larger than the former.[28] Therefore, **although the errors of measurement in the dependent variable still give unbiased estimates of the parameters and their variances, the estimated variances are now larger than in the case where there are no such errors of measurement.**

Errors of Measurement in the Explanatory Variable *X*

Now assume that instead of Eq. (13.5.1), we have the following model:

$$Y_i = \alpha + \beta X_i^* + u_i \tag{13.5.6}$$

where $Y_i =$ current consumption expenditure
$X_i^* =$ permanent income
$u_i =$ disturbance term (equation error)

[27]This phrase is due to Milton Friedman. See also Exercise 13.8.

[28]But note that this variance is still unbiased because under the stated conditions the composite error term $v_i = u_i + \varepsilon_i$ still satisfies the assumptions underlying the method of least squares.

Suppose instead of observing X_i^*, we observe

$$X_i = X_i^* + w_i \tag{13.5.7}$$

where w_i represents errors of measurement in X_i^*. Therefore, instead of estimating Eq. (13.5.6), we estimate

$$\begin{aligned} Y_i &= \alpha + \beta(X_i - w_i) + u_i \\ &= \alpha + \beta X_i + (u_i - \beta w_i) \\ &= \alpha + \beta X_i + z_i \end{aligned} \tag{13.5.8}$$

where $z_i = u_i - \beta w_i$, a compound of equation and measurement errors.

Now even if we assume that w_i has zero mean, is serially independent, and is uncorrelated with u_i, we can no longer assume that the composite error term z_i is independent of the explanatory variable X_i because (assuming $E[z_i] = 0$)

$$\begin{aligned} \operatorname{cov}(z_i, X_i) &= E[z_i - E(z_i)][X_i - E(X_i)] \\ &= E(u_i - \beta w_i)(w_i) \qquad \text{using (13.5.7)} \\ &= E(-\beta w_i^2) \\ &= -\beta\sigma_w^2 \end{aligned} \tag{13.5.9}$$

Thus, the explanatory variable and the error term in Eq. (13.5.8) are correlated, which violates the crucial assumption of the classical linear regression model that the explanatory variable is uncorrelated with the stochastic disturbance term. If this assumption is violated, it can be shown that the *OLS estimators are not only biased but also inconsistent, that is, they remain biased even if the sample size n increases indefinitely.*[29]

For model (13.5.8), it is shown in Appendix 13A, Section 13A.3 that

$$\operatorname{plim}\hat{\beta} = \beta\left[\frac{1}{1 + \sigma_w^2/\sigma_{X^*}^2}\right] \tag{13.5.10}$$

where σ_w^2 and $\sigma_{X^*}^2$ are variances of w_i and X^*, respectively, and where plim $\hat{\beta}$ means the probability limit of β.

Since the term inside the brackets is expected to be less than 1 (why?), Eq. (13.5.10) shows that even if the sample size increases indefinitely, $\hat{\beta}$ will not converge to β. Actually, if β is assumed positive, $\hat{\beta}$ will underestimate β, that is, it is biased toward zero. Of course, if there are no measurement errors in X (i.e., $\sigma_w^2 = 0$), $\hat{\beta}$ will provide a consistent estimator of β.

Therefore, measurement errors pose a serious problem when they are present in the explanatory variable(s) because they make consistent estimation of the parameters impossible. Of course, as we saw, if they are present only in the dependent variable, the estimators remain unbiased and hence they are consistent too. If errors of measurement are present in the explanatory variable(s), what is the solution? The answer is not easy. At one extreme, we can assume that if σ_w^2 is small compared to $\sigma_{X^*}^2$, for all practical purposes we can "assume away" the problem and proceed with the usual OLS estimation. Of course, the rub

[29]As shown in **Appendix A**, $\hat{\beta}$ is a consistent estimator of β if, as n increases indefinitely, the sampling distribution of $\hat{\beta}$ will ultimately collapse to the true β. Technically, this is stated as $\operatorname{plim}_{n\to\infty}\hat{\beta} = \beta$. As noted in **Appendix A**, consistency is a large-sample property and is often used to study the behavior of an estimator when its finite or small-sample properties (e.g., unbiasedness) cannot be determined.

here is that we cannot readily observe or measure σ_w^2 and $\sigma_{X^*}^2$ and therefore there is no way to judge their relative magnitudes.

One other suggested remedy is the use of **instrumental** or **proxy variables** that, although highly correlated with the original X variables, are uncorrelated with the equation and measurement error terms (i.e., u_i and w_i). If such proxy variables can be found, then one can obtain a consistent estimate of β. But this task is much easier said than done. In practice it is not easy to find good proxies; we are often in the situation of complaining about the bad weather without being able to do much about it. Besides, it is not easy to find out if the selected instrumental variable is in fact independent of the error terms u_i and w_i.

In the literature there are other suggestions to solve the problem.[30] But most of them are specific to the given situation and are based on restrictive assumptions. There is really no satisfactory answer to the measurement errors problem. That is why it is so crucial to measure the data as accurately as possible.

EXAMPLE 13.2
An Example

We conclude this section with an example constructed to highlight the preceding points. Table 13.2 gives hypothetical data on true consumption expenditure Y^*, true income X^*, measured consumption Y, and measured income X. The table also explains how these variables were measured.[31]

Measurement Errors in the Dependent Variable Y Only. Based on the given data, the true consumption function is

$$\begin{aligned} \hat{Y}_i^* &= 25.00 \quad + \quad 0.6000X_i^* \\ &\quad (10.477) \qquad (0.0584) \\ t &= (2.3861) \quad (10.276) \\ &\qquad\qquad R^2 = 0.9296 \end{aligned} \tag{13.5.11}$$

TABLE 13.2 Hypothetical Data on Y^* (True Consumption Expenditure), X^* (True Income), Y (Measured Consumption Expenditure), and X (Measured Income); All Data in Dollars

Y^*	X^*	Y	X	ε	w	u
75.4666	80.00	67.6011	80.0940	−7.8655	0.0940	2.4666
74.9801	100.00	75.4438	91.5721	0.4636	−8.4279	−10.0199
102.8242	120.00	109.6956	112.1406	6.8714	2.1406	5.8242
125.7651	140.00	129.4159	145.5969	3.6509	5.5969	16.7651
106.5035	160.00	104.2388	168.5579	−2.2647	8.5579	−14.4965
131.4318	180.00	125.8319	171.4793	−5.5999	−8.5207	−1.5682
149.3693	200.00	153.9926	203.5366	4.6233	3.5366	4.3693
143.8628	220.00	152.9208	222.8533	9.0579	2.8533	−13.1372
177.5218	240.00	176.3344	232.9879	−1.1874	−7.0120	8.5218
182.2748	260.00	174.5252	261.1813	−7.7496	1.1813	1.2748

Note: The data on X^* are assumed to be given. In deriving the other variables the assumptions made were as follows: (1) $E(u_i) = E(\varepsilon_i) = E(w_i) = 0$; (2) cov $(X, u) =$ cov $(X, \varepsilon) =$ cov $(u, \varepsilon) =$ cov $(w, u) =$ cov $(\varepsilon, w) = 0$; (3) $\sigma_u^2 = 100$, $\sigma_\varepsilon^2 = 36$, and $\sigma_w^2 = 36$; and (4) $Y_i^* = 25 + 0.6X_i^* + u_i$, $Y_i = Y_i^* + \varepsilon_i$, and $X_i = X_i^* + w_i$.

(*Continued*)

[30]See Thomas B. Fomby, R. Carter Hill, and Stanley R. Johnson, *Advanced Econometric Methods*, Springer-Verlag, New York, 1984, pp. 273–277. See also Kennedy, op. cit., pp. 138–140, for a discussion of weighted regression as well as instrumental variables. See also: G. S. Maddala, *Introduction to Econometrics*, 3d ed., John Wiley & Sons, New York, 2001, pp. 437–462, and Quirino Paris, "Robust Estimators of Errors-in-Variables Models: Part I," Working Paper No. 04–007, 200, Department of Agricultural and Resource Economics, University of California at Davis, August 2004.

[31]I am indebted to Kenneth J. White for constructing this example. See his *Computer Handbook Using SHAZAM*, for use with Damodar Gujarati, *Basic Econometrics*, September 1985, pp. 117–121.

EXAMPLE 13.2 *(Continued)*

whereas, if we use Y_i instead of Y_i^*, we obtain

$$\begin{aligned} \hat{Y}_i &= 25.00 \quad + 0.6000X_i^* \\ &\quad (12.218) \quad (0.0681) \\ t &= (2.0461) \quad (8.8118) \\ &\qquad R^2 = 0.9066 \end{aligned} \tag{13.5.12}$$

As these results show, and according to the theory, the estimated coefficients remain the same. The only effect of errors of measurement in the dependent variable is that the estimated standard errors of the coefficients tend to be larger (see Eq. [13.5.5]), which is clearly seen in Eq. (13.5.12). In passing, note that the regression coefficients in Eqs. (13.5.11) and (13.5.12) are the same because the sample was generated to match the assumptions of the measurement error model.

Errors of Measurement in *X*. We know that the true regression is Eq. (13.5.11). Suppose now that instead of using X_i^* we use X_i. (*Note:* In reality X_i^* is rarely observable.) The regression results are as follows:

$$\begin{aligned} \hat{Y}_i^* &= 25.992 \quad + 0.5942X_i \\ &\quad (11.0810) \quad (0.0617) \\ t &= (2.3457) \quad (9.6270) \\ &\qquad R^2 = 0.9205 \end{aligned} \tag{13.5.13}$$

These results are in accord with the theory—when there are measurement errors in the explanatory variable(s), the estimated coefficients are biased. Fortunately, in this example the bias is rather small—from Eq. (13.5.10) it is evident that the bias depends on $\sigma_w^2/\sigma_{X^*}^2$, and in generating the data it was assumed that $\sigma_w^2 = 36$ and $\sigma_{X^*}^2 = 3667$, thus making the bias factor rather small, about 0.98 percent ($= 36/3667$).

We leave it to the reader to find out what happens when there are errors of measurement in both Y and X, that is, if we regress Y_i on X_i rather than Y_i^* on X_i^* (see Exercise 13.23).

13.6 Incorrect Specification of the Stochastic Error Term

A common problem facing a researcher is the specification of the error term u_i that enters the regression model. Since the error term is not directly observable, there is no easy way to determine the form in which it enters the model. To see this, let us return to the models given in Eqs. (13.2.8) and (13.2.9). For simplicity of exposition, we have assumed that there is no intercept in the model. We further assume that u_i in Eq. (13.2.8) is such that ln u_i satisfies the usual OLS assumptions.

If we assume that Eq. (13.2.8) is the "correct" model but estimate Eq. (13.2.9), what are the consequences? It is shown in Appendix 13.A, Section 13A.4, that if $\ln u_i \sim N(0, \sigma^2)$, then

$$u_i \sim \text{log normal}\left[e^{\sigma^2/2}, e^{\sigma^2}\left(e^{\sigma^2} - 1\right)\right] \tag{13.6.1}$$

As a result,

$$E(\hat{\alpha}) = \beta e^{\sigma^2/2} \tag{13.6.2}$$

where e is the base of the natural logarithm.

As you can see, $\hat{\alpha}$ is a biased estimator, as its average value is not equal to the true β. We will have more to say about the specification of the stochastic error term in the chapter on nonlinear-in-the-parameter regression models.

13.7 Nested versus Non-Nested Models

In carrying out specification testing, it is useful to distinguish between **nested** and **non-nested models.** To distinguish between the two, consider the following models:

$$\text{Model A:} \quad Y_i = \beta_1 + \beta_2 X_{2i} + \beta_3 X_{3i} + \beta_4 X_{4i} + \beta_5 X_{5i} + u_i$$

$$\text{Model B:} \quad Y_i = \beta_1 + \beta_2 X_{2i} + \beta_3 X_{3i} + u_i$$

We say that Model B is nested in Model A because it is a special case of Model A: If we estimate Model A and test the hypothesis that $\beta_4 = \beta_5 = 0$ and do not reject it on the basis of, say, the F test,[32] Model A reduces to Model B. If we add variable X_4 to Model B, then Model A will reduce to Model B if β_5 is zero; here we will use the t test to test the hypothesis that the coefficient of X_5 is zero.

Without calling them such, the specification error tests that we have discussed previously and the restricted F test that we discussed in Chapter 8 are essentially tests of nested hypothesis.

Now consider the following models:

$$\text{Model C:} \quad Y_i = \alpha_1 + \alpha_2 X_{2i} + \alpha_3 X_{3i} + u_i$$

$$\text{Model D:} \quad Y_i = \beta_1 + \beta_2 Z_{2i} + \beta_3 Z_{3i} + v_i$$

where the X's and Z's are different variables. We say that Models C and D are **non-nested** because one cannot be derived as a special case of the other. In economics, as in other sciences, more than one competing theory may explain a phenomenon. Thus, the monetarists would emphasize the role of money in explaining changes in GDP, whereas the Keynesians may explain them by changes in government expenditure.

It may be noted here that one can allow Models C and D to contain regressors that are common to both. For example, X_3 could be included in Model D and Z_2 could be included in Model C. Even then these are non-nested models, because Model C does not contain Z_3 and Model D does not contain X_2.

Even if the same variables enter the model, the functional form may make two models non-nested. For example, consider the model:

$$\text{Model E:} \quad Y_i = \beta_1 + \beta_2 \ln Z_{2i} + \beta_3 \ln Z_{3i} + w_i$$

Models D and E are non-nested, as one cannot be derived as a special case of the other.

Since we already have looked at tests of nested models (t and F tests), in the following section we discuss some of the tests of non-nested models, which earlier we called model mis-specification errors.

[32] More generally, one can use the likelihood ratio test, or the Wald test or the Lagrange Multiplier test, which were discussed briefly in Chapter 8.

13.8 Tests of Non-Nested Hypotheses

According to Harvey,[33] there are two approaches to testing non-nested hypotheses: (1) the **discrimination approach,** where given two or more competing models, one chooses a model based on some criteria of goodness of fit, and (2) the **discerning approach** (our terminology) where, in investigating one model, we take into account information provided by other models. We consider these approaches briefly.

The Discrimination Approach

Consider Models C and D in Section 3.7. Since both models involve the same dependent variable, we can choose between two (or more) models based on some goodness-of-fit criterion, such as R^2 or adjusted R^2, which we have already discussed. But keep in mind that in comparing two or more models, the regressand must be the same. Besides these criteria, there are other criteria that are also used. These include **Akaike's information criterion (AIC), Schwarz's information criterion (SIC),** and **Mallows's C_p criterion.** We discuss these criteria in Section 13.9. Most modern statistical software packages have one or more of these criteria built into their regression routines. In the last section of this chapter, we will illustrate these criteria using an extended example. On the basis of one or more of these criteria a model is finally selected that has the highest $\bar{R}^2$ or the lowest value of AIC or SIC, etc.

The Discerning Approach

The Non-Nested F Test or Encompassing F Test

Consider Models C and D introduced in Section 3.7. How do we choose between the two models? For this purpose suppose we estimate the following nested or *hybrid* model:

$$\text{Model F:} \qquad Y_i = \lambda_1 + \lambda_2 X_{2i} + \lambda_3 X_{3i} + \lambda_4 Z_{2i} + \lambda_5 Z_{3i} + u_i$$

Notice that Model F *nests* or *encompasses* Models C and D. But note that C is not nested in D and D is not nested in C, so they are non-nested models.

Now if Model C is correct, $\lambda_4 = \lambda_5 = 0$, whereas Model D is correct if $\lambda_2 = \lambda_3 = 0$. This testing can be done by the usual F test, hence the name non-nested F test.

However, there are problems with this testing procedure. *First,* if the X's and the Z's are highly correlated, then, as noted in the chapter on multicollinearity, it is quite likely that one or more of the λ's are individually statistically insignificant, although on the basis of the F test one can reject the hypothesis that all the slope coefficients are simultaneously zero. In this case, we have no way of deciding whether Model C or Model D is the correct model. *Second,* there is another problem. Suppose we choose Model C as the *reference hypothesis* or model, and find that all its coefficients are significant. Now we add Z_2 or Z_3 or both to the model and find, using the F test, that their incremental contribution to the explained sum of squares (ESS) is statistically insignificant. Therefore, we decide to choose Model C.

But suppose we had instead chosen Model D as the reference model and found that all its coefficients were statistically significant. But when we add X_2 or X_3 or both to this model, we find, again using the F test, that their incremental contribution to ESS is insignificant. Therefore, we would have chosen model D as the correct model. Hence, "the choice of the reference hypothesis could determine the outcome of the choice model,"[34] especially if severe multicollinearity is present in the competing regressors. *Finally,* the artificially nested model F may not have any economic meaning.

[33]Andrew Harvey, *The Econometric Analysis of Time Series,* 2d ed., The MIT Press, Cambridge, Mass., 1990, Chapter 5.

[34]Thomas B. Fomby, R. Carter Hill, and Stanley R. Johnson, *Advanced Econometric Methods,* Springer Verlag, New York, 1984, p. 416.

EXAMPLE 13.3
An Illustrative Example: The St. Louis Model

To determine whether changes in nominal GNP can be explained by changes in the money supply (monetarism) or by changes in government expenditure (Keynesianism), we consider the following models:

$$\dot{Y}_t = \alpha + \beta_0 \dot{M}_t + \beta_1 \dot{M}_{t-1} + \beta_2 \dot{M}_{t-2} + \beta_3 \dot{M}_{t-3} + \beta_4 \dot{M}_{t-4} + u_{1t}$$

$$= \alpha + \sum_{i=0}^{4} \beta_i \dot{M}_{t-i} + u_{1t} \tag{13.8.1}$$

$$\dot{Y}_t = \gamma + \lambda_0 \dot{E}_t + \lambda_1 \dot{E}_{t-1} + \lambda_2 \dot{E}_{t-2} + \lambda_3 \dot{E}_{t-3} + \lambda_4 \dot{E}_{t-4} + u_{2t}$$

$$= \gamma + \sum_{i=0}^{4} \lambda_i \dot{E}_{t-i} + u_{2t} \tag{13.8.2}$$

where $\dot{Y}_t$ = rate of growth in nominal GNP at time t
$\dot{M}_t$ = rate of growth in the money supply (M_1 version) at time t
$\dot{E}_t$ = rate of growth in full, or high, employment government expenditure at time t

In passing, note that Eqs. (13.8.1) and (13.8.2) are examples of **distributed-lag models,** a topic thoroughly discussed in Chapter 17. For the time being, simply note that the effect of a unit change in the money supply or government expenditure on GNP is distributed over a period of time and is not instantaneous.

Since a priori it may be difficult to decide between the two competing models, let us enmesh the two models as shown below:

$$\dot{Y}_t = \text{constant} + \sum_{i=0}^{4} \beta_i \dot{M}_{t-i} + \sum_{i=0}^{4} \lambda_i \dot{E}_{t-i} + u_{3t} \tag{13.8.3}$$

This nested model is one form in which the famous (Federal Reserve Bank of) St. Louis model, a pro-monetary-school bank, has been expressed and estimated. The results of this model for the period 1953–I to 1976–IV for the United States are as follows (t ratios in parentheses):[35]

(13.8.4)

Coefficient	Estimate	Coefficient	Estimate
β_0	0.40 (2.96)	λ_0	0.08 (2.26)
β_1	0.41 (5.26)	λ_1	0.06 (2.52)
β_2	0.25 (2.14)	λ_2	0.00 (0.02)
β_3	0.06 (0.71)	λ_3	−0.06 (−2.20)
β_4	−0.05 (−0.37)	λ_4	−0.07 (−1.83)
$\sum_{i=0}^{4} \beta_i$	1.06 (5.59)	$\sum_{i=0}^{4} \lambda_i$	0.03 (0.40)

$R^2 = 0.40$
$d = 1.78$

What do these results suggest about the superiority of one model over the other? If we consider the cumulative effect of a unit change in $\dot{M}$ and $\dot{E}$ on $\dot{Y}$, we obtain, respectively, $\sum_{i=0}^{4} \beta_i = 1.06$ and $\sum_{i=0}^{4} \lambda_i = 0.03$, the former being statistically significant and the latter not. This comparison would tend to support the monetarist claim that it is changes in the money supply that determine changes in the (nominal) GNP. It is left as an exercise for the reader to critically evaluate this claim.

[35]See Keith M. Carlson, "Does the St. Louis Equation Now Believe in Fiscal Policy?" *Review, Federal Reserve Bank of St. Louis,* vol. 60, no. 2, February 1978, p. 17, table IV.

Davidson–MacKinnon J Test[36]

Because of the problems just listed in the non-nested F testing procedure, alternatives have been suggested. One is the **Davidson–MacKinnon *J* test.** To illustrate this test, suppose we want to compare hypothesis or Model C with hypothesis or Model D. The ***J* test** proceeds as follows:

1. We estimate Model D and from it we obtain the estimated Y values, $\hat{Y}_i^D$.

2. We add the predicted Y value in Step 1 as an additional regressor to Model C and estimate the following model:

$$Y_i = \alpha_1 + \alpha_2 X_{2i} + \alpha_3 X_{3i} + \alpha_4 \hat{Y}_i^D + u_i \tag{13.8.5}$$

where the $\hat{Y}_i^D$ values are obtained from Step 1. This model is an example of the **encompassing principle,** as in the Hendry methodology.

3. Using the t test, test the hypothesis that $\alpha_4 = 0$.

4. If the hypothesis that $\alpha_4 = 0$ is not rejected, we can accept (i.e., not reject) Model C as the true model because $\hat{Y}_i^D$ included in Eq. (13.8.5), which represents the influence of variables not included in Model C, has no additional explanatory power beyond that contributed by Model C. In other words, Model C *encompasses* Model D in the sense that the latter model does not contain any additional information that will improve the performance of Model C. By the same token, if the null hypothesis is rejected, Model C cannot be the true model (why?).

5. Now we reverse the roles of hypotheses, or Models C and D. We now estimate Model C first, use the estimated Y values from this model as the regressor in Eq. (13.8.5), repeat Step 4, and decide whether to accept Model D over Model C. More specifically, we estimate the following model:

$$Y_i = \beta_1 + \beta_2 Z_{2i} + \beta_3 Z_{3i} + \beta_4 \hat{Y}_i^C + u_i \tag{13.8.6}$$

where $\hat{Y}_i^C$ are the estimated Y values from Model C. We now test the hypothesis that $\beta_4 = 0$. If this hypothesis is not rejected, we choose Model D over C. If the hypothesis that $\beta_4 = 0$ is rejected, we choose C over D, as the latter does not improve over the performance of C.

Although it is intuitively appealing, the J test has some problems. Since the tests given in Eqs. (13.8.5) and (13.8.6) are performed independently, we have the following likely outcomes:

	Hypothesis: $\alpha_4 = 0$	
Hypothesis: $\beta_4 = 0$	**Do Not Reject**	**Reject**
Do not reject	Accept both C and D	Accept D, reject C
Reject	Accept C, reject D	Reject both C and D

As this table shows, we will not be able to get a clear answer if the J testing procedure leads to the acceptance or rejection of both models. In case both models are rejected, neither model helps us to explain the behavior of Y. Similarly, if both models are accepted, as Kmenta notes, "the data are apparently not rich enough to discriminate between the two hypotheses [models]."[37]

[36] R. Davidson and J. G. MacKinnon, "Several Tests for Model Specification in the Presence of Alternative Hypotheses," *Econometrica,* vol. 49, 1981, pp. 781–793.

[37] Jan Kmenta, op. cit., p. 597.

Another problem with the J test is that when we use the t statistic to test the significance of the estimated Y variable in models (13.8.5) and (13.8.6), the t statistic has the standard normal distribution only asymptotically, that is, in large samples. Therefore, the J test may not be very powerful (in the statistical sense) in small samples because it tends to reject the true hypothesis or model more frequently than it ought to.

EXAMPLE 13.4
Personal Consumption Expenditure and Disposable Personal Income

To illustrate the J test, consider the data given in Table 13.3. This table gives data on per capita personal consumption expenditure (PPCE) and per capita disposable personal income (PDPI), both measured in current (2008) dollars for the United States for the period 1970–2005. Consider the following rival models:

$$\text{Model A:} \quad \text{PPCE}_t = \alpha_1 + \alpha_2 \text{PDPI}_t + \alpha_3 \text{PDPI}_{t-1} + u_t \tag{13.8.7}$$

$$\text{Model B:} \quad \text{PPCE}_t = \beta_1 + \beta_2 \text{PDPI}_t + \beta_3 \text{PCPE}_{t-1} + u_t \tag{13.8.8}$$

Model A states that PPCE depends on PDPI in the current and previous time period; this model is an example of what is known as the **distributed-lag model** (see Chapter 17). Model B postulates that PPCE depends on current PDPI as well as PPCE in the previous time period; this model represents what is known as the **autoregressive model** (see Chapter 17 again). The reason for introducing the lagged value of PPCE in this model is to reflect inertia or habit persistence.

The results of estimating these models separately were as follows:

$$\text{Model A:} \quad \widehat{\text{PPCE}}_t = -606.6347 + 0.6170\ \text{PDPI}_t + 0.3530\ \text{PDPI}_{t-1}$$
$$t = \quad (-3.8334) \quad (2.5706) \quad (1.4377) \tag{13.8.9}$$
$$R^2 = 0.9983 \qquad d = 0.2161$$

$$\text{Model B:} \quad \widehat{\text{PPCE}}_t = 76.8947 + 0.2074\ \text{PDPI}_t + 0.8104\ \text{PPCE}_{t-1}$$
$$t = (0.7256) \quad (2.6734) \quad (9.7343) \tag{13.8.10}$$
$$R^2 = 0.9996 \qquad d - 0.9732$$

TABLE 13.3
Per Capita Personal Consumption Expenditure (PPCE) and per Capita Personal Disposable Income (PDPI), U.S., 1970–2005

Source: *Economic Report of the President*, 2007.

Year	PPCE	PDPI	Year	PPCE	PDPI
1970	3,162	3,587	1988	13,685	15,297
1971	3,379	3,860	1989	14,546	16,257
1972	3,671	4,140	1990	15,349	17,131
1973	4,022	4,616	1991	15,722	17,609
1974	4,364	5,010	1992	16,485	18,494
1975	4,789	5,498	1993	17,204	18,872
1976	5,282	5,972	1994	18,004	19,555
1977	5,804	6,517	1995	18,665	20,287
1978	6,417	7,224	1996	19,490	21,091
1979	7,073	7,967	1997	20,323	21,940
1980	7,716	8,822	1998	21,291	23,161
1981	8,439	9,765	1999	22,491	23,968
1982	8,945	10,426	2000	23,862	25,472
1983	9,775	11,131	2001	24,722	26,235
1984	10,589	12,319	2002	25,501	27,164
1985	11,406	13,037	2003	26,463	28,039
1986	12,048	13,649	2004	27,937	29,536
1987	12,766	14,241	2005	29,468	30,458

(Continued)

EXAMPLE 13.4 *(Continued)*

If one were to choose between these two models on the basis of the discrimination approach, using the highest R^2 criterion, one would probably choose Model B (13.8.10) because it is just slightly higher than Model A (13.8.9). Also, in Model B (13.8.10), both variables are individually statistically significant, whereas in Model A (13.8.9) only the current PDPI is statistically significant (there might be a collinearity problem, though). For predictive purposes, there is not much difference between the two estimated R^2 values, though.

To apply the *J* test, suppose we assume Model A is the null hypothesis, or the maintained model, and Model B is the alternative hypothesis. Following the *J* test steps discussed earlier, we use the estimated PPCE values from model (13.8.10) as an additional regressor in Model A. The following is the outcome from this regression:

$$\widehat{\text{PPCE}}_t = -35.17 + 0.2762\,\text{PDPI}_t - 0.5141\,\text{PDPI}_{t-1} + 1.2351\,\widehat{\text{PPCE}}_t^B$$
$$t = (-0.43) \quad (2.60) \quad (-4.05) \quad (12.06) \tag{13.8.11}$$
$$R^2 = 1.00 \quad d = 1.5205$$

where $\widehat{\text{PPCE}}_t^B$ on the right-hand side of Eq. (13.8.11) represents the estimated PPCE values from the original Model B (13.8.10). Since the coefficient of this variable is statistically significant with a very high *t*-statistic of 12.06, following the *J* test procedure we have to reject Model A in favor of Model B.

Now we will assume Model B is the maintained hypothesis and Model A is the alternative. Following the exact same procedure, we obtain the following results:

$$\widehat{\text{PPCE}}_t = -823.7 + 1.4309\,\text{PDPI}_t + 1.0009\,\text{PPCE}_{t-1} - 1.4563\,\widehat{\text{PPCE}}_t^A$$
$$t = (-3.45) \quad (4.64) \quad (12.06) \quad (-4.05) \tag{13.8.12}$$
$$R^2 = 1.00 \quad d = 1.5205$$

where $\widehat{\text{PPCE}}_t^A$ on the right-hand side of Eq. (13.8.12) represents the estimated PPCE values from the original Model A (13.8.9). In this regression, the coefficient of $\widehat{\text{PPCE}}_t^A$ is also statistically significant with a *t*-statistic of −4.05. This result suggests that we should now reject Model B in favor of Model A.

All this tells us is that neither model is particularly useful in explaining the behavior of per capita personal consumption expenditure in the United States over the period 1970–2005. Of course, we have considered only two competing models. In reality, there may be more than two models. The *J* test procedure can be extended to multiple model comparisons, although the analysis can quickly become complex.

This example shows very vividly why the CLRM assumes that the regression model used in the analysis is correctly specified. Obviously, in developing a model it is crucial to pay very careful attention to the phenomenon being modeled.

Other Tests of Model Selection

The *J* test just discussed is only one of a group of tests of model selection. There is the **Cox test,** the **JA test,** the **P test,** the **Mizon–Richard encompassing test,** and variants of these tests. Obviously, we cannot hope to discuss these specialized tests, for which the reader may want to consult the references cited in the various footnotes.[38]

[38]See also Badi H. Baltagi, *Econometrics,* Springer, New York, 1998, pp. 209–222.

13.9 Model Selection Criteria

In this section we discuss several criteria that have been used to choose among competing models and/or to compare models for forecasting purposes. Here we distinguish between **in-sample** forecasting and **out-of-sample** forecasting. In-sample forecasting essentially tells us how the chosen model fits the data in a given sample. Out-of-sample forecasting is concerned with determining how a fitted model forecasts future values of the regressand, given the values of the regressors.

Several criteria are used for this purpose. In particular, we discuss these criteria: (1) R^2, (2) adjusted $R^2 (= \bar{R}^2)$, (3) Akaike's information criterion (AIC), (4) Schwarz's information criterion (SIC), (5) Mallows's C_p criterion, and (6) forecast χ^2 (chi-square). All these criteria aim at minimizing the residual sum of squares (RSS) (or increasing the R^2 value). However, except for the first criterion, criteria (2), (3), (4), and (5) impose a penalty for including an increasingly large number of regressors. Thus there is a trade-off between goodness of fit of the model and its complexity (as judged by the number of regressors).

The R^2 Criterion

We know that one of the measures of goodness of fit of a regression model is R^2, which, as we know, is defined as:

$$R^2 = \frac{\text{ESS}}{\text{TSS}} = 1 - \frac{\text{RSS}}{\text{TSS}} \tag{13.9.1}$$

R^2, thus defined, of necessity lies between 0 and 1. The closer it is to 1, the better is the fit. But there are problems with R^2. *First,* it measures *in-sample* goodness of fit in the sense of how close an estimated Y value is to its actual value in the given sample. There is no guarantee that it will forecast well *out-of-sample* observations. *Second,* in comparing two or more R^2's, the dependent variable, or regressand, must be the same. *Third,* and more importantly, an R^2 cannot fall when more variables are added to the model. Therefore, there is every temptation to play the game of "maximizing the R^2" by simply adding more variables to the model. Of course, adding more variables to the model may increase R^2 but it may also increase the variance of forecast error.

Adjusted R^2

As a penalty for adding regressors to increase the R^2 value, Henry Theil developed the adjusted R^2, denoted by $\bar{R}^2$, which we studied in Chapter 7. Recall that

$$\bar{R}^2 = 1 - \frac{\text{RSS}/(n-k)}{\text{TSS}/(n-1)} = 1 - (1 - R^2)\frac{n-1}{n-k} \tag{13.9.2}$$

As you can see from this formula, $\bar{R}^2 \le R^2$, showing how the adjusted R^2 penalizes for adding more regressors. As we noted in Chapter 8, unlike R^2, the adjusted R^2 will increase only if the absolute t value of the added variable is greater than 1. For comparative purposes, therefore, $\bar{R}^2$ is a better measure than R^2. But again keep in mind that the regressand must be the same for the comparison to be valid.

Akaike's Information Criterion (AIC)

The idea of imposing a penalty for adding regressors to the model has been carried further in the AIC criterion, which is defined as:

$$\text{AIC} = e^{2k/n}\frac{\sum \hat{u}_i^2}{n} = e^{2k/n}\frac{\text{RSS}}{\text{n}} \tag{13.9.3}$$

where k is the number of regressors (including the intercept) and n is the number of observations. For mathematical convenience, Eq. (13.9.3) is written as

$$\ln \text{AIC} = \left(\frac{2k}{n}\right) + \ln\left(\frac{\text{RSS}}{n}\right) \tag{13.9.4}$$

where ln AIC = natural log of AIC and $2k/n$ = penalty factor. Some textbooks and software packages define AIC only in terms of its log transform so there is no need to put ln before AIC. As you see from this formula, AIC imposes a harsher penalty than $\bar{R}^2$ for adding more regressors. In comparing two or more models, the model with the lowest value of AIC is preferred. One advantage of AIC is that it is useful for not only in-sample but also out-of-sample forecasting performance of a regression model. Also, it is useful for both nested and non-nested models. It also has been used to determine the lag length in an AR(p) model.

Schwarz's Information Criterion (SIC)

Similar in spirit to the AIC, the SIC criterion is defined as:

$$\text{SIC} = n^{k/n}\frac{\sum \hat{u}^2}{n} = n^{k/n}\frac{\text{RSS}}{n} \tag{13.9.5}$$

or in log-form:

$$\ln \text{SIC} = \frac{k}{n}\ln n + \ln\left(\frac{\text{RSS}}{\text{n}}\right) \tag{13.9.6}$$

where $[(k/n)\ln n]$ is the penalty factor. SIC imposes a harsher penalty than AIC, as is obvious from comparing Eq. (13.9.6) to Eq. (13.9.4). Like AIC, the lower the value of SIC, the better the model. Again, like AIC, SIC can be used to compare in-sample or out-of-sample forecasting performance of a model.

Mallows's C_p Criterion

Suppose we have a model consisting of k regressors, including the intercept. Let $\hat{\sigma}^2$ as usual be the estimator of the true σ^2. But suppose that we only choose p regressors ($p \leq k$) and obtain the RSS from the regression using these p regressors. Let RSS_p denote the residual sum of squares using the p regressors. Now C. P. Mallows has developed the following criterion for model selection, known as the C_p criterion:

$$C_p = \frac{\text{RSS}_p}{\hat{\sigma}^2} - (n - 2p) \tag{13.9.7}$$

where n is the number of observations.

We know that $E(\hat{\sigma}^2)$ is an unbiased estimator of the true σ^2. Now, if the model with p regressors is adequate in that it does not suffer from lack of fit, it can be shown[39] that $E(\text{RSS}_p) = (n - p)\sigma^2$. In consequence, it is true *approximately* that

$$E(C_p) \approx \frac{(n - p)\sigma^2}{\sigma^2} - (n - 2p) \approx p \tag{13.9.8}$$

In choosing a model according to the C_p criterion, we would look for a model that has a low C_p value, about equal to p. In other words, following the principle of parsimony, we will choose a model with p regressors ($p < k$) that gives a fairly good fit to the data.

In practice, one usually plots C_p computed from Eq. (13.9.7) against p. An "adequate" model will show up as a point close to the $C_p = p$ line, as can be seen from Figure 13.3. As this figure shows, Model A may be preferable to Model B, as it is closer to the $C_p = p$ line than Model B.

A Word of Caution about Model Selection Criteria

We have discussed several model selection criteria. But one should look at these criteria as an adjunct to the various specification tests we have discussed in this chapter. Some of the criteria discussed above are purely descriptive and may not have strong theoretical properties. Some of them may even be open to the charge of data mining. Nonetheless, they are so frequently used by the practitioner that the reader should be aware of them. No one of these criteria is necessarily superior to the others.[40] Most modern software packages now

FIGURE 13.3
Mallows's C_p plot.

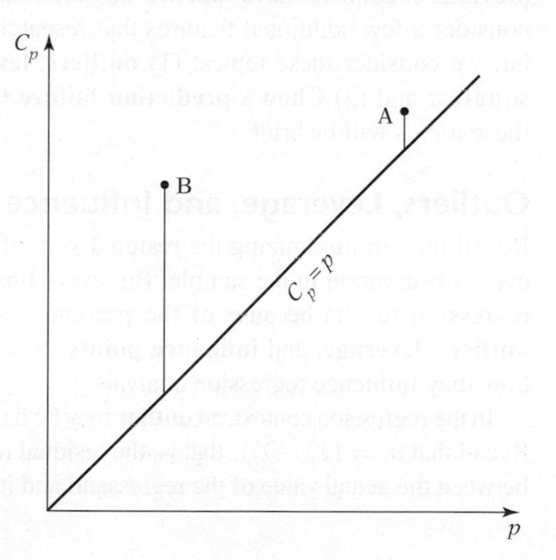

[39] Norman D. Draper and Harry Smith, *Applied Regression Analysis,* 3d ed., John Wiley & Sons, New York, 1998, p. 332. See this book for some worked examples of C_p.

[40] For a useful discussion on this topic, see Francis X. Diebold, *Elements of Forecasting,* 2d ed., South Western Publishing, 2001, pp. 83–89. On balance, Diebold recommends the SIC criterion.

include R^2, adjusted R^2, AIC, and SIC. Mallows's C_p is not routinely given, although it can be easily computed from its definition.

Forecast Chi-Square (χ^2)

Suppose we have a regression model based on n observations and suppose we want to use it to forecast the (mean) values of the regressand for an additional t observations. As noted elsewhere, it is a good idea to save part of the sample data to see how the estimated model forecasts the observations not included in the sample, the postsample period.

Now the forecast χ^2 test is defined as follows:

$$\text{Forecast, } \chi^2 = \frac{\sum_{n+1}^{n+t} \hat{u}_i^2}{\hat{\sigma}^2} \tag{13.9.9}$$

where $\hat{u}_i$ is the forecast error made for period $i\ (= n+1, n+2, \ldots, +n+t)$, using the parameters obtained from the fitted regression and the values of the regressors in the post-sample period. $\hat{\sigma}^2$ is the usual OLS estimator of σ^2 based on the fitted regression.

If we hypothesize that the parameter values have not changed between the sample and postsample periods, it can be shown that the statistic given in Eq. (13.9.9) follows the chi-square distribution with t degrees of freedom, where t is the number of periods for which the forecast is made. As Charemza and Deadman note, the forecast χ^2 test has *weak statistical power*, meaning that the probability that the test will correctly reject a false null hypothesis is low and therefore the test should be used as a signal rather than a definitive test.[41]

13.10 Additional Topics in Econometric Modeling

As noted in the introduction to this chapter, the topic of econometric modeling and diagnostic testing is so vast and evolving that specialized books are written on this topic. In the previous section we have touched on some major themes in this area. In this section we consider a few additional features that researchers may find useful in practice. In particular, we consider these topics: (1) **outliers, leverage, and influence;** (2) **recursive least squares;** and (3) **Chow's prediction failure test.** Of necessity the discussion of each of these topics will be brief.

Outliers, Leverage, and Influence[42]

Recall that, in minimizing the residual sum of squares (RSS), OLS gives equal weight to every observation in the sample. But every observation may not have equal impact on the regression results because of the presence of three types of special data points called **outliers, leverage,** and **influence points.** It is important that we know what they are and how they influence regression analysis.

In the regression context, an **outlier** may be defined as an observation with a "large residual." Recall that $\hat{u}_i = (Y_i - \hat{Y}_i)$, that is, the residual represents the difference (positive or negative) between the actual value of the regressand and its value estimated from the regression model.

[41]Wojciech W. Charemza and Derek F. Deadman, *New Directions in Econometric Practice: A General to Specific Modelling, Cointegration and Vector Autoregression,* 2d ed., Edward Elgar Publishers, 1997, p. 30. See also pp. 250–252 for their views on various model selection criteria.

[42]The following discussion is influenced by Chandan Mukherjee, Howard White, and Marc Wyuts, *Econometrics and Data Analysis for Developing Countries,* Routledge, New York, 1998, pp. 137–148.

FIGURE 13.4 In each subfigure, the solid line gives the OLS line for all the data and the broken line gives the OLS line with the outlier, denoted by an ⊛, omitted. In (*a*), the outlier is near the mean value of *X* and has low leverage and little influence on the regression coefficients. In (*b*), the outlier is far away from the mean value of *X* and has high leverage as well as substantial influence on the regression coefficients. In (*c*), the outlier has high leverage but low influence on the regression coefficients because it is in line with the rest of the observations.

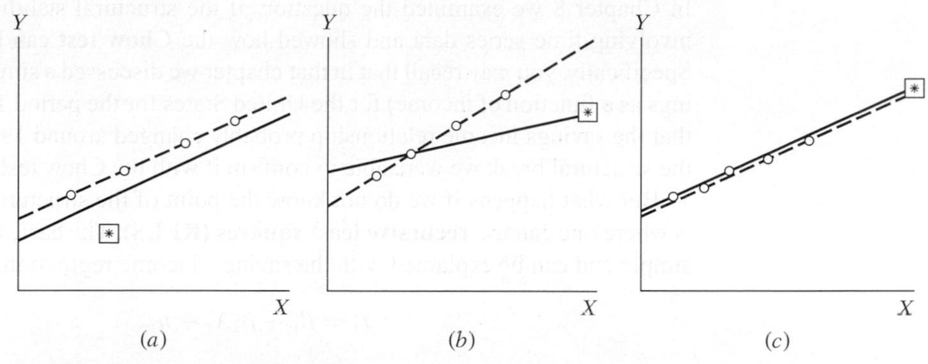

Source: Adapted from John Fox, op. cit., p. 268.

When we say that a residual is large, it is in comparison with the other residuals and very often such a large residual catches our attention immediately because of its rather large vertical distance from the estimated regression line. Note that in a data set there may be more than one outlier. We have already encountered an example of this in Exercise 11.22, where you were asked to regress percent change in stock prices (Y) on percent change in consumer prices (X) for a sample of 20 countries. One observation, that relating to Chile, was an outlier.

A data point is said to exert (high) **leverage** if it is disproportionately distant from the bulk of the values of a regressor(s). Why does a leverage point matter? It matters because it is capable of pulling the regression line toward itself, thus distorting the slope of the regression line. If this actually happens, then we call such a leverage (data) point an **influential point.** The removal of such a data point from the sample can dramatically affect the regression line. Returning to Exercise 11.22, you will see that if you regress Y on X including the observation for Chile, the slope coefficient is positive and "highly statistically significant." But if you drop the observation for Chile, the slope coefficient is practically zero. Thus the Chilean observation has leverage and is also an influential observation.

To further clarify the nature of outliers, leverage, and influence points, consider the diagram in Figure 13.4, which is self-explanatory.[43]

How do we handle such data points? Should we just drop them and confine our attention to the remaining data points? According to Draper and Smith:

> Automatic rejection of outliers is not always a wise procedure. Sometimes the outlier is providing information that other data points cannot due to the fact that it arises from an unusual combination of circumstances which may be of vital interest and requires further investigation rather than rejection. As a general rule, outliers should be rejected out of hand only if they can be traced to causes such as errors of recording the observations or setting up the apparatus [in a physical experiment]. Otherwise, careful investigation is in order.[44]

[43]Adapted from John Fox, *Applied Regression Analysis, Linear Models, and Related Methods*, Sage Publications, California, 1997, p. 268.

[44]Norman R. Draper and Harry Smith, op. cit., p. 76.

What are some of the tests that one can use to detect outliers and leverage points? There are several tests discussed in the literature, but we will not discuss them here because that will take us far afield.[45] Software packages such as SHAZAM and MICROFIT have routines to detect outliers, leverage, and influential points.

Recursive Least Squares

In Chapter 8 we examined the question of the structural stability of a regression model involving time series data and showed how the **Chow test** can be used for this purpose. Specifically, you may recall that in that chapter we discussed a simple savings function (savings as a function of income) for the United States for the period 1970–2005. There we saw that the savings income relationship probably changed around 1982. Knowing the point of the structural break we were able to confirm it with the Chow test.

But what happens if we do not know the point of the structural break (or breaks)? This is where one can use **recursive least squares (RELS).** The basic idea behind RELS is very simple and can be explained with the savings–income regression.

$$Y_t = \beta_1 + \beta_2 X_t + u_t$$

where $Y =$ savings and $X =$ income and where the sample is for the period 1970–2005. (See the data in Table 8.11.)

Suppose we first use the data for 1970–1974 and estimate the savings function, obtaining the estimates of β_1 and β_2. Then we use the data for 1970–1975 and again estimate the savings function and obtain the estimates of the two parameters. Then we use the data for 1970–1976 and re-estimate the savings model. In this fashion we go on adding an additional data point on Y and X until we exhaust the entire sample. As you can imagine, each regression run will give you a new set of estimates of β_1 and β_2. If you plot the estimated values of these parameters against each iteration, you will see how the values of estimated parameters change. If the model under consideration is structurally stable, the changes in the estimated values of the two parameters will be small and essentially random. However, if the estimated values of the parameters change significantly, it would indicate a structural break. RELS is thus a useful routine with time series data since time is ordered chronologically. It is also a useful diagnostic tool in cross-sectional data where the data are ordered by some "size" or "scale" variable, such as the employment or asset size of the firm. In Exercise 13.30 you are asked to apply RELS to the savings data given in Table 8.11.

Software packages such as SHAZAM, *EViews,* and MICROFIT now do recursive least-squares estimates routinely. RELS also generates **recursive residuals** on which several diagnostic tests have been based.[46]

Chow's Prediction Failure Test

We have already discussed Chow's test of structural stability in Chapter 8. Chow has shown that his test can be modified to test the predictive power of a regression model. Again, we will revert to the U.S. savings–income regression for the period 1970–1995.

[45]Here are some accessible sources: Alvin C. Rencher, *Linear Models in Statistics,* John Wiley & Sons, New York, 2000, pp. 219–224; A. C. Atkinson, *Plots, Transformations and Regression: An Introduction to Graphical Methods of Diagnostic Regression Analysis,* Oxford University Press, New York, 1985, Chapter 3; Ashis Sen and Muni Srivastava, *Regression Analysis: Theory, Methods, and Applications,* Springer-Verlag, New York, 1990, Chapter 8; and John Fox, op. cit., Chapter 11.

[46]For details, see Jack Johnston and John DiNardo, *Econometric Methods,* 4th ed., McGraw-Hill, New York, 1997, pp. 117–121.

Suppose we estimate the savings–income regression for the period 1970–1981, obtaining $\hat{\beta}_{1,70-81}$ and $\hat{\beta}_{2,70-81}$, which are the estimated intercept and slope coefficients based on the data for 1970–1981. Now using the actual values of income for the period 1982–1995 and the intercept and slope values for the period 1970–1981, we predict the values of savings for each of 1982–1995 years. The logic here is that if there is no serious structural change in the parameter values, the values of savings estimated for 1982–1995, based on the parameter estimates for the earlier period, should not be very different from the actual values of savings prevailing in the latter period. Of course, if there is a vast difference between the actual and predicted values of savings for the latter period, it will cast doubts on the stability of the savings–income relation for the entire data period.

Whether the difference between the actual and estimated savings value is large or small can be tested by the F test as follows:

$$F = \frac{\left(\sum \hat{u}_t^{*2} - \sum \hat{u}_t^2\right)/n_2}{\left(\sum \hat{u}_t^2\right)/(n_1 - k)} \tag{13.10.1}$$

where n_1 = number of observations in the first period (1970–1981) on which the initial regression is based, n_2 = number of observations in the second or forecast period, $\sum \hat{u}_t^{*2}$ = RSS when the equation is estimated for all the observations $(n_1 + n_2)$, and $\sum \hat{u}_t^2$ = RSS when the equation is estimated for the first n_1 observations, and k is the number of parameters estimated (two in the present instance). If the errors are independent, and identically, normally distributed, the F statistic given in Eq. (13.10.1) follows the F distribution with n_2 and n_1 df, respectively. In Exercise 13.31 you are asked to apply Chow's predictive failure test to find out if the savings–income relation has in fact changed. In passing, note the similarity between this test and the forecast χ^2 test discussed previously.

Missing Data

In applied work it is not uncommon to find that sometimes observations are missing from the sample data. For example, in time series data there may be gaps in the data because of special circumstances. During the Second World War, data on some macro variables were not available or were not published for strategic reasons. In cross-section data it is not uncommon to find that information on some variables for some individuals is missing, especially in data collected from questionnaire-type surveys. In panel data also, over time some respondents drop out or do not provide information on all the questions.

Whatever the reason, missing data is a problem that every researcher faces from time to time. The question is how we deal with the missing data. Is there any way to **impute values** to the missing observations?

This is not an easy question to answer. Although there are some complicated solutions suggested in the literature, we will not pursue them here because of their complexity.[47] However, we will discuss two cases.[48] In the first case, the reasons for the missing data are independent of the available observations, which are called by Darnell the "ignorable case." In the second case, not only are the available data incomplete, but the missing observations may be systematically related to the available data. This is a more serious case, for it may be the result of *self-selection bias,* that is, the observed data are not truly randomly collected.

[47]For a thorough, but rather advanced, treatment of the subject, see A. Colin Cameron and Pravin K. Trivedi, *Microeconometrics: Methods and Applications,* Cambridge University Press, New York, 2005, Chapter 27, pp. 923–941.

[48]The following discussion is based on Adrian C. Darnell, *A Dictionary of Econometrics,* Edward Elgar Publishing, Lyne, U.K., 1994, pp. 256–258.

In the ignorable case, we may simply ignore the missing observations and use the available observations. Most statistical packages do this automatically. Of course, in this case the sample size is reduced and we may not be able to get precise estimates of the regression coefficients. We might use the available data to shed some light on the missing observations, however. Here we consider three possibilities.

1. Out of a total number of observations of N, we have complete data on N_1 ($N_1 < N$) for both the regressand and k regressors denoted by $\boldsymbol{Y}_1$ and $\boldsymbol{X}_1$, respectively. ($\boldsymbol{Y}_1$ is vector of N_1 observations and $\boldsymbol{X}_1$ is a row vector of k regressors).
2. For some observations ($N_2 < N$) there are complete data on the regressand, denoted by $\boldsymbol{Y}_2$, but incomplete observations on some $\boldsymbol{X}_2$ (again these are vectors).
3. For some observations ($N_3 < N$), there are no data on $\boldsymbol{Y}$, but complete data on X, denoted by $\boldsymbol{X}_3$.

In the first case, regression of $\boldsymbol{Y}_1$ on $\boldsymbol{X}_1$ will produce estimates of the regression coefficients that are unbiased but they may not be efficient because we ignore N_2 and N_3 observations. The other two cases are rather complicated and we leave it for the reader to follow the references for solutions.[49]

13.11 Concluding Examples

We conclude this chapter with two examples that illustrate one or more points raised in the chapter. The first example on wage determination uses cross-section data and the second example, which considers the real consumption function for the U.S., uses time series data.

1. A Model of Hourly Wage Determination

To examine what factors determine hourly wages, we consider a Mincer-type wage model, which has become popular with labor economists. This model has the following form:[50]

$$\ln \text{wage}_i = \beta_1 + \beta_2 \text{Edu}_i + \beta_3 \text{Exp}_i + \beta_4 \text{Fe}_i + \beta_5 \text{NW}_i + \beta_6 \text{UN}_i + \beta_7 \text{WK}_i + u_i \tag{13.11.1}$$

Where ln wage = natural log of hourly wage ($), Edu = education in years, Exp = labor market experience, Fe = 1 if female, 0 otherwise, NW = 1 if non-white, 0 otherwise, UN = 1 if in union, 0 otherwise, and WK = 1 for non-hourly paid workers, 0 otherwise. For the non-hourly paid workers, the hourly wage is computed as weekly earnings divided by the usual hours worked.

There are many more variables that could be added to this model. Some of these variables are ethnic origin, marital status, number of children under age 6, and wealth or non-labor income. For now, we will work with the model shown in Eq. (13.11.1).

The data consist of 1,289 persons interviewed in March 1985 as a part of the *Current Population Survey (CPS)* periodically conducted by the U.S. Census Bureau. These data were originally collected by Paul Rudd.[51]

[49]Besides the references already cited, see A. A. Afifi, and R. M. Elashoff, "Missing Observations in Multivariate Statistics," *Journal of the American Statistical Association,* vol. 61, 1966, pp. 595–604, and vol. 62, 1967, pp. 10–29.

[50]See J. Mincer, *School, Experience and Earnings,* Columbia University Press, New York, 1974.

[51]Paul A. Rudd, *An Introduction to Classical Econometric Theory,* Oxford University Press, New York, 2000. We have not included data on age because it is highly collinear with job experience.

A priori, we would expect education and experience to have a positive impact on wages. The dummy variables Fe and NW are expected to have a negative impact on wages if there is some kind of discrimination and UN is expected to have a positive impact because of uncertainty of income.

When all the dummy variables take a value of zero, Eq. (13.11.1) reduces to

$$\ln \text{wage}_i = \beta_1 + \beta_2 \text{Edu}_i + \beta_3 \text{Exp}_i + u_i \qquad (13.11.2)$$

which is the wage function for a non-unionized white male worker who is on an hourly wage rate. This is the base, or *reference,* category.

Let us now present the regression results and then discuss them.

TABLE 13.4 ***EViews* Regression Results Based on Equation (13.11.1)**

Dependent Variable: LW
Method: Least Squares
Sample: 1-1,289
Included observations: 1,289

	Coefficient	Std. Error	*t* Statistic	Prob.
C	1.037880	0.074370	13.95563	0.0000
EDU	0.084037	0.005110	16.44509	0.0000
EXP	0.011152	0.001163	9.591954	0.0000
FE	-0.234934	0.026071	-9.011170	0.0000
NW	-0.124447	0.036340	-3.424498	0.0006
UN	0.207508	0.036265	5.721963	0.0000
WK	0.228725	0.028939	7.903647	0.0000

R-squared	0.376053	Mean dependent var.	2.342416
Adjusted *R*-squared	0.373133	S.D. dependent var.	0.586356
S.E. of regression	0.464247	Akaike info criterion	1.308614
Sum squared resid.	276.3030	Schwarz criterion	1.336645
Log likelihood	-836.4018	Hannan-Quinn criter.	1.319136
F-statistic	128.7771	Durbin-Watson stat.	1.977004
Prob. (*F*-statistic)	0.000000		

The first thing to notice is that all the estimated coefficients are *individually* highly significant, for the *p*-values are so low. The *F* is also very high, suggesting that collectively, also, all the variables are statistically important.

Compared to the reference worker, the average wage of a female worker and a non-white worker is lower. Union workers and those who are paid weekly, on average, make more wages.

How adequate is model (13.11.1), given the variables we have considered? Is it possible that non-white female workers earn less than white workers? Is it possible that non-white female non-union workers earn less than white female non-union workers? In other words, are there any interaction effects between the quantitative regressors and the dummy variables?

Statistical packages have routines to answer such questions. For instance, *EViews* has such a facility. After a model is estimated, if you think that some variables can be added to the model but you are not sure of their importance, you can run the *test of omitted variables*.

To show this, suppose we estimate Eq. (13.11.1) and now want to find out if the products of Fe and NW, FE and UN, and FE and WK should be added to the model to take into account the interaction between the explanatory variables. Using the *EViews 6* routine, we obtain the following answer: The *null hypothesis* is that these three added variables have no effect on the estimated model.

As you would suspect, we can use the F test (discussed in Chapter 8) to assess the incremental, or marginal, contribution of the added variables and test the null hypothesis. For our example, the results are as follows:

TABLE 13.5
Partial *EViews* Results Using Interactions

Omitted Variables: FE*NW FE*UN FE*WK			
F-statistic	0.805344	Prob. *F* (3,1279)	0.4909
Log likelihood ratio	2.432625	Prob. chi-square (3)	0.4876

We do not reject the null hypothesis that the interaction between female and non-white, female and union, and female and weekly wage earners, collectively, has no significant impact on the estimated model given in Table 13.4, for the estimated F value of 0.8053 is not statistically significant, the p value being about 49 percent.

We leave it for the reader to try other combinations of the regressors to assess their contribution to the original model.

Before proceeding further, the model (13.11.1) suggests that the influence of experience on log wages is linear, that is, holding other variables constant, the relative increase in wages (remember the regressand is in log form), remains the same for every year's increase in job experience. This assumption may be true over some years of experience, but as basic labor economics suggests, as workers get older, the rate of wage increase decreases. To see if this is the case in our example, we added the squared experience term to our initial model and obtained the following results:

TABLE 13.6
***EViews* Results with Experience Squared**

Dependent Variable: LW
Method: Least Squares
Sample: 1-1,289
Included observations: 1,289

	Coefficient	Std. Error	*t* Statistic	Prob.
C	0.912279	0.075151	12.13922	0.0000
EDU	0.079867	0.005051	15.81218	0.0000
EXP	0.036659	0.003800	9.647230	0.0000
FE	-0.228848	0.025606	-8.937218	0.0000
NW	-0.121805	0.035673	-3.414458	0.0007
UN	0.199957	0.035614	5.614579	0.0000
WK	0.222549	0.028420	7.830675	0.0000
EXP*EXP	-0.000611	8.68E-05	-7.037304	0.0000

R-squared	0.399277	Mean dependent var.	2.342416
Adjusted *R*-squared	0.395995	S.D. dependent var.	0.586356
S.E. of regression	0.455703	Akaike info criterion	1.272234
Sum squared resid.	266.0186	Schwarz criterion	1.304269
Log likelihood	-811.9549	Hannan-Quinn criter.	1.284259
F-statistic	121.6331	Durbin-Watson stat.	1.971753
Prob. (*F*-statistic)	0.000000		

The squared experience term is not only negative but it is also highly statistically significant. It also accords with labor market behavior; over time, the rate of growth of wages slows down $\left(\frac{\partial lw}{\partial \text{EXP}} = 0.0366 - 0.0012\text{EXP}\right)$.

We take this opportunity to discuss the Akaike and Schwarz criteria. Like R^2, these are tests of the goodness of fit of the estimated model; the difference is that under the R^2 criterion, the higher its value, the better the model explains the behavior of the regressand. On the other hand, under the Akaike and Schwarz criteria, the lower the value of these statistics, the better is the model.

Of course, all these criteria are meaningful if we want to compare two or more models. Thus, if you compare the model in Table 13.4 with the model in Table 13.6, which has the experience-squared as an additional regressor, we see that the model in Table 13.6 is preferable to the one in Table 13.4 on the basis of the three criteria.

Incidentally, note that in both models the R^2 values seem "low," but such low values are typically observed in cross-section data with a large number of observations. However, note that this "low" R^2 value is statistically significant, since in both models the computed F statistic is highly significant (recall the relationship between F and R^2 discussed in Chapter 8).

Let us continue with the expanded model given in Table 13.6. Although the model looks satisfactory, let us explore a couple of points. First, since we are dealing with cross-section data, there is every chance that the model suffers from heteroscedasticity. So, we need to find out if this is the case. We applied several of the tests of heteroscedasticity discussed in Chapter 11 and found that the model does in fact suffer from heteroscedasticity. The reader should verify this assertion.

To correct for the observed heteroscedasticity, we can obtain *White's heteroscedasticity-consistent standard errors,* which were discussed in Chapter 11. The results are given in the following table.

TABLE 13.7
***EViews* Results Using White's Corrected STD Errors**

Dependent Variable: LW
Method: Least Squares
Sample: 1-1,289
Included observations: 1,289
White's Heteroscedasticity-Consistent Standard Errors and Covariance

	Coefficient	Std. Error	*t* Statistic	Prob.
C	0.912279	0.077524	11.76777	0.0000
EDU	0.079867	0.005640	14.15988	0.0000
EXP	0.036659	0.003789	9.675724	0.0000
FE	-0.228848	0.025764	-8.882625	0.0000
NW	-0.121805	0.033698	-3.614573	0.0003
UN	0.199957	0.029985	6.668458	0.0000
WK	0.222549	0.031301	7.110051	0.0000
EXP*EXP	-0.000611	9.44E-05	-6.470218	0.0000

R-squared	0.399277	Mean dependent var.	2.342416
Adjusted *R*-squared	0.395995	S.D. dependent var.	0.586356
S.E. of regression	0.455703	Akaike info criterion	1.272234
Sum squared resid.	266.0186	Schwarz criterion	1.304269
Log likelihood	-811.9549	Hannan-Quinn criter.	1.284259
F-statistic	121.6331	Durbin-Watson stat.	1.971753
Prob. (*F*-statistic)	0.000000		

As you would expect, there are some changes in the estimated standard errors, although this does not change the conclusion that all the regressors are important, both individually as well as collectively, in explaining the behavior of relative wages.

Let us now examine if the error terms are normally distributed. The histogram of the residuals obtained from the model in Table 13.7 is shown in Figure 13.5. The Jarque–Bera

FIGURE 13.5 A histogram of the residuals obtained from the regression in Table 13.7

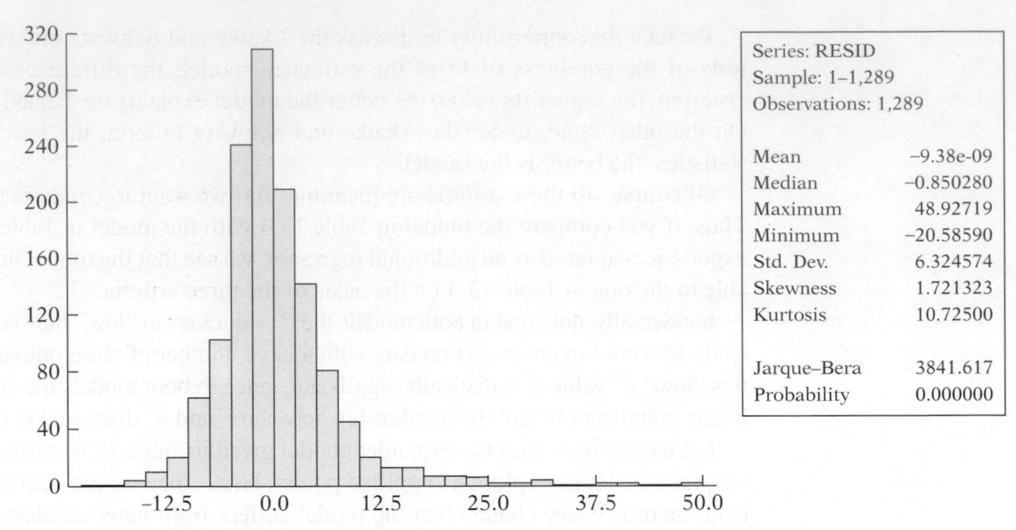

statistic rejects the hypothesis that the errors are normally distributed, for the JB statistic is high and the p value is practically zero: Note that for a normally distributed variable, the skewness and kurtosis coefficients are, respectively, 0 and 3.

Now what? Our hypothesis testing procedure thus far has rested on the assumption that the disturbance, or error, term in the regression model is normally distributed. Does this mean that we cannot legitimately use the t and F tests to test hypotheses in our wage regression?

The answer is **no.** As noted in the chapter, the OLS estimators are asymptotically normally distributed with the caveat noted in the chapter, namely that the error term has finite variance, is homoscedastic, and the mean value of the error term, given the values of the explanatory variables, is zero. As a result, we can continue to use the usual t and F tests, provided the sample is reasonably large. In passing it may be noted that we did not need the normality assumption to obtain OLS estimators. Even without the normality assumption the OLS estimators are best linear unbiased estimators (BLUE) under the Gauss–Markov assumptions.

How large is a large sample? There is no definitive answer to this question, but the sample size of 1,289 observations in our wage regression seems reasonably large.

Are there any "outliers" in our wage regression? Some idea about this can be gleaned from the graph in Figure 13.6, which gives the actual and estimated values of the dependent

FIGURE 13.6 Residuals vs estimated values of the dependent variable, ln wage

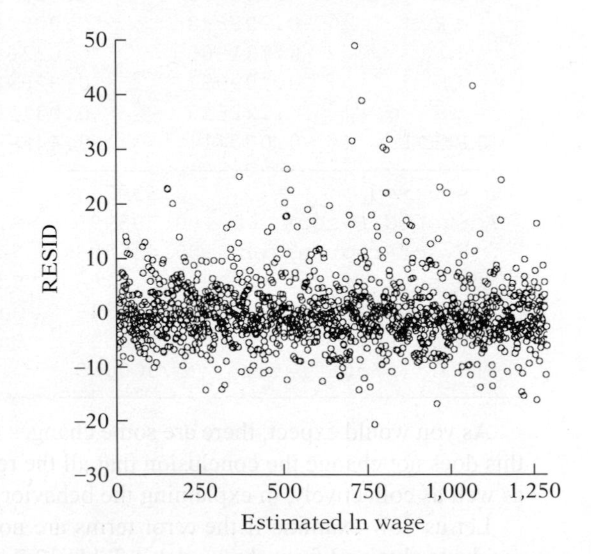

variable (ln wage) and the residuals, which are the differences between the actual and estimated values of the regressand.

Although the mean value of the residuals is always zero (why?), the graph in Figure 13.6 shows that there are several residuals that seem large (in absolute value) compared with the bulk of the residuals. It is possible that there are outliers in the data. We provide the raw statistics on the three quantitative variables in Table 13.8 to aid the reader in deciding whether there are indeed outliers.

TABLE 13.8

Sample: 1-1,289

	W	EDU	EXP
Mean	12.36585	13.14507	18.78976
Median	10.08000	12.00000	18.00000
Maximum	64.08000	20.00000	56.00000
Minimum	0.840000	0.000000	0.000000
Std. Dev.	7.896350	2.813823	11.66284
Skewness	1.848114	0.290381	0.375669
Kurtosis	7.836565	5.977464	2.327946
Jarque-Bera	1990.134	494.2552	54.57664
Probability	0.000000	0.000000	0.000000
Sum	15939.58	16944.00	24220.00
Sum Sq. Dev.	80309.82	10197.87	175196.0
Observations	1,289	1,289	1,289

2. Real Consumption Function for the United States, 1947–2000

In Chapter 10 we considered the consumption function for the U.S. for the years 1947–2000. The specific form of the consumption function we considered was:

$$\ln \text{TC}_t = \beta_1 + \beta_2 \ln \text{YD}_t + \beta_3 \ln \text{W} + \beta_4 \text{Interest}_t + u_t \qquad (13.11.3)$$

Where TC, YD, W, and Interest are, respectively, total consumption expenditure, personal disposable income, wealth, and interest rate, all in real terms. The results based on our data are as follows:

TABLE 13.9
Results of Regression Equation (13.11.3)

Method: Least Squares
Sample: 1947-2000
Included observations: 54

	Coefficient	Std. Error	*t* Statistic	Prob.
C	-0.467711	0.042778	-10.93343	0.0000
LOG(YD)	0.804873	0.017498	45.99836	0.0000
LOG(WEALTH)	0.201270	0.017593	11.44060	0.0000
INTEREST	-0.002689	0.000762	-3.529265	0.0009

R-squared	0.999560	Mean dependent var.	7.826093
Adjusted *R*-squared	0.999533	S.D. dependent var.	0.552368
S.E. of regression	0.011934	Akaike info criterion	-5.947703
Sum squared resid.	0.007121	Schwarz criterion	-5.800371
Log likelihood	164.5880	Hannan-Quinn criter.	-5.890883
F-statistc	37832.59	Durbin-Watson stat.	1.289219
Prob. (*F*-statistic)	0.000000		

Since TC, YD, and Wealth enter in logarithmic form, the estimated slope coefficients of YD and Wealth are, respectively, income and wealth elasticities. As you would expect, these elasticities are positive and are highly statistically significant. Numerically, the income and wealth elasticities are about 0.80 and 0.20. The coefficient of the interest rate variable represents semielasticity (why?). Holding other variables constant, the results show that if the interest rate goes up by 1 percentage point, on average, real consumption expenditure goes down by about 0.27 percent. Note that the estimated semielasticity is also highly statistically significant.

Look at some of the summary statistics. The R^2 value is very high, almost reaching 100 percent. The F value is also highly statistically significant, suggesting that, not only individually, but also collectively, all the explanatory variables have a significant impact on consumption expenditure.

The Durbin–Watson statistic, however, suggests that errors in the model are serially correlated. If we consult the Durbin–Watson tables (Table D.5 in Appendix D), we see that for 55 observations (the closest number to 54) and three explanatory variables, the lower and upper 5 percent critical d values are 1.452 and 1.681. Since the observed d in our example, 1.2892, is below the lower critical d values, we may conclude that the errors in our consumption function are positively correlated. This should not be a surprising finding, for most time series regressions suffer from autocorrelation.

But before we accept this conclusion, let us find out if there are any specification errors. As we know, sometimes autocorrelation may be apparent because we have omitted some important variables. To see if this is the case, we consider the regression obtained in Table 13.10.

TABLE 13.10

Dependent Variable: LTC
Method: Least Squares
Sample: 1947–2000
Included observations: 54

	Coefficient	Std. Error	*t* Statistic	Prob.
C	2.689644	0.566034	4.751737	0.0000
LYD	0.512836	0.054056	9.487076	0.0000
LW	-0.205281	0.074068	-2.771510	0.0079
INTEREST	-0.001162	0.000661	-1.759143	0.0848
LYD*LW	0.039901	0.007141	5.587986	0.0000

R-squared	0.999731	Mean dependent var.	7.826093
Adjusted *R*-squared	0.999709	S.D. dependent var.	0.552368
S.E. of regression	0.009421	Akaike info criterion	-6.403689
Sum squared resid.	0.004349	Schwarz criterion	-6.219524
Log likelihood	177.8996	Hannan-Quinn criter.	-6.332663
F-statistic	45534.94	Durbin-Watson Stat.	1.530268
Prob. (*F*-statistic)	0.000000		

The additional variable in this model is the interaction of the logs of disposable income and wealth. This interaction term is highly significant. Notice that now the interest variable has become less significant (p value of about 8 percent), although it retains its negative sign. But now the Durbin–Watson d value has increased from about 1.28 to about 1.53.

The 5 percent critical d values now are 1.378 and 1.721. The observed d value of 1.53 lies between these values, suggesting that, on the basis of the Durbin–Watson statistic, we cannot determine whether or not we have autocorrelation. However, the observed d value is closer to the upper limit *d* value. As noted in the chapter on autocorrelation, some authors suggest using the upper limit of the *d* statistic as approximately the true significance limit; therefore, if the computed *d* value is below the upper limit, there is evidence of positive autocorrelation. By that criterion, in the present instance we can conclude that our model suffers from positive autocorrelation.

We also applied the Breusch–Godfrey test of autocorrelation that we discussed in Chapter 12. Adding the two lagged terms of the estimated residuals in Equation (12.6.15) to the model in Table 13.9, we obtained the following results:

TABLE 13.11

Breusch-Godfrey Serial Correlation LM Test:

F-statistic	3.254131	Prob. *F*(2,48)	0.0473
Obs**R*-squared	6.447576	Prob. chi-square (2)	0.0398

Dependent Variable: RESID
Method: Least Squares
Sample: 1947–2000
Included observations: 54
Presample missing value lagged residuals set to zero.

	Coefficient	Std. Error	*t* Statistic	Prob.
C	-0.006514	0.041528	-0.156851	0.8760
LYD	-0.004197	0.017158	-0.244619	0.8078
LW	0.004191	0.017271	0.242674	0.8093
INTEREST	0.000116	0.000736	0.156964	0.8759
RESID(-1)	0.385190	0.151581	2.541147	0.0143
RESID(-2)	-0.165609	0.154695	-1.070556	0.2897

R-squared	0.119400	Mean dependent var.	-9.02E-17
Adjusted *R* squared	0.027670	S.D. dependent var.	0.011591
S.E. of regression	0.011430	Akaike info criterion	-6.000781
Sum squared resid.	0.006271	Schwarz criterion	-5.779782
Log likelihood	168.0211	Hannan-Quinn criter.	-5.915550
F-statistic	1.301653	Durbin-Watson Stat.	1.848014
Prob. (*F*-statistic)	0.279040		

The *F* reported at the top tests the hypothesis that the two lagged residuals included in the model have zero values. This hypothesis is rejected because the *F* is significant at about the 5 percent level.

To sum up, it seems that there is autocorrelation in the error term. We can apply one or more procedures discussed in Chapter 12 to remove autocorrelation. But to save space, we leave that task to the reader.

In Table 13.12 we report the results of regression analysis that present the HAC or Newey–West standard errors that take into account the autocorrelation. Our sample size of 54 observations is large enough to use the HAC standard errors.

If you compare these results with those given in Table 13.9, you will observe that the regression coefficients remain the same, but that the standard errors are somewhat different.

In this chapter we discussed Chow's prediction failure test. We have a sample period that extends from 1947 to 2000. Over this period, we have had several business cycles, mostly of short durations. For example, there was a recession in 1990 and another one in 2000. Is

TABLE 13.12

Dependent Variable: LTC
Method: Least Squares
Sample: 1947-2000
Included observations: 54
Newey-West HAC Standard Errors and Covariance (lag truncation = 3)

	Coefficient	Std. Error	*t* Statistic	Prob.
C	-0.467714	0.043937	-10.64516	0.0000
LYD	0.804871	0.017117	47.02132	0.0000
LW	0.201272	0.015447	13.02988	0.0000
INTEREST	-0.002689	0.000880	-3.056306	0.0036

R-squared	0.999560	Mean dependent var.	7.826093
Adjusted *R*-squared	0.999533	S.D. dependent var.	0.552368
S.E. of regression	0.011934	Akaike info criterion	-5.947707
Sum squared resid.	0.007121	Schwarz criterion	-5.800374
Log likelihood	164.5881	Hannan-Quinn criter.	-5.890886
F-statistic	37832.71	Durbin-Watson Stat.	1.289237
Prob. (*F*-statistic)	0.000000		

the behavior of consumer expenditure in relation to income, wealth, and the interest rate different during recessions?

To shed light on this question, let us consider the 1990 recession and apply Chow's prediction failure test. The details of this test have already been discussed in the chapter. Using Chow's predictive failure test in *EViews,* version 6, we obtain the results given in Table 13.13.

TABLE 13.13
Chow's Test of Predictive Failure

Chow's Forecast Test: Forecast from 1991 to 2000

F-statistic	1.957745	Prob. *F* (10,40)	0.0652
Log likelihood ratio	21.51348	Prob. chi-square (10)	0.0178

Dependent Variable: LTC
Method: Least Squares
Sample: 1947–1990
Included observations: 44

	Coefficient	Std. Error	*t* Statistic	Prob.
C	-0.287952	0.095089	-3.028236	0.0043
LYD	0.853172	0.028473	29.96474	0.0000
LW	0.141513	0.033085	4.277239	0.0001
INTEREST	-0.002060	0.000804	-2.562790	0.0143

R-squared	0.999496	Mean dependent var.	7.659729
Adjusted *R*-squared	0.999458	S.D. dependent var.	0.469580
S.E. of regression	0.010933	Akaike info criterion	-6.107640
Sum squared resid.	0.004781	Schwarz criterion	-5.945441
Log likelihood	138.3681	Hannan-Quinn criter.	-6.047489
F-statistic	26430.49	Durbin-Watson Stat.	1.262748
Prob. (*F*-statistic)	0.000000		

The F statistic given in the top portion of Table 13.13 suggests that there probably is not a substantial difference in the consumption function pre- and post-1990, for its p value is not significant at the 5 percent level. But if you choose the 10 percent level of significance, the F value is statistically significant.

We can look at this problem differently. In Chapter 8 we discussed a test of parameter stability. To see if there has been any statistically significant change in the consumption function regression coefficients, we used the Chow test discussed in Section 8.7 of Chapter 8 and obtained the results given in Table 13.14.

TABLE 13.14
Chow's Test of Parameter Stability

Chow Breakpoint Test: 1990
Null Hypothesis: No breaks at specified breakpoints
Varying regressors: All equation variables
Equation Sample: 1947-2000

F-statistic	4.254054	Prob. *F*(4,46)	0.0052
Log likelihood ratio	16.99654	Prob. chi-square (4)	0.0019
Wald statistic	17.01622	Prob. chi-square (4)	0.0019

Apparently, it seems that the consumption function pre- and post-1990 are statistically different, for the computed F statistic, following Eq. (8.7.4), is highly statistically significant because the p value is only 0.0052.

The reader is encouraged to apply Chow's parameter stability and predictive failure tests to determine if the consumption function pre- and post-2000 has changed. To do this, you will have to extend the data beyond 2000. Also note that to apply these tests the number of observations must be greater than the number of coefficients estimated.

We have exhausted all of the diagnostic tests that we can apply to our consumption data. But the analysis provided thus far should give you a fairly good idea about how one can apply the various tests.

13.12 Non-Normal Errors and Stochastic Regressors

In this section we discuss two topics that are of a somewhat advanced nature, namely, non-normal distribution of the error term, and stochastic, or random, regressors and their practical importance.

1. What Happens If the Error Term Is Not Normally Distributed?

In the *classical normal linear regression model* (CNLRM) discussed in Chapter 4, we assumed that the error term u follows the normal distribution. We invoked the **central limit theorem (CLT)** to justify the normality assumption. Because of this assumption, we were able to establish that the OLS estimators are also normally distributed. As a result, we were able to do hypothesis testing using the t and F tests regardless of the sample size. We also discussed using the **Jarque–Bera** and **Anderson–Darling** normality tests to find out if the estimated errors are normally distributed in any practical application.

What happens if the errors are *not* normally distributed? It can be stated that the OLS estimators are still BLUE, that is, they are unbiased and in the class of linear estimators they show minimum variance. Intuitively, this should not be surprising, for to establish the Gauss–Markov (BLUE) theorem we did not need the normality assumption.

Then what is the problem?

The problem is that we need the **sampling,** or **probability, distributions** of the OLS estimators. Without that we cannot engage in any kind of hypothesis testing regarding the true values of these estimators. As shown in Chapters 3 and 7, the OLS estimators are linear funtions of the dependent variable Y, and Y itself is a linear function of the stochastic error term u, assuming that the explanatory variables are non-stochastic, or fixed in repeated sampling. Ultimately, then, we need the probability distribution of u.

As noted above, the *classical normal linear regression model* (CNLRM) assumes that the error term follows the normal distribution (with zero mean and constant variance). Using the **central limit theorem (CLT)** to justify the normality of the error term, we were able to show that the OLS estimators themselves are normally distributed with means and variance discussed in Chapters 4 and 7. This in turn allowed us to use the t and F statistics in hypothesis testing in small, or finite, samples as well as in large samples. Therefore, the role of the normality assumption is very critical, especially in small samples.

But what if we cannot maintain the normality assumption on the basis of various normality tests? What then? We have two choices. The first is **bootstrapping** and the second is to invoke **large,** or **asymptotic, sample theory.**

A discussion of bootstrapping, which is gradually seeping into applied econometrics, will take us far afield. The basic idea underlying bootstrapping is to *churn* (or regurgitate) a given sample over and over again and then obtain the sampling distributions of the parameters of interest (OLS estimators for our purpose). How this is done in practice is best left for references.[52] By the way, the term bootstrapping comes from the commonly used expression, "to pull oneself up by one's own bootstrap."

The other approach to deal with non-normal error terms is to use asymptotic, or large sample theory. As a matter of fact, a glimpse of this was given in Appendix 3A.7 in Chapter 3, where we showed that the OLS estimators are **consistent.** As discussed in **Appendix A,** an estimator is consistent if it approaches the true value of the estimator as the sample size gets larger and larger (see Figure A.11 in Appendix A).

But how does that help us in hypothesis testing? Can we still use the t and F tests? It can be shown that under the Gauss–Markov assumptions the OLS estimators are **asymptotically normally distributed** with the means and variances discussed in Chapters 4 and 7.[53] As a result, the t and F tests developed under the normality assumption are *approximately* valid in large samples. The approximation becomes quite good as the sample size increases.[54]

2. Stochastic Explanatory Variables

In Chapter 3 we introduced the classical linear (in parameter) regression model under some simplifying assumptions. One of the assumptions was that the explanatory variables, or regressors, were either fixed or non-stochastic, or if stochastic, they were independent of the error term. We called the former case the *fixed regressor case* and the latter the *random regressor case.*

[52]For an informal discussion, see Christopher Z. Mooney and Robert D. Duval, *Bootstrapping: A Nonparametric Approach to Statistical Inference,* Sage University Press, California, 1993. For a more formal textbook discussion, see Russell Davidson and James G. MacKinnon, *Econometric Theory and Methods,* Oxford University Press, New York, 2004, pp. 159–166.

[53]Recall the Gauss–Markov assumptions, namely, the expected value of the error term is zero, the error term and each of the explanatory variables are independent, the error variance is homoscedastic, and there is no autocorrelation in the error term. It is also assumed that the variance-covariance matrix of the explanatory variables is finite. We can also relax the condition of independence between the error term and the regressors and assume the weaker condition that they are uncorrelated.

[54]The proof of asymptotic normality of OLS estimators is beyond the scope of this book. See James H. Stock and Mark W. Watson, *Introduction to Econometrics,* 2d ed., Pearson/Addison Wesley, Boston, 2007, pp. 710–711.

In the *fixed regressor case,* we already know the properties of the OLS estimators (see Chapters 5 and 8). In the *random regressor case,* if we proceed with the assumption that our analysis is *conditional* on the given values of the regressors, the properties of OLS estimators that we have studied under the fixed regressor case continue to hold true.

If in the random regressor case we assume that these regressors and the error term are independently distributed, the OLS estimators are still unbiased but they are no longer efficient.[55]

Things get complicated if the error term is not normally distributed, or regressors are stochastic, or both. Here it is difficult to make any general statements regarding the finite-sample properties of the OLS estimators. However, under certain conditions, we can invoke the central limit theorem to establish the asymptotic normality of OLS estimators. Although beyond the scope of this book, the proofs can be found elsewhere.[56]

13.13 A Word to the Practitioner

We have covered a lot of ground in this chapter. There is no question that model building is an art as well as a science. A practical researcher may be bewildered by theoretical niceties and an array of diagnostic tools. But it is well to keep in mind Martin Feldstein's caution that "The applied econometrician, like the theorist, soon discovers from experience that a useful model is not one that is 'true' or 'realistic' but one that is parsimonious, plausible and informative."[57]

Peter Kennedy of Simon Fraser University in Canada advocates the following "Ten Commandments of Applied Econometrics":[58]

1. Thou shalt use common sense and economic theory.
2. Thou shalt ask the right questions (i.e., put relevance before mathematical elegance).
3. Thou shalt know the context (do not perform ignorant statistical analysis).
4. Thou shalt inspect the data.
5. Thou shalt not worship complexity. Use the **KISS principle,** that is, *keep it stochastically simple.*
6. Thou shalt look long and hard at thy results.
7. Thou shalt beware the costs of data mining.
8. Thou shalt be willing to compromise (do not worship textbook prescriptions).
9. Thou shalt not confuse significance with substance (do not confuse statistical significance with practical significance).
10. Thou shalt confess in the presence of sensitivity (that is, anticipate criticism).

You may want to read Kennedy's paper fully to appreciate the conviction with which he advocates the above ten commandments. Some of these commandments may sound tongue-in-cheek, but there is a grain of truth in each.

[55]For technical details, see William H. Greene, *Econometric Analysis,* 6th ed., Pearson/Prentice-Hall, New Jersey, 2008, pp. 49–50.

[56]See Greene, op. cit.

[57]Martin S. Feldstein, "Inflation, Tax Rules and Investment: Some Econometric Evidence," *Econometrica,* vol. 30, 1982, p. 829.

[58]Peter Kennedy, op. cit., pp. 17–18.

Summary and Conclusions

1. The assumption of the CLRM that the econometric model used in analysis is correctly specified has two meanings. One, there are no **equation specification errors,** and two, there are no **model specification errors.** In this chapter the major focus was on equation specification errors.
2. The equation specification errors discussed in this chapter were (1) omission of an important variable(s), (2) inclusion of a superfluous variable(s), (3) adoption of the wrong function form, (4) incorrect specification of the error term u_i, and (5) errors of measurement in the regressand and regressors.
3. When legitimate variables are omitted from a model, the consequences can be very serious: The OLS estimators of the variables retained in the model are not only biased but inconsistent as well. Additionally, the variances and standard errors of these coefficients are incorrectly estimated, thereby vitiating the usual hypothesis-testing procedures.
4. The consequences of including irrelevant variables in the model are fortunately less serious: The estimators of the coefficients of the relevant as well as "irrelevant" variables remain unbiased as well as consistent, and the error variance σ^2 remains correctly estimated. The only problem is that the estimated variances tend to be larger than necessary, thereby making for less precise estimation of the parameters. That is, the confidence intervals tend to be larger than necessary.
5. To detect equation specification errors, we considered several tests, such as (1) examination of residuals, (2) the Durbin–Watson d statistic, (3) Ramsey's RESET test, and (4) the Lagrange multiplier test.
6. A special kind of specification error is errors of measurement in the values of the regressand and regressors. If there are errors of measurement in the regressand only, the OLS estimators are unbiased as well as consistent but they are less efficient. If there are errors of measurement in the regressors, the OLS estimators are biased as well as inconsistent.
7. Even if errors of measurement are detected or suspected, the remedies are often not easy. The use of instrumental or proxy variables is theoretically attractive but not always practical. Thus it is very important in practice that the researcher be careful in stating the sources of his/her data, how they were collected, what definitions were used, etc. Data collected by official agencies often come with several footnotes and the researcher should bring those to the attention of the reader.
8. Model mis-specification errors can be as serious as equation specification errors. In particular, we distinguished between nested and non-nested models. To decide on the appropriate model we discussed the non-nested, or encompassing, F test and the Davidson–MacKinnon J test and pointed out the limitations of each test.
9. In choosing an empirical model in practice researchers have used a variety of criteria. We discussed some of these, such as the Akaike and Schwarz information criteria, Mallows's C_p criterion, and forecast χ^2 criterion. We discussed the advantages and disadvantages of these criteria and also warned the reader that these criteria are not absolute but are adjunct to a careful specification analysis.
10. We also discussed these additional topics: (1) outliers, leverage, and influence; (2) recursive least squares; and (3) Chow's prediction failure test. We discussed the role of each in applied work.
11. We discussed briefly two special cases, namely, non-normality of the stochastic error term and random regressors and the role of asymptotic, or large, sample theory in situations where small, or finite, sample properties of OLS estimators canot be established.

12. We concluded this chapter by discussing Peter Kennedy's "ten commandments of applied econometrics." The point of these commandments is to ask the researcher to look beyond the purely technical aspects of econometrics.

EXERCISES

Questions

13.1. Refer to the demand function for chicken estimated in Eq. (8.6.23). Considering the attributes of a good model discussed in Section 13.1, could you say that this demand function is "correctly" specified?

13.2. Suppose that the true model is

$$Y_i = \beta_1 X_i + u_i \tag{1}$$

but instead of fitting this regression through the origin you routinely fit the usual intercept-present model:

$$Y_i = \alpha_0 + \alpha_1 X_i + v_i \tag{2}$$

Assess the consequences of this specification error.

13.3. Continue with Exercise 13.2 but assume that it is model (2) that is the truth. Discuss the consequences of fitting the mis-specified model (1).

13.4. Suppose that the "true" model is

$$Y_i = \beta_1 + \beta_2 X_{2i} + u_t \tag{1}$$

but we add an "irrelevant" variable X_3 to the model (irrelevant in the sense that the true β_3 coefficient attached to the variable X_3 is zero) and estimate

$$Y_i = \beta_1 + \beta_2 X_{2i} + \beta_3 X_{3i} + v_i \tag{2}$$

a. Would the R^2 and the adjusted R^2 for model (2) be larger than that for model (1)?

b. Are the estimates of β_1 and β_2 obtained from model (2) unbiased?

c. Does the inclusion of the "irrelevant" variable X_3 affect the variances of $\hat{\beta}_1$ and $\hat{\beta}_2$?

13.5. Consider the following "true" (Cobb–Douglas) production function:

$$\ln Y_i = \alpha_0 + \alpha_1 \ln L_{1i} + \alpha_2 \ln L_{2i} + \alpha_3 \ln K_i + u_i$$

where Y = output
L_1 = production labor
L_2 = nonproduction labor
K = capital

But suppose the regression actually used in empirical investigation is

$$\ln Y_i = \beta_0 + \beta_1 \ln L_{1i} + \beta_2 \ln K_i + u_i$$

On the assumption that you have cross-sectional data on the relevant variables,

a. Will $E(\hat{\beta}_1) = \alpha_1$ and $E(\hat{\beta}_2) = \alpha_3$?

b. Will the answer in (*a*) hold if it is known that L_2 is an *irrelevant* input in the production function? Show the necessary derivations.

13.6. Refer to Eqs. (13.3.4) and (13.3.5). As you can see, $\hat{\alpha}_2$, although biased, has a smaller variance than $\hat{\beta}_2$, which is unbiased. How would you decide on the trade-off between bias and smaller variance? *Hint:* The MSE (mean-square error) for the two estimators is expressed as

$$\text{MSE}(\hat{\alpha}_2) = \left(\sigma^2 \Big/ \sum x_{2i}^2\right) + \beta_3^2 b_{32}^2$$

$$= \text{sampling variance} + \text{square of bias}$$

$$\text{MSE}(\hat{\beta}_2) = \sigma^2 \Big/ \sum x_2^2 (1 - r_{23}^2)$$

On MSE, see **Appendix A.**

13.7. Show that β estimated from either Eq. (13.5.1) or Eq. (13.5.3) provides an unbiased estimate of true β.

13.8. Following Friedman's permanent income hypothesis, we may write

$$Y_i^* = \alpha + \beta X_i^* \qquad (1)$$

where Y_i^* = "permanent" consumption expenditure and X_i^* = "permanent" income. Instead of observing the "permanent" variables, we observe

$$Y_i = Y_i^* + u_i$$

$$X_i = X_i^* + v_i$$

where Y_i and X_i are the quantities that can be observed or measured and where u_i and v_i are measurement errors in Y^* and X^*, respectively.

Using the observable quantities, we can write the consumption function as

$$Y_i = \alpha + \beta(X_i - v_i) + u_i$$

$$= \alpha + \beta X_i + (u_i - \beta v_i) \qquad (2)$$

Assuming that (1) $E(u_i) = E(v_i) = 0$, (2) $\text{var}(u_i) = \sigma_u^2$ and $\text{var}(v_i) = \sigma_v^2$, (3) $\text{cov}(Y_i^*, u_i) = 0$, $\text{cov}(X_i^*, v_i) = 0$, and (4) $\text{cov}(u_i, X_i^*) = \text{cov}(v_i, Y_i^*) = \text{cov}(u_i, v_i) = 0$, show that in large samples β estimated from Eq. (2) can be expressed as

$$\text{plim}(\hat{\beta}) = \frac{\beta}{1 + (\sigma_v^2/\sigma_{X^*}^2)}$$

a. What can you say about the nature of the bias in $\hat{\beta}$?

b. If the sample size increases indefinitely, will the estimated β tend toward equality with the true β?

13.9. *Capital asset pricing model.* The capital asset pricing model (CAPM) of modern investment theory postulates the following relationship between the average rate of return of a security (common stock), measured over a certain period, and the volatility of the security, called the *beta coefficient* (volatility is measure of risk):

$$\bar{R}_i = \alpha_1 + \alpha_2(\beta_i) + u_i \qquad (1)$$

where $\bar{R}_i$ = average rate of return of security i

β_i = true beta coefficient of security i

u_i = stochastic disturbance term

The true β_i is not directly observable but is measured as follows:

$$r_{it} = \alpha_1 + \beta^* r_{m_t} + e_t \qquad (2)$$

where r_{it} = rate of return of security i for time t

r_{m_t} = market rate of return for time t (this rate is the rate of return on some broad market index, such as the S&P index of industrial securities)

e_t = residual term

and where β^* is an estimate of the "true" beta coefficient. In practice, therefore, instead of estimating Eq. (1), one estimates

$$\bar{R}_i = \alpha_1 + \alpha_2(\beta_i^*) + u_i \tag{3}$$

where β_i^* are obtained from the regression (2). But since β_i^* are estimated, the relationship between true β and β^* can be written as

$$\beta_i^* = \beta_i + v_i \tag{4}$$

where v_i can be called the *error of measurement.*

a. What will be the effect of this error of measurement on the estimate of α_2?

b. Will the α_2 estimated from Eq. (3) provide an unbiased estimate of true α_2? If not, is it a consistent estimate of α_2? If not, what remedial measures do you suggest?

13.10. Consider the model

$$Y_i = \beta_1 + \beta_2 X_{2i} + u_i \tag{1}$$

To find out whether this model is mis-specified because it omits the variable X_3 from the model, you decide to regress the residuals obtained from model (1) on the variable X_3 only. (*Note:* There is an intercept in this regression.) The Lagrange multiplier (LM) test, however, requires you to regress the residuals from model (1) on both X_2 and X_3 and a constant. Why is your procedure likely to be inappropriate?*

13.11. Consider the model

$$Y_i = \beta_1 + \beta_2 X_i^* + u_i$$

In practice we measure X_i^* by X_i such that

a. $X_i = X_i^* + 5$

b. $X_i = 3X_i^*$

c. $X_i = (X_i^* + \varepsilon_i)$, where ε_i is a purely random term with the usual properties

What will be the effect of these measurement errors on estimates of true β_1 and β_2?

13.12. Refer to the regression Eqs. (13.3.1) and (13.3.2). In a manner similar to Eq. (13.3.3) show that

$$E(\hat{\alpha}_1) = \beta_1 + \beta_3(\bar{X}_3 - b_{32}\bar{X}_2)$$

where b_{32} is the slope coefficient in the regression of the omitted variable X_3 on the included variable X_2.

13.13. Critically evaluate the following view expressed by Leamer:†

> My interest in metastatistics [i.e., theory of inference actually drawn from data] stems from my observations of economists at work. The opinion that econometric theory is

*See Maddala, op. cit., p. 477.

†Edward E. Leamer, *Specification Searches: Ad Hoc Inference with Nonexperimental Data*, John Wiley & Sons, New York, 1978, p. vi.

> irrelevant is held by an embarrassingly large share of the economic profession. The wide gap between econometric theory and econometric practice might be expected to cause professional tension. In fact, a calm equilibrium permeates our journals and our [professional] meetings. We comfortably divide ourselves into a celibate priesthood of statistical theorists, on the one hand, and a legion of inveterate sinner-data analysts, on the other. The priests are empowered to draw up lists of sins and are revered for the special talents they display. Sinners are not expected to avoid sins; they need only confess their errors openly.

13.14. Evaluate the following statement made by Henry Theil:*

> Given the present state of the art, the most sensible procedure is to interpret confidence coefficients and significance limits liberally when confidence intervals and test statistics are computed from the final regression of a regression strategy in the conventional way. That is, a 95 percent confidence coefficient may actually be an 80 percent confidence coefficient and a 1 percent significance level may actually be a 10 percent level.

13.15. Commenting on the econometric methodology practiced in the 1950s and early 1960s, Blaug stated:†

> . . . much of it [i.e., empirical research] is like playing tennis with the net down: instead of attempting to refute testable predictions, modern economists all too frequently are satisfied to demonstrate that the real world conforms to their predictions, thus replacing falsification [à la Popper], which is difficult, with verification, which is easy.

Do you agree with this view? You may want to peruse Blaug's book to learn more about his views.

13.16. According to Blaug, "There is no logic of proof but there is logic of disproof."‡ What does he mean by this?

13.17. Refer to the St. Louis model discussed in the text. Keeping in mind the problems associated with the nested F test, critically evaluate the results presented in regression (13.8.4).

13.18. Suppose the true model is

$$Y_i = \beta_1 + \beta_2 X_i + \beta_2 X_i^2 + \beta_3 X_i^3 + u_i$$

but you estimate

$$Y_i = \alpha_1 + \alpha_2 X_i + v_i$$

If you use observations of Y at $X = -3, -2, -1, 0, 1, 2, 3$, and estimate the "incorrect" model, what bias will result in these estimates?§

13.19. To see if the variable X_i^2 belongs in the model $Y_i = \beta_1 + \beta_2 X_i + u_i$, Ramsey's RESET test would estimate the linear model, obtaining the estimated Y_i values from this model [i.e., $\hat{Y}_i = \hat{\beta}_1 + \hat{\beta}_2 X_i$] and then estimating the model $Y_i = \alpha_1 + \alpha_2 X_i + \alpha_3 \hat{Y}_i^2 + v_i$ and testing the significance of α_3. Prove that, if $\hat{\alpha}_3$ turns out to be statistically significant in the preceding (RESET) equation, it is the same thing as estimating

*Henry Theil, *Principles of Econometrics,* John Wiley & Sons, New York, 1971, pp. 605–606.

†M. Blaug, *The Methodology of Economics. Or How Economists Explain,* Cambridge University Press, New York, 1980, p. 256.

‡Ibid., p. 14.

§Adapted from G. A. F., Sebeir, *Linear Regression Analysis,* John Wiley & Sons, New York, 1977, p. 176.

the following model directly: $Y_i = \beta_1 + \beta_2 X_i + \beta_3 X_i^2 + u_i$. (*Hint:* Substitute for $\hat{Y}_i$ in the RESET regression.)*

13.20. State with reason whether the following statements are true or false.†

a. An observation can be influential but not an outlier.

b. An observation can be an outlier but not influential.

c. An observation can be both influential and an outlier.

d. If in the model $Y_i = \beta_1 + \beta_2 X_i + \beta_3 X_i^2 + u_i \hat{\beta}_3$ turns out to be statistically significant, we should retain the linear term X_i even if $\hat{\beta}_2$ is statistically insignificant.

e. If you estimate the model $Y_i = \beta_1 + \beta_2 X_{2i} + \beta_3 X_{3i} + u_i$ or $Y_i = \alpha_1 + \beta_2 x_{2i} + \beta_3 x_{3i} + u_i$ by OLS, the estimated regression line is the same, where $x_{2i} = (X_{2i} - \bar{X}_2)$ and $x_{3i} = (X_{3i} - \bar{X}_3)$.

Empirical Exercises

13.21. Use the data for the demand for chicken given in Exercise 7.19. Suppose you are told that the true demand function is

$$\ln Y_t = \beta_1 + \beta_2 \ln X_{2t} + \beta_3 \ln X_{3t} + \beta_6 \ln X_{6t} + u_t \tag{1}$$

but you think differently and estimate the following demand function:

$$\ln Y_t = \alpha_1 + \alpha_2 \ln X_{2t} + \alpha_3 \ln X_{3t} + v_t \tag{2}$$

where Y = per capita consumption of chickens (lb)

X_2 = real disposable per capita income

X_3 = real retail price of chickens

X_6 = composite real price of chicken substitutes

a. Carry out RESET and LM tests of specification errors, assuming the demand function (1) just given is the truth.

b. Suppose $\hat{\beta}_6$ in Eq. (1) turns out to be statistically insignificant. Does that mean there is no specification error if we fit Eq. (2) to the data?

c. If $\hat{\beta}_6$ turns out to be insignificant, does that mean one should not introduce the price of a substitute product(s) as an argument in the demand function?

13.22. Continue with Exercise 13.21. Strictly for pedagogical purposes, assume that model (2) is the true demand function.

a. If we now estimate model (1), what type of specification error is committed in this instance?

b. What are the theoretical consequences of this specification error? Illustrate with the data at hand.

13.23. The true model is

$$Y_i^* = \beta_1 + \beta_2 X_i^* + u_i \tag{1}$$

but because of errors of measurement you estimate

$$Y_i = \alpha_1 + \alpha_2 X_i + v_i \tag{2}$$

where $Y_i = Y_i^* + \varepsilon_i$ and $X_i = X_i^* + w_i$, where ε_i and w_i are measurement errors.

*Adapted from Kerry Peterson, op. cit., pp. 184–185.

†Adapted from Norman R. Draper and Harry Smith, op. cit., pp. 606–607.

Using the data given in Table 13.2, document the consequences of estimating model (2) instead of the true model (1).

13.24. *Monte Carlo experiment.*[*] Ten individuals had weekly permanent income as follows: \$200, 220, 240, 260, 280, 300, 320, 340, 380, and 400. Permanent consumption (Y_i^*) was related to permanent income X_i^* as

$$Y_i^* = 0.8X_i^* \tag{1}$$

Each of these individuals had transitory income equal to 100 times a random number u_i drawn from a normal population with mean $= 0$ and $\sigma^2 = 1$ (i.e., standard normal variable). Assume that there is no transitory component in consumption. Thus, measured consumption and permanent consumption are the same.

a. Draw 10 random numbers from a normal population with zero mean and unit variance and obtain 10 numbers for measured income $X_i (= X_i^* + 100u_i)$.

b. Regress permanent (= measured) consumption on measured income using the data obtained in (*a*) and compare your results with those shown in Eq. (1). A priori, the intercept should be zero (why?). Is that the case? Why or why not?

c. Repeat (*a*) 100 times and obtain 100 regressions as shown in (*b*) and compare your results with the true regression (1). What general conclusions do you draw?

13.25. Refer to Exercise 8.26. With the definitions of the variables given there, consider the following two models to explain Y:

$$\text{Model A:} \quad Y_t = \alpha_1 + \alpha_2 X_{3t} + \alpha_3 X_{4t} + \alpha_4 X_{6t} + u_t$$

$$\text{Model B:} \quad Y_t = \beta_1 + \beta_2 X_{2t} + \beta_3 X_{5t} + \beta_4 X_{6t} + u_t$$

Using the nested F test, how will you choose between the two models?

13.26. Continue with Exercise 13.25. Using the J test, how would you decide between the two models?

13.27. Refer to Exercise 7.19, which is concerned with the demand for chicken in the United States. There you were given five models.

a. What is the difference between model 1 and model 2? If model 2 is correct and you estimate model 1, what kind of error is committed? Which test would you apply—equation specification error or model selection error? Show the necessary calculations.

b. Between models 1 and 5, which would you choose? Which test(s) do you use and why?

13.28. Refer to Table 8.11, which gives data on personal savings (Y) and personal disposable income (X) for the period 1970–2005. Now consider the following models:

$$\text{Model A:} \quad Y_t = \alpha_1 + \alpha_2 X_t + \alpha_3 X_{t-1} + u_t$$

$$\text{Model B:} \quad Y_t = \beta_1 + \beta_2 X_t + \beta_3 Y_{t-1} + u_t$$

How would you choose between these two models? State clearly the test procedure(s) you use and show all the calculations. Suppose someone contends that the interest rate variable belongs in the savings function. How would you test this? Collect data on the 3-month treasury bill rate as a proxy for the interest and demonstrate your answer.

[*] Adapted from Christopher Dougherty, *Introduction to Econometrics,* Oxford University Press, New York, 1992, pp. 253–256.

13.29. Use the data in Exercise 13.28. To familiarize yourself with recursive least squares, estimate the savings functions for 1970–1981, 1970–1985, 1970–1990, and 1970–1995. Comment on the stability of estimated coefficients in the savings functions.

13.30. Continue with Exercise 13.29, but now use the updated data in Table 8.10.

a. Suppose you estimate the savings function for 1970–1981. Using the parameters thus estimated and the personal disposable income data from 1982–2000, estimate the predicted savings for the latter period and use Chow's prediction failure test to find out if it rejects the hypothesis that the savings function between the two time periods has not changed.

b. Now estimate the savings function for the data from 2000–2005. Compare the results to the function for the 1982–2000 period using the same method as above (Chow's prediction failure test). Is there a significant change in the savings function between the two periods?

13.31. *Omission of a variable in the K-variable regression model.* Refer to Eq. (13.3.3), which shows the bias in omitting the variable X_3 from the model $Y_i = \beta_1 + \beta_2 X_{2i} + \beta_3 X_{3i} + u_i$. This can be generalized as follows: In the k-variable model $Y_i = \beta_1 + \beta_2 X_{2i} + \cdots + \beta_k X_{ki} + u_i$, suppose we omit the variable X_k. Then it can be shown that the omitted variable bias of the slope coefficient of included variable X_j is:

$$E(\hat{\beta}_j) = \beta_j + \beta_k b_{kj} \qquad j = 2, 3, \ldots, (k-1)$$

where b_{kj} is the (partial) slope coefficient of X_j in the auxiliary regression of the excluded variable X_k on all the explanatory variables included in the model.*

Refer to Exercise 13.21. Find out the bias of the coefficients in Eq. (1) if we excluded the variable $\ln X_6$ from the model. Is this exclusion serious? Show the necessary calculations.

Appendix 13A

13A.1 The Proof that $E(b_{12}) = \beta_2 + \beta_3 b_{32}$ [Equation (13.3.3)]

In the deviation form the three-variable population regression model can be written as

$$y_i = \beta_2 x_{2i} + \beta_3 x_{3i} + (u_i - \bar{u}) \tag{1}$$

First multiplying by x_2 and then by x_3, the usual normal equations are

$$\sum y_i x_{2i} = \beta_2 \sum x_{2i}^2 + \beta_3 \sum x_{2i} x_{3i} + \sum x_{2i}(u_i - \bar{u}) \tag{2}$$

$$\sum y_i x_{3i} = \beta_2 \sum x_{2i} x_{3i} + \beta_3 \sum x_{3i}^2 + \sum x_{3i}(u_i - \bar{u}) \tag{3}$$

Dividing Eq. (2) by $\sum x_{2i}^2$ on both sides, we obtain

$$\frac{\sum y_i x_{2i}}{\sum x_{2i}^2} = \beta_2 + \beta_3 \frac{\sum x_{2i} x_{3i}}{\sum x_{2i}^2} + \frac{\sum x_{2i}(u_i - \bar{u})}{\sum x_{2i}^2} \tag{4}$$

*This can be generalized to the case where more than one relevant X variable is excluded from the model. On this, see Chandan Mukherjee et al., op. cit., p. 215.

Now recalling that

$$b_{12} = \frac{\sum y_i x_{2i}}{\sum x_{2i}^2}$$

$$b_{32} = \frac{\sum x_{2i} x_{3i}}{\sum x_{2i}^2}$$

Eq. (4) can be written as

$$b_{12} = \beta_2 + \beta_3 b_{32} + \frac{\sum x_{2i}(u_i - \bar{u})}{\sum x_{2i}^2} \tag{5}$$

Taking the expected value of Eq. (5) on both sides, we finally obtain

$$E(b_{12}) = \beta_2 + \beta_3 b_{32} \tag{6}$$

where use is made of the facts that (*a*) for a given sample, b_{32} is a known fixed quantity, (*b*) β_2 and β_3 are constants, and (*c*) u_i is uncorrelated with X_{2i} (as well as X_{3i}).

13A.2 The Consequences of Including an Irrelevant Variable: The Unbiasedness Property

For the true model (13.3.6), we have

$$\hat{\beta}_2 = \frac{\sum y x_2}{\sum x_2^2} \tag{1}$$

and we know that it is unbiased.

For the model (13.3.7), we obtain

$$\hat{\alpha}_2 = \frac{\left(\sum y x_2\right)\left(\sum x_3^2\right) - \left(\sum y x_3\right)\left(\sum x_2 x_3\right)}{\sum x_2^2 \sum x_3^2 - \left(\sum x_2 x_3\right)^2} \tag{2}$$

Now the true model in deviation form is

$$y_i = \beta_2 x_2 + (u_i - \bar{u}) \tag{3}$$

Substituting for y_i from model (3) into model (2) and simplifying, we obtain

$$\begin{aligned} E(\hat{\alpha}_2) &= \beta_2 \frac{\sum x_2^2 \sum x_3^2 - \left(\sum x_2 x_3\right)^2}{\sum x_2^2 \sum x_3^2 - \left(\sum x_2 x_3\right)^2} \\ &= \beta_2 \end{aligned} \tag{4}$$

that is, $\hat{\alpha}_2$ remains unbiased.

We also obtain

$$\hat{\alpha}_3 = \frac{\left(\sum y x_3\right)\left(\sum x_2^2\right) - \left(\sum y x_2\right)\left(\sum x_2 x_3\right)}{\sum x_2^2 \sum x_3^2 - \left(\sum x_2 x_3\right)^2} \tag{5}$$

Substituting for y_i from model (3) into model (5) and simplifying, we obtain

$$E(\hat{\alpha}_3) = \beta_2 \frac{\left[\left(\sum x_2 x_3\right)\left(\sum x_2^2\right) - \left(\sum x_2 x_3\right)\left(\sum x_2^2\right)\right]}{\sum x_2^2 \sum x_3^2 - \left(\sum x_2 x_3\right)^2} \tag{6}$$

$$= 0$$

which is its value in the true model since X_3 is absent from the true model.

13A.3 The Proof of Equation (13.5.10)

We have

$$Y = \alpha + \beta X_i^* + u_i \tag{1}$$

$$X_i = X_i^* + w_i \tag{2}$$

Therefore, in deviation form we obtain

$$y_i = \beta x_i^* + (u_i - \bar{u}) \tag{3}$$

$$x_i = x_i^* + (w_i - \bar{w}) \tag{4}$$

Now when we use

$$Y_i = \alpha + \beta X_i + u_i \tag{5}$$

we obtain

$$\hat{\beta} = \frac{\sum yx}{\sum x^2}$$

$$= \frac{\sum[\beta x^* + (u - \bar{u})][x^* + (w - \bar{w})]}{\sum[x^* + (w - \bar{w})]^2} \quad \text{using (3) and (4)}$$

$$= \frac{\beta \sum x^{*2} + \beta \sum x^*(w - \bar{w}) + \sum x^*(u - \bar{u}) + \sum(u - \bar{u})(w - \bar{w})}{\sum x^{*2} + 2\sum x^*(w - \bar{w}) + \sum(w - \bar{w})^2}$$

Since we cannot take expectation of this expression because the expectation of the ratio of two variables is not equal to the ratio of their expectations (*note:* the expectations operator E is a linear operator), first we divide each term of the numerator and the denominator by n and take the probability limit, plim (see **Appendix A** for details of plim), of

$$\hat{\beta} = \frac{(1/n)\left[\beta \sum x^{*2} + \beta \sum x^*(w - \bar{w}) + \sum x^*(u - \bar{u}) + \sum(u - \bar{u})(w - \bar{w})\right]}{(1/n)\left[\sum x^{*2} + 2\sum x^*(w - \bar{w}) + \sum(w - \bar{w})^2\right]}$$

Now the probability limit of the ratio of two variables is the ratio of their probability limits. Applying this rule and taking plim of each term, we obtain

$$\text{plim}\,\hat{\beta} = \frac{\beta \sigma_{X^*}^2}{\sigma_{X^*}^2 + \sigma_w^2}$$

where $\sigma_{X^*}^2$ and σ_w^2 are variances of X^* and w as sample size increases indefinitely and where we have used the fact that as the sample size increases indefinitely there is no correlation between the errors u and w as well as between them and the true X^*. From the preceding expression, we finally obtain

$$\text{plim}\,\hat{\beta} = \beta \left[\frac{1}{1 + \left(\sigma_w^2 / \sigma_{X^*}^2\right)}\right]$$

which is the required result.

13A.4 The Proof of Equation (13.6.2)

Since there is no intercept in the model, the estimate of α, according to the formula for the regression through the origin, is as follows:

$$\hat{\alpha} = \frac{\sum X_i Y_i}{\sum X_i^2} \tag{1}$$

Substituting for Y from the true model (13.2.8), we obtain

$$\hat{\alpha} = \frac{\sum X_i(\beta X_i u_i)}{\sum X_i^2} = \beta \frac{\sum X_i^2 u_i}{\sum X_i^2} \tag{2}$$

Statistical theory shows that if $\ln u_i \sim N(0, \sigma^2)$ then

$$u_i = \text{log normal}\left[e^{\sigma^2/2},\ e^{\sigma^2}\left(e^{\sigma^2-1}\right)\right] \tag{3}$$

Therefore,

$$\begin{aligned} E(\hat{\alpha}) &= \beta E\left(\frac{\sum X_i^2 u_i}{\sum X_i^2}\right) \\ &= \beta\left(E\frac{\left(X_1^2 u_1 + X_2^2 u_2 + \cdots + X_n^2 u_n\right)}{\sum X_i^2}\right) \\ &= \beta e^{\sigma^2/2}\left(\frac{\sum X_i^2}{\sum X_i^2}\right) = \beta e^{\sigma^2/2} \end{aligned}$$

where use is made of the fact that the X's are nonstochastic and each u_i has an expected value of $e^{\sigma^2/2}$.

Since $E(\hat{\alpha}) \neq \beta$, $\hat{\alpha}$ is a biased estimator of β.

Part 3

Topics in Econometrics

In **Part 1** we introduced the classical linear regression model with all its assumptions. In **Part 2** we examined in detail the consequences that ensue when one or more of the assumptions are not satisfied and what can be done about them. In **Part 3** we study some selected but commonly encountered econometric techniques. In particular, we discuss these topics: (1) nonlinear-in-the-parameter regression models, (2) qualitative response regression models, (3) panel data regression models, and (4) dynamic econometric models.

In Chapter 14, we consider models that are *intrinsically* nonlinear in the parameters. With the ready availability of software packages, it is no longer a big challenge to estimate such models. Although the underlying mathematics may elude some readers, the basic ideas of nonlinear-in-the-parameter regression models can be explained intuitively. With suitable examples, this chapter shows how such models are estimated and interpreted.

In Chapter 15, we consider regression models in which the dependent variable is qualitative in nature. This chapter therefore complements Chapter 9, where we discussed models in which the explanatory variables were qualitative in nature. The basic thrust of this chapter is on developing models in which the regressand is of the yes or no type. Since ordinary least squares (OLS) poses several problems in estimating such models, several alternatives have been developed. In this chapter we consider two such alternatives, namely, the **logit model** and the **probit model.** This chapter also discusses several variants of the qualitative response models, such as the **Tobit model** and the **Poisson regression model.** Several extensions of the qualitative response models are also briefly discussed, such as the **ordered probit, ordered logit,** and **multinomial logit.**

In Chapter 16 we discuss **panel data regression models.** Such models combine time series and cross-section observations. Although by combining such observations we increase the sample size, panel data regression models pose several estimation challenges. In this chapter we discuss only the essentials of such models and guide the reader to the appropriate resources for further study.

In Chapter 17, we consider regression models that include current as well as past, or lagged, values of the explanatory variables in addition to models that include the lagged value(s) of the dependent variable as one of the explanatory variables. These models are called, respectively, **distributed lag** and **autoregressive models.** Although such models are extremely useful in empirical econometrics, they pose some special estimating problems because they violate one or more assumptions of the classical regression model. We consider these special problems in the context of the Koyck, the adaptive-expectations (AE), and the partial-adjustment models. We also note the criticism leveled against the AE model by the advocates of the so-called rational expectations (RE) school.

Chapter 14

Nonlinear Regression Models

The major emphasis of this book is on linear regression models, that is, models that are linear in the parameters and/or models that can be transformed so that they are linear in the parameters. On occasions, however, for theoretical or empirical reasons we have to consider models that are nonlinear in the parameters.[1] In this chapter we take a look at such models and study their special features.

14.1 Intrinsically Linear and Intrinsically Nonlinear Regression Models

When we started our discussion of linear regression models in Chapter 2, we stated that our concern in this book is basically with models that are linear in the parameters; they may or may not be linear in the variables. If you refer to Table 2.3, you will see that a model that is linear in the parameters as well as the variables is a linear regression model and so is a model that is linear in the parameters but nonlinear in the variables. On the other hand, if a model is nonlinear in the parameters it is a nonlinear (in-the-parameter) regression model whether the variables of such a model are linear or not.

However, one has to be careful here, for some models look nonlinear in the parameters but are **inherently** or **intrinsically** linear because with suitable transformation they can be made linear-in-the-parameter regression models. But if such models cannot be linearized in the parameters, they are called **intrinsically nonlinear regression models.** *From now on when we talk about a nonlinear regression model, we mean that it is intrinsically nonlinear.* For brevity, we will call them **NLRM.**

To drive home the distinction between the two, let us revisit Exercises 2.6 and 2.7. In Exercise 2.6, Models **a, b, c,** and **e** are linear regression models because they are all linear in the parameters. Model **d** is a mixed bag, for β_2 is linear but not $\ln \beta_1$. But if we let $\alpha = \ln \beta_1$, then this model is linear in α and β_2.

In Exercise 2.7, Models **d** and **e** are intrinsically nonlinear because there is no simple way to linearize them. Model **c** is obviously a linear regression model. What about Models **a**

[1]We noted in Chapter 4 that under the assumption of normally distributed error term, the OLS estimators are not only BLUE but are BUE (best unbiased estimator) in the entire class of estimators, linear or not. But if we drop the assumption of normality, as Davidson and MacKinnon note, it is possible to obtain nonlinear and/or biased estimators that may perform better than the OLS estimators. See Russell Davidson and James G. MacKinnon, *Estimation and Inference in Econometrics,* Oxford University Press, New York, 1993, p. 161.

and **b**? Taking the logarithms on both sides of **a,** we obtain $\ln Y_i = \beta_1 + \beta_2 X_i + u_i$, which is linear in the parameters. Hence Model **a** is *intrinsically* a linear regression model. Model **b** is an example of the **logistic (probability) distribution function,** and we will study this in Chapter 15. On the surface, it seems that this is a nonlinear regression model. But a simple mathematical trick will render it a linear regression model, namely,

$$\ln\left(\frac{1 - Y_i}{Y_i}\right) = \beta_1 + \beta_2 X_i + u_i \tag{14.1.1}$$

Therefore, Model **b** is intrinsically linear. We will see the utility of models like Eq. (14.1.1) in the next chapter.

Consider now the famous **Cobb–Douglas (C–D) production function.** Letting Y = output, X_2 = labor input, and X_3 = capital input, we will write this function in three different ways:

$$Y_i = \beta_1 X_{2i}^{\beta_2} X_{3i}^{\beta_3} e^{u_i} \tag{14.1.2}$$

or,

$$\ln Y_i = \alpha + \beta_2 \ln X_{2i} + \beta_3 \ln X_{3i} + u_i \tag{14.1.2a}$$

where $\alpha = \ln \beta_1$. Thus in this format the C–D function is intrinsically linear.

Now consider this version of the C–D function:

$$Y_i = \beta_1 X_{2i}^{\beta_2} X_{3i}^{\beta_3} u_i \tag{14.1.3}$$

or,

$$\ln Y_i = \alpha + \beta_2 \ln X_{2i} + \beta_3 \ln X_{3i} + \ln u_i \tag{14.1.3a}$$

where $\alpha = \ln \beta_1$. This model too is linear in the parameters.

But now consider the following version of the C–D function:

$$Y_i = \beta_1 X_{2i}^{\beta_2} X_{3i}^{\beta_3} + u_i \tag{14.1.4}$$

As we just noted, C–D versions (14.1.2*a*) and (14.1.3*a*) are intrinsically linear (in the parameter) regression models, but there is no way to transform Eq. (14.1.4) so that the transformed model can be made linear in the parameters.[2] Therefore, Eq. (14.1.4) is intrinsically a nonlinear regression model.

Another well-known but intrinsically nonlinear function is the **constant elasticity of substitution (CES)** production function of which the Cobb–Douglas production is a special case. The CES production takes the following form:

$$Y_i = A\left[\delta K_i^{-\beta} + (1 - \delta) L_i^{-\beta}\right]^{-1/\beta} \tag{14.1.5}$$

where Y = output, K = capital input, L = labor input, A = scale parameter, δ = distribution parameter ($0 < \delta < 1$), and β = substitution parameter ($\beta \geq -1$).[3] No matter in what form you enter the stochastic error term u_i in this production function, there is no way to make it a linear (in parameter) regression model. It is intrinsically a nonlinear regression model.

[2]If you try to log-transform the model, it will not work because $\ln(A + B) \neq \ln A + \ln B$.

[3]For properties of the CES production function, see Michael D. Intriligator, Ronald Bodkin, and Cheng Hsiao, *Econometric Models, Techniques, and Applications,* 2d ed., Prentice Hall, 1996, pp. 294–295.

14.2 Estimation of Linear and Nonlinear Regression Models

To see the difference in estimating linear and nonlinear regression models, consider the following two models:

$$Y_i = \beta_1 + \beta_2 X_i + u_i \tag{14.2.1}$$

$$Y_i = \beta_1 e^{\beta_2 X_i} + u_i \tag{14.2.2}$$

By now you know that Eq. (14.2.1) is a linear regression model, whereas Eq. (14.2.2) is a nonlinear regression model. Regression (14.2.2) is known as the **exponential regression model** and is often used to measure the growth of a variable, such as population, GDP, or money supply.

Suppose we consider estimating the parameters of the two models by ordinary least squares (OLS). In OLS we minimize the residual sum of squares (RSS), which for model (14.2.1) is:

$$\sum \hat{u}_i^2 = \sum (Y_i - \hat{\beta}_1 - \hat{\beta}_2 X_i)^2 \tag{14.2.3}$$

where as usual $\hat{\beta}_1$ and $\hat{\beta}_2$ are the OLS estimators of the true β's. Differentiating the preceding expression with respect to the two unknowns, we obtain the **normal equations** shown in Eqs. (3.1.4) and (3.1.5). Solving these equations simultaneously, we obtain the OLS estimators given in Eqs. (3.1.6) and (3.1.7). Observe very carefully that in these equations the unknowns (β's) are on the left-hand side and the knowns (X and Y) are on the right-hand side. As a result we get explicit solutions of the two unknowns in terms of our data.

Now see what happens if we try to minimize the RSS of Eq. (14.2.2). As shown in Appendix 14A, Section 14A.1, the normal equations corresponding to Eqs. (3.1.4) and (3.1.5) are as follows:

$$\sum Y_i e^{\hat{\beta}_2 X_i} = \beta_1 e^{2\hat{\beta}_2 X_i} \tag{14.2.4}$$

$$\sum Y_i X_i e^{\hat{\beta}_2 X_i} = \hat{\beta}_1 \sum X_i e^{2\hat{\beta}_2 X_i} \tag{14.2.5}$$

Unlike the normal equations in the case of the linear regression model, the normal equations for nonlinear regression have the unknowns (the $\hat{\beta}$'s) both on the left- and right-hand sides of the equations. As a consequence, we *cannot obtain explicit solutions* of the unknowns in terms of the known quantities. To put it differently, the unknowns are expressed in terms of themselves and the data! Therefore, although we can apply the method of least squares to estimate the parameters of the nonlinear regression models, we cannot obtain explicit solutions of the unknowns. Incidentally, OLS applied to a nonlinear regression model is called **nonlinear least squares (NLLS).** So, what is the solution? We take this question up next.

14.3 Estimating Nonlinear Regression Models: The Trial-and-Error Method

To set the stage, let us consider a concrete example. The data in Table 14.1 relates to the management fees that a leading mutual fund in the United States pays to its investment advisors to manage its assets. The fees paid depend on the net asset value of the fund. As you can see, the higher the net asset value of the fund, the lower are the advisory fees, which can be seen clearly from Figure 14.1.

TABLE 14.1
Advisory Fees Charged and Asset Size

	Fee, %	Asset*
1	0.520	0.5
2	0.508	5.0
3	0.484	10
4	0.46	15
5	0.4398	20
6	0.4238	25
7	0.4115	30
8	0.402	35
9	0.3944	40
10	0.388	45
11	0.3825	55
12	0.3738	60

*Asset represents net asset value, billions of dollars.

FIGURE 14.1
Relationship of advisory fees to fund assets.

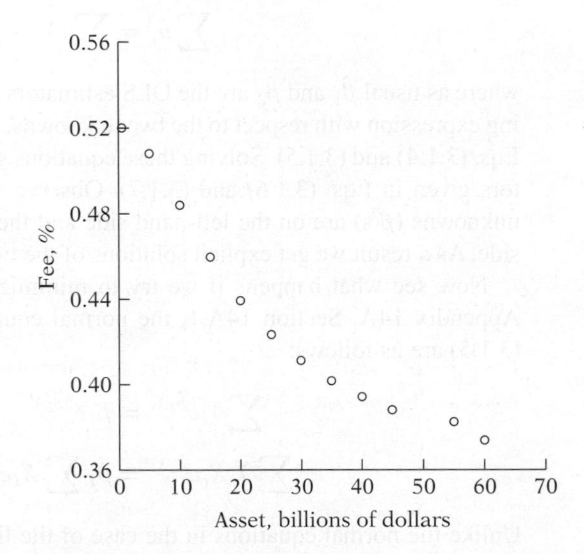

To see how the exponential regression model in Eq. (14.2.2) fits the data given in Table 14.1, we can proceed by trial and error. Suppose we assume that initially $\beta_1 = 0.45$ and $\beta_2 = 0.01$. These are pure guesses, sometimes based on prior experience or prior empirical work or obtained by just fitting a linear regression model even though it may not be appropriate. At this stage do not worry about how these values are obtained.

Since we know the values of β_1 and β_2, we can write Eq. (14.2.2) as:

$$u_i = Y_i - \beta_1 e^{\beta_2 X_i} = Y_i - 0.45e^{0.01X_i} \tag{14.3.1}$$

Therefore,

$$\sum u_i^2 = \sum (Y_i - 0.45e^{0.01X_i})^2 \tag{14.3.2}$$

Since Y, X, β_1, and β_2 are known, we can easily find the *error sum of squares* in Eq. (14.3.2).[4] Remember that in OLS our objective is to find those values of the unknown parameters that will make the error sum of squares as small as possible. This will happen if the estimated

[4]Note that we call $\sum u_i^2$ the error sum of squares and not the usual residual sum of squares because the values of the parameters are assumed to be known.

Y values from the model are as close as possible to the actual Y values. With the given values, we obtain $\sum u_i^2 = 0.3044$. But how do we know that this is the least possible error sum of squares that we can obtain? What happens if you choose another value for β_1 and β_2, say, 0.50 and -0.01, respectively? Repeating the procedure just laid down, we find that we now obtain $\sum u_i^2 = 0.0073$. Obviously, this error sum of squares is much smaller than the one obtained before, namely, 0.3044. But how do we know that we have reached the lowest possible error sum of squares, if by choosing yet another set of values for the β's, we will obtain yet another error sum of squares?

As you can see, such a trial-and-error, or **iterative,** process can be easily implemented. And if one has infinite time and infinite patience, the trial-and-error process *may* ultimately produce values of β_1 and β_2 that may guarantee the lowest possible error sum of squares. But you might ask, how did we go from ($\beta_1 = 0.45$; $\beta_2 = 0.01$) to ($\beta_1 = 0.50$; $\beta_2 = -0.01$)? Clearly, we need some kind of *algorithm* that will tell us how we go from one set of values of the unknowns to another set before we stop. Fortunately such algorithms are available, and we discuss them in the next section.

14.4 Approaches to Estimating Nonlinear Regression Models

There are several approaches, or algorithms, to NLRMs: (1) direct search or trial and error, (2) direct optimization, and (3) iterative linearization.[5]

Direct Search or Trial-and-Error or Derivative-Free Method

In the previous section we showed how this method works. Although intuitively appealing because it does not require the use of calculus methods as the other methods do, this method is generally not used. *First,* if an NLRM involves several parameters, the method becomes very cumbersome and computationally expensive. For example, if an NLRM involves 5 parameters and 25 alternative values for each parameter are considered, you will have to compute the error sum of squares $(25)^5 = 9{,}765{,}625$ times! *Second,* there is no guarantee that the final set of parameter values you have selected will necessarily give you the absolute minimum error sum of squares. In the language of calculus, you may obtain a local and not an absolute minimum. In fact, no method guarantees a global minimum.

Direct Optimization

In direct optimization we differentiate the error sum of squares with respect to each unknown coefficient, or parameter, set the resulting equation to zero, and solve the resulting normal equations simultaneously. We have already seen this in Eqs. (14.2.4) and (14.2.5). But as you can see from these equations, they cannot be solved explicitly or *analytically.* Some iterative routine is therefore called for. One routine is called the **method of steepest descent.** We will not discuss the technical details of this method as they are somewhat involved, but the reader can find the details in the references. Like the method of trial and error, the method of steepest descent also involves selecting initial trial values of the unknown parameters but then it proceeds more systematically than the hit-or-miss or trial-and-error method. One disadvantage of this method is that it may converge to the final values of the parameters extremely slowly.

[5]The following discussion leans heavily on these sources: Robert S. Pindyck and Daniel L. Rubinfeld, *Econometric Models and Economic Forecasts,* 4th ed., McGraw-Hill, 1998, Chapter 10; Norman R. Draper and Harry Smith, *Applied Regression Analysis,* 3d ed., John Wiley & Sons, 1998, Chapter 24; Arthur S. Goldberger, *A Course in Econometrics,* Harvard University Press, 1991, Chapter 29; Russell Davidson and James MacKinnon, op. cit., pp. 201–207; John Fox, *Applied Regression Analysis, Linear Models, and Related Methods,* Sage Publications, 1997, pp. 393–400; and Ronald Gallant, *Nonlinear Statistical Models,* John Wiley and Sons, 1987.

Iterative Linearization Method

In this method we linearize a nonlinear equation around some initial values of the parameters. The linearized equation is then estimated by OLS and the initially chosen values are adjusted. These adjusted values are used to *relinearize* the model, and again we estimate it by OLS and readjust the estimated values. This process is continued until there is no substantial change in the estimated values from the last couple of iterations. The main technique used in linearizing a nonlinear equation is the **Taylor series expansion** from calculus. Rudimentary details of this method are given in Appendix 14A, Section 14A.2. Estimating NLRM using Taylor series expansion is systematized in two algorithms, known as the **Gauss–Newton iterative method** and the **Newton–Raphson iterative method.** Since one or both of these methods are now incorporated in several computer packages, and since a discussion of their technical details will take us far beyond the scope of this book, there is no need to dwell on them here.[6] In the next section we discuss some examples using these methods.

14.5 Illustrative Examples

EXAMPLE 14.1
Mutual Fund Advisory Fees

Refer to the data given in Table 14.1 and the NLRM (14.2.2). Using the *EViews 6* nonlinear regression routine, which uses the linearization method,[7] we obtained the following regression results; the coefficients, their standard errors, and their *t* values are given in a tabular form:

Variable	Coefficient	Std. Error	*t* Value	*p* Value
Intercept	0.5089	0.0074	68.2246	0.0000
Asset	−0.0059	0.00048	−12.3150	0.0000

$$R^2 = 0.9385 \qquad d = 0.3493$$

From these results, we can write the estimated model as:

$$\widehat{\text{Fee}}_i = 0.5089\,\text{Asset}^{-0.0059} \tag{14.5.1}$$

Before we discuss these results, it may be noted that if you do not supply the initial values of the parameters to start the linearization process, *EViews* will do it on its own. It took *EViews* five iterations to obtain the results shown in Eq. (14.5.1). However, you can supply your own initial values to start the process. To demonstrate, we chose the initial value of $\beta_1 = 0.45$ and $\beta_2 = 0.01$. We obtained the same results as in Eq. (14.5.1) but it took eight iterations. *It is important to note that fewer iterations will be required if your initial values are not very far from the final values.* In some cases you can choose the initial values of the parameters by simply running an OLS regression of the regressand on the regressor(s), simply ignoring the nonlinearities. For instance, using the data in Table 14.1, if you were to regress fee on assets, the OLS estimate of β_1 is 0.5028 and that of β_2 is −0.002, which

[6]There is another method that is sometimes used, called the **Marquard method,** which is a compromise between the method of steepest descent and the linearization (or Taylor series) method. The interested reader may consult the references for the details of this method.

[7]*EViews* provides three options: quadratic hill climbing, Newton–Raphson, and Berndt–Hall–Hall–Hausman. The default option is quadratic hill climbing, which is a variation of the Newton–Raphson method.

EXAMPLE 14.1 *(Continued)*

are much closer to the final values given in Eq. (14.5.1). (For the technical details, see Appendix 14A, Section 14A.3.)

Now about the properties of nonlinear least squares (NLLS) estimators. You may recall that, in the case of linear regression models with normally distributed error terms, we were able to develop exact inference procedures (i.e., test hypotheses) using the *t*, *F*, and χ^2 tests in small as well as large samples. Unfortunately, this is not the case with NLRMs, even with normally distributed error terms. *The NLLS estimators are not normally distributed, are not unbiased, and do not have minimum variance* in finite, or small, samples. As a result, we cannot use the *t* test (to test the significance of an individual coefficient) or the *F* test (to test the overall significance of the estimated regression) because we cannot obtain an unbiased estimate of the error variance σ^2 from the estimated residuals. Furthermore, the residuals (the difference between the actual *Y* values and the estimated *Y* values from the NLRM) do not necessarily sum to zero, ESS and RSS do not necessarily add up to the TSS, and therefore $R^2 = \text{ESS}/\text{TSS}$ may not be a meaningful descriptive statistic for such models. However, we can compute R^2 as:

$$R^2 = 1 - \frac{\sum \hat{u}_i^2}{\sum (Y_i - \bar{Y})^2} \tag{14.5.2}$$

where Y = regressand and $\hat{u}_i = Y_i - \hat{Y}_i$, where $\hat{Y}_i$ are the estimated Y values from the (fitted) NLRM.

Consequently, inferences about the regression parameters in nonlinear regression are usually based on large-sample theory. This theory tells us that the least-squares and maximum likelihood estimators for nonlinear regression models with normal error terms, when the sample size is large, are approximately normally distributed and almost unbiased, and have almost minimum variance. This large-sample theory also applies when the error terms are not normally distributed.[8]

In short, then, all inference procedures in NLRM are large sample, or asymptotic. Returning to Example 14.1, the *t* statistics given in Eq. (14.5.1) are meaningful only if interpreted in the large-sample context. In that sense, we can say that estimated coefficients shown in Eq. (14.5.1) are individually statistically significant. Of course, our sample in the present instance is rather small.

Returning to Eq. (14.5.1), how do we find out the rate of change of Y (= fee) with respect to X (asset size)? Using the basic rules of derivatives, the reader can see that the rate of change of Y with respect to X is:

$$\frac{dY}{dX} = \beta_1 \beta_2 e^{\beta_2 X} = (-0.0059)(0.5089)e^{-0.0059X} \tag{14.5.3}$$

As can be seen, the rate of change of fee depends on the value of the assets. For example, if $X = 20$ (million), the expected rate of change in the fees charged can be seen from Eq. (14.5.3) to be about -0.0031 percent. Of course, this answer will change depending on the X value used in the computation. Judged by the R^2 as computed from Eq. (14.5.2), the R^2 value of 0.9385 suggests that the chosen NLRM fits the data in Table 14.1 quite well. The estimated Durbin–Watson value of 0.3493 may suggest that there is autocorrelation or possibly model specification error. Although there are procedures to take care of these problems as well as the problem of heteroscedasticity in NLRM, we will not pursue these topics here. The interested reader may consult the references.

[8]John Neter, Michael H. Kutner, Christopher J. Nachtsheim, and William Wasserman, *Applied Regression Analysis,* 3d ed., Irwin, 1996, pp. 548–549.

EXAMPLE 14.2
The Cobb–Douglas Production Function of the Mexican Economy

Refer to the data given in Exercise 14.9 (Table 14.3). These data refer to the Mexican economy for years 1955–1974. We will see if the NLRM given in Eq. (14.1.4) fits the data, noting that Y = output, X_2 = labor input, and X_3 = capital input. Using *EViews 6*, we obtained the following regression results, after 32 iterations.

Variable	Coefficient	Std. Error	*t* Value	*p* Value
Intercept	0.5292	0.2712	1.9511	0.0677
Labor	0.1810	0.1412	1.2814	0.2173
Capital	0.8827	0.0708	12.4658	0.0000

$$R^2 = 0.9942 \qquad d = 0.2899$$

Therefore, the estimated Cobb–Douglas production function is:

$$\widehat{\text{GDP}}_t = 0.5292\text{Labor}_t^{0.1810}\text{Capital}_t^{0.8827} \tag{14.5.4}$$

Interpreted asymptotically, the equation shows that only the coefficient of the capital input is significant in this model. In Exercise 14.9 you are asked to compare these results with those obtained from the multiplicative Cobb–Douglas production function as given in Eq. (14.1.2).

EXAMPLE 14.3
Growth of U.S. Population, 1970–2007

The Table in Exercise 14.8 gives data on total U.S. population for the period 1970–2007. A **logistic model** of the following type is often used to measure the growth of some populations, human beings, bacteria, etc.:

$$Y_t = \frac{\beta_1}{1 + e^{(\beta_2 + \beta_3^t)}} + u_t \tag{14.5.5}$$

Where Y = population, in millions; t = time, measured chronologically; and the β's are the parameters.

This model is nonlinear in the parameters; there is no simple way to convert it into a model that is linear in the parameters. So we will need to use one of the nonlinear estimation methods to estimate the parameters. Notice an interesting feature of this model: Although there are only two variables in the model, population and time, there are three unknown parameters, which shows that in a NLRM there can be more parameters than variables.

An attempt to fit Eq. (14.5.5) to our data was not successful, as all the estimated coefficients were statistically insignificant. This is probably not surprising, for if we plot population against time, we obtain Figure 14.2.

FIGURE 14.2
Population versus Year.

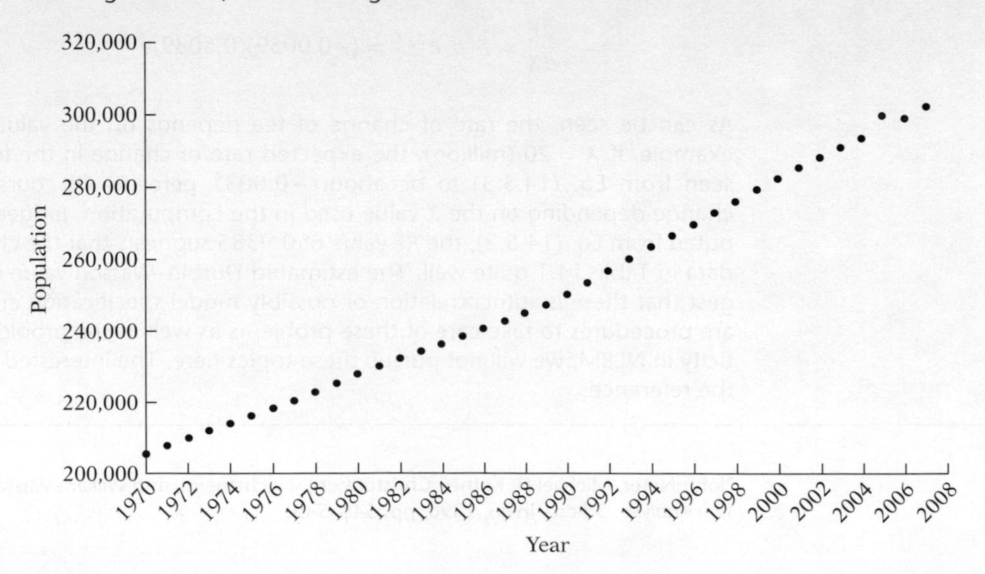

EXAMPLE 14.3
(*Continued*)

This figure shows that there is an almost linear relationship between the two variables. If we plot the *logarithm* of population against time, we obtain the following figure:

FIGURE 14.3
Logarithm of Population versus Year.

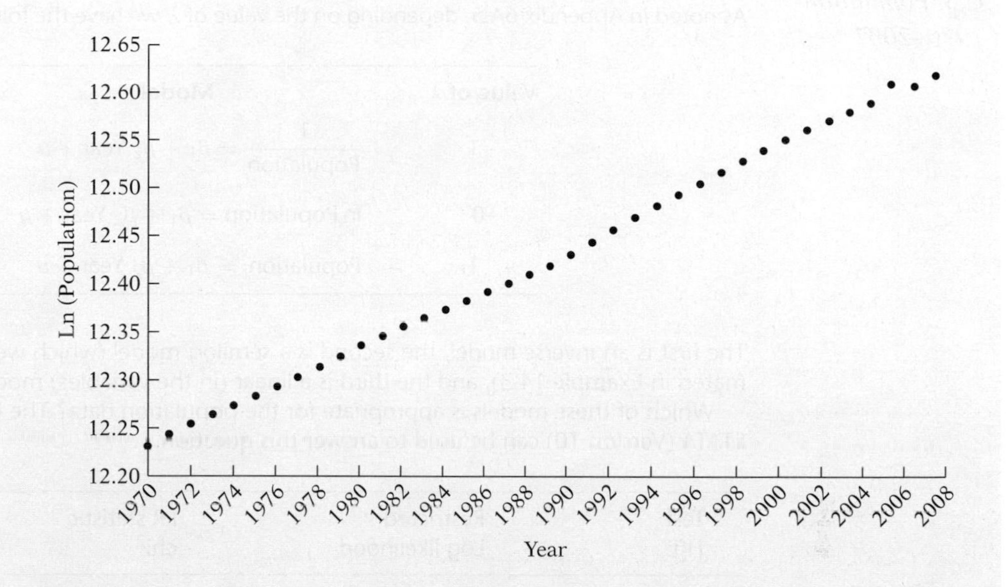

The slope of this figure (multiplied by 100) gives us the growth rate of population (why?).

As a matter of fact, if we regress the log of population on time, we get the following results:

Dependent Variable: LPOPULATION
Method: Least Squares
Sample: 1970–2007
Included observations: 38

	Coefficient	Std. Error	*t*-Statistic	Prob.
C	-8.710413	0.147737	-58.95892	0.0000
YEAR	0.010628	7.43E-05	143.0568	0.0000

R-squared	0.998244	Mean dependent var.	12.42405
Adjusted *R*-squared	0.998195	S.D. dependent var.	0.118217
S.E. of regression	0.005022	Akaike info criterion	-7.698713
Sum squared resid.	0.000908	Schwarz criterion	-7.612525
Log likelihood	148.2756	Hannan-Quinn criter.	-7.668048
F-statistic	20465.26	Durbin-Watson stat.	0.366006
Prob. (*F*-statistic)	0.000000		

This table shows that, over the period 1970–2007, the U.S. population has been growing at the rate of about 1.06 percent per year. The R^2 value of 0.998 suggests that there is almost a perfect fit.

This example brings out an important point that sometimes a linear (in the parameter) model might be preferable to a nonlinear (in the parameter) model.

EXAMPLE 14.4

Box-Cox Transformation: U.S. Population 1970–2007

In Appendix 6A.5 we briefly considered the Box-Cox transformation. Let us continue with Example 14.3 but assume the following model:

$$\text{Population}^{\lambda} = \beta_1 + \beta_2 \text{ Year} + u$$

As noted in Appendix 6A.5, depending on the value of λ we have the following possibilities:

Value of λ	**Model**
−1	$\frac{1}{\text{Population}} = \beta_1 + \beta_2 \text{ Year} + u$
0	$\ln \text{Population} = \beta_1 + \beta_2 \text{ Year} + u$
1	$\text{Population}_i = \beta_1 + \beta_2 \text{ Year} + u$

The first is an inverse model, the second is a semilog model (which we have already estimated in Example 14.3), and the third is a linear (in the variables) model.

Which of these models is appropriate for the population data? The Box-Cox routine in STATA (Version 10) can be used to answer this question:

Test H0:	Restricted Log likelihood	LR statistic chi^2	*p*-value Prob > chi^2
$\theta = -1$	−444.42475	0.14	0.707
$\theta = 0$	−444.38813	0.07	0.794
$\theta = 1$	−444.75684	0.81	0.369

Note: In our notation, theta (θ) is the same thing as lamda (λ). The table shows that on the basis of the likelihood ratio (LR) test, we cannot reject any of these λ values as possible values for power of population; that is, in the present example, linear, inverse and semilog models are equal candidates to depict the behavior of population over the sample period 1970–2007. Therefore, we present the results of all three models:

Dependent variable	Intercept	Slope	R^2
1/Population	0.000089	−4.28e-08	0.9986
	t (166.14)	(−1568.10)	
ln Population	−8.7104	0.0106	0.9982
	t (−58.96)	(143.06)	
Population	−5042627	2661.825	0.9928
	t (−66.92)	(70.24)	

In all of these models the estimated coefficients are all highly statistically significant. But note that the R^2 values are not directly comparable because the dependent variables in the three models are different.

This example shows how nonlinear estimation techniques can be applied in concrete situations.

Summary and Conclusions

The main points discussed in this chapter can be summarized as follows:

1. Although linear regression models predominate theory and practice, there are occasions where nonlinear-in-the-parameter regression models (NLRM) are useful.
2. The mathematics underlying linear regression models is comparatively simple in that one can obtain explicit, or analytical, solutions of the coefficients of such models. The small-sample and large-sample theory of inference of such models is well established.
3. In contrast, for intrinsically nonlinear regression models (NLRM), parameter values cannot be obtained explicitly. They have to be estimated numerically, that is, by iterative procedures.
4. There are several methods of obtaining estimates of NLRMs, such as (1) trial and error, (2) nonlinear least squares (NLLS), and (3) linearization through Taylor series expansion.
5. Computer packages now have built-in routines, such as Gauss–Newton, Newton Raphson, and Marquard. These are all iterative routines.
6. NLLS estimators do not possess optimal properties in finite samples, but in large samples they do have such properties. Therefore, the results of NLLS in small samples must be interpreted carefully.
7. Autocorrelation, heteroscedasticity, and model specification problems can plague NLRM, as they do linear regression models.
8. We illustrated the NLLS with several examples. With the ready availability of user-friendly software packages, estimation of NLRM should no longer be a mystery. Therefore, the reader should not shy away from such models whenever theoretical or practical reasons dictate their use. As a matter of fact, if you refer to Exercise 12.10, you will see from Eq. (1) that it is intrinsically a nonlinear regression model that should be estimated as such.

EXERCISES

Questions

14.1. What is meant by intrinsically linear and intrinsically nonlinear regression models? Give some examples.

14.2. Since the error term in the Cobb–Douglas production function can be entered multiplicatively or additively, how would you decide between the two?

14.3. What is the difference between OLS and nonlinear least-squares (NLLS) estimation?

14.4. The relationship between pressure and temperature in saturated steam can be expressed as:*

$$Y = \beta_1(10)^{\beta_2 t/(\gamma+t)} + u_t$$

where Y = pressure and t = temperature. Using the method of nonlinear least squares (NLLS), obtain the *normal equations* for this model.

*Adapted from Draper and Smith, op. cit., p. 554.

14.5. State whether the following statements are true or false. Give your reasoning.

a. Statistical inference in NLLS regression cannot be made on the basis of the usual t, F, and χ^2 tests even if the error term is assumed to be normally distributed.

b. The coefficient of determination (R^2) is not a particularly meaningful number for an NLRM.

14.6. How would you linearize the CES production function discussed in the chapter? Show the necessary steps.

14.7. Models that describe the behavior of a variable over time are called growth models. Such models are used in a variety of fields, such as economics, biology, botany, ecology, and demography. Growth models can take a variety of forms, both linear and nonlinear. Consider the following models, where Y is the variable whose growth we want to measure; t is time, measured chronologically; and u_t is the stochastic error term.

a. $Y_t = \beta_1 + \beta_2 t + u_t$

b. $\ln Y_t = \beta_1 + \beta_2 t + u_t$

c. Logistic growth model: $Y_t = \frac{\beta_1}{1 + \beta_2 e^{-\beta_3 t}} + u_t$

d. Gompertz growth model: $Y_t = \beta_1 e^{-\beta_2 e^{-\beta_3 t}} + u_t$

Find out the properties of these models by considering the growth of Y in relation to time.

Empirical Exercises

14.8. The data in Table 14.2 gives U.S. population, in millions of persons, for the period 1970–2007. Fit the growth models given in Exercise 14.7 and decide which model gives a better fit. Interpret the parameters of the model.

14.9. Table 14.3 gives data on real GDP, labor, and capital for Mexico for the period 1955–1974. See if the multiplicative Cobb–Douglas production function given in Eq. (14.1.2*a*) fits these data. Compare your results with those obtained from fitting the additive Cobb–Douglas production function given in Eq. (14.1.4), whose results are given in Example 14.2. Which is a better fit?

TABLE 14.2
U.S. Population (Millions)

Source: *Economic Report of the President,* 2008.

Year	Population	Year	Population
1970	205,052	1989	247,342
1971	207,661	1990	250,132
1972	209,896	1991	253,493
1973	211,909	1992	256,894
1974	213,854	1993	260,255
1975	215,973	1994	263,436
1976	218,035	1995	266,557
1977	220,239	1996	269,667
1978	222,585	1997	272,912
1979	225,055	1998	276,115
1980	227,726	1999	279,295
1981	229,966	2000	282,407
1982	232,188	2001	285,339
1983	234,307	2002	288,189
1984	236,348	2003	290,941
1985	238,466	2004	293,609
1986	240,651	2005	299,801
1987	242,804	2006	299,157
1988	245,021	2007	302,405

TABLE 14.3 Production Function Data for the Mexican Economy

Observation	GDP	Labor	Capital	Observation	GDP	Labor	Capital
1955	114,043	8,310	182,113	1965	212,323	11,746	315,715
1956	120,410	8,529	193,749	1966	226,977	11,521	337,642
1957	129,187	8,738	205,192	1967	241,194	11,540	363,599
1958	134,705	8,952	215,130	1968	260,881	12,066	391,847
1959	139,960	9,171	225,021	1969	277,498	12,297	422,382
1960	150,511	9,569	237,026	1970	296,530	12,955	455,049
1961	157,897	9,527	248,897	1971	306,712	13,338	484,677
1962	165,286	9,662	260,661	1972	329,030	13,738	520,553
1963	178,491	10,334	275,466	1973	354,057	15,924	561,531
1964	199,457	10,981	295,378	1974	374,977	14,154	609,825

Notes: GDP is in millions of 1960 pesos.
Labor is in thousands of people.
Capital is in millions of 1960 pesos.

Source: Victor J. Elias, *Sources of Growth: A Study of Seven Latin American Economies,* International Center for Economic Growth, ICS Press, San Francisco, 1992, Tables E-5, E-12, E-14.

Appendix 14A

14A.1 Derivation of Equations (14.2.4) and (14.2.5)

Write Eq. (14.2.2) as

$$u_i = Y_i - \beta_1 e^{\beta_2 X_i} \tag{1}$$

Therefore,

$$\sum u_i^2 = \sum (Y_i - \beta_1 e^{\beta_2 X_i})^2 \tag{2}$$

The error sum of squares is thus a function of β_1 and β_2, since the values of Y and X are known. Therefore, to minimize the error sum of squares, we have to partially differentiate it with respect to the two unknowns, which gives:

$$\frac{\partial \sum u_i^2}{\partial \beta_1} = 2\sum (Y_i - \beta_1 e^{\beta_2 X_i})(-1e^{\beta_2 X_i}) \tag{3}$$

$$\frac{\partial \sum u_i^2}{\partial \beta_2} = 2\sum (Y_i - \beta_1 e^{\beta_2 X_i})(-\beta_1 e^{\beta_2 X_i} X_i) \tag{4}$$

By the first-order condition of optimization, setting the preceding equations to zero and solving them simultaneously, we obtain Eqs. (14.2.4) and (14.2.5). Note that in differentiating the error sum of squares we have used the chain rule.

14A.2 The Linearization Method

Students familiar with calculus will recall **Taylor's theorem,** which states that any arbitrary function $f(X)$ that is continuous and has a continuous nth-order derivative can be approximated around point $X = X_0$ by a polynomial function and a remainder as follows:

$$f(X) = \frac{f(X_0)}{0!} + \frac{f'(X_0)(X - X_0)}{1!} + \frac{f''(X_0)(X - X_0)^2}{2!} + \cdots + \frac{f^n(X_0)(X - X_0)^n}{n!} + R \tag{1}$$

where $f'(X_0)$ is the first derivative of $f(X)$ evaluated at $X = X_0$, $f''(X_0)$ is the second derivative of $f(X)$ evaluated at $X = X_0$ and so on, where $n!$ (read n factorial) stands for $n(n-1)(n-2)\ldots 1$ with the convention that $0! = 1$, and R stands for the remainder. If we take $n = 1$, we get a linear approximation; choosing $n = 2$, we get a second-degree polynomial approximation. As you can expect, the higher the order of the polynomial, the better the approximation to the original function. The series given in Eq. (1) is called **Taylor's series expansion of $f(X)$ around the point $X = X_0$.** As an example, consider the function:

$$Y = f(X) = \alpha_1 + \alpha_2 X + \alpha_3 X^2 + \alpha_4 X^3$$

Suppose we want to approximate it at $X = 0$. We now obtain:

$$f(0) = \alpha_1 \qquad f'(0) = \alpha_2 \qquad f''(0) = 2\alpha_3 \qquad f'''(0) = 6\alpha_4$$

Hence we can obtain the following approximations:

First order: $$Y = \alpha_1 + \frac{f'(0)}{1!} = \alpha_1 + a_2 X + \text{remainder}\,(= \alpha_3 X^2 + \alpha_4 X^3)$$

Second order: $$Y = f(0) + \frac{f'(0)}{1!}X + \frac{f''(0)}{2!}X^2$$
$$= \alpha_1 + \alpha_2 X + \alpha_3 X^2 + \text{remainder}\,(= \alpha_4 X^3)$$

Third order: $$Y = \alpha_1 + \alpha_2 X + \alpha_3 X^2 + \alpha_4 X^3$$

The third-order approximation reproduces the original equation exactly.

The objective of Taylor series approximation is usually to choose a lower-order polynomial in the hope that the remainder term will be inconsequential. It is often used to approximate a nonlinear function by a linear function, by dropping the higher-order terms.

The Taylor series approximation can be easily extended to a function containing more than one X. For example, consider the following function:

$$Y = f(X, Z) \tag{2}$$

and suppose we want to expand it around $X = a$ and $Z = b$. Taylor's theorem shows that

$$\begin{aligned} f(x, z) &= f(a, b) + f_x(a, b)(x - a) \\ &\quad + f_z(a, b)f(z - b) + \frac{1}{2!}[f_{xx}(a, b)(x - a)^2 \\ &\quad - 2f_{xz}(a, b)(x - a)(z - b) + f_{zz}(a, b)(z - b)^2] + \cdots \end{aligned} \tag{3}$$

where f_x = partial derivative of the function with respect to (w.r.t.) X, f_{xx} = second partial derivative of the function w.r.t. X and similarly for the variable Z. If we want a linear approximation to the function, we will use the first two terms in Eq. (3), if we want a quadratic, or second-degree, approximation, we will use the first three terms in Eq. (3), and so on.

14A.3 Linear Approximation of the Exponential Function Given in Equation (14.2.2)

The function under consideration is:

$$Y = f(\beta_1, \beta_2) = \beta_1 e^{\beta_2 X} \tag{1}$$

Note: For ease of manipulation, we have dropped the observation subscript.

Remember that in this function the unknowns are the β coefficients. Let us linearize this function at $\beta_1 = \beta_1^*$ and $\beta_2 = \beta_2^*$, where the starred quantities are *given fixed values.* To *linearize* this, we proceed as follows:

$$Y = f(\beta_1, \beta_2) = f(\beta_1^*, \beta_2^*) + f_{\beta_1}(\beta_1^*, \beta_2^*)(\beta_1 - \beta_1^*) + f_{\beta_2}(\beta_1^*, \beta_2^*)(\beta_2 - \beta_2^*) \tag{2}$$

where f_{β_1} and f_{β_2} are the partial derivatives of the function (1) with respect to the unknowns and these derivatives will be evaluated at the (assumed) starred values of the unknown parameters. Note that we are using only the first derivatives in the preceding expression, since we are linearizing the function. Now assume that $\beta_1^* = 0.45$ and $\beta_2^* = 0.01$, which are pure guess–estimates of the true coefficients. Now

$$f(\beta_1^* = 0.45, \beta_2^* = 0.01) = 0.45e^{0.01X_i}$$
$$f_{\beta_1} = e^{\beta_2 X_i} \quad \text{and} \quad f_{\beta_2} = \beta_1 X_i e^{\beta_2 X_i} \tag{3}$$

by the standard rules of differentiation. Evaluating these derivatives at the given values and reverting to Eq. (2), we obtain:

$$Y_i = 0.45e^{0.01X_i} + e^{0.01X_i}(\beta_1 - 0.45) + (0.45)X_i e^{0.01X_i}(\beta_2 - 0.01) \tag{4}$$

which we write as:

$$(Y_i - 0.45e^{0.01X_i}) = e^{0.01X_i}\alpha_1 + 0.45X_i e^{0.01X_i}\alpha_2 \tag{5}$$

where

$$\alpha_1 = (\beta_1 - 0.45) \quad \text{and} \quad \alpha_2 = (\beta_2 - 0.01) \tag{6}$$

Now let $Y_i^* = (Y_i - 0.45e^{0.01X_i})$, $X_1 = e^{0.01X_i}$, and $X_{2i} = 0.45X_i e^{0.01X_i}$. Using these definitions and adding the error term u_i, we can finally write Eq. (5) as:

$$Y_i^* = \alpha_1 X_{1i} + \alpha_2 X_{2i} + u_i \tag{7}$$

Lo and behold, we now have a linear regression model. Since Y_i^*, X_{1i}, and X_{2i} can be readily computed from the data, we can easily estimate Eq. (7) by OLS and obtain the values of α_1 and α_2. Then, from Eq. (6), we obtain:

$$\beta_1 = \hat{\alpha}_1 + 0.45 \quad \text{and} \quad \beta_2 = \hat{\alpha}_2 + 0.01 \tag{8}$$

Call these values β_1^{**} and β_2^{**}, respectively. Using these (revised) values, we can start the iterative process given in Eq. (2), obtaining yet another set of values of the β coefficients. We can go on iterating (or linearizing) in this fashion until there is no substantial change in the values of the β coefficients. In Example 14.1, it took five iterations, but for the Mexican Cobb–Douglas example (Example 14.2), it took 32 iterations. But the underlying logic behind these iterations is the procedure just illustrated.

For the mutual fund fee structure example in Section 14.3, the Y^*, X_1, and X_2 as given in Eq. (6) are as shown in Table 14.4; the basic data are given in Table 14.1. From these values, the regression results corresponding to Eq. (7) are:

Dependent variable: Y*
Method: Least squares

Variable	Coefficient	Std. Error	*t*-Statistic	Prob.
X_1	0.022739	0.014126	1.609705	0.1385
X_2	-0.010693	0.000790	-13.52990	0.0000

R^2 = 0.968324 Durbin-Watson *d* statistic = 0.308883

Now using Eq. (8), the reader can verify that

$$\beta_1^* = 0.4727 \quad \text{and} \quad \beta_2^* = -0.00069 \tag{9}$$

TABLE 14.4

Y^*	X_1	X_2
0.067744	1.005013	0.226128
0.034928	1.051271	2.365360
−0.013327	1.105171	4.973269
−0.062825	1.161834	7.842381
−0.109831	1.221403	10.99262
−0.154011	1.284025	14.44529
−0.195936	1.349859	18.22309
−0.236580	1.419068	22.35031
−0.276921	1.491825	26.85284
−0.317740	1.568312	31.75832
−0.397464	1.733253	42.89801
−0.446153	1.822119	49.19721

Contrast these numbers with the initial guesses of 0.45 and 0.01, respectively, for the two parameters. Using the new estimates given in Eq. (9), you can start the iterative procedure once more and go on iterating until there is "convergence" in the sense that the final round of the estimates does not differ much from the round before that. Of course, you will require fewer iterations if your initial guess is closer to the final values. Also, notice that we have used only the linear term in Taylor's series expansion. If you were to use the quadratic or higher-order terms in the expansion, perhaps you would reach the final values much quicker. But in many applications the linear approximation has proved to be quite good.

Chapter 15

Qualitative Response Regression Models

In all the regression models that we have considered so far, we have implicitly assumed that the regressand, the dependent variable, or the *response* variable Y is quantitative, whereas the explanatory variables are either quantitative, qualitative (or dummy), or a mixture thereof. In fact, in Chapter 9, on dummy variables, we saw how the dummy regressors are introduced in a regression model and what role they play in specific situations.

In this chapter we consider several models in which the regressand itself is qualitative in nature. Although increasingly used in various areas of social sciences and medical research, qualitative response regression models pose interesting estimation and interpretation challenges. In this chapter we only touch on some of the major themes in this area, leaving the details to more specialized books.[1]

15.1 The Nature of Qualitative Response Models

Suppose we want to study the labor force participation (LFP) decision of adult males. Since an adult is either in the labor force or not, LFP is a *yes* or *no* decision. Hence, the response variable, or regressand, can take only two values, say, 1 if the person is in the labor force and 0 if he or she is not. In other words, the regressand is a **binary,** or **dichotomous, variable.** Labor economics research suggests that the LFP decision is a function of the unemployment rate, average wage rate, education, family income, etc.

As another example, consider U.S. presidential elections. Assume that there are two political parties, Democratic and Republican. The dependent variable here is vote choice between the two political parties. Suppose we let $Y = 1$, if the vote is for a Democratic candidate, and $Y = 0$, if the vote is for a Republican candidate. A considerable amount of research on this topic has been done by the economist Ray Fair of Yale University and several political scientists.[2] Some of the variables used in the vote choice are growth rate of GDP, unemployment and inflation rates, whether the candidate is running for reelection, etc.

[1] At the introductory level, the reader may find the following sources very useful. Daniel A. Powers and Yu Xie, *Statistical Methods for Categorical Data Analysis,* Academic Press, 2000; John H. Aldrich and Forrest Nelson, *Linear Probability, Logit, and Probit Models,* Sage Publications, 1984; and Tim Futing Liao, *Interpreting Probability Models: Logit, Probit and Other Generalized Linear Models,* Sage Publications, 1994. For a very comprehensive review of the literature, see G. S. Maddala, *Limited-Dependent and Qualitative Variables in Econometrics,* Cambridge University Press, 1983.

[2] See, for example, Ray Fair, "Econometrics and Presidential Elections," *Journal of Economic Perspective,* Summer 1996, pp. 89–102, and Michael S. Lewis-Beck, *Economics and Elections: The Major Western Democracies,* University of Michigan Press, Ann Arbor, 1980.

For the present purposes, the important thing to note is that the regressand is a qualitative variable.

One can think of several other examples where the regressand is qualitative in nature. Thus, a family either owns a house or it does not, it has disability insurance or it does not, both husband and wife are in the labor force or only one spouse is. Similarly, a certain drug is effective in curing an illness or it is not. A firm decides to declare a stock dividend or not, a senator decides to vote for a tax cut or not, a U.S. president decides to veto a bill or accept it, etc.

We do not have to restrict our response variable to yes/no or dichotomous categories only. Returning to our presidential elections example, suppose there are three parties, Democratic, Republican, and Independent. The response variable here is **trichotomous.** In general, we can have a **polychotomous** (or **multiple-category**) response variable.

What we plan to do is to first consider the dichotomous regressand and then consider various extensions of the basic model. But before we do that, it is important to note a fundamental difference between a regression model where the regressand Y is quantitative and a model where it is qualitative.

In a model where Y is quantitative, our objective is to estimate its expected, or mean, value given the values of the regressors. In terms of Chapter 2, what we want is $E(Y_i \mid X_{1i}, X_{2i}, \ldots, X_{ki})$, where the X's are regressors, both quantitative and qualitative. In models where Y is qualitative, our objective is to find the probability of something happening, such as voting for a Democratic candidate, or owning a house, or belonging to a union, or participating in a sport, etc. Hence, qualitative response regression models are often known as *probability models*.

In the rest of this chapter, we seek answers to the following questions:

1. How do we estimate qualitative response regression models? Can we simply estimate them with the usual OLS procedures?
2. Are there special inference problems? In other words, is the hypothesis testing procedure any different from the ones we have learned so far?
3. If a regressand is qualitative, how can we measure the goodness of fit of such models? Is the conventionally computed R^2 of any value in such models?
4. Once we go beyond the dichotomous regressand case, how do we estimate and interpret the polychotomous regression models? Also, how do we handle models in which the regressand is **ordinal,** that is, an ordered categorical variable, such as schooling (less than 8 years, 8 to 11 years, 12 years, and 13 or more years), or the regressand is **nominal** where there is no inherent ordering, such as ethnicity (Black, White, Hispanic, Asian, and other)?
5. How do we model phenomena such as the number of visits to one's physician per year, the number of patents received by a firm in a given year, the number of articles published by a college professor in a year, the number of telephone calls received in a span of 5 minutes, or the number of cars passing through a toll booth in a span of 5 minutes? Such phenomena, called **count data,** or **rare event** data, are an example of the **Poisson** (probability) process.

In this chapter we provide answers to some of these questions at the elementary level, for some of the topics are quite advanced and require more background in mathematics and statistics than assumed in this book. References cited in the various footnotes may be consulted for further details.

We start our study of qualitative response models by first considering the **binary response** regression model. There are four approaches to developing a probability model for a binary response variable:

1. The **linear probability model (LPM)**

2. The **logit model**
3. The **probit model**
4. The **tobit model**

Because of its comparative simplicity, and because it can be estimated by ordinary least squares (OLS), we will first consider the LPM, leaving the other two models for subsequent sections.

15.2 The Linear Probability Model (LPM)

To fix ideas, consider the following regression model:

$$Y_i = \beta_1 + \beta_2 X_i + u_i \tag{15.2.1}$$

where X = family income and $Y = 1$ if the family owns a house and 0 if it does not own a house.

Model (15.2.1) looks like a typical linear regression model but because the regressand is binary, or dichotomous, it is called a **linear probability model (LPM).** This is because the conditional expectation of Y_i given X_i, $E(Y_i \mid X_i)$, can be interpreted as the *conditional probability* that the event will occur given X_i, that is, $\Pr(Y_i = 1 \mid X_i)$. Thus, in our example, $E(Y_i \mid X_i)$ gives the probability of a family owning a house and whose income is the given amount X_i.

The justification of the name LPM for models like Eq. (15.2.1) can be seen as follows: Assuming $E(u_i) = 0$, as usual (to obtain unbiased estimators), we obtain

$$E(Y_i \mid X_i) = \beta_1 + \beta_2 X_i \tag{15.2.2}$$

Now, if P_i = probability that $Y_i = 1$ (that is, the event occurs), and $(1 - P_i)$ = probability that $Y_i = 0$ (that is, the event does not occur), the variable Y_i has the following (probability) distribution:

Y_i	Probability
0	$1 - P_i$
1	P_i
Total	1

That is, Y_i follows the **Bernoulli probability distribution.**

Now, by the definition of mathematical expectation, we obtain:

$$E(Y_i) = 0(1 - P_i) + 1(P_i) = P_i \tag{15.2.3}$$

Comparing Eq. (15.2.2) with Eq. (15.2.3), we can equate

$$E(Y_i \mid X_i) = \beta_1 + \beta_2 X_i = P_i \tag{15.2.4}$$

that is, the conditional expectation of the model (15.2.1) can, in fact, be interpreted as the conditional probability of Y_i. In general, the expectation of a Bernoulli random variable is the probability that the random variable equals 1. In passing note that if there are n independent trials, each with a probability p of success and probability $(1 - p)$ of failure, and X of these trials represent the number of successes, then X is said to follow the **binomial distribution.** The mean of the binomial distribution is np and its variance is $np(1 - p)$. The term *success* is defined in the context of the problem.

Since the probability P_i must lie between 0 and 1, we have the restriction

$$0 \leq E(Y_i \mid X_i) \leq 1 \tag{15.2.5}$$

that is, the conditional expectation (or conditional probability) must lie between 0 and 1.

From the preceding discussion it would seem that OLS can be easily extended to binary dependent variable regression models. So, perhaps there is nothing new here. Unfortunately, this is not the case, for the LPM poses several problems, which are as follows:

Non-Normality of the Disturbances u_i

Although OLS does not require the disturbances (u_i) to be normally distributed, we assumed them to be so distributed for the purpose of statistical inference.[3] But the assumption of normality for u_i is not tenable for the LPMs because, like Y_i, the disturbances u_i also take only two values; that is, they also follow the Bernoulli distribution. This can be seen clearly if we write Eq. (15.2.1) as

$$u_i = Y_i - \beta_1 - \beta_2 X_i \tag{15.2.6}$$

The probability distribution of u_i is

	u_i	Probability
When $Y_i = 1$	$1 - \beta_1 - \beta_2 X_i$	P_i
When $Y_i = 0$	$-\beta_1 - \beta_2 X_i$	$(1 - P_i)$

(15.2.7)

Obviously, u_i cannot be assumed to be normally distributed; they follow the Bernoulli distribution.

But the nonfulfillment of the normality assumption may not be so critical as it appears because we know that the OLS point estimates still remain unbiased (recall that, if the objective is point estimation, the normality assumption is not necessary). Besides, as the sample size increases indefinitely, statistical theory shows that the OLS estimators tend to be normally distributed generally.[4] As a result, in large samples the statistical inference of the LPM will follow the usual OLS procedure under the normality assumption.

Heteroscedastic Variances of the Disturbances

Even if $E(u_i) = 0$ and $\text{cov}(u_i, u_j) = 0$ for $i \neq j$ (i.e., no serial correlation), it can no longer be maintained that in the LPM the disturbances are homoscedastic. This is, however, not surprising. As statistical theory shows, for a Bernoulli distribution the theoretical mean and variance are, respectively, p and $p(1 - p)$, where p is the probability of success (i.e., something happening), showing that the variance is a function of the mean. Hence the error variance is heteroscedastic.

For the distribution of the error term given in Eq. (15.2.7), applying the definition of variance, the reader should verify that (see Exercise 15.10)

$$\text{var}(u_i) = P_i(1 - P_i) \tag{15.2.8}$$

[3]Recall that we have recommended that the normality assumption be checked in an application by suitable normality tests, such as the Jarque–Bera test.

[4]The proof is based on the central limit theorem and may be found in E. Malinvaud, *Statistical Methods of Econometrics*, Rand McNally, Chicago, 1966, pp. 195–197. If the regressors are deemed stochastic and are jointly normally distributed, the F and t tests can still be used even though the disturbances are non-normal. Also keep in mind that as the sample size increases indefinitely, the binomial distribution converges to the normal distribution.

That is, the variance of the error term in the LPM is heteroscedastic. Since $P_i = E(Y_i \mid X_i) = \beta_1 + \beta_2 X_i$, the variance of u_i ultimately depends on the values of X and hence is not homoscedastic.

We already know that, in the presence of heteroscedasticity, the OLS estimators, although unbiased, are not efficient; that is, they do not have minimum variance. But the problem of heteroscedasticity, like the problem of non-normality, is not insurmountable. In Chapter 11 we discussed several methods of handling the heteroscedasticity problem. Since the variance of u_i depends on $E(Y_i \mid X_i)$, one way to resolve the heteroscedasticity problem is to transform the model (15.2.1) by dividing it through by

$$\sqrt{E(Y_i|X_i)[1 - E(Y_i|X_i)]} = \sqrt{P_i(1 - P_i)} = \text{say } \sqrt{w_i}$$

that is,

$$\frac{Y_i}{\sqrt{w_i}} = \frac{\beta_1}{\sqrt{w_i}} + \beta_2 \frac{X_i}{\sqrt{w_i}} + \frac{u_i}{\sqrt{w_i}} \tag{15.2.9}$$

As you can readily verify, the transformed error term in Eq. (15.2.9) is homoscedastic. Therefore, after estimating Eq. (15.2.1), we can now estimate Eq. (15.2.9) by OLS, which is nothing but the *weighted least squares* (WLS) with w_i serving as the weights.

In theory, what we have just described is fine. But in practice the true $E(Y_i \mid X_i)$ is unknown; hence the weights w_i are unknown. To estimate w_i, we can use the following two-step procedure:[5]

Step 1. Run the OLS regression (15.2.1) despite the heteroscedasticity problem and obtain $\hat{Y}_i$ = estimate of the true $E(Y_i \mid X_i)$. Then obtain $\hat{w}_i = \hat{Y}_i(1 - \hat{Y}_i)$, the estimate of w_i.

Step 2. Use the estimated w_i to transform the data as shown in Eq. (15.2.9) and estimate the transformed equation by OLS (i.e., weighted least squares).

Although we will illustrate this procedure for our example shortly, it may be noted that we can use White's heteroscedasticity-corrected standard errors to deal with heteroscedasticity, provided the sample is reasonably large.

Even if we correct for heteroscedasticity, we first need to address another problem that plagues LPM.

Nonfulfillment of $0 \leq E(Y_i \mid X_i) \leq 1$

Since $E(Y_i \mid X_i)$ in the linear probability models measures the conditional probability of the event Y occurring given X, it must necessarily lie between 0 and 1. Although this is true a priori, there is no guarantee that $\hat{Y}_i$, the estimators of $E(Y_i \mid X_i)$, will necessarily fulfill this restriction, *and this is the real problem with the OLS estimation of the LPM.* This happens because OLS does not take into account the restriction that $0 \leq E(Y_i) \leq 1$ (an inequality restriction). There are two ways of finding out whether the estimated $\hat{Y}_i$ lie between 0 and 1. One is to estimate the LPM by the usual OLS method and find out whether the estimated $\hat{Y}_i$ lie between 0 and 1. If some are less than 0 (that is, negative), $\hat{Y}_i$ is assumed to be zero for those cases; if they are greater than 1, they are assumed to be 1. The second procedure is to devise an estimating technique that will guarantee that the estimated conditional probabilities $\hat{Y}_i$ will lie between 0 and 1. The logit and probit models discussed later will guarantee that the estimated probabilities will indeed lie between the logical limits 0 and 1.

[5]For the justification of this procedure, see Arthur S. Goldberger, *Econometric Theory,* John Wiley & Sons, New York, 1964, pp. 249–250. The justification is basically a large-sample one that we discussed under the topic of feasible or estimated generalized least squares in the chapter on heteroscedasticity (see Sec. 11.6).

Questionable Value of R^2 as a Measure of Goodness of Fit

The conventionally computed R^2 is of limited value in the dichotomous response models. To see why, consider Figure 15.1. Corresponding to a given X, Y is either 0 or 1. Therefore, all the Y values will either lie along the X axis or along the line corresponding to 1. Therefore, generally no LPM is expected to fit such a scatter well, whether it is the *unconstrained LPM* (Figure 15.1*a*) or the *truncated* or *constrained LPM* (Figure 15.1*b*), an LPM estimated in such a way that it will not fall outside the logical band 0–1. As a result, the conventionally computed R^2 is likely to be much lower than 1 for such models. In most practical applications the R^2 ranges between 0.2 to 0.6. R^2 in such models will be high, say, in excess of 0.8 only when the actual scatter is very closely clustered around points A and B (Figure 15.1*c*), for in that case it is easy to fix the straight line by joining the two points A and B. In this case the predicted Y_i will be very close to either 0 or 1.

FIGURE 15.1 Linear probability models.

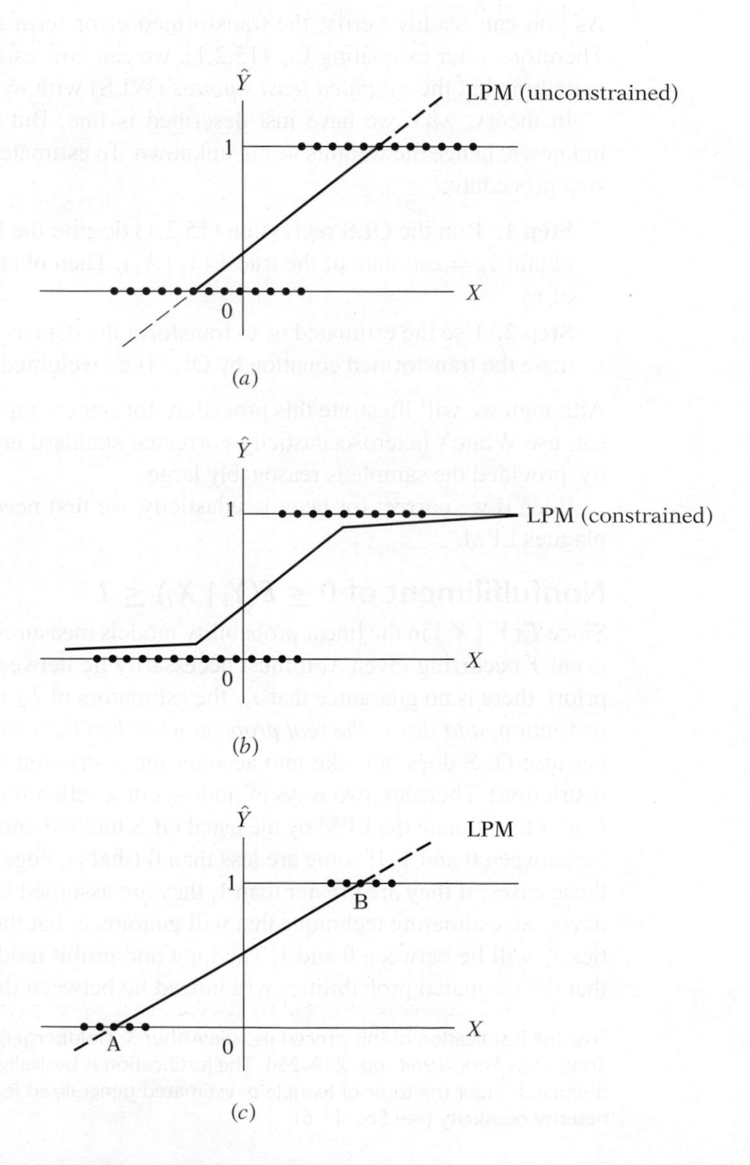

For these reasons John Aldrich and Forrest Nelson contend that "use of the coefficient of determination as a summary statistic should be avoided in models with qualitative dependent variable[s]."[6]

EXAMPLE 15.1

LPM: A Numerical Example

To illustrate some of the points made about the LPM in this section, we present a numerical example. Table 15.1 gives invented data on home ownership Y (1 = owns a house, 0 = does not own a house) and family income X (thousands of dollars) for 40 families. From these data the LPM estimated by OLS was as follows:

$$\begin{aligned} \hat{Y}_i &= -0.9457 + 0.1021X_i \\ &\quad\ (0.1228) \quad (0.0082) \\ t &= (-7.6984) \quad (12.515) \qquad R^2 = 0.8048 \end{aligned} \tag{15.2.10}$$

First, let us interpret this regression. The intercept of −0.9457 gives the "probability" that a family with zero income will own a house. Since this value is negative, and since probability cannot be negative, we treat this value as zero, which is sensible in the present instance.[7] The slope value of 0.1021 means that for a unit change in income (here $1,000), on the average the probability of owning a house increases by 0.1021 or about 10 percent. Of course, given a particular level of income, we can estimate the actual probability of owning a house from Eq. (15.2.10). Thus, for $X = 12$ ($12,000), the estimated probability of owning a house is

$$\begin{aligned} (\hat{Y}_i \mid X = 12) &= -0.9457 + 12(0.1021) \\ &= 0.2795 \end{aligned}$$

TABLE 15.1 **Hypothetical Data on Home Ownership ($Y = 1$ If owns home, 0 Otherwise) and Income X (Thousands of dollars)**

Family	Y	X	Family	Y	X
1	0	8	21	1	22
2	1	16	22	1	16
3	1	18	23	0	12
4	0	11	24	0	11
5	0	12	25	1	16
6	1	19	26	0	11
7	1	20	27	1	20
8	0	13	28	1	18
9	0	9	29	0	11
10	0	10	30	0	10
11	1	17	31	1	17
12	1	18	32	0	13
13	0	14	33	1	21
14	1	20	34	1	20
15	0	6	35	0	11
16	1	19	36	0	8
17	1	16	37	1	17
18	0	10	38	1	16
19	0	8	39	0	7
20	1	18	40	1	17

(Continued)

[6] Aldrich and Nelson, op. cit., p. 15. For other measures of goodness of fit in models involving dummy regressands, see T. Amemiya, "Qualitative Response Models," *Journal of Economic Literature*, vol. 19, 1981, pp. 331–354.

[7] One can loosely interpret the highly negative value as near improbability of owning a house when income is zero.

EXAMPLE 15.1 (*Continued*)

That is, the probability that a family with an income of $12,000 will own a house is about 28 percent. Table 15.2 shows the estimated probabilities, $\hat{Y}_i$, for the various income levels listed in the table. The most noticeable feature of this table is that six estimated values are negative and six values are in excess of 1, demonstrating clearly the point made earlier that, although $E(Y_i \mid X_i)$ is positive and less than 1, their estimators, $\hat{Y}_i$, need not be necessarily positive or less than 1. This is one reason that the LPM is not the recommended model when the dependent variable is dichotomous.

Even if the estimated Y_i were all positive and less than 1, the LPM still suffers from the problem of heteroscedasticity, which can be seen readily from Eq. (15.2.8). As a consequence, we cannot trust the estimated standard errors reported in Eq. (15.2.10). (Why?) But we can use the weighted least-squares (WLS) procedure discussed earlier to obtain more efficient estimates of the standard errors. The necessary weights, $\hat{w}_i$, required for the application of WLS are also shown in Table 15.2. But note that since some Y_i are negative and some are in excess of one, the $\hat{w}_i$ corresponding to these values will be negative. Thus, we cannot use these observations in WLS (why?), thereby reducing the number of observations, from 40 to 28 in the present example.[8] Omitting these observations, the WLS regression is

$$\frac{\hat{Y}_i}{\sqrt{\hat{w}_i}} = -1.2456\frac{1}{\sqrt{\hat{w}_i}} + 0.1196\frac{X_i}{\sqrt{\hat{w}_i}} \tag{15.2.11}$$

$$\begin{aligned} &\quad\ (0.1206) \qquad\quad (0.0069) \\ t = &\ (-10.332) \qquad\ (17.454) \qquad R^2 = 0.9214 \end{aligned}$$

TABLE 15.2 Actual Y, Estimated Y, and Weights w_i for the Home Ownership Example

Y_i	$\hat{Y}_i$	$\hat{w}_i$‡	$\sqrt{\hat{w}_i}$	Y_i	$\hat{Y}_i$	$\hat{w}_i$‡	$\sqrt{\hat{w}_i}$
0	−0.129*			1	1.301†		
1	0.688	0.2146	0.4633	1	0.688	0.2147	0.4633
1	0.893	0.0956	0.3091	0	0.280	0.2016	0.4990
0	0.178	0.1463	0.3825	0	0.178	0.1463	0.3825
0	0.280	0.2016	0.4490	1	0.688	0.2147	0.4633
1	0.995	0.00498	0.0705	0	0.178	0.1463	0.3825
1	1.098†			1	1.097†		
0	0.382	0.2361	0.4859	1	0.893	0.0956	0.3091
0	−0.0265*			0	0.178	0.1463	0.3825
0	0.076	0.0702	0.2650	0	0.076	0.0702	0.2650
1	0.791	0.1653	0.4066	1	0.791	0.1653	0.4055
1	0.893	0.0956	0.3091	0	0.382	0.2361	0.4859
0	0.484	0.2497	0.4997	1	1.199†		
1	1.097†			1	1.097†		
0	−0.333*			0	0.178	0.1463	0.3825
1	0.995	0.00498	0.0705	0	−0.129*		
1	0.688	0.2147	0.4633	1	0.791	0.1653	0.4066
0	0.076	0.0702	0.2650	1	0.688	0.2147	0.4633
0	−0.129*			0	−0.231*		
1	0.893	0.0956	0.3091	1	0.791	0.1653	0.4066

* Treated as zero to avoid probabilities being negative.
† Treated as unity to avoid probabilities exceeding one.
‡ $\hat{Y}_i(1 - \hat{Y}_i)$

[8]To avoid the loss of the degrees of freedom, we could let $\hat{Y}_i = 0.01$ when the estimated Y_i are negative and $\hat{Y}_i = 0.99$ when they are in excess of or equal to 1. See Exercise 15.1.

EXAMPLE 15.1
(Continued)

These results show that, compared with Eq. (15.2.10), the estimated standard errors are smaller and, correspondingly, the estimated t ratios (in absolute value) are larger. But one should take this result with a grain of salt since in estimating Eq. (15.2.11) we had to drop 12 observations. Also, since w_i are estimated, the usual statistical hypothesis-testing procedures are, strictly speaking, valid in the large samples (see Chapter 11).

15.3 Applications of LPM

Until the availability of readily accessible computer packages to estimate the logit and probit models (to be discussed shortly), the LPM was used quite extensively because of its simplicity. We now illustrate some of these applications.

EXAMPLE 15.2
Cohen–Rea–Lerman Study[9]

In a study prepared for the U.S. Department of Labor, Cohen, Rea, and Lerman were interested in examining the labor-force participation of various categories of labor as a function of several socioeconomic–demographic variables. In all their regressions, the dependent variable is a dummy, taking a value of 1 if a person is in the labor force, 0 if he or she is not. In Table 15.3 we reproduce one of their several dummy-dependent variable regressions.

Before interpreting the results, note these features: The preceding regression was estimated by using the OLS. To correct for heteroscedasticity, the authors used the two-step procedure outlined previously in some of their regressions but found that the standard errors of the estimates thus obtained did not differ materially from those obtained without correction for heteroscedasticity. Perhaps this result is due to the sheer size of the sample, namely, about 25,000. Because of this large sample size, the estimated t values may be tested for statistical significance by the usual OLS procedure even though the error term takes dichotomous values. The estimated R^2 of 0.175 may seem rather low, but in view of the large sample size, this R^2 is still significant on the basis of the F test (See Section 8.4). Finally, notice how the authors have blended quantitative and qualitative variables and how they have taken into account the interaction effects.

Turning to the interpretations of the findings, we see that each slope coefficient gives the rate of change in the conditional probability of the event occurring for a given unit change in the value of the explanatory variable. For instance, the coefficient of −0.2753 attached to the variable "age 65 and over" means, holding all other factors constant, the probability of participation in the labor force by women in this age group is smaller by about 27 percent (as compared with the base category of women aged 22 to 54). By the same token, the coefficient of 0.3061 attached to the variable "16 or more years of schooling" means, holding all other factors constant, the probability of women with this much education participating in the labor force is higher by about 31 percent (as compared with women with less than 5 years of schooling, the base category).

Now consider the **interaction term** marital status and age. The table shows that the labor-force participation probability is higher by some 29 percent for those women who were never married (as compared with the base category) and smaller by about 28 percent for those women who are 65 and over (again in relation to the base category). But the probability of participation of women who were never married and are 65 or over is smaller by about 20 percent as compared with the base category. This implies that women aged 65 and over but never married are likely to participate in the labor force more than those who are aged 65 and over and are married or fall into the "other" category.

(*Continued*)

[9] Malcolm S. Cohen, Samuel A. Rea, Jr., and Robert I. Lerman, *A Micro Model of Labor Supply*, BLS Staff Paper 4, U.S. Department of Labor, 1970.

EXAMPLE 15.2 *(Continued)*

TABLE 15.3 Labor-Force Participation

Regression of women, age 22 and over, living in largest 96 standard metropolitan statistical areas (SMSA) (dependent variable: in or out of labor force during 1966)

Explanatory Variable		Coefficient	t Ratio
Constant		0.4368	15.4
Marital status			
Married, spouse present		—	—
Married, other		0.1523	13.8
Never married		0.2915	22.0
Age			
22–54		—	—
55–64		−0.0594	−5.7
65 and over		−0.2753	−9.0
Years of schooling			
0–4		—	—
5–8		0.1255	5.8
9–11		0.1704	7.9
12–15		0.2231	10.6
16 and over		0.3061	13.3
Unemployment rate (1966), %			
Under 2.5		—	—
2.5–3.4		−0.0213	−1.6
3.5–4.0		−0.0269	−2.0
4.1–5.0		−0.0291	−2.2
5.1 and over		−0.0311	−2.4
Employment change (1965–1966), %			
Under 3.5		—	—
3.5–6.49		0.0301	3.2
6.5 and over		0.0529	5.1
Relative employment opportunities, %			
Under 62		—	—
62–73.9		0.0381	3.2
74 and over		0.0571	3.2
FILOW, $			
Less than 1,500 and negative		—	—
1,500–7,499		−0.1451	−15.4
7,500 and over		−0.2455	−24.4
Interaction (marital status and age)			
Marital status	Age		
Other	55–64	−0.0406	−2.1
Other	65 and over	−0.1391	−7.4
Never married	55–64	−0.1104	−3.3
Never married	65 and over	−0.2045	−6.4
Interaction (age and years of schooling completed)			
Age	Years of schooling		
65 and over	5–8	−0.0885	−2.8
65 and over	9–11	−0.0848	−2.4
65 and over	12–15	−0.1288	−4.0
65 and over	16 and over	−0.1628	−3.6
		$R^2 = 0.175$	
No. of observations = 25,153			

Note: — indicates the base or omitted category.

FILOW: family income less own wage and salary income.

Source: Malcolm S. Cohen, Samuel A. Rea, Jr., and Robert I. Lerman, *A Micro Model of Labor Supply,* BLS Staff Paper 4, U.S. Department of Labor, 1970, Table F-6, pp. 212–213.

EXAMPLE 15.2 *(Continued)*

Following this procedure, the reader can easily interpret the rest of the coefficients given in Table 15.3. From the given information, it is easy to obtain the estimates of the conditional probabilities of labor-force participation of the various categories. Thus, if we want to find the probability for married women (other), aged 22 to 54, with 12 to 15 years of schooling, with an unemployment rate of 2.5 to 3.4 percent, employment change of 3.5 to 6.49 percent, relative employment opportunities of 74 percent and over, and with FILOW of $7,500 and over, we obtain

$$0.4368 + 0.1523 + 0.2231 - 0.0213 + 0.0301 + 0.0571 - 0.2455 = 0.6326$$

In other words, the probability of labor-force participation by women with the preceding characteristics is estimated to be about 63 percent.

EXAMPLE 15.3 *Predicting a Bond Rating*

Based on a pooled time series and cross-sectional data of 200 Aa (high-quality) and Baa (medium-quality) bonds over the period 1961–1966, Joseph Cappelleri estimated the following bond rating prediction model.[10]

$$Y_i = \beta_1 + \beta_2 X_{2i}^2 + \beta_3 X_{3i} + \beta_4 X_{4i} + \beta_5 X_{5i} + u_i$$

where Y_i = 1 if the bond rating is Aa (Moody's rating)
= 0 if the bond rating is Baa (Moody's rating)
X_2 = debt capitalization ratio, a measure of leverage

$$= \frac{\text{dollar value of long-term debt}}{\text{dollar value of total capitalization}} \cdot 100$$

X_3 = profit rate

$$= \frac{\text{dollar value of after-tax income}}{\text{dollar value of net total assets}} \cdot 100$$

X_4 = standard deviation of the profit rate, a measure of profit rate variability
X_5 = net total assets (thousands of dollars), a measure of size

A priori, β_2 and β_4 are expected to be negative (why?) and β_3 and β_5 are expected to be positive.

After correcting for heteroscedasticity and first-order autocorrelation, Cappelleri obtained the following results:[11]

$$\begin{aligned} \hat{Y}_i = &\ 0.6860 - 0.0179X_{2i}^2 + 0.0486X_{3i} + 0.0572X_{4i} + 0.378(E\text{-}7)X_5 \\ &(0.1775)\quad (0.0024)\qquad (0.0486)\qquad (0.0178)\qquad (0.039)(E\text{-}8) \end{aligned} \tag{15.3.1}$$

$$R^2 = 0.6933$$

Note: 0.378 (*E*-7) means 0.0000000378, etc.

All but the coefficient of X_4 have the correct signs. It is left to finance students to rationalize why the profit rate variability coefficient has a positive sign, for one would expect that the greater the variability in profits, the less likely it is Moody's would give an Aa rating, other things remaining the same.

The interpretation of the regression is straightforward. For example, 0.0486 attached to X_3 means that, other things being the same, a 1 percentage point increase in the profit rate will lead on average to about a 0.05 increase in the probability of a bond getting the Aa rating. Similarly, the higher the squared leveraged ratio, the lower by 0.02 is the probability of a bond being classified as an Aa bond per unit increase in this ratio.

[10] Joseph Cappelleri, "Predicting a Bond Rating," unpublished term paper, C.U.N.Y. The model used in the paper is a modification of the model used by Thomas F. Pogue and Robert M. Soldofsky, "What Is in a Bond Rating?" *Journal of Financial and Quantitative Analysis*, June 1969, pp. 201–228.

[11] Some of the estimated probabilities before correcting for heteroscedasticity were negative and some were in excess of 1; in these cases they were assumed to be 0.01 and 0.99, respectively, to facilitate the computation of the weights w_i.

EXAMPLE 15.4 *Who Holds a Debit Card?*

Like credit cards, debit cards are now used extensively by consumers. Vendors prefer them because when you use a debit card, the amount of your purchase is automatically deducted from your checking or other designated account. To find out what factors determine the use of the debit card, we obtained data on 60 customers and considered the following model:[12]

$$Y_i = \beta_1 + \beta_2 X_{2i} + \beta_3 X_{3i} + \beta_4 X_{4i} + u_i$$

where $Y = 1$ for debit card holder, 0 otherwise; $X_2 =$ account balance in dollars; $X_3 =$ number of ATM transactions; $X_4 = 1$ if interest is received on the account, 0 otherwise.

Since the linear probability model (LPM) exhibits heteroscedasticity, we present the usual OLS results and the OLS results corrected for heteroscedasticity in a tabular form.

Variable	Coefficient	Coefficient*
Constant	0.3631	0.3631
	(0.1796)**	(0.1604)**
Balance	0.00028**	0.00028**
	(0.00015)	(0.00014)
ATM	−0.0269	−0.0269
	(0.208)	(0.0202)
Interest	−0.3019**	−0.3019**
	(0.1448)	(0.1353)
R^2	0.1056	(0.1056)

Note: *denotes heteroscedasticity-corrected standard errors.
**significant at about 5% level.

As these results show, those who have higher account balances will tend to hold a debit card. The higher the interest rate paid on account balances, the less the tendency to hold a debit card. Although the ATM variable is not significant, note that it has a negative sign. This is perhaps due to ATM transaction fees.

There is not a vast difference between the estimated standard errors with and without heteroscedasticity correction. To save space, we have not presented the fitted values (i.e., the estimated probabilities), but they all were within the limits of 0 and 1. However, there is no guarantee that this will happen in every case.

15.4 Alternatives to LPM

As we have seen, the LPM is plagued by several problems, such as (1) non-normality of u_i, (2) heteroscedasticity of u_i, (3) possibility of $\hat{Y}_i$ lying outside the 0–1 range, and (4) the generally lower R^2 values. But these problems are surmountable. For example, we can use WLS to resolve the heteroscedasticity problem or increase the sample size to minimize the non-normality problem. By resorting to restricted least-squares or mathematical programming techniques we can even make the estimated probabilities lie in the 0–1 interval.

But even then the fundamental problem with the LPM is that it is not logically a very attractive model because it assumes that $P_i = E(Y = 1 \mid X)$ increases linearly with X, that is, the marginal or incremental effect of X remains constant throughout. Thus, in our home ownership example we found that as X increases by a unit ($1,000), the probability of

[12]The data used in the analysis are obtained from Douglas A. Lind, William G. Marchal, and Robert D. Mason, *Statistical Techniques in Business and Economics,* 11th Ed., McGraw-Hill, 2002, Appendix *N*, pp. 775–776. We have not used all the variables used by the authors.

FIGURE 15.2
A cumulative distribution function (CDF).

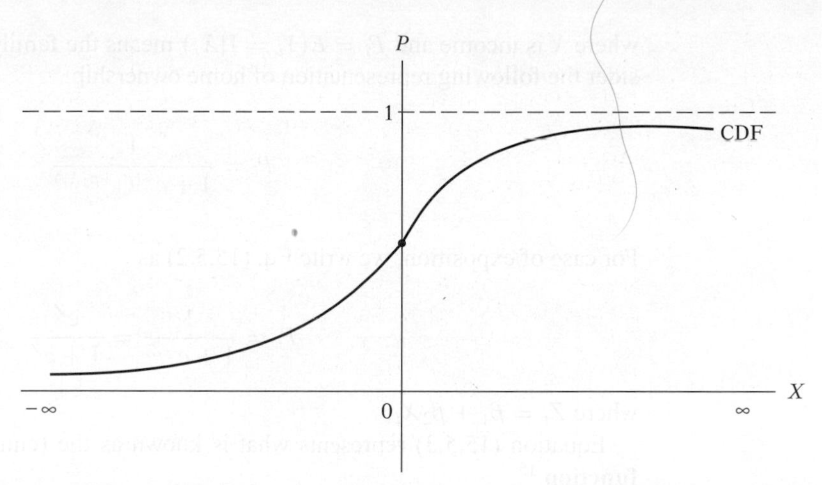

owning a house increases by the same constant amount of 0.10. This is so whether the income level is \$8,000, \$10,000, \$18,000, or \$22,000. This seems patently unrealistic. In reality one would expect that P_i is nonlinearly related to X_i: At very low income a family will not own a house but at a sufficiently high level of income, say, X^*, it most likely will own a house. Any increase in income beyond X^* will have little effect on the probability of owning a house. Thus, at both ends of the income distribution, the probability of owning a house will be virtually unaffected by a small increase in X.

Therefore, what we need is a (probability) model that has these two features: (1) As X_i increases, $P_i = E(Y = 1 \mid X)$ increases but never steps outside the 0–1 interval, and (2) the relationship between P_i and X_i is nonlinear, that is, "one which approaches zero at slower and slower rates as X_i gets small and approaches one at slower and slower rates as X_i gets very large."[13]

Geometrically, the model we want would look something like Figure 15.2. Notice in this model that the probability lies between 0 and 1 and that it varies nonlinearly with X.

The reader will realize that the sigmoid, or S-shaped, curve in the figure very much resembles the **cumulative distribution function** (CDF) of a random variable.[14] Therefore, one can easily use the CDF to model regressions where the response variable is dichotomous, taking 0–1 values. The practical question now is, which CDF? For although all CDFs are S shaped, for each random variable there is a unique CDF. For historical as well as practical reasons, the CDFs commonly chosen to represent the 0–1 response models are (1) the logistic and (2) the normal, the former giving rise to the **logit** model and the latter to the **probit** (or **normit**) model.

Although a detailed discussion of the logit and probit models is beyond the scope of this book, we will indicate somewhat informally how one estimates such models and how one interprets them.

15.5 The Logit Model

We will continue with our home ownership example to explain the basic ideas underlying the logit model. Recall that in explaining home ownership in relation to income, the LPM was

$$P_i = \beta_1 + \beta_2 X_i \tag{15.5.1}$$

[13] John Aldrich and Forrest Nelson, op. cit., p. 26.

[14] As discussed in **Appendix A**, the CDF of a random variable X is simply the probability that it takes a value less than or equal to x_0, where x_0 is some specified numerical value of X. In short, $F(X)$, the CDF of X, is $F(X = x_0) = P(X \leq x_0)$.

where X is income and $P_i = E(Y_i = 1|X_i)$ means the family owns a house. But now consider the following representation of home ownership:

$$P_i = \frac{1}{1 + e^{-(\beta_1 + \beta_2 X_i)}} \tag{15.5.2}$$

For ease of exposition, we write Eq. (15.5.2) as

$$P_i = \frac{1}{1 + e^{-Z_i}} = \frac{e^Z}{1 + e^Z} \tag{15.5.3}$$

where $Z_i = \beta_1 + \beta_2 X_i$.

Equation (15.5.3) represents what is known as the (cumulative) **logistic distribution function.**[15]

It is easy to verify that as Z_i ranges from $-\infty$ to $+\infty$, P_i ranges between 0 and 1 and that P_i is nonlinearly related to Z_i (i.e., X_i), thus satisfying the two requirements considered earlier.[16] But it seems that in satisfying these requirements, we have created an estimation problem because P_i is nonlinear not only in X but also in the β's as can be seen clearly from Eq. (15.5.2). This means that we cannot use the familiar OLS procedure to estimate the parameters.[17] But this problem is more apparent than real because Eq. (15.5.2) can be linearized, which can be shown as follows.

If P_i, the probability of owning a house, is given by Eq. (15.5.3), then $(1 - P_i)$, the probability of not owning a house, is

$$1 - P_i = \frac{1}{1 + e^{Z_i}} \tag{15.5.4}$$

Therefore, we can write

$$\frac{P_i}{1 - P_i} = \frac{1 + e^{Z_i}}{1 + e^{-Z_i}} = e^{Z_i} \tag{15.5.5}$$

Now $P_i/(1 - P_i)$ is simply the **odds ratio** in favor of owning a house—the ratio of the probability that a family will own a house to the probability that it will not own a house. Thus, if $P_i = 0.8$, it means that odds are 4 to 1 in favor of the family owning a house.

Now if we take the natural log of Eq. (15.5.5), we obtain a very interesting result, namely,

$$\begin{aligned} L_i = \ln\left(\frac{P_i}{1 - P_i}\right) &= Z_i \\ &= \beta_1 + \beta_2 X_i \end{aligned} \tag{15.5.6}$$

[15]The logistic model has been used extensively in analyzing growth phenomena, such as population, GNP, money supply, etc. For theoretical and practical details of logit and probit models, see J. S. Kramer, *The Logit Model for Economists*, Edward Arnold Publishers, London, 1991; and G. S. Maddala, op. cit.

[16]Note that as $Z_i \to +\infty$, e^{-Z_i} tends to zero and as $Z_i \to -\infty$, e^{-Z_i} increases indefinitely. Recall that $e = 2.71828$.

[17]Of course, one could use nonlinear estimation techniques discussed in Chapter 14. See also Section 15.8.

that is, L, the log of the odds ratio, is not only linear in X, but also (from the estimation viewpoint) linear in the parameters.[18] L is called the **logit,** and hence the name **logit model** for models like Eq. (15.5.6).

Notice these features of the logit model.

1. As P goes from 0 to 1 (i.e., as Z varies from $-\infty$ to $+\infty$), the logit L goes from $-\infty$ to $+\infty$. That is, although the probabilities (of necessity) lie between 0 and 1, the logits are not so bounded.

2. Although L is linear in X, the probabilities themselves are not. This property is in contrast with the LPM model (15.5.1) where the probabilities increase linearly with X.[19]

3. Although we have included only a single X variable, or regressor, in the preceding model, one can add as many regressors as may be dictated by the underlying theory.

4. If L, the logit, is positive, it means that when the value of the regressor(s) increases, the odds that the regressand equals 1 (meaning some event of interest happens) increases. If L is negative, the odds that the regressand equals 1 decreases as the value of X increases. To put it differently, the logit becomes negative and increasingly large in magnitude as the odds ratio decreases from 1 to 0 and becomes increasingly large and positive as the odds ratio increases from 1 to infinity.[20]

5. More formally, the interpretation of the logit model given in Eq. (15.5.6) is as follows: β_2, the slope, measures the change in L for a unit change in X, that is, it tells how the log-odds in favor of owning a house change as income changes by a unit, say, $1,000. The intercept β_1 is the value of the log-odds in favor of owning a house if income is zero. Like most interpretations of intercepts, this interpretation may not have any physical meaning.

6. Given a certain level of income, say, X^*, if we actually want to estimate not the odds in favor of owning a house but the probability of owning a house itself, this can be done directly from Eq. (15.5.3) once the estimates of β_1 and β_2 are available. This, however, raises the most important question: How do we estimate β_1 and β_2 in the first place? The answer is given in the next section.

7. Whereas the LPM assumes that P_i is linearly related to X_i, the logit model assumes that the log of the odds ratio is linearly related to X_i.

15.6 Estimation of the Logit Model

For estimation purposes, we write Eq. (15.5.6) as follows:

$$L_i = \ln\left(\frac{P_i}{1 - P_i}\right) = \beta_1 + \beta_2 X_i + u_i \tag{15.6.1}$$

We will discuss the properties of the stochastic error term u_i shortly.

[18]Recall that the linearity assumption of OLS does not require that the X variable be necessarily linear. So we can have X^2, X^3, etc., as regressors in the model. For our purpose, it is linearity in the parameters that is crucial.

[19]Using calculus, it can be shown that $dP/dX = \beta_2 P(1 - P)$, which shows that the rate of change in probability with respect to X involves not only β_2 but also the level of probability from which the change is measured (but more on this in Section 15.7). In passing, note that the effect of a unit change in X_i on P is greatest when $P = 0.5$ and least when P is close to 0 or 1.

[20]This point is due to David Garson.

To estimate Eq. (15.6.1), we need, apart from X_i, the values of the regressand, or logit, L_i. This depends on the type of data we have for analysis. We distinguish two types of data: (1) *data at the individual, or micro, level,* and (2) *grouped or replicated data.*

Data at the Individual Level

If we have data on individual families, as in the case of Table 15.1, OLS estimation of Eq. (15.6.1) is infeasible. This is easy to see. In terms of the data given in Table 15.1, $P_i = 1$ if a family owns a house and $P_i = 0$ if it does not own a house. But if we put these values directly into the logit L_i, we obtain:

$$L_i = \ln\left(\frac{1}{0}\right) \quad \text{if a family own a house}$$

$$L_i = \ln\left(\frac{0}{1}\right) \quad \text{if a family does not own a house}$$

Obviously, these expressions are meaningless. Therefore, if we have data at the micro, or individual, level, we cannot estimate Eq. (15.6.1) by the standard OLS routine. In this situation we may have to resort to the **maximum-likelihood (ML)** method to estimate the parameters. Although the rudiments of this method were discussed in the appendix to Chapter 4, its application in the present context will be discussed in Appendix 15A, Section 15A.1, for the benefit of readers who would like to learn more about it.[21] Software packages, such as MICROFIT, *EViews*, LIMDEP, SHAZAM, PC-GIVE, STATA, and MINITAB, have built-in routines to estimate the logit model at the individual level. We will illustrate the use of the ML method later in the chapter.

Grouped or Replicated Data

Now consider the data given in Table 15.4. This table gives data on several families *grouped* or *replicated* (repeat observations) according to income level and the number of families owning a house at each income level. Corresponding to each income level X_i, there are N_i families, n_i among whom are home owners ($n_i \le N_i$). Therefore, if we compute

$$\hat{P}_i = \frac{n_i}{N_i} \tag{15.6.2}$$

TABLE 15.4
Hypothetical Data on X_i (Income), N_i (Number of Families at Income X_i), and n_i (Number of Families Owning a House)

X (thousands of dollars)	N_i	n_i
6	40	8
8	50	12
10	60	18
13	80	28
15	100	45
20	70	36
25	65	39
30	50	33
35	40	30
40	25	20

[21]For a comparatively simple discussion of maximum likelihood in the context of the logit model, see John Aldrich and Forrest Nelson, op. cit., pp. 49–54. See also, Alfred Demarsi, *Logit Modeling: Practical Applications,* Sage Publications, Newbury Park, Calif., 1992.

that is, the *relative frequency,* we can use it as an estimate of the true P_i corresponding to each X_i. If N_i is fairly large, $\hat{P}_i$ will be a reasonably good estimate of P_i.[22] Using the estimated P_i, we can obtain the estimated logit as

$$\hat{L}_i = \ln\left(\frac{\hat{P}_i}{1-\hat{P}_i}\right) = \hat{\beta}_1 + \hat{\beta}_2 X_i \tag{15.6.3}$$

which will be a fairly good estimate of the true logit L_i if the number of observations N_i at each X_i is reasonably large.

In short, given the *grouped* or *replicated* data, such as Table 15.4, one can obtain the data on the dependent variable, the logits, to estimate the model (15.6.1). Can we then apply OLS to Eq. (15.6.3) and estimate the parameters in the usual fashion? The answer is, not quite, since we have not yet said anything about the properties of the stochastic disturbance term. It can be shown that if N_i is fairly large and if each observation in a given income class X_i is distributed independently as a binomial variable, then

$$u_i \sim N\left[0, \frac{1}{N_i P_i(1-P_i)}\right] \tag{15.6.4}$$

that is, u_i follows the normal distribution with zero mean and variance equal to $1/[N_i P_i(1-P_i)]$.[23]

Therefore, as in the case of the LPM, the disturbance term in the logit model is heteroscedastic. Thus, instead of using OLS we will have to use the weighted least squares (WLS). For empirical purposes, however, we will replace the unknown P_i by $\hat{P}_i$ and use

$$\hat{\sigma}^2 = \frac{1}{N_i \hat{P}_i(1-\hat{P}_i)} \tag{15.6.5}$$

as estimator of σ^2.

We now describe the various steps in estimating the logit regression in Eq. (15.6.1):

1. For each income level X, compute the probability of owning a house as $\hat{P}_i = n_i/N_i$.
2. For each X_i, obtain the logit as[24]

$$\hat{L}_i = \ln[\hat{P}_i/(1-\hat{P}_i)]$$

3. To resolve the problem of heteroscedasticity, transform Eq. (15.6.1) as follows:[25]

$$\sqrt{w_i}L_i = \beta_1\sqrt{w_i} + \beta_2\sqrt{w_i}X_i + \sqrt{w_i}u_i \tag{15.6.6}$$

[22]From elementary statistics recall that the probability of an event is the limit of the relative frequency as the sample size becomes infinitely large.

[23]As shown in elementary probability theory, $\hat{P}_i$, the proportion of successes (here, owning a house), follows the binomial distribution with mean equal to true P_i and variance equal to $P_i(1-P_i)/N_i$; and as N_i increases indefinitely the binomial distribution approximates the normal distribution. The distributional properties of u_i given in Eq. (15.6.4) follow from this basic theory. For details, see Henry Theil, "On the Relationships Involving Qualitative Variables," *American Journal of Sociology*, vol. 76, July 1970, pp. 103–154.

[24]Since $\hat{P}_i = n_i/N_i$, L_i can be alternatively expressed as $\hat{L}_i = \ln n_i/(N_i - n_i)$. In passing it should be noted that to avoid $\hat{P}_i$ taking the value of 0 or 1, in practice $\hat{L}_i$ is measured as $\hat{L}_i = \ln(n_i + \frac{1}{2})/(N_i - n_i + \frac{1}{2}) = \ln(\hat{P}_i + 1/2N_i)/(1 - \hat{P}_i + 1/2N_i)$. It is recommended as a rule of thumb that N_i be at least 5 at each value of X_i. For additional details, see D. R. Cox, *Analysis of Binary Data*, Methuen, London, 1970, p. 33.

[25]If we estimate Eq. (15.6.1) disregarding heteroscedasticity, the estimators, although unbiased, will not be efficient, as we know from Chapter 11.

which we write as

$$L_i^* = \beta_1\sqrt{w_i} + \beta_2 X_i^* + v_i \tag{15.6.7}$$

where the weights $w_i = N_i\hat{P}_i(1-\hat{P}_i)$; L_i^* = transformed or weighted L_i; X_i^* = transformed or weighted X_i; and v_i = transformed error term. It is easy to verify that the transformed error term v_i is homoscedastic, keeping in mind that the original error variance is $\sigma_u^2 = 1/[N_i P_i(1-P_i)]$.

4. Estimate Eq. (15.6.6) by OLS—recall that WLS is OLS on the transformed data. Notice that in Eq. (15.6.6) there is no intercept term introduced explicitly (why?). Therefore, one will have to use the regression through the origin routine to estimate Eq. (15.6.6).
5. Establish confidence intervals and/or test hypotheses in the usual OLS framework, *but keep in mind that all the conclusions will be valid strictly speaking only if the sample is reasonably large* (why?). Therefore, in small samples, the estimated results should be interpreted carefully.

15.7 The Grouped Logit (Glogit) Model: A Numerical Example

To illustrate the theory just discussed, we will use the data given in Table 15.4. Since the data in the table are grouped, the logit model based on this data will be called a grouped logit model, glogit, for short. The necessary raw data and other relevant calculations necessary to implement glogit are given in Table 15.5. The results of the weighted least-squares regression (15.6.7) based on the data given in Table 15.5 are as follows: Note that there is no intercept in Eq. (15.6.7); hence the regression-through-the-origin procedure is appropriate here.

$$\begin{aligned}
\hat{L}_i^* &= \quad -1.59474\sqrt{w_i} + \quad 0.07862X_i^* \\
\text{se} &= \quad (0.11046) \qquad\qquad (0.00539) \\
t &= (-14.43619) \qquad\quad (14.56675) \qquad R^2 = 0.9642
\end{aligned} \tag{15.7.1}$$

The R^2 is the squared correlation coefficient between actual and estimated L_i^*. L_i^* and X_i^* are weighted L_i and X_i, as shown in Eq. (15.6.6). Although we have shown the calculations of the grouped logit in Table 15.5 for pedagogical reasons, this can be done easily by invoking the **glogit** (grouped logit) command in STATA.

Interpretation of the Estimated Logit Model

How do we interpret Eq. (15.7.1)? There are various ways, some intuitive and some not:

Logit Interpretation

As Eq. (15.7.1) shows, the estimated slope coefficient suggests that for a unit ($1,000) increase in weighted income, the weighted log of the odds in favor of owning a house goes up by 0.08 units. This mechanical interpretation, however, is not very appealing.

Odds Interpretation

Remember that $L_i = \ln[P_i/(1-P_i)]$. Therefore, taking the antilog of the estimated logit, we get $P_i/(1-P_i)$, that is, the odds ratio. Hence, taking the antilog of Eq. (15.7.1),

TABLE 15.5 Data to Estimate the Logit Model of Home Ownership

X (thousands of dollars)	N_i	n_i	$\hat{P}_i$	$1-\hat{P}_i$	$\frac{\hat{P}_i}{1-\hat{P}_i}$	$\hat{L}_i = \ln\left(\frac{\hat{P}_i}{1-\hat{P}_i}\right)$	$N_i\hat{P}_i(1-\hat{P}_i) = w_i$	$\sqrt{w_i} = \sqrt{N_i\hat{P}_i(1-\hat{P}_i)}$	$\hat{L}_i^* = \hat{L}_i\sqrt{w_i}$	$\hat{X}_i^* = \hat{X}_i\sqrt{w_i}$
(1)	(2)	(3)	(4) = (3) ÷ (2)	(5)	(6)	(7)	(8)	(9) = $\sqrt{(8)}$	(10) = (7)(9)	(11) = (1)(9)
6	40	8	0.20	0.80	0.25	−1.3863	6.40	2.5298	−3.5071	15.1788
8	50	12	0.24	0.76	0.32	−1.1526	9.12	3.0199	−3.4807	24.1592
10	60	18	0.30	0.70	0.43	−0.8472	12.60	3.5496	−3.0072	35.4960
13	80	28	0.35	0.65	0.54	−0.6190	18.20	4.2661	−2.6407	55.4593
15	100	45	0.45	0.55	0.82	−0.2007	24.75	4.9749	−0.9985	74.6235
20	70	36	0.51	0.49	1.04	0.0570	17.49	4.1816	0.1673	83.6506
25	65	39	0.60	0.40	1.50	0.4054	15.60	3.9497	1.6012	98.7425
30	50	33	0.66	0.34	1.94	0.6633	11.20	3.3496	2.2218	100.4880
35	40	30	0.75	0.25	3.0	1.0986	7.50	2.7386	3.0086	95.8405
40	25	20	0.80	0.20	4.0	1.3863	4.00	2.000	2.7726	80.0000

we obtain:

$$\frac{\hat{P}_i}{1-\hat{P}_i} = e^{-1.59474\sqrt{w_i}+0.07862X_i^*}$$
$$= e^{-1.59474\sqrt{w_i}} \cdot e^{0.07862X_i^*} \tag{15.7.2}$$

Using a calculator, you can easily verify that $e^{0.07862} = 1.0817$. This means that for a unit increase in weighted income, the (weighted) odds in favor of owning a house increases by 1.0817 or about 8.17 percent. *In general, if you take the antilog of the jth slope coefficient (in case there is more than one regressor in the model), subtract 1 from it, and multiply the result by 100, you will get the percent change in the odds for a unit increase in the jth regressor.*

Incidentally, if you want to carry the analysis in terms of unweighted logit, all you have to do is divide the estimated L_i^* by $\sqrt{w_i}$. Table 15.6 gives the estimated weighted and unweighted logits for each observation and some other data, which we will discuss shortly.

Computing Probabilities

Since the language of logit and odds ratio may be unfamiliar to some, we can always compute the probability of owning a house at a certain level of income. Suppose we want to compute this probability at $X = 20$ ($20,000). Plugging this value into Eq. (15.7.1), we obtain: $\hat{L}_i^* = -0.09311$ and dividing this by $\sqrt{w_i} = 4.1816$ (see Table 15.5), we obtain $\hat{L}_i = -0.02226$. Therefore, at the income level of $20,000, we have

$$-0.02199 = \ln\left(\frac{\hat{P}_i}{1-\hat{P}_i}\right)$$

Therefore,

$$\frac{\hat{P}}{1-\hat{P}_i} = e^{-0.02199} = 0.97825$$

Solving this for

$$\hat{P}_i = \frac{e^{-0.02199}}{1+e^{-0.02199}}$$

TABLE 15.6
Lstar, Xstar, Estimated Lstar, Probability, and Change in Probability*

Lstar	Xstar	ELstar	Logit	Probability, $\hat{P}$	Change in Probability†
−3.50710	15.1788	−2.84096	−1.12299	0.24545	0.01456
−3.48070	24.15920	−2.91648	−0.96575	0.27572	0.01570
−3.48070	35.49600	−2.86988	−0.80850	0.30821	0.01676
−2.64070	55.45930	−2.44293	−0.57263	0.36063	0.01813
−0.99850	74.62350	−2.06652	−0.41538	0.39762	0.01883
0.16730	83.65060	−0.09311	−0.02226	0.49443	0.01965
1.60120	98.74250	1.46472	0.37984	0.59166	0.01899
2.22118	100.48800	2.55896	0.76396	0.68221	0.01704
3.00860	95.84050	3.16794	1.15677	0.76074	0.01431
2.77260	80.00000	3.10038	1.55019	0.82494	0.01135

*Lstar and Xstar are from Table 15.5. ELstar is the estimated Lstar. Logit is the unweighted logit. Probability is the estimated probability of owning a house. Change in probability is the change per unit change in income.
†Computed from $\hat{\beta}_2\hat{P}(1-\hat{P}) = 0.07862\hat{P}(1-\hat{P})$.

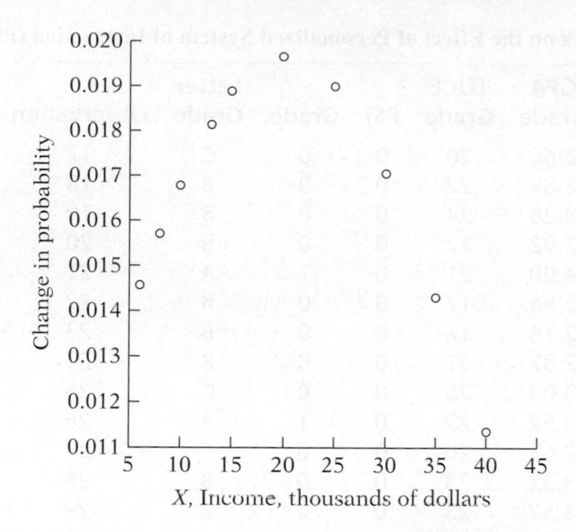

FIGURE 15.3 Change in probability in relation to income.

the reader can see that the estimated probability is 0.4945. That is, given the income of \$20,000, the probability of a family owning a house is about 49 percent. Table 15.6 shows the probabilities thus computed at various income levels. As this table shows, the probability of house ownership increases with income, but not linearly as with the LPM model.

Computing the Rate of Change of Probability

As you can gather from Table 15.6, the probability of owning a house depends on the income level. How can we compute the rate of change of probabilities as income varies? As noted in footnote 19, that depends not only on the estimated slope coefficient β_2 but also on the level of the probability from which the change is measured; the latter of course depends on the income level at which the probability is computed.

To illustrate, suppose we want to measure the change in the probability of owning a house at the income level \$20,000. Then, from footnote 19 the change in probability for a unit increase in income from the level 20 (thousand) is: $\hat{\beta}(1-\hat{P})\hat{P} = 0.07862(0.5056)(0.4944) = 0.01965$.

It is left as an exercise for the reader to show that at income level \$40,000, the change in probability is 0.01135. Table 15.6 shows the change in probability of owning a house at various income levels; these probabilities are also depicted in Figure 15.3.

To conclude our discussion of the glogit model, we present the results based on OLS, or unweighted regression, for the home ownership example:

$$
\begin{aligned}
\hat{L}_i &= -1.6587 + 0.0792X_i \\
\text{se} &= \quad (0.0958) \quad (0.0041) \\
t &= (-17.32) \qquad (19.11) \qquad r^2 = 0.9786
\end{aligned}
\tag{15.7.3}
$$

We leave it to the reader to compare this regression with the weighted least-squares regression given by Eq. (15.7.1).

15.8 The Logit Model for Ungrouped or Individual Data

To set the stage, consider the data given in Table 15.7. Letting $Y = 1$ if a student's final grade in an intermediate microeconomics course was A and $Y = 0$ if the final grade was a B or a C, Spector and Mazzeo used grade point average (GPA), TUCE, and

TABLE 15.7 Data on the Effect of Personalized System of Instruction (PSI) on Course Grades

Observation	GPA Grade	TUCE Grade	PSI	Grade	Letter Grade	Observation	GPA Grade	TUCE Grade	PSI	Grade	Letter Grade
1	2.66	20	0	0	C	17	2.75	25	0	0	C
2	2.89	22	0	0	B	18	2.83	19	0	0	C
3	3.28	24	0	0	B	19	3.12	23	1	0	B
4	2.92	12	0	0	B	20	3.16	25	1	1	A
5	4.00	21	0	1	A	21	2.06	22	1	0	C
6	2.86	17	0	0	B	22	3.62	28	1	1	A
7	2.76	17	0	0	B	23	2.89	14	1	0	C
8	2.87	21	0	0	B	24	3.51	26	1	0	B
9	3.03	25	0	0	C	25	3.54	24	1	1	A
10	3.92	29	0	1	A	26	2.83	27	1	1	A
11	2.63	20	0	0	C	27	3.39	17	1	1	A
12	3.32	23	0	0	B	28	2.67	24	1	0	B
13	3.57	23	0	0	B	29	3.65	21	1	1	A
14	3.26	25	0	1	A	30	4.00	23	1	1	A
15	3.53	26	0	0	B	31	3.10	21	1	0	C
16	2.74	19	0	0	B	32	2.39	19	1	1	A

Notes: Grade $Y = 1$ if the final grade is A
$= 0$ if the final grade is B or C
TUCE = score on an examination given at the beginning of the term to test entering knowledge of macroeconomics
PSI = 1 if the new teaching method is used
= 0 otherwise
GPA = the entering grade point average

Source: L. Spector and M. Mazzeo, "Probit Analysis and Economic Education," *Journal of Economic Education,* vol. 11, 1980, pp. 37–44.

Personalized System of Instruction (PSI) as the grade predictors. The logit model here can be written as:

$$L_i = \ln\left(\frac{P_i}{1 - P_i}\right) = \beta_1 + \beta_2 \text{GPA}_i + \beta_3 \text{TUCE}_i + \beta_4 \text{PSI}_i + u_i \quad \textbf{(15.8.1)}$$

As we noted in Section 15.6, we cannot simply put $P_i = 1$ if a family owns a house, and zero if it does not own a house. Here neither OLS nor weighted least squares (WLS) is helpful. We have to resort to nonlinear estimating procedures using the method of maximum likelihood. The details of this method are given in Appendix 15A, Section 15A.1. Since most modern statistical packages have routines to estimate logit models on the basis of ungrouped data, we will present the results of model (15.8.1) using the data given in Table 15.7 and show how to interpret the results. The results are given in Table 15.8 in tabular form and are obtained by using *EViews 6.* Before interpreting these results, some general observations are in order.

1. Since we are using the method of maximum likelihood, which is generally a large-sample method, the estimated standard errors are *asymptotic.*

2. As a result, instead of using the t statistic to evaluate the statistical significance of a coefficient, we use the (standard normal) Z statistic. So inferences are based on the normal table. Recall that if the sample size is reasonably large, the t distribution converges to the normal distribution.

3. As noted earlier, the conventional measure of goodness of fit, R^2, is not particularly meaningful in binary regressand models. Measures similar to R^2, called **pseudo R^2**, are

TABLE 15.8
Regression Results of Equation (15.8.1)

Dependent Variable: Grade
Method: ML-Binary Logit
Convergence achieved after 5 iterations

Variable	Coefficient	Std. Error	Z Statistic	Probability
C	-13.0213	4.931	-2.6405	0.0082
GPA	2.8261	1.2629	2.2377	0.0252
TUCE	0.0951	0.1415	0.67223	0.5014
PSI	2.3786	1.0645	2.2345	0.0255

McFadden $R^2 = 0.3740$ LR statistic (3 df) = 15.40419

available, and there are a variety of them.[26] *EViews* presents one such measure, the McFadden R^2, denoted by R^2_{McF}, whose value in our example is 0.3740.[27] Like R^2, R^2_{McF} also ranges between 0 and 1. Another comparatively simple measure of goodness of fit is the **count R^2**, which is defined as:

$$\textbf{Count } R^2 = \frac{\text{number of correct predictions}}{\text{total number of observations}} \tag{15.8.2}$$

Since the regressand in the logit model takes a value of 1 or zero, if the predicted probability is greater than 0.5, we classify that as 1, but if it is less than 0.5, we classify that as 0. We then count the number of correct predictions and compute the R^2 as given in Eq. (15.8.2). We will illustrate this shortly.

It should be noted, however, that in binary regressand models, goodness of fit is of secondary importance. What matters is the expected signs of the regression coefficients and their statistical and/or practical significance.

4. To test the null hypothesis that all the slope coefficients are simultaneously equal to zero, the equivalent of the F test in the linear regression model is the **likelihood ratio (LR) statistic.** Given the null hypothesis, the LR statistic follows the χ^2 distribution with df equal to the number of explanatory variables, three in the present example. (*Note:* Exclude the intercept term in computing the df.)

Now let us interpret the regression results given in Eq. (15.8.1). Each slope coefficient in this equation is a *partial slope* coefficient and measures the change in the estimated logit for a unit change in the value of the given regressor (holding other regressors constant). Thus, the GPA coefficient of 2.8261 means, with other variables held constant, that if GPA increases by a unit, on average the estimated logit increases by about 2.83 units, suggesting a positive relationship between the two. As you can see, all the other regressors have a positive effect on the logit, although statistically the effect of TUCE is not significant. However, together all the regressors have a significant impact on the final grade, as the LR statistic is 15.40 with a p value of about 0.0015, which is very small.

As noted previously, a more meaningful interpretation is in terms of odds, which are obtained by taking the antilog of the various slope coefficients. Thus, if you take the antilog of the PSI coefficient of 2.3786 you will get 10.7897 ($\approx e^{2.3786}$). This suggests that

[26]For an accessible discussion, see J. Scott Long, *Regression Models for Categorical and Limited Dependent Variables,* Sage Publications, Newbury Park, California, 1997, pp. 102–113.

[27]Technically, this is defined as: $1 - (\text{LLF}_{ur}/\text{LLF}_r)$, where LLF_{ur} is the unrestricted log likelihood function where all regressors are included in the model and LLF_r is the restricted log likelihood function where only the intercept is included in the model. Conceptually, LLF_{ur} is equivalent to RSS and LLF_r is equivalent to TSS of the linear regression model.

TABLE 15.9
Actual and Fitted Values Based on Regression in Table 15.8

Observation	Actual	Fitted	Residual	Residual Plot
1	0	0.02658	−0.02658	
2	0	0.05950	−0.05950	
3	0	0.18726	−0.18726	
4	0	0.02590	−0.02590	
5	1	0.56989	0.43011	
6	0	0.03486	−0.03486	
7	0	0.02650	−0.02650	
8	0	0.05156	−0.05156	
9	0	0.11113	−0.11113	
10	1	0.69351	0.30649	
11	0	0.02447	−0.02447	
12	0	0.19000	−0.19000	
13	0	0.32224	−0.32224	
*14	1	0.19321	0.80679	
15	0	0.36099	−0.36099	
16	0	0.03018	−0.03018	
17	0	0.05363	−0.05363	
18	0	0.03859	−0.03859	
*19	0	0.58987	−0.58987	
20	1	0.66079	0.33921	
21	0	0.06138	−0.06138	
22	1	0.90485	0.09515	
23	0	0.24177	−0.24177	
*24	0	0.85209	−0.85209	
25	1	0.83829	0.16171	
*26	1	0.48113	0.51887	
27	1	0.63542	0.36458	
28	0	0.30722	−0.30722	
29	1	0.84170	0.15830	
30	1	0.94534	0.05466	
*31	0	0.52912	−0.52912	
*32	1	0.11103	0.88897	

*Incorrect predictions.

students who are exposed to the new method of teaching are more than 10 times as likely to get an A than students who are not exposed to it, other things remaining the same.

Suppose we want to compute the actual probability of a student getting an A grade. Consider student number 10 in Table 15.7. Putting the actual data for this student in the estimated logit model given in Table 15.8, the reader can check that the estimated logit value for this student is 0.8178. Using Eq. (15.5.2), the reader can easily check that the estimated probability is 0.69351. Since this student's actual final grade was an A, and since our logit model assigns a probability of 1 to a student who gets an A, the estimated probability of 0.69351 is not exactly 1 but close to it.

Recall the count R^2 defined earlier. Table 15.9 gives you the actual and predicted values of the regressand for our illustrative example. From this table you can observe that, out of 32 observations, there were 6 incorrect predictions (students 14, 19, 24, 26, 31, and 32). Hence the count R^2 value is $26/32 = 0.8125$, whereas the McFadden R^2 value is 0.3740. Although these two values are not directly comparable, they give you some idea about the orders of magnitude. Besides, one should not overplay the importance of goodness of fit in models where the regressand is dichotomous.

EXAMPLE 15.5

Who Owns a Debit Card? Logit Analysis

We have already seen the results of the linear probability model (LPM) applied to the bank debit card data, so let us see how the logit model does. The results are as follows:

```
Dependent Variable: DEBIT
Method: ML-Binary Logit (Quadratic hill climbing)
Sample: 1-60
Included observations: 60
Convergence achieved after 4 iterations
Covariance matrix computed using second derivatives
```

Variable	Coefficient	Std. Error	z-Statistic	Prob.
C	-0.574900	0.785787	-0.731624	0.4644
Balance	0.001248	0.000697	1.789897	0.0735
ATM	-0.120225	0.093984	-1.279205	0.2008
Interest	-1.352086	0.680988	-1.985478	0.0471

McFadden R-squared	0.080471	Mean dependent var.	0.433333
S.D. dependent var.	0.499717	S.E. of regression	0.486274
Akaike info criterion	1.391675	Sum squared resid.	13.24192
Schwarz criterion	1.531298	Log likelihood	-37.75024
Hannan-Quinn criter.	1.446289	Restr. log likelihood	-41.05391
LR statistic	6.607325	Avg. log likelihood	-0.629171
Prob. (LR statistic)	0.085525		
Obs. with Dep = 0	34	Total obs.	60
Obs. with Dep = 1	26		

The positive sign of Balance and the negative signs of ATM and Interest are similar to the LPM, although we cannot directly compare the two. The interpretation of the coefficients in the logit model is different from the LPM. Here, for example, if the interest rate goes up by 1 percentage point, the logit goes down by about 1.35, holding other variables constant. If we take the anti log of −1.352086, we get about 0.2587. This means that if interest rate is paid on account balances, on average only about one-fourth of the customers are likely to hold debit cards.

From the estimated LR statistic we see that collectively the three variables are statistically significant at about the 8.5 percent level. If we use the conventional 5 percent significance level, then these variables are only marginally significant.

The McFadden R^2 value is quite low. Using the data, the reader can find out the value of the count R^2.

As noted earlier, unlike the LPM, the slope coefficients do not give us the rate of change of probability for a unit change in the regressor. We have to calculate them as shown in Table 15.6. Fortunately, this manual task is not necessary, for statistical packages like STATA can do this routinely. For our example, the results are as follows:

Marginal effects after logit

$$Y = \Pr(\text{debit})\ (\text{predict}) = .42512423$$

Variable	dy/dx	Std. Error	z	p > |z|	[95% C.I.	]	x
Balance	.000305	.00017	1.79	0.073	-.000029	.000639	1499.87
Interest*	-.2993972	.12919	-2.32	0.020	-.552595	−.046199	.266667
ATM	-.0293822	.02297	-1.28	0.201	-.074396	.015631	10.3

*dy/dx is for discrete change of dummy variable from 0 to 1.

(Continued)

EXAMPLE 15.5 *(Continued)*

The coefficient of 0.000305 suggests that customers with higher balances have a 0.03 percent higher probability of owning a debit card, but if the interest rate goes up by 1 percentage point, the probability of owning a debit card goes down by about 30 percent. The coefficient of ATM, although statistically insignificant, suggests that if ATM transactions go up by a unit, the probability of owning a debit card goes down by about 2.9 percent.

15.9 The Probit Model

As we have noted, to explain the behavior of a dichotomous dependent variable we will have to use a suitably chosen cumulative distribution function (CDF). The logit model uses the cumulative logistic function, as shown in Eq. (15.5.2). But this is not the only CDF that one can use. In some applications, the normal CDF has been found useful. The estimating model that emerges from the normal CDF[28] is popularly known as the **probit model,** although sometimes it is also known as the **normit model.** In principle one could substitute the normal CDF in place of the logistic CDF in Eq. (15.5.2) and proceed as in Section 16.5. Instead of following this route, we will present the probit model based on utility theory, or rational choice perspective on behavior, as developed by McFadden.[29]

To motivate the probit model, assume that in our home ownership example the decision of the ith family to own a house or not depends on an *unobservable* **utility index** I_i (also known as a **latent variable**), that is determined by one or more explanatory variables, say income X_i, in such a way that the larger the value of the index I_i, the greater the probability of a family owning a house. We express the index I_i as

$$I_i = \beta_1 + \beta_2 X_i \tag{15.9.1}$$

where X_i is the income of the ith family.

How is the (unobservable) index related to the actual decision to own a house? As before, let $Y = 1$ if the family owns a house and $Y = 0$ if it does not. Now it is reasonable to assume that there is a **critical** or **threshold level** of the index, call it I_i^*, such that if I_i exceeds I_i^*, the family will own a house, otherwise it will not. The threshold I_i^*, like I_i, is not observable, but if we assume that it is normally distributed with the same mean and variance, it is possible not only to estimate the parameters of the index given in Eq. (15.9.1) but also to get some information about the unobservable index itself. This calculation is as follows.

Given the assumption of normality, the probability that I_i^* is less than or equal to I_i can be computed from the standardized normal CDF as:[30]

$$P_i = P(Y = 1 \mid X) = P(I_i^* \leq I_i) = P(Z_i \leq \beta_1 + \beta_2 X_i) = F(\beta_1 + \beta_2 X_i) \tag{15.9.2}$$

[28]See **Appendix A** for a discussion of the normal CDF. Briefly, if a variable X follows the normal distribution with mean μ and variance σ^2, its PDF is

$$f(X) = \frac{1}{\sqrt{2\sigma^2\pi}} e^{-(X-\mu)^2/2\sigma^2}$$

and its CDF is

$$F(X) = \int_{-\infty}^{X_0} \frac{1}{\sqrt{2\sigma^2\pi}} e^{-(X-\mu)^2/2\sigma^2}$$

where X_0 is some specified value of X.

[29]D. McFadden, "Conditional Logit Analysis of Qualitative Choice Behavior," in P. Zarembka (ed.), *Frontiers in Econometrics,* Academic Press, New York, 1973.

[30]A normal distribution with zero mean and unit (= 1) variance is known as a standard or standardized normal variable (see **Appendix A**).

FIGURE 15.4
Probit model: (*a*) given I_i, read P_i from the ordinate; (*b*) given P_i, read I_i from the abscissa.

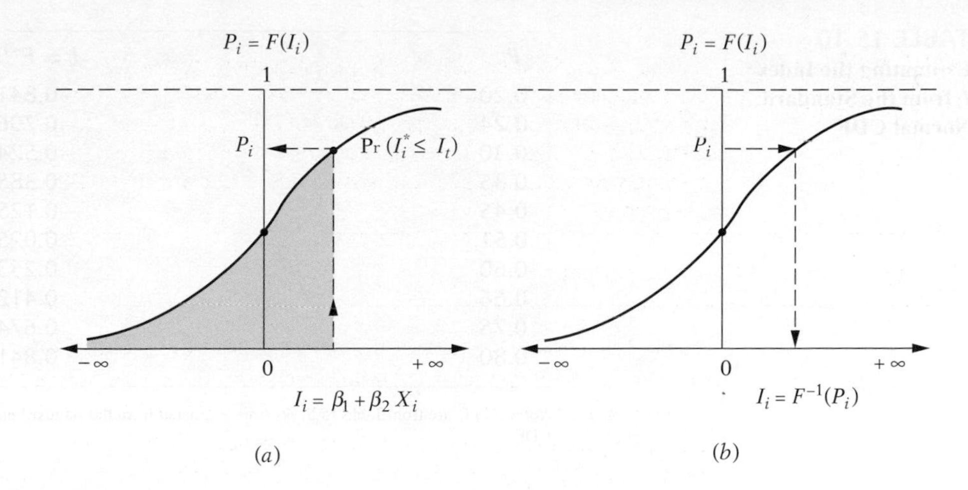

where $P(Y = 1 \mid X)$ means the probability that an event occurs given the value(s) of the X, or explanatory, variable(s) and where Z_i is the standard normal variable, i.e., $Z \sim N(0, \sigma^2)$. F is the standard normal CDF, which written explicitly in the present context is:

$$F(I_i) = \frac{1}{\sqrt{2\pi}} \int_{-\infty}^{I_i} e^{-z^2/2}\, dz$$
$$= \frac{1}{\sqrt{2\pi}} \int_{-\infty}^{\beta_1+\beta_2 X_i} e^{-z^2/2}\, dz \tag{15.9.3}$$

Since P represents the probability that an event will occur, here the probability of owning a house, it is measured by the area of the standard normal curve from $-\infty$ to I_i as shown in Figure 15.4*a*.

Now to obtain information on I_i, the utility index, as well as on β_1 and β_2, we take the inverse of Eq. (15.9.2) to obtain:

$$I_i = F^{-1}(I_i) = F^{-1}(P_i)$$
$$= \beta_1 + \beta_2 X_i \tag{15.9.4}$$

where F^{-1} is the inverse of the normal CDF. What all this means can be made clear from Figure 15.4. In panel (*a*) of this figure we obtain from the ordinate the (cumulative) probability of owning a house given $I_i^* \le I_i$, whereas in panel (*b*) we obtain from the abscissa the value of I_i given the value of P_i, which is simply the reverse of the former.

But how do we actually go about obtaining the index I_i as well as estimating β_1 and β_2? As in the case of the logit model, the answer depends on whether we have grouped data or ungrouped data. We consider the two cases individually.

Probit Estimation with Grouped Data: gprobit

We will use the same data that we used for glogit, which is given in Table 15.4. Since we already have $\hat{P}_i$, the relative frequency (the empirical measure of probability) of owning a house at various income levels as shown in Table 15.5, we can use it to obtain I_i from the normal CDF as shown in Table 15.10, or from Figure 15.5.

TABLE 15.10
Estimating the Index I_i from the Standard Normal CDF

$\hat{P}_i$	$I_i = F^{-1}(\hat{P}_i)$
0.20	−0.8416
0.24	−0.7063
0.30	−0.5244
0.35	−0.3853
0.45	−0.1257
0.51	0.0251
0.60	0.2533
0.66	0.4125
0.75	0.6745
0.80	0.8416

Notes: (1) $\hat{P}_i$ are from Table 15.5; (2) I_i are estimated from the standard normal CDF.

FIGURE 15.5
Normal CDF.

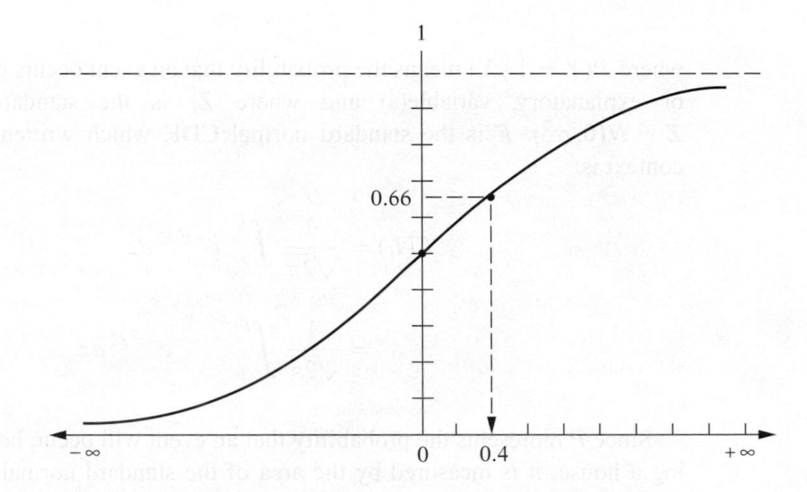

Once we have the estimated I_i, estimating β_1 and β_2 is relatively straightforward, as we show shortly. In passing, note that in the language of probit analysis the unobservable utility index I_i is known as the **normal equivalent deviate** (n.e.d.) or simply **normit.** Since the n.e.d. or I_i will be negative whenever $P_i < 0.5$, in practice the number 5 is added to the n.e.d. and the result is called a probit.

EXAMPLE 15.6
Illustration of Gprobit Using Housing Example

Let us continue with our housing example. We have already presented the results of the glogit model for this example. The grouped probit (gprobit) results of the same data are as follows:

Using the n.e.d. ($= I$) given in Table 15.10, the regression results are as shown in Table 15.11.[31] The regression results based on the probits ($=$ n.e.d. $+ 5$) are as shown in Table 15.12.

Except for the intercept term, these results are identical with those given in the previous table. But this should not be surprising. (Why?)

[31]The following results are not corrected for heteroscedasticity. See Exercise 15.12 for the appropriate procedure to correct heteroscedasticity.

EXAMPLE 15.6
(Continued)

TABLE 15.11

Dependent Variable: *I*

Variable	Coefficient	Std. Error	*t*-Statistic	Probability
C	-1.0166	0.0572	-17.7473	1.0397E-07
Income	0.04846	0.00247	19.5585	4.8547E-08

R^2 = 0.97951   Durbin-Watson statistic = 0.91384

TABLE 15.12

Dependent Variable: Probit

Variable	Coefficient	Std. Error	*t*-Statistic	Probability
C	3.9833	0.05728	69.5336	2.03737E-12
Income	0.04846	0.00247	19.5585	4.8547E-08

R^2 = 0.9795   Durbin Watson statistic = 0.9138

Note: These results are not corrected for heteroscedasticity (see Exercise 15.12).

Interpretation of the Probit Estimates in Table 15.11

How do we interpret the preceding results? Suppose we want to find out the effect of a unit change in X (income measured in thousands of dollars) on the probability that $Y = 1$, that is, a family purchases a house. To do this, look at Eq. (15.9.2). We want to take the derivative of this function with respect to X (that is, the rate of change of the probability with respect to income). It turns out that this derivative is:

$$\frac{dP_i}{dX_i} = f(\beta_1 + \beta_2 X_i)\beta_2 \tag{15.9.5}$$ [32]

where $f(\beta_1 + \beta_2 X_i)$ is the standard normal probability density function evaluated at $\beta_1 + \beta_2 X_i$. As you will realize, this evaluation will depend on the particular value of the X variables. Let us take a value of X from Table 15.5, say, $X = 6$ (thousand dollars). Using the estimated values of the parameters given in Table 15.11, we thus want to find the normal density function at $f[-1.0166 + 0.04846(6)] = f(-0.72548)$. If you refer to the normal distribution tables, you will find that for $Z = -0.72548$, the normal density is about 0.3066.[33] Now multiplying this value by the estimated slope coefficient of 0.04846, we obtain 0.01485. This means that starting with an income level of $6,000, if the income goes up by $1,000, the probability of a family purchasing a house goes up by about 1.4 percent. (Compare this result with that given in Table 15.6.)

As you can see from the preceding discussion, compared with the LPM and logit models, the computation of changes in probability using the probit model is a bit tedious.

Instead of computing changes in probability, suppose you want to find the estimated probabilities from the fitted gprobit model. This can be done easily. Using the data in

[32]We use the chain rule of derivatives:

$$\frac{dP_i}{dX_i} = \frac{dF(t)}{dt} \cdot \frac{dt}{dX}$$

where $t = \beta_1 + \beta_2 X_i$.

[33]Note that the standard normal Z can range from $-\infty$ to $+\infty$, but the density function $f(Z)$ is always positive.

Table 15.11 and inserting the values of X from Table 15.5, the reader can check that the estimated n.i.d. values (to two digits) are as follows:

X	6	8	10	13	15	20	25	30	35	40
Estimated n.i.d.	−0.72	−0.63	−0.53	−0.39	−0.29	−0.05	0.19	0.43	0.68	0.92

Now statistical packages such as MINITAB can easily compute the (cumulative) probabilities associated with the various n.i.d.'s. For example, corresponding to an n.i.d. value −0.63, the estimated probability is 0.2647 and, corresponding to an n.i.d. value of 0.43, the estimated probability is 0.6691. If you compare these estimates with the actual values given in Table 15.5, you will find that the two are fairly close, suggesting that the fitted model is quite good. Graphically, what we have just done is already shown in Figure 15.4.

The Probit Model for Ungrouped or Individual Data

Let us revisit Table 15.7, which gives data on 32 individuals about their final grade in an intermediate microeconomics course in relation to the variables GPA, TUCE, and PSI. The results of the logit regression are given in Table 15.8. Let us see what the probit results look like. Notice that as in the case of the logit model for individual data, we will have to use a nonlinear estimating procedure based on the method of maximum likelihood. The regression results calculated by *EViews 6* are given in Table 15.13.

"Qualitatively," the results of the probit model are comparable with those obtained from the logit model in that GPA and PSI are individually statistically significant. Collectively, all the coefficients are statistically significant, since the value of the LR statistic is 15.5458 with a p value of 0.0014. For reasons discussed in the next sections, we cannot directly compare the logit and probit regression coefficients.

For comparative purposes, we present the results based on the linear probability model (LPM) for the grade data in Table 15.14. Again, qualitatively, the LPM results are similar

TABLE 15.13

Dependent Variable: grade
Method: ML–Binary probit
Convergence achieved after 5 iterations

Variable	Coefficient	Std. Error	Z-Statistic	Probability
C	-7.4523	2.5424	-2.9311	0.0033
GPA	1.6258	0.6938	2.3430	0.0191
TUCE	0.0517	0.0838	0.6166	0.5374
PSI	1.4263	5950	2.3970	0.0165

LR statistic (3 df) = 15.5458   McFadden R^2 = 0.3774
Probability (LR stat) = 0.0014

TABLE 15.14

Dependent Variable: grade

Variable	Coefficient	Std. Error	t-Statistic	Probability
C	-1.4980	0.5238	-2.8594	0.0079
GPA	0.4638	0.1619	2.8640	0.0078
TUCE	0.0104	0.0194	0.5386	0.5943
PSI	0.3785	0.1391	2.7200	0.0110

R^2 = 0.4159   Durbin-Watson d = 2.3464   F-statistic = 6.6456

to the logit and probit models in that GPA and PSI are individually statistically significant but TUCE is not. Also, together the explanatory variables have a significant impact on grade, as the F value of 6.6456 is statistically significant because its p value is only 0.0015.

The Marginal Effect of a Unit Change in the Value of a Regressor in the Various Regression Models

In the *linear regression model,* the slope coefficient measures the change in the average value of the regressand for a unit change in the value of a regressor, with all other variables held constant.

In the *LPM*, the slope coefficient measures directly the change in the probability of an event occurring as the result of a unit change in the value of a regressor, with the effect of all other variables held constant.

In the *logit model* the slope coefficient of a variable gives the change in the log of the odds associated with a unit change in that variable, again holding all other variables constant. But as noted previously, for the logit model the rate of change in the probability of an event happening is given by $\beta_j P_i(1 - P_i)$, where β_j is the (partial regression) coefficient of the *j*th regressor. But in evaluating P_i, all the variables included in the analysis are involved.

In the *probit model,* as we saw earlier, the rate of change in the probability is somewhat complicated and is given by $\beta_j f(Z_i)$, where $f(Z_i)$ is the density function of the standard normal variable and $Z_i = \beta_1 + \beta_2 X_{2i} + \cdots + \beta_k X_{ki}$, that is, the regression model used in the analysis.

Thus, in both the logit and probit models all the regressors are involved in computing the changes in probability, whereas in the LPM only the *j*th regressor is involved. This difference may be one reason for the early popularity of the LPM model. Statistical packages, such as STATA, have made the task of finding the rate of change of probability for the logit and probit models much easier. So now there is no need to choose LPM just because of its simplicity.

15.10 Logit and Probit Models

Although for our grade example LPM, logit, and probit give qualitatively similar results, we will confine our attention to logit and probit models because of the problems with the LPM noted earlier. Between logit and probit, which model is preferable? In most applications the models are quite similar, the main difference being that the logistic distribution has slightly fatter tails, which can be seen from Figure 15.6. That is to say, the conditional probability P_i approaches 0 or 1 at a slower rate in logit than in probit. This can be seen more clearly from Table 15.15. Therefore, there is no compelling reason to choose one over the other. In practice many researchers choose the logit model because of its comparative mathematical simplicity.

Though the models are similar, one has to be careful in interpreting the coefficients estimated by the two models. For example, for our grade example, the coefficient of GPA of 1.6258 of the probit model (see Table 15.13) and 2.8261 of the logit model (see Table 15.8) are not directly comparable. The reason is that, although the standard logistic (the basis of logit) and the standard normal distributions (the basis of probit) both have a mean value of zero, their variances are different; 1 for the standard normal (as we already know) and $\pi^2/3$ for the logistic distribution, where $\pi \approx 22/7$. Therefore, if you multiply the probit coefficient by about 1.81 (which is approximately $= \pi/\sqrt{3}$), you will get approximately the logit coefficient. For our example, the probit coefficient of GPA is 1.6258. Multiplying this by 1.81, we obtain 2.94, which is close to the logit coefficient. Alternatively, if you multiply a logit coefficient by 0.55 $(= 1/1.81)$, you will get the probit

FIGURE 15.6
Logit and probit cumulative distributions.

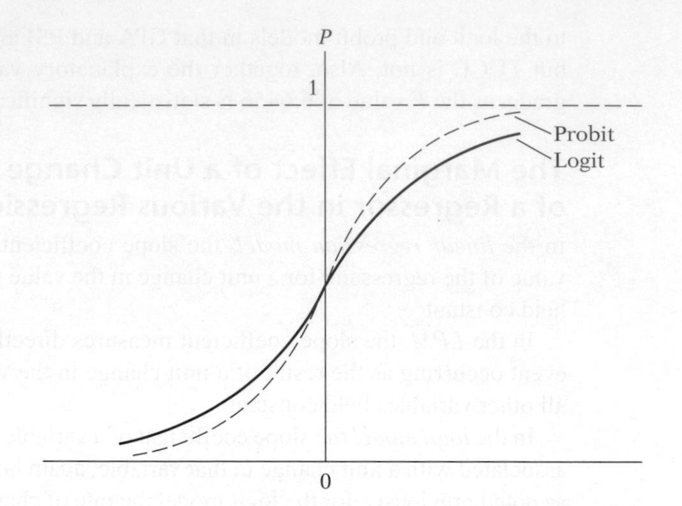

TABLE 15.15
Values of Cumulative Probability Functions

	Cumulative Normal	Cumulative Logistic
Z	$P_1(Z) = \frac{1}{\sqrt{2\pi}}\int_{-\infty}^{z} e^{-s^2/2}ds$	$P_2(Z) = \frac{1}{1+e^{-z}}$
−3.0	0.0013	0.0474
−2.0	0.0228	0.1192
−1.5	0.0668	0.1824
−1.0	0.1587	0.2689
−0.5	0.3085	0.3775
0	0.5000	0.5000
0.5	0.6915	0.6225
1.0	0.8413	0.7311
1.5	0.9332	0.8176
2.0	0.9772	0.8808
3.0	0.9987	0.9526

coefficient. Amemiya, however, suggests multiplying a logit estimate by 0.625 to get a better estimate of the corresponding probit estimate.[34] Conversely, multiplying a probit coefficient by 1.6 ($= 1/0.625$) gives the corresponding logit coefficient.

Incidentally, Amemiya has also shown that the coefficients of LPM and logit models are related as follows:

$$\beta_{\text{LPM}} = 0.25\beta_{\text{logit}} \qquad \text{except for intercept}$$

and

$$\beta_{\text{LPM}} = 0.25\beta_{\text{logit}} + 0.5 \qquad \text{for intercept}$$

We leave it to the reader to find out if these approximations hold for our grade example.

To conclude our discussion of LPM, logit, and probit models, we consider an extended example.

[34] T. Amemiya, "Qualitative Response Model: A Survey," *Journal of Economic Literature,* vol. 19, 1981, pp. 481–536.

EXAMPLE 15.7

To Smoke or Not to Smoke

To find out what factors determine whether or not a person becomes a smoker, we obtained data on 1,196 individuals.[35] For each individual, there is information on education, age, income, and the price of cigarettes in 1979. The dependent variable is smoker, with 1-smokers and 0-nonsmokers. Further analysis will be examined by Exercise 15.20 and the data can be found in Table 15.28 on the textbook website. For comparative purposes, we present the results based on LPM, logit, and probit models in a tabular form (see Table 15.16). These results have been obtained from STATA version 10.

TABLE 15.16

Variables	LPM	Logit	Probit
Constant	1.1230	2.7450	1.7019
	(5.96)	(3.31)	(3.33)
Age	−0.0047	−0.0208	−0.0129
	(−5.70)	(−5.58)	(−5.66)
Education	−0.0206	−0.0909	−0.0562
	(−4.47)	(−4.40)	(−4.45)
Income	1.03e–0.6	4.72e–06	2.72e–06
	(0.63)	(0.66)	(0.62)
Pcigs79	−0.0051	−0.0223	−0.0137
	(−1.80)	(−1.79)	(−1.79)
R^2	0.0388	0.0297	0.0301

Notes: Figures in the parentheses are t ratios for LPM and z ratios for logit and probit. For logit and probit, the R^2 values are pseudo R^2 values.

Although the coefficients of the three models are not directly comparable, qualitatively they are similar. Thus, age, education, and price of cigarettes have a negative impact on smoking and income has positive impact. Statistically, the income effect is zero and the price effect is significant at about an 8 percent level. In Exercise 15.20, you are asked to apply the conversion factor to render the various coefficients comparable.

In Table 15.17 we present the *marginal effect* of each variable on the probability of smoking for each model type.

TABLE 15.17

Variables	LPM	Logit	Probit
Age	−0.0047	−0.0048	−0.0049
Education	−0.0206	−0.0213	−0.0213
Income	1.03e–06	1.11e–06	1.03e–06
Pcigs79	−0.0051	−0.0052	−0.0052

Note: Except for income, the estimated coefficients are highly statistically significant for age and education, and significant at about the 8 percent level for the price of cigarettes.

As you will recognize, the marginal effect of a variable on the probability of smoking for LPM is directly obtained from the estimated regression coefficients, but for the logit and probit models they have to be computed as discussed in the chapter.

It is interesting that the marginal effects are quite similar for the three models. For example, if the level of education goes up, on average, the probability of someone becoming a smoker goes down by about 2 percent.

[35]These data are from Michael P. Murray, *Econometrics: A Modern Introduction,* Pearson/Addison-Wesley, Boston, 2006, and can be downloaded from www.aw-bc.com/murray.

15.11 The Tobit Model

An extension of the probit model is the **tobit model** originally developed by James Tobin, the Nobel laureate economist. To explain this model, we continue with our home ownership example. In the probit model our concern was with estimating the probability of owning a house as a function of some socioeconomic variables. In the tobit model our interest is in finding out the amount of money a person or family spends on a house in relation to socioeconomic variables. Now we face a dilemma: If a consumer does not purchase a house, obviously we have no data on housing expenditure for such consumers; we have such data only on consumers who actually purchase a house.

Thus consumers are divided into two groups, one consisting of, say, n_1 consumers about whom we have information on the regressors (say, income, mortgage interest rate, number of people in the family, etc.) as well as the regressand (amount of expenditure on housing) and another consisting of n_2 consumers about whom we have information only on the regressors but not on the regressand. A sample in which information on the regressand is available only for some observations is known as a **censored sample.**[36] Therefore, the tobit model is also known as a censored regression model. Some authors call such models **limited dependent variable regression models** because of the restriction put on the values taken by the regressand.

Statistically, we can express the tobit model as

$$\begin{aligned} Y_i &= \beta_1 + \beta_2 X_i + u_i \qquad &\text{if RHS} > 0 \\ &= 0 &\text{otherwise} \end{aligned} \tag{15.11.1}$$

where RHS = right-hand side. *Note:* Additional X variables can be easily added to the model.

Can we estimate regression (15.11.1) using only n_1 observations and not worry about the remaining n_2 observations? The answer is no, for the OLS estimates of the parameters obtained from the subset of n_1 observations will be *biased as well as inconsistent;* that is, they are biased even asymptotically.[37]

To see this, consider Figure 15.7. As the figure shows, if Y is not observed (because of censoring), all such observations ($= n_2$), denoted by crosses, will lie on the horizontal axis. If Y is observed, the observations ($= n_1$), denoted by dots, will lie in the X–Y plane. It is intuitively clear that if we estimate a regression line based on the n_1 observations only, the resulting intercept and slope coefficients are bound to be different than if all the $(n_1 + n_2)$ observations were taken into account.

How then does one estimate tobit, or censored regression, models, such as Eq. (15.11.1)? The actual mechanics involves the method of maximum likelihood, which is rather involved and is beyond the scope of this book. But the reader can get more information about the ML method from the references.[38]

[36]A censored sample should be distinguished from a **truncated sample** in which information on the regressors is available only if the regressand is observed. We will not pursue this topic here, but the interested reader may consult William H. Greene, *Econometric Analysis,* Prentice Hall, 4th ed., Englewood Cliffs, NJ, Chapter 19. For an intuitive discussion, see Peter Kennedy, *A Guide to Econometrics,* The MIT Press, Cambridge, Mass., 4th ed., 1998, Chapter 16.

[37]The bias arises from the fact that if we consider only the n_1 observations and omit the others, there is no guarantee that $E(u_i)$ will be necessarily zero. And without $E(u_i) = 0$ we cannot guarantee that the OLS estimates will be unbiased. This bias can be readily seen from the discussion in Appendix 3A, Eqs. (4) and (5).

[38]See Greene, op. cit. A somewhat less technical discussion can be found in Richard Breen, *Regression Models: Censored, Sample Selected or Truncated Data,* Sage Publications, Newbury Park, California, 1996.

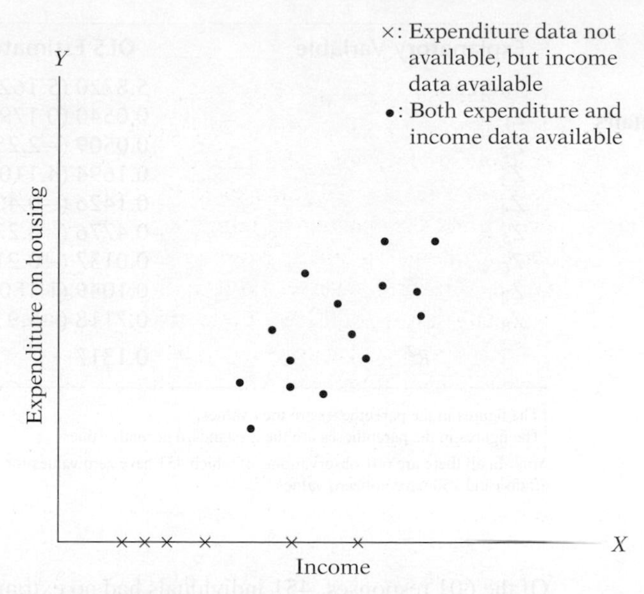

FIGURE 15.7
Plot of amount of money consumer spends in buying a house versus income.

James Heckman has proposed an alternative to the ML method, which is comparatively simple.[39] This alternative consists of a two-step estimating procedure. In step 1, we first estimate the probability of a consumer owning a house, which is done on the basis of the probit model. In step 2, we estimate the model (15.11.1) by adding to it a variable (called the **inverse Mills ratio** or the **hazard rate**) that is derived from the probit estimate. For the actual mechanics, see the Heckman article. The Heckman procedure yields consistent estimates of the parameters of Eq. (15.11.1), but they are not as efficient as the ML estimates. Since most modern statistical software packages have the ML routine, it may be preferable to use these packages rather than the Heckman two-step procedure.

Illustration of the Tobit Model: Ray Fair's Model of Extramarital Affairs[40]

In an interesting and theoretically innovative article, Ray Fair collected a sample of 601 men and women then married for the first time and analyzed their responses to a question about extramarital affairs.[41] The variables used in this study are defined as follows:

Y = number of affairs in the past year, 0, 1, 2, 3, 4–10 (coded as 7)
Z_1 = 0 for female and 1 for male
Z_2 = age
Z_3 = number of years married
Z_4 = children: 0 if no children and 1 if children
Z_5 = religiousness on a scale of 1 to 5, 1 being antireligion
Z_6 = education, years: grade school = 9; high school = 12, Ph.D. or other = 20
Z_7 = occupation, "Hollingshead" scale, 1–7
Z_8 = self-rating of marriage, 1 = very unhappy, 5 = very happy

[39] J. J. Heckman, "Sample Selection Bias as a Specification Error," *Econometrica,* vol. 47, pp. 153–161.

[40] Ray Fair, "A Theory of Extramarital Affairs," *Journal of Political Economy,* vol. 86, 1978, pp. 45–61. For the article and the data, see http://fairmodel.econ.yale.edu/rayfair/pdf/1978DAT.ZIP.

[41] In 1969 *Psychology Today* published a 101-question survey on sex and asked its readers to mail in their answers. In the July 1970 issue of the magazine the survey results were discussed on the basis of about 2,000 replies that were collected in electronic form. Ray Fair extracted the sample of 601 from these replies.

TABLE 15.18
OLS and Tobit Estimates of Extramarital Affairs

Explanatory Variable	OLS Estimate	Tobit Estimate
Intercept	5.8720 (5.1622)*	7.6084 (1.9479)†
Z_1	0.0540 (0.1799)	0.9457 (0.8898)
Z_2	−0.0509 (−2.2536)	−0.1926 (−2.3799)
Z_3	0.1694 (4.1109)	0.5331 (3.6368)
Z_4	−0.1426 (−0.4072)	1.0191 (0.7965)
Z_5	−0.4776 (−4.2747)	−1.6990 (−4.1906)
Z_6	−0.0137 (−0.2143)	0.0253 (0.1113)
Z_7	0.1049 (1.1803)	0.2129 (0.6631)
Z_8	−0.7118 (−5.9319)	−2.2732 (−5.4724)
R^2	0.1317	0.1515

*The figures in the parentheses are the t values.
†The figures in the parentheses are the Z (standard normal) values.
Note: In all there are 601 observations, of which 451 have zero values for the dependent variable (number of extramarital affairs) and 150 have nonzero values.

Of the 601 responses, 451 individuals had no extramarital affairs, and 150 individuals had one or more affairs.

In terms of Figure 15.7, if we plot the number of affairs on the vertical axis and, say, education on the horizontal axis, there will be 451 observations lying along the horizontal axis. Thus, we have a censored sample, and a tobit model may be appropriate.

Table 15.18 gives estimates of the preceding model using both (the inappropriate) OLS and (the appropriate) ML procedures. As you can see, OLS includes 451 individuals who had no affairs and 150 who had one or more affairs. The ML method takes this into account explicitly but the OLS method does not, thus the difference between the two estimates. For reasons already discussed, one should rely on the ML and not the OLS estimates. The coefficients in the two models can be interpreted like any other regression coefficients. The negative coefficient of Z_8 (marital happiness) means that the higher the marital happiness, the lower is the incidence of extramarital affairs, perhaps an unsurprising finding.

In passing, note that if we are interested in the probability of extramarital affairs and not in the number of such affairs, we can use the probit model assigning $Y = 0$ for individuals who did not have any affairs and $Y = 1$ for those who had such affairs, giving the results shown in Table 15.19. With the knowledge of probit modeling, readers should be able to interpret the probit results given in this table on their own.

15.12 Modeling Count Data: The Poisson Regression Model

There are many phenomena where the regressand is of the **count type,** such as the number of vacations taken by a family per year, the number of patents received by a firm per year, the number of visits to a dentist or a doctor per year, the number of visits to a grocery store per week, the number of parking or speeding tickets received per year, the number of days stayed in a hospital in a given period, the number of cars passing through a toll booth in a span of, say, 5 minutes, and so on. The underlying variable in each case is discrete, taking only a finite number of values. Sometimes count data can also refer to *rare,* or *infrequent,* occurrences, such as getting hit by lightning in a span of a week, winning more than one lottery within 2 weeks, or having two or more heart attacks in a span of 4 weeks. How do we model such phenomena?

TABLE 15.19

Dependent Variable: YSTAR
Method: ML–Binary probit
Sample: 1-601
Included observations: 601
Convergence achieved after 5 iterations

Variable	Coefficient	Std. Error	Z Statistic	Probability
C	0.779402	0.512549	1.520638	0.1284
Z_1	0.173457	0.137991	1.257015	0.2087
Z_2	-0.024584	0.010418	-2.359844	0.0183
Z_3	0.054343	0.018809	2.889278	0.0039
Z_4	0.216644	0.165168	1.311657	0.1896
Z_5	-0.185468	0.051626	-3.592551	0.0003
Z_6	0.011262	0.029517	0.381556	0.7028
Z_7	0.013669	0.041404	0.330129	0.7413
Z_8	-0.271791	0.053475	-5.082608	0.0000

Mean dependent var.	0.249584	S.D. dependent var.	0.433133
S.E. of regression	0.410279	Akaike info criterion	1.045581
Sum squared resid.	99.65088	Schwarz criterion	1.111453
Log likelihood	-305.1980	Hannan-Quinn criter.	1.071224
Restr. log likelihood	-337.6885	Avg. log likelihood	-0.507817
LR statistic (8 df)	64.98107	McFadden R-squared	0.096215
Probability (LR stat)	4.87E-11		

Obs. with Dep = 0	451	Total obs.	601
Obs. with Dep = 1	150		

Just as the Bernoulli distribution was chosen to model the yes/no decision in the linear probability model, the probability distribution that is specifically suited for count data is the **Poisson** probability distribution. The pdf of the Poisson distribution is given by:[42]

$$f(Y_i) = \frac{\mu^Y e^{-\mu}}{Y!} \qquad Y = 0, 1, 2, \ldots \tag{15.12.1}$$

where $f(Y)$ denotes the probability that the variable Y takes non-negative integer values, and where $Y!$ (read Y factorial) stands for $Y! = Y \times (Y-1) \times (Y-2) \times 2 \times 1$. It can be proved that

$$E(Y) = \mu \tag{15.12.2}$$

$$\text{var}(Y) = \mu \tag{15.12.3}$$

Notice an interesting feature of the Poisson distribution: *Its variance is the same as its mean value.*

The Poisson regression model may be written as:

$$Y_i = E(Y_i) + u_i = \mu_i + u_i \tag{15.12.4}$$

[42]See any standard book on statistics for the details of this distribution.

where the Y's are independently distributed as Poisson random variables with mean μ_i for each individual expressed as

$$\mu_i = E(Y_i) = \beta_1 + \beta_2 X_{2i} + \beta_3 X_{3_i} + \cdots + \beta_k X_{ki} \quad (15.12.5)$$

where the X's are some of the variables that might affect the mean value. For example, if our count variable is the number of visits to the Metropolitan Museum of Art in New York in a given year, this number will depend on variables such as income of the consumer, admission price, distance from the museum, and parking fees.

For estimation purposes, we write the model as:

$$Y_i = \frac{\mu^Y e^{-\mu}}{Y!} + u_i \quad (15.12.6)$$

with μ replaced by Eq. (5.12.5). As you can readily see, the resulting regression model will be nonlinear in the parameters, necessitating nonlinear regression estimation discussed in the previous chapter. Let us consider a concrete example to see how all this works out.

EXAMPLE 15.8

An Illustrative Example: Geriatric Study of Frequency of Falls

The data used here were collected by Neter et al.[43] The data relate to 100 individuals 65 years of age and older. The objective of the study was to record the number of falls ($= Y$) suffered by these individuals in relation to gender ($X_2 = 0$ female and 1 for male), a balance index (X_3), and a strength index (X_4). The higher the balance index, the more stable is the subject, and the higher the strength index, the stronger is the subject. To find out if education or education plus aerobic exercise has any effect on the number of falls, the authors introduced an additional variable (X_1), called the *intervention* variable, such that $X_1 = 0$ if only education and $X_1 = 1$ if education plus aerobic exercise training. The subjects were randomly assigned to the two intervention methods.

Using *EViews 6*, we obtained the output in Table 15.20.

TABLE 15.20

Dependent Variable: Y
Sample: 1-100
Convergence achieved after 7 iterations
Y=EXP(C(0)+C(1)*X1+C(2)*X2+C(3)*X3+C(4)*X4)

	Coefficient	Std. Error	t-Statistic	Probability
C(0)	0.37020	0.3459	1.0701	0.2873
C(1)	-1.10036	0.1705	-6.4525	0.0000
C(2)	-0.02194	0.1105	-0.1985	0.8430
C(3)	0.01066	0.0027	3.9483	0.0001
C(4)	0.00927	0.00414	2.2380	0.0275

R^2 = 0.4857 Adjusted R^2 = 0.4640
Log likelihood = -197.2096 Durbin-Watson statistic = 1.7358

Note: EXP( ) means e (the base of natural logarithm) raised by the expression in ( ).

[43]John Neter, Michael H. Kutner, Christopher J. Nachtsheim, and William Wasserman, *Applied Regression Models,* Irwin, 3d ed., Chicago, 1996. The data were obtained from the data disk included in the book and refer to Exercise 14.28.

EXAMPLE 15.8 *(Continued)*

Interpretation of Results. Keep in mind that what we have obtained in Table 15.20 is the estimated mean value for the ith individual, $\hat{\mu}_i$; that is, what we have estimated is:

$$\hat{\mu}_i = e^{0.3702-1.100366X_{1i}-0.02194X_{2i}+0.0106X_{3i}+0.00927X_{4i}} \tag{15.12.7}$$

To find the actual mean value for the ith subject, we need to put the values of the various X variables for that subject. For example, subject 99 had these values: $Y = 4$, $X_1 = 0$, $X_2 = 1$, $X_3 = 50$, and $X_4 = 56$. Putting these values in Eq. (15.12.7), we obtain $\hat{\mu}_{99} = 3.3538$ as the estimated mean value for the 99th subject. The actual Y value for this individual was 4.

Now if we want to find out the probability that a subject similar to subject 99 has less than 5 falls per year, we can obtain it as follows:

$$\begin{aligned} P(Y < 5) &= P(Y = 0) + P(Y = 1) + P(Y = 2) + P(Y = 3) + P(Y = 4) \\ &= \frac{(3.3538)^0 e^{-3.3538}}{0!} + \frac{(3.3538)^1 e^{-3.3538}}{1!} + \frac{(3.3538)^2 e^{-3.3538}}{2!} \\ &\quad + \frac{(3.3538)^3 e^{-3.3538}}{3!} + \frac{(3.3538)^4 e^{-3.3538}}{4!} \\ &= 0.7491 \end{aligned}$$

We can also find out the marginal, or partial, effect of a regressor on the mean value of Y as follows. In terms of our illustrative example, suppose we want to find out the effect of a unit increase in the strength index (X_4) on mean Y. Since

$$\mu = e^{C_0+C_1X_{1i}+C_2X_{2i}+C_3X_{3i}+C_4X_{4i}} \tag{15.12.8}$$

we want to find $\partial\mu/\partial X_4$. Using the chain rule of calculus, it can be easily shown that this is equal to

$$\frac{\partial\mu}{\partial X_4} = C_4 e^{C_0+C_1X_{1i}+C_2X_{2i}+C_3X_{3i}+C_4X_{4i}} = C_4\mu \tag{15.12.9}$$

That is, the rate of change of the mean value with respect to a regressor is equal to the coefficient of that regressor times the mean value. Of course, the mean value μ will depend on the values taken by all the regressors in the model. This is similar to the logit and probit models we discussed earlier, where the marginal contribution of a variable also depended on the values taken by all the variables in the model.

Returning to the statistical significance of the individual coefficients, we see that the intercept and variable X_2 are individually statistically insignificant. But note that the standard errors given in the table are asymptotic and hence the t values are to be interpreted asymptotically. As noted previously, generally the results of all nonlinear iterative estimating procedures have validity in large samples only.

In concluding our discussion of the Poisson regression model, it may be noted that the model makes restrictive assumptions in that the mean and the variance of the Poisson process are the same and that the probability of an occurrence is constant at any point in time.

15.13 Further Topics in Qualitative Response Regression Models

As noted at the outset, the topic of qualitative response regression models is vast. What we have presented in this chapter are some of the basic models in this area. For those who want to pursue this topic further, we discuss below very briefly some other models in this area. We will not pursue them here, for that would take us far away from the scope of this book.

Ordinal Logit and Probit Models

In the bivariate logit and probit models we were interested in modeling a yes or no response variable. But often the response variable, or regressand, can have more than two outcomes and very often these outcomes are **ordinal** in nature; that is, they cannot be expressed on an interval scale. Frequently, in survey-type research the responses are on a Likert-type scale, such as "strongly agree," "somewhat agree," or "strongly disagree." Or the responses in an educational survey may be "less than high school," "high school," "college," or "professional degrees." Very often these responses are coded as 0 (less than high school), 1 (high school), 2 (college), 3 (postgraduate). These are ordinal scales in that there is clear ranking among the categories but we cannot say that 2 (college education) is twice 1 (high school education) or 3 (postgraduate education) is three times 1 (high school education).

To study phenomena such as the preceding, one can extend the bivariate logit and probit models to take into account multiple ranked categories. The arithmetic gets quite involved as we have to use multistage normal and logistic probability distributions to allow for the various ranked categories. For the underlying mathematics and some of the applications, the reader may consult the Greene and Maddala texts cited earlier. At a comparatively intuitive level, the reader may consult the Liao monograph.[44] Software packages such as LIMDEP, *EViews*, STATA, and SHAZAM have routines to estimate ordered logit and probit models.

Multinomial Logit and Probit Models

In the ordered probit and logit models the response variable has more than two ordered, or ranked, categories. But there are situations where the regressand is unordered. Take, for example, the choice of transportation mode to work. The choices may be bicycle, motorbike, car, bus, or train. Although these are categorical responses, there is no ranking or order here; they are essentially nominal in character. For another example, consider occupational classifications, such as unskilled, semiskilled, and highly skilled. Again, there is no order here. Similarly, occupational choices such as self-employed, working for a private firm, working for a local government, and working for the federal government are essentially nominal in character.

The techniques of multinomial logit or probit models can be employed to study such nominal categories. Again, the mathematics gets a little involved. The references cited previously will give the essentials of these techniques. And the statistical packages cited earlier can be used to implement such models, if their use is required in specific cases.

Duration Models

Consider questions such as these: (1) What determines the duration of unemployment spells? (2) What determines the life of a light bulb? (3) What factors determine the duration of a strike? (4) What determines the survival time of an HIV-positive patient?

Subjects such as these are the topic of duration models, popularly known as **survival analysis** or **time-to-event data analysis.** In each of the examples cited above, the key variable is the length of time or spell length, which is modeled as a random variable. Again the mathematics involves the CDFs and PDFs of appropriate probability distributions. Although the technical details can be tedious, there are accessible books on this subject.[45]

[44] Tim Futing Liao, op. cit.

[45] See, for example, David W. Hosmer, Jr., and Stanley Lemeshow, *Applied Survival Analysis*, John Wiley & Sons, New York, 1999.

Statistical packages such as STATA and LIMDEP can easily estimate such duration models. These packages have worked examples to aid the researcher in the use of such models.

Summary and Conclusions

1. Qualitative response regression models refer to models in which the response, or regressand, variable is not quantitative or an interval scale.
2. The simplest possible qualitative response regression model is the binary model in which the regressand is of the yes/no or presence/absence type.
3. The simplest possible binary regression model is the linear probability model (LPM) in which the binary response variable is regressed on the relevant explanatory variables by using the standard OLS methodology. Simplicity may not be a virtue here, for the LPM suffers from several estimation problems. Even if some of the estimation problems can be overcome, the fundamental weakness of the LPM is that it assumes that the probability of something happening increases linearly with the level of the regressor. This very restrictive assumption can be avoided if we use the logit and probit models.
4. In the logit model the dependent variable is the log of the odds ratio, which is a linear function of the regressors. The probability function that underlies the logit model is the logistic distribution. If the data are available in grouped form, we can use OLS to estimate the parameters of the logit model, provided we take into account explicitly the heteroscedastic nature of the error term. If the data are available at the individual, or micro, level, nonlinear-in-the-parameter estimating procedures are called for.
5. If we choose the normal distribution as the appropriate probability distribution, then we can use the probit model. This model is mathematically a bit difficult as it involves integrals. But for all practical purposes, both logit and probit models give similar results. In practice, the choice therefore depends on the ease of computation, which is not a serious problem with sophisticated statistical packages that are now readily available.
6. If the response variable is of the count type, the model that is most frequently used in applied work is the Poisson regression model, which is based on the Poisson probability distribution.
7. A model that is closely related to the probit model is the tobit model, also known as a censored regression model. In this model, the response variable is observed only if a certain condition(s) is met. Thus, the question of how much one spends on a car is meaningful only if one decides to buy a car to begin with. However, Maddala notes that the tobit model is "applicable only in those cases where the latent variable [i.e., the basic variable underlying a phenomenon] can, in principle, take negative values and the observed zero values are a consequence of censoring and nonobservability."[46]
8. There are various extensions of the binary response regression models. These include ordered probit and logit and nominal probit and logit models. The philosophy underlying these models is the same as the simpler logit and probit models, although the mathematics gets rather complicated.
9. Finally, we considered briefly the so-called duration models in which the duration of a phenomenon, such as unemployment or sickness, depends on several factors. In such models, the length, or the spell of duration, becomes the variable of research interest.

[46] G. S. Maddala, *Introduction to Econometrics,* 2d ed., Macmillan, New York, 1992, p. 342.

EXERCISES

Questions

15.1. Refer to the data given in Table 15.2. If $\hat{Y}_i$ is negative, assume it to be equal to 0.01 and if it is greater than 1, assume it to be equal to 0.99. Recalculate the weights w_i and estimate the LPM using WLS. Compare your results with those given in Eq. (15.2.11) and comment.

15.2. For the home ownership data given in Table 15.1, the maximum likelihood estimates of the logit model are as follows:

$$\hat{L}_i = \ln\left(\frac{\hat{P}_i}{1-\hat{P}_i}\right) = -493.54 + \quad 32.96 \text{ income}$$
$$t = \quad (-0.000008)(0.000008)$$

Comment on these results, bearing in mind that all values of income above 16 (thousand dollars) correspond to $Y = 1$ and all values of income below 16 correspond to $Y = 0$. A priori, what would you expect in such a situation?

15.3. In studying the purchase of durable goods Y ($Y = 1$ if purchased, $Y = 0$ if no purchase) as a function of several variables for a total of 762 households, Janet A. Fisher* obtained the following LPM results:

Explanatory Variable	Coefficient	Standard Error
Constant	0.1411	—
1957 disposable income, X_1	0.0251	0.0118
(Disposable income $= X_1)^2$, X_2	−0.0004	0.0004
Checking accounts, X_3	−0.0051	0.0108
Savings accounts, X_4	0.0013	0.0047
U.S. savings bonds, X_5	−0.0079	0.0067
Housing status: rent, X_6	−0.0469	0.0937
Housing status: own, X_7	0.0136	0.0712
Monthly rent, X_8	−0.7540	1.0983
Monthly mortgage payments, X_9	−0.9809	0.5162
Personal noninstallment debt, X_{10}	−0.0367	0.0326
Age, X_{11}	0.0046	0.0084
Age squared, X_{12}	−0.0001	0.0001
Marital status, X_{13} (1 = married)	0.1760	0.0501
Number of children, X_{14}	0.0398	0.0358
(Number of children $= X_{14})^2$, X_{15}	−0.0036	0.0072
Purchase plans, X_{16} (1 = planned; 0 otherwise)	0.1760	0.0384
	$R^2 = 0.1336$	

Notes: All financial variables are in thousands of dollars.
Housing status: Rent (1 if rents; 0 otherwise).
Housing status: Own (1 if owns; 0 otherwise).

Source: Janet A. Fisher, "An Analysis of Consumer Goods Expenditure," *The Review of Economics and Statistics,* vol. 64, no. 1, Table 1, 1962, p. 67.

a. Comment generally on the fit of the equation.

b. How would you interpret the coefficient of −0.0051 attached to the checking accounts variable? How would you rationalize the negative sign for this variable?

c. What is the rationale behind introducing the age-squared and number of children-squared variables? Why is the sign negative in both cases?

*"An Analysis of Consumer Goods Expenditure," *The Review of Economics and Statistics,* vol. 64, no. 1, 1962, pp. 64–71.

d. Assuming values of zero for all but the income variable, find out the conditional probability of a household whose income is \$20,000 purchasing a durable good.

e. Estimate the conditional probability of owning durable good(s), given: $X_1 =$ \$15,000, $X_3 =$ \$3,000, $X_4 =$ \$5,000, $X_6 = 0$, $X_7 = 1$, $X_8 =$ \$500, $X_9 =$ \$300, $X_{10} = 0, X_{11} = 35, X_{13} = 1, X_{14} = 2, X_{16} = 0$.

15.4. The R^2 value in the labor-force participation regression given in Table 15.3 is 0.175, which is rather low. Can you test this value for statistical significance? Which test do you use and why? Comment in general on the value of R^2 in such models.

15.5. Estimate the probabilities of owning a house at the various income levels underlying the regression (15.7.1). Plot them against income and comment on the resulting relationship.

*15.6. In the probit regression given in Table 15.11 show that the intercept is equal to $-\mu_x/\sigma_x$ and the slope is equal to $1/\sigma_x$, where μ_x and σ_x are the mean and standard deviation of *X*.

15.7. From data for 54 standard metropolitan statistical areas (SMSA), Demaris estimated the following logit model to explain high murder rate versus low murder rate:**

$$\begin{aligned} \ln \hat{O}_i &= 1.1387 + 0.0014P_i + 0.0561C_i - 0.4050R_i \\ \text{se} &= \qquad\qquad (0.0009) \quad (0.0227) \quad (0.1568) \end{aligned}$$

where $O =$ the odds of a high murder rate, $P =$ 1980 population size in thousands, $C =$ population growth rate from 1970 to 1980, $R =$ reading quotient, and the se are the asymptotic standard errors.

a. How would you interpret the various coefficients?

b. Which of the coefficients are individually statistically significant?

c. What is the effect of a unit increase in the reading quotient on the odds of having a higher murder rate?

d. What is the effect of a percentage point increase in the population growth rate on the odds of having a higher murder rate?

15.8. Compare and comment on the OLS and WLS regressions in Eqs. (15.7.3) and (15.7.1).

Empirical Exercises

15.9. From the household budget survey of 1980 of the Dutch Central Bureau of Statistics, J. S. Cramer obtained the following logit model based on a sample of 2,820 households. (The results given here are based on the method of maximum likelihood and are after the third iteration.)† The purpose of the logit model was to determine car ownership as a function of (logarithm of) income. Car ownership was a binary variable: $Y = 1$ if a household owns a car, zero otherwise.

$$\begin{aligned} \hat{L}_i &= -2.77231 + 0.347582 \ln \text{Income} \\ t &= (-3.35) \qquad (4.05) \\ \chi^2&(1\ \text{df}) = 16.681\ (p \text{ value} = 0.0000) \end{aligned}$$

where $\hat{L}_i =$ estimated logit and where ln Income is the logarithm of income. The χ^2 measures the goodness of fit of the model.

*Optional.

**Demaris, op. cit., p. 46.

†J. S. Cramer, *An Introduction to the Logit Model for Economist,* 2d ed., published and distributed by Timberlake Consultants Ltd., 2001, p. 33. These results are reproduced from the statistical package PC-GIVE 10 published by Timberlake Consultants, p. 51.

a. Interpret the estimated logit model.

b. From the estimated logit model, how would you obtain the expression for the probability of car ownership?

c. What is the probability that a household with an income of $20,000 will own a car? And at an income level of $25,000? What is the rate of change of probability at the income level of $20,000?

d. Comment on the statistical significance of the estimated logit model.

15.10. Establish Eq. (15.2.8).

15.11. In an important study of college graduation rates of all high school matriculants and Black-only matriculants, Bowen and Bok obtained the results in Table 15.21, based on the logit model.*

TABLE 15.21 **Logistic Regression Model Predicting Graduation Rates, 1989 Entering Cohort**

	All Matriculants			Black Only		
Variable	Parameter Estimate	Standard Error	Odds Ratio	Parameter Estimate	Standard Error	Odds Ratio
Intercept	0.957	0.052	—	0.455	0.112	—
Female	**0.280**	0.031	1.323	**0.265**	0.101	1.303
Black	**−0.513**	0.056	0.599			
Hispanic	**−0.350**	0.080	0.705			
Asian	**0.122**	0.055	1.130			
Other race	**−0.330**	0.104	0.719			
SAT > 1,299	**0.331**	0.059	1.393	0.128	0.248	1.137
SAT 1,200–1,299	**0.253**	0.055	1.288	0.232	0.179	1.261
SAT 1,100–1,199	**0.350**	0.053	1.420	0.308	0.149	1.361
SAT 1,000–1,099	**0.192**	0.054	1.211	0.141	0.136	1.151
SAT not available	**−0.330**	0.127	0.719	0.048	0.349	1.050
Top 10% of high school class	**0.342**	0.036	1.407	**0.315**	0.117	1.370
High school class rank not available	−0.065	0.046	0.937	−0.065	0.148	0.937
High socioeconomic status (SES)	**0.283**	0.036	1.327	**0.557**	0.175	1.746
Low SES	**−0.385**	0.079	0.680	**−0.305**	0.143	0.737
SES not available	**0.110**	0.050	1.116	0.031	0.172	1.031
SEL-1	**1.092**	0.058	2.979	**0.712**	0.161	2.038
SEL-2	**0.193**	0.036	1.212	**0.280**	0.119	1.323
Women's college	**−0.299**	0.069	0.742	0.158	0.269	1.171
Number of observations	32,524			2,354		
−2 log likelihood						
Restricted	31,553			2,667		
Unrestricted	30,160			2,569		
Chi square	1,393 with 18 d.f.			98 with 14 d.f.		

Notes: Bold coefficients are significant at the .05 level; other coefficients are not. The omitted categories in the model are White, male, SAT < 1,000, bottom 90% of high school class, middle SES, SEL-3, coed institution. Graduation rates are 6-year, first-school graduation rates, as defined in the notes to Appendix Table D.3.1. Institutional selectivity categories are as defined in the notes to Appendix Table D.3.1. See **Appendix B** for definition of socioeconomic status (SES).

SEL-1 = institutions with mean combined SAT scores of 1,300 and above.

SEL-2 = institutions with mean combined SAT scores between 1,150 and 1,299.

SEL-3 = institutions with mean combined SAT scores below 1,150.

Source: Bowen and Bok, op. cit., p. 381.

*William G. Bowen and Derek Bok, *The Shape of the River: Long Term Consequences of Considering Race in College and University Admissions,* Princeton University Press, Princeton, NJ, 1998, p. 381.

a. What general conclusion do you draw about graduation rates of all matriculants and black-only matriculants?

b. The *odds ratio* is the ratio of two odds. Compare two groups of all matriculants, one with a SAT score of greater than 1,299 and the other with a SAT score of less than 1,000 (the base category). The odds ratio of 1.393 means the odds of matriculants in the first category graduating from college are 39 percent higher than those in the latter category. Do the various odds ratios shown in the table accord with a priori expectations?

c. What can you say about the statistical significance of the estimated parameters? What about the overall significance of the estimated model?

15.12. In the probit model given in Table 15.11 the disturbance u_i has this variance:

$$\sigma_u^2 = \frac{P_i(1 - P_i)}{N_i f_i^2}$$

where f_i is the standard normal density function evaluated at $F^{-1}(P_i)$.

a. Given the preceding variance of u_i, how would you transform the model in Table 15.10 to make the resulting error term homoscedastic?

b. Use the data in Table 15.10 to show the transformed data.

c. Estimate the probit model based on the transformed data and compare the results with those based on the original data.

15.13. Since R^2 as a measure of goodness of fit is not particularly well suited for the dichotomous dependent variable models, one suggested alternative is the χ^2 test described below:

$$\chi^2 = \sum_{i=1}^{G} \frac{N_i(\hat{P}_i - P_i^*)^2}{P_i^*(1 - P_i^*)}$$

where N_i = number of observations in the ith cell

$\hat{P}_i$ = actual probability of the event occurring ($= n_i/N_i$)

P_I^* = estimated probability

G = number of cells (i.e., the number of levels at which X_i is measured, e.g., 10 in Table 15.4)

It can be shown that, for large samples, χ^2 is distributed according to the χ^2 distribution with $(G - k)$ df, where k is the number of parameters in the estimating model $(k < G)$.

Apply the preceding χ^2 test to regression (15.7.1) and comment on the resulting goodness of fit and compare it with the reported R^2 value.

15.14. Table 15.22 gives data on the results of spraying rotenone of different concentrations on the chrysanthemum aphis in batches of approximately fifty. Develop a suitable model to express the probability of death as a function of the log of X, the log of dosage, and comment on the results. Also compute the χ^2 test of fit discussed in Exercise 15.13.

15.15. Thirteen applicants to a graduate program had quantitative and verbal scores on the GRE as listed in Table 15.23. Six students were admitted to the program.

a. Use the LPM to predict the probability of admission to the program based on quantitative and verbal scores in the GRE.

b. Is this a satisfactory model? If not, what alternative(s) do you suggest?

TABLE 15.22
Toxicity Study and Rotenone on Chrysanthemum Aphis

Source: D. J. Fennet, *Probit Analysis,* Cambridge University Press, London, 1964.

Concentration, Milligrams per Liter		Total,	Death,	
X	log (X)	N_i	n_i	$\hat{P}_i = n_i/N_i$
2.6	0.4150	50	6	0.120
3.8	0.5797	48	16	0.333
5.1	0.7076	46	24	0.522
7.7	0.8865	49	42	0.857
10.2	1.0086	50	44	0.880

TABLE 15.23
GRE Scores

Source: Donald F. Morrison, *Applied Linear Statistical Methods,* Prentice-Hall, Inc., Englewood Cliffs, NJ, 1983, p. 279 (adapted).

	GRE Aptitude Test Scores		Admitted to Graduate Program
Student Number	Quantitative, Q	Verbal, V	(Yes = 1, No = 0)
1	760	550	1
2	600	350	0
3	720	320	0
4	710	630	1
5	530	430	0
6	650	570	0
7	800	500	1
8	650	680	1
9	520	660	0
10	800	250	0
11	670	480	0
12	670	520	1
13	780	710	1

15.16. To study the effectiveness of a price discount coupon on a six-pack of a soft drink, Douglas Montgomery and Elizabeth Peck collected the data shown in Table 15.24. A sample of 5,500 consumers was randomly assigned to the eleven discount categories shown in the table, 500 per category. The response variable is whether or not consumers redeemed the coupon within one month.

a. See if the logit model fits the data, treating the redemption rate as the dependent variable and price discount as the explanatory variable.

b. See if the probit model does as well as the logit model.

TABLE 15.24
Price of Soda with Discount Coupon

Source: Douglas C. Montgomery and Elizabeth A. Peck, *Introduction to Linear Regression Analysis,* John Wiley & Sons, New York, 1982, p. 243 (notation changed).

Price Discount X, ¢	Sample Size N_i	Number of Coupons Redeemed n_i
5	500	100
7	500	122
9	500	147
11	500	176
13	500	211
15	500	244
17	500	277
19	500	310
21	500	343
23	500	372
25	500	391

c. What is the predicted redemption rate if the price discount was 17 cents?

d. Estimate the price discount for which 70 percent of the coupons will be redeemed.

15.17. To find out who has a bank account (checking, savings, etc.) and who doesn't, John Caskey and Andrew Peterson estimated a probit model for the years 1977 and 1989, using data on U.S. households. The results are given in Table 15.25. The values of the slope coefficients given in the table measure the implied effect of a unit change in a regressor on the probability that a household has a bank account, these marginal effects being calculated at the mean values of the regressors included in the model.

a. For 1977, what is the effect of marital status on ownership of a bank account? And for 1989? Do these results make economic sense?

b. Why is the coefficient for the *minority* variable negative for both 1977 and 1989?

c. How can you rationalize the negative sign for the number of children variable?

d. What does the chi-square statistic given in the table suggest? (*Hint:* See Exercise 15.13.)

TABLE 15.25 Probit Regressions Where Dependent Variable Is Ownership of a Deposit Account

	1977 Data		1989 Data	
	Coefficients	Implied Slope	Coefficients	Implied Slope
Constant	−1.06 (3.3)*		−2.20 (6.8)*	
Income (thousands 1991 $)	0.030 (6.9)	0.002	0.025 (6.8)	0.002
Married	0.127 (0.8)	0.008	0.235 (1.7)	0.023
Number of children	0.131 (3.6)	−0.009	−0.084 (2.0)	−0.008
Age of head of household (HH)	0.006 (1.7)	0.0004	0.021 (6.3)	0.002
Education of HH	0.121 (7.4)	0.008	0.128 (7.7)	0.012
Male HH	−0.078 (0.5)	−0.005	−0.144 (0.9)	−0.011
Minority	−0.750 (6.8)	−0.050	−0.600 (6.5)	−0.058
Employed	0.186 (1.6)	0.012	0.402 (3.6)	0.039
Homeowner	0.520 (4.7)	0.035	0.522 (5.3)	0.051
Log likelihood	−430.7		−526.0	
Chi-square statistic (H_0: All coefficients except constant equal zero)	408		602	
Number of observations	2,025		2,091	
Percentage in sample with correct predictions	91		90	

*Numbers in parentheses are *t* statistics.

Source: John P. Caskey and Andrew Peterson, "Who Has a Bank Account and Who Doesn't: 1977 and 1989," Research Working Paper 93-10, Federal Reserve Bank of Kansas City, October 1993.

15.18. *Monte Carlo study*. As an aid to understanding the probit model, William Becker and Donald Waldman assumed the following:*

$$E(Y \mid X) = -1 + 3X$$

Then, letting $Y_i = -1 + 3X + \varepsilon_i$, where ε_i is assumed standard normal (i.e., zero mean and unit variance), they generated a sample of 35 observations as shown in Table 15.26.

a. From the data on Y and X given in this table, can you estimate an LPM? Remember that the true $E(Y \mid X) = -1 + 3X$.

b. Given $X = 0.48$, estimate $E(Y \mid X = 0.48)$ and compare it with the true $E(Y \mid X = 0.48)$. Note $\bar{X} = 0.48$.

c. Using the data on Y^* and X given in Table 15.26, estimate a probit model. You may use any statistical package you want. The authors' estimated probit model is the following:

$$\hat{Y}_i^* = -0.969 + 2.764X_i$$

Find out the $P(Y^* = 1 \mid X = 0.48)$, that is, $P(Y_1 > 0 \mid X = 0.48)$. See if your answer agrees with the authors' answer of 0.64.

d. The sample standard deviation of the X values given in Table 15.26 is 0.31. What is the predicted change in probability if X is one standard deviation above the mean value, that is, what is $P(Y^* = 1 \mid X = 0.79)$? The authors' answer is 0.25.

TABLE 15.26
Hypothetical Data Set Generated by the Model $Y = -1 + 3X + \varepsilon$ and $Y^* = 1$ If $Y > 0$

Source: William E. Becker and Donald M. Waldman, "A Graphical Interpretation of Probit Coefficients," *Journal of Economic Education,* Fall 1989, Table 1, p. 373.

Y	Y*	X	Y	Y*	X
−0.3786	0	0.29	−0.3753	0	0.56
1.1974	1	0.59	1.9701	1	0.61
−0.4648	0	0.14	−0.4054	0	0.17
1.1400	1	0.81	2.4416	1	0.89
0.3188	1	0.35	0.8150	1	0.65
2.2013	1	1.00	−0.1223	0	0.23
2.4473	1	0.80	0.1428	1	0.26
0.1153	1	0.40	−0.6681	0	0.64
0.4110	1	0.07	1.8286	1	0.67
2.6950	1	0.87	−0.6459	0	0.26
2.2009	1	0.98	2.9784	1	0.63
0.6389	1	0.28	−2.3326	0	0.09
4.3192	1	0.99	0.8056	1	0.54
−1.9906	0	0.04	−0.8983	0	0.74
−0.9021	0	0.37	−0.2355	0	0.17
0.9433	1	0.94	1.1429	1	0.57
−3.2235	0	0.04	−0.2965	0	0.18
0.1690	1	0.07			

*William E. Becker and Donald M. Waldman, "A Graphical Interpretation of Probit Coefficients," *Journal of Economic Education,* vol. 20, no. 4, Fall 1989, pp. 371–378.

15.19. Table 15.27 on the textbook website gives data for 2,000 women regarding work (1 = a woman works, 0 = otherwise), age, marital status (1 = married, 0 = otherwise), number of children, and education (number of years of schooling). Out of a total of 2,000 women, 657 were recorded as not being wage earners.

a. Using these data, estimate the linear probability model (LPM).

b. Using the same data, estimate a logit model and obtain the marginal effects of the various variables.

c. Repeat (*b*) for the probit model.

d. Which model would you choose? Why?

15.20. For the smokers example discussed in the text (see Section 15.10) download the data from the textbook website in Table 15.28. See if the product of education and income (i.e., the interaction effect) has any effect on the probability of becoming a smoker.

15.21. Download the data set Benign, which is Table 15.29, from the textbook website. The variable cancer is a dummy variable, where 1 = had breast cancer and 0 = did not have breast cancer.* Using the variables age (= age of subject), HIGD (= highest grade completed in school), CHK (= 0 if subject did not undergo regular medical checkups and = 1 if subject did undergo regular checkups), AGPI (= age at first pregnancy), miscarriages (= number of miscarriages), and weight (= weight of subject), perform a logistic regression to conclude if these variables are statistically useful for predicting whether a woman will contract breast cancer or not.

Appendix 15A

15A.1 Maximum Likelihood Estimation of the Logit and Probit Models for Individual (Ungrouped) Data†

As in the text, assume that we are interested in estimating the probability that an individual owns a house, given the individual's income X. We assume that this probability can be expressed by the logistic function (15.5.2), which is reproduced below for convenience.

$$P_i = \frac{1}{1 + e^{-(\beta_1 + \beta_2 X_i)}} \tag{1}$$

We do not actually observe P_i, but only observe the outcome $Y = 1$, if an individual owns a house, and $Y = 0$, if the individual does not own a house.

Since each Y_i is a Bernoulli random variable, we can write

$$\Pr(Y_i = 1) = P_i \tag{2}$$

$$\Pr(Y_i = 0) = (1 - P_i) \tag{3}$$

*Data are provided on 50 women who were diagnosed as having benign breast disease and 150 age-matched controls, with three controls per case. Trained interviewers administered a standardized structured questionnaire to collect information from each subject (see Pastides, et al. [1983] and Pastides, et al. [1985]).

†The following discussion leans heavily on John Neter, Michael H. Kutner, Christopher J. Nachsteim, and William Wasserman, *Applied Linear Statistical Models,* 4th ed., Irwin, 1996, pp. 573–574.

Suppose we have a *random sample* of n observations. Letting $f_i(Y_i)$ denote the probability that $Y_i =$ 1 or 0, the joint probability of observing the n Y values, i.e., $f(Y_1, Y_2, \ldots, Y_n)$ is given as:

$$f(Y_1, Y_2, \ldots, Y_n) = \prod_{1}^{n} f_i(Y_i) = \prod_{1}^{n} P_i^{Y_i}(1 - P_i)^{1-Y_i} \tag{4}$$

where $\prod$ is the product operator. Note that we can write the joint probability density function as a product of individual density functions because each Y_i is drawn independently and each Y_i has the same (logistic) density function. The joint probability given in Eq. (4) is known as the **likelihood function (LF).**

Equation (4) is a little awkward to manipulate. But if we take its natural logarithm, we obtain what is called the **log likelihood function (LLF):**

$$\begin{aligned} \ln f(Y_1, Y_2, \ldots, Y_n) &= \sum_{1}^{n} [Y_i \ln P_i + (1 - Y_i) \ln (1 - P_i)] \\ &= \sum_{1}^{n} [Y_i \ln P_i - Y_i \ln (1 - P_i) + \ln (1 - P_i)] \\ &= \sum_{1}^{n} \left[Y_i \ln \left(\frac{P_i}{1 - P_i} \right) \right] + \sum_{1}^{n} \ln (1 - P_i) \end{aligned} \tag{5}$$

From Eq. (1) it is easy to verify that

$$(1 - P_i) = \frac{1}{1 + e^{\beta_1 + \beta_2 X_i}} \tag{6}$$

as well as

$$\ln \left(\frac{P_i}{1 - P_i} \right) = \beta_1 + \beta_2 X_i \tag{7}$$

Using Eqs. (6) and (7), we can write the LLF (5) as:

$$\ln f(Y_1, Y_2, \ldots, Y_n) = \sum_{1}^{n} Y_i(\beta_1 + \beta_2 X_i) - \sum_{1}^{n} \ln \left[1 + e^{(\beta_1 + \beta_2 X_i)} \right] \tag{8}$$

As you can see from Eq. (8), the log likelihood function is a function of the parameters β_1 and β_2, since the X_i are known.

In ML our objective is to maximize the LF (or LLF), that is, to obtain the values of the unknown parameters in such a manner that the probability of observing the given Y's is as high (maximum) as possible. For this purpose, we differentiate Eq. (8) partially with respect to each unknown, set the resulting expressions to zero, and solve the resulting expressions. One can then apply the second-order condition of maximization to verify that the values of the parameters we have obtained do in fact maximize the LF.

So, you have to differentiate Eq. (8) with respect to β_1 and β_2 and proceed as indicated. As you will quickly realize, the resulting expressions become highly nonlinear in the parameters and no explicit solutions can be obtained. That is why we will have to use one of the methods of nonlinear estimation discussed in the previous chapter to obtain numerical solutions. Once the numerical values of β_1 and β_2 are obtained, we can easily estimate Eq. (1).

The ML procedure for the probit model is similar to that for the logit model, except that in Eq. (1) we use the normal CDF rather than the logistic CDF. The resulting expression becomes rather complicated, but the general idea is the same. So, we will not pursue it any further.

Chapter 16

Panel Data Regression Models

In Chapter 1 we discussed briefly the types of data that are generally available for empirical analysis, namely, **time series, cross section,** and **panel.** In time series data we observe the values of one or more variables over a period of time (e.g., GDP for several quarters or years). In cross-section data, values of one or more variables are collected for several sample units, or subjects, at the same point in time (e.g., crime rates for 50 states in the United States for a given year). In panel data the same cross-sectional unit (say a family or a firm or a state) is surveyed over time. In short, panel data have space as well as time dimensions.

We have already seen an example of this in Table 1.1, which gives data on eggs produced and their prices for 50 states in the United States for years 1990 and 1991. For any given year, the data on eggs and their prices represent a cross-sectional sample. For any given state, there are two time series observations on eggs and their prices. Thus, we have in all 100 (pooled) observations on eggs produced and their prices.

Another example of panel data was given in Table 1.2, which gives data on investment, value of the firm, and capital stock for four companies for the period 1935–1954. The data for each company over the period 1935–1954 constitute *time series data,* with 20 observations; data, for all four companies for a given year is an example of *cross-section data,* with only four observations; and data for all the companies for all the years is an example of *panel data,* with a total of 80 observations.

There are other names for panel data, such as **pooled data** (pooling of time series and cross-sectional observations), **combination of time series and cross-section data, micropanel data, longitudinal data** (a study over time of a variable or group of subjects), **event history analysis** (studying the movement over time of subjects through successive states or conditions), and **cohort analysis** (e.g., following the career path of 1965 graduates of a business school). Although there are subtle variations, all these names essentially connote movement over time of cross-sectional units. We will therefore use the term panel data in a generic sense to include one or more of these terms. And we will call regression models based on such data **panel data regression models.**

Panel data are now being used increasingly in economic research. Some of the well-known panel data sets are:

1. The **Panel Study of Income Dynamics (PSID)** conducted by the Institute of Social Research at the University of Michigan. Started in 1968, each year the Institute collects data on some 5,000 families about various socioeconomic and demographic variables.

2. The Bureau of the Census of the Department of Commerce conducts a survey similar to PSID, called the **Survey of Income and Program Participation (SIPP).** Four times a year respondents are interviewed about their economic condition.
3. The **German Socio-Economic Panel (GESOEP)** studied 1,761 individuals every year between 1984 and 2002. Information on year of birth, gender, life satisfaction, marital status, individual labor earnings, and annual hours of work was collected for each individual for the period 1984 to 2002.

There are also many other surveys that are conducted by various governmental agencies, such as:

Household, Income and Labor Dynamics in Australia Survey (HILDA)
British Household Panel Survey (BHPS)
Korean Labor and Income Panel Study (KLIPS)

At the outset a warning is in order: The topic of panel data regressions is vast, and some of the mathematics and statistics involved are quite complicated. We only hope to touch on some of the essentials of the panel data regression models, leaving the details for the references.[1] But be forewarned that some of these references are highly technical. Fortunately, user-friendly software packages such as LIMDEP, PC-GIVE, SAS, STATA, SHAZAM, and *EViews,* among others, have made the task of actually implementing panel data regressions quite easy.

16.1 Why Panel Data?

What are the advantages of panel data over cross-section or time series data? Baltagi lists the following advantages of panel data:[2]

1. Since panel data relate to individuals, firms, states, countries, etc., over time, there is bound to be *heterogeneity* in these units. The techniques of panel data estimation can take such heterogeneity explicitly into account by allowing for subject-specific variables, as we shall show shortly. We use the term **subject** in a generic sense to include microunits such as individuals, firms, states, and countries.
2. By combining time series of cross-section observations, panel data gives "more informative data, more variability, less collinearity among variables, more degrees of freedom and more efficiency."
3. By studying the repeated cross section of observations, panel data are better suited to study the dynamics of change. Spells of unemployment, job turnover, and labor mobility are better studied with panel data.
4. Panel data can better detect and measure effects that simply cannot be observed in pure cross-section or pure time series data. For example, the effects of minimum wage laws

[1]Some of the references are G. Chamberlain, "Panel Data," in *Handbook of Econometrics,* vol. II; Z. Griliches and M. D. Intriligator, eds., North-Holland Publishers, 1984, Chapter 22; C. Hsiao, *Analysis of Panel Data,* Cambridge University Press, 1986; G. G. Judge, R. C. Hill, W. E. Griffiths, H. Lutkepohl, and T. C. Lee, *Introduction to the Theory and Practice of Econometrics,* 2d ed., John Wiley & Sons, New York, 1985, Chapter 11; W. H. Greene, *Econometric Analysis,* 6th ed., Prentice-Hall, Englewood Cliffs, NJ, 2008, Chapter 9; Badi H. Baltagi, *Econometric Analysis of Panel Data,* John Wiley and Sons, New York, 1995; and J. M. Wooldridge, *Econometric Analysis of Cross Section and Panel Data,* MIT Press, Cambridge, Mass., 1999. For a detailed treatment of the subject with empirical applications, see Edward W. Frees, *Longitudinal and Panel Data: Analysis and Applications in the Social Sciences,* Cambridge University Press, New York, 2004.

[2]Baltagi, op. cit., pp. 3–6.

on employment and earnings can be better studied if we include successive waves of minimum wage increases in the federal and/or state minimum wages.

5. Panel data enables us to study more complicated behavioral models. For example, phenomena such as economies of scale and technological change can be better handled by panel data than by pure cross-section or pure time series data.
6. By making data available for several thousand units, panel data can minimize the bias that might result if we aggregate individuals or firms into broad aggregates.

In short, panel data can enrich empirical analysis in ways that may not be possible if we use only cross-section or time series data. This is not to suggest that there are no problems with panel data modeling. We will discuss them after we cover some theory and discuss some examples.

16.2 Panel Data: An Illustrative Example

To set the stage, let us consider a concrete example. Consider the data given as Table 16.1 on the textbook website, which were originally collected by Professor Moshe Kim and are reproduced from William Greene.[3] The data analyzes the costs of six airline firms for the period 1970–1984, for a total of 90 panel data observations.

The variables are defined as: I = airline id; T = year id; Q = output, in revenue passenger miles, an index number; C = total cost, in \$1,000; PF = fuel price; and LF = load factor, the average capacity utilization of the fleet.

Suppose we are interested in finding out how total cost (C) behaves in relation to output (Q), fuel price (PF), and load factor (LF). In short, we wish to estimate an airline cost function.

How do we go about estimating this function? Of course, we can estimate the cost function for each airline using the data for 1970–1984 (i.e., a time series regression). This can be accomplished with the usual ordinary least squares (OLS) procedure. We will have in all six cost functions, one for each airline. But then we neglect the information about the other airlines which operate in the same (regulatory) environment.

We can also estimate a cross-section cost function (i.e., a cross-section regression). We will have in all 15 cross-section regressions, one for each year. But this would not make much sense in the present context, for we have only six observations per year and there are three explanatory variables (plus the intercept term); we will have very few degrees of freedom to do a meaningful analysis. Also, we will not "exploit" the panel nature of our data.

Incidentally, the panel data in our example is called a **balanced panel;** a panel is said to be balanced if each subject (firm, individuals, etc.) has the same number of observations. If each entity has a different number of observations, then we have an **unbalanced panel.** For most of this chapter, we will deal with balanced panels. In the panel data literature you will also come across the terms **short panel** and **long panel.** In a short panel the number of cross-sectional subjects, N, is greater than the number of time periods, T. In a long panel, it is T that is greater than N. As we discuss later, the estimating techniques can depend on whether we have a short panel or a long one.

What, then, are the options? There are four possibilities:

1. **Pooled OLS model.** We simply pool all 90 observations and estimate a "grand" regression, neglecting the cross-section and time series nature of our data.
2. The **fixed effects least squares dummy variable (LSDV) model.** Here we pool all 90 observations, but allow each cross-section unit (i.e., airline in our example) to have its own (intercept) dummy variable.

[3]William H. Greene, *Econometric Analysis,* 6th ed., 2008. Data are located at http://pages.stern.nyu.edu/~wgreen/Text/econometricanalysis.htm.

3. The **fixed effects within-group model.** Here also we pool all 90 observations, but for each airline we express each variable as a deviation from its mean value and then estimate an OLS regression on such *mean-corrected* or "de-meaned" values.
4. The **random effects model (REM).** Unlike the LSDV model, in which we allow each airline to have its own (fixed) intercept value, we assume that the intercept values are a random drawing from a much bigger population of airlines.

We now discuss each of these methods using the data given in Table 16.1. (See textbook website.)

16.3 Pooled OLS Regression or Constant Coefficients Model

Consider the following model:

$$C_{it} = \beta_1 + \beta_2 Q_{it} + \beta_3 PF_{it} + \beta_4 LF_{it} + u_{it} \tag{16.3.1}$$
$$i = 1, 2, \ldots, 6$$
$$t = 1, 2, \ldots, 15$$

where i is ith subject and t is the time period for the variables we defined previously. We have chosen the linear cost function for illustrative purposes, but in Exercise 16.10 you are asked to estimate a log–linear, or double-log function, in which case the slope coefficients will give the elasticity estimates.

Notice that we have pooled together all 90 observations, but note that we are assuming the regression coefficients are the same for all the airlines. That is, there is no distinction between the airlines—one airline is as good as the other, an assumption that may be difficult to maintain.

It is assumed that the explanatory variables are nonstochastic. If they are stochastic, they are uncorrelated with the error term. Sometimes it is assumed that the explanatory variables are **strictly exogenous.** *A variable is said to be strictly exogenous if it does not depend on current, past, and future values of the error term* u_{it}.

It is also assumed that the error term is $u_{it} \sim iid(0, \sigma_u^2)$, that is, it is independently and identically distributed with zero mean and constant variance. For the purpose of hypothesis testing, it may be assumed that the error term is also normally distributed. Notice the double-subscripted notation in Eq. (16.3.1), which should be self-explanatory.

Let us first present the results of the estimated equation (16.3.1) and then discuss some of the problems with this model. The regression results based on *EViews,* Version 6 are presented in Table 16.2.

If you examine the results of the **pooled regression** and apply the conventional criteria, you will see that all the regression coefficients are not only highly statistically significant but are also in accord with prior expectations and that the R^2 value is very high. The only "fly in the ointment" is that the estimated Durbin–Watson statistic is quite low, suggesting that perhaps there is autocorrelation and/or spatial correlation in the data. Of course, as we know, a low Durbin–Watson could also be due to specification errors.

The major problem with this model is that it does not distinguish between the various airlines nor does it tell us whether the response of total cost to the explanatory variables over time is the same for all the airlines. In other words, by lumping together different airlines at different times we *camouflage* the **heterogeneity** (individuality or uniqueness) that may exist among the airlines. Another way of stating this is that the individuality of each subject is subsumed in the disturbance term u_{it}. As a consequence, it is quite possible that the error term may be correlated with some of the regressors included in the model. If that is the case, the estimated coefficients in Eq. (16.3.1) may be biased as well as inconsistent.

TABLE 16.2

Dependent Variable: *C*
Method: Least Squares
Included observations: 90

	Coefficient	Std. Error	*t* Statistic	Prob.
C (intercept)	1158559.	360592.7	3.212930	0.0018
Q	2026114.	61806.95	32.78134	0.0000
PF	1.225348	0.103722	11.81380	0.0000
LF	-3065753.	696327.3	-4.402747	0.0000

R-squared	0.946093	Mean dependent var.	1122524.
Adjusted *R*-squared	0.944213	S.D. dependent var.	1192075.
S.E. of regression	281559.5	*F*-statistic	503.1176
Sum squared resid.	6.82E+12	Prob. (*F*-statistic)	0.000000
		Durbin-Watson	0.434162

Recall that one of the important assumptions of the classical linear regression model is that there is no correlation between the regressors and the disturbance or error term.

To see how the error term may be correlated with the regressors, let us consider the following revision of model (16.3.1):

$$C_{it} = \beta_1 + \beta_2 PF_{it} + \beta_3 LF_{it} + \beta_4 M_{it} + u_{it} \tag{16.3.2}$$

where the additional variable $M =$ management philosophy or management quality. Of the variables included in Eq. (16.3.2), only the variable M is **time-invariant** (or **time-constant**) because it varies among subjects but is constant over time for a given subject (airline).

Although it is time-invariant, the variable M is not directly observable and therefore we cannot measure its contribution to the cost function. We can, however, do this indirectly if we write Eq. (16.3.2) as

$$C_{it} = \beta_1 + \beta_2 PF_{it} + \beta_3 LF_{it} + \alpha_i + u_{it} \tag{16.3.3}$$

where α_i, called the **unobserved,** or **heterogeneity, effect,** reflects the impact of M on cost. Note that for simplicity we have shown only the unobserved effect of M on cost, but in reality there may be more such unobserved effects, for example, the nature of ownership (privately owned or publicly owned), whether it is a minority-owned company, whether the CEO is a man or a woman, etc. Although such variables may differ among the subjects (airlines), they will probably remain the same for any given subject over the sample period.

Since α_i is not directly observable, why not consider it random and include it in the error term u_{it}, and thereby consider the composite error term $v_{it} = \alpha_i + u_{it}$? We now write Eq. (16.3.3) as:

$$C_{it} = \beta_1 + \beta_2 PF_{it} + \beta_3 LF_{it} + v_{it} \tag{16.3.4}$$

But if the α_i term included in the error term v_{it} is correlated with any of the regressors in Eq. (16.3.4), we have a violation of one of the key assumptions of the classical linear regression model—namely, that the error term is not correlated with the regressors. As we know in this situation, the OLS estimates are not only biased but they are also inconsistent.

There is a real possibility that the unobservable α_i is correlated with one or more of the regressors. For example, the management of one airline may be astute enough to buy future contracts of the fuel price to avoid severe price fluctuations. This will have the effect of lowering the cost of airline services. As a result of this correlation, it can be shown that $\text{cov}\,(v_{it}, v_{is}) = \sigma_u^2;\ t \neq s$, which is non-zero, and therefore, the (unobserved) heterogeneity induces *autocorrelation* and we will have to pay attention to it. We will show later how this problem can be handled.

The question, therefore, is how we account for the unobservable, or heterogeneity, effect(s) so that we can obtain consistent and/or efficient estimates of the parameters of the variables of prime interest, which are output, fuel price, and load factor in our case. Our prime interest may not be in obtaining the impact of the unobservable variables because they remain the same for a given subject. That is why such unobservable, or heterogeneity, effects are called **nuisance parameters.** How then do we proceed? It is to this question we now turn.

16.4 The Fixed Effect Least-Squares Dummy Variable (LSDV) Model

The least-squares dummy variable (LSDV) model allows for heterogeneity among subjects by allowing each entity to have its own intercept value, as shown in model (16.4.1). Again, we continue with our airlines example.

$$C_{it} = \beta_{1i} + \beta_2 Q_{it} + \beta_3 PF_{it} + \beta_4 LF_{it} + u_{it} \qquad (16.4.1)$$

$$i = 1, 2 \ldots, 6$$

$$t = 1, 2, \ldots, 15$$

Notice that we have put the subscript i on the intercept term to suggest that the intercepts of the six airlines may be different. The difference may be due to special features of each airline, such as managerial style, managerial philosophy, or the type of market each airline is serving.

In the literature, model (16.4.1) is known as the **fixed effects (regression) model (FEM).** The term "fixed effects" is due to the fact that, although the intercept may differ across subjects (here the six airlines), each entity's intercept does not vary over time, that is, it is **time-invariant.** Notice that if we were to write the intercept as β_{1it}, it would suggest that the intercept of each entity or individual is **time-variant.** It may be noted that the FEM given in Eq. (16.4.1) assumes that the (slope) coefficients of the regressors do not vary across individuals or over time.

Before proceeding further, it may be useful to visualize the difference between the pooled regression model and the LSDV model. For simplicity assume that we want to regress total cost on output only. In Figure 16.1 we show this cost function estimated for two airline companies separately, as well as the cost function if we pool the data for the two

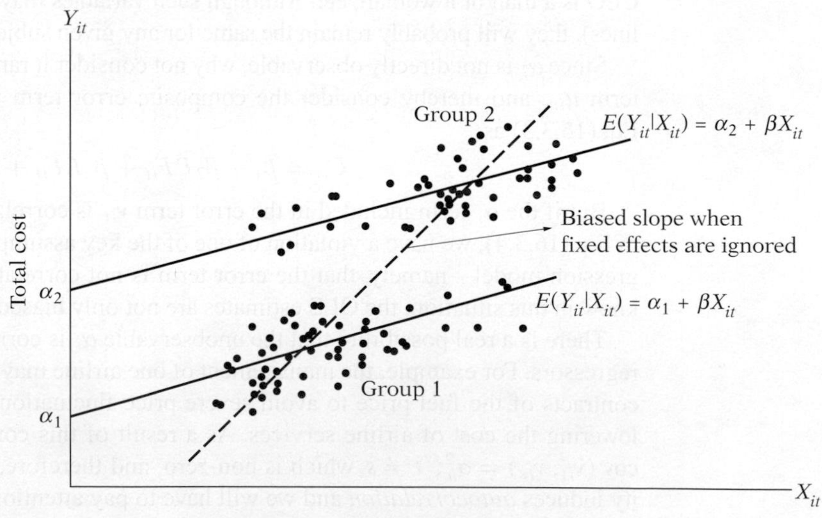

FIGURE 16.1 Bias from ignoring fixed effects.

companies; this is equivalent to neglecting the fixed effects.[4] You can see from Figure 16.1 how the pooled regression can bias the slope estimate.

How do we actually allow for the (fixed effect) intercept to vary among the airlines? We can easily do this by using the dummy variable technique, particularly the **differential intercept dummy technique,** which we learned in Chapter 9. Now we write Eq. (16.4.1) as:

$$C_{it} = \alpha_1 + \alpha_2 D_{2i} + \alpha_3 D_{3i} + \alpha_4 D_{4i} + \alpha_5 D_{5i} + \alpha_6 D_{6i} + \beta_2 Q_{it} + \beta_3 PF_{it} + \beta_4 LF_{it} + u_{it} \tag{16.4.2}$$

where $D_{2i} = 1$ for airline 2, 0 otherwise; $D_{3i} = 1$ for airline 3, 0 otherwise; and so on. Notice that since we have six airlines, we have introduced only five dummy variables to avoid falling into the **dummy-variable trap** (i.e., the situation of perfect collinearity). Here we are treating airline 1 as the base, or reference, category. Of course, you can choose any airline as the reference point. As a result, the intercept α_1 is the intercept value of airline 1 and the other α coefficients represent by how much the intercept values of the other airlines differ from the intercept value of the first airline. Thus, α_2 tells by how much the intercept value of the second airline differs from α_1. The sum $(\alpha_1 + \alpha_2)$ gives the actual value of the intercept for airline 2. The intercept values of the other airlines can be computed similarly. *Keep in mind that if you want to introduce a dummy for each airline, you will have to drop the (common) intercept; otherwise, you will fall into the dummy-variable trap.*

The results of the model (16.4.2) for our data are presented in Table 16.3.

The first thing to notice about these results is that all the differential intercept coefficients are individually highly statistically significant, suggesting that perhaps the six airlines are heterogeneous and, therefore, the pooled regression results given in Table 16.2 may be suspect. The values of the slope coefficients given in Tables 16.2 and 16.3 are also different, again casting some doubt on the results given in Table 16.2. It seems model (16.4.1) is better than model (16.3.1). In passing, note that OLS applied to a fixed effect model produces estimators that are called **fixed effect estimators.**

TABLE 16.3

Dependent Variable: TC
Method: Least Squares
Sample: 1-90
Included observations: 90

	Coefficient	Std. Error	*t* Statistic	Prob.
C ($=\alpha_1$)	-131236.0	350777.1	-0.374129	0.7093
Q	3319023.	171354.1	19.36939	0.0000
PF	0.773071	0.097319	7.943676	0.0000
LF	-3797368.	613773.1	-6.186924	0.0000
DUM2	601733.2	100895.7	5.963913	0.0000
DUM3	1337180.	186171.0	7.182538	0.0000
DUM4	1777592.	213162.9	8.339126	0.0000
DUM5	1828252.	231229.7	7.906651	0.0000
DUM6	1706474.	228300.9	7.474672	0.0000

R-squared	0.971642	Mean dependent var.	1122524.
Adjusted *R*-squared	0.968841	S.D. dependent var.	1192075.
S.E. of regression	210422.8	*F*-statistics	346.9188
Sum squared resid.	3.59E+12	Prob. (*F*-statistic)	0.000000
Log likelihood	-1226.082	Durbin-Watson stat.	0.693288

[4] Adapted from the unpublished notes of Alan Duncan.

We can provide a formal test of the two models. In relation to model (16.4.1), model (16.3.1) is a *restricted* model in that it imposes a common intercept for all the airlines. Therefore, we can use the **restricted F test** discussed in Chapter 8. Using formula (8.6.10), the reader can check that in the present case the F value is:

$$F = \frac{(0.971642 - 0.946093)/5}{(1 - 0.971642)/81} \approx 14.99$$

Note: The restricted and unrestricted R^2 values are obtained from Tables 16.1 and 16.2. Also note that the number of restrictions is 5 (why?).

The null hypothesis here is that all the differential intercepts are equal to zero. The computed F value for 5 numerator and 81 denominator df is highly statistically significant. Therefore, we reject the null hypothesis that all the (differential) intercepts are zero. If the F value were not statistically significant, we would have concluded that there is no difference in the intercepts of the six airlines. In this case, we would have pooled all 90 of the observations, as we did in the pooled regression given in Table 16.2.

Model (16.4.1) is known as a **one-way fixed effects** model because we have allowed the intercepts to differ between airlines. But we can also allow for **time effect** if we believe that the cost function changes over time because of factors such as technological changes, changes in government regulation and/or tax policies, and other such effects. Such a time effect can be easily accounted for if we introduce time dummies, one for each year from 1970 to 1984. Since we have data for 15 years, we can introduce 14 time dummies (why?) and extend model (16.4.1) by adding these variables. If we do that, the model that emerges is called a **two-way fixed effects model** because we have allowed for both individual and time effects.

In the present example, if we add the time dummies, we will have in all 23 coefficients to estimate—the common intercept, five airlines dummies, 14 time dummies, and three slope coefficients. As you can see, we will consume several degrees of freedom. Furthermore, if we decide to allow the slope coefficients to differ among the companies, we can interact the five firm (airline) dummies with each of the three explanatory variables and introduce **differential slope dummy coefficients.** Then we will have to estimate 15 additional coefficients (five dummies interacted with three explanatory variables). As if this is not enough, if we interact the 14 time dummies with the three explanatory variables, we will have in all 42 additional coefficients to estimate. As you can see, we will not have any degrees of freedom left.

A Caution in the Use of the Fixed Effect LSDV Model

As the preceding discussion suggests, the LSDV model has several problems that need to be borne in mind:

First, if you introduce too many dummy variables, you will run up against the degrees of freedom problem. That is, you will lack enough observations to do a meaningful statistical analysis. *Second,* with many dummy variables in the model, both individual and interactive or multiplicative, there is always the possibility of multicollinearity, which might make precise estimation of one or more parameters difficult.

Third, in some situations the LSDV may not be able to identify the impact of time-invariant variables. Suppose we want to estimate a wage function for a group of workers using panel data. Besides wage, a wage function may include age, experience, and education as explanatory variables. Suppose we also decide to add sex, color, and ethnicity as additional variables in the model. Since these variables will not change over time for an individual subject, the LSDV approach may not be able to identify the impact of such time-invariant variables on wages. To put it differently, the subject-specific intercepts absorb all heterogeneity that may exist in the dependent and explanatory variables. Incidentally, the time-invariant variables are sometimes called **nuisance variables** or **lurking variables.**

Fourth, we have to think carefully about the error term u_{it}. The results we have presented in Eqs. (16.3.1) and (16.4.1) are based on the assumption that the error term follows the classical assumptions, namely, $u_{it} \sim N(0, \sigma^2)$. Since the index i refers to cross-section observations and t to time series observations, the classical assumption for u_{it} may have to be modified. There are several possibilities, including:

1. We can assume that the error variance is the same for all cross-section units or we can assume that the error variance is heteroscedastic.[5]
2. For each entity, we can assume that there is no autocorrelation over time. Thus, in our illustrative example, we can assume that the error term of the cost function for airline #1 is non-autocorrelated, or we can assume that it is autocorrelated, say, of the AR(1) type.
3. For a given time, it is possible that the error term for airline #1 is correlated with the error term for, say, airline #2.[6] Or we can assume that there is no such correlation.

There are also other combinations and permutations of the error term. As you will quickly realize, allowing one or more of these possibilities will make the analysis that much more complicated. (Space and mathematical demands preclude us from considering all the possibilities. The references in footnote 1 discuss some of these topics.) Some of these problems may be alleviated, however, if we consider the alternatives discussed in the next two sections.

16.5 The Fixed-Effect Within-Group (WG) Estimator

One way to estimate a pooled regression is to eliminate the fixed effect, β_{1i}, by expressing the values of the dependent and explanatory variables for each airline as deviations from their respective mean values. Thus, for airline #1 we will obtain the sample mean values of TC, Q, PF, and LF, ($\overline{TC}$, $\overline{Q}$, $\overline{PF}$, and $\overline{LF}$, respectively) and subtract them from the individual values of these variables. The resulting values are called "de-meaned" or *mean-corrected* values. We do this for each airline and then pool all the (90) mean-corrected values and run an OLS regression.

Letting tc_{it}, q_{it}, pf_{it}, and lf_{it} represent the mean-corrected values, we now run the regression:

$$tc_{it} = \beta_2 q_{it} + \beta_3 pf_{it} + \beta_4 lf_{it} + u_{it} \tag{16.5.1}$$

where $i = 1, 2, \ldots, 6$, and $t = 1, 2, \ldots, 15$. Note that Eq. (16.5.1) *does not* have an intercept term (why?).

Returning to our example, we obtain the results in Table 16.4. *Note:* The prefix DM means that the values are mean-corrected or expressed as deviations from their sample means.

Note the difference between the pooled regression given in Table 16.2 and the pooled regression in Table 16.4. The former simply ignores the heterogeneity among the six airlines, whereas the latter takes it into account, not by the dummy variable method, but by eliminating it by differencing sample observations around their sample means. The difference between the two is obvious, as shown in Figure 16.2.

It can be shown that the WG estimator produces *consistent estimates* of the slope coefficients, whereas the ordinary pooled regression may not. It should be added, however,

[5]STATA provides heteroscedasticity-corrected standard errors in the panel data regression models.

[6]This leads to the so-called **seemingly unrelated regression (SURE) model,** originally proposed by Arnold Zellner. See A. Zellner, "An Efficient Method of Estimating Seemingly Unrelated Regressions and Tests for Aggregation Bias," *Journal of the American Statistical Association,* vol. 57, 1962, pp. 348–368.

TABLE 16.4

Dependent Variable: DMTC
Method: Least Squares
Sample: 1-90
Included observations: 90

	Coefficient	Std. Error	*t* Statistic	Prob.
DMQ	3319023.	165339.8	20.07396	0.0000
DMPF	0.773071	0.093903	8.232630	0.0000
DMLF	-3797368.	592230.5	-6.411976	0.0000

R-squared	0.929366	Mean dependent var.	2.59E-11
Adjusted *R*-squared	0.927743	S.D. dependent var.	755325.8
S.E. of regression	203037.2	Durbin-Watson stat.	0.693287
Sum squared resid.	3.59E+12		

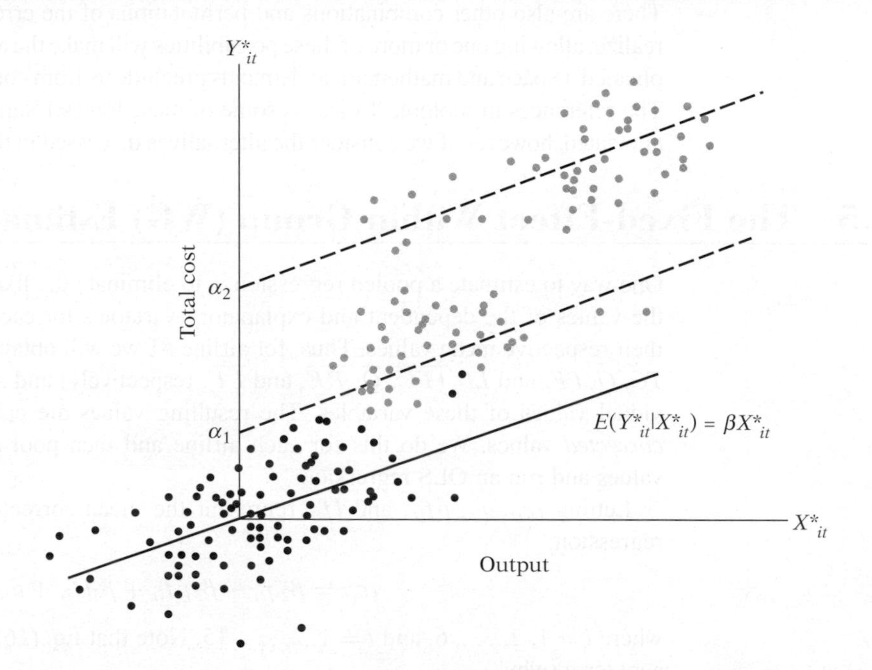

FIGURE 16.2
The within-groups estimator.

Source: Alan Duncan, "Cross-Section and Panel Data Econometrics," unpublished lecture notes (adapted).

that WG estimators, although consistent, are inefficient (i.e., have larger variances) compared to the ordinary pooled regression results.[7] Observe that the slope coefficients of the Q, PF, and LF are identical in Tables 16.3 and 16.4. *This is because mathematically the two models are identical.* Incidentally, the regression coefficients estimated by the WG method are called *WG estimators.*

One disadvantage of the WG estimator can be explained with the following wage regression model:

$$W_{it} = \beta_{1i} + \beta_2 \text{Experience}_{it} + \beta_3 \text{Age}_{it} + \beta_4 \text{Gender}_{it} + \beta_5 \text{Education}_{it} + \beta_6 \text{Race}_{it} \tag{16.5.2}$$

In this wage function, variables such as gender, education, and race are time-invariant. If we use the WG estimators, these time-invariant variables will be wiped out (because of

[7]The reason for this is that when we express variables as deviations from their mean values, the variation in these mean-corrected values will be much smaller than the variation in the original values of the variables. In that case, the variation in the disturbance term u_{it} may be relatively large, thus leading to higher standard errors of the estimated coefficients.

differencing). As a result, we will not know how wage reacts to these time-invariant variables.[8] But this is the price we have to pay to avoid the correlation between the error term (α_i included in v_{it}) and the explanatory variables.

Another disadvantage of the WG estimator is that, "... it may distort the parameter values and can certainly remove any long run effects."[9] *In general, when we difference a variable, we remove the long-run component from that variable.* What is left is the short-run value of that variable. We will discuss this further when we discuss time series econometrics later in the book.

In using LSDV we obtained direct estimates of the intercepts for each airline. How can we obtain the estimates of the intercepts using the WG method? For the airlines example, they are obtained as follows:

$$\hat{\alpha}_i = \bar{C}_i - \hat{\beta}_2 \bar{Q}_i - \hat{\beta}_3 \overline{PF}_i - \hat{\beta}_4 \overline{LF} \tag{16.5.3}$$

where bars over the variables denote the sample mean values of the variables for the ith airline.

That is, we obtain the intercept value of the ith airline by subtracting from the mean value of the dependent variable the mean values of the explanatory variables for that airline times the estimated slope coefficients from the WG estimators. Note that the estimated slope coefficients remain the same for all of the airlines, as shown in Table 16.4. It may be noted that the intercept estimated in Eq. (16.5.3) is similar to the intercept we estimate in the standard linear regression model, which can be see from Eq. (7.4.21). We leave it for the reader to find the intercepts of the six airlines in the manner shown and verify that they are the same as the intercept values derived in Table 16.3, save for the rounding errors.

It may be noted that the estimated intercept of each airline represents the *subject-specific* characteristics of each airline, but we will not be able to identify these characteristics individually. Thus, the α_1 intercept for airline #1 represents the management philosophy of that airline, the composition of its board of directors, the personality of the CEO, the gender of the CEO, etc. All these heterogeneity characteristics are subsumed in the intercept value. As we will see later, such characteristics can be included in the *random effects model.*

In passing, we note that an alternative to the WG estimator is the **first-difference method.** In the WG method, we express each variable as a deviation from that variable's mean value. In the first-difference method, for each subject we take successive differences of the variables. Thus, for airline #1 we subtract the first observation of TC from the second observation of TC, the second observation of TC from the third observation of TC, and so on. We do this for each of the remaining variables and repeat this process for the remaining five airlines. After this process we have only 14 observations for each airline, since the first observation has no previous value. As a result, we now have 84 observations instead of the original 90 observations. We then regress the first-differenced values of the TC variable on the first-differenced values of the explanatory variables as follows:

$$\begin{aligned} \Delta TC_{it} &= \beta_2 \Delta Q_{it} + \beta_3 \Delta PF_{it} + \beta_4 \Delta LF_{it} + (u_{it} - u_{i,t-1}) \\ i &= 1, 2, \ldots, 6 \\ t &= 1, 2, \ldots, 84 \end{aligned} \tag{16.5.4}$$

where $\Delta = (TC_{it} - TC_{i,\,t-1})$. As noted in Chapter 11, Δ is called the first difference operator.[10]

[8] This is also true of the LSDV model.

[9] Dimitrios Asteriou and Stephen G. Hall, *Applied Econometrics: A Modern Approach,* Palgrave Macmillan, New York, 2007, p. 347.

[10] Notice that Eq. (16.5.3) has no intercept term (why?), but we can include it if there is a trend variable in the original model.

In passing, note that the original disturbance term is now replaced by the difference between the current and previous values of the disturbance term. If the original disturbance term is not autocorrelated, the transformed disturbance *is,* and therefore it poses the kinds of estimation problems that we discussed in Chapter 11. However, if the explanatory variables are **strictly exogenous,** the first difference estimator is unbiased, given the values of the explanatory variables. Also note that the first-difference method has the same disadvantages as the WG method in that the explanatory variables that remain fixed over time for an individual are wiped out in the first-difference transformation.

It may be pointed out that the first difference and fixed effects estimators are the same when we have only two time periods, but if there are more than two periods, these estimators differ. The reasons for this are rather involved and the interested reader may consult the references.[11] It is left as an exercise for the reader to apply the first difference method to our airlines example and compare the results with the other fixed effects estimators.

16.6 The Random Effects Model (REM)

Commenting on fixed effect, or LSDV, modeling, Kmenta writes:[12]

> An obvious question in connection with the covariance [i.e., LSDV] model is whether the inclusion of the dummy variables—and the consequent loss of the number of degrees of freedom—is really necessary. The reasoning underlying the covariance model is that in specifying the regression model we have failed to include relevant explanatory variables that do not change over time (and possibly others that do change over time but have the same value for all cross-sectional units), and that the inclusion of dummy variables is a *coverup of our ignorance.*

If the dummy variables do in fact represent a lack of knowledge about the (true) model, why not express this ignorance through the disturbance term? This is precisely the approach suggested by the proponents of the so-called **error components model (ECM)** or **random effects model (REM),** which we will now illustrate with our airline cost function.

The basic idea is to start with Eq. (16.4.1):

$$TC_{it} = \beta_{1i} + \beta_2 Q_{it} + \beta_3 PF_{it} + \beta_4 LF_{it} + u_{it} \tag{16.6.1}$$

Instead of treating β_{1i} as fixed, we assume that it is a random variable with a mean value of β_1 (no subscript *i* here). The intercept value for an individual company can be expressed as

$$\beta_{1i} = \beta_1 + \varepsilon_i \tag{16.6.2}$$

where ε_i is a random error term with a mean value of zero and a variance of σ_ε^2.

What we are essentially saying is that the six firms included in our sample are a drawing from a much larger universe of such companies and that they have a common mean value for the intercept ($= \beta_1$). The individual differences in the intercept values of each company are reflected in the error term ε_i.

Substituting Eq. (16.6.2) into Eq. (16.6.1), we obtain:

$$\begin{aligned} TC_{it} &= \beta_1 + \beta_2 Q_{it} + \beta_3 PF_{it} + \beta_4 LF_{it} + \varepsilon_i + u_{it} \\ &= \beta_1 + \beta_2 Q_{it} + \beta_3 PF_{it} + \beta_4 LF_{it} + w_{it} \end{aligned} \tag{16.6.3}$$

where

$$w_{it} = \varepsilon_i + u_{it} \tag{16.6.4}$$

[11] See in particular Jeffrey M. Wooldridge, *Econometric Analysis of Cross Section and Panel Data,* MIT Press, Cambridge, Mass., 2002, pp. 279–283.

[12] Jan Kmenta, *Elements of Econometrics,* 2d ed., Macmillan, New York, 1986, p. 633.

The composite error term w_{it} consists of two components: ε_i, which is the cross-section, or individual-specific, error component, and u_{it}, which is the combined time series and cross-section error component and is sometimes called the **idiosyncratic term** because it varies over cross-section (i.e., subject) as well as time. The *error components model* (ECM) is so named because the composite error term consists of two (or more) error components.

The usual assumptions made by the ECM are that

$$\begin{aligned} &\varepsilon_i \sim N(0, \sigma_\varepsilon^2) \\ &u_{it} \sim N(0, \sigma_u^2) \\ &E(\varepsilon_i u_{it}) = 0; \quad E(\varepsilon_i \varepsilon_j) = 0 \quad (i \neq j) \\ &E(u_{it} u_{is}) = E(u_{ij} u_{ij}) = E(u_{it} u_{js}) = 0 \quad (i \neq j; t \neq s) \end{aligned} \tag{16.6.5}$$

that is, the individual error components are not correlated with each other and are not autocorrelated across both cross-section and time series units. *It is also very important to note that w_{it} is not correlated with any of the explanatory variables included in the model.* Since ε_i is a component of w_{it}, it is possible that the latter is correlated with the explantory variables. If that is indeed the case, the ECM will result in inconsistent estimation of the regression coefficients. Shortly, we will discuss the **Hausman test,** which will tell us in a given application if w_{it} is correlated with the explanatory variables, that is, whether ECM is the appropriate model.

Notice carefully the difference between FEM and ECM. In FEM each cross-sectional unit has its own (fixed) intercept value, in all N such values for N cross-sectional units. In ECM, on the other hand, the (common) intercept represents the *mean value* of all the (cross-sectional) intercepts and the error component ε_i represents the (random) deviation of individual intercept from this mean value. Keep in mind, however, that ε_i is not directly observable; it is what is known as an **unobservable,** or **latent, variable.**

As a result of the assumptions stated in Eq. (16.6.5), it follows that

$$E(w_{it}) = 0 \tag{16.6.6}$$

$$\operatorname{var}(w_{it}) = \sigma_\varepsilon^2 + \sigma_u^2 \tag{16.6.7}$$

Now if $\sigma_\varepsilon^2 = 0$, there is no difference between models (16.3.1) and (16.6.3) and we can simply pool all the (cross-sectional and time series) observations and run the pooled regression, as we did in Eq. (16.3.1). This is true because in this situation there are either no subject-specific effects or they have all been accounted for in the explanatory variables.

As Eq. (16.6.7) shows, the error term is homoscedastic. However, it can be shown that w_{it} and $w_{is} (t \neq s)$ are correlated; that is, the error terms of a given cross-sectional unit at two different points in time are correlated. The correlation coefficient, corr (w_{it}, w_{is}), is as follows:

$$\rho = \operatorname{corr}(w_{it}, w_{is}) = \frac{\sigma_\varepsilon^2}{\sigma_\varepsilon^2 + \sigma_u^2}; \quad t \neq s \tag{16.6.8}$$

Notice two special features of the preceding correlation coefficient. *First,* for any given cross-sectional unit, the value of the correlation between error terms at two different times remains the same no matter how far apart the two time periods are, as is clear from Eq. (16.6.8). This is in strong contrast to the first-order [AR(1)] scheme that we discussed in Chapter 12, where we found that the correlation between periods declines over time. *Second,* the correlation structure given in Eq. (16.6.8) remains the same for all cross-sectional units; that is, it is identical for all subjects.

If we do not take this correlation structure into account, and estimate Eq. (16.6.3) by OLS, the resulting estimators will be inefficient. The most appropriate method here is the method of **generalized least squares (GLS).**

TABLE 16.5

Dependent Variable: TC
Method: Panel EGLS (Cross-section random effects)
Sample: 1-15
Periods included: 15
Cross-sections included: 6
Total panel (balanced) observations: 90
Swamy and Arora estimator of component variances

	Coefficient	Std. Error	*t* Statistic	Prob.
C	107429.3	303966.2	3.534251	0.0007
Q	2288588.	88172.77	25.95572	0.0000
PF	1.123591	0.083298	13.48877	0.0000
LF	-3084994.	584373.2	-5.279151	0.0000

Effects Specification

	S.D.	Rho
Cross-section random	107411.2	0.2067
Idiosyncratic random	210422.8	0.7933

	Firm	Effect
1	1.000000	-270615.0
2	2.000000	-87061.32
3	3.000000	-21338.40
4	4.000000	187142.9
5	5.000000	134488.9
6	6.000000	57383.00

We will not discuss the mathematics of GLS in the present context because of its complexity.[13] Since most modern statistical software packages now have routines to estimate ECM (as well as FEM), we will present the results for our illustrative example only. But before we do that, it may be noted that we can easily extend Eq. (16.4.2) to allow for a random error component to take into account variation over time (see Exercise 16.6).

The results of ECM estimation of the airline cost function are presented in Table 16.5. Notice these features of the REM. The (average) intercept value is 107429.3. The (differential) intercept values of the six entities are given at the bottom of the regression results. Firm number 1, for example, has an intercept value which is 270615 units lower than the common intercept value of 107429.3; the actual value of the intercept for this airline is then −163185.7. On the other hand, the intercept value of firm number 6 is higher by 57383 units than the common intercept value; the actual intercept value for this airline is (107429.3 + 57383), or 164812.3. The intercept values for the other airlines can be derived similarly. However, note that if you add the (differential) intercept values of all the six airlines, the sum is 0, as it should be (why?).

If you compare the results of the fixed-effect and random-effect regressions, you will see that there are substantial differences between the two. The important question now is: Which results are reliable? Or, to put it differently, which should be the choice between the two models? We can apply the *Hausman test* to shed light on this question.

The null hypothesis underlying the Hausman test is that the FEM and ECM estimators do not differ substantially. The test statistic developed by Hausman has an asymptotic χ^2

[13]See Kmenta, op. cit., pp. 625–630.

TABLE 16.6

Correlated Random Effects—Hausman Test
Equation: Untitled
Test cross-section random effects

Test Summary	Chi-Sq. Statistic	Chi-Sq. d.f.	Prob.
Cross-section random	49.619687	3	0.0000

Cross-section random effects test comparisons:

Variable	Fixed	Random	Var(Diff.)	Prob.
Q	3319023.28	2288587.95	21587779733.	0.0000
PF	0.773071	1.123591	0.002532	0.0000
LF	-3797367.59	-3084994.0	35225469544.	0.0001

distribution. If the null hypothesis is rejected, the conclusion is that the ECM is not appropriate because the random effects are probably correlated with one or more regressors. In this case, FEM is preferred to ECM. For our example, the results of the Hausman test are as shown in Table 16.6.

The Hausman test clearly rejects the null hypothesis, for the estimated χ^2 value for 3 df is highly significant; if the null hypothesis were true, the probability of obtaining a chi-square value of as much as 49.62 or greater would be practically zero. As a result, we can reject the ECM (REM) in favor of FEM. Incidentally, the last part of the preceding table compares the fixed-effect and random-effect coefficients of each variable and, as the last column shows, in the present example the differences are statistically significant.

Breusch and Pagan Lagrange Multiplier Test[14]

Besides the Hausman test, we can also use the Breusch-Pagan (BP) test to test the hypothesis that there are no random effects, i.e., σ_u^2 in Eq. (16.6.7) is zero. This test is built into software packages such as STATA. Under the null hypothesis, BP follows a chi-square distribution with 1 df; there is only 1 df because we are testing the single hypothesis that $\sigma_u^2 = 0$. We will not present the formula underlying the test, for it is rather complicated.

Turning to our airlines example, an application of the BP test produces a chi-square value of 0.61. With 1 df, the p value of obtaining a chi-square value of 0.61 or greater is about 43 percent. Therefore, we do not reject the null hypothesis. In other words, the random effects model is not appropriate in the present example. The BP test thus reinforces the Hausman test, which also found that the random effects model is not appropriate for our airlines example.

16.7 Properties of Various Estimators[15]

We have discussed several methods of estimating (linear) panel regression models, namely, pooled estimators, fixed effects estimators that include least squares dummy variable (LSDV) estimators, fixed-effect within-group estimators, first-difference estimators, and random effects estimators. What are their statistical properties? Since panel data generally involve a large number of observations, we will concentrate on the consistency property of these estimators.

[14]T. Breusch and A. R. Pagan, "The Lagrange Multiplier Test and Its Application to Model Specification in Econometrics," *Review of Economic Studies,* vol. 47, 1980, pp. 239–253.

[15]The following discussion draws on A. Colin Cameron and Pravin K. Trivedi, *Microeconometrics: Methods and Applications,* Cambridge University Press, Cambridge, New York, 2005, Chapter 21.

Pooled Estimators

Assuming the slope coefficients are constant across subjects, if the error term in Eq. (16.3.1) is uncorrelated with the regressors, pooled estimators are consistent. However, as noted earlier, the error terms are likely to be correlated over time for a given subject. Therefore, **panel-corrected standard errors** must be used for hypothesis testing. Make sure the statistical package you use has this facility, otherwise the computed standard errors may be underestimated. It should be noted that if the fixed effects model is appropriate but we use the pooled estimator, the estimated coefficients will be inconsistent.

Fixed Effects Estimators

Even if it is assumed that the underlying model is pooled or random, the fixed effects estimators are always consistent.

Random Effects Estimators

The random effects model is consistent even if the true model is the pooled estimator. However, if the true model is fixed effects, the random effects estimator is inconsistent.

For proofs and further details about these properties, refer to the textbooks of Cameron and Trivedi, Greene, and Wooldridge cited in the footnotes.

16.8 Fixed Effects versus Random Effects Model: Some Guidelines

The challenge facing a researcher is: Which model is better, FEM or ECM? The answer to this question hinges around the assumption we make about the likely correlation between the individual, or cross-section specific, error component ε_i and the X regressors.

If it is assumed that ε_i and the X's are uncorrelated, ECM may be appropriate, whereas if ε_i and the X's are correlated, FEM may be appropriate.

The assumption underlying ECM is that the ε_i are random drawings from a much larger population, but sometimes this may not be so. For example, suppose we want to study the crime rate across the 50 states in the United States. Obviously, in this case, the assumption that the 50 states are a random sample is not tenable.

Keeping this fundamental difference in the two approaches in mind, what more can we say about the choice between FEM and ECM? Here the observations made by Judge et al. may be helpful:[16]

1. If T (the number of time series data) is large and N (the number of cross-sectional units) is small, there is likely to be little difference in the values of the parameters estimated by FEM and ECM. Hence the choice here is based on computational convenience. On this score, FEM may be preferable.
2. When N is large and T is small (i.e., a short panel), the estimates obtained by the two methods can differ significantly. Recall that in ECM $\beta_{1i} = \beta_1 + \varepsilon_i$, where ε_i is the cross-sectional random component, whereas in FEM we treat β_{1i} as fixed and not random. In the latter case, statistical inference is conditional on the observed cross-sectional units in the sample. This is appropriate if we strongly believe that the individual, or cross-sectional, units in our sample are not random drawings from a larger sample. In that case, FEM is appropriate. If the cross-sectional units in the sample are regarded as random drawings, however, then ECM is appropriate, for in that case statistical inference is unconditional.
3. If the individual error component ε_i and one or more regressors are correlated, then the ECM estimators are biased, whereas those obtained from FEM are unbiased.

[16]Judge et al., op. cit., pp. 489–491.

4. If N is large and T is small, and if the assumptions underlying ECM hold, ECM estimators are more efficient than FEM.
5. Unlike FEM, ECM can estimate coefficients of time-invariant variables such as gender and ethnicity. The FEM does control for such time-invariant variables, but it cannot estimate them directly, as is clear from the LSDV or within-group estimator models. On the other hand, FEM controls for *all* time-invariant variables (why?), whereas ECM can estimate only such time-invariant variables as are explicitly introduced in the model.

Despite the Hausman test, it is important to keep in mind the warning sounded by Johnston and DiNardo. In deciding between fixed effects or random effects models, they argue that, " . . . there is no simple rule to help the researcher navigate past the Scylla of fixed effects and the Charybdis of measurement error and dynamic selection. Although they are an improvement over cross-section data, panel data do not provide a cure-all for all of an econometrician's problems."[17]

16.9 Panel Data Regressions: Some Concluding Comments

As noted at the outset, the topic of panel data modeling is vast and complex. We have barely scratched the surface. The following are among the many topics we have not discussed.

1. Hypothesis testing with panel data.
2. Heteroscedasticity and autocorrelation in ECM.
3. Unbalanced panel data.
4. Dynamic panel data models in which the lagged value(s) of the regressand appears as an explanatory variable.
5. Simultaneous equations involving panel data.
6. Qualitative dependent variables and panel data.
7. Unit roots in panel data (on unit roots, see Chapter 21).

One or more of these topics can be found in the references cited in this chapter, and the reader is urged to consult them to learn more about this topic. These references also cite several empirical studies in various areas of business and economics that have used panel data regression models. The beginner is well-advised to read some of these applications to get a feel for how researchers have actually implemented such models.[18]

16.10 Some Illustrative Examples

EXAMPLE 16.1 *Productivity and Public Investment*

To find out why productivity has declined and what the role of public investment is, Alicia Munnell studied productivity data in 48 continental United States for 17 years from 1970 to 1986, for a total of 816 observations.[19] Using these data, we estimated the pooled regression in Table 16.7. Note that this regression does not take into account the panel nature of the data.

The dependent variable in this model is GSP (gross state product), and the explanatory variables are: PRIVCAP (private capital), PUBCAP (public capital), WATER (water utility capital), and UNEMP (unemployment rate). Note: L stands for natural log.

(Continued)

[17]Jack Johnston and John DiNardo, *Econometric Methods,* 4th ed., McGraw-Hill, 1997, p. 403.

[18]For further details and concrete applications, see Paul D. Allison, *Fixed Effects Regression Methods for Longitudinal Data, Using SAS,* SAS Institute, Cary, North Carolina, 2005.

[19]The Munnell data can be found at www.aw-bc.com/murray.

EXAMPLE 16.1 (*Continued*)

TABLE 16.7

Dependent Variable: LGSP
Method: Panel Least Squares
Sample: 1970–1986
Periods included: 17
Cross-sections included: 48
Total panel (balanced) observations: 816

	Coefficient	Std. Error	*t* Statistic	Prob.
C	0.907604	0.091328	9.937854	0.0000
LPRIVCAP	0.376011	0.027753	13.54847	0.0000
LPUBCAP	0.351478	0.016162	21.74758	0.0000
LWATER	0.312959	0.018739	16.70062	0.0000
LUNEMP	-0.069886	0.015092	-4.630528	0.0000

R-squared	0.981624	Mean dependent var.	10.50885
Adjusted *R*-squared	0.981533	S.D. dependent var.	1.021132
S.E. of regression	0.138765	*F*-statistic	10830.51
Sum squared resid.	15.61630	Prob. (*F*-statistic)	0.000000
Log likelihood	456.2346	Durbin-Watson stat.	0.063016

All the variables have the expected signs and all are individually, as well as collectively, statistically significant, assuming all the assumptions of the classical linear regression model hold true.

To take into account the panel dimension of the data, in Table 16.8 we estimated a fixed effects model using 47 dummies for the 48 states to avoid falling into the dummy-variable

TABLE 16.8

Dependent Variable: LGSP
Method: Panel Least Squares
Sample: 1970–1986
Periods included: 17
Cross-sections included: 48
Total panel (balanced) observations: 816

	Coefficient	Std. Error	*t* Statistic	Prob.
C	-0.033235	0.208648	-0.159286	0.8735
LPRIVCAP	0.267096	0.037015	7.215864	0.0000
LPUBCAP	0.714094	0.026520	26.92636	0.0000
LWATER	0.088272	0.021581	4.090291	0.0000
LUNEMP	-0.138854	0.007851	-17.68611	0.0000

Effects Specification

Cross-section fixed (dummy variables)

R-squared	0.997634	Mean dependent var.	10.50885
Adjusted *R*-squared	0.997476	S.D. dependent var.	1.021132
S.E. of regression	0.051303	*F*-statistic	6315.897
Sum squared resid.	2.010854	Prob. (*F*-statistic)	0.000000
Log likelihood	1292.535	Durbin-Watson stat.	0.520682

EXAMPLE 16.1
(Continued)

TABLE 16.9

Dependent Variable: LGSP
Method: Panel EGLS (Cross-section random effects)

Sample: 1970-1986
Periods included: 17
Cross-sections included: 48
Total panel (balanced) observations: 816
Swamy and Arora estimator of component variances

	Coefficient	Std. Error	*t* Statistic	Prob.
C	-0.046176	0.161637	-0.285680	0.7752
*L*PRIVCAP	0.313980	0.029740	10.55760	0.0000
*L*PUBCAP	0.641926	0.023330	27.51514	0.0000
*L*WATER	0.130768	0.020281	6.447875	0.0000
LUNEMP	-0.139820	0.007442	-18.78669	0.0000

Effects Specification

	S.D.	Rho
Cross-section random	0.130128	0.8655
Idiosyncratic random	0.051303	0.1345

trap. To save space, we only present the estimated regression coefficients and not the individual dummy coefficients. But it should be added that all of the 47 state dummies were individually highly statistically significant.

You can see that there are substantial differences between the pooled regression and the fixed-effects regression, casting doubt on the results of the pooled regression.

To see if the random effects model is more appropriate in this case, we present the results of the random effects regression model in Table 16.9.

To choose between the two models, we use the Hausman test, which gives the results shown in Table 16.10.

Since the estimated chi-square value is highly statistically significant, we reject the hypothesis that there is no significant difference in the estimated coefficients of the two models. It seems there is correlation between the error term and one or more regressors. Hence, we can reject the random effects model in favor of the fixed effects model. Note, however, as the last part of Table 16.10 shows, not all coefficients differ in the two models. For example, there is not a statistically significant difference in the values of the *L*UNEMP coefficient in the two models.

TABLE 16.10

Test Summary	Chi-Sq. Statistic	Chi-Sq. d.f.	Prob.
Cross-section random	42.458353	4	0.0000

Cross-section random effects test comparisons:

Variable	Fixed	Random	Var (Diff.)	Prob.
*L*PRIVCAP	0.267096	0.313980	0.000486	0.0334
*L*PUBCAP	0.714094	0.641926	0.000159	0.0000
*L*WATER	0.088272	0.130768	0.000054	0.0000
*L*UNEMP	-0.138854	-0.139820	0.000006	0.6993

EXAMPLE 16.2
Demand for Electricity in the USA

In their article, Maddala et al. considered the demand for residential electricity and natural gas in 49 states in the USA for the period 1970–1990; Hawaii was not included in the analysis.[20] They collected data on several variables; these data can be found on the book's website. In this example, we will only consider the demand for residential electricity. We first present the results based on the fixed effects estimation (Table 16.11) and then the random effects estimation (Table 16.12), followed by a comparison of the two models.

TABLE 16.11

Dependent Variable: Log(ESRCBPC)
Method: Panel Least Squares

Sample: 1971–1990
Periods included: 20
Cross-sections included: 49
Total panel (balanced) observations: 980

	Coefficient	Std. Error	*t* Statistic	Prob.
C	-12.55760	0.363436	-34.55249	0.0000
Log(RESRCD)	-0.628967	0.029089	-21.62236	0.0000
Log(YDPC)	1.062439	0.040280	26.37663	0.0000

Effects Specification

Cross-section fixed (dummy variables)

R-squared	0.757600	Mean dependent var.	-4.536187
Adjusted *R*-squared	0.744553	S.D. dependent var.	0.316205
S.E. of regression	0.159816	Akaike info criterion	-0.778954
Sum squared resid.	23.72762	Schwarz criterion	-0.524602
Log likelihood	432.6876	Hannan-Quinn criter.	-0.682188
F-statistic	58.07007	Durbin-Watson stat.	0.404314
Prob. (*F*-statistic)	0.000000		

where Log(ESRCBPC) = natural log of residential electricity consumption per capita (in billion btu), Log(RESRCD) = natural log of real 1987 electricity price, and Log(YDPC) = natural log of real 1987 disposable income per capita.

Since this is a double-log model, the estimated slope coefficients represent elasticities. Thus, holding other things the same, if real per capita income goes up by 1 percent, the mean consumption of electricity goes up by about 1 percent. Likewise, holding other things constant, if the real price of electricity goes up by 1 percent, the average consumption of electricity goes down by about 0.6 percent. All the estimated elasticities are statistically significant.

The results of the random error model are as shown in Table 16.12.

It seems that there is not much difference in the two models. But we can use the Hausman test to find out if this is so. The results of this test are as shown in Table 16.13.

Although the coefficients of the two models in Tables 16.11 and 16.12 look quite similar, the Hausman test shows that this is not the case. The chi-square value is highly statistically significant. Therefore, we can choose the fixed effects model over the random

[20] G. S. Maddala, Robert P. Trost, Hongyi Li, and Frederick Joutz, "Estimation of Short-run and Long-run Elasticities of Demand from Panel Data Using Shrikdage Estimators," *Journal of Business and Economic Statistics,* vol. 15, no. 1, January 1997, pp. 90–100.

EXAMPLE 16.2
(Continued)

TABLE 16.12

Dependent Variable: Log(ESRCBPC)
Method: Panel EGLS (Cross-section random effects)

Sample: 1971-1990
Periods included: 20
Cross-sections included: 49
Total panel (balanced) observations: 980
Swamy and Arora estimator of component variances

	Coefficient	Std. Error	*t* Statistic	Prob.
C	-11.68536	0.353285	-33.07631	0.0000
Log(RESRCD)	-0.665570	0.028088	-23.69612	0.0000
Log(YDPC)	0.980877	0.039257	24.98617	0.0000

Effects Specification

	S.D.	Rho
Cross-section random	0.123560	0.3741
Idiosyncratic random	0.159816	0.6259

Weighted Statistics

R-squared	0.462591	Mean dependent var.	-1.260296
Adjusted *R*-squared	0.461491	S.D. dependent var.	0.229066
S.E. of regression	0.168096	Sum squared resid.	27.60641
F-statistic	420.4906	Durbin-Watson stat.	0.345453
Prob. (*F*-statistic)	0.000000		

Unweighted Statistics

R-squared	0.267681	Mean dependent var.	-4.536187
Sum squared resid.	71.68384	Durbin-Watson stat.	0.133039

TABLE 16.13

Correlated Random Effects—Hausman Test
Equation: Untitled
Test cross-section random effects

Test Summary	Chi-Sq. Statistic	Chi-Sq. d.f.	Prob.
Cross-section random	105.865216	2	0.0000

Cross-section random effects test comparisons:

Variable	Fixed	Random	Var (Diff.)	Prob.
Log(RESRCD)	-0.628967	-0.665570	0.000057	0.0000
Log(YDPC)	1.062439	0.980877	0.000081	0.0000

effects model. *This example brings out the important point that when the sample size is large, in our case 980 observations, even small differences in the estimated coefficients of the two models can be statistically significant.* Thus, the coefficients of the Log(RESRCD) variable in the two models look reasonably close, but statistically they are not.

EXAMPLE 16.3 *Beer Consumption, Income and Beer Tax*

To assess the impact of beer tax on beer consumption, Philip Cook investigated the relationship between the two, after allowing for the effect of income.[21] His data pertain to 50 states and Washington, D.C, for the period 1975–2000. In this example we study the relationship of per capita beer sales to tax rate and income, all at the state level. We present the results of pooled OLS, fixed effects, and random effects models in tabular form in Table 16.14. The dependent variable is per capita beer sales.

These results are interesting. As per economic theory, we would expect a negative relationship between beer consumption and beer taxes, which is the case for the three models. The negative income effect on beer consumption would suggest that beer is an **inferior good.** An inferior good is one whose demand decreases as consumers' income rises. Maybe when their income rises, consumers prefer champagne!

For our purpose, what is interesting is the difference in the estimated coefficients. Apparently there is not much difference in estimated coefficients between FEM and ECM. As a matter of fact, the Hausman test produces a chi-square value of 3.4, which is not significant for 2 df at the 5 percent level; the p value is 0.1783.

The results based on OLS, however, are vastly different. The coefficient of the beer tax variable, in absolute value, is much smaller than that obtained from FEM or ECM. The income variable, although it has the negative sign, is not statistically significant, whereas the other two models show that it is highly significant.

This example shows very vividly what could happen if we neglect the panel structure of the data and estimate a pooled regression.

TABLE 16.14

Variable	OLS	FEM	REM
Constant	1.4192	1.7617	1.7542
	(24.37)	(52.23)	(39.22)
Beer tax	−0.0067	−0.0183	−0.0181
	(−2.13)	(−9.67)	(−9.69)
Income	$-3.54(e^{-6})$	−0.000020	−0.000019
	(−1.12)	(−9.17)	(−9.10)
R^2	0.0062	0.0052	0.0052

Notes: Figures in parentheses are the estimated t ratios. $-3.54(e^{-6}) = -0.00000354$.

Summary and Conclusions

1. Panel regression models are based on panel data. Panel data consist of observations on the same cross-sectional, or individual, units over several time periods.
2. There are several advantages to using panel data. First, they increase the sample size considerably. Second, by studying repeated cross-section observations, panel data are better suited to study the dynamics of change. Third, panel data enable us to study more complicated behavioral models.
3. Despite their substantial advantages, panel data pose several estimation and inference problems. Since such data involve both cross-section and time dimensions, problems that plague cross-sectional data (e.g., heteroscedasticity) and time series data (e.g., autocorrelation) need to be addressed. There are some additional problems as well, such as cross-correlation in individual units at the same point in time.

[21]The data used here are obtained from the website of Michael P. Murphy, *Econometrics: A Modern Introduction,* Pearson/Addison Wesley, Boston, 2006, but the original data were collected by Philip Cook for his book, *Paying the Tab: The Costs and Benefits of Alcohol Control,* Princeton University Press, Princeton, New Jersey, 2007.

4. There are several estimation techniques to address one or more of these problems. The two most prominent are (1) the fixed effects model (FEM) and (2) the random effects model (REM), or error components model (ECM).
5. In FEM, the intercept in the regression model is allowed to differ among individuals in recognition of the fact that each individual, or cross-sectional, unit may have some special characteristics of its own. To take into account the differing intercepts, one can use dummy variables. The FEM using dummy variables is known as the least-squares dummy variable (LSDV) model. FEM is appropriate in situations where the individual-specific intercept may be correlated with one or more regressors. A disadvantage of LSDV is that it consumes a lot of degrees of freedom when the number of cross-sectional units, N, is very large, in which case we have to introduce N dummies (but suppress the common intercept term).
6. An alternative to FEM is ECM. In ECM it is assumed that the intercept of an individual unit is a random drawing from a much larger population with a constant mean value. The individual intercept is then expressed as a deviation from this constant mean value. One advantage of ECM over FEM is that it is economical in degrees of freedom, as we do not have to estimate N cross-sectional intercepts. We need only to estimate the mean value of the intercept and its variance. ECM is appropriate in situations where the (random) intercept of each cross-sectional unit is uncorrelated with the regressors. Another advantage of ECM is that we can introduce variables such as gender, religion, and ethnicity, which remain constant for a given subject. In FEM we cannot do that because all such variables are colinear with the subject-specific intercept. Moreover, if we use the within-group estimator or first-difference estimator, all such time-invariance will be swept out.
7. The Hausman test can be used to decide between FEM and ECM. We can also use the Breusch–Pagan test to see if ECM is appropriate.
8. Despite its increasing popularity in applied research, and despite the increasing availability of such data, panel data regressions may not be appropriate in every situation. One has to use some practical judgment in each case.
9. There are some specific problems with panel data that need to be borne in mind. The most serious is the problem of attrition, whereby, for one reason or another, subjects of the panel drop out over time so that over subsequent surveys (or cross-sections) fewer original subjects remain in the panel. Even if there is no attrition, over time subjects may refuse or be unwilling to answer some questions.

EXERCISES

Questions

16.1. What are the special features of (*a*) cross-section data, (*b*) time series data, and (*c*) panel data?

16.2. What is meant by a fixed effects model (FEM)? Since panel data have both time and space dimensions, how does FEM allow for both dimensions?

16.3. What is meant by an error components model (ECM)? How does it differ from FEM? When is ECM appropriate? And when is FEM appropriate?

16.4. Is there a difference between LSDV, within-estimator, and first-difference models?

16.5. When are panel data regression models inappropriate? Give examples.

16.6. How would you extend model (16.4.2) to allow for a time error component? Write down the model explicitly.

16.7. Refer to the data on eggs produced and their prices given in Table 1.1. Which model may be appropriate here, FEM or ECM? Why?

16.8. For the investment data given in Table 1.2, which model would you choose—FEM or REM? Why?

16.9. Based on the Michigan Income Dynamics Study, Hausman attempted to estimate a wage, or earnings, model using a sample of 629 high school graduates, who were followed for a period of six years, thus giving in all 3,774 observations. The dependent variable in this study was logarithm of wage, and the explanatory variables were: age (divided into several age groups); unemployment in the previous year; poor health in the previous year; self-employment; region of residence (for graduate from the South, South = 1 and 0 otherwise) and area of residence (for a graduate from rural area, Rural = 1 and 0 otherwise). Hausman used both FEM and ECM. The results are given in Table 16.15 (standard errors in parentheses).

TABLE 16.15
Wage Equations (Dependent Variable: Log Wage)

Variable	Fixed Effects	Random Effects
1. Age 1 (20–35)	0.0557 (0.0042)	0.0393 (0.0033)
2. Age 2 (35–45)	0.0351 (0.0051)	0.0092 (0.0036)
3. Age 3 (45–55)	0.0209 (0.0055)	−0.0007 (0.0042)
4. Age 4 (55–65)	0.0209 (0.0078)	−0.0097 (0.0060)
5. Age 5 (65–)	−0.0171 (0.0155)	−0.0423 (0.0121)
6. Unemployed previous year	−0.0042 (0.0153)	−0.0277 (0.0151)
7. Poor health previous year	−0.0204 (0.0221)	−0.0250 (0.0215)
8. Self-employment	−0.2190 (0.0297)	−0.2670 (0.0263)
9. South	−0.1569 (0.0656)	−0.0324 (0.0333)
10. Rural	−0.0101 (0.0317)	−0.1215 (0.0237)
11. Constant	—	0.8499 (0.0433)
S^2	0.0567	0.0694
Degrees of freedom	3,135	3,763

Source: Reproduced from Cheng Hsiao, *Analysis of Panel Data,* Cambridge University Press, 1986, p. 42. Original source: J. A. Hausman, "Specification Tests in Econometrics," *Econometrica,* vol. 46, 1978, pp. 1251–1271.

a. Do the results make economic sense?

b. Is there a vast difference in the results produced by the two models? If so, what might account for these differences?

c. On the basis of the data given in the table, which model, if any, would you choose?

Empirical Exercises

16.10. Refer to the airline example discussed in the text. Instead of the linear model given in Eq. (16.4.2), estimate a log–linear regression model and compare your results with those given in Table 16.2.

16.11. Refer to the data in Table 1.1.

a. Let $Y =$ eggs produced (in millions) and $X =$ price of eggs (cents per dozen). Estimate the model for the years 1990 and 1991 separately.

b. Pool the observations for the two years and estimate the pooled regression. What assumptions are you making in pooling the data?

c. Use the fixed effects model, distinguishing the two years, and present the regression results.

d. Can you use the fixed effects model, distinguishing the 50 states? Why or why not?

e. Would it make sense to distinguish both the state effect and the year effect? If so, how many dummy variables would you have to introduce?

f. Would the error components model be appropriate to model the production of eggs? Why or why not? See if you can estimate such a model using, say, *EViews.*

16.12. Continue with Exercise 16.11. Before deciding to run the pooled regression, you want to find out whether the data are "poolable." For this purpose you decide to use the Chow test discussed in Chapter 8. Show the necessary calculations involved and determine if the pooled regression makes any sense.

16.13. Use the investment data given in Table 1.6.

a. Estimate the Grunfeld investment function for each company individually.

b. Now pool the data for all the companies and estimate the Grunfeld investment function by OLS.

c. Use LSDV to estimate the investment function and compare your results with the pooled regression estimated in (*b*).

d. How would you decide between the pooled regression and the LSDV regression? Show the necessary calculations.

16.14. Table 16.16 gives data on the hourly compensation rate in manufacturing in U.S. dollars, Y (%), and the civilian unemployment rate, X (index, 1992 = 100), for Canada, the United Kingdom, and the United States for the period 1980–2006. Consider the model:

$$Y_{it} = \beta_1 + \beta_2 X_{it} + u_{it} \tag{1}$$

TABLE 16.16 Unemployment Rate and Hourly Compensation in Manufacturing, in the United States, Canada, and the United Kingdom, 1980–2006.

Source: *Economic Report of the President*, January 2008, Table B-109.

Year	COMP_U.S.	UN_U.S.	COMP_CAN	UN_CAN	COMP_U.K.	UN_U.K.
1980	55.9	7.1	49.0	7.3	47.1	6.9
1981	61.6	7.6	53.8	7.3	47.5	9.7
1982	67.2	9.7	60.1	10.7	45.1	10.8
1983	69.3	9.6	64.3	11.6	41.9	11.5
1984	71.6	7.5	65.0	10.9	39.8	11.8
1985	75.3	7.2	65.0	10.2	42.3	11.4
1986	78.8	7.0	64.9	9.3	52.0	11.4
1987	81.3	6.2	69.6	8.4	64.5	10.5
1988	84.1	5.5	78.5	7.4	74.8	8.6
1989	86.6	5.3	85.5	7.1	73.5	7.3
		5.6				
1990	90.5		92.4	7.7	89.6	7.1
1991	95.6	6.8	100.7	9.8	99.9	8.9
1992	100.0	7.5	100.0	10.6	100.0	10.0
1993	102.0	6.9	94.8	10.8	88.8	10.4
		6.1				
1994	105.3		92.1	9.6	92.8	8.7
1995	107.3	5.6	93.9	8.6	97.3	8.7
1996	109.3	5.4	95.9	8.8	96.0	8.1
1997	112.2	4.9	96.7	8.4	104.1	7.0
1998	118.7	4.5	94.9	7.7	113.8	6.3
1999	123.4	4.2	96.8	7.0	117.5	6.0
2000	134.7	4.0	100.0	6.1	114.8	5.5
2001	137.8	4.7	98.9	6.5	114.7	5.1
2002	147.8	5.8	101.0	7.0	126.8	5.2
2003	158.2	6.0	116.7	6.9	145.2	5.0
2004	161.5	5.5	127.1	6.4	171.4	4.8
2005	168.3	5.1	141.8	6.0	177.4	4.8
2006	172.4	4.6	155.5	5.5	192.3	5.5

Notes: UN = Unemployment rate %.
COMP = *Index of hourly compensation in U. S. dollars, 1992–100.*
CAN = Canada.

a. A priori, what is the expected relationship between Y and X? Why?

b. Estimate the model given in Eq. (1) for each country.

c. Estimate the model, pooling all of the 81 observations.

d. Estimate the fixed effects model.

e. Estimate the error components model.

f. Which is a better model, FEM or ECM? Justify your answer (*Hint:* Apply the Hausman Test).

16.15. Baltagi and Griffin considered the following gasoline demand function:*

$$\ln Y_{it} = \beta_1 + \beta_2 \ln X_{2it} + \beta_3 \ln X_{3it} + \beta_4 \ln X_{4it} + u_{it}$$

Where $Y =$ gasoline consumption per car; $X_2 =$ real income per capita, $X_3 =$ real gasoline price, $X_4 =$ number of cars per capita, $i =$ country code, in all 18 OECD countries, and $t =$ time (annual observations from 1960–1978). *Note:* Values in table are logged already.

a. Estimate the above demand function pooling the data for all 18 of the countries (a total of 342 observations).

b. Estimate a fixed effects model using the same data.

c. Estimate a random components model using the same data.

d. From your analysis, which model best describes the gasoline demand in the 18 OECD countries? Justify your answer.

16.16. The article by Subhayu Bandyopadhyay and Howard J. Wall, "The Determinants of Aid in the Post-Cold War Era," *Review,* Federal Reserve Bank of St. Louis, November/December 2007, vol. 89, number 6, pp. 533–547, uses panel data to estimate the responsiveness of aid to recipient countries' economic and physical needs, civil/political rights, and government effectiveness. The data are for 135 countries for three years. The article and data can be found at: http://research.stlouisfed.org/publications/review/past/2007 in the November/December Vol. 89, No. 10 section. The data can also be found on the textbook website in Table 16.18. Estimate the authors' model (given on page 534 of their article) using a random effects estimator. Compare your results with those of the pooled and fixed effects estimators given by the authors in Table 2 of their article. Which model is appropriate here, fixed effects or random effects? Why?

16.17. Refer to the airlines example discussed in the text. For each airline, estimate a time series logarithmic cost function. How do these regressions compare with the fixed effects and random effects models discussed in the chapter? Would you also estimate 15 cross-section logarithmic cost functions? Why or why not?

*B. H. Baltagi and J. M. Griffin, "Gasoline Demand in the OECD: An Application of Pooling and Testing Procedures," *European Economic Review,* vol. 22, 1983, pp. 117–137. The data for 18 OECD countries for the years 1960–1978 can be obtained from: http://www.wiley.com/legacy/wileychi/baltagi/supp/Gasoline.dat, or from the textbook website, Table 16.17.

Chapter 17

Dynamic Econometric Models: Autoregressive and Distributed-Lag Models

In regression analysis involving time series data, if the regression model includes not only the current but also the lagged (past) values of the explanatory variables (the X's), it is called a **distributed-lag model.** If the model includes one or more lagged values of the dependent variable among its explanatory variables, it is called an **autoregressive model.** Thus,

$$Y_t = \alpha + \beta_0 X_t + \beta_1 X_{t-1} + \beta_2 X_{t-2} + u_t$$

represents a distributed-lag model, whereas

$$Y_t = \alpha + \beta X_t + \gamma Y_{t-1} + u_t$$

is an example of an autoregressive model. The latter are also known as **dynamic models** since they portray the time path of the dependent variable in relation to its past value(s).

Autoregressive and distributed-lag models are used extensively in econometric analysis, and in this chapter we take a close look at such models with a view to finding out the following:

1. What is the role of lags in economics?
2. What are the reasons for the lags?
3. Is there any theoretical justification for the commonly used lagged models in empirical econometrics?
4. What is the relationship, if any, between autoregressive and distributed-lag models? Can one be derived from the other?
5. What are some of the statistical problems involved in estimating such models?
6. Does a lead–lag relationship between variables imply causality? If so, how does one measure it?

17.1 The Role of "Time," or "Lag," in Economics

In economics the dependence of a variable Y (the dependent variable) on another variable(s) X (the explanatory variable) is rarely instantaneous. Very often, Y responds to X with a lapse of time. Such a lapse of time is called a *lag*. To illustrate the nature of the lag, we consider several examples.

EXAMPLE 17.1
The Consumption Function

Suppose a person receives a salary increase of \$2,000 in annual pay, and suppose that this is a "permanent" increase in the sense that the increase in salary is maintained. What will be the effect of this increase in income on the person's annual consumption expenditure?

Following such a gain in income, people usually do not rush to spend all the increase immediately. Thus, our recipient may decide to increase consumption expenditure by \$800 in the first year following the salary increase in income, by another \$600 in the next year, and by another \$400 in the following year, saving the remainder. By the end of the third year, the person's annual consumption expenditure will be increased by \$1,800. We can thus write the consumption function as

$$Y_t = \text{constant} + 0.4X_t + 0.3X_{t-1} + 0.2X_{t-2} + u_t \quad (17.1.1)$$

where Y is consumption expenditure and X is income.

Equation (17.1.1) shows that the effect of an increase in income of \$2,000 is spread, or distributed, over a period of 3 years. Models such as Eq. (17.1.1) are therefore called **distributed-lag models** because the effect of a given cause (income) is spread over a number of time periods. Geometrically, the distributed-lag model (17.1.1) is shown in Figure 17.1, or alternatively, in Figure 17.2.

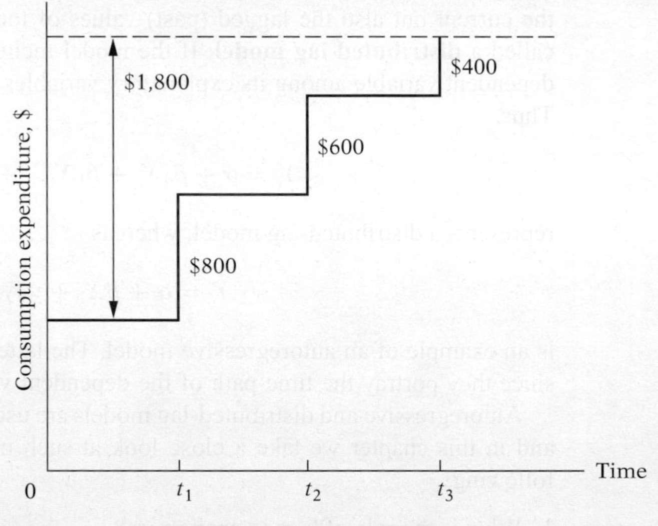

FIGURE 17.1
Example of distributed lags.

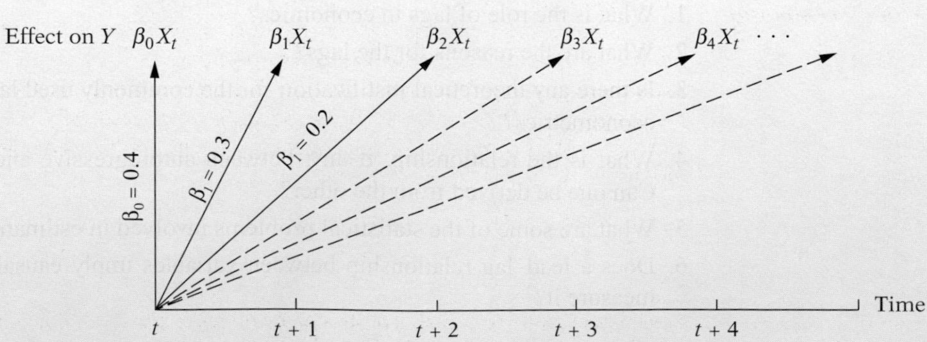

FIGURE 17.2
The effect of a unit change in X at time t on Y at time t and subsequent time periods.

More generally we may write

$$Y_t = \alpha + \beta_0 X_t + \beta_1 X_{t-1} + \beta_2 X_{t-2} + \cdots + \beta_k X_{t-k} + u_t \tag{17.1.2}$$

which is a distributed-lag model with a finite lag of k time periods. The coefficient β_0 is known as the **short-run,** or **impact, multiplier** because it gives the change in the mean value of Y following a unit change in X in the same time period.[1] If the change in X is maintained at the same level thereafter, then $(\beta_0 + \beta_1)$ gives the change in (the mean value of) Y in the next period, $(\beta_0 + \beta_1 + \beta_2)$ in the following period, and so on. These partial sums are called **interim,** or **intermediate, multipliers.** Finally, after k periods we obtain

$$\sum_{i=0}^{k} \beta_i = \beta_0 + \beta_1 + \beta_2 + \cdots + \beta_k = \beta \tag{17.1.3}$$

which is known as the **long-run,** or **total, distributed-lag multiplier,** provided the sum β exists (to be discussed elsewhere).

If we define

$$\beta_i^* = \frac{\beta_i}{\sum \beta_i} = \frac{\beta_i}{\beta} \tag{17.1.4}$$

we obtain "standardized" β_i. Partial sums of the standardized β_i then give the proportion of the long-run, or total, impact felt by a certain time period.

Returning to the consumption regression (17.1.1), we see that the short-run multiplier, which is nothing but the short-run marginal propensity to consume (MPC), is 0.4, whereas the long-run multiplier, which is the long-run marginal propensity to consume, is $0.4 + 0.3 + 0.2 = 0.9$. That is, following a \$1 increase in income, the consumer will increase his or her level of consumption by about 40 cents in the year of increase, by another 30 cents in the next year, and by yet another 20 cents in the following year. The long-run impact of an increase of \$1 in income is thus 90 cents. If we divide each β_i by 0.9, we obtain, respectively, 0.44, 0.33, and 0.23, which indicate that 44 percent of the total impact of a unit change in X on Y is felt immediately, 77 percent after one year, and 100 percent by the end of the second year.

EXAMPLE 17.2

Creation of Bank Money (Demand Deposits)

Suppose the Federal Reserve System pours \$1,000 of new money into the banking system by buying government securities. What will be the total amount of bank money, or demand deposits, that will be generated ultimately?

Following the fractional reserve system, if we assume that the law requires banks to keep a 20 percent reserve backing for the deposits they create, then by the well-known multiplier process the total amount of demand deposits that will be generated will be equal to \$1,000[1/(1 − 0.8)] = \$5,000. Of course, \$5,000 in demand deposits will not be created overnight. The process takes time, which can be shown schematically in Figure 17.3.

(Continued)

[1]Technically, β_0 is the partial derivative of Y with respect to X_t, β_1 that with respect to X_{t-1}, β_2 that with respect to X_{t-2}, and so forth. Symbolically, $\partial Y_t / \partial X_{t-k} = \beta_k$.

EXAMPLE 17.2 *(Continued)*

FIGURE 17.3 Cumulative expansion in bank deposits (initial reserve $1,000 and 20 percent reserve requirement).

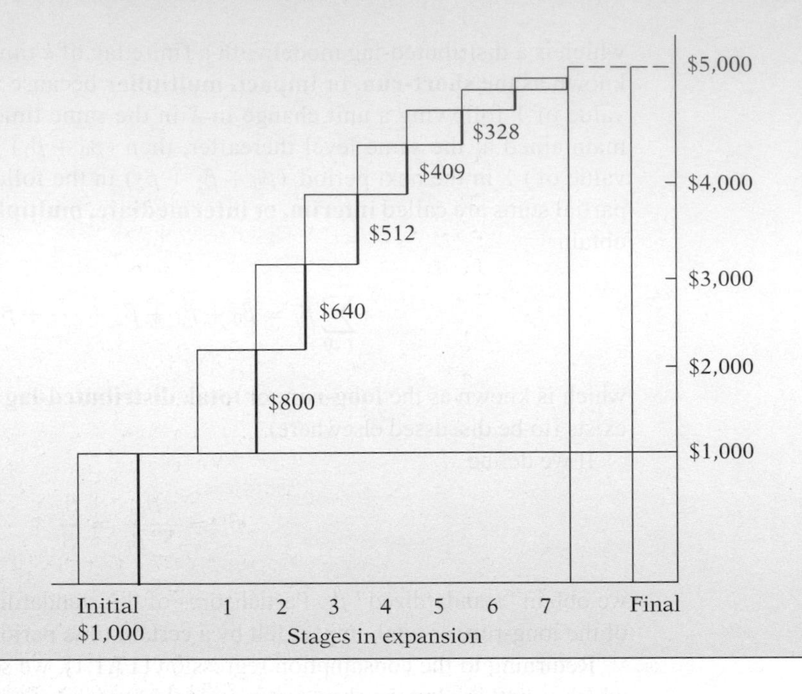

EXAMPLE 17.3 *Link between Money and Prices*

According to the monetarists, inflation is essentially a monetary phenomenon in the sense that a continuous increase in the general price level is due to the rate of expansion in money supply far in excess of the amount of money actually demanded by the economic units. Of course, this link between inflation and changes in money supply is not instantaneous. Studies have shown that the lag between the two is anywhere from 3 to about 20 quarters. The results of one such study are shown in Table 17.1,[2] where we see the effect of a 1 percent change in the M1B money supply (= currency + checkable deposits at financial institutions) is felt over a period of 20 quarters. The long-run impact of a 1 percent change in the money supply on inflation is about 1 ($= \sum m_i$), which is statistically significant, whereas the short-run impact is about 0.04, which is not significant, although the intermediate multipliers seem to be generally significant. Incidentally, note that since P and M are both in percent forms, the m_i (β_i in our usual notation) give the elasticity of P with respect to M, that is, the percent response of prices to a 1 percent increase in the money supply. Thus, $m_0 = 0.041$ means that for a 1 percent increase in the money supply the short-run elasticity of prices is about 0.04 percent. The long-term elasticity is 1.03 percent, implying that in the long run a 1 percent increase in the money supply is reflected by just about the same percentage increase in the prices. In short, a 1 percent increase in the money supply is accompanied in the long run by a 1 percent increase in the inflation rate.

[2]Keith M. Carlson, "The Lag from Money to Prices," *Review,* Federal Reserve Bank of St. Louis, October 1980, Table 1, p. 4.

EXAMPLE 17.3 *(Continued)*

TABLE 17.1 Estimate of Money–Price Equation: Original Specification

Sample period: 1955–I to 1969–IV: $m_{21} = 0$

$$\dot{P} = \underset{(0.395)}{-0.146} + \sum_{i=0}^{20} m_i \dot{M}_{-i}$$

	Coeff.	$\lvert t \rvert$		Coeff.	$\lvert t \rvert$		Coeff.	$\lvert t \rvert$
m_0	0.041	1.276	m_8	0.048	3.249	m_{16}	0.069	3.943
m_1	0.034	1.538	m_9	0.054	3.783	m_{17}	0.062	3.712
m_2	0.030	1.903	m_{10}	0.059	4.305	m_{18}	0.053	3.511
m_3	0.029	2.171	m_{11}	0.065	4.673	m_{19}	0.039	3.338
m_4	0.030	2.235	m_{12}	0.069	4.795	m_{20}	0.022	3.191
m_5	0.033	2.294	m_{13}	0.072	4.694	$\sum m_i$	1.031	7.870
m_6	0.037	2.475	m_{14}	0.073	4.468	**Mean lag**	10.959	5.634
m_7	0.042	2.798	m_{15}	0.072	4.202			

$\bar{R}^2$ 0.525 se 1.066 D.W. 2.00

Notation: $\dot{P}$ = compounded annual rate of change of GNP deflator.
$\dot{M}$ = compounded annual rate of change of M1B.

Source: Keith M. Carlson, "The Lag from Money to Prices," *Review,* Federal Reserve Bank of St. Louis, October 1980, Table 1, p. 4.

EXAMPLE 17.4 *Lag between R&D Expenditure and Productivity*

The decision to invest in research and development (R&D) expenditure and its ultimate payoff in terms of increased productivity involve considerable lag, actually several lags, such as, ". . . the lag between the investment of funds and the time inventions actually begin to appear, the lag between the invention of an idea or device and its development up to a commercially applicable stage, and the lag which is introduced by the process of diffusion: it takes time before all the old machines are replaced by the better new ones."[3]

EXAMPLE 17.5 *The J Curve of International Economics*

Students of international economics are familiar with what is called the *J curve,* which shows the relationship between trade balance and depreciation of currency. Following depreciation of a country's currency (e.g., due to devaluation), initially the trade balance deteriorates but eventually it improves, assuming other things are the same. The curve is as shown in Figure 17.4.

FIGURE 17.4
The *J* curve.
Source: Paul R. Krugman and Maurice Obstfeld, *International Economics: Theory and Practice,* 3d ed., Harper Collins, New York, 1994, p. 465.

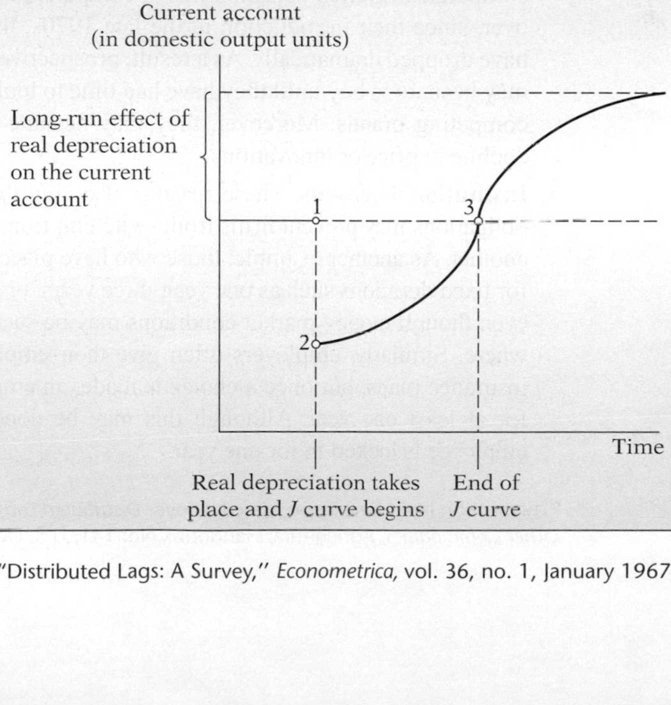

[3]Zvi Griliches, "Distributed Lags: A Survey," *Econometrica,* vol. 36, no. 1, January 1967, pp. 16–49.

EXAMPLE 17.6
The Accelerator Model of Investment

In its simplest form, the acceleration principle of investment theory states that investment is proportional to changes in output. Symbolically,

$$I_t = \beta(X_t - X_{t-1}) \qquad \beta > 0 \tag{17.1.5}$$

where I_t is investment at time t, X_t is output at time t, and X_{t-1} is output at time $(t - 1)$.

The preceding examples are only a sample of the use of lag in economics. Undoubtedly, the reader can produce several examples from his or her own experience.

17.2 The Reasons for Lags[4]

Although the examples cited in Section 17.1 point out the nature of lagged phenomena, they do not fully explain why lags occur. There are three main reasons:

1. **Psychological reasons.** As a result of the force of habit (inertia), people do not change their consumption habits immediately following a price decrease or an income increase perhaps because the process of change may involve some immediate disutility. Thus, those who become instant millionaires by winning lotteries may not change the lifestyles to which they were accustomed for a long time because they may not know how to react to such a windfall gain immediately. Of course, given reasonable time, they may learn to live with their newly acquired fortune. Also, people may not know whether a change is "permanent" or "transitory." Thus, my reaction to an increase in my income will depend on whether or not the increase is permanent. If it is only a nonrecurring increase and in succeeding periods my income returns to its previous level, I may save the entire increase, whereas someone else in my position might decide to "live it up."
2. **Technological reasons.** Suppose the price of capital relative to labor declines, making substitution of capital for labor economically feasible. Of course, addition of capital takes time (the gestation period). Moreover, if the drop in price is expected to be temporary, firms may not rush to substitute capital for labor, especially if they expect that after the temporary drop the price of capital may increase beyond its previous level. Sometimes, imperfect knowledge also accounts for lags. At present the market for personal computers is glutted with all kinds of computers with varying features and prices. Moreover, since their introduction in the late 1970s, the prices of most personal computers have dropped dramatically. As a result, prospective consumers for the personal computer may hesitate to buy until they have had time to look into the features and prices of all the competing brands. Moreover, they may hesitate to buy in the expectation of further decline in price or innovations.
3. **Institutional reasons.** These reasons also contribute to lags. For example, contractual obligations may prevent firms from switching from one source of labor or raw material to another. As another example, those who have placed funds in long-term savings accounts for fixed durations such as one year, three years, or seven years are essentially "locked in" even though money market conditions may be such that higher yields are available elsewhere. Similarly, employers often give their employees a choice among several health insurance plans, but once a choice is made, an employee may not switch to another plan for at least one year. Although this may be done for administrative convenience, the employee is locked in for one year.

[4]This section leans heavily on Marc Nerlove, *Distributed Lags and Demand Analysis for Agricultural and Other Commodities,* Agricultural Handbook No. 141, U.S. Department of Agriculture, June 1958.

For the reasons just discussed, lag occupies a central role in economics. This is clearly reflected in the short-run–long-run methodology of economics. It is for this reason we say that short-run price or income elasticities are generally smaller (in absolute value) than the corresponding long-run elasticities or that short-run marginal propensity to consume is generally smaller than long-run marginal propensity to consume.

17.3 Estimation of Distributed-Lag Models

Granted that distributed-lag models play a highly useful role in economics, how does one estimate such models? Specifically, suppose we have the following distributed-lag model in one explanatory variable:[5]

$$Y_t = \alpha + \beta_0 X_t + \beta_1 X_{t-1} + \beta_2 X_{t-2} + \cdots + u_t \tag{17.3.1}$$

where we have not defined the length of the lag, that is, how far back into the past we want to go. Such a model is called an **infinite (lag) model,** whereas a model of the type shown in Eq. (17.1.2) is called a **finite (lag) distributed-lag model** because the length of the lag k is specified. We shall continue to use Eq. (17.3.1) because it is easy to handle mathematically, as we shall see.[6]

How do we estimate the α and β's of Eq. (17.3.1)? We may adopt two approaches: (1) ad hoc estimation and (2) a priori restrictions on the β's by assuming that the β's follow some systematic pattern. We shall consider ad hoc estimation in this section and the other approach in Section 17.4.

Ad Hoc Estimation of Distributed-Lag Models

Since the explanatory variable X_t is assumed to be nonstochastic (or at least uncorrelated with the disturbance term u_t), X_{t-1}, X_{t-2}, and so on, are nonstochastic, too. Therefore, in principle, the ordinary least squares (OLS) can be applied to Eq. (17.3.1). This is the approach taken by Alt[7] and Tinbergen.[8] They suggest that to estimate Eq. (17.3.1) one may proceed *sequentially;* that is, first regress Y_t on X_t, then regress Y_t on X_t and X_{t-1}, then regress Y_t on X_t, X_{t-1}, and X_{t-2}, and so on. This sequential procedure stops when the regression coefficients of the lagged variables start becoming statistically insignificant and/or the coefficient of at least one of the variables changes signs from positive to negative or vice versa. Following this precept, Alt regressed fuel oil consumption Y on new orders X. Based on the quarterly data for the period 1930–1939, the results were as follows:

$$\begin{aligned}
\hat{Y}_t &= 8.37 + 0.171X_t \\
\hat{Y}_t &= 8.27 + 0.111X_t + 0.064X_{t-1} \\
\hat{Y}_t &= 8.27 + 0.109X_t + 0.071X_{t-1} - 0.055X_{t-2} \\
\hat{Y}_t &= 8.32 + 0.108X_t + 0.063X_{t-1} + 0.022X_{t-2} - 0.020X_{t-3}
\end{aligned}$$

[5]If there is more than one explanatory variable in the model, each variable may have a lagged effect on Y. For simplicity only, we assume one explanatory variable.

[6]In practice, however, the coefficients of the distant X values are expected to have a negligible effect on Y.

[7]F. F. Alt, "Distributed Lags," *Econometrica,* vol. 10, 1942, pp. 113–128.

[8]J. Tinbergen, "Long-Term Foreign Trade Elasticities," *Metroeconomica,* vol. 1, 1949, pp. 174–185.

Alt chose the second regression as the "best" one because in the last two equations the sign of X_{t-2} was not stable and in the last equation the sign of X_{t-3} was negative, which may be difficult to interpret economically.

Although seemingly straightforward, ad hoc estimation suffers from many drawbacks, such as the following:

1. There is no a priori guide as to what is the maximum length of the lag.[9]
2. As one estimates successive lags, there are fewer degrees of freedom left, making statistical inference somewhat shaky. Economists are not usually that lucky to have a long series of data so that they can go on estimating numerous lags.
3. More importantly, in economic time series data, successive values (lags) tend to be highly correlated; hence multicollinearity rears its ugly head. As noted in Chapter 10, multicollinearity leads to imprecise estimation; that is, the standard errors tend to be large in relation to the estimated coefficients. As a result, based on the routinely computed t ratios, we may tend to declare (erroneously), that a lagged coefficient(s) is statistically insignificant.
4. The sequential search for the lag length opens the researcher to the charge of **data mining.** Also, as we noted in Section 13.4, the nominal and true level of significance to test statistical hypotheses becomes an important issue in such sequential searches (see Eq. [13.4.2]).

In view of the preceding problems, the ad hoc estimation procedure has very little to recommend it. Clearly, some prior or theoretical considerations must be brought to bear upon the various β's if we are to make headway with the estimation problem.

17.4 The Koyck Approach to Distributed-Lag Models

Koyck has proposed an ingenious method of estimating distributed-lag models. Suppose we start with the infinite lag distributed-lag model (17.3.1). *Assuming that the β's are all of the same sign*, Koyck assumes that they decline geometrically as follows.[10]

$$\beta_k = \beta_0 \lambda^k \qquad k = 0, 1, \ldots \tag{17.4.1}$$

(17.4.1)[11]

where λ, such that $0 < \lambda < 1$, is known as the *rate of decline,* or *decay,* of the distributed lag and where $1 - \lambda$ is known as the *speed of adjustment.*

What Eq. (17.4.1) postulates is that each successive β coefficient is numerically less than each preceding β (this statement follows since $\lambda < 1$), implying that as one goes back into the distant past, the effect of that lag on Y_t becomes progressively smaller, a quite plausible assumption. After all, current and recent past incomes are expected to affect current consumption expenditure more heavily than income in the distant past. Geometrically, the Koyck scheme is depicted in Figure 17.5.

As this figure shows, the value of the lag coefficient β_k depends, apart from the common β_0, on the value of λ. The closer λ is to 1, the slower the rate of decline in β_k, whereas the

[9]If the lag length, k, is incorrectly specified, we will have to contend with the problem of misspecification errors discussed in Chapter. 13. Also keep in mind the warning about **data mining.**

[10]L. M. Koyck, *Distributed Lags and Investment Analysis,* North Holland Publishing Company, Amsterdam, 1954.

[11]Sometimes this is also written as

$$\beta_k = \beta_0(1 - \lambda)\lambda^k \qquad k = 0, 1, \ldots$$

for reasons given in footnote 12.

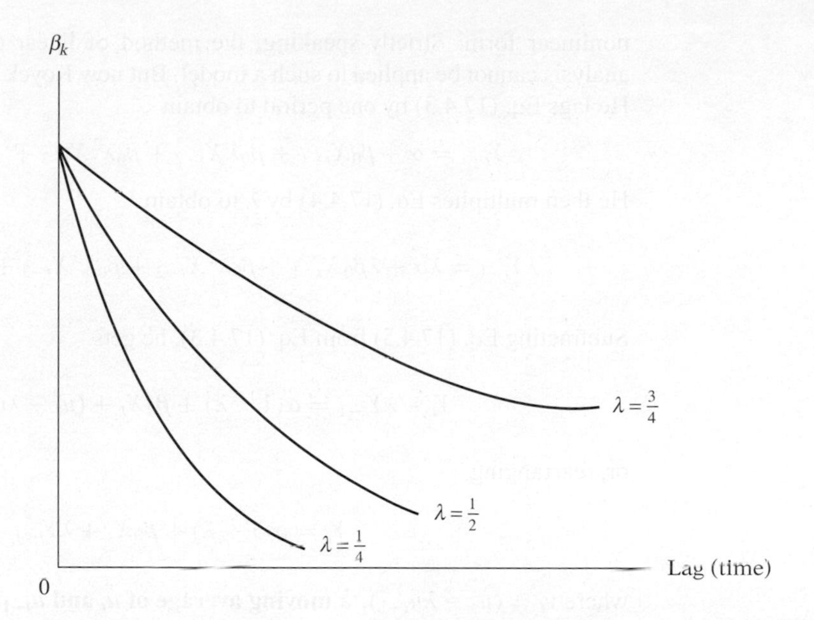

FIGURE 17.5
Koyck scheme (declining geometric distribution).

closer it is to zero, the more rapid the decline in β_k. In the former case, distant past values of X will exert sizable impact on Y_t, whereas in the latter case their influence on Y_t will peter out quickly. This pattern can be seen clearly from the following illustration:

λ	β_0	β_1	β_2	β_3	β_4	β_5	$\cdots$	β_{10}
0.75	β_0	$0.75\beta_0$	$0.56\beta_0$	$0.42\beta_0$	$0.32\beta_0$	$0.24\beta_0$	$\cdots$	$0.06\beta_0$
0.25	β_0	$0.25\beta_0$	$0.06\beta_0$	$0.02\beta_0$	$0.004\beta_0$	$0.001\beta_0$	$\cdots$	0.0

Note these features of the Koyck scheme: (1) By assuming nonnegative values for λ, Koyck rules out the β's from changing sign; (2) by assuming $\lambda < 1$, he gives lesser weight to the distant β's than the current ones; and (3) he ensures that the sum of the β's, which gives the long-run multiplier, is finite, namely,

$$\sum_{k=0}^{\infty} \beta_k = \beta_0 \left(\frac{1}{1-\lambda} \right) \tag{17.4.2}$$[12]

As a result of Eq. (17.4.1), the infinite lag model (17.3.1) may be written as

$$Y_t = \alpha + \beta_0 X_t + \beta_0 \lambda X_{t-1} + \beta_0 \lambda^2 X_{t-2} + \cdots + u_t \tag{17.4.3}$$

As it stands, the model is still not amenable to easy estimation since a large (literally infinite) number of parameters remain to be estimated and the parameter λ enters in a highly

[12]This is because

$$\sum \beta_k = \beta_0 (1 + \lambda + \lambda^2 + \lambda^3 + \cdots) = \beta_0 \left(\frac{1}{1-\lambda} \right)$$

since the expression in the parentheses on the right side is an infinite geometric series whose sum is $1/(1-\lambda)$ provided $0 < \lambda < 1$. In passing, note that if β_k is as defined in footnote 11, $\sum \beta_k = \beta_0(1-\lambda)/(1-\lambda) = \beta_0$, thus ensuring that the weights $(1-\lambda)\lambda^k$ sum to 1.

nonlinear form: Strictly speaking, the method of linear (in the parameters) regression analysis cannot be applied to such a model. But now Koyck suggests an ingenious way out. He lags Eq. (17.4.3) by one period to obtain

$$Y_{t-1} = \alpha + \beta_0 X_{t-1} + \beta_0 \lambda X_{t-2} + \beta_0 \lambda^2 X_{t-3} + \cdots + u_{t-1} \tag{17.4.4}$$

He then multiplies Eq. (17.4.4) by λ to obtain

$$\lambda Y_{t-1} = \lambda\alpha + \lambda\beta_0 X_{t-1} + \beta_0 \lambda^2 X_{t-2} + \beta_0 \lambda^3 X_{t-3} + \cdots + \lambda u_{t-1} \tag{17.4.5}$$

Subtracting Eq. (17.4.5) from Eq. (17.4.3), he gets

$$Y_t - \lambda Y_{t-1} = \alpha(1-\lambda) + \beta_0 X_t + (u_t - \lambda u_{t-1}) \tag{17.4.6}$$

or, rearranging,

$$Y_t = \alpha(1-\lambda) + \beta_0 X_t + \lambda Y_{t-1} + v_t \tag{17.4.7}$$

where $v_t = (u_t - \lambda u_{t-1})$, a **moving average of u_t and u_{t-1}.**

The procedure just described is known as the **Koyck transformation.** Comparing Eq. (17.4.7) with Eq. (17.3.1), we see the tremendous simplification accomplished by Koyck. Whereas before we had to estimate α and an infinite number of β's, we now have to estimate only three unknowns: α, β_0, and λ. Now there is no reason to expect multicollinearity. In a sense, multicollinearity is resolved by replacing X_{t-1}, $X_{t-2}, \ldots,$ by a single variable, namely, Y_{t-1}. But note the following features of the Koyck transformation:

1. We started with a distributed-lag model but ended up with an autoregressive model because Y_{t-1} appears as one of the explanatory variables. This transformation shows how one can "convert" a distributed-lag model into an autoregressive model.
2. The appearance of Y_{t-1} is likely to create some statistical problems. Y_{t-1}, like Y_t, is stochastic, which means that we have a stochastic explanatory variable in the model. Recall that the classical least-squares theory is predicated on the assumption that the explanatory variables either are nonstochastic or, if stochastic, are distributed independently of the stochastic disturbance term. Hence, we must find out if Y_{t-1} satisfies this assumption. (We shall return to this point in Section 17.8.)
3. In the original model (17.3.1) the disturbance term was u_t, whereas in the transformed model it is $v_t = (u_t - \lambda u_{t-1})$. The statistical properties of v_t depend on what is assumed about the statistical properties of u_t, for, as shown later, if the original u_t's are serially uncorrelated, the v_t's are serially correlated. Therefore, we may have to face up to the serial correlation problem in addition to the stochastic explanatory variable Y_{t-1}. We shall do that in Section 17.8.
4. The presence of lagged Y violates one of the assumptions underlying the Durbin–Watson d test. Therefore, we will have to develop an alternative to test for serial correlation in the presence of lagged Y. One alternative is the **Durbin h test,** which is discussed in Section 17.10.

As we saw in Eq. (17.1.4), the partial sums of the standardized β_i tell us the proportion of the long-run, or total, impact felt by a certain time period. In practice, though, the **mean** or **median lag** is often used to characterize the nature of the lag structure of a distributed-lag model.

The Median Lag

The median lag is the time required for the first half, or 50 percent, of the total change in Y following a unit sustained change in X. For the Koyck model, the median lag is as follows (see Exercise 17.6):

$$\text{Koyck model: Median lag} = -\frac{\log 2}{\log \lambda} \tag{17.4.8}$$

Thus, if $\lambda = 0.2$ the median lag is 0.4306, but if $\lambda = 0.8$ the median lag is 3.1067. Verbally, in the former case 50 percent of the total change in Y is accomplished in less than half a period, whereas in the latter case it takes more than 3 periods to accomplish the 50 percent change. But this contrast should not be surprising, for as we know, the higher the value of λ the lower the speed of adjustment, and the lower the value of λ the greater the speed of adjustment.

The Mean Lag

Provided all β_k are positive, the mean, or average, lag is defined as

$$\text{Mean lag} = \frac{\sum_0^\infty k\beta_k}{\sum_0^\infty \beta_k} \tag{17.4.9}$$

which is simply the weighted average of all the lags involved, with the respective β coefficients serving as weights. In short, it is a **lag-weighted average** of time. For the Koyck model the mean lag is (see Exercise 17.7)

$$\text{Koyck model: Mean lag} = \frac{\lambda}{1-\lambda} \tag{17.4.10}$$

Thus, if $\lambda = \frac{1}{2}$, the mean lag is 1.

From the preceding discussion it is clear that the median and mean lags serve as a summary measure of the speed with which Y responds to X. In the example given in Table 17.1 the mean lag is about 11 quarters, showing that it takes quite some time, on the average, for the effect of changes in the money supply to be felt on price changes.

EXAMPLE 17.7 *Per Capita Personal Consumption Expenditure (PPCE) and Per Capita Disposable Income (PPDI)*

This example examines PPCE in relation to PPDI, both expressed in 2000 dollars, for the United States for the period 1959–2006. As an illustration of the Koyck model, consider the data given in Table 17.2. Regression of PPCE on PPDI and lagged PPCE gives the results shown in Table 17.3.

The consumption function in this table can be called the short-run consumption function. We will derive the long-run consumption function shortly.

Using the estimated value of λ, we can compute the distributed lag coefficients. If $\beta_0 \approx 0.2139$, $\beta_1 = (0.2139)(0.7971) \approx 0.1704$, $\beta_2 = (0.2139)(0.7971)^2 \approx 0.0231$, and so on, which are short- and medium-term multipliers. Finally, using Eq. (17.4.2), we can obtain the long-run multiplier, that is, the total impact of change in income on consumption after all lagged effects are taken into account, which in the present example becomes

$$\sum_0^\infty \beta_k = \beta_0\left(\frac{1}{1-\lambda}\right) = (0.2139)\left(\frac{1}{1-0.7971}\right) \approx 1.0537$$

(Continued)

EXAMPLE 17.7 (Continued)

TABLE 17.2 PPCE and PPDI, 1959–2006

Year	PPCE	PPDI	Year	PPCE	PPDI
1959	8,776	9,685	1983	15,656	17,828
1960	8,873	9,735	1984	16,343	19,011
1961	8,873	9,901	1985	17,040	19,476
1962	9,170	10,227	1986	17,570	19,906
1963	9,412	10,455	1987	17,994	20,072
1964	9,839	11,061	1988	18,554	20,740
1965	10,331	11,594	1989	18,898	21,120
1966	10,793	12,065	1990	19,067	21,281
1967	10,994	12,457	1991	18,848	21,109
1968	11,510	12,892	1992	19,208	21,548
1969	11,820	13,163	1993	19,593	21,493
1970	11,955	13,563	1994	20,082	21,812
1971	12,256	14,001	1995	20,382	22,153
1972	12,868	14,512	1996	20,835	22,546
1973	13,371	15,345	1997	21,365	23,065
1974	13,148	15,094	1998	22,183	24,131
1975	13,320	15,291	1999	23,050	24,564
1976	13,919	15,738	2000	23,860	25,469
1977	14,364	16,128	2001	24,205	25,687
1978	14,837	16,704	2002	24,612	26,217
1979	15,030	16,931	2003	25,043	26,535
1980	14,816	16,940	2004	25,711	27,232
1981	14,879	17,217	2005	26,277	27,436
1982	14,944	17,418	2006	26,828	28,005

Notes: PPCE = per capita personal consumption expenditure in chained 2000 dollars.
PPDI = per capita personal disposable income in chained 2000 dollars.

Source: *Economic Report of the President,* 2007, Table B-31.

TABLE 17.3

Dependent Variable: PPCE
Method: Least Squares
Sample (adjusted): 1960-2006
Included observations: 47 after adjustments

	Coefficient	Std. Error	t Statistic	Prob.
C	-252.9190	157.3517	-1.607348	0.1151
PPDI	0.213890	0.070617	3.028892	0.0041
PPCE(-1)	0.797146	0.073308	10.87389	0.0000

R-squared	0.998216	Mean dependent var.	16691.28
Adjusted *R*-squared	0.998134	S.D. dependent var.	5205.873
S.E. of regression	224.8504	Akaike info criterion	13.73045
Sum squared resid.	2224539.	Schwarz criterion	13.84854
Log likelihood	-319.6656	Hannan-Quinn criter.	13.77489
F-statistic	12306.99	Durbin-Watson stat.	0.961921
Prob. (*F*-statistic)	0.000000	Durbin h = 3.8269*	

*The calculation of Durbin h is discussed in Section 17.10.

EXAMPLE 17.7 *(Continued)*

In words, a sustained increase of a dollar in PPDI will eventually lead to about 1.05 dollars increase in PPCE, the immediate, or short-run impact being only 21 cents.

The long-run consumption function can now be written as:

$$\text{PPCE}_t = -1247.1351 + 1.0537\text{PPDI}_t$$

This is obtained by dividing the short-run consumption function given in Table 17.3 by 0.2029 on both sides and dropping the lagged PPDI term.[13]

In the long run the marginal propensity to consume (MPC) is about 1. This means that when consumers have had time to adjust to a dollar's increase in PPDI, they will increase their PPCE by almost a dollar. In the short run, however, as Table 17.3 shows, the MPC is only about 21 cents. What is the reason for such a difference between the short- and long-run MPC?

The answer can be found in the median and mean lags. Given $\lambda = 0.7971$, the median lag is

$$\frac{\log(2)}{\log \lambda} = \frac{\log(2)}{\log(0.7971)} = 3.0589$$

and the mean lag is

$$\frac{\lambda}{1-\lambda} = 3.9285$$

It seems real PPCE adjusts to real PPDI with a substantial lag: Recall that the larger the value of λ (between 0 and 1), the longer it takes for the full impact of a change in the value of the explanatory variable to be felt on the dependent variable.

17.5 Rationalization of the Koyck Model: The Adaptive Expectations Model

Although very neat, the Koyck model (17.4.7) is ad hoc since it was obtained by a purely algebraic process; it is devoid of any theoretical underpinning. But this gap can be filled if we start from a different perspective. Suppose we postulate the following model:

$$Y_t = \beta_0 + \beta_1 X_t^* + u_t \tag{17.5.1}$$

where Y = demand for money (real cash balances)
X^* = equilibrium, optimum, expected long-run or normal rate of interest
u = error term

Equation (17.5.1) postulates that the demand for money is a function of *expected* (i.e., anticipated) rate of interest.

Since the expectational variable X^* is not directly observable, let us propose the following hypothesis about how expectations are formed:

$$X_t^* - X_{t-1}^* = \gamma(X_t - X_{t-1}^*) \qquad (17.5.2)^{14}$$

[13]In equilibrium all PPCE values will be the same. Therefore, $\text{PPCE}_t = \text{PPCE}_{t-1}$. Making this substitution, you should get the long-run consumption function.

[14]Sometimes the model is expressed as

$$X_t^* - X_{t-1}^* = \gamma(X_{t-1} - X_{t-1}^*)$$

where γ, such that $0 < \gamma \le 1$, is known as the **coefficient of expectation.** Hypothesis (17.5.2) is known as the **adaptive expectation, progressive expectation,** or **error learning** hypothesis, popularized by Cagan[15] and Friedman.[16]

What Eq. (17.5.2) implies is that "economic agents will adapt their expectations in the light of past experience and that in particular they will learn from their mistakes."[17] More specifically, Eq. (17.5.2) states that expectations are revised each period by a fraction γ of the gap between the current value of the variable and its previous expected value. Thus, for our model this would mean that expectations about interest rates are revised each period by a fraction γ of the discrepancy between the rate of interest observed in the current period and what its anticipated value had been in the previous period. Another way of stating this would be to write Eq. (17.5.2) as

$$X_t^* = \gamma X_t + (1-\gamma)X_{t-1}^* \tag{17.5.3}$$

which shows that the expected value of the rate of interest at time t is a weighted average of the actual value of the interest rate at time t and its value expected in the previous period, with weights of γ and $1-\gamma$, respectively. If $\gamma = 1$, $X_t^* = X_t$, meaning that expectations are realized immediately and fully, that is, in the same time period. If, on the other hand, $\gamma = 0$, $X_t^* = X_{t-1}^*$, meaning that expectations are static, that is, "conditions prevailing today will be maintained in all subsequent periods. Expected future values then become identified with current values."[18]

Substituting Eq. (17.5.3) into Eq. (17.5.1), we obtain

$$\begin{aligned} Y_t &= \beta_0 + \beta_1[\gamma X_t + (1-\gamma)X_{t-1}^*] + u_t \\ &= \beta_0 + \beta_1\gamma X_t + \beta_1(1-\gamma)X_{t-1}^* + u_t \end{aligned} \tag{17.5.4}$$

Now lag Eq. (17.5.1) one period, multiply it by $1-\gamma$, and subtract the product from Eq. (17.5.4). After simple algebraic manipulations, we obtain

$$\begin{aligned} Y_t &= \gamma\beta_0 + \gamma\beta_1 X_t + (1-\gamma)Y_{t-1} + u_t - (1-\gamma)u_{t-1} \\ &= \gamma\beta_0 + \gamma\beta_1 X_t + (1-\gamma)Y_{t-1} + v_t \end{aligned} \tag{17.5.5}$$

where $v_t = u_t - (1-\gamma)u_{t-1}$.

Before proceeding any further, let us note the difference between Eq. (17.5.1) and Eq. (17.5.5). In the former, β_1 measures the average response of Y to a unit change in X^*, the equilibrium or long-run value of X. In Eq. (17.5.5), on the other hand, $\gamma\beta_1$ measures the average response of Y to a unit change in the actual or observed value of X. These responses will not be the same unless, of course, $\gamma = 1$, that is, the current and long-run values of X are the same. In practice, we first estimate Eq. (17.5.5). Once an estimate of γ is obtained from the coefficient of lagged Y, we can easily compute β_1 by simply dividing the coefficient of X_t $(= \gamma\beta_1)$ by γ.

[15]P. Cagan, "The Monetary Dynamics of Hyperinflations," in M. Friedman (ed.), *Studies in the Quantity Theory of Money,* University of Chicago Press, Chicago, 1956.

[16]Milton Friedman, *A Theory of the Consumption Function,* National Bureau of Economic Research, Princeton University Press, Princeton, NJ, 1957.

[17]G. K. Shaw, *Rational Expectations: An Elementary Exposition,* St. Martin's Press, New York, 1984, p. 25.

[18]Ibid., pp. 19–20.

The similarity between the adaptive expectations model (17.5.5) and the Koyck model (17.4.7) should be readily apparent although the interpretations of the coefficients in the two models are different. Note that like the Koyck model, the adaptive expectations model is autoregressive and its error term is similar to the Koyck error term. We shall return to the estimation of the adaptive expectations model in Section 17.8 and to some examples in Section 17.12. Now that we have sketched the adaptive expectations (AE) model, how realistic is it? It is true that it is more appealing than the purely algebraic Koyck approach, but is the AE hypothesis reasonable? In favor of the AE hypothesis one can say the following:

> It provides a fairly simple means of modelling expectations in economic theory whilst postulating a mode of behaviour upon the part of economic agents which seems eminently sensible. The belief that people learn from experience is obviously a more sensible starting point than the implicit assumption that they are totally devoid of memory, characteristic of static expectations thesis. Moreover, the assertion that more distant experiences exert a lesser effect than more recent experience would accord with common sense and would appear to be amply confirmed by simple observation.[19]

Until the advent of the **rational expectations (RE) hypothesis,** initially put forward by J. Muth and later propagated by Robert Lucas and Thomas Sargent, the AE hypothesis was quite popular in empirical economics. The proponents of the RE hypothesis contend that the AE hypothesis is inadequate because it relies solely on the past values of a variable in formulating expectations,[20] whereas the RE hypothesis assumes that "individual economic agents use *current available* and *relevant* information in forming their expectations and do not rely purely upon past experience."[21] In short, the RE hypothesis contends that "expectations are 'rational' in the sense that they efficiently incorporate *all* information available at the time the expectation is formulated"[22] and not just the past information.

The criticism directed by the RE proponents against the AE hypothesis is well-taken, although there are many critics of the RE hypothesis itself.[23] This is not the place to get bogged down with this rather heady material. Perhaps one could agree with Stephen McNees that, "At best, the adaptive expectations assumption can be defended only as a 'working hypothesis' proxying for a more complex, perhaps changing expectations formulation mechanism."[24]

EXAMPLE 17.8
Example 17.7 Revisited

Since the Koyck transformation underlies the adaptive expectations model, the results presented in Table 17.3 can also be interpreted in terms of Equation (17.5.5). Thus $\hat{\gamma}\,\hat{\beta}_0 = -252.9190$; $\hat{\gamma}\,\hat{\beta}_1 = 0.21389$, and $(1-\hat{\gamma}) = 0.797146$. So the expectation coefficient $\hat{\gamma} \approx 0.2028$, and, following the preceding discussion about the AE model, we can say that about 20 percent of the discrepancy between actual and expected PPDI is eliminated within a year.

[19]Ibid., p. 27.

[20]Like the Koyck model, it can be shown that, under AE, expectations of a variable are an exponentially weighted average of past values of that variable.

[21]G. K. Shaw, op. cit., p. 47. For additional details of the RE hypothesis, see Steven M. Sheffrin, *Rational Expectations,* Cambridge University Press, New York, 1983.

[22]Stephen K. McNees, "The Phillips Curve: Forward- or Backward-Looking?" *New England Economic Review,* July–August 1979, p. 50.

[23]For a recent critical appraisal of the RE hypothesis, see Michael C. Lovell, "Test of the Rational Expectations Hypothesis," *American Economic Review,* March 1966, pp. 110–124.

[24]Stephen K. McNees, op. cit., p. 50.

17.6 Another Rationalization of the Koyck Model: The Stock Adjustment, or Partial Adjustment, Model

The adaptive expectations model is one way of rationalizing the Koyck model. Another rationalization is provided by Marc Nerlove in the so-called **stock adjustment** or **partial adjustment model (PAM).**[25] To illustrate this model, consider the **flexible accelerator model** of economic theory, which assumes that there is an *equilibrium*, *optimal*, *desired*, or *long-run* amount of capital stock needed to produce a given output under the given state of technology, rate of interest, etc. For simplicity assume that this desired level of capital Y_t^* is a linear function of output X as follows:

$$Y_t^* = \beta_0 + \beta_1 X_t + u_t \tag{17.6.1}$$

Since the desired level of capital is not directly observable, Nerlove postulates the following hypothesis, known as the **partial adjustment,** or **stock adjustment, hypothesis:**

$$Y_t - Y_{t-1} = \delta(Y_t^* - Y_{t-1}) \qquad (17.6.2)^{26}$$

where δ, such that $0 < \delta \le 1$, is known as the **coefficient of adjustment** and where $Y_t - Y_{t-1}$ = actual change and $(Y_t^* - Y_{t-1})$ = desired change.

Since $Y_t - Y_{t-1}$, the change in capital stock between two periods, is nothing but investment, Eq. (17.6.2) can alternatively be written as

$$I_t = \delta(Y_t^* - Y_{t-1}) \tag{17.6.3}$$

where I_t = investment in time period t.

Equation (17.6.2) postulates that the actual change in capital stock (investment) in any given time period t is some fraction δ of the desired change for that period. If $\delta = 1$, it means that the actual stock of capital is equal to the desired stock; that is, actual stock adjusts to the desired stock instantaneously (in the same time period). However, if $\delta = 0$, it means that nothing changes since actual stock at time t is the same as that observed in the previous time period. Typically, δ is expected to lie between these extremes since adjustment to the desired stock of capital is likely to be incomplete because of rigidity, inertia, contractual obligations, etc.—hence the name **partial adjustment model.** Note that the adjustment mechanism (17.6.2) alternatively can be written as

$$Y_t = \delta Y_t^* + (1 - \delta)Y_{t-1} \tag{17.6.4}$$

showing that the observed capital stock at time t is a weighted average of the desired capital stock at that time and the capital stock existing in the previous time period, δ and $(1 - \delta)$ being the weights. Now substitution of Eq. (17.6.1) into Eq. (17.6.4) gives

$$\begin{aligned} Y_t &= \delta(\beta_0 + \beta_1 X_t + u_t) + (1 - \delta)Y_{t-1} \\ &= \delta\beta_0 + \delta\beta_1 X_t + (1 - \delta)Y_{t-1} + \delta u_t \end{aligned} \tag{17.6.5}$$

[25]Marc Nerlove, *Distributed Lags and Demand Analysis for Agricultural and Other Commodities,* op. cit.

[26]Some authors do not add the stochastic disturbance term u_t to the relation (17.6.1) but add it to this relation, believing that if the former is truly an equilibrium relation, there is no scope for the error term, whereas the adjustment mechanism can be imperfect and may require the disturbance term. In passing, note that Eq. (17.6.2) is sometimes also written as

$$Y_t - Y_{t-1} = \delta(Y_{t-1}^* - Y_{t-1})$$

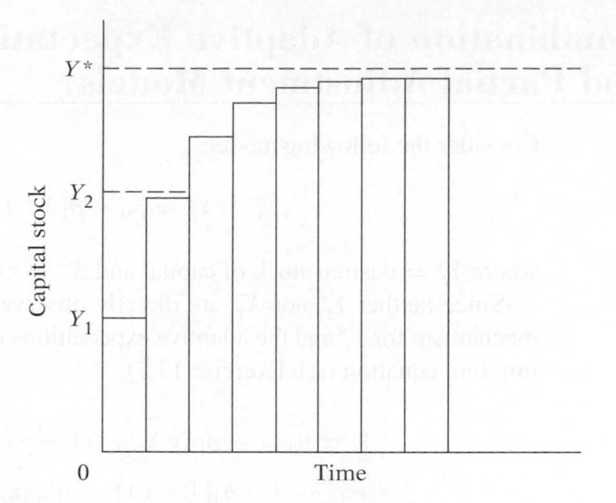

FIGURE 17.6 The gradual adjustment of the capital stock.

This model is called the **partial adjustment model (PAM).**

Since Eq. (17.6.1) represents the long-run, or equilibrium, demand for capital stock, Eq. (17.6.5) can be called the *short-run* demand function for capital stock since in the short run the existing capital stock may not necessarily be equal to its long-run level. Once we estimate the short-run function (17.6.5) and obtain the estimate of the adjustment coefficient δ (from the coefficient of Y_{t-1}), we can easily derive the long-run function by simply dividing $\delta\beta_0$ and $\delta\beta_1$ by δ and omitting the lagged Y term, which will then give Eq. (17.6.1).

Geometrically, the partial adjustment model can be shown as in Figure 17.6.[27] In this figure Y^* is the desired capital stock and Y_1 the current actual capital stock. For illustrative purposes assume that $\delta = 0.5$. This implies that the firm plans to close half the gap between the actual and the desired stock of capital each period. Thus, in the first period it moves to Y_2, with investment equal to $(Y_2 - Y_1)$, which in turn is equal to half of $(Y^* - Y_1)$. In each subsequent period it closes half the gap between the capital stock at the beginning of the period and the desired capital stock Y^*.

The partial adjustment model resembles both the Koyck and adaptive expectations models in that it is autoregressive. But it has a much simpler disturbance term: the original disturbance term u_t multiplied by a constant δ. But bear in mind that although similar in appearance, the adaptive expectations and partial adjustment models are conceptually very different. The former is based on uncertainty (about the future course of prices, interest rates, etc.), whereas the latter is due to technical or institutional rigidities, inertia, cost of change, etc. However, both of these models are theoretically much sounder than the Koyck model.

Since in appearance the adaptive expectations and partial adjustment models are indistinguishable, the γ coefficient of 0.2028 of the adaptive expectations model can also be interpreted as the δ coefficient of the stock adjustment model if we assume that the latter model is operative in the present case (i.e., it is the desired or expected PPCE that is linearly related to the current PDPI).

The important point to keep in mind is that since Koyck, adaptive expectations, and stock adjustment models—apart from the difference in the appearance of the error term—yield the same final estimating model, a researcher must be extremely careful in telling the reader which model he or she is using and why. Thus, researchers must specify the theoretical underpinning of their model.

[27]This is adapted from Figure 7.4 from Rudiger Dornbusch and Stanley Fischer, *Macroeconomics,* 3d ed., McGraw-Hill, New York, 1984, p. 216.

*17.7 Combination of Adaptive Expectations and Partial Adjustment Models

Consider the following model:

$$Y_t^* = \beta_0 + \beta_1 X_t^* + u_t \tag{17.7.1}$$

where Y_t^* = desired stock of capital and X_t^* = expected level of output.

Since neither Y_t^* nor X_t^* are directly observable, one could use the partial adjustment mechanism for Y_t^* and the adaptive expectations model for X_t^* to arrive at the following estimating equation (see Exercise 17.2):

$$\begin{aligned} Y_t &= \beta_0\delta\gamma + \beta_1\delta\gamma X_t + [(1-\gamma) + (1-\delta)]Y_{t-1} \\ &\quad - (1-\delta)(1-\gamma)Y_{t-2} + [\delta u_t - \delta(1-\gamma)u_{t-1}] \\ &= \alpha_0 + \alpha_1 X_t + \alpha_2 Y_{t-1} + \alpha_3 Y_{t-2} + v_t \end{aligned} \tag{17.7.2}$$

where $v_t = \delta[u_t - (1-\gamma)u_{t-1}]$. This model too is autoregressive, the only difference from the purely adaptive expectations model being that Y_{t-2} appears along with Y_{t-1} as an explanatory variable. Like Koyck and the AE models, the error term in Eq. (17.7.2) follows a moving average process. Another feature of this model is that although the model is linear in the α's, it is nonlinear in the original parameters.

A celebrated application of Eq. (17.7.1) has been Friedman's permanent income hypothesis, which states that "permanent" or long-run consumption is a function of "permanent" or long-run income.[28]

The estimation of Eq. (17.7.2) presents the same estimation problems as the Koyck or the AE model in that all these models are autoregressive with similar error structures. In addition, Eq. (17.7.2) involves some nonlinear estimation problems that we consider briefly in Exercise 17.10, but do not delve into in this book.

17.8 Estimation of Autoregressive Models

From our discussion thus far we have the following three models:

Koyck

$$Y_t = \alpha(1-\lambda) + \beta_0 X_t + \lambda Y_{t-1} + v_t \tag{17.4.7}$$

Adaptive expectations

$$Y_t = \gamma\beta_0 + \gamma\beta_1 X_t + (1-\gamma)Y_{t-1} + [u_t - (1-\gamma)u_{t-1}] \tag{17.5.5}$$

Partial adjustment

$$Y_t = \delta\beta_0 + \delta\beta_1 X_t + (1-\delta)Y_{t-1} + \delta u_t \tag{17.6.5}$$

*Optional.

[28]Milton Friedman, *A Theory of Consumption Function,* Princeton University Press, Princeton, N.J., 1957.

All these models have the following common form:

$$Y_t = \alpha_0 + \alpha_1 X_t + \alpha_2 Y_{t-1} + v_t \tag{17.8.1}$$

that is, they are all autoregressive in nature. Therefore, we must now look at the estimation problem of such models, because the classical least-squares theory may not be directly applicable to them. **The reason is twofold: the presence of stochastic explanatory variables and the possibility of serial correlation.**

Now, as noted previously, for the application of the classical least-squares theory, it must be shown that the stochastic explanatory variable Y_{t-1} is distributed independently of the disturbance term v_t. To determine whether this is so, it is essential to know the properties of v_t. If we assume that the original disturbance term u_t satisfies all the classical assumptions, such as $E(u_t) = 0$, var $(u_t) = \sigma^2$ (the assumption of homoscedasticity), and cov $(u_t, u_{t+s}) = 0$ for $s \neq 0$ (the assumption of no autocorrelation), v_t may not inherit all these properties. Consider, for example, the error term in the Koyck model, which is $v_t = (u_t - \lambda u_{t-1})$. Given the assumptions about u_t, we can easily show that v_t is serially correlated because

$$E(v_t v_{t-1}) = -\lambda\sigma^2 \tag{17.8.2}$$[29]

which is nonzero (unless λ happens to be zero). And since Y_{t-1} appears in the Koyck model as an explanatory variable, it is bound to be correlated with v_t (via the presence of u_{t-1} in it). As a matter of fact, it can be shown that

$$\text{cov}\,[Y_{t-1}, (u_t - \lambda u_{t-1})] = -\lambda\sigma^2 \tag{17.8.3}$$

which is the same as Eq. (17.8.2). The reader can verify that the same holds true of the adaptive expectations model.

What is the implication of the finding that in the Koyck model as well as the adaptive expectations model the stochastic explanatory variable Y_{t-1} is correlated with the error term v_t? As noted previously, **if an explanatory variable in a regression model is correlated with the stochastic disturbance term, the OLS estimators are not only biased but also not even consistent; that is, even if the sample size is increased indefinitely, the estimators do not approximate their true population values.**[30] **Therefore, estimation of the Koyck and adaptive expectations models by the usual OLS procedure may yield seriously misleading results.**

The partial adjustment model is different, however. In this model $v_t = \delta u_t$, where $0 < \delta \leq 1$. Therefore, if u_t satisfies the assumptions of the classical linear regression model given previously, so will δu_t. Thus, OLS estimation of the partial adjustment model will yield consistent estimates although the estimates tend to be biased (in finite or small samples).[31] Intuitively, the reason for consistency is this: Although Y_{t-1} depends on u_{t-1}

[29] $E(v_t v_{t-1}) = E(u_t - \lambda u_{t-1})(u_{t-1} - \lambda u_{t-2})$
$= -\lambda E(u_{t-1})^2$ since covariances between u's are zero by assumption
$= -\lambda\sigma^2$

[30] The proof is beyond the scope of this book and may be found in Griliches, op. cit., pp. 36–38. However, see Chapter 18 for an outline of the proof in another context. See also Asatoshi Maeshiro, "Teaching Regressions with a Lagged Dependent Variable and Autocorrelated Disturbances," *The Journal of Economic Education,* Winter 1996, vol. 27, no. 1, pp. 72–84.

[31] For proof, see J. Johnston, *Econometric Methods,* 3d ed., McGraw-Hill, New York, 1984, pp. 360–362. See also H. E. Doran and J. W. B. Guise, *Single Equation Methods in Econometrics: Applied Regression Analysis,* University of New England Teaching Monograph Series 3, Armidale, NSW, Australia, 1984, pp. 236–244.

and all the previous disturbance terms, it is not related to the current error term u_t. Therefore, as long as u_t is serially independent, Y_{t-1} will also be independent or at least uncorrelated with u_t, thereby satisfying an important assumption of OLS, namely, noncorrelation between the explanatory variable(s) and the stochastic disturbance term.

Although OLS estimation of the stock, or partial, adjustment model provides consistent estimation because of the simple structure of the error term in such a model, one should not assume that it applies rather than the Koyck or adaptive expectations model.[32] The reader is strongly advised against doing so. A model should be chosen on the basis of strong theoretical considerations, not simply because it leads to easy statistical estimation. Every model should be considered on its own merit, paying due attention to the stochastic disturbances appearing therein. If in models such as the Koyck or adaptive expectations model OLS cannot be straightforwardly applied, methods need to be devised to resolve the estimation problem. Several alternative estimation methods are available although some of them may be computationally tedious. In the following section we consider one such method.

17.9 The Method of Instrumental Variables (IV)

The reason why OLS cannot be applied to the Koyck or adaptive expectations model is that the explanatory variable Y_{t-1} tends to be correlated with the error term v_t. If somehow this correlation can be removed, one can apply OLS to obtain consistent estimates, as noted previously. (*Note:* There will be some small sample bias.) How can this be accomplished? Liviatan has proposed the following solution.[33]

Let us suppose that we find a *proxy* for Y_{t-1} that is highly correlated with Y_{t-1} but is uncorrelated with v_t, where v_t is the error term appearing in the Koyck or adaptive expectations model. Such a proxy is called an **instrumental variable (IV).**[34] Liviatan suggests X_{t-1} as the instrumental variable for Y_{t-1} and further suggests that the parameters of the regression (17.8.1) can be obtained by solving the following normal equations:

$$
\begin{aligned}
\sum Y_t &= n\hat{\alpha}_0 + \hat{\alpha}_1 \sum X_t + \hat{\alpha}_2 \sum Y_{t-1} \\
\sum Y_t X_t &= \hat{\alpha}_0 \sum X_t + \hat{\alpha}_1 \sum X_t^2 + \hat{\alpha}_2 \sum Y_{t-1} X_t \\
\sum Y_t X_{t-1} &= \hat{\alpha}_0 \sum X_{t-1} + \hat{\alpha}_1 \sum X_t X_{t-1} + \hat{\alpha}_2 \sum Y_{t-1} X_{t-1}
\end{aligned}
\tag{17.9.1}
$$

Notice that if we were to apply OLS directly to Eq. (17.8.1), the usual OLS normal equations would be (see Section 7.4):

$$
\begin{aligned}
\sum Y_t &= n\hat{\alpha}_0 + \hat{\alpha}_1 \sum X_t + \hat{\alpha}_2 \sum Y_{t-1} \\
\sum Y_t X_t &= \hat{\alpha}_0 \sum X_t + \hat{\alpha}_1 \sum X_t^2 + \hat{\alpha}_2 \sum Y_{t-1} X_t \\
\sum Y_t Y_{t-1} &= \hat{\alpha}_0 \sum Y_{t-1} + \hat{\alpha}_1 \sum X_t Y_{t-1} + \hat{\alpha}_2 \sum Y_{t-1}^2
\end{aligned}
\tag{17.9.2}
$$

The difference between the two sets of normal equations should be readily apparent. Liviatan has shown that the α's estimated from Eq. (17.9.1) are consistent, whereas those

[32]Also, as J. Johnston notes (op. cit., p. 350), "[the] pattern of adjustment [suggested by the partial adjustment model] . . . may sometimes be implausible."

[33]N. Liviatan, "Consistent Estimation of Distributed Lags," *International Economic Review,* vol. 4, January 1963, pp. 44–52.

[34]Such instrumental variables are used frequently in simultaneous equation models (see Chapter 20).

estimated from Eq. (17.9.2) may not be consistent because Y_{t-1} and v_t [$= u_t - \lambda u_{t-1}$ or $u_t - (1-\gamma)u_{t-1}$] may be correlated whereas X_t and X_{t-1} are uncorrelated with v_t. (Why?)

Although easy to apply in practice once a suitable proxy is found, the Liviatan technique is likely to suffer from the multicollinearity problem because X_t and X_{t-1}, which enter in the normal equations of (17.9.1), are likely to be highly correlated (as noted in Chapter 12, most economic time series typically exhibit a high degree of correlation between successive values). The implication, then, is that although the Liviatan procedure yields consistent estimates, the estimators are likely to be inefficient.[35]

Before we move on, the obvious question is: How does one find a "good" proxy for Y_{t-1} in such a way that, although highly correlated with Y_{t-1}, it is uncorrelated with v_t? There are some suggestions in the literature, which we take up by way of an exercise (see Exercise 17.5). But it must be stated that finding good proxies is not always easy, in which case the IV method is of little practical use and one may have to resort to maximum likelihood estimation techniques, which are beyond the scope of this book.[36]

Is there a test one can use to find out if the chosen instrument(s) is valid? Dennis Sargan has developed a test, dubbed the **SARG test,** for this purpose. The test is described in Appendix 17A, Section 17A.1.

17.10 Detecting Autocorrelation in Autoregressive Models: Durbin *h* Test

As we have seen, the likely serial correlation in the errors v_t make the estimation problem in the autoregressive model rather complex: In the stock adjustment model the error term v_t did not have (first-order) serial correlation if the error term u_t in the original model was serially uncorrelated, whereas in the Koyck and adaptive expectations models v_t was serially correlated even if u_t was serially independent. The question, then, is: How does one know if there is serial correlation in the error term appearing in the autoregressive models?

As noted in Chapter 12, the Durbin–Watson d statistic may not be used to detect (first-order) serial correlation in autoregressive models, because the computed d value in such models generally tends toward 2, which is the value of d expected in a truly random sequence. In other words, if we routinely compute the d statistic for such models, there is a built-in bias against discovering (first-order) serial correlation. Despite this, many researchers compute the d value for want of anything better. However, Durbin himself has proposed a *large-sample* test of first-order serial correlation in autoregressive models.[37] This test is called the ***h* statistic.**

We have already discussed the Durbin *h test* in Exercise 12.36. For convenience, we reproduce the h statistic (with a slight change in notation):

$$h = \hat{\rho}\sqrt{\frac{n}{1 - n[\mathrm{var}(\hat{\alpha}_2)]}} \tag{17.10.1}$$

[35]To see how the efficiency of the estimators can be improved, consult Lawrence R. Klien, *A Textbook of Econometrics,* 2d ed., Prentice-Hall, Englewood Cliffs, NJ., 1974, p. 99. See also William H. Greene, *Econometric Analysis,* Macmillan, 2d ed., New York, 1993, pp. 535–538.

[36]For a condensed discussion of the ML methods, see J. Johnston, op. cit., pp. 366–371, as well as Appendix 4A and Appendix 15A.

[37]J. Durbin, "Testing for Serial Correlation in Least-Squares Regression When Some of the Regressors Are Lagged Dependent Variables," *Econometrica,* vol. 38, 1970, pp. 410–421.

where n is the sample size, $\text{var}(\hat{\alpha}_2)$ is the variance of the lagged $Y_t\ (= Y_{t-1})$ coefficient in Eq. (17.8.1), and $\hat{\rho}$ is an estimate of the first-order serial correlation ρ, first discussed in Chapter 12.

As noted in Exercise 12.36, for a large sample, Durbin has shown that, under the null hypothesis that $\rho = 0$, the h statistic of Eq. (17.10.1) follows the standard normal distribution. That is,

$$h_{\text{asy}} \sim N(0, 1) \tag{17.10.2}$$

where asy means asymptotically.

In practice, as noted in Chapter 12, one can estimate ρ as

$$\hat{\rho} \approx 1 - \frac{d}{2} \tag{17.10.3}$$

It is interesting to observe that although we cannot use the Durbin d to test for autocorrelation in autoregressive models, we can use it as an input in computing the h statistic.

Let us illustrate the use of the h statistic with our Example 17.7. In this example, $n = 47$, $\hat{\rho} \approx (1 - d/2) = 0.5190$ (*note:* $d = 0.9619$), and $\text{var}(\hat{\alpha}_2) = \text{var}(\text{PPCE}_{t-1}) = (0.0733)^2 = 0.0053$. Putting these values in Eq. (17.10.1), we obtain:

$$h = 0.5190\sqrt{\frac{47}{1 - 47(0.0053)}} = 4.1061 \tag{17.10.4}$$

Since this h value has the standard normal distribution under the null hypothesis, the probability of obtaining such a high h value is very small. Recall that the probability that a standard normal variate exceeds the value of ± 3 is extremely small. In the present example our conclusion, then, is that there is (positive) autocorrelation. Of course, bear in mind that h follows the standard normal distribution asymptotically. Our sample of 47 observations is reasonably large.

Note these features of the h statistic.

1. It does not matter how many X variables or how many lagged values of Y are included in the regression model. To compute h, we need consider only the variance of the coefficient of lagged Y_{t-1}.
2. The test is not applicable if $[n\ \text{var}(\hat{\alpha}_2)]$ exceeds 1. (Why?) In practice, though, this does not usually happen.
3. Since the test is a large-sample test, its application in small samples is not strictly justified, as shown by Inder[38] and Kiviet.[39] It has been suggested that the Breusch–Godfrey (BG) test, also known as the Lagrange multiplier test, discussed in Chapter 12 is statistically more powerful not only in the large samples but also in finite, or small, samples and is therefore preferable to the h test.[40]

The conclusion based on the h test that our model suffers from autocorrelation is confirmed by the Breusch–Godfrey (BG) test, which is shown in Equation (12.6.17). Using the seven lagged values of the residuals estimated from the regression shown in Table 17.3,

[38] B. Inder, "An Approximation to the Null Distribution of the Durbin–Watson Statistic in Models Containing Lagged Dependent Variables," *Econometric Theory,* vol. 2, no. 3, 1986, pp. 413–428.

[39] J. F. Kiviet, "On the Vigour of Some Misspecification Tests for Modelling Dynamic Relationships," *Review of Economic Studies,* vol. 53, no. 173, 1986, pp. 241–262.

[40] Gabor Korosi, Laszlo Matyas, and Istvan P. Szekely, *Practical Econometrics,* Ashgate Publishing Company, Brookfield, Vermont, 1992, p. 92.

TABLE 17.4

Dependent Variable: PCE
Method: Least Squares
Sample (adjusted): 1960–2006
Included observations: 47 after adjustments
Newey-West HAC Standard Errors & Covariance (lag truncation = 3)

	Coefficient	Std. Error	*t* Statistic	Prob.
C	-252.9190	168.4610	-1.501350	0.1404
PPDI	0.213890	0.051245	4.173888	0.0001
PPCE(-1)	0.797146	0.051825	15.38148	0.0000

R-squared	0.998216	Mean dependent var.	16691.28
Adjusted *R*-squared	0.998134	S.D. dependent var.	5205.873
S.E. of regression	224.8504	Akaike info criterion	13.73045
Sum squared resid.	2224539.	Schwarz criterion	13.84854
Log likelihood	-319.6656	Hannan-Quinn criter.	13.77489
F-statistic	12306.99	Durbin-Watson stat.	0.961921
Prob. (*F*-statistic)	0.000000		

the BG test shown in Eq. (12.6.18) obtained a χ^2 value of 15.3869. For seven degrees of freedom (the number of lagged residuals used in the BG test), the probability of obtaining a chi-square value of as much as 15.38 or greater is about 3 percent, which is quite low.

For this reason, we need to correct the standard errors shown in Table 17.3, which can be done by the Newey–West HAC procedure discussed in Chapter 12. The results are as shown in Table 17.4.

It seems OLS underestimates the standard errors of the regression coefficients.

17.11 A Numerical Example: The Demand for Money in Canada, 1979–I to 1988–IV

To illustrate the use of the models we have discussed thus far, consider one of the earlier empirical applications, namely, the demand for money (or real cash balances). In particular, consider the following model.[41]

$$M_t^* = \beta_0 R_t^{\beta_1} Y_t^{\beta_2} e^{u_t} \tag{17.11.1}$$

where M_t^* = desired, or long-run, demand for money (real cash balances)
R_t = long-term interest rate, %
Y_t = aggregate real national income

For statistical estimation, Eq. (17.11.1) may be expressed conveniently in log form as

$$\ln M_t^* = \ln \beta_0 + \beta_1 \ln R_t + \beta_2 \ln Y_t + u_t \tag{17.11.2}$$

[41]For a similar model, see Gregory C. Chow, "On the Long-Run and Short-Run Demand for Money," *Journal of Political Economy,* vol. 74, no. 2, 1966, pp. 111–131. Note that one advantage of the multiplicative function is that the exponents of the variables give direct estimates of elasticities (see Chapter 6).

Since the desired demand variable is not directly observable, let us assume the stock adjustment hypothesis, namely,

$$\frac{M_t}{M_{t-1}} = \left(\frac{M_t^*}{M_{t-1}}\right)^{\delta} \qquad 0 < \delta \leq 1 \tag{17.11.3}$$

Equation (17.11.3) states that a constant percentage (why?) of the discrepancy between the actual and desired real cash balances is eliminated within a single period (year). In log form, Eq. (17.11.3) may be expressed as

$$\ln M_t - \ln M_{t-1} = \delta(\ln M_t^* - \ln M_{t-1}) \tag{17.11.4}$$

Substituting $\ln M_t^*$ from Eq. (17.11.2) into Eq. (17.11.4) and rearranging, we obtain

$$\ln M_t = \delta \ln \beta_0 + \beta_1 \delta \ln R_t + \beta_2 \delta \ln Y_t + (1 - \delta) \ln M_{t-1} + \delta u_t \tag{17.11.5}$$ [42]

which may be called the *short-run demand function* for money. (Why?)

As an illustration of the short-term and long-term demand for real cash balances, consider the data given in Table 17.5. These quarterly data pertain to Canada for the period 1979 to 1988. The variables are defined as follows: M [as defined by M1 money supply, Canadian dollars (C$), millions], P (implicit price deflator, 1981 = 100), GDP at constant 1981 prices (C$, millions), and R (90-day prime corporate rate of interest, %).[43] M1 was deflated by P to obtain figures for real cash balances. A priori, real money demand is expected to be positively related to GDP (positive income effect) and negatively related to R (the higher the interest rate, the higher the opportunity cost of holding money, as M1 money pays very little interest, if any).

The regression results were as follows:[44]

$$\begin{aligned}
\widehat{\ln M_t} &= 0.8561 - 0.0634 \ln R_t - 0.0237 \ln \text{GDP}_t + 0.9607 \ln M_{t-1} \\
\text{se} &= (0.5101) \quad (0.0131) \quad (0.0366) \quad (0.0414) \\
t &= (1.6782) \quad (-4.8134) \quad (-0.6466) \quad (23.1972) \\
R^2 &= 0.9482 \quad d = 2.4582 \quad F = 213.7234
\end{aligned} \tag{17.11.6}$$

The estimated short-run demand function shows that the short-run interest elasticity has the correct sign and that it is statistically quite significant, as its p value is almost zero. The short-run income elasticity is surprisingly negative, although statistically it is not different from zero. The coefficient of adjustment is $\delta = (1 - 0.9607) = 0.0393$, implying that only about 4 percent of the discrepancy between the desired and actual real cash balances is eliminated in a quarter, a rather slow adjustment.

[42] In passing, note that this model is essentially nonlinear in the parameters. Therefore, although OLS may give an unbiased estimate of, say, $\beta_1\delta$ taken together, it may not give unbiased estimates of β_1 and δ individually, especially if the sample is small.

[43] These data are obtained from B. Bhaskar Rao, ed., *Cointegration for the Applied Economist,* St. Martin's Press, New York, 1994, pp. 210–213. The original data is from 1956–I to 1988–IV, but for illustration purposes we begin our analysis from the first quarter of 1979.

[44] Note this feature of the estimated standard errors. The standard error of, say, the coefficient of $\ln R_t$ refers to the standard error of $\widehat{\beta_1\delta}$, an estimator of $\beta_1\delta$. There is no simple way to obtain the standard errors of $\hat{\beta}_1$ and $\hat{\delta}$ individually from the standard error of $\widehat{\beta_1\delta}$, especially if the sample is relatively small. For large samples, however, individual standard errors of $\hat{\beta}_1$ and $\hat{\delta}$ can be obtained approximately, but the computations are involved. See Jan Kmenta, *Elements of Econometrics,* Macmillan, New York, 1971, p. 444.

TABLE 17.5
Money, Interest Rate, Price Index, and GDP, Canada

Source: Rao, op. cit., pp. 210–213.

Observation	M1	*R*	*P*	GDP
1979–1	22,175.00	11.13333	0.77947	334,800
1979–2	22,841.00	11.16667	0.80861	336,708
1979–3	23,461.00	11.80000	0.82649	340,096
1979–4	23,427.00	14.18333	0.84863	341,844
1980–1	23,811.00	14.38333	0.86693	342,776
1980–2	23,612.33	12.98333	0.88950	342,264
1980–3	24,543.00	10.71667	0.91553	340,716
1980–4	25,638.66	14.53333	0.93743	347,780
1981–1	25,316.00	17.13333	0.96523	354,836
1981–2	25,501.33	18.56667	0.98774	359,352
1981–3	25,382.33	21.01666	1.01314	356,152
1981–4	24,753.00	16.61665	1.03410	353,636
1982–1	25,094.33	15.35000	1.05743	349,568
1982–2	25,253.66	16.04999	1.07748	345,284
1982–3	24,936.66	14.31667	1.09666	343,028
1982–4	25,553.00	10.88333	1.11641	340,292
1983–1	26,755.33	9.616670	1.12303	346,072
1983–2	27,412.00	9.316670	1.13395	353,860
1983–3	28,403.33	9.333330	1.14721	359,544
1983–4	28,402.33	9.550000	1.16059	362,304
1984–1	28,715.66	10.08333	1.17117	368,280
1984–2	28,996.33	11.45000	1.17406	376,768
1984–3	28,479.33	12.45000	1.17795	381,016
1984–4	28,669.00	10.76667	1.18438	385,396
1985–1	29,018.66	10.51667	1.18990	390,240
1985–2	29,398.66	9.666670	1.20625	391,580
1985–3	30,203.66	9.033330	1.21492	396,384
1985–4	31,059.33	9.016670	1.21805	405,308
1986–1	30,745.33	11.03333	1.22408	405,680
1986–2	30,477.66	8.733330	1.22856	408,116
1986–3	31,563.66	8.466670	1.23916	409,160
1986–4	32,800.66	8.400000	1.25368	409,616
1987–1	33,958.33	7.250000	1.27117	416,484
1987–2	35,795.66	8.300000	1.28429	422,916
1987–3	35,878.66	9.300000	1.29599	429,980
1987–4	36,336.00	8.700000	1.31001	436,264
1988–1	36,480.33	8.616670	1.32325	440,592
1988–2	37,108.66	9.133330	1.33219	446,680
1988–3	38,423.00	10.05000	1.35065	450,328
1988–4	38,480.66	10.83333	1.36648	453,516

Notes: M1 = C\$, millions.
P = implicit price deflator (1981 = 100).
R = 90-day prime corporate interest rate, %.
GDP = C\$, millions (1981 prices).

To get back to the long-run demand function (17.11.2), all that needs to be done is to divide the short-run demand function through by δ (why?) and drop the $\ln M_{t-1}$ term. The results are:

$$\widehat{\ln M_t^*} = 21.7888 - 1.6132 \ln R_t - 0.6030 \ln \text{GDP} \qquad (17.11.7)^{45}$$

[45]Note that we have not presented the standard errors of the estimated coefficients for reasons discussed in footnote 44.

As can be seen, the long-run interest elasticity of demand for money is substantially greater (in absolute terms) than the corresponding short-run elasticity, which is also true of the income elasticity, although in the present instance its economic and statistical significance is dubious.

Note that the estimated Durbin–Watson d is 2.4582, which is close to 2. This substantiates our previous remark that in the autoregressive models the computed d is generally close to 2. Therefore, we should not trust the computed d to find out whether there was serial correlation in our data. The sample size in our case is 40 observations, which may be reasonably large to apply the h test. In the present case, the reader can verify that the estimated h value is -1.5008, which is not significant at the 5 percent level, perhaps suggesting that there is no first-order autocorrelation in the error term.

17.12 Illustrative Examples

In this section we present a few examples of distributed lag models to show how researchers have used them in empirical studies.

EXAMPLE 17.9

The Fed and the Real Rate of Interest

To assess the effect of M_1 (currency + checkable deposits) growth on Aaa bond real interest rate measure, G. J. Santoni and Courtenay C. Stone[46] estimated, using monthly data, the following distributed lag model for the United States.

$$r_t = \text{constant} + \sum_{i=0}^{11} a_i \dot{M}_{t-i} + u_i \tag{17.12.1}$$

where r_t = Moody's Index of Aaa bond yield minus the average annual rate of change in the seasonally adjusted consumer price index over the prior 36 months, which is used as the measure of real interest rate, and $\dot{M}_t$ = monthly M_1 growth.

According to the "neutrality of money doctrine," real economic variables—such as output, employment, economic growth, and the real rate of interest—are not influenced permanently by money growth and, therefore, are essentially unaffected by monetary policy. . . . Given this argument, the Federal Reserve has no permanent influence over the real rate of interest whatsoever.[47]

If this doctrine is valid, then one should expect the distributed lag coefficients a_i as well as their sum to be statistically indifferent from zero. To find out whether this is the case, the authors estimated Eq. (17.12.1) for two different time periods, February 1951 to September 1979 and October 1979 to November 1982, the latter to take into account the change in the Fed's monetary policy, which since October 1979 has paid more attention to the rate of growth of the money supply than to the rate of interest, which was the policy in the earlier period. Their regression results are presented in Table 17.6. The results seem to support the "neutrality of money doctrine," since for the period February 1951 to September 1979 the current as well as lagged money growth had no statistically significant effect on the real interest rate measure. For the latter period, too, the neutrality doctrine seems to hold since $\sum a_i$ is not statistically different from zero; only the coefficient a_1 is significant, but it has the wrong sign. (Why?)

[46]"The Fed and the Real Rate of Interest," *Review*, Federal Reserve Bank of St. Louis, December 1982, pp. 8–18.

[47]Ibid. p. 15.

EXAMPLE 17.9 *(Continued)*

TABLE 17.6 Influence of Monthly M1 Growth on an Aaa Bond Real Interest Rate Measure: February 1951 to November 1982

$$r = \text{constant} + \sum_{i=0}^{11} a_i \dot{M}1_{t-1}$$

	February 1951 to September 1979		October 1979 to November 1982	
	Coefficient	$\lvert t\rvert$*	Coefficient	$\lvert t\rvert$*
Constant	1.4885†	2.068	1.0360	0.801
a_0	−0.00088	0.388	0.00840	1.014
a_1	0.00171	0.510	0.03960†	3.419
a_2	0.00170	0.423	0.03112	2.003
a_3	0.00233	0.542	0.02719	1.502
a_4	−0.00249	0.553	0.00901	0.423
a_5	−0.00160	0.348	0.01940	0.863
a_6	0.00292	0.631	0.02411	1.056
a_7	0.00253	0.556	0.01446	0.666
a_8	0.00000	0.001	−0.00036	0.019
a_9	0.00074	0.181	−0.00499	0.301
a_{10}	0.00016	0.045	−0.01126	0.888
a_{11}	0.00025	0.107	−0.00178	0.211
$\sum a_i$	0.00737	0.221	0.1549	0.926
$\bar{R}^2$	0.9826		0.8662	
D-W	2.07		2.04	
RH01	1.27†	24.536	1.40†	9.838
RH02	−0.28†	5.410	−0.48†	3.373
NOB	344.		38.	
SER (= RSS)	0.1548		0.3899	

*$\lvert t\rvert$ = absolute t value.

†Significantly different from zero at the 0.05 level.

Source: G. J. Santoni and Courtenay C. Stone, "The Fed and the Real Rate of Interest," *Review*, Federal Reserve Bank of St. Louis, December 1982, p. 16.

EXAMPLE 17.10 *The Short- and Long-Run Aggregate Consumption for Sri Lanka, 1967–1993*

Suppose consumption C is linearly related to permanent income X^*:

$$C_t = \beta_1 + \beta_2 X_t^* + u_t \qquad \textbf{(17.12.2)}$$

Since X_t^* is not directly observable, we need to specify the mechanism that generates permanent income. Suppose we adopt the adaptive expectations hypothesis specified in Eq. (17.5.2). Using Eq. (17.5.2) and simplifying, we obtain the following estimating equation (cf. 17.5.5):

$$C_t = \alpha_1 + \alpha_2 X_t + \alpha_3 C_{t-1} + v_t \qquad \textbf{(17.12.3)}$$

where
$$\alpha_1 = \gamma\beta_1$$
$$\alpha_2 = \gamma\beta_2$$
$$\alpha_3 = (1-\gamma)$$
$$v_t = [u_t - (1-\gamma)u_{t-1}]$$

As we know, β_2 gives the mean response of consumption to, say, a \$1 increase in permanent income, whereas α_2 gives the mean response of consumption to a \$1 increase in current income.

(Continued)

EXAMPLE 17.10 *(Continued)*

From annual data for Sri Lanka for the period 1967–1993 given in Table 17.7, the following regression results were obtained:[48]

$$
\begin{aligned}
\hat{C} &= 1038.403 \quad + 0.4043X_t + 0.5009C_{t-1} \\
\text{se} &= (2501.455) \quad (0.0919) \quad (0.1213) \\
t &= \quad (0.4151) \quad (4.3979) \quad (4.1293) \\
R^2 &= 0.9912 \quad d = 1.4162 \quad F = 1298.466
\end{aligned}
\tag{17.12.4}
$$

where $C =$ private consumption expenditure, and $X =$ GDP, both at constant prices. We also introduced real interest rate in the model, but it was not statistically significant.

The results show that the short-run marginal propensity to consume (MPC) is 0.4043, suggesting that a 1 rupee increase in the current or observed real income (as measured by real GDP) would increase mean consumption by about 0.40 rupee. But if the increase in income is sustained, then eventually the MPC out of the permanent income will be $\beta_2 = \gamma\beta_2/\gamma = 0.4043/0.4991 = 0.8100$, or about 0.81 rupee. In other words, when consumers have had time to adjust to the 1 rupee change in income, they will increase their consumption ultimately by about 0.81 rupee.

Now suppose that our consumption function were

$$
C_t^* = \beta_1 + \beta_2 X_t + u_t \tag{17.12.5}
$$

In this formulation permanent or long-run consumption C_t is a linear function of the current or observed income. Since C_t^* is not directly observable, let us invoke the partial adjustment model (17.6.2). Using this model, and after algebraic manipulations, we obtain

$$
\begin{aligned}
C_t &= \delta\beta_1 + \delta\beta_2 X_t + (1 - \delta)C_{t-1} + \delta u_t \\
&= \alpha_1 + \alpha_2 X_t + \alpha_3 C_{t-1} + v_t
\end{aligned}
\tag{17.12.6}
$$

In appearance, this model is indistinguishable from the adaptive expectations model (17.12.3). Therefore, the regression results given in (17.12.4) are equally applicable here. However, there is a major difference in the interpretation of the two models, not to mention the estimation problem associated with the autoregressive and possibly serially correlated

TABLE 17.7
Private Consumption Expenditure and GDP, Sri Lanka

Source: See footnote 48.

Observation	PCON	GDP	Observation	PCON	GDP
1967	61,284	78,221	1981	120,477	152,846
1968	68,814	83,326	1982	133,868	164,318
1969	76,766	90,490	1983	148,004	172,414
1970	73,576	92,692	1984	149,735	178,433
1971	73,256	94,814	1985	155,200	185,753
1972	67,502	92,590	1986	154,165	192,059
1973	78,832	101,419	1987	155,445	191,288
1974	80,240	105,267	1988	157,199	196,055
1975	84,477	112,149	1989	158,576	202,477
1976	86,038	116,078	1990	169,238	223,225
1977	96,275	122,040	1991	179,001	233,231
1978	101,292	128,578	1992	183,687	242,762
1979	105,448	136,851	1993	198,273	259,555
1980	114,570	144,734			

Notes: PCON = private consumption expenditure.
GDP = gross domestic product.

[48]The data are obtained from the data disk in Chandan Mukherjee, Howard White, and Marc Wuyts, *Econometrics and Data Analysis for Developing Countries*, Routledge, New York, 1998. The original data are from World Bank's World Tables.

EXAMPLE 17.10 *(Continued)*

model (17.12.3). The model (17.12.5) is the long-run, or equilibrium, consumption function, whereas the model (17.12.6) is the short-run consumption function. β_2 measures the long-run MPC, whereas $\alpha_2\,(=\delta\beta_2)$ gives the short-run MPC; the former can be obtained from the latter by dividing it by δ, the coefficient of adjustment.

Returning to (17.12.4), we can now interpret 0.4043 as the short-run MPC. Since $\delta = 0.4991$, the long-run MPC is 0.81. Note that the adjustment coefficient of about 0.50 suggests that in any given time period consumers only adjust their consumption one-half of the way toward its desired or long-run level.

This example brings out the crucial point that in appearance the adaptive expectations and the partial adjustment models, or the Koyck model for that matter, are so similar that by just looking at the estimated regression, such as Eq. (17.12.4), one cannot tell which is the correct specification. That is why it is so vital that one specify the theoretical underpinning of the model chosen for empirical analysis and then proceed appropriately. If habit or inertia characterizes consumption behavior, then the partial adjustment model is appropriate. On the other hand, if consumption behavior is forward-looking in the sense that it is based on expected future income, then the adaptive expectations model is appropriate. If it is the latter, then, one will have to pay close attention to the estimation problem to obtain consistent estimators. In the former case, the OLS will provide consistent estimators, provided the usual OLS assumptions are fulfilled.

17.13 The Almon Approach to Distributed-Lag Models: The Almon or Polynomial Distributed Lag (PDL)[49]

Although used extensively in practice, the Koyck distributed-lag model is based on the assumption that the β coefficients decline geometrically as the lag lengthens (see Figure 17.5). This assumption may be too restrictive in some situations. Consider, for example, Figure 17.7.

In Figure 17.7*a* it is assumed that the β's increase at first and then decrease, whereas in Figure 17.7*c* it is assumed that they follow a cyclical pattern. Obviously, the Koyck scheme of distributed-lag models will not work in these cases. However, after looking at Figures 17.7*a* and *c*, it seems that one can express β_i as a function of *i*, the length of the lag (time), and fit suitable curves to reflect the functional relationship between the two, as indicated in Figures 17.7*b* and *d*. This approach is precisely the one suggested by Shirley Almon. To illustrate her technique, let us revert to the finite distributed-lag model considered previously, namely,

$$Y_t = \alpha + \beta_0 X_t + \beta_1 X_{t-1} + \beta_2 X_{t-2} + \cdots + \beta_k X_{t-k} + u_t \qquad (17.1.2)$$

which may be written more compactly as

$$Y_t = \alpha + \sum_{i=0}^{k} \beta_i X_{t-i} + u_t \qquad (17.13.1)$$

Following a theorem in mathematics known as **Weierstrass' theorem,** Almon assumes that β_i can be approximated by a suitable-degree polynomial in *i*, the length of the lag.[50] For instance, if the lag scheme shown in Figure 17.7*a* applies, we can write

$$\beta_i = a_0 + a_1 i + a_2 i^2 \qquad (17.13.2)$$

[49] Shirley Almon, "The Distributed Lag between Capital Appropriations and Expenditures," *Econometrica,* vol. 33, January 1965, pp. 178–196.

[50] Broadly speaking, the theorem states that on a finite closed interval any continuous function may be approximated uniformly by a polynomial of a suitable degree.

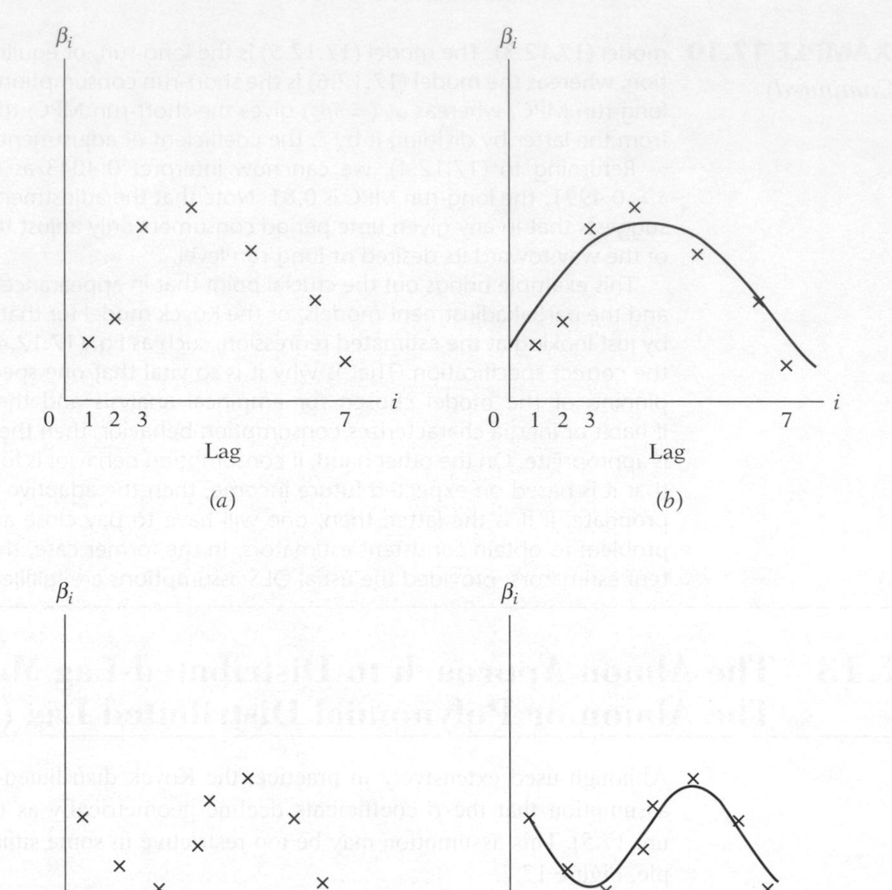

FIGURE 17.7
Almon polynomial-lag scheme.

which is a quadratic, or second-degree, polynomial in i (see Figure 17.7*b*). However, if the β's follow the pattern of Figure 17.7*c*, we can write

$$\beta_i = a_0 + a_1 i + a_2 i^2 + a_3 i^3 \tag{17.13.3}$$

which is a third-degree polynomial in i (see Figure 17.7*d*). More generally, we may write

$$\beta_i = a_0 + a_1 i + a_2 i^2 + \cdots + a_m i^m \tag{17.13.4}$$

which is an mth-degree polynomial in i. It is assumed that m (the degree of the polynomial) is less than k (the maximum length of the lag).

To explain how the Almon scheme works, let us assume that the β's follow the pattern shown in Figure 17.7*a* and, therefore, the second-degree polynomial approximation is appropriate. Substituting Eq. (17.13.2) into Eq. (17.13.1), we obtain

$$\begin{aligned} Y_t &= \alpha + \sum_{i=0}^{k} (a_0 + a_1 i + a_2 i^2) X_{t-i} + u_t \\ &= \alpha + a_0 \sum_{i=0}^{k} X_{t-i} + a_1 \sum_{i=0}^{k} i X_{t-i} + a_2 \sum_{i=0}^{k} i^2 X_{t-i} + u_t \end{aligned} \tag{17.13.5}$$

Defining

$$Z_{0t} = \sum_{i=0}^{k} X_{t-i}$$

$$Z_{1t} = \sum_{i=0}^{k} i X_{t-i} \tag{17.13.6}$$

$$Z_{2t} = \sum_{i=0}^{k} i^2 X_{t-i}$$

we may write Eq. (17.13.5) as

$$Y_t = \alpha + a_0 Z_{0t} + a_1 Z_{1t} + a_2 Z_{2t} + u_t \tag{17.13.7}$$

In the Almon scheme Y is regressed on the constructed variables Z, not the original X variables. Note that Eq. (17.13.7) can be estimated by the usual OLS procedure. The estimates of α and a_i thus obtained will have all the desirable statistical properties provided the stochastic disturbance term u satisfies the assumptions of the classical linear regression model. In this respect, the Almon technique has a distinct advantage over the Koyck method because, as we have seen, the latter has some serious estimation problems that result from the presence of the stochastic explanatory variable Y_{t-1} and its likely correlation with the disturbance term.

Once the a's are estimated from Eq. (17.13.7), the original β's can be estimated from Eq. (17.13.2) (or more generally from Eq. [17.13.4]) as follows:

$$\begin{aligned} \hat{\beta}_0 &= \hat{a}_0 \\ \hat{\beta}_1 &= \hat{a}_0 + \hat{a}_1 + \hat{a}_2 \\ \hat{\beta}_2 &= \hat{a}_0 + 2\hat{a}_1 + 4\hat{a}_2 \\ \hat{\beta}_3 &= \hat{a}_0 + 3\hat{a}_1 + 9\hat{a}_2 \\ &\cdots\cdots\cdots\cdots \\ \hat{\beta}_k &= \hat{a}_0 + k\hat{a}_1 + k^2\hat{a}_2 \end{aligned} \tag{17.13.8}$$

Before we apply the Almon technique, we must resolve the following practical problems.

1. The maximum length of the lag k must be specified in advance. Here perhaps one can follow the advice of Davidson and MacKinnon:

> The best approach is probably to settle the question of lag length first, by starting with a very large value of q [the lag length] and then seeing whether the fit of the model deteriorates significantly when it is reduced without imposing any restrictions on the shape of the distributed lag.[51]

Remember that if there is some "true" lag length, choosing fewer lags will lead to the "omission of relevant variable bias," whose consequences, as we saw in Chapter 13, can be very serious. On the other hand, choosing more lags than necessary will lead to the "inclusion of irrelevant variable bias," whose consequences are less serious; the coefficients can be consistently estimated by OLS, although their variances may be less efficient.

[51]Russell Davidson and James G. MacKinnon, *Estimation and Inference in Econometrics,* Oxford University Press, New York, 1993, pp. 675–676.

One can use the *Akaike* or *Schwarz information criterion* discussed in Chapter 13 to choose the appropriate lag length. These criteria can also be used to discuss the appropriate degree of the polynomial in addition to the discussion in point 2.

2. Having specified k, we must also specify the degree of the polynomial m. Generally, the degree of the polynomial should be at least one more than the number of turning points in the curve relating β_i to i. Thus, in Figure 17.7*a* there is only one turning point; hence a second-degree polynomial will be a good approximation. In Figure 17.7*c* there are two turning points; hence a third-degree polynomial will provide a good approximation. A priori, however, one may not know the number of turning points, and therefore, the choice of m is largely subjective. However, theory may suggest a particular shape in some cases. In practice, one hopes that a fairly low-degree polynomial (say, $m = 2$ or 3) will give good results. Having chosen a particular value of m, if we want to find out whether a higher-degree polynomial will give a better fit, we can proceed as follows.

Suppose we must decide between the second- and third-degree polynomials. For the second-degree polynomial the estimating equation is as given by Eq. (17.13.7). For the third-degree polynomial the corresponding equation is

$$Y_t = \alpha + a_0 Z_{0t} + a_1 Z_{1t} + a_2 Z_{2t} + a_3 Z_{3t} + u_t \tag{17.13.9}$$

where $Z_{3t} = \sum_{i=0}^{k} i^3 X_{t-i}$. After running regression (17.13.9), if we find that a_2 is statistically significant but a_3 is not, we may assume that the second-degree polynomial provides a reasonably good approximation.

Alternatively, as Davidson and MacKinnon suggest, "After q [the lag length] is determined, one can then attempt to determine d [the degree of the polynomial] once again starting with a large value and then reducing it."[52]

However, we must beware of the problem of multicollinearity, which is likely to arise because of the way the Z's are constructed from the X's, as shown in Eq. (17.13.6) (see also Eq. [17.13.10]). As shown in Chapter 10, in cases of serious multicollinearity, $\hat{a}_3$ may turn out to be statistically insignificant, not because the true a_3 is zero, but simply because the sample at hand does not allow us to assess the separate impact of Z_3 on Y. Therefore, in our illustration, before we accept the conclusion that the third-degree polynomial is not the correct choice, we must make sure that the multicollinearity problem is not serious enough, which can be done by applying the techniques discussed in Chapter 10.

3. Once m and k are specified, the Z's can be readily constructed. For instance, if $m = 2$ and $k = 5$, the Z's are

$$\begin{aligned}
Z_{0t} &= \sum_{i=0}^{5} X_{t-i} = (X_t + X_{t-1} + X_{t-2} + X_{t-3} + X_{t-4} + X_{t-5}) \\
Z_{1t} &= \sum_{i=0}^{5} i X_{t-i} = (X_{t-1} + 2X_{t-2} + 3X_{t-3} + 4X_{t-4} + 5X_{t-5}) \\
Z_{2t} &= \sum_{i=0}^{5} i^2 X_{t-i} = (X_{t-1} + 4X_{t-2} + 9X_{t-3} + 16X_{t-4} + 25X_{t-5})
\end{aligned} \tag{17.13.10}$$

Notice that the Z's are linear combinations of the original X's. Also notice why the Z's are likely to exhibit multicollinearity.

[52]Ibid., pp. 675–676.

Before proceeding to a numerical example, note the advantages of the Almon method. First, it provides a flexible method of incorporating a variety of lag structures (see Exercise 17.17). The Koyck technique, on the other hand, is quite rigid in that it assumes that the β's decline geometrically. Second, unlike the Koyck technique, in the Almon method we do not have to worry about the presence of the lagged dependent variable as an explanatory variable in the model and the problems it creates for estimation. Finally, if a sufficiently low-degree polynomial can be fitted, the number of coefficients to be estimated (the a's) is considerably smaller than the original number of coefficients (the β's).

But let us re-emphasize the problems with the Almon technique. First, the degree of the polynomial as well as the maximum value of the lag is largely a subjective decision. Second, for reasons noted previously, the Z variables are likely to exhibit multicollinearity. Therefore, in models like Eq. (17.13.9) the estimated a's are likely to show large standard errors (relative to the values of these coefficients), thereby rendering one or more such coefficients statistically insignificant on the basis of the conventional t test. But this does not necessarily mean that one or more of the original $\hat{\beta}$ coefficients will also be statistically insignificant. (The proof of this statement is slightly involved but is suggested in Exercise 17.18.) As a result, the multicollinearity problem may not be as serious as one might think. Besides, as we know, in cases of multicollinearity even if we cannot estimate an individual coefficient precisely, a linear combination of such coefficients (the **estimable function**) can be estimated more precisely.

EXAMPLE 17.11 *Illustration of the Almon Distributed-Lag Model*

To illustrate the Almon technique, Table 17.8 gives data on inventories Y and sales X for the United States for the period 1954–1999.

For illustrative purposes, assume that inventories depend on sales in the current year and in the preceding 3 years as follows:

$$Y_t = \alpha + \beta_0 X_t + \beta_1 X_{t-1} + \beta_2 X_{t-2} + \beta_3 X_{t-3} + u_t \quad \textbf{(17.13.11)}$$

Furthermore, assume that β_i can be approximated by a second-degree polynomial as shown in Eq. (17.13.2). Then, following Eq. (17.13.7), we may write

$$Y_t = \alpha + a_0 Z_{0t} + a_1 Z_{1t} + a_2 Z_{2t} + u_t \quad \textbf{(17.13.12)}$$

where

$$\begin{aligned} Z_{0t} &= \sum_{i=0}^{3} X_{t-i} = (X_t + X_{t-1} + X_{t-2} + X_{t-3}) \\ Z_{1t} &= \sum_{i=0}^{3} i X_{t-i} = (X_{t-1} + 2X_{t-2} + 3X_{t-3}) \\ Z_{2t} &= \sum_{i=0}^{3} i^2 X_{t-i} = (X_{t-1} + 4X_{t-2} + 9X_{t-3}) \end{aligned} \quad \textbf{(17.13.13)}$$

The Z variables thus constructed are shown in Table 17.8. Using the data on Y and the Z's, we obtain the following regression:

$$\begin{aligned} \hat{Y}_t &= 25{,}845.06 \quad + 1.1149Z_{0t} \quad - \quad 0.3713Z_{1t} \quad - \quad 0.0600Z_{2t} \\ \text{se} &= \quad (6596.998) \quad (0.5381) \quad (1.3743) \quad (0.4549) \\ t &= \quad (3.9177) \quad (2.0718) \quad (-0.2702) \quad (-0.1319) \\ & R^2 = 0.9755 \quad d = 0.1643 \quad F = 517.7656 \end{aligned} \quad \textbf{(17.13.14)}$$

Note: Since we are using a 3-year lag, the total number of observations has been reduced from 46 to 43.

(Continued)

EXAMPLE 17.11 (*Continued*)

TABLE 17.8 Inventories *Y* and Sales *X*, U.S. Manufacturing, and Constructed *Z*'s

Observation	Inventory	Sales	Z_0	Z_1	Z_2
1954	41,612	23,355	NA	NA	NA
1955	45,069	26,480	NA	NA	NA
1956	50,642	27,740	NA	NA	NA
1957	51,871	28,736	106,311	150,765	343,855
1958	50,203	27,248	110,204	163,656	378,016
1959	52,913	30,286	114,010	167,940	391,852
1960	53,786	30,878	117,148	170,990	397,902
1961	54,871	30,922	119,334	173,194	397,254
1962	58,172	33,358	125,444	183,536	427,008
1963	60,029	35,058	130,216	187,836	434,948
1964	63,410	37,331	136,669	194,540	446,788
1965	68,207	40,995	146,742	207,521	477,785
1966	77,986	44,870	158,254	220,831	505,841
1967	84,646	46,486	169,682	238,853	544,829
1968	90,560	50,229	182,580	259,211	594,921
1969	98,145	53,501	195,086	277,811	640,003
1970	101,599	52,805	203,021	293,417	672,791
1971	102,567	55,906	212,441	310,494	718,870
1972	108,121	63,027	225,239	322,019	748,635
1973	124,499	72,931	244,669	333,254	761,896
1974	157,625	84,790	276,654	366,703	828,193
1975	159,708	86,589	307,337	419,733	943,757
1976	174,636	98,797	343,107	474,962	1,082,128
1977	188,378	113,201	383,377	526,345	1,208,263
1978	211,691	126,905	425,492	570,562	1,287,690
1979	242,157	143,936	482,839	649,698	1,468,882
1980	265,215	154,391	538,433	737,349	1,670,365
1981	283,413	168,129	593,361	822,978	1,872,280
1982	311,852	163,351	629,807	908,719	2,081,117
1983	312,379	172,547	658,418	962,782	2,225,386
1984	339,516	190,682	694,709	1,003,636	2,339,112
1985	334,749	194,538	721,118	1,025,829	2,351,029
1986	322,654	194,657	752,424	1,093,543	2,510,189
1987	338,109	206,326	786,203	1,155,779	2,688,947
1988	369,374	224,619	820,140	1,179,254	2,735,796
1989	391,212	236,698	862,300	1,221,242	2,801,836
1990	405,073	242,686	910,329	1,304,914	2,992,108
1991	390,905	239,847	943,850	1,389,939	3,211,049
1992	382,510	250,394	969,625	1,435,313	3,340,873
1993	384,039	260,635	993,562	1,458,146	3,393,956
1994	404,877	279,002	1,029,878	1,480,964	3,420,834
1995	430,985	299,555	1,089,586	1,551,454	3,575,088
1996	436,729	309,622	1,148,814	1,639,464	3,761,278
1997	456,133	327,452	1,215,631	1,745,738	4,018,860
1998	466,798	337,687	1,274,316	1,845,361	4,261,935
1999	470,377	354,961	1,329,722	1,921,457	4,434,093

Note: Y and *X* are in millions of dollars, seasonally adjusted.

Source: *Economic Report of the President*, 2001, Table B-57, p. 340. The *Z*'s are as shown in Eq. (17.13.13).

EXAMPLE 17.11 (*Continued*)

A brief comment on the preceding results is in order. Of the three Z variables, only Z_0 is individually statistically significant at the 5 percent level, but the others are not, yet the F value is so high that we can reject the null hypothesis that collectively the Z's have no effect on Y. As you may suspect, this might very well be due to multicollinearity. Also, note that the computed d value is very low. This does not necessarily mean that the residuals suffer from autocorrelation. More likely, the low d value suggests that the model we have used is probably mis-specified. We will comment on this shortly.

From the estimated a's given in Eq. (17.13.3), we can easily estimate the original β's easily, as shown in Eq. (17.13.8). In the present example, the results are as follows:

$$\begin{aligned}\hat{\beta}_0 &= \hat{a}_0 = 1.1149\\ \hat{\beta}_1 &= (\hat{a}_0 + \hat{a}_1 + \hat{a}_2) = 0.6836\\ \hat{\beta}_2 &= (\hat{a}_0 + 2\hat{a}_1 + 4\hat{a}_2) = 0.1321\\ \hat{\beta}_3 &= (\hat{a}_0 + 3\hat{a}_1 + 9\hat{a}_2) = -0.5394\end{aligned} \tag{17.13.15}$$

Thus, the estimated distributed-lag model corresponding to Eq. (17.13.11) is:

$$\begin{aligned}\hat{Y}_t = {} & 25{,}845.0 && + 1.1150X_0 && + 0.6836X_{t-1} && + 0.1321X_{t-2} && - 0.5394X_{t-3}\\ \text{se} = {} & (6596.99) && (0.5381) && (0.4672) && (0.4656) && (0.5656)\\ t = {} & (3.9177) && (2.0718) && (1.4630) && (0.2837) && (-0.9537)\end{aligned} \tag{17.13.16}$$

Geometrically, the estimated β_i is as shown in Figure 17.8.

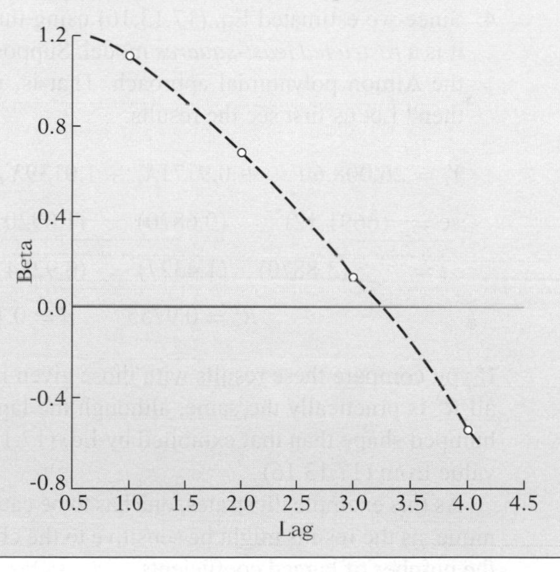

FIGURE 17.8 Lag structure of the illustrative example.

Our illustrative example may be used to point out a few additional features of the Almon lag procedure:

1. The standard errors of the a coefficients are directly obtainable from the OLS regression (17.13.14), but the standard errors of some of the $\hat{\beta}$ coefficients, the objective of primary interest, cannot be so obtained. But they can be obtained from the standard errors of the estimated a coefficients by using a well-known formula from statistics, which is given in Exercise 17.18. Of course, there is no need to do this manually, for most statistical packages can do this routinely. The standard errors given in Eq. (17.13.15) were obtained from *EViews 6*.

2. The $\hat{\beta}$'s obtained in Eq. (17.13.16) are called *unrestricted estimates* in the sense that no a priori restrictions are placed on them. In some situations, however, one may want to impose the so-called **endpoint restrictions** on the β's by assuming that β_0 and β_k (the current and kth lagged coefficient) are zero. Because of psychological, institutional, or technical reasons, the value of the explanatory variable in the current period may not have any impact on the current value of the regressand, thereby justifying the zero value for β_0. By the same token, beyond a certain time the kth lagged coefficient may not have any impact on the regressand, thus supporting the assumption that β_k is zero. In our inventory example (Example 17.11), the coefficient of X_{t-3} had a negative sign, which may not make economic sense. Hence, one may want to constrain that coefficient to zero.[53] Of course, you do not have to constrain both ends; you could put restriction only on the first coefficient, called near-end restriction, or on the last coefficient, called far-end restriction. For our inventory example, this is illustrated in Exercise 17.28. Sometimes the β's are estimated with the restriction that their sum is 1. But one should not put such restrictions mindlessly because such restrictions also affect the values of the other (unconstrained) lagged coefficients.
3. Since the choice of the number of lagged coefficients as well as the degree of the polynomial is at the discretion of the modeler, some trial and error is inevitable, the charge of data mining notwithstanding. Here is where the **Akaike and Schwarz information criteria** discussed in Chapter 13 may come in handy.
4. Since we estimated Eq. (17.13.16) using three lags and the second-degree polynomial, it is a *restricted least-squares* model. Suppose we decide to use three lags but do not use the Almon polynomial approach. That is, we estimate Eq. (17.13.11) by OLS. What then? Let us first see the results:

$$\begin{aligned}
\hat{Y}_t &= 26{,}008.60 \quad + 0.9771X_t + 1.0139X_{t-1} - 0.2022\,X_{t-2} - 0.3935X_{t-3} \\
\text{se} &= \quad (6691.12) \quad (0.6820) \quad (1.0920) \quad (1.1021) \quad (0.7186) \\
t &= \quad (3.8870) \quad (1.4327) \quad (0.9284) \quad (-0.1835) \quad (-0.5476) \\
& \qquad R^2 = 0.9755 \qquad d = 0.1571 \qquad F = 379.51
\end{aligned} \tag{17.13.17}$$

If you compare these results with those given in Eq. (17.13.16), you will see that the overall R^2 is practically the same, although the lagged pattern in (17.13.17) shows more of a humped shape than that exhibited by Eq. (17.13.16). It is left to the reader to verify the R^2 value from (17.13.16).

As this example illustrates, one has to be careful in using the Almon distributed lag technique, as the results might be sensitive to the choice of the degree of the polynomial and/or the number of lagged coefficients.

17.14 Causality in Economics: The Granger Causality Test[54]

Back in Section 1.4 we noted that, although regression analysis deals with the dependence of one variable on other variables, it does not necessarily imply causation. In other words, the existence of a relationship between variables does not prove causality or the direction

[53]For a concrete application, see D. B. Batten and Daniel Thornton, "Polynomial Distributed Lags and the Estimation of the St. Louis Equation," *Review*, Federal Reserve Bank of St. Louis, April 1983, pp. 13–25.

[54]There is another test of causality that is sometimes used, the so-called **Sims test of causality.** We discuss it by way of an exercise.

of influence. But in regressions involving time series data, the situation may be somewhat different because, as one author puts it,

> . . . time does not run backward. That is, if event A happens before event B, then it is *possible* that A is causing B. However, it is not *possible* that B is causing A. In other words, events in the past can cause events to happen today. Future events cannot.[55] [Emphasis added.]

This is roughly the idea behind the so-called Granger causality test.[56] But it should be noted clearly that the question of causality is deeply philosophical with all kinds of controversies. At one extreme are people who believe that "everything causes everything," and at the other extreme are people who deny the existence of causation whatsoever.[57] The econometrician Edward Leamer prefers the term **precedence** over causality. Francis Diebold prefers the term **predictive causality.** As he writes:

> . . . the statement "y_i causes y_j" is just shorthand for the more precise, but long-winded, statement, "y_i contains useful information for predicting y_j (in the linear least squares sense), over and above the past histories of the other variables in the system." To save space, we simply say that y_i causes y_j.[58]

The Granger Test

To explain the Granger test, we will consider the often asked question in macroeconomics: Is it GDP that "causes" the money supply M (GDP $\rightarrow M$)? Or is it the money supply M that causes GDP ($M \rightarrow$ GDP)? (where the arrow points to the direction of causality). The Granger causality test assumes that the information relevant to the prediction of the respective variables, GDP and M, is contained solely in the time series data on these variables. The test involves estimating the following pair of regressions:

$$\text{GDP}_t = \sum_{i=1}^{n} \alpha_i M_{t-i} + \sum_{j=1}^{n} \beta_j \text{GDP}_{t-j} + u_{1t} \tag{17.14.1}$$

$$M_t = \sum_{i=1}^{n} \lambda_i M_{t-i} + \sum_{j=1}^{n} \delta_j \text{GDP}_{t-j} + u_{2t} \tag{17.14.2}$$

where it is assumed that the disturbances u_{1t} and u_{2t} are uncorrelated. In passing, note that, since we have two variables, we are dealing with **bilateral causality.** In the chapters on time series econometrics, we will extend this to multivariable causality through the technique of **vector autoregression (VAR).**

Equation (17.14.1) postulates that current GDP is related to past values of itself as well as that of M, and Eq. (17.14.2) postulates a similar behavior for M. Note that these regressions can

[55] Gary Koop, *Analysis of Economic Data,* John Wiley & Sons, New York, 2000, p. 175.

[56] C. W. J. Granger, "Investigating Causal Relations by Econometric Models and Cross-Spectral Methods," *Econometrica,* July 1969, pp. 424–438. Although popularly known as the Granger causality test, it is appropriate to call it the **Wiener–Granger causality test,** for it was earlier suggested by Wiener. See N. Wiener, "The Theory of Prediction," in E. F. Beckenback, ed., *Modern Mathematics for Engineers,* McGraw-Hill, New York, 1956, pp. 165–190.

[57] For an excellent discussion of this topic, see Arnold Zellner, "Causality and Econometrics," *Carnegie-Rochester Conference Series,* 10, K. Brunner and A. H. Meltzer, eds., North Holland Publishing Company, Amsterdam, 1979, pp. 9–50.

[58] Francis X. Diebold, *Elements of Forecasting,* South Western Publishing, 2d ed., 2001, p. 254.

be cast in growth forms, $\dot{GDP}$ and $\dot{M}$, where a dot over a variable indicates its growth rate. We now distinguish four cases:

1. *Unidirectional causality from M to GDP* is indicated if the estimated coefficients on the lagged M in Eq. (17.14.1) are statistically different from zero as a group and the set of estimated coefficients on the lagged GDP in Eq. (17.14.2) is not statistically different from zero.
2. Conversely, *unidirectional causality from GDP to M* exists if the set of lagged M coefficients in Eq. (17.14.1) is not statistically different from zero and the set of the lagged GDP coefficients in Eq. (17.14.2) is statistically different from zero.
3. *Feedback,* or *bilateral causality,* is suggested when the sets of M and GDP coefficients are statistically significantly different from zero in both regressions.
4. Finally, *independence* is suggested when the sets of M and GDP coefficients are not statistically significant in either of the regressions.

More generally, since the future cannot predict the past, if variable X (Granger) causes variable Y, then changes in X should *precede* changes in Y. Therefore, in a regression of Y on other variables (including its own past values) if we include past or lagged values of X and it significantly improves the prediction of Y, then we can say that X (Granger) causes Y. A similar definition applies if Y (Granger) causes X.

The steps involved in implementing the Granger causality test are as follows. We illustrate these steps with the GDP-money example given in Eq. (17.14.1).

1. Regress current GDP on all lagged GDP terms and other variables, if any, but *do not* include the lagged M variables in this regression. As per Chapter 8, this is the restricted regression. From this regression obtain the restricted residual sum of squares, RSS_R.
2. Now run the regression including the lagged M terms. In the language of Chapter 8, this is the unrestricted regression. From this regression obtain the unrestricted residual sum of squares, RSS_{UR}.
3. The null hypothesis is H_0: $\alpha_i = 0$, $i = 1, 2, \ldots, n$, that is, lagged M terms do not belong in the regression.
4. To test this hypothesis, we apply the F test given by Eq. (8.7.9), namely,

$$F = \frac{(\text{RSS}_R - \text{RSS}_{\text{UR}})/m}{\text{RSS}_{\text{UR}}/(n-k)} \tag{8.7.9}$$

   which follows the F distribution with m and $(n - k)$ df. In the present case m is equal to the number of lagged M terms and k is the number of parameters estimated in the unrestricted regression.
5. If the computed F value exceeds the critical F value at the chosen level of significance, we reject the null hypothesis, in which case the lagged M terms belong in the regression. This is another way of saying that M causes GDP.
6. Steps 1 to 5 can be repeated to test the model (17.14.2), that is, whether GDP causes M.

Before we illustrate the Granger causality test, there are several things that need to be noted:

1. It is assumed that the two variables, GDP and M, are *stationary*. We have already discussed the concept of stationarity in intuitive terms before and will discuss it more formally in Chapter 21. Sometimes taking the first differences of the variables makes them stationary, if they are not already stationary in the level form.

2. The number of lagged terms to be introduced in the causality tests is an important practical question. As in the case of the distributed-lag models, we may have to use the *Akaike or Schwarz information criterion* to make the choice. But it should be added that the *direction of causality may depend critically on the number of lagged terms included.*
3. We have assumed that the error terms entering the causality test are uncorrelated. If this is not the case, appropriate transformation, as discussed in Chapter 12, may have to be taken.[59]
4. Since our interest is in testing for causality, one need not present the estimated coefficients of models (17.14.1) and (17.14.2) explicitly (to save space); just the results of the F test given in Eq. (8.7.9) will suffice.
5. One has to guard against "spurious" causality. In our GDP-money example, suppose we consider interest rate, say the short-term interest rate. It is quite possible that money "Granger-causes" the interest rate and the interest rate in turn "Granger-causes" GDP. Therefore, if we do not account for the interest rate, and find that it is money that causes GDP, then, the observed causality between GDP and money may be spurious.[60] As noted previously, one way of dealing with this is to consider a multiple-equation system, such as **vector autoregression (VAR),** which we will discuss in some length in Chapter 22.

EXAMPLE 17.12 *Causality between Money and Income*

R. W. Hafer used the Granger test to find out the nature of causality between GNP (rather than GDP) and M for the United States for the period 1960–I to 1980–IV. Instead of using the gross values of these variables, he used their growth rates, $\dot{\text{GNP}}$ and $\dot{M}$, and used four lags of each variable in the two regressions given previously. The results were as follows:[61] The null hypothesis in each case is that the variable under consideration does not "Granger-cause" the other variable.

Direction of Causality	F Value	Decision
$\dot{M} \rightarrow \dot{\text{GNP}}$	2.68	Reject
$\dot{\text{GNP}} \rightarrow \dot{M}$	0.56	Do not reject

These results suggest that the direction of causality is from money growth to GNP growth since the estimated F is significant at the 5 percent level; the critical F value is 2.50 (for 4 and 71 df). On the other hand, there is no "reverse causation" from GNP growth to money growth, since the F value is statistically insignificant.

EXAMPLE 17.13 *Causality between Money and Interest Rate in Canada*

Refer to the Canadian data given in Table 17.5. Suppose we want to find out if there is any causality between money supply and interest rate in Canada for the quarterly periods of 1979–1988. To show that the Granger causality test depends critically on the number of lagged terms introduced in the model, we present below the results of the F test using several (quarterly) lags. In each case, the null hypothesis is that interest rate does *not* (Granger-) cause money supply and vice versa.

(Continued)

[59]For further details, see Wojciech W. Charemza and Derek F. Deadman, *New Directions in Econometric Practice: General to Specific Modelling, Cointegration and Vector Autoregression,* 3d ed., Edward Elgar Publishing, 1997, Chapter 6.

[60]On this, see J. H. Stock and M. W. Watson, "Interpreting the Evidence on Money-Income Causality," *Journal of Econometrics,* vol. 40, 1989, pp. 783–820.

[61]R. W. Hafer, "The Role of Fiscal Policy in the St. Louis Equation," *Review,* Federal Reserve Bank of St. Louis, January 1982, pp. 17–22. See his footnote 12 for the details of the procedure.

EXAMPLE 17.13 *(Continued)*

Direction of Causality	Number of Lags	*F* Value	Decision
$R \rightarrow M$	2	12.92	Reject
$M \rightarrow R$	2	3.22	Reject
$R \rightarrow M$	4	5.59	Reject
$M \rightarrow R$	4	2.45	Reject (at 7%)
$R \rightarrow M$	6	3.5163	Reject
$M \rightarrow R$	6	2.71	Reject
$R \rightarrow M$	8	1.40	Do not reject
$M \rightarrow R$	8	1.62	Do not reject

Note these features of the preceding results of the *F* test: Up to six lags, there is bilateral causality between money supply and interest rate. However, at eight lags, there is no statistically discernible relationship between the two variables. This reinforces the point made earlier that the outcome of the Granger test is sensitive to the number of lags introduced in the model.

EXAMPLE 17.14 *Causality between GDP Growth Rate and Gross Savings Rate in Nine East Asian Countries*

A study of the bilateral causality between GDP growth rate (g) and gross savings rate (s) showed the results given in Table 17.9.[62] For comparison, the results for the United States are also presented in the table. By and large, the results presented in Table 17.9 show that for most East Asian countries the causality runs from the GDP growth rate to the gross savings rate. By contrast, for the United States for the period 1950–1988 up to lag 3, causality ran in both directions, but for lags 4 and 5, the causality ran from the GDP growth rate to the savings rate but not the other way round.

TABLE 17.9
Tests of Bivariate Granger Causality between the Real Per Capita GDP Growth Rate and the Gross Savings Rate

Source: World Bank, *The East Asian Miracle: Economic Growth and Public Policy,* Oxford University Press, New York, 1993, p. 244, (Table A5-2). The original source is Robert Summers and Alan Heston, "The Penn World Tables (Mark 5): An Expanded Set of International Comparisons, 1950–88," *Quarterly Journal of Economics,* vol. 105, no. 2, 1991.

Economy, Years	Years of Lags	Lagged Right-hand Side Variable Savings	Growth	Economy, Years	Years of Lags	Lagged Right-hand Side Variable Savings	Growth
Hong Kong, 1960–88	1	Sig	Sig	Philippines, 1950–88	1	NS	Sig
	2	Sig	Sig		2	NS	Sig
	3	Sig	Sig		3	NS	Sig
	4	Sig	Sig		4	NS	Sig
	5	Sig	Sig		5	NS	Sig
Indonesia, 1965	1	Sig	Sig	Singapore, 1960–88	1	NS	NS
	2	NS	Sig		2	NS	NS
	3	NS	Sig		3	NS	NS
	4	NS	Sig		4	Sig	NS
	5	NS	Sig		5	Sig	NS
Japan, 1950–88	1	NS	Sig	Taiwan, China, 1950–88	1	Sig	Sig
	2	NS	Sig		2	NS	Sig
	3	NS	Sig		3	NS	Sig
	4	NS	Sig		4	NS	Sig
	5	NS	Sig		5	NS	Sig
Korea, Rep. of, 1955–88	1	Sig	Sig	Thailand, 1950–88	1	NS	Sig
	2	NS	Sig		2	NS	Sig
	3	NS	Sig		3	NS	Sig
	4	NS	Sig		4	NS	Sig
	5	NS	Sig		5	NS	Sig
Malaysia, 1955–88	1	Sig	Sig	United States, 1950–88	1	Sig	Sig
	2	Sig	Sig		2	Sig	Sig
	3	NS	NS		3	Sig	Sig
	4	NS	NS		4	NS	Sig
	5	NS	Sig		5	NS	Sig

Sig: Significant; NS: Not significant.
Note: Growth is real per capita GDP growth at 1985 international prices.

[62]These results are obtained from *The East Asian Miracle: Economic Growth and Public Policy,* published for the World Bank by Oxford University Press, 1993, p. 244.

EXAMPLE 17.14 *(Continued)*

To conclude our discussion of Granger causality, keep in mind that the question we are examining is whether *statistically* one can detect the direction of causality when *temporally* there is a lead–lag relationship between two variables. If causality is established, it suggests that one can use a variable to better predict the other variable than simply the past history of that other variable. In the case of the East Asian economies, it seems that we can better predict the gross savings rate by considering the lagged values of the GDP growth rate than merely the lagged values of the gross savings rate.

*A Note on Causality and Exogeneity

As we will study in the chapters on simultaneous-equation models in **Part 4** of this text, economic variables are often classified into two broad categories, **endogenous** and **exogenous.** Loosely speaking, endogenous variables are the equivalent of the dependent variable in the single-equation regression model and exogenous variables are the equivalent of the X variables, or regressors, in such a model, provided the X variables are uncorrelated with the error term in that equation.[63]

Now we raise an interesting question: Suppose in a Granger causality test we find that an X variable (Granger-) causes a Y variable without being caused by the latter (i.e., no bilateral causality). Can we then treat the X variable as exogenous? In other words, can we use Granger causality (or noncausality) to establish exogeneity?

To answer this question, we need to distinguish three types of exogeneity: (1) weak, (2) strong, and (3) super. To keep the exposition simple, suppose we consider only two variables, Y_t and X_t, and further suppose we regress Y_t on X_t. We say that X_t is *weakly exogenous* if Y_t also does not explain X_t. In this case estimation and testing of the regression model can be done, conditional on the values of X_t. As a matter of fact, going back to Chapter 2, you will realize that our regression modeling was conditional on the values of the X variables. X_t is said to be *strongly* exogenous if current and lagged Y values do not explain it (i.e., no feedback relationship). And X_t is *super-exogenous* if the parameters in the regression of Y on X do not change even if the X values change; that is, the parameter values are invariant to changes in the value(s) of X. If that is in fact the case, then, the famous "Lucas critique" may lose its force.[64]

The reason for distinguishing the three types of exogeneity is that, "In general, weak exogeneity is all that is needed for estimating and testing, strong exogeneity is necessary for forecasting and super exogeneity for policy analysis."[65]

Returning to Granger causality, if a variable, say Y, does not cause another variable, say X, can we then assume that the latter is exogenous? Unfortunately, the answer is not straightforward. If we are talking about weak exogeneity, it can be shown that *Granger causality is neither necessary nor sufficient to establish exogeneity.* On the other hand, Granger causality is necessary (but not sufficient) for strong exogeneity. The proofs of these statements are beyond the scope of this book.[66] For our purpose, then, it is better to

*Optional.

[63]Of course, if the explanatory variables include one or more lagged terms of the endogenous variable, this requirement may not be fulfilled.

[64]The Nobel laureate Robert Lucas put forth the proposition that existing relations between economic variables may change when policy changes, in which case the estimated parameters from a regression model will be of little value for prediction. On this, see Oliver Blanchard, *Macroeconomics,* Prentice Hall, 1997, pp. 371–372.

[65]Keith Cuthbertson, Stephen G. Hall, and Mark P. Taylor, *Applied Econometric Techniques,* University of Michigan Press, 1992, p. 100.

[66]For a comparatively simple discussion, see G. S. Maddala, *Introduction to Econometrics,* 2d ed., Macmillan, New York, 1992, pp. 394–395, and also David F. Hendry, *Dynamic Econometrics,* Oxford University Press, New York, 1995, Chapter 5.

keep the concepts of Granger causality and exogeneity separate and treat the former as a useful descriptive tool for time series data. In Chapter 19 we will discuss a test that can be used to find out if a variable can be treated as exogenous.

Summary and Conclusions

1. For psychological, technological, and institutional reasons, a regressand may respond to a regressor(s) with a time lag. Regression models that take into account time lags are known as **dynamic** or **lagged regression models.**
2. There are two types of lagged models: **distributed-lag** and **autoregressive.** In the former, the current and lagged values of regressors are explanatory variables. In the latter, the lagged value(s) of the regressand appears as an explanatory variable(s).
3. A purely distributed-lag model can be estimated by OLS, but in that case there is the problem of multicollinearity since successive lagged values of a regressor tend to be correlated.
4. As a result, some shortcut methods have been devised. These include the Koyck, the adaptive expectations, and partial adjustment mechanisms, the first being a purely algebraic approach and the other two being based on economic principles.
5. A unique feature of the **Koyck, adaptive expectations,** and **partial adjustment models** is that they all are autoregressive in nature in that the lagged value(s) of the regressand appears as one of the explanatory variables.
6. Autoregressiveness poses estimation challenges; if the lagged regressand is correlated with the error term, OLS estimators of such models are not only biased but also are inconsistent. Bias and inconsistency are the case with the Koyck and the adaptive expectations models; the partial adjustment model is different in that it can be consistently estimated by OLS despite the presence of the lagged regressand.
7. To estimate the Koyck and adaptive expectations models consistently, the most popular method is the **method of instrumental variable.** The instrumental variable is a proxy variable for the lagged regressand but with the property that it is uncorrelated with the error term.
8. An alternative to the lagged regression models just discussed is the **Almon polynomial distributed-lag model,** which avoids the estimation problems associated with the autoregressive models. The major problem with the Almon approach, however, is that one must *prespecify* both the lag length and the degree of the polynomial. There are both formal and informal methods of resolving the choice of the lag length and the degree of the polynomial.
9. Despite the estimation problems, which can be surmounted, the distributed and autoregressive models have proved extremely useful in empirical economics because they make the otherwise static economic theory a dynamic one by taking into account explicitly the role of time. Such models help us to distinguish between the short- and the long-run responses of the dependent variable to a unit change in the value of the explanatory variable(s). Thus, for estimating short- and long-run price, income, substitution, and other elasticities these models have proved to be highly useful.[67]
10. Because of the lags involved, distributed and/or autoregressive models raise the topic of causality in economic variables. In applied work, **Granger causality** modeling has

[67]For applications of these models, see Arnold C. Harberger, ed., *The Demand for Durable Goods,* University of Chicago Press, Chicago, 1960.

received considerable attention. But one has to exercise great caution in using the Granger methodology because it is very sensitive to the lag length used in the model.

11. Even if a variable (X) "Granger-causes" another variable (Y), it does not mean that X is exogenous. We distinguished three types of exogeneity—weak, strong, and super—and pointed out the importance of the distinction.

EXERCISES

Questions

17.1. Explain with a brief reason whether the following statements are true, false, or uncertain:

a. All econometric models are essentially dynamic.

b. The Koyck model will not make much sense if some of the distributed-lag coefficients are positive and some are negative.

c. If the Koyck and adaptive expectations models are estimated by OLS, the estimators will be biased but consistent.

d. In the partial adjustment model, OLS estimators are biased in finite samples.

e. In the presence of a stochastic regressor(s) and an autocorrelated error term, the method of instrumental variables will produce unbiased as well as consistent estimates.

f. In the presence of a lagged regressand as a regressor, the Durbin–Watson d statistic to detect autocorrelation is practically useless.

g. The Durbin h test is valid in both large and small samples.

h. The Granger test is a test of precedence rather than a test of causality.

17.2. Establish Eq. (17.7.2).

17.3. Prove Eq. (17.8.3).

17.4. Assume that prices are formed according to the following adaptive expectations hypothesis:

$$P_t^* = \gamma P_{t-1} + (1 - \gamma) P_{t-1}^*$$

where P^* is the expected price and P the actual price.

Complete the following table, assuming $\gamma = 0.5$:*

Period	P*	P
$t-3$	100	110
$t-2$		125
$t-1$		155
t		185
$t+1$		—

17.5. Consider the model

$$Y_t = \alpha + \beta_1 X_{1t} + \beta_2 X_{2t} + \beta_3 Y_{t-1} + v_t$$

*Adapted from G. K. Shaw, op. cit., p. 26.

Suppose Y_{t-1} and v_t are correlated. To remove the correlation, suppose we use the following instrumental variable approach: First regress Y_t on X_{1t} and X_{2t} and obtain the estimated $\hat{Y}_t$ from this regression. Then regress

$$Y_t = \alpha + \beta_1 X_{1t} + \beta_2 X_{2t} + \beta_3 \hat{Y}_{t-1} + v_t$$

where $\hat{Y}_{t-1}$ are estimated from the first-stage regression.

a. How does this procedure remove the correlation between Y_{t-1} and v_t in the original model?

b. What are the advantages of the recommended procedure over the Liviatan approach?

*17.6. *a.* Establish (17.4.8).

b. Evaluate the median lag for $\lambda = 0.2, 0.4, 0.6, 0.8$.

c. Is there any systematic relationship between the value of λ and the value of the median lag?

17.7. *a.* Prove that for the Koyck model, the mean lag is as shown in Eq. (17.4.10).

b. If λ is relatively large, what are its implications?

17.8. Using the formula for the mean lag given in Eq. (17.4.9), verify the mean lag of 10.959 quarters reported in the illustration of Table 17.1.

17.9. Suppose

$$M_t = \alpha + \beta_1 Y_t^* + \beta_2 R_t^* + u_t$$

where M = demand for real cash balances, Y^* = expected real income, and R^* = expected interest rate. Assume that expectations are formulated as follows:

$$Y_t^* = \gamma_1 Y_t + (1 - \gamma_1) Y_{t-1}^*$$
$$R_t^* = \gamma_2 R_t + (1 - \gamma_2) R_{t-1}^*$$

where γ_1 and γ_2 are coefficients of expectation, both lying between 0 and 1.

a. How would you express M_t in terms of the observable quantities?

b. What estimation problems do you foresee?

*17.10. If you estimate Eq. (17.7.2) by OLS, can you derive estimates of the original parameters? What problems do you foresee? (For details, see Roger N. Waud.)†

17.11. *Serial correlation model.* Consider the following model:

$$Y_t = \alpha + \beta X_t + u_t$$

Assume that u_t follows the Markov first-order autoregressive scheme given in Chapter 12, namely,

$$u_t = \rho u_{t-1} + \varepsilon_t$$

where ρ is the coefficient of (first-order) autocorrelation and where ε_t satisfies all the assumptions of the classical OLS. Then, as shown in Chapter 12, the model

$$Y_t = \alpha(1 - \rho) + \beta(X_t - \rho X_{t-1}) + \rho Y_{t-1} + \varepsilon_t$$

will have a serially independent error term, making OLS estimation possible. But this model, called the **serial correlation model,** very much resembles the Koyck,

*Optional.

†"Misspecification in the 'Partial Adjustment' and 'Adaptive Expectations' Models," *International Economic Review,* vol. 9, no. 2, June 1968, pp. 204–217.

adaptive expectations, and partial adjustment models. How would you know in any given situation which of the preceding models is appropriate?*

17.12. Consider the Koyck (or, for that matter, the adaptive expectations) model given in Eq. (17.4.7), namely,

$$Y_t = \alpha(1-\lambda) + \beta_0 X_t + \lambda Y_{t-1} + (u_t - \lambda u_{t-1})$$

Suppose in the original model u_t follows the first-order autoregressive scheme $u_t - \rho u_{1-t} = \varepsilon_t$, where ρ is the coefficient of autocorrelation and where ε_t satisfies all the classical OLS assumptions.

a. If $\rho = \lambda$, can the Koyck model be estimated by OLS?

b. Will the estimates thus obtained be unbiased? Consistent? Why or why not?

c. How reasonable is it to assume that $\rho = \lambda$?

17.13. *Triangular, or arithmetic, distributed-lag model.*† This model assumes that the stimulus (explanatory variable) exerts its greatest impact in the current time period and then declines by equal decrements to zero as one goes into the distant past. Geometrically, it is shown in Figure 17.9. Following this distribution, suppose we run the following succession of regressions:

$$Y_t = \alpha + \beta\left(\frac{2X_t + X_{t-1}}{3}\right)$$

$$Y_t = \alpha + \beta\left(\frac{3X_t + 2X_{t-1} + X_{t-2}}{6}\right)$$

$$Y_t = \alpha + \beta\left(\frac{4X_t + 3X_{t-1} + 2X_{t-2} + X_{t-1}}{10}\right)$$

etc., and choose the regression that gives the highest R^2 as the "best" regression. Comment on this strategy.

FIGURE 17.9
Triangular or arithmetic lag scheme (Fisher's).

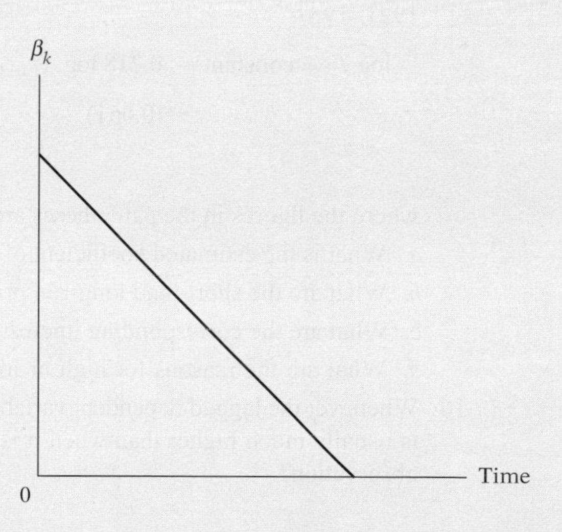

*For a discussion of the serial correlation model, see Zvi Griliches, "Distributed Lags: A Survey," *Econometrica,* vol. 35, no. 1, January 1967, p. 34.

†This model was proposed by Irving Fisher in "Note on a Short-Cut Method for Calculating Distributed Lags," *International Statistical Bulletin,* 1937, pp. 323–328.

17.14. From the quarterly data for the period 1950–1960, F. P. R. Brechling obtained the following demand function for labor for the British economy (the figures in parentheses are standard errors):*

$$\hat{\dot{E}}_t = \underset{(2.61)}{14.22} + \underset{(0.014)}{0.172Q_t} - \underset{(0.015)}{0.028t} - \underset{(0.0002)}{0.0007t^2} - \underset{(0.033)}{0.297E_{t-1}}$$

$$\bar{R}^2 = 0.76 \qquad d = 1.37$$

where $\dot{E}_t = (E_t - E_{t-1})$
Q = output
t = time

The preceding equation was based on the assumption that the desired level of employment E_t^* is a function of output, time, and time squared and on the hypothesis that $E_t - E_{t-1} = \delta(E_t^* - E_{t-1})$, where δ, the coefficient of adjustment, lies between 0 and 1.

a. Interpret the preceding regression.
b. What is the value of δ?
c. Derive the long-run demand function for labor from the estimated short-run demand function.
d. How would you test for serial correlation in the preceding model?

17.15. In studying the farm demand for tractors, Griliches used the following model:†

$$T_t^* = \alpha X_{1,t-1}^{\beta_1} X_{2,t-1}^{\beta_2}$$

where T^* = desired stock of tractors
X_1 = relative price of tractors
X_2 = interest rate

Using the stock adjustment model, he obtained the following results for the period 1921–1957:

$$\widehat{\log T_t} = \text{constant} - \underset{(0.051)}{0.218 \log X_{1,t-1}} - \underset{(0.170)}{0.855 \log X_{2,t-1}} + \underset{(0.035)}{0.864 \log T_{t-1}}$$

$$R^2 = 0.987$$

where the figures in the parentheses are the estimated standard errors.

a. What is the estimated coefficient of adjustment?
b. What are the short- and long-run price elasticities?
c. What are the corresponding interest elasticities?
d. What are the reasons for high or low rate of adjustment in the present model?

17.16. Whenever the lagged dependent variable appears as an explanatory variable, the R^2 is usually much higher than when it is not included. What are the reasons for this observation?

*F. P. R. Brechling, "The Relationship between Output and Employment in British Manufacturing Industries," *Review of Economic Studies,* vol. 32, July 1965.

†Zvi Griliches, "The Demand for a Durable Input: Farm Tractors in the United States, 1921–1957," in Arnold C. Harberger, ed., *The Demand for Durable Goods,* University of Chicago Press, Chicago, 1960.

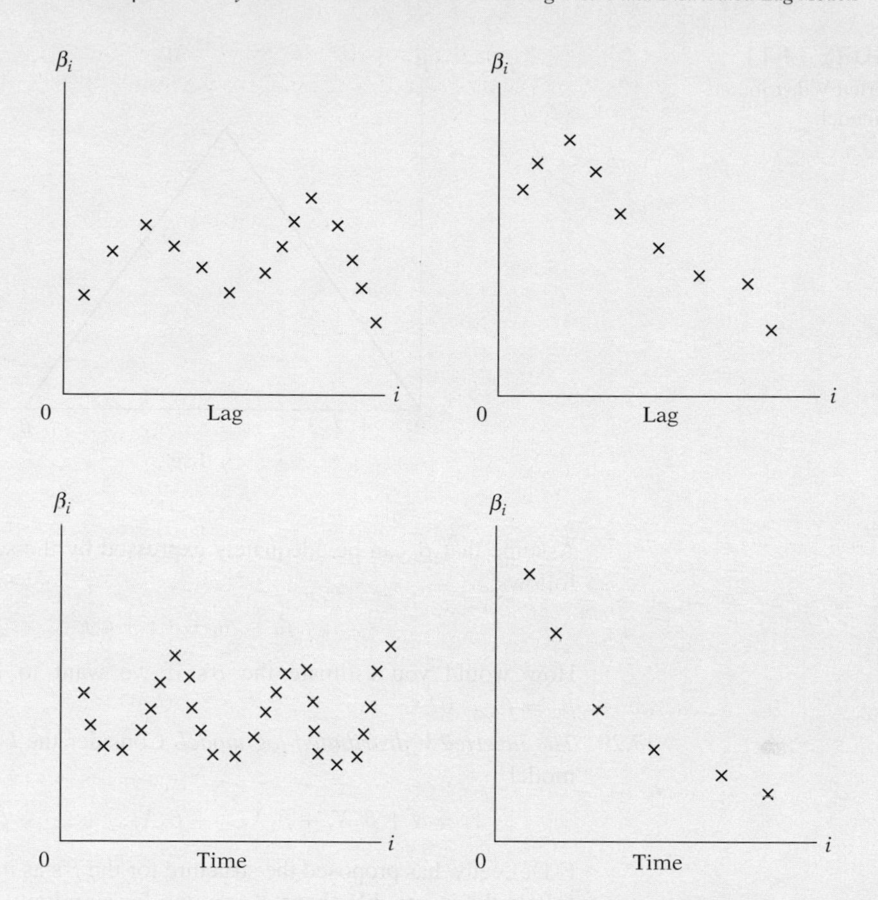

FIGURE 17.10
Hypothetical lag structures.

17.17. Consider the lag patterns in Figure 17.10. What degree polynomials would you fit to the lag structures and why?

17.18. Consider Eq. (17.13.4):

$$\beta_i = a_0 + a_1 i + a_2 i^2 + \cdots + a_m i^m$$

To obtain the variance of $\hat{\beta}_i$ from the variances of $\hat{a}_i$, we use the following formula:

$$\begin{aligned} \text{var}\,(\hat{\beta}_i) &= \text{var}\,(\hat{a}_0 + \hat{a}_1 i + \hat{a}_2 i^2 + \cdots + \hat{a}_m i^m) \\ &= \sum_{j=0}^{m} i^{2j}\,\text{var}\,(\hat{a}_j) + 2\sum_{j<p} i^{(j+p)}\,\text{cov}\,(\hat{a}_j \hat{a}_p) \end{aligned}$$

a. Using the preceding formula, find the variance of $\hat{\beta}_i$ expressed as

$$\hat{\beta}_i = \hat{a}_0 + \hat{a}_1 i + \hat{a}_2 i^2$$
$$\hat{\beta}_i = \hat{a}_0 + \hat{a}_1 i + \hat{a}_2 i^2 + \hat{a}_3 i^3$$

b. If the variances of $\hat{a}_i$ are large relative to themselves, will the variance of $\hat{\beta}_i$ be large also? Why or why not?

17.19. Consider the following distributed-lag model:

$$Y_t = \alpha + \beta_0 X_t + \beta_1 X_{t-1} + \beta_2 X_{t-2} + \beta_3 X_{t-3} + \beta_4 X_{t-4} + u_t$$

FIGURE 17.11
Inverted V distributed-lag model.

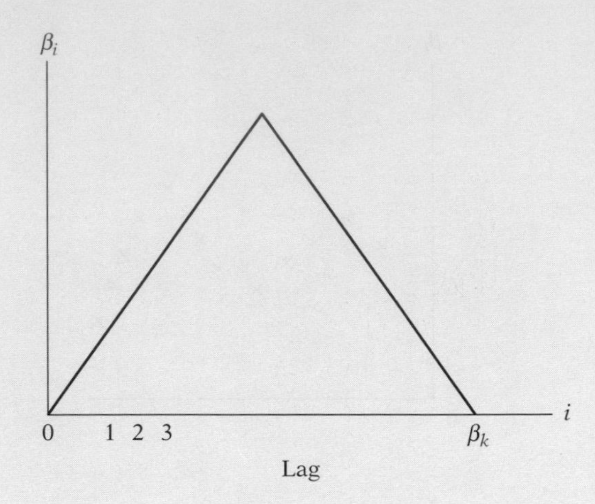

Assume that β_i can be adequately expressed by the second-degree polynomial as follows:

$$\beta_i = a_0 + a_1 i + a_2 i^2$$

How would you estimate the β's if we want to impose the restriction that $\beta_0 = \beta_4 = 0$?

17.20. *The inverted V distributed-lag model.* Consider the k-period finite distributed-lag model

$$Y_t = \alpha + \beta_0 X_t + \beta_1 X_{t-1} + \beta_2 X_{t-2} + \cdots + \beta_k X_{t-k} + u_t$$

F. DeLeeuw has proposed the structure for the β's as in Figure 17.11, where the β's follow the inverted V shape. Assuming for simplicity that k (the maximum length of the lag) is an even number, and further assuming that β_0 and β_k are zero, DeLeeuw suggests the following scheme for the β's:*

$$\begin{aligned} \beta_i &= i\beta & 0 \le i \le \frac{k}{2} \\ &= (k - i)\beta & \frac{k}{2} \le i < k \end{aligned}$$

How would you use the DeLeeuw scheme to estimate the parameters of the preceding k-period distributed-lag model?

17.21. Refer to Exercise 12.15. Since the d value shown there is of little use in detecting (first-order) autocorrelation (why?), how would you test for autocorrelation in this case?

Empirical Exercises

17.22. Consider the following model:

$$Y_i^* = \alpha + \beta_0 X_t + u_t$$

where Y^* = desired, or long-run, business expenditure for new plant and equipment, X_t = sales, and t = time. Using the stock adjustment model, estimate the

*See his article, "The Demand for Capital Goods by Manufacturers: A Study of Quarterly Time Series," *Econometrica*, vol. 30, no. 3, July 1962, pp. 407–423.

TABLE 17.10
Investment in Fixed Plant and Equipment in Manufacturing Y and Manufacturing Sales X_2 in Billions of Dollars, Seasonally Adjusted, United States, 1970–1991

Source: *Economic Report of the President*, 1993. Data on Y from Table B-52, p. 407; data on X_2 from Table 8-53, p. 408.

Year	Plant Expenditure, Y	Sales, X_2	Year	Plant Expenditure, Y	Sales, X_2
1970	36.99	52.805	1981	128.68	168.129
1971	33.60	55.906	1982	123.97	163.351
1972	35.42	63.027	1983	117.35	172.547
1973	42.35	72.931	1984	139.61	190.682
1974	52.48	84.790	1985	152.88	194.538
1975	53.66	86.589	1986	137.95	194.657
1976	58.53	98.797	1987	141.06	206.326
1977	67.48	113.201	1988	163.45	223.541
1978	78.13	126.905	1989	183.80	232.724
1979	95.13	143.936	1990	192.61	239.459
1980	112.60	154.391	1991	182.81	235.142

parameters of the long- and short-run demand function for expenditure on new plant and equipment given in Table 17.10.

How would you find out if there is serial correlation in the data?

17.23. Use the data of Exercise 17.22 but consider the following model:

$$Y_i^* = \beta_0 X_t^{\beta_1} e^{u_t}$$

Using the stock adjustment model (why?), estimate the short- and long-run elasticities of expenditure on new plant and equipment with respect to sales. Compare your results with those for Exercise 17.22. Which model would you choose and why? Is there serial correlation in the data? How do you know?

17.24. Use the data of Exercise 17.22 but assume that

$$Y_t = \alpha + \beta X_t^* + u_t$$

where X_t^* are the desired sales. Estimate the parameters of this model and compare the results with those obtained in Exercise 17.22. How would you decide which is the appropriate model? On the basis of the h statistic, would you conclude there is serial correlation in the data?

17.25. Suppose someone convinces you that the relationship between business expenditure for new plant and equipment and sales is as follows:

$$Y_t^* = \alpha + \beta X_t^* + u_t$$

where Y^* is desired expenditure and X^* is desired or expected sales. Use the data given in Exercise 17.22 to estimate this model and comment on your results.

17.26. Using the data given in Exercise 17.22, determine whether plant expenditure Granger-causes sales or whether sales Granger-cause plant expenditure. Use up to six lags and comment on your results. What important conclusion do you draw from this exercise?

17.27. Assume that sales in Exercise 17.22 has a distributed-lag effect on expenditure on plant and equipment. Fit a suitable Almon lag model to the data.

17.28. Reestimate Eq. (17.13.16) imposing (1) near-end restriction, (2) far-end restriction, and (3) both end restrictions and compare your results given in Eq. (17.13.16). What general conclusion do you draw?

TABLE 17.11 Investments, Sales, and Interest Rate, United States, 1960–1999

Observation	Investment	Sales	Interest	Observation	Investment	Sales	Interest
1960	4.9	60,827	4.41	1980	69.6	327,233	11.94
1961	5.2	61,159	4.35	1981	82.4	355,822	14.17
1962	5.7	65,662	4.33	1982	88.9	347,625	13.79
1963	6.5	68,995	4.26	1983	100.8	369,286	12.04
1964	7.3	73,682	4.40	1984	121.7	410,124	12.71
1965	8.5	80,283	4.49	1985	130.8	422,583	11.37
1966	10.6	87,187	5.13	1986	137.6	430,419	9.02
1967	11.2	90,820	5.51	1987	141.9	457,735	9.38
1968	11.9	96,685	6.18	1988	155.9	497,157	9.71
1969	14.6	105,690	7.03	1989	173.0	527,039	9.26
1970	16.7	108,221	8.04	1990	176.1	545,909	9.32
1971	17.3	116,895	7.39	1991	181.4	542,815	8.77
1972	19.3	131,081	7.21	1992	197.5	567,176	8.14
1973	23.0	153,677	7.44	1993	215.0	595,628	7.22
1974	26.8	177,912	8.57	1994	233.7	639,163	7.96
1975	28.2	182,198	8.83	1995	262.0	684,982	7.59
1976	32.4	204,150	8.43	1996	287.3	718,113	7.37
1977	38.6	229,513	8.02	1997	325.2	753,445	7.26
1978	48.3	260,320	8.73	1998	367.4	779,413	6.53
1979	58.6	297,701	9.63	1999	433.0	833,079	7.04

Notes: Investment = private fixed investment in information processing equipment and software, billions of dollars, seasonally adjusted.
Sales = sales in total manufacturing and trade, millions of dollars, seasonally adjusted.
Interest = Moody's Aaa corporate bond rate, %.

Source: *Economic Report of the President,* 2001, Tables B-18, B-57, and B-73.

17.29. Table 17.11 gives data on private fixed investment in information processing and equipment (Y, in billions of dollars), sales in total manufacturing and trade (X_2, in millions of dollars), and interest rate (X_3, Moody's Aaa corporate bond rate, percent); data on Y and X_2 are seasonally adjusted.

a. Test for bilateral causality between Y and X_2, paying careful attention to the lag length.

b. Test for bilateral causality between Y and X_3, again paying careful attention to the lag length.

c. To allow for the distributed lag effect of sales on investment, suppose you decide to use the Almon lag technique. Show the estimated model, after paying due attention to the length of the lag as well as the degree of the polynomial.

17.30. Table 17.12 gives data on indexes of real compensation per hour (Y) and output per hour (X_2), with both indexes to base 1992 = 100, in the business sector of the U.S. economy for the period 1960–1999, as well as the civilian unemployment rate (X_3) for the same period.

a. How would you decide whether it is wage compensation that determines labor productivity or the other way round?

b. Develop a suitable model to test your conjecture in (*a*), providing the usual statistics.

c. Do you think the unemployment rate has any effect on wage compensation, and if so, how would you take that into account? Show the necessary statistical analysis.

TABLE 17.12 Compensation, Productivity and Unemployment Rate, United States, 1960–1999

Observation	COMP	PRODUCT	UNRate	Observation	COMP	PRODUCT	UNRate
1960	60.0	48.8	5.5	1980	89.5	80.4	7.1
1961	61.8	50.6	6.7	1981	89.5	82.0	7.6
1962	63.9	52.9	5.5	1982	90.9	81.7	9.7
1963	65.4	55.0	5.7	1983	91.0	84.6	9.6
1964	67.9	57.5	5.2	1984	91.3	87.0	7.5
1965	69.4	59.6	4.5	1985	92.7	88.7	7.2
1966	71.9	62.0	3.8	1986	95.8	91.4	7.0
1967	73.8	63.4	3.8	1987	96.3	91.9	6.2
1968	76.3	65.4	3.6	1988	97.3	93.0	5.5
1969	77.4	65.7	3.5	1989	95.9	93.9	5.3
1970	78.9	67.0	4.9	1990	96.5	95.2	5.6
1971	80.4	69.9	5.9	1991	97.5	96.3	6.8
1972	82.7	72.2	5.6	1992	100.0	100.0	7.5
1973	84.5	74.5	4.9	1993	99.9	100.5	6.9
1974	83.5	73.2	5.6	1994	99.7	101.9	6.1
1975	84.4	75.8	8.5	1995	99.3	102.6	5.6
1976	86.8	78.5	7.7	1996	99.7	105.4	5.4
1977	87.9	79.8	7.1	1997	100.4	107.6	4.9
1978	89.5	80.7	6.1	1998	104.3	110.5	4.5
1979	89.7	80.7	5.8	1999	107.3	114.0	4.2

Notes: COMP = index of real compensation per hour (1992 = 100).
PRODUCT = index of output per hour (1992 = 100).
UNRate = civilian unemployment rate, %.

Source: *Economic Report of the President,* 2001, Table B-49, p. 332.

17.31. In a test of Granger causality, Christopher Sims exploits the fact that the future cannot cause the present.* To decide whether a variable Y causes a variable X, Sims suggests estimating the following pair of equations:

$$Y_t = \alpha_1 + \sum_{i=1}^{i=n} \beta_i X_{t-i} + \sum_{i=1}^{i=m} \gamma_i Y_{t-i} + \sum_{i=1}^{i=p} \lambda_i X_{t+i} + u_{1t} \tag{1}$$

$$X_t = \alpha_2 + \sum_{i=1}^{i=n} \delta_i X_{t-i} + \sum_{i=1}^{i=m} \theta_i Y_{t-i} + \sum_{i=1}^{i=p} \omega_i Y_{t+i} + u_{2t} \tag{2}$$

These regressions include the lagged, current, and future, or **lead,** values of the regressors; terms such as X_{t+1}, X_{t+2}, etc., are called **lead terms.**

If Y is to Granger-cause X, then there must be some relationship between Y and the lead, or future, values of X. Therefore, instead of testing that $\Sigma\beta_i = 0$, we should test $\Sigma\lambda_i = 0$ in Eq. (1). If we reject this hypothesis, the causality then runs from Y to X, and not from X to Y, because the future cannot cause the present. Similar comments apply to Equation (2).

*C. A. Sims, "Money, Income, and Causality," *American Economic Review,* vol. 62, 1972, pp. 540–552.

TABLE 17.13
Macroeconomic Data for the Greek Economy, 1960–1995

Source: H. R. Seddighi, K. A. Lawler, and A. V. Katos, *Econometrics: A Practical Approach,* Routledge, London, 2000, p. 158.

Year	PC	PDI	Grossinv	GNP	LTI
1960	107808	117179	29121	145458	8
1961	115147	127599	31476	161802	8
1962	120050	135007	34128	164674	8
1963	126115	142128	35996	181534	8.25
1964	137192	159649	43445	196586	9
1965	147707	172756	49003	214922	9
1966	157687	182366	50567	228040	9
1967	167528	195611	49770	240791	9
1968	179025	204470	60397	257226	8.75
1969	190089	222638	71653	282168	8
1970	206813	246819	70663	304420	8
1971	217212	269249	80558	327723	8
1972	232312	297266	92977	356886	8
1973	250057	335522	100093	383916	9
1974	251650	310231	74500	369325	11.83
1975	266884	327521	74660	390000	11.88
1976	281066	350427	79750	415491	11.5
1977	293928	366730	85950	431164	12
1978	310640	390189	91100	458675	13.46
1979	318817	406857	99121	476048	16.71
1980	319341	401942	92705	485108	21.25
1981	325851	419669	85750	484259	21.33
1982	338507	421716	84100	483879	20.5
1983	339425	417930	83000	481198	20.5
1984	345194	434696	78300	490881	20.5
1985	358671	456576	82360	502258	20.5
1986	361026	439654	77234	507199	20.5
1987	365473	438454	73315	505713	21.82
1988	378488	476345	79831	529460	22.89
1989	394942	492334	87873	546572	23.26
1990	403194	495939	96139	546982	27.62
1991	412458	513173	91726	566586	29.45
1992	420028	502520	93140	568582	28.71
1993	420585	523066	91292	569724	28.56
1994	426893	520728	93073	579846	27.44
1995	433723	518407	98470	588691	23.05

Note: All nominal data are expressed at constant market prices of year 1970 in millions of drachmas. Private disposable income is deflated by the consumption price deflator.

To carry out the Sims test, we estimate Eq. (1) without the lead terms (call it *restricted regression*) and then estimate Eq. (1) with the lead terms (call it *unrestricted regression*). Then we carry out the F test as indicated in Equation (8.7.9). If the F statistic is significant (say, at the 5% level), then we conclude that it is Y that Granger-causes X. Similar comments apply to Equation (2).

Which test do we choose—Granger or Sims? We can apply both tests.* The one factor that is in favor of the Granger test is that it uses fewer degrees of freedom

*The choice between Granger and Sims causality tests is not clear. For further discussion of these tests, see G. Chamberlain, "The General Equivalence of Granger and Sims Causality," *Econometrica,* vol. 50, 1982, pp. 569–582.

because it does not use the lead terms. If the sample is not sufficiently large, we will have to use the Sims test cautiously.

Refer to the data given in Exercise 12.34. For pedagogical purposes, apply the Sims test of causality to determine whether it is sales that causes plant expenditure or vice versa. Use the last four years' data as the lead terms in your analysis.

17.32. Table 17.13 gives some macroeconomic data for the Greek economy for the years 1960–1995.

Consider the following consumption function:

$$\ln \text{PC}_t^* = \beta_1 + \beta_2 \ln \text{PDI}_t + \beta_3 \text{LTI}_t + u_t$$

Where PC_t^* = real desired private consumption expenditure at time t; PDI_t = real private disposable income at time t; LTI_t = long-term interest rate at time t; and ln stands for natural logarithm.

a. From the data given in Table 17.13, estimate the previous consumption function, stating clearly how you measured the real desired private consumption expenditure.

b. What econometric problems did you encounter in estimating the preceding consumption function? How did you resolve them? Explain fully.

17.33. Using the data in Table 17.13, develop a suitable model to explain the behavior of gross real investment in the Greek economy for the period 1960–1995. Look up any textbook on macroeconomics for the accelerator model of investment.

Appendix 17A

17A.1 The Sargan Test for the Validity of Instruments

Suppose we use an instrumental variable(s) to replace an explanatory variable(s) that is correlated with the error term. How valid is the instrumental variable(s), that is, how do we know that the instruments chosen are independent of the error term? Sargan has developed a statistic, dubbed SARG, to test the validity of the instruments used in instrumental variable(s) (IV).* The steps involved in SARG are as follows:†

1. Divide the variables included in a regression equation into two groups, those that are independent of the error term (say, $X_1, X_2, \ldots, X_p$) and those that are not independent of the error term (say, $Z_1, Z_2, \ldots, Z_q$).
2. Let $W_1, W_2, \ldots, W_s$ be the instruments chosen for the Z variables in 1, where $s > q$.
3. Estimate the original regression, replacing the Z's by the W's, that is, estimate the original regression by IV and obtain the residuals, say, $\hat{u}$.
4. Regress $\hat{u}$ on a constant, all the X variables and all the W variables but exclude all the Z variables. Obtain R^2 from this regression.
5. Now compute the SARG statistic, defined as:

$$\text{SARG} = (n - k)R^2 \sim \chi^2_{s-q} \tag{17A.1.1}$$

*J. D. Sargan, "Wages and Prices in the United Kingdom: A Study in Econometric Methodology," in P. E. Hart, G. Mills, and J. K. Whitaker (eds.) *Econometric Analysis for National Economic Planning,* Butterworths, London, 1964.

†The following discussion leans on H. R. Seddighi, K. A. Lawler, and A. V. Katos, *Econometrics: A Practical Approach,* Routledge, New York, 2000, pp. 155–156.

Where $n =$ the number of observations and k is the number of coefficients in the original regression equation. Under the null hypothesis that the instruments are exogenous, Sargan has shown the SARG test asymptotically has the χ^2 distribution with $(s - q)$ degrees of freedom, where s is the number of instruments (i.e., the variables in W) and q is the number of regressors in the original equation. If the computed chi-square value in an application is statistically significant, we reject the validity of the instruments. If it is not statistically significant, we can accept the chosen instrument as valid. It should be emphasized that $s > q$, that is, the number of instruments must be greater than q. If that is not the case (i.e., $s \leq q$), the SARG test is not valid.

6. The null hypothesis is that all (W) instruments are valid. If the computed chi-square exceeds the critical chi-square value, we reject the null hypothesis, which means that at least one instrument is correlated with the error term and therefore the IV estimates based on the chosen instruments are not valid.

Simultaneous-Equation Models and Time Series Econometrics

Part 4

A casual look at the published empirical work in business and economics will reveal that many economic relationships are of the single-equation type. That is why we devoted the first three parts of this book to the discussion of single-equation regression models. In such models, one variable (the dependent variable Y) is expressed as a linear function of one or more other variables (the explanatory variables, the X's). In such models an implicit assumption is that the cause-and-effect relationship, if any, between Y and the X's is unidirectional: The explanatory variables are the *cause* and the dependent variable is the *effect.*

However, there are situations where there is a two-way flow of influence among economic variables; that is, one economic variable affects another economic variable(s) and is, in turn, affected by it (them). Thus, in the regression of money M on the rate of interest r, the single-equation methodology assumes implicitly that the rate of interest is fixed (say, by the Federal Reserve System) and tries to find out the response of money demanded to the changes in the level of the interest rate. But what happens if the rate of interest depends on the demand for money? In this case, the conditional regression analysis made in this book thus far may not be appropriate because now M depends on r and r depends on M. Thus, we need to consider two equations, one relating M to r and another relating r to M. And this leads us to consider simultaneous-equation models, models in which there is more than one regression equation, one for each interdependent variable.

In **Part 4** we present a very elementary and often heuristic introduction to the complex subject of **simultaneous-equation models,** the details being left for the references.

In Chapter 18, we provide several examples of simultaneous-equation models and show why the method of ordinary least squares considered previously is generally inapplicable in estimating the parameters of each of the equations in the model.

In Chapter 19, we consider the so-called **identification problem.** If in a system of simultaneous equations containing two or more equations it is not possible to obtain numerical values of each parameter in each equation because the equations are *observationally indistinguishable,* or look too much like one another, then we have the identification problem. Thus, in the regression of quantity Q on price P, is the resulting equation a demand function or a supply function (for Q and P enter into both functions)? Therefore, if we have data on Q and P only and no other information, it will be difficult if not impossible to identify the regression as the demand or supply function. It is essential to resolve the identification problem before we proceed to estimation because if we do not know what we are estimating, estimation per se is meaningless. In Chapter 19 we offer various methods of solving the identification problem.

In Chapter 20, we consider several estimation methods that are designed specifically for estimating the simultaneous-equation models and consider their merits and limitations.

Chapter 18

Simultaneous-Equation Models

In this and the following two chapters we discuss the simultaneous-equation models. In particular, we discuss their special features, their estimation, and some of the statistical problems associated with them.

18.1 The Nature of Simultaneous-Equation Models

In **Parts 1** to **3** of this text we were concerned exclusively with single-equation models, i.e., models in which there was a single dependent variable Y and one or more explanatory variables, the X's. In such models the emphasis was on estimating and/or predicting the average value of Y conditional upon the fixed values of the X variables. The cause-and-effect relationship, if any, in such models therefore ran from the X's to the Y.

But in many situations, such a one-way or unidirectional cause-and-effect relationship is not meaningful. This occurs if Y is determined by the X's, and some of the X's are, in turn, determined by Y. In short, there is a two-way, or simultaneous, relationship between Y and (some of) the X's, which makes the distinction between *dependent* and *explanatory* variables of dubious value. It is better to lump together a set of variables that can be determined simultaneously by the remaining set of variables—precisely what is done in simultaneous-equation models. In such models there is more than one equation—one for each of the *mutually,* or *jointly,* dependent or **endogenous variables.**[1] And unlike the single-equation models, in the simultaneous-equation models one may not estimate the parameters of a single equation without taking into account information provided by other equations in the system.

What happens if the parameters of each equation are estimated by applying, say, the method of ordinary least squares (OLS), disregarding other equations in the system? Recall that one of the crucial assumptions of the method of OLS is that the explanatory X variables are either nonstochastic or, if stochastic (random), distributed independently of the stochastic disturbance term. If neither of these conditions is met, then, as shown later, the least-squares estimators are not only biased but also inconsistent; that is, as the sample size

[1] In the context of the simultaneous-equation models, the jointly dependent variables are called **endogenous variables** and the variables that are truly nonstochastic or can be so regarded are called the **exogenous,** or **predetermined, variables.** (More on this in Chapter 19.)

increases indefinitely, the estimators do not converge to their true (population) values. Thus, in the following hypothetical system of equations,[2]

$$Y_{1i} = \beta_{10} + \beta_{12} Y_{2i} + \gamma_{11} X_{1i} + u_{1i} \quad (18.1.1)$$

$$Y_{2i} = \beta_{20} + \beta_{21} Y_{1i} + \gamma_{21} X_{1i} + u_{2i} \quad (18.1.2)$$

where Y_1 and Y_2 are mutually dependent, or endogenous, variables and X_1 is an exogenous variable and where u_1 and u_2 are the stochastic disturbance terms, the variables Y_1 and Y_2 are both stochastic. Therefore, unless it can be shown that the stochastic explanatory variable Y_2 in Eq. (18.1.1) is distributed independently of u_1 and the stochastic explanatory variable Y_1 in Eq. (18.1.2) is distributed independently of u_2, application of the classical OLS to these equations individually will lead to inconsistent estimates.

In the remainder of this chapter we give a few examples of simultaneous-equation models and show the bias involved in the direct application of the least-squares method to such models. After discussing the so-called identification problem in Chapter 19, in Chapter 20 we discuss some of the special methods developed to handle the simultaneous-equation models.

18.2 Examples of Simultaneous-Equation Models

EXAMPLE 18.1

Demand-and-Supply Model

As is well known, the price P of a commodity and the quantity Q sold are determined by the intersection of the demand-and-supply curves for that commodity. Thus, assuming for simplicity that the demand-and-supply curves are linear and adding the stochastic disturbance terms u_1 and u_2, we may write the empirical demand-and-supply functions as:

$$\text{Demand function:} \quad Q_t^d = \alpha_0 + \alpha_1 P_t + u_{1t} \quad \alpha_1 < 0 \quad (18.2.1)$$

$$\text{Supply function:} \quad Q_t^s = \beta_0 + \beta_1 P_t + u_{2t} \quad \beta_1 > 0 \quad (18.2.2)$$

$$\text{Equilibrium condition:} \quad Q_t^d = Q_t^s$$

where Q^d = quantity demanded
Q^s = quantity supplied
t = time

and the α's and β's are the parameters. A priori, α_1 is expected to be negative (downward-sloping demand curve), and β_1 is expected to be positive (upward-sloping supply curve).

Now it is not too difficult to see that P and Q are jointly dependent variables. If, for example, u_{1t} in Eq. (18.2.1) changes because of changes in other variables affecting Q_t^d (such as income, wealth, and tastes), the demand curve will shift upward if u_{1t} is positive and downward if u_{1t} is negative. These shifts are shown in Figure 18.1.

As the figure shows, a shift in the demand curve changes both P and Q. Similarly, a change in u_{2t} (because of strikes, weather, import or export restrictions, etc.) will shift the supply curve, again affecting both P and Q. Because of this simultaneous dependence between Q and P, u_{1t} and P_t in Eq. (18.2.1) and u_{2t} and P_t in Eq. (18.2.2) cannot be independent. Therefore, a regression of Q on P as in Eq. (18.2.1) would violate an important assumption of the classical linear regression model, namely, the assumption of no correlation between the explanatory variable(s) and the disturbance term.

[2] These economical but self-explanatory notations will be generalized to more than two equations in Chapter 19.

EXAMPLE 18.1
(Continued)

FIGURE 18.1 Interdependence of price and quantity.

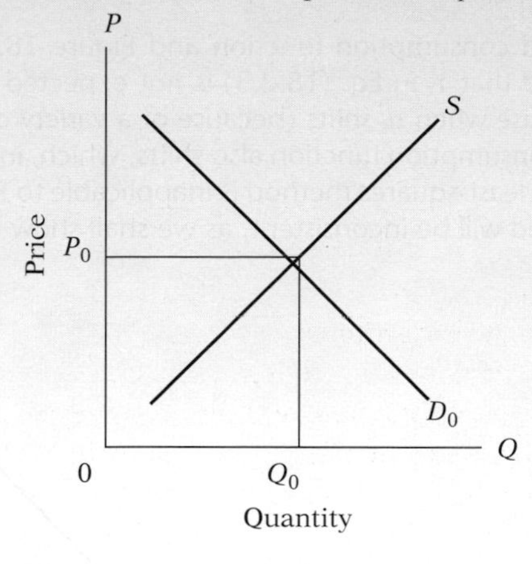

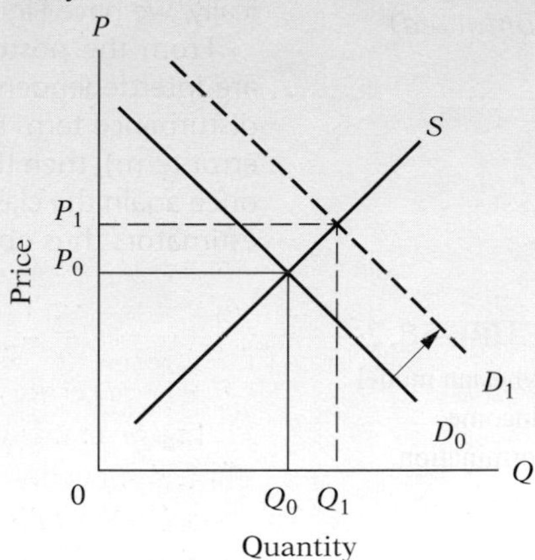

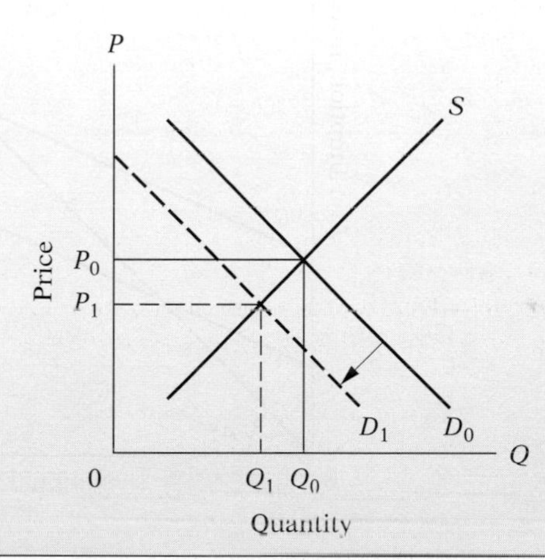

EXAMPLE 18.2
Keynesian Model of Income Determination

Consider the simple Keynesian model of income determination:

$$\text{Consumption function:} \quad C_t = \beta_0 + \beta_1 Y_t + u_t \qquad 0 < \beta_1 < 1 \qquad \textbf{(18.2.3)}$$

$$\text{Income identity:} \quad Y_t = C_t + I_t (= S_t) \qquad \textbf{(18.2.4)}$$

where C = consumption expenditure
Y = income
I = investment (assumed exogenous)
S = savings
t = time
u = stochastic disturbance term
β_0 and β_1 = parameters

The parameter β_1 is known as the *marginal propensity to consume* (MPC) (the amount of extra consumption expenditure resulting from an extra dollar of income). From economic theory, β_1 is expected to lie between 0 and 1. Equation (18.2.3) is the (stochastic) consumption function; and Eq. (18.2.4) is the national income identity, signifying that total income is equal to total consumption expenditure plus total investment expenditure, it

(Continued)

EXAMPLE 18.2 *(Continued)*

being understood that total investment expenditure is equal to total savings. Diagrammatically, we have Figure 18.2.

From the postulated consumption function and Figure 18.2 it is clear that C and Y are interdependent and that Y_t in Eq. (18.2.3) is not expected to be independent of the disturbance term because when u_t shifts (because of a variety of factors subsumed in the error term), then the consumption function also shifts, which, in turn, affects Y_t. Therefore, once again the classical least-squares method is inapplicable to Eq. (18.2.3). If applied, the estimators thus obtained will be inconsistent, as we shall show later.

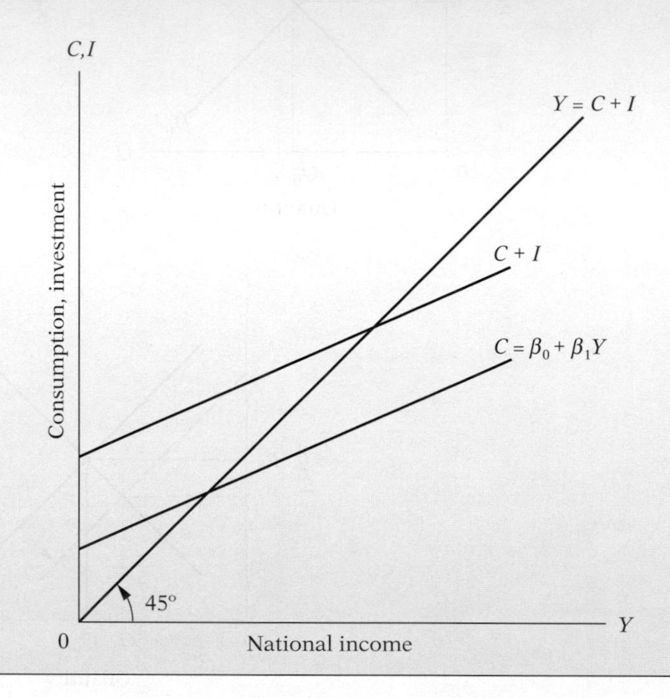

FIGURE 18.2 Keynesian model of income determination.

EXAMPLE 18.3 *Wage–Price Models*

Consider the following Phillips-type model of money-wage and price determination:

$$\dot{W}_t = \alpha_0 + \alpha_1 \text{UN}_t + \alpha_2 \dot{P}_t + u_{1t} \tag{18.2.5}$$

$$\dot{P}_t = \beta_0 + \beta_1 \dot{W}_t + \beta_2 \dot{R}_t + \beta_3 \dot{M}_t + u_{2t} \tag{18.2.6}$$

where $\dot{W}$ = rate of change of money wages
UN = unemployment rate, %
$\dot{P}$ = rate of change of prices
$\dot{R}$ = rate of change of cost of capital
$\dot{M}$ = rate of change of price of imported raw material
t = time
u_1, u_2 = stochastic disturbances

Since the price variable $\dot{P}$ enters into the wage equation and the wage variable $\dot{W}$ enters into the price equation, the two variables are jointly dependent. Therefore, these stochastic explanatory variables are expected to be correlated with the relevant stochastic disturbances, once again rendering the classical OLS method inapplicable to estimate the parameters of the two equations individually.

EXAMPLE 18.4
The IS Model of Macroeconomics

The celebrated IS, or goods market equilibrium, model of macroeconomics[3] in its nonstochastic form can be expressed as:

Consumption function:	$C_t = \beta_0 + \beta_1 Y_{dt}$	$0 < \beta_1 < 1$	**(18.2.7)**
Tax function:	$T_t = \alpha_0 + \alpha_1 Y_t$	$0 < \alpha_1 < 1$	**(18.2.8)**
Investment function:	$I_t = \gamma_0 + \gamma_1 r_t$		**(18.2.9)**
Definition:	$Y_{dt} = Y_t - T_t$		**(18.2.10)**
Government expenditure:	$G_t = \bar{G}$		**(18.2.11)**
National income identity:	$Y_t = C_t + I_t + G_t$		**(18.2.12)**

where Y = national income
C = consumption spending
I = planned or desired net investment
$\bar{G}$ = given level of government expenditure
T = taxes
Y_d = disposable income
r = interest rate

If you substitute Eqs. (18.2.10) and (18.2.8) into Eq. (18.2.7) and substitute the resulting equation for C and Eqs. (18.2.9) and (18.2.11) into Eq. (18.2.12), you should obtain the IS equation:

$$Y_t = \pi_0 + \pi_1 r_t \tag{18.2.13}$$

where

$$\pi_0 = \frac{\beta_0 - \alpha_0\beta_1 + \gamma_0 + \bar{G}}{1 - \beta_1(1 - \alpha_1)}$$
$$\pi_1 = \frac{1}{1 - \beta_1(1 - \alpha_1)} \tag{18.2.14}$$

Equation (18.2.13) is the equation of the IS, or goods market equilibrium, that is, it gives the combinations of the interest rate and level of income such that the goods market clears or is in equilibrium. Geometrically, the IS curve is shown in Figure 18.3.

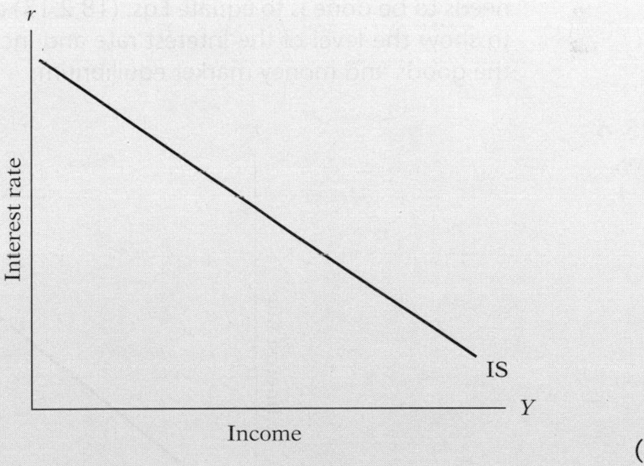

FIGURE 18.3 The IS curve.

(*Continued*)

[3]"The goods market equilibrium schedule, or IS schedule, shows combinations of interest rates and levels of output such that planned spending equals income." See Rudiger Dornbusch and Stanley Fischer, *Macroeconomics*, 3d ed., McGraw-Hill, New York, 1984, p. 102. Note that for simplicity we have assumed away the foreign trade sector.

EXAMPLE 18.4
(Continued)

What would happen if we were to estimate, say, the consumption function (18.2.7) in isolation? Could we obtain unbiased and/or consistent estimates of β_0 and β_1? Such a result is unlikely because consumption depends on disposable income, which depends on national income Y, but the latter depends on r and $\bar{G}$ as well as the other parameters entering in π_0. Therefore, unless we take into account all these influences, a simple regression of C on Y_d is bound to give biased and/or inconsistent estimates of β_0 and β_1.

EXAMPLE 18.5
The LM Model

The other half of the famous IS–LM paradigm is the LM, or money market equilibrium, relation, which gives the combinations of the interest rate and level of income such that the money market is cleared, that is, the demand for money is equal to its supply. Algebraically, the model, in the nonstochastic form, may be expressed as:

$$\text{Money demand function:} \quad M_t^d = a + bY_t - cr_t \tag{18.2.15}$$

$$\text{Money supply function:} \quad M_t^s = \bar{M} \tag{18.2.16}$$

$$\text{Equilibrium condition:} \quad M_t^d = M_t^s \tag{18.2.17}$$

where Y = income, r = interest rate, and $\bar{M}$ = assumed level of money supply, say, determined by the Fed.

Equating the money demand and supply functions and simplifying, we obtain the LM equation:

$$Y_t = \lambda_0 + \lambda_1 \bar{M} + \lambda_2 r_t \tag{18.2.18}$$

where

$$\begin{aligned} \lambda_0 &= -a/b \\ \lambda_1 &= 1/b \\ \lambda_2 &= c/b \end{aligned} \tag{18.2.19}$$

For a given $M = \bar{M}$, the LM curve representing the relation (18.2.18) is as shown in Figure 18.4.

The IS and LM curves show, respectively, that a whole array of interest rates is consistent with goods market equilibrium and a whole array of interest rates is compatible with equilibrium in the money market. Of course, only one interest rate and one level of income will be consistent simultaneously with the two equilibria. To obtain these, all that needs to be done is to equate Eqs. (18.2.13) and (18.2.18). In Exercise 18.4 you are asked to show the level of the interest rate and income that is simultaneously compatible with the goods and money market equilibrium.

FIGURE 18.4
The LM curve.

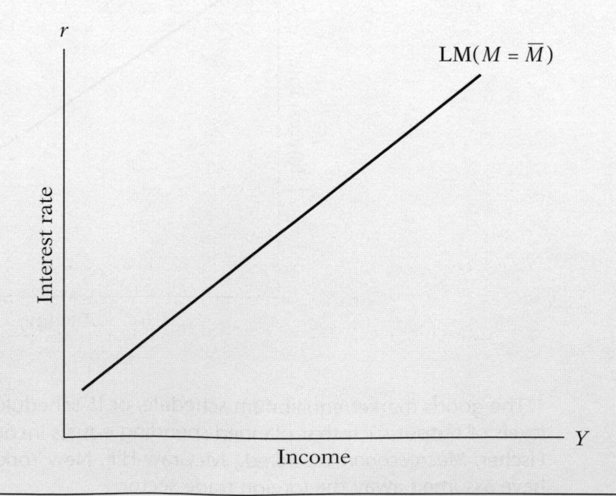

EXAMPLE 18.6
Econometric Models

An extensive use of simultaneous-equation models has been made in the econometric models built by several econometricians. An early pioneer in this field was Professor Lawrence Klein of the Wharton School of the University of Pennsylvania. His initial model, known as **Klein's model I**, is as follows:

$$\begin{aligned}
&\textit{Consumption function:} && C_t = \beta_0 + \beta_1 P_t + \beta_2 (W + W')_t + \beta_3 P_{t-1} + u_{1t} \\
&\textit{Investment function:} && I_t = \beta_4 + \beta_5 P_t + \beta_6 P_{t-1} + \beta_7 K_{t-1} + u_{2t} \\
&\textit{Demand for labor:} && W_t = \beta_8 + \beta_9 (Y + T - W')_t \\
& && \qquad + \beta_{10}(Y + T - W')_{t-1} + \beta_{11} t + u_{3t} \\
&\textit{Identity:} && Y_t + T_t = C_t + I_t + G_t \\
&\textit{Identity:} && Y_t = W_t' + W_t + P_t \\
&\textit{Identity:} && K_t = K_{t-1} + I_t
\end{aligned} \tag{18.2.20}$$

where
C = consumption expenditure
I = investment expenditure
G = government expenditure
P = profits
W = private wage bill
W' = government wage bill
K = capital stock
T = taxes
Y = income after tax
t = time
u_1, u_2, and u_3 = stochastic disturbances[4]

In the preceding model the variables C, I, W, Y, P, and K are treated as jointly dependent, or endogenous, variables and the variables P_{t-1}, K_{t-1}, and Y_{t-1} are treated as predetermined.[5] In all, there are six equations (including the three identities) to study the interdependence of six endogenous variables.

In Chapter 20 we shall see how such econometric models are estimated. For the time being, note that because of the interdependence among the endogenous variables, in general they are not independent of the stochastic disturbance terms, which therefore makes it inappropriate to apply the method of OLS to an individual equation in the system. As shown in Section 18.3, the estimators thus obtained are inconsistent; they do not converge to their true population values even when the sample size is very large.

18.3 The Simultaneous-Equation Bias: Inconsistency of OLS Estimators

As stated previously, the method of least squares may not be applied to estimate a single equation embedded in a system of simultaneous equations if one or more of the explanatory variables are correlated with the disturbance term in that equation because the estimators thus obtained are inconsistent. To show this, let us revert to the simple Keynesian

[4] L. R. Klein, *Economic Fluctuations in the United States, 1921–1941*, John Wiley & Sons, New York, 1950.

[5] The model builder will have to specify which of the variables in a model are endogenous and which are predetermined. K_{t-1} and Y_{t-1} are predetermined because at time t their values are known. (More on this in Chapter 19.)

model of income determination given in Example 18.2. Suppose that we want to estimate the parameters of the consumption function (18.2.3). Assuming that $E(u_t) = 0$, $E(u_t^2) = \sigma^2$, $E(u_t u_{t+j}) = 0$ (for $j \neq 0$), and $\text{cov}(I_t, u_t) = 0$, which are the assumptions of the classical linear regression model, we first show that Y_t and u_t in (18.2.3) are correlated and then prove that $\hat{\beta}_1$ is an inconsistent estimator of β_1.

To prove that Y_t and u_t are correlated, we proceed as follows. Substitute Eq. (18.2.3) into Eq. (18.2.4) to obtain

$$Y_t = \beta_0 + \beta_1 Y_t + u_t + I_t$$

that is,

$$Y_t = \frac{\beta_0}{1-\beta_1} + \frac{1}{1-\beta_1} I_t + \frac{1}{1-\beta_1} u_t \tag{18.3.1}$$

Now

$$E(Y_t) = \frac{\beta_0}{1-\beta_1} + \frac{1}{1-\beta_1} I_t \tag{18.3.2}$$

where use is made of the fact that $E(u_t) = 0$ and that I_t being exogenous, or predetermined (because it is fixed in advance), has as its expected value I_t.

Therefore, subtracting Eq. (18.3.2) from Eq. (18.3.1) results in

$$Y_t - E(Y_t) = \frac{u_t}{1-\beta_1} \tag{18.3.3}$$

Moreover,

$$u_t - E(u_t) = u_t \qquad \text{(Why?)} \tag{18.3.4}$$

whence

$$\begin{aligned} \text{cov}(Y_t, u_t) &= E[Y_t - E(Y_t)][u_t - E(u_t)] \\ &= \frac{E(u_t^2)}{1-\beta_1} \qquad \text{from Eqs. (18.3.3) and (18.3.4)} \\ &= \frac{\sigma^2}{1-\beta_1} \end{aligned} \tag{18.3.5}$$

Since σ^2 is positive by assumption (why?), the covariance between Y and u given in Eq. (18.3.5) is bound to be different from zero.[6] As a result, Y_t and u_t in Eq. (18.2.3) are expected to be correlated, which violates the assumption of the classical linear regression model that the disturbances are independent or at least uncorrelated with the explanatory variables. As noted previously, the OLS estimators in this situation are inconsistent.

To show that the OLS estimator $\hat{\beta}_1$ is an inconsistent estimator of β_1 because of correlation between Y_t and u_t, we proceed as follows:

$$\begin{aligned} \hat{\beta}_1 &= \frac{\sum (C_t - \bar{C})(Y_t - \bar{Y})}{\sum (Y_t - \bar{Y})^2} \\ &= \frac{\sum c_t y_t}{\sum y_t^2} \\ &= \frac{\sum C_t y_t}{\sum y_t^2} \end{aligned} \tag{18.3.6}$$

[6] It will be greater than zero as long as β_1, the MPC, lies between 0 and 1, and it will be negative if β_1 is greater than unity. Of course, a value of MPC greater than unity would not make much economic sense. In reality therefore the covariance between Y_t and u_t is expected to be positive.

where the lowercase letters, as usual, indicate deviations from the (sample) mean values. Substituting for C_t from Eq. (18.2.3), we obtain

$$\begin{aligned}\hat{\beta}_1 &= \frac{\sum(\beta_0 + \beta_1 Y_t + u_t)y_t}{\sum y_t^2} \\ &= \beta_1 + \frac{\sum y_t u_t}{\sum y_t^2}\end{aligned} \tag{18.3.7}$$

where in the last step use is made of the fact that $\sum y_t = 0$ and $(\sum Y_t y_t / \sum y_t^2) = 1$ (why?).

If we take the expectation of Eq. (18.3.7) on both sides, we obtain

$$E(\hat{\beta}_1) = \beta_1 + E\left[\frac{\sum y_t u_t}{\sum y_t^2}\right] \tag{18.3.8}$$

Unfortunately, we cannot evaluate $E(\sum y_t u_t / \sum y_t^2)$ since the expectations operator is a linear operator. [*Note:* $E(A/B) \neq E(A)/E(B)$.] But intuitively it should be clear that unless the term $(\sum y_t u_t / \sum y_t^2)$ is zero, $\hat{\beta}_1$ is a biased estimator of β_1. But have we not shown in Eq. (18.3.5) that the covariance between Y and u is nonzero and therefore would $\hat{\beta}_1$ not be biased? The answer is, not quite, since cov (Y_t, u_t), a population concept, is not quite $\sum y_t u_t$, which is a sample measure, although as the sample size increases indefinitely the latter will tend toward the former. But if the sample size increases indefinitely, then we can resort to the concept of consistent estimator and find out what happens to $\hat{\beta}_1$ as n, the sample size, increases indefinitely. In short, when we cannot explicitly evaluate the expected value of an estimator, as in Eq. (18.3.8), we can turn our attention to its behavior in the large sample.

Now an estimator is said to be consistent if its **probability limit,**[7] or **plim** for short, is equal to its true (population) value. Therefore, to show that $\hat{\beta}_1$ of Eq. (18.3.7) is inconsistent, we must show that its plim is not equal to the true β_1. Applying the rules of probability limit to Eq. (18.3.7), we obtain:[8]

$$\begin{aligned}\text{plim}\,(\hat{\beta}_1) &= \text{plim}\,(\beta_1) + \text{plim}\left(\frac{\sum y_t u_t}{\sum y_t^2}\right) \\ &= \text{plim}\,(\beta_1) + \text{plim}\left(\frac{\sum y_t u_t / n}{\sum y_t^2 / n}\right) \\ &= \beta_1 + \frac{\text{plim}\,(\sum y_t u_t / n)}{\text{plim}\,(\sum y_t^2 / n)}\end{aligned} \tag{18.3.9}$$

where in the second step we have divided $\sum y_t u_t$ and $\sum y_t^2$ by the total number of observations in the sample n so that the quantities in the parentheses are now the sample covariance between Y and u and the sample variance of Y, respectively.

In words, Eq. (18.3.9) states that the probability limit of $\hat{\beta}_1$ is equal to true β_1 plus the ratio of the plim of the sample covariance between Y and u to the plim of the sample variance of Y. Now as the sample size n increases indefinitely, one would expect the sample covariance between Y and u to approximate the true population covariance $E[Y_t - E(Y_t)][u_t - E(u_t)]$, which from Eq. (18.3.5) is equal to $[\sigma^2/(1 - \beta_1)]$. Similarly, as n tends to infinity, the sample

[7]See **Appendix A** for the definition of probability limit.

[8]As stated in **Appendix A,** the plim of a constant (for example, β_1) is the same constant and the plim of $(A/B) = \text{plim}\,(A)/\text{plim}\,(B)$. Note, however, that $E(A/B) \neq E(A)/E(B)$.

variance of Y will approximate its population variance, say σ_Y^2. Therefore, Eq. (18.3.9) may be written as

$$\begin{aligned}\text{plim}\,(\hat{\beta}_1) &= \beta_1 + \frac{\sigma^2/(1-\beta_1)}{\sigma_Y^2} \\ &= \beta_1 + \frac{1}{1-\beta_1}\left(\frac{\sigma^2}{\sigma_Y^2}\right)\end{aligned} \tag{18.3.10}$$

Given that $0 < \beta_1 < 1$ and that σ^2 and σ_Y^2 are both positive, it is obvious from Eq. (18.3.10) that plim $(\hat{\beta}_1)$ will always be greater than β_1; that is, $\hat{\beta}_1$ will overestimate the true β_1.[9] In other words, $\hat{\beta}_1$ is a biased estimator, and the bias will not disappear no matter how large the sample size.

18.4 The Simultaneous-Equation Bias: A Numerical Example

To demonstrate some of the points made in the preceding section, let us return to the simple Keynesian model of income determination given in Example 18.2 and carry out the following **Monte Carlo** study.[10] Assume that the values of investment I are as shown in column 3 of Table 18.1. Further assume that

$$\begin{aligned} E(u_t) &= 0 \\ E(u_t u_{t+j}) &= 0 \qquad (j \neq 0) \\ \text{var}\,(u_t) &= \sigma^2 = 0.04 \\ \text{cov}\,(u_t, I_t) &= 0 \end{aligned}$$

The u_t thus generated are shown in column 4.

For the consumption function (18.2.3) assume that the values of the true parameters are known and are $\beta_0 = 2$ and $\beta_1 = 0.8$.

From the assumed values of β_0 and β_1 and the generated values of u_t we can generate the values of income Y_t from Eq. (18.3.1), which are shown in column 1 of Table 18.1. Once Y_t are known, and knowing β_0, β_1, and u_t, one can easily generate the values of consumption C_t from Eq. (18.2.3). The C's thus generated are given in column 2.

Since the true β_0 and β_1 are known, and since our sample errors are exactly the same as the "true" errors (because of the way we designed the Monte Carlo study), if we use the data of Table 18.1 to regress C_t on Y_t we should obtain $\beta_0 = 2$ and $\beta_1 = 0.8$, if OLS were unbiased. But from Eq. (18.3.7) we know that this will not be the case if the regressor Y_t and the disturbance u_t are correlated. Now it is not too difficult to verify from our data that the (sample) covariance between Y_t and u_t is $\sum y_t u_t = 3.8$ and that $\sum y_t^2 = 184$. Then, as Eq. (18.3.7) shows, we should have

$$\begin{aligned}\hat{\beta}_1 &= \beta_1 + \frac{\sum y_t u_t}{\sum y_t^2} \\ &= 0.8 + \frac{3.8}{184} \\ &= 0.82065\end{aligned} \tag{18.4.1}$$

That is, $\hat{\beta}_1$ is upward-biased by 0.02065.

[9] In general, however, the direction of the bias will depend on the structure of the particular model and the true values of the regression coefficients.

[10] This is borrowed from Kenneth J. White, Nancy G. Horsman, and Justin B. Wyatt, *SHAZAM: Computer Handbook for Econometrics for Use with Basic Econometrics*, McGraw-Hill, New York, 1985, pp. 131–134.

TABLE 18.1

Y_t (1)	C_t (2)	I_t (3)	u_t (4)
18.15697	16.15697	2.0	−0.3686055
19.59980	17.59980	2.0	−0.8004084E-01
21.93468	19.73468	2.2	0.1869357
21.55145	19.35145	2.2	0.1102906
21.88427	19.48427	2.4	−0.2314535E-01
22.42648	20.02648	2.4	0.8529544E-01
25.40940	22.80940	2.6	0.4818807
22.69523	20.09523	2.6	−0.6095481E-01
24.36465	21.56465	2.8	0.7292983E-01
24.39334	21.59334	2.8	0.7866819E-01
24.09215	21.09215	3.0	−0.1815703
24.87450	21.87450	3.0	−0.2509900E-01
25.31580	22.11580	3.2	−0.1368398
26.30465	23.10465	3.2	0.6092946E-01
25.78235	22.38235	3.4	−0.2435298
26.08018	22.68018	3.4	−0.1839638
27.24440	23.64440	3.6	−0.1511200
28.00963	24.40963	3.6	0.1926739E-02
30.89301	27.09301	3.8	0.3786015
28.98706	25.18706	3.8	−0.2588852E-02

Source: Kenneth J. White, Nancy G. Horsman, and Justin B. Wyatt, *SHAZAM: Computer Handbook for Econometrics for Use with Damodar Gujarati: Basic Econometrics,* September 1985, p. 132.

Now let us regress C_t on Y_t, using the data given in Table 18.1. The regression results are

$$\begin{aligned} \hat{C}_t &= 1.4940 + 0.82065Y_t \\ \text{se} &= (0.35413) \quad (0.01434) \\ t &= (4.2188) \quad (57.209) \qquad R^2 = 0.9945 \end{aligned} \tag{18.4.2}$$

As expected, the estimated β_1 is precisely the one predicted by Eq. (18.4.1). In passing, note that the estimated β_0 too is biased.

In general, the amount of the bias in $\hat{\beta}_1$ depends on β_1, σ^2 and var (Y) and, in particular, on the degree of covariance between Y and u.[11] As Kenneth White et al. note, "This is what simultaneous equation bias is all about. In contrast to single equation models, we can no longer assume that variables on the right hand side of the equation are uncorrelated with the error term."[12] Bear in mind that this bias remains even in large samples.

In view of the potentially serious consequences of applying OLS in simultaneous-equation models, is there a test of simultaneity that can tell us whether in a given instance we have the simultaneity problem? One version of the **Hausman specification test** can be used for this purpose, which we discuss in Chapter 19.

[11]See Eq. (18.3.5).

[12]Op. cit., pp. 133–134.

Summary and Conclusions

1. In contrast to single-equation models, in simultaneous-equation models more than one dependent, or **endogenous,** variable is involved, necessitating as many equations as the number of endogenous variables.
2. A unique feature of simultaneous-equation models is that the endogenous variable (i.e., regressand) in one equation may appear as an explanatory variable (i.e., regressor) in another equation of the system.
3. As a consequence, such an **endogenous explanatory variable** becomes stochastic and is usually correlated with the disturbance term of the equation in which it appears as an explanatory variable.
4. In this situation the classical OLS method may not be applied because the estimators thus obtained are not consistent, that is, they do not converge to their true population values no matter how large the sample size.
5. The Monte Carlo example presented in the text shows the nature of the bias involved in applying OLS to estimate the parameters of a regression equation in which the regressor is correlated with the disturbance term, which is typically the case in simultaneous-equation models.
6. Since simultaneous-equation models are used frequently, especially in econometric models, alternative estimating techniques have been developed by various authors. These are discussed in Chapter 20, after the topic of the **identification problem** is considered in Chapter 19, a topic logically prior to estimation.

EXERCISES

Questions

18.1. Develop a simultaneous-equation model for the supply of and demand for dentists in the United States. Specify the endogenous and exogenous variables in the model.

18.2. Develop a simple model of the demand for and supply of money in the United States and compare your model with those developed by K. Brunner and A. H. Meltzer* and R. Tiegen.†

18.3. *a.* For the demand-and-supply model of Example 18.1, obtain the expression for the probability limit of $\hat{\alpha}_1$.

b. Under what conditions will this probability limit be equal to the true α_1?

18.4. For the IS-LM model discussed in the text, find the level of interest rate and income that is simultaneously compatible with the goods and money market equilibrium.

18.5. To study the relationship between inflation and yield on common stock, Bruno Oudet‡ used the following model:

$$R_{bt} = \alpha_1 + \alpha_2 R_{st} + \alpha_3 R_{bt-1} + \alpha_4 L_t + \alpha_5 Y_t + \alpha_6 \text{NIS}_t + \alpha_7 I_t + u_{1t}$$

$$R_{st} = \beta_1 + \beta_2 R_{bt} + \beta_3 R_{bt-1} + \beta_4 L_t + \beta_5 Y_t + \beta_6 \text{NIS}_t + \beta_7 E_t + u_{2t}$$

*"Some Further Evidence on Supply and Demand Functions for Money," *Journal of Finance,* vol. 19, May 1964, pp. 240–283.

†"Demand and Supply Functions for Money in the United States," *Econometrica,* vol. 32, no. 4, October 1964, pp. 476–509.

‡Bruno A. Oudet, "The Variation of the Return on Stocks in Periods of Inflation," *Journal of Financial and Quantitative Analysis,* vol. 8, no. 2, March 1973, pp. 247–258.

where L = real per capita monetary base
Y = real per capita income
I = the expected rate of inflation
NIS = a new issue variable
E = expected end-of-period stock returns, proxied by lagged stock price ratios
R_{bt} = bond yield
R_{st} = common stock returns

a. Offer a theoretical justification for this model and see if your reasoning agrees with that of Oudet.

b. Which are the endogenous variables in the model? Which are the exogenous variables?

c. How would you treat the lagged R_{bt}—endogenous or exogenous?

18.6. In their article, "A Model of the Distribution of Branded Personal Products in Jamaica,"* John U. Farley and Harold J. Levitt developed the following model (the personal products considered were shaving cream, skin cream, sanitary napkins, and toothpaste):

$$Y_{1i} = \alpha_1 + \beta_1 Y_{2i} + \beta_2 Y_{3i} + \beta_3 Y_{4i} + u_{1i}$$
$$Y_{2i} = \alpha_2 + \beta_4 Y_{1i} + \beta_5 Y_{5i} + \gamma_1 X_{1i} + \gamma_2 X_{2i} + u_{2i}$$
$$Y_{3i} = \alpha_3 + \beta_6 Y_{2i} + \gamma_3 X_{3i} + u_{3i}$$
$$Y_{4i} = \alpha_4 + \beta_7 Y_{2i} + \gamma_4 X_{4i} + u_{4i}$$
$$Y_{5i} = \alpha_5 + \beta_8 Y_{2i} + \beta_9 Y_{3i} + \beta_{10} Y_{4i} + u_{5i}$$

where Y_1 = percent of stores stocking the product
Y_2 = sales in units per month
Y_3 = index of direct contact with importer and manufacturer for the product
Y_4 = index of wholesale activity in the area
Y_5 = index of depth of brand stocking for the product (i.e., average number of brands of the product stocked by stores carrying the product)
X_1 = target population for the product
X_2 = income per capita in the parish where the area is
X_3 = distance from the population center of gravity to Kingston
X_4 = distance from population center to nearest wholesale town

a. Can you identify the endogenous and exogenous variables in the preceding model?

b. Can one or more equations in the model be estimated by the method of least squares? Why or why not?

18.7. To study the relationship between advertising expenditure and sales of cigarettes, Frank Bass used the following model:†

$$Y_{1t} = \alpha_1 + \beta_1 Y_{3t} + \beta_2 Y_{4t} + \gamma_1 X_{1t} + \gamma_2 X_{2t} + u_{1t}$$
$$Y_{2t} = \alpha_2 + \beta_3 Y_{3t} + \beta_4 Y_{4t} + \gamma_3 X_{1t} + \gamma_4 X_{2t} + u_{2t}$$
$$Y_{3t} = \alpha_3 + \beta_5 Y_{1t} + \beta_6 Y_{2t} + u_{3t}$$
$$Y_{4t} = \alpha_4 + \beta_7 Y_{1t} + \beta_8 Y_{2t} + u_{4t}$$

**Journal of Marketing Research,* November 1968, pp. 362–368.

†"A Simultaneous Equation Regression Study of Advertising and Sales of Cigarettes," *Journal of Marketing Research,* vol. 6, August 1969, pp. 291–300.

where Y_1 = logarithm of sales of filter cigarettes (number of cigarettes) divided by population over age 20
Y_2 = logarithm of sales of nonfilter cigarettes (number of cigarettes) divided by population over age 20
Y_3 = logarithm of advertising dollars for filter cigarettes divided by population over age 20 divided by advertising price index
Y_4 = logarithm of advertising dollars for nonfilter cigarettes divided by population over age 20 divided by advertising price index
X_1 = logarithm of disposable personal income divided by population over age 20 divided by consumer price index
X_2 = logarithm of price per package of nonfilter cigarettes divided by consumer price index

a. In the preceding model the Y's are endogenous and the X's are exogenous. Why does the author assume X_2 to be exogenous?

b. If X_2 is treated as an endogenous variable, how would you modify the preceding model?

18.8. G. Menges developed the following econometric model for the West German economy:*

$$Y_t = \beta_0 + \beta_1 Y_{t-1} + \beta_2 I_t + u_{1t}$$

$$I_t = \beta_3 + \beta_4 Y_t + \beta_5 Q_t + u_{2t}$$

$$C_t = \beta_6 + \beta_7 Y_t + \beta_8 C_{t-1} + \beta_9 P_t + u_{3t}$$

$$Q_t = \beta_{10} + \beta_{11} Q_{t-1} + \beta_{12} R_t + u_{4t}$$

where Y = national income
I = net capital formation
C = personal consumption
Q = profits
P = cost of living index
R = industrial productivity
t = time
u = stochastic disturbances

a. Which of the variables would you regard as endogenous and which as exogenous?

b. Is there any equation in the system that can be estimated by the single-equation least-squares method?

c. What is the reason behind including the variable P in the consumption function?

18.9. L. E. Gallaway and P. E. Smith developed a simple model for the United States economy, which is as follows:†

$$Y_t = C_t + I_t + G_t$$

$$C_t = \beta_1 + \beta_2 \text{YD}_{t-1} + \beta_3 M_t + u_{1t}$$

$$I_t = \beta_4 + \beta_5 (Y_{t-1} - Y_{t-2}) + \beta_6 Z_{t-1} + u_{2t}$$

$$G_t = \beta_7 + \beta_8 G_{t-1} + u_{3t}$$

*G. Menges, "Ein Ökonometriches Modell der Bundesrepublik Deutschland (Vier Strukturgleichungen)," I.F.O. Studien, vol. 5, 1959, pp. 1–22.

†"A Quarterly Econometric Model of the United States," *Journal of American Statistical Association*, vol. 56, 1961, pp. 379–383.

where Y = gross national product
C = personal consumption expenditure
I = gross private domestic investment
G = government expenditure plus net foreign investment
YD = disposable, or after-tax, income
M = money supply at the beginning of the quarter
Z = property income before taxes
t = time
u_1, u_2, and u_3 = stochastic disturbances

All variables are measured in the first-difference form.

From the quarterly data from 1948–1957, the authors applied the least-squares method to each equation individually and obtained the following results:

$$\hat{C}_t = 0.09 + 0.43\text{YD}_{t-1} + 0.23M_t \qquad R^2 = 0.23$$

$$\hat{I}_t = 0.08 + 0.43(Y_{t-1} - Y_{t-2}) + 0.48Z_t \qquad R^2 = 0.40$$

$$\hat{G}_t = 0.13 + 0.67G_{t-1} \qquad R^2 = 0.42$$

a. How would you justify the use of the single-equation least-squares method in this case?

b. Why are the R^2 values rather low?

Empirical Exercises

18.10. Table 18.2 gives you data on Y (gross domestic product), I (gross private domestic investment), and C (personal consumption expenditure) for the United States for the period 1970–2006. All data are in 1996 billions of dollars. Assume that C is linearly related to Y as in the simple Keynesian model of income determination of Example 18.2. Obtain OLS estimates of the parameters of the consumption function. Save the results for another look at the same data using the methods developed in Chapter 20.

18.11. Using the data given in Exercise 18.10, regress gross domestic investment I on GDP and save the results for further examination in a later chapter.

18.12. Consider the macroeconomics identity

$$C + I = Y \qquad (= \text{GDP})$$

As before, assume that

$$C_t = \beta_0 + \beta_1 Y_t + u_t$$

and, following the **accelerator model** of macroeconomics, let

$$I_t = \alpha_0 + \alpha_1(Y_t - Y_{t-1}) + v_t$$

where u and v are error terms. From the data given in Exercise 18.10, estimate the accelerator model and save the results for further study.

18.13. *Supply and demand for gas.* Table 18.3, found on the textbook website, gives data on some of the variables that determine demand for and supply of gasoline in the U.S. from January 1978 to August 2002.* The variables are: pricegas (cents per

*These data are taken from the website of Stephen J. Schmidt, *Econometrics,* McGraw-Hill, New York, 2005. See www.mhhe.com/economics.

TABLE 18.2 Personal Consumption Expenditure, Gross Private Domestic Investment, and GDP, United States, 1970–2006 (billions of 1996 dollars)

Observation	C	I	Y	Observation	C	I	Y
1970	2,451.9	427.1	3,771.9	1989	4,675.0	926.2	6,981.4
1971	2,545.5	475.7	3,898.6	1990	4,770.3	895.1	7,112.5
1972	2,701.3	532.1	4,105.0	1991	4,778.4	822.2	7,100.5
1973	2,833.8	594.4	4,341.5	1992	4,934.8	889.0	7,336.6
1974	2,812.3	550.6	4,319.6	1993	5,099.8	968.3	7,532.7
1975	2,876.9	453.1	4,311.2	1994	5,290.7	1,099.6	7,835.5
1976	3,035.5	544.7	4,540.9	1995	5,433.5	1,134.0	8,031.7
1977	3,164.1	627.0	4,750.5	1996	5,619.4	1,234.3	8,328.9
1978	3,303.1	702.6	5,015.0	1997	5,831.8	1,387.7	8,703.5
1979	3,383.4	725.0	5,173.4	1998	6,125.8	1,524.1	9,066.9
1980	3,374.1	645.3	5,161.7	1999	6,438.6	1,642.6	9,470.3
1981	3,422.2	704.9	5,291.7	2000	6,739.4	1,735.5	9,817.0
1982	3,470.3	606.0	5,189.3	2001	6,910.4	1,598.4	9,890.7
1983	3,668.6	662.5	5,423.8	2002	7,099.3	1,557.1	10,048.8
1984	3,863.3	857.7	5,813.6	2003	7,295.3	1,613.1	10,301.0
1985	4,064.0	849.7	6,053.7	2004	7,561.4	1,770.2	10,675.8
1986	4,228.9	843.9	6,263.6	2005	7,803.6	1,869.3	11,003.4
1987	4,369.8	870.0	6,475.1	2006	8,044.1	1,919.5	11,319.4
1988	4,546.9	890.5	6,742.7				

Notes: C = personal consumption expenditure.
I = gross private domestic investment.
Y = gross domestic product.

Source: *Economic Report of the President,* 2008, Table B-2.

gallon); quantgas (thousands of barrels per day, unleaded); persincome (personal income, billions of dollars); and car sales (millions of cars per year).

a. Develop a suitable supply-and-demand model for gasoline consumption.

b. Which variables in the model in (*a*) are endogenous and which are exogenous?

c. If you estimate the demand-and-supply functions that you have developed by OLS, will your results be reliable? Why or why not?

d. Save the OLS estimates of your demand-and-supply functions for another look after we discuss Chapter 20.

18.14. Table 18.4, found on the textbook website, gives macroeconomic data on several variables for the U.S. economy for the quarterly periods 1951–I to 2000–IV.* The variables are as follows: *Year* = date; *Qtr* = quarter; *Realgdp* = real GDP (billions of dollars); *Realcons* = real consumption expenditure; *Realinvs* = real investment by private sector; *Realgovt* = real government expenditure; *Realdpi* = real disposable personal income; *CPI_U* = consumer price index; *M*1 = nominal money stock; *Tbilrate* = quarterly average of month-end 90-day T-bill rate; *Pop* = population, millions, interpolate of year-end figures using constant growth rate per quarter; *Infl* = rate of inflation (first observation is missing); and *Realint* = expost real interest rate = *Tbilrate–Infl* (first observation missing).

Using these data, develop a simple macroeconomic model of the U.S. economy. You will be asked to estimate this model in Chapter 20.

*These data are originally from the Department of Commerce, Bureau of Economic Analysis, and from www.economagic.com, and are reproduced from William H. Greene, *Econometric Analysis,* 6th ed., 2008, Table F5.1, p.1083.

Chapter 19

The Identification Problem

In this chapter we consider the nature and significance of the identification problem. The crux of the identification problem is as follows: Recall the demand-and-supply model introduced in Section 18.2. Suppose that we have time series data on Q and P only and no additional information (such as income of the consumer, price prevailing in the previous period, and weather condition). The identification problem then consists in seeking an answer to this question: Given only the data on P and Q, how do we know whether we are estimating the demand function or the supply function? Alternatively, if we *think* we are fitting a demand function, how do we guarantee that it is, in fact, the demand function that we are estimating and not something else?

A moment's reflection will reveal that an answer to the preceding question is necessary before one proceeds to estimate the parameters of our demand function. In this chapter we shall show how the identification problem is resolved. We first introduce a few notations and definitions and then illustrate the identification problem with several examples. This is followed by the rules that may be used to find out whether an equation in a simultaneous-equation model is identified, that is, whether it is the relationship that we are actually estimating, be it the demand or supply function or something else.

19.1 Notations and Definitions

To facilitate our discussion, we introduce the following notations and definitions.

The general M equations model in M endogenous, or jointly dependent, variables may be written as Eq. (19.1.1):

$$\begin{aligned}
Y_{1t} &= \beta_{12}Y_{2t} + \beta_{13}Y_{3t} + \cdots + \beta_{1M}Y_{Mt} \\
&\qquad + \gamma_{11}X_{1t} + \gamma_{12}X_{2t} + \cdots + \gamma_{1K}X_{Kt} + u_{1t} \\
Y_{2t} &= \beta_{21}Y_{1t} + \beta_{23}Y_{3t} + \cdots + \beta_{2M}Y_{Mt} \\
&\qquad + \gamma_{21}X_{1t} + \gamma_{22}X_{2t} + \cdots + \gamma_{2K}X_{Kt} + u_{2t} \\
Y_{3t} &= \beta_{31}Y_{1t} + \beta_{32}Y_{2t} + \cdots + \beta_{3M}Y_{Mt} \\
&\qquad + \gamma_{31}X_{1t} + \gamma_{32}X_{2t} + \cdots + \gamma_{3K}X_{Kt} + u_{3t} \\
&\cdots\cdots\cdots\cdots\cdots\cdots\cdots\cdots\cdots\cdots\cdots\cdots \\
Y_{MT} &= \beta_{M1}Y_{1t} + \beta_{M2}Y_{2t} + \cdots + \beta_{M,M-1}Y_{M-1,t} \\
&\qquad + \gamma_{M1}X_{1t} + \gamma_{M2}X_{2t} + \cdots + \gamma_{MK}X_{Kt} + u_{Mt}
\end{aligned} \tag{19.1.1}$$

where $Y_1, Y_2, \ldots, Y_M = M$ endogenous, or jointly dependent, variables
$X_1, X_2, \ldots, X_K = K$ predetermined variables (one of these X variables may take a value of unity to allow for the intercept term in each equation)
$u_1, u_2, \ldots, u_M = M$ stochastic disturbances
$t = 1, 2, \ldots, T =$ total number of observations
β's = coefficients of the endogenous variables
γ's = coefficients of the predetermined variables

In passing, note that not each and every variable need appear in each equation. As a matter of fact, we see in Section 19.2 that this must not be the case if an equation is to be identified.

As Eq. (19.1.1) shows, the variables entering a simultaneous-equation model are of two types: **endogenous,** that is, those (whose values are) determined within the model; and **predetermined,** that is, those (whose values are) determined outside the model. The endogenous variables are regarded as stochastic, whereas the predetermined variables are treated as nonstochastic.

The predetermined variables are divided into two categories: **exogenous,** current as well as lagged, and **lagged endogenous.** Thus, X_{1t} is a current (present-time) exogenous variable, whereas $X_{1(t-1)}$ is a lagged exogenous variable, with a lag of one time period. $Y_{(t-1)}$ is a lagged endogenous variable with a lag of one time period, but since the value of $Y_{1(t-1)}$ is known at the current time t, it is regarded as nonstochastic, hence, a predetermined variable.[1] In short, current exogenous, lagged exogenous, and lagged endogenous variables are deemed predetermined; their values are not determined by the model in the current time period.

It is up to the model builder to specify which variables are endogenous and which are predetermined. Although (noneconomic) variables, such as temperature and rainfall, are clearly exogenous or predetermined, the model builder must exercise great care in classifying economic variables as endogenous or predetermined: He or she must defend the classification on a priori or theoretical grounds. However, later in the chapter we provide a statistical test of exogeneity.

The equations appearing in (19.1.1) are known as the **structural,** or **behavioral,** equations because they may portray the structure (of an economic model) of an economy or the behavior of an economic agent (e.g., consumer or producer). The β's and γ's are known as the **structural parameters** or **coefficients.**

From the structural equations one can solve for the M endogenous variables and derive the **reduced-form equations** and the associated **reduced-form coefficients. A reduced-form equation is one that expresses an endogenous variable solely in terms of the predetermined variables and the stochastic disturbances.** To illustrate, consider the Keynesian model of income determination encountered in Chapter 18:

Consumption function: $$C_t = \beta_0 + \beta_1 Y_t + u_t \qquad 0 < \beta_1 < 1 \tag{18.2.3}$$

Income identity: $$Y_t = C_t + I_t \tag{18.2.4}$$

In this model C (consumption) and Y (income) are the endogenous variables and I (investment expenditure) is treated as an exogenous variable. Both these equations are structural equations, Eq. (18.2.4) being an identity. As usual, the MPC β_1 is assumed to lie between 0 and 1.

If Eq. (18.2.3) is substituted into Eq. (18.2.4), we obtain, after simple algebraic manipulation,

$$Y_t = \Pi_0 + \Pi_1 I_t + w_t \tag{19.1.2}$$

[1] It is assumed implicitly here that the stochastic disturbances, the u's, are serially uncorrelated. If this is not the case, Y_{t-1} will be correlated with the current period disturbance term u_t. Hence, we cannot treat it as predetermined.

where

$$\Pi_0 = \frac{\beta_0}{1 - \beta_1}$$
$$\Pi_1 = \frac{1}{1 - \beta_1} \tag{19.1.3}$$
$$w_t = \frac{u_t}{1 - \beta_1}$$

Equation (19.1.2) is a **reduced-form equation;** it expresses the endogenous variable Y solely as a function of the exogenous (or predetermined) variable I and the stochastic disturbance term u. Π_0 and Π_1 are the associated **reduced-form coefficients.** Notice that these reduced-form coefficients are nonlinear combinations of the structural coefficient(s).

Substituting the value of Y from Eq. (19.1.2) into C of Eq. (18.2.3), we obtain another reduced-form equation:

$$C_t = \Pi_2 + \Pi_3 I_t + w_t \tag{19.1.4}$$

where

$$\Pi_2 = \frac{\beta_0}{1 - \beta_1} \qquad \Pi_3 = \frac{\beta_1}{1 - \beta_1}$$
$$w_t = \frac{u_t}{1 - \beta_1} \tag{19.1.5}$$

The reduced-form coefficients, such as Π_1 and Π_3, are also known as **impact,** or **short-run, multipliers,** because they measure the immediate impact on the endogenous variable of a unit change in the value of the exogenous variable.[2] If in the preceding Keynesian model the investment expenditure is increased by, say, \$1 and if the MPC is assumed to be 0.8, then from Eq. (19.1.3) we obtain $\Pi_1 = 5$. This result means that increasing the investment by \$1 will immediately (i.e., in the current time period) lead to an increase in income of \$5, that is, a fivefold increase. Similarly, under the assumed conditions, Eq. (19.1.5) shows that $\Pi_3 = 4$, meaning that \$1 increase in investment expenditure will lead immediately to \$4 increase in consumption expenditure.

In the context of econometric models, equations such as Eq. (18.2.4) or $Q_t^d = Q_t^s$ (quantity demanded equal to quantity supplied) are known as the *equilibrium conditions*. Identity (18.2.4) states that aggregate income Y must be equal to aggregate consumption (i.e., consumption expenditure plus investment expenditure). When equilibrium is achieved, the endogenous variables assume their equilibrium values.[3]

Notice an interesting feature of the reduced-form equations. Since only the predetermined variables and stochastic disturbances appear on the right sides of these equations, and since the predetermined variables are assumed to be uncorrelated with the disturbance terms, the OLS method can be applied to estimate the coefficients of the reduced-form equations (the Π's). From the estimated reduced-form coefficients one may estimate the structural coefficients (the β's), as shown later. This procedure is known as **indirect least squares** (ILS), and the estimated structural coefficients are called ILS estimates.

[2]In econometric models the exogenous variables play a crucial role. Very often, such variables are under the direct control of the government. Examples are the rate of personal and corporate taxes, subsidies, unemployment compensation, etc.

[3]For details, see Jan Kmenta, *Elements of Econometrics,* 2d ed., Macmillan, New York, 1986, pp. 723–731.

We shall study the ILS method in greater detail in Chapter 20. In the meantime, note that since the reduced-form coefficients can be estimated by the OLS method, and since these coefficients are combinations of the structural coefficients, the possibility exists that the structural coefficients can be "retrieved" from the reduced-form coefficients, and it is in the estimation of the structural parameters that we may be ultimately interested. How does one retrieve the structural coefficients from the reduced-form coefficients? The answer is given in Section 19.2, an answer that brings out the crux of the identification problem.

19.2 The Identification Problem

By the **identification problem** we mean whether numerical estimates of the parameters of a structural equation can be obtained from the estimated reduced-form coefficients. If this can be done, we say that the particular equation is *identified*. If this cannot be done, then we say that the equation under consideration is *unidentified,* or *underidentified.*

An identified equation may be either *exactly* (or fully or just) *identified* or *overidentified*. It is said to be exactly identified if unique numerical values of the structural parameters can be obtained. It is said to be overidentified if more than one numerical value can be obtained for some of the parameters of the structural equations. The circumstances under which each of these cases occurs will be shown in the following discussion.

The identification problem arises because different sets of structural coefficients may be compatible with the same set of data. To put the matter differently, a given reduced-form equation may be compatible with different structural equations or different hypotheses (models), and it may be difficult to tell which particular hypothesis (model) we are investigating. In the remainder of this section we consider several examples to show the nature of the identification problem.

Underidentification

Consider once again the demand-and-supply model (18.2.1) and (18.2.2), together with the market-clearing, or equilibrium, condition that demand is equal to supply. By the equilibrium condition, we obtain

$$\alpha_0 + \alpha_1 P_t + u_{1t} = \beta_0 + \beta_1 P_t + u_{2t} \tag{19.2.1}$$

Solving Eq. (19.2.1), we obtain the equilibrium price

$$P_t = \Pi_0 + v_t \tag{19.2.2}$$

where

$$\Pi_0 = \frac{\beta_0 - \alpha_0}{\alpha_1 - \beta_1} \tag{19.2.3}$$

$$v_t = \frac{u_{2t} - u_{1t}}{\alpha_1 - \beta_1} \tag{19.2.4}$$

Substituting P_t from Eq. (19.2.2) into Eq. (18.2.1) or (18.2.2), we obtain the following equilibrium quantity:

$$Q_t = \Pi_1 + w_t \tag{19.2.5}$$

where

$$\Pi_1 = \frac{\alpha_1\beta_0 - \alpha_0\beta_1}{\alpha_1 - \beta_1} \tag{19.2.6}$$

$$w_t = \frac{\alpha_1 u_{2t} - \beta_1 u_{1t}}{\alpha_1 - \beta_1} \tag{19.2.7}$$

Incidentally, note that the error terms v_t and w_t are linear combinations of the original error terms u_1 and u_2.

Equations (19.2.2) and (19.2.5) are reduced-form equations. Now our demand-and-supply model contains four structural coefficients α_0, α_1, β_0, and β_1, but there is no unique way of estimating them. Why? The answer lies in the two reduced-form coefficients given in Eqs. (19.2.3) and (19.2.6). These reduced-form coefficients contain all four structural parameters, but there is no way in which the four structural unknowns can be estimated from only two reduced-form coefficients. Recall from high school algebra that to estimate four unknowns we must have four (independent) equations, and, in general, to estimate k unknowns we must have k (independent) equations. Incidentally, if we run the reduced-form regression (19.2.2) and (19.2.5), we will see that there are no explanatory variables, only the *constants,* and these *constants* will simply give the mean values of P and Q (why?).

What all this means is that, given time series data on P (price) and Q (quantity) and no other information, there is no way the researcher can guarantee whether he or she is estimating the demand function or the supply function. That is, a given P_t and Q_t represent simply the point of intersection of the appropriate demand-and-supply curves because of the equilibrium condition that demand is equal to supply. To see this clearly, consider the scattergram shown in Figure 19.1.

Figure 19.1*a* gives a few scatterpoints relating Q to P. Each scatterpoint represents the intersection of a demand and a supply curve, as shown in Figure 19.1*b*. Now consider a single point, such as that shown in Figure 19.1*c*. There is no way we can be sure which demand-and-supply curve of a whole family of curves shown in that panel generated that point. Clearly, some additional information about the nature of the demand-and-supply curves is needed. For example, if the demand curve shifts over time because of change in income,

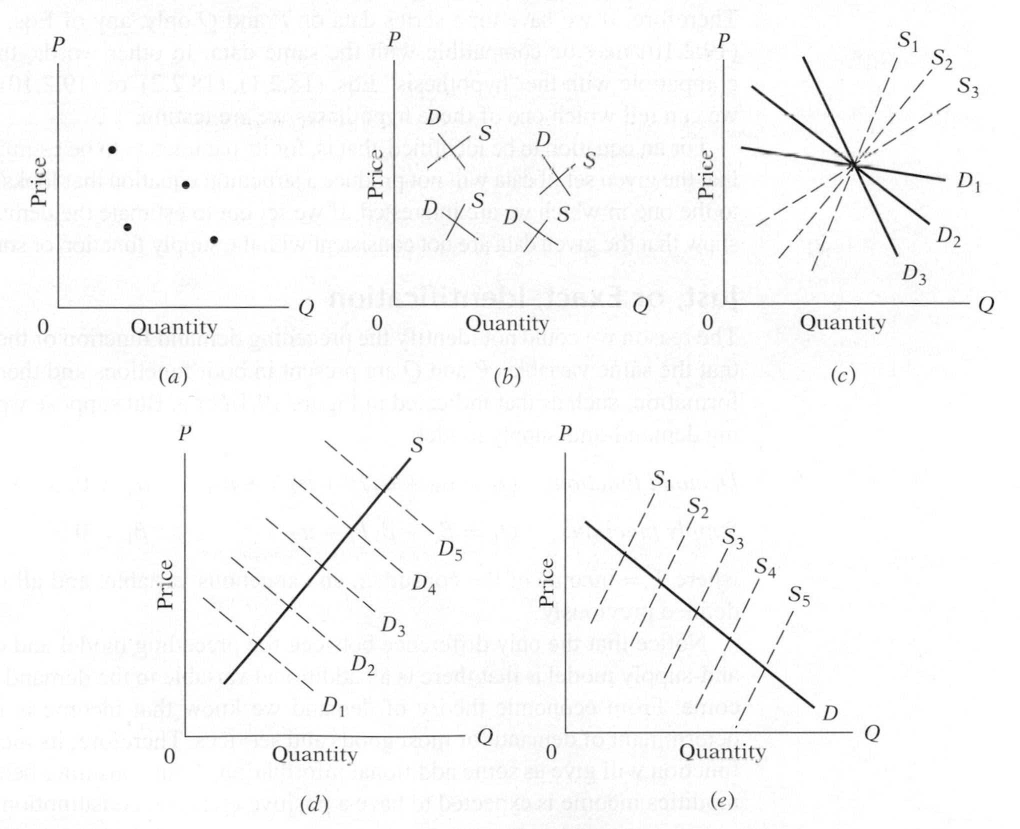

FIGURE 19.1 Hypothetical supply-and-demand functions and the identification problem.

tastes, etc., but the supply curve remains relatively stable, as in Figure 19.1*d*, the scatterpoints trace out a supply curve. In this situation, we say that the supply curve is identified. By the same token, if the supply curve shifts over time because of changes in weather conditions (in the case of agricultural commodities) or other extraneous factors but the demand curve remains relatively stable, as in Figure 19.1*e*, the scatterpoints trace out a demand curve. In this case, we say that the demand curve is identified.

There is an alternative and perhaps more illuminating way of looking at the identification problem. Suppose we multiply Eq. (18.2.1) by λ $(0 \le \lambda \le 1)$ and Eq. (18.2.2) by $1 - \lambda$ to obtain the following equations (*note:* we drop the superscripts on Q):

$$\lambda Q_t = \lambda\alpha_0 + \lambda\alpha_1 P_t + \lambda u_{1t} \tag{19.2.8}$$

$$(1-\lambda)Q_t = (1-\lambda)\beta_0 + (1-\lambda)\beta_1 P_t + (1-\lambda)u_{2t} \tag{19.2.9}$$

Adding these two equations gives the following *linear combination* of the original demand-and-supply equations:

$$Q_t = \gamma_0 + \gamma_1 P_t + w_t \tag{19.2.10}$$

where

$$\begin{aligned} \gamma_0 &= \lambda\alpha_0 + (1-\lambda)\beta_0 \\ \gamma_1 &= \lambda\alpha_1 + (1-\lambda)\beta_1 \\ w_t &= \lambda u_{1t} + (1-\lambda)u_{2t} \end{aligned} \tag{19.2.11}$$

The "bogus," or "mongrel," equation (19.2.10) is *observationally indistinguishable* from either Eq. (18.2.1) or Eq. (18.2.2) because they involve the regression of Q and P. Therefore, if we have time series data on P and Q only, any of Eqs. (18.2.1), (18.2.2), or (19.2.10) may be compatible with the same data. In other words, the same data may be compatible with the "hypothesis" Eqs. (18.2.1), (18.2.2), or (19.2.10), and there is no way we can tell which one of these hypotheses we are testing.

For an equation to be identified, that is, for its parameters to be estimated, it must be shown that the given set of data will not produce a structural equation that looks similar in appearance to the one in which we are interested. If we set out to estimate the demand function, we must show that the given data are not consistent with the supply function or some mongrel equation.

Just, or Exact, Identification

The reason we could not identify the preceding demand function or the supply function was that the same variables P and Q are present in both functions and there is no additional information, such as that indicated in Figure 19.1*d* or *e*. But suppose we consider the following demand-and-supply model:

Demand function: $$Q_t = \alpha_0 + \alpha_1 P_t + \alpha_2 I_t + u_{1t} \qquad \alpha_1 < 0, \alpha_2 > 0 \tag{19.2.12}$$

Supply function: $$Q_t = \beta_0 + \beta_1 P_t + u_{2t} \qquad \beta_1 > 0 \tag{19.2.13}$$

where I = income of the consumer, an exogenous variable, and all other variables are as defined previously.

Notice that the only difference between the preceding model and our original demand-and-supply model is that there is an additional variable in the demand function, namely, income. From economic theory of demand we know that income is usually an important determinant of demand for most goods and services. Therefore, its inclusion in the demand function will give us some additional information about consumer behavior. For most commodities income is expected to have a positive effect on consumption ($\alpha_2 > 0$).

Using the market-clearing mechanism, quantity demanded = quantity supplied, we have

$$\alpha_0 + \alpha_1 P_t + \alpha_2 I_t + u_{1t} = \beta_0 + \beta_1 P_t + u_{2t} \tag{19.2.14}$$

Solving Eq. (19.2.14) provides the following equilibrium value of P_t:

$$P_t = \Pi_0 + \Pi_1 I_t + v_t \tag{19.2.15}$$

where the reduced-form coefficients are

$$\begin{aligned} \Pi_0 &= \frac{\beta_0 - \alpha_0}{\alpha_1 - \beta_1} \\ \Pi_1 &= -\frac{\alpha_2}{\alpha_1 - \beta_1} \end{aligned} \tag{19.2.16}$$

and

$$v_t = \frac{u_{2t} - u_{1t}}{\alpha_1 - \beta_1}$$

Substituting the equilibrium value of P_t into the preceding demand or supply function, we obtain the following equilibrium quantity:

$$Q_t = \Pi_2 + \Pi_3 I_t + w_t \tag{19.2.17}$$

where

$$\begin{aligned} \Pi_2 &= \frac{\alpha_1 \beta_0 - \alpha_0 \beta_1}{\alpha_1 - \beta_1} \\ \Pi_3 &= -\frac{\alpha_2 \beta_1}{\alpha_1 - \beta_1} \end{aligned} \tag{19.2.18}$$

and

$$w_t = \frac{\alpha_1 u_{2t} - \beta_1 u_{1t}}{\alpha_1 - \beta_1}$$

Since Eqs. (19.2.15) and (19.2.17) are both reduced-form equations, the ordinary least squares (OLS) method can be applied to estimate their parameters. Now the demand-and-supply model (19.2.12) and (19.2.13) contains five structural coefficients—$\alpha_0, \alpha_1, \alpha_2, \beta_0$ and β_1. But there are only four equations to estimate them, namely, the four reduced-form coefficients Π_0, Π_1, Π_2, and Π_3 given in Eqs. (19.2.16) and (19.2.18). Hence, unique solution of all the structural coefficients is not possible. But it can be readily shown that the parameters of the supply function can be identified (estimated) because

$$\begin{aligned} \beta_0 &= \Pi_2 - \beta_1 \Pi_0 \\ \beta_1 &= \frac{\Pi_3}{\Pi_1} \end{aligned} \tag{19.2.19}$$

But there is no unique way of estimating the parameters of the demand function; therefore, it remains underidentified. Incidentally, note that the structural coefficient β_1 is a nonlinear function of the reduced-form coefficients, which poses some problems when it comes to estimating the standard error of the estimated β_1, as we shall see in Chapter 20.

To verify that the demand function (19.2.12) cannot be identified (estimated), let us multiply it by λ $(0 \le \lambda \le 1)$ and (19.2.13) by $1 - \lambda$ and add them up to obtain the following "mongrel" equation:

$$Q_t = \gamma_0 + \gamma_1 P_t + \gamma_2 I_t + w_t \tag{19.2.20}$$

where

$$\gamma_0 = \lambda\alpha_0 + (1-\lambda)\beta_0$$
$$\gamma_1 = \lambda\alpha_1 + (1-\lambda)\beta_1 \qquad (19.2.21)$$
$$\gamma_2 = \lambda\alpha_2$$

and

$$w_t = \lambda u_{1t} + (1-\lambda)u_{2t}$$

Equation (19.2.20) is observationally indistinguishable from the demand function (19.2.12) although it is distinguishable from the supply function (19.2.13), which does not contain the variable I as an explanatory variable. Hence, the demand function remains unidentified.

Notice an interesting fact: It is the presence of an additional variable in the demand function that enables us to identify the supply function! Why? The inclusion of the income variable in the demand equation provides us some additional information about the variability of the function, as indicated in Figure 19.1*d*. The figure shows how the intersection of the stable supply curve with the shifting demand curve (on account of changes in income) enables us to trace (identify) the supply curve. As will be shown shortly, very often the identifiability of an equation depends on whether it excludes one or more variables that are included in other equations in the model.

But suppose we consider the following demand-and-supply model:

$$\textit{Demand function:} \quad Q_t = \alpha_0 + \alpha_1 P_t + \alpha_2 I_t + u_{1t} \qquad \alpha_1 < 0, \alpha_2 > 0 \qquad (19.2.12)$$

$$\textit{Supply function:} \quad Q_t = \beta_0 + \beta_1 P_t + \beta_2 P_{t-1} + u_{2t} \qquad \beta_1 > 0, \beta_2 > 0 \qquad (19.2.22)$$

where the demand function remains as before but the supply function includes an additional explanatory variable, price lagged one period. The supply function postulates that the quantity of a commodity supplied depends on its current and previous period's price, a model often used to explain the supply of many agricultural commodities. Note that P_{t-1} is a predetermined variable because its value is known at time t.

By the market-clearing mechanism we have

$$\alpha_0 + \alpha_1 P_t + \alpha_2 I_t + u_{1t} = \beta_0 + \beta_1 P_t + \beta_2 P_{t-1} + u_{2t} \qquad (19.2.23)$$

Solving this equation, we obtain the following equilibrium price:

$$P_t = \Pi_0 + \Pi_1 I_t + \Pi_2 P_{t-1} + v_t \qquad (19.2.24)$$

where

$$\Pi_0 = \frac{\beta_0 - \alpha_0}{\alpha_1 - \beta_1}$$
$$\Pi_1 = -\frac{\alpha_2}{\alpha_1 - \beta_1}$$
$$\Pi_2 = \frac{\beta_2}{\alpha_1 - \beta_1} \qquad (19.2.25)$$
$$v_t = \frac{u_{2t} - u_{1t}}{\alpha_1 - \beta_1}$$

Substituting the equilibrium price into the demand or supply equation, we obtain the corresponding equilibrium quantity:

$$Q_t = \Pi_3 + \Pi_4 I_t + \Pi_5 P_{t-1} + w_t \tag{19.2.26}$$

where the reduced-form coefficients are

$$\Pi_3 = \frac{\alpha_1\beta_0 - \alpha_0\beta_1}{\alpha_1 - \beta_1}$$

$$\Pi_4 = -\frac{\alpha_2\beta_1}{\alpha_1 - \beta_1} \tag{19.2.27}$$

$$\Pi_5 = \frac{\alpha_1\beta_2}{\alpha_1 - \beta_1}$$

and

$$w_t = \frac{\alpha_1 u_{2t} - \beta_1 u_{1t}}{\alpha_1 - \beta_1}$$

The demand-and-supply model given in Eqs. (19.2.12) and (19.2.22) contains six structural coefficients—$\alpha_0, \alpha_1, \alpha_2, \beta_0, \beta_1$, and β_2—and there are six reduced-form coefficients—$\Pi_0, \Pi_1, \Pi_2, \Pi_3, \Pi_4$, and Π_5—to estimate them. Thus, we have six equations in six unknowns, and normally we should be able to obtain unique estimates. Therefore, the parameters of both the demand-and-supply equations can be identified, and the system as a whole can be identified. (In Exercise 19.2 the reader is asked to express the six structural coefficients in terms of the six reduced-form coefficients given previously to show that unique estimation of the model is possible.)

To check that the preceding demand-and-supply functions are identified, we can also resort to the device of multiplying the demand equation (19.2.12) by λ $(0 \le \lambda \le 1)$ and the supply equation (19.2.22) by $1 - \lambda$ and add them to obtain a mongrel equation. This mongrel equation will contain both the predetermined variables I_t and P_{t-1}; hence, it will be observationally different from the demand as well as the supply equation because the former does not contain P_{t-1} and the latter does not contain I_t.

Overidentification

For certain goods and services, income as well as wealth of the consumer is an important determinant of demand. Therefore, let us modify the demand function (19.2.12) as follows, keeping the supply function as before:

Demand function: $$Q_t = \alpha_0 + \alpha_1 P_t + \alpha_2 I_t + \alpha_3 R_t + u_{1t} \tag{19.2.28}$$

Supply function: $$Q_t = \beta_0 + \beta_1 P_t + \beta_2 P_{t-1} + u_{2t} \tag{19.2.22}$$

where in addition to the variables already defined, R represents wealth; for most goods and services, wealth, like income, is expected to have a positive effect on consumption.

Equating demand to supply, we obtain the following equilibrium price and quantity:

$$P_t = \Pi_0 + \Pi_1 I_t + \Pi_2 R_t + \Pi_3 P_{t-1} + v_t \tag{19.2.29}$$

$$Q_t = \Pi_4 + \Pi_5 I_t + \Pi_6 R_t + \Pi_7 P_{t-1} + w_t \tag{19.2.30}$$

where

$$\Pi_0 = \frac{\beta_0 - \alpha_0}{\alpha_1 - \beta_1} \qquad \Pi_1 = -\frac{\alpha_2}{\alpha_1 - \beta_1}$$

$$\Pi_2 = -\frac{\alpha_3}{\alpha_1 - \beta_1} \qquad \Pi_3 = \frac{\beta_2}{\alpha_1 - \beta_1}$$

$$\Pi_4 = \frac{\alpha_1\beta_0 - \alpha_0\beta_1}{\alpha_1 - \beta_1} \qquad \Pi_5 = -\frac{\alpha_2\beta_1}{\alpha_1 - \beta_1} \tag{19.2.31}$$

$$\Pi_6 = -\frac{\alpha_3\beta_1}{\alpha_1 - \beta_1} \qquad \Pi_7 = \frac{\alpha_1\beta_2}{\alpha_1 - \beta_1}$$

$$w_t = \frac{\alpha_1 u_{2t} - \beta_1 u_{1t}}{\alpha_1 - \beta_1} \qquad v_t = \frac{u_{2t} - u_{1t}}{\alpha_1 - \beta_1}$$

The preceding demand-and-supply model contains seven structural coefficients, but there are eight equations to estimate them—the eight reduced-form coefficients given in Eq. (19.2.31); that is, the number of equations is greater than the number of unknowns. As a result, unique estimation of all the parameters of our model is not possible, which can be shown easily. From the preceding reduced-form coefficients, we can obtain

$$\beta_1 = \frac{\Pi_6}{\Pi_2} \tag{19.2.32}$$

or

$$\beta_1 = \frac{\Pi_5}{\Pi_1} \tag{19.2.33}$$

that is, there are two estimates of the price coefficient in the supply function, and there is no guarantee that these two values or solutions will be identical.[4] Moreover, since β_1 appears in the denominators of all the reduced-form coefficients, the ambiguity in the estimation of β_1 will be transmitted to other estimates too.

Why was the supply function identified in the system (19.2.12) and (19.2.22) but not in the system (19.2.28) and (19.2.22), although in both cases the supply function remains the same? The answer is that we have "too much," or an **oversufficiency of information,** to identify the supply curve. This situation is the opposite of the case of underidentification, where there is too little information. The oversufficiency of the information results from the fact that in the model (19.2.12) and (19.2.22) the exclusion of the income variable from the supply function was enough to identify it, but in the model (19.2.28) and (19.2.22) the supply function excludes not only the income variable but also the wealth variable. In other words, in the latter model we put "too many" restrictions on the supply function by requiring it to exclude more variables than necessary to identify it. However, this situation does not imply that overidentification is necessarily bad because we shall see in Chapter 20 how we can handle the problem of too much information, or too many restrictions.

We have now exhausted all the cases. As the preceding discussion shows, an equation in a simultaneous-equation model may be underidentified or identified (either over- or just). The model as a whole is identified if each equation in it is identified. To secure identification, we resort to the reduced-form equations. But in Section 19.3, we consider an alternative and perhaps less time-consuming method of determining whether or not an equation in a simultaneous-equation model is identified.

[4]Notice the difference between under- and overidentification. In the former case, it is impossible to obtain estimates of the structural parameters, whereas in the latter case, there may be several estimates of one or more structural coefficients.

19.3 Rules for Identification

As the examples in Section 19.2 show, in principle it is possible to resort to the reduced-form equations to determine the identification of an equation in a system of simultaneous equations. But these examples also show how time-consuming and laborious the process can be. Fortunately, it is not essential to use this procedure. The so-called **order and rank conditions of identification** lighten the task by providing a systematic routine.

To understand the order and rank conditions, we introduce the following notations:

M = number of endogenous variables in the model
m = number of endogenous variables in a given equation
K = number of predetermined variables in the model including the intercept
k = number of predetermined variables in a given equation

The Order Condition of Identifiability[5]

A necessary (but not sufficient) condition of identification, known as the **order condition,** may be stated in two different but equivalent ways as follows (the necessary as well as sufficient condition of identification will be presented shortly):

Definition 19.1 In a model of M simultaneous equations, in order for an equation to be identified, it must exclude *at least* $M - 1$ variables (endogenous as well as predetermined) appearing in the model. If it excludes exactly $M - 1$ variables, the equation is just identified. If it excludes more than $M - 1$ variables, it is overidentified.

Definition 19.2 In a model of M simultaneous equations, in order for an equation to be identified, the number of predetermined variables excluded from the equation must not be less than the number of endogenous variables included in that equation less 1, that is,

$$K - k \geq m - 1 \tag{19.3.1}$$

If $K - k = m - 1$, the equation is just identified, but if $K - k > m - 1$, it is overidentified.

In Exercise 19.1 the reader is asked to prove that the preceding two definitions of identification are equivalent.

To illustrate the order condition, let us revert to our previous examples.

EXAMPLE 19.1

$$\text{Demand function:} \quad Q_t^d = \alpha_0 + \alpha_1 P_t + u_{1t} \tag{18.2.1}$$

$$\text{Supply function:} \quad Q_t^s = \beta_0 + \beta_1 P_t + u_{2t} \tag{18.2.2}$$

This model has two endogenous variables P and Q and no predetermined variables. To be identified, each of these equations must exclude at least $M - 1 = 1$ variable. Since this is not the case, neither equation is identified.

EXAMPLE 19.2

$$\text{Demand function:} \quad Q_t^d = \alpha_0 + \alpha_1 P_t + \alpha_2 I_t + u_{1t} \tag{19.2.12}$$

$$\text{Supply function:} \quad Q_t^s = \beta_0 + \beta_1 P_t + u_{2t} \tag{19.2.13}$$

In this model Q and P are endogenous and I is exogenous. Applying the order condition given in Eq. (19.3.1), we see that the demand function is unidentified. On the other hand, the supply function is just identified because it excludes exactly $M - 1 = 1$ variable I_t.

[5]The term **order** refers to the order of a matrix, that is, the number of rows and columns present in a matrix. See **Appendix B.**

EXAMPLE 19.3

Demand function: $Q_t^d = \alpha_0 + \alpha_1 P_t + \alpha_2 I_t + u_{1t}$ **(19.2.12)**

Supply function: $Q_t^s = \beta_0 + \beta_1 P_t + \beta_2 P_{t-1} + u_{2t}$ **(19.2.22)**

Given that P_t and Q_t are endogenous and I_t and P_{t-1} are predetermined, Eq. (19.2.12) excludes exactly one variable P_{t-1} and Eq. (19.2.22) also excludes exactly one variable I_t. Hence each equation is identified by the order condition. Therefore, the model as a whole is identified.

EXAMPLE 19.4

Demand function: $Q_t^d = \alpha_0 + \alpha_1 P_t + \alpha_2 I_t + \alpha_3 R_t + u_{1t}$ **(19.2.28)**

Supply function: $Q_t^s = \beta_0 + \beta_1 P_t + \beta_2 P_{t-1} + u_{2t}$ **(19.2.22)**

In this model P_t and Q_t are endogenous and I_t, R_t, and P_{t-1} are predetermined. The demand function excludes exactly one variable P_{t-1}, and hence by the order condition it is exactly identified. But the supply function excludes two variables I_t and R_t, and hence it is overidentified. As noted before, in this case there are two ways of estimating β_1, the coefficient of the price variable.

Notice a slight complication here. By the order condition the demand function is identified. But if we try to estimate the parameters of this equation from the reduced-form coefficients given in Eq. (19.2.31), the estimates will not be unique because β_1, which enters into the computations, takes two values and we shall have to decide which of these values is appropriate. But this complication can be obviated because it is shown in Chapter 20 that in cases of overidentification the method of indirect least squares is not appropriate and should be discarded in favor of other methods. One such method is **two-stage least squares**, which we shall discuss fully in Chapter 20.

As the previous examples show, identification of an equation in a model of simultaneous equations is possible if that equation excludes one or more variables that are present elsewhere in the model. This situation is known as the *exclusion* (of variables) *criterion,* or the *zero restrictions criterion* (the coefficients of variables not appearing in an equation are assumed to have zero values). This criterion is by far the most commonly used method of securing or determining identification of an equation. But notice that the zero restrictions criterion is based on a priori or theoretical expectations that certain variables do not appear in a given equation. It is up to the researcher to spell out clearly why he or she does expect certain variables to appear in some equations and not in others.

The Rank Condition of Identifiability[6]

The order condition discussed previously is *a necessary but not sufficient* condition for identification; that is, even if it is satisfied, it may happen that an equation is not identified. Thus, in Example 19.2, the supply equation was identified by the order condition because it excluded the income variable I_t, which appeared in the demand function. But identification is accomplished only if α_2, the coefficient of I_t in the demand function, is not zero, that is, if the income variable not only probably but actually does enter the demand function.

More generally, even if the order condition $K - k \geq m - 1$ is satisfied by an equation, it may be unidentified because the predetermined variables excluded from this equation but present in the model may not all be independent so that there may not be one-to-one correspondence between the structural coefficients (the β's) and the reduced-form coefficients

[6]The term **rank** refers to the rank of a matrix and is given by the largest-order square matrix (contained in the given matrix) whose determinant is nonzero. Alternatively, the rank of a matrix is the largest number of linearly independent rows or columns of that matrix. See **Appendix B.**

(the Π's). That is, we may not be able to estimate the structural parameters from the reduced-form coefficients, as we shall show shortly. Therefore, we need both a necessary and sufficient condition for identification. This is provided by the *rank condition* of identification, which may be stated as follows:

Rank Condition of Identification In a model containing M equations in M endogenous variables, an equation is identified if and only if *at least* one nonzero determinant of order $(M-1)(M-1)$ can be constructed from the coefficients of the variables (both endogenous and predetermined) excluded from that particular equation but included in the other equations of the model.

As an illustration of the rank condition of identification, consider the following hypothetical system of simultaneous equations in which the Y variables are endogenous and the X variables are predetermined.[7]

$$Y_{1t} - \beta_{10} - \beta_{12}Y_{2t} - \beta_{13}Y_{3t} - \gamma_{11}X_{1t} = u_{1t} \tag{19.3.2}$$

$$Y_{2t} - \beta_{20} - \beta_{23}Y_{3t} - \gamma_{21}X_{1t} - \gamma_{22}X_{2t} = u_{2t} \tag{19.3.3}$$

$$Y_{3t} - \beta_{30} - \beta_{31}Y_{1t} - \gamma_{31}X_{1t} - \gamma_{32}X_{2t} = u_{3t} \tag{19.3.4}$$

$$Y_{4t} - \beta_{40} - \beta_{41}Y_{1t} - \beta_{42}Y_{2t} - \gamma_{43}X_{3t} = u_{4t} \tag{19.3.5}$$

To facilitate identification, let us write the preceding system in Table 19.1, which is self-explanatory.

Let us first apply the order condition of identification, as shown in Table 19.2. By the order condition each equation is identified. Let us recheck with the rank condition. Consider the first equation, which excludes variables Y_4, X_2, and X_3 (this is represented by zeros in the first row of Table 19.1). For this equation to be identified, we must obtain at

TABLE 19.1

	Coefficients of the Variables							
Equation No.	1	Y_1	Y_2	Y_3	Y_4	X_1	X_2	X_3
(19.3.2)	$-\beta_{10}$	1	$-\beta_{12}$	$-\beta_{13}$	0	$-\gamma_{11}$	0	0
(19.3.3)	$-\beta_{20}$	0	1	$-\beta_{23}$	0	$-\gamma_{21}$	$-\gamma_{22}$	0
(19.3.4)	$-\beta_{30}$	$-\beta_{31}$	0	1	0	$-\gamma_{31}$	$-\gamma_{32}$	0
(19.3.5)	$-\beta_{40}$	$-\beta_{41}$	$-\beta_{42}$	0	1	0	0	$-\gamma_{43}$

TABLE 19.2

Equation No.	No. of Predetermined Variables Excluded, $(K-k)$	No. of Endogenous Variables Included, Less One, $(m-1)$	Identified?
(19.3.2)	2	2	Exactly
(19.3.3)	1	1	Exactly
(19.3.4)	1	1	Exactly
(19.3.5)	2	2	Exactly

[7] The simultaneous-equation system presented in Eq. (19.1.1) may be shown in the following alternative form, which may be convenient for matrix manipulations.

least one nonzero determinant of order 3×3 from the coefficients of the variables excluded from this equation but included in other equations. To obtain the determinant we first obtain the relevant matrix of coefficients of variables Y_4, X_2, and X_3 included in the other equations. In the present case there is only one such matrix, call it **A**, defined as follows:

$$\mathbf{A} = \begin{bmatrix} 0 & -\gamma_{22} & 0 \\ 0 & -\gamma_{32} & 0 \\ 1 & 0 & -\gamma_{43} \end{bmatrix} \tag{19.3.6}$$

It can be seen that the determinant of this matrix is zero:

$$\det \mathbf{A} = \begin{vmatrix} 0 & -\gamma_{22} & 0 \\ 0 & -\gamma_{32} & 0 \\ 1 & 0 & -\gamma_{43} \end{vmatrix} \tag{19.3.7}$$

Since the determinant is zero, the rank of the matrix (19.3.6), denoted by $\rho(\mathbf{A})$, is less than 3. Therefore, Eq. (19.3.2) does not satisfy the rank condition and hence is not identified.

As noted, the rank condition is both a necessary and sufficient condition for identification. Therefore, although the order condition shows that Eq. (19.3.2) is identified, the rank condition shows that it is not. Apparently, the columns or rows of the matrix **A** given in Eq. (19.3.6) are not (linearly) independent, meaning that there is some relationship between the variables Y_4, X_2, and X_3. As a result, we may not have enough information to estimate the parameters of equation (19.3.2); the reduced-form equations for the preceding model will show that it is not possible to obtain the structural coefficients of that equation from the reduced-form coefficients. The reader should verify that by the rank condition Eqs. (19.3.3) and (19.3.4) are also unidentified but Eq. (19.3.5) is identified.

As the preceding discussion shows, *the rank condition tells us whether the equation under consideration is identified or not, whereas the order condition tells us if it is exactly identified or overidentified.*

To apply the rank condition one may proceed as follows:

1. Write down the system in a tabular form, as shown in Table 19.1.
2. Strike out the coefficients of the row in which the equation under consideration appears.
3. Also strike out the columns corresponding to those coefficients in step (2) which are nonzero.
4. The entries left in the table will then give only the coefficients of the variables included in the system but not in the equation under consideration. From these entries form all possible matrices, like **A**, of order $M - 1$ and obtain the corresponding determinants. If at least one nonvanishing or nonzero determinant can be found, the equation in question is (just or over-) identified. The rank of the matrix, say, **A**, in this case is exactly equal to $M - 1$. If all the possible $(M - 1)(M - 1)$ determinants are zero, the rank of the matrix **A** is less than $M - 1$ and the equation under investigation is not identified.

Our discussion of the order and rank conditions of identification leads to the following general principles of identifiability of a structural equation in a system of M simultaneous equations:

1. If $K - k > m - 1$ and the rank of the **A** matrix is $M - 1$, the equation is overidentified.
2. If $K - k = m - 1$ and the rank of the matrix **A** is $M - 1$, the equation is exactly identified.
3. If $K - k \geq m - 1$ and the rank of the matrix **A** is less than $M - 1$, the equation is underidentified.
4. If $K - k < m - 1$, the structural equation is unidentified. The rank of the **A** matrix in this case is bound to be less than $M - 1$. (Why?)

Henceforth, when we talk about identification we mean exact identification or overidentification. There is no point in considering unidentified, or underidentified, equations because no matter how extensive the data, the structural parameters cannot be estimated. Besides, most simultaneous-equation systems in economics and finance are overidentified rather than underidentified, so we need not worry too much about underidentification. However, as shown in Chapter 20, parameters of overidentified as well as just identified equations can be estimated.

Which condition should one use in practice: Order or rank? For large simultaneous-equation models, applying the rank condition is a formidable task. Therefore, as Harvey notes,

> Fortunately, the order condition is usually sufficient to ensure identifiability, and although it is important to be aware of the rank condition, a failure to verify it will rarely result in disaster.[8]

*19.4 A Test of Simultaneity[9]

If there is no simultaneous equation, or **simultaneity problem,** the OLS estimators produce consistent and efficient estimators. On the other hand, if there is simultaneity, OLS estimators are not even consistent. In the presence of simultaneity, as we will show in Chapter 20, the methods of **two-stage least squares (2SLS)** and **instrumental variables (IV)** will give estimators that are consistent and efficient. Oddly, if we apply these alternative methods when there is in fact no simultaneity, these methods yield estimators that are consistent but not efficient (i.e., with smaller variance). This discussion suggests that we should check for the simultaneity problem before we discard OLS in favor of the alternatives.

As we showed earlier, the simultaneity problem arises because some of the regressors are endogenous and are therefore likely to be correlated with the disturbance, or error, term. Therefore, *a test of simultaneity is essentially a test of whether (an endogenous) regressor is correlated with the error term.* If it is, the simultaneity problem exists, in which case alternatives to OLS must be found; if it is not, we can use OLS. To find out which is the case in a concrete situation, we can use Hausman's specification error test.

Hausman Specification Test

A version of the Hausman specification error test that can be used for testing the simultaneity problem can be explained as follows:[10]

To fix ideas, consider the following two-equation model:

$$\textit{Demand function:} \quad Q_t^d = \alpha_0 + \alpha_1 P_t + \alpha_2 I_t + \alpha_3 R_t + u_{1t} \tag{19.4.1}$$

$$\textit{Supply function:} \quad Q_t^s = \beta_0 + \beta_1 P_t + u_{2t} \tag{19.4.2}$$

where P = price
Q = quantity
I = income
R = wealth
u's = error terms

Assume that I and R are exogenous. Of course, P and Q are endogenous.

*Optional.

[8]Andrew Harvey, *The Econometric Analysis of Time Series,* 2d ed., The MIT Press, Cambridge, Mass., 1990, p. 328.

[9]The following discussion draws from Robert S. Pindyck and Daniel L. Rubinfeld, *Econometric Models and Economic Forecasts,* 3d ed., McGraw-Hill, New York, 1991, pp. 303–305.

[10]J. A. Hausman, "Specification Tests in Econometrics," *Econometrica,* vol. 46, November 1976, pp. 1251–1271. See also A. Nakamura and M. Nakamura, "On the Relationship among Several Specification Error Tests Presented by Durbin, Wu, and Hausman," *Econometrica,* vol. 49, November 1981, pp. 1583–1588.

Now consider the supply function (19.4.2). If there is no simultaneity problem (i.e., P and Q are mutually independent), P_t and u_{2t} should be uncorrelated (why?). On the other hand, if there is simultaneity, P_t and u_{2t} will be correlated. To find out which is the case, the Hausman test proceeds as follows:

First, from Eqs. (19.4.1) and (19.4.2) we obtain the following reduced-form equations:

$$P_t = \Pi_0 + \Pi_1 I_t + \Pi_2 R_t + v_t \tag{19.4.3}$$

$$Q_t = \Pi_3 + \Pi_4 I_t + \Pi_5 R_t + w_t \tag{19.4.4}$$

where v and w are the reduced-form error terms. Estimating Eq. (19.4.3) by OLS we obtain

$$\hat{P}_t = \hat{\Pi}_0 + \hat{\Pi}_1 I_t + \hat{\Pi}_2 R_t \tag{19.4.5}$$

Therefore,

$$P_t = \hat{P}_t + \hat{v}_t \tag{19.4.6}$$

where $\hat{P}_t$ are estimated P_t and $\hat{v}_t$ are the estimated residuals. Now consider the following equation:

$$Q_t = \beta_0 + \beta_1 \hat{P}_t + \beta_1 \hat{v}_t + u_{2t} \tag{19.4.7}$$

Note: The coefficients of P_t and v_t are the same. The difference between this equation and the original supply equation is that it includes the additional variable $\hat{v}_t$, the residual from regression (19.4.3).

Now, if the null hypothesis is that there is no simultaneity, that is, P_t is not an endogenous variable, the correlation between $\hat{v}_t$ and u_{2t} should be zero, asymptotically. Thus, if we run the regression (19.4.7) and find that the coefficient of v_t in Eq. (19.4.7) is statistically zero, we can conclude that there is no simultaneity problem. Of course, this conclusion will be reversed if we find this coefficient to be statistically significant. In passing, note that Hausman's simultaneity test is also known as the *Hausman test of endogeneity:* In the present example we want to find out if P_t is endogenous. If it is, we have the simultaneity problem.

Essentially, then, the Hausman test involves the following steps:

Step 1. Regress P_t on I_t and R_t to obtain $\hat{v}_t$.

Step 2. Regress Q_t on $\hat{P}_t$ and $\hat{v}_t$ and perform a t test on the coefficient of $\hat{v}_t$. If it is significant, do not reject the hypothesis of simultaneity; otherwise, reject it.[11] For efficient estimation, however, Pindyck and Rubinfeld suggest regressing Q_t on P_t and $\hat{v}_t$.[12]

There are alternative ways to apply the Hausman test, which are given by way of an exercise.

EXAMPLE 19.5 *Pindyck–Rubinfeld Model of Public Spending*[13]

To study the behavior of U.S. state and local government expenditure, the authors developed the following simultaneous-equation model:

$$\text{EXP} = \beta_1 + \beta_2 \text{AID} + \beta_3 \text{INC} + \beta_4 \text{POP} + u_i \tag{19.4.8}$$

$$\text{AID} = \delta_1 + \delta_2 \text{EXP} + \delta_3 \text{PS} + v_i \tag{19.4.9}$$

where
EXP = state and local government public expenditures
AID = level of federal grants-in-aid
INC = income of states
POP = state population
PS = population of primary and secondary school children
u and v = error terms

In this model, INC, POP, and PS are regarded as exogenous.

[11] If more than one endogenous regressor is involved, we will have to use the F test.

[12] Pindyck and Rubinfeld, op. cit., p. 304. *Note:* The regressor is P_t and *not* $\hat{P}_t$.

[13] Pindyck and Rubinfeld, op. cit., pp. 176–177. Notations slightly altered.

EXAMPLE 19.5 (*Continued*)

Because of the possibility of simultaneity between EXP and AID, the authors first regress AID on INC, POP, and PS (i.e., the reduced-form regression). Let the error term in this regression be w_i. From this regression the calculated residual is $\hat{w}_i$. The authors then regress EXP on AID, INC, POP, and $\hat{w}_i$, to obtain the following results:

$$\begin{aligned} \widehat{\text{EXP}} &= -89.41 + 4.50\text{AID} + 0.00013\text{INC} - 0.518\text{POP} - 1.39\hat{w}_i \\ t &= (-1.04) \quad (5.89) \quad (3.06) \quad (-4.63) \quad (-1.73) \\ & R^2 = 0.99 \end{aligned} \tag{19.4.10}$$

[14]

At the 5 percent level of significance, the coefficient of $\hat{w}_i$ is not statistically significant, and therefore, at this level, there is no simultaneity problem. However, at the 10 percent level of significance, it is statistically significant, raising the possibility that the simultaneity problem is present.

Incidentally, the OLS estimation of Eq. (19.4.8) is as follows:

$$\begin{aligned} \widehat{\text{EXP}} &= -46.81 + 3.24\text{AID} + 0.00019\text{INC} - 0.597\text{POP} \\ t &= (-0.56) \quad (13.64) \quad (8.12) \quad (-5.71) \\ & R^2 = 0.993 \end{aligned} \tag{19.4.11}$$

Notice an interesting feature of the results given in Eqs. (19.4.10) and (19.4.11): When simultaneity is explicitly taken into account, the AID variable is less significant although numerically it is greater in magnitude.

*19.5 Tests for Exogeneity

We noted earlier that it is the researcher's responsibility to specify which variables are endogenous and which are exogenous. This will depend on the problem at hand and the a priori information the researcher has. But is it possible to develop a statistical test of exogeneity, in the manner of Granger's causality test?

The Hausman test discussed in Section 19.4 can be utilized to answer this question. Suppose we have a three-equation model in three endogenous variables, Y_1, Y_2, and Y_3, and suppose there are three exogenous variables, X_1, X_2, and X_3. Further, suppose that the first equation of the model is

$$Y_{1i} = \beta_0 + \beta_2 Y_{2i} + \beta_3 Y_{3i} + \alpha_1 X_{1i} + u_{1i} \tag{19.5.1}$$

If Y_2 and Y_3 are truly endogenous, we cannot estimate Eq. (19.5.1) by OLS (why?). But how do we find that out? We can proceed as follows. We obtain the reduced-form equations for Y_2 and Y_3 (*Note:* the reduced-form equations will have only predetermined variables on the right-hand side). From these reduced-form equations, we obtain $\hat{Y}_{2i}$ and $\hat{Y}_{3i}$, the predicted values of Y_{2i} and Y_{3i}, respectively. Then in the spirit of the Hausman test discussed earlier, we can estimate the following equation by OLS:

$$Y_{1i} = \beta_0 + \beta_2 Y_{2i} + \beta_3 Y_{3i} + \alpha_1 X_{1i} + \lambda_2 \hat{Y}_{2i} + \lambda_3 \hat{Y}_{3i} + u_{1i} \tag{19.5.2}$$

Using the F test, we test the hypothesis that $\lambda_2 = \lambda_3 = 0$. If this hypothesis is rejected, Y_2 and Y_3 can be deemed endogenous, but if it is not rejected, they can be treated as exogenous. For a concrete example, see Exercise 19.16.

*Optional.

[14]As in footnote 12, the authors use AID rather than $\widehat{\text{AID}}$ as the regressor.

Summary and Conclusions

1. The problem of identification precedes the problem of estimation.
2. The identification problem asks whether one can obtain unique numerical estimates of the structural coefficients from the estimated reduced-form coefficients.
3. If this can be done, an equation in a system of simultaneous equations is identified. If this cannot be done, that equation is un- or under-identified.
4. An identified equation can be just identified or overidentified. In the former case, unique values of structural coefficients can be obtained; in the latter, there may be more than one value for one or more structural parameters.
5. The identification problem arises because the same set of data may be compatible with different sets of structural coefficients, that is, different models. Thus, in the regression of price on quantity only, it is difficult to tell whether one is estimating the supply function or the demand function, because price and quantity enter both equations.
6. To assess the identifiability of a structural equation, one may apply the technique of **reduced-form equations,** which expresses an endogenous variable solely as a function of predetermined variables.
7. However, this time-consuming procedure can be avoided by resorting to either the **order condition** or the **rank condition** of identification. Although the order condition is easy to apply, it provides only a necessary condition for identification. On the other hand, the rank condition is both a necessary and sufficient condition for identification. If the rank condition is satisfied, the order condition is satisfied, too, although the converse is not true. In practice, though, the order condition is generally adequate to ensure identifiability.
8. In the presence of simultaneity, OLS is generally not applicable, as was shown in Chapter 18. But if one wants to use it nonetheless, it is imperative to test for simultaneity explicitly. The **Hausman specification test** can be used for this purpose.
9. Although in practice deciding whether a variable is endogenous or exogenous is a matter of judgment, one can use the Hausman specification test to determine whether a variable or group of variables is endogenous or exogenous.
10. Although they are in the same family, the concepts of causality and exogeneity are different and one may not necessarily imply the other. In practice it is better to keep those concepts separate (see Section 17.14).

EXERCISES

Questions

19.1. Show that the two definitions of the order condition of identification (see Section 19.3) are equivalent.

19.2. Deduce the structural coefficients from the reduced-form coefficients given in Eqs. (19.2.25) and (19.2.27).

19.3. Obtain the reduced form of the following models and determine in each case whether the structural equations are unidentified, just identified, or overidentified:

a. Chap. 18, Example 18.2.

b. Chap. 18, Example 18.3.

c. Chap. 18, Example 18.6.

19.4. Check the identifiability of the models of Exercise 19.3 by applying both the order and rank conditions of identification.

19.5. In the model (19.2.22) of the text it was shown that the supply equation was overidentified. What restrictions, if any, on the structural parameters will make this equation just identified? Justify the restrictions you impose.

19.6. From the model

$$Y_{1t} = \beta_{10} + \beta_{12}Y_{2t} + \gamma_{11}X_{1t} + u_{1t}$$
$$Y_{2t} = \beta_{20} + \beta_{21}Y_{1t} + \gamma_{22}X_{2t} + u_{2t}$$

the following reduced-form equations are obtained:

$$Y_{1t} = \Pi_{10} + \Pi_{11}X_{1t} + \Pi_{12}X_{2t} + w_t$$
$$Y_{2t} = \Pi_{20} + \Pi_{21}X_{1t} + \Pi_{22}X_{2t} + v_t$$

a. Are the structural equations identified?

b. What happens to identification if it is known a priori that $\gamma_{11} = 0$?

19.7. Refer to Exercise 19.6. The estimated reduced-form equations are as follows:

$$Y_{1t} = 4 + 3X_{1t} + 8X_{2t}$$
$$Y_{2t} = 2 + 6X_{1t} + 10X_{2t}$$

a. Obtain the values of the structural parameters.

b. How would you test the null hypothesis that $\gamma_{11} = 0$?

19.8. The model

$$Y_{1t} = \beta_{10} + \beta_{12}Y_{2t} + \gamma_{11}X_{1t} + u_{1t}$$
$$Y_{2t} = \beta_{20} + \beta_{21}Y_{1t} + u_{2t}$$

produces the following reduced-form equations:

$$Y_{1t} = 4 + 8X_{1t}$$
$$Y_{2t} = 2 + 12X_{1t}$$

a. Which structural coefficients, if any, can be estimated from the reduced-form coefficients? Demonstrate your contention.

b. How does the answer to *(a)* change if it is known a priori that (1) $\beta_{12} = 0$ and (2) $\beta_{10} = 0$?

19.9. Determine whether the structural equations of the model given in Exercise 18.8 are identified.

19.10. Refer to Exercise 18.7 and find out which structural equations can be identified.

19.11. Table 19.3 is a model in five equations with five endogenous variables Y and four exogenous variables X:

TABLE 19.3

	Coefficients of the Variables								
Equation No.	Y_1	Y_2	Y_3	Y_4	Y_5	X_1	X_2	X_3	X_4
1	1	β_{12}	0	β_{14}	0	γ_{11}	0	0	γ_{14}
2	0	1	β_{23}	β_{24}	0	0	γ_{22}	γ_{23}	0
3	β_{31}	0	1	β_{34}	β_{35}	0	0	γ_{33}	γ_{34}
4	0	β_{42}	0	1	0	γ_{41}	0	γ_{43}	0
5	β_{51}	0	0	β_{54}	1	0	γ_{52}	γ_{53}	0

Determine the identifiability of each equation with the aid of the order and rank conditions of identifications.

19.12. Consider the following extended Keynesian model of income determination:

Consumption function: $C_t = \beta_1 + \beta_2 Y_t - \beta_3 T_t + u_{1t}$

Investment function: $I_t = \alpha_0 + \alpha_1 Y_{t-1} + u_{2t}$

Taxation function: $T_t = \gamma_0 + \gamma_1 Y_t + u_{3t}$

Income identity: $Y_t = C_t + I_t + G_t$

where C = consumption expenditure
Y = income
I = investment
T = taxes
G = government expenditure
u's = the disturbance terms

In the model the endogenous variables are C, I, T, and Y and the predetermined variables are G and Y_{t-1}.

By applying the order condition, check the identifiability of each of the equations in the system and of the system as a whole. What would happen if r_t, the interest rate, assumed to be exogenous, were to appear on the right-hand side of the investment function?

19.13. Refer to the data given in Table 18.1 of Chapter 18. Using these data, estimate the reduced-form regressions (19.1.2) and (19.1.4). Can you estimate β_0 and β_1? Show your calculations. Is the model identified? Why or why not?

19.14. Suppose we propose yet another definition of the order condition of identifiability:

$$K \geq m + k - 1$$

which states that the number of predetermined variables in the system can be no less than the number of unknown coefficients in the equation to be identified. Show that this definition is equivalent to the two other definitions of the order condition given in the text.

19.15. A simplified version of Suits's model of the watermelon market is as follows:*

Demand equation: $P_t = \alpha_0 + \alpha_1(Q_t/N_t) + \alpha_2(Y_t/N_t) + \alpha_3 F_t + u_{1t}$

Crop supply function: $Q_t = \beta_0 + \beta_1(P_t/W_t) + \beta_2 P_{t-1} + \beta_3 C_{t-1} + \beta_4 T_{t-1} + u_{2t}$

where P = price
(Q/N) = per capita quantity demanded
(Y/N) = per capita income
F_t = freight costs
(P/W) = price relative to the farm wage rate
C = price of cotton
T = price of other vegetables
N = population

P and Q are the endogenous variables.

a. Obtain the reduced form.

b. Determine whether the demand, the supply, or both functions are identified.

Empirical Exercises

19.16. Consider the following demand-and-supply model for money:

Money demand: $M_t^d = \beta_0 + \beta_1 Y_t + \beta_2 R_t + \beta_3 P_t + u_{1t}$

Money supply: $M_t^s = \alpha_0 + \alpha_1 Y_t + u_{2t}$

*D. B. Suits, "An Econometric Model of the Watermelon Market," *Journal of Farm Economics,* vol. 37, 1955, pp. 237–251.

TABLE 19.4
Money, GDP, Interest Rate, and Consumer Price Index, United States, 1970–2006

Source: *Economic Report of the President,* 2007, Tables B-2, B-60, B-69, B-73.

Observation	M_2	GDP	TBRATE	CPI
1970	626.5	3,771.9	6.458	38.8
1971	710.3	3,898.6	4.348	40.5
1972	802.3	4,105.0	4.071	41.8
1973	855.5	4,341.5	7.041	44.4
1974	902.1	4,319.6	7.886	49.3
1975	1,016.2	4,311.2	5.838	53.8
1976	1,152.0	4,540.9	4.989	56.9
1977	1,270.3	4,750.5	5.265	60.6
1978	1,366.0	5,015.0	7.221	65.2
1979	1,473.7	5,173.4	10.041	72.6
1980	1,599.8	5,161.7	11.506	82.4
1981	1,755.5	5,291.7	14.029	90.9
1982	1,910.1	5,189.3	10.686	96.5
1983	2,126.4	5,423.8	8.63	99.6
1984	2,309.8	5,813.6	9.58	103.9
1985	2,495.5	6,053.7	7.48	107.6
1986	2,732.2	6,263.6	5.98	109.6
1987	2,831.3	6,475.1	5.82	113.6
1988	2,994.3	6,742.7	6.69	118.3
1989	3,158.3	6,981.4	8.12	124.0
1990	3,277.7	7,112.5	7.51	130.7
1991	3,378.3	7,100.5	5.42	136.2
1992	3,431.8	7,336.6	3.45	140.3
1993	3,482.5	7,532.7	3.02	144.5
1994	3,498.5	7,835.5	4.29	148.2
1995	3,641.7	8,031.7	5.51	152.4
1996	3,820.5	8,328.9	5.02	156.9
1997	4,035.0	8,703.5	5.07	160.5
1998	4,381.8	9,066.9	4.81	163.0
1999	4,639.2	9,470.3	4.66	166.6
2000	4,921.7	9,817.0	5.85	172.2
2001	5,433.5	9,890.7	3.45	177.1
2002	5,779.2	10,048.8	1.62	179.9
2003	6,071.2	10,301.0	1.02	184.0
2004	6,421.6	10,675.8	1.38	188.9
2005	6,691.7	11,003.4	3.16	195.3
2006	7,035.5	11,319.4	4.73	201.6

Notes: $M_2 = M_2$ Money supply (billions of dollars).
GDP = gross domestic product (billions of dollars).
TBRATE = 3-month Treasury bill rate, %.
CPI = Consumer Price Index (1982–1984 = 100).

where M = money
Y = income
R = rate of interest
P = price
u's = error terms

Assume that R and P are exogenous and M and Y are endogenous. Table 19.4 gives data on M (M_2 definition), Y (GDP), R (3-month Treasury bill rate) and P (Consumer Price Index), for the United States for 1970–2006.

a. Is the demand function identified?
b. Is the supply function identified?
c. Obtain the expressions for the reduced-form equations for *M* and *Y*.
d. Apply the test of simultaneity to the supply function.
e. How would we find out if *Y* in the money supply function is in fact endogenous?

19.17. The Hausman test discussed in the text can also be conducted in the following way. Consider Eq. (19.4.7):

$$Q_t = \beta_0 + \beta_1 P_t + \beta_1 v_t + u_{2t}$$

a. Since P_t and v_t have the same coefficients, how would you test that in a given application that is indeed the case? What are the implications of this?
b. Since P_t is uncorrelated with u_{2t} by design (why?), one way to find out if P_t is exogenous is to see if v_t is correlated with u_{2t}. How would you go about testing this? Which test do you use? (*Hint:* Substitute P_t from [19.4.6] into Eq. [19.4.7].)

Chapter 20

Simultaneous-Equation Methods

Having discussed the nature of the simultaneous-equation models in the previous two chapters, in this chapter we turn to the problem of estimation of the parameters of such models. At the outset it may be noted that the estimation problem is rather complex because there are a variety of estimation techniques with varying statistical properties. In view of the introductory nature of this text, we shall consider only a few of these techniques. Our discussion will be simple and often heuristic, the finer points being left to the references.

20.1 Approaches to Estimation

If we consider the general M equations model in M endogenous variables given in Eq. (19.1.1), we may adopt two approaches to estimate the structural equations, namely, single-equation methods, also known as **limited information methods,** and system methods, also known as **full information methods.** In the single-equation methods to be considered shortly, we estimate each equation in the system (of simultaneous equations) individually, taking into account any restrictions placed on that equation (such as exclusion of some variables) without worrying about the restrictions on the other equations in the system,[1] hence the name *limited information methods.* In the system methods, on the other hand, we estimate all the equations in the model simultaneously, taking due account of all restrictions on such equations by the omission or absence of some variables (recall that for identification such restrictions are essential), hence the name *full information methods*.

As an example, consider the following four-equations model:

$$
\begin{aligned}
Y_{1t} &= \beta_{10} + \phantom{\beta_{31}Y_{1t} +} + \beta_{12}Y_{2t} + \beta_{13}Y_{3t} + \phantom{\beta_{34}Y_{4t}} + \gamma_{11}X_{1t} + \phantom{\gamma_{43}X_{3t}} + u_{1t} \\
Y_{2t} &= \beta_{20} + \phantom{\beta_{31}Y_{1t} + \beta_{12}Y_{2t}} + \beta_{23}Y_{3t} + \gamma_{21}X_{1t} + \gamma_{22}X_{2t} + u_{2t} \\
Y_{3t} &= \beta_{30} + \beta_{31}Y_{1t} + \phantom{\beta_{12}Y_{2t}} + \beta_{34}Y_{4t} + \gamma_{31}X_{1t} + \gamma_{32}X_{2t} + u_{3t} \\
Y_{4t} &= \beta_{40} + \phantom{\beta_{31}Y_{1t}} + \beta_{42}Y_{2t} \phantom{+ \beta_{34}Y_{4t} + \gamma_{31}X_{1t}} + \gamma_{43}X_{3t} + u_{4t}
\end{aligned}
\tag{20.1.1}
$$

[1]For the purpose of identification, however, information provided by other equations will have to be taken into account. But as noted in Chapter 19, estimation is possible only in the case of (fully or over-) identified equations. In this chapter we assume that the identification problem is solved using the techniques of Chapter 19.

where the Y's are the endogenous variables and the X's are the exogenous variables. If we are interested in estimating, say, the third equation, the single-equation methods will consider this equation only, noting that variables Y_2 and X_3 are excluded from it. In the systems methods, on the other hand, we try to estimate all four equations simultaneously, taking into account all the restrictions imposed on the various equations of the system.

To preserve the spirit of simultaneous-equation models, ideally one should use the systems method, such as the **full information maximum likelihood (FIML) method.**[2] In practice, however, such methods are not commonly used for a variety of reasons. First, the computational burden is enormous. For example, the comparatively small (20 equations) 1955 Klein–Goldberger model of the U.S. economy had 151 nonzero coefficients, of which the authors estimated only 51 coefficients using the time series data. The Brookings-Social Science Research Council (SSRC) econometric model of the U.S. economy published in 1965 initially had 150 equations.[3] Although such elaborate models may furnish finer details of the various sectors of the economy, the computations are a stupendous task even in these days of high-speed computers, not to mention the cost involved. Second, the systems methods, such as FIML, lead to solutions that are highly nonlinear in the parameters and are therefore often difficult to determine. Third, if there is a specification error (say, a wrong functional form or exclusion of relevant variables) in one or more equations of the system, that error is transmitted to the rest of the system. As a result, the systems methods become very sensitive to specification errors.

In practice, therefore, single-equation methods are often used. As Klein puts it,

> Single equation methods, in the context of a simultaneous system, may be less sensitive to specification error in the sense that those parts of the system that are correctly specified may not be affected appreciably by errors in specification in another part.[4]

In the rest of the chapter we shall deal with single-equation methods only. Specifically, we shall discuss the following single-equation methods:

1. Ordinary least squares (OLS)
2. Indirect least squares (ILS)
3. Two-stage least squares (2SLS)

20.2 Recursive Models and Ordinary Least Squares

We saw in Chapter 18 that, because of the interdependence between the stochastic disturbance term and the endogenous explanatory variable(s), the OLS method is inappropriate for the estimation of an equation in a system of simultaneous equations. If applied erroneously, then, as we saw in Section 18.3, the estimators are not only biased (in small samples) but also inconsistent; that is, the bias does not disappear no matter how large the sample size. There is, however, one situation where OLS can be applied appropriately even in the context of simultaneous equations. This is the case of the **recursive, triangular,** or

[2]For a simple discussion of this method, see Carl F. Christ, *Econometric Models and Methods,* John Wiley & Sons, New York, 1966, pp. 395–401.

[3]James S. Duesenberry, Gary Fromm, Lawrence R. Klein, and Edwin Kuh, eds., *A Quarterly Model of the United States Economy,* Rand McNally, Chicago, 1965.

[4]Lawrence R. Klein, *A Textbook of Econometrics,* 2d ed., Prentice Hall, Englewood Cliffs, NJ, 1974, p. 150.

causal models. To see the nature of these models, consider the following three-equation system:

$$\begin{aligned} Y_{1t} &= \beta_{10} \qquad\qquad\qquad\qquad\;\; + \gamma_{11}X_{1t} + \gamma_{12}X_{2t} + u_{1t} \\ Y_{2t} &= \beta_{20} + \beta_{21}Y_{1t} \qquad\qquad\; + \gamma_{21}X_{1t} + \gamma_{22}X_{2t} + u_{2t} \\ Y_{3t} &= \beta_{30} + \beta_{31}Y_{1t} + \beta_{32}Y_{2t} + \gamma_{31}X_{1t} + \gamma_{32}X_{2t} + u_{3t} \end{aligned} \tag{20.2.1}$$

where, as usual, the Y's and the X's are, respectively, the endogenous and exogenous variables. The disturbances are such that

$$\text{cov}\,(u_{1t}, u_{2t}) = \text{cov}\,(u_{1t}, u_{3t}) = \text{cov}\,(u_{2t}, u_{3t}) = 0$$

that is, the same-period disturbances in different equations are uncorrelated (technically, this is the assumption of **zero contemporaneous correlation**).

Now consider the first equation of (20.2.1). Since it contains only the exogenous variables on the right-hand side and since by assumption they are uncorrelated with the disturbance term u_{1t}, this equation satisfies the critical assumption of the classical OLS, namely, uncorrelatedness between the explanatory variables and the stochastic disturbances. Hence, OLS can be applied straightforwardly to this equation. Next consider the second equation of (20.2.1), which contains the endogenous variable Y_1 as an explanatory variable along with the nonstochastic X's. Now OLS can also be applied to this equation, provided Y_{1t} and u_{2t} are uncorrelated. Is this so? The answer is yes because u_1, which affects Y_1, is by assumption uncorrelated with u_2. Therefore, for all practical purposes, Y_1 is a predetermined variable insofar as Y_2 is concerned. Hence, one can proceed with OLS estimation of this equation. Carrying this argument a step further, we can also apply OLS to the third equation in (20.2.1) because both Y_1 and Y_2 are uncorrelated with u_3.

Thus, in the recursive system OLS can be applied to each equation separately. Actually, we do not have a simultaneous-equation problem in this situation. From the structure of such systems, it is clear that there is no interdependence among the endogenous variables. Thus, Y_1 affects Y_2, but Y_2 does not affect Y_1. Similarly, Y_1 and Y_2 influence Y_3 without, in turn, being influenced by Y_3. In other words, each equation exhibits a unilateral causal dependence, hence the name causal models.[5] Schematically, we have Figure 20.1.

FIGURE 20.1
Recursive model.

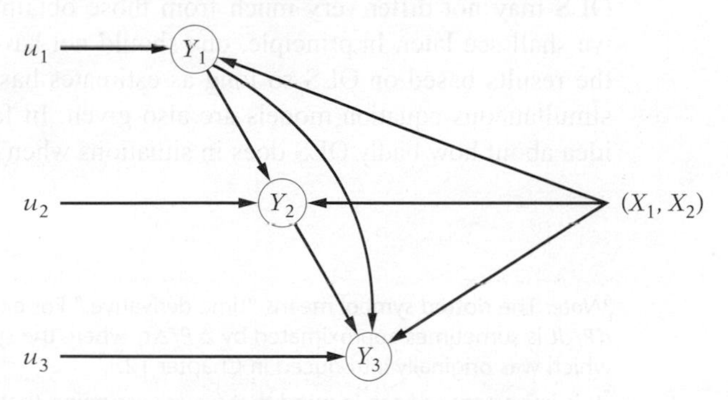

[5]The alternative name *triangular* stems from the fact that if we form the matrix of the coefficients of the endogenous variables given in Eq. (20.2.1), we obtain the following triangular matrix:

$$\begin{array}{l} \\ \text{Equation 1} \\ \text{Equation 2} \\ \text{Equation 3} \end{array} \begin{array}{c} \begin{array}{ccc} Y_1 & Y_2 & Y_3 \end{array} \\ \begin{bmatrix} 1 & 0 & 0 \\ \beta_{21} & 1 & 0 \\ \beta_{31} & \beta_{32} & 1 \end{bmatrix} \end{array}$$

Note that the entries above the main diagonal are zeros (why?).

As an example of a recursive system, one may postulate the following model of wage and price determination:

$$\text{Price equation:} \quad \dot{P}_t = \beta_{10} + \beta_{11}\dot{W}_{t-1} + \beta_{12}\dot{R}_t + \beta_{13}\dot{M}_t + \beta_{14}\dot{L}_t + u_{1t}$$

$$\text{Wage equation:} \quad \dot{W}_t = \beta_{20} + \beta_{21}\text{UN}_t + \beta_{32}\dot{P}_t + u_{2t} \tag{20.2.2}$$

where $\dot{P}$ = rate of change of price per unit of output
$\dot{W}$ = rate of change of wages per employee
$\dot{R}$ = rate of change of price of capital
$\dot{M}$ = rate of change of import prices
$\dot{L}$ = rate of change of labor productivity
UN = unemployment rate, %[6]

The price equation postulates that the rate of change of price in the current period is a function of the rates of change in the prices of capital and of raw material, the rate of change in labor productivity, and the rate of change in wages in the previous period. The wage equation shows that the rate of change in wages in the current period is determined by the current period rate of change in price and the unemployment rate. It is clear that the causal chain runs from $\dot{W}_{t-1} \rightarrow \dot{P}_t \rightarrow \dot{W}_t$, and hence OLS may be applied to estimate the parameters of the two equations individually.

Although recursive models have proved to be useful, most simultaneous-equation models do not exhibit such a unilateral cause-and-effect relationship. Therefore, OLS, in general, is inappropriate to estimate a single equation in the context of a simultaneous-equation model.[7]

There are some who argue that, although OLS is generally inapplicable to simultaneous-equation models, one can use it, if only as a standard or norm of comparison. That is, one can estimate a structural equation by OLS, with the resulting properties of biasedness, inconsistency, etc. Then the same equation may be estimated by other methods especially designed to handle the simultaneity problem and the results of the two methods compared, at least qualitatively. In many applications the results of the inappropriately applied OLS may not differ very much from those obtained by more sophisticated methods, as we shall see later. In principle, one should not have much objection to the production of the results based on OLS so long as estimates based on alternative methods devised for simultaneous-equation models are also given. In fact, this approach might give us some idea about how badly OLS does in situations when it is applied inappropriately.[8]

[6]*Note:* The dotted symbol means "time derivative." For example, $\dot{P} = dP/dt$. For discrete time series, dP/dt is sometimes approximated by $\Delta P/\Delta t$, where the symbol Δ is the first difference operator, which was originally introduced in Chapter 12.

[7]It is important to keep in mind that we are assuming that the disturbances across equations are contemporaneously uncorrelated. If this is not the case, we may have to resort to the Zellner SURE (seemingly unrelated regressions) estimation technique to estimate the parameters of the recursive system. See A. Zellner, "An Efficient Method of Estimating Seemingly Unrelated Regressions and Tests for Aggregation Bias," *Journal of the American Statistical Association,* vol. 57, 1962, pp. 348–368.

[8]It may also be noted that in small samples the alternative estimators, like the OLS estimators, are also biased. But the OLS estimator has the "virtue" that it has minimum variance among these alternative estimators. But this is true of small samples only.

20.3 Estimation of a Just Identified Equation: The Method of Indirect Least Squares (ILS)

For a just or exactly identified structural equation, the method of obtaining the estimates of the structural coefficients from the OLS estimates of the reduced-form coefficients is known as the **method of indirect least squares (ILS),** and the estimates thus obtained are known as the **indirect least-squares estimates.** ILS involves the following three steps:

Step 1. We first obtain the reduced-form equations. As noted in Chapter 19, these reduced-form equations are obtained from the structural equations in such a manner that the dependent variable in each equation is the only endogenous variable and is a function solely of the predetermined (exogenous or lagged endogenous) variables and the stochastic error term(s).

Step 2. We apply OLS to the reduced-form equations individually. This operation is permissible since the explanatory variables in these equations are predetermined and hence uncorrelated with the stochastic disturbances. The estimates thus obtained are consistent.[9]

Step 3. We obtain estimates of the original structural coefficients from the estimated reduced-form coefficients obtained in Step 2. As noted in Chapter 19, if an equation is exactly identified, there is a one-to-one correspondence between the structural and reduced-form coefficients; that is, one can derive unique estimates of the former from the latter.

As this three-step procedure indicates, the name ILS derives from the fact that structural coefficients (the object of primary enquiry in most cases) are obtained indirectly from the OLS estimates of the reduced-form coefficients.

An Illustrative Example

Consider the demand-and-supply model introduced in Section 19.2, which for convenience is given below with a slight change in notation:

$$\text{Demand function:} \quad Q_t = \alpha_0 + \alpha_1 P_t + \alpha_2 X_t + u_{1t} \tag{20.3.1}$$

$$\text{Supply function:} \quad Q_t = \beta_0 + \beta_1 P_t + u_{2t} \tag{20.3.2}$$

where Q = quantity
P = price
X = income or expenditure

Assume that X is exogenous. As noted previously, the supply function is exactly identified whereas the demand function is not identified.

The reduced-form equations corresponding to the preceding structural equations are

$$P_t = \Pi_0 + \Pi_1 X_t + w_t \tag{20.3.3}$$

$$Q_t = \Pi_2 + \Pi_3 X_t + v_t \tag{20.3.4}$$

[9]In addition to being consistent, the estimates "may be best unbiased and/or asymptotically efficient, depending respectively upon whether (*i*) the z's [= X's] are exogenous and not merely predetermined [i.e., do not contain lagged values of endogenous variables] and/or (*ii*) the distribution of the disturbances is normal." See W. C. Hood and Tjalling C. Koopmans, *Studies in Econometric Method,* John Wiley & Sons, New York, 1953, p. 133.

where the Π's are the reduced-form coefficients and are (nonlinear) combinations of the structural coefficients, as shown in Eqs. (19.2.16) and (19.2.18), and where w and v are linear combinations of the structural disturbances u_1 and u_2.

Notice that each reduced-form equation contains only one endogenous variable, which is the dependent variable and which is a function solely of the exogenous variable X (income) and the stochastic disturbances. Hence, the parameters of the preceding reduced-form equations may be estimated by OLS. These estimates are

$$\hat{\Pi}_1 = \frac{\sum p_t x_t}{\sum x_t^2} \tag{20.3.5}$$

$$\hat{\Pi}_0 = \bar{P} - \hat{\Pi}_1 \bar{X} \tag{20.3.6}$$

$$\hat{\Pi}_3 = \frac{\sum q_t x_t}{\sum x_t^2} \tag{20.3.7}$$

$$\hat{\Pi}_2 = \bar{Q} - \hat{\Pi}_3 \bar{X} \tag{20.3.8}$$

where the lowercase letters, as usual, denote deviations from sample means and where $\bar{Q}$ and $\bar{P}$ are the sample mean values of Q and P. As noted previously, the $\hat{\Pi}_i$'s are consistent estimators and under appropriate assumptions are also minimum variance unbiased or asymptotically efficient (see footnote 9).

Since our primary objective is to determine the structural coefficients, let us see if we can estimate them from the reduced-form coefficients. Now as shown in Section 19.2, the supply function is exactly identified. Therefore, its parameters can be estimated uniquely from the reduced-form coefficients as follows:

$$\beta_0 = \Pi_2 - \beta_1 \Pi_0 \quad \text{and} \quad \beta_1 = \frac{\Pi_3}{\Pi_1}$$

Hence, the estimates of these parameters can be obtained from the estimates of the reduced-form coefficients as

$$\hat{\beta}_0 = \hat{\Pi}_2 - \hat{\beta}_1 \hat{\Pi}_0 \tag{20.3.9}$$

$$\hat{\beta}_1 = \frac{\hat{\Pi}_3}{\hat{\Pi}_1} \tag{20.3.10}$$

which are the ILS estimators. Note that the parameters of the demand function cannot be thus estimated (however, see Exercise 20.13).

To give some numerical results, we obtained the data shown in Table 20.1. First we estimate the reduced-form equations, regressing separately price and quantity on per capita real consumption expenditure. The results are as follows:

$$\begin{aligned} \hat{P}_t &= 90.9601 + 0.0007X_t \\ \text{se} &= (4.0517) \quad (0.0002) \\ t &= (22.4499) \quad (3.0060) \qquad R^2 = (0.2440) \end{aligned} \tag{20.3.11}$$

$$\begin{aligned} \hat{Q}_t &= 59.7618 + 0.0020X_t \\ \text{se} &= (1.5600) \quad (0.00009) \\ t &= (38.3080) \quad (20.9273) \qquad R^2 = 0.9399 \end{aligned} \tag{20.3.12}$$

Using Eqs. (20.3.9) and (20.3.10), we obtain these ILS estimates:

$$\hat{\beta}_0 = -183.7043 \tag{20.3.13}$$

$$\hat{\beta}_1 = 2.6766 \tag{20.3.14}$$

TABLE 20.1
Crop Production, Crop Prices, and per Capita Personal Consumption Expenditures, 2007 Dollars, United States, 1975–2004

Source: *Economic Report of the President*, 2007. Data on Q (Table B-99), on P (Table B-101), and on X (Table B-31).

Observation	Index of Crop Production (1996 = 100), Q	Index of Crop Prices Received by Farmers (1990–1992 = 100), P	Real per Capita Personal Consumption Expenditure, X
1975	66	88	4,789
1976	67	87	5,282
1977	71	83	5,804
1978	73	89	6,417
1979	78	98	7,073
1980	75	107	7,716
1981	81	111	8,439
1982	82	98	8,945
1983	71	108	9,775
1984	81	111	10,589
1985	85	98	11,406
1986	82	87	12,048
1987	84	86	12,766
1988	80	104	13,685
1989	86	109	14,546
1990	90	103	15,349
1991	90	101	15,722
1992	96	101	16,485
1993	91	102	17,204
1994	101	105	18,004
1995	96	112	18,665
1996	100	127	19,490
1997	104	115	20,323
1998	105	107	21,291
1999	108	97	22,491
2000	108	96	23,862
2001	108	99	24,722
2002	107	105	25,501
2003	108	111	26,463
2004	112	117	27,937

Therefore, the estimated ILS regression is[10]

$$\hat{Q}_t = -183.7043 + 2.6766P_t \tag{20.3.15}$$

For comparison, we give the results of the (inappropriately applied) OLS regression of Q on P:

$$\begin{aligned} \hat{Q}_t &= \;\; 20.89 + \;\; 0.673P_t \\ \text{se} &= (23.04) \quad (0.2246) \\ t &= \;\; (0.91) \quad\; (2.99) \qquad R^2 = 0.2430 \end{aligned} \tag{20.3.16}$$

These results show how OLS can distort the "true" picture when it is applied in inappropriate situations.

[10]We have not presented the standard errors of the estimated structural coefficients because, as noted previously, these coefficients are generally nonlinear functions of the reduced-form coefficients and there is no simple method of estimating their standard errors from the standard errors of the reduced-form coefficients. For large-sample size, however, standard errors of the structural coefficients can be obtained approximately. For details, see Jan Kmenta, *Elements of Econometrics*, Macmillan, New York, 1971, p. 444.

Properties of ILS Estimators

We have seen that the estimators of the reduced-form coefficients are consistent and under appropriate assumptions also best unbiased or asymptotically efficient (see footnote 9). Do these properties carry over to the ILS estimators? It can be shown that the ILS estimators inherit all the asymptotic properties of the reduced-form estimators, such as consistency and asymptotic efficiency. But (the small sample) properties such as unbiasedness do not generally hold true. It is shown in Appendix 20A, Section 20A.1, that the ILS estimators $\hat{\beta}_0$ and $\hat{\beta}_1$ of the supply function given previously are biased but the bias disappears as the sample size increases indefinitely (that is, the estimators are consistent).[11]

20.4 Estimation of an Overidentified Equation: The Method of Two-Stage Least Squares (2SLS)

Consider the following model:

$$\text{Income function:} \quad Y_{1t} = \beta_{10} + \quad + \beta_{11}Y_{2t} + \gamma_{11}X_{1t} + \gamma_{12}X_{2t} + u_{1t} \tag{20.4.1}$$

$$\text{Money supply function:} \quad Y_{2t} = \beta_{20} + \beta_{21}Y_{1t} \quad + u_{2t} \tag{20.4.2}$$

where Y_1 = income
Y_2 = stock of money
X_1 = investment expenditure
X_2 = government expenditure on goods and services

The variables X_1 and X_2 are exogenous.

The income equation, a hybrid of quantity-theory–Keynesian approaches to income determination, states that income is determined by money supply, investment expenditure, and government expenditure. The *money supply function* postulates that the stock of money is determined (by the Federal Reserve System) on the basis of the level of income. Obviously, we have a simultaneous-equation problem, which can be checked by the simultaneity test discussed in Chapter 19.

Applying the order condition of identification, we can see that the income equation is underidentified whereas the money supply equation is overidentified. There is not much that can be done about the income equation short of changing the model specification. The overidentified money supply function may not be estimated by ILS because there are two estimates of β_{21} (the reader should verify this via the reduced-form coefficients).

As a matter of practice, one may apply OLS to the money supply equation, but the estimates thus obtained will be inconsistent in view of the likely correlation between the stochastic explanatory variable Y_1 and the stochastic disturbance term u_2. Suppose, however, we find a "proxy" for the stochastic explanatory variable Y_1 such that, although "resembling" Y_1 (in the sense that it is highly correlated with Y_1), it is uncorrelated with u_2. Such a proxy is also known as an **instrumental variable** (see Chapter 17). If one can find such a proxy, OLS can be used straightforwardly to estimate the money supply function.

[11] Intuitively this can be seen as follows: $E(\hat{\beta}_1) = \beta_1$ if $E(\hat{\Pi}_3/\hat{\Pi}_1) = (\Pi_3/\Pi_1)$. Now even if $E(\hat{\Pi}_3) = \Pi_3$ and $E(\hat{\Pi}_1), = \Pi_1$, it can be shown that $E(\hat{\Pi}_3/\hat{\Pi}_1) \neq E(\hat{\Pi}_3)/E(\hat{\Pi}_1)$; that is, the expectation of the ratio of two variables is not equal to the ratio of the expectations of the two variables. However, as shown in Appendix 20A.1, plim $(\hat{\Pi}_3/\hat{\Pi}_1)$ = plim $(\hat{\Pi}_3)$/plim $(\hat{\Pi}_1) = \Pi_3/\Pi_1$ since $\hat{\Pi}_3$ and $\hat{\Pi}_1$ are consistent estimators.

But how does one obtain such an instrumental variable? One answer is provided by the **two-stage least squares** (2SLS), developed independently by Henri Theil[12] and Robert Basmann.[13] As the name indicates, the method involves two successive applications of OLS. The process is as follows:

Stage 1. To get rid of the likely correlation between Y_1 and u_2, regress first Y_1 on *all* the predetermined variables in the *whole system,* not just that equation. In the present case, this means regressing Y_1 on X_1 and X_2 as follows:

$$Y_{1t} = \hat{\Pi}_0 + \hat{\Pi}_1 X_{1t} + \hat{\Pi}_2 X_{2t} + \hat{u}_t \tag{20.4.3}$$

where $\hat{u}_t$ are the usual OLS residuals. From Eq. (20.4.3) we obtain

$$\hat{Y}_{1t} = \hat{\Pi}_0 + \hat{\Pi}_1 X_{1t} + \hat{\Pi}_2 X_{2t} \tag{20.4.4}$$

where $\hat{Y}_{1t}$ is an estimate of the mean value of Y conditional upon the fixed X's. Note that Eq. (20.4.3) is nothing but a reduced-form regression because only the exogenous or predetermined variables appear on the right-hand side.

Equation (20.4.3) can now be expressed as

$$Y_{1t} = \hat{Y}_{1t} + \hat{u}_t \tag{20.4.5}$$

which shows that the stochastic Y_1 consists of two parts: $\hat{Y}_{1t}$, which is a linear combination of the nonstochastic X's, and a random component $\hat{u}_t$. Following the OLS theory, $\hat{Y}_{1t}$ and $\hat{u}_t$ are uncorrelated. (Why?)

Stage 2. The overidentified money supply equation can now be written as

$$\begin{aligned} Y_{2t} &= \beta_{20} + \beta_{21}(\hat{Y}_{1t} + \hat{u}_t) + u_{2t} \\ &= \beta_{20} + \beta_{21}\hat{Y}_{1t} + (u_{2t} + \beta_{21}\hat{u}_t) \\ &= \beta_{20} + \beta_{21}\hat{Y}_{1t} + u_t^* \end{aligned} \tag{20.4.6}$$

where $u_t^* = u_{2t} + \beta_{21}\hat{u}_t$.

Comparing Eq. (20.4.6) with Eq. (20.4.2), we see that they are very similar in appearance, the only difference being that Y_1 is replaced by $\hat{Y}_1$. What is the advantage of Eq. (20.4.6)? It can be shown that although Y_1 in the original money supply equation is correlated or likely to be correlated with the disturbance term u_2 (hence rendering OLS inappropriate), $\hat{Y}_{1t}$ in Eq. (20.4.6) is uncorrelated with u_t^* *asymptotically,* that is, in the large sample (or more accurately, as the sample size increases indefinitely). As a result, OLS can be applied to Eq. (20.4.6), which will give consistent estimates of the parameters of the money supply function.[14]

[12]Henri Theil, "Repeated Least-Squares Applied to Complete Equation Systems," The Hague: The Central Planning Bureau, The Netherlands, 1953 (mimeographed).

[13]Robert L. Basmann, "A Generalized Classical Method of Linear Estimation of Coefficients in a Structural Equation," *Econometrica,* vol. 25, 1957, pp. 77–83.

[14]But note that in small samples $\hat{Y}_{1t}$ is likely to be correlated with u_i^*. The reason is as follows: From Eq. (20.4.4) we see that $\hat{Y}_{1t}$ is a weighted linear combination of the predetermined X's, with $\hat{\Pi}$'s as the weights. Now even if the predetermined variables are truly nonstochastic, the $\hat{\Pi}$'s, being estimators, are stochastic. Therefore, $\hat{Y}_{1t}$ is stochastic too. Now from our discussion of the reduced-form equations and indirect least-squares estimation, it is clear that the reduced-coefficients, the $\hat{\Pi}$'s, are functions of the stochastic disturbances, such as u_2. And since $\hat{Y}_{1t}$ depends on the $\hat{\Pi}$'s, it is likely to be correlated with u_2, which is a component of u_t^*. As a result, $\hat{Y}_{1t}$ is expected to be correlated with u_t^*. But as noted previously, this correlation disappears as the sample size tends to infinity. The upshot of all this is that in small samples the 2SLS procedure may lead to biased estimation.

As this two-stage procedure indicates, the basic idea behind 2SLS is to "purify" the stochastic explanatory variable Y_1 of the influence of the stochastic disturbance u_2. This goal is accomplished by performing the reduced-form regression of Y_1 on all the predetermined variables in the system (Stage 1), obtaining the estimates $\hat{Y}_{1t}$ and replacing Y_{1t} in the original equation by the estimated $\hat{Y}_{1t}$, and then applying OLS to the equation thus transformed (Stage 2). The estimators thus obtained are consistent; that is, they converge to their true values as the sample size increases indefinitely.

To illustrate 2SLS further, let us modify the income–money supply model as follows:

$$Y_{1t} = \beta_{10} + \beta_{12}Y_{2t} + \gamma_{11}X_{1t} + \gamma_{12}X_{2t} + u_{1t} \tag{20.4.7}$$

$$Y_{2t} = \beta_{20} + \beta_{21}Y_{1t} + \gamma_{23}X_{3t} + \gamma_{24}X_{4t} + u_{2t} \tag{20.4.8}$$

where, in addition to the variables already defined, X_3 = income in the previous time period and X_4 = money supply in the previous period. Both X_3 and X_4 are predetermined.

It can be readily verified that both Eqs. (20.4.7) and (20.4.8) are overidentified. To apply 2SLS, we proceed as follows: In Stage 1 we regress the endogenous variables on *all* the predetermined variables in the system. Thus,

$$Y_{1t} = \hat{\Pi}_{10} + \hat{\Pi}_{11}X_{1t} + \hat{\Pi}_{12}X_{2t} + \hat{\Pi}_{13}X_{3t} + \hat{\Pi}_{14}X_{4t} + \hat{u}_{1t} \tag{20.4.9}$$

$$Y_{2t} = \hat{\Pi}_{20} + \hat{\Pi}_{21}X_{1t} + \hat{\Pi}_{22}X_{2t} + \hat{\Pi}_{23}X_{3t} + \hat{\Pi}_{24}X_{4t} + \hat{u}_{2t} \tag{20.4.10}$$

In Stage 2 we replace Y_1 and Y_2 in the original (structural) equations by their estimated values from the preceding two regressions and then run the OLS regressions as follows:

$$Y_{1t} = \beta_{10} + \beta_{12}\hat{Y}_{2t} + \gamma_{11}X_{1t} + \gamma_{12}X_{2t} + u^*_{1t} \tag{20.4.11}$$

$$Y_{2t} = \beta_{20} + \beta_{21}\hat{Y}_{1t} + \gamma_{23}X_{3t} + \gamma_{24}X_{4t} + u^*_{2t} \tag{20.4.12}$$

where $u^*_{1t} = u_{1t} + \beta_{12}\hat{u}_{2t}$ and $\hat{u}^*_{2t} = u_{2t} + \beta_{21}\hat{u}_{1t}$. The estimates thus obtained will be consistent.

Note the following features of 2SLS.

1. It can be applied to an individual equation in the system without directly taking into account any other equation(s) in the system. Hence, for solving econometric models involving a large number of equations, 2SLS offers an economical method. For this reason the method has been used extensively in practice.
2. Unlike ILS, which provides multiple estimates of parameters in the overidentified equations, 2SLS provides only one estimate per parameter.
3. It is easy to apply because all one needs to know is the total number of exogenous or predetermined variables in the system without knowing any other variables in the system.
4. Although specially designed to handle overidentified equations, the method can also be applied to exactly identified equations. But then ILS and 2SLS will give identical estimates. (Why?)
5. If the R^2 values in the reduced-form regressions (that is, Stage 1 regressions) are very high, say, in excess of 0.8, the classical OLS estimates and 2SLS estimates will be very close. But this result should not be surprising because if the R^2 value in the first stage is very high, it means that the estimated values of the endogenous variables are very close to their actual values, and hence the latter are less likely to be correlated with the stochastic disturbances in the original structural equations. (Why?)[15] If, however, the

[15]In the extreme case of $R^2 = 1$ in the first-stage regression, the endogenous explanatory variable in the original (overidentified) equation will be practically nonstochastic (why?).

R^2 values in the first-stage regressions are very low, the 2SLS estimates will be practically meaningless because we shall be replacing the original Y's in the second-stage regressions by the estimated $\hat{Y}$'s from the first-stage regressions, which will essentially represent the disturbances in the first-stage regressions. In other words, in this case, the $\hat{Y}$'s will be very poor proxies for the original Y's.

6. Notice that in reporting the ILS regression in Eq. (20.3.15) we did not state the standard errors of the estimated coefficients (for reasons explained in footnote 10). But we can do this for the 2SLS estimates because the structural coefficients are directly estimated from the second-stage (OLS) regressions. There is, however, a caution to be exercised. The estimated standard errors in the second-stage regressions need to be modified because, as can be seen from Eq. (20.4.6), the error term u_t^* is, in fact, the original error term u_{2t} plus $\beta_{21}\hat{u}_t$. Hence, the variance of u_t^* is not exactly equal to the variance of the original u_{2t}. However, the modification required can be easily effected by the formula given in Appendix 20A, Section 20A.2.
7. In using the 2SLS, bear in mind the following remarks of Henri Theil:

> The statistical justification of the 2SLS is of the large-sample type. When there are no lagged endogenous variables, . . . the 2SLS coefficient estimators are consistent if the exogenous variables are constant in repeated samples and if the disturbance[s] [appearing in the various behavioral or structural equations] . . . are independently and identically distributed with zero means and finite variances. . . . If these two conditions are satisfied, the sampling distribution of 2SLS coefficient estimators becomes approximately normal for large samples. . . .
>
> When the equation system contains lagged endogenous variables, the consistency and large-sample normality of the 2SLS coefficient estimators require an additional condition, . . . that as the sample increases the mean square of the values taken by each lagged endogenous variable converges in probability to a positive limit. . . .
>
> If [the disturbances appearing in the various structural equations are] *not* independently distributed, lagged endogenous variables are not independent of the current operation of the equation system . . . , which means these variables are not really predetermined. If these variables are nevertheless treated as predetermined in the 2SLS procedure, the resulting estimators are not consistent.[16]

20.5 2SLS: A Numerical Example

To illustrate the 2SLS method, consider the income–money supply model given previously in Eqs. (20.4.1) and (20.4.2). As shown, the money supply equation is overidentified. To estimate the parameters of this equation, we resort to the two-stage least-squares method. The data required for analysis are given in Table 20.2; this table also gives some data that are required to answer some of the questions given in the exercises.

Stage 1 Regression

We first regress the stochastic explanatory variable income Y_1, represented by GDP, on the predetermined variables private investment X_1 and government expenditure X_2, obtaining the following results:

$$\begin{aligned} \hat{Y}_{1t} &= 2689.848 \quad + \quad 1.8700X_{1t} + \quad 2.0343X_{2t} \\ \text{se} &= \quad (67.9874) \qquad (0.1717) \qquad (0.1075) \\ t &= \quad (39.5639) \qquad (10.8938) \qquad (18.9295) \qquad R^2 = 0.9964 \end{aligned} \tag{20.5.1}$$

[16]Henri Theil, *Introduction to Econometrics,* Prentice Hall, Englewood Cliffs, NJ, 1978, pp. 341–342.

TABLE 20.2
GDP, M2, FEDEXP, TB6, USA, 1970–2005

Source: *Economic Report of the President*, 2007. Tables B-2, B-69, B-84, and B-73.

Observation	GDP (Y_1)	M2 (Y_2)	GPDI (X_1)	FEDEXP (X_2)	TB6 (X_3)
1970	3,771.9	626.5	427.1	201.1	6.562
1971	3,898.6	710.3	475.7	220.0	4.511
1972	4,105.0	802.3	532.1	244.4	4.466
1973	4,341.5	855.5	594.4	261.7	7.178
1974	4,319.6	902.1	550.6	293.3	7.926
1975	4,311.2	1,016.2	453.1	346.2	6.122
1976	4,540.9	1,152.0	544.7	374.3	5.266
1977	4,750.5	1,270.3	627.0	407.5	5.510
1978	5,015.0	1,366.0	702.6	450.0	7.572
1979	5,173.4	1,473.7	725.0	497.5	10.017
1980	5,161.7	1,599.8	645.3	585.7	11.374
1981	5,291.7	1,755.4	704.9	672.7	13.776
1982	5,189.3	1,910.3	606.0	748.5	11.084
1983	5,423.8	2,126.5	662.5	815.4	8.75
1984	5,813.6	2,310.0	857.7	877.1	9.80
1985	6,053.7	2,495.7	849.7	948.2	7.66
1986	6,263.6	2,732.4	843.9	1,006.0	6.03
1987	6,475.1	2,831.4	870.0	1,041.6	6.05
1988	6,742.7	2,994.5	890.5	1,092.7	6.92
1989	6,981.4	3,158.5	926.2	1,167.5	8.04
1990	7,112.5	3,278.6	895.1	1,253.5	7.47
1991	7,100.5	3,379.1	822.2	1,315.0	5.49
1992	7,336.6	3,432.5	889.0	1,444.6	3.57
1993	7,532.7	3,484.0	968.3	1,496.0	3.14
1994	7,835.5	3,497.5	1,099.6	1,533.1	4.66
1995	8,031.7	3,640.4	1,134.0	1,603.5	5.59
1996	8,328.9	3,815.1	1,234.3	1,665.8	5.09
1997	8,703.5	4,031.6	1,387.7	1,708.9	5.18
1998	9,066.9	4,379.0	1,524.1	1,734.9	4.85
1999	9,470.3	4,641.1	1,642.6	1,787.6	4.76
2000	9,817.0	4,920.9	1,735.5	1,864.4	5.92
2001	9,890.7	5,430.3	1,598.4	1,969.5	3.39
2002	10,048.8	5,774.1	1,557.1	2,101.1	1.69
2003	10,301.0	6,062.0	1,613.1	2,252.1	1.06
2004	10,703.5	6,411.7	1,770.6	2,383.0	1.58
2005	11,048.6	6,669.4	1,866.3	2,555.9	3.40

Notes: Y_1 = GDP = gross domestic product (billions of chained 2000 dollars).
Y_2 = M2 = M2 money supply (billions of dollars).
X_1 = GPDI = gross private domestic investment (billions of chained 2000 dollars).
X_2 = FEDEXP = Federal government expenditure (billions of dollars).
X_3 = TB6 = 6-month Treasury bill rate (%).

Stage 2 Regression

We now estimate the money supply function (20.4.2), replacing the endogenous variable Y_1 by Y_1 estimated from Eq. (20.5.1) ($= \hat{Y}_1$). The results are as follows:

$$\begin{aligned} \hat{Y}_{2t} &= -2440.180 \quad + \quad 0.7920\hat{Y}_{1t} \\ \text{se} &= \quad (127.3720) \qquad (0.0178) \\ t &= \quad (-19.1579) \qquad (44.5246) \qquad R^2 = 0.9831 \end{aligned} \tag{20.5.2}$$

As we pointed out previously, the estimated standard errors given in Eq. (20.5.2) need to be corrected in the manner suggested in Appendix 20.A, Section 20A.2. Effecting this correction (most econometric packages can do it now), we obtain the following results:

$$\begin{aligned} \hat{Y}_{2t} &= -2440.180 \quad + \quad 0.7920\hat{Y}_{1t} \\ \text{se} &= \quad (126.9598) \qquad (0.0212) \\ t &= \quad (-17.3149) \qquad (37.3057) \qquad R^2 = 0.9803 \end{aligned} \tag{20.5.3}$$

As noted in Appendix 20A, Section 20A.2, the standard errors given in Eq. (20.5.3) do not differ much from those given in Eq. (20.5.2) because the R^2 in Stage 1 regression is very high.

OLS Regression

For comparison, we give the regression of money stock on income as shown in Eq. (20.4.2) without "purging" the stochastic Y_{1t} of the influence of the stochastic disturbance term.

$$\begin{aligned} \hat{Y}_{2t} &= \quad 2195.468 \quad + \quad 0.7911Y_{1t} \\ \text{se} &= \quad (126.6460) \qquad (0.0211) \\ t &= \quad (-17.3354) \qquad (37.3812) \qquad R^2 = 0.9803 \end{aligned} \tag{20.5.4}$$

Comparing the "inappropriate" OLS results with the Stage 2 regression, we see that the two regressions are virtually the same. Does this mean that the 2SLS procedure is worthless? Not at all. That in the present situation the two results are practically identical should not be surprising because, as noted previously, the R^2 value in the first stage is very high, thus making the estimated $\hat{Y}_{1t}$ virtually identical with the actual Y_{1t}. Therefore, in this case the OLS and second-stage regressions will be more or less similar. But there is no guarantee that this will happen in every application. An implication, then, is that in overidentified equations one should not accept the classical OLS procedure without checking the second-stage regression(s).

Simultaneity between GDP and Money Supply

Let us find out if GDP (Y_1) and money supply (Y_2) are mutually dependent. For this purpose we use the Hausman test of simultaneity discussed in Chapter 19.

First we regress GDP on X_1 (investment expenditure) and X_2 (government expenditure), the exogenous variables in the system (i.e., we estimate the reduced-form regression). From this regression we obtain the estimated GDP and the residuals $\hat{v}_t$, as suggested in Eq. (19.4.7). Then we regress money supply on estimated GDP and v_t to obtain the following results:

$$\begin{aligned} \hat{Y}_{2t} &= -2198.297 \quad + \quad 0.7915\hat{Y}_{1t} + \ 0.6984\hat{v}_t \\ \text{se} &= \quad (129.0548) \qquad (0.0215) \qquad (0.2970) \\ t &= \quad (-17.0338) \qquad (36.70016) \qquad (2.3511) \end{aligned} \tag{20.5.5}$$

Since the t value of $\hat{v}_t$ is statistically significant (the p value is 0.0263), we cannot reject the hypothesis of simultaneity between money supply and GDP, which should not be surprising. (*Note:* Strictly speaking, this conclusion is valid only in large samples; technically, it is only valid as the sample size increases indefinitely.)

Hypothesis Testing

Suppose we want to test the hypothesis that income has no effect on money demand. Can we test this hypothesis with the usual t test from the estimated regression (20.5.2)? Yes, provided the sample is large and provided we correct the standard errors as shown in Eq. (20.5.3), we can use the t test to test the significance of an individual coefficient and the F test to test joint significance of two or more coefficients, using formula (8.4.7).[17]

What happens if the error term in a structural equation is autocorrelated and/or correlated with the error term in another structural equation in the system? A full answer to this question will take us beyond the scope of the book and is better left for the references (see the reference given in footnote 7). Nevertheless, estimation techniques (such as Zellner's SURE technique) do exist to handle these complications.

To conclude the discussion of our numerical example, it may be added that the various steps involved in the application of 2SLS are now routinely handled by software packages such as STATA and *EViews*. It was only for pedagogical reason we showed the details of 2SLS. See Exercise 20.15.

20.6 Illustrative Examples

In this section we consider some applications of the simultaneous-equation methods.

EXAMPLE 20.1

Advertising, Concentration, and Price Margins

To study the interrelationships among advertising, concentration (as measured by the concentration ratio), and price-cost margins, Allyn D. Strickland and Leonard W. Weiss formulated the following three-equation model.[18]

Advertising intensity function:

$$\text{Ad}/S = a_0 + a_1 M + a_2(\text{CD}/S) + a_3 C + a_4 C^2 + a_5 \text{Gr} + a_6 \text{Dur} \tag{20.6.1}$$

Concentration function:

$$C = b_0 + b_1(\text{Ad}/S) + b_2(\text{MES}/S) \tag{20.6.2}$$

Price-cost margin function:

$$M = c_0 + c_1(K/S) + c_2 \text{Gr} + c_3 C + c_4 \text{GD} + c_5(\text{Ad}/S) + c_6(\text{MES}/S) \tag{20.6.3}$$

where
Ad = advertising expense
S = value of shipments
C = four-firm concentration ratio
CD = consumer demand
MES = minimum efficient scale
M = price/cost margin
Gr = annual rate of growth of industrial production
Dur = dummy variable for durable goods industry
K = capital stock
GD = measure of geographic dispersion of output

[17]But take this precaution: The restricted and unrestricted RSS in the numerator must be calculated using predicted Y (as in Stage 2 of 2SLS) and the RSS in the denominator is calculated using actual rather than predicted values of the regressors. For an accessible discussion of this point, see T. Dudley Wallace and J. Lew Silver, *Econometrics: An Introduction*, Addison–Wesley, Reading, Mass., 1988, Sec. 8.5.

[18]See their "Advertising, Concentration, and Price-Cost Margins," *Journal of Political Economy*, vol. 84, no. 5, 1976, pp. 1109–1121.

EXAMPLE 20.1 *(Continued)*

By the order conditions for identifiability, Eq. (20.6.2) is overidentified, whereas Eqs. (20.6.1) and (20.6.3) are exactly identified.

The data for the analysis came largely from the 1963 Census of Manufacturers and covered 408 of the 417 four-digit manufacturing industries. The three equations were first estimated by OLS, yielding the results shown in Table 20.3. To correct for the simultaneous-equation bias, the authors reestimated the model using 2SLS. The ensuing results are given in Table 20.4. We leave it to the reader to compare the two results.

TABLE 20.3
OLS Estimates of Three Equations (*t* ratios in parentheses)

	Dependent Variable		
	Ad/*S* Eq. (20.6.1)	*C* Eq. (20.6.2)	*M* Eq. (20.6.3)
Constant	−0.0314 (−7.45)	0.2638 (25.93)	0.1682 (17.15)
C	0.0554 (3.56)	—	0.0629 (2.89)
C^2	−0.0568 (−3.38)	—	—
M	0.1123 (9.84)	—	—
CD/*S*	0.0257 (8.94)	—	—
Gr	0.0387 (1.64)	—	0.2255 (2.61)
Dur	−0.0021 (−1.11)	—	—
Ad/*S*	—	1.1613 (3.3)	1.6536 (11.00)
MES/*S*	—	4.1852 (18.99)	0.0686 (0.54)
K/*S*	—	—	0.1123 (8.03)
GD	—	—	−0.0003 (−2.90)
R^2	0.374	0.485	0.402
df	401	405	401

TABLE 20.4
Two-Stage Least-Squares Estimates of Three Equations (*t* ratios in parentheses)

	Dependent Variable		
	Ad/*S* Eq. (20.6.1)	*C* Eq. (20.6.2)	*M* Eq. (20.6.3)
Constant	−0.0245 (−3.86)	0.2591 (21.30)	0.1736 (14.66)
C	0.0737 (2.84)	—	0.0377 (0.93)
C^2	−0.0643 (−2.64)	—	—
M	0.0544 (2.01)	—	—
CD/*S*	0.0269 (8.96)	—	—
Gr	0.0539 (2.09)	—	0.2336 (2.61)
Dur	−0.0018 (−0.93)	—	—
Ad/*S*	—	1.5347 (2.42)	1.6256 (5.52)
MES/*S*	—	4.169 (18.84)	0.1720 (0.92)
K/*S*	—	—	0.1165 (7.30)
GD	—	—	−0.0003 (−2.79)

EXAMPLE 20.2 *Klein's Model I*

In Example 18.6 we discussed briefly the pioneering model of Klein. Initially, the model was estimated for the period 1920–1941. The underlying data are given in Table 20.5; and OLS, reduced-form, and 2SLS estimates are given in Table 20.6. We leave it to the reader to interpret these results.

(Continued)

EXAMPLE 20.2 *(Continued)*

TABLE 20.5 **Underlying Data for Klein's Model I**

Year	C^*	P	W	I	K_{-1}	X	W'	G	T
1920	39.8	12.7	28.8	2.7	180.1	44.9	2.2	2.4	3.4
1921	41.9	12.4	25.5	−0.2	182.8	45.6	2.7	3.9	7.7
1922	45.0	16.9	29.3	1.9	182.6	50.1	2.9	3.2	3.9
1923	49.2	18.4	34.1	5.2	184.5	57.2	2.9	2.8	4.7
1924	50.6	19.4	33.9	3.0	189.7	57.1	3.1	3.5	3.8
1925	52.6	20.1	35.4	5.1	192.7	61.0	3.2	3.3	5.5
1926	55.1	19.6	37.4	5.6	197.8	64.0	3.3	3.3	7.0
1927	56.2	19.8	37.9	4.2	203.4	64.4	3.6	4.0	6.7
1928	57.3	21.1	39.2	3.0	207.6	64.5	3.7	4.2	4.2
1929	57.8	21.7	41.3	5.1	210.6	67.0	4.0	4.1	4.0
1930	55.0	15.6	37.9	1.0	215.7	61.2	4.2	5.2	7.7
1931	50.9	11.4	34.5	−3.4	216.7	53.4	4.8	5.9	7.5
1932	45.6	7.0	29.0	−6.2	213.3	44.3	5.3	4.9	8.3
1933	46.5	11.2	28.5	−5.1	207.1	45.1	5.6	3.7	5.4
1934	48.7	12.3	30.6	−3.0	202.0	49.7	6.0	4.0	6.8
1935	51.3	14.0	33.2	−1.3	199.0	54.4	6.1	4.4	7.2
1936	57.7	17.6	36.8	2.1	197.7	62.7	7.4	2.9	8.3
1937	58.7	17.3	41.0	2.0	199.8	65.0	6.7	4.3	6.7
1938	57.5	15.3	38.2	−1.9	201.8	60.9	7.7	5.3	7.4
1939	61.6	19.0	41.6	1.3	199.9	69.5	7.8	6.6	8.9
1940	65.0	21.1	45.0	3.3	201.2	75.7	8.0	7.4	9.6
1941	69.7	23.5	53.3	4.9	204.5	88.4	8.5	13.8	11.6

*Interpretation of column heads is listed in Example 18.6.

Source: These data are taken from G. S. Maddala, *Econometrics,* McGraw-Hill, New York, 1977, p. 238.

TABLE 20.6* **OLS, Reduced-Form and 2SLS Estimates of Klein's Model I**

Source: G. S. Maddala, *Econometrics,* McGraw-Hill, New York, 1977, p. 242.

OLS:

$$\hat{C} = \underset{(1.203)}{16.237} + \underset{(0.091)}{0.193}P + \underset{(0.040)}{0.796}(W + W') + \underset{(0.090)}{0.089}P_{-1} \qquad \bar{R}^2 = 0.978 \quad DW = 1.367$$

$$\hat{I} = \underset{(5.465)}{10.125} + \underset{(0.097)}{0.479}P + \underset{(0.100)}{0.333}P_{-1} - \underset{(0.026)}{0.112}K_{-1} \qquad \bar{R}^2 = 0.919 \quad DW = 1.810$$

$$\hat{W} = \underset{(1.151)}{0.064} + \underset{(0.032)}{0.439}X + \underset{(0.037)}{0.146}X_{-1} + \underset{(0.031)}{0.130}t \qquad \bar{R}^2 = 0.985 \quad DW = 1.958$$

Reduced-form:

$$\hat{P} = \underset{(10.870)}{46.383} + \underset{(0.444)}{0.813}P_{-1} - \underset{(0.067)}{0.213}K_{-1} + \underset{(0.252)}{0.015}X_{-1} + \underset{(0.154)}{0.297}t - \underset{(0.385)}{0.926}T + \underset{(0.373)}{0.443}G$$

$$\bar{R}^2 = 0.753 \quad DW = 1.854$$

$$\widehat{W + W'} = \underset{(8.787)}{40.278} + \underset{(0.359)}{0.823}P_{-1} - \underset{(0.054)}{0.144}K_{-1} + \underset{(0.204)}{0.115}X_{-1} + \underset{(0.124)}{0.881}t - \underset{(0.311)}{0.567}T + \underset{(0.302)}{0.859}G$$

$$\bar{R}^2 = 0.949 \quad DW = 2.395$$

$$\hat{X} = \underset{(18.860)}{78.281} + \underset{(0.771)}{1.724}P_{-1} - \underset{(0.110)}{0.319}K_{-1} + \underset{(0.438)}{0.094}X_{-1} + \underset{(0.267)}{0.878}t - \underset{(0.669)}{0.565}T + \underset{(0.648)}{1.317}G$$

$$\bar{R}^2 = 0.882 \quad DW = 2.049$$

2SLS:

$$\hat{C} = \underset{(1.464)}{16.543} + \underset{(0.130)}{0.019}P + \underset{(0.044)}{0.810}(W + W') + \underset{(0.118)}{0.214}P_{-1} \qquad \bar{R}^2 = 0.9726$$

$$\hat{I} = \underset{(8.361)}{20.284} + \underset{(0.191)}{0.149}P + \underset{(0.180)}{0.616}P_{-1} - \underset{(0.040)}{0.157}K_{-1} \qquad \bar{R}^2 = 0.8643$$

$$\hat{W} = \underset{(1.894)}{0.065} + \underset{(0.065)}{0.438}X + \underset{(0.070)}{0.146}X_{-1} + \underset{(0.053)}{0.130}t \qquad \bar{R}^2 = 0.9852$$

*Interpretation of variables is listed in Example 18.6 (standard errors in parentheses).

EXAMPLE 20.3

The Capital Asset Pricing Model Expressed as a Recursive System

In a rather unusual application of recursive simultaneous-equation modeling, Cheng F. Lee and W. P. Lloyd[19] estimated the following model for the oil industry:

$$
\begin{aligned}
R_{1t} &= \alpha_1 + \gamma_1 M_t + u_{1t} \\
R_{2t} &= \alpha_2 + \beta_{21} R_{1t} + \gamma_2 M_t + u_{2t} \\
R_{3t} &= \alpha_3 + \beta_{31} R_{1t} + \beta_{32} R_{2t} + \gamma_3 M_t + u_{3t} \\
R_{4t} &= \alpha_4 + \beta_{41} R_{1t} + \beta_{42} R_{2t} + \beta_{43} R_{3t} + \gamma_4 M_t + u_{4t} \\
R_{5t} &= \alpha_5 + \beta_{51} R_{1t} + \beta_{52} R_{2t} + \beta_{53} R_{3t} + \beta_{54} R_{4t} + \gamma_5 M_t + u_{5t} \\
R_{6t} &= \alpha_6 + \beta_{61} R_{1t} + \beta_{62} R_{2t} + \beta_{63} R_{3t} + \beta_{64} R_{4t} + \beta_{65} R_{5t} + \gamma_6 M_t + u_{6t} \\
R_{7t} &= \alpha_7 + \beta_{71} R_{1t} + \beta_{72} R_{2t} + \beta_{73} R_{3t} + \beta_{74} R_{4t} + \beta_{75} R_{5t} + \beta_{76} R_{6t} + \gamma_7 M_t + u_{7t}
\end{aligned}
$$

where R_1 = rate of return on security 1 (= Imperial Oil)
R_2 = rate of return on security 2 (= Sun Oil)
⋮
R_7 = rate of return on security 7 (= Standard of Indiana)
M_t = rate of return on the market index
u_{it} = disturbances ($i = 1, 2, \ldots, 7$)

Before we present the results, the obvious question is: How do we choose which is security 1, which is security 2, and so on? Lee and Lloyd answer this question purely empirically. They regress the rate of return on security i on the rates of return of the remaining six securities and observe the resulting R^2. Thus, there will be seven such regressions. Then they order the estimated R^2 values, from the lowest to the highest. The security having the lowest R^2 is designated as security 1 and the one having the highest R^2 is designated as security 7. The idea behind this is intuitively simple. If the R^2 of the rate of return of, say, Imperial Oil, is lowest with respect to the other six securities, it would suggest that this security is affected least by the movements in the returns of the other securities. Therefore, the causal ordering, if any, runs from this security to the others and there is no feedback from the other securities.

Although one may object to such a purely empirical approach to causal ordering, let us present their empirical results nonetheless, which are given in Table 20.7.

In Exercise 5.5 we introduced the *characteristic line* of modern investment theory, which is simply the regression of the rate of return on security i on the market rate of return. The slope coefficient, known as the *beta coefficient*, is a measure of the volatility of the security's return. What the Lee–Lloyd regression results suggest is that there are significant intra-industry relationships between security returns, apart from the common market influence represented by the market portfolio. Thus, Standard of Indiana's return depends not only on the market rate of return but also on the rates of return on Shell Oil, Phillips Petroleum, and Union Oil. To put the matter differently, the movement in the rate of return on Standard of Indiana can be better explained if in addition to the market rate of return we also consider the rates of return experienced by Shell Oil, Phillips Petroleum, and Union Oil.

(Continued)

[19]"The Capital Asset Pricing Model Expressed as a Recursive System: An Empirical Investigation," *Journal of Financial and Quantitative Analysis,* June 1976, pp. 237–249.

EXAMPLE 20.3
(Continued)

TABLE 20.7 **Recursive System Estimates for the Oil Industry**

	Linear Form Dependent Variables						
	Standard of Indiana	**Shell Oil**	**Phillips Petroleum**	**Union Oil**	**Standard of Ohio**	**Sun Oil**	**Imperial Oil**
Standard of Indiana							
Shell Oil	0.2100*						
	(2.859)						
Phillips Petroleum	0.2293*	0.0791					
	(2.176)	(1.065)					
Union Oil	0.1754*	0.2171*	0.2225*				
	(2.472)	(3.177)	(2.337)				
Standard of Ohio	−0.0794	0.0147	0.4248*	0.1468*			
	(−1.294)	(0.235)	(5.501)	(1.735)			
Sun Oil	0.1249	0.1710*	0.0472	0.1339	0.0499		
	(1.343)	(1.843)	(0.355)	(0.908)	(0.271)		
Imperial Oil	−0.1077	0.0526	0.0354	0.1580	−0.2541*	0.0828	
	(−1.412)	(0.6804)	(0.319)	(1.290)	(−1.691)	(0.971)	
Constant	0.0868	−0.0384	−0.0127	−0.2034	0.3009	0.2013	0.3710*
	(0.681)	(1.296)	(−0.068)	(0.986)	(1.204)	(1.399)	(2.161)
Market index	0.3681*	0.4997*	0.2884	0.7609*	0.9089*	0.7161*	0.6432*
	(2.165)	(3.039)	(1.232)	(3.069)	(3.094)	(4.783)	(3.774)
R^2	0.5020	0.4658	0.4106	0.2532	0.0985	0.2404	0.1247
Durbin–Watson	2.1083	2.4714	2.2306	2.3468	2.2181	2.3109	1.9592

*Denotes significance at 0.10 level or better for two-tailed test.
Note: The *t* values appear in parentheses beneath the coefficients.
Source: Cheng F. Lee and W. P. Lloyd, op. cit., Table 3b.

EXAMPLE 20.4
Revised Form of St. Louis Model[20]

The well-known, and often controversial, St. Louis model originally developed in the late 1960s has been revised from time to time. One such revision is given in Table 20.8, and the empirical results based on this revised model are given in Table 20.9. (*Note:* A dot over a variable means the growth rate of that variable.) The model basically consists of Eqs. (1), (2), (4), and (5) in Table 20.8, the other equations representing the definitions. Equation (1) was estimated by OLS. Equations (1), (2), and (4) were estimated using the Almon distributed-lag method with (endpoint) constraints on the coefficients. Where relevant, the equations were corrected for first-order (ρ_1) and/or second-order (ρ_2) serial correlation.

Examining the results, we observe that it is the rate of growth in the money supply that primarily determines the rate of growth of (nominal) GNP and not the rate of growth in high-employment expenditures. The sum of the M coefficients is 1.06, suggesting that a 1 percent (sustained) increase in the money supply on the average leads to about 1.06 percent increase in the nominal GNP. On the other hand, the sum of the E coefficients, about 0.05, suggests that a change in high-employment government expenditure has little impact on the rate of growth of nominal GNP. It is left to the reader to interpret the results of the other regressions reported in Table 20.9.

[20]Federal Reserve Bank of St. Louis, *Review,* May 1982, p. 14.

EXAMPLE 20.4 *(Continued)*

TABLE 20.8 The St. Louis Model

(1) $\dot{Y}_1 = C1 + \sum_{i=0}^{4} CM_i(\dot{M}_{t-i}) + \sum_{i=0}^{4} CE(\dot{E}_{t-i}) + \varepsilon 1_t$

(2) $\dot{P}_t = C2 + \sum_{i=1}^{4} CPE_i(\dot{PE}_{t-i}) + \sum_{i=0}^{5} CD_i(\dot{X}_{t-i} - \dot{XF}^*_{t-i1})$
$+ CPA(\dot{PA}_t) + CDUM1(DUM1) + CDUM2(DUM2) + \varepsilon 2_t$

(3) $\dot{PA}_t = \sum_{i=1}^{21} CPRL_i(\dot{P}_{t-i})$

(4) $RL_t = C3 + \sum_{i=0}^{20} CPRL_i(\dot{P}_{t-i}) + \varepsilon 3_t$

(5) $U_t - UF_t = CG(GAP_t) + CG1(GAP_{t-1}) + \varepsilon 4_t$

(6) $Y_t = (P_t/100)(X_t)$

(7) $\dot{Y}_t = [(Y_t/Y_{t-i})^4 - 1]100$

(8) $\dot{X}_t = [(X_t/X_{t-i})^4 - 1]100$

(9) $\dot{P}_t = [(P_t/P_{t-i})^4 - 1]100$

(10) $GAP_t = [(XF_t/X_t)/XF_t]100$

(11) $\dot{XF}^*_t = [(XF_t/X_{t-1})^4 - 1]100$

Y = nominal GNP
M = money stock (M1)
E = high employment expenditures
P = GNP deflator (1972 = 100)
PE = relative price of energy
X = output in 1972 dollars
XF = potential output (Rasche/Tatom)
RL = corporate bond rate
U = unemployment rate
UF = unemployment rate at full employment
DUM1 = control dummy (1971–III to 1973–I – 1; 0 elsewhere)
DUM2 = postcontrol dummy (1973–II to 1975–I = 1; 0 elsewhere)

Source: Federal Reserve Bank of St. Louis, *Review,* May 1982, p. 14.

TABLE 20.9
In-Sample Estimation: 1960–I to 1980–IV (absolute value of *t* statistic in parentheses)

Source: Federal Reserve Bank of St. Louis, *Review,* May 1982, p. 14.

(1)
$$\hat{\dot{Y}}_t = \underset{(2.15)}{2.44} + \underset{(3.38)}{0.40\dot{M}_t} + \underset{(5.06)}{0.39\dot{M}_{t-1}} + \underset{(2.18)}{0.22\dot{M}_{t-2}} + \underset{(0.82)}{0.06\dot{M}_{t-3}} - \underset{(0.11)}{0.01\dot{M}_{t-4}}$$
$$+ \underset{(1.46)}{0.06\dot{E}_t} + \underset{(0.63)}{0.02\dot{E}_{t-1}} - \underset{(0.57)}{0.02\dot{E}_{t-2}} - \underset{(0.52)}{0.02\dot{E}_{t-3}} + \underset{(0.34)}{0.01\dot{E}_{t-4}}$$
$R^2 = 0.39$ se = 3.50 DW = 2.02

(2)
$$\hat{\dot{P}}_t = \underset{(2.53)}{0.96} + \underset{(0.75)}{0.01\dot{PE}_{t-1}} + \underset{(1.96)}{0.04\dot{PE}_{t-2}} - \underset{(0.73)}{0.01\dot{PE}_{t-3}} + \underset{(1.38)}{0.02\dot{PE}_{t-4}}$$
$$- \underset{(0.18)}{0.00(\dot{X}_t - \dot{XF}^*_t)} + \underset{(1.43)}{0.01(\dot{X}_{t-1} - \dot{XF}^*_{t-1})} + \underset{(4.63)}{0.02(\dot{X}_{t-2} - \dot{XF}^*_{t-2})}$$
$$+ \underset{(3.00)}{0.02(\dot{X}_{t-3} - \dot{XF}^*_{t-3})} + \underset{(2.42)}{0.02(\dot{X}_{t-4} - \dot{XF}^*_{t-4})} + \underset{(2.16)}{0.01(\dot{X}_{t-5} - \dot{XF}^*_{t-5})}$$
$$+ \underset{(10.49)}{1.03(\dot{PA}_t)} - \underset{(1.02)}{0.61(DUM1_t)} + \underset{(2.71)}{1.65(DUM2_t)}$$
$R^2 = 0.80$ se = 1.28 DW = 1.97 $\hat{\rho} = 0.12$

(4)
$$\widehat{RL}_t = \underset{(3.12)}{2.97} + \underset{(5.22)}{0.96} \sum_{i=0}^{20} \dot{P}_{t-i}$$
$R^2 = 0.32$ se = 0.33 DW = 1.76 $\hat{\rho} = 0.94$

(5)
$$\widehat{U_t - UF_t} = \underset{(11.89)}{0.28(GAP_t)} + \underset{(6.31)}{0.14(GAP_{t-1})}$$
$R^2 = 0.63$ se = 0.17 DW = 1.95 $\hat{\rho}_1 = 1.43$ $\hat{\rho}_2 = 0.52$

Summary and Conclusions

1. Assuming that an equation in a simultaneous-equation model is identified (either exactly or over-), we have several methods to estimate it.
2. These methods fall into two broad categories: *Single-equation methods* and *systems methods*.
3. For reasons of economy, specification errors, etc., the single-equation methods are by far the most popular. A unique feature of these methods is that one can estimate a single-equation in a multiequation model without worrying too much about other equations in the system. (*Note:* For identification purposes, however, the other equations in the system count.)
4. Three commonly used single-equation methods are **OLS, ILS,** and **2SLS.**
5. Although OLS is, in general, inappropriate in the context of simultaneous-equation models, it can be applied to the so-called **recursive models** where there is a definite but unidirectional cause-and-effect relationship among the endogenous variables.
6. The method of ILS is suited for just or exactly identified equations. In this method OLS is applied to the reduced-form equation, and it is from the reduced-form coefficients that one estimates the original structural coefficients.
7. The method of 2SLS is especially designed for overidentified equations, although it can also be applied to exactly identified equations. But then the results of 2SLS and ILS are identical. The basic idea behind 2SLS is to replace the (stochastic) endogenous explanatory variable by a linear combination of the predetermined variables in the model and use this combination as the explanatory variable in lieu of the original endogenous variable. The 2SLS method thus resembles the **instrumental variable method** of estimation in that the linear combination of the predetermined variables serves as an instrument, or proxy, for the endogenous regressor.
8. A noteworthy feature of both ILS and 2SLS is that the estimates obtained are consistent, that is, as the sample size increases indefinitely, the estimates converge to their true population values. The estimates may not satisfy small-sample properties, such as unbiasedness and minimum variance. Therefore, the results obtained by applying these methods to small samples and the inferences drawn from them should be interpreted with due caution.

EXERCISES

Questions

20.1. State whether each of the following statements is true or false:

a. The method of OLS is not applicable to estimate a structural equation in a simultaneous-equation model.

b. In case an equation is not identified, 2SLS is not applicable.

c. The problem of simultaneity does not arise in a recursive simultaneous-equation model.

d. The problems of simultaneity and exogeneity mean the same thing.

e. The 2SLS and other methods of estimating structural equations have desirable statistical properties only in large samples.

f. There is no such thing as an R^2 for the simultaneous-equation model as a whole.

**g.* The 2SLS and other methods of estimating structural equations are not applicable if the equation errors are autocorrelated and/or are correlated across equations.

h. If an equation is exactly identified, ILS and 2SLS give identical results.

*Optional.

20.2. Why is it unnecessary to apply the two-stage least-squares method to exactly identified equations?

20.3. Consider the following modified Keynesian model of income determination:

$$C_t = \beta_{10} + \beta_{11} Y_t + u_{1t}$$
$$I_t = \beta_{20} + \beta_{21} Y_t + \beta_{22} Y_{t-1} + u_{2t}$$
$$Y_t = C_t + I_t + G_t$$

where $C =$ consumption expenditure
$I =$ investment expenditure
$Y =$ income
$G =$ government expenditure
G_t and Y_{t-1} are assumed predetermined

a. Obtain the reduced-form equations and determine which of the preceding equations are identified (either just or over-).

b. Which method will you use to estimate the parameters of the overidentified equation and of the exactly identified equation? Justify your answer.

20.4. Consider the following results:*

$$OLS: \ \widehat{\dot{W}_t} = 0.276 + 0.258\dot{P}_t + 0.046\dot{P}_{t-1} + 4.959V_t \qquad R^2 = 0.924$$

$$OLS: \ \widehat{\dot{P}_t} = 2.693 + 0.232\dot{W}_t - 0.544\dot{X}_t + 0.247\dot{M}_t + 0.064\dot{M}_{t-1} \quad R^2 = 0.982$$

$$2SLS: \ \widehat{\dot{W}_t} = 0.272 + 0.257\dot{P}_t + 0.046\dot{P}_{t-1} + 4.966V_t \qquad R^2 = 0.920$$

$$2SLS: \ \widehat{\dot{P}_t} = 2.686 + 0.233\dot{W}_t - 0.544\dot{X}_t + 0.246\dot{M}_t + 0.046\dot{M}_{t-1} \quad R^2 = 0.981$$

where $\dot{W}_t$, $\dot{P}_t$, $\dot{M}_t$, and $\dot{X}_t$ are percentage changes in earnings, prices, import prices, and labor productivity (all percentage changes are over the previous year), respectively, and where V_t represents unfilled job vacancies (percentage of total number of employees).

"Since the OLS and 2SLS results are practically identical, 2SLS is meaningless." Comment.

†20.5. Assume that production is characterized by the Cobb–Douglas production function

$$Q_i = AK_i^{\alpha} L_i^{\beta}$$

where $Q =$ output
$K =$ capital input
$L =$ labor input
A, α, and $\beta =$ parameters
$i = i$th firm

Given the price of final output P, the price of labor W, and the price of capital R, and assuming profit maximization, we obtain the following empirical model of production:

Production function:

$$\ln Q_i = \ln A + \alpha \ln K_i + \beta \ln L_i + \ln u_{1i} \qquad (1)$$

*Source: *Prices and Earnings in 1951–1969: An Econometric Assessment,* Department of Employment, United Kingdom, Her Majesty's Stationery Office, London, 1971, p. 30.

†Optional.

Marginal product of labor function:

$$\ln Q_i = -\ln \beta + \ln L_i + \ln \frac{W}{P} + \ln u_{2i} \tag{2}$$

Marginal product of capital function:

$$\ln Q_i = -\ln \alpha + \ln K_i + \ln \frac{R}{P} + \ln u_{3i} \tag{3}$$

where u_1, u_2, and u_3 are stochastic disturbances.

In the preceding model there are three equations in three endogenous variables Q, L, and K. P, R, and W are exogenous.

a. What problems do you encounter in estimating the model if $\alpha + \beta = 1$, that is, when there are constant returns to scale?

b. Even if $\alpha + \beta \neq 1$, can you estimate the equations? Answer by considering the identifiability of the system.

c. If the system is not identified, what can be done to make it identifiable?

Note: Equations (2) and (3) are obtained by differentiating Q with respect to labor and capital, respectively, setting them equal to W/P and R/P, transforming the resulting expressions into logarithms, and adding (the logarithm of) the disturbance terms.

20.6. Consider the following demand-and-supply model for money:

$$\textit{Demand for money:} \quad M_t^d = \beta_0 + \beta_1 Y_1 + \beta_2 R_t + \beta_3 P_t + u_{1t}$$

$$\textit{Supply of money:} \quad M_t^s = \alpha_0 + \alpha_1 Y_t + u_{2t}$$

where M = money
Y = income
R = rate of interest
P = price

Assume that R and P are predetermined.

a. Is the demand function identified?

b. Is the supply function identified?

c. Which method would you use to estimate the parameters of the identified equation(s)? Why?

d. Suppose we modify the supply function by adding the explanatory variables Y_{t-1} and M_{t-1}. What happens to the identification problem? Would you still use the method you used in (*c*)? Why or why not?

20.7. Refer to Exercise 18.10. For the two-equation system there obtain the reduced-form equations and estimate their parameters. Estimate the indirect least-squares regression of consumption on income and compare your results with the OLS regression.

Empirical Exercises

20.8. Consider the following model:

$$R_t = \beta_0 + \beta_1 M_t + \beta_2 Y_t + u_{1t}$$

$$Y_t = \alpha_0 + \alpha_1 R_t + u_{2t}$$

where M_t (money supply) is exogenous, R_t is the interest rate, and Y_t is GDP.

a. How would you justify the model?

b. Are the equations identified?

c. Using the data given in Table 20.2, estimate the parameters of the identified equations. Justify the method(s) you use.

20.9. Suppose we change the model in Exercise 20.8 as follows:

$$R_t = \beta_0 + \beta_1 M_t + \beta_2 Y_t + \beta_3 Y_{t-1} + u_{1t}$$
$$Y_t = \alpha_0 + \alpha_1 R_t + u_{2t}$$

a. Find out if the system is identified.

b. Using the data given in Table 20.2, estimate the parameters of the identified equation(s).

20.10. Consider the following model:

$$R_t = \beta_0 + \beta_1 M_t + \beta_2 Y_t + u_{1t}$$
$$Y_t = \alpha_0 + \alpha_1 R_t + \alpha_2 I_t + u_{2t}$$

where the variables are as defined in Exercise 20.8. Treating I (domestic investment) and M exogenously, determine the identification of the system. Using the data given in Table 20.2, estimate the parameters of the identified equation(s).

20.11. Suppose we change the model of Exercise 20.10 as follows:

$$R_t = \beta_0 + \beta_1 M_t + \beta_2 Y_t + u_{1t}$$
$$Y_t = \alpha_0 + \alpha_1 R_t + \alpha_2 I_t + u_{2t}$$
$$I_t = \gamma_0 + \gamma_1 R_t + u_{3t}$$

Assume that M is determined exogenously.

a. Find out which of the equations are identified.

b. Estimate the parameters of the identified equation(s) using the data given in Table 20.2. Justify your method(s).

20.12. Verify the standard errors reported in Eq. (20.5.3).

20.13. Return to the demand-and-supply model given in Eqs. (20.3.1) and (20.3.2). Suppose the supply function is altered as follows:

$$Q_t = \beta_0 + \beta_1 P_{t-1} + u_{2t}$$

where P_{t-1} is the price prevailing in the previous period.

a. If X (expenditure) and P_{t-1} are predetermined, is there a simultaneity problem?

b. If there is, are the demand and supply functions each identified? If they are, obtain their reduced-form equations and estimate them from the data given in Table 20.1.

c. From the reduced-form coefficients, can you derive the structural coefficients? Show the necessary computations.

20.14. *Class Exercise:* Consider the following simple macroeconomic model for the U.S. economy, say, for the period 1960–1999.*

Private consumption function:

$$C_t = \alpha_0 + \alpha_1 Y_t + \alpha_2 C_{t-1} + u_{1t} \qquad \alpha_1 > 0,\ 0 < \alpha_2 < 1$$

Private gross investment function:

$$I_t = \beta_0 + \beta_1 Y_t + \beta_2 R_t + \beta_3 I_{t-1} + u_{2t} \qquad \beta_1 > 0,\ \beta_2 < 0,\ 0 < \beta_3 < 1$$

A money demand function:

$$R_t = \lambda_0 + \lambda_1 Y_t + \lambda_2 M_{t-1} + \lambda_3 P_t + \lambda_4 R_{t-1} + u_{3t}$$
$$\lambda_1 > 0,\ \lambda_2 < 0,\ \lambda_3 > 0,\ 0 < \lambda_4 < 1$$

*Adapted from H. R. Seddighi, K. A. Lawler, and A. V. Katos, *Econometrics: A Practical Approach*, Routledge, New York, 2000, p. 204.

Income identity:

$$Y_t = C_t + I_t + G_t$$

where C = real private consumption; I = real gross private investment, G = real government expenditure, Y = real GDP, M = M2 money supply at current prices, R = long-term interest rate (%), and P = Consumer Price Index. The endogenous variables are C, I, R, and Y. The predetermined variables are: $C_{t-1}, I_{t-1}, M_{t-1}, P_t, R_{t-1}$, and G_t plus the intercept term. The u's are the error terms.

a. Using the order condition of identification, determine which of the four equations are identified, either exact or over-.

b. Which method(s) do you use to estimate the identified equations?

c. Obtain suitable data from government and/or private sources, estimate the model, and comment on your results.

20.15. In this exercise we examine data for 534 workers obtained from the Current Population Survey (CPS) for 1985. The data can be found as Table 20.10 on the textbook website.* The variables in this table are defined as follows:

W = wages \$, per hour; occup = occupation; sector = 1 for manufacturing, 2 for construction, 0 for other; union = 1 if union member, 0 otherwise; educ = years of schooling; exper = work experience in years; age = age in years; sex = 1 for female; marital status = 1 if married; race = 1 for other, 2 for Hispanic, 3 for white; region = 1 if lives in the South.

Consider the following simple wage determination model:

$$\ln W = \beta_1 + \beta_2 \text{Educ} + \beta_3 \text{Exper} + \beta_4 \text{Exper}^2 + u_i \qquad (1)$$

a. Suppose education, like wages, is endogenous. How would you find out that in Equation (1) education is in fact endogenous? Use the data given in the table in your analysis.

b. Does the Hausman test support your analysis in (*a*)? Explain fully.

20.16. *Class Exercise:* Consider the following demand-and-supply model for loans of commercial banks to businesses:

$$\textit{Demand: } Q_t^d = \alpha_1 + \alpha_2 R_t + \alpha_2 \text{RD}_t + \alpha_4 \text{IPI}_t + u_{1t}$$

$$\textit{Supply: } Q_t^s = \beta_1 + \beta_2 R_t + \beta_3 \text{RS}_t + \beta_4 \text{TBD}_t + u_{2t}$$

Where Q = total commercial bank loans (\$billion); R = average prime rate; RS = 3-month Treasury bill rate; RD = AAA corporate bond rate; IPI = Index of Industrial Production; and TBD = total bank deposits.

a. Collect data on these variables for the period 1980–2007 from various sources, such as www.economagic.com, the website of the Federal Reserve Bank of St. Louis, or any other source.

b. Are the demand and supply functions identified? List which variables are endogenous and which are exogenous.

c. How would you go about estimating the demand and supply functions listed above? Show the necessary calculations.

d. Why are both R and RS included in the model? What is the role of IPI in the model?

*Data can be found on the Web, at http://lib.stat.cmu.edu/datasets/cps_85_wages.

Appendix 20A

20A.1 Bias in the Indirect Least-Squares Estimators

To show that the ILS estimators, although consistent, are biased, we use the demand-and-supply model given in Eqs. (20.3.1) and (20.3.2). From Eq. (20.3.10) we obtain

$$\hat{\beta}_1 = \frac{\hat{\Pi}_3}{\hat{\Pi}_1}$$

Now

$$\hat{\Pi}_3 = \frac{\sum q_t x_t}{\sum x_t^2} \qquad \text{from Eq. (20.3.7)}$$

and

$$\hat{\Pi}_1 = \frac{\sum p_t x_t}{\sum x_t^2} \qquad \text{from Eq. (20.3.5)}$$

Therefore, on substitution, we obtain

$$\hat{\beta}_1 = \frac{\sum q_t x_t}{\sum p_t x_t} \tag{1}$$

Using Eqs. (20.3.3) and (20.3.4), we obtain

$$p_t = \Pi_1 x_t + (w_t - \bar{w}) \tag{2}$$

$$q_t = \Pi_3 x_t + (v_t - \bar{v}) \tag{3}$$

where $\bar{w}$ and $\bar{v}$ are the mean values of w_t and v_t, respectively.

Substituting Eqs. (2) and (3) into Eq. (1), we obtain

$$\begin{aligned} \hat{\beta}_1 &= \frac{\Pi_3 \sum x_t^2 + \sum (v_t - \bar{v}) x_t}{\Pi_1 \sum x_t^2 + \sum (w_t - \bar{w}) x_t} \\ &= \frac{\Pi_3 + \sum (v_t - \bar{v}) x_t / \sum x_t^2}{\Pi_1 + \sum (w_t - \bar{w}) x_t / \sum x_t^2} \end{aligned} \tag{4}$$

Since the expectation operator E is a linear operator, we cannot take the expectation of Eq. (4), although it is clear that $\hat{\beta}_1 \neq (\Pi_3/\Pi_1)$ generally. (Why?)

But as the sample size tends to infinity, we can obtain

$$\text{plim}\,(\hat{\beta}_1) = \frac{\text{plim}\,\Pi_3 + \text{plim}\,\sum (v_t - \bar{v}) x_t / \sum x_t^2}{\text{plim}\,\Pi_1 + \text{plim}\,\sum (w_t - \bar{w}) x_t / \sum x_t^2} \tag{5}$$

where use is made of the properties of plim, namely, that

$$\text{plim}\,(A + B) = \text{plim}\,A + \text{plim}\,B \text{ and plim}\left(\frac{A}{B}\right) = \frac{\text{plim}\,A}{\text{plim}\,B}$$

Now as the sample size is increased indefinitely, the second term in both the denominator and the numerator of Eq. (5) tends to zero (why?), yielding

$$\text{plim}\,(\hat{\beta}_1) = \frac{\Pi_3}{\Pi_1} \tag{6}$$

showing that, although biased, $\hat{\beta}_1$ is a consistent estimator of β_1.

20A.2 Estimation of Standard Errors of 2SLS Estimators

The purpose of this appendix is to show that the standard errors of the estimates obtained from the second-page regression of the 2SLS procedure, using the formula applicable in OLS estimation, are not the "proper" estimates of the "true" standard errors. To see this, we use the income–money supply model given in Eqs. (20.4.1) and (20.4.2). We estimate the parameters of the overidentified money supply function from the second-stage regression as

$$Y_{2t} = \beta_{20} + \beta_{21}\hat{Y}_{1t} + u_t^* \tag{20.4.6}$$

where

$$u_t^* = u_{2t} + \beta_{21}\hat{u}_t \tag{7}$$

Now when we run regression (20.4.6), the standard error of, say, $\hat{\beta}_{21}$ is obtained from the following expression:

$$\text{var}(\hat{\beta}_{21}) = \frac{\hat{\sigma}_{u^*}^2}{\sum \hat{y}_{1t}^2} \tag{8}$$

where

$$\hat{\sigma}_{u^*}^2 = \frac{\sum(\hat{u}_t^*)^2}{n-2} = \frac{\sum(Y_{2t} - \hat{\beta}_{20} - \hat{\beta}_{21}\hat{Y}_{1t})^2}{n-2} \tag{9}$$

But $\sigma_{u^*}^2$ is not the same thing as $\hat{\sigma}_{u_2}^2$, where the latter is an unbiased estimate of the true variance of u_2. This difference can be readily verified from Eq. (7). To obtain the true (as defined previously) $\hat{\sigma}_{u_2}^2$, we proceed as follows:

$$\hat{u}_{2t} = Y_{2t} - \hat{\beta}_{20} - \hat{\beta}_{21}Y_{1t}$$

where $\hat{\beta}_{20}$ and $\hat{\beta}_{21}$ are the estimates from the second-stage regression. Hence,

$$\hat{\sigma}_{u_2}^2 = \frac{\sum(Y_{2t} - \hat{\beta}_{20} - \hat{\beta}_{21}Y_{1t})^2}{n-2} \tag{10}$$

Note the difference between Eqs. (9) and (10): In Eq. (10) we use actual Y_1 rather than the estimated Y_1 from the first-stage regression.

Having estimated Eq. (10), the easiest way to correct the standard errors of coefficients estimated in the second-stage regression is to multiply each one of them by $\hat{\sigma}_{u_2}/\hat{\sigma}_{u_{\ddagger}^*}$. Note that if Y_{1t} and $\hat{Y}_{1t}$ are very close, that is, the R^2 in the first-stage regression is very high, the correction factor $\hat{\sigma}_{u_2}/\hat{\sigma}_{u^*}$ will be close to 1, in which case the estimated standard errors in the second-stage regression may be taken as the true estimates. But in other situations, we shall have to use the preceding correction factor.

Chapter 21

Time Series Econometrics: Some Basic Concepts

We noted in Chapter 1 that one of the important types of data used in empirical analysis is **time series** data. In this and the following chapter we take a closer look at such data not only because of the frequency with which they are used in practice but also because they pose several challenges to econometricians and practitioners.

First, empirical work based on time series data assumes that the underlying time series is **stationary.** Although we have discussed the concept of stationarity intuitively in Chapter 1, we discuss it more fully in this chapter. More specifically, we will try to find out what stationarity means and why one should worry about it.

Second, in Chapter 12, on autocorrelation, we discussed several causes of autocorrelation. Sometimes autocorrelation results because the underlying time series is nonstationary.

Third, in regressing a time series variable on another time series variable(s), one often obtains a very high R^2 (in excess of 0.9) even though there is no meaningful relationship between the two variables. Sometimes we expect no relationship between two variables, yet a regression of one on the other variable often shows a significant relationship. This situation exemplifies the problem of **spurious,** or **nonsense, regression,** whose nature will be explored shortly. It is therefore very important to find out if the relationship between economic variables is spurious or nonsensical. We will see in this chapter how spurious regressions can arise if time series are not stationary.

Fourth, some financial time series, such as stock prices, exhibit what is known as the **random walk phenomenon.** This means the best prediction of the price of a stock, say IBM, tomorrow is equal to its price today plus a purely random shock (or error term). If this were in fact the case, forecasting asset prices would be a futile exercise.

Fifth, regression models involving time series data are often used for forecasting. In view of the preceding discussion, we would like to know if such forecasting is valid if the underlying time series are not stationary.

Finally, causality tests (recall the Granger and Sims causality tests discussed in Chapter 17) assume that the time series involved in analysis are stationary. Therefore, tests of stationarity should precede tests of causality.

At the outset a disclaimer is in order. The topic of time series analysis is so vast and evolving and some of the mathematics underlying the various techniques of time series analysis is so involved that the best we hope to achieve in an introductory text like this is to give the reader a glimpse of some of the fundamental concepts of time series analysis. For those who want to pursue this topic further, we provide references.[1]

21.1 A Look at Selected U.S. Economic Time Series

To set the ball rolling, and to give the reader a feel for the somewhat esoteric concepts of time series analysis to be developed in this chapter, it might be useful to consider several U.S. economic time series of general interest. The time series we consider are:

DPI = real disposable personal income (billions of dollars)
GDP = gross domestic product (billions of dollars)
PCE = real personal consumption expenditure (billions of dollars)
CP = corporate profits (billions of dollars)
Dividend = dividends, (billions of dollars)

The time period covered is from 1947–I to 2007–IV, for a total of 244 quarters, and all data are seasonally adjusted at the annual rate. All the data are collected from FRED, the economic website of the Federal Reserve Bank of St. Louis. GDP, DPI, and PCE are in constant dollars, here 2000 dollars. CP and Dividend are in nominal dollars.

To save space, the raw data are posted on the book's website. But to get some idea of these data, we have plotted them in the following two figures. Figure 21.1 is a plot of the data of logarithms of GDP, DPI, and PCE and Figure 21.2 presents the logs of the other two time series (CP and Dividend). It is common practice to plot the log of a time series to get a glimpse of the growth rate of such a series. A visual plot of the data is usually the first step in the analysis of time series. In these figures the letter L denotes the natural logarithm.

The first impression we get from these two figures is that all these time series seem to be "trending" upward, albeit with fluctuations. Suppose we want to speculate on the shape of these curves beyond the sample period, say for all the quarters of 2008.[2] We can do that if we know the statistical, or stochastic, mechanism, or the **data generating process (DGP)** that generated these curves. But what is that mechanism? To answer this and related questions, we need to study some "new" vocabulary that has been developed by time series analysts, to which we now turn.

[1]At the introductory level, these references may be helpful: Gary Koop, *Analysis of Economic Data,* John Wiley & Sons, New York, 2000; Jeff B. Cromwell, Walter C. Labys, and Michel Terraza, *Univariate Tests for Time Series Models,* Sage Publications, California, Ansbury Park, 1994; Jeff B. Cromwell, Michael H. Hannan, Walter C. Labys, and Michel Terraza, *Multivariate Tests for Time Series Models,* Sage Publications, California, Ansbury Park, 1994; and H. R. Seddighi, K. A. Lawler, and A. V. Katos, *Econometrics: A Practical Approach,* Routledge, New York, 2000. At the intermediate level, see Walter Enders, *Applied Econometric Time Series,* John Wiley & Sons, New York, 1995; Kerry Patterson, *An Introduction to Applied Econometrics: A Time Series Approach,* St. Martin's Press, New York, 2000; T. C. Mills, *The Econometric Modelling of Financial Time Series,* 2d ed., Cambridge University Press, New York, 1999; Marno Verbeek, *A Guide to Modern Econometrics,* John Wiley & Sons, New York, 2000; and Wojciech W. Charemza and Derek F. Deadman, *New Directions in Econometric Practice: General to Specific Modelling and Vector Autoregression,* 2d ed., Edward Elgar Publisher, New York, 1997. At the advanced level, see J. D. Hamilton, *Time Series Analysis,* Princeton University Press, Princeton, NJ, 1994, and G. S. Maddala and In-Moo Kim, *Unit Roots, Cointegration, and Structural Change,* Cambridge University Press, 1998. At the applied level, see B. Bhaskara Rao, ed., *Cointegration for the Applied Economist,* St. Martin's Press, New York, 1994, and Chandan Mukherjee, Howard White, and Marc Wuyts, *Econometrics and Data Analysis for Developing Countries,* Routledge, New York, 1998.

[2]Of course, we have the actual data for this period now and could compare it with the data that is "predicted" on the basis of the earlier period.

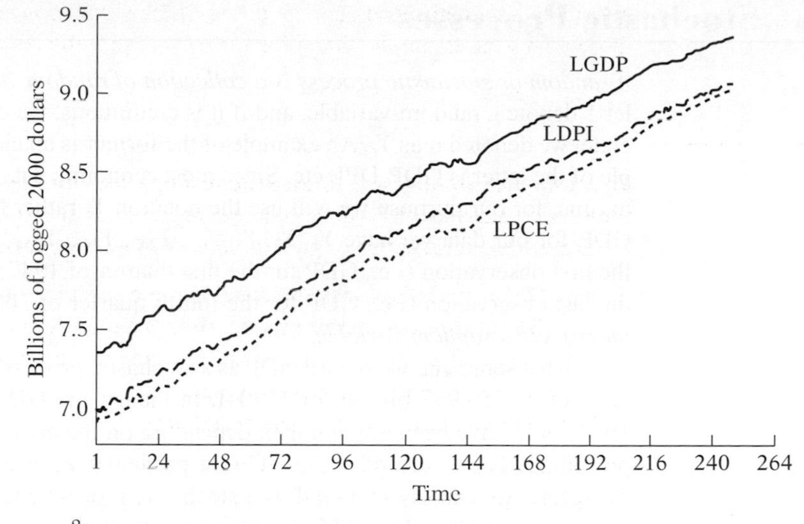

FIGURE 21.1 Logarithms of real GDP, DPI, and PCE, United States, 1947–2007 (quarterly, $ billions).

Note: In the figure the letter L denotes natural logarithm.

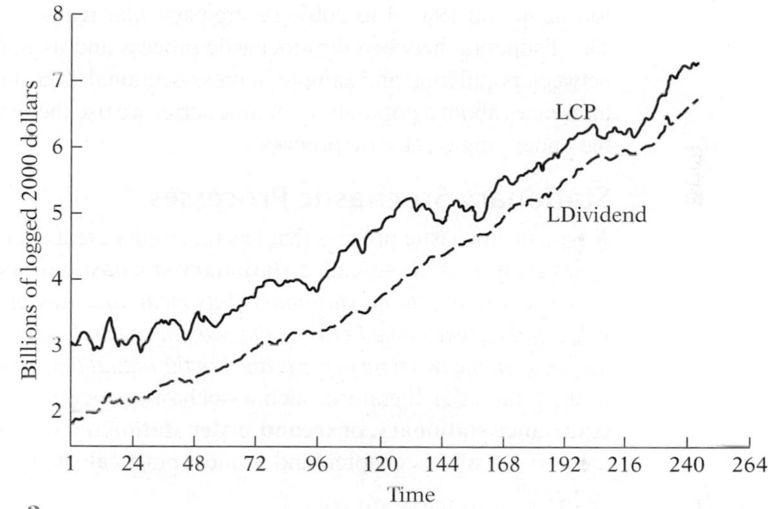

FIGURE 21.2 Logarithms of corporate profits (CP) and dividends, United States, 1947–2007 (quarterly, $ billions).

Note: L denotes logarithm.

21.2 Key Concepts[3]

What is this vocabulary? It consists of concepts such as these:

1. Stochastic processes
2. Stationarity processes
3. Purely random processes
4. Nonstationary processes
5. Integrated variables
6. Random walk models
7. Cointegration
8. Deterministic and stochastic trends
9. Unit root tests

In what follows we will discuss each of these concepts. Our discussion will often be heuristic. Wherever possible and helpful, we will provide appropriate examples.

[3]The following discussion is based on Maddala et al., op. cit., Charemza et al., op. cit., and Carol Alexander, *Market Models: A Guide to Financial Data Analysis*, John Wiley & Sons, New York, 2001.

21.3 Stochastic Processes

A random or stochastic process is a collection of random variables ordered in time.[4] If we let Y denote a random variable, and if it is continuous, we denote it as $Y(t)$, but if it is discrete, we denoted it as Y_t. An example of the former is an electrocardiogram, and an example of the latter is GDP, DPI, etc. Since most economic data are collected at discrete points in time, for our purpose we will use the notation Y_t rather than $Y(t)$. If we let Y represent GDP, for our data we have $Y_1, Y_2, Y_3, \ldots, Y_{242}, Y_{243}, Y_{244}$, where the subscript 1 denotes the first observation (i.e., GDP for the first quarter of 1947) and the subscript 244 denotes the last observation (i.e., GDP for the fourth quarter of 2007). *Keep in mind that each of these Y's is a random variable.*

In what sense can we regard GDP as a stochastic process? Consider for instance the real GDP of $3,759.997 billion for 1970–I. In theory, the GDP figure for the first quarter of 1970 could have been any number, depending on the economic and political climate then prevailing. The figure of 3,759.997 is a particular **realization** of all such possibilities.[5] Therefore, we can say that GDP is a stochastic process and the actual values we observed for the period 1947–I to 2007–IV are particular realizations of that process (i.e., sample). The distinction between the stochastic process and its realization is akin to the distinction between population and sample in cross-sectional data. Just as we use sample data to draw inferences about a population, in time series we use the realization to draw inferences about the underlying stochastic process.

Stationary Stochastic Processes

A type of stochastic process that has received a great deal of attention and scrutiny by time series analysts is the so-called **stationary stochastic process.** Broadly speaking, *a stochastic process is said to be stationary if its mean and variance are constant over time and the value of the covariance between the two time periods depends only on the distance or gap or lag between the two time periods and not the actual time at which the covariance is computed.* In the time series literature, such a stochastic process is known as a **weakly stationary,** or **covariance stationary,** or **second-order stationary,** or **wide sense, stochastic process.** For the purpose of this chapter, and in most practical situations, this type of stationarity often suffices.[6]

To explain weak stationarity, let Y_t be a stochastic time series with these properties:

$$\text{Mean:} \quad E(Y_t) = \mu \tag{21.3.1}$$

$$\text{Variance:} \quad \operatorname{var}(Y_t) = E(Y_t - \mu)^2 = \sigma^2 \tag{21.3.2}$$

$$\text{Covariance:} \quad \gamma_k = E[(Y_t - \mu)(Y_{t+k} - \mu)] \tag{21.3.3}$$

where γ_k, the covariance (or autocovariance) at lag k, is the covariance between the values of Y_t and Y_{t+k}, that is, between two Y values k periods apart. If $k = 0$, we obtain γ_0, which

[4]The term "stochastic" comes from the Greek word "stokhos," which means a target or bull's-eye. If you have ever thrown darts on a dart board with the aim of hitting the bull's-eye, how often did you hit the bull's-eye? Out of a hundred darts you may be lucky to hit the bull's-eye only a few times; at other times the darts will be spread randomly around the bull's-eye.

[5]You can think of the value of $3,759.997 billion as the mean value of all possible values of GDP for the first quarter of 1970.

[6]A time series is strictly stationary if *all* the moments of its probability distribution and not just the first two (i.e., mean and variance) are invariant over time. If, however, the stationary process is normal, the weakly stationary stochastic process is also strictly stationary, for the normal stochastic process is fully specified by its two moments, the mean and the variance.

is simply the variance of $Y\,(=\sigma^2)$; if $k=1$, γ_1 is the covariance between two adjacent values of Y, the type of covariance we encountered in Chapter 12 (recall the Markov first-order autoregressive scheme).

Suppose we shift the origin of Y from Y_t to Y_{t+m} (say, from the first quarter of 1947 to the first quarter of 1952 for our GDP data). Now if Y_t is to be stationary, the mean, variance, and autocovariances of Y_{t+m} must be the same as those of Y_t. *In short, if a time series is stationary, its mean, variance, and autocovariance (at various lags) remain the same no matter at what point we measure them; that is, they are time invariant.* Such a time series will tend to return to its mean (called **mean reversion**) and fluctuations around this mean (measured by its variance) will have a broadly constant amplitude.[7] To put it differently, a stationary process will not drift too far away from its mean value because of the finite variance. As we shall see shortly, this is not the case with nonstationary stochastic processes. It should be noted that for a stationary process the speed of mean reversion depends on the autocovariances; it is quick if the autocovariances are small and slow when they are large, as we will show shortly.

If a time series is not stationary in the sense just defined, it is called a **nonstationary time series** (keep in mind we are talking only about weak stationarity). In other words, a nonstationary time series will have a *time-varying mean or a time-varying variance or both.*

Why are stationary time series so important? Because if a time series is nonstationary, we can study its behavior only for the time period under consideration. Each set of time series data will therefore be for a particular episode. As a consequence, it is not possible to generalize it to other time periods. Therefore, for the purpose of forecasting, such (nonstationary) time series may be of little practical value.

How do we know that a particular time series is stationary? In particular, are the time series shown in Figures 21.1 and 21.2 stationary? We will take this important topic up in Sections 21.8 and 21.9, where we will consider several tests of stationarity. But if we depend on common sense, it would seem that the time series depicted in Figures 21.1 and 21.2 are nonstationary, at least in the mean values. But more on this later.

Before we move on, we mention a special type of stochastic process (or time series), namely, a **purely random,** or **white noise, process.** We call a stochastic process purely random if it has zero mean, constant variance σ^2, and is serially uncorrelated.[8] You may recall that the error term u_t, entering the classical normal linear regression model that we discussed in **Part 1** of this book, was assumed to be a white noise process, which we denoted as $u_t \sim \text{IIDN}(0, \sigma^2)$; that is, u_t is independently and identically distributed as a normal distribution with zero mean and constant variance. Such a process is called a **Gaussian white noise process.**

Nonstationary Stochastic Processes

Although our interest is in stationary time series, one often encounters nonstationary time series, the classic example being the **random walk model** (RWM).[9] It is often said that asset prices, such as stock prices or exchange rates, follow a random walk; that is, they are nonstationary. We distinguish two types of random walks: (1) random walk without drift (i.e., no constant or intercept term) and (2) random walk with drift (i.e., a constant term is present).

[7]This point has been made by Keith Cuthbertson, Stephen G. Hall, and Mark P. Taylor, *Applied Econometric Techniques,* The University of Michigan Press, 1995, p. 130.

[8]If it is also independent, such a process is called **strictly white noise.**

[9]The term random walk is often compared with a drunkard's walk. Leaving a bar, the drunkard moves a random distance u_t at time t, and, continuing to walk indefinitely, will eventually drift farther and farther away from the bar. The same is said about stock prices. Today's stock price is equal to yesterday's stock price plus a random shock.

Random Walk without Drift

Suppose u_t is a white noise error term with mean 0 and variance σ^2. Then the series Y_t is said to be a random walk if

$$Y_t = Y_{t-1} + u_t \tag{21.3.4}$$

In the random walk model, as Eq. (21.3.4) shows, the value of Y at time t is equal to its value at time $(t - 1)$ plus a random shock; thus it is an AR(1) model in the language of Chapters 12 and 17. We can think of Eq. (21.3.4) as a regression of Y at time t on its value lagged one period. Believers in the **efficient capital market hypothesis** argue that stock prices are essentially random and therefore there is no scope for profitable speculation in the stock market: If one could predict tomorrow's price on the basis of today's price, we would all be millionaires.

Now from Eq. (21.3.4) we can write

$$Y_1 = Y_0 + u_1$$

$$Y_2 = Y_1 + u_2 = Y_0 + u_1 + u_2$$

$$Y_3 = Y_2 + u_3 = Y_0 + u_1 + u_2 + u_3$$

In general, if the process started at some time 0 with a value of Y_0, we have

$$Y_t = Y_0 + \sum u_t \tag{21.3.5}$$

Therefore,

$$E(Y_t) = E\left(Y_0 + \sum u_t\right) = Y_0 \quad \text{(why?)} \tag{21.3.6}$$

In like fashion, it can be shown that

$$\operatorname{var}(Y_t) = t\sigma^2 \tag{21.3.7}$$

As the preceding expression shows, the mean of Y is equal to its initial, or starting, value, which is constant, but as t increases, its variance increases indefinitely, thus violating a condition of stationarity. In short, the RWM without drift is a nonstationary stochastic process. In practice Y_0 is often set at zero, in which case $E(Y_t) = 0$.

An interesting feature of the RWM is the *persistence of random shocks* (i.e., random errors), which is clear from Eq. (21.3.5): Y_t is the sum of initial Y_0 plus the sum of random shocks. As a result, the impact of a particular shock does not die away. For example, if $u_2 = 2$ rather than $u_2 = 0$, then all Y_t's from Y_2 onward will be 2 units higher and the effect of this shock never dies out. That is why random walk is said to have an *infinite memory*. As Kerry Patterson notes, random walk remembers the shock forever;[10] that is, it has infinite memory. The sum $\sum u_t$ is also known as a **stochastic trend,** about which more will be said shortly.

Interestingly, if you write Eq. (21.3.4) as

$$(Y_t - Y_{t-1}) = \Delta Y_t = u_t \tag{21.3.8}$$

where Δ is the first difference operator that we discussed in Chapter 12, it is easy to show that, while Y_t is nonstationary, its first difference is stationary. In other words, the first differences of a random walk time series are stationary. But we will have more to say about this later.

[10] Kerry Patterson, op cit., Chapter 6.

Random Walk with Drift

Let us modify Eq. (21.3.4) as follows:

$$Y_t = \delta + Y_{t-1} + u_t \tag{21.3.9}$$

where δ is known as the **drift parameter.** The name drift comes from the fact that if we write the preceding equation as

$$Y_t - Y_{t-1} = \Delta Y_t = \delta + u_t \tag{21.3.10}$$

it shows that Y_t drifts upward or downward, depending on δ being positive or negative. Note that model (21.3.9) is also an AR(1) model.

Following the procedure discussed for random walk without drift, it can be shown that for the random walk with drift model (21.3.9),

$$E(Y_t) = Y_0 + t \cdot \delta \tag{21.3.11}$$

$$\text{var}(Y_t) = t\sigma^2 \tag{21.3.12}$$

As you can see, for RWM with drift the mean as well as the variance increases over time, again violating the conditions of (weak) stationarity. In short, RWM, with or without drift, is a nonstationary stochastic process.

To give a glimpse of the random walk with and without drift, we conducted two simulations as follows:

$$Y_t = Y_0 + u_t \tag{21.3.13}$$

where u_t are white noise error terms such that each $u_t \sim N(0, 1)$; that is, each u_t follows the standard normal distribution. From a random number generator, we obtained 500 values of u and generated Y_t as shown in Eq. (21.3.13). We assumed $Y_0 = 0$. Thus, Eq. (21.3.13) is an RWM without drift.

Now consider

$$Y_t = \delta + Y_0 + u_t \tag{21.3.14}$$

which is RWM with drift. We assumed u_t and Y_0 as in Eq. (21.3.13) and assumed that $\delta = 2$.

The graphs of models (21.3.13) and (21.3.14), respectively, are in Figures 21.3 and 21.4. The reader can compare these two diagrams in light of our discussion of the RWM with and without drift.

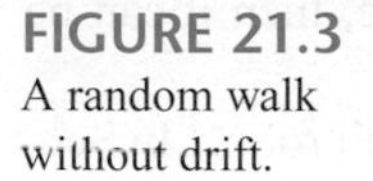

FIGURE 21.3 A random walk without drift.

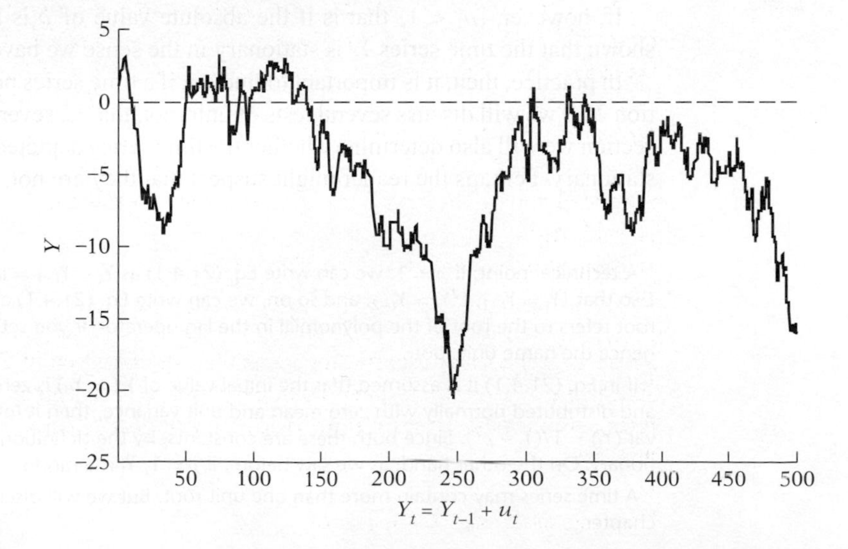

FIGURE 21.4
A random walk with drift.

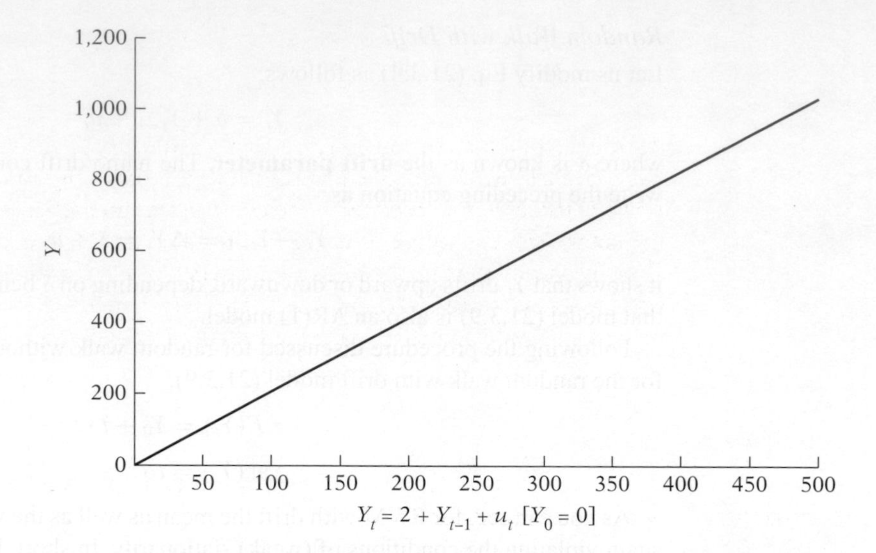

The random walk model is an example of what is known in the literature as a **unit root process.** Since this term has gained tremendous currency in the time series literature, we next explain what a unit root process is.

21.4 Unit Root Stochastic Process

Let us write the RWM (21.3.4) as:

$$Y_t = \rho Y_{t-1} + u_t \qquad -1 \leq \rho \leq 1 \tag{21.4.1}$$

This model resembles the Markov first-order autoregressive model that we discussed in the chapter on autocorrelation. If $\rho = 1$, Eq. (21.4.1) becomes a RWM (without drift). If ρ is in fact 1, we face what is known as the **unit root problem,** that is, a situation of nonstationarity; we already know that in this case the variance of Y_t is not stationary. The name unit root is due to the fact that $\rho = 1$.[11] *Thus the terms nonstationarity, random walk, unit root, and stochastic trend can be treated synonymously.*

If, however, $|\rho| < 1$, that is if the absolute value of ρ is less than one, then it can be shown that the time series Y_t is stationary in the sense we have defined it.[12]

In practice, then, it is important to find out if a time series possesses a unit root.[13] In Section 21.9 we will discuss several tests of unit root, that is, several tests of stationarity. In that section we will also determine whether the time series depicted in Figures 21.1 and 21.2 are stationary. Perhaps the reader might suspect that they are not. But we shall see.

[11]A technical point: If $\rho = 1$, we can write Eq. (21.4.1) as $Y_t - Y_{t-1} = u_t$. Now using the **lag operator** L so that $LY_t = Y_{t-1}$, $L^2Y_t = Y_{t-2}$, and so on, we can write Eq. (21.4.1) as $(1 - L)Y_t = u_t$. The term unit root refers to the root of the polynomial in the lag operator. If you set $(1 - L) = 0$, we obtain, $L = 1$, hence the name unit root.

[12]If in Eq. (21.4.1) it is assumed that the initial value of Y ($= Y_0$) is zero, $|\rho| < 1$, and u_t is white noise and distributed normally with zero mean and unit variance, then it follows that $E(Y_t) = 0$ and $\text{var}(Y_t) = 1/(1 - \rho^2)$. Since both these are constants, by the definition of weak stationarity, Y_t is stationary. On the other hand, as we saw before, if $\rho = 1$, Y_t is a random walk or nonstationary.

[13]A time series may contain more than one unit root. But we will discuss this situation later in the chapter.

21.5 Trend Stationary (TS) and Difference Stationary (DS) Stochastic Processes

The distinction between stationary and nonstationary stochastic processes (or time series) has a crucial bearing on whether the trend (the slow long-run evolution of the time series under consideration) observed in the constructed time series in Figures 21.3 and 21.4 or in the actual economic time series of Figures 21.1 and 21.2 is **deterministic** or **stochastic.** Broadly speaking, if the trend in a time series is a deterministic function of time, such as time, time-squared etc., we call it a deterministic trend, whereas if it is not predictable, we call it a stochastic trend. To make the definition more formal, consider the following model of the time series Y_t.

$$Y_t = \beta_1 + \beta_2 t + \beta_3 Y_{t-1} + u_t \tag{21.5.1}$$

where u_t is a white noise error term and where t is time measured chronologically. Now we have the following possibilities:

Pure random walk: If in Eq. (21.5.1) $\beta_1 = 0$, $\beta_2 = 0$, $\beta_3 = 1$, we get

$$Y_t = Y_{t-1} + u_t \tag{21.5.2}$$

which is nothing but a RWM without drift and is therefore nonstationary. But note that, if we write Eq. (21.5.2) as

$$\Delta Y_t = (Y_t - Y_{t-1}) = u_t \tag{21.3.8}$$

it becomes stationary, as noted before. Hence, a RWM without drift is a **difference stationary process (DSP).**

Random walk with drift: If in Eq. (21.5.1) $\beta_1 \neq 0$, $\beta_2 = 0$, $\beta_3 = 1$, we get

$$Y_t = \beta_1 + Y_{t-1} + u_t \tag{21.5.3}$$

which is a random walk with drift and is therefore nonstationary. If we write it as

$$(Y_t - Y_{t-1}) = \Delta Y_t = \beta_1 + u_t \tag{21.5.3a}$$

this means Y_t will exhibit a positive ($\beta_1 > 0$) or negative ($\beta_1 < 0$) trend (see Figure 21.4). Such a trend is called a **stochastic trend.** Equation (21.5.3*a*) is a DSP process because the nonstationarity in Y_t can be eliminated by taking first differences of the time series. Remember that u_t in Eq. (21.5.3*a*) is a white noise error term.

Deterministic trend: If in Eq. (21.5.1), $\beta_1 \neq 0$, $\beta_2 \neq 0$, $\beta_3 = 0$, we obtain

$$Y_t = \beta_1 + \beta_2 t + u_t \tag{21.5.4}$$

which is called a **trend stationary process (TSP).** Although the mean of Y_t is $\beta_1 + \beta_2 t$, which is not constant, its variance ($= \sigma^2$) is. Once the values of β_1 and β_2 are known, the mean can be forecast perfectly. Therefore, if we subtract the mean of Y_t from Y_t, the resulting series will be stationary, hence the name **trend stationary.** This procedure of removing the (deterministic) trend is called **detrending.**

Random walk with drift and deterministic trend: If in Eq. (21.5.1), $\beta_1 \neq 0$, $\beta_2 \neq 0$, $\beta_3 = 1$, we obtain:

$$Y_t = \beta_1 + \beta_2 t + Y_{t-1} + u_t \tag{21.5.5}$$

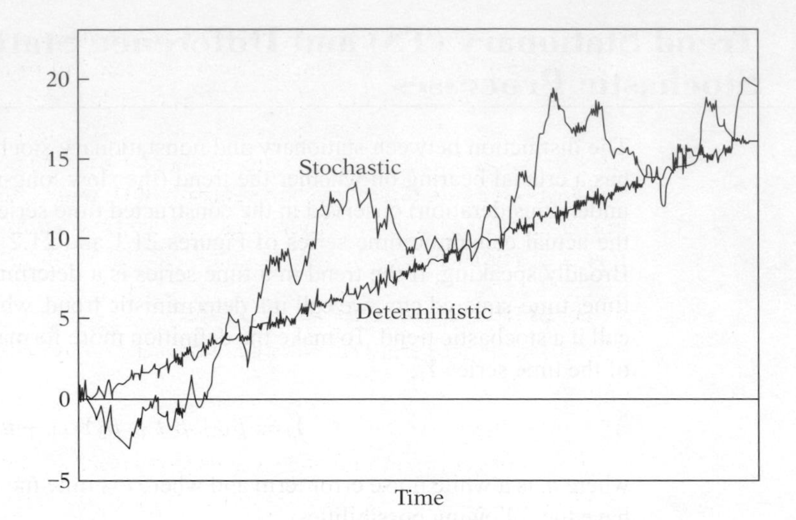

FIGURE 21.5 Deterministic versus stochastic trend.

Source: Charemza et al., op. cit., p. 91.

in which case we have a random walk with drift and a deterministic trend, which can be seen if we write this equation as

$$\Delta Y_t = \beta_1 + \beta_2 t + u_t \tag{21.5.5a}$$

which means that Y_t is nonstationary.

Deterministic trend with stationary AR(1) component: If in Eq. (21.5.1) $\beta_1 \neq 0$, $\beta_2 \neq 0$, $\beta_3 < 1$, then we get

$$Y_t = \beta_1 + \beta_2 t + \beta_3 Y_{t-1} + u_t \tag{21.5.6}$$

which is stationary around the deterministic trend.

To see the difference between stochastic and deterministic trends, consider Figure 21.5.[14] The series named stochastic in this figure is generated by an RWM with drift: $Y_t = 0.5 + Y_{t-1} + u_t$, where 500 values of u_t were generated from a standard normal distribution and where the initial value of Y was set at 1. The series named deterministic is generated as follows: $Y_t = 0.5t + u_t$, where u_t were generated as above and where t is time measured chronologically.

As you can see from Figure 21.5, in the case of the deterministic trend, the deviations from the trend line (which represents the nonstationary mean) are purely random and they die out quickly; they do not contribute to the long-run development of the time series, which is determined by the trend component $0.5t$. In the case of the stochastic trend, on the other hand, the random component u_t affects the long-run course of the series Y_t.

21.6 Integrated Stochastic Processes

The random walk model is but a specific case of a more general class of stochastic processes known as **integrated processes.** Recall that the RWM without drift is nonstationary, but its first difference, as shown in Eq. (21.3.8), is stationary. Therefore, we call the RWM without drift **integrated of order 1,** denoted as $I(1)$. Similarly, if a time series has to be differenced twice (i.e., take the first difference of the first differences) to make it stationary, we call such a time series **integrated of order 2.**[15] In general, if a (nonstationary) time

[14]The following discussion is based on Wojciech W. Charemza et al., op. cit., pp. 89–91.

[15]For example if Y_t is $I(2)$, then $\Delta\Delta Y_t = \Delta(Y_t - Y_{t-1}) = \Delta Y_t - \Delta Y_{t-1} = Y_t - 2Y_{t-1} + Y_{t-2}$ will become stationary. But note that $\Delta\Delta Y_t = \Delta^2 Y_t \neq Y_t - Y_{t-2}$.

series has to be differenced d times to make it stationary, that time series is said to be **integrated of order d.** A time series Y_t integrated of order d is denoted as $Y_t \sim I(d)$. If a time series Y_t is stationary to begin with (i.e., it does not require any differencing), it is said to be integrated of order zero, denoted by $Y_t \sim I(0)$. Thus, we will use the terms "stationary time series" and "time series integrated of order zero" to mean the same thing.

Most economic time series are generally $I(1)$; that is, they generally become stationary only after taking their first differences. Are the time series shown in Figures 21.1 and 21.2 $I(1)$ or of higher order? We will examine them in Sections 21.8 and 21.9.

Properties of Integrated Series

The following properties of integrated time series may be noted: Let X_t, Y_t, and Z_t be three time series.

1. If $X_t \sim I(0)$ and $Y_t \sim I(1)$, then $Z_t = (X_t + Y_t) = I(1)$; that is, a linear combination or sum of stationary and nonstationary time series is nonstationary.
2. If $X_t \sim I(d)$, then $Z_t = (a + bX_t) = I(d)$, where a and b are constants. That is, a linear combination of an $I(d)$ series is also $I(d)$. Thus, if $X_t \sim I(0)$, then $Z_t = (a + bX_t) \sim I(0)$.
3. If $X_t \sim I(d_1)$ and $Y_t \sim I(d_2)$, then $Z_t = (aX_t + bY_t) \sim I(d_2)$, where $d_1 < d_2$.
4. If $X_t \sim I(d)$ and $Y_t \sim I(d)$, then $Z_t = (aX_t + bY_t) \sim I(d^*)$; d^* is generally equal to d, but in some cases $d^* < d$ (see the topic of cointegration in Section 21.11).

As you can see from the preceding statements, one has to pay careful attention in combining two or more time series that are integrated of different order.

To see why this is important, consider the two-variable regression model discussed in Chapter 3, namely, $Y_t = \beta_1 + \beta_2 X_t + u_t$. Under the classical OLS assumptions, we know that

$$\hat{\beta}_2 = \frac{\sum x_t y_t}{\sum x_t^2} \tag{21.6.1}$$

where the small letters, as usual, indicate deviation from mean values. Suppose Y_t is $I(0)$, but X_t is $I(1)$; that is, the former is stationary and the latter is not. Since X_t is nonstationary, its variance will increase indefinitely, thus dominating the numerator term in Eq. (21.6.1) with the result that $\hat{\beta}_2$ will converge to zero asymptotically (i.e., in large samples) and it will not even have an asymptotic distribution.[16]

21.7 The Phenomenon of Spurious Regression

To see why stationary time series are so important, consider the following two random walk models:

$$Y_t = Y_{t-1} + u_t \tag{21.7.1}$$

$$X_t = X_{t-1} + v_t \tag{21.7.2}$$

where we generated 500 observations of u_t from $u_t \sim N(0, 1)$ and 500 observations of v_t from $v_t \sim N(0, 1)$ and assumed that the initial values of both Y and X were zero. We also assumed that u_t and v_t are serially uncorrelated as well as mutually uncorrelated. As you know by now, both these time series are nonstationary; that is, they are $I(1)$ or exhibit stochastic trends.

[16]This point is due to Maddala et al., op. cit., p. 26.

Suppose we regress Y_t on X_t. Since Y_t and X_t are uncorrelated $I(1)$ processes, the R^2 from the regression of Y on X should tend to zero; that is, there should not be any relationship between the two variables. But wait till you see the regression results:

Variable	Coefficient	Std. Error	t Statistic
C	-13.2556	0.6203	-21.36856
X	0.3376	0.0443	7.61223
	R^2 = 0.1044	d = 0.0121	

As you can see, the coefficient of X is highly statistically significant, and, although the R^2 value is low, it is statistically significantly different from zero. From these results, you may be tempted to conclude that there is a significant statistical relationship between Y and X, whereas a priori there should be none. This is in a nutshell the **phenomenon of spurious** or **nonsense regression,** first discovered by Yule.[17] Yule showed that (spurious) correlation could persist in nonstationary time series even if the sample is very large. That there is something wrong in the preceding regression is suggested by the extremely low Durbin–Watson d value, which suggests very strong first-order autocorrelation. According to Granger and Newbold, *an* $R^2 > d$ *is a good rule of thumb to suspect that the estimated regression is spurious,* as in the example above. It may be added that the R^2 and the t statistic from such a spurious regression are misleading, and the t statistics are not distributed as (Student's) t distribution and, therefore, cannot be used for testing hypotheses about the parameters.

That the regression results presented above are meaningless can be easily seen from regressing the first differences of $Y_t\,(= \Delta Y_t)$ on the first differences of $X_t\,(= \Delta X_t)$; remember that although Y_t and X_t are nonstationary, their first differences are stationary. In such a regression you will find that R^2 is practically zero, as it should be, and the Durbin–Watson d is about 2. In Exercise 21.24 you are asked to run this regression and verify the statement just made.

Although dramatic, this example is a strong reminder that one should be extremely wary of conducting regression analyses based on time series that exhibit stochastic trends. And one should therefore be extremely cautious in reading too much into the regression results based on $I(1)$ variables. For an example, see Exercise 21.26. To some extent, this is true of time series subject to deterministic trends, an example of which is given in Exercise 21.25.

21.8 Tests of Stationarity

By now the reader probably has a good idea about the nature of stationary stochastic processes and their importance. In practice we face two important questions: (1) How do we find out if a given time series is stationary? (2) If we find that a given time series is not stationary, is there a way that it can be made stationary? We take up the first question in this section and discuss the second question in Section 21.10.

Before we proceed, keep in mind that we are primarily concerned with weak, or covariance, stationarity.

Although there are several tests of stationarity, we discuss only those that are prominently discussed in the literature. In this section we discuss two tests: (1) graphical analysis and

[17]G. U. Yule, "Why Do We Sometimes Get Nonsense Correlations Between Time Series? A Study in Sampling and the Nature of Time Series," *Journal of the Royal Statistical Society,* vol. 89, 1926, pp. 1–64. For extensive Monte Carlo simulations on spurious regression see C. W. J. Granger and P. Newbold, "Spurious Regressions in Econometrics," *Journal of Econometrics,* vol. 2, 1974, pp. 111–120.

(2) the correlogram test. Because of the importance attached to it in the recent past, we discuss the *unit root test* in the next section. We illustrate these tests with appropriate examples.

1. Graphical Analysis

As noted earlier, before one pursues formal tests, it is always advisable to plot the time series under study, as we have done in Figures 21.1 and 21.2 for the U.S. economic time series data posted on the book's website. Such plots give an initial clue about the likely nature of the time series. Take, for instance, the GDP time series shown in Figure 21.1. You will see that over the period of study the log of GDP has been increasing, that is, showing an upward trend, suggesting perhaps that the mean of the log of GDP has been changing. This perhaps suggests that the log of the GDP series is not stationary. This is also more or less true of the other U.S. economic time series shown in Figure 21.2. Such an intuitive feel is the starting point of more formal tests of stationarity.

2. Autocorrelation Function (ACF) and Correlogram

One simple test of stationarity is based on the so-called **autocorrelation function (ACF).** The ACF at lag k, denoted by ρ_k, is defined as

$$\rho_k = \frac{\gamma_k}{\gamma_0} = \frac{\text{covariance at lag } k}{\text{variance}} \tag{21.8.1}$$

where covariance at lag k and variance are as defined before. Note that if $k = 0$, $\rho_0 = 1$ (why?)

Since both covariance and variance are measured in the same units of measurement, ρ_k is a *unitless,* or *pure, number.* It lies between -1 and $+1$, as any correlation coefficient does. If we plot ρ_k against k, the graph we obtain is known as the **population correlogram.**

Since in practice we only have a realization (i.e., sample) of a stochastic process, we can only compute the **sample autocorrelation function (SAFC),** $\hat{\rho}_k$. To compute this, we must first compute the **sample covariance** at lag k, $\hat{\gamma}_k$, and the **sample variance,** $\hat{\gamma}_0$, which are defined as:[18]

$$\hat{\gamma}_k = \frac{\sum(Y_t - \bar{Y})(Y_{t+k} - \bar{Y})}{n} \tag{21.8.2}$$

$$\hat{\gamma}_0 = \frac{\sum(Y_t - \bar{Y})^2}{n} \tag{21.8.3}$$

where n is the sample size and $\bar{Y}$ is the sample mean.

Therefore, the sample autocorrelation function at lag k is:

$$\hat{\rho}_k = \frac{\hat{\gamma}_k}{\hat{\gamma}_0} \tag{21.8.4}$$

which is simply the ratio of sample covariance (at lag k) to sample variance. A plot of $\hat{\rho}_k$ against k is known as the **sample correlogram.**

How does a sample correlogram enable us to find out if a particular time series is stationary? For this purpose, let us first present the sample correlograms of a purely white noise

[18]Strictly speaking, we should divide the sample covariance at lag k by $(n - k)$ and the sample variance by $(n - 1)$ rather than by n (why?), where n is the sample size.

FIGURE 21.6 Correlogram of white noise error term u. AC = autocorrelation, PAC = partial autocorrelation (see Chapter 22), Q-Stat = Q statistic, Prob = probability.

Sample: 2 500
Included observations: 499

Autocorrelation	Partial Correlation		AC	PAC	Q-Stat	Prob
		1	−0.022	−0.022	0.2335	0.629
		2	−0.019	−0.020	0.4247	0.809
		3	−0.009	−0.010	0.4640	0.927
		4	−0.031	−0.031	0.9372	0.919
		5	−0.070	−0.072	3.4186	0.636
		6	−0.008	−0.013	3.4493	0.751
		7	0.048	0.045	4.6411	0.704
		8	−0.069	−0.070	7.0385	0.532
		9	0.022	0.017	7.2956	0.606
		10	−0.004	−0.011	7.3059	0.696
		11	0.024	0.025	7.6102	0.748
		12	0.024	0.027	7.8993	0.793
		13	0.026	0.021	8.2502	0.827
		14	−0.047	−0.046	9.3726	0.806
		15	−0.037	−0.030	10.074	0.815
		16	−0.026	−0.031	10.429	0.843
		17	−0.029	−0.024	10.865	0.863
		18	−0.043	−0.050	11.807	0.857
		19	0.038	0.028	12.575	0.860
		20	0.099	0.093	17.739	0.605
		21	0.001	0.007	17.739	0.665
		22	0.065	0.060	19.923	0.588
		23	0.053	0.055	21.404	0.556
		24	−0.017	−0.004	21.553	0.606
		25	−0.024	−0.005	21.850	0.644
		26	−0.008	−0.008	21.885	0.695
		27	−0.036	−0.027	22.587	0.707
		28	0.053	0.072	24.068	0.678
		29	−0.004	−0.011	24.077	0.725
		30	−0.026	−0.025	24.445	0.752

random process and of a random walk process. Return to the driftless RWM (21.3.13). There we generated a sample of 500 error terms, the u's, from the standard normal distribution. The correlogram of these 500 purely random error terms is as shown in Figure 21.6; we have shown this correlogram up to 30 lags. We will comment shortly on how one chooses the lag length.

For the time being, just look at the column labeled AC, which is the sample autocorrelation function, and the first diagram on the left, labeled Autocorrelation. The solid vertical line in this diagram represents the zero axis; observations to the right of the line are positive values and those to the left of the line are negative values. As is very clear from this diagram, for a purely white noise process the autocorrelations at various lags hover around zero. *This is the picture of a correlogram of a stationary time series.* Thus, if the correlogram of an actual (economic) time series resembles the correlogram of a white noise time series, we can say that time series is probably stationary.

FIGURE 21.7
Correlogram of a random walk time series. See Figure 21.6 for definitions.

Sample: 2 500
Included observations: 499

Autocorrelation	Partial Correlation		AC	PAC	Q-Stat	Prob
		1	0.992	0.992	493.86	0.000
		2	0.984	0.000	980.68	0.000
		3	0.976	0.030	1461.1	0.000
		4	0.969	0.005	1935.1	0.000
		5	0.961	−0.059	2402.0	0.000
		6	0.953	0.050	2862.7	0.000
		7	0.946	0.004	3317.3	0.000
		8	0.939	0.040	3766.4	0.000
		9	0.932	−0.009	4210.1	0.000
		10	0.927	0.055	4649.1	0.000
		11	0.921	0.018	5083.9	0.000
		12	0.916	0.039	5514.9	0.000
		13	0.912	0.002	5942.4	0.000
		14	0.908	0.056	6367.0	0.000
		15	0.905	0.061	6789.8	0.000
		16	0.902	0.000	7210.6	0.000
		17	0.899	0.006	7629.4	0.000
		18	0.896	0.030	8046.7	0.000
		19	0.894	0.053	8463.1	0.000
		20	0.892	0.013	8878.7	0.000
		21	0.890	−0.041	9292.6	0.000
		22	0.886	−0.040	9704.1	0.000
		23	0.882	−0.044	10113.	0.000
		24	0.878	−0.012	10518.	0.000
		25	0.873	−0.023	10920.	0.000
		26	0.867	−0.041	11317.	0.000
		27	0.860	−0.055	11709.	0.000
		28	0.853	−0.045	12095.	0.000
		29	0.846	−0.010	12476.	0.000
		30	0.839	0.008	12851.	0.000
		31	0.832	−0.006	13221.	0.000
		32	0.825	0.003	13586.	0.000
		33	0.819	−0.006	13946.	0.000

Now look at the correlogram of a random walk series, as generated, say, by Eq. (21.3.13). The picture is as shown in Figure 21.7. The most striking feature of this correlogram is that the autocorrelation coefficients at various lags are very high even up to a lag of 33 quarters. As a matter of fact, if we consider lags of up to 60 quarters, the autocorrelation coefficients are quite high; the coefficient is about 0.7 at lag 60. Figure 21.7 is the typical correlogram of a nonstationary time series: The autocorrelation coefficient starts at a very high value and declines very slowly toward zero as the lag lengthens.

Now let us take a concrete economic example. Let us examine the correlogram of the LGDP time series plotted using the U.S. economic times series data posted on the book's website (see Section 21.1). The correlogram up to 36 lags is shown in Figure 21.8. The LGDP correlogram up to 36 lags also shows a pattern similar to the correlogram of the random walk

FIGURE 21.8 Correlogram of U.S. LGDP, 1947–I to 2007–IV. See Figure 21.6 for definitions.

Sample: 1947–I 2007–IV
Included observations: 244

Autocorrelation	Partial Correlation		AC	PAC	Q-Stat	Prob
		1	0.977	0.977	235.73	0.000
		2	0.954	−0.009	461.43	0.000
		3	0.931	−0.010	677.31	0.000
		4	0.908	−0.006	883.67	0.000
		5	0.886	−0.003	1080.9	0.000
		6	0.864	−0.001	1269.3	0.000
		7	0.843	−0.006	1449.3	0.000
		8	0.822	−0.006	1621.0	0.000
		9	0.801	−0.010	1784.6	0.000
		10	0.780	−0.004	1940.6	0.000
		11	0.759	−0.007	2089.0	0.000
		12	0.738	−0.013	2230.0	0.000
		13	0.718	0.003	2364.1	0.000
		14	0.699	−0.005	2491.5	0.000
		15	0.679	−0.001	2612.4	0.000
		16	0.660	−0.004	2727.2	0.000
		17	0.642	−0.002	2836.2	0.000
		18	0.624	0.002	2939.6	0.000
		19	0.607	0.003	3037.8	0.000
		20	0.590	−0.003	3130.9	0.000
		21	0.573	−0.003	3219.3	0.000
		22	0.557	−0.003	3303.1	0.000
		23	0.541	−0.001	3382.5	0.000
		24	0.526	0.007	3457.9	0.000
		25	0.511	0.002	3529.4	0.000
		26	0.496	−0.005	3597.2	0.000
		27	0.482	−0.011	3661.4	0.000
		28	0.467	−0.009	3722.0	0.000
		29	0.453	−0.005	3779.2	0.000
		30	0.438	−0.006	3833.1	0.000
		31	0.424	−0.005	3883.9	0.000
		32	0.411	0.004	3931.6	0.000
		33	0.398	0.004	3976.7	0.000
		34	0.385	−0.001	4019.1	0.000
		35	0.373	−0.009	4058.9	0.000
		36	0.360	−0.010	4096.3	0.000

model in Figure 21.7. The autocorrelation coefficient starts at a very high value at lag 1 (0.977) and declines very slowly. Thus it seems that the LGDP time series is nonstationary. If you plot the correlograms of the other U.S. economic time series shown in Figures 21.1 and 21.2, you will also see a similar pattern, leading to the conclusion that all these time series are nonstationary; they may be nonstationary in mean or variance or both.

Two practical questions may be posed here. First, how do we choose the lag length to compute the ACF? Second, how do you decide whether a correlation coefficient at a certain lag is statistically significant? The answer follows.

The Choice of Lag Length

This is basically an empirical question. A rule of thumb is to compute ACF up to one-third to one-quarter the length of the time series. Since for our economic data we have 244 quarterly observations, by this rule lags of 61 to 81 quarters will do. To save space, we have only shown 36 lags in the ACF graph in Figure 21.8. The best practical advice is to start with sufficiently large lags and then reduce them by some statistical criterion, such as the *Akaike* or *Schwarz information criterion* that we discussed in Chapter 13. Alternatively, one can use the following statistical tests.

Statistical Significance of Autocorrelation Coefficients

Consider, for instance, the correlogram of the LGDP time series given in Figure 21.8. How do we decide whether the correlation coefficient of 0.780 at lag 10 (quarters) is statistically significant? The statistical significance of any $\hat{\rho}_k$ can be judged by its standard error. Bartlett has shown that if a time series is purely random, that is, it exhibits white noise (see Figure 21.6), the sample autocorrelation coefficients $\hat{\rho}_k$ are *approximately*[19]

$$\hat{\rho}_k \sim N(0, 1/n) \tag{21.8.5}$$

that is, in large samples the sample autocorrelation coefficients are normally distributed with zero mean and variance equal to one over the sample size. Since we have 244 observations, the variance is $1/244 \approx 0.0041$ and the standard error is $\sqrt{0.0041} \approx 0.0640$. Then following the properties of the standard normal distribution, the 95 percent confidence interval for any (population) ρ_k is:

$$\hat{\rho}_k + 1.96(0.0640) = \hat{\rho}_k \pm 0.1254 \tag{21.8.6}$$

In other words,

$$\text{Prob}\,(\hat{\rho}_k - 0.1254 \le \rho_k \le \hat{\rho}_k + 0.1254) = 0.95 \tag{21.8.7}$$

If the preceding interval includes the value of zero, we do not reject the hypothesis that the true ρ_k is zero, but if this interval does not include 0, we reject the hypothesis that the true ρ_k is zero. Applying this to the estimated value of $\hat{\rho}_{10} = 0.873$, the reader can verify that the 95 percent confidence interval for true ρ_{10} is (0.873 ± 0.1254) or $(0.7476, 0.9984)$.[20] Obviously, this interval does not include the value of zero, suggesting that we are 95 percent confident that the true ρ_{10} is significantly different from zero.[21] As you can check, even at lag 20 the estimated ρ_{20} is statistically significant at the 5 percent level.

Instead of testing the statistical significance of any individual autocorrelation coefficient, we can test the *joint hypothesis* that all the ρ_k up to certain lags are simultaneously equal to zero. This can be done by using the ***Q* statistic** developed by Box and Pierce, which is defined as[22]

$$Q = n\sum_{k=1}^{m} \hat{\rho}_k^2 \tag{21.8.8}$$

[19]M. S. Bartlett, "On the Theoretical Specification of Sampling Properties of Autocorrelated Time Series," *Journal of the Royal Statistical Society,* Series B, vol. 27, 1946, pp. 27–41.

[20]Our sample size of 244 observations is reasonably large to use the normal approximation.

[21]Alternatively, if you divide the estimated value of any ρ_k by the standard error of $(\sqrt{1/n})$, for sufficiently large n, you will obtain the standard Z value, whose probability can be easily obtained from the standard normal table. Thus for the estimated $\rho_{10} = 0.780$, the Z value is $0.780/0.1066 = 7.32$ (approx.). If the true ρ_{10} were in fact zero, the probability of obtaining a Z value of as much as 7.32 or greater is very small, thus rejecting the hypothesis that the true ρ_{10} is zero.

[22] G. E. P. Box and D. A. Pierce, "Distribution of Residual Autocorrelations in Autoregressive Integrated Moving Average Time Series Models," *Journal of the American Statistical Association*, vol. 65, 1970, pp. 1509–1526.

where n = sample size and m = lag length. The Q statistic is often used as a test of whether a time series is white noise. In large samples, it is *approximately* distributed as the chi-square distribution with m df. In an application, if the computed Q exceeds the critical Q value from the chi-square distribution at the chosen level of significance, one can reject the null hypothesis that all the (true) ρ_k are zero; at least some of them must be nonzero.

A variant of the Box–Pierce Q statistic is the **Ljung–Box (LB) statistic,** which is defined as[23]

$$\text{LB} = n(n+2)\sum_{k=1}^{m}\left(\frac{\hat{\rho}_k^2}{n-k}\right) \sim \chi^2 m \tag{21.8.9}$$

Although in large samples both Q and LB statistics follow the chi-square distribution with m df, the LB statistic has been found to have better (more powerful, in the statistical sense) small-sample properties than the Q statistic.[24]

Returning to the LGDP example given in Figure 21.8, the value of the Q statistic up to lag 36 is about 4096. The probability of obtaining such a Q value under the null hypothesis that the sum of 36 squared estimated autocorrelation coefficients is zero is practically zero, as the last column of that figures shows. Therefore, the conclusion is that the LGDP time series is probably nonstationary, therefore reinforcing our hunch from Figure 21.1 that the LGDP series may be nonstationary. In Exercise 21.16 you are asked to confirm that the other four U.S. economic time series are also nonstationary.

21.9 The Unit Root Test

A test of stationarity (or nonstationarity) that has become widely popular over the past several years is the **unit root test.** We will first explain it, then illustrate it, and then consider some of its limitations.

The starting point is the unit root (stochastic) process that we discussed in Section 21.4. We start with

$$Y_t = \rho Y_{t-1} + u_t \qquad -1 \leq \rho \leq 1 \tag{21.4.1}$$

where u_t is a white noise error term.

We know that if $\rho = 1$, that is, in the case of the unit root, Eq. (21.4.1) becomes a random walk model without drift, which we know is a nonstationary stochastic process. Therefore, why not simply regress Y_t on its (one-period) lagged value Y_{t-1} and find out if the estimated ρ is statistically equal to 1? If it is, then Y_t is nonstationary. This is the general idea behind the unit root test of stationarity.

However, we cannot estimate Eq. (21.4.1) by OLS and test the hypothesis that $\rho = 1$ by the usual t test because that test is severely biased in the case of a unit root. Therefore, we manipulate Eq. (21.4.1) as follows: Subtract Y_{t-1} from both sides of Eq. (21.4.1) to obtain:

$$\begin{aligned} Y_t - Y_{t-1} &= \rho Y_{t-1} - Y_{t-1} + u_t \\ &= (\rho - 1)Y_{t-1} + u_t \end{aligned} \tag{21.9.1}$$

which can be alternatively written as:

$$\Delta Y_t = \delta Y_{t-1} + u_t \tag{21.9.2}$$

where $\delta = (\rho - 1)$ and Δ, as usual, is the first difference operator.

[23] G. M. Ljung and G. E. P. Box, "On a Measure of Lack of Fit in Time Series Models," *Biometrika*, vol. 66, 1978, pp. 66–72.

[24] The Q and LB statistics may not be appropriate in every case. For a critique, see Maddala et al., op. cit., p. 19.

In practice, therefore, instead of estimating Eq. (21.4.1), we estimate Eq. (21.9.2) and test the (null) hypothesis that $\delta = 0$, the alternative hypothesis being that $\delta < 0$ (see footnote 25). If $\delta = 0$, then $\rho = 1$, that is we have a unit root, meaning the time series under consideration is nonstationary.

Before we proceed to estimate Eq. (21.9.2), it may be noted that if $\delta = 0$, Eq. (21.9.2) will become

$$\Delta Y_t = (Y_t - Y_{t-1}) = u_t \tag{21.9.3}$$

Since u_t is a white noise error term, it is stationary, which means that the first differences of a random walk time series are stationary, a point we have already made before.

Now let us turn to the estimation of Eq. (21.9.2). This is simple enough; all we have to do is to take the first differences of Y_t and regress them on Y_{t-1} and see if the estimated slope coefficient in this regression ($= \hat{\delta}$) is zero or not. If it is zero, we conclude that Y_t is nonstationary. But if it is negative, we conclude that Y_t is stationary.[25] The only question is which test we use to find out if the estimated coefficient of Y_{t-1} in Eq. (21.9.2) is zero or not. You might be tempted to say, why not use the usual *t* test? Unfortunately, under the null hypothesis that $\delta = 0$ (i.e., $\rho = 1$), the *t* value of the estimated coefficient of Y_{t-1} does not follow the *t* distribution even in large samples; that is, it does not have an asymptotic normal distribution.

What is the alternative? Dickey and Fuller have shown that under the null hypothesis that $\delta = 0$, the estimated *t* value of the coefficient of Y_{t-1} in Eq. (21.9.2) follows the **τ (tau) statistic.**[26] These authors have computed the critical values of the *tau statistic* on the basis of Monte Carlo simulations. A sample of these critical values is given in **Appendix D,** Table D.7. The table is limited, but MacKinnon has prepared more extensive tables, which are now incorporated in several econometric packages.[27] In the literature the **tau statistic or test** is known as the **Dickey–Fuller (DF) test,** in honor of its discoverers. Interestingly, if the hypothesis that $\delta = 0$ is rejected (i.e., the time series is stationary), we can use the usual (Student's) *t* test. Keep in mind that the Dickey–Fuller test is one-sided because the alternative hypothesis is that $\delta < 0$ (or $\rho < 1$).

The actual procedure of implementing the DF test involves several decisions. In discussing the nature of the unit root process in Sections 21.4 and 21.5, we noted that a random walk process may have no drift, or it may have drift, or it may have both deterministic and stochastic trends. To allow for the various possibilities, the DF test is estimated in three different forms, that is, under three different null hypotheses.

Y_t is a random walk: $$\Delta Y_t = \delta Y_{t-1} + u_t \tag{21.9.2}$$

Y_t is a random walk with drift: $$\Delta Y_t = \beta_1 + \delta Y_{t-1} + u_t \tag{21.9.4}$$

Y_t is a random walk with drift around a deterministic trend: $$\Delta Y_t = \beta_1 + \beta_2 t + \delta Y_{t-1} + u_t \tag{21.9.5}$$

[25] Since $\delta = (\rho - 1)$, for stationarity ρ must be less than one. For this to happen δ must be negative.

[26] D. A. Dickey and W. A. Fuller, "Distribution of the Estimators for Autoregressive Time Series with a Unit Root," *Journal of the American Statistical Association,* vol. 74, 1979, pp. 427–431. See also W. A. Fuller, *Introduction to Statistical Time Series,* John Wiley & Sons, New York, 1976.

[27] J. G. MacKinnon, "Critical Values of Cointegration Tests," in R. E. Engle and C. W. J. Granger, eds., *Long-Run Economic Relationships: Readings in Cointegration,* Chapter 13, Oxford University Press, New York, 1991.

where t is the time or trend variable. In each case the hypotheses are:

Null hypothesis: $H_0 : \delta = 0$ (i.e., there is a unit root or the time series is nonstationary, or it has a stochastic trend).

Alternative hypothesis: $H_1 : \delta < 0$ (i.e., the time series is stationary, possibly around a deterministic trend).[28]

If the null hypothesis is rejected, it means either (1) Y_t is stationary with zero mean, in the case of Eq. (21.9.2), or (2) Y_t is stationary with nonzero mean, in the case of Eq. (21.9.4). In the case of Eq. (21.9.5), we can test for $\delta < 0$ (i.e., no stochastic trend) and $\alpha \neq 0$ (i.e., the existence of a deterministic trend) simultaneously, using the F test, but using the critical values tabulated by Dickey and Fuller. It may be noted that a time series may contain both a stochastic and a deterministic trend.

It is extremely important to note that the critical values of the tau test to test the hypothesis that $\delta = 0$ are different for each of the preceding three specifications of the DF test, which can be seen clearly from **Appendix D,** Table D.7. Moreover, if, say, specification (21.9.4) is correct, but we estimate Eq. (21.9.2), we will be committing a specification error, whose consequences we already know from Chapter 13. The same is true if we estimate Eq. (21.9.4) rather than the true Eq. (21.9.5). Of course, there is no way of knowing which specification is correct to begin with. Some trial and error is inevitable, data mining notwithstanding.

The actual estimation procedure is as follows: Estimate Eq. (21.9.2), or Eq. (21.9.3), or Eq. (21.9.4) by OLS; divide the estimated coefficient of Y_{t-1} in each case by its standard error to compute the (τ) tau statistic; and refer to the DF tables (or any statistical package). If the computed absolute value of the tau statistic ($|\tau|$) exceeds the *absolute* DF or MacKinnon critical tau values, we reject the hypothesis that $\delta = 0$, in which case the time series is stationary. On the other hand, if the computed $|\tau|$ does not exceed the absolute critical tau value, we do not reject the null hypothesis, in which case the time series is nonstationary. Make sure that you use the appropriate critical τ values. In most applications the tau value will be negative. Therefore, alternatively we can say that if the computed (negative) tau value is smaller than (i.e., more negative than) the critical tau value, we reject the null hypothesis (i.e., the time series is stationary) otherwise, we do not reject it (i.e., the time series is nonstationary).

Let us return to the U.S. GDP time series. For this series, the results of the three regressions (21.9.2), (21.9.4), and (21.9.5) are as follows: The dependent variable in each case is $\Delta Y_t = \Delta \text{LGDP}_t$, where LGDP is the logarithm of real GDP.

$$\begin{aligned} \widehat{\Delta \text{LGDP}}_t &= 0.000968\text{LGDP}_{t-1} \\ t &= (12.9270) \qquad R^2 = 0.0147 \qquad d = 1.3194 \end{aligned} \tag{21.9.6}$$

$$\begin{aligned} \widehat{\Delta \text{LGDP}}_t &= 0.0221 - 0.00165\text{LGDP}_{t-1} \\ t &= (2.4342) \quad (-1.5294) \qquad R^2 = 0.0096 \qquad d = 1.3484 \end{aligned} \tag{21.9.7}$$

$$\begin{aligned} \widehat{\Delta \text{LGDP}}_t &= 0.2092 + 0.0002t - 0.0269\text{LGDP}_{t-1} \\ t &= (1.8991) \quad (1.7040) \quad (-1.8102) \\ & R^2 = 0.0215 \qquad d = 1.3308 \end{aligned} \tag{21.9.8}$$

[28]We rule out the possibility that $\delta > 0$, because in that case $\rho > 1$, in which case the underlying time series will be explosive.

Our primary interest in all these regressions is in the $t(=\tau)$ value of the LGDP_{t-1} coefficient. If you look at Table D.7 in **Appendix D,** you will see that the 5 percent critical tau values for sample size 250 (the closest number to our sample of 244 observations) are -1.95 (no intercept, no trend), -2.88 (intercept but no trend), and -3.43 (intercept as well as trend). *EViews* and other statistical packages provide critical values for the sample size used in the analysis.

Before we examine the results, we have to decide which of the three models may be appropriate. We should rule out model (21.9.6) because the coefficient of LGDP_{t-1}, which is equal to δ is positive. But since $\delta = (\rho - 1)$, a positive δ would imply that $\rho > 1$. Although a theoretical possibility, we rule this out because in this case the LGDP time series would be explosive.[29] That leaves us with models (21.9.7) and (21.9.8). In both cases the estimated δ coefficient is negative, implying that the estimated ρ is less than 1. For these two models, the estimated ρ values are 0.9984 and 0.9731, respectively. The only question now is if these values are statistically significantly below 1 for us to declare that the GDP time series is stationary.

For model (21.9.7) the estimated τ value is -1.5294, whereas the 5 percent critical τ value, as noted above, is -2.88. Since, in *absolute* terms, the former is smaller than the latter, our conclusion is that the LGDP time series is not stationary.[30]

The story is the same for model (21.9.8). The computed τ value of -1.8102, in absolute terms, is smaller than the 5 percent critical value of -3.43.

Therefore, on the basis of graphical analysis, the correlogram, and the Dickey–Fuller test, the conclusion is that for the quarterly periods of 1947 to 2007, the U.S. LGDP time series was nonstationary; i.e., it contained a unit root, or it had a stochastic trend.

The Augmented Dickey–Fuller (ADF) Test

In conducting the DF test as in Eqs. (21.9.2), (21.9.4), and (21.9.5), it was assumed that the error term u_t was uncorrelated. But in case the u_t are correlated, Dickey and Fuller have developed another test, known as the **augmented Dickey–Fuller (ADF) test.** This test is conducted by "augmenting" the preceding three equations by adding the lagged values of the dependent variable ΔY_t. To be specific, suppose we use Eq. (21.9.5). The ADF test here consists of estimating the following regression:

$$\Delta Y_t = \beta_1 + \beta_2 t + \delta Y_{t-1} + \sum_{i=1}^{m} \alpha_i \Delta Y_{t-i} + \varepsilon_t \qquad \textbf{(21.9.9)}$$

where ε_t is a pure white noise error term and where $\Delta Y_{t-1} = (Y_{t-1} - Y_{t-2})$, $\Delta Y_{t-2} = (Y_{t-2} - Y_{t-3})$, etc. The number of lagged difference terms to include is often determined empirically, the idea being to include enough terms so that the error term in Eq. (21.9.9) is serially uncorrelated, so that we can obtain an unbiased estimate of δ, the coefficient of lagged Y_{t-1}. *EViews 6* has an option that automatically selects the lag length based on Akaike, Schwarz, and other information criteria. In ADF we still test whether $\delta = 0$ and the ADF test follows the same asymptotic distribution as the DF statistic, so the same critical values can be used.

To give a glimpse of this procedure, we estimated Eq. (21.9.9) for the LGDP series. Since we have quarterly data, we decided to use four lags. The results of the ADF regression are as follows:[31]

[29]More technically, since Eq. (21.9.2) is a first-order difference equation, the so-called stability condition requires that $|\rho| < 1$.

[30]Another way of stating this is that the computed τ value should be more negative than the critical τ value, which is not the case here. Hence the conclusion stays. Since in general δ is expected to be negative, the estimated τ statistic will have a negative sign. Therefore, a large negative τ value is generally an indication of stationarity.

[31]Higher-order lagged differences were considered but they were insignificant.

$$\widehat{\Delta \text{LGDP}_t} = 0.2677 + 0.0003t - 0.0352\text{LGDP}_{t-1} + 0.2990\Delta\text{LGDP}_{t-1} + 0.1451\Delta\text{LGDP}_{t-2} - 0.0621\Delta\text{LGDP}_{t-3} - 0.0876\Delta\text{LGDP}_t$$
$$t = (2.4130) \quad (2.2561) \quad (-2.3443) \qquad (4.6255) \qquad (2.1575) \qquad (-0.9205) \qquad (-1.3438)$$
$$R^2 = 0.1617 \qquad d = 2.0075 \tag{21.9.10}$$

The $t\ (= \tau)$ value of the lagged LGDP_{t-1} coefficient $(= \delta)$ is -2.3443, which in absolute terms is much less than even the 10 percent critical τ value of -3.1378, again suggesting that even after taking care of possible autocorrelation in the error term, the LGDP series is nonstationary. (*Note:* The @trend command in *EViews* automatically generates the time or trend variable.)

Could this be the result of our choosing only four lagged values of ΔLGDP? We used the Schwarz criterion using 14 lagged values of ΔLGDP, which gave the tau value δ of -1.8102. Even then, this tau value was not significant at the 10 percent level (the critical tau value at this level was -3.1376). It seems logged GDP is nonstationary.

Testing the Significance of More than One Coefficient: The *F* Test

Suppose we estimate model (21.9.5) and test the hypothesis that $\beta_1 = \beta_2 = 0$, that is, the model is RWM without drift and trend. To test this joint hypothesis, we can use the *restricted F* test discussed in Chapter 8. That is, we estimate Eq. (21.9.5) (the unrestricted regression) and then estimate Eq. (21.9.5) again, dropping the intercept and trend. Then we use the restricted F test as shown in Eq. (8.6.9), except that we cannot use the conventional F table to get the critical F values. As they did with the τ statistic, Dickey and Fuller have developed critical F values for this situation, a sample of which is given in **Appendix D,** Table D.7. An example is presented in Exercise 21.27.

The Phillips–Perron (PP) Unit Root Tests[32]

An important assumption of the DF test is that the error terms u_t are independently and identically distributed. The ADF test adjusts the DF test to take care of possible serial correlation in the error terms by adding the lagged difference terms of the regressand. Phillips and Perron use *nonparametric statistical methods* to take care of the serial correlation in the error terms without adding lagged difference terms. Since the asymptotic distribution of the PP test is the same as the ADF test statistic, we will not pursue this topic here.

Testing for Structural Changes

The macroeconomic data introduced in Section 21.1 (see the book's website for the actual data) are for the period 1947–2007, a period of 61 years. In this period the U.S. economy experienced several business cycles of varying durations. Business cycles are marked by periods of recessions and periods of expansions. It is quite likely that one business cycle is different from another, which may reflect **structural breaks** or **structural changes** in the economy.

For instance, take the first oil embargo in 1973. It quadrupled oil prices. Prices again increased substantially after the second oil embargo in 1979. Naturally, these shocks will affect economic behavior. Therefore, if we were to regress personal consumption expenditure (PCE) on disposable personal income (DPI), the intercept, the slope, or both are likely to change from one business cycle to another (recall the Chow test of structural breaks). This is what is meant by structural changes.

[32] P. C. B. Phillips and P. Perron, "Testing for a Unit Root in Time Series Regression," *Biometrika,* vol. 75, 1988, pp. 335–346. The PP test is now included in several software packages.

Perron, for instance, has argued that the standard tests of the unit root hypothesis may not be reliable in the presence of structural changes.[33] There are ways to test for structural changes and to account for them, the simplest involving the use of dummy variables. But a discussion of the various tests of structural breaks will take us far afield and is best left for the references.[34] However, see Exercise 21.28.

A Critique of the Unit Root Tests[35]

We have discussed several unit root tests and there are several more. The question is: Why are there so many unit root tests? The answer lies in the **size** and **power** of these tests. By size of a test we mean the level of significance (i.e., the probability of committing a Type I error) and by power of a test we mean the probability of rejecting the null hypothesis when it is false. The power of a test is calculated by subtracting the probability of a Type II error from 1; Type II error is the probability of accepting a false null hypothesis. The maximum power is 1. Most unit root tests are based on the null hypothesis that the time series under consideration has a unit root; that is, it is nonstationary. The alternative hypothesis is that the time series is stationary.

Size of Test

You will recall from Chapter 13 the distinction we made between the nominal and the true levels of significance. The DF test is sensitive to the way it is conducted. Remember that we discussed three varieties of the DF test: (1) a pure random walk, (2) a random walk with drift, and (3) a random walk with drift and trend. If, for example, the true model is (1) but we estimate (2), and conclude that, say, on the 5 percent level that the time series is stationary, this conclusion may be wrong because the true level of significance in this case is much larger than 5 percent.[36] The size distortion could also result from excluding moving average (MA) components from the model (on moving average, see Chapter 22).

Power of Test

Most tests of the DF type have low power; that is, they tend to accept the null of unit root more frequently than is warranted. That is, these tests may find a unit root even when none exists. There are several reasons for this. *First,* the power depends on the (time) *span* of the data more than the mere size of the sample. For a given sample size n, the power is greater when the span is large. Thus, a unit root test(s) based on 30 observations over a span of 30 years may have more power than one based on, say, 100 observations over a span of 100 days. *Second,* if $\rho \approx 1$ but not exactly 1, the unit root test may declare such a time series nonstationary. *Third,* these types of tests assume a single unit root; that is, they assume that the given time series is $I(1)$. But if a time series is integrated of order higher than 1, say, $I(2)$, there will be more than one unit root. In the latter case one may use the **Dickey–Pantula test.**[37] *Fourth,* if there are structural breaks in a time series (see the chapter on dummy variables) due to, say, the OPEC oil embargoes, the unit root tests may not catch them.

In applying the unit root tests one should therefore keep in mind the limitations of the tests. Of course, there have been modifications of these tests by Perron and Ng, Elliot,

[33] P. Perron, "The Great Crash, the Oil Price Shock and the Unit Root Hypothesis," *Econometrica,* vol. 57, 1989, pp. 1361–1401.

[34] For an accessible discussion, see James H. Stock and Mark W. Watson, *Introduction to Econometrics,* 2d ed., Pearson/Addison-Wesley, Boston, 2007, pp. 565–571. For a more thorough discussion, see G. S. Maddala and In-Moo Kim, *Unit Roots, Cointegration, and Structural Change,* Cambridge University Press, New York, 1998.

[35] For detailed discussion, see Terrence C. Mills, op. cit., pp. 87–88.

[36] For a Monte Carlo experiment about this, see Charemza et al., op. cit., p. 114.

[37] D. A. Dickey and S. Pantula, "Determining the Order of Differencing in Autoregressive Processes," *Journal of Business and Economic Statistics,* vol. 5, 1987, pp. 455–461.

Rothenberg and Stock, Fuller, and Leybourne.[38] Because of this, Maddala and Kim advocate that the traditional DF, ADF, and PP tests should be discarded. As econometric software packages incorporate the new tests, that may very well happen. But it should be added that as yet there is no uniformly powerful test of the unit root hypothesis.

21.10 Transforming Nonstationary Time Series

Now that we know the problems associated with nonstationary time series, the practical question is what to do. To avoid the spurious regression problem that may arise from regressing a nonstationary time series on one or more nonstationary time series, we have to transform nonstationary time series to make them stationary. The transformation method depends on whether the time series are difference stationary (DSP) or trend stationary (TSP). We consider each of these methods in turn.

Difference-Stationary Processes

If a time series has a unit root, the first differences of such time series are stationary.[39] Therefore, the solution here is to take the first differences of the time series.

Returning to our U.S. LGDP time series, we have already seen that it has a unit root. Let us now see what happens if we take the first differences of the LGDP series.

Let $\Delta \text{LGDP}_t = (\text{LGDP}_t - \text{LGDP}_{t-1})$. For convenience, let $D_t = \Delta \text{LGDP}_t$. Now consider the following regression:

$$\begin{aligned} \widehat{\Delta D_t} &= \quad 0.00557 - \quad 0.6711 D_{t-1} \\ t &= (7.1407) \quad (-11.0204) \\ & \qquad R^2 = 0.3360 \qquad d = 2.0542 \end{aligned} \tag{21.10.1}$$

The 1 percent critical DF τ value is -3.4574. Since the computed $\tau\,(= t)$ of -11.0204 is more negative than the critical value, we conclude that the first-differenced LGDP is stationary; that is, it is $I(0)$. It is as shown in Figure 21.9. If you compare Figure 21.9 with Figure 21.1, you will see the obvious difference between the two.

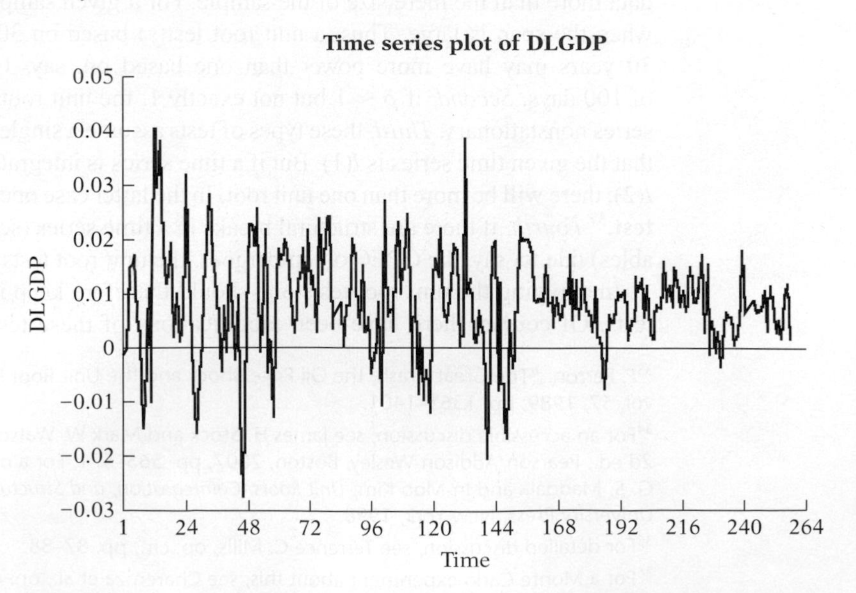

FIGURE 21.9 First differences of logs of U.S. GDP, 1947–2007 (quarterly).

[38] A discussion of these tests can be found in Maddala et al., op. cit., Chapter 4.

[39] If a time series is $I(2)$, it will contain two unit roots, in which case we will have to difference it twice. If it is $I(d)$, it has to be differenced d times, where d is any integer.

Trend-Stationary Processes

As we have seen in Figure 21.5, a TSP is stationary around the trend line. Hence, the simplest way to make such a time series stationary is to regress it on time and the residuals from this regression will then be stationary. In other words, run the following regression:

$$Y_t = \beta_1 + \beta_2 t + u_t \tag{21.10.2}$$

where Y_t is the time series under study and where t is the trend variable measured chronologically.

Now

$$\hat{u}_t = (Y_t - \hat{\beta}_1 - \hat{\beta}_2 t) \tag{21.10.3}$$

will be stationary. $\hat{u}_t$ is known as a (linearly) **detrended time series.**

It is important to note that the trend may be nonlinear. For example, it could be

$$Y_t = \beta_1 + \beta_2 t + \beta_3 t^2 + u_t \tag{21.10.4}$$

which is a quadratic trend series. If that is the case, the residuals from Eq. (21.10.4) will now be (quadratically) detrended time series.

It should be pointed out that if a time series is DSP but we treat it as TSP, this is called **underdifferencing.** On the other hand, if a time series is TSP but we treat it as DSP, this is called **overdifferencing.** The consequences of these types of specification errors can be serious, depending on how one handles the serial correlation properties of the resulting error terms.[40]

To see what happens if we confuse a TSP series with a DSP series or vice versa, Figure 21.10 shows the first-differenced LGDP and the residuals of LGDP estimated from the TSP regression (21.10.2):

FIGURE 21.10 First differences (delta LGDP) and deviations from trend (RESI1) for logged GDP, 1947–2007 (quarterly).

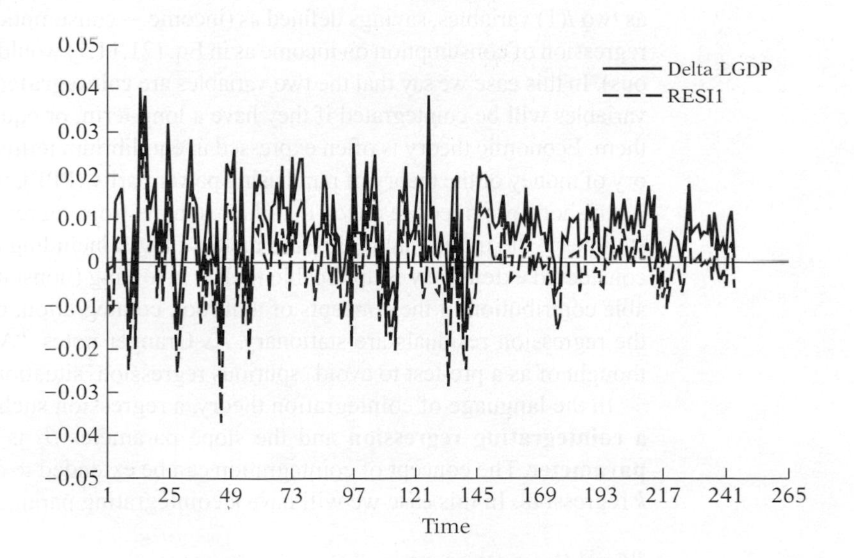

[40]For a detailed discussion of this, see Maddala et al., op. cit., Section 2.7.

A look at this figure tells us that the first differences of real logged DGP are stationary (as confirmed by regression (21.10.1) but the residuals from the trend line (RESI1) are not.

In summary, ". . . it is very important to apply the right sort of stationarity transform to the data, if they are not already stationary. Most financial markets generate price, rate or yield data that are non-stationary because of stochastic rather than a deterministic trend. It is hardly ever appropriate to detrend the data by fitting a trend line and taking deviations. Instead the data should be detrended by taking first differences, usually of the log price or rates, because then the transformed stationary data will correspond to market returns."[41]

21.11 Cointegration: Regression of a Unit Root Time Series on Another Unit Root Time Series

We have warned that the regression of a nonstationary time series on another nonstationary time series may produce a spurious regression. Let us suppose that we consider the LPCE and LDPI time series data introduced in Section 21.1 (see the book's website for the actual data). Subjecting these time series individually to unit root analysis, you will find that they both are $I(1)$; that is, they contain a stochastic trend. It is quite possible that the two series *share the same common trend* so that the regression of one on the other will not be necessarily spurious.

To be specific, we use the U.S. economic time series data (see Section 21.1 and the book's website) and run the following regression of LPCE on LDPI:

$$\text{LPCE}_t = \beta_1 + \beta_2 \text{LDPI}_t + u_t \tag{21.11.1}$$

where L denotes logarithm. β_2 is the elasticity of real personal consumption expenditure with respect to real disposable personal income. For illustrative purposes, we will call it *consumption elasticity.* Let us write this as:

$$u_t = \text{LPCE}_t - \beta_1 - \beta_2 \text{LDPI}_t \tag{21.11.2}$$

Suppose we now subject u_t to unit root analysis and find that it is stationary; that is, it is $I(0)$. This is an interesting situation, for although LPCE_t and LDPI_t are individually $I(1)$, that is, they have stochastic trends, their linear combination (21.11.2) is $I(0)$. So to speak, the linear combination cancels out the stochastic trends in the two series. If you take consumption and income as two $I(1)$ variables, savings defined as (income − consumption) could be $I(0)$. As a result, a regression of consumption on income as in Eq. (21.11.1) would be meaningful (i.e., not spurious). In this case we say that the two variables are **cointegrated.** Economically speaking, two variables will be cointegrated if they have a long-term, or equilibrium, relationship between them. Economic theory is often expressed in equilibrium terms, such as Fisher's quantity theory of money or the theory of purchasing power parity (PPP), just to name a few.

In short, provided we check that the residuals from regressions like (21.11.1) are $I(0)$ or stationary, the traditional regression methodology (including the t and F tests) that we have considered extensively is applicable to data involving (nonstationary) time series. The valuable contribution of the concepts of unit root, cointegration, etc. is to force us to find out if the regression residuals are stationary. As Granger notes, "A test for cointegration can be thought of as a pre-test to avoid 'spurious regression' situations."[42]

In the language of cointegration theory, a regression such as Eq. (21.11.1) is known as a **cointegrating regression** and the slope parameter β_2 is known as the **cointegrating parameter.** The concept of cointegration can be extended to a regression model containing k regressors. In this case we will have k cointegrating parameters.

[41] Carol Alexander, op. cit., p. 324.

[42] C. W. J. Granger, "Developments in the Study of Co-Integrated Economic Variables," *Oxford Bulletin of Economics and Statistics,* vol. 48, 1986, p. 226.

Testing for Cointegration

A number of methods for testing cointegration have been proposed in the literature. We consider here a comparatively simple method, namely the DF or ADF unit root test on the residuals estimated from the cointegrating regression.[43]

Engle–Granger (EG) or Augmented Engle–Granger (AEG) Test

We already know how to apply the DF or ADF unit root tests. All we have to do is estimate a regression like Eq. (21.11.1), obtain the residuals, and use the DF or ADF tests.[44] There is one precaution to exercise, however. Since the estimated u_t are based on the *estimated* cointegrating parameter β_2, the DF and ADF critical significance values are not quite appropriate. Engle and Granger have calculated these values, which can be found in the references.[45] Therefore, the DF and ADF tests in the present context are known as **Engle–Granger (EG)** and **augmented Engle–Granger (AEG)** tests. However, several software packages now present these critical values along with other outputs.

Let us illustrate these tests. Using the data introduced in Section 21.1 and found on the book's website, we first regressed LPCEC on LDPIC and obtained the following regression:

$$\begin{aligned} \widehat{\text{LPCE}}_t &= -0.1942 + 1.0114\text{LDPI}_t \\ t &= (-8.2328) \quad (348.5429) \\ R^2 &= 0.9980 \quad d = 0.1558 \end{aligned} \tag{21.11.3}$$

Since LPCE and LDPI are individually nonstationary, there is the possibility that this regression is spurious. But when we performed a unit root test on the residuals obtained from Eq. (21.11.3), we obtained the following results:

$$\begin{aligned} \widehat{\Delta\hat{u}_t} &= -0.0764\hat{u}_{t-1} \\ t &= (-3.0458) \\ R^2 &= 0.0369 \quad d = 2.5389 \end{aligned} \tag{21.11.4}$$

The Engle–Granger asymptotic 5 percent and 10 percent critical values are about −3.34 and −3.04, respectively. Therefore, the residuals from the regression are not stationary at the 5 percent level. It would be difficult to accept this reason, for economic theory suggests that there should be a stable relationship between PCE and DPI.

Let us reestimate Eq. (21.11.3) including the trend variable and then see if the residuals from this equation are stationary. We present the results first and then discuss what may be going on.

$$\begin{aligned} \widehat{\text{LPCE}}_t &= 2.8130 + 0.0037_t + 0.5844\text{LDPI}_t \\ t &= (21.3491) \quad (22.9394) \quad (31.2754) \\ R^2 &= 0.9994 \quad d = 0.2956 \end{aligned} \tag{21.11.3a}$$

[43]There is this difference between tests for unit roots and tests for cointegration. As David A. Dickey, Dennis W. Jansen, and Daniel I. Thornton observe, "Tests for unit roots are performed on univariate [i.e., single] time series. In contrast, cointegration deals with the relationship among a group of variables, where (unconditionally) each has a unit root." See their article, "A Primer on Cointegration with an Application to Money and Income," *Economic Review,* Federal Reserve Bank of St. Louis, March–April 1991, p. 59. As the name suggests, this article is an excellent introduction to cointegration testing.

[44]If PCE and DPI are not cointegrated, any linear combination of them will be nonstationary and, therefore, the u_t will also be nonstationary.

[45]R. F. Engle and C. W. Granger, "Co-integration and Error Correction: Representation, Estimation and Testing," *Econometrica,* vol. 55, 1987, pp. 251–276.

To see if the residuals from this regression are stationary, we obtained the following results (compare with Eq. [21.11.4]):

$$\widehat{\Delta u_t} = -0.1498\hat{u}_{t-1}$$
$$t = (-4.4545) \qquad \textbf{(21.11.4a)}$$
$$R^2 = 0.0758 \qquad d = 2.3931$$

Note: $\hat{u}_t$ is the residual from Eq. (21.11.3*a*).

The DF test now shows that these residuals are stationary. Even if we use ADF with several lags, the residuals are still stationary.

What is going on here? Although the residuals from regression (21.11.4*a*) are stationary, that is, they are $I(0)$, they are stationary around a deterministic time trend, the trend here being linear. That is, the residuals are $I(0)$ plus a linear trend. As noted earlier, a time series may contain both a deterministic and a stochastic trend.

Before we proceed further, it should be noted that our time series data cover a long period of time (61 years). It is quite possible that because of structural changes in the U.S. economy over this period, our results and conclusions are likely to differ. In Exercise 21.28 you are asked to check for this possibility.

Cointegration and Error Correction Mechanism (ECM)

We just showed that, allowing for the (linear) trend, LPCE and LDPI seem to be cointegrated, that is, there is a long-term, or equilibrium, relationship between the two. Of course, in the short-run there may be disequilibrium. Therefore, we can treat the error term in the following equation as the "equilibrium error." And we can use this error term to tie the short-run behavior of PCE to its long-run value:

$$u_t = \text{LPCE}_t - \beta_1 - \beta_2\text{LDPI} - \beta_3 t \qquad \textbf{(21.11.5)}$$

The **error correction mechanism (ECM)** first used by Sargan[46] and later popularized by Engle and Granger corrects for disequilibrium. An important theorem, known as the **Granger representation theorem,** states that if two variables Y and X are cointegrated, the relationship between the two can be expressed as ECM. To see what this means, let us revert to our PCE–DPI example. Now consider the following model:

$$\Delta\text{LPCE}_t = \alpha_0 + \alpha_1\Delta\text{LDPI}_t + \alpha_2 u_{t-1} + \varepsilon_t \qquad \textbf{(21.11.6)}$$

where ε_t is a white noise error term and u_{t-1} is the lagged value of the error term in Eq. (21.11.5).

ECM equation (21.11.5) states that ΔLPCE depends on ΔLDPI and also on the equilibrium error term.[47] If the latter is nonzero, then the model is out of equilibrium. Suppose ΔLDPI is zero and u_{t-1} is positive. This means LPCE_{t-1} is too high to be in equilibrium, that is, LPCE_{t-1} is above its equilibrium value of $(\alpha_0 + \alpha_1\text{LDPI}_{t-1})$. Since α_2 is expected to be negative, the term $\alpha_2 u_{t-1}$ is negative and, therefore, ΔLPCE_t will be negative to restore the equilibrium. That is, if LPCE_t is above its equilibrium value, it will start falling in the next period to correct the equilibrium error; hence the name ECM. By the same token, if u_{t-1} is negative (i.e., LPCE is below its equilibrium value), $\alpha_2 u_{t-1}$ will be positive, which will cause ΔLPCE_t to be positive, leading LPCE_t to rise in period t. Thus, the absolute value of α_2 decides how quickly the equilibrium is restored. In practice, we estimate u_{t-1} by

[46] J. D. Sargan, "Wages and Prices in the United Kingdom: A Study in Econometric Methodology," in K. F. Wallis and D. F. Hendry, eds., *Quantitative Economics and Econometric Analysis,* Basil Blackwell, Oxford, U.K., 1984.

[47] The following discussion is based on Gary Koop, op. cit., pp. 159–160 and Kerry Peterson, op. cit., Section 8.5.

$\hat{u}_{t-1} = (\text{LPCE}_t - \hat{\beta}_1 - \hat{\beta}_2\text{LDPI} - \hat{\beta}_3 t)$. Keep in mind that the error correction coefficient α_2 is expected to be negative (why?).

Returning to our illustrative example, the empirical counterpart of Eq. (21.11.6) is:

$$\widehat{\Delta\text{LPCE}_t} = 0.0061 + 0.2967\Delta\text{LDPI}_t - 0.1223\hat{u}_{t-1}$$
$$t = (9.6753) \quad (6.2282) \quad (-3.8461) \tag{21.11.7}$$
$$R^2 = 0.1658 \quad d = 2.1496$$

Statistically, the ECM term is significant, suggesting that PCE adjusts to DPI with a lag; only about 12 percent of the discrepancy between long-term and short-term PCE is corrected within a quarter.

From regression (21.11.7) we see that the short-run consumption elasticity is about 0.29. The long-run elasticity is about 0.58, which can be seen from Eq. (21.11.3*a*).

Before we conclude this section, the caution sounded by S. G. Hall is worth remembering:

> While the concept of cointegration is clearly an important theoretical underpinning of the error correction model there are still a number of problems surrounding its practical application; the critical values and small sample performance of many of these tests are unknown for a wide range of models; informed inspection of the correlogram may still be an important tool.[48]

21.12 Some Economic Applications

We conclude this chapter by considering some concrete examples.

EXAMPLE 21.1 *M1 Monthly Money Supply in the United States, January 1959 to March 1, 2008*

Figure 21.11 shows the M1 money supply for the United States from January 1959 to March 1, 2008. From our knowledge of stationarity, it seems that the M1 money supply time series is nonstationary, which can be confirmed by unit root analysis. (*Note:* To save

FIGURE 21.11 U.S. money supply over 1959:01 to 2008:03.

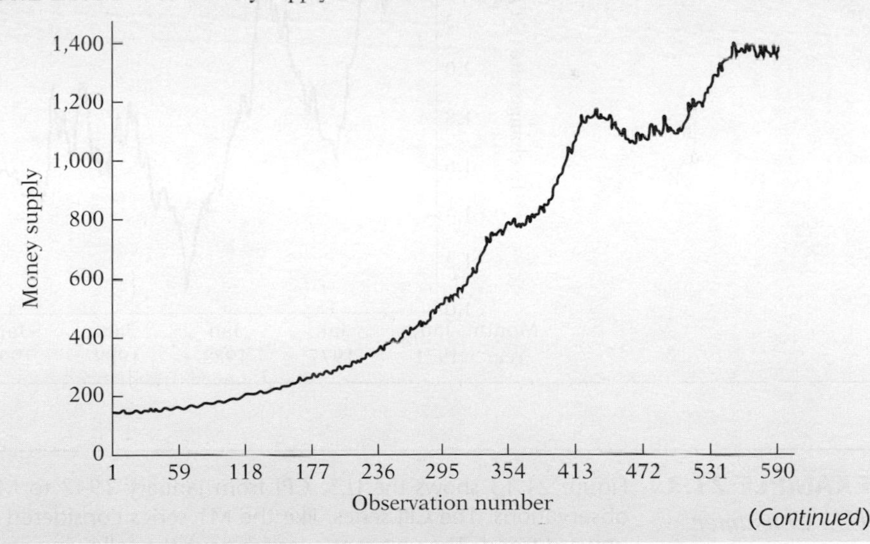

(Continued)

[48] S. G. Hall, "An Application of the Granger and Engle Two-Step Estimation Procedure to the United Kingdom Aggregate Wage Data," *Oxford Bulletin of Economics and Statistics,* vol. 48, no. 3, August 1986, p. 238. See also John Y. Campbell and Pierre Perron, "Pitfalls and Opportunities: What Macroeconomists Should Know about Unit Roots," NBER (National Bureau of Economic Research) *Macroeconomics Annual 1991,* pp. 141–219.

EXAMPLE 21.1 *(Continued)*

space, we have not given the actual data, which can be obtained from the Federal Reserve Board or the Federal Reserve Bank of St. Louis.)

$$\Delta\hat{M}_t = -0.1347 + 0.0293t - 0.0102M_{t-1}$$
$$t = (-0.14) \quad (2.62) \quad (-2.30) \tag{21.12.1}$$
$$R^2 = 0.0130 \quad d = 2.2325$$

The 1, 5, and 10 percent critical τ values are −3.9811, −3.4210, and −3.1329. Since the t value of −2.30 is less negative than any of these critical values, the conclusion is that the M1 time series is nonstationary; that is, it contains a unit root or it is $I(1)$. Even when several lagged values of ΔM_t (à la ADF) were introduced, the conclusion did not change. On the other hand, the first differences of the M1 money supply were found to be stationary (check this out).

EXAMPLE 21.2 *The U.S./U.K. Exchange Rate: January 1971 to April 2008*

Figure 21.12 gives the graph of the ($/£) exchange rate from January 1971 to April 2008, for a total of 286 observations. By now you should be able to spot this time series as nonstationary. Carrying out the unit root tests, we obtained the following τ statistics: −0.82 (no intercept, no trend), −1.96 (intercept), and −1.33 (intercept and trend). Each of these statistics, in absolute value, was less than its critical τ value from the appropriate DF tables, thus confirming the graphical impression that the U.S./U.K. exchange rate time series is nonstationary.

FIGURE 21.12 U.S./U.K. exchange rate: January 1971 to April 2008.

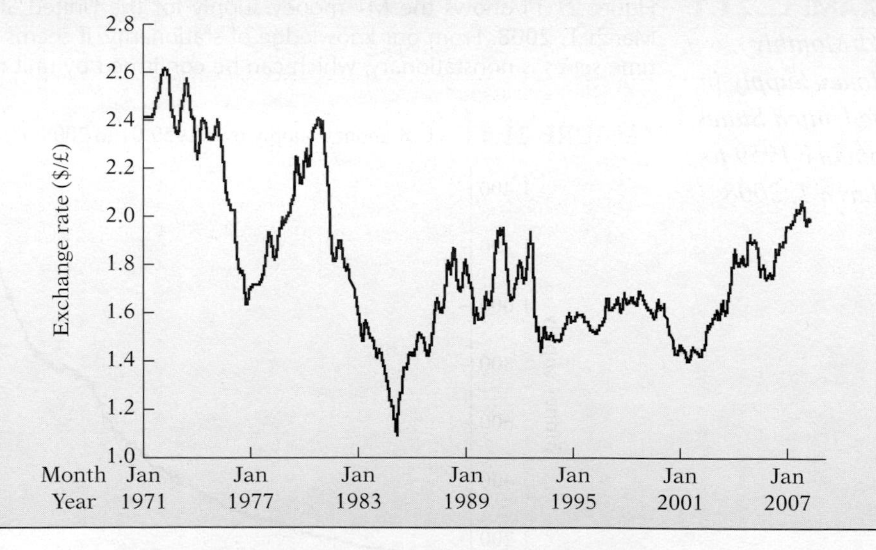

EXAMPLE 21.3 *U.S. Consumer Price Index (CPI), January 1947 to March 2008*

Figure 21.13 shows the U.S. CPI from January 1947 to March 2008 for a total of 733 observations. The CPI series, like the M1 series considered previously, shows a sustained upward trend. The unit root exercise gave the following results:

$$\widehat{\Delta\text{CPI}}_t = -0.01082 + 0.00068t - 0.00096\text{CPI}_{t-1} + 0.40669\Delta\text{CPI}_{t-1}$$
$$t = (-0.54) \quad (4.27) \quad (-1.77) \quad (12.03) \tag{21.12.2}$$
$$R^2 = 0.3570 \quad d = 1.9295$$

EXAMPLE 21.3
(Continued)

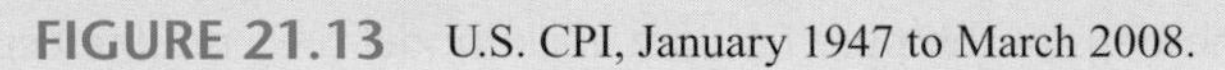

FIGURE 21.13 U.S. CPI, January 1947 to March 2008.

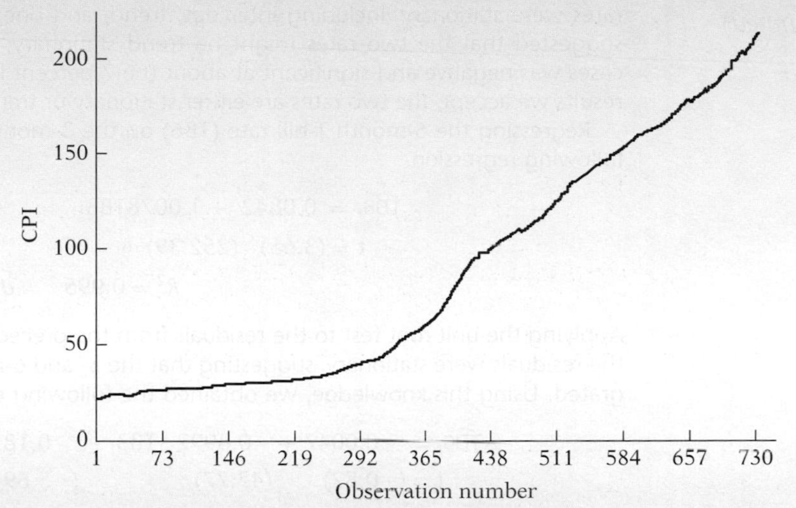

The $t\ (=\tau)$ value of CPI_{t-1} is -1.77. The 10 percent critical value is -3.1317. Since, in absolute terms, the computed τ is less than the critical τ, the conclusion is that CPI is not a stationary time series. We can characterize it as having a stochastic trend (why?). However, if you take the first differences of the CPI series, you will find them to be stationary. Hence CPI is a difference-stationary (DS) time series.

EXAMPLE 21.4
Are 3-Month and 6-Month Treasury Bill Rates Cointegrated?

Figure 21.14 plots (constant maturity) 3-month and 6-month U.S. Treasury bill (T-bill) rates from January 1982 to March 2008, for a total of 315 observations. Does the graph show that the two rates are cointegrated; that is, is there an equilibrium relationship between the two? From financial theory, we would expect that to be the case, otherwise arbitrageurs will exploit any discrepancy between the short and the long rates. First of all, let us see if the two time series are stationary.

FIGURE 21.14
Three- and six-month Treasury bill rates (constant maturity).

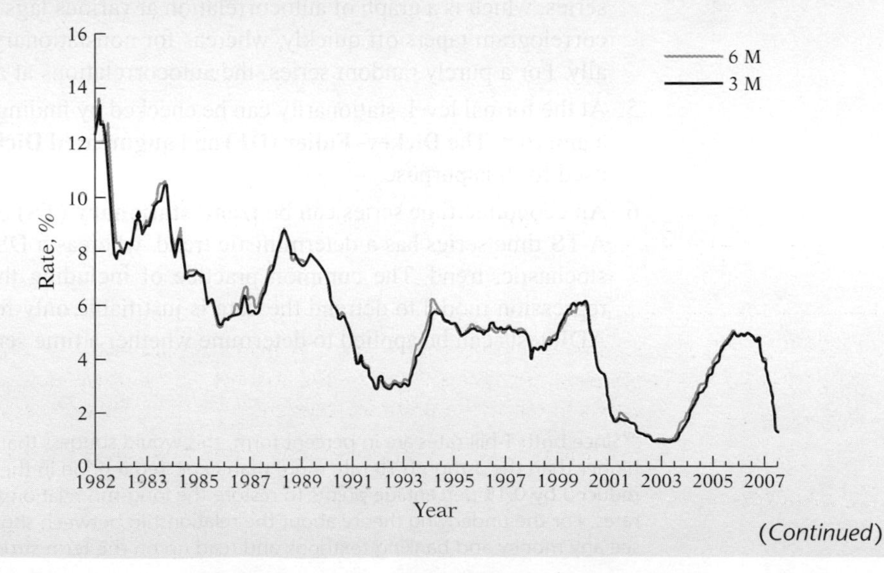

(Continued)

EXAMPLE 21.4 *(Continued)*

On the basis of the pure random walk model (i.e., no intercept, no trend), both the rates were stationary. Including intercept, trend, and one lagged difference, the results suggested that the two rates might be trend stationary; the trend coefficient in both cases was negative and significant at about the 7 percent level. So, depending on which results we accept, the two rates are either stationary or trend stationary.

Regressing the 6-month T-bill rate (TB6) on the 3-month T-bill rate, we obtained the following regression.

$$\begin{aligned}\widehat{TB6}_t &= 0.0842 + 1.0078TB3_t \\ t &= (3.65) \quad (252.39) \\ & \qquad R^2 = 0.995 \qquad d = 0.4035\end{aligned} \tag{21.12.3}$$

Applying the unit root test to the residuals from the preceding regression, we found that the residuals were stationary, suggesting that the 3- and 6-month T-bill rates were cointegrated. Using this knowledge, we obtained the following error correction model (ECM):

$$\begin{aligned}\Delta\widehat{TB6}_t &= -0.0047 + 0.8992\Delta TB3_t - 0.1855\hat{u}_{t-1} \\ t &= (-0.82) \qquad (47.77) \qquad (-5.69) \\ & \qquad R^2 = 0.880 \qquad d = 1.5376\end{aligned} \tag{21.12.4}$$

where $\hat{u}_{t-1}$ is the lagged value of the error correction term from the preceding period. As these results show, 0.19 of the discrepancy in the two rates in the previous month is eliminated this month.[49] Besides, short-run changes in the 3-month T-bill rate are quickly reflected in the 6-month T-bill rate, as the slope coefficient between the two is 0.8992. This should not be a surprising finding in view of the efficiency of the U.S. money markets.

Summary and Conclusions

1. Regression analysis based on time series data implicitly assumes that the underlying time series are stationary. The classical *t* tests, *F* tests, etc., are based on this assumption.
2. In practice most economic time series are nonstationary.
3. A stochastic process is said to be **weakly stationary** if its mean, variance, and autocovariances are constant over time (i.e., they are time-invariant).
4. At the informal level, weak stationarity can be tested by the **correlogram** of a time series, which is a graph of autocorrelation at various lags. For stationary time series, the correlogram tapers off quickly, whereas for nonstationary time series it dies off gradually. For a purely random series, the autocorrelations at all lags 1 and greater are zero.
5. At the formal level, stationarity can be checked by finding out if the time series contains a unit root. The **Dickey–Fuller (DF)** and **augmented Dickey–Fuller (ADF)** tests can be used for this purpose.
6. An economic time series can be **trend stationary (TS)** or **difference stationary (DS).** A TS time series has a deterministic trend, whereas a DS time series has a variable, or stochastic, trend. The common practice of including the time or trend variable in a regression model to detrend the data is justifiable only for TS time series. The DF and ADF tests can be applied to determine whether a time series is TS or DS.

[49]Since both T-bill rates are in percent form, this would suggest that if the 6-month TB rate was higher than the 3-month TB rate more than expected a priori in the last month, this month it will be reduced by 0.19 percentage points to restore the long-run relationship between the two interest rates. For the underlying theory about the relationship between short- and long-run interest rates, see any money and banking textbook and read up on the term structure of interest rates.

7. Regression of one time series variable on one or more time series variables often can give nonsensical or spurious results. This phenomenon is known as **spurious regression.** One way to guard against it is to find out if the time series are cointegrated.
8. **Cointegration** means that despite being individually nonstationary, a linear combination of two or more time series can be stationary. The **Engle–Granger (EG)** and the **augmented Engle–Granger (AEG)** tests can be used to find out if two or more time series are cointegrated.
9. Cointegration of two (or more) time series suggests that there is a long-run, or equilibrium, relationship between them.
10. The **error correction mechanism (ECM)** developed by Engle and Granger is a means of reconciling the short-run behavior of an economic variable with its long-run behavior.
11. The field of time series econometrics is evolving. The established results and tests are in some cases tentative and a lot more work remains. An important question that needs an answer is why some economic time series are stationary and others are nonstationary.

EXERCISES

Questions

21.1. What is meant by weak stationarity?

21.2. What is meant by an integrated time series?

21.3. What is the meaning of a unit root?

21.4. If a time series is $I(3)$, how many times would you have to difference it to make it stationary?

21.5. What are Dickey–Fuller (DF) and augmented DF tests?

21.6. What are Engle–Granger (EG) and augmented EG tests?

21.7. What is the meaning of cointegration?

21.8. What is the difference, if any, between tests of unit roots and tests of cointegration?

21.9. What is spurious regression?

21.10. What is the connection between cointegration and spurious regression?

21.11. What is the difference between a deterministic trend and a stochastic trend?

21.12. What is meant by a trend-stationary process (TSP) and a difference-stationary process (DSP)?

21.13. What is a random walk (model)?

21.14. "For a random walk stochastic process, the variance is infinite." Do you agree? Why?

21.15. What is the error correction mechanism (ECM)? What is its relationship with cointegration?

Empirical Exercises

21.16. Using the U.S. economic time series data posted on the book's website, obtain sample correlograms up to 36 lags for the time series LPCE, LDPI, LCP(profits), and LDIVIDENDS. What general pattern do you see? Intuitively, which one(s) of these time series seems to be stationary?

21.17. For each of the time series of Exercise 21.16, use the DF test to find out if these series contain a unit root. If a unit root exists, how would you characterize such a time series?

21.18. Continue with Exercise 21.17. How would you decide if the ADF test is more appropriate than the DF test?

21.19. Consider the dividends and profits time series given in the U.S. economic time series data posted on the book's website. Since dividends depend on profits, consider the following simple model:

$$\text{LDIVIDENDS}_t = \beta_1 + \beta_2\text{LCP} + u_t$$

a. Would you expect this regression to suffer from the spurious regression phenomenon? Why?

b. Are the logged Dividends and logged Profits time series cointegrated? How do you test for this explicitly? If, after testing, you find that they are cointegrated, would your answer in (*a*) change?

c. Employ the error correction mechanism (ECM) to study the short- and long-run behavior of dividends in relation to profits.

d. If you examine the LDIVIDENDS and LCP series individually, do they exhibit stochastic or deterministic trends? What tests do you use?

**e.* Assume LDIVIDENDS and LCP are cointegrated. Then, instead of regressing dividends on profits, you regress profits on dividends. Is such a regression valid?

21.20. Take the first differences of the time series given in the U.S. economic time series data posted on the book's website and plot them. Also obtain a correlogram of each time series up to 36 lags. What strikes you about these correlograms?

21.21. Instead of regressing LDIVIDENDS on LCP in level form, suppose you regress the first difference of LDIVIDENDS on the first difference of LCP. Would you include the intercept in this regression? Why or why not? Show the calculations.

21.22. Continue with the previous exercise. How would you test the first-difference regression for stationarity? In the present example, what would you expect a priori and why? Show all the calculations.

21.23. From the U.K. private sector housing starts (X) for the period 1948 to 1984, Terence Mills obtained the following regression results:[†]

$$\begin{aligned} \widehat{\Delta X_t} &= 31.03 \quad - \quad 0.188X_{t-1} \\ \text{se} &= (12.50) \qquad (0.080) \\ (t =)\tau & \qquad\qquad\quad (-2.35) \end{aligned}$$

Note: The 5 percent critical τ value is -2.95 and the 10 percent critical τ value is -2.60.

a. On the basis of these results, is the housing starts time series stationary or nonstationary? Alternatively, is there a unit root in this time series? How do you know?

b. If you were to use the usual t test, is the observed t value statistically significant? On this basis, would you have concluded that this time series is stationary?

c. Now consider the following regression results:

$$\begin{aligned} \widehat{\Delta^2 X_t} &= 4.76 \quad - 1.39\Delta X_{t-1} + 0.313\Delta^2 X_{t-1} \\ \text{se} &= (5.06) \quad (0.236) \qquad (0.163) \\ (t =)\tau & \qquad\quad (-5.89) \end{aligned}$$

*Optional.

[†]Terence C. Mills, op. cit., p. 127. Notation slightly altered.

where Δ^2 is the second difference operator, that is, the first difference of the first difference. The estimated τ value is now statistically significant. What can you say now about the stationarity of the time series in question?

Note: The purpose of the preceding regression is to find out if there is a **second unit root** in the time series.

21.24. Generate two random walk series as indicated in Eqs. (21.7.1) and (21.7.2) and regress one on the other. Repeat this exercise but now use their first differences and verify that in this regression the R^2 value is about zero and the Durbin–Watson d is close to 2.

21.25. To show that two variables, each with deterministic trend, can lead to spurious regression, Charemza et al. obtained the following regression based on 30 observations:*

$$\hat{Y}_t = 5.92 + 0.030X_t$$
$$t = (9.9) \quad (21.2)$$
$$R^2 = 0.92 \qquad d = 0.06$$

where $Y_1 = 1, Y_2 = 2, \ldots, Y_n = n$ and $X_1 = 1, X_2 = 4, \ldots, X_n = n^2$.

a. What kind of trend does Y exhibit? and X?

b. Plot the two variables and plot the regression line. What general conclusion do you draw from this plot?

21.26. From the data for the period 1971–I to 1988–IV for Canada, the following regression results were obtained:

1. $$\widehat{\ln \text{M1}_t} = -10.2571 + 1.5975 \ln \text{GDP}_t$$
$$t = (-12.9422) \quad (25.8865)$$
$$R^2 = 0.9463 \qquad d = 0.3254$$

2. $$\widehat{\Delta \ln \text{M1}_t} = 0.0095 + 0.5833 \Delta \ln \text{GDP}_t$$
$$t = (2.4957) \quad (1.8958)$$
$$R^2 = 0.0885 \qquad d = 1.7399$$

3. $$\Delta \hat{u}_t = -0.1958 \hat{u}_{t-1}$$
$$(t = \tau) \; (-2.2521)$$
$$R^2 = 0.1118 \qquad d = 1.4767$$

where M1 = M1 money supply, GDP = gross domestic product, both measured in billions of Canadian dollars, ln is natural log, and $\hat{u}_t$ represent the estimated residuals from regression (1).

a. Interpret regressions (1) and (2).

b. Do you suspect that regression (1) is spurious? Why?

c. Is regression (2) spurious? How do you know?

d. From the results of regression (3), would you change your conclusion in (*b*)? Why?

*Charemza et al., op. cit., p. 93.

e. Now consider the following regression:

$$\widehat{\Delta \ln M1_t} = 0.0084 + 0.7340 \Delta \ln GDP_t - 0.0811 \hat{u}_{t-1}$$
$$t = (2.0496) \quad (2.0636) \quad (-0.8537)$$
$$R^2 = 0.1066 \qquad d = 1.6697$$

What does this regression tell you? Does this help you decide if regression (1) is spurious or not?

21.27. The following regressions are based on the CPI data for the United States for the period 1960–2007, for a total of 48 annual observations:

1.
$$\widehat{\Delta CPI_t} = 0.0334 CPI_{t-1}$$
$$t = (12.37)$$
$$R^2 = 0.0703 \qquad d = 0.3663 \qquad RSS = 206.65$$

2.
$$\widehat{\Delta CPI_t} = 1.8662 + 0.0192 CPI_{t-1}$$
$$t = (3.27) \quad (3.86)$$
$$R^2 = 0.249 \qquad d = 0.4462 \qquad RSS = 166.921$$

3.
$$\widehat{\Delta CPI_t} = 1.1611 + 0.5344t - 0.1077 CPI_{t-1}$$
$$t = (2.37) \quad (4.80) \quad (-4.02)$$
$$R^2 = 0.507 \qquad d = 0.6071 \qquad RSS = 109.608$$

where RSS = residual sum of squares.

a. Examining the preceding regressions, what can you say about stationarity of the CPI time series?

b. How would you choose among the three models?

c. Equation (1) is Eq. (3) minus the intercept and trend. Which test would you use to decide if the implied restrictions of model (1) are valid? (*Hint:* Use the Dickey–Fuller t and F tests. Use the approximate values given in **Appendix D,** Table D.7.)

21.28. As noted in the text, there may be several structural breaks in the U.S. economic time series dataset introduced in Section 21.1. Dummy variables are a good way of incorporating these shifts in the data.

a. Using dummy variables to designate three different periods related to the oil embargoes in 1973 and 1979, regress the log of personal consumption expenditures (LPCE) on the log of disposable personal income (LDPI). Has there been a change in the results? What is your decision about the unit root hypothesis now?

b. Several websites list the official economic cycles that may have affected the U.S. economic time series data discussed in Section 21.1. See, for example, http://www.nber.org/cycles/cyclesmain.html. Using the information here, create dummy variables indicating some of the major cycles and check the results of regressing LPCE on LDPI. Has there been a change?

Chapter 22

Time Series Econometrics: Forecasting

We noted in the **Introduction** that forecasting is an important part of econometric analysis, for some people probably the most important. How do we forecast economic variables, such as GDP, inflation, exchange rates, stock prices, unemployment rates, and myriad other economic variables? In this chapter we discuss two methods of forecasting that have become quite popular: (1) **autoregressive integrated moving average (ARIMA),** popularly known as the **Box–Jenkins** methodology,[1] and (2) **vector autoregression (VAR).**

In this chapter we also discuss the special problems involved in forecasting prices of financial assets, such as stock prices and exchange rates. These asset prices are characterized by the phenomenon known as **volatility clustering,** that is, periods in which they exhibit wide swings for an extended time period followed by a period of comparative tranquility. One only has to look at the Dow Jones Index in the recent past. The so-called **autoregressive conditional heteroscedasticity (ARCH)** or **generalized autoregressive conditional heteroscedasticity (GARCH)** models can capture such volatility clustering.

The topic of economic forecasting is vast, and specialized books have been written on this subject. Our objective in this chapter is to give the reader just a glimpse of this subject. The interested reader may consult the references for further study. Fortunately, most modern econometric packages have user-friendly introductions to several techniques discussed in this chapter.

The linkage between this chapter and the previous chapter is that the forecasting methods discussed below assume that the underlying time series are stationary or they can be made stationary with appropriate transformations. As we progress through this chapter, you will see the use of the several concepts that we introduced in the last chapter.

22.1 Approaches to Economic Forecasting

Broadly speaking, there are five approaches to economic forecasting based on time series data: (1) exponential smoothing methods, (2) single-equation regression models, (3) simultaneous-equation regression models, (4) autoregressive integrated moving average (ARIMA) models, and (5) vector autoregression (VAR) models.

[1] G. P. E. Box and G. M. Jenkins, *Time Series Analysis: Forecasting and Control,* revised ed., Holden Day, San Francisco, 1978.

Exponential Smoothing Methods[2]

These are essentially methods of fitting a suitable curve to historical data of a given time series. There are a variety of these methods, such as *single exponential smoothing, Holt's linear method, Holt–Winters' method,* and their variations. Although still used in several areas of business and economic forecasting, these are now supplemented (supplanted?) by the other four methods that follow. We will not discuss exponential smoothing methods in this chapter, for that would take us far afield.

Single-Equation Regression Models

The bulk of this book has been devoted to single-equation regression models. As an example of a single-equation model, consider the demand function for automobiles. On the basis of economic theory, we postulate that the demand for automobiles is a function of automobile prices, advertising expenditure, income of the consumer, interest rate (as a measure of the cost of borrowing), and other relevant variables (e.g., family size, travel distance to work). From time series data, we estimate an appropriate model of auto demand (either linear, log–linear, or nonlinear), which can be used for forecasting demand for autos in the future. Of course, as noted in Chapter 5, forecasting errors increase rapidly if we go too far out in the future.

Simultaneous-Equation Regression Models[3]

In Chapters 18, 19, and 20 we considered simultaneous-equation models. In their heyday during the 1960s and 1970s, elaborate models of the U.S. economy based on simultaneous equations dominated economic forecasting. But since then the glamor of such forecasting models has subsided because of their poor forecasting performance, especially since the 1973 and 1979 oil price shocks (due to OPEC oil embargoes) and also because of the so-called **Lucas critique.**[4] The thrust of this critique, as you may recall, is that the parameters estimated from an econometric model are dependent on the policy prevailing at the time the model was estimated and will change if there is a policy change. In short, the estimated parameters are not invariant in the presence of policy changes.

For example, in October 1979 the Fed changed its monetary policy dramatically. Instead of targeting interest rates, it announced it would henceforth monitor the rate of growth of the money supply. With such a pronounced change, an econometric model estimated from past data will have little forecasting value in the new regime. These days the Fed's emphasis has changed from controlling the money supply to controlling the short-term interest rate (the federal funds rate).

ARIMA Models

The publication by Box and Jenkins of *Time Series Analysis: Forecasting and Control* (op. cit.) ushered in a new generation of forecasting tools. Popularly known as the Box–Jenkins (BJ) methodology, but technically known as the ARIMA methodology, the emphasis of these methods is not on constructing single-equation or simultaneous-equation models but on analyzing the probabilistic, or stochastic, properties of economic time series

[2]For a comparatively simple exposition of these methods, see Spyros Makridakis, Steven C. Wheelwright, and Rob J. Hyndman, *Forecasting Methods and Applications,* 3d ed., John Wiley & Sons, New York, 1998.

[3]For a textbook treatment of the use of simultaneous-equation models in forecasting, see Robert S. Pindyck and Daniel L. Rubinfeld, *Econometric Models & Economic Forecasts,* 4th ed., McGraw-Hill, New York, 1998, Part III.

[4]Robert E. Lucas, "Econometric Policy Evaluation: A Critique," in Carnegie–Rochester Conference Series, *The Phillips Curve,* North-Holland, Amsterdam, 1976, pp. 19–46. This article, among others, earned Lucas a Nobel Prize in economics.

on their own under the philosophy *let the data speak for themselves*. Unlike the regression models, in which Y_t is explained by k regressors $X_1, X_2, X_3, \ldots, X_k$, the BJ-type time series models allow Y_t to be explained by past, or lagged, values of Y itself and stochastic error terms. For this reason, ARIMA models are sometimes called *atheoretic* models because they are not derived from any economic theory—and economic theories are often the basis of simultaneous-equation models.

In passing, note that our emphasis in this chapter is on *univariate* ARIMA models, that is, ARIMA models pertaining to a single time series. But the analysis can be extended to multivariate ARIMA models.

VAR Models

VAR methodology superficially resembles simultaneous-equation modeling in that we consider several endogenous variables together. But each endogenous variable is explained by its lagged, or past, values and the lagged values of all other endogenous variables in the model; usually, there are no exogenous variables in the model.

In the rest of this chapter we discuss the fundamentals of Box–Jenkins and VAR approaches to economic forecasting. Our discussion is elementary and heuristic. The reader wishing to pursue this subject further is advised to consult the references.[5]

22.2 AR, MA, and ARIMA Modeling of Time Series Data

To introduce several ideas, some old and some new, let us work with the GDP time series data for the United States introduced in Section 21.1 (see the book's website for the actual data). A plot of this time series is already given in Figures 21.1 (undifferenced logged GDP) and 21.9 (first-differenced LGDP); recall that LGDP in level form is nonstationary but in the (first) differenced form it is stationary.

If a time series is stationary, we can model it in a variety of ways.

An Autoregressive (AR) Process

Let Y_t represent the logged GDP at time t. If we model Y_t as

$$(Y_t - \delta) = \alpha_1(Y_{t-1} - \delta) + u_t \tag{22.2.1}$$

where δ is the mean of Y and where u_t is an uncorrelated random error term with zero mean and constant variance σ^2 (i.e., it is *white noise*), then we say that Y_t follows a **first-order autoregressive,** or **AR(1),** stochastic process, which we have already encountered in Chapter 12. Here the value of Y at time t depends on its value in the previous time period and a random term; the Y values are expressed as deviations from their mean value. In other words, this model says that the forecast value of Y at time t is simply some proportion $(= \alpha_1)$ of its value at time $(t - 1)$ plus a random shock or disturbance at time t; again the Y values are expressed around their mean values.

But if we consider this model,

$$(Y_t - \delta) = \alpha_1(Y_{t-1} - \delta) + \alpha_3(Y_{t-2} - \delta) + u_t \tag{22.2.2}$$

[5]See Pindyck and Rubinfeld, op. cit., Part 3; Alan Pankratz, *Forecasting with Dynamic Regression Models,* John Wiley & Sons, New York, 1991 (this is an applied book); and Andrew Harvey, *The Econometric Analysis of Time Series,* The MIT Press, 2d ed., Cambridge, Mass., 1990 (this is a rather advanced book). A thorough but accessible discussion can also be found in Terence C. Mills, *Time Series Techniques for Economists,* Cambridge University Press, New York, 1990.

then we say that Y_t follows a **second-order autoregressive,** or **AR(2),** process. That is, the value of Y at time t depends on its value in the previous two time periods, the Y values being expressed around their mean value δ.

In general, we can have

$$(Y_t - \delta) = \alpha_1(Y_{t-1} - \delta) + \alpha_2(Y_{t-2} - \delta) + \cdots + \alpha_p(Y_{t-p} - \delta) + u_t \quad (22.2.3)$$

in which case Y_t is a ***p*****th-order autoregressive,** or **AR(*p*),** process.

Notice that in all the preceding models only the current and previous Y values are involved; there are no other regressors. In this sense, we say that the "data speak for themselves." They are a kind of *reduced form model* that we encountered in our discussion of the simultaneous-equation models.

A Moving Average (MA) Process

The AR process just discussed is not the only mechanism that may have generated Y. Suppose we model Y as follows:

$$Y_t = \mu + \beta_0 u_t + \beta_1 u_{t-1} \quad (22.2.4)$$

where μ is a constant and u, as before, is the white noise stochastic error term. Here Y at time t is equal to a constant plus a moving average of the current and past error terms. Thus, in the present case, we say that Y follows a **first-order moving average,** or an **MA(1),** process.

But if Y follows the expression

$$Y_t = \mu + \beta_0 u_t + \beta_1 u_{t-1} + \beta_2 u_{t-2} \quad (22.2.5)$$

then it is an **MA(2)** process. More generally,

$$Y_t = \mu + \beta_0 u_t + \beta_1 u_{t-1} + \beta_2 u_{t-2} + \cdots + \beta_q u_{t-q} \quad (22.2.6)$$

is an **MA(*q*)** process. In short, a moving average process is simply a linear combination of white noise error terms.

An Autoregressive and Moving Average (ARMA) Process

Of course, it is quite likely that Y has characteristics of both AR and MA and is therefore *ARMA*. Thus, Y_t follows an **ARMA(1, 1)** process if it can be written as

$$Y_t = \theta + \alpha_1 Y_{t-1} + \beta_0 u_t + \beta_1 u_{t-1} \quad (22.2.7)$$

because there is one autoregressive and one moving average term. In Eq. (22.2.7) θ represents a constant term.

In general, in an **ARMA(*p*, *q*)** process, there will be p autoregressive and q moving average terms.

An Autoregressive Integrated Moving Average (ARIMA) Process

The time series models we have already discussed are based on the assumption that the time series involved are (weakly) stationary in the sense defined in Chapter 21. Briefly, the mean and variance for a weakly stationary time series are constant and its covariance is time-invariant. But we know that many economic time series are nonstationary, that is, they are *integrated;* for example, the economic time series introduced in Section 21.1 of Chapter 21 are integrated.

But we also saw in Chapter 21 that if a time series is integrated of order 1 (i.e., it is $I[1]$), its first differences are $I(0)$, that is, stationary. Similarly, if a time series is $I(2)$, its second difference is $I(0)$. In general, if a time series is $I(d)$, after differencing it d times we obtain an $I(0)$ series.

Therefore, if we have to difference a time series d times to make it stationary and then apply the ARMA(p, q) model to it, we say that the original time series is **ARIMA(p, d, q)**, that is, it is an **autoregressive integrated moving average** time series, where p denotes the number of autoregressive terms, d the number of times the series has to be differenced before it becomes stationary, and q the number of moving average terms. Thus, an ARIMA(2, 1, 2) time series has to be differenced once ($d = 1$) before it becomes stationary and the (first-differenced) stationary time series can be modeled as an ARMA(2, 2) process, that is, it has two AR and two MA terms. Of course, if $d = 0$ (i.e., a series is stationary to begin with), ARIMA(p, $d = 0$, q) = ARMA(p, q). Note that an ARIMA(p, 0, 0) process means a purely AR(p) stationary process; an ARIMA(0, 0, q) means a purely MA(q) stationary process. Given the values of p, d, and q, one can tell what process is being modeled.

The important point to note is that to use the Box–Jenkins methodology, we must have either a stationary time series or a time series that is stationary after one or more differencings. The reason for assuming stationarity can be explained as follows:

> The objective of B–J [Box–Jenkins] is to identify and estimate a statistical model which can be interpreted as having generated the sample data. If this estimated model is then to be used for forecasting we must assume that the features of this model are constant through time, and particularly over future time periods. Thus the simple reason for requiring stationary data is that any model which is inferred from these data can itself be interpreted as stationary or stable, therefore providing [a] valid basis for forecasting.[6]

22.3 The Box–Jenkins (BJ) Methodology

The million-dollar question obviously is: Looking at a time series, such as the U.S. LGDP series in Figure 21.1, how does one know whether it follows a purely AR process (and if so, what is the value of p) or a purely MA process (and if so, what is the value of q) or an ARMA process (and if so, what are the values of p and q) or an ARIMA process, in which case we must know the values of p, d, and q. The BJ methodology comes in handy in answering the preceding question. The method consists of four steps:

Step 1. Identification. That is, find out the appropriate values of p, d, and q. We will show shortly how the **correlogram** and **partial correlogram** aid in this task.

Step 2. Estimation. Having identified the appropriate p and q values, the next stage is to estimate the parameters of the autoregressive and moving average terms included in the model. Sometimes this calculation can be done by simple least squares but sometimes we will have to resort to nonlinear (in parameter) estimation methods. Since this task is now routinely handled by several statistical packages, we do not have to worry about the actual mathematics of estimation; the enterprising student may consult the references on that.

Step 3. Diagnostic checking. Having chosen a particular ARIMA model, and having estimated its parameters, we next see whether the chosen model fits the data reasonably well, for it is possible that another ARIMA model might do the job as well. This is why Box–Jenkins ARIMA modeling is more an art than a science; considerable skill is required to choose the right ARIMA model. One simple test of the chosen model is to see if the residuals estimated from this model are white noise; if they are, we can accept the particular fit; if not, we must start over. **Thus, the BJ methodology is an iterative process** (see Figure 22.1).

[6]Michael Pokorny, *An Introduction to Econometrics,* Basil Blackwell, New York, 1987, p. 343.

FIGURE 22.1
The Box–Jenkins methodology.

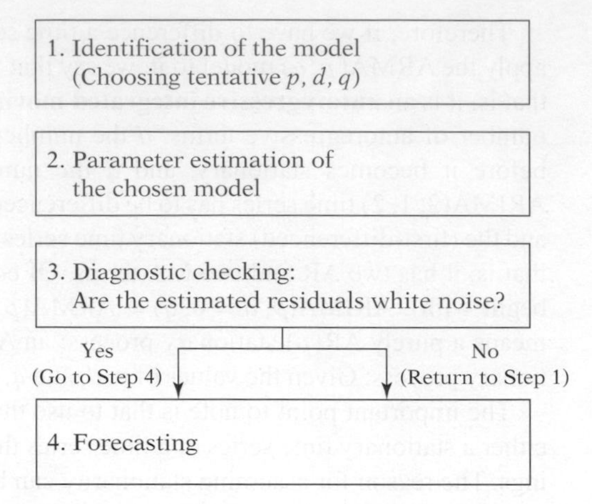

Step 4. Forecasting. One of the reasons for the popularity of the ARIMA modeling is its success in forecasting. In many cases, the forecasts obtained by this method are more reliable than those obtained from the traditional econometric modeling, particularly for short-term forecasts. Of course, each case must be checked.

With this general discussion, let us look at these four steps in some detail. Throughout, we will use the GDP data introduced in Section 21.1 (see the book's website for the actual data) to illustrate the various points.

22.4 Identification

The chief tools in identification are the **autocorrelation function (ACF),** the **partial autocorrelation function (PACF),** and the resulting **correlograms,** which are simply the plots of ACFs and PACFs against the lag length.

In the previous chapter we defined the (population) ACF (ρ_k) and the sample ACF ($\hat{\rho}_k$). The concept of partial autocorrelation is analogous to the concept of partial regression coefficient. In the k-variable multiple regression model, the kth regression coefficient β_k measures the rate of change in the mean value of the regressand for a unit change in the kth regressor X_k, holding the influence of all other regressors constant.

In similar fashion, the **partial autocorrelation** ρ_{kk} measures correlation between (time series) observations that are k time periods apart after controlling for correlations at intermediate lags (i.e., lags less than k). In other words, partial autocorrelation is the correlation between Y_t and Y_{t-k} after removing the effect of the intermediate Y's.[7] In Section 7.11 we already introduced the concept of partial correlation in the regression context and showed its relation to simple correlations. Such partial correlations are now routinely computed by most statistical packages.

In Figure 22.2 we show the correlogram (panel *a*) and partial correlogram (panel *b*) of the LGDP series. From this figure, two facts stand out: First, the ACF declines very slowly; as shown in Figure 21.8, ACF up to about 22 lags are individually statistically significantly different from zero, for they all are outside the 95 percent confidence bounds. Second, after the second lag, the PACF drops dramatically, and most PACFs after lag 2 are statistically insignificant, save for maybe lag 13.

[7]In time series data a large proportion of correlation between Y_t and Y_{t-k} may be due to the correlations they have with the intervening lags $Y_{t-1}, Y_{t-2}, \ldots, Y_{t-k+1}$. The partial correlation ρ_{kk} removes the influence of these intervening variables.

FIGURE 22.2
(*a*) Correlogram and (*b*) partial correlogram, for LGDP, United States, 1947–I to 2007–IV.

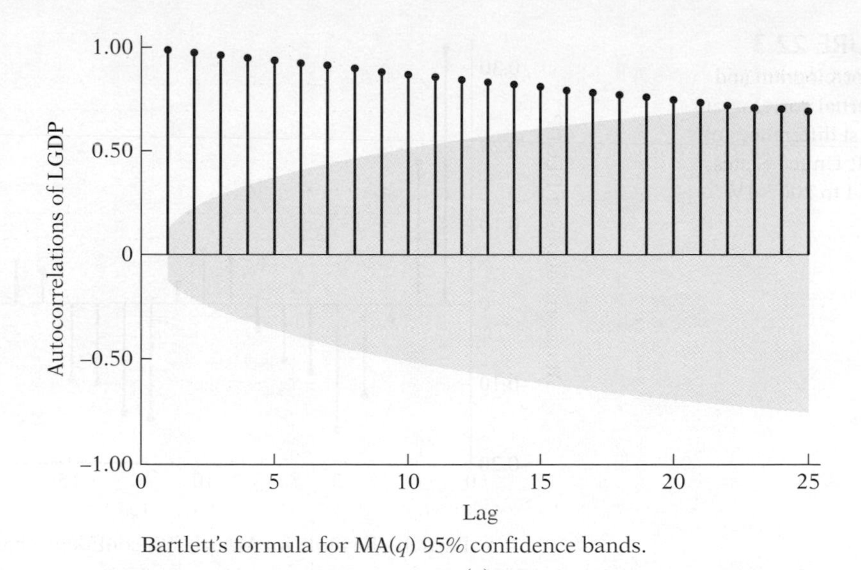

(*a*)

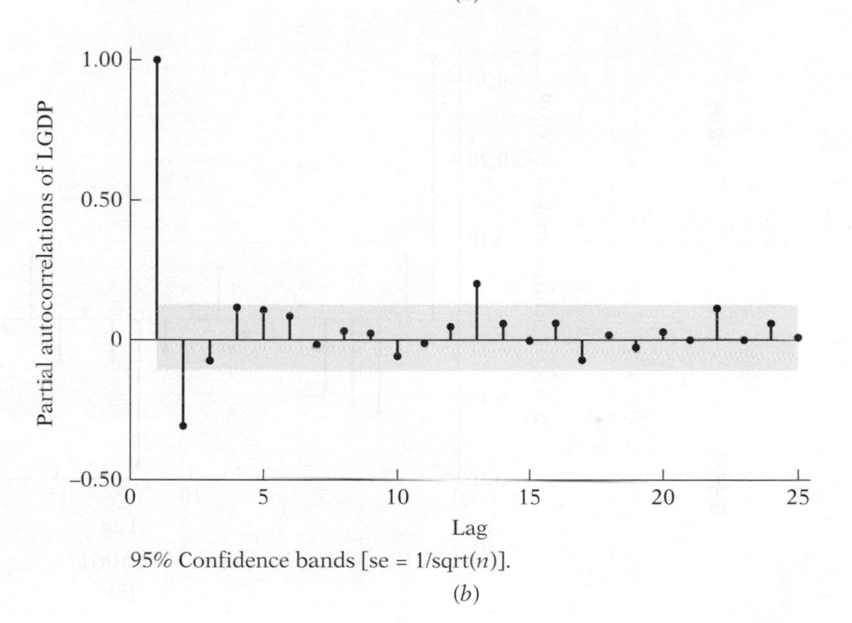

(*b*)

Since the U.S. LGDP time series is not stationary, we have to make it stationary before we can apply the Box–Jenkins methodology. In Figure 21.9 we plotted the first differences of LGDP. Unlike Figure 21.1, we do not observe any trend in this series, perhaps suggesting that the first-differenced LGDP time series is stationary.[8] A formal application of the **Dickey–Fuller unit root test** shows that that is indeed the case. We can also see this visually from the estimated ACF and PACF correlograms given in panels (*a*) and (*b*) of Figure 22.3. Now we have a much different pattern of ACF and PACF. The ACFs at lags 1, 2, and 5 seem statistically different from zero; recall from Chapter 21 that the approximate 95 percent confidence limits for ρ_k are -0.1254 and $+0.1254$. (*Note:* As discussed in Chapter 21, these

[8]It is hard to tell whether the variance of this series is stationary, especially around 1979–1980. The oil embargo of 1979 and a significant change in the Fed's monetary policy in 1979 may have something to do with our difficulty.

FIGURE 22.3
(*a*) Correlogram and (*b*) partial correlogram for first differences of LGDP, United States, 1947–I to 2007–IV.

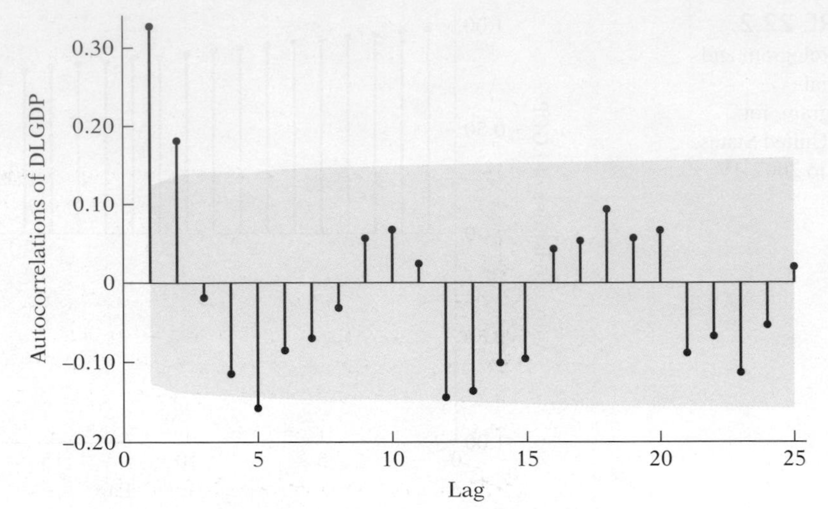

(*a*)

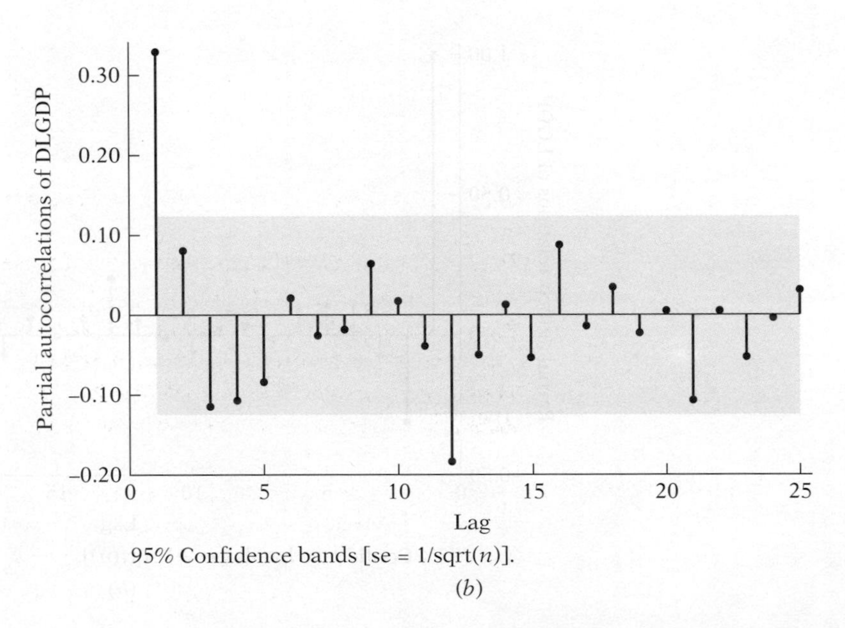

(*b*)

confidence limits are asymptotic and so can be considered approximate.) But at all other lags, they are not statistically different from zero. For the partial autocorrelations, only lags 1 and 12 seem to be statistically different from zero.

Now how do the correlograms given in Figure 22.3 enable us to find the ARMA pattern of the LGDP time series? (*Note:* We will consider only the first-differenced LGDP series because it is stationary.) One way of accomplishing this is to consider the ACF and PACF and the associated correlograms of a selected number of ARMA processes, such as AR(1), AR(2), MA(1), MA(2), ARMA(1, 1), ARIMA(2, 2), and so on. Since each of these stochastic processes exhibits typical patterns of ACF and PACF, if the time series under study fits one of these patterns we can identify the time series with that process. Of course, we will have to apply diagnostic tests to find out if the chosen ARMA model is reasonably accurate.

To study the properties of the various standard ARIMA processes would consume a lot of space. What we plan to do is to give general guidelines (see Table 22.1); the references can give the details of the various stochastic processes.

TABLE 22.1
Theoretical Patterns of ACF and PACF

Type of Model	Typical Pattern of ACF	Typical Pattern of PACF
AR(p)	Decays exponentially or with damped sine wave pattern or both	Significant spikes through lags p
MA(q)	Significant spikes through lags q	Declines exponentially
ARMA(p, q)	Exponential decay	Exponential decay

Note: The terms *exponential* and *geometric decay* mean the same things (recall our discussion of the Koyck distributed lag).

FIGURE 22.4 ACF and PACF of selected stochastic processes: (a) AR(2): $\alpha_1 = 0.5$, $\alpha_2 = 0.3$; (b) MA(2): $\beta_1 = 0.5$, $\beta_2 = 0.3$; (c) ARMA(1, 1): $\alpha_1 = 0.5$, $\beta_1 = 0.5$.

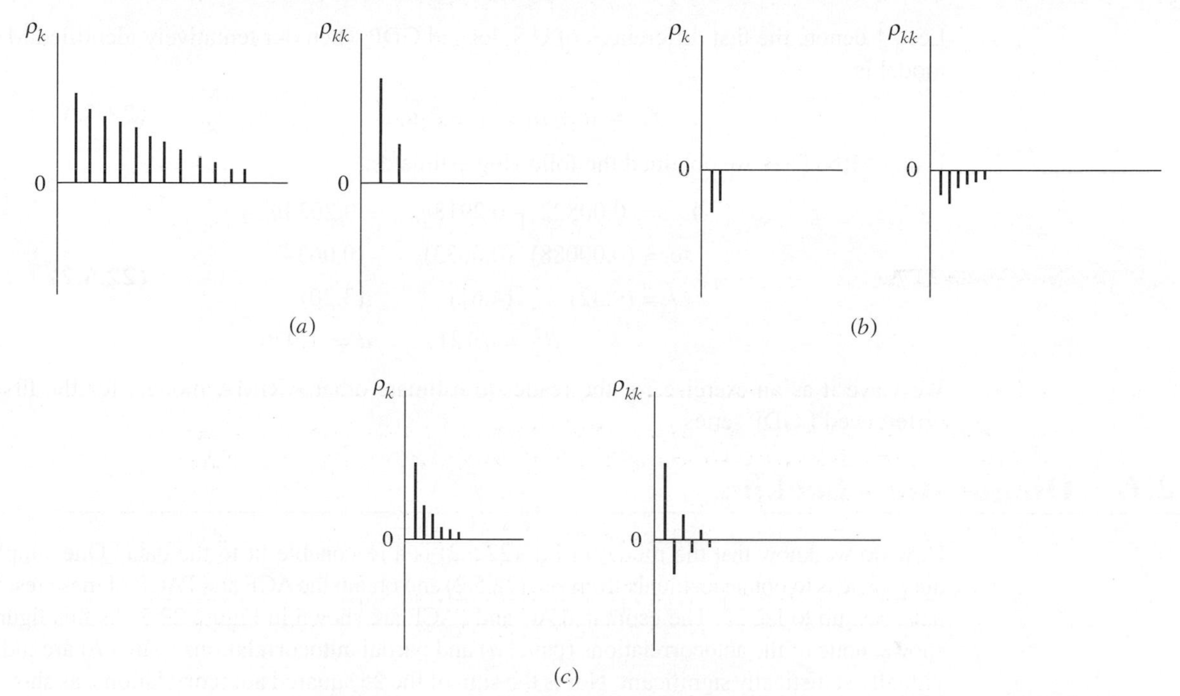

Notice that the ACFs and PACFs of AR(p) and MA(q) processes have opposite patterns; in the AR(p) case the AC declines geometrically or exponentially but the PACF cuts off after a certain number of lags, whereas the opposite happens to an MA(q) process.

Geometrically, these patterns are shown in Figure 22.4.

A Warning

Since in practice we do not observe the theoretical ACFs and PACFs and rely on their sample counterparts, the estimated ACFs and PACFs will not match exactly their theoretical counterparts. What we are looking for is the resemblance between theoretical and sample ACFs and PACFs so that they can point us in the right direction in constructing ARIMA models. And that is why ARIMA modeling requires a great deal of skill, which of course comes from practice.

ARIMA Identification of U.S. GDP

Returning to the correlogram and partial correlogram of the stationary (after first-differencing) U.S. LGDP for 1947–I to 2007–IV given in Figure 22.3, what do we see?

Remembering that the ACF and PACF are sample quantities, we do not have a nice pattern as suggested in Table 22.1. The autocorrelations (panel *a*) decline for the first two lags and then, with the exception of lag 5, the rest of them are not statistically different from zero (the gray area shown in the figures gives the approximate 95 percent confidence limits). The partial autocorrelations (panel *b*) with spikes at lags 1 and 12 seem statistically significant but the rest are not; if the partial correlation coefficient were significant only at lag 1, we could have identified this as an AR(1) model. Let us therefore assume that the process that generated the (first-differenced) LGDP series is an MA(2) process. Keep in mind that unless the ACF and PACF are not well-defined, it is hard to choose a model without trial and error. The reader is encouraged to try other ARIMA models on the first-differenced LGDP series.

22.5 Estimation of the ARIMA Model

Let Y_t^* denote the first differences of U.S. logged GDP. Then our tentatively identified MA model is

$$Y_t^* = \mu + \beta_1 u_{t-1} + \beta_2 u_{t-2} \tag{22.5.1}$$

Using MINITAB, we obtained the following estimates:

$$\begin{aligned} \hat{Y}_t^* &= 0.00822 + 0.2918u_{t-1} + 0.2024u_{t-2} \\ \text{se} &= (0.00088) \quad (0.0633) \qquad (0.0634) \\ t &= (9.32) \qquad (4.61) \qquad (3.20) \\ & \qquad R^2 = 0.1217 \qquad d = 1.9705 \end{aligned} \tag{22.5.2}$$

We leave it as an exercise for the reader to estimate other ARIMA models for the first-differenced LGDP series.

22.6 Diagnostic Checking

How do we know that the model in Eq. (22.5.2) is a reasonable fit to the data? One simple diagnostic is to obtain residuals from Eq. (22.5.2) and obtain the ACF and PACF of these residuals, say, up to lag 25. The estimated AC and PACF are shown in Figure 22.5. As this figure shows, none of the autocorrelations (panel *a*) and partial autocorrelations (panel *b*) are individually statistically significant. Nor is the sum of the 25 squared autocorrelations, as shown by the Box–Pierce Q and Ljung–Box (LB) statistics (see Chapter 21), statistically significant. In other words, the correlograms of both autocorrelation and partial autocorrelation give the impression that the residuals estimated from Eq. (22.5.2) are purely random. Hence, there may not be any need to look for another ARIMA model.

22.7 Forecasting

Remember that the GDP data are for the period 1974–I to 2007–IV. Suppose, on the basis of model (22.5.2), we want to forecast LGDP for the first four quarters of 2008. But in Eq. (22.5.2) the dependent variable is *change* in the LGDP over the previous quarter. Therefore, if we use Eq. (22.5.2), what we can obtain are the forecasts of LGDP changes between the first quarter of 2008 and the fourth quarter of 2007, the second quarter of 2008 over the first quarter of 2008, etc.

To obtain the forecast of LGDP level rather than its changes, we can "undo" the first-difference transformation that we had used to obtain the changes. (More technically, we *integrate* the first-differenced series.) Thus, to obtain the forecast value of LGDP (not ΔLGDP) for 2008–I, we rewrite model (22.5.1) as

$$Y_{2008-\text{I}} - Y_{2007-\text{IV}} = \mu + \beta_1 u_{2007-\text{IV}} + \beta_2 u_{2007-\text{III}} + u_{2008-\text{I}} \tag{22.7.1}$$

FIGURE 22.5
(*a*) Correlogram and (*b*) partial correlogram for residuals of MA(2) model for the first differences of LGDP, United States, 1947–I to 2007–IV.

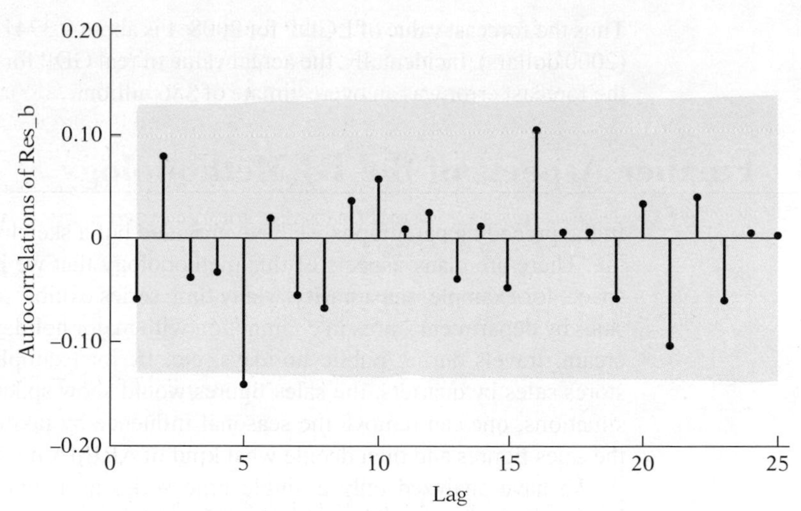

(*a*)

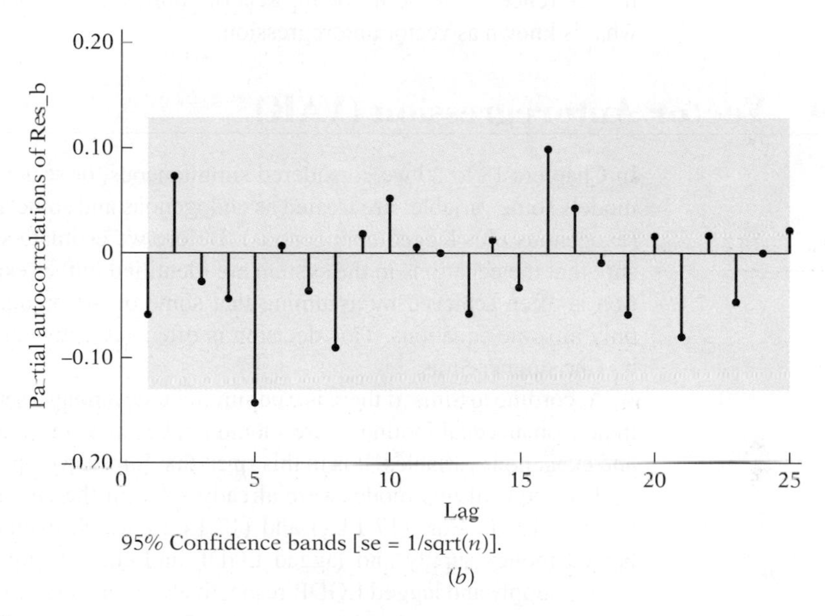

(*b*)

That is,

$$Y_{2008\text{–I}} = \mu + \beta_1 u_{2007\text{–IV}} + \beta_2 u_{2007\text{–III}} + u_{2008\text{–I}} + Y_{2007\text{–IV}} \qquad \textbf{(22.7.2)}$$

The values of μ, β_1, and β_2 are already known from the estimated regression (22.5.2). The value of $u_{2008\text{–I}}$ is assumed to be zero (why?). Therefore, we can easily obtain the forecast value of $Y_{2008\text{–I}}$. The numerical estimate of this forecast value is:[9]

$$\begin{aligned} Y_{2008\text{–I}} &= 0.00822 + (0.2918)u_{2007\text{–IV}} + (0.2024)(u_{2007\text{–III}}) + Y_{2007\text{–IV}} \\ &= 0.00822 + (0.2918)(0.00853) + (0.2024)(-0.00399) + 9.3653 \\ &= 9.3741(\text{approx.}) \end{aligned}$$

[9]Although standard computer packages do this computation routinely, we show the detailed calculations to illustrate the mechanics involved.

Thus the forecast value of LGDP for 2008–I is about 9.3741, which is about $11,779 billion (2000 dollars). Incidentally, the actual value of real GDP for 2008–I was $11,693.09 billion; the forecast error was an overestimate of $86 billion.

22.8 Further Aspects of the BJ Methodology

In the preceding paragraphs we have provided but a sketchy introduction to the BJ modeling. There are many aspects of this methodology that we have not considered for lack of space, for example, **seasonality.** Many time series exhibit seasonal behavior. Examples are sales by department stores in conjunction with major holidays, seasonal consumption of ice cream, travels during public holidays, etc. If, for example, we had data on department stores sales by quarters, the sales figures would show spikes in the fourth quarter. In such situations, one can remove the seasonal influence by taking fourth-quarter differences of the sales figures and then decide what kind of ARIMA model to fit.

We have analyzed only a single time series at a time. But nothing prevents the BJ methodology from being extended to the simultaneous study of two or more time series. A foray into that topic would take us far afield. The interested reader may want to consult the references.[10] In the following section, however, we discuss this topic in the context of what is known as vector autoregression.

22.9 Vector Autoregression (VAR)

In Chapters 18 to 20 we considered simultaneous, or structural, equation models. In such models some variables are treated as endogenous and some as exogenous or predetermined (exogenous plus lagged endogenous). Before we estimate such models, we have to make sure that the equations in the system are identified (either exactly or over-). This identification is often achieved by assuming that some of the predetermined variables are present only in some equations. This decision is often subjective and has been severely criticized by Christopher Sims.[11]

According to Sims, if there is true simultaneity among a set of variables, they should all be treated on an equal footing; there should not be any a priori distinction between endogenous and exogenous variables. It is in this spirit that Sims developed his **VAR** model.

The seeds of this model were already sown in the Granger causality test discussed in Chapter 17. In Eqs. (17.14.1) and (17.14.2), which explain current LGDP in terms of lagged money supply and lagged LGDP and current money supply in terms of lagged money supply and lagged LGDP, respectively, we are essentially treating LGDP and money supply as a pair of endogenous variables. There are no exogenous variables in this system.

Similarly, in Example 17.13 we examined the nature of causality between money and interest rate in Canada. In the money equation, only the lagged values of money and interest rate appear, and in the interest rate equation only the lagged values of interest rate and money appear.

Both these examples are illustrations of **vector autoregressive models;** the term autoregressive is due to the appearance of the lagged value of the dependent variable on the right-hand side and the term vector is due to the fact that we are dealing with a vector of two (or more) variables.

[10]For an accessible treatment of this subject, see Terence C. Mills, op. cit., Part III.

[11]C. A. Sims, "Macroeconomics and Reality," *Econometrica*, vol. 48, 1980, pp. 1–48.

Estimation or VAR

Returning to the Canadian money–interest rate example, we saw that when we introduced six lags of each variable as regressors, we could not reject the hypothesis that there was bilateral causality between money (M_1) and interest rate, R (90-day corporate interest rate). That is, M_1 affects R and R affects M_1. These kinds of situations are ideally suited for the application of VAR.

To explain how a VAR is estimated, we will continue with the preceding example. For now we assume that each equation contains k lag values of M (as measured by M_1) and R. In this case, one can estimate each of the following equations by OLS.[12]

$$M_{1t} = \alpha + \sum_{j=1}^{k} \beta_j M_{t-j} + \sum_{j=1}^{k} \gamma_j R_{t-j} + u_{1t} \tag{22.9.1}$$

$$R_t = \alpha' + \sum_{j=1}^{k} \theta_j M_{t-j} + \sum_{j=1}^{k} \gamma_j R_{t-j} + u_{2t} \tag{22.9.2}$$

where the u's are the stochastic error terms, called **impulses** or **innovations** or **shocks** in the language of VAR.

Before we estimate Eqs. (22.9.1) and (22.9.2) we have to decide on the maximum lag length, k. This is an empirical question. We have 40 observations in all. Including too many lagged terms will consume degrees of freedom, not to mention introducing the possibility of multicollinearity. Including too few lags will lead to specification errors. One way of deciding this question is to use a criterion like the Akaike or Schwarz and choose that model that gives the lowest values of these criteria. There is no question that some trial and error is inevitable.

To illustrate the mechanics, we initially used four lags ($k = 4$) of each variable and using *EViews 6* we obtained the estimates of the parameters of the preceding two equations, which are given in Table 22.2. Note that although our sample runs from 1979–I to 1988–IV, we used the sample for the period 1980–I to 1987–IV and saved the last four observations to check the forecasting accuracy of the fitted VAR.

Since the preceding equations are OLS regressions, the output of the regression given in Table 22.2 is to be interpreted in the usual fashion. Of course, with several lags of the same variables, each estimated coefficient will not be statistically significant, possibly because of multicollinearity. But collectively, they may be significant on the basis of the standard F test.

Let us examine the results presented in Table 22.2. First consider the M_1 regression. Individually, only M_1 at lag 1 and R at lags 1 and 2 are statistically significant. But the F value is so high that we cannot reject the hypothesis that collectively all the lagged terms are statistically significant. Turning to the interest rate regression, we see that all of the four lagged money terms are individually statistically significant (at the 10 percent or better level), whereas only the 1-period lagged interest rate variable is significant.

For comparative purposes, we present in Table 22.3 the VAR results based on only 2 lags of each endogenous variable. Here you will see that in the money regression the 1-period-lagged money variable and both lagged interest rate terms are individually statistically significant. In the interest rate regression, both lagged money terms (at about the 5 percent level) and one lagged interest term are individually significant.

[12]One can use the **SURE** (seemingly unrelated regression) technique to estimate the two equations together. However, since each regression contains the same number of lagged endogenous variables, the OLS estimation of each equation separately produces identical (and efficient) estimates.

TABLE 22.2
Vector Autoregression Estimates Based on 4 Lags

Sample (adjusted): 1980–I to 1987–IV
Included observations: 32 after adjusting endpoints
Standard errors in ( ) and *t* statistics in [ ]

	M_1	R
M_1 (−1)	1.076737 (0.20174) [5.33733]	0.001282 (0.00067) [1.90083]
M_1 (−2)	0.173433 (0.31444) [0.55157]	−0.002140 (0.00105) [−2.03584]
M_1 (−3)	−0.366465 (0.34687) [−1.05648]	0.002176 (0.00116) [1.87699]
M_1 (−4)	0.077602 (0.20789) [0.37329]	−0.001479 (0.00069) [−2.12855]
R (−1)	−275.0293 (57.2174) [−4.80675]	1.139310 (0.19127) [5.95670]
R (−2)	227.1750 (95.3947) [2.38142]	−0.309053 (0.31888) [−0.96917]
R (−3)	8.511851 (96.9176) [0.08783]	0.052361 (0.32397) [0.16162]
R (−4)	−50.19926 (64.7554) [−0.77521]	0.001076 (0.21646) [0.00497]
C	2413.827 (1622.65) [1.48759]	4.919000 (5.42416) [0.90687]
R^2	0.988154	0.852890
Adj. R^2	0.984034	0.801721
Sum square residuals	4820241.	53.86233
SE equation	457.7944	1.530307
F statistic	239.8315	16.66815
Log likelihood	−236.1676	−53.73716
Akaike A/C	15.32298	3.921073
Schwarz SC	15.73521	4.333311
Mean dependent	28514.53	11.67292
SD dependent	3623.058	3.436688
Determinant residual covariance	490782.3	
Log likelihood (df adjusted)	−300.4722	
Akaike information criterion	19.90451	
Schwarz criterion	20.72899	

If we have to make a choice between the model given in Table 22.2 and that given in Table 22.3, which would we choose? The Akaike and Schwarz information values for the model in Table 22.2 are, respectively, 15.32 and 15.73, whereas the corresponding values for Table 22.3 are 15.10 and 15.33. Since the lower values of Akaike and Schwarz statistics, the better the model, on that basis it seems the more parsimonious model given in Table 22.3 is preferable. We also considered 6 lags of each of the endogenous variables and found that the values of Akaike and Schwarz statistics were 15.37 and 15.98, respectively. Again, the choice seems to be the model with two lagged terms of each endogenous variable, that is, the model in Table 22.3.

Forecasting with VAR

Suppose we choose the model given in Table 22.3. We can use it for the purpose of forecasting the values of M_1 and R. Remember that our data covers the period 1979–I to 1988–IV, but we have not used the values for 1988 in estimating the VAR models. Now suppose we want to forecast the value of M_1 for 1988–I, that is, the first quarter of 1988. The forecast value for 1988–I can be obtained as follows:

$$\begin{aligned}\hat{M}_{1988\text{–I}} = {} & 1451.977 + 1.0375M_{1987\text{–IV}} - 0.0446M_{1987\text{–III}} \\ & - 234.8850R_{1987\text{–IV}} + 160.1560R_{1987\text{–III}}\end{aligned}$$

TABLE 22.3
Vector Autoregression Estimates Based on 2 Lags

Sample (adjusted): 1979–III to 1987–IV
Included observations: 34 after adjusting endpoints
Standard errors in ( ) and *t* statistics in [ ]

	M_1	R
M_1 (−1)	1.037537 (0.16048) [6.46509]	0.001091 (0.00059) [1.85825]
M_1 (−2)	−0.044661 (0.15591) [−0.28646]	−0.001255 (0.00057) [−2.19871]
R (−1)	−234.8850 (45.5224) [−5.15977]	1.069081 (0.16660) [6.41708]
R (−2)	160.1560 (48.5283) [3.30026]	−0.223364 (0.17760) [−1.25768]
C	1451.977 (1185.59) [1.22468]	5.796434 (4.33894) [1.33591]
R^2	0.988198	0.806660
Adj. R^2	0.986571	0.779993
Sum square residuals	5373510.	71.97054
SE equation	430.4573	1.575355
F statistic	607.0720	30.24878
Log likelihood	−251.7446	−60.99215
Akaike A/C	15.10263	3.881891
Schwarz SC	15.32709	4.106356
Mean dependent	28216.26	11.75049
SD dependent	3714.506	3.358613
Determinant residual covariance	458485.4	
Log likelihood (df adjusted)	−318.0944	
Akaike information criterion	19.29967	
Schwarz criterion	19.74860	

where the coefficient values are obtained from Table 22.3. Now using the appropriate values of M_1 and R from Table 17.5, the forecast value of money for the first quarter of 1988 can be seen to be 36,996 (millions of Canadian dollars). The actual value of M_1 for 1988–I was 36,480, which means that our model overpredicted the actual value by about 516 (millions of dollars), which is about 1.4 percent of the actual M_1 for 1988–I. Of course, these estimates will change, depending on how many lagged values we consider in the VAR model. It is left as an exercise for the reader to forecast the value of R for the first quarter of 1988 and compare it with its actual value for that quarter.

VAR and Causality

You may recall that we discussed the topic of causality in Chapter 17. There we considered the Granger and Sims tests of causality. Is there any connection between VAR and causality? In Chapter 17 (Section 17.14) we saw that up to 2, 4, and 6 lags there was bilateral causality between M_1 and R, but at lag 8 there was no causality between the two variables. Thus, the results are mixed. Now you may recall from Chapter 21 the Granger representation theorem. One of the implications of this theorem is that if two variables, say, X_t and Y_t are cointegrated and each is individually $I(1)$, that is, integrated of order 1 (i.e., each is individually nonstationary), then either X_t must Granger-cause Y_t or Y_t must Granger-cause X_t.

In our illustrative example this means if M_1 and R are individually $I(1)$, but are cointegrated, then either M_1 must Granger-cause R or R must Granger-cause M_1. This means we must first find out if the two variables are $I(1)$ individually and then find out if they are cointegrated. If this is not the case, then the whole question of causality may become moot. In Exercise 22.22, the reader is asked to find out if the two variables are nonstationary but are cointegrated. If you do the exercise, you will find that there is some *weak* evidence of cointegration between M_1 and R, which is why the causality tests discussed in Section 17.14 were equivocal.

Some Problems with VAR Modeling

The advocates of VAR emphasize these virtues of the method: (1) The method is simple; one does not have to worry about determining which variables are endogenous and which ones are exogenous. All variables in VAR are endogenous.[13] (2) Estimation is simple; that is, the usual OLS method can be applied to each equation separately. (3) The forecasts obtained by this method are in many cases better than those obtained from the more complex simultaneous-equation models.[14]

But the critics of VAR modeling point out the following problems:

1. Unlike simultaneous-equation models, a VAR model is *a-theoretic* because it uses less prior information. Recall that in simultaneous-equation models exclusion or inclusion of certain variables plays a crucial role in the identification of the model.

2. Because of its emphasis on forecasting, VAR models are less suited for policy analysis.

3. The biggest practical challenge in VAR modeling is to choose the appropriate lag length. Suppose you have a three-variable VAR model and you decide to include eight lags of each variable in each equation. You will have 24 lagged parameters in each equation plus the constant term, for a total of 25 parameters. Unless the sample size is large, estimating that many parameters will consume a lot of degrees of freedom with all the problems associated with that.[15]

4. Strictly speaking, in an m-variable VAR model, all the m variables should be (jointly) stationary. If that is not the case, we will have to transform the data appropriately (e.g., by first-differencing). As Harvey notes, the results from the transformed data may be unsatisfactory. He further notes that "The usual approach adopted by VAR *aficionados* is therefore to work in levels, even if some of these series are nonstationary. In this case, it is important to recognize the effect of unit roots on the distribution of estimators."[16] Worse yet, if the model contains a mix of $I(0)$ and $I(1)$ variables, that is, a mix of stationary and nonstationary variables, transforming the data will not be easy.

However, Cuthbertson argues that, ". . . cointegration analysis indicates that a VAR *solely* in first differences is misspecified, if there are some cointegrating vectors present among the $I(1)$ series. Put another way, a VAR solely in first differences omits potentially important

[13]Sometimes purely exogenous variables are included to allow for trend and seasonal factors.

[14]See, for example, T. Kinal and J. B. Ratner, "Regional Forecasting Models with Vector Autoregression: The Case of New York State," Discussion Paper #155, Department of Economics, State University of New York at Albany, 1982.

[15]If we have an m-equation VAR model with p lagged values of the m variables, in all we have to estimate $(m + pm^2)$ parameters.

[16]Andrew Harvey, *The Econometric Analysis of Time Series,* The MIT Press, 2d ed., Cambridge, Mass., 1990, p. 83.

stationary variables (i.e., the error-correction, cointegrating vectors) and hence parameter estimates may suffer from omitted variables bias."[17]

5. Since the individual coefficients in the estimated VAR models are often difficult to interpret, the practitioners of this technique often estimate the so-called **impulse response function (IRF).** The IRF traces out the response of the dependent variable in the VAR system to shocks in the error terms, such as u_1 and u_2 in Eqs. (22.9.1) and (22.9.2). Suppose u_1 in the M_1 equation increases by a value of one standard deviation. Such a shock or change will change M_1 in the current as well as future periods. But since M_1 appears in the R regression, the change in u_1 will also have an impact on R. Similarly, a change of one standard deviation in u_2 of the R equation will have an impact on M_1. The IRF traces out the impact of such shocks for several periods in the future. Although the utility of such IRF analysis has been questioned by researchers, it is the centerpiece of VAR analysis.[18]

For a comparison of the performance of VAR with other forecasting techniques, the reader may consult the references.[19]

An Application of VAR: A VAR Model of the Texas Economy

To test the conventional wisdom, "As the oil patch goes, so goes the Texas economy," Thomas Fomby and Joseph Hirschberg developed a three-variable VAR model of the Texas economy for the period 1974–I to 1988–I.[20] The three variables considered were (1) percentage change in real price of oil, (2) percentage change in Texas nonagricultural employment, and (3) percentage change in nonagricultural employment in the rest of the United States. The authors introduced the constant term and two lagged values of each variable in each equation. Therefore, the number of parameters estimated in each equation was seven. The results of the OLS estimation of the VAR model are given in Table 22.4. The F tests given in this table are to test the hypothesis that collectively the various lagged coefficients are zero. Thus, the F test for the x variable (percentage change in real price of oil) shows that both the lagged terms of x are statistically different from zero; the probability of obtaining an F value of 12.5536 under the null hypothesis that they are both simultaneously equal to zero is very low, about 0.00004. On the other hand, collectively, the two lagged y values (percentage change in Texas nonagricultural employment) are not significantly different from zero to explain x; the F value is only 1.36. All other F statistics are to be interpreted similarly.

On the basis of these and other results presented in their paper, Fomby and Hirschberg conclude that the conventional wisdom about the Texas economy is not quite accurate, for after the initial instability resulting from OPEC oil shocks, the Texas economy is now less dependent on fluctuations in the price of oil.

[17]Keith Cuthbertson, *Quantitative Financial Economics: Stocks, Bonds and Foreign Exchange,* John Wiley & Sons, New York, 2002, p.436.

[18]D. E. Runkle, "Vector Autoregression and Reality," *Journal of Business and Economic Statistics,* vol. 5, 1987, pp. 437–454.

[19]S. McNees, "Forecasting Accuracy of Alternative Techniques: A Comparison of U.S. Macroeconomic Forecasts," *Journal of Business and Economic Statistics,* vol. 4, 1986, pp. 5–15; and E. Mahmoud, "Accuracy in Forecasting: A Survey," *Journal of Forecasting,* vol. 3, 1984, pp. 139–159.

[20]Thomas B. Fomby and Joseph G. Hirschberg, "Texas in Transition: Dependence on Oil and the National Economy," *Economic Review,* Federal Reserve Bank of Dallas, January 1989, pp. 11–28.

TABLE 22.4
Estimation Results for Second-Order* Texas VAR System: 1974–I to 1988–I

Source: *Economic Review,* Federal Reserve Bank of Dallas, January 1989, p. 21.

Dependent variable: x (percentage change in real price of oil)

Variable	Lag	Coefficient	Standard error	Significance level
x	1	0.7054	0.1409	0.8305E−5
x	2	−0.3351	0.1500	0.3027E−1
y	1	−1.3525	2.7013	0.6189
y	2	3.4371	2.4344	0.1645
z	1	3.4566	2.8048	0.2239
z	2	−4.8703	2.7500	0.8304E−1
Constant	0	−0.9983E−2	0.1696E−1	0.5589

$\bar{R}^2 = 0.2982$; $Q(21) = 8.2618$ ($P = 0.9939$)

Tests for joint significance, dependent variable = x

Variable	F-statistic	Significance level
x	12.5536	0.4283E−4
y	1.3646	0.2654
z	1.5693	0.2188

Dependent variable: y (percentage change in Texas nonagricultural employment)

Variable	Lag	Coefficient	Standard error	Significance level
x	1	0.2228E−1	0.8759E−2	0.1430E−1
x	2	−0.1883E−2	0.9322E−2	0.8407
y	1	0.6462	0.1678	0.3554E−3
y	2	0.4234E−1	0.1512	0.7807
z	1	0.2655	0.1742	0.1342
z	2	−0.1715	0.1708	0.3205
Constant	0	−0.1602E−2	0.1053E−1	0.1351

$\bar{R}^2 = 0.6316$; $Q(21) = 21.5900$ ($P = 0.4234$)

Tests for joint significance, dependent variable = y

Variable	F-statistic	Significance level
x	3.6283	0.3424E−4
y	19.1440	0.8287E−6
z	1.1684	0.3197

Dependent variable: z (percentage change in nonagricultural employment in rest of United States)

Variable	Lag	Coefficient	Standard error	Significance level
x	1	−0.8330E−2	0.6849E−2	0.2299
x	2	0.3635E−2	0.7289E−2	0.6202
y	1	0.3849	0.1312	0.5170E−2
y	2	−0.4805	0.1182	0.1828E−2
z	1	0.7226	0.1362	0.3004E−5
z	2	−0.1366E−1	0.1336	0.9190
Constant	0	−0.2387E−2	0.8241E−3	0.5701E−2

$\bar{R}^2 = 0.6503$; $Q(21) = 15.6182$ ($P = 0.7907$)

Tests for joint significance, dependent variable = z

Variable	F-statistic	Significance level
x	0.7396	0.4827
y	8.2714	0.8360E−3
z	27.9609	0.1000E−7

*Two-lagged terms of each variable.

22.10 Measuring Volatility in Financial Time Series: The ARCH and GARCH Models

As noted in the introduction to this chapter, financial time series, such as stock prices, exchange rates, inflation rates, etc., often exhibit the phenomenon of **volatility clustering,** that is, periods in which their prices show wide swings for an extended time period followed by periods in which there is relative calm. As Philip Franses notes:

> Since such [financial time series] data reflect the result of trading among buyers and sellers at, for example, stock markets, various sources of news and other exogenous economic events may have an impact on the time series pattern of asset prices. Given that news can lead to various interpretations, and also given that specific economic events like an oil crisis can last for some time, we often observe that large positive and large negative observations in financial time series tend to appear in clusters.[21]

Knowledge of volatility is of crucial importance in many areas. For example, considerable macroeconometric work has been done in studying the variability of inflation over time. For some decision makers, inflation in itself may not be bad, but its variability is bad because it makes financial planning difficult.

The same is true of importers, exporters, and traders in foreign exchange markets, for variability in the exchange rates means huge losses or profits. Investors in the stock market are obviously interested in the volatility of stock prices, for high volatility could mean huge losses or gains and hence greater uncertainty. In volatile markets it is difficult for companies to raise capital in the capital markets.

How do we model financial time series that may experience such volatility? For example, how do we model times series of stock prices, exchange rates, inflation, etc.? A characteristic of most of these financial time series is that in their *level form* they are random walks; that is, they are nonstationary. On the other hand, in the first difference form, they are generally stationary, as we saw in the case of GDP series in the previous chapter, even though GDP is not strictly a financial time series.

Therefore, instead of modeling the levels of financial time series, why not model their first differences? But these first differences often exhibit wide swings, or **volatility,** suggesting that the variance of financial time series varies over time. How can we model such "varying variance"? This is where the so-called **autoregressive conditional heteroscedasticity (ARCH)** model originally developed by Engle comes in handy.[22]

As the name suggests, heteroscedasticity, or unequal variance, may have an autoregressive structure in that heteroscedasticity observed over different periods may be autocorrelated. To see what all this means, let us consider a concrete example.

EXAMPLE 22.1
U.S./U.K. Exchange Rate: An Example

Figure 22.6 gives *logs* of the monthly U.S./U.K. exchange rate (dollars per pound) for the period 1971–2007, for a total of 444 monthly observations. As you can see from this figure, there are considerable ups and downs in the exchange rate over the sample period. To see this more vividly, in Figure 22.7 we plot the changes in the logs of the exchange

(Continued)

[21] Philip Hans Franses, *Time Series Models for Business and Economic Forecasting,* Cambridge University Press, New York, 1998, p. 155.

[22] R. Engle, "Autoregressive Conditional Heteroscedasticity with Estimates of the Variance of United Kingdom Inflation," *Econometrica,* vol. 50. no. 1, 1982, pp. 987–1007. See also A. Bera and M. Higgins, "ARCH Models: Properties, Estimation and Testing," *Journal of Economic Surveys,* vol. 7, 1993, pp. 305–366.

EXAMPLE 22.1 (*Continued*)

FIGURE 22.6 Log of U.S./U.K. exchange rate, 1971–2007 (monthly)

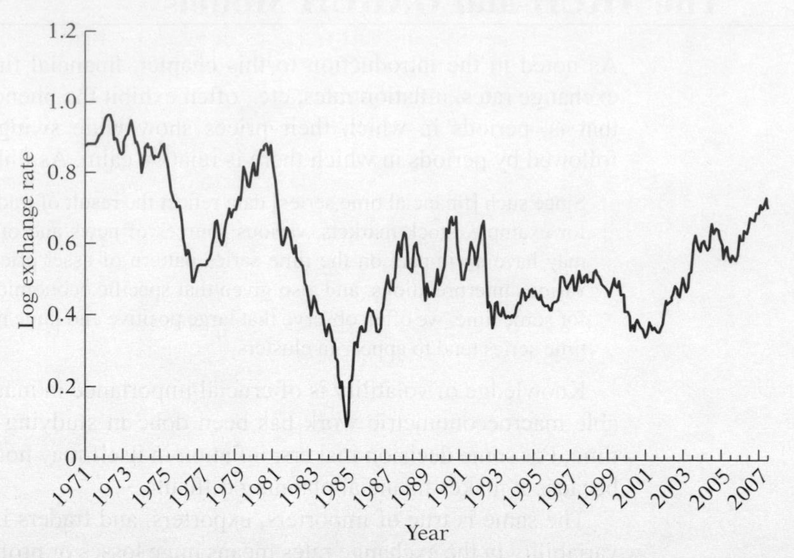

FIGURE 22.7 Change in the log of U.S./U.K. exchange rate.

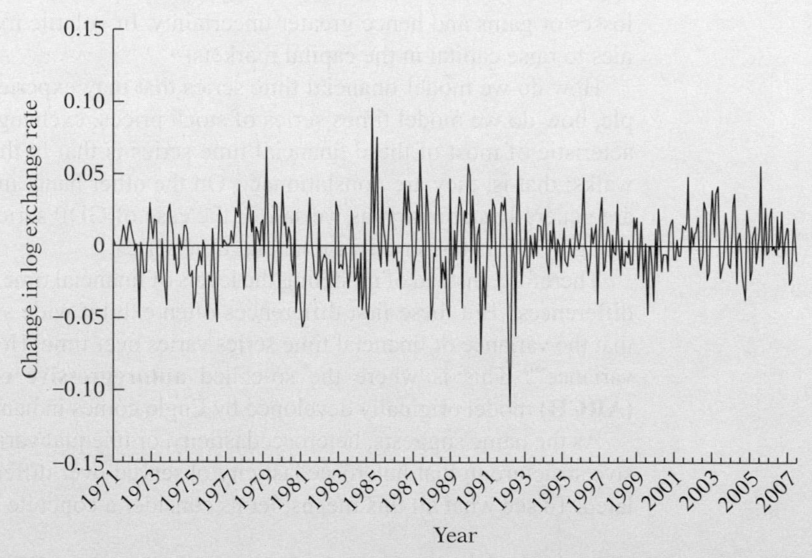

rate; note that changes in the log of a variable denote relative changes, which, if multiplied by 100, give percentage changes. As you can observe, the relative changes in the U.S./U.K. exchange rate show periods of wide swings for some time periods and periods of rather moderate swings in other time periods, thus exemplifying the phenomenon of volatility clustering.

Now the practical question is: How do we statistically measure volatility? Let us illustrate this with our exchange rate example.

Let $Y_t =$ U.S./U.K. exchange rate

$Y_t^* =$ log of Y_t

$dY_t^* = Y_t^* - Y_{t-1}^* =$ relative change in the exchange rate

$d\bar{Y}_t^* =$ mean of dY_t^*

$X_t = dY_t^* - d\bar{Y}_t^*$

EXAMPLE 22.1 (*Continued*)

Thus, X_t is the mean-adjusted relative change in the exchange rate. Now we can use X_t^2 as a measure of volatility. Being a squared quantity, its value will be high in periods when there are big changes in the prices of financial assets and its value will be comparatively small when there are modest changes in the prices of financial assets.[23]

Accepting X_t^2 as a measure of volatility, how do we know if it changes over time? Suppose we consider the following AR(1), or ARIMA (1, 0, 0), model:

$$X_t^2 = \beta_0 + \beta_1 X_{t-1}^2 + u_t \tag{22.10.1}$$

This model postulates that volatility in the current period is related to its value in the previous period plus a white noise error term. If β_1 is positive, it suggests that if volatility was high in the previous period, it will continue to be high in the current period, indicating volatility clustering. If β_1 is zero, then there is no volatility clustering. The statistical significance of the estimated β_2 can be judged by the usual t test.

There is nothing to prevent us from considering an AR(p) model of volatility such that

$$X_t^2 = \beta_0 + \beta_1 X_{t-1}^2 + \beta_2 X_{t-2}^2 + \cdots + \beta_p X_{t-p}^2 + u_t \tag{22.10.2}$$

This model suggests that volatility in the current period is related to volatility in the past p periods, the value of p being an empirical question. This empirical question can be resolved by one or more of the model selection criteria that we discussed in Chapter 13 (e.g., the Akaike information measure). We can test the significance of any individual β coefficient by the t test and the collective significance of two or more coefficients by the usual F test.

Model (22.10.1) is an example of an **ARCH(1)** model and Eq. (22.10.2) is called an **ARCH(*p*)** model, where p represents the number of autoregressive terms in the model.

Before proceeding further, let us illustrate the ARCH model with the U.S./U.K. exchange rate data. The results of the ARCH(1) model were as follows.

$$\begin{aligned} X_t^2 &= 0.00043 + 0.23036 X_{t-1}^2 \\ t &= (7.71) \qquad (4.97) \\ & \qquad R^2 = 0.0531 \qquad d = 1.9933 \end{aligned} \tag{22.10.3}$$

where X_t^2 is as defined before.

Since the coefficient of the lagged term is highly significant (p value of about 0.000), it seems volatility clustering is present in the present instance. We tried higher-order ARCH models, but only the AR(1) model turned out to be significant.

How would we test for the ARCH effect in a regression model in general that is based on time series data? To be more specific, let us consider the k-variable linear regression model:

$$Y_t = \beta_1 + \beta_2 X_{2t} + \cdots + \beta_k X_{kt} + u_t \tag{22.10.4}$$

and assume that *conditional* on the information available at time $(t-1)$, the disturbance term is distributed as

$$u_t \sim N\left[0, \left(\alpha_0 + \alpha_1 u_{t-1}^2\right)\right] \tag{22.10.5}$$

(*Continued*)

[23]You might wonder why we do not use the variance of $X_t = \sum X_t^2/n$ as a measure of volatility. This is because we want to take into account changing volatility of asset prices over time. If we use the variance of X_t, it will only be a single value for a given data set.

EXAMPLE 22.1 *(Continued)*

that is, u_t is normally distributed with zero mean and

$$\operatorname{var}(u_t) = \left(\alpha_0 + \alpha_1 u_{t-1}^2\right) \quad \textbf{(22.10.6)}$$

that is, the variance of u_t follows an ARCH(1) process.

The normality of u_t is not new to us. What is new is that the variance of u at time t is dependent on the squared disturbance at time $(t-1)$, thus giving the appearance of serial correlation.[24] Of course, the error variance may depend not only on one lagged term of the squared error term but also on several lagged squared terms as follows:

$$\operatorname{var}(u_t) = \sigma_t^2 = \alpha_0 + \alpha_1 u_{t-1}^2 + \alpha_2 u_{t-2}^2 + \cdots + \alpha_p u_{t-p}^2 \quad \textbf{(22.10.7)}$$

If there is no autocorrelation in the error variance, we have

$$H_0\colon \alpha_1 = \alpha_2 = \cdots = \alpha_p = 0 \quad \textbf{(22.10.8)}$$

in which case $\operatorname{var}(u_t) = \alpha_0$, and we do not have the ARCH effect.

Since we do not directly observe σ_t^2, Engle has shown that running the following regression can easily test the preceding null hypothesis:

$$\hat{u}_t^2 = \hat{\alpha}_0 + \hat{\alpha}_1 \hat{u}_{t-1}^2 + \hat{\alpha}_2 \hat{u}_{t-2}^2 + \cdots + \hat{\alpha}_p \hat{u}_{t-p}^2 \quad \textbf{(22.10.9)}$$

where $\hat{u}_t$, as usual, denotes the OLS residuals obtained from the original regression model (22.10.4).

One can test the null hypothesis H_0 by the usual F test, or alternatively, by computing nR^2, where R^2 is the coefficient of determination from the auxiliary regression (22.10.9). It can be shown that

$$nR_{\text{asy}}^2 \sim \chi_p^2 \quad \textbf{(22.10.10)}$$

that is, in large samples nR^2 follows the chi-square distribution with df equal to the number of autoregressive terms in the auxiliary regression.

Before we proceed to illustrate, make sure that you do not confuse autocorrelation of the error term as discussed in Chapter 12 and the ARCH model. In the ARCH model it is the (conditional) variance of u_t that depends on the (squared) previous error terms, thus giving the impression of autocorrelation.

EXAMPLE 22.2 *New York Stock Exchange Price Changes*

As a further illustration of the ARCH effect, Figure 22.8 presents monthly percentage change in the NYSE (New York Stock Exchange) Index for the period 1966–2002.[25] It is evident from this graph that the percent price changes in the NYSE Index exhibit considerable volatility. Notice especially the wide swing around the 1987 crash in stock prices.

To capture the volatility in the stock return seen in the figure, let us consider a very simple model:

$$Y_t = \beta_1 + u_t \quad \textbf{(22.10.11)}$$

where Y_t = percent change in the NYSE stock index and u_t = random error term.

[24] A technical note: Remember that for our classical linear model the variance of u_t was assumed to be σ^2, which in the present context becomes unconditional variance. If $\alpha_1 < 1$, the stability condition, we can write $\sigma^2 = \alpha_0 + \alpha_1\sigma^2$; that is, $\sigma^2 = \alpha_0/(1-\alpha_1)$. This shows that the unconditional variance of u does not depend on t, but does depend on the ARCH parameter α_1.

[25] This graph and the regression results presented in this example are based on the data collected by Gary Koop, *Analysis of Economic Data,* John Wiley & Sons, New York, 2000 (data from the data disk). The monthly percentage change in the stock price index can be regarded as a rate of return on the index.

EXAMPLE 22.2 (*Continued*)

FIGURE 22.8 Monthly percent change in the NYSE Price Index, 1966–2002.

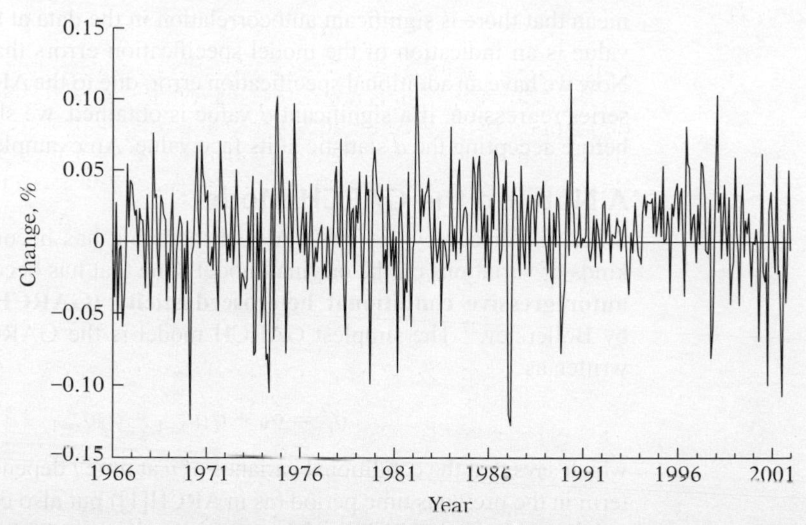

Notice that besides the intercept, there is no other explanatory variable in the model. From the data, we obtained the following OLS regression:

$$\begin{aligned} \hat{Y}_t &= 0.00574 \\ t &= (3.36) \\ d &= 1.4915 \end{aligned} \tag{22.10.12}$$

What does this intercept denote? It is simply the average percent rate of return on the NYSE index, or the mean value of Y_t (can you verify this?). Thus over the sample period the average monthly return on the NYSE index was about 0.00574 percent.

Now we obtain the residuals from the preceding regression and estimate the ARCH(1) model, which gave the following results:

$$\begin{aligned} \widehat{\hat{u}_t^2} &= 0.000007 + 0.25406\hat{u}_{t-1}^2 \\ t &= (0.000) \qquad (5.52) \\ & \qquad R^2 = 0.0645 \qquad d = 1.9464 \end{aligned} \tag{22.10.13}$$

where $\hat{u}_t$ is the estimated residual from regression (22.10.12).

Since the lagged squared disturbance term is statistically significant (p value of about 0.000), it seems the error variances are correlated; that is, there is an ARCH effect. We tried higher-order ARCH models but only ARCH(1) was statistically significant.

What to Do If ARCH Is Present

Recall that we have discussed several methods of correcting for heteroscedasticity, which basically involved applying OLS to transformed data. Remember that OLS applied to transformed data is generalized least squares (GLS). If the ARCH effect is found, we will have to use GLS. We will not pursue the technical details, for they are beyond the scope of this book.[26] Fortunately, software packages such as *EViews*, SHAZAM, MICROFIT, and PC-GIVE now have user-friendly routines to estimate such models.

[26]Consult Russell Davidson and James G. MacKinnon, *Estimation and Inference in Econometrics*, Oxford University Press, New York, 1993, Section 16.4 and William H. Greene, *Econometric Analysis*, 4th ed., Prentice Hall, Englewood Cliffs, NJ, 2000, Section 18.5.

A Word on the Durbin–Watson *d* and the ARCH Effect

We have reminded the reader several times that a significant d statistic may not always mean that there is significant autocorrelation in the data at hand. Very often a significant d value is an indication of the model specification errors that we discussed in Chapter 13. Now we have an additional specification error, due to the ARCH effect. Therefore, in a time series regression, if a significant d value is obtained, we should test for the ARCH effect before accepting the d statistic at its face value. An example is given in Exercise 22.23.

A Note on the GARCH Model

Since its "discovery" in 1982, ARCH modeling has become a growth industry, with all kinds of variations on the original model. One that has become popular is the **generalized autoregressive conditional heteroscedasticity (GARCH)** model, originally proposed by Bollerslev.[27] The simplest GARCH model is the GARCH(1, 1) model, which can be written as:

$$\sigma_t^2 = \alpha_0 + \alpha_1 u_{t-1}^2 + \alpha_2 \sigma_{t-1}^2 \tag{22.10.14}$$

which says that the conditional variance of u at time t depends not only on the squared error term in the previous time period (as in ARCH[1]) but also on its conditional variance in the previous time period. This model can be generalized to a GARCH(p, q) model in which there are p lagged terms of the squared error term and q terms of the lagged conditional variances.

We will not pursue the technical details of these models, as they are involved, except to point out that a GARCH(1, 1) model is equivalent to an ARCH(2) model and a GARCH(p, q) model is equivalent to an ARCH($p + q$) model.[28]

For our U.S./U.K. exchange rate and NYSE stock return examples, we have already stated that an ARCH(2) model was not significant, suggesting that perhaps a GARCH(1, 1) model is not appropriate in these cases.

22.11 Concluding Examples

We conclude this chapter by considering a few additional examples that illustrate some of the points we have made in this chapter.

EXAMPLE 22.3

The Relationship between the Help-Wanted Index (HWI) and the Unemployment Rate (UN) from January 1969 to January 2000

To study causality between HWI and UN, two indicators of labor market conditions in the United States, Marc A. Giammatteo considered the following regression model:[29]

$$\text{HWI}_t = \alpha_0 + \sum_{i=1}^{25} \alpha_i \text{UN}_{t-i} + \sum_{j}^{25} \beta_j \text{HWI}_{t-j} \tag{22.11.1}$$

$$\text{UN}_t = \alpha_0 + \sum_{i=1}^{25} \lambda_i \text{UN}_{t-i} + \sum_{j=1}^{25} \delta_j \text{HWI}_{t-j} \tag{22.11.2}$$

To save space we will not present the actual regression results, but the main conclusion that emerges from this study is that there is bilateral causality between the two labor market indicators and this conclusion did not change when the lag length was varied. The data on HWI and UN are given on the textbook website as Table 22.5.

[27] T. Bollerslev, "Generalized Autoregressive Conditional Heteroscedasticity," *Journal of Econometrics*, vol. 31, 1986, pp. 307–326.

[28] For details, see Davidson and MacKinnon, op. cit., pp. 558–560.

[29] Marc A. Giammatteo (West Point, Class of 2000), "The Relationship between the Help Wanted Index and the Unemployment Rate," unpublished term paper. (Notations altered to conform to our notation.)

EXAMPLE 22.4
ARIMA Modeling of the Yen/Dollar Exchange Rate: January 1971 to April 2008

The yen/dollar exchange rate (¥/$) is a key exchange rate. From the logarithms of the monthly ¥/$, it was found that in the level form this exchange rate showed the typical pattern of a nonstationary time series. But examining the first differences, it was found that they were stationary; the graph here pretty much resembles Figure 22.8.

Unit root analysis confirmed that the first differences of the logs of ¥/$ were stationary. After examining the correlogram of the log first differences, we estimated the following MA(1) model:

$$\begin{aligned} \hat{Y}_t &= -0.0028 - 0.3300u_{t-1} \\ t &= (-1.71) \quad (-7.32) \\ R^2 &= 0.1012 \quad d = 1.9808 \end{aligned} \tag{22.11.3}$$

where Y_t = first differences of the logs of ¥/$ and u = a white noise error term.

To save space, we have provided the data underlying the preceding analysis on the textbook website in Table 22.6. Using these data, the reader is urged to try other models and compare their forecasting performances.

EXAMPLE 22.5
ARCH Model of the U.S. Inflation Rate: January 1947 to March 2008

To see if the ARCH effect is present in the U.S. inflation rate as measured by the CPI, we obtained CPI data from January 1947 to March 2008. The plot of the logarithms of the CPI showed that the time series was nonstationary. But the plot of the first differences of the logs of the CPI, as shown in Figure 22.9, shows considerable volatility even though the first differences are stationary.

Following the procedure outlined in regressions (22.10.12) and (22.10.13), we first regressed the logged first differences of CPI on a constant and obtained residuals from this equation. Squaring these residuals, we obtained the following ARCH(2) model:

$$\begin{aligned} \widehat{\hat{u}_t^2} &= 0.000028 + 0.12125\hat{u}_{t-1}^2 + 0.08718\hat{u}_{t-2}^2 \\ t &= (5.42) \qquad (3.34) \qquad (2.41) \\ & R^2 = 0.026 \quad d = 2.0214 \end{aligned} \tag{22.11.4}$$

FIGURE 22.9 First differences of the logs of CPI.

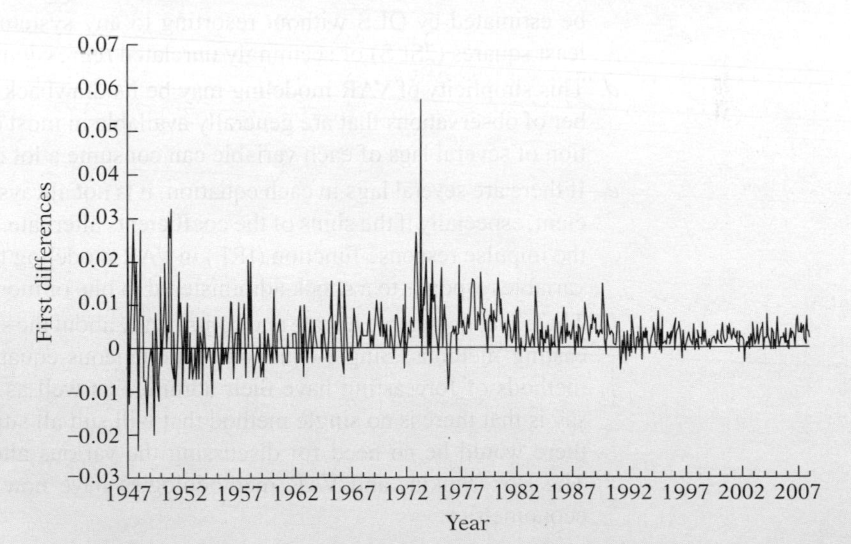

(Continued)

EXAMPLE 22.5 (*Continued*)

As you can see, there is quite a bit of persistence in the volatility, as volatility in the current month depends on volatility in the preceding 2 months. The reader is advised to obtain CPI data from government sources and try to see if another model, preferably a GARCH model, does a better job.

Summary and Conclusions

1. Box–Jenkins and VAR approaches to economic forecasting are alternatives to traditional single- and simultaneous-equation models.
2. To forecast the values of a time series, the basic Box–Jenkins strategy is as follows:
   a. First examine the series for stationarity. This step can be done by computing the autocorrelation function (ACF) and the partial autocorrelation function (PACF) or by a formal unit root analysis. The correlograms associated with ACF and PACF are often good visual diagnostic tools.
   b. If the time series is not stationary, difference it one or more times to achieve stationarity.
   c. The ACF and PACF of the stationary time series are then computed to find out if the series is purely autoregressive or purely of the moving average type or a mixture of the two. From broad guidelines given in Table 22.1 one can then determine the values of p and q in the ARMA process to be fitted. At this stage the chosen ARMA(p, q) model is tentative.
   d. The tentative model is then estimated.
   e. The residuals from this tentative model are examined to find out if they are white noise. If they are, the tentative model is probably a good approximation to the underlying stochastic process. If they are not, the process is started all over again. Therefore, the Box–Jenkins method is iterative.
   f. The model finally selected can be used for forecasting.
3. The VAR approach to forecasting considers several time series at a time. The distinguishing features of VAR are as follows:
   a. It is a truly simultaneous system in that all variables are regarded as endogenous.
   b. In VAR modeling the value of a variable is expressed as a linear function of the past, or lagged, values of that variable and all other variables included in the model.
   c. If each equation contains the same number of lagged variables in the system, it can be estimated by OLS without resorting to any systems method, such as two-stage least squares (2SLS) or seemingly unrelated regressions (SURE).
   d. This simplicity of VAR modeling may be its drawback. In view of the limited number of observations that are generally available in most economic analyses, introduction of several lags of each variable can consume a lot of degrees of freedom.[30]
   e. If there are several lags in each equation, it is not always easy to interpret each coefficient, especially if the signs of the coefficients alternate. For this reason one examines the impulse response function (IRF) in VAR modeling to find out how the dependent variable responds to a shock administered to one or more equations in the system.
   f. There is considerable debate and controversy about the superiority of the various forecasting methods. Single-equation, simultaneous-equation, Box–Jenkins, and VAR methods of forecasting have their admirers as well as their detractors. All one can say is that there is no single method that will suit all situations. If that were the case, there would be no need for discussing the various alternatives. One thing is sure: The Box–Jenkins and VAR methodologies have now become an integral part of econometrics.

[30]Followers of Bayesian statistics believe that this problem can be minimized. See R. Litterman, "A Statistical Approach to Economic Forecasting," *Journal of Business and Economic Statistics*, vol. 4, 1986, pp. 1–4.

4. We also considered in this chapter a special class of models, ARCH and GARCH, which are especially useful in analyzing financial time series, such as stock prices, inflation rates, and exchange rates. A distinguishing feature of these models is that the error variance may be correlated over time because of the phenomenon of volatility clustering. In this connection we also pointed out that in many cases a significant Durbin–Watson *d* may in fact be due to the ARCH or GARCH effect.
5. There are variants of ARCH and GARCH models, but we have not considered them in this chapter due to space constraints. Some of these other models are: **GARCH-M** (GARCH in mean), **TGARCH** (threshold GARCH), and **EGARCH** (exponential GARCH). A discussion of these models can be found in the references.[31]

EXERCISES

Questions

22.1. What are the major methods of economic forecasting?

22.2. What are the major differences between simultaneous-equation and Box–Jenkins approaches to economic forecasting?

22.3. Outline the major steps involved in the application of the Box–Jenkins approach to forecasting.

22.4. What happens if Box–Jenkins techniques are applied to time series that are nonstationary?

22.5. What are the differences between Box–Jenkins and VAR approaches to economic forecasting?

22.6. In what sense is VAR atheoretic?

22.7. "If the primary object is forecasting, VAR will do the job." Critically evaluate this statement.

22.8. Since the number of lags to be introduced in a VAR model can be a subjective question, how does one decide how many lags to introduce in a concrete application?

22.9. Comment on this statement: "Box–Jenkins and VAR are prime examples of measurement without theory."

22.10. What is the connection, if any, between Granger causality tests and VAR modeling?

Empirical Exercises

22.11. Consider the data on log DPI (personal disposable income) introduced in Section 21.1 (see the book's website for the actual data). Suppose you want to fit a suitable ARIMA model to these data. Outline the steps involved in carrying out this task.

22.12. Repeat Exercise 22.11 for the LPCE (personal consumption expenditure) data introduced in Section 21.1 (again, see the book's website for the actual data).

22.13. Repeat Exercise 22.11 for the LCP.

22.14. Repeat Exercise 22.11 for the LDNIDENDS.

22.15. In Section 13.9 you were introduced to the Schwarz Information criterion (SIC) to determine lag length. How would you use this criterion to determine the appropriate lag length in a VAR model?

22.16. Using the data on LPCE and LDPI introduced in Section 21.1 (see the book's website for the actual data), develop a bivariate VAR model for the period 1970–I to 2006–IV. Use this model to forecast the values of these variables for the four quarters of 2007 and compare the forecast values with the actual values given in the dataset.

[31]See Walter Enders, *Applied Econometric Time Series,* 2d ed., John Wiley & Sons, New York, 2004. For an application-oriented discussion, see Dimitrios Asteriou and Stephen Hall, *Applied Econometrics: A Modern Approach,* revised edition, Palgrave/Macmillan, New York, 2007, Chapter 14.

22.17. Repeat Exercise 22.16, using the data on LDIVIDENDS and LCP.

*22.18. Refer to any statistical package and estimate the impulse response function for a period of up to 8 lags for the VAR model that you developed in Exercise 22.16.

22.19. Repeat Exercise 22.18 for the VAR model that you developed in Exercise 22.17.

22.20. Refer to the VAR regression results given in Table 22.4. From the various F tests reported in the three regressions given there, what can you say about the nature of causality in the three variables?

22.21. Continuing with Exercise 20.20, can you guess why the authors chose to express the three variables in the model in percentage change form rather than using the levels of these variables? (*Hint:* Stationarity.)

22.22. Using the Canadian data given in Table 17.5, find out if M_1 and R are stationary random variables. If not, are they cointegrated? Show the necessary calculations.

22.23. Continue with the data given in Table 17.5. Now consider the following simple model of money demand in Canada:

$$\ln M_{1t} = \beta_1 + \beta_2 \ln \text{GDP}_t + \beta_3 \ln R_t + u_t$$

a. How would you interpret the parameters of this model?

b. Obtain the residuals from this model and find out if there is any ARCH effect.

22.24. Refer to the ARCH(2) model given in Eq. (22.11.4). Using the same data we estimated the following ARCH(1) model:

$$\widehat{\hat{u}_t^2} = 0.00000078 + 0.3737\hat{u}_{t-1}^2$$
$$t = (7.5843) \qquad (10.2351)$$
$$R^2 = 0.1397 \qquad d = 1.9896$$

How would you choose between the two models? Show the necessary calculations.

22.25. Table 22.7 gives data on three-month (TB3M) and six-month (TB6M) Treasury bill rates from January 1, 1982, to March 2008, for a total of 315 monthly observations. The data can be found on the textbook's website.

a. Plot the two time series in the same diagram. What do you see?

b. Do a formal unit root analysis to find out if these time series are stationary.

c. Are the two time series cointegrated? How do you know? Show the necessary calculations.

d. What is the economic meaning of *cointegration* in the present context? If the two series are not cointegrated, what are the economic implications?

e. If you want to estimate a VAR model, say, with four lags of each variable, do you have to use the first differences of the two series or can you do the analysis in levels of the two series? Justify your answer.

22.26. *Class Exercise:* Pick a stock market index of your choosing and obtain *daily* data on the value of the chosen index for five years to find out if the stock index is characterized by ARCH effects.

22.27. *Class Exercise:* Collect data on inflation and unemployment rates in the U.S. for the quarterly periods in 1980–2007 and develop and estimate a VAR model for the two variables. To compute the inflation rate, use CPI (consumer price index) and use the civilian unemployment rate for the unemployment rate. Pay careful attention to the stationarity of these variables. Also, find out if one variable Granger-causes the other variable. Present all your calculations.

*Optional.

Appendix

A Review of Some Statistical Concepts

This appendix provides a very sketchy introduction to some of the statistical concepts encountered in the text. The discussion is nonrigorous, and no proofs are given because several excellent books on statistics do that job very well. Some of these books are listed at the end of this appendix.

A.1 Summation and Product Operators

The Greek capital letter $\sum$ (sigma) is used to indicate summation. Thus,

$$\sum_{i=1}^{n} x_i = x_1 + x_2 + \cdots + x_n$$

Some of the important properties of the summation operator $\sum$ are

1. $\sum_{i=1}^{n} k = nk$, where k is constant. Thus, $\sum_{i=1}^{4} 3 = 4 \cdot 3 = 12$.
2. $\sum_{i=1}^{n} kx_i = k\sum_{i=1}^{n} x_i$, where k is a constant.
3. $\sum_{i=1}^{n} (a + bx_i) = na + b\sum_{i=1}^{n} x_i$, where a and b are constants and where use is made of properties 1 and 2 above.
4. $\sum_{i=1}^{n} (x_i + y_i) = \sum_{i=1}^{n} x_i + \sum_{i=1}^{n} y_i$.

The summation operator can also be extended to multiple sums. Thus, $\sum\sum$, the double summation operator, is defined as

$$\begin{aligned}\sum_{i=1}^{n}\sum_{j=1}^{m} x_{ij} &= \sum_{i=1}^{n} (x_{i1} + x_{i2} + \cdots + x_{im})\\ &= (x_{11} + x_{21} + \cdots + x_{n1}) + (x_{12} + x_{22} + \cdots + x_{n2})\\ &\quad + \cdots + (x_{1m} + x_{2m} + \cdots + x_{nm})\end{aligned}$$

Some of the properties of $\sum\sum$ are

1. $\sum_{i=1}^{n}\sum_{j=1}^{m} x_{ij} = \sum_{j=1}^{m}\sum_{i=1}^{n} x_{ij}$; that is, the order in which the double summation is performed is interchangeable.
2. $\sum_{i=1}^{n}\sum_{j=1}^{m} x_i y_j = \sum_{i=1}^{n} x_i \sum_{j=1}^{m} y_j$.

3. $\sum_{i=1}^{n}\sum_{j=1}^{m}(x_{ij}+y_{ij}) = \sum_{i=1}^{n}\sum_{j=1}^{m}x_{ij} + \sum_{i=1}^{n}\sum_{j=1}^{m}y_{ij}$.
4. $\left[\sum_{i=1}^{n}x_i\right]^2 = \sum_{i=1}^{n}x_i^2 + 2\sum_{i=1}^{n-1}\sum_{j=i+1}^{n}x_i x_j = \sum_{i=1}^{n}x_i^2 + 2\sum_{i<j}x_i x_j$.

The product operator Π is defined as

$$\prod_{i=1}^{n} x_i = x_1 \cdot x_2 \cdots x_n$$

Thus,

$$\prod_{i=1}^{3} x_i = x_1 \cdot x_2 \cdot x_3$$

A.2 Sample Space, Sample Points, and Events

The set of all possible outcomes of a random, or chance, experiment is called the **population,** or **sample space,** and each member of this sample space is called a **sample point.** Thus, in the experiment of tossing two coins, the sample space consists of these four possible outcomes: *HH*, *HT*, *TH*, and *TT*, where *HH* means a head on the first toss and also a head on the second toss, *HT* means a head on the first toss and a tail on the second toss, and so on. Each of the preceding occurrences constitutes a sample point.

An **event** is a subset of the sample space. Thus, if we let *A* denote the occurrence of one head and one tail, then, of the preceding possible outcomes, only two belong to *A*, namely *HT* and *TH*. In this case *A* constitutes an event. Similarly, the occurrence of two heads in a toss of two coins is an event. Events are said to be **mutually exclusive** if the occurrence of one event precludes the occurrence of another event. If in the preceding example *HH* occurs, the occurrence of the event *HT* at the same time is not possible. Events are said to be (collectively) **exhaustive** if they exhaust all the possible outcomes of an experiment. Thus, in the example, the events (a) two heads, (b) two tails, and (c) one tail, one head exhaust all the outcomes; hence they are (collectively) exhaustive events.

A.3 Probability and Random Variables

Probability

Let *A* be an event in a sample space. By *P*(*A*), the probability of the event *A*, we mean the proportion of times the event *A* will occur in repeated trials of an experiment. Alternatively, in a total of *n* possible equally likely outcomes of an experiment, if *m* of them are favorable to the occurrence of the event *A*, we define the ratio *m*/*n* as the **relative frequency** of *A*. For large values of *n*, this relative frequency will provide a very good approximation of the probability of *A*.

Properties of Probability

P(*A*) is a real-valued function[1] and has these properties:

1. $0 \le P(A) \le 1$ for every *A*.
2. If $A, B, C, \ldots$ constitute an exhaustive set of events, then $P(A+B+C+\cdots) = 1$, where $A+B+C$ means *A* or *B* or *C*, and so forth.
3. If $A, B, C, \ldots$ are mutually exclusive events, then

$$P(A+B+C+\cdots) = P(A) + P(B) + P(C) + \cdots$$

[1] A function whose domain and range are subsets of real numbers is commonly referred to as a real-valued function. For details, see Alpha C. Chiang, *Fundamental Methods of Mathematical Economics,* 3d ed., McGraw-Hill, 1984, Chapter 2.

EXAMPLE 1 Consider the experiment of throwing a die numbered 1 through 6. The sample space consists of the outcomes 1, 2, 3, 4, 5, and 6. These six events therefore exhaust the entire sample space. The probability of any one of these numbers showing up is 1/6 since there are six equally likely outcomes and any one of them has an equal chance of showing up. Since 1, 2, 3, 4, 5, and 6 form an exhaustive set of events, $P(1+2+3+4+5+6) = 1$ where 1, 2, 3, ... means the probability of number 1 or number 2 or number 3, etc. And since 1, 2, ..., 6 are mutually exclusive events in that two numbers cannot occur simultaneously, $P(1+2+3+4+5+6) = P(1) + P(2) + \cdots + P(6) = 1$.

Random Variables

A variable whose value is determined by the outcome of a chance experiment is called a **random variable** (rv). Random variables are usually denoted by the capital letters X, Y, Z, and so on, and the values taken by them are denoted by small letters x, y, z, and so on.

A random variable may be either **discrete** or **continuous.** A discrete rv takes on only a finite (or countably infinite) number of values.[2] For example, in throwing two dice, each numbered 1 to 6, if we define the random variable X as the sum of the numbers showing on the dice, then X will take one of these values: 2, 3, 4, 5, 6, 7, 8, 9, 10, 11, or 12. Hence it is a discrete random variable. A continuous rv, on the other hand, is one that can take on any value in some interval of values. Thus, the height of an individual is a continuous variable—in the range, say, 60 to 65 inches it can take any value, depending on the precision of measurement.

A.4 Probability Density Function (PDF)

Probability Density Function of a Discrete Random Variable

Let X be a discrete rv taking distinct values $x_1, x_2, \ldots, x_n, \ldots$. Then the function

$$
\begin{aligned}
f(x) &= P(X = x_i) \qquad \text{for } i = 1, 2, \ldots, n, \ldots \\
&= 0 \qquad \text{for } x \neq x_i
\end{aligned}
$$

is called the **discrete probability density function** (PDF) of X, where $P(X = x_i)$ means the probability that the discrete rv X takes the value of x_i.

EXAMPLE 2 In a throw of two dice, the random variable X, the sum of the numbers shown on two dice, can take one of the 11 values shown. The PDF of this variable can be shown to be as follows (see also Figure A.1):

$$
\begin{array}{lccccccccccc}
x = & 2 & 3 & 4 & 5 & 6 & 7 & 8 & 9 & 10 & 11 & 12 \\
f(x) = & \left(\frac{1}{36}\right) & \left(\frac{2}{36}\right) & \left(\frac{3}{36}\right) & \left(\frac{4}{36}\right) & \left(\frac{5}{36}\right) & \left(\frac{6}{36}\right) & \left(\frac{5}{36}\right) & \left(\frac{4}{36}\right) & \left(\frac{3}{36}\right) & \left(\frac{2}{36}\right) & \left(\frac{1}{36}\right)
\end{array}
$$

These probabilities can be easily verified. In all there are 36 possible outcomes, of which one is favorable to number 2, two are favorable to number 3 (since the sum 3 can occur either as 1 on the first die and 2 on the second die or 2 on the first die and 1 on the second die), and so on.

(Continued)

[2]For a simple discussion of the notion of countably infinite sets, see R. G. D. Allen, *Basic Mathematics,* Macmillan, London, 1964, p. 104.

EXAMPLE 2 (*Continued*)

FIGURE A.1 Density function of the discrete random variable of Example 2.

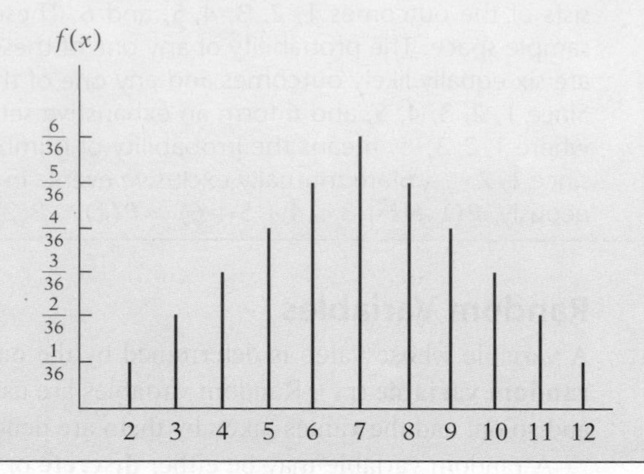

Probability Density Function of a Continuous Random Variable

Let X be a continuous rv. Then $f(x)$ is said to be the PDF of X if the following conditions are satisfied:

$$f(x) \geq 0$$

$$\int_{-\infty}^{\infty} f(x)\,dx = 1$$

$$\int_{a}^{b} f(x)\,dx = P(a \leq x \leq b)$$

where $f(x)\,dx$ is known as the *probability element* (the probability associated with a small interval of a continuous variable) and where $P(a \leq x \leq b)$ means the probability that X lies in the interval a to b. Geometrically, we have Figure A.2.

For a continuous rv, in contrast with a discrete rv, the probability that X takes a specific value is zero;[3] probability for such a variable is measurable only over a given range or interval, such as (a, b) shown in Figure A.2.

EXAMPLE 3

Consider the following density function:

$$f(x) = \frac{1}{9}x^2 \qquad 0 \leq x \leq 3$$

It can be readily verified that $f(x) \geq 0$ for all x in the range 0 to 3 and that $\int_0^3 \frac{1}{9}x^2 dx = 1$. (*Note:* The integral is $(\frac{1}{27}x^3 \,|_0^3) = 1$.) If we want to evaluate the above PDF between, say, 0 and 1, we obtain $\int_0^1 \frac{1}{9}x^2 dx = (\frac{1}{27}x^3 \,|_0^1) = \frac{1}{27}$; that is, the probability that x lies between 0 and 1 is 1/27.

FIGURE A.2 Density function of a continuous random variable.

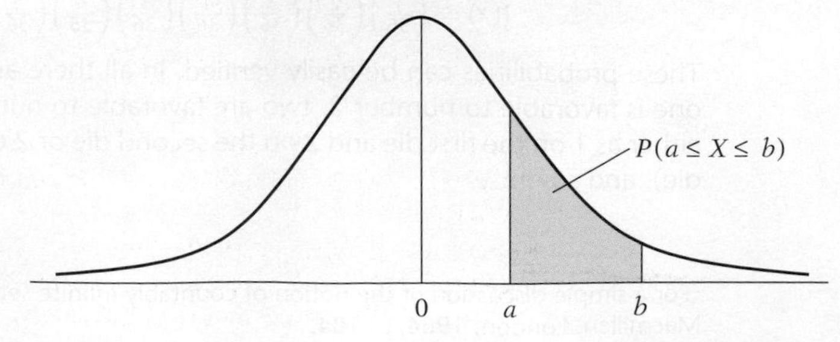

[3] *Note:* $\int_a^a f(x)\,dx = 0$.

Joint Probability Density Functions

Discrete Joint PDF

Let X and Y be two discrete random variables. Then the function

$$\begin{aligned} f(x, y) &= P(X = x \text{ and } Y = y) \\ &= 0 \qquad \text{when } X \neq x \text{ and } Y \neq y \end{aligned}$$

is known as the **discrete joint probability density function** and gives the (joint) probability that X takes the value of x and Y takes the value of y.

EXAMPLE 4

The following table gives the joint PDF of the discrete variables X and Y.

		X			
		−2	0	2	3
Y	3	0.27	0.08	0.16	0
	6	0	0.04	0.10	0.35

This table tells us that the probability that X takes the value of −2 while Y simultaneously takes the value of 3 is 0.27 and that the probability that X takes the value of 3 while Y takes the value of 6 is 0.35, and so on.

Marginal Probability Density Function

In relation to $f(x, y)$, $f(x)$ and $f(y)$ are called **individual,** or **marginal,** probability density functions. These marginal PDFs are derived as follows:

$$f(x) = \sum_y f(x, y) \qquad \text{marginal PDF of } X$$

$$f(y) = \sum_x f(x, y) \qquad \text{marginal PDF of } Y$$

where, for example, $\sum_y$ means the sum over all values of Y and $\sum_x$ means the sum over all values of X.

EXAMPLE 5

Consider the data given in Example 4. The marginal PDF of X is obtained as follows:

$$f(x = -2) = \sum_y f(x, y) = 0.27 + 0 = 0.27$$

$$f(x = 0) = \sum_y f(x, y) = 0.08 + 0.04 = 0.12$$

$$f(x = 2) = \sum_y f(x, y) = 0.16 + 0.10 = 0.26$$

$$f(x = 3) = \sum_y f(x, y) = 0 + 0.35 = 0.35$$

Likewise, the marginal PDF of Y is obtained as

$$f(y = 3) = \sum_x f(x, y) = 0.27 + 0.08 + 0.16 + 0 = 0.51$$

$$f(y = 6) = \sum_x f(x, y) = 0 + 0.04 + 0.10 + 0.35 = 0.49$$

As this example shows, to obtain the marginal PDF of X we add the column numbers, and to obtain the marginal PDF of Y we add the row numbers. Notice that $\sum_x f(x)$ over all values of X is 1, as is $\sum_y f(y)$ over all values of Y (why?).

Conditional PDF

As noted in Chapter 2, in regression analysis we are often interested in studying the behavior of one variable conditional upon the value(s) of another variable(s). This can be done by considering the conditional PDF. The function

$$f(x \mid y) = P(X = x \mid Y = y)$$

is known as the **conditional PDF** of X; it gives the probability that X takes on the value of x given that Y has assumed the value y. Similarly,

$$f(y \mid x) = P(Y = y \mid X = x)$$

which gives the *conditional PDF of Y.*

The conditional PDFs may be obtained as follows:

$$f(x \mid y) = \frac{f(x, y)}{f(y)} \qquad \text{conditional PDF of } X$$

$$f(y \mid x) = \frac{f(x, y)}{f(x)} \qquad \text{conditional PDF of } Y$$

As the preceding expressions show, the conditional PDF of one variable can be expressed as the ratio of the joint PDF to the marginal PDF of another (conditioning) variable.

EXAMPLE 6

Continuing with Examples 4 and 5, let us compute the following conditional probabilities:

$$f(X = -2 \mid Y = 3) = \frac{f(X = -2, Y = 3)}{f(Y = 3)} = 0.27/0.51 = 0.53$$

Notice that the unconditional probability $f(X = -2)$ is 0.27, but if Y has assumed the value of 3, the probability that X takes the value of -2 is 0.53.

$$f(X = 2 \mid Y = 6) = \frac{f(X = 2, Y = 6)}{f(Y = 6)} = 0.10/0.49 = 0.20$$

Again note that the unconditional probability that X takes the value of 2 is 0.26, which is different from 0.20, which is its value if Y assumes the value of 6.

Statistical Independence

Two random variables X and Y are statistically independent if and only if

$$f(x, y) = f(x)f(y)$$

that is, if the joint PDF can be expressed as the product of the marginal PDFs.

EXAMPLE 7

A bag contains three balls numbered 1, 2, and 3. Two balls are drawn at random, with replacement, from the bag (i.e., the first ball drawn is replaced before the second is drawn). Let X denote the number of the first ball drawn and Y the number of the second ball drawn. The following table gives the joint PDF of X and Y.

EXAMPLE 7
(Continued)

		X		
		1	2	3
	1	$\frac{1}{9}$	$\frac{1}{9}$	$\frac{1}{9}$
Y	2	$\frac{1}{9}$	$\frac{1}{9}$	$\frac{1}{9}$
	3	$\frac{1}{9}$	$\frac{1}{9}$	$\frac{1}{9}$

Now $f(X=1, Y=1) = \frac{1}{9}$, $f(X=1) = \frac{1}{3}$ (obtained by summing the first column), and $f(y=1) = \frac{1}{3}$ (obtained by summing the first row). Since $f(X, Y) = f(X)f(Y)$ in this example we can say that the two variables are statistically independent. It can be easily checked that for any other combination of X and Y values given in the above table the joint PDF factors into individual PDFs.

It can be shown that the X and Y variables given in Example 4 are not statistically independent since the product of the two marginal PDFs is not equal to the joint PDF. (*Note:* $f(X, Y) = f(X)f(Y)$ must be true for all combinations of X and Y if the two variables are to be statistically independent.)

Continuous Joint PDF

The PDF $f(x, y)$ of two continuous variables X and Y is such that

$$f(x, y) \geq 0$$

$$\int_{-\infty}^{\infty}\int_{-\infty}^{\infty} f(x, y)\,dx\,dy = 1$$

$$\int_{c}^{d}\int_{a}^{b} f(x, y)\,dx\,dy = P(a \leq x \leq b, c \leq y \leq d)$$

EXAMPLE 8

Consider the following PDF

$$f(x, y) = 2 - x - y \qquad 0 \leq x \leq 1; 0 \leq y \leq 1$$

It is obvious that $f(x, y) \geq 0$. Moreover[4]

$$\int_{0}^{1}\int_{0}^{1} (2 - x - y)\,dx\,dy = 1$$

The marginal PDF of X and Y can be obtained as

$$f(x) = \int_{-\infty}^{\infty} f(x, y)\,dy \qquad \text{marginal PDF of } X$$

$$f(y) = \int_{-\infty}^{\infty} f(x, y)\,dx \qquad \text{marginal PDF of } Y$$

4

$$\int_{0}^{1}\left[\int_{0}^{1}(2 - x - y)\,dx\right]dy = \int_{0}^{1}\left[\left(2x - \frac{x^2}{2} - xy\right)\Big|_{0}^{1}\right]dy$$
$$= \int_{0}^{1}\left(\frac{3}{2} - y\right)dy$$
$$= \left(\frac{3}{2}y - \frac{y^2}{2}\right)\Big|_{0}^{1} = 1$$

Note: The expression $(\frac{3}{2}y - y^2/2)|_0^1$ means the expression in the parentheses is to be evaluated at the upper limit value of 1 and the lower limit value of 0; the latter value is subtracted from the former to obtain the value of the integral. Thus, in the preceding example the limits are $(\frac{3}{2} - \frac{1}{2})$ at $y = 1$ and 0 at $y = 0$, giving the value of the integral as 1.

EXAMPLE 9

The two marginal PDFs of the joint PDF given in Example 8 are as follows:

$$f(x) = \int_0^1 f(x, y)dy = \int_0^1 (2 - x - y)dy$$

$$\left(2y - xy - \frac{y^2}{2}\right)\Bigg|_0^1 = \frac{3}{2} - x \qquad 0 \leq x \leq 1$$

$$f(y) = \int_0^1 (2 - x - y)dx$$

$$\left(2x - xy - \frac{x^2}{2}\right)\Bigg|_0^1 = \frac{3}{2} - y \qquad 0 \leq y \leq 1$$

To see if the two variables of Example 8 are statistically independent, we need to find out if $f(x, y) = f(x)f(y)$. Since $(2 - x - y) \neq (\frac{3}{2} - x)(\frac{3}{2} - y)$, we can say that the two variables are not statistically independent.

A.5 Characteristics of Probability Distributions

A probability distribution can often be summarized in terms of a few of its characteristics, known as the **moments** of the distribution. Two of the most widely used moments are the **mean,** or **expected value,** and the **variance.**

Expected Value

The expected value of a discrete rv X, denoted by $E(X)$, is defined as follows:

$$E(X) = \sum_x xf(x)$$

where $\sum_x$ means the sum over all values of X and where $f(x)$ is the (discrete) PDF of X.

EXAMPLE 10

Consider the probability distribution of the sum of two numbers in the throw of two dice given in Example 2. (See Figure A.1.) Multiplying the various X values given there by their probabilities and summing over all the observations, we obtain:

$$E(X) = 2\left(\tfrac{1}{36}\right) + 3\left(\tfrac{2}{26}\right) + 4\left(\tfrac{3}{36}\right) + \cdots + 12\left(\tfrac{1}{36}\right)$$
$$= 7$$

which is the average value of the sum of numbers observed in a throw of two dice.

EXAMPLE 11

Estimate $E(X)$ and $E(Y)$ for the data given in Example 4. We have seen that

x	−2	0	2	3
$f(x)$	0.27	0.12	0.26	0.35

Therefore,

$$E(X) = \sum_x xf(x)$$
$$= (-2)(0.27) + (0)(0.12) + (2)(0.26) + (3)(0.35)$$
$$= 1.03$$

EXAMPLE 11 *(Continued)*

Similarly,

y	3	6
$f(y)$	0.51	0.49

$$
\begin{aligned}
E(Y) &= \sum_y y f(y) \\
&= (3)(0.51) + (6)(0.49) \\
&= 4.47
\end{aligned}
$$

The expected value of a continuous rv is defined as

$$E(X) = \int_{-\infty}^{\infty} x f(x) dx$$

The only difference between this case and the expected value of a discrete rv is that we replace the summation symbol by the integral symbol.

EXAMPLE 12

Let us find out the expected value of the continuous PDF given in Example 3.

$$
\begin{aligned}
F(X) &= \int_0^3 x\left(\frac{x^2}{9}\right) dx \\
&= \frac{1}{9}\left[\left(\frac{x^4}{4}\right)\right]_0^3 \\
&= \frac{9}{4} \\
&= 2.25
\end{aligned}
$$

Properties of Expected Values

1. The expected value of a constant is the constant itself. Thus, if b is a constant, $E(b) = b$.
2. If a and b are constants,

$$E(aX + b) = aE(X) + b$$

This can be generalized. If $X_1, X_2, \ldots, X_N$ are N random variables and $a_1, a_2, \ldots, a_N$ and b are constants, then

$$E(a_1X_1 + a_2X_2 + \cdots + a_NX_N + b) = a_1E(X_1) + a_2E(X_2) + \cdots + a_NE(X_N) + b$$

3. If X and Y are *independent* random variables, then

$$E(XY) = E(X)E(Y)$$

That is, the expectation of the product XY is the product of the (individual) expectations of X and Y.

However, note that

$$E\left(\frac{X}{Y}\right) \neq \frac{E(X)}{E(Y)}$$

even if X and Y are independent.

4. If X is a random variable with PDF $f(x)$ and if $g(X)$ is any function of X, then

$$E[g(X)] = \sum_x g(X)f(x) \qquad \text{if } X \text{ is discrete}$$

$$= \int_{-\infty}^{\infty} g(X)f(x)\,dx \qquad \text{if } X \text{ is continuous}$$

Thus, if $g(X) = X^2$,

$$E(X^2) = \sum_x x^2 f(X) \qquad \text{if } X \text{ is discrete}$$

$$= \int_{-\infty}^{\infty} x^2 f(X)\,dx \qquad \text{if } X \text{ is continuous}$$

EXAMPLE 13 Consider the following PDF:

x	-2	1	2
$f(x)$	$\frac{5}{8}$	$\frac{1}{8}$	$\frac{2}{8}$

Then

$$E(X) = -2\left(\tfrac{5}{8}\right) + 1\left(\tfrac{1}{8}\right) + 2\left(\tfrac{2}{8}\right)$$

$$= -\tfrac{5}{8}$$

and

$$E(X^2) = 4\left(\tfrac{5}{8}\right) + 1\left(\tfrac{1}{8}\right) + 4\left(\tfrac{2}{8}\right)$$

$$= \tfrac{29}{8}$$

Variance

Let X be a random variable and let $E(X) = \mu$. The distribution, or spread, of the X values around the expected value can be measured by the variance, which is defined as

$$\text{var}\,(X) = \sigma_X^2 = E(X - \mu)^2$$

The positive square root of σ_X^2, σ_X, is defined as the **standard deviation** of X. The variance or standard deviation gives an indication of how closely or widely the individual X values are spread around their mean value.

The variance defined previously is computed as follows:

$$\text{var}\,(X) = \sum_x (X - \mu)^2 f(x) \qquad \text{if } X \text{ is a discrete rv}$$

$$= \int_{-\infty}^{\infty} (X - \mu)^2 f(x)\,dx \qquad \text{if } X \text{ is a continuous rv}$$

For computational convenience, the variance formula given above can also be expressed as

$$\text{var}\,(X) = \sigma_x^2 = E(X - \mu)^2$$

$$= E(X^2) - \mu^2$$

$$= E(X^2) - [E(X)]^2$$

Applying this formula, it can be seen that the variance of the random variable given in Example 13 is $\frac{29}{8} - (-\frac{5}{8})^2 = \frac{207}{64} = 3.23$.

EXAMPLE 14 Let us find the variance of the random variable given in Example 3.

$$\operatorname{var}(X) = E(X^2) - [E(X)]^2$$

Now

$$\begin{aligned} E(X^2) &= \int_0^3 x^2 \left(\frac{x^2}{9}\right) dx \\ &= \int_0^3 \frac{x^4}{9} dx \\ &= \frac{1}{9}\left[\frac{x^5}{5}\right]_0^3 \\ &= 243/45 \\ &= 27/5 \end{aligned}$$

Since $E(X) = \frac{9}{4}$ (see Example 12), we finally have

$$\begin{aligned} \operatorname{var}(X) &= 243/45 - \left(\tfrac{9}{4}\right)^2 \\ &= 243/720 = 0.34 \end{aligned}$$

Properties of Variance

1. $E(X - \mu)^2 = E(X^2) - \mu^2$, as noted before.
2. The variance of a constant is zero.
3. If a and b are constants, then

$$\operatorname{var}(aX + b) = a^2 \operatorname{var}(X)$$

4. If X and Y are *independent* random variables, then

$$\operatorname{var}(X + Y) = \operatorname{var}(X) + \operatorname{var}(Y)$$

$$\operatorname{var}(X - Y) = \operatorname{var}(X) + \operatorname{var}(Y)$$

This can be generalized to more than two independent variables.

5. If X and Y are *independent* rv's and a and b are constants, then

$$\operatorname{var}(aX + bY) = a^2 \operatorname{var}(X) + b^2 \operatorname{var}(Y)$$

Covariance

Let X and Y be two rv's with means μ_x and μ_y, respectively. Then the **covariance** between the two variables is defined as

$$\operatorname{cov}(X, Y) = E\{(X - \mu_x)(Y - \mu_y)\} = E(XY) - \mu_x \mu_y$$

It can be readily seen that the variance of a variable is the covariance of that variable with itself.

The covariance is computed as follows:

$$\begin{aligned} \operatorname{cov}(X, Y) &= \sum_y \sum_x (X - \mu_x)(Y - \mu_y) f(x, y) \\ &= \sum_y \sum_x XY f(x, y) - \mu_x \mu_y \end{aligned}$$

if X and Y are discrete random variables, and

$$\begin{aligned}\operatorname{cov}(X, Y) &= \int_{-\infty}^{\infty}\int_{-\infty}^{\infty}(X-\mu_x)(Y-\mu_y)f(x, y)\,dx\,dy \\ &= \int_{-\infty}^{\infty}\int_{-\infty}^{\infty} XYf(x, y)\,dx\,dy - \mu_x\,\mu_y\end{aligned}$$

if X and Y are continuous random variables.

Properties of Covariance

1. If X and Y are independent, their covariance is zero, for

$$\begin{aligned}\operatorname{cov}(X, Y) &= E(XY) - \mu_x\mu_y \\ &= \mu_x\mu_y - \mu_x\mu_y \qquad \text{since } E(XY) = E(X)E(Y) = \mu_x\mu_y \text{ when } X \text{ and } Y \text{ are independent} \\ &= 0\end{aligned}$$

2.

$$\operatorname{cov}(a + bX, c + dY) = bd\operatorname{cov}(X, Y)$$

where a, b, c, and d are constants.

EXAMPLE 15 Let us find out the covariance between discrete random variables X and Y whose joint PDF is as shown in Example 4. From Example 11 we already know that $\mu_x = E(X) = 1.03$ and $\mu_y = E(Y) = 4.47$.

$$\begin{aligned}E(XY) &= \sum_y\sum_x XYf(x, y) \\ &= (-2)(3)(0.27) + (0)(3)(0.08) + (2)(3)(0.16) + (3)(3)(0) \\ &\quad + (-2)(6)(0) + (0)(6)(0.04) + (2)(6)(0.10) + (3)(6)(0.35) \\ &= 6.84\end{aligned}$$

Therefore,

$$\begin{aligned}\operatorname{cov}(X, Y) &= E(XY) - \mu_x\mu_y \\ &= 6.84 - (1.03)(4.47) \\ &= 2.24\end{aligned}$$

Correlation Coefficient

The (population) correlation coefficient ρ (rho) is defined as

$$\rho = \frac{\operatorname{cov}(X, Y)}{\sqrt{\{\operatorname{var}(X)\operatorname{var}(Y)\}}} = \frac{\operatorname{cov}(X, Y)}{\sigma_x\sigma_y}$$

Thus defined, ρ is a measure of *linear* association between two variables and lies between -1 and $+1$, -1 indicating perfect negative association and $+1$ indicating perfect positive association.

From the preceding formula, it can be seen that

$$\operatorname{cov}(X, Y) = \rho\sigma_x\sigma_y$$

EXAMPLE 16 Estimate the coefficient of correlation for the data of Example 4.

From the PDFs given in Example 11 it can be easily shown that $\sigma_x = 2.05$ and $\sigma_y = 1.50$. We have already shown that $\text{cov}(X, Y) = 2.24$. Therefore, applying the preceding formula we estimate ρ as $2.24/(2.05)(1.50) = 0.73$.

Variances of Correlated Variables

Let X and Y be two rv's. Then

$$\begin{aligned}\text{var}(X+Y) &= \text{var}(X) + \text{var}(Y) + 2\,\text{cov}(X, Y)\\ &= \text{var}(X) + \text{var}(Y) + 2\rho\sigma_x\sigma_y\\ \text{var}(X-Y) &= \text{var}(X) + \text{var}(Y) - 2\,\text{cov}(X, Y)\\ &= \text{var}(X) + \text{var}(Y) - 2\rho\sigma_x\sigma_y\end{aligned}$$

If, however, X and Y are independent, $\text{cov}(X, Y)$ is zero, in which case the $\text{var}(X+Y)$ and $\text{var}(X-Y)$ are both equal to $\text{var}(X) + \text{var}(Y)$, as noted previously.

The preceding results can be generalized as follows. Let $\sum_{i=1}^{n} X_i = X_1 + X_2 + \cdots + X_n$, then the variance of the linear combination $\sum X_i$ is

$$\begin{aligned}\text{var}\left(\sum_{i=1}^{n} X_i\right) &= \sum_{i=1}^{n} \text{var}\, X_i + 2\sum_{i<j}\sum \text{cov}(X_i, X_j)\\ &= \sum_{i=1}^{n} \text{var}\, X_i + 2\sum_{i<j}\sum \rho_{ij}\sigma_i\sigma_j\end{aligned}$$

where ρ_{ij} is the correlation coefficient between X_i and X_j and where σ_i and σ_j are the standard deviations of X_i and X_j.

Thus,

$$\begin{aligned}\text{var}(X_1+X_2+X_3) &= \text{var}\, X_1 + \text{var}\, X_2 + \text{var}\, X_3 + 2\,\text{cov}(X_1, X_2)\\ &\quad + 2\,\text{cov}(X_1, X_3) + 2\,\text{cov}(X_2, X_3)\\ &= \text{var}\, X_1 + \text{var}\, X_2 + \text{var}\, X_3 + 2\rho_{12}\sigma_1\sigma_2\\ &\quad + 2\rho_{13}\sigma_1\sigma_3 + 2\rho_{23}\sigma_2\sigma_3\end{aligned}$$

where σ_1, σ_2, and σ_3 are, respectively, the standard deviations of X_1, X_2, and X_3 and where ρ_{12} is the correlation coefficient between X_1 and X_2, ρ_{13} that between X_1 and X_3, and ρ_{23} that between X_2 and X_3.

Conditional Expectation and Conditional Variance

Let $f(x, y)$ be the joint PDF of random variables X and Y. The conditional expectation of X, given $Y = y$, is defined as

$$\begin{aligned}E(X \mid Y = y) &= \sum_x x f(x \mid Y = y) &&\text{if } X \text{ is discrete}\\ &= \int_{-\infty}^{\infty} x f(x \mid Y = y)\, dx &&\text{if } X \text{ is continuous}\end{aligned}$$

where $E(X \mid Y = y)$ means the conditional expectation of X given $Y = y$ and where $f(x \mid Y = y)$ is the conditional PDF of X. The conditional expectation of Y, $E(Y \mid X = x)$, is defined similarly.

Conditional Expectation

Note that $E(X \mid Y)$ is a random variable because it is a function of the conditioning variable Y. However, $E(X \mid Y = y)$, where y is a specific value of Y, is a constant.

Conditional Variance

The conditional variance of X given $Y = y$ is defined as

$$\begin{aligned}
\text{var}\,(X \mid Y = y) &= E\{[X - E(X \mid Y = y)]^2 \mid Y = y\} \\
&= \sum_x [X - E(X \mid Y = y)]^2 f(x \mid Y = y) \qquad \text{if } X \text{ is discrete} \\
&= \int_{-\infty}^{\infty} [X - E(X \mid Y = y)]^2 f(x \mid Y = y)\, dx \qquad \text{if } X \text{ is continuous}
\end{aligned}$$

EXAMPLE 17 Compute $E(Y \mid X = 2)$ and $\text{var}\,(Y \mid X = 2)$ for the data given in Example 4.

$$\begin{aligned}
E(Y \mid X = 2) &= \sum_Y Y f(Y = y \mid X = 2) \\
&= 3f(Y = 3 \mid X = 2) + 6f(Y = 6 \mid X = 2) \\
&= 3(0.16/0.26) + 6(0.10/0.26) \\
&= 4.15
\end{aligned}$$

Note: $f(Y = 3 \mid X = 2) = f(Y = 3, X = 2)/f(X = 2) = 0.16/0.26$, and $f(Y = 6 \mid X = 2) = f(Y = 6, X = 2)/f(X = 2) = 0.10/0.26$, so

$$\begin{aligned}
\text{var}\,(Y \mid X = 2) &= \sum_Y [Y - E(Y \mid X = 2)]^2 f(Y \mid X = 2) \\
&= (3 - 4.15)^2(0.16/0.26) + (6 - 4.15)^2(0.10/0.26) \\
&= 2.13
\end{aligned}$$

Properties of Conditional Expectation and Conditional Variance

1. If $f(X)$ is a function of X, then $E(f(X) \mid X) = f(X)$, that is, the function of X behaves as a constant in computation of its expectation conditional on X. Thus, $[E(X^3 \mid X)] = E(X^3)$; this is because, if X is known, X^3 is also known.
2. If $f(X)$ and $g(X)$ are functions of X, then

$$E[f(X)Y + g(X) \mid X] = f(X)E(Y \mid X) + g(X)$$

For example, $E[XY + cX^2 \mid X] = XE(Y \mid X) + cX^2$, where c is a constant.

3. If X and Y are independent, $E(Y \mid X) = E(Y)$. That is, if X and Y are independent random variables, then the conditional expectation of Y, given X, is the same as the unconditional expectation of Y.

4. **The law of iterated expectations.** It is interesting to note the following relation between the unconditional expectation of a random variable Y, $E(Y)$, and its conditional expectation based on another random variable X, $E(Y \mid X)$:

$$E(Y) = E_X[E(Y \mid X)]$$

This is known as the law of iterated expectations, which in the present context states that the marginal, or unconditional, expectation of Y is equal to the expectation of its conditional expectation, the symbol E_X denoting that the expectation is taken over the values of X. Put simply, this law states that if we first obtain $E(Y \mid X)$ as a function of X and take its expected value over the distribution of X values, you wind up with $E(Y)$, the unconditional expectation of Y. The reader can verify this using the data given in Example 4.

An implication of the law of iterated expectations is that if the conditional mean of Y given X (i.e., $E[Y|X]$) is zero, then the (unconditional) mean of Y is also zero. This follows immediately because in that case

$$E[E(Y|X)] = E[0] = 0$$

5. If X and Y are independent, then $\text{var}(Y \mid X) = \text{var}(Y)$.
6. $\text{var}(Y) = E[\text{var}(Y \mid X)] + \text{var}[E(Y \mid X)]$; that is, the (unconditional) variance of Y is equal to expectation of the conditional variance of Y plus the variance of the conditional expectation of Y.

Higher Moments of Probability Distributions

Although mean, variance, and covariance are the most frequently used summary measures of univariate and multivariate PDFs, we occasionally need to consider higher moments of the PDFs, such as the third and the fourth moments. The third and fourth moments of a univariate PDF $f(x)$ around its mean value (μ) are defined as

$$\text{Third moment:} \quad E(X - \mu)^3$$

$$\text{Fourth moment:} \quad E(X - \mu)^4$$

In general, the rth moment about the mean is defined as

$$r\text{th moment:} \quad E(X - \mu)^r$$

The third and fourth moments of a distribution are often used in studying the "shape" of a probability distribution, in particular, its **skewness,** S (i.e., lack of symmetry) and **kurtosis,** K (i.e., tallness or flatness), as shown in Figure A.3.

One measure of skewness is defined as

$$S = \frac{E(X - \mu)^3}{\sigma^3} = \frac{\text{third moment about the mean}}{\text{cube of the standard deviation}}$$

A commonly used measure of kurtosis is given by

$$K = \frac{E(X - \mu)^4}{[E(X - \mu)^2]^2} = \frac{\text{fourth moment about the mean}}{\text{square of the second moment}}$$

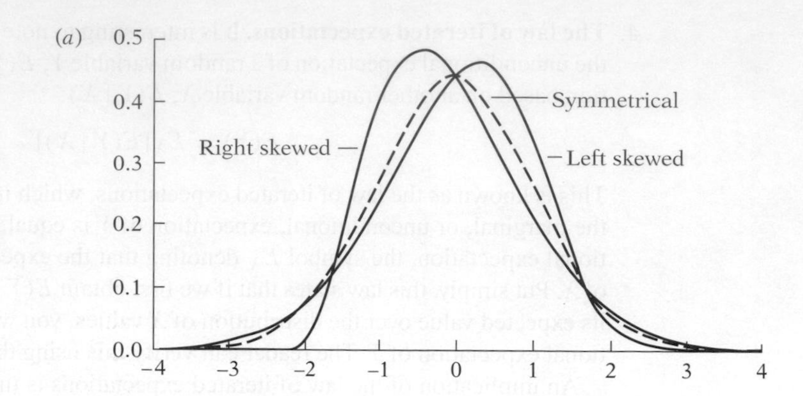

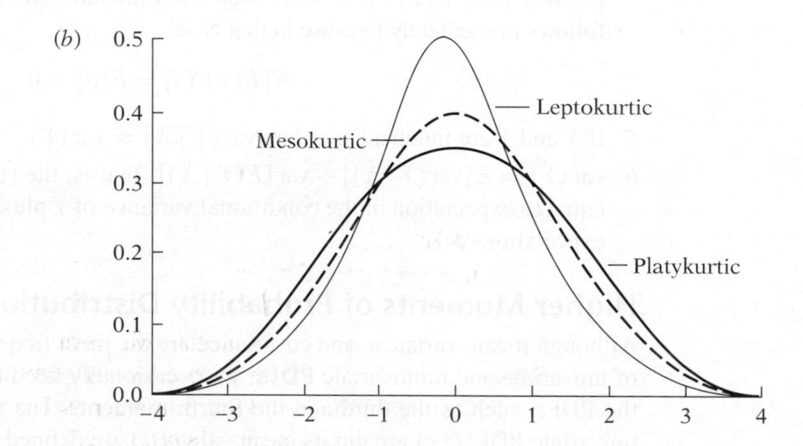

FIGURE A.3 (*a*) Skewness; (*b*) kurtosis.

PDFs with values of K less than 3 are called **platykurtic** (fat or short-tailed), and those with values greater than 3 are called **leptokurtic** (slim or long-tailed). See Figure A.3. A PDF with a kurtosis value of 3 is known as **mesokurtic,** of which the normal distribution is the prime example. (See the discussion of the normal distribution in Section A.6.)

We will show shortly how the measures of skewness and kurtosis can be combined to determine whether a random variable follows a normal distribution. Recall that our hypothesis-testing procedure, as in the t and F tests, is based on the assumption (at least in small or finite samples) that the underlying distribution of the variable (or sample statistic) is normal. It is therefore very important to find out in concrete applications whether this assumption is fulfilled.

A.6 Some Important Theoretical Probability Distributions

In the text extensive use is made of the following probability distributions.

Normal Distribution

The best known of all the theoretical probability distributions is the normal distribution, whose bell-shaped picture is familiar to anyone with a modicum of statistical knowledge.

A (continuous) random variable X is said to be normally distributed if its PDF has the following form:

$$f(x) = \frac{1}{\sigma\sqrt{2\pi}} \exp\left(-\frac{1}{2}\frac{(x-\mu)^2}{\sigma^2}\right) \qquad -\infty < x < \infty$$

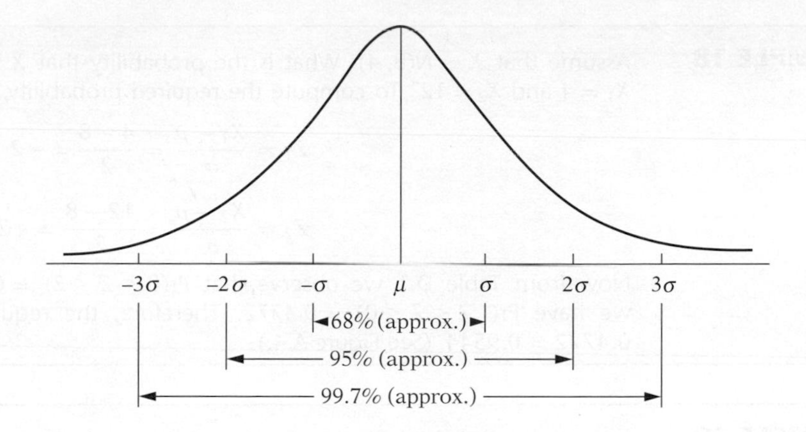

FIGURE A.4 Areas under the normal curve.

where μ and σ^2, known as the *parameters of the distribution,* are, respectively, the mean and the variance of the distribution. The properties of this distribution are as follows:

1. It is symmetrical around its mean value.
2. Approximately 68 percent of the area under the normal curve lies between the values of $\mu \pm \sigma$, about 95 percent of the area lies between $\mu \pm 2\sigma$, and about 99.7 percent of the area lies between $\mu \pm 3\sigma$, as shown in Figure A.4.
3. The normal distribution depends on the two parameters μ and σ^2, so once these are specified, one can find the probability that X will lie within a certain interval by using the PDF of the normal distribution. But this task can be lightened considerably by referring to Table D.1 of **Appendix D.** To use this table, we convert the given normally distributed variable X with mean μ and σ^2 into a **standardized normal variable** Z by the following transformation:

$$Z = \frac{x - \mu}{\sigma}$$

An important property of any standardized variable is that its mean value is zero and its variance is unity. Thus Z has zero mean and unit variance. Substituting z into the normal PDF given previously, we obtain

$$f(Z) = \frac{1}{\sqrt{2\pi}} \exp\left(-\frac{1}{2}Z^2\right)$$

which is the PDF of the standardized normal variable. The probabilities given in **Appendix D,** Table D.1, are based on this standardized normal variable.

By convention, we denote a normally distributed variable as

$$X \sim N(\mu, \sigma^2)$$

where $\sim$ means "distributed as," N stands for the normal distribution, and the quantities in the parentheses are the two parameters of the normal distribution, namely, the mean and the variance. Following this convention,

$$X \sim N(0, 1)$$

means X is a normally distributed variable with zero mean and unit variance. In other words, it is a standardized normal variable Z.

EXAMPLE 18

Assume that $X \sim N(8, 4)$. What is the probability that X will assume a value between $X_1 = 4$ and $X_2 = 12$? To compute the required probability, we compute the Z values as

$$Z_1 = \frac{X_1 - \mu}{\sigma} = \frac{4 - 8}{2} = -2$$

$$Z_2 = \frac{X_2 - \mu}{\sigma} = \frac{12 - 8}{2} = +2$$

Now from Table D.1 we observe that $\Pr(0 \leq Z \leq 2) = 0.4772$. Then, by symmetry, we have $\Pr(-2 \leq Z \leq 0) = 0.4772$. Therefore, the required probability is $0.4772 + 0.4772 = 0.9544$. (See Figure A.4.)

EXAMPLE 19

What is the probability that in the preceding example X exceeds 12?

The probability that X exceeds 12 is the same as the probability that Z exceeds 2. From Table D.1 it is obvious that this probability is (0.5 – 0.4772) or 0.0228.

4. Let $X_1 \sim N(\mu_1, \sigma_1^2)$ and $X_2 \sim N(\mu_2, \sigma_2^2)$ and assume that they are independent. Now consider the linear combination

$$Y = aX_1 + bX_2$$

where a and b are constants. Then it can be shown that

$$Y \sim N\left[(a\mu_1 + b\mu_2), \left(a^2\sigma_1^2 + b^2\sigma_2^2\right)\right]$$

This result, which states that *a linear combination of normally distributed variables is itself normally distributed,* can be easily generalized to a linear combination of more than two normally distributed variables.

5. **Central limit theorem.** Let $X_1, X_2, \ldots, X_n$ denote n independent random variables, all of which have the same PDF with mean $= \mu$ and variance $= \sigma^2$. Let $\bar{X} = \sum X_i/n$ (i.e., the sample mean). Then as n increases indefinitely (i.e., $n \to \infty$),

$$\underset{n \to \infty}{\bar{X}} \sim N\left(\mu, \frac{\sigma^2}{n}\right)$$

That is, $\bar{X}$ approaches the normal distribution with mean μ and variance σ^2/n. Notice that this result holds true regardless of the form of the PDF. As a result, it follows that

$$z = \frac{\bar{X} - \mu}{\sigma/\sqrt{n}} = \frac{\sqrt{n}(\bar{X} - u)}{\sigma} \sim N(0, 1)$$

That is, Z is a standardized normal variable.

6. The third and fourth moments of the normal distribution around the mean value are as follows:

$$\text{Third moment:} \quad E(X - \mu)^3 = 0$$

$$\text{Fourth moment:} \quad E(X - \mu)^4 = 3\sigma^4$$

Note: All odd-powered moments about the mean value of a normally distributed variable are zero.

7. As a result, and following the measures of skewness and kurtosis discussed earlier, for a normal PDF skewness = 0 and kurtosis = 3; that is, a normal distribution is symmetric

and mesokurtic. Therefore, a simple test of normality is to find out whether the computed values of skewness and kurtosis depart from the norms of 0 and 3. This is in fact the logic underlying the **Jarque–Bera (JB) test of normality** discussed in the text:

$$\text{JB} = n\left[\frac{S^2}{6} + \frac{(K-3)^2}{24}\right] \tag{5.12.1}$$

where S stands for skewness and K for kurtosis. Under the null hypothesis of normality, JB is distributed as a **chi-square** statistic with 2 df.

8. The mean and the variance of a normally distributed random variable are independent in that one is not a function of the other.
9. If X and Y are jointly normally distributed, then they are independent if, and only if, the covariance between them [i.e., cov (X, Y)] is zero. (See Exercise 4.1.)

The χ^2 (Chi-Square) Distribution

Let $Z_1, Z_2, \ldots, Z_k$ be *independent* standardized normal variables (i.e., normal variables with zero mean and unit variance). Then the quantity

$$Z = \sum_{i=1}^{k} Z_i^2$$

is said to possess the χ^2 distribution with k degrees of freedom (df), where the term df means the number of independent quantities in the previous sum. A chi-square-distributed variable is denoted by χ_k^2, where the subscript k indicates the df. Geometrically, the chi-square distribution appears in Figure A.5.

Properties of the χ^2 distribution are as follows:

1. As Figure A.5 shows, the χ^2 distribution is a skewed distribution, the degree of the skewness depending on the df. For comparatively few df, the distribution is highly skewed to the right; but as the number of df increases, the distribution becomes increasingly symmetrical. As a matter of fact, for df in excess of 100, the variable

$$\sqrt{2\chi^2} - \sqrt{(2k-1)}$$

can be treated as a standardized normal variable, where k is the df.

FIGURE A.5
Density function of the χ^2 variable.

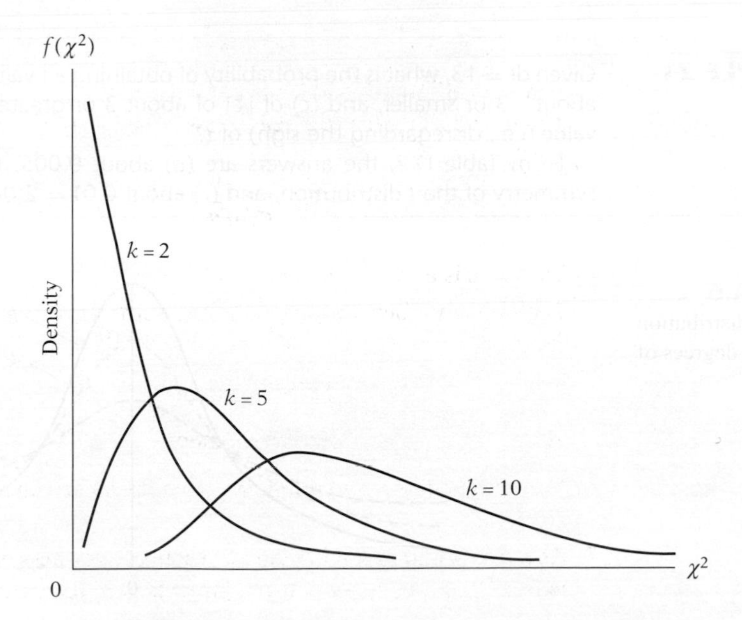

2. The mean of the chi-square distribution is k, and its variance is $2k$, where k is the df.
3. If Z_1 and Z_2 are two independent chi-square variables with k_1 and k_2 df, then the sum $Z_1 + Z_2$ is also a chi-square variable with df $= k_1 + k_2$.

EXAMPLE 20

What is the probability of obtaining a χ^2 value of 40 or greater, given the df of 20?

As Table D.4 shows, the probability of obtaining a χ^2 value of 39.9968 or greater (20 df) is 0.005. Therefore, the probability of obtaining a χ^2 value of 40 or greater is less than 0.005, a rather small probability.

Student's *t* Distribution

If Z_1 is a standardized normal variable [that is, $Z_1 \sim N(0, 1)$] and another variable Z_2 follows the chi-square distribution with k df and is distributed independently of Z_1, then the variable defined as

$$t = \frac{Z_1}{\sqrt{(Z_2/k)}} = \frac{Z_1\sqrt{k}}{\sqrt{Z_2}}$$

follows Student's t distribution with k df. A t-distributed variable is often designated as t_k, where the subscript k denotes the df. Geometrically, the t distribution is shown in Figure A.6.

Properties of the Student's t distribution are as follows:

1. As Figure A.6 shows, the t distribution, like the normal distribution, is symmetrical, but it is flatter than the normal distribution. But as the df increase, the t distribution approximates the normal distribution.
2. The mean of the t distribution is zero, and its variance is $k/(k-2)$.

The t distribution is tabulated in Table D.2.

EXAMPLE 21

Given df = 13, what is the probability of obtaining a t value (*a*) of about 3 or greater, (*b*) of about −3 or smaller, and (*c*) of $|t|$ of about 3 or greater, where $|t|$ means the absolute value (i.e., disregarding the sign) of t?

From Table D.2, the answers are (*a*) about 0.005, (*b*) about 0.005 because of the symmetry of the t distribution, and (*c*) about 0.01 = 2(0.005).

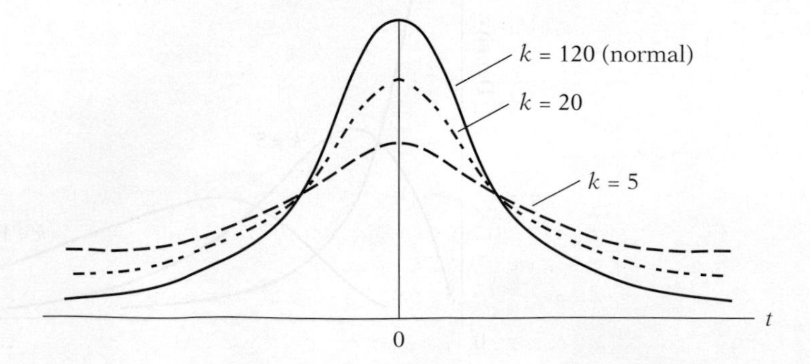

FIGURE A.6 Student's t distribution for selected degrees of freedom.

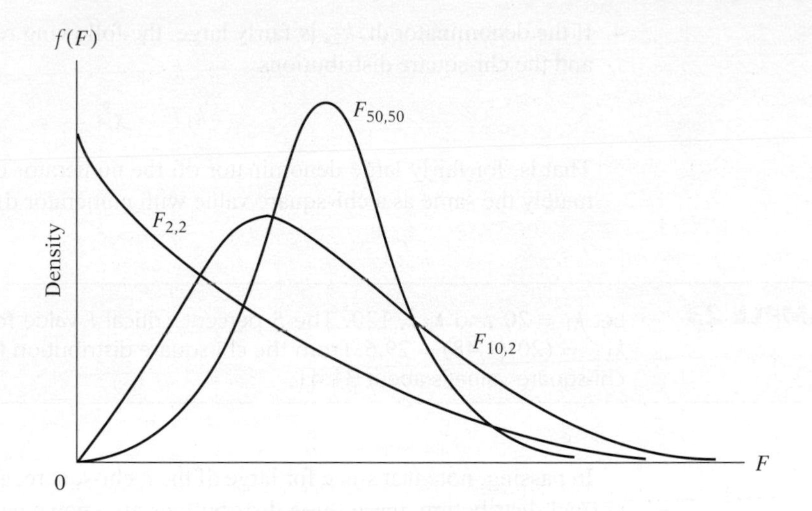

FIGURE A.7 F distribution for various degrees of freedom.

The *F* Distribution

If Z_1 and Z_2 are independently distributed chi-square variables with k_1 and k_2 df, respectively, the variable

$$F = \frac{Z_1/k_1}{Z_2/k_2}$$

follows (Fisher's) *F* distribution with k_1 and k_2 df. An *F*-distributed variable is denoted by F_{k_1,k_2} where the subscripts indicate the df associated with the two *Z* variables, k_1 being called the *numerator df* and k_2 the *denominator df*. Geometrically, the *F* distribution is shown in Figure A.7.

The *F* distribution has the following properties:

1. Like the chi-square distribution, the *F* distribution is skewed to the right. But it can be shown that as k_1 and k_2 become large, the *F* distribution approaches the normal distribution.
2. The mean value of an *F*-distributed variable is $k_2/(k_2 - 2)$, which is defined for $k_2 > 2$, and its variance is

$$\frac{2k_2^2(k_1 + k_2 - 2)}{k_1(k_2 - 2)^2(k_2 - 4)}$$

which is defined for $k_2 > 4$.

3. The square of a *t*-distributed random variable with *k* df has an *F* distribution with 1 and *k* df. Symbolically,

$$t_k^2 = F_{1,k}$$

EXAMPLE 22 Given $k_1 = 10$ and $k_2 = 8$, what is the probability of obtaining an *F* value (*a*) of 3.4 or greater and (*b*) of 5.8 or greater?

As Table D.3 shows, these probabilities are (*a*) approximately 0.05 and (*b*) approximately 0.01.

4. If the denominator df, k_2, is fairly large, the following relationship holds between the F and the chi-square distributions:

$$k_1 F \sim \chi^2_{k1}$$

That is, for fairly large denominator df, the numerator df times the F value is approximately the same as a chi-square value with numerator df.

EXAMPLE 23 Let $k_1 = 20$ and $k_2 = 120$. The 5 percent critical F value for these df is 1.48. Therefore, $k_1 F = (20)(1.48) = 29.6$. From the chi-square distribution for 20 df, the 5 percent critical chi-square value is about 31.41.

In passing, note that since for large df the t, chi-square, and F distributions approach the normal distribution, these three distributions are known as the *distributions related to the normal distribution.*

The Bernoulli Binomial Distribution

A random variable X is said to follow a distribution named after Bernoulli (a Swiss mathematician) if its probability density (or mass) function (PDF) is:

$$P(X = 0) = 1 - p$$

$$P(X = 1) = p$$

where p, $0 \leq p \leq 1$, is the probability that some event is a "success," such as the probability of obtaining a head in a toss of a coin. For such a variable,

$$E(X) = [1 \times p(X = 1) + 0 \times p(X = 0)] = p$$

$$\text{var}(X) = pq$$

where $q = (1 - p)$, that is, the probability of a "failure."

Binomial Distribution

The binomial distribution is the generalization of the Bernoulli distribution. Let n denote the number of independent trials, each of which results in a "success" with probability p and a "failure" with a probability $q = (1 - p)$. If X represents the number of successes in the n trials, then X is said to follow the binomial distribution whose PDF is:

$$f(X) = \binom{n}{x} p^x (1 - p)^{n-x}$$

where x represents the number of successes in n trials and where

$$\binom{n}{x} = \frac{n!}{x!(n - x)!}$$

where $n!$, read as n factorial, means $n(n - 1)(n - 2) \cdots 1$.

The binomial is a two-parameter distribution, n and p. For this distribution,

$$E(X) = np$$

$$\text{var}(X) = np(1 - p) = npq$$

For example, if you toss a coin 100 times and want to find out the probability of obtaining 60 heads, you put $p = 0.5$, $n = 100$ and $x = 60$ in the above formula. Computer routines exist to evaluate such probabilities.

You can see how the binomial distribution is a generalization of the Bernoulli distribution.

The Poisson Distribution

A random X variable is said to have the Poisson distribution if its PDF is:

$$f(X) = \frac{e^{-\lambda}\lambda^x}{x!} \qquad \text{for } x = 0, 1, 2, \ldots, \lambda > 0$$

The Poisson distribution depends on a single parameter, λ. A distinguishing feature of the Poisson distribution is that its variance is equal to its expected value, which is λ. That is,

$$E(X) = \text{var}(X) = \lambda$$

The Poisson model, as we saw in the chapter on nonlinear regression models, is used to model rare or infrequent phenomena, such as the number of phone calls received in a span of, say, 5 minutes, or the number of speeding tickets received in a span of an hour, or the number of patents received by a firm, say, in a year.

A.7 Statistical Inference: Estimation

In Section A.6 we considered several theoretical probability distributions. Very often we know or are willing to assume that a random variable X follows a particular probability distribution but do not know the value(s) of the parameter(s) of the distribution. For example, if X follows the normal distribution, we may want to know the value of its two parameters, namely, the mean and the variance. To estimate the unknowns, the usual procedure is to assume that we have a **random sample** of size n from the known probability distribution and use the sample data to estimate the unknown parameters.[5] This is known as the **problem of estimation.** In this section, we take a closer look at this problem. The problem of estimation can be broken down into two categories: point estimation and interval estimation.

Point Estimation

To fix the ideas, let X be a random variable with PDF $f(x; \theta)$, where θ is the parameter of the distribution (for simplicity of discussion only, we are assuming that there is only one unknown parameter; our discussion can be readily generalized). Assume that we know the functional form—that is, we know the theoretical PDF, such as the t distribution—but do not know the value of θ. Therefore, we draw a random sample of size n from this known PDF and then develop a function of the sample values such that

$$\hat{\theta} = f(x_1, x_2, \ldots, x_n)$$

provides us an estimate of the true θ. $\hat{\theta}$ is known as a **statistic,** or an **estimator,** and a particular numerical value taken by the estimator is known as an **estimate.** Note that $\hat{\theta}$ can be

[5]Let $X_1, X_2, \ldots, X_n$ be n random variables with joint PDF $f(x_1, x_2, \ldots, x_n)$. If we can write

$$f(x_1, x_2, \ldots, x_n) = f(x_1)\,f(x_2)\cdots f(x_n)$$

where $f(x)$ is the common PDF of each X, then $x_1, x_2, \ldots, x_n$ are said to constitute a random sample of size n from a population with PDF $f(x_n)$.

treated as a random variable because it is a function of the sample data. $\hat{\theta}$ provides us with a rule, or formula, that tells us how we may estimate the true θ. Thus, if we let

$$\hat{\theta} = \frac{1}{n}(x_1 + x_2 + \cdots + x_n) = \bar{X}$$

where $\bar{X}$ is the sample mean, then $\bar{X}$ is an estimator of the true mean value, say, μ. If in a specific case $\bar{X} = 50$, this provides an *estimate of* μ. The estimator $\hat{\theta}$ obtained previously is known as a **point estimator** because it provides only a single (point) estimate of θ.

Interval Estimation

Instead of obtaining only a single estimate of θ, suppose we obtain two estimates of θ by constructing two estimators $\hat{\theta}_1(x_1, x_2, \ldots, x_n)$ and $\hat{\theta}_2(x_1, x_2, \ldots, x_n)$, and say with some confidence (i.e., probability) that the interval between $\hat{\theta}_1$ and $\hat{\theta}_2$ includes the true θ. Thus, in interval estimation, in contrast with point estimation, we provide a range of possible values within which the true θ may lie.

The key concept underlying interval estimation is the notion of the **sampling,** or **probability distribution, of an estimator.** For example, it can be shown that if a variable X is normally distributed, then the sample mean $\bar{X}$ is also normally distributed with mean = μ (the true mean) and variance = σ^2/n, where n is the sample size. In other words, the sampling, or probability, distribution of the estimator $\bar{X}$ is $\bar{X} \sim N(\mu, \sigma^2/n)$. As a result, if we construct the interval

$$\bar{X} \pm 2\frac{\sigma}{\sqrt{n}}$$

and say that the probability is approximately 0.95, or 95 percent, that intervals like it will include the true μ, we are in fact constructing an interval estimator for μ. Note that the interval given previously is random since it is based on $\bar{X}$, which will vary from sample to sample.

More generally, in interval estimation we construct two estimators $\hat{\theta}_1$ and $\hat{\theta}_2$, both functions of the sample X values, such that

$$\Pr(\hat{\theta}_1 \leq \theta \leq \hat{\theta}_2) = 1 - \alpha \qquad 0 < \alpha < 1$$

That is, we can state that the probability is $1 - \alpha$ that the interval from $\hat{\theta}_1$ to $\hat{\theta}_2$ contains the true θ. This interval is known as a **confidence interval** of size $1 - \alpha$ for θ, $1 - \alpha$ being known as the **confidence coefficient.** If $\alpha = 0.05$, then $1 - \alpha = 0.95$, meaning that if we construct a confidence interval with a confidence coefficient of 0.95, then in repeated such constructions resulting from repeated sampling we shall be right in 95 out of 100 cases if we maintain that the interval contains the true θ. When the confidence coefficient is 0.95, we often say that we have a 95 percent confidence interval. In general, if the confidence coefficient is $1 - \alpha$, we say that we have a $100(1 - \alpha)\%$ confidence interval. Note that α is known as the **level of significance,** or the probability of committing a Type I error. This topic is discussed in Section A.8.

EXAMPLE 24

Suppose that the distribution of height of men in a population is normally distributed with mean = μ inches and $\sigma = 2.5$ inches. A sample of 100 men drawn randomly from this population had an average height of 67 inches. Establish a 95 percent confidence interval for the mean height (= μ) in the population as a whole.

As noted, $\bar{X} \sim N(\mu, \sigma^2/n)$, which in this case becomes $\bar{X} \sim N(\mu, 2.5^2/100)$. From Table D.1 one can see that

$$\bar{X} - 1.96\left(\frac{\sigma}{\sqrt{n}}\right) \leq \mu \leq \bar{X} + 1.96\frac{\sigma}{\sqrt{n}}$$

EXAMPLE 24 *(Continued)*

covers 95 percent of the area under the normal curve. Therefore, the preceding interval provides a 95 percent confidence interval for μ. Plugging in the given values of $\bar{X}$, σ, and n, we obtain the 95 percent confidence interval as

$$66.51 \leq \mu \leq 67.49$$

In repeated such measurements, intervals thus established will include the true μ with 95 percent confidence. A technical point may be noted here. Although we can say that the probability that the random interval $[\bar{X} \pm 1.96(\sigma/\sqrt{n})]$ includes μ is 95 percent, we *cannot* say that the probability is 95 percent that the particular interval (66.51, 67.49) includes μ. Once this interval is fixed, the probability that it will include μ is either 0 or 1. What we can say is that if we construct 100 such intervals, 95 out of the 100 intervals will include the true μ; we cannot guarantee that one particular interval will necessarily include μ.

Methods of Estimation

Broadly speaking, there are three methods of parameter estimation: (1) least squares (LS), (2) maximum likelihood (ML), and (3) method of moments (MOM) and its extension, the generalized method of moments (GMM). We have devoted considerable time to illustrate the LS method. In Chapter 4 we introduced the ML method in the regression context. But the method is of much broader application.

The key idea behind the ML is the **likelihood function.** To illustrate this, suppose the random variable X has PDF $f(X,\theta)$ which depends on a single parameter θ. We know the PDF (e.g., Bernoulli or binomial) but do not know the parameter value. Suppose we obtain a random sample of nX values. The joint PDF of these n values is:

$$g(x_1, x_2, \ldots, x_n; \theta)$$

Because it is a random sample, we can write the preceding joint PDF as a product of the individual PDF as

$$g(x_1, x_2, \ldots, x_n; \theta) = f(x_1; \theta) f(x_2; \theta) \cdots f(x_n; \theta)$$

The joint PDF has a dual interpretation. If θ is known, we interpret it as the joint probability of observing the given sample values. On the other hand, we can treat it as a function of θ for given values of $x_1, x_2, \ldots, x_n$. On the latter interpretation, we call the joint PDF the **likelihood function (LF)** and write it as

$$L(\theta; x_1, x_2, \ldots, x_n) = f(x_1; \theta) f(x_2; \theta) \cdots f(x_n; \theta)$$

Observe the role reversal of θ in the joint probability density function and the likelihood function.

The ML estimator of θ is that value of θ that maximizes the (sample) likelihood function, L. For mathematical convenience, we often take the log of the likelihood, called the **log-likelihood function (log L).** Following the calculus rules of maximization, we differentiate the log-likelihood function with respect to the unknown and equate the resulting derivative to zero. The resulting value of the estimator is called the **maximum-likelihood estimator.** One can apply the second-order condition of maximization to assure that the value we have obtained is in fact the maximum value.

In case there is more than one unknown parameter, we differentiate the log-likelihood function with respect to each unknown, set the resulting expressions to zero, and solve them simultaneously to obtain the values of the unknown parameters. We have already shown this for the multiple regression model (see Chapter 4, Appendix 4A.1).

EXAMPLE 25 Assume that the random variable X follows the Poisson distribution with the mean value of λ. Suppose $x_1, x_2, \ldots, x_n$ are independent Poisson random variables each with mean λ. Suppose we want to find out the ML estimator of λ. The likelihood function here is:

$$L(x_1, x_2, \ldots, x_n; \lambda) = \frac{e^{-\lambda}\lambda^{x_1}}{x_1!}\frac{e^{-\lambda}\lambda^{x_2}}{x_2!}\cdots\frac{e^{-\lambda}\lambda^{x_n}}{x_n!}$$
$$= \frac{e^{-n\lambda}\lambda^{\Sigma x_i}}{x_1!x_2!\cdots x_n!}$$

This is a rather unwieldy expression, but if we take its log, it becomes

$$\log(x_1, x_2, \ldots, x_n; \lambda) = -n\lambda + \sum x_i \log\lambda - \log c$$

where $\log c = \prod x_i!$. Differentiating the preceding expression with respect to λ, we obtain $(-n + (\sum x_i)/\lambda)$. By setting this last expression to zero, we obtain $\lambda_{ml} = (\sum x_i)/n = \bar{X}$, which is the ML estimator of the unknown λ.

The Method of Moments

We have given a glimpse of MOM in Exercise 3.4 in the so-called **analogy principle** in which the sample moments try to duplicate the properties of their population counterparts. The generalized method of moments (GMM), which is a generalization of MOM, is now becoming more popular, but not at the introductory level. Hence we will not pursue it here.

The desirable statistical properties fall into two categories: small-sample, or finite-sample, properties and large-sample, or asymptotic, properties. Underlying both of these sets of properties is the notion that an estimator has a sampling, or probability, distribution.

Small-Sample Properties

Unbiasedness

An estimator $\hat{\theta}$ is said to be an unbiased estimator of θ if the expected value of $\hat{\theta}$ is equal to the true θ; that is,

$$E(\hat{\theta}) = \theta$$

or

$$E(\hat{\theta}) - \theta = 0$$

If this equality does not hold, then the estimator is said to be biased, and the bias is calculated as

$$\text{bias}(\hat{\theta}) = E(\hat{\theta}) - \theta$$

Of course, if $E(\hat{\theta}) = \theta$—that is, $\hat{\theta}$ is an unbiased estimator—the bias is zero.

Geometrically, the situation is as depicted in Figure A.8. In passing, note that unbiasedness is a property of repeated sampling, not of any given sample: Keeping the sample size fixed, we draw several samples, each time obtaining an estimate of the unknown parameter. The average value of these estimates is expected to be equal to the true value if the estimator is unbiased.

Minimum Variance

$\hat{\theta}_1$ is said to be a minimum-variance estimator of θ if the variance of $\hat{\theta}_1$ is smaller than or at most equal to the variance of $\hat{\theta}_2$, which is any other estimator of θ. Geometrically, we have

FIGURE A.8 Biased and unbiased estimators.

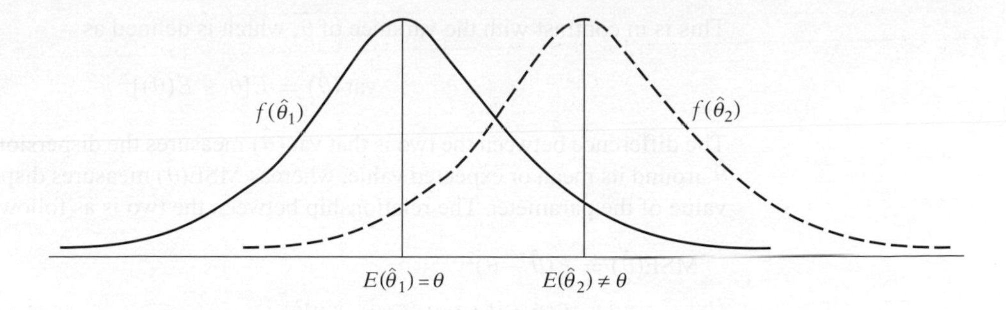

FIGURE A.9 Distribution of three estimators of θ.

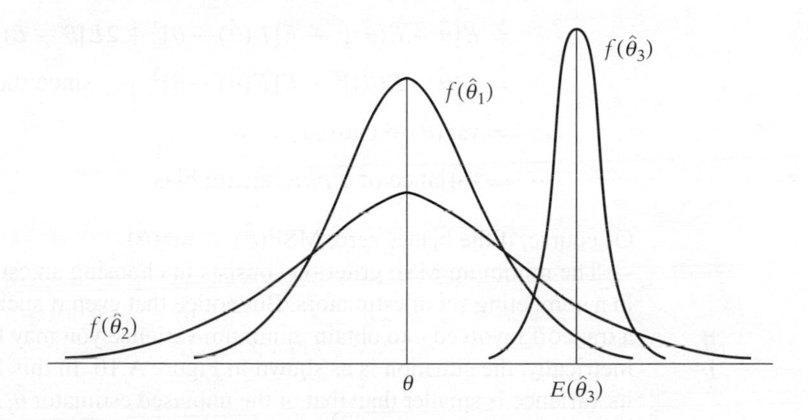

Figure A.9, which shows three estimators of θ, namely $\hat{\theta}_1$, $\hat{\theta}_2$, and $\hat{\theta}_3$, and their probability distributions. As shown, the variance of $\hat{\theta}_3$ is smaller than that of either $\hat{\theta}_1$ or $\hat{\theta}_2$. Hence, assuming only the three possible estimators, in this case $\hat{\theta}_3$ is a minimum-variance estimator. But note that $\hat{\theta}_3$ is a biased estimator (why?).

Best Unbiased, or Efficient, Estimator

If $\hat{\theta}_1$ and $\hat{\theta}_2$ are two *unbiased* estimators of θ, and the variance of $\hat{\theta}_1$ is smaller than or at most equal to the variance of $\hat{\theta}_2$, then $\hat{\theta}_1$ is a **minimum-variance unbiased,** or **best unbiased,** or **efficient, estimator.** Thus, in Figure A.9, of the two unbiased estimators $\hat{\theta}_1$ and $\hat{\theta}_2$, $\hat{\theta}_1$ is best unbiased, or efficient.

Linearity

An estimator $\hat{\theta}$ is said to be a linear estimator of θ if it is a linear function of the sample observations. Thus, the sample mean defined as

$$\bar{X} = \frac{1}{n}\sum X_i = \frac{1}{n}(x_1 + x_2 + \cdots + x_n)$$

is a linear estimator because it is a linear function of the X values.

Best Linear Unbiased Estimator (BLUE)

If $\hat{\theta}$ is linear, is unbiased, and has minimum variance in the class of all linear unbiased estimators of θ, then it is called a **best linear unbiased estimator,** or **BLUE** for short.

Minimum Mean-Square-Error (MSE) Estimator

The MSE of an estimator $\hat{\theta}$ is defined as

$$\text{MSE}(\hat{\theta}) = E(\hat{\theta} - \theta)^2$$

This is in contrast with the variance of $\hat{\theta}$, which is defined as

$$\text{var}(\hat{\theta}) = E[\hat{\theta} - E(\hat{\theta})]^2$$

The difference between the two is that var $(\hat{\theta})$ measures the dispersion of the distribution of $\hat{\theta}$ around its mean or expected value, whereas MSE$(\hat{\theta})$ measures dispersion around the true value of the parameter. The relationship between the two is as follows:

$$\begin{aligned}
\text{MSE}(\hat{\theta}) &= E(\hat{\theta} - \theta)^2 \\
&= E[\hat{\theta} - E(\hat{\theta}) + E(\hat{\theta}) - \theta]^2 \\
&= E[\hat{\theta} - E(\hat{\theta})]^2 + E[E(\hat{\theta}) - \theta]^2 + 2E[\hat{\theta} - E(\hat{\theta})][E(\hat{\theta}) - \theta] \\
&= E[\hat{\theta} - E(\hat{\theta})]^2 + E[E(\hat{\theta}) - \theta]^2 \qquad \text{since the last term is zero}^6 \\
&= \text{var}(\hat{\theta}) + \text{bias}(\hat{\theta})^2 \\
&= \text{variance of } \hat{\theta} \textit{ plus } \text{square bias}
\end{aligned}$$

Of course, if the bias is zero, MSE$(\hat{\theta}) = \text{var}(\hat{\theta})$.

The minimum MSE criterion consists in choosing an estimator whose MSE is the least in a competing set of estimators. But notice that even if such an estimator is found, there is a tradeoff involved—to obtain minimum variance you may have to accept some bias. Geometrically, the situation is as shown in Figure A.10. In this figure, $\hat{\theta}_2$ is slightly biased, but its variance is smaller than that of the unbiased estimator $\hat{\theta}_1$. In practice, however, the minimum MSE criterion is used when the best unbiased criterion is incapable of producing estimators with smaller variances.

Large-Sample Properties

It often happens that an estimator does not satisfy one or more of the desirable statistical properties in small samples. But as the sample size increases indefinitely, the estimator possesses several desirable statistical properties. These properties are known as the **large-sample,** or **asymptotic, properties.**

FIGURE A.10
Tradeoff between bias and variance.

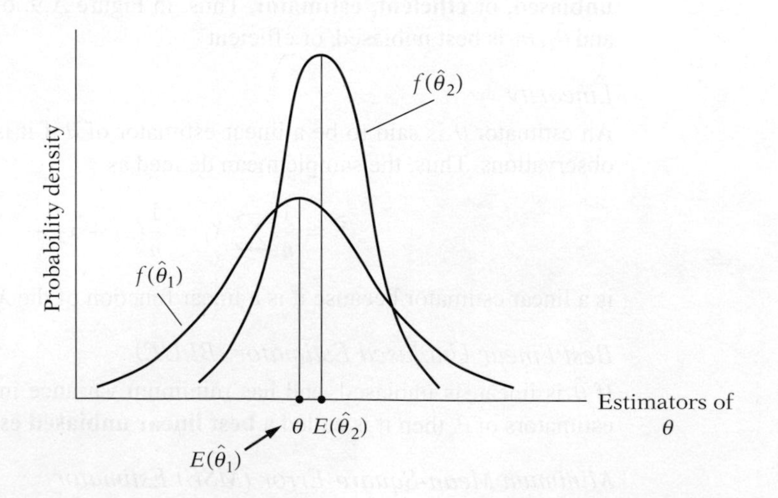

[6]The last term can be written as $2\{[E(\hat{\theta})]^2 - [E(\hat{\theta})]^2 - \theta E(\hat{\theta}) + \theta E(\hat{\theta})\} = 0$. Also note that $E[E(\hat{\theta}) - \theta]^2 = [E(\hat{\theta}) - \theta]^2$, since the expected value of a constant is simply the constant itself.

Asymptotic Unbiasedness

An estimator $\hat{\theta}$ is said to be an asymptotically unbiased estimator of θ if

$$\lim_{n\to\infty} E(\hat{\theta}_n) = \theta$$

where $\hat{\theta}_n$ means that the estimator is based on a sample size of n and where lim means limit and $n \to \infty$ means that n increases indefinitely. In words, $\hat{\theta}$ is an asymptotically unbiased estimator of θ if its expected, or mean, value approaches the true value as the sample size gets larger and larger. As an example, consider the following measure of the sample variance of a random variable X:

$$S^2 = \frac{\sum(X_i - \bar{X})^2}{n}$$

It can be shown that

$$E(S^2) = \sigma^2\left(1 - \frac{1}{n}\right)$$

where σ^2 is the true variance. It is obvious that in a small sample S^2 is biased, but as n increases indefinitely, $E(S^2)$ approaches true σ^2; hence it is asymptotically unbiased.

Consistency

$\hat{\theta}$ is said to be a consistent estimator if it approaches the true value θ as the sample size gets larger and larger. Figure A.11 illustrates this property.

In this figure we have the distribution of $\hat{\theta}$ based on sample sizes of 25, 50, 80, and 100. As the figure shows, $\hat{\theta}$ based on $n = 25$ is biased since its sampling distribution is not centered on the true θ. But as n increases, the distribution of $\hat{\theta}$ not only tends to be more closely centered on θ (i.e., $\hat{\theta}$ becomes less biased) but its variance also becomes smaller. If in the limit (i.e., when n increases indefinitely) the distribution of $\hat{\theta}$ collapses to the single point θ, that is, if the distribution of $\hat{\theta}$ has zero spread, or variance, we say that $\hat{\theta}$ is a **consistent estimator** of θ.

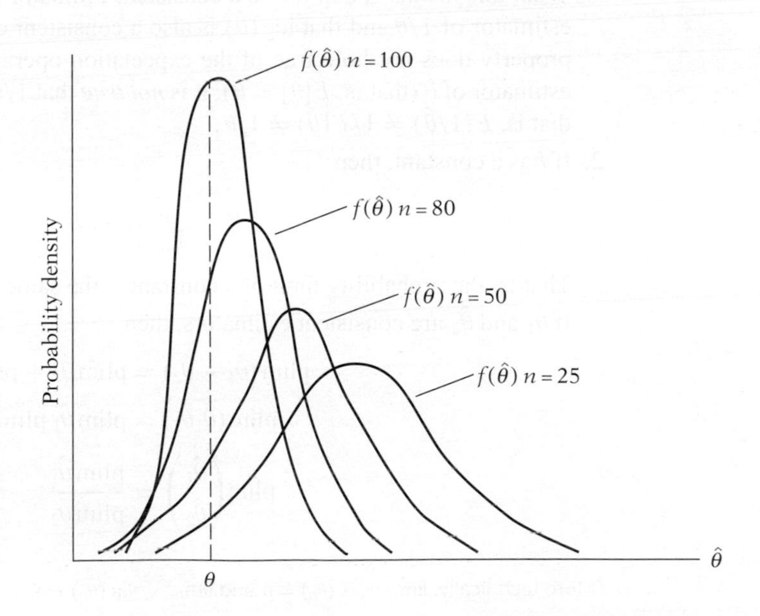

FIGURE A.11 The distribution of $\hat{\theta}$ as sample size increases.

More formally, an estimator $\hat{\theta}$ is said to be a consistent estimator of θ if the probability that the absolute value of the difference between $\hat{\theta}$ and θ is less than δ (an arbitrarily small positive quantity) approaches unity. Symbolically,

$$\lim_{n\to\infty} P\{|\hat{\theta} - \theta| < \delta\} = 1 \qquad \delta > 0$$

where P stands for probability. This is often expressed as

$$\underset{n\to\infty}{\text{plim}}\, \hat{\theta} = \theta$$

where plim means probability limit.

Note that the properties of unbiasedness and consistency are conceptually very different. The property of unbiasedness can hold for any sample size, whereas consistency is strictly a large-sample property.

A *sufficient condition* for consistency is that the bias and variance both tend to zero as the sample size increases indefinitely.[7] Alternatively, a sufficient condition for consistency is that the MSE($\hat{\theta}$) tends to zero as n increases indefinitely. (For MSE[$\hat{\theta}$], see the discussion presented previously.)

EXAMPLE 26

Let $X_1, X_2, \ldots, X_n$ be a random sample from a distribution with mean μ and variance σ^2. Show that the sample mean $\bar{X}$ is a consistent estimator of μ.

From elementary statistics it is known that $E(\bar{X}) = \mu$ and $\text{var}(\bar{X}) = \sigma^2/n$. Since $E(\bar{X}) = \mu$ regardless of the sample size, it is unbiased. Moreover, as n increases indefinitely, $\text{var}(\bar{X})$ tends toward zero. Hence, $\bar{X}$ is a consistent estimator of μ.

The following rules about probability limits are noteworthy.

1. *Invariance (Slutsky property).* If $\hat{\theta}$ is a consistent estimator of θ and if $h(\hat{\theta})$ is any continuous function of $\hat{\theta}$, then

$$\underset{n\to\infty}{\text{plim}}\, h(\hat{\theta}) = h(\theta)$$

What this means is that if $\hat{\theta}$ is a consistent estimator of θ, then $1/\hat{\theta}$ is also a consistent estimator of $1/\theta$ and that $\log(\hat{\theta})$ is also a consistent estimator of $\log(\theta)$. Note that this property does not hold true of the expectation operator E; that is, if $\hat{\theta}$ is an unbiased estimator of θ (that is, $E[\hat{\theta}] = \theta$), it is *not true* that $1/\hat{\theta}$ is an unbiased estimator of $1/\theta$; that is, $E(1/\hat{\theta}) \neq 1/E(\hat{\theta}) \neq 1/\theta$.

2. If b is a constant, then

$$\underset{n\to\infty}{\text{plim}}\, b = b$$

That is, the probability limit of a constant is the same constant.

3. If $\hat{\theta}_1$ and $\hat{\theta}_2$ are consistent estimators, then

$$\text{plim}\,(\hat{\theta}_1 + \hat{\theta}_2) = \text{plim}\,\hat{\theta}_1 + \text{plim}\,\hat{\theta}_2$$

$$\text{plim}\,(\hat{\theta}_1\hat{\theta}_2) = \text{plim}\,\hat{\theta}_1\ \text{plim}\,\hat{\theta}_2$$

$$\text{plim}\left(\frac{\hat{\theta}_1}{\hat{\theta}_2}\right) = \frac{\text{plim}\,\hat{\theta}_1}{\text{plim}\,\hat{\theta}_2}$$

[7]More technically, $\lim_{n\to\infty} E(\hat{\theta}_n) = \theta$ and $\lim_{n\to\infty} \text{var}(\hat{\theta}_n) = 0$.

The last two properties, in general, do not hold true of the expectation operator E. Thus, $E(\hat{\theta}_1/\hat{\theta}_2) \neq E(\hat{\theta}_1)/E(\hat{\theta}_2)$. Similarly, $E(\hat{\theta}_1\hat{\theta}_2) \neq E(\hat{\theta}_1)E(\hat{\theta}_2)$. If, however, $\hat{\theta}_1$ and $\hat{\theta}_2$ are independently distributed, $E(\hat{\theta}_1\hat{\theta}_2) = E(\hat{\theta}_1)E(\hat{\theta}_2)$, as noted previously.

Asymptotic Efficiency

Let $\hat{\theta}$ be an estimator of θ. The variance of the asymptotic distribution of $\hat{\theta}$ is called the **asymptotic variance** of $\hat{\theta}$. If $\hat{\theta}$ is consistent and its asymptotic variance is smaller than the asymptotic variance of all other consistent estimators of θ, $\hat{\theta}$ is called **asymptotically efficient.**

Asymptotic Normality

An estimator $\hat{\theta}$ is said to be asymptotically normally distributed if its sampling distribution tends to approach the normal distribution as the sample size n increases indefinitely. For example, statistical theory shows that if $X_1, X_2, \ldots, X_n$ are independent normally distributed variables with the same mean μ and the same variance σ^2, the sample mean $\bar{X}$ is also normally distributed with mean μ and variance σ^2/n in small as well as large samples. But if the X_i are independent with mean μ and variance σ^2 but are not necessarily from the normal distribution, then the sample mean $\bar{X}$ is asymptotically normally distributed with mean μ and variance σ^2/n; that is, as the sample size n increases indefinitely, the sample mean tends to be normally distributed with mean μ and variance σ^2/n. That is in fact the central limit theorem discussed previously.

A.8 Statistical Inference: Hypothesis Testing

Estimation and hypothesis testing constitute the twin branches of classical statistical inference. Having examined the problem of estimation, we briefly look at the problem of testing statistical hypotheses.

The problem of hypothesis testing may be stated as follows. Assume that we have an rv X with a known PDF $f(x;\theta)$, where θ is the parameter of the distribution. Having obtained a random sample of size n, we obtain the point estimator $\hat{\theta}$. Since the true θ is rarely known, we raise the question: Is the estimator $\hat{\theta}$ "compatible" with some hypothesized value of θ, say, $\theta = \theta^*$, where θ^* is a specific numerical value of θ? In other words, could our sample have come from the PDF $f(x;\theta) = \theta^*$? In the language of hypothesis testing $\theta = \theta^*$ is called the **null** (or maintained) **hypothesis** and is generally denoted by H_0. The null hypothesis is tested against an **alternative hypothesis,** denoted by H_1, which, for example, may state that $\theta \neq \theta^*$. (*Note:* In some textbooks, H_0 and H_1 are designated by H_1 and H_2, respectively.)

The null hypothesis and the alternative hypothesis can be **simple** or **composite.** A hypothesis is called *simple* if it specifies the value(s) of the parameter(s) of the distribution; otherwise it is called a *composite* hypothesis. Thus, if $X \sim N(\mu, \sigma^2)$ and we state that

$$H_0\colon \mu = 15 \qquad \text{and} \qquad \sigma = 2$$

it is a simple hypothesis, whereas

$$H_0\colon \mu = 15 \qquad \text{and} \qquad \sigma > 2$$

is a composite hypothesis because here the value of σ is not specified.

To test the null hypothesis (i.e., to test its validity), we use the sample information to obtain what is known as the **test statistic.** Very often this test statistic turns out to be the point estimator of the unknown parameter. Then we try to find out the *sampling,* or *probability, distribution* of the test statistic and use the **confidence interval** or **test of significance** approach to test the null hypothesis. The mechanics are illustrated below.

To fix the ideas, let us revert to Example 24, which was concerned with the height (X) of men in a population. We are told that

$$X_i \sim N(\mu, \sigma^2) = N(\mu, 2.5^2)$$

$$\bar{X} = 67 \qquad n = 100$$

Let us assume that

$$H_0: \mu = \mu^* = 69$$

$$H_1: \mu \neq 69$$

The question is: Could the sample with $\bar{X} = 67$, the test statistic, have come from the population with the mean value of 69? Intuitively, we may not reject the null hypothesis if $\bar{X}$ is "sufficiently close" to μ^*; otherwise we may reject it in favor of the alternative hypothesis. But how do we decide that $\bar{X}$ is "sufficiently close" to μ^*? We can adopt two approaches, (1) confidence interval and (2) test of significance, both leading to identical conclusions in any specific application.

The Confidence Interval Approach

Since $X_i \sim N(\mu, \sigma^2)$, we know that the test statistic $\bar{X}$ is distributed as

$$\bar{X} \sim N(\mu, \sigma^2/n)$$

Since we know the probability distribution of $\bar{X}$, why not establish, say, a $100(1-\alpha)$ confidence interval for μ based on $\bar{X}$ and see whether this confidence interval includes $\mu = \mu^*$? If it does, we may not reject the null hypothesis; if it does not, we may reject the null hypothesis. Thus, if $\alpha = 0.05$, we will have a 95 percent confidence interval and if this confidence interval includes μ^*, we may not reject the null hypothesis—95 out of 100 intervals thus established are likely to include μ^*.

The actual mechanics are as follows: since $\bar{X} \sim N(\mu, \sigma^2/n)$, it follows that

$$Z_i = \frac{\bar{X} - \mu}{\sigma/\sqrt{n}} \sim N(0, 1)$$

that is, a standard normal variable. Then from the normal distribution table we know that

$$\Pr(-1.96 \leq Z_i \leq 1.96) = 0.95$$

That is,

$$\Pr\left(-1.96 \leq \frac{\bar{X} - \mu}{\sigma/\sqrt{n}} \leq 1.96\right) = 0.95$$

which, on rearrangement, gives

$$\Pr\left[\bar{X} - 1.96\frac{\sigma}{\sqrt{n}} \leq \mu \leq \bar{X} + 1.96\frac{\sigma}{\sqrt{n}}\right] = 0.95$$

This is a 95 percent confidence interval for μ. Once this interval has been established, the test of the null hypothesis is simple. All that we have to do is to see whether $\mu = \mu^*$ lies in this interval. If it does, we may not reject the null hypothesis; if it does not, we may reject it.

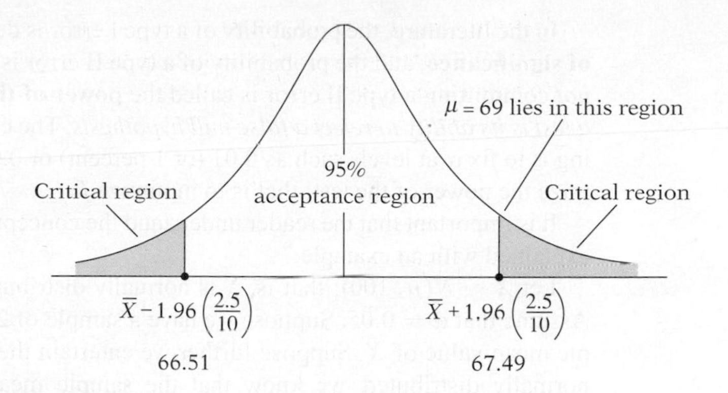

FIGURE A.12
95 percent confidence interval for μ.

Returning to Example 24, we have already established a 95 percent confidence interval for μ, which is

$$66.51 \le \mu \le 67.49$$

This interval obviously does not include $\mu = 69$. Therefore, we can reject the null hypothesis that the true μ is 69 with a 95 percent confidence coefficient. Geometrically, the situation is as depicted in Figure A.12.

In the language of hypothesis testing, the confidence interval that we have established is called the **acceptance region** and the area(s) outside the acceptance region is (are) called the **critical region(s),** or **region(s) of rejection** of the null hypothesis. The lower and upper limits of the acceptance region (which demarcate it from the rejection regions) are called the **critical values.** In this language of hypothesis testing, if the hypothesized value falls inside the acceptance region, one may not reject the null hypothesis; otherwise one may reject it.

It is important to note that in deciding to reject or not reject H_0, we are likely to commit two types of errors: (1) we may reject H_0 when it is, in fact, true; this is called a **type I error** (thus, in the preceding example $\bar{X} = 67$ could have come from the population with a mean value of 69), or (2) we may not reject H_0 when it is, in fact, false; this is called a **type II error.** Therefore, a hypothesis test does not establish the value of true μ. It merely provides a means of deciding whether we may act as if $\mu = \mu^*$.

Type I and Type II Errors

Schematically, we have

	State of Nature	
Decision	**H_0 Is True**	**H_0 Is False**
Reject	Type I error	No error
Do not reject	No error	Type II error

Ideally, we would like to minimize both type I and type II errors. But unfortunately, for any given sample size, it is not possible to minimize both the errors simultaneously. The classical approach to this problem, embodied in the work of Neyman and Pearson, is to assume that a type I error is likely to be more serious in practice than a type II error. Therefore, one should try to keep the probability of committing a type I error at a fairly low level, such as 0.01 or 0.05, and then try to minimize the probability of having a type II error as much as possible.

In the literature, the probability of a type I error is designated as α and is called the **level of significance,** and the probability of a type II error is designated as β. The probability of *not* committing a type II error is called the **power of the test.** *Put differently, the power of a test is its ability to reject a false null hypothesis.* The classical approach to hypothesis testing is to fix α at levels such as 0.01 (or 1 percent) or 0.05 (5 percent) and then try to maximize the power of the test; that is to minimize β.

It is important that the reader understand the concept of the power of a test, which is best explained with an example.[8]

Let $X \sim N(\mu, 100)$; that is, X is normally distributed with mean μ and variance 100. Assume that $\alpha = 0.05$. Suppose we have a sample of 25 observations, which gives a sample mean value of $\bar{X}$. Suppose further we entertain the hypothesis H_0: $\mu = 50$. Since X is normally distributed, we know that the sample mean is also normally distributed as: $\bar{X} \sim N(\mu, 100/25)$. Hence under the stated null hypothesis that $\mu = 50$, the 95 percent confidence interval for $\bar{X}$ is $(\mu \pm 1.96(\sqrt{100/25}) = \mu \pm 3.92$, that is, (46.08 to 53.92). Therefore, the critical region consists of all values of $\bar{X}$ less than 46.08 or greater than 53.92. That is, we will reject the null hypothesis that the true mean is 50 if a sample mean value is found below 46.08 or greater than 53.92.

But what is the probability that $\bar{X}$ will lie in the preceding critical region(s) if the true μ has a value different from 50? Suppose there are three alternative hypotheses: $\mu = 48$, $\mu = 52$, and $\mu = 56$. If any of these alternatives is true, it will be the actual mean of the distribution of X. The standard error is unchanged for the three alternatives since σ^2 is still assumed to be 100.

The shaded areas in Figure A.13 show the probabilities that $\bar{X}$ will fall in the critical region if each of the alternative hypotheses is true. As you can check, these probabilities

FIGURE A.13 Distribution of $\bar{X}$ when $N = 25$, $\sigma = 10$, and $\mu = 48, 50, 52$, or 56. Under H: $\mu = 50$, the critical region with $\alpha = 0.05$ is $\bar{X} < 46.1$ and $\bar{X} > 53.9$. The shaded area indicates the probability that $\bar{X}$ will fall into the critical region. This probability is:

0.17 if $\mu = 48$	0.17 if $\mu = 52$
0.05 if $\mu = 50$	0.85 if $\mu = 56$

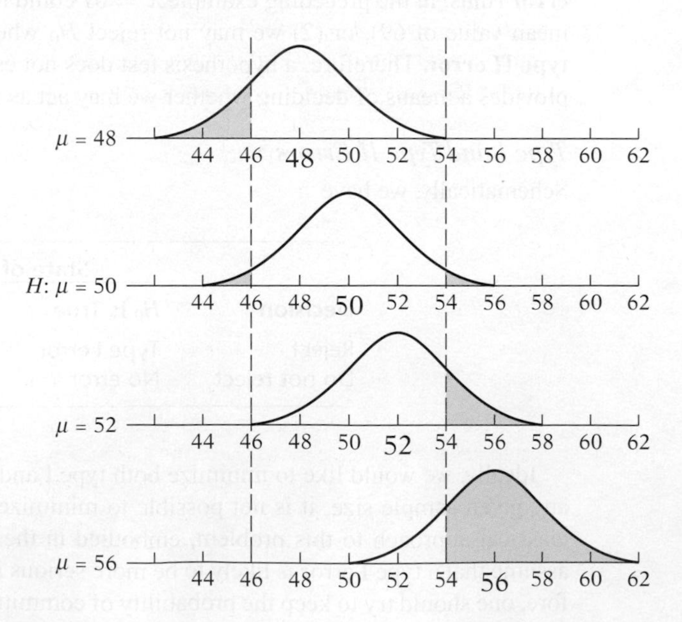

[8]The following discussion and the figures are based on Helen M. Walker and Joseph Lev, *Statistical Inference,* Holt, Rinehart and Winston, New York, 1953, pp. 161–162.

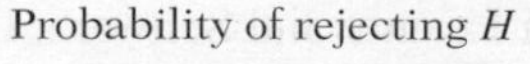

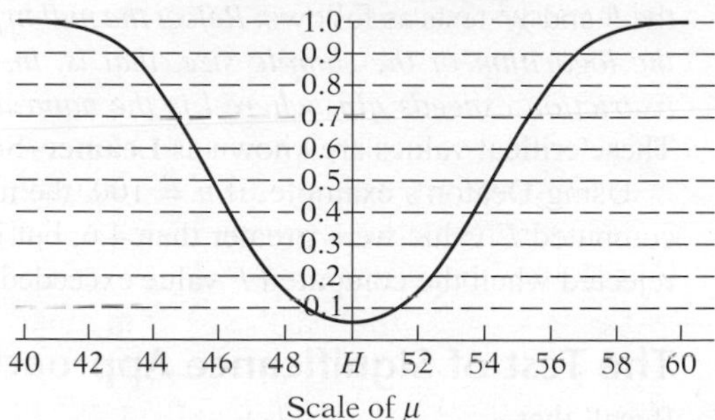

FIGURE A.14
Power function of test of hypothesis $\mu = 50$ when $N = 25$, $\sigma = 10$, and $\alpha = 0.05$.

are 0.17 (for $\mu = 48$), 0.05 (for $\mu = 50$), 0.17 (for $\mu = 52$) and 0.85 (for $\mu = 56$). As you can see from this figure, whenever the true value of μ differs substantially from the hypothesis under consideration (which here is $\mu = 50$), the probability of rejecting the hypothesis is high but when the true value is not very different from the value given under the null hypothesis, the probability of rejection is small. Intuitively, this should make sense if the null and alternative hypotheses are very closely bunched.

This can be seen further if you consider Figure A.14, which is called the **power function graph;** the curve shown there is called the **power curve.**

The reader will by now realize that the confidence coefficient $(1 - \alpha)$ discussed earlier is simply 1 minus the probability of committing a type I error. Thus a 95 percent confidence coefficient means that we are prepared to accept at the most a 5 percent probability of committing a type I error—we do not want to reject the true hypothesis by more than 5 out of 100 times.

The p Value, or Exact Level of Significance

Instead of preselecting α at arbitrary levels, such as 1, 5, or 10 percent, one can obtain the ***p* (probability) value,** or **exact level of significance** of a test statistic. The p value is defined as *the lowest significance level at which a null hypothesis can be rejected.*

Suppose that in an application involving 20 df we obtain a t value of 3.552. Now the p value, or the exact probability, of obtaining a t value of 3.552 or greater can be seen from Table D.2 as 0.001 (one-tailed) or 0.002 (two-tailed). We can say that the observed t value of 3.552 is statistically significant at the 0.001 or 0.002 level, depending on whether we are using a one-tail or two-tail test.

Several statistical packages now routinely print out the p value of the estimated test statistics. Therefore, the reader is advised to give the p value wherever possible.

Sample Size and Hypothesis Tests

In survey-type data involving hundreds of observations, the null hypothesis seems to be rejected more frequently than in small samples. It is worth quoting Angus Deaton here:

> As the sample size increases, and provided we are using a consistent estimation procedure, our estimates will be closer to the truth, and less dispersed around it, so that discrepancies that are undetectable with small sample size will lead to rejection in large samples. Large sample sizes are like greater resolving power on a telescope; features that are not visible from a distance become more and more sharply delineated as the magnification is turned up.[9]

[9]Angus Deaton, *The Analysis of Household Surveys: A Microeconometric Approach to Development Policy,* The Johns Hopkins University Press, Baltimore, 2000, p. 130.

Following Leamer and Schwarz, Deaton suggests adjusting the standard critical values of the F and χ^2 tests as follows: *Reject the null hypothesis when the computed F value exceeds the logarithm of the sample size, that is, ln, and when the computed χ^2 statistic for q restriction exceeds* ***qln****, where l is the natural logarithm and where n is the sample size.* These critical values are known as **Leamer–Schwarz** critical values.

Using Deaton's example, if $n = 100$, the null hypothesis would be rejected only if the computed F value were greater than 4.6, but if $n = 10{,}000$, the null hypothesis would be rejected when the computed F value exceeded 9.2.

The Test of Significance Approach

Recall that

$$Z_i = \frac{\bar{X} - \mu}{\sigma/\sqrt{n}} \sim N(0, 1)$$

In any given application, $\bar{X}$ and n are known (or can be estimated), but the true μ and σ are not known. But if σ is specified and we assume (under H_0) that $\mu = \mu^*$, a specific numerical value, then Z_i can be directly computed and we can easily look at the normal distribution table to find the probability of obtaining the computed Z value. If this probability is small, say, less than 5 percent or 1 percent, we can reject the null hypothesis—if the hypothesis were true, the chances of obtaining the particular Z value should be very high. This is the general idea behind the test of significance approach to hypothesis testing. The key idea here is the test statistic (here the Z statistic) and its probability distribution under the assumed value $\mu = \mu^*$. Appropriately, in the present case, the test is known as the ***Z* test,** since we use the Z (standardized normal) value.

Returning to our example, if $\mu = \mu^* = 69$, the Z statistic becomes

$$\begin{aligned} Z &= \frac{\bar{X} - \mu^*}{\sigma/\sqrt{n}} \\ &= \frac{67 - 69}{2.5/\sqrt{100}} \\ &= -2/0.25 = -8 \end{aligned}$$

If we look at the normal distribution table (Table D.1), we see that the probability of obtaining such a Z value is extremely small. (*Note:* The probability of a Z value exceeding 3 or -3 is about 0.001. Therefore, the probability of Z exceeding 8 is even smaller.) Therefore, we can reject the null hypothesis that $\mu = 69$; given this value, our chance of obtaining $\bar{X}$ of 67 is extremely small. We therefore doubt that our sample came from the population with a mean value of 69. Diagrammatically, the situation is depicted in Figure A.15.

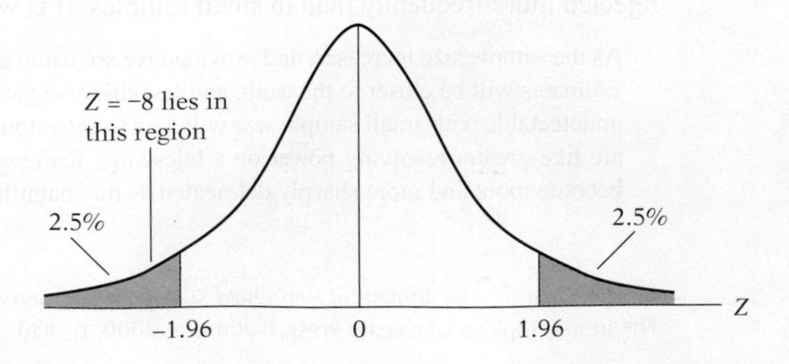

FIGURE A.15 The distribution of the Z statistic.

In the language of test of significance, when we say that a test (statistic) is significant, we generally mean that we can reject the null hypothesis. And the test statistic is regarded as significant if the probability of our obtaining it is equal to or less than α, the probability of committing a type I error. Thus if $\alpha = 0.05$, we know that the probability of obtaining a Z value of -1.96 or 1.96 is 5 percent (or 2.5 percent in each tail of the standardized normal distribution). In our illustrative example Z was -8. Hence the probability of obtaining such a Z value is much smaller than 2.5 percent, well below our prespecified probability of committing a type I error. That is why the computed value of $Z = -8$ is statistically significant; that is, we reject the null hypothesis that the true μ^* is 69. Of course, we reached the same conclusion using the confidence interval approach to hypothesis testing.

We now summarize the steps involved in testing a statistical hypothesis:

Step 1. State the null hypothesis H_0 and the alternative hypothesis H_1 (e.g., $H_0\colon \mu = 69$ and $H_1\colon \mu \neq 69$).

Step 2. Select the test statistic (e.g., $\bar{X}$).

Step 3. Determine the probability distribution of the test statistic (e.g.,$\bar{X} \sim N(\mu, \sigma^2/n)$.

Step 4. Choose the level of significance (i.e., the probability of committing a type I error) α.

Step 5. Using the probability distribution of the test statistic, establish a $100(1-\alpha)\%$ confidence interval. If the value of the parameter under the null hypothesis (e.g., $\mu = \mu^* = 69$) lies in this confidence region, the region of acceptance, do not reject the null hypothesis. But if it falls outside this interval (i.e., it falls into the region of rejection), you may reject the null hypothesis. Keep in mind that in not rejecting or rejecting a null hypothesis you are taking a chance of being wrong α percent of the time.

References

For the details of the material covered in this appendix, the reader may consult the following references:

Hoel, Paul G., *Introduction to Mathematical Statistics,* 4th ed., John Wiley & Sons, New York, 1974. This book provides a fairly simple introduction to various aspects of mathematical statistics.

Freund, John E., and Ronald E. Walpole, *Mathematical Statistics,* 3d ed., Prentice Hall, Englewood Cliffs, NJ, 1980. Another introductory textbook in mathematical statistics.

Mood, Alexander M., Franklin A. Graybill, and Duane C. Boes, *Introduction to the Theory of Statistics,* 3d ed., McGraw-Hill, New York, 1974. This is a comprehensive introduction to the theory of statistics but is somewhat more difficult than the preceding two textbooks.

Newbold, Paul, *Statistics for Business and Economics,* Prentice Hall, Englewood Cliffs, NJ, 1984. A comprehensive nonmathematical introduction to statistics with lots of worked-out problems.

Appendix B

Rudiments of Matrix Algebra

This appendix offers the essentials of matrix algebra required to understand Appendix C and some of the material in Chapter 18. The discussion is nonrigorous, and no proofs are given. For proofs and further details, the reader may consult the references.

B.1 Definitions

Matrix

A matrix is a rectangular array of numbers or elements arranged in rows and columns. More precisely, a matrix of **order,** or **dimension,** M by N (written as $M \times N$) is a set of $M \times N$ elements arranged in M rows and N columns. Thus, letting boldface letters denote matrices, an $(M \times N)$ matrix $\mathbf{A}$ may be expressed as

$$\mathbf{A} = [a_{ij}] = \begin{bmatrix} a_{11} & a_{12} & a_{13} & \cdots & a_{1N} \\ a_{21} & a_{22} & a_{23} & \cdots & a_{2N} \\ \cdots & \cdots & \cdots & \cdots & \cdots \\ a_{M1} & a_{M2} & a_{M3} & \cdots & a_{MN} \end{bmatrix}$$

where a_{ij} is the element appearing in the ith row and the jth column of $\mathbf{A}$ and where $[a_{ij}]$ is a shorthand expression for the matrix $\mathbf{A}$ whose typical element is a_{ij}. The order, or dimension, of a matrix—that is, the number of rows and columns—is often written underneath the matrix for easy reference.

$$\underset{2\times 3}{\mathbf{A}} = \begin{bmatrix} 2 & 3 & 5 \\ 6 & 1 & 3 \end{bmatrix} \qquad \underset{3\times 3}{\mathbf{B}} = \begin{bmatrix} 1 & 5 & 7 \\ -1 & 0 & 4 \\ 8 & 9 & 11 \end{bmatrix}$$

Scalar

A scalar is a single (real) number. Alternatively, a scalar is a 1×1 matrix.

Column Vector

A matrix consisting of M rows and only one column is called a **column vector.** Letting the boldface lowercase letters denote vectors, an example of a column vector is

$$\underset{4\times 1}{\mathbf{x}} = \begin{bmatrix} 3 \\ 4 \\ 5 \\ 9 \end{bmatrix}$$

Row Vector

A matrix consisting of only one row and N columns is called a **row vector.**

$$\underset{1\times 4}{\mathbf{x}} = [1 \quad 2 \quad 5 \quad -4] \qquad \underset{1\times 5}{\mathbf{y}} = [0 \quad 5 \quad -9 \quad 6 \quad 10]$$

Transposition

The transpose of an $M \times N$ matrix $\mathbf{A}$, denoted by $\mathbf{A}'$ (read as $\mathbf{A}$ prime or $\mathbf{A}$ transpose) is an $N \times M$ matrix obtained by interchanging the rows and columns of $\mathbf{A}$; that is, the ith row of $\mathbf{A}$ becomes the ith column of $\mathbf{A}'$. For example,

$$\underset{3\times 2}{\mathbf{A}} = \begin{bmatrix} 4 & 5 \\ 3 & 1 \\ 5 & 0 \end{bmatrix} \qquad \underset{2\times 3}{\mathbf{A}'} = \begin{bmatrix} 4 & 3 & 5 \\ 5 & 1 & 0 \end{bmatrix}$$

Since a vector is a special type of matrix, the transpose of a row vector is a column vector and the transpose of a column vector is a row vector. Thus

$$\mathbf{x} = \begin{bmatrix} 4 \\ 5 \\ 6 \end{bmatrix} \quad \text{and} \quad \mathbf{x}' = [4 \quad 5 \quad 6]$$

We shall follow the convention of indicating the row vectors by primes.

Submatrix

Given any $M \times N$ matrix $\mathbf{A}$, if all but r rows and s columns of $\mathbf{A}$ are deleted, the resulting matrix of order $r \times s$ is called a **submatrix** of $\mathbf{A}$. Thus, if

$$\underset{3\times 3}{\mathbf{A}} = \begin{bmatrix} 3 & 5 & 7 \\ 8 & 2 & 1 \\ 3 & 2 & 1 \end{bmatrix}$$

and we delete the third row and the third column of $\mathbf{A}$, we obtain

$$\underset{2\times 2}{\mathbf{B}} = \begin{bmatrix} 3 & 5 \\ 8 & 2 \end{bmatrix}$$

which is a submatrix of $\mathbf{A}$ whose order is 2×2.

B.2 Types of Matrices

Square Matrix

A matrix that has the same number of rows as columns is called a **square matrix.**

$$\mathbf{A} = \begin{bmatrix} 3 & 4 \\ 5 & 6 \end{bmatrix} \qquad \mathbf{B} = \begin{bmatrix} 3 & 5 & 8 \\ 7 & 3 & 1 \\ 4 & 5 & 0 \end{bmatrix}$$

Diagonal Matrix

A square matrix with at least one nonzero element on the main diagonal (running from the upper-left-hand corner to the lower-right-hand corner) and zeros elsewhere is called a **diagonal matrix.**

$$\underset{2\times 2}{\mathbf{A}} = \begin{bmatrix} 2 & 0 \\ 0 & 3 \end{bmatrix} \qquad \underset{3\times 3}{\mathbf{B}} = \begin{bmatrix} -2 & 0 & 0 \\ 0 & 5 & 0 \\ 0 & 0 & 1 \end{bmatrix}$$

Scalar Matrix

A diagonal matrix whose diagonal elements are all equal is called a **scalar matrix.** An example is the variance-covariance matrix of the population disturbance of the classical linear regression model given in Equation (C.2.3), namely,

$$\text{var-cov}(\mathbf{u}) = \begin{bmatrix} \sigma^2 & 0 & 0 & 0 & 0 \\ 0 & \sigma^2 & 0 & 0 & 0 \\ 0 & 0 & \sigma^2 & 0 & 0 \\ 0 & 0 & 0 & \sigma^2 & 0 \\ 0 & 0 & 0 & 0 & \sigma^2 \end{bmatrix}$$

Identity, or Unit, Matrix

A diagonal matrix whose diagonal elements are all 1 is called an **identity,** or **unit, matrix** and is denoted by **I**. It is a special kind of scalar matrix.

$$\underset{3\times 3}{\mathbf{I}} = \begin{bmatrix} 1 & 0 & 0 \\ 0 & 1 & 0 \\ 0 & 0 & 1 \end{bmatrix} \qquad \underset{4\times 4}{\mathbf{I}} = \begin{bmatrix} 1 & 0 & 0 & 0 \\ 0 & 1 & 0 & 0 \\ 0 & 0 & 1 & 0 \\ 0 & 0 & 0 & 1 \end{bmatrix}$$

Symmetric Matrix

A square matrix whose elements above the main diagonal are mirror images of the elements below the main diagonal is called a **symmetric matrix.** Alternatively, a symmetric matrix is such that its transpose is equal to itself; that is, $\mathbf{A} = \mathbf{A}'$. That is, the element a_{ij} of **A** is equal to the element a_{ji} of $\mathbf{A}'$. An example is the variance-covariance matrix given in Equation (C.2.2). Another example is the correlation matrix given in (C.5.1).

Null Matrix

A matrix whose elements are all zero is called a **null matrix** and is denoted by **0**.

Null Vector

A row or column vector whose elements are all zero is called a **null vector** and is also denoted by **0**.

Equal Matrices

Two matrices **A** and **B** are said to be equal if they are of the same order and their corresponding elements are equal; that is, $a_{ij} = b_{ij}$ for all i and j. For example, the matrices

$$\underset{3\times 3}{\mathbf{A}} = \begin{bmatrix} 3 & 4 & 5 \\ 0 & -1 & 2 \\ 5 & 1 & 3 \end{bmatrix} \quad \text{and} \quad \underset{3\times 3}{\mathbf{B}} = \begin{bmatrix} 3 & 4 & 5 \\ 0 & -1 & 2 \\ 5 & 1 & 3 \end{bmatrix}$$

are equal; that is $\mathbf{A} = \mathbf{B}$.

B.3 Matrix Operations

Matrix Addition

Let $\mathbf{A} = [a_{ij}]$ and $\mathbf{B} = [b_{ij}]$. If **A** and **B** are of the same order, we define matrix addition as

$$\mathbf{A} + \mathbf{B} = \mathbf{C}$$

where $\mathbf{C}$ is of the same order as $\mathbf{A}$ and $\mathbf{B}$ and is obtained as $c_{ij} = a_{ij} + b_{ij}$ for all i and j; that is, $\mathbf{C}$ is obtained by adding the corresponding elements of $\mathbf{A}$ and $\mathbf{B}$. If such addition can be effected, $\mathbf{A}$ and $\mathbf{B}$ are said to be *conformable* for addition. For example, if

$$\mathbf{A} = \begin{bmatrix} 2 & 3 & 4 & 5 \\ 6 & 7 & 8 & 9 \end{bmatrix} \quad \text{and} \quad \mathbf{B} = \begin{bmatrix} 1 & 0 & -1 & 3 \\ -2 & 0 & 1 & 5 \end{bmatrix}$$

and $\mathbf{C} = \mathbf{A} + \mathbf{B}$, then

$$\mathbf{C} = \begin{bmatrix} 3 & 3 & 3 & 8 \\ 4 & 7 & 9 & 14 \end{bmatrix}$$

Matrix Subtraction

Matrix subtraction follows the same principle as matrix addition except that $\mathbf{C} = \mathbf{A} - \mathbf{B}$; that is, we subtract the elements of $\mathbf{B}$ from the corresponding elements of $\mathbf{A}$ to obtain $\mathbf{C}$, provided $\mathbf{A}$ and $\mathbf{B}$ are of the same order.

Scalar Multiplication

To multiply a matrix $\mathbf{A}$ by a scalar λ (a real number), we multiply each element of the matrix by λ:

$$\lambda\mathbf{A} = [\lambda a_{ij}]$$

For example, if $\lambda = 2$ and

$$\mathbf{A} = \begin{bmatrix} -3 & 5 \\ 8 & 7 \end{bmatrix}$$

then

$$\lambda\mathbf{A} = \begin{bmatrix} -6 & 10 \\ 16 & 14 \end{bmatrix}$$

Matrix Multiplication

Let $\mathbf{A}$ be $M \times N$ and $\mathbf{B}$ be $N \times P$. Then the product $\mathbf{AB}$ (in that order) is defined to be a new matrix $\mathbf{C}$ of order $M \times P$ such that

$$c_{ij} = \sum_{k=1}^{N} a_{ik} b_{kj} \qquad \begin{array}{l} i = 1, 2, \ldots, M \\ j = 1, 2, \ldots, P \end{array}$$

That is, the element in the ith row and the jth column of $\mathbf{C}$ is obtained by multiplying the elements of the ith row of $\mathbf{A}$ by the corresponding elements of the jth column of $\mathbf{B}$ and summing over all terms; this is known as the *row by column* rule of multiplication. Thus, to obtain c_{11}, the element in the first row and the first column of $\mathbf{C}$, we multiply the elements in the first row of $\mathbf{A}$ by the corresponding elements in the first column of $\mathbf{B}$ and sum over all terms. Similarly, to obtain c_{12}, we multiply the elements in the first row of $\mathbf{A}$ by the corresponding elements in the second column of $\mathbf{B}$ and sum over all terms, and so on.

Note that for multiplication to exist, matrices $\mathbf{A}$ and $\mathbf{B}$ must be conformable with respect to multiplication; that is, the number of columns in $\mathbf{A}$ must be equal to the number of rows in $\mathbf{B}$. If, for example,

$$\underset{2\times3}{\mathbf{A}} = \begin{bmatrix} 3 & 4 & 7 \\ 5 & 6 & 1 \end{bmatrix} \quad \text{and} \quad \underset{3\times2}{\mathbf{B}} = \begin{bmatrix} 2 & 1 \\ 3 & 5 \\ 6 & 2 \end{bmatrix}$$

$$\mathbf{AB} = \underset{2\times2}{\mathbf{C}} = \begin{bmatrix} (3\times2)+(4\times3)+(7\times6) & (3\times1)+(4\times5)+(7\times2) \\ (5\times2)+(6\times3)+(1\times6) & (5\times1)+(6\times5)+(1\times2) \end{bmatrix}$$

$$= \begin{bmatrix} 60 & 37 \\ 34 & 37 \end{bmatrix}$$

But if

$$\underset{2\times 3}{\mathbf{A}} = \begin{bmatrix} 3 & 4 & 7 \\ 5 & 6 & 1 \end{bmatrix} \quad \text{and} \quad \underset{2\times 2}{\mathbf{B}} = \begin{bmatrix} 2 & 3 \\ 5 & 6 \end{bmatrix}$$

the product **AB** is not defined since **A** and **B** are not conformable with respect to multiplication.

Properties of Matrix Multiplication

1. Matrix multiplication is not necessarily *commutative;* that is, in general, $\mathbf{AB} \neq \mathbf{BA}$. Therefore, the order in which the matrices are multiplied is very important. **AB** means that **A** is *postmultiplied* by **B** or **B** is *premultiplied* by **A**.
2. Even if **AB** and **BA** exist, the resulting matrices may not be of the same order. Thus, if **A** is $M \times N$ and **B** is $N \times M$, **AB** is $M \times M$ whereas **BA** is $N \times N$, hence of different order.
3. Even if **A** and **B** are both square matrices, so that **AB** and **BA** are both defined, the resulting matrices will not be necessarily equal. For example, if

$$\mathbf{A} = \begin{bmatrix} 4 & 7 \\ 3 & 2 \end{bmatrix} \quad \text{and} \quad \mathbf{B} = \begin{bmatrix} 1 & 5 \\ 6 & 8 \end{bmatrix}$$

then

$$\mathbf{AB} = \begin{bmatrix} 46 & 76 \\ 15 & 31 \end{bmatrix} \quad \text{and} \quad \mathbf{BA} = \begin{bmatrix} 19 & 17 \\ 48 & 58 \end{bmatrix}$$

and $\mathbf{AB} \neq \mathbf{BA}$. An example of $\mathbf{AB} = \mathbf{BA}$ is when both **A** and **B** are identity matrices.

4. A row vector postmultiplied by a column vector is a scalar. Thus, consider the ordinary least-squares residuals $\hat{u}_1, \hat{u}_2, \ldots, \hat{u}_n$. Letting **u** be a column vector and $\mathbf{u}'$ be a row vector, we have

$$\begin{aligned} \hat{\mathbf{u}}'\hat{\mathbf{u}} &= [\hat{u}_1 \quad \hat{u}_2 \quad \hat{u}_3 \quad \cdots \quad \hat{u}_n] \begin{bmatrix} \hat{u}_1 \\ \hat{u}_2 \\ \hat{u}_3 \\ \vdots \\ \hat{u}_n \end{bmatrix} \\ &= \hat{u}_1^2 + \hat{u}_2^2 + \hat{u}_3^2 + \cdots + \hat{u}_n'^2 \\ &= \sum \hat{u}_i^2 \quad \text{a scalar [see Eq. (C.3.5)]} \end{aligned}$$

5. A column vector postmultiplied by a row vector is a matrix. As an example, consider the population disturbances of the classical linear regression model, namely, $u_1, u_2, \ldots, u_n$. Letting **u** be a column vector and $\mathbf{u}'$ a row vector, we obtain

$$\begin{aligned} \mathbf{uu}' &= \begin{bmatrix} u_1 \\ u_2 \\ u_3 \\ \vdots \\ u_n \end{bmatrix} [u_1 \quad u_2 \quad u_3 \quad \cdots \quad u_n] \\ &= \begin{bmatrix} u_1^2 & u_1u_2 & u_1u_3 & \cdots & u_1u_n \\ u_2u_1 & u_2^2 & u_2u_3 & \cdots & u_2u_n \\ \cdots & \cdots & \cdots & \cdots & \cdots \\ u_nu_1 & u_nu_2 & u_nu_3 & \cdots & u_n^2 \end{bmatrix} \end{aligned}$$

which is a matrix of order $n \times n$. Note that the preceding matrix is symmetrical.

6. A matrix postmultiplied by a column vector is a column vector.
7. A row vector postmultiplied by a matrix is a row vector.
8. Matrix multiplication is *associative;* that is, $(\mathbf{AB})\mathbf{C} = \mathbf{A}(\mathbf{BC})$, where $\mathbf{A}$ is $M \times N$, $\mathbf{B}$ is $N \times P$, and $\mathbf{C}$ is $P \times K$.
9. Matrix multiplication is distributive with respect to addition; that is, $\mathbf{A}(\mathbf{B} + \mathbf{C}) = \mathbf{AB} + \mathbf{AC}$ and $(\mathbf{B} + \mathbf{C})\mathbf{A} = \mathbf{BA} + \mathbf{CA}$.

Matrix Transposition

We have already defined the process of matrix transposition as interchanging the rows and the columns of a matrix (or a vector). We now state some of the properties of transposition.

1. The transpose of a transposed matrix is the original matrix itself. Thus, $(\mathbf{A}')' = \mathbf{A}$.
2. If $\mathbf{A}$ and $\mathbf{B}$ are conformable for addition, then $\mathbf{C} = \mathbf{A} + \mathbf{B}$ and $\mathbf{C}' = (\mathbf{A} + \mathbf{B})' = \mathbf{A}' + \mathbf{B}'$. That is, the transpose of the sum of two matrices is the sum of their transposes.
3. If $\mathbf{AB}$ is defined, then $(\mathbf{AB})' = \mathbf{B}'\mathbf{A}'$. That is, the transpose of the product of two matrices is the product of their transposes in the reverse order. This can be generalized: $(\mathbf{ABCD})' = \mathbf{D}'\mathbf{C}'\mathbf{B}'\mathbf{A}'$.
4. The transpose of an identity matrix $\mathbf{I}$ is the identity matrix itself; that is $\mathbf{I}' = \mathbf{I}$.
5. The transpose of a scalar is the scalar itself. Thus, if λ is a scalar, $\lambda' = \lambda$.
6. The transpose of $(\lambda\mathbf{A})'$ is $\lambda\mathbf{A}'$ where λ is a scalar. [*Note:* $(\lambda\mathbf{A})' = \mathbf{A}'\lambda' = \mathbf{A}'\lambda = \lambda\mathbf{A}'$.]
7. If $\mathbf{A}$ is a square matrix such that $\mathbf{A} = \mathbf{A}'$, then $\mathbf{A}$ is a symmetric matrix. (See the definition of symmetric matrix given in Section B.2.)

Matrix Inversion

An inverse of a square matrix $\mathbf{A}$, denoted by $\mathbf{A}^{-1}$ (read $\mathbf{A}$ inverse), if it exists, is a unique square matrix such that

$$\mathbf{AA}^{-1} = \mathbf{A}^{-1}\mathbf{A} = \mathbf{I}$$

where $\mathbf{I}$ is an identity matrix whose order is the same as that of $\mathbf{A}$. For example

$$\mathbf{A} = \begin{bmatrix} 2 & 4 \\ 6 & 8 \end{bmatrix} \qquad \mathbf{A}^{-1} = \begin{bmatrix} -1 & \frac{1}{2} \\ \frac{6}{8} & -\frac{1}{4} \end{bmatrix} \qquad \mathbf{AA}^{-1} = \begin{bmatrix} 1 & 0 \\ 0 & 1 \end{bmatrix} = \mathbf{I}$$

We shall see how $\mathbf{A}^{-1}$ is computed after we study the topic of determinants. In the meantime, note these properties of the inverse.

1. $(\mathbf{AB})^{-1} = \mathbf{B}^{-1}\mathbf{A}^{-1}$; that is, the inverse of the product of two matrices is the product of their inverses in the reverse order.
2. $(\mathbf{A}^{-1})' = (\mathbf{A}')^{-1}$; that is, the transpose of $\mathbf{A}$ inverse is the inverse of $\mathbf{A}$ transpose.

B.4 Determinants

To every square matrix, $\mathbf{A}$, there corresponds a number (scalar) known as the determinant of the matrix, which is denoted by det $\mathbf{A}$ or by the symbol $|\mathbf{A}|$, where $|\;|$ means "the determinant of." Note that a matrix per se has no numerical value, but the determinant of a matrix is a number.

$$\mathbf{A} = \begin{bmatrix} 1 & 3 & -7 \\ 2 & 5 & 0 \\ 3 & 8 & 6 \end{bmatrix} \qquad |\mathbf{A}| = \begin{vmatrix} 1 & 3 & -7 \\ 2 & 5 & 0 \\ 3 & 8 & 6 \end{vmatrix}$$

The $|\mathbf{A}|$ in this example is called a determinant of order 3 because it is associated with a matrix of order 3×3.

Evaluation of a Determinant

The process of finding the value of a determinant is known as the *evaluation, expansion,* or *reduction* of the determinant. This is done by manipulating the entries of the matrix in a well-defined manner.

Evaluation of a 2 × 2 Determinant

If

$$\mathbf{A} = \begin{bmatrix} a_{11} & a_{12} \\ a_{21} & a_{22} \end{bmatrix}$$

its determinant is evaluated as follows:

$$|\mathbf{A}| = \begin{vmatrix} a_{11} & a_{12} \\ a_{21} & a_{22} \end{vmatrix} = a_{11}a_{22} - a_{12}a_{21}$$

which is obtained by cross-multiplying the elements on the main diagonal and subtracting from it the cross-multiplication of the elements on the other diagonal of matrix **A**, as indicated by the arrows.

Evaluation of a 3 × 3 Determinant

If

$$\mathbf{A} = \begin{bmatrix} a_{11} & a_{12} & a_{13} \\ a_{21} & a_{22} & a_{23} \\ a_{31} & a_{32} & a_{33} \end{bmatrix}$$

then

$$|\mathbf{A}| = a_{11}a_{22}a_{33} - a_{11}a_{23}a_{32} + a_{12}a_{23}a_{31} - a_{12}a_{21}a_{33} + a_{13}a_{21}a_{32} - a_{13}a_{22}a_{31}$$

A careful examination of the evaluation of a 3×3 determinant shows:

1. Each term in the expansion of the determinant contains one and only one element from each row and each column.
2. The number of elements in each term is the same as the number of rows (or columns) in the matrix. Thus, a 2×2 determinant has two elements in each term of its expansion, a 3×3 determinant has three elements in each term of its expansion, and so on.
3. The terms in the expansion alternate in sign from + to −.
4. A 2×2 determinant has two terms in its expansion, and a 3×3 determinant has six terms in its expansion. The general rule is: The determinant of order $N \times N$ has $N! = N(N-1)(N-2)\cdots 3 \cdot 2 \cdot 1$ terms in its expansion, where $N!$ is read "N factorial." Following this rule, a determinant of order 5×5 will have $5 \cdot 4 \cdot 3 \cdot 2 \cdot 1 = 120$ terms in its expansion.[1]

Properties of Determinants

1. A matrix whose determinantal value is zero is called a **singular matrix,** whereas a matrix with a nonzero determinant is called a **nonsingular matrix.** The inverse of a matrix as defined before does not exist for a singular matrix.

[1]To evaluate the determinant of an $N \times N$ matrix, **A**, see the references

2. If all the elements of any row of **A** are zero, its determinant is zero. Thus,

$$|\mathbf{A}| = \begin{vmatrix} 0 & 0 & 0 \\ 3 & 4 & 5 \\ 6 & 7 & 8 \end{vmatrix} = 0$$

3. $|\mathbf{A}'| = |\mathbf{A}|$; that is, the determinants of **A** and **A** transpose are the same.
4. Interchanging any two rows or any two columns of a matrix **A** changes the sign of $|\mathbf{A}|$.

EXAMPLE 1

If

$$\mathbf{A} = \begin{bmatrix} 6 & 9 \\ -1 & 4 \end{bmatrix} \quad \text{and} \quad \mathbf{B} = \begin{bmatrix} -1 & 4 \\ 6 & 9 \end{bmatrix}$$

where **B** is obtained by interchanging the rows of **A**, then

$$|\mathbf{A}| = 24 - (-9) \quad \text{and} \quad |\mathbf{B}| = -9 - (24)$$
$$= 33 \qquad\qquad = -33$$

5. If every element of a row or a column of **A** is multiplied by a scalar λ, then $|\mathbf{A}|$ is multiplied by λ.

EXAMPLE 2

If

$$\lambda = 5 \quad \text{and} \quad \mathbf{A} = \begin{bmatrix} 5 & -8 \\ 2 & 4 \end{bmatrix}$$

and we multiply the first row of **A** by 5 to obtain

$$\mathbf{B} = \begin{bmatrix} 25 & -40 \\ 2 & 4 \end{bmatrix}$$

it can be seen that $|\mathbf{A}| = 36$ and $|\mathbf{B}| = 180$, which is $5\,|\mathbf{A}|$.

6. If two rows or columns of a matrix are identical, its determinant is zero.
7. If one row or a column of a matrix is a multiple of another row or column of that matrix, its determinant is zero. Thus, if

$$\mathbf{A} = \begin{bmatrix} 4 & 8 \\ 2 & 4 \end{bmatrix}$$

where the first row of **A** is twice its second row, $|\mathbf{A}| = 0$. More generally, if any row (column) of a matrix is a linear combination of other rows (columns), its determinant is zero.

8. $|\mathbf{AB}| = |\mathbf{A}||\mathbf{B}|$; that is, the determinant of the product of two matrices is the product of their (individual) determinants.

Rank of a Matrix

The rank of a matrix is the order of the largest square submatrix whose determinant is not zero.

EXAMPLE 3

$$\mathbf{A} = \begin{bmatrix} 3 & 6 & 6 \\ 0 & 4 & 5 \\ 3 & 2 & 1 \end{bmatrix}$$

It can be seen that $|\mathbf{A}| = 0$. In other words, **A** is a singular matrix. Hence although its order is 3×3, its rank is less than 3. Actually, it is 2, because we can find a 2×2 submatrix whose determinant is not zero. For example, if we delete the first row and the first column of **A**, we obtain

$$\mathbf{B} = \begin{bmatrix} 4 & 5 \\ 2 & 1 \end{bmatrix}$$

whose determinant is -6, which is nonzero. Hence the rank of **A** is 2. As noted previously, the inverse of a singular matrix does not exist. Therefore, for an $N \times N$ matrix **A**, its rank must be N for its inverse to exist; if it is less than N, **A** is singular.

Minor

If the ith row and jth column of an $N \times N$ matrix **A** are deleted, the determinant of the resulting submatrix is called the **minor** of the element a_{ij} (the element at the intersection of the ith row and the jth column) and is denoted by $|\mathbf{M}_{ij}|$.

EXAMPLE 4

$$\mathbf{A} = \begin{bmatrix} a_{11} & a_{12} & a_{13} \\ a_{21} & a_{22} & a_{23} \\ a_{31} & a_{32} & a_{33} \end{bmatrix}$$

The minor of a_{11} is

$$|\mathbf{M}_{11}| = \begin{vmatrix} a_{22} & a_{23} \\ a_{32} & a_{33} \end{vmatrix} = a_{22}a_{33} - a_{23}a_{32}$$

Similarly, the minor of a_{21} is

$$|\mathbf{M}_{21}| = \begin{vmatrix} a_{12} & a_{13} \\ a_{32} & a_{33} \end{vmatrix} = a_{12}a_{33} - a_{13}a_{32}$$

The minors of other elements of **A** can be found similarly.

Cofactor

The cofactor of the element a_{ij} of an $N \times N$ matrix **A**, denoted by c_{ij}, is defined as

$$c_{ij} = (-1)^{i+j}|\mathbf{M_{ij}}|$$

In other words, a cofactor is a *signed* minor, the sign being positive if $i + j$ is even and being negative if $i + j$ is odd. Thus, the cofactor of the element a_{11} of the 3×3 matrix **A** given previously is $a_{22}a_{33} - a_{23}a_{32}$, whereas the cofactor of the element a_{21} is $-(a_{12}a_{33} - a_{13}a_{32})$ since the sum of the subscripts 2 and 1 is 3, which is an odd number.

Cofactor Matrix

Replacing the elements a_{ij} of a matrix **A** by their cofactors, we obtain a matrix known as the **cofactor matrix** of **A**, denoted by (cof **A**).

Adjoint Matrix

The adjoint matrix, written as (adj **A**), is the transpose of the cofactor matrix; that is, (adj **A**) = (cof **A**)′.

B.5 Finding the Inverse of a Square Matrix

If **A** is square and nonsingular (that is, $|\mathbf{A}| \neq 0$), its inverse $\mathbf{A}^{-1}$ can be found as follows:

$$\mathbf{A}^{-1} = \frac{1}{|\mathbf{A}|}(\text{adj } \mathbf{A})$$

The steps involved in the computation are as follows:

1. Find the determinant of **A**. If it is nonzero, proceed to step 2.
2. Replace each element a_{ij} of **A** by its cofactor to obtain the cofactor matrix.
3. Transpose the cofactor matrix to obtain the adjoint matrix.
4. Divide each element of the adjoint matrix by $|\mathbf{A}|$.

EXAMPLE 5 Find the inverse of the matrix

$$\mathbf{A} = \begin{bmatrix} 1 & 2 & 3 \\ 5 & 7 & 4 \\ 2 & 1 & 3 \end{bmatrix}$$

Step 1. We first find the determinant of the matrix. Applying the rules of expanding a 3×3 determinant given previously, we obtain $|\mathbf{A}| = -24$.

Step 2. We now obtain the cofactor matrix, say, **C**:

$$\mathbf{C} = \begin{bmatrix} \begin{vmatrix} 7 & 4 \\ 1 & 3 \end{vmatrix} & -\begin{vmatrix} 5 & 4 \\ 2 & 3 \end{vmatrix} & \begin{vmatrix} 5 & 7 \\ 2 & 1 \end{vmatrix} \\ -\begin{vmatrix} 2 & 3 \\ 1 & 3 \end{vmatrix} & \begin{vmatrix} 1 & 3 \\ 2 & 3 \end{vmatrix} & -\begin{vmatrix} 1 & 2 \\ 2 & 1 \end{vmatrix} \\ \begin{vmatrix} 2 & 3 \\ 7 & 4 \end{vmatrix} & -\begin{vmatrix} 1 & 3 \\ 5 & 4 \end{vmatrix} & \begin{vmatrix} 1 & 2 \\ 5 & 7 \end{vmatrix} \end{bmatrix}$$

$$= \begin{bmatrix} 17 & -7 & -9 \\ -3 & -3 & 3 \\ -13 & 11 & -3 \end{bmatrix}$$

Step 3. Transposing the preceding cofactor matrix, we obtain the following adjoint matrix:

$$(\text{adj } \mathbf{A}) = \begin{bmatrix} 17 & -3 & -13 \\ -7 & -3 & 11 \\ -9 & 3 & -3 \end{bmatrix}$$

Step 4. We now divide the elements of (adj **A**) by the determinantal value of -24 to obtain

$$\mathbf{A}^{-1} = -\frac{1}{24}\begin{bmatrix} 17 & -3 & -13 \\ -7 & -3 & 11 \\ -9 & 3 & -3 \end{bmatrix}$$

$$= \begin{bmatrix} -\frac{17}{24} & \frac{3}{24} & \frac{13}{24} \\ \frac{7}{24} & \frac{3}{24} & -\frac{11}{24} \\ \frac{9}{24} & -\frac{3}{24} & \frac{3}{24} \end{bmatrix}$$

It can be readily verified that

$$\mathbf{AA}^{-1} = \begin{bmatrix} 1 & 0 & 0 \\ 0 & 1 & 0 \\ 0 & 0 & 1 \end{bmatrix}$$

which is an identity matrix. The reader should verify that for the illustrative example given in Appendix C (see Section C.10) the inverse of the $\mathbf{X}'\mathbf{X}$ matrix is as shown in Eq. (C.10.5).

B.6 Matrix Differentiation

To follow the material in Appendix CA, Section CA.2, we need some rules regarding matrix differentiation.

RULE 1

If $\mathbf{a}' = [a_1 \quad a_2 \quad \cdots \quad a_n]$ is a row vector of numbers, and

$$\mathbf{x} = \begin{bmatrix} x_1 \\ x_2 \\ \vdots \\ x_n \end{bmatrix}$$

is a column vector of the variables $x_1, x_2, \ldots, x_n$, then

$$\frac{\partial(\mathbf{a}'\mathbf{x})}{\partial \mathbf{x}} = \mathbf{a} = \begin{bmatrix} a_1 \\ a_2 \\ \vdots \\ a_n \end{bmatrix}$$

RULE 2

Consider the matrix $\mathbf{x}'\mathbf{A}\mathbf{x}$ such that

$$\mathbf{x}'\mathbf{A}\mathbf{x} = [x_1 \quad x_2 \quad \cdots \quad x_n] \begin{bmatrix} a_{11} & a_{12} & \cdots & a_{1n} \\ a_{21} & a_{22} & \cdots & a_{2n} \\ \cdots & \cdots & \cdots & \cdots \\ a_{n1} & a_{n2} & & a_{nn} \end{bmatrix} \begin{bmatrix} x_1 \\ x_2 \\ \vdots \\ x_n \end{bmatrix}$$

Then

$$\frac{\partial(\mathbf{x}'\mathbf{A}\mathbf{x})}{\partial \mathbf{x}} = 2\mathbf{A}\mathbf{x}$$

which is a column vector of n elements, or

$$\frac{\partial(\mathbf{x}'\mathbf{A}\mathbf{x})}{\partial \mathbf{x}} = 2\mathbf{x}'\mathbf{A}$$

which is a row vector of n elements.

References

Chiang, Alpha C., *Fundamental Methods of Mathematical Economics,* 3d ed., McGraw-Hill, New York, 1984, chapters 4 and 5. This is an elementary discussion.

Hadley, G., *Linear Algebra,* Addison-Wesley, Reading, Mass., 1961. This is an advanced discussion.

Appendix C

The Matrix Approach to Linear Regression Model

This appendix presents the classical linear regression model involving k variables (Y and $X_2, X_3, \ldots, X_k$) in matrix algebra notation. Conceptually, the k-variable model is a logical extension of the two- and three-variable models considered thus far in this text. Therefore, this appendix presents very few new concepts save for the matrix notation.[1]

A great advantage of matrix algebra over scalar algebra (elementary algebra dealing with scalars or real numbers) is that it provides a compact method of handling regression models involving any number of variables; once the k-variable model is formulated and solved in matrix notation, the solution applies to one, two, three, or any number of variables.

C.1 The k-Variable Linear Regression Model

If we generalize the two- and three-variable linear regression models, the k-variable population regression function (PRF) model involving the dependent variable Y and $k - 1$ explanatory variables $X_2, X_3, \ldots, X_k$ may be written as

$$\text{PRF:}\quad Y_i = \beta_1 + \beta_2 X_{2i} + \beta_3 X_{3i} + \cdots + \beta_k X_{ki} + u_i \qquad i = 1, 2, 3, \ldots, n \tag{C.1.1}$$

where β_1 = the intercept, β_2 to β_k = partial slope coefficients, u = stochastic disturbance term, and i = ith observation, n being the size of the population. The PRF (C.1.1) is to be interpreted in the usual manner: It gives the mean or expected value of Y conditional upon the fixed (in repeated sampling) values of $X_2, X_3, \ldots, X_k$, that is, $E(Y \mid X_{2i}, X_{3i}, \ldots, X_{ki})$.

[1]Readers not familiar with matrix algebra should review **Appendix B** before proceeding any further. **Appendix B** provides the essentials of matrix algebra needed to follow this appendix.

Equation (C.1.1) is a shorthand expression for the following set of n simultaneous equations:

$$\begin{aligned} Y_1 &= \beta_1 + \beta_2 X_{21} + \beta_3 X_{31} + \cdots + \beta_k X_{k1} + u_1 \\ Y_2 &= \beta_1 + \beta_2 X_{22} + \beta_3 X_{32} + \cdots + \beta_k X_{k2} + u_2 \\ &\cdots\cdots\cdots\cdots\cdots\cdots\cdots\cdots\cdots\cdots \\ Y_n &= \beta_1 + \beta_2 X_{2n} + \beta_3 X_{3n} + \cdots + \beta_k X_{kn} + u_n \end{aligned} \tag{C.1.2}$$

Let us write the system of equations (C.1.2) in an alternative but more illuminating way as follows:[2]

$$\begin{bmatrix} Y_1 \\ Y_2 \\ \vdots \\ Y_n \end{bmatrix} = \begin{bmatrix} 1 & X_{21} & X_{31} & \cdots & X_{k1} \\ 1 & X_{22} & X_{32} & \cdots & X_{k2} \\ \vdots & \vdots & \vdots & \ddots & \vdots \\ 1 & X_{2n} & X_{3n} & \cdots & X_{kn} \end{bmatrix} \begin{bmatrix} \beta_1 \\ \beta_2 \\ \vdots \\ \beta_k \end{bmatrix} + \begin{bmatrix} u_1 \\ u_2 \\ \vdots \\ u_n \end{bmatrix} \tag{C.1.3}$$

$$\underset{n \times 1}{\mathbf{y}} = \underset{n \times k}{\mathbf{X}} \quad \underset{k \times 1}{\boldsymbol{\beta}} + \underset{n \times 1}{\mathbf{u}}$$

where $\mathbf{y} = n \times 1$ column vector of observations on the dependent variable Y
$\mathbf{X} = n \times k$ matrix giving n observations on $k - 1$ variables X_2 to X_k, the first column of 1's representing the intercept term (this matrix is also known as the **data matrix**)
$\boldsymbol{\beta} = k \times 1$ column vector of the unknown parameters $\beta_1, \beta_2, \ldots, \beta_k$
$\mathbf{u} = n \times 1$ column vector of n disturbances u_i

Using the rules of matrix multiplication and addition, the reader should verify that systems (C.1.2) and (C.1.3) are equivalent.

System (C.1.3) is known as the *matrix representation of the general (k-variable) linear regression model*. It can be written more compactly as

$$\underset{n \times 1}{\mathbf{y}} = \underset{n \times k}{\mathbf{X}} \; \underset{k \times 1}{\boldsymbol{\beta}} + \underset{n \times 1}{\mathbf{u}} \tag{C.1.4}$$

Where there is no confusion about the dimensions or orders of the matrix **X** and the vectors **y**, **β**, and **u**, Eq. (C.1.4) may be written simply as

$$\mathbf{y} = \mathbf{X}\boldsymbol{\beta} + \mathbf{u} \tag{C.1.5}$$

As an illustration of the matrix representation, consider the two-variable consumption–income model considered in Chapter 3, namely, $Y_i = \beta_1 + \beta_2 X_i + u_i$, where Y is consumption expenditure and X is income. Using the data given in Table 3.2, we may write the

[2]Following the notation introduced in **Appendix B**, we shall represent vectors by lowercase boldfaced letters and matrices by uppercase boldfaced letters.

matrix formulation as

$$\begin{bmatrix} 70 \\ 65 \\ 90 \\ 95 \\ 110 \\ 115 \\ 120 \\ 140 \\ 155 \\ 150 \end{bmatrix} = \begin{bmatrix} 1 & 80 \\ 1 & 100 \\ 1 & 120 \\ 1 & 140 \\ 1 & 160 \\ 1 & 180 \\ 1 & 200 \\ 1 & 220 \\ 1 & 240 \\ 1 & 260 \end{bmatrix} \begin{bmatrix} \beta_1 \\ \beta_2 \end{bmatrix} + \begin{bmatrix} u_1 \\ u_2 \\ u_3 \\ u_4 \\ u_5 \\ u_6 \\ u_7 \\ u_8 \\ u_9 \\ u_{10} \end{bmatrix} \tag{C.1.6}$$

$$\underset{10 \times 1}{\mathbf{y}} = \underset{10 \times 2}{\mathbf{X}} \; \underset{2 \times 1}{\boldsymbol{\beta}} + \underset{10 \times 1}{\mathbf{u}}$$

As in the two- and three-variable cases, our objective is to estimate the parameters of the multiple regression (C.1.1) and to draw inferences about them from the data at hand. In matrix notation this amounts to estimating $\boldsymbol{\beta}$ and drawing inferences about this $\boldsymbol{\beta}$. For the purpose of estimation, we may use the method of ordinary least squares (OLS) or the method of maximum likelihood (ML). But as noted before, these two methods yield identical estimates of the regression coefficients.[3] Therefore, we shall confine our attention to the method of OLS.

C.2 Assumptions of the Classical Linear Regression Model in Matrix Notation

The assumptions underlying the classical linear regression model are given in Table C.1; they are presented both in scalar notation and in matrix notation. Assumption 1 given in Eq. (C.2.1) means that the expected value of the disturbance vector $\mathbf{u}$, that is, of each of its elements, is zero. More explicitly, $E(\mathbf{u}) = \mathbf{0}$ means

$$E \begin{bmatrix} u_1 \\ u_2 \\ \vdots \\ u_n \end{bmatrix} = \begin{bmatrix} E(u_1) \\ E(u_2) \\ \vdots \\ E(u_n) \end{bmatrix} = \begin{bmatrix} 0 \\ 0 \\ \vdots \\ 0 \end{bmatrix} \tag{C.2.1}$$

Assumption 2 (Eq. [C.2.2]) is a compact way of expressing the two assumptions given in Eqs. (3.2.5) and (3.2.2) by the scalar notation. To see this, we can write

$$E(\mathbf{uu}') = E \begin{bmatrix} u_1 \\ u_2 \\ \vdots \\ u_n \end{bmatrix} [u_1 \quad u_2 \quad \cdots \quad u_n]$$

[3]The proof that this is so in the *k*-variable case can be found in the footnote reference given in Chapter 4.

TABLE C.1 Assumptions of the Classical Linear Regression Model

Scalar Notation		Matrix Notation
1. $E(u_i) = 0$, for each i	(3.2.1)	1. $E(\mathbf{u}) = \mathbf{0}$ where $\mathbf{u}$ and $\mathbf{0}$ are $n \times 1$ column vectors, $\mathbf{0}$ being a null vector
2. $E(u_i u_j) = 0 \quad i \neq j$	(3.2.5)	2. $E(\mathbf{uu}') = \sigma^2\mathbf{I}$ where $\mathbf{I}$ is an $n \times n$ identity matrix
$\quad = \sigma^2 \quad i = j$	(3.2.2)	
3. $X_2, X_3, \ldots, X_k$ are nonstochastic or fixed		3. The $n \times k$ matrix $\mathbf{X}$ is nonstochastic, that is, it consists of a set of fixed numbers
4. There is no exact linear relationship among the X variables, that is, no multicollinearity	(7.1.9)	4. The rank of $\mathbf{X}$ is $p(\mathbf{X}) = k$, where k is the number of columns in $\mathbf{X}$ and k is less than the number of observations, n
5. For hypothesis testing, $u_i \sim N(0, \sigma^2)$	(4.2.4)	5. The $\mathbf{u}$ vector has a multivariate normal distribution, i.e., $\mathbf{u} \sim N(\mathbf{0}, \sigma^2\mathbf{I})$

where $\mathbf{u}'$ is the transpose of the column vector $\mathbf{u}$, or a row vector. Performing the multiplication, we obtain

$$E(\mathbf{uu}') = E\begin{bmatrix} u_1^2 & u_1u_2 & \cdots & u_1u_n \\ u_2u_1 & u_2^2 & \cdots & u_2u_n \\ \cdots & \cdots & \cdots & \cdots \\ u_nu_1 & u_nu_2 & \cdots & u_n^2 \end{bmatrix}$$

Applying the expectations operator E to each element of the preceding matrix, we obtain

$$E(\mathbf{uu}') = \begin{bmatrix} E(u_1^2) & E(u_1u_2) & \cdots & E(u_1u_n) \\ E(u_2u_1) & E(u_2^2) & \cdots & E(u_2u_n) \\ \cdots & \cdots & \cdots & \cdots \\ E(u_nu_1) & E(u_nu_2) & \cdots & E(u_n^2) \end{bmatrix} \tag{C.2.2}$$

Because of the assumptions of homoscedasticity and no serial correlation, matrix (C.2.2) reduces to

$$E(\mathbf{uu}') = \begin{bmatrix} \sigma^2 & 0 & 0 & \cdots & 0 \\ 0 & \sigma^2 & 0 & \cdots & 0 \\ \cdots & \cdots & \cdots & \cdots & \cdots \\ 0 & 0 & 0 & \cdots & \sigma^2 \end{bmatrix}$$

$$= \sigma^2\begin{bmatrix} 1 & 0 & 0 & \cdots & 0 \\ 0 & 1 & 0 & \cdots & 0 \\ \cdots & \cdots & \cdots & \cdots & \cdots \\ 0 & 0 & 0 & \cdots & 1 \end{bmatrix} \tag{C.2.3}$$

$$= \sigma^2\mathbf{I}$$

where $\mathbf{I}$ is an $n \times n$ identity matrix.

Matrix (C.2.2) (and its representation given in Eq. [C.2.3]) is called the **variance-covariance matrix** of the disturbances u_i; the elements on the main diagonal of this matrix (running from the upper left corner to the lower right corner) give the variances, and the elements off the main diagonal give the covariances.[4] Note that the variance–covariance matrix is **symmetric:** The elements above and below the main diagonal are reflections of one another.

Assumption 3 in Table C.1 states that the $n \times k$ matrix $\mathbf{X}$ is nonstochastic; that is, it consists of fixed numbers. As noted previously, our regression analysis is conditional regression analysis, conditional upon the fixed values of the X variables.

Assumption 4 states that the $\mathbf{X}$ matrix has full column rank equal to k, the number of columns in the matrix. This means that the columns of the X matrix are linearly independent; that is, there is no **exact linear relationship** among the X variables. In other words there is no multicollinearity. In scalar notation this is equivalent to saying that there exists no set of numbers $\lambda_1, \lambda_2, \ldots, \lambda_k$ not all zero such that (cf. Eq. [7.1.8])

$$\lambda_1 X_{1i} + \lambda_2 X_{2i} + \cdots + \lambda_k X_{ki} = 0 \qquad \text{(C.2.4)}$$

where $X_{1i} = 1$ for all i (to allow for the column of 1's in the $\mathbf{X}$ matrix). In matrix notation, Eq. (C.2.4) can be represented as

$$\boldsymbol{\lambda}'\mathbf{x} = 0 \qquad \text{(C.2.5)}$$

where $\boldsymbol{\lambda}'$ is a $1 \times k$ row vector and $\mathbf{x}$ is a $k \times 1$ column vector.

If an exact linear relationship such as Eq. (C.2.4) exists, the variables are said to be collinear. If, on the other hand, Eq. (C.2.4) holds true only if $\lambda_1 = \lambda_2 = \lambda_3 = \cdots = 0$, then the X variables are said to be linearly independent. An intuitive reason for the *no multicollinearity* assumption was given in Chapter 7, and we explored this assumption further in Chapter 10.

C.3 OLS Estimation

To obtain the OLS estimate of $\boldsymbol{\beta}$, let us first write the k-variable sample regression function (SRF):

$$Y_i = \hat{\beta}_1 + \hat{\beta}_2 X_{2i} + \hat{\beta}_3 X_{3i} + \cdots + \hat{\beta}_k X_{ki} + \hat{u}_i \qquad \text{(C.3.1)}$$

which can be written more compactly in matrix notation as

$$\mathbf{y} = \mathbf{X}\hat{\boldsymbol{\beta}} + \hat{\mathbf{u}} \qquad \text{(C.3.2)}$$

and in matrix form as

$$\begin{bmatrix} Y_1 \\ Y_2 \\ \vdots \\ Y_n \end{bmatrix} = \begin{bmatrix} 1 & X_{21} & X_{31} & \cdots & X_{k1} \\ 1 & X_{22} & X_{32} & \cdots & X_{k2} \\ \cdots & \cdots & \cdots & \cdots & \cdots \\ 1 & X_{2n} & X_{3n} & \cdots & X_{kn} \end{bmatrix} \begin{bmatrix} \hat{\beta}_1 \\ \hat{\beta}_2 \\ \vdots \\ \hat{\beta}_k \end{bmatrix} + \begin{bmatrix} \hat{u}_1 \\ \hat{u}_2 \\ \vdots \\ \hat{u}_n \end{bmatrix} \qquad \text{(C.3.3)}$$

$$\underset{n \times 1}{\mathbf{y}} = \underset{n \times k}{\mathbf{X}} \; \underset{k \times 1}{\hat{\boldsymbol{\beta}}} + \underset{n \times 1}{\hat{\mathbf{u}}}$$

where $\hat{\boldsymbol{\beta}}$ is a k-element column vector of the OLS estimators of the regression coefficients and where $\hat{\mathbf{u}}$ is an $n \times 1$ column vector of n residuals.

[4]By definition, the variance of $u_i = E[u_i - E(u_i)]^2$ and the covariance between u_i and $u_j = E[u_i - E(u_i)][u_j - E(u_j)]$. But because of the assumption $E(u_i) = 0$ for each i, we have the variance-covariance matrix (C.2.3).

As in the two- and three-variable models, in the k-variable case the OLS estimators are obtained by minimizing

$$\sum \hat{u}_i^2 = \sum (Y_i - \hat{\beta}_1 - \hat{\beta}_2 X_{2i} - \cdots - \hat{\beta}_k X_{ki})^2 \tag{C.3.4}$$

where $\sum \hat{u}_i^2$ is the residual sum of squares (RSS). In matrix notation, this amounts to minimizing $\hat{\mathbf{u}}'\hat{\mathbf{u}}$ since

$$\hat{\mathbf{u}}'\hat{\mathbf{u}} = [\hat{u}_1 \quad \hat{u}_2 \quad \cdots \quad \hat{u}_n] \begin{bmatrix} \hat{u}_1 \\ \hat{u}_2 \\ \vdots \\ \hat{u}_n \end{bmatrix} = \hat{u}_1^2 + \hat{u}_2^2 + \cdots + \hat{u}_n^2 = \sum \hat{u}_i^2 \tag{C.3.5}$$

Now from Eq. (C.3.2) we obtain

$$\hat{\mathbf{u}} = \mathbf{y} - \mathbf{X}\hat{\boldsymbol{\beta}} \tag{C.3.6}$$

Therefore,

$$\begin{aligned} \hat{\mathbf{u}}'\hat{\mathbf{u}} &= (\mathbf{y} - \mathbf{X}\hat{\boldsymbol{\beta}})'(\mathbf{y} - \mathbf{X}\hat{\boldsymbol{\beta}}) \\ &= \mathbf{y}'\mathbf{y} - 2\hat{\boldsymbol{\beta}}'\mathbf{X}'\mathbf{y} + \hat{\boldsymbol{\beta}}'\mathbf{X}'\mathbf{X}\hat{\boldsymbol{\beta}} \end{aligned} \tag{C.3.7}$$

where use is made of the properties of the transpose of a matrix, namely, $(\mathbf{X}\hat{\boldsymbol{\beta}})' = \hat{\boldsymbol{\beta}}'\mathbf{X}'$; and since $\hat{\boldsymbol{\beta}}'\mathbf{X}'\mathbf{y}$ is a scalar (a real number), it is equal to its transpose $\mathbf{y}'\mathbf{X}\hat{\boldsymbol{\beta}}$.

Equation (C.3.7) is the matrix representation of (C.3.4). In scalar notation, the method of OLS consists in so estimating $\beta_1, \beta_2, \ldots, \beta_k$ that $\sum \hat{u}_i^2$ is as small as possible. This is done by differentiating Eq. (C.3.4) partially with respect to $\hat{\beta}_1, \hat{\beta}_2, \ldots, \hat{\beta}_k$ and setting the resulting expressions to zero. This process yields k simultaneous equations in k unknowns, the normal equations of the least-squares theory. As shown in Appendix CA, Section CA.1, these equations are as follows:

$$\begin{aligned} n\hat{\beta}_1 + \hat{\beta}_2 \sum X_{2i} + \hat{\beta}_3 \sum X_{3i} + \cdots + \hat{\beta}_k \sum X_{ki} &= \sum Y_i \\ \hat{\beta}_1 \sum X_{2i} + \hat{\beta}_2 \sum X_{2i}^2 + \hat{\beta}_3 \sum X_{2i}X_{3i} + \cdots + \hat{\beta}_k \sum X_{2i}X_{ki} &= \sum X_{2i}Y_i \\ \hat{\beta}_1 \sum X_{3i} + \hat{\beta}_2 \sum X_{3i}X_{2i} + \hat{\beta}_3 \sum X_{3i}^2 + \cdots + \hat{\beta}_k \sum X_{3i}X_{ki} &= \sum X_{3i}Y_i \\ \cdots\cdots\cdots\cdots\cdots\cdots\cdots\cdots\cdots\cdots\cdots\cdots\cdots\cdots & \\ \hat{\beta}_1 \sum X_{ki} + \hat{\beta}_2 \sum X_{ki}X_{2i} + \hat{\beta}_3 \sum X_{ki}X_{3i} + \cdots + \hat{\beta}_k \sum X_{ki}^2 &= \sum X_{ki}Y_i \end{aligned}$$

(C.3.8)[5]

In matrix form, Eq. (C.3.8) can be represented as

$$\underbrace{\begin{bmatrix} n & \sum X_{2i} & \sum X_{3i} & \cdots & \sum X_{ki} \\ \sum X_{2i} & \sum X_{2i}^2 & \sum X_{2i}X_{3i} & \cdots & \sum X_{2i}X_{ki} \\ \sum X_{3i} & \sum X_{3i}X_{2i} & \sum X_{3i}^2 & \cdots & \sum X_{3i}X_{ki} \\ \cdots & \cdots & \cdots & \cdots & \cdots \\ \sum X_{ki} & \sum X_{ki}X_{2i} & \sum X_{ki}X_{3i} & \cdots & \sum X_{ki}^2 \end{bmatrix}}_{(\mathbf{X}'\mathbf{X})} \underbrace{\begin{bmatrix} \hat{\beta}_1 \\ \hat{\beta}_2 \\ \hat{\beta}_3 \\ \vdots \\ \hat{\beta}_k \end{bmatrix}}_{\hat{\boldsymbol{\beta}}} = \underbrace{\begin{bmatrix} 1 & 1 & \cdots & 1 \\ X_{21} & X_{22} & \cdots & X_{2n} \\ X_{31} & X_{32} & \cdots & X_{3n} \\ \cdots & \cdots & \cdots & \cdots \\ X_{k1} & X_{k2} & \cdots & X_{kn} \end{bmatrix}}_{\mathbf{X}'} \underbrace{\begin{bmatrix} Y_1 \\ Y_2 \\ Y_3 \\ \vdots \\ Y_n \end{bmatrix}}_{\mathbf{y}} \tag{C.3.9}$$

[5]These equations can be remembered easily. Start with the equation $Y_i = \hat{\beta}_1 + \hat{\beta}_2 X_{2i} + \hat{\beta}_3 X_{3i} + \cdots + \hat{\beta}_k X_{ki}$. Summing this equation over the n values gives the first equation in (C.3.8); multiplying it by X_2 on both sides and summing over n gives the second equation; multiplying it by X_3 on both sides and summing over n gives the third equation; and so on. In passing, note that the first equation in (C.3.8) gives at once $\hat{\beta}_1 = \bar{Y} - \hat{\beta}_2 \bar{X}_2 - \cdots - \hat{\beta}_k \bar{X}_k$ (cf. [7.4.6]).

or, more compactly, as

$$(\mathbf{X}'\mathbf{X})\hat{\boldsymbol{\beta}} = \mathbf{X}'\mathbf{y} \tag{C.3.10}$$

Note these features of the $(\mathbf{X}'\mathbf{X})$ matrix: (1) It gives the raw sums of squares and cross products of the X variables, one of which is the intercept term taking the value of 1 for each observation. The elements on the main diagonal give the raw sums of squares, and those off the main diagonal give the raw sums of cross products (by *raw* we mean in original units of measurement). (2) It is symmetrical since the cross product between X_{2i} and X_{3i} is the same as that between X_{3i} and X_{2i}. (3) It is of order $(k \times k)$, that is, k rows and k columns.

In Eq. (C.3.10) the known quantities are $(\mathbf{X}'\mathbf{X})$ and $(\mathbf{X}'\mathbf{y})$ (the cross product between the X variables and y) and the unknown is $\hat{\boldsymbol{\beta}}$. Now using matrix algebra, if the inverse of $(\mathbf{X}'\mathbf{X})$ exists, say, $(\mathbf{X}'\mathbf{X})^{-1}$, then premultiplying both sides of Eq. (C.3.10) by this inverse, we obtain

$$(\mathbf{X}'\mathbf{X})^{-1}(\mathbf{X}'\mathbf{X})\hat{\boldsymbol{\beta}} = (\mathbf{X}'\mathbf{X})^{-1}\mathbf{X}'\mathbf{y}$$

But since $(\mathbf{X}'\mathbf{X})^{-1}(\mathbf{X}'\mathbf{X}) = \mathbf{I}$, an identity matrix of order $k \times k$, we get

$$\mathbf{I}\hat{\boldsymbol{\beta}} = (\mathbf{X}'\mathbf{X})^{-1}\mathbf{X}'\mathbf{y}$$

or

$$\underset{k \times 1}{\hat{\boldsymbol{\beta}}} = \underset{k \times k}{(\mathbf{X}'\mathbf{X})^{-1}} \; \underset{(k \times n)}{\mathbf{X}'} \; \underset{(n \times 1)}{\mathbf{y}} \tag{C.3.11}$$

Equation (C.3.11) is a fundamental result of the OLS theory in matrix notation. It shows how the $\hat{\boldsymbol{\beta}}$ vector can be estimated from the given data. Although Eq. (C.3.11) was obtained from Eq. (C.3.9), it can be obtained directly from Eq. (C.3.7) by differentiating $\hat{\mathbf{u}}'\hat{\mathbf{u}}$ with respect to $\hat{\boldsymbol{\beta}}$. The proof is given in Appendix CA, Section CA.2.

An Illustration

As an illustration of the matrix methods developed so far, let us work a consumption–income example using the data in Eq. (C.1.6). For the two-variable case we have

$$\hat{\boldsymbol{\beta}} = \begin{bmatrix} \hat{\beta}_1 \\ \hat{\beta}_2 \end{bmatrix}$$

$$(\mathbf{X}'\mathbf{X}) = \begin{bmatrix} 1 & 1 & 1 & \cdots & 1 \\ X_1 & X_2 & X_3 & \cdots & X_n \end{bmatrix} \begin{bmatrix} 1 & X_1 \\ 1 & X_2 \\ 1 & X_3 \\ \cdots & \cdots \\ 1 & X_N \end{bmatrix} = \begin{bmatrix} n & \sum X_i \\ \sum X_i & \sum X_i^2 \end{bmatrix}$$

and

$$\mathbf{X}'\mathbf{y} = \begin{bmatrix} 1 & 1 & 1 & \cdots & 1 \\ X_1 & X_2 & X_3 & \cdots & X_n \end{bmatrix} \begin{bmatrix} Y_1 \\ Y_2 \\ Y_3 \\ \vdots \\ Y_n \end{bmatrix} = \begin{bmatrix} \sum Y_i \\ \sum X_i Y_i \end{bmatrix}$$

Using the data given in Eq. (C.1.6), we obtain

$$\mathbf{X}'\mathbf{X} = \begin{bmatrix} 10 & 1700 \\ 1700 & 322000 \end{bmatrix}$$

and

$$\mathbf{X}'\mathbf{y} = \begin{bmatrix} 1110 \\ 205500 \end{bmatrix}$$

Using the rules of matrix inversion given in **Appendix B, Section B.3,** we can see that the inverse of the preceding ($\mathbf{X}'\mathbf{X}$) matrix is

$$\mathbf{X}'\mathbf{X}^{-1} = \begin{bmatrix} 0.97576 & -0.005152 \\ -0.005152 & 0.0000303 \end{bmatrix}$$

Therefore,

$$\hat{\boldsymbol{\beta}} = \begin{bmatrix} \hat{\beta}_1 \\ \hat{\beta}_2 \end{bmatrix} = \begin{bmatrix} 0.97576 & -0.005152 \\ -0.005152 & 0.0000303 \end{bmatrix} \begin{bmatrix} 1110 \\ 205500 \end{bmatrix}$$

$$= \begin{bmatrix} 24.4545 \\ 0.5079 \end{bmatrix}$$

Using the computer, we obtained $\hat{\beta}_1 = 24.4545$ and $\hat{\beta}_2 = 0.5091$. The difference between the two estimates is due to the rounding errors. In passing, note that in working on a desk calculator it is essential to obtain results to several significant digits to minimize the rounding errors.

Variance-Covariance Matrix of $\hat{\boldsymbol{\beta}}$

Matrix methods enable us to develop formulas not only for the variance of $\hat{\beta}_i$, any given element of $\hat{\boldsymbol{\beta}}$, but also for the covariance between any two elements of $\hat{\boldsymbol{\beta}}$, say, $\hat{\beta}_i$ and $\hat{\beta}_j$. We need these variances and covariances for the purpose of statistical inference.

By definition, the variance-covariance matrix of $\hat{\boldsymbol{\beta}}$ is (compare Eq. [C.2.2])

$$\text{var-cov}\,(\hat{\boldsymbol{\beta}}) = E\{[\hat{\boldsymbol{\beta}} - E(\hat{\boldsymbol{\beta}})][\hat{\boldsymbol{\beta}} - E(\hat{\boldsymbol{\beta}})]'\}$$

which can be written explicitly as

$$\text{var-cov}\,(\hat{\boldsymbol{\beta}}) = \begin{bmatrix} \text{var}\,(\hat{\beta}_1) & \text{cov}\,(\hat{\beta}_1, \hat{\beta}_2) & \cdots & \text{cov}\,(\hat{\beta}_1, \hat{\beta}_k) \\ \text{cov}\,(\hat{\beta}_2, \hat{\beta}_1) & \text{var}\,(\hat{\beta}_2) & \cdots & \text{cov}\,(\hat{\beta}_2, \hat{\beta}_k) \\ \cdots & \cdots & \cdots & \cdots \\ \text{cov}\,(\hat{\beta}_k, \hat{\beta}_1) & \text{cov}\,(\hat{\beta}_k, \hat{\beta}_2) & \cdots & \text{var}\,(\hat{\beta}_k) \end{bmatrix} \tag{C.3.12}$$

It is shown in Appendix CA, Section CA.3, that the preceding variance-covariance matrix can be obtained from the following formula:

$$\text{var-cov}\,(\hat{\boldsymbol{\beta}}) = \sigma^2(\mathbf{X}'\mathbf{X})^{-1} \tag{C.3.13}$$

where σ^2 is the homoscedastic variance of u_i and $(\mathbf{X}'\mathbf{X})^{-1}$ is the inverse matrix appearing in Eq. (C.3.11), which gives the OLS estimator $\hat{\boldsymbol{\beta}}$.

In the two- and three-variable linear regression models an unbiased estimator of σ^2 was given by $\hat{\sigma}^2 = \sum \hat{u}_i^2/(n-2)$ and $\hat{\sigma}^2 = \sum \hat{u}_i^2/(n-3)$, respectively. In the k-variable case, the corresponding formula is

$$\hat{\sigma}^2 = \frac{\sum \hat{u}_i^2}{n-k} = \frac{\hat{\mathbf{u}}'\hat{\mathbf{u}}}{n-k} \tag{C.3.14}$$

where there are now $n-k$ df. (Why?)

Although in principle $\hat{\mathbf{u}}'\hat{\mathbf{u}}$ can be computed from the estimated residuals, in practice it can be obtained directly as follows. Recalling that $\sum \hat{u}_i^2$ (= RSS) = TSS − ESS, in the two-variable case we may write

$$\sum \hat{u}_i^2 = \sum y_i^2 - \hat{\beta}_2^2 \sum x_i^2 \tag{3.3.6}$$

and in the three-variable case

$$\sum \hat{u}_i^2 = \sum y_i^2 - \hat{\beta}_2 \sum y_i x_{2i} - \hat{\beta}_3 \sum y_i x_{3i} \tag{7.4.19}$$

By extending this principle, it can be seen that for the k-variable model

$$\sum \hat{u}_i^2 = \sum y_i^2 - \hat{\beta}_2 \sum y_i x_{2i} - \cdots - \hat{\beta}_k \sum y_i x_{ki} \tag{C.3.15}$$

In matrix notation,

$$\text{TSS: } \sum y_i^2 = \mathbf{y}'\mathbf{y} - n\bar{Y}^2 \tag{C.3.16}$$

$$\text{ESS: } \hat{\beta}_2 \sum y_i x_{2i} + \cdots + \hat{\beta}_k \sum y_i x_{ki} = \hat{\boldsymbol{\beta}}'\mathbf{X}'\mathbf{y} - n\bar{Y}^2 \tag{C.3.17}$$

where the term $n\bar{Y}^2$ is known as the correction for mean.[6] Therefore,

$$\hat{\mathbf{u}}'\hat{\mathbf{u}} = \mathbf{y}'\mathbf{y} - \hat{\boldsymbol{\beta}}'\mathbf{X}'\mathbf{y} \tag{C.3.18}$$

Once $\hat{\mathbf{u}}'\hat{\mathbf{u}}$ is obtained, $\hat{\sigma}^2$ can be easily computed from Eq. (C.3.14), which, in turn, will enable us to estimate the variance-covariance matrix (C.3.13).

For our illustrative example,

$$\begin{aligned}\hat{\mathbf{u}}'\hat{\mathbf{u}} &= 132100 - [24.4545 \quad 0.5091]\begin{bmatrix}1110\\205500\end{bmatrix}\\ &= 337.373\end{aligned}$$

Hence, $\hat{\sigma}^2 = (337.273/8) = 42.1591$, which is approximately the value obtained previously in Chapter 3.

[6] *Note:* $\sum y_i^2 = \sum (Y_i - \bar{Y})^2 = \sum Y_i^2 - n\bar{Y}^2 = \mathbf{y}'\mathbf{y} - n\bar{Y}^2$. Therefore, without the correction term, $\mathbf{y}'\mathbf{y}$ will give simply the raw sum of squares, not the sum of squared deviations.

Properties of OLS Vector $\hat{\boldsymbol{\beta}}$

In the two- and three-variable cases we know that the OLS estimators are linear and unbiased, and in the class of all linear unbiased estimators they have minimum variance (the Gauss–Markov property). In short, the OLS estimators are best linear unbiased estimators (BLUE). This property extends to the entire $\hat{\boldsymbol{\beta}}$ vector; that is, $\hat{\boldsymbol{\beta}}$ is linear (each of its elements is a linear function of Y, the dependent variable). $E(\hat{\boldsymbol{\beta}}) = \boldsymbol{\beta}$, that is, the expected value of each element of $\hat{\boldsymbol{\beta}}$ is equal to the corresponding element of the true $\boldsymbol{\beta}$, and in the class of all linear unbiased estimators of $\boldsymbol{\beta}$, the OLS estimator $\hat{\boldsymbol{\beta}}$ has minimum variance.

The proof is given in Appendix CA, Section CA.4. As stated in the introduction, the k-variable case is in most cases a straight extension of the two- and three-variable cases.

C.4 The Coefficient of Determination R^2 in Matrix Notation

The coefficient of determination R^2 has been defined as

$$R^2 = \frac{\text{ESS}}{\text{TSS}}$$

In the two-variable case,

$$R^2 = \frac{\hat{\beta}_2^2 \sum x_i^2}{\sum y_i^2} \tag{3.5.6}$$

and in the three-variable case

$$R^2 = \frac{\hat{\beta}_2 \sum y_i x_{2i} + \hat{\beta}_3 \sum y_i x_{3i}}{\sum y_i^2} \tag{7.5.5}$$

Generalizing, we obtain for the k-variable case

$$R^2 = \frac{\hat{\beta}_2 \sum y_i x_{2i} + \hat{\beta}_3 \sum y_i x_{3i} + \cdots + \hat{\beta}_k \sum y_i x_{ki}}{\sum y_i^2} \tag{C.4.1}$$

By using Eqs. (C.3.16) and (C.3.17), Eq. (C.4.1) can be written as

$$R^2 = \frac{\hat{\boldsymbol{\beta}}'\mathbf{X}'\mathbf{y} - n\bar{Y}^2}{\mathbf{y}'\mathbf{y} - n\bar{Y}^2} \tag{C.4.2}$$

which gives the matrix representation of R^2.

For our illustrative example,

$$\begin{aligned}\hat{\boldsymbol{\beta}}'\mathbf{X}'\mathbf{y} &= [24.3571 \quad 0.5079]\begin{bmatrix} 1{,}110 \\ 205{,}500 \end{bmatrix} \\ &= 131{,}409.831 \\ \mathbf{y}'\mathbf{y} &= 132{,}100\end{aligned}$$

and

$$n\bar{Y}^2 = 123{,}210$$

Plugging these values into Eq. (C.4.2), we see that $R^2 = 0.9224$, which is about the same as obtained before, save for the rounding errors.

C.5 The Correlation Matrix

In the previous chapters we came across the zero-order, or simple, correlation coefficients r_{12}, r_{13}, r_{23}, and the partial, or first-order, correlations $r_{12.3}, r_{13.2}, r_{23.1}$, and their interrelationships. In the k-variable case, we shall have in all $k(k-1)/2$ zero-order correlation coefficients. (Why?) These $k(k-1)/2$ correlations can be put into a matrix, called the **correlation matrix *R*** as follows:

$$
\begin{aligned}
R &= \begin{bmatrix} r_{11} & r_{12} & r_{13} & \cdots & r_{1k} \\ r_{21} & r_{22} & r_{23} & \cdots & r_{2k} \\ \cdots & \cdots & \cdots & \cdots & \cdots \\ r_{k1} & r_{k2} & r_{k3} & \cdots & r_{kk} \end{bmatrix} \\
&= \begin{bmatrix} 1 & r_{12} & r_{13} & \cdots & r_{1k} \\ r_{21} & 1 & r_{23} & \cdots & r_{2k} \\ \cdots & \cdots & \cdots & \cdots & \cdots \\ r_{k1} & r_{k2} & r_{k3} & \cdots & 1 \end{bmatrix}
\end{aligned}
\tag{C.5.1}
$$

where the subscript 1, as before, denotes the dependent variable Y (r_{12} means correlation coefficient between Y and X_2, and so on) and where use is made of the fact that the coefficient of correlation of a variable with respect to itself is always 1 ($r_{11} = r_{22} = \cdots = r_{kk} = 1$).

From the correlation matrix R one can obtain correlation coefficients of first order (see Chapter 7) and of higher order such as $r_{12.34\ldots k}$. (See Exercise C.4.) Many computer programs routinely compute the R matrix. We have used the correlation matrix in Chapter 10.

C.6 Hypothesis Testing about Individual Regression Coefficients in Matrix Notation

For reasons spelled out in the previous chapters, if our objective is inference as well as estimation, we shall have to assume that the disturbances u_i follow some probability distribution. Also for reasons given previously, in regression analysis we usually assume that each u_i follows the normal distribution with zero mean and constant variance σ^2. In matrix notation, we have

$$\mathbf{u} \sim N(\mathbf{0}, \sigma^2\mathbf{I}) \tag{C.6.1}$$

where **u** and **0** are $n \times 1$ column vectors and **I** is an $n \times n$ identity matrix, **0** being the **null vector.**

Given the normality assumption, we know that in two- and three-variable linear regression models (1) the OLS estimators $\hat{\beta}_i$ and the ML estimators $\tilde{\beta}_i$ are identical, but the ML estimator $\tilde{\sigma}^2$ is biased, although this bias can be removed by using the unbiased OLS estimator $\hat{\sigma}^2$; and (2) the OLS estimators $\hat{\beta}_i$ are also normally distributed. Generalizing, in the k-variable case we can show that

$$\hat{\boldsymbol{\beta}} \sim N[\boldsymbol{\beta}, \sigma^2(\mathbf{X}'\mathbf{X})^{-1}] \tag{C.6.2}$$

that is, each element of $\hat{\boldsymbol{\beta}}$ is normally distributed with mean equal to the corresponding element of true $\boldsymbol{\beta}$ and the variance given by σ^2 times the appropriate diagonal element of the inverse matrix $(\mathbf{X}'\mathbf{X})^{-1}$.

Since in practice σ^2 is unknown, it is estimated by $\hat{\sigma}^2$. Then by the usual shift to the t distribution, it follows that each element of $\hat{\boldsymbol{\beta}}$ follows the t distribution with $n - k$ df. Symbolically,

$$t = \frac{\hat{\beta}_i - \beta_i}{\text{se}(\hat{\beta}_i)} \tag{C.6.3}$$

with $n - k$ df, where $\hat{\beta}_i$ is any element of $\hat{\boldsymbol{\beta}}$.

The t distribution can therefore be used to test hypotheses about the true β_i as well as to establish confidence intervals about it. The actual mechanics have already been illustrated in Chapters 5 and 8. For a fully worked example, see Section C.10.

C.7 Testing the Overall Significance of Regression: Analysis of Variance in Matrix Notation

In Chapter 8 we developed the ANOVA technique (1) to test the overall significance of the estimated regression, that is, to test the null hypothesis that the true (partial) slope coefficients are simultaneously equal to zero, and (2) to assess the incremental contribution of an explanatory variable. The ANOVA technique can be easily extended to the k-variable case. Recall that the ANOVA technique consists of decomposing the TSS into two components: the ESS and the RSS. The matrix expressions for these three sums of squares are already given in Eqs. (C.3.16), (C.3.17), and (C.3.18), respectively. The degrees of freedom associated with these sums of squares are $n - 1$, $k - 1$, and $n - k$, respectively. (Why?) Then, following Chapter 8, Table 8.1, we can set up Table C.2.

Assuming that the disturbances u_i are normally distributed and the null hypothesis is $\beta_2 = \beta_3 = \cdots = \beta_k = 0$, and following Chapter 8, one can show that

$$F = \frac{(\hat{\boldsymbol{\beta}}'\mathbf{X}'\mathbf{y} - n\bar{Y}^2)/(k-1)}{(\mathbf{y}'\mathbf{y} - \hat{\boldsymbol{\beta}}'\mathbf{X}'\mathbf{y})/(n-k)} \tag{C.7.1}$$

follows the F distribution with $k - 1$ and $n - k$ df.

In Chapter 8 we saw that, under the assumptions stated previously, there is a close relationship between F and R^2, namely,

$$F = \frac{R^2/(k-1)}{(1 - R^2)/(n-k)} \tag{8.4.11}$$

Therefore, the ANOVA Table C.2 can be expressed as Table C.3. One advantage of Table C.3 over Table C.2 is that the entire analysis can be done in terms of R^2; one need not consider the term $(\mathbf{y}'\mathbf{y} - n\bar{Y}^2)$, for it drops out in the F ratio.

TABLE C.2 Matrix Formulation of the ANOVA Table for k-Variable Linear Regression Model

Source of Variation	SS	df	MSS
Due to regression (that is, due to $X_2, X_3, \ldots, X_k$)	$\hat{\boldsymbol{\beta}}'\mathbf{X}'\mathbf{y} - n\bar{Y}^2$	$k-1$	$\dfrac{\hat{\boldsymbol{\beta}}\mathbf{X}'\mathbf{y} - n\bar{Y}^2}{k-1}$
Due to residuals	$\mathbf{y}'\mathbf{y} - \hat{\boldsymbol{\beta}}'\mathbf{X}'\mathbf{y}$	$n-k$	$\dfrac{\mathbf{y}'\mathbf{y} - \hat{\boldsymbol{\beta}}'\mathbf{X}'\mathbf{y}}{n-k}$
Total	$\mathbf{y}'\mathbf{y} - n\bar{Y}^2$	$n-1$	

TABLE C.3
***k*-Variable ANOVA Table in Matrix Form in Terms of R^2**

Source of Variation	SS	df	MSS
Due to regression (that is, due to $X_2, X_3, \ldots, X_k$)	$R^2(\mathbf{y}'\mathbf{y} - n\bar{Y}^2)$	$k-1$	$\dfrac{R^2(\mathbf{y}'\mathbf{y} - n\bar{Y}^2)}{k-1}$
Due to residuals	$(1-R^2)(\mathbf{y}'\mathbf{y} - n\bar{Y}^2)$	$n-k$	$\dfrac{(1-R^2)(\mathbf{y}'\mathbf{y} - n\bar{Y}^2)}{n-k}$
Total	$\mathbf{y}'\mathbf{y} - n\bar{Y}^2$	$n-1$	

C.8 Testing Linear Restrictions: General *F* Testing Using Matrix Notation

In Section 8.6 we introduced the general F test to test the validity of linear restrictions imposed on one or more parameters of the k-variable linear regression model. The appropriate test was given in (8.6.9) (or its equivalent, Eq. [8.6.10]). The matrix counterpart of (8.6.9) can be easily derived.

Let

$\hat{\mathbf{u}}_R$ = the residual vector from the restricted least-squares regression

$\hat{\mathbf{u}}_{UR}$ = the residual vector from the unrestricted least-squares regression

Then

$\hat{\mathbf{u}}_R'\hat{\mathbf{u}}_R = \sum \hat{u}_R^2$ = RSS from the restricted regression

$\hat{\mathbf{u}}_{UR}'\hat{\mathbf{u}}_{UR} = \sum \hat{u}_{UR}^2$ = RSS from the unrestricted regression

m = number of linear restrictions

k = number of parameters (including the intercept) in the unrestricted regression

n = number of observations

The matrix counterpart of Eq. (8.6.9) is then

$$F = \frac{(\hat{\mathbf{u}}_R'\hat{\mathbf{u}}_R - \hat{\mathbf{u}}_{UR}'\hat{\mathbf{u}}_{UR})/m}{(\hat{\mathbf{u}}_{UR}'\hat{\mathbf{u}}_{UR})/(n-k)} \tag{C.8.1}$$

which follows the F distribution with $(m, n-k)$ df. As usual, if the computed F value from Eq. (C.8.1) exceeds the critical F value, we can reject the restricted regression; otherwise, we do not reject it.

C.9 Prediction Using Multiple Regression: Matrix Formulation

In Section 8.8 we discussed, using scalar notation, how the estimated multiple regression can be used for predicting (1) the mean and (2) individual values of Y, given the values of the X regressors. In this section we show how to express these predictions in matrix form. We also present the formulas to estimate the variances and standard errors of the predicted values; in Chapter 8 we noted that these formulas are better handled in matrix notation, for the scalar or algebraic expressions of these formulas become rather unwieldy.

Mean Prediction

Let

$$\mathbf{X}_0 = \begin{bmatrix} 1 \\ X_{02} \\ X_{03} \\ \vdots \\ X_{0k} \end{bmatrix} \tag{C.9.1}$$

be the vector of values of the X variables for which we wish to predict $\hat{Y}_0$, the mean prediction of Y.

Now the estimated multiple regression, in scalar form, is

$$\hat{Y}_i = \hat{\beta}_1 + \hat{\beta}_2 X_{2i} + \hat{\beta}_3 X_{3i} + \cdots + \hat{\beta}_k X_{ki} + u_i \tag{C.9.2}$$

which in matrix notation can be written compactly as

$$\hat{Y}_i = \mathbf{x}_i' \hat{\boldsymbol{\beta}} \tag{C.9.3}$$

where $\mathbf{x}_i' = [1 \; X_{2i} \; X_{3i} \; \cdots \; X_{ki}]$ and

$$\hat{\boldsymbol{\beta}} = \begin{bmatrix} \hat{\beta}_1 \\ \hat{\beta}_2 \\ \vdots \\ \hat{\beta}_k \end{bmatrix}$$

Equation (C.9.2) or (C.9.3) is of course the mean prediction of Y_i corresponding to given $\mathbf{x}_i'$.

If $\mathbf{x}_i'$ is as given in Eq. (C.9.1), Eq. (C.9.3) becomes

$$(\hat{Y}_i \mid \mathbf{x}_0') = \mathbf{x}_0' \hat{\boldsymbol{\beta}} \tag{C.9.4}$$

where, of course, the values of $\mathbf{x}_0$ are specified. Note that Eq. (C.9.4) gives an unbiased prediction of $E(Y_i \mid \mathbf{x}_0')$, since $E(x_0' \hat{\boldsymbol{\beta}}) = \mathbf{x}_0' \hat{\boldsymbol{\beta}}$. (Why?)

Variance of Mean Prediction

The formula to estimate the variance of $(\hat{Y}_0 \mid \mathbf{x}_0')$ is as follows:[7]

$$\operatorname{var}(\hat{Y}_0 \mid \mathbf{x}_0') = \sigma^2 \mathbf{x}_0' (\mathbf{X}'\mathbf{X})^{-1} \mathbf{x}_0 \tag{C.9.5}$$

where σ^2 is the variance of u_i, $\mathbf{x}_0'$ are the given values of the X variables for which we wish to predict, and $(\mathbf{X}'\mathbf{X})$ is the matrix given in Eq. (C.3.9). In practice, we replace σ^2 by its unbiased estimator $\hat{\sigma}^2$.

We will illustrate mean prediction and its variance in the next section.

Individual Prediction

As pointed out in Chapters 5 and 8, the individual prediction of Y ($= Y_0$) is also given by Eq. (C.9.3) or more specifically by Eq. (C.9.4). The difference between mean and individual predictions lies in their variances.

Variance of Individual Prediction

The formula for the variance of an individual prediction is as follows:[8]

$$\operatorname{var}(Y_0 \mid \mathbf{x}_0) = \sigma^2 [1 + \mathbf{x}_0' (\mathbf{X}'\mathbf{X})^{-1} \mathbf{x}_0] \tag{C.9.6}$$

where $\operatorname{var}(Y_0 \mid \mathbf{x}_0)$ stands for $E[Y_0 - \hat{Y}_0 \mid X]^2$. In practice we replace σ^2 by its unbiased estimator $\hat{\sigma}^2$. We illustrate this formula in the next section.

[7]For derivation, see J. Johnston, *Econometrics Methods,* McGraw-Hill, 3d ed., New York, 1984, pp. 195–196.

[8]Ibid.

C.10 Summary of the Matrix Approach: An Illustrative Example

Consider the data given in Table C.4. These data pertain to per capita personal consumption expenditure (PPCE) and per capital personal disposable income (PPDI) and time or the trend variable. By including the trend variable in the model, we are trying to find out the relationship of PPCE to PPDI net of the trend variable (which may represent a host of other factors, such as technology, change in tastes, etc.).

For empirical purposes, therefore, the regression model is

$$Y_i = \hat{\beta}_1 + \hat{\beta}_2 X_{2i} + \hat{\beta}_3 X_{3i} + \hat{u}_i \tag{C.10.1}$$

where Y = per capita consumption expenditure, X_2 = per capita disposable income, and X_3 = time. The data required to run the regression (C.10.1) are given in Table C.4.

In matrix notation, our problem may be shown as follows:

$$\begin{bmatrix} 1673 \\ 1688 \\ 1666 \\ 1735 \\ 1749 \\ 1756 \\ 1815 \\ 1867 \\ 1948 \\ 2048 \\ 2128 \\ 2165 \\ 2257 \\ 2316 \\ 2324 \end{bmatrix} = \begin{bmatrix} 1 & 1839 & 1 \\ 1 & 1844 & 2 \\ 1 & 1831 & 3 \\ 1 & 1881 & 4 \\ 1 & 1883 & 5 \\ 1 & 1910 & 6 \\ 1 & 1969 & 7 \\ 1 & 2016 & 8 \\ 1 & 2126 & 9 \\ 1 & 2239 & 10 \\ 1 & 2336 & 11 \\ 1 & 2404 & 12 \\ 1 & 2487 & 13 \\ 1 & 2535 & 14 \\ 1 & 2595 & 15 \end{bmatrix} \begin{bmatrix} \hat{\beta}_1 \\ \hat{\beta}_2 \\ \hat{\beta}_3 \end{bmatrix} + \begin{bmatrix} \hat{u}_1 \\ \hat{u}_2 \\ \hat{u}_3 \\ \hat{u}_4 \\ \hat{u}_5 \\ \hat{u}_6 \\ \hat{u}_7 \\ \hat{u}_8 \\ \hat{u}_9 \\ \hat{u}_{10} \\ \hat{u}_{11} \\ \hat{u}_{12} \\ \hat{u}_{13} \\ \hat{u}_{14} \\ \hat{u}_{15} \end{bmatrix} \tag{C.10.2}$$

$$\underset{15 \times 1}{\mathbf{y}} = \underset{15 \times 3}{\mathbf{X}} \quad \underset{3 \times 1}{\hat{\boldsymbol{\beta}}} + \underset{15 \times 1}{\hat{\mathbf{u}}}$$

TABLE C.4 Per Capita Personal Consumption Expenditure (PPCE) and Per Capita Personal Disposable Income (PPDI) in the United States, 1956–1970, in 1958 Dollars

PPCE, Y	PPDI, X_2	Time, X_3	PPCE, Y	PPDI, X_2	Time, X_3
1673	1839	1 (= 1956)	1948	2126	9
1688	1844	2	2048	2239	10
1666	1831	3	2128	2336	11
1735	1881	4	2165	2404	12
1749	1883	5	2257	2487	13
1756	1910	6	2316	2535	14
1815	1969	7	2324	2595	15 (= 1970)
1867	2016	8			

Source: *Economic Report of the President*, January 1972, Table B-16.

From the preceding data we obtain the following quantities:

$$\bar{Y} = 1942.333 \qquad \bar{X}_2 = 2126.333 \qquad \bar{X}_3 = 8.0$$

$$\sum (Y_i - \bar{Y})^2 = 830{,}121.333$$

$$\sum (X_{2i} - \bar{X}_2)^2 = 1{,}103{,}111.333 \qquad \sum (X_{3i} - \bar{X}_3)^2 = 280.0$$

$$\mathbf{X}'\mathbf{X} = \begin{bmatrix} 1 & 1 & 1 & \cdots & 1 \\ X_{21} & X_{22} & X_{23} & \cdots & X_{2n} \\ X_{31} & X_{32} & X_{33} & \cdots & X_{3n} \end{bmatrix} \begin{bmatrix} 1 & X_{21} & X_{31} \\ 1 & X_{22} & X_{32} \\ 1 & X_{23} & X_{33} \\ \vdots & \vdots & \vdots \\ 1 & X_{2n} & X_{3n} \end{bmatrix}$$

$$= \begin{bmatrix} n & \sum X_{2i} & \sum X_{3i} \\ \sum X_{2i} & \sum X_{2i}^2 & \sum X_{2i}X_{3i} \\ \sum X_{3i} & \sum X_{2i}X_{3i} & \sum X_{3i}^2 \end{bmatrix}$$

$$= \begin{bmatrix} 15 & 31{,}895 & 120 \\ 31{,}895 & 68{,}922.513 & 272{,}144 \\ 120 & 272{,}144 & 1240 \end{bmatrix} \tag{C.10.3}$$

$$\mathbf{X}'\mathbf{y} = \begin{bmatrix} 29{,}135 \\ 62{,}905{,}821 \\ 247{,}934 \end{bmatrix} \tag{C.10.4}$$

Using the rules of matrix inversion given in **Appendix B,** one can see that

$$(\mathbf{X}'\mathbf{X})^{-1} = \begin{bmatrix} 37.232491 & -0.0225082 & 1.336707 \\ -0.0225082 & 0.0000137 & -0.0008319 \\ 1.336707 & -0.0008319 & 0.054034 \end{bmatrix} \tag{C.10.5}$$

Therefore,

$$\hat{\boldsymbol{\beta}} = (\mathbf{X}'\mathbf{X})^{-1}\mathbf{X}'\mathbf{y} = \begin{bmatrix} 300.28625 \\ 0.74198 \\ 8.04356 \end{bmatrix} \tag{C.10.6}$$

The residual sum of squares can now be computed as

$$\begin{aligned} \sum \hat{u}_i^2 &= \hat{\mathbf{u}}'\hat{\mathbf{u}} \\ &= \mathbf{y}'\mathbf{y} - \hat{\boldsymbol{\beta}}'\mathbf{X}'\mathbf{y} \\ &= 57{,}420{,}003 - [300.28625 \quad 0.74198 \quad 8.04356] \begin{bmatrix} 29{,}135 \\ 62{,}905{,}821 \\ 247{,}934 \end{bmatrix} \\ &= 1976.85574 \end{aligned} \tag{C.10.7}$$

whence we obtain

$$\hat{\sigma}^2 = \frac{\hat{\mathbf{u}}'\hat{\mathbf{u}}}{12} = 164.73797 \tag{C.10.8}$$

The variance-covariance matrix for $\hat{\boldsymbol{\beta}}$ can therefore be shown as

$$\text{var-cov}\,(\hat{\boldsymbol{\beta}}) = \hat{\sigma}^2(\mathbf{X}'\mathbf{X})^{-1} = \begin{bmatrix} 6133.650 & -3.70794 & 220.20634 \\ -3.70794 & 0.00226 & -0.13705 \\ 220.20634 & -0.13705 & 8.90155 \end{bmatrix} \tag{C.10.9}$$

The diagonal elements of this matrix give the variances of $\hat{\beta}_1$, $\hat{\beta}_2$, and $\hat{\beta}_3$, respectively, and their positive square roots give the corresponding standard errors.

From the previous data, it can be readily verified that

$$\text{ESS: } \hat{\boldsymbol{\beta}}'\mathbf{X}'\mathbf{y} - n\bar{Y}^2 = 828{,}144.47786 \tag{C.10.10}$$

$$\text{TSS: } \mathbf{y}'\mathbf{y} - n\bar{Y}^2 = 830{,}121.333 \tag{C.10.11}$$

Therefore,

$$\begin{aligned} R^2 &= \frac{\hat{\boldsymbol{\beta}}'\mathbf{X}'\mathbf{y} - n\bar{Y}^2}{\mathbf{y}'\mathbf{y} - n\bar{Y}^2} \\ &= \frac{828{,}144.47786}{830{,}121.333} \\ &= 0.99761 \end{aligned} \tag{C.10.12}$$

Applying Eq. (7.8.4) the **adjusted coefficient of determination** can be seen to be

$$\bar{R}^2 = 0.99722 \tag{C.10.13}$$

Collecting our results thus far, we have

$$\begin{aligned} \hat{Y}_i &= 300.28625 \quad + \ 0.74198X_{2i} \ + 8.04356X_{3i} \\ &\quad\ (78.31763) \quad (0.04753) \qquad (2.98354) \\ t &= \ \ (3.83421) \quad (15.60956) \qquad (2.69598) \\ R^2 &= 0.99761 \qquad \bar{R}^2 = 0.99722 \qquad \text{df} = 12 \end{aligned} \tag{C.10.14}$$

The interpretation of Eq. (C.10.14) is this: If both X_2 and X_3 are fixed at zero value, the average value of per capita personal consumption expenditure is estimated at about \$300. As usual, this mechanical interpretation of the intercept should be taken with a grain of salt. The partial regression coefficient of 0.74198 means that, holding all other variables constant, an increase in per capita income of, say, a dollar is accompanied by an increase in the mean per capita personal consumption expenditure of about 74 cents. In short, the marginal propensity to consume is estimated to be about 0.74, or 74 percent. Similarly, holding all other variables constant, the mean per capita personal consumption expenditure increased at the rate of about \$8 per year during the period of the study, 1956–1970. The R^2 value of 0.9976 shows that the two explanatory variables accounted for over 99 percent of the variation in per capita consumption expenditure in the United States over the period 1956–1970. Although $\bar{R}^2$ dips slightly, it is still very high.

Turning to the statistical significance of the estimated coefficients, we see from Eq. (C.10.14) that each of the estimated coefficients is *individually* statistically significant at, say, the 5 percent level of significance: The ratios of the estimated coefficients to their standard errors (that is, t ratios) are 3.83421, 15.61077, and 2.69598, respectively. Using a two-tail t test at the 5 percent level of significance, we see that the critical t value for 12 df is 2.179. Each of the computed t values exceeds this critical value. Hence, individually we may reject the null hypothesis that the true population value of the relevant coefficient is zero.

As noted previously, we cannot apply the usual t test to test the hypothesis that $\beta_2 = \beta_3 = 0$ simultaneously because the t-test procedure assumes that an independent sample is drawn every time the t test is applied. If the same sample is used to test hypotheses about β_2 and β_3 simultaneously, it is likely that the estimators $\hat{\beta}_2$ and $\hat{\beta}_3$ are correlated, thus

TABLE C.5
The ANOVA Table for the Data of Table C.4

Source of Variation	SS	df	MSS
Due to X_2, X_3	828,144.47786	2	414,072.3893
Due to residuals	1,976.85574	12	164.73797
Total	830,121.33360	14	

violating the assumption underlying the t-test procedure.[9] As a matter of fact, a look at the variance-covariance matrix of $\hat{\boldsymbol{\beta}}$ given in Eq. (C.10.9) shows that the estimators $\hat{\beta}_2$ and $\hat{\beta}_3$ are negatively correlated (the covariance between the two is -0.13705). Hence we cannot use the t test to test the null hypothesis that $\beta_2 = \beta_3 = 0$.

But recall that a null hypothesis like $\beta_2 = \beta_3 = 0$, simultaneously, can be tested by the analysis of variance technique and the attendant F test, which were introduced in Chapter 8. For our problem, the analysis of variance table is Table C.5. Under the usual assumptions, we obtain

$$F = \frac{414{,}072.3893}{164.73797} = 2513.52 \tag{C.10.15}$$

which is distributed as the F distribution with 2 and 12 df. The computed F value is obviously highly significant; we can reject the null hypothesis that $\beta_2 = \beta_3 = 0$, that is, that per capita personal consumption expenditure is not linearly related to per capita disposable income and trend.

In Section C.9 we discussed the mechanics of forecasting, mean as well as individual. Assume that for 1971 the PPDI figure is \$2,610 and we wish to forecast the PPCE corresponding to this figure. Then, the mean as well as individual forecast of PPCE for 1971 is the same and is given as

$$\begin{aligned}(\text{PPCE}_{1971} \mid \text{PPDI}_{1971}, X_3 = 16) &= \mathbf{x}'_{1971}\hat{\boldsymbol{\beta}} \\ &= [1 \quad 2610 \quad 16]\begin{bmatrix} 300.28625 \\ 0.74198 \\ 8.04356 \end{bmatrix} \\ &= 2365.55\end{aligned} \tag{C.10.16}$$

where use is made of Eq. (C.9.3).

The variances of $\hat{Y}_{1971}$ and Y_{1971}, as we know from Section C.9, are different and are as follows:

$$\begin{aligned}\text{var}(\hat{Y}_{1971} \mid \mathbf{x}'_{1971}) &= \hat{\sigma}^2[\mathbf{x}'_{1971}(\mathbf{X}'\mathbf{X})^{-1}\mathbf{x}_{1971}] \\ &= 164.73797[1 \quad 2610 \quad 16](\mathbf{X}'\mathbf{X})^{-1}\begin{bmatrix} 1 \\ 2610 \\ 16 \end{bmatrix}\end{aligned} \tag{C.10.17}$$

where $(\mathbf{X}'\mathbf{X})^{-1}$ is as shown in Eq. (C.10.5). Substituting this into Eq. (C.10.17), the reader should verify that

$$\text{var}(\hat{Y}_{1971} \mid \mathbf{x}'_{1971}) = 48.6426 \tag{C.10.18}$$

[9] See Section 8.4 for details.

and therefore

$$\text{se}\,(\hat{Y}_{1971} \mid \mathbf{x}_{1971}) = 6.9744$$

We leave it to the reader to verify, using Eq. (C.9.6), that

$$\text{var}\,(Y_{1971} \mid \mathbf{x}'_{1971}) = 213.3806 \tag{C.10.19}$$

and

$$\text{se}\,(Y_{1971} \mid \mathbf{x}'_{1971}) = 14.6076$$

Note: $\text{var}\,(Y_{1971} \mid \mathbf{x}'_{1971}) = E[Y_{1971} - \hat{Y}_{1971} \mid \mathbf{x}'_{1971}]^2$.

In Section C.5 we introduced the correlation matrix $\boldsymbol{R}$. For our data, the correlation matrix is as follows:

$$\begin{array}{cc} & \begin{array}{ccc} Y & X_2 & X_3 \end{array} \\ R = \begin{array}{c} Y \\ X_2 \\ X_3 \end{array} & \begin{bmatrix} 1 & 0.9980 & 0.9743 \\ 0.9980 & 1 & 0.9664 \\ 0.9743 & 0.9664 & 1 \end{bmatrix} \end{array} \tag{C.10.20}$$

Note that in Eq. (C.10.20) we have bordered the correlation matrix by the variables of the model so that we can readily identify which variables are involved in the computation of the correlation coefficient. Thus, the coefficient 0.9980 in the first row of matrix (C.10.20) tells us that it is the correlation coefficient between Y and X_2 (that is, r_{12}). From the zero-order correlations given in the correlation matrix (C.10.20) one can easily derive the first-order correlation coefficients. (See Exercise C.7.)

C.11 Generalized Least Squares (GLS)

On several occasions we have mentioned that OLS is a special case of GLS. To see this, return to Eq. (C.2.2). To take into account heteroscedastic variances (the elements on the main diagonal of Eq. [C.2.2]) and autocorrelations in the error terms (the elements off the main diagonal of Eq. [C.2.2]), assume that

$$\text{E}(\mathbf{uu}') = \sigma^2\mathbf{V} \tag{C.11.1}$$

where $\mathbf{V}$ is a known $n \times n$ matrix.

Therefore, if our model is:

$$\mathbf{y} = \mathbf{X}\boldsymbol{\beta} + \mathbf{u}$$

where $E(\mathbf{u}) = \mathbf{0}$ and $\text{var-cov}\,(\mathbf{u}) = \sigma^2\mathbf{V}$. In case σ^2 is unknown, which is typically the case, $\mathbf{V}$ then represents the assumed structure of variances and covariances among the random errors u_t.

Under the stated condition of the variance-covariance of the error terms, it can be shown that

$$\boldsymbol{\beta}^{\text{gls}} = (\mathbf{X}'\mathbf{V}^{-1}\mathbf{X})^{-1}\mathbf{X}'\mathbf{V}^{-1}\mathbf{y} \tag{C.11.2}$$

$\boldsymbol{\beta}^{\text{gls}}$ is known as the **generalized least-squares (GLS) estimator** of $\boldsymbol{\beta}$.

It can also be shown that

$$\text{var-cov}\,(\boldsymbol{\beta}^{\text{gls}}) = \sigma^2(\mathbf{X}'\mathbf{V}^{-1}\mathbf{X})^{-1} \tag{C.11.3}$$

It can be proved that $\boldsymbol{\beta}^{\text{gls}}$ is the best linear unbiased estimator of $\boldsymbol{\beta}$.

If it is assumed that the variance of each error term is the same constant σ^2 and the error terms are mutually uncorrelated, then the **V** matrix reduces to the identity matrix, as shown in Eq. (C.2.3). If the error terms are mutually uncorrelated but they have different (i.e., heteroscedastic) variances, then the **V** matrix will be diagonal with the unequal variances along the main diagonal. Of course, if there is heteroscedasticity as well as autocorrelation, then the **V** matrix will have entries on the main diagonal as well as on the off diagonal.

The real problem in practice is that we do not know σ^2 as well as the true variances and covariances (i.e., the structure of the **V** matrix). As a solution, we can use the method of **estimated (or feasible) generalized least squares (EGLS).** Here we first estimate our model by OLS, disregarding the problems of heteroscedasticity and/or autocorrelation. We obtain the residuals from this model and form the (estimated) variance-covariance matrix of the error term by replacing the entries in the expression just before Eq. (C.2.2) by the estimated u, namely, $\hat{u}$. It can be shown that EGLS estimators are consistent estimators of GLS. Symbolically,

$$\boldsymbol{\beta}^{\text{egls}} = (\mathbf{X}'\hat{\mathbf{V}}^{-1}\mathbf{X})^{-1}(\mathbf{X}'\hat{\mathbf{V}}^{-1}\mathbf{y}) \tag{C.11.4}$$

$$\text{var-cov}\,(\boldsymbol{\beta}^{\text{egls}}) = \sigma^2(\mathbf{X}'\hat{\mathbf{V}}^{-1}\mathbf{X})^{-1} \tag{C.11.5}$$

where $\hat{\mathbf{V}}$ is an estimate of **V**.

C.12 Summary and Conclusions

The primary purpose of this appendix was to introduce the matrix approach to the classical linear regression model. Although very few new concepts of regression analysis were introduced, the matrix notation provides a compact method of dealing with linear regression models involving any number of variables.

In concluding this appendix, note that if the Y and X variables are measured in the deviation form, that is, as deviations from their sample means, there are a few changes in the formulas presented previously. These changes are listed in Table C.6.[10] As this table shows, in

TABLE C.6 ***k*-Variable Regression Model in Original Units and in the Deviation Form***

Original Units		Deviation Form	
$\mathbf{y} = \mathbf{X}\hat{\boldsymbol{\beta}} + \hat{\mathbf{u}}$	(C.3.2)	$\mathbf{y} = \mathbf{X}\hat{\boldsymbol{\beta}} + \hat{\mathbf{u}}$ The column of 1's in the **X** matrix drops out. (Why?)	
$\hat{\boldsymbol{\beta}} = (\mathbf{X}'\mathbf{X})^{-1}\mathbf{X}'\mathbf{y}$	(C.3.11)	Same	
$\text{var-cov}\,(\hat{\boldsymbol{\beta}}) = \sigma^2(\mathbf{X}'\mathbf{X})^{-1}$	(C.3.13)	Same	
$\hat{\mathbf{u}}'\hat{\mathbf{u}} = \mathbf{y}'\mathbf{y} - \hat{\boldsymbol{\beta}}'\mathbf{X}'\mathbf{y}$	(C.3.18)	Same	
$\sum y_i^2 = \mathbf{y}'\mathbf{y} - n\bar{Y}^2$	(C.3.16)	$\sum y_i^2 = \mathbf{y}'\mathbf{y}$	(C.12.1)
$\text{ESS} = \hat{\boldsymbol{\beta}}'\mathbf{X}'\mathbf{y} - n\bar{Y}^2$	(C.3.17)	$\text{ESS} = \boldsymbol{\beta}'\mathbf{X}'\mathbf{y}$	(C.12.2)
$R^2 = \dfrac{\hat{\boldsymbol{\beta}}'\mathbf{X}'\mathbf{y} - n\bar{Y}^2}{\mathbf{y}'\mathbf{y} - n\bar{Y}^2}$	(C.4.2)	$R^2 = \dfrac{\hat{\boldsymbol{\beta}}'\mathbf{X}'\mathbf{y}}{\mathbf{y}'\mathbf{y}}$	(C.12.3)

*Note that although in both cases the symbols for the matrices and vectors are the same, in the deviation form the elements of the matrices and vectors are assumed to be deviations rather than the raw data. Note also that in the deviation form $\hat{\boldsymbol{\beta}}$ is of order $k-1$ and the var-cov $(\hat{\boldsymbol{\beta}})$ is of order $(k-1)(k-1)$.

[10] In these days of high-speed computers there may not be need for the deviation form. But it simplifies formulas and therefore calculations if one is working with a desk calculator and dealing with large numbers.

the deviation form the correction for mean $n\bar{Y}^2$ drops out from the TSS and ESS. (Why?) This loss results in a change for the formula for R^2. Otherwise, most of the formulas developed in the original units of measurement hold true for the deviation form.

EXERCISES

C.1. For the illustrative example discussed in Section C.10 the $\mathbf{X}'\mathbf{X}$ and $\mathbf{X}'\mathbf{y}$ using the data in the deviation form are as follows:

$$\mathbf{X}'\mathbf{X} = \begin{bmatrix} 1{,}103{,}111.333 & 16{,}984 \\ 16{,}984 & 280 \end{bmatrix}$$

$$\mathbf{X}'\mathbf{y} = \begin{bmatrix} 955{,}099.333 \\ 14{,}854.000 \end{bmatrix}$$

a. Estimate β_2 and β_3.

b. How would you estimate β_1?

c. Obtain the variance of $\hat{\beta}_2$ and $\hat{\beta}_3$ and their covariances.

d. Obtain R^2 and $\bar{R}^2$.

e. Comparing your results with those given in Section C.10, what do you find are the advantages of the deviation form?

C.2. Refer to Exercise 22.23. Using the data given therein, set up the appropriate $(\mathbf{X}'\mathbf{X})$ matrix and the $\mathbf{X}'\mathbf{y}$ vector and estimate the parameter vector $\boldsymbol{\beta}$ and its variance-covariance matrix. Also obtain R^2. How would you test the hypothesis that the elasticities of M1 with respect to GDP and interest rate R are numerically the same?

C.3. *Testing the equality of two regression coefficients.* Suppose that you are given the following regression model:

$$Y_i = \beta_1 + \beta_2 X_{2i} + \beta_3 X_{3i} + u_i$$

and you want to test the hypothesis that $\beta_2 = \beta_3$. If we assume that the u_i are normally distributed, it can be shown that

$$t = \frac{\hat{\beta}_2 - \hat{\beta}_3}{\sqrt{\operatorname{var}(\hat{\beta}_2) + \operatorname{var}(\hat{\beta}_3) - 2\operatorname{cov}(\hat{\beta}_2, \hat{\beta}_3)}}$$

follows the t distribution with $n - 3$ df (see Section 8.5). (In general, for the k-variable case the df are $n - k$.) Therefore, the preceding t test can be used to test the null hypothesis $\beta_2 = \beta_3$.

Apply the preceding t test to test the hypothesis that the true values of β_2 and β_3 in the regression (C.10.14) are identical.

Hint: Use the var-cov matrix of $\boldsymbol{\beta}$ given in Eq. (C.10.9).

C.4. *Expressing higher-order correlations in terms of lower-order correlations.* Correlation coefficients of order p can be expressed in terms of correlation coefficients of order $p - 1$ by the following **reduction formula:**

$$r_{12.345\ldots p} = \frac{r_{12.345\ldots(p-1)} - [r_{1p.345\ldots(p-1)} r_{2p.345\ldots(p-1)}]}{\sqrt{[1 - r^2_{1p.345\ldots(p-1)}]}\sqrt{[1 - r^2_{2p.345\ldots(p-1)}]}}$$

Thus,

$$r_{12.3} = \frac{r_{12} - r_{13}r_{23}}{\sqrt{1 - r_{13}^2}\sqrt{1 - r_{23}^2}}$$

as found in Chapter 7.

You are given the following correlation matrix:

$$\mathbf{R} = \begin{matrix} \\ Y \\ X_2 \\ X_3 \\ X_4 \\ X_5 \end{matrix} \begin{matrix} Y & X_2 & X_3 & X_4 & X_5 \\ \end{matrix} \begin{bmatrix} 1 & 0.44 & -0.34 & -0.31 & -0.14 \\ & 1 & 0.25 & -0.19 & -0.35 \\ & & 1 & 0.44 & 0.33 \\ & & & 1 & 0.85 \\ & & & & 1 \end{bmatrix}$$

Find the following:

a. $r_{12.345}$ *b.* $r_{12.34}$ *c.* $r_{12.3}$

d. $r_{13.245}$ *e.* $r_{13.24}$ *f.* $r_{13.2}$

C.5. *Expressing higher-order regression coefficients in terms of lower-order regression coefficients.* A regression coefficient of order p can be expressed in terms of a regression coefficient of order $p - 1$ by the following reduction formula:

$$\hat{\beta}_{12.345\ldots p} = \frac{\hat{\beta}_{12.345\ldots(p-1)} - \left[\hat{\beta}_{1p.345\ldots(p-1)}\hat{\beta}_{p2.345\ldots(p-1)}\right]}{1 - \hat{\beta}_{2p.345\ldots(p-1)}\hat{\beta}_{p2.345\ldots(p-1)}}$$

Thus,

$$\hat{\beta}_{12.3} = \frac{\hat{\beta}_{12} - \hat{\beta}_{13}\hat{\beta}_{32}}{1 - \hat{\beta}_{23}\hat{\beta}_{32}}$$

where $\beta_{12.3}$ is the slope coefficient in the regression of y on X_2 holding X_3 constant. Similarly, $\beta_{12.34}$ is the slope coefficient in the regression of Y on X_2 holding X_3 and X_4 constant, and so on.

Using the preceding formula, find expressions for the following regression coefficients in terms of lower-order regression coefficients: $\hat{\beta}_{12.3456}$, $\hat{\beta}_{12.345}$, and $\hat{\beta}_{12.34}$.

C.6. Establish the following identity:

$$\hat{\beta}_{12.3}\hat{\beta}_{23.1}\hat{\beta}_{31.2} = r_{12.3}r_{23.1}r_{31.2}$$

C.7. For the correlation matrix $\boldsymbol{R}$ given in Eq. (C.10.20) find all the first-order partial correlation coefficients.

C.8. In studying the variation in crime rates in certain large cities in the United States, Ogburn obtained the following data:*

$$\begin{matrix} \bar{Y} = 19.9 & S_1 = 7.9 \\ \bar{X}_2 = 49.2 & S_2 = 1.3 \\ \bar{X}_3 = 10.2 & S_3 = 4.6 \\ \bar{X}_4 = 481.4 & S_4 = 74.4 \\ \bar{X}_5 = 41.6 & S_5 = 10.8 \end{matrix} \qquad \boldsymbol{R} = \begin{matrix} Y \\ X_2 \\ X_3 \\ X_4 \\ X_5 \end{matrix} \overset{\begin{matrix} Y & X_2 & X_3 & X_4 & X_5 \end{matrix}}{\begin{bmatrix} 1 & 0.44 & -0.34 & -0.31 & -0.14 \\ & 1 & 0.25 & -0.19 & -0.35 \\ & & 1 & 0.44 & 0.33 \\ & & & 1 & 0.85 \\ & & & & 1 \end{bmatrix}}$$

*W. F. Ogburn, "Factors in the Variation of Crime among Cities," *Journal of American Statistical Association,* vol. 30, 1935, p. 12.

where Y = crime rate, number of known offenses per thousand of population
X_2 = percentage of male inhabitants
X_3 = percentage of total inhabitants who are foreign-born males
X_4 = number of children under 5 years of age per thousand married women between ages 15 and 44 years
X_5 = church membership, number of church members 13 years of age and over per 100 of total population 13 years of age and over; S_1 to S_5 are the sample standard deviations of variables Y through X_5 and $\boldsymbol{R}$ is the correlation matrix

a. Treating Y as the dependent variable, obtain the regression of Y on the four X variables and interpret the estimated regression.

b. Obtain $r_{12.3}$, $r_{14.35}$, and $r_{15.34}$.

c. Obtain R^2 and test the hypothesis that all partial slope coefficients are simultaneously equal to zero.

C.9. The following table gives data on output and total cost of production of a commodity in the short run. (See Example 7.4.)

Output	Total Cost, $
1	193
2	226
3	240
4	244
5	257
6	260
7	274
8	297
9	350
10	420

To test whether the preceding data suggest the U-shaped average and marginal cost curves typically encountered in the short run, one can use the following model:

$$Y_i = \beta_1 + \beta_2 X_i + \beta_3 X_i^2 + \beta_4 X_i^3 + u_i$$

where Y = total cost and X = output. The additional explanatory variables X_i^2 and X_i^3 are derived from X.

a. Express the data in the deviation form and obtain $(\mathbf{X'X})$, $(\mathbf{X'y})$, and $(\mathbf{X'X})^{-1}$.

b. Estimate β_2, β_3, and β_4.

c. Estimate the var-cov matrix of $\hat{\boldsymbol{\beta}}$.

d. Estimate β_1. Interpret $\hat{\beta}_1$ in the context of the problem.

e. Obtain R^2 and $\bar{R}^2$.

f. A priori, what are the signs of β_2, β_3, and β_4? Why?

g. From the total cost function given previously obtain expressions for the marginal and average cost functions.

h. Fit the average and marginal cost functions to the data and comment on the fit.

i. If $\beta_3 = \beta_4 = 0$, what is the nature of the marginal cost function? How would you test the hypothesis that $\beta_3 = \beta_4 = 0$?

j. How would you derive the total variable cost and average variable cost functions from the given data?

TABLE C.7
Labor Force Participation Experience of the Urban Poor: Census Tracts, New York City, 1970

Source: Census Tracts: New York, Bureau of the Census, U.S. Department of Commerce, 1970.

Tract No.	% in Labor Force, Y*	Mean Family Income, X_2†	Mean Family Size, X_3	Unemployment Rate, X_4‡
137	64.3	1,998	2.95	4.4
139	45.4	1,114	3.40	3.4
141	26.6	1,942	3.72	1.1
142	87.5	1,998	4.43	3.1
143	71.3	2,026	3.82	7.7
145	82.4	1,853	3.90	5.0
147	26.3	1,666	3.32	6.2
149	61.6	1,434	3.80	5.4
151	52.9	1,513	3.49	12.2
153	64.7	2,008	3.85	4.8
155	64.9	1,704	4.69	2.9
157	70.5	1,525	3.89	4.8
159	87.2	1,842	3.53	3.9
161	81.2	1,735	4.96	7.2
163	67.9	1,639	3.68	3.6

*Y = family heads under 65 years old.
†X_2 = dollars.
‡X_4 = percent of civilian labor force unemployed.

C.10. In order to study the labor force participation of urban poor families (families earning less than $3,943 in 1969), the data in Table C.7 were obtained from the 1970 Census of Population.

a. Using the regression model $Y_i = \beta_1 + \beta_2 X_{2i} + \beta_3 X_{3i} + \beta_4 X_{4i} + u_i$, obtain the estimates of the regression coefficients and interpret your results.

b. A priori, what are the expected signs of the regression coefficients in the preceding model and why?

c. How would you test the hypothesis that the overall unemployment rate has no effect on the labor force participation of the urban poor in the census tracts given in the accompanying table?

d. Should any variables be dropped from the preceding model? Why?

e. What other variables would you consider for inclusion in the model?

C.11. In an application of the Cobb–Douglas production function the following results were obtained:

$$\widehat{\ln Y_i} = 2.3542 + \underset{(0.3022)}{0.9576} \ln X_{2i} + \underset{(0.3571)}{0.8242} \ln X_{3i}$$

$$R^2 = 0.8432 \qquad \text{df} = 12$$

where Y = output, X_2 = labor input, and X_3 = capital input, and where the figures in parentheses are the estimated standard errors.

a. As noted in Chapter 7, the coefficients of the labor and capital inputs in the preceding equation give the elasticities of output with respect to labor and capital. Test the hypothesis that these elasticities are *individually* equal to unity.

b. Test the hypothesis that the labor and capital elasticities are equal, assuming (*i*) the covariance between the estimated labor and capital coefficients is zero, and (*ii*) it is −0.0972.

c. How would you test the overall significance of the preceding regression equation?

*C.12. Express the likelihood function for the k-variable regression model in matrix notation and show that $\tilde{\boldsymbol{\beta}}$, the vector of maximum likelihood estimators, is identical to $\hat{\boldsymbol{\beta}}$, the vector of OLS estimators of the k-variable regression model.

C.13. *Regression using standardized variables.* Consider the following sample regression functions (SRFs):

$$Y_i = \hat{\beta}_1 + \hat{\beta}_2 X_{2i} + \hat{\beta}_3 X_{3i} + \hat{u}_i \tag{1}$$

$$Y_i^* = b_1 + b_2 X_{2i}^* + b_3 X_{3i}^* + \hat{u}_i^* \tag{2}$$

where

$$Y_i^* = \frac{Y_i - \bar{Y}}{s_Y}$$

$$X_{2i}^* = \frac{X_{2i} - \bar{X}_2}{s_2}$$

$$X_{3i}^* = \frac{X_{3i} - \bar{X}_3}{s_3}$$

where the s's denote the sample standard deviations. As noted in Chapter 6, Section 6.3, the starred variables above are known as the *standardized variables*. These variables have zero means and unit ($=1$) standard deviations. Expressing all the variables in the deviation form, show the following for model (2):

a. $\mathbf{X'X} = \begin{bmatrix} 1 & r_{23} \\ r_{23} & 1 \end{bmatrix} n$

b. $\mathbf{X'y} = \begin{bmatrix} r_{12} \\ r_{13} \end{bmatrix} n$

c. $\mathbf{X'X}^{-1} = \dfrac{1}{n(1 - r_{23}^2)} \begin{bmatrix} 1 & -r_{23} \\ -r_{23} & 1 \end{bmatrix}$

d. $\hat{\boldsymbol{\beta}} = \begin{bmatrix} b_2 \\ b_3 \end{bmatrix} = \dfrac{1}{1 - r_{23}^2} \begin{bmatrix} r_{12} - r_{23} r_{13} \\ r_{13} - r_{23} r_{12} \end{bmatrix}$

e. $b_1 = 0$

Also establish the relationship between the b's and the $\hat{\beta}$'s.

(Note that in the preceding relations n denotes the sample size; r_{12}, r_{13}, and r_{23} denote the correlations between Y and X_2, between Y and X_3, and between X_2 and X_3, respectively.)

C.14. Verify Eqs. (C.10.18) and (C.10.19).

*C.15. *Constrained least-squares.* Assume

$$\mathbf{y} = \mathbf{X}\boldsymbol{\beta} + \mathbf{u} \tag{1}$$

which we want to estimate subject to a set of equality restrictions or constraints:

$$\mathbf{R}\boldsymbol{\beta} = \mathbf{r} \tag{2}$$

where $\mathbf{R}$ is a *known* matrix of order qxk ($q \leq k$) and $\mathbf{r}$ is a *known* vector of q elements. To illustrate, suppose our model is

$$Y_i = \beta_1 + \beta_2 X_{2i} + \beta_3 X_{3i} + \beta_4 X_{4i} + \beta_5 X_{5i} + u_i \tag{3}$$

*Optional.

and suppose we want to estimate this model subject to these restrictions:

$$\begin{aligned} \beta_2 - \beta_3 &= 0 \\ \beta_4 + \beta_5 &= 1 \end{aligned} \tag{4}$$

We can use some of the techniques discussed in Chapter 8 to incorporate these restrictions (e.g., $\beta_2 = \beta_3$ and $\beta_4 = 1 - \beta_5$, thus removing β_2 and β_4 from the model) and test for the validity of these restrictions by the F test discussed there. But a more direct way of estimating Eq. (3) incorporating the restrictions (4) directly in the estimating procedure is first to express the restrictions in the form of Eq. (2), which in the present case becomes

$$\mathbf{R} = \begin{bmatrix} 0 & 1 & -1 & 0 & 0 \\ 0 & 0 & 0 & 1 & 1 \end{bmatrix} \qquad \mathbf{r} = \begin{bmatrix} 0 \\ 1 \end{bmatrix} \tag{5}$$

Letting $\boldsymbol{\beta}^*$ denote the restricted least-squares or constrained least-squares estimator, one can show that $\boldsymbol{\beta}^*$ can be estimated by the following formula:*

$$\hat{\boldsymbol{\beta}}^* = \hat{\boldsymbol{\beta}} + (\mathbf{X}'\mathbf{X})^{-1}\mathbf{R}'[\mathbf{R}(\mathbf{X}'\mathbf{X})^{-1}\mathbf{R}']^{-1}(\mathbf{r} - \mathbf{R}) \tag{6}$$

where $\hat{\boldsymbol{\beta}}$ is the usual (unconstrained) estimator estimated from the usual formula $(\mathbf{X}'\mathbf{X})^{-1}\mathbf{X}'\mathbf{y}$.

a. What is the β vector in Eq. (3)?

b. Given this β vector, verify that the **R** matrix and **r** vector given in Eq. (5) do in fact incorporate the restrictions in Eq. (4).

c. Write down the **R** and **r** in the following cases:

(*i*) $\beta_2 = \beta_3 = \beta_4 = 2$

(*ii*) $\beta_2 = \beta_3$ and $\beta_4 = \beta_5$

(*iii*) $\beta_2 - 3\beta_3 = 5\beta_4$

(*iv*) $\beta_2 + 3\beta_3 = 0$

d. When will $\hat{\boldsymbol{\beta}}^* = \hat{\boldsymbol{\beta}}$?

Appendix CA

CA.1 Derivation of *k* Normal or Simultaneous Equations

Differentiating

$$\sum \hat{u}_i^2 = \sum (Y_i - \hat{\beta}_1 - \hat{\beta}_2 X_{2i} - \cdots - \hat{\beta}_k X_{ki})^2$$

partially with respect to $\hat{\beta}_1, \hat{\beta}_2, \ldots, \hat{\beta}_k$, we obtain

$$\frac{\partial \sum \hat{u}_i^2}{\partial \hat{\beta}_1} = 2\sum (Y_i - \hat{\beta}_1 - \hat{\beta}_2 X_{2i} - \cdots - \hat{\beta}_k X_{ki})(-1)$$

$$\frac{\partial \sum \hat{u}_i^2}{\partial \hat{\beta}_2} = 2\sum (Y_i - \hat{\beta}_1 - \hat{\beta}_2 X_{2i} - \cdots - \hat{\beta}_k X_{ki})(-X_{2i})$$

....

$$\frac{\partial \sum \hat{u}_i^2}{\partial \hat{\beta}_k} = 2\sum (Y_i - \hat{\beta}_1 - \hat{\beta}_2 X_{ki} - \cdots - \hat{\beta}_k X_{ki})(-X_{ki})$$

Setting the preceding partial derivatives equal to zero and rearranging the terms, we obtain the k normal equations given in Eq. (C.3.8).

*See J. Johnston, op. cit., p. 205.

CA.2 Matrix Derivation of Normal Equations

From Eq. (C.3.7) we obtain

$$\hat{\mathbf{u}}'\hat{\mathbf{u}} = \mathbf{y}'\mathbf{y} - 2\hat{\boldsymbol{\beta}}'\mathbf{X}'\mathbf{y} + \hat{\boldsymbol{\beta}}'\mathbf{X}'\mathbf{X}\hat{\boldsymbol{\beta}}$$

Using the rules of matrix differentiation given in **Appendix B, Section B.6,** we obtain

$$\frac{\partial(\hat{\mathbf{u}}'\hat{\mathbf{u}})}{\partial\hat{\boldsymbol{\beta}}} = -2\mathbf{X}'\mathbf{y} + 2\mathbf{X}'\mathbf{X}\hat{\boldsymbol{\beta}}$$

Setting the preceding equation to zero gives

$$(\mathbf{X}'\mathbf{X})\hat{\boldsymbol{\beta}} = \mathbf{X}'\mathbf{y}$$

whence $\hat{\boldsymbol{\beta}} = (\mathbf{X}'\mathbf{X})^{-1}\mathbf{X}'\mathbf{y}$, provided the inverse exists.

CA.3 Variance–Covariance Matrix of $\hat{\boldsymbol{\beta}}$

From Eq. (C.3.11) we obtain

$$\hat{\boldsymbol{\beta}} = (\mathbf{X}'\mathbf{X})^{-1}\mathbf{X}'\mathbf{y}$$

Substituting $\mathbf{y} = \mathbf{X}\boldsymbol{\beta} + \mathbf{u}$ into the preceding expression gives

$$\begin{aligned}\hat{\boldsymbol{\beta}} &= (\mathbf{X}'\mathbf{X})^{-1}\mathbf{X}'(\mathbf{X}\boldsymbol{\beta} + \mathbf{u}) \\ &= (\mathbf{X}'\mathbf{X})^{-1}\mathbf{X}'\mathbf{X}\boldsymbol{\beta} + (\mathbf{X}'\mathbf{X})^{-1}\mathbf{X}'\mathbf{u} \qquad (1) \\ &= \boldsymbol{\beta} + (\mathbf{X}'\mathbf{X})^{-1}\mathbf{X}'\mathbf{u}\end{aligned}$$

Therefore,

$$\hat{\boldsymbol{\beta}} - \boldsymbol{\beta} = (\mathbf{X}'\mathbf{X})^{-1}\mathbf{X}'\mathbf{u} \qquad (2)$$

By definition

$$\begin{aligned}\text{var-cov}(\hat{\boldsymbol{\beta}}) &= E[(\hat{\boldsymbol{\beta}} - \boldsymbol{\beta})(\hat{\boldsymbol{\beta}} - \boldsymbol{\beta})'] \\ &= E\{[(\mathbf{X}'\mathbf{X})^{-1}\mathbf{X}'\mathbf{u}][(\mathbf{X}'\mathbf{X})^{-1}\mathbf{X}'\mathbf{u}]'\} \qquad (3) \\ &= E[(\mathbf{X}'\mathbf{X})^{-1}\mathbf{X}'\mathbf{u}\mathbf{u}'\mathbf{X}(\mathbf{X}'\mathbf{X})^{-1}]\end{aligned}$$

where in the last step use is made of the fact that $(\mathbf{AB})' = \mathbf{B}'\mathbf{A}'$.

Noting that the X's are nonstochastic, on taking expectation of Eq. (3) we obtain

$$\begin{aligned}\text{var-cov}(\hat{\boldsymbol{\beta}}) &= (\mathbf{X}'\mathbf{X})^{-1}\mathbf{X}'E(\mathbf{u}\mathbf{u}')\mathbf{X}(\mathbf{X}'\mathbf{X})^{-1} \\ &= (\mathbf{X}'\mathbf{X})^{-1}\mathbf{X}'\sigma^2\mathbf{I}\mathbf{X}(\mathbf{X}'\mathbf{X})^{-1} \\ &= \sigma^2(\mathbf{X}'\mathbf{X})^{-1}\end{aligned}$$

which is the result given in Eq. (C.3.13). Note that in deriving the preceding result use is made of the assumption that $E(\mathbf{u}\mathbf{u}') = \sigma^2\mathbf{I}$.

CA.4 BLUE Property of OLS Estimators

From Eq. (C.3.11) we have

$$\hat{\boldsymbol{\beta}} = (\mathbf{X}'\mathbf{X})^{-1}\mathbf{X}'\mathbf{y} \qquad (1)$$

Since $(\mathbf{X}'\mathbf{X})^{-1}\mathbf{X}'$ is a matrix of fixed numbers, $\hat{\boldsymbol{\beta}}$ is a linear function of Y. Hence, by definition it is a linear estimator.

Recall that the PRF is

$$\mathbf{y} = \mathbf{X}\boldsymbol{\beta} + \mathbf{u} \tag{2}$$

Substituting this into Eq. (1), we obtain

$$\hat{\boldsymbol{\beta}} = (\mathbf{X}'\mathbf{X})^{-1}\mathbf{X}'(\mathbf{X}\boldsymbol{\beta} + \mathbf{u}) \tag{3}$$

$$= \boldsymbol{\beta} + (\mathbf{X}'\mathbf{X})^{-1}\mathbf{X}'\mathbf{u} \tag{4}$$

since $(\mathbf{X}'\mathbf{X})^{-1}\mathbf{X}'\mathbf{X} = \mathbf{I}$.

Taking expectation of Eq. (4) gives

$$E(\hat{\boldsymbol{\beta}}) = E(\boldsymbol{\beta}) + (\mathbf{X}'\mathbf{X})^{-1}\mathbf{X}'E(\mathbf{u})$$

$$= \boldsymbol{\beta} \tag{5}$$

since $E(\boldsymbol{\beta}) = \boldsymbol{\beta}$ (why?) and $E(\mathbf{u}) = \mathbf{0}$ by assumption, which shows that $\hat{\boldsymbol{\beta}}$ is an unbiased estimator of $\boldsymbol{\beta}$.

Let $\hat{\boldsymbol{\beta}}^*$ be any other linear estimator of $\boldsymbol{\beta}$, which can be written as

$$\boldsymbol{\beta}^* = [(\mathbf{X}'\mathbf{X})^{-1}\mathbf{X}' + \mathbf{C}]\mathbf{y} \tag{6}$$

where $\mathbf{C}$ is a matrix of constants.

Substituting for $\mathbf{y}$ from Eq. (2) into Eq. (6), we get

$$\hat{\boldsymbol{\beta}}^* = [(\mathbf{X}'\mathbf{X})^{-1}\mathbf{X}' + \mathbf{C}](\mathbf{X}\boldsymbol{\beta} + \mathbf{u})$$

$$= \boldsymbol{\beta} + \mathbf{C}\mathbf{X}\boldsymbol{\beta} + (\mathbf{X}'\mathbf{X})^{-1}\mathbf{X}'\mathbf{u} + \mathbf{C}\mathbf{u} \tag{7}$$

Now if $\hat{\boldsymbol{\beta}}^*$ is to be an unbiased estimator of $\boldsymbol{\beta}$, we must have

$$\mathbf{C}\mathbf{X} = 0 \qquad \text{(Why?)} \tag{8}$$

Using Eq. (8), Eq. (7) can be written as

$$\hat{\boldsymbol{\beta}}^* - \boldsymbol{\beta} = (\mathbf{X}'\mathbf{X})^{-1}\mathbf{X}'\mathbf{u} + \mathbf{C}\mathbf{u} \tag{9}$$

By definition, the var-cov $(\hat{\boldsymbol{\beta}}^*)$ is

$$E(\hat{\boldsymbol{\beta}}^* - \boldsymbol{\beta})(\hat{\boldsymbol{\beta}}^* - \boldsymbol{\beta})' = E[(\mathbf{X}'\mathbf{X})^{-1}\mathbf{X}'\mathbf{u} + \mathbf{C}\mathbf{u}][(\mathbf{X}'\mathbf{X})^{-1}\mathbf{X}'\mathbf{u} + \mathbf{C}\mathbf{u}]' \tag{10}$$

Making use of the properties of matrix inversion and transposition and after algebraic simplification, we obtain

$$\text{var-cov}\,(\hat{\boldsymbol{\beta}}^*) = \sigma^2(\mathbf{X}'\mathbf{X})^{-1} + \sigma^2\mathbf{C}\mathbf{C}'$$

$$= \text{var-cov}\,(\hat{\boldsymbol{\beta}}) + \sigma^2\mathbf{C}\mathbf{C}' \tag{11}$$

which shows that the variance-covariance matrix of the alternative unbiased linear estimator $\hat{\boldsymbol{\beta}}^*$ is equal to the variance-covariance matrix of the OLS estimator $\hat{\boldsymbol{\beta}}$ plus σ^2 times $\mathbf{C}\mathbf{C}'$, which is a positive semidefinite* matrix. Hence the variances of a given element of $\hat{\boldsymbol{\beta}}^*$ must necessarily be equal to or greater than the corresponding element of $\hat{\boldsymbol{\beta}}$, which shows that $\hat{\boldsymbol{\beta}}$ is BLUE. Of course, if $\mathbf{C}$ is a null matrix, i.e., $\mathbf{C} = \mathbf{0}$, then $\hat{\boldsymbol{\beta}}^* = \hat{\boldsymbol{\beta}}$, which is another way of saying that if we have found a BLUE estimator, it must be the least-squares estimator $\hat{\boldsymbol{\beta}}$.

*See references in **Appendix B.**

Appendix D

Statistical Tables

TABLE D.1
Areas Under the Standardized Normal Distribution

Example

$\Pr(0 \leq Z \leq 1.96) = 0.4750$

$\Pr(Z \geq 1.96) = 0.5 - 0.4750 = 0.025$

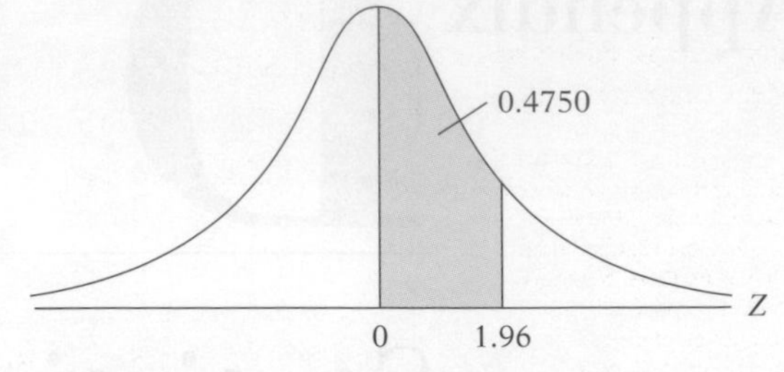

Z	.00	.01	.02	.03	.04	.05	.06	.07	.08	.09
0.0	.0000	.0040	.0080	.0120	.0160	.0199	.0239	.0279	.0319	.0359
0.1	.0398	.0438	.0478	.0517	.0557	.0596	.0636	.0675	.0714	.0753
0.2	.0793	.0832	.0871	.0910	.0948	.0987	.1026	.1064	.1103	.1141
0.3	.1179	.1217	.1255	.1293	.1331	.1368	.1406	.1443	.1480	.1517
0.4	.1554	.1591	.1628	.1664	.1700	.1736	.1772	.1808	.1844	.1879
0.5	.1915	.1950	.1985	.2019	.2054	.2088	.2123	.2157	.2190	.2224
0.6	.2257	.2291	.2324	.2357	.2389	.2422	.2454	.2486	.2517	.2549
0.7	.2580	.2611	.2642	.2673	.2704	.2734	.2764	.2794	.2823	.2852
0.8	.2881	.2910	.2939	.2967	.2995	.3023	.3051	.3078	.3106	.3133
0.9	.3159	.3186	.3212	.3238	.3264	.3289	.3315	.3340	.3365	.3389
1.0	.3413	.3438	.3461	.3485	.3508	.3531	.3554	.3577	.3599	.3621
1.1	.3643	.3665	.3686	.3708	.3729	.3749	.3770	.3790	.3810	.3830
1.2	.3849	.3869	.3888	.3907	.3925	.3944	.3962	.3980	.3997	.4015
1.3	.4032	.4049	.4066	.4082	.4099	.4115	.4131	.4147	.4162	.4177
1.4	.4192	.4207	.4222	.4236	.4251	.4265	.4279	.4292	.4306	.4319
1.5	.4332	.4345	.4357	.4370	.4382	.4394	.4406	.4418	.4429	.4441
1.6	.4452	.4463	.4474	.4484	.4495	.4505	.4515	.4525	.4535	.4545
1.7	.4454	.4564	.4573	.4582	.4591	.4599	.4608	.4616	.4625	.4633
1.8	.4641	.4649	.4656	.4664	.4671	.4678	.4686	.4693	.4699	.4706
1.9	.4713	.4719	.4726	.4732	.4738	.4744	.4750	.4756	.4761	.4767
2.0	.4772	.4778	.4783	.4788	.4793	.4798	.4803	.4808	.4812	.4817
2.1	.4821	.4826	.4830	.4834	.4838	.4842	.4846	.4850	.4854	.4857
2.2	.4861	.4864	.4868	.4871	.4875	.4878	.4881	.4884	.4887	.4890
2.3	.4893	.4896	.4898	.4901	.4904	.4906	.4909	.4911	.4913	.4916
2.4	.4918	.4920	.4922	.4925	.4927	.4929	.4931	.4932	.4934	.4936
2.5	.4938	.4940	.4941	.4943	.4945	.4946	.4948	.4949	.4951	.4952
2.6	.4953	.4955	.4956	.4957	.4959	.4960	.4961	.4962	.4963	.4964
2.7	.4965	.4966	.4967	.4968	.4969	.4970	.4971	.4972	.4973	.4974
2.8	.4974	.4975	.4976	.4977	.4977	.4978	.4979	.4979	.4980	.4981
2.9	.4981	.4982	.4982	.4983	.4984	.4984	.4985	.4985	.4986	.4986
3.0	.4987	.4987	.4987	.4988	.4988	.4989	.4989	.4989	.4990	.4990

Note: This table gives the area in the right-hand tail of the distribution (i.e., $Z \geq 0$). But since the normal distribution is symmetrical about $Z = 0$, the area in the left-hand tail is the same as the area in the corresponding right-hand tail. For example, $P(-1.96 \leq Z \leq 0) = 0.4750$. Therefore, $P(-1.96 \leq Z \leq 1.96) = 2(0.4750) = 0.95$.

TABLE D.2

Percentage Points of the *t* Distribution

Source: From E. S. Pearson and H. O. Hartley, eds., *Biometrika Tables for Statisticians,* vol. 1, 3d ed., table 12, Cambridge University Press, New York, 1966. Reproduced by permission of the editors and trustees of *Biometrika.*

Example

$\Pr(t > 2.086) = 0.025$

$\Pr(t > 1.725) = 0.05$ for df = 20

$\Pr(|t| > 1.725) = 0.10$

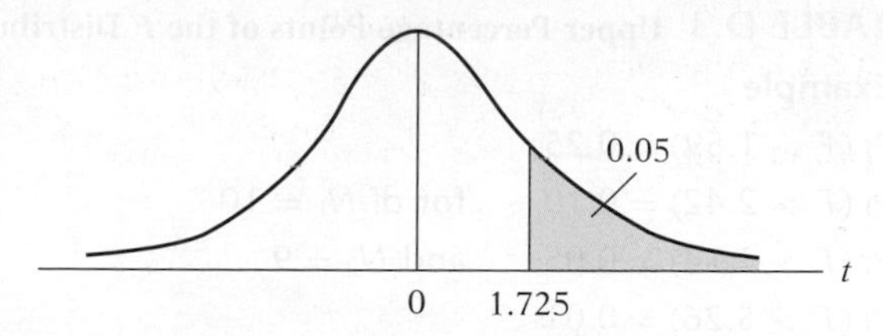

df \ Pr	0.25 0.50	0.10 0.20	0.05 0.10	0.025 0.05	0.01 0.02	0.005 0.010	0.001 0.002
1	1.000	3.078	6.314	12.706	31.821	63.657	318.31
2	0.816	1.886	2.920	4.303	6.965	9.925	22.327
3	0.765	1.638	2.353	3.182	4.541	5.841	10.214
4	0.741	1.533	2.132	2.776	3.747	4.604	7.173
5	0.727	1.476	2.015	2.571	3.365	4.032	5.893
6	0.718	1.440	1.943	2.447	3.143	3.707	5.208
7	0.711	1.415	1.895	2.365	2.998	3.499	4.785
8	0.706	1.397	1.860	2.306	2.896	3.355	4.501
9	0.703	1.383	1.833	2.262	2.821	3.250	4.297
10	0.700	1.372	1.812	2.228	2.764	3.169	4.144
11	0.697	1.363	1.796	2.201	2.718	3.106	4.025
12	0.695	1.356	1.782	2.179	2.681	3.055	3.930
13	0.694	1.350	1.771	2.160	2.650	3.012	3.852
14	0.692	1.345	1.761	2.145	2.624	2.977	3.787
15	0.691	1.341	1.753	2.131	2.602	2.947	3.733
16	0.690	1.337	1.746	2.120	2.583	2.921	3.686
17	0.689	1.333	1.740	2.110	2.567	2.898	3.646
18	0.688	1.330	1.734	2.101	2.552	2.878	3.610
19	0.688	1.328	1.729	2.093	2.539	2.861	3.579
20	0.687	1.325	1.725	2.086	2.528	2.845	3.552
21	0.686	1.323	1.721	2.080	2.518	2.831	3.527
22	0.686	1.321	1.717	2.074	2.508	2.819	3.505
23	0.685	1.319	1.714	2.069	2.500	2.807	3.485
24	0.685	1.318	1.711	2.064	2.492	2.797	3.467
25	0.684	1.316	1.708	2.060	2.485	2.787	3.450
26	0.684	1.315	1.706	2.056	2.479	2.779	3.435
27	0.684	1.314	1.703	2.052	2.473	2.771	3.421
28	0.683	1.313	1.701	2.048	2.467	2.763	3.408
29	0.683	1.311	1.699	2.045	2.462	2.756	3.396
30	0.683	1.310	1.697	2.042	2.457	2.750	3.385
40	0.681	1.303	1.684	2.021	2.423	2.704	3.307
60	0.679	1.296	1.671	2.000	2.390	2.660	3.232
120	0.677	1.289	1.658	1.980	2.358	2.617	3.160
∞	0.674	1.282	1.645	1.960	2.326	2.576	3.090

Note: The smaller probability shown at the head of each column is the area in one tail; the larger probability is the area in both tails.

TABLE D.3 Upper Percentage Points of the F Distribution

Example

$\Pr(F > 1.59) = 0.25$

$\Pr(F > 2.42) = 0.10$ for df $N_1 = 10$

$\Pr(F > 3.14) = 0.05$ and $N_2 = 9$

$\Pr(F > 5.26) = 0.01$

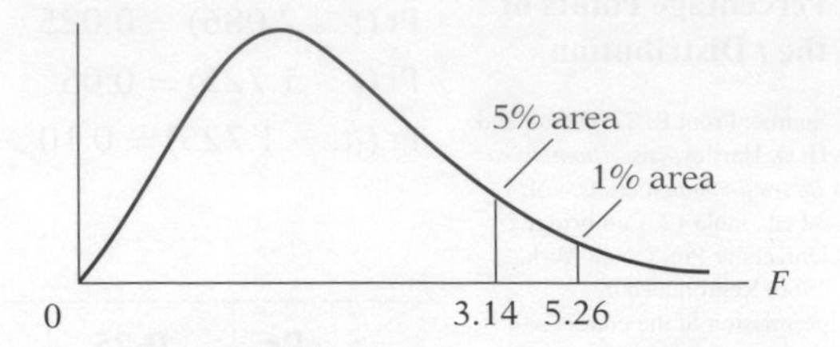

df for denominator N_2		df for numerator N_1											
	Pr	1	2	3	4	5	6	7	8	9	10	11	12
1	.25	5.83	7.50	8.20	8.58	8.82	8.98	9.10	9.19	9.26	9.32	9.36	9.41
	.10	39.9	49.5	53.6	55.8	57.2	58.2	58.9	59.4	59.9	60.2	60.5	60.7
	.05	161	200	216	225	230	234	237	239	241	242	243	244
2	.25	2.57	3.00	3.15	3.23	3.28	3.31	3.34	3.35	3.37	3.38	3.39	3.39
	.10	8.53	9.00	9.16	9.24	9.29	9.33	9.35	9.37	9.38	9.39	9.40	9.41
	.05	18.5	19.0	19.2	19.2	19.3	19.3	19.4	19.4	19.4	19.4	19.4	19.4
	.01	98.5	99.0	99.2	99.2	99.3	99.3	99.4	99.4	99.4	99.4	99.4	99.4
3	.25	2.02	2.28	2.36	2.39	2.41	2.42	2.43	2.44	2.44	2.44	2.45	2.45
	.10	5.54	5.46	5.39	5.34	5.31	5.28	5.27	5.25	5.24	5.23	5.22	5.22
	.05	10.1	9.55	9.28	9.12	9.01	8.94	8.89	8.85	8.81	8.79	8.76	8.74
	.01	34.1	30.8	29.5	28.7	28.2	27.9	27.7	27.5	27.3	27.2	27.1	27.1
4	.25	1.81	2.00	2.05	2.06	2.07	2.08	2.08	2.08	2.08	2.08	2.08	2.08
	.10	4.54	4.32	4.19	4.11	4.05	4.01	3.98	3.95	3.94	3.92	3.91	3.90
	.05	7.71	6.94	6.59	6.39	6.26	6.16	6.09	6.04	6.00	5.96	5.94	5.91
	.01	21.2	18.0	16.7	16.0	15.5	15.2	15.0	14.8	14.7	14.5	14.4	14.4
5	.25	1.69	1.85	1.88	1.89	1.89	1.89	1.89	1.89	1.89	1.89	1.89	1.89
	.10	4.06	3.78	3.62	3.52	3.45	3.40	3.37	3.34	3.32	3.30	3.28	3.27
	.05	6.61	5.79	5.41	5.19	5.05	4.95	4.88	4.82	4.77	4.74	4.71	4.68
	.01	16.3	13.3	12.1	11.4	11.0	10.7	10.5	10.3	10.2	10.1	9.96	9.89
6	.25	1.62	1.76	1.78	1.79	1.79	1.78	1.78	1.78	1.77	1.77	1.77	1.77
	.10	3.78	3.46	3.29	3.18	3.11	3.05	3.01	2.98	2.96	2.94	2.92	2.90
	.05	5.99	5.14	4.76	4.53	4.39	4.28	4.21	4.15	4.10	4.06	4.03	4.00
	.01	13.7	10.9	9.78	9.15	8.75	8.47	8.26	8.10	7.98	7.87	7.79	7.72
7	.25	1.57	1.70	1.72	1.72	1.71	1.71	1.70	1.70	1.69	1.69	1.69	1.68
	.10	3.59	3.26	3.07	2.96	2.88	2.83	2.78	2.75	2.72	2.70	2.68	2.67
	.05	5.59	4.74	4.35	4.12	3.97	3.87	3.79	3.73	3.68	3.64	3.60	3.57
	.01	12.2	9.55	8.45	7.85	7.46	7.19	6.99	6.84	6.72	6.62	6.54	6.47
8	.25	1.54	1.66	1.67	1.66	1.66	1.65	1.64	1.64	1.63	1.63	1.63	1.62
	.10	3.46	3.11	2.92	2.81	2.73	2.67	2.62	2.59	2.56	2.54	2.52	2.50
	.05	5.32	4.46	4.07	3.84	3.69	3.58	3.50	3.44	3.39	3.35	3.31	3.28
	.01	11.3	8.65	7.59	7.01	6.63	6.37	6.18	6.03	5.91	5.81	5.73	5.67
9	.25	1.51	1.62	1.63	1.63	1.62	1.61	1.60	1.60	1.59	1.59	1.58	1.58
	.10	3.36	3.01	2.81	2.69	2.61	2.55	2.51	2.47	2.44	2.42	2.40	2.38
	.05	5.12	4.26	3.86	3.63	3.48	3.37	3.29	3.23	3.18	3.14	3.10	3.07
	.01	10.6	8.02	6.99	6.42	6.06	5.80	5.61	5.47	5.35	5.26	5.18	5.11

Source: From E. S. Pearson and H. O. Hartley, eds., *Biometrika Tables for Statisticians,* vol. 1, 3d ed., table 18, Cambridge University Press, New York, 1966. Reproduced by permission of the editors and trustees of *Biometrika*.

df for numerator N_1													df for denominator N_2
15	20	24	30	40	50	60	100	120	200	500	∞	Pr	
9.49	9.58	9.63	9.67	9.71	9.74	9.76	9.78	9.80	9.82	9.84	9.85	.25	
61.2	61.7	62.0	62.3	62.5	62.7	62.8	63.0	63.1	63.2	63.3	63.3	.10	1
246	248	249	250	251	252	252	253	253	254	254	254	.05	
3.41	3.43	3.43	3.44	3.45	3.45	3.46	3.47	3.47	3.48	3.48	3.48	.25	
9.42	9.44	9.45	9.46	9.47	9.47	9.47	9.48	9.48	9.49	9.49	9.49	.10	2
19.4	19.4	19.5	19.5	19.5	19.5	19.5	19.5	19.5	19.5	19.5	19.5	.05	
99.4	99.4	99.5	99.5	99.5	99.5	99.5	99.5	99.5	99.5	99.5	99.5	.01	
2.46	2.46	2.46	2.47	2.47	2.47	2.47	2.47	2.47	2.47	2.47	2.47	.25	
5.20	5.18	5.18	5.17	5.16	5.15	5.15	5.14	5.14	5.14	5.14	5.13	.10	3
8.70	8.66	8.64	8.62	8.59	8.58	8.57	8.55	8.55	8.54	8.53	8.53	.05	
26.9	26.7	26.6	26.5	26.4	26.4	26.3	26.2	26.2	26.2	26.1	26.1	.01	
2.08	2.08	2.08	2.08	2.08	2.08	2.08	2.08	2.08	2.08	2.08	2.08	.25	
3.87	3.84	3.83	3.82	3.80	3.80	3.79	3.78	3.78	3.77	3.76	3.76	.10	4
5.86	5.80	5.77	5.75	5.72	5.70	5.69	5.66	5.66	5.65	5.64	5.63	.05	
14.2	14.0	13.9	13.8	13.7	13.7	13.7	13.6	13.6	13.5	13.5	13.5	.01	
1.89	1.88	1.88	1.88	1.88	1.88	1.87	1.87	1.87	1.87	1.87	1.87	.25	
3.24	3.21	3.19	3.17	3.16	3.15	3.14	3.13	3.12	3.12	3.11	3.10	.10	5
4.62	4.56	4.53	4.50	4.46	4.44	4.43	4.41	4.40	4.39	4.37	4.36	.05	
9.72	9.55	9.47	9.38	9.29	9.24	9.20	9.13	9.11	9.08	9.04	9.02	.01	
1.76	1.76	1.75	1.75	1.75	1.75	1.74	1.74	1.74	1.74	1.74	1.74	.25	
2.87	2.84	2.82	2.80	2.78	2.77	2.76	2.75	2.74	2.73	2.73	2.72	.10	6
3.94	3.87	3.84	3.81	3.77	3.75	3.74	3.71	3.70	3.69	3.68	3.67	.05	
7.56	7.40	7.31	7.23	7.14	7.09	7.06	6.99	6.97	6.93	6.90	6.88	.01	
1.68	1.67	1.67	1.66	1.66	1.66	1.65	1.65	1.65	1.65	1.65	1.65	.25	
2.63	2.59	2.58	2.56	2.54	2.52	2.51	2.50	2.49	2.48	2.48	2.47	.10	7
3.51	3.44	3.41	3.38	3.34	3.32	3.30	3.27	3.27	3.25	3.24	3.23	.05	
6.31	6.16	6.07	5.99	5.91	5.86	5.82	5.75	5.74	5.70	5.67	5.65	.01	
1.62	1.61	1.60	1.60	1.59	1.59	1.59	1.58	1.58	1.58	1.58	1.58	.25	
2.46	2.42	2.40	2.38	2.36	2.35	2.34	2.32	2.32	2.31	2.30	2.29	.10	8
3.22	3.15	3.12	3.08	3.04	2.02	3.01	2.97	2.97	2.95	2.94	2.93	.05	
5.52	5.36	5.28	5.20	5.12	5.07	5.03	4.96	4.95	4.91	4.88	4.86	.01	
1.57	1.56	1.56	1.55	1.55	1.54	1.54	1.53	1.53	1.53	1.53	1.53	.25	
2.34	2.30	2.28	2.25	2.23	2.22	2.21	2.19	2.18	2.17	2.17	2.16	.10	9
3.01	2.94	2.90	2.86	2.83	2.80	2.79	2.76	2.75	2.73	2.72	2.71	.05	
4.96	4.81	4.73	4.65	4.57	4.52	4.48	4.42	4.40	4.36	4.33	4.31	.01	

(*Continued*)

TABLE D.3 Upper Percentage Points of the *F* Distribution (*Continued*)

df for denominator N_2		df for numerator N_1											
	Pr	1	2	3	4	5	6	7	8	9	10	11	12
10	.25	1.49	1.60	1.60	1.59	1.59	1.58	1.57	1.56	1.56	1.55	1.55	1.54
	.10	3.29	2.92	2.73	2.61	2.52	2.46	2.41	2.38	2.35	2.32	2.30	2.28
	.05	4.96	4.10	3.71	3.48	3.33	3.22	3.14	3.07	3.02	2.98	2.94	2.91
	.01	10.0	7.56	6.55	5.99	5.64	5.39	5.20	5.06	4.94	4.85	4.77	4.71
11	.25	1.47	1.58	1.58	1.57	1.56	1.55	1.54	1.53	1.53	1.52	1.52	1.51
	.10	3.23	2.86	2.66	2.54	2.45	2.39	2.34	2.30	2.27	2.25	2.23	2.21
	.05	4.84	3.98	3.59	3.36	3.20	3.09	3.01	2.95	2.90	2.85	2.82	2.79
	.01	9.65	7.21	6.22	5.67	5.32	5.07	4.89	4.74	4.63	4.54	4.46	4.40
12	.25	1.46	1.56	1.56	1.55	1.54	1.53	1.52	1.51	1.51	1.50	1.50	1.49
	.10	3.18	2.81	2.61	2.48	2.39	2.33	2.28	2.24	2.21	2.19	2.17	2.15
	.05	4.75	3.89	3.49	3.26	3.11	3.00	2.91	2.85	2.80	2.75	2.72	2.69
	.01	9.33	6.93	5.95	5.41	5.06	4.82	4.64	4.50	4.39	4.30	4.22	4.16
13	.25	1.45	1.55	1.55	1.53	1.52	1.51	1.50	1.49	1.49	1.48	1.47	1.47
	.10	3.14	2.76	2.56	2.43	2.35	2.28	2.23	2.20	2.16	2.14	2.12	2.10
	.05	4.67	3.81	3.41	3.18	3.03	2.92	2.83	2.77	2.71	2.67	2.63	2.60
	.01	9.07	6.70	5.74	5.21	4.86	4.62	4.44	4.30	4.19	4.10	4.02	3.96
14	.25	1.44	1.53	1.53	1.52	1.51	1.50	1.49	1.48	1.47	1.46	1.46	1.45
	.10	3.10	2.73	2.52	2.39	2.31	2.24	2.19	2.15	2.12	2.10	2.08	2.05
	.05	4.60	3.74	3.34	3.11	2.96	2.85	2.76	2.70	2.65	2.60	2.57	2.53
	.01	8.86	6.51	5.56	5.04	4.69	4.46	4.28	4.14	4.03	3.94	3.86	3.80
15	.25	1.43	1.52	1.52	1.51	1.49	1.48	1.47	1.46	1.46	1.45	1.44	1.44
	.10	3.07	2.70	2.49	2.36	2.27	2.21	2.16	2.12	2.09	2.06	2.04	2.02
	.05	4.54	3.68	3.29	3.06	2.90	2.79	2.71	2.64	2.59	2.54	2.51	2.48
	.01	8.68	6.36	5.42	4.89	4.56	4.32	4.14	4.00	3.89	3.80	3.73	3.67
16	.25	1.42	1.51	1.51	1.50	1.48	1.47	1.46	1.45	1.44	1.44	1.44	1.43
	.10	3.05	2.67	2.46	2.33	2.24	2.18	2.13	2.09	2.06	2.03	2.01	1.99
	.05	4.49	3.63	3.24	3.01	2.85	2.74	2.66	2.59	2.54	2.49	2.46	2.42
	.01	8.53	6.23	5.29	4.77	4.44	4.20	4.03	3.89	3.78	3.69	3.62	3.55
17	.25	1.42	1.51	1.50	1.49	1.47	1.46	1.45	1.44	1.43	1.43	1.42	1.41
	.10	3.03	2.64	2.44	2.31	2.22	2.15	2.10	2.06	2.03	2.00	1.98	1.96
	.05	4.45	3.59	3.20	2.96	2.81	2.70	2.61	2.55	2.49	2.45	2.41	2.38
	.01	8.40	6.11	5.18	4.67	4.34	4.10	3.93	3.79	3.68	3.59	3.52	3.46
18	.25	1.41	1.50	1.49	1.48	1.46	1.45	1.44	1.43	1.42	1.42	1.41	1.40
	.10	3.01	2.62	2.42	2.29	2.20	2.13	2.08	2.04	2.00	1.98	1.96	1.93
	.05	4.41	3.55	3.16	2.93	2.77	2.66	2.58	2.51	2.46	2.41	2.37	2.34
	.01	8.29	6.01	5.09	4.58	4.25	4.01	3.84	3.71	3.60	3.51	3.43	3.37
19	.25	1.41	1.49	1.49	1.47	1.46	1.44	1.43	1.42	1.41	1.41	1.40	1.40
	.10	2.99	2.61	2.40	2.27	2.18	2.11	2.06	2.02	1.98	1.96	1.94	1.91
	.05	4.38	3.52	3.13	2.90	2.74	2.63	2.54	2.48	2.42	2.38	2.34	2.31
	.01	8.18	5.93	5.01	4.50	4.17	3.94	3.77	3.63	3.52	3.43	3.36	3.30
20	.25	1.40	1.49	1.48	1.46	1.45	1.44	1.43	1.42	1.41	1.40	1.39	1.39
	.10	2.97	2.59	2.38	2.25	2.16	2.09	2.04	2.00	1.96	1.94	1.92	1.89
	.05	4.35	3.49	3.10	2.87	2.71	2.60	2.51	2.45	2.39	2.35	2.31	2.28
	.01	8.10	5.85	4.94	4.43	4.10	3.87	3.70	3.56	3.46	3.37	3.29	3.23

df for numerator N_1													df for denom-inator N_2
15	20	24	30	40	50	60	100	120	200	500	∞	Pr	
1.53	1.52	1.52	1.51	1.51	1.50	1.50	1.49	1.49	1.49	1.48	1.48	.25	10
2.24	2.20	2.18	2.16	2.13	2.12	2.11	2.09	2.08	2.07	2.06	2.06	.10	
2.85	2.77	2.74	2.70	2.66	2.64	2.62	2.59	2.58	2.56	2.55	2.54	.05	
4.56	4.41	4.33	4.25	4.17	4.12	4.08	4.01	4.00	3.96	3.93	3.91	.01	
1.50	1.49	1.49	1.48	1.47	1.47	1.47	1.46	1.46	1.46	1.45	1.45	.25	11
2.17	2.12	2.10	2.08	2.05	2.04	2.03	2.00	2.00	1.99	1.98	1.97	.10	
2.72	2.65	2.61	2.57	2.53	2.51	2.49	2.46	2.45	2.43	2.42	2.40	.05	
4.25	4.10	4.02	3.94	3.86	3.81	3.78	3.71	3.69	3.66	3.62	3.60	.01	
1.48	1.47	1.46	1.45	1.45	1.44	1.44	1.43	1.43	1.43	1.42	1.42	.25	12
2.10	2.06	2.04	2.01	1.99	1.97	1.96	1.94	1.93	1.92	1.91	1.90	.10	
2.62	2.54	2.51	2.47	2.43	2.40	2.38	2.35	2.34	2.32	2.31	2.30	.05	
4.01	3.86	3.78	3.70	3.62	3.57	3.54	3.47	3.45	3.41	3.38	3.36	.01	
1.46	1.45	1.44	1.43	1.42	1.42	1.42	1.41	1.41	1.40	1.40	1.40	.25	13
2.05	2.01	1.98	1.96	1.93	1.92	1.90	1.88	1.88	1.86	1.85	1.85	.10	
2.53	2.46	2.42	2.38	2.34	2.31	2.30	2.26	2.25	2.23	2.22	2.21	.05	
3.82	3.66	3.59	3.51	3.43	3.38	3.34	3.27	3.25	3.22	3.19	3.17	.01	
1.44	1.43	1.42	1.41	1.41	1.40	1.40	1.39	1.39	1.39	1.38	1.38	.25	14
2.01	1.96	1.94	1.91	1.89	1.87	1.86	1.83	1.83	1.82	1.80	1.80	.10	
2.46	2.39	2.35	2.31	2.27	2.24	2.22	2.19	2.18	2.16	2.14	2.13	.05	
3.66	3.51	3.43	3.35	3.27	3.22	3.18	3.11	3.09	3.06	3.03	3.00	.01	
1.43	1.41	1.41	1.40	1.39	1.39	1.38	1.38	1.37	1.37	1.36	1.36	.25	15
1.97	1.92	1.90	1.87	1.85	1.83	1.82	1.79	1.79	1.77	1.76	1.76	.10	
2.40	2.33	2.29	2.25	2.20	2.18	2.16	2.12	2.11	2.10	2.08	2.07	.05	
3.52	3.37	3.29	3.21	3.13	3.08	3.05	2.98	2.96	2.92	2.89	2.87	.01	
1.41	1.40	1.39	1.38	1.37	1.37	1.36	1.36	1.35	1.35	1.34	1.34	.25	16
1.94	1.89	1.87	1.84	1.81	1.79	1.78	1.76	1.75	1.74	1.73	1.72	.10	
2.35	2.28	2.24	2.19	2.15	2.12	2.11	2.07	2.06	2.04	2.02	2.01	.05	
3.41	3.26	3.18	3.10	3.02	2.97	2.93	2.86	2.84	2.81	2.78	2.75	.01	
1.40	1.39	1.38	1.37	1.36	1.35	1.35	1.34	1.34	1.34	1.33	1.33	.25	17
1.91	1.86	1.84	1.81	1.78	1.76	1.75	1.73	1.72	1.71	1.69	1.69	.10	
2.31	2.23	2.19	2.15	2.10	2.08	2.06	2.02	2.01	1.99	1.97	1.96	.05	
3.31	3.16	3.08	3.00	2.92	2.87	2.83	2.76	2.75	2.71	2.68	2.65	.01	
1.39	1.38	1.37	1.36	1.35	1.34	1.34	1.33	1.33	1.32	1.32	1.32	.25	18
1.89	1.84	1.81	1.78	1.75	1.74	1.72	1.70	1.69	1.68	1.67	1.66	.10	
2.27	2.19	2.15	2.11	2.06	2.04	2.02	1.98	1.97	1.95	1.93	1.92	.05	
3.23	3.08	3.00	2.92	2.84	2.78	2.75	2.68	2.66	2.62	2.59	2.57	.01	
1.38	1.37	1.36	1.35	1.34	1.33	1.33	1.32	1.32	1.31	1.31	1.30	.25	19
1.86	1.81	1.79	1.76	1.73	1.71	1.70	1.67	1.67	1.65	1.64	1.63	.10	
2.23	2.16	2.11	2.07	2.03	2.00	1.98	1.94	1.93	1.91	1.89	1.88	.05	
3.15	3.00	2.92	2.84	2.76	2.71	2.67	2.60	2.58	2.55	2.51	2.49	.01	
1.37	1.36	1.35	1.34	1.33	1.33	1.32	1.31	1.31	1.30	1.30	1.29	.25	20
1.84	1.79	1.77	1.74	1.71	1.69	1.68	1.65	1.64	1.63	1.62	1.61	.10	
2.20	2.12	2.08	2.04	1.99	1.97	1.95	1.91	1.90	1.88	1.86	1.84	.05	
3.09	2.94	2.86	2.78	2.69	2.64	2.61	2.54	2.52	2.48	2.44	2.42	.01	

(*Continued*)

TABLE D.3 Upper Percentage Points of the *F* Distribution (*Continued*)

df for denominator N_2	df for numerator N_1												
	Pr	1	2	3	4	5	6	7	8	9	10	11	12
22	.25	1.40	1.48	1.47	1.45	1.44	1.42	1.41	1.40	1.39	1.39	1.38	1.37
	.10	2.95	2.56	2.35	2.22	2.13	2.06	2.01	1.97	1.93	1.90	1.88	1.86
	.05	4.30	3.44	3.05	2.82	2.66	2.55	2.46	2.40	2.34	2.30	2.26	2.23
	.01	7.95	5.72	4.82	4.31	3.99	3.76	3.59	3.45	3.35	3.26	3.18	3.12
24	.25	1.39	1.47	1.46	1.44	1.43	1.41	1.40	1.39	1.38	1.38	1.37	1.36
	.10	2.93	2.54	2.33	2.19	2.10	2.04	1.98	1.94	1.91	1.88	1.85	1.83
	.05	4.26	3.40	3.01	2.78	2.62	2.51	2.42	2.36	2.30	2.25	2.21	2.18
	.01	7.82	5.61	4.72	4.22	3.90	3.67	3.50	3.36	3.26	3.17	3.09	3.03
26	.25	1.38	1.46	1.45	1.44	1.42	1.41	1.39	1.38	1.37	1.37	1.36	1.35
	.10	2.91	2.52	2.31	2.17	2.08	2.01	1.96	1.92	1.88	1.86	1.84	1.81
	.05	4.23	3.37	2.98	2.74	2.59	2.47	2.39	2.32	2.27	2.22	2.18	2.15
	.01	7.72	5.53	4.64	4.14	3.82	3.59	3.42	3.29	3.18	3.09	3.02	2.96
28	.25	1.38	1.46	1.45	1.43	1.41	1.40	1.39	1.38	1.37	1.36	1.35	1.34
	.10	2.89	2.50	2.29	2.16	2.06	2.00	1.94	1.90	1.87	1.84	1.81	1.79
	.05	4.20	3.34	2.95	2.71	2.56	2.45	2.36	2.29	2.24	2.19	2.15	2.12
	.01	7.64	5.45	4.57	4.07	3.75	3.53	3.36	3.23	3.12	3.03	2.96	2.90
30	.25	1.38	1.45	1.44	1.42	1.41	1.39	1.38	1.37	1.36	1.35	1.35	1.34
	.10	2.88	2.49	2.28	2.14	2.05	1.98	1.93	1.88	1.85	1.82	1.79	1.77
	.05	4.17	3.32	2.92	2.69	2.53	2.42	2.33	2.27	2.21	2.16	2.13	2.09
	.01	7.56	5.39	4.51	4.02	3.70	3.47	3.30	3.17	3.07	2.98	2.91	2.84
40	.25	1.36	1.44	1.42	1.40	1.39	1.37	1.36	1.35	1.34	1.33	1.32	1.31
	.10	2.84	2.44	2.23	2.09	2.00	1.93	1.87	1.83	1.79	1.76	1.73	1.71
	.05	4.08	3.23	2.84	2.61	2.45	2.34	2.25	2.18	2.12	2.08	2.04	2.00
	.01	7.31	5.18	4.31	3.83	3.51	3.29	3.12	2.99	2.89	2.80	2.73	2.66
60	.25	1.35	1.42	1.41	1.38	1.37	1.35	1.33	1.32	1.31	1.30	1.29	1.29
	.10	2.79	2.39	2.18	2.04	1.95	1.87	1.82	1.77	1.74	1.71	1.68	1.66
	.05	4.00	3.15	2.76	2.53	2.37	2.25	2.17	2.10	2.04	1.99	1.95	1.92
	.01	7.08	4.98	4.13	3.65	3.34	3.12	2.95	2.82	2.72	2.63	2.56	2.50
120	.25	1.34	1.40	1.39	1.37	1.35	1.33	1.31	1.30	1.29	1.28	1.27	1.26
	.10	2.75	2.35	2.13	1.99	1.90	1.82	1.77	1.72	1.68	1.65	1.62	1.60
	.05	3.92	3.07	2.68	2.45	2.29	2.17	2.09	2.02	1.96	1.91	1.87	1.83
	.01	6.85	4.79	3.95	3.48	3.17	2.96	2.79	2.66	2.56	2.47	2.40	2.34
200	.25	1.33	1.39	1.38	1.36	1.34	1.32	1.31	1.29	1.28	1.27	1.26	1.25
	.10	2.73	2.33	2.11	1.97	1.88	1.80	1.75	1.70	1.66	1.63	1.60	1.57
	.05	3.89	3.04	2.65	2.42	2.26	2.14	2.06	1.98	1.93	1.88	1.84	1.80
	.01	6.76	4.71	3.88	3.41	3.11	2.89	2.73	2.60	2.50	2.41	2.34	2.27
∞	.25	1.32	1.39	1.37	1.35	1.33	1.31	1.29	1.28	1.27	1.25	1.24	1.24
	.10	2.71	2.30	2.08	1.94	1.85	1.77	1.72	1.67	1.63	1.60	1.57	1.55
	.05	3.84	3.00	2.60	2.37	2.21	2.10	2.01	1.94	1.88	1.83	1.79	1.75
	.01	6.63	4.61	3.78	3.32	3.02	2.80	2.64	2.51	2.41	2.32	2.25	2.18

df for numerator N_1													df for denom-inator N_2
15	20	24	30	40	50	60	100	120	200	500	∞	Pr	
1.36	1.34	1.33	1.32	1.31	1.31	1.30	1.30	1.30	1.29	1.29	1.28	.25	22
1.81	1.76	1.73	1.70	1.67	1.65	1.64	1.61	1.60	1.59	1.58	1.57	.10	
2.15	2.07	2.03	1.98	1.94	1.91	1.89	1.85	1.84	1.82	1.80	1.78	.05	
2.98	2.83	2.75	2.67	2.58	2.53	2.50	2.42	2.40	2.36	2.33	2.31	.01	
1.35	1.33	1.32	1.31	1.30	1.29	1.29	1.28	1.28	1.27	1.27	1.26	.25	24
1.78	1.73	1.70	1.67	1.64	1.62	1.61	1.58	1.57	1.56	1.54	1.53	.10	
2.11	2.03	1.98	1.94	1.89	1.86	1.84	1.80	1.79	1.77	1.75	1.73	.05	
2.89	2.74	2.66	2.58	2.49	2.44	2.40	2.33	2.31	2.27	2.24	2.21	.01	
1.34	1.32	1.31	1.30	1.29	1.28	1.28	1.26	1.26	1.26	1.25	1.25	.25	26
1.76	1.71	1.68	1.65	1.61	1.59	1.58	1.55	1.54	1.53	1.51	1.50	.10	
2.07	1.99	1.95	1.90	1.85	1.82	1.80	1.76	1.75	1.73	1.71	1.69	.05	
2.81	2.66	2.58	2.50	2.42	2.36	2.33	2.25	2.23	2.19	2.16	2.13	.01	
1.33	1.31	1.30	1.29	1.28	1.27	1.27	1.26	1.25	1.25	1.24	1.24	.25	28
1.74	1.69	1.66	1.63	1.59	1.57	1.56	1.53	1.52	1.50	1.49	1.48	.10	
2.04	1.96	1.91	1.87	1.82	1.79	1.77	1.73	1.71	1.69	1.67	1.65	.05	
2.75	2.60	2.52	2.44	2.35	2.30	2.26	2.19	2.17	2.13	2.09	2.06	.01	
1.32	1.30	1.29	1.28	1.27	1.26	1.26	1.25	1.24	1.24	1.23	1.23	.25	30
1.72	1.67	1.64	1.61	1.57	1.55	1.54	1.51	1.50	1.48	1.47	1.46	.10	
2.01	1.93	1.89	1.84	1.79	1.76	1.74	1.70	1.68	1.66	1.64	1.62	.05	
2.70	2.55	2.47	2.39	2.30	2.25	2.21	2.13	2.11	2.07	2.03	2.01	.01	
1.30	1.28	1.26	1.25	1.24	1.23	1.22	1.21	1.21	1.20	1.19	1.19	.25	40
1.66	1.61	1.57	1.54	1.51	1.48	1.47	1.43	1.42	1.41	1.39	1.38	.10	
1.92	1.84	1.79	1.74	1.69	1.66	1.64	1.59	1.58	1.55	1.53	1.51	.05	
2.52	2.37	2.29	2.20	2.11	2.06	2.02	1.94	1.92	1.87	1.83	1.80	.01	
1.27	1.25	1.24	1.22	1.21	1.20	1.19	1.17	1.17	1.16	1.15	1.15	.25	60
1.60	1.54	1.51	1.48	1.44	1.41	1.40	1.36	1.35	1.33	1.31	1.29	.10	
1.84	1.75	1.70	1.65	1.59	1.56	1.53	1.48	1.47	1.44	1.41	1.39	.05	
2.35	2.20	2.12	2.03	1.94	1.88	1.84	1.75	1.73	1.68	1.63	1.60	.01	
1.24	1.22	1.21	1.19	1.18	1.17	1.16	1.14	1.13	1.12	1.11	1.10	.25	120
1.55	1.48	1.45	1.41	1.37	1.34	1.32	1.27	1.26	1.24	1.21	1.19	.10	
1.75	1.66	1.61	1.55	1.50	1.46	1.43	1.37	1.35	1.32	1.28	1.25	.05	
2.19	2.03	1.95	1.86	1.76	1.70	1.66	1.56	1.53	1.48	1.42	1.38	.01	
1.23	1.21	1.20	1.18	1.16	1.14	1.12	1.11	1.10	1.09	1.08	1.06	.25	200
1.52	1.46	1.42	1.38	1.34	1.31	1.28	1.24	1.22	1.20	1.17	1.14	.10	
1.72	1.62	1.57	1.52	1.46	1.41	1.39	1.32	1.29	1.26	1.22	1.19	.05	
2.13	1.97	1.89	1.79	1.69	1.63	1.58	1.48	1.44	1.39	1.33	1.28	.01	
1.22	1.19	1.18	1.16	1.14	1.13	1.12	1.09	1.08	1.07	1.04	1.00	.25	∞
1.49	1.42	1.38	1.34	1.30	1.26	1.24	1.18	1.17	1.13	1.08	1.00	.10	
1.67	1.57	1.52	1.46	1.39	1.35	1.32	1.24	1.22	1.17	1.11	1.00	.05	
2.04	1.88	1.79	1.70	1.59	1.52	1.47	1.36	1.32	1.25	1.15	1.00	.01	

TABLE D.4
Upper Percentage Points of the χ^2 Distribution

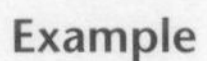

Example

$\Pr(\chi^2 > 10.85) = 0.95$

$\Pr(\chi^2 > 23.83) = 0.25$ for df = 20

$\Pr(\chi^2 > 31.41) = 0.05$

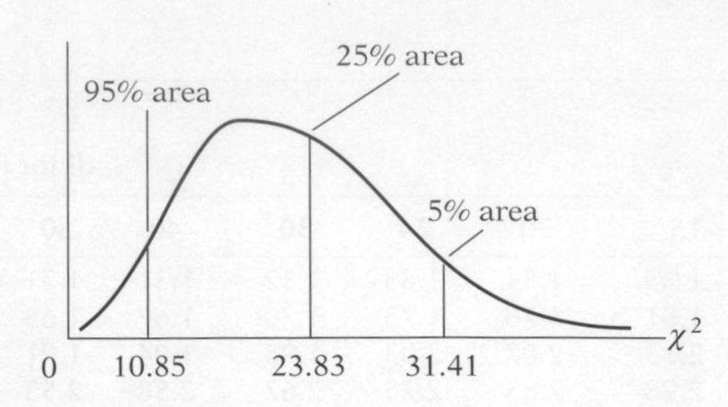

Degrees of freedom \ Pr	.995	.990	.975	.950	.900
1	392704×10^{-10}	157088×10^{-9}	982069×10^{-9}	393214×10^{-8}	.0157908
2	.0100251	.0201007	.0506356	.102587	.210720
3	.0717212	.114832	.215795	.351846	.584375
4	.206990	.297110	.484419	.710721	1.063623
5	.411740	.554300	.831211	1.145476	1.61031
6	.675727	.872085	1.237347	1.63539	2.20413
7	.989265	1.239043	1.68987	2.16735	2.83311
8	1.344419	1.646482	2.17973	2.73264	3.48954
9	1.734926	2.087912	2.70039	3.32511	4.16816
10	2.15585	2.55821	3.24697	3.94030	4.86518
11	2.60321	3.05347	3.81575	4.57481	5.57779
12	3.07382	3.57056	4.40379	5.22603	6.30380
13	3.56503	4.10691	5.00874	5.89186	7.04150
14	4.07468	4.66043	5.62872	6.57063	7.78953
15	4.60094	5.22935	6.26214	7.26094	8.54675
16	5.14224	5.81221	6.90766	7.96164	9.31223
17	5.69724	6.40776	7.56418	8.67176	10.0852
18	6.26481	7.01491	8.23075	9.39046	10.8649
19	6.84398	7.63273	8.90655	10.1170	11.6509
20	7.43386	8.26040	9.59083	10.8508	12.4426
21	8.03366	8.89720	10.28293	11.5913	13.2396
22	8.64272	9.54249	10.9823	12.3380	14.0415
23	9.26042	10.19567	11.6885	13.0905	14.8479
24	9.88623	10.8564	12.4011	13.8484	15.6587
25	10.5197	11.5240	13.1197	14.6114	16.4734
26	11.1603	12.1981	13.8439	15.3791	17.2919
27	11.8076	12.8786	14.5733	16.1513	18.1138
28	12.4613	13.5648	15.3079	16.9279	18.9392
29	13.1211	14.2565	16.0471	17.7083	19.7677
30	13.7867	14.9535	16.7908	18.4926	20.5992
40	20.7065	22.1643	24.4331	26.5093	29.0505
50	27.9907	29.7067	32.3574	34.7642	37.6886
60	35.5346	37.4848	40.4817	43.1879	46.4589
70	43.2752	45.4418	48.7576	51.7393	55.3290
80	51.1720	53.5400	57.1532	60.3915	64.2778
90	59.1963	61.7541	65.6466	69.1260	73.2912
100*	67.3276	70.0648	74.2219	77.9295	82.3581

*For df greater than 100 the expression $\sqrt{2\chi^2} - \sqrt{(2k-1)} = Z$ follows the standardized normal distribution, where k represents the degrees of freedom.

.750	.500	.250	.100	.050	.025	.010	.005
.1015308	.454937	1.32330	2.70554	3.84146	5.02389	6.63490	7.87944
.575364	1.38629	2.77259	4.60517	5.99147	7.37776	9.21034	10.5966
1.212534	2.36597	4.10835	6.25139	7.81473	9.34840	11.3449	12.8381
1.92255	3.35670	5.38527	7.77944	9.48773	11.1433	13.2767	14.8602
2.67460	4.35146	6.62568	9.23635	11.0705	12.8325	15.0863	16.7496
3.45460	5.34812	7.84080	10.6446	12.5916	14.4494	16.8119	18.5476
4.25485	6.34581	9.03715	12.0170	14.0671	16.0128	18.4753	20.2777
5.07064	7.34412	10.2188	13.3616	15.5073	17.5346	20.0902	21.9550
5.89883	8.34283	11.3887	14.6837	16.9190	19.0228	21.6660	23.5893
6.73720	9.34182	12.5489	15.9871	18.3070	20.4831	23.2093	25.1882
7.58412	10.3410	13.7007	17.2750	19.6751	21.9200	24.7250	26.7569
8.43842	11.3403	14.8454	18.5494	21.0261	23.3367	26.2170	28.2995
9.29906	12.3398	15.9839	19.8119	22.3621	24.7356	27.6883	29.8194
10.1653	13.3393	17.1170	21.0642	23.6848	26.1190	29.1413	31.3193
11.0365	14.3389	18.2451	22.3072	24.9958	27.4884	30.5779	32.8013
11.9122	15.3385	19.3688	23.5418	26.2962	28.8454	31.9999	34.2672
12.7919	16.3381	20.4887	24.7690	27.5871	30.1910	33.4087	35.7185
13.6753	17.3379	21.6049	25.9894	28.8693	31.5264	34.8053	37.1564
14.5620	18.3376	22.7178	27.2036	30.1435	32.8523	36.1908	38.5822
15.4518	19.3374	23.8277	28.4120	31.4104	34.1696	37.5662	39.9968
16.3444	20.3372	24.9348	29.6151	32.6705	35.4789	38.9321	41.4010
17.2396	21.3370	26.0393	30.8133	33.9244	36.7807	40.2894	42.7956
18.1373	22.3369	27.1413	32.0069	35.1725	38.0757	41.6384	44.1813
19.0372	23.3367	28.2412	33.1963	36.4151	39.3641	42.9798	45.5585
19.9393	24.3366	29.3389	34.3816	37.6525	40.6465	44.3141	46.9278
20.8434	25.3364	30.4345	35.5631	38.8852	41.9232	45.6417	48.2899
21.7494	26.3363	31.5284	36.7412	40.1133	43.1944	46.9630	49.6449
22.6572	27.3363	32.6205	37.9159	41.3372	44.4607	48.2782	50.9933
23.5666	28.3362	33.7109	39.0875	42.5569	45.7222	49.5879	52.3356
24.4776	29.3360	34.7998	40.2560	43.7729	46.9792	50.8922	53.6720
33.6603	39.3354	45.6160	51.8050	55.7585	59.3417	63.6907	66.7659
42.9421	49.3349	56.3336	63.1671	67.5048	71.4202	76.1539	79.4900
52.2938	59.3347	66.9814	74.3970	79.0819	83.2976	88.3794	91.9517
61.6983	69.3344	77.5766	85.5271	90.5312	95.0231	100.425	104.215
71.1445	79.3343	88.1303	96.5782	101.879	106.629	112.329	116.321
80.6247	89.3342	98.6499	107.565	113.145	118.136	124.116	128.299
90.1332	99.3341	109.141	118.498	124.342	129.561	135.807	140.169

Source: Abridged from E. S. Pearson and H. O. Hartley, eds., *Biometrika Tables for Statisticians,* vol. 1, 3d ed., table 8, Cambridge University Press, New York, 1966. Reproduced by permission of the editors and trustees of *Biometrika*.

TABLE D.5A Durbin–Watson d Statistic: Significance Points of d_L and d_U at 0.05 Level of Significance

	$k'=1$		$k'=2$		$k'=3$		$k'=4$		$k'=5$		$k'=6$		$k'=7$		$k'=8$		$k'=9$		$k'=10$	
n	d_L	d_U	d_L	d_U	d_L	d_U	d_L	d_U	d_L	d_U	d_L	d_U	d_L	d_U	d_L	d_U	d_L	d_U	d_L	d_U
6	0.610	1.400	—	—	—	—	—	—	—	—	—	—	—	—	—	—	—	—	—	—
7	0.700	1.356	0.467	1.896	—	—	—	—	—	—	—	—	—	—	—	—	—	—	—	—
8	0.763	1.332	0.559	1.777	0.368	2.287	—	—	—	—	—	—	—	—	—	—	—	—	—	—
9	0.824	1.320	0.629	1.699	0.455	2.128	0.296	2.588	—	—	—	—	—	—	—	—	—	—	—	—
10	0.879	1.320	0.697	1.641	0.525	2.016	0.376	2.414	0.243	2.822	—	—	—	—	—	—	—	—	—	—
11	0.927	1.324	0.658	1.604	0.595	1.928	0.444	2.283	0.316	2.645	0.203	3.005	—	—	—	—	—	—	—	—
12	0.971	1.331	0.812	1.579	0.658	1.864	0.512	2.177	0.379	2.506	0.268	2.832	0.171	3.149	—	—	—	—	—	—
13	1.010	1.340	0.861	1.562	0.715	1.816	0.574	2.094	0.445	2.390	0.328	2.692	0.230	2.985	0.147	3.266	—	—	—	—
14	1.045	1.350	0.905	1.551	0.767	1.779	0.632	2.030	0.505	2.296	0.389	2.572	0.286	2.848	0.200	3.111	0.127	3.360	—	—
15	1.077	1.361	0.946	1.543	0.814	1.750	0.685	1.977	0.562	2.220	0.447	2.472	0.343	2.727	0.251	2.979	0.175	3.216	0.111	3.438
16	1.106	1.371	0.982	1.539	0.857	1.728	0.734	1.935	0.615	2.157	0.502	2.388	0.398	2.624	0.304	2.860	0.222	3.090	0.155	3.304
17	1.133	1.381	1.015	1.536	0.897	1.710	0.779	1.900	0.664	2.104	0.554	2.318	0.451	2.537	0.356	2.757	0.272	2.975	0.198	3.184
18	1.158	1.391	1.046	1.535	0.933	1.696	0.820	1.872	0.710	2.060	0.603	2.257	0.502	2.461	0.407	2.667	0.321	2.873	0.244	3.073
19	1.180	1.401	1.074	1.536	0.967	1.685	0.859	1.848	0.752	2.023	0.649	2.206	0.549	2.396	0.456	2.589	0.369	2.783	0.290	2.974
20	1.201	1.411	1.100	1.537	0.998	1.676	0.894	1.828	0.792	1.991	0.692	2.162	0.595	2.339	0.502	2.521	0.416	2.704	0.336	2.885
21	1.221	1.420	1.125	1.538	1.026	1.669	0.927	1.812	0.829	1.964	0.732	2.124	0.637	2.290	0.547	2.460	0.461	2.633	0.380	2.806
22	1.239	1.429	1.147	1.541	1.053	1.664	0.958	1.797	0.863	1.940	0.769	2.090	0.677	2.246	0.588	2.407	0.504	2.571	0.424	2.734
23	1.257	1.437	1.168	1.543	1.078	1.660	0.986	1.785	0.895	1.920	0.804	2.061	0.715	2.208	0.628	2.360	0.545	2.514	0.465	2.670
24	1.273	1.446	1.188	1.546	1.101	1.656	1.013	1.775	0.925	1.902	0.837	2.035	0.751	2.174	0.666	2.318	0.584	2.464	0.506	2.613
25	1.288	1.454	1.206	1.550	1.123	1.654	1.038	1.767	0.953	1.886	0.868	2.012	0.784	2.144	0.702	2.280	0.621	2.419	0.544	2.560
26	1.302	1.461	1.224	1.553	1.143	1.652	1.062	1.759	0.979	1.873	0.897	1.992	0.816	2.117	0.735	2.246	0.657	2.379	0.581	2.513
27	1.316	1.469	1.240	1.556	1.162	1.651	1.084	1.753	1.004	1.861	0.925	1.974	0.845	2.093	0.767	2.216	0.691	2.342	0.616	2.470
28	1.328	1.476	1.255	1.560	1.181	1.650	1.104	1.747	1.028	1.850	0.951	1.958	0.874	2.071	0.798	2.188	0.723	2.309	0.650	2.431
29	1.341	1.483	1.270	1.563	1.198	1.650	1.124	1.743	1.050	1.841	0.975	1.944	0.900	2.052	0.826	2.164	0.753	2.278	0.682	2.396
30	1.352	1.489	1.284	1.567	1.214	1.650	1.143	1.739	1.071	1.833	0.998	1.931	0.926	2.034	0.854	2.141	0.782	2.251	0.712	2.363
31	1.363	1.496	1.297	1.570	1.229	1.650	1.160	1.735	1.090	1.825	1.020	1.920	0.950	2.018	0.879	2.120	0.810	2.226	0.741	2.333
32	1.373	1.502	1.309	1.574	1.244	1.650	1.177	1.732	1.109	1.819	1.041	1.909	0.972	2.004	0.904	2.102	0.836	2.203	0.769	2.306
33	1.383	1.508	1.321	1.577	1.258	1.651	1.193	1.730	1.127	1.813	1.061	1.900	0.994	1.991	0.927	2.085	0.861	2.181	0.795	2.281
34	1.393	1.514	1.333	1.580	1.271	1.652	1.208	1.728	1.144	1.808	1.080	1.891	1.015	1.979	0.950	2.069	0.885	2.162	0.821	2.257
35	1.402	1.519	1.343	1.584	1.283	1.653	1.222	1.726	1.160	1.803	1.097	1.884	1.034	1.967	0.971	2.054	0.908	2.144	0.845	2.236
36	1.411	1.525	1.354	1.587	1.295	1.654	1.236	1.724	1.175	1.799	1.114	1.877	1.053	1.957	0.991	2.041	0.930	2.127	0.868	2.216
37	1.419	1.530	1.364	1.590	1.307	1.655	1.249	1.723	1.190	1.795	1.131	1.870	1.071	1.948	1.011	2.029	0.951	2.112	0.891	2.198
38	1.427	1.535	1.373	1.594	1.318	1.656	1.261	1.722	1.204	1.792	1.146	1.864	1.088	1.939	1.029	2.017	0.970	2.098	0.912	2.180
39	1.435	1.540	1.382	1.597	1.328	1.658	1.273	1.722	1.218	1.789	1.161	1.859	1.104	1.932	1.047	2.007	0.990	2.085	0.932	2.164
40	1.442	1.544	1.391	1.600	1.338	1.659	1.285	1.721	1.230	1.786	1.175	1.854	1.120	1.924	1.064	1.997	1.008	2.072	0.952	2.149
45	1.475	1.566	1.430	1.615	1.383	1.666	1.336	1.720	1.287	1.776	1.238	1.835	1.189	1.895	1.139	1.958	1.089	2.022	1.038	2.088
50	1.503	1.585	1.462	1.628	1.421	1.674	1.378	1.721	1.335	1.771	1.291	1.822	1.246	1.875	1.201	1.930	1.156	1.986	1.110	2.044
55	1.528	1.601	1.490	1.641	1.452	1.681	1.414	1.724	1.374	1.768	1.334	1.814	1.294	1.861	1.253	1.909	1.212	1.959	1.170	2.010
60	1.549	1.616	1.514	1.652	1.480	1.689	1.444	1.727	1.408	1.767	1.372	1.808	1.335	1.850	1.298	1.894	1.260	1.939	1.222	1.984
65	1.567	1.629	1.536	1.662	1.503	1.696	1.471	1.731	1.438	1.767	1.404	1.805	1.370	1.843	1.336	1.882	1.301	1.923	1.266	1.964
70	1.583	1.641	1.554	1.672	1.525	1.703	1.494	1.735	1.464	1.768	1.433	1.802	1.401	1.837	1.369	1.873	1.337	1.910	1.305	1.948
75	1.598	1.652	1.571	1.680	1.543	1.709	1.515	1.739	1.487	1.770	1.458	1.801	1.428	1.834	1.399	1.867	1.369	1.901	1.339	1.935
80	1.611	1.662	1.586	1.688	1.560	1.715	1.534	1.743	1.507	1.772	1.480	1.801	1.453	1.831	1.425	1.861	1.397	1.893	1.369	1.925
85	1.624	1.671	1.600	1.696	1.575	1.721	1.550	1.747	1.525	1.774	1.500	1.801	1.474	1.829	1.448	1.857	1.422	1.886	1.396	1.916
90	1.635	1.679	1.612	1.703	1.589	1.726	1.566	1.751	1.542	1.776	1.518	1.801	1.494	1.827	1.469	1.854	1.445	1.881	1.420	1.909
95	1.645	1.687	1.623	1.709	1.602	1.732	1.579	1.755	1.557	1.778	1.535	1.802	1.512	1.827	1.489	1.852	1.465	1.877	1.442	1.903
100	1.654	1.694	1.634	1.715	1.613	1.736	1.592	1.758	1.571	1.780	1.550	1.803	1.528	1.826	1.506	1.850	1.484	1.874	1.462	1.898
150	1.720	1.746	1.706	1.760	1.693	1.774	1.679	1.788	1.665	1.802	1.651	1.817	1.637	1.832	1.622	1.847	1.608	1.862	1.594	1.877
200	1.758	1.778	1.748	1.789	1.738	1.799	1.728	1.810	1.718	1.820	1.707	1.831	1.697	1.841	1.686	1.852	1.675	1.863	1.665	1.874

	$k'=11$		$k'=12$		$k'=13$		$k'=14$		$k'=15$		$k'=16$		$k'=17$		$k'=18$		$k'=19$		$k'=20$	
n	d_L	d_U	d_L	d_U	d_l	d_U	d_L	d_U	d_L	d_U	d_L	d_U	d_L	d_U	d_L	d_U	d_L	d_U	d_L	d_U
16	0.098	3.503	—	—	—	—	—	—	—	—	—	—	—	—	—	—	—	—	—	—
17	0.138	3.378	0.087	3.557	—	—	—	—	—	—	—	—	—	—	—	—	—	—	—	—
18	0.177	3.265	0.123	3.441	0.078	3.603	—	—	—	—	—	—	—	—	—	—	—	—	—	—
19	0.220	3.159	0.160	3.335	0.111	3.496	0.070	3.642	—	—	—	—	—	—	—	—	—	—	—	—
20	0.263	3.063	0.200	3.234	0.145	3.395	0.100	3.542	0.063	3.676	—	—	—	—	—	—	—	—	—	—
21	0.307	2.976	0.240	3.141	0.182	3.300	0.132	3.448	0.091	3.583	0.058	3.705	—	—	—	—	—	—	—	—
22	0.349	2.897	0.281	3.057	0.220	3.211	0.166	3.358	0.120	3.495	0.083	3.619	0.052	3.731	—	—	—	—	—	—
23	0.391	2.826	0.322	2.979	0.259	3.128	0.202	3.272	0.153	3.409	0.110	3.535	0.076	3.650	0.048	3.753	—	—	—	—
24	0.431	2.761	0.362	2.908	0.297	3.053	0.239	3.193	0.186	3.327	0.141	3.454	0.101	3.572	0.070	3.678	0.044	3.773	—	—
25	0.470	2.702	0.400	2.844	0.335	2.983	0.275	3.119	0.221	3.251	0.172	3.376	0.130	3.494	0.094	3.604	0.065	3.702	0.041	3.790
26	0.508	2.649	0.438	2.784	0.373	2.919	0.312	3.051	0.256	3.179	0.205	3.303	0.160	3.420	0.120	3.531	0.087	3.632	0.060	3.724
27	0.544	2.600	0.475	2.730	0.409	2.859	0.348	2.987	0.291	3.112	0.238	3.233	0.191	3.349	0.149	3.460	0.112	3.563	0.081	3.658
28	0.578	2.555	0.510	2.680	0.445	2.805	0.383	2.928	0.325	3.050	0.271	3.168	0.222	3.283	0.178	3.392	0.138	3.495	0.104	3.592
29	0.612	2.515	0.544	2.634	0.479	2.755	0.418	2.874	0.359	2.992	0.305	3.107	0.254	3.219	0.208	3.327	0.166	3.431	0.129	3.528
30	0.643	2.477	0.577	2.592	0.512	2.708	0.451	2.823	0.392	2.937	0.337	3.050	0.286	3.160	0.238	3.266	0.195	3.368	0.156	3.465
31	0.674	2.443	0.608	2.553	0.545	2.665	0.484	2.776	0.425	2.887	0.370	2.996	0.317	3.103	0.269	3.208	0.224	3.309	0.183	3.406
32	0.703	2.411	0.638	2.517	0.576	2.625	0.515	2.733	0.457	2.840	0.401	2.946	0.349	3.050	0.299	3.153	0.253	3.252	0.211	3.348
33	0.731	2.382	0.668	2.484	0.606	2.588	0.546	2.692	0.488	2.796	0.432	2.899	0.379	3.000	0.329	3.100	0.283	3.198	0.239	3.293
34	0.758	2.355	0.695	2.454	0.634	2.554	0.575	2.654	0.518	2.754	0.462	2.854	0.409	2.954	0.359	3.051	0.312	3.147	0.267	3.240
35	0.783	2.330	0.722	2.425	0.662	2.521	0.604	2.619	0.547	2.716	0.492	2.813	0.439	2.910	0.388	3.005	0.340	3.099	0.295	3.190
36	0.808	2.306	0.748	2.398	0.689	2.492	0.631	2.586	0.575	2.680	0.520	2.774	0.467	2.868	0.417	2.961	0.369	3.053	0.323	3.142
37	0.831	2.285	0.772	2.374	0.714	2.464	0.657	2.555	0.602	2.646	0.548	2.738	0.495	2.829	0.445	2.920	0.397	3.009	0.351	3.097
38	0.854	2.265	0.796	2.351	0.739	2.438	0.683	2.526	0.628	2.614	0.575	2.703	0.522	2.792	0.472	2.880	0.424	2.968	0.378	3.054
39	0.875	2.246	0.819	2.329	0.763	2.413	0.707	2.499	0.653	2.585	0.600	2.671	0.549	2.757	0.499	2.843	0.451	2.929	0.404	3.013
40	0.896	2.228	0.840	2.309	0.785	2.391	0.731	2.473	0.678	2.557	0.626	2.641	0.575	2.724	0.525	2.808	0.477	2.892	0.430	2.974
45	0.988	2.156	0.938	2.225	0.887	2.296	0.838	2.367	0.788	2.439	0.740	2.512	0.692	2.586	0.644	2.659	0.598	2.733	0.553	2.807
50	1.064	2.103	1.019	2.163	0.973	2.225	0.927	2.287	0.882	2.350	0.836	2.414	0.792	2.479	0.747	2.544	0.703	2.610	0.660	2.675
55	1.129	2.062	1.087	2.116	1.045	2.170	1.003	2.225	0.961	2.281	0.919	2.338	0.877	2.396	0.836	2.454	0.795	2.512	0.754	2.571
60	1.184	2.031	1.145	2.079	1.106	2.127	1.068	2.177	1.029	2.227	0.990	2.278	0.951	2.330	0.913	2.382	0.874	2.434	0.836	2.487
65	1.231	2.006	1.195	2.049	1.160	2.093	1.124	2.138	1.088	2.183	1.052	2.229	1.016	2.276	0.980	2.323	0.944	2.371	0.908	2.419
70	1.272	1.986	1.239	2.026	1.206	2.066	1.172	2.106	1.139	2.148	1.105	2.189	1.072	2.232	1.038	2.275	1.005	2.318	0.971	2.362
75	1.308	1.970	1.277	2.006	1.247	2.043	1.215	2.080	1.184	2.118	1.153	2.156	1.121	2.195	1.090	2.235	1.058	2.275	1.027	2.315
80	1.340	1.957	1.311	1.991	1.283	2.024	1.253	2.059	1.224	2.093	1.195	2.129	1.165	2.165	1.136	2.201	1.106	2.238	1.076	2.275
85	1.369	1.946	1.342	1.977	1.315	2.009	1.287	2.040	1.260	2.073	1.232	2.105	1.205	2.139	1.177	2.172	1.149	2.206	1.121	2.241
90	1.395	1.937	1.369	1.966	1.344	1.995	1.318	2.025	1.292	2.055	1.266	2.085	1.240	2.116	1.213	2.148	1.187	2.179	1.160	2.211
95	1.418	1.929	1.394	1.956	1.370	1.984	1.345	2.012	1.321	2.040	1.296	2.068	1.271	2.097	1.247	2.126	1.222	2.156	1.197	2.186
100	1.439	1.923	1.416	1.948	1.393	1.974	1.371	2.000	1.347	2.026	1.324	2.053	1.301	2.080	1.277	2.108	1.253	2.135	1.229	2.164
150	1.579	1.892	1.564	1.908	1.550	1.924	1.535	1.940	1.519	1.956	1.504	1.972	1.489	1.989	1.474	2.006	1.458	2.023	1.443	2.040
200	1.654	1.885	1.643	1.896	1.632	1.908	1.621	1.919	1.610	1.931	1.599	1.943	1.588	1.955	1.576	1.967	1.565	1.979	1.554	1.991

Note: n = number of observations, k' = number of explanatory variables excluding the constant term.

Source: This table is an extension of the original Durbin–Watson table and is reproduced from N. E. Savin and K. J. White, "The Durbin-Watson Test for Serial Correlation with Extreme Small Samples or Many Regressors," *Econometrica,* vol. 45, November 1977, pp. 1989–96 and as corrected by R. W. Farebrother, *Econometrica,* vol. 48, September 1980, p. 1554. Reprinted by permission of the Econometric Society.

EXAMPLE 1

If $n = 40$ and $k' = 4$, $d_L = 1.285$ and $d_U = 1.721$. If a computed d value is less than 1.285, there is evidence of positive first-order serial correlation; if it is greater than 1.721, there is no evidence of positive first-order serial correlation; but if d lies between the lower and the upper limit, there is inconclusive evidence regarding the presence or absence of positive first-order serial correlation.

TABLE D.5B **Durbin–Watson *d* Statistic: Significance Points of d_L and d_U at 0.01 Level of Significance**

	$k'=1$		$k'=2$		$k'=3$		$k'=4$		$k'=5$		$k'=6$		$k'=7$		$k'=8$		$k'=9$		$k'=10$	
n	d_L	d_U	d_L	d_U	d_L	d_U	d_L	d_U	d_L	d_U	d_L	d_U	d_L	d_U	d_L	d_U	d_L	d_U	d_L	d_U
6	0.390	1.142	—	—	—	—	—	—	—	—	—	—	—	—	—	—	—	—	—	—
7	0.435	1.036	0.294	1.676	—	—	—	—	—	—	—	—	—	—	—	—	—	—	—	—
8	0.497	1.003	0.345	1.489	0.229	2.102	—	—	—	—	—	—	—	—	—	—	—	—	—	—
9	0.554	0.998	0.408	1.389	0.279	1.875	0.183	2.433	—	—	—	—	—	—	—	—	—	—	—	—
10	0.604	1.001	0.466	1.333	0.340	1.733	0.230	2.193	0.150	2.690	—	—	—	—	—	—	—	—	—	—
11	0.653	1.010	0.519	1.297	0.396	1.640	0.286	2.030	0.193	2.453	0.124	2.892	—	—	—	—	—	—	—	—
12	0.697	1.023	0.569	1.274	0.449	1.575	0.339	1.913	0.244	2.280	0.164	2.665	0.105	3.053	—	—	—	—	—	—
13	0.738	1.038	0.616	1.261	0.499	1.526	0.391	1.826	0.294	2.150	0.211	2.490	0.140	2.838	0.090	3.182	—	—	—	—
14	0.776	1.054	0.660	1.254	0.547	1.490	0.441	1.757	0.343	2.049	0.257	2.354	0.183	2.667	0.122	2.981	0.078	3.287	—	—
15	0.811	1.070	0.700	1.252	0.591	1.464	0.488	1.704	0.391	1.967	0.303	2.244	0.226	2.530	0.161	2.817	0.107	3.101	0.068	3.374
16	0.844	1.086	0.737	1.252	0.633	1.446	0.532	1.663	0.437	1.900	0.349	2.153	0.269	2.416	0.200	2.681	0.142	2.944	0.094	3.201
17	0.874	1.102	0.772	1.255	0.672	1.432	0.574	1.630	0.480	1.847	0.393	2.078	0.313	2.319	0.241	2.566	0.179	2.811	0.127	3.053
18	0.902	1.118	0.805	1.259	0.708	1.422	0.613	1.604	0.522	1.803	0.435	2.015	0.355	2.238	0.282	2.467	0.216	2.697	0.160	2.925
19	0.928	1.132	0.835	1.265	0.742	1.415	0.650	1.584	0.561	1.767	0.476	1.963	0.396	2.169	0.322	2.381	0.255	2.597	0.196	2.813
20	0.952	1.147	0.863	1.271	0.773	1.411	0.685	1.567	0.598	1.737	0.515	1.918	0.436	2.110	0.362	2.308	0.294	2.510	0.232	2.714
21	0.975	1.161	0.890	1.277	0.803	1.408	0.718	1.554	0.633	1.712	0.552	1.881	0.474	2.059	0.400	2.244	0.331	2.434	0.268	2.625
22	0.997	1.174	0.914	1.284	0.831	1.407	0.748	1.543	0.667	1.691	0.587	1.849	0.510	2.015	0.437	2.188	0.368	2.367	0.304	2.548
23	1.018	1.187	0.938	1.291	0.858	1.407	0.777	1.534	0.698	1.673	0.620	1.821	0.545	1.977	0.473	2.140	0.404	2.308	0.340	2.479
24	1.037	1.199	0.960	1.298	0.882	1.407	0.805	1.528	0.728	1.658	0.652	1.797	0.578	1.944	0.507	2.097	0.439	2.255	0.375	2.417
25	1.055	1.211	0.981	1.305	0.906	1.409	0.831	1.523	0.756	1.645	0.682	1.776	0.610	1.915	0.540	2.059	0.473	2.209	0.409	2.362
26	1.072	1.222	1.001	1.312	0.928	1.411	0.855	1.518	0.783	1.635	0.711	1.759	0.640	1.889	0.572	2.026	0.505	2.168	0.441	2.313
27	1.089	1.233	1.019	1.319	0.949	1.413	0.878	1.515	0.808	1.626	0.738	1.743	0.669	1.867	0.602	1.997	0.536	2.131	0.473	2.269
28	1.104	1.244	1.037	1.325	0.969	1.415	0.900	1.513	0.832	1.618	0.764	1.729	0.696	1.847	0.630	1.970	0.566	2.098	0.504	2.229
29	1.119	1.254	1.054	1.332	0.988	1.418	0.921	1.512	0.855	1.611	0.788	1.718	0.723	1.830	0.658	1.947	0.595	2.068	0.533	2.193
30	1.133	1.263	1.070	1.339	1.006	1.421	0.941	1.511	0.877	1.606	0.812	1.707	0.748	1.814	0.684	1.925	0.622	2.041	0.562	2.160
31	1.147	1.273	1.085	1.345	1.023	1.425	0.960	1.510	0.897	1.601	0.834	1.698	0.772	1.800	0.710	1.906	0.649	2.017	0.589	2.131
32	1.160	1.282	1.100	1.352	1.040	1.428	0.979	1.510	0.917	1.597	0.856	1.690	0.794	1.788	0.734	1.889	0.674	1.995	0.615	2.104
33	1.172	1.291	1.114	1.358	1.055	1.432	0.996	1.510	0.936	1.594	0.876	1.683	0.816	1.776	0.757	1.874	0.698	1.975	0.641	2.080
34	1.184	1.299	1.128	1.364	1.070	1.435	1.012	1.511	0.954	1.591	0.896	1.677	0.837	1.766	0.779	1.860	0.722	1.957	0.665	2.057
35	1.195	1.307	1.140	1.370	1.085	1.439	1.028	1.512	0.971	1.589	0.914	1.671	0.857	1.757	0.800	1.847	0.744	1.940	0.689	2.037
36	1.206	1.315	1.153	1.376	1.098	1.442	1.043	1.513	0.988	1.588	0.932	1.666	0.877	1.749	0.821	1.836	0.766	1.925	0.711	2.018
37	1.217	1.323	1.165	1.382	1.112	1.446	1.058	1.514	1.004	1.586	0.950	1.662	0.895	1.742	0.841	1.825	0.787	1.911	0.733	2.001
38	1.227	1.330	1.176	1.388	1.124	1.449	1.072	1.515	1.019	1.585	0.966	1.658	0.913	1.735	0.860	1.816	0.807	1.899	0.754	1.985
39	1.237	1.337	1.187	1.393	1.137	1.453	1.085	1.517	1.034	1.584	0.982	1.655	0.930	1.729	0.878	1.807	0.826	1.887	0.774	1.970
40	1.246	1.344	1.198	1.398	1.148	1.457	1.098	1.518	1.048	1.584	0.997	1.652	0.946	1.724	0.895	1.799	0.844	1.876	0.749	1.956
45	1.288	1.376	1.245	1.423	1.201	1.474	1.156	1.528	1.111	1.584	1.065	1.643	1.019	1.704	0.974	1.768	0.927	1.834	0.881	1.902
50	1.324	1.403	1.285	1.446	1.245	1.491	1.205	1.538	1.164	1.587	1.123	1.639	1.081	1.692	1.039	1.748	0.997	1.805	0.955	1.864
55	1.356	1.427	1.320	1.466	1.284	1.506	1.247	1.548	1.209	1.592	1.172	1.638	1.134	1.685	1.095	1.734	1.057	1.785	1.018	1.837
60	1.383	1.449	1.350	1.484	1.317	1.520	1.283	1.558	1.249	1.598	1.214	1.639	1.179	1.682	1.144	1.726	1.108	1.771	1.072	1.817
65	1.407	1.468	1.377	1.500	1.346	1.534	1.315	1.568	1.283	1.604	1.251	1.642	1.218	1.680	1.186	1.720	1.153	1.761	1.120	1.802
70	1.429	1.485	1.400	1.515	1.372	1.546	1.343	1.578	1.313	1.611	1.283	1.645	1.253	1.680	1.223	1.716	1.192	1.754	1.162	1.792
75	1.448	1.501	1.422	1.529	1.395	1.557	1.368	1.587	1.340	1.617	1.313	1.649	1.284	1.682	1.256	1.714	1.227	1.748	1.199	1.783
80	1.466	1.515	1.441	1.541	1.416	1.568	1.390	1.595	1.364	1.624	1.338	1.653	1.312	1.683	1.285	1.714	1.259	1.745	1.232	1.777
85	1.482	1.528	1.458	1.553	1.435	1.578	1.411	1.603	1.386	1.630	1.362	1.657	1.337	1.685	1.312	1.714	1.287	1.743	1.262	1.773
90	1.496	1.540	1.474	1.563	1.452	1.587	1.429	1.611	1.406	1.636	1.383	1.661	1.360	1.687	1.336	1.714	1.312	1.741	1.288	1.769
95	1.510	1.552	1.489	1.573	1.468	1.596	1.446	1.618	1.425	1.642	1.403	1.666	1.381	1.690	1.358	1.715	1.336	1.741	1.313	1.767
100	1.522	1.562	1.503	1.583	1.482	1.604	1.462	1.625	1.441	1.647	1.421	1.670	1.400	1.693	1.378	1.717	1.357	1.741	1.335	1.765
150	1.611	1.637	1.598	1.651	1.584	1.665	1.571	1.679	1.557	1.693	1.543	1.708	1.530	1.722	1.515	1.737	1.501	1.752	1.486	1.767
200	1.664	1.684	1.653	1.693	1.643	1.704	1.633	1.715	1.623	1.725	1.613	1.735	1.603	1.746	1.592	1.757	1.582	1.768	1.571	1.779

	$k'=11$		$k'=12$		$k'=13$		$k'=14$		$k'=15$		$k'=16$		$k'=17$		$k'=18$		$k'=19$		$k'=20$	
n	d_L	d_U	d_L	d_U	d_L	d_U	d_L	d_U	d_L	d_U	d_L	d_U	d_L	d_U	d_L	d_U	d_L	d_U	d_L	d_U
16	0.060	3.446	—	—	—	—	—	—	—	—	—	—	—	—	—	—	—	—	—	—
17	0.084	3.286	0.053	3.506	—	—	—	—	—	—	—	—	—	—	—	—	—	—	—	—
18	0.113	3.146	0.075	3.358	0.047	3.357	—	—	—	—	—	—	—	—	—	—	—	—	—	—
19	0.145	3.023	0.102	3.227	0.067	3.420	0.043	3.601	—	—	—	—	—	—	—	—	—	—	—	—
20	0.178	2.914	0.131	3.109	0.092	3.297	0.061	3.474	0.038	3.639	—	—	—	—	—	—	—	—	—	—
21	0.212	2.817	0.162	3.004	0.119	3.185	0.084	3.358	0.055	3.521	0.035	3.671	—	—	—	—	—	—	—	—
22	0.246	2.729	0.194	2.909	0.148	3.084	0.109	3.252	0.077	3.412	0.050	3.562	0.032	3.700	—	—	—	—	—	—
23	0.281	2.651	0.227	2.822	0.178	2.991	0.136	3.155	0.100	3.311	0.070	3.459	0.046	3.597	0.029	3.725	—	—	—	—
24	0.315	2.580	0.260	2.744	0.209	2.906	0.165	3.065	0.125	3.218	0.092	3.363	0.065	3.501	0.043	3.629	0.027	3.747	—	—
25	0.348	2.517	0.292	2.674	0.240	2.829	0.194	2.982	0.152	3.131	0.116	3.274	0.085	3.410	0.060	3.538	0.039	3.657	0.025	3.766
26	0.381	2.460	0.324	2.610	0.272	2.758	0.224	2.906	0.180	3.050	0.141	3.191	0.107	3.325	0.079	3.452	0.055	3.572	0.036	3.682
27	0.413	2.409	0.356	2.552	0.303	2.694	0.253	2.836	0.208	2.976	0.167	3.113	0.131	3.245	0.100	3.371	0.073	3.490	0.051	3.602
28	0.444	2.363	0.387	2.499	0.333	2.635	0.283	2.772	0.237	2.907	0.194	3.040	0.156	3.169	0.122	3.294	0.093	3.412	0.068	3.524
29	0.474	2.321	0.417	2.451	0.363	2.582	0.313	2.713	0.266	2.843	0.222	2.972	0.182	3.098	0.146	3.220	0.114	3.338	0.087	3.450
30	0.503	2.283	0.447	2.407	0.393	2.533	0.342	2.659	0.294	2.785	0.249	2.909	0.208	3.032	0.171	3.152	0.137	3.267	0.107	3.379
31	0.531	2.248	0.475	2.367	0.422	2.487	0.371	2.609	0.322	2.730	0.277	2.851	0.234	2.970	0.196	3.087	0.160	3.201	0.128	3.311
32	0.558	2.216	0.503	2.330	0.450	2.446	0.399	2.563	0.350	2.680	0.304	2.797	0.261	2.912	0.221	3.026	0.184	3.137	0.151	3.246
33	0.585	2.187	0.530	2.296	0.477	2.408	0.426	2.520	0.377	2.633	0.331	2.746	0.287	2.858	0.246	2.969	0.209	3.078	0.174	3.184
34	0.610	2.160	0.556	2.266	0.503	2.373	0.452	2.481	0.404	2.590	0.357	2.699	0.313	2.808	0.272	2.915	0.233	3.022	0.197	3.126
35	0.634	2.136	0.581	2.237	0.529	2.340	0.478	2.444	0.430	2.550	0.383	2.655	0.339	2.761	0.297	2.865	0.257	2.969	0.221	3.071
36	0.658	2.113	0.605	2.210	0.554	2.310	0.504	2.410	0.455	2.512	0.409	2.614	0.364	2.717	0.322	2.818	0.282	2.919	0.244	3.019
37	0.680	2.092	0.628	2.186	0.578	2.282	0.528	2.379	0.480	2.477	0.434	2.576	0.389	2.675	0.347	2.774	0.306	2.872	0.268	2.969
38	0.702	2.073	0.651	2.164	0.601	2.256	0.552	2.350	0.504	2.445	0.458	2.540	0.414	2.637	0.371	2.733	0.330	2.828	0.291	2.923
39	0.723	2.055	0.673	2.143	0.623	2.232	0.575	2.323	0.528	2.414	0.482	2.507	0.438	2.600	0.395	2.694	0.354	2.787	0.315	2.879
40	0.744	2.039	0.694	2.123	0.645	2.210	0.597	2.297	0.551	2.386	0.505	2.476	0.461	2.566	0.418	2.657	0.377	2.748	0.338	2.838
45	0.835	1.972	0.790	2.044	0.744	2.118	0.700	2.193	0.655	2.269	0.612	2.346	0.570	2.424	0.528	2.503	0.488	2.582	0.448	2.661
50	0.913	1.925	0.871	1.987	0.829	2.051	0.787	2.116	0.746	2.182	0.705	2.250	0.665	2.318	0.625	2.387	0.586	2.456	0.548	2.526
55	0.979	1.891	0.940	1.945	0.902	2.002	0.863	2.059	0.825	2.117	0.786	2.176	0.748	2.237	0.711	2.298	0.674	2.359	0.637	2.421
60	1.037	1.865	1.001	1.914	0.965	1.964	0.929	2.015	0.893	2.067	0.857	2.120	0.822	2.173	0.786	2.227	0.751	2.283	0.716	2.338
65	1.087	1.845	1.053	1.889	1.020	1.934	0.986	1.980	0.953	2.027	0.919	2.075	0.886	2.123	0.852	2.172	0.819	2.221	0.786	2.272
70	1.131	1.831	1.099	1.870	1.068	1.911	1.037	1.953	1.005	1.995	0.974	2.038	0.943	2.082	0.911	2.127	0.880	2.172	0.849	2.217
75	1.170	1.819	1.141	1.856	1.111	1.893	1.082	1.931	1.052	1.970	1.023	2.009	0.993	2.049	0.964	2.090	0.934	2.131	0.905	2.172
80	1.205	1.810	1.177	1.844	1.150	1.878	1.122	1.913	1.094	1.949	1.066	1.984	1.039	2.022	1.011	2.059	0.983	2.097	0.955	2.135
85	1.236	1.803	1.210	1.834	1.184	1.866	1.158	1.898	1.132	1.931	1.106	1.965	1.080	1.999	1.053	2.033	1.027	2.068	1.000	2.104
90	1.264	1.798	1.240	1.827	1.215	1.856	1.191	1.886	1.166	1.917	1.141	1.948	1.116	1.979	1.091	2.012	1.066	2.044	1.041	2.077
95	1.290	1.793	1.267	1.821	1.244	1.848	1.221	1.876	1.197	1.905	1.174	1.934	1.150	1.963	1.126	1.993	1.102	2.023	1.079	2.054
100	1.314	1.790	1.292	1.816	1.270	1.841	1.248	1.868	1.225	1.895	1.203	1.922	1.181	1.949	1.158	1.977	1.136	2.006	1.113	2.034
150	1.473	1.783	1.458	1.799	1.444	1.814	1.429	1.830	1.414	1.847	1.400	1.863	1.385	1.880	1.370	1.897	1.355	1.913	1.340	1.931
200	1.561	1.791	1.550	1.801	1.539	1.813	1.528	1.824	1.518	1.836	1.507	1.847	1.495	1.860	1.484	1.871	1.474	1.883	1.462	1.896

Note: n = number of observations.
k' = number of explanatory variables excluding the constant term.

Source: Savin and White, op. cit., by permission of the Econometric Society.

TABLE D.6A Critical Values of Runs in the Runs Test

	N_2																		
N_1	2	3	4	5	6	7	8	9	10	11	12	13	14	15	16	17	18	19	20
2											2	2	2	2	2	2	2	2	2
3					2	2	2	2	2	2	2	2	2	3	3	3	3	3	3
4				2	2	2	3	3	3	3	3	3	3	3	4	4	4	4	4
5			2	2	3	3	3	3	3	4	4	4	4	4	4	4	5	5	5
6		2	2	3	3	3	3	4	4	4	4	5	5	5	5	5	5	6	6
7		2	2	3	3	3	4	4	5	5	5	5	5	6	6	6	6	6	6
8		2	3	3	3	4	4	5	5	5	6	6	6	6	6	7	7	7	7
9		2	3	3	4	4	5	5	5	6	6	6	7	7	7	7	8	8	8
10		2	3	3	4	5	5	5	6	6	7	7	7	7	8	8	8	8	9
11		2	3	4	4	5	5	6	6	7	7	7	8	8	8	9	9	9	9
12	2	2	3	4	4	5	6	6	7	7	7	8	8	8	9	9	9	10	10
13	2	2	3	4	5	5	6	6	7	7	8	8	9	9	9	10	10	10	10
14	2	2	3	4	5	5	6	7	7	8	8	9	9	9	10	10	10	11	11
15	2	3	3	4	5	6	6	7	7	8	8	9	9	10	10	11	11	11	12
16	2	3	4	4	5	6	6	7	8	8	9	9	10	10	11	11	11	12	12
17	2	3	4	4	5	6	7	7	8	9	9	10	10	11	11	11	12	12	13
18	2	3	4	5	5	6	7	8	8	9	9	10	10	11	11	12	12	13	13
19	2	3	4	5	6	6	7	8	8	9	10	10	11	11	12	12	13	13	13
20	2	3	4	5	6	6	7	8	9	9	10	10	11	12	12	13	13	13	14

Note: Tables D.6A and D.6B give the critical values of runs n for various values of N_1 (+ symbol) and N_2 (− symbol). For the one-sample runs test, any value of n that is equal to or smaller than that shown in Table D.6A or equal to or larger than that shown in Table D.6B is significant at the 0.05 level.

Source: Sidney Siegel, *Nonparametric Statistics for the Behavioral Sciences,* McGraw-Hill Book Company, New York, 1956, table F, pp. 252–253. The tables have been adapted by Siegel from the original source: Frieda S. Swed and C. Eisenhart, "Tables for Testing Randomness of Grouping in a Sequence of Alternatives," *Annals of Mathematical Statistics,* vol. 14, 1943. Used by permission of McGraw-Hill Book Company and *Annals of Mathematical Statistics*.

TABLE D.6B Critical Values of Runs in the Runs Test

	N_2																		
N_1	2	3	4	5	6	7	8	9	10	11	12	13	14	15	16	17	18	19	20
2																			
3																			
4				9	9														
5			9	10	10	11	11												
6			9	10	11	12	12	13	13	13	13								
7				11	12	13	13	14	14	14	14	15	15	15					
8				11	12	13	14	14	15	15	16	16	16	16	17	17	17	17	17
9					13	14	14	15	16	16	16	17	17	18	18	18	18	18	18
10					13	14	15	16	16	17	17	18	18	18	19	19	19	20	20
11					13	14	15	16	17	17	18	19	19	19	20	20	20	21	21
12					13	14	16	16	17	18	19	19	20	20	21	21	21	22	22
13						15	16	17	18	19	19	20	20	21	21	22	22	23	23
14						15	16	17	18	19	20	20	21	22	22	23	23	23	24
15						15	16	18	18	19	20	21	22	22	23	23	24	24	25
16							17	18	19	20	21	21	22	23	23	24	25	25	25
17							17	18	19	20	21	22	23	23	24	25	25	26	26
18							17	18	19	20	21	22	23	24	25	25	26	26	27
19							17	18	20	21	22	23	23	24	25	26	26	27	27
20							17	18	20	21	22	23	24	25	25	26	27	27	28

EXAMPLE 2

In a sequence of 30 observations consisting of 20 + signs (= N_1) and 10 − signs (= N_2), the critical values of runs at the 0.05 level of significance are 9 and 20, as shown by Tables D.6A and D.6B, respectively. Therefore, if in an application it is found that the number of runs is equal to or less than 9 or equal to or greater than 20, one can reject (at the 0.05 level of significance) the hypothesis that the observed sequence is random.

TABLE D.7 1% and 5% Critical Dickey–Fuller t (= τ) and F Values for Unit Root Tests

Sample Size	t_{nc}^*		t_c^*		t_{ct}^*		$F^\dagger$		$F^\ddagger$	
	1%	5%	1%	5%	1%	5%	1%	5%	1%	5%
25	−2.66	−1.95	−3.75	−3.00	−4.38	−3.60	10.61	7.24	8.21	5.68
50	−2.62	−1.95	−3.58	−2.93	−4.15	−3.50	9.31	6.73	7.02	5.13
100	−2.60	−1.95	−3.51	−2.89	−4.04	−3.45	8.73	6.49	6.50	4.88
250	−2.58	−1.95	−3.46	−2.88	−3.99	−3.43	8.43	6.34	6.22	4.75
500	−2.58	−1.95	−3.44	−2.87	−3.98	−3.42	8.34	6.30	6.15	4.71
∞	−2.58	−1.95	−3.43	−2.86	−3.96	−3.41	8.27	6.25	6.09	4.68

*Subscripts nc, c, and ct denote, respectively, that there is no constant, a constant, and a constant and trend term in the regression Eq. (21.9.5).

†The critical F values are for the joint hypothesis that the constant and δ terms in Eq. (21.9.5) are simultaneously equal to zero.

‡The critical F values are for the joint hypothesis that the constant, trend, and δ terms in Eq. (21.9.5) are simultaneously equal to zero.

Source: Adapted from W. A. Fuller, *Introduction to Statistical Time Series,* John Wiley & Sons, New York, 1976, p. 373 (for the τ test), and D. A. Dickey and W. A. Fuller, "Likelihood Ratio Statistics for Autoregressive Time Series with a Unit Root," *Econometrica,* vol. 49, 1981, p. 1063.

Appendix 

Computer Output of EViews, MINITAB, Excel, and STATA

In this appendix we show the computer output of *EViews*, MINITAB, Excel, and STATA, which are some of the popularly used statistical packages for regression and related statistical routines. We use the data given in Table E.1 from the textbook website to illustrate the output of these packages. Table E.1 gives data on the civilian labor force participation rate (CLFPR), the civilian unemployment rate (CUNR), and real average hourly earnings in 1982 dollars (AHE82) for the U.S. economy for the period 1980 to 2002.

Although in many respects the basic regression output is similar in all these packages, there are differences in how they present their results. Some packages give results to several digits, whereas some others approximate them to four or five digits. Some packages give analysis of variance (ANOVA) tables directly, whereas for some other packages they need to be derived. There are also differences in some of the summary statistics presented by the various packages. It is beyond the scope of this appendix to enumerate all the differences in these statistical packages. You can consult the websites of these packages for further information.

E.1 *EViews*

Using Version 6 of *EViews,* we regressed CLFPR on CUNR and AHE82 and obtained the results shown in Figure E.1.

This is the standard format in which *EViews* results are presented. The first part of this figure gives the regression coefficients, their estimated standard errors, the t values under the null hypothesis that the corresponding population values of these coefficients are zero, and the p values of these t values. This is followed by R^2 and adjusted R^2. The other summary output in the first part relates to the standard error of the regression, residual sum of squares (RSS), and the F value to test the hypothesis that the (true) values of all the slope coefficients are simultaneously equal to zero. Akaike information and Schwartz criteria are often used to choose between competing models. The lower the value of these criteria, the better the model is. The method of maximum likelihood (ML) is an alternative to the method of least squares. Just as in OLS we find those estimators that minimize

FIGURE E.1
EViews output of civilian labor force participation regression.

Dependent Variable: CLFPR
Method: Least Squares
Sample: 1980–2002
Included observations: 23

Variable	Coefficient	Std. Error	*t*-Statistic	Prob.
C	80.90133	4.756195	17.00967	0.0000
CUNR	−0.671348	0.082720	−8.115928	0.0000
AHE82	−1.404244	0.608615	−2.307278	0.0319

R-squared	0.772765	Mean dependent var	65.89565
Adjusted R-squared	0.750042	S.D. dependent var	1.168713
S.E. of regression	0.584308	Akaike info criterion	1.884330
Sum squared resid	6.828312	Schwarz criterion	2.032438
Log likelihood	−18.66979	*F*-statistic	34.00731
Durbin–Watson stat	0.787625	Prob(*F*-statistic)	0.000000

Obs	Actual	Fitted	Residual	Residual Plot
1980	63.8000	65.2097	−1.40974	
1981	63.9000	65.0004	−1.10044	
1982	64.0000	63.6047	0.39535	
1983	64.0000	63.5173	0.48268	
1984	64.4000	64.9131	−0.51311	
1985	64.8000	65.1566	−0.35664	
1986	65.3000	65.2347	0.06526	
1987	65.6000	65.8842	−0.28416	
1988	65.9000	66.4103	−0.51027	
1989	66.5000	66.6148	−0.11476	
1990	66.5000	66.5819	−0.08186	
1991	66.2000	65.8745	0.32546	
1992	66.4000	65.4608	0.93923	
1993	66.3000	65.8917	0.40834	
1994	66.6000	66.4147	0.18530	
1995	66.6000	66.7644	−0.16441	
1996	66.8000	66.8425	−0.04251	
1997	67.1000	67.0097	0.09032	
1998	67.1000	66.9974	0.10263	
1999	67.1000	67.0443	0.05569	
2000	67.2000	67.1364	0.06355	
2001	56.9000	66.4589	0.44105	
2002	66.6000	65.5770	1.02304	

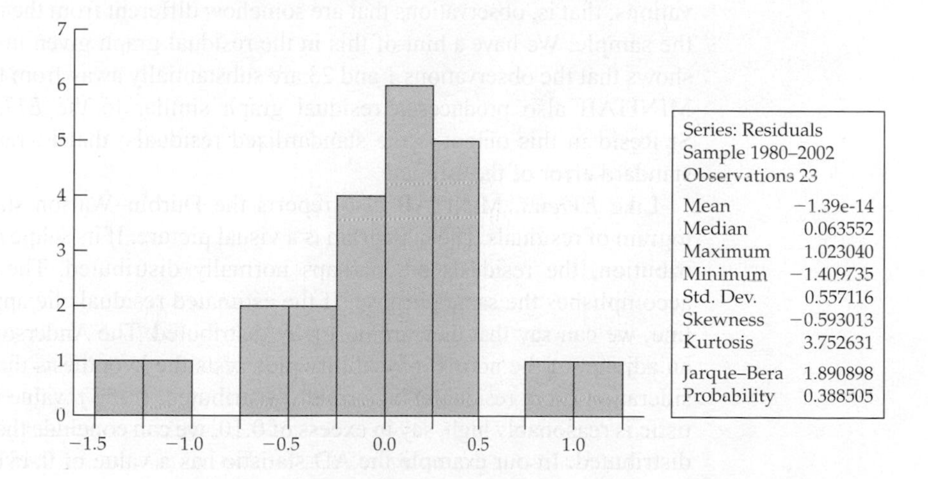

the error sum of squares, in ML we try to find those estimators that maximize the possibility of observing the sample at hand. Under the normality assumption of the error term, OLS and ML give identical estimates of the regression coefficients. The Durbin–Watson statistic is used to find out if there is first-order serial correlation in the error terms.

The second part of the *EViews* output gives the actual and fitted values of the dependent variable and the difference between the two, which represent the residuals. These residuals are plotted alongside this output with a vertical line denoting zero. Points to the right of the vertical line are positive residuals and those to the left represent negative residuals.

The third part of the output gives the histogram of the residuals along with their summary statistics. It gives the Jarque–Bera (JB) statistic to test for the normality of the error terms and also gives the probability of obtaining the stated statistics. The higher the probability of obtaining the observed JB statistic, the greater is the evidence in favor of the null hypothesis that the error terms are normally distributed.

Note that *EViews* does not give directly the analysis-of-variance (ANOVA) table, but it can be constructed easily from the data on the residual sum of squares, the total sum of squares (which will have to be derived from the standard deviation of the dependent variable), and their associated degrees of freedom. The F value given from this exercise should be equal to the F value reported in the first part of the table.

E.2 MINITAB

Using Version 15 of MINITAB, and using the same data, we obtained the regression results shown in Figure E.2.

MINITAB first reports the estimated multiple regression. This is followed by a list of predictor (i.e., explanatory) variables, the estimated regression coefficients, their standard errors, the $T (= t)$ values, and the p values. In this output S represents the standard error of the estimate, and R^2 and adjusted R^2 values are given in percent form.

This is followed by the usual ANOVA table. One characteristic feature of the ANOVA table is that it breaks down the regression, or explained, sum of squares among predictors. Thus of the total regression, sum of squares of 23.226, the share of CUNR is 21.404 and that of AHE82 is 1.822, suggesting that relatively, CUNR has more impact on CLFPR than AHE82.

A unique feature of the MINITAB regression output is that it reports "unusual" observations; that is, observations that are somehow different from the rest of the observations in the sample. We have a hint of this in the residual graph given in the *EViews* output, for it shows that the observations 1 and 23 are substantially away from the zero line shown there. MINITAB also produces a residual graph similar to the *EViews* residual graph. The St Resid in this output is the standardized residuals; that is, residuals divided by S, the standard error of the estimate.

Like *EViews,* MINITAB also reports the Durbin–Watson statistic and gives the histogram of residuals. The histogram is a visual picture. If its shape resembles the normal distribution, the residuals are perhaps normally distributed. The normal probability plot accomplishes the same purpose. If the estimated residuals lie approximately on a straight line, we can say that they are normally distributed. The Anderson–Darling (AD) statistic, an adjunct of the normal probability plot, tests the hypothesis that the variable under consideration (here residuals) is normally distributed. If the p value of the calculated AD statistic is reasonably high, say in excess of 0.10, we can conclude that the variable is normally distributed. In our example the AD statistic has a value of 0.481 with a p value of about 0.21 or 21 percent. So we can conclude that the residuals obtained from the regression model are normally distributed.

FIGURE E.2 MINITAB output of civilian labor force participation rate.

Regression Analysis: CLFPR versus CUNR, AHE82

The regression equation is
CLFPR = 81.0 − 0.672 CUNR − 1.41 AHE82

Predictor	Coef	SE Coef	T	P
Constant	80.951	4.770	16.97	0.000
CUNR	−0.67163	0.08270	−8.12	0.000
AHE82	−1.4104	0.6103	−2.31	0.032

S = 0.584117   R-Sq = 77.3%   R-Sq(adj) = 75.0%

Analysis of Variance

Source	DF	SS	MS	F	P
Regression	2	23.226	11.613	34.04	0.000
Residual Error	20	6.824	0.341		
Total	22	30.050			

Source	DF	Seq SS
CUNR	1	21.404
AHE82	1	1.822

Unusual Observations

Obs	CUNR	CLFPR	Fit	SE Fit	Residual	St Resid
1	7.10	63.800	65.209	0.155	−1.409	−2.50*R*
23	5.80	66.600	65.575	0.307	1.025	2.06*R*

R denotes an observation with a large standardized residual.

Durbin–Watson statistic = 0.787065

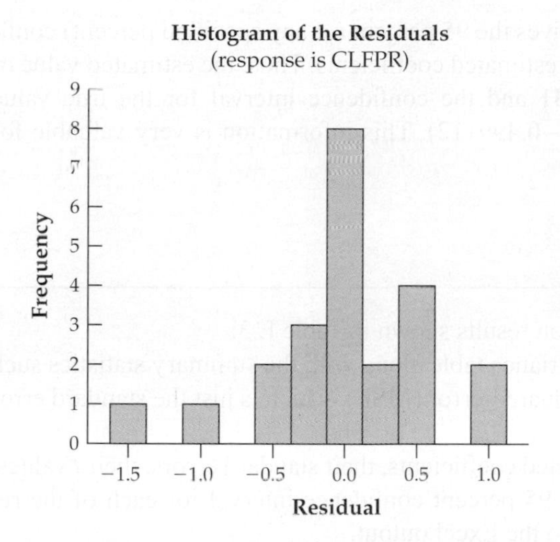

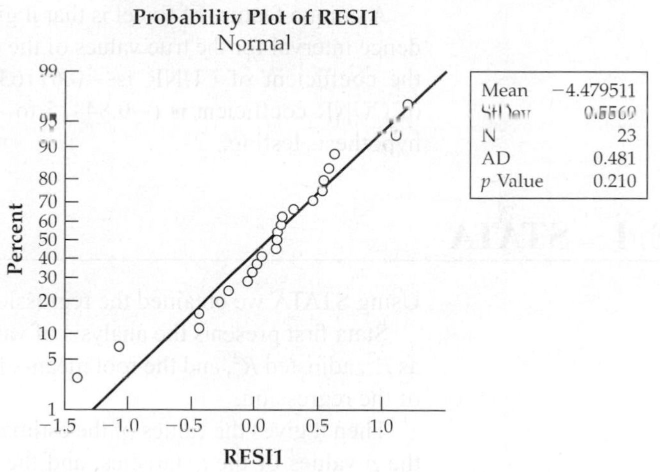

E.3 Excel

Using Microsoft Excel we obtained the regression output shown in Table E.2.

Excel first presents summary statistics, such as R^2, multiple R, which is the (positive) square root of R, adjusted R^2, and the standard error of the estimate. Then it presents the ANOVA table. After that it presents the estimated coefficients, their standard errors, the t values of the estimated coefficients and their p values. It also gives the actual and estimated

TABLE E.2
Excel Output of Civilian Labor Force Participation Rate

Summary Output

Regression Statistics	
Multiple *R*	0.879155
R Square	0.772914
Adjusted *R*	0.750205
Standard E	0.584117
Observation	23

ANOVA

	df	SS	MS	*F*	Significance *F*
Regression	2	23.22572	11.61286	34.03611	3.65E-07
Residual	20	6.823846	0.341192		
Total	22	30.04957			

	Coefficient	Standard Err	*t* Stat	*p*-value	Lower 95%	Upper 95%
Intercept	80.95122	4.770337	16.96971	2.42E-13	71.00047	90.90196
CUNR	−0.671631	0.082705	−8.120845	9.24E-08	−0.84415	−0.499112
AHE82	−1.410432	0.610348	−2.310867	0.031626	−2.683594	−0.13727

values of the dependent variable and the residual graph as well as the normal probability plot.

A unique feature of Excel is that it gives the 95 percent (or any specified percent) confidence interval for the true values of the estimated coefficients. Thus, the estimated value of the coefficient of CUNR is −0.671631 and the confidence interval for the true value of CUNR coefficient is (−0.84415 to −0.499112). This information is very valuable for hypothesis testing.

E.4 STATA

Using STATA we obtained the regression results shown in Table E.3.

Stata first presents the analysis of variance table along with the summary statistics such as R^2, adjusted R^2, and the root mean-squared-error (MSE), which is just the standard error of the regression.

Then it gives the values of the estimated coefficients, their standard errors, their t values, the p values of the t statistics, and the 95 percent confidence interval for each of the regression coefficients, which is similar to the Excel output.

E.5 Concluding Comments

We have given just the basic output of these packages for our example. But it may be noted that packages such as *EViews* and STATA are very comprehensive and contain many of the econometric techniques discussed in this text. Once you know how to access these packages, running various subroutines is a matter of practice. If you wish to pursue econometrics further, you may want to buy one or more of these packages.

TABLE E.3
STATA Output of Civilian Labor Force Participation Rate

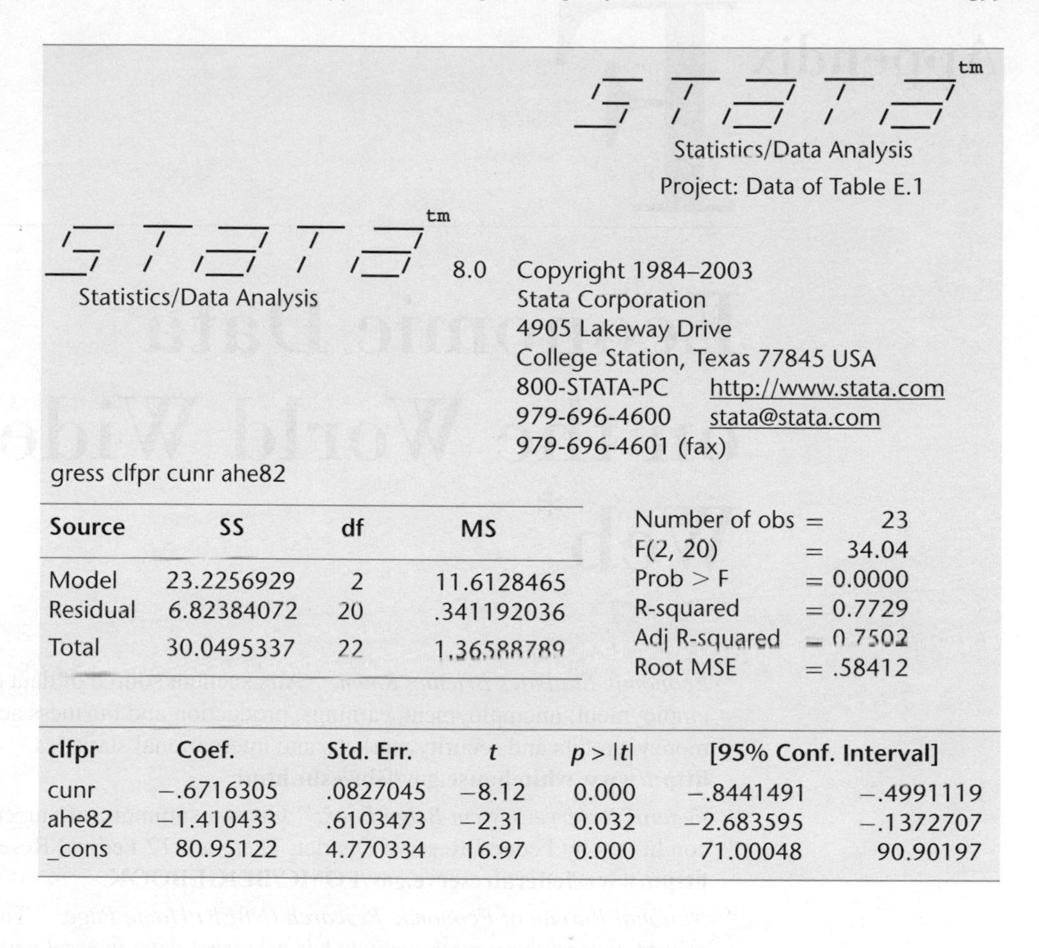

STATA tm
Statistics/Data Analysis
Project: Data of Table E.1

STATA tm 8.0
Statistics/Data Analysis

Copyright 1984–2003
Stata Corporation
4905 Lakeway Drive
College Station, Texas 77845 USA
800-STATA-PC http://www.stata.com
979-696-4600 stata@stata.com
979-696-4601 (fax)

gress clfpr cunr ahe82

Source	SS	df	MS
Model	23.2256929	2	11.6128465
Residual	6.82384072	20	.341192036
Total	30.0495337	22	1.36588789

Number of obs	= 23
F(2, 20)	= 34.04
Prob > F	= 0.0000
R-squared	= 0.7729
Adj R-squared	= 0.7502
Root MSE	= .58412

clfpr	Coef.	Std. Err.	t	$p > \|t\|$	[95% Conf.	Interval]
cunr	−.6716305	.0827045	−8.12	0.000	−.8441491	−.4991119
ahe82	−1.410433	.6103473	−2.31	0.032	−2.683595	−.1372707
_cons	80.95122	4.770334	16.97	0.000	71.00048	90.90197

References

www.eviews.com
www.stata.com
www.minitab.com
Microsoft Excel

R. Carter Hill, William E. Griffiths, George G. Judge, *Using Excel for Undergraduate Econometrics,* John Wiley & Sons, New York, 2001.

Appendix F

Economic Data on the World Wide Web*

Economic Statistics Briefing Room: An excellent source of data on output, income, employment, unemployment, earnings, production and business activity, prices and money, credits and security markets, and international statistics.
http://www.whitehouse.gov/fsbr/esbr.html

Federal Reserve System Beige Book: Gives a summary of current economic conditions by Federal Reserve District. There are 12 Federal Reserve Districts.
http://www.federalreserve.gov/FOMC/BEIGEBOOK

National Bureau of Economic Research (NBER) Home Page: This highly regarded private economic research institute has extensive data on asset prices, labor, productivity, money supply, business cycle indicators, etc. NBER has many links to other Web sites.
http://www.nber.org

Panel Study: Provides data on longitudinal survey of representative sample of U.S. individuals and families. These data have been collected annually since 1968.
http://psidonline.isr.umich.edu/

Resources for Economists on the Internet: Very comprehensive source of information and data on many economic activities with links to many Web sites. A very valuable source for academic and nonacademic economists.
http://rfe.org/

American Stock Exchange: Information on some 700 companies listed on the second largest stock market.
http://www.amex.com/

Bureau of Economic Analysis (BEA) Home Page: This agency of the U.S. Department of Commerce, which publishes the *Survey of Current Business,* is an excellent source of data on all kinds of economic activities.
http://www.bea.gov/

*Adapted from *Annual Editions: Microeconomics 98/99,* ed. Don Cole, Dushkin/McGraw-Hill, Connecticut, 1998. It should be noted that this list is by no means exhaustive. The sources listed here are updated continually.

CIA Publications: This source includes the *World Fact Book* (annual) and *Handbook of International Statistics.*
http://www.cia.gov/library/publications

Energy Information Administration (DOE): Economic information and data on each fuel category.
http://www.eia.doe.gov/

FRED Database: Federal Reserve Bank of St. Louis publishes historical economic and social data, which include interest rates, monetary and business indicators, exchange rates, etc.
http://research.stlouisfed.org/fred2/

International Trade Administration: Offers many Web links to trade statistics, cross-country programs, etc.
http://trade.gov/index.asp

STAT-USA Databases: The National Trade Data Bank provides the most comprehensive source of international trade data and export promotion information. There is also extensive data on demographic, political, and socioeconomic conditions for several countries.
http://www.stat-usa.gov/

Statistical Resources on the Web/Economics: An excellent source of statistics collated from various federal bureaus, economic indicators, the Federal Reserve Board, data on consumer price, and Web links to other sources.
http://www.lib.umich.edu/govdocs/stats.html

Bureau of Labor Statistics: The home page provides data related to various aspects of employment, unemployment, and earnings, as well as links to other statistical Web sites.
http://www.stats.bls.gov/

U.S. Census Bureau Home Page: Prime source of social, demographic, and economic data on income, employment, income distribution, and poverty.
http://www.census.gov/

General Social Survey: Annual personal interview survey data on U.S. households that began in 1972. More than 35,000 have responded to some 2,500 different questions covering a variety of data.
http://www.norc.org/GSS+website/

Institute for Research on Poverty: Data collected by nonpartisan and nonprofit university-based research center on a variety of questions relating to poverty and social inequality.
http://www.irp.wisc.edu/

Social Security Administration: The official Web site of the Social Security Administration with a variety of data.
http://www.ssa.gov/

Selected Bibliography

Introductory

Frank, C. R., Jr., *Statistics and Econometrics,* Holt, Rinehart and Winston, New York, 1971.

Goldberger, Arthur S., *Introductory Econometrics,* Harvard University Press, 1998.

Gujarati, Damodar N., *Essentials of Econometrics,* 3d ed., McGraw-Hill, New York, 2006.

Halcoussis, Dennis, *Understanding Econometrics,* Thomson, 2005.

Hill, Carter, William Griffiths, and George Judge, *Undergraduate Econometrics,* John Wiley & Sons, New York, 2001.

Hu, Teh-Wei, *Econometrics: An Introductory Analysis,* University Park Press, Baltimore, 1973.

Katz, David A., *Econometric Theory and Applications,* Prentice Hall, Englewood Cliffs, NJ, 1982.

Klein, Lawrence R., *An Introduction to Econometrics,* Prentice Hall, Englewood Cliffs, NJ, 1962.

Koop, Gary, *Analysis of Economic Data,* John Wiley & Sons, New York, 2000.

Schmidt, Stephen J., *Econometrics,* McGraw-Hill, New York, 2005.

Walters, A. A., *An Introduction to Econometrics,* Macmillan, London, 1968.

Intermediate

Aigner, D. J., *Basic Econometrics,* Prentice Hall, Englewood Cliffs, NJ, 1971.

Dhrymes, Phoebus J., *Introductory Econometrics,* Springer-Verlag, New York, 1978.

Dielman, Terry E., *Applied Regression Analysis for Business and Economics,* PWS-Kent, Boston, 1991.

Dougherty, Christopher, *Introduction to Econometrics,* 3d ed., Oxford University Press, Oxford, 2007.

Draper, N. R., and H. Smith, *Applied Regression Analysis,* 3d ed., John Wiley & Sons, New York, 1998.

Dutta, M., *Econometric Methods,* South-Western Publishing Company, Cincinnati, 1975.

Goldberger, A. S., *Topics in Regression Analysis,* Macmillan, New York, 1968.

Griffiths, William E., R. Carter Hill, and George G. Judge, *Learning and Practicing Econometrics,* John Wiley & Sons, New York, 1993.

Harris, Richard, and Robert Sollis, *Applied Time Series Modelling and Forecasting,* John Wiley & Sons, England, 2003.

Heij, Christiaan, Paul deBoer, Philip Hans Franses, Teun Kloek, and Herman K. van Djik, *Econometric Methods with Applications in Business and Economics,* Oxford University Press, New York, 2004.

Huang, D. S., *Regression and Econometric Methods,* John Wiley & Sons, New York, 1970.

Judge, George G., R. Carter Hill, William E. Griffiths, Helmut Lütkepohl, and Tsoung-Chao Lee, *Introduction to the Theory and Practice of Econometrics,* John Wiley & Sons, New York, 1982.

Kelejian, H. A., and W. E. Oates, *Introduction to Econometrics: Principles and Applications,* 2d ed., Harper & Row, New York, 1981.

Koutsoyiannis, A., *Theory of Econometrics,* Harper & Row, New York, 1973.

Maddala, G. S., *Introduction to Econometrics,* 3d ed., John Wiley & Sons, New York, 2001.

Mark, Stewart B., and Kenneth F. Wallis, *Introductory Econometrics,* 2d ed., John Wiley & Sons, New York, 1981. A Halsted Press Book.

Murphy, James L., *Introductory Econometrics,* Richard D. Irwin, Homewood, IL., 1973.

Nachane, Dilip M., *Econometrics: Theoretical Foundations and Empirical Perspectives,* Oxford University Press, New Delhi, 2006.

Netter, J., and W. Wasserman, *Applied Linear Statistical Models,* Richard D. Irwin, Homewood, IL., 1974.

Pindyck, R. S., and D. L. Rubinfeld, *Econometric Models and Econometric Forecasts,* 4th ed., McGraw-Hill, New York, 1990.

Sprent, Peter, *Models in Regression and Related Topics,* Methuen, London, 1969.

Stock, James H., and Mark W. Watson, *Introduction to Econometrics,* 2d ed., Pearson/Addison-Wesley, Boston, 2007.

Tintner, Gerhard, *Econometrics,* John Wiley & Sons (science ed.), New York, 1965.

Valavanis, Stefan, *Econometrics: An Introduction to Maximum-Likelihood Methods,* McGraw-Hill, New York, 1959.

Verbeek, Marno, *A Guide to Modern Econometrics,* John Wiley & Sons, New York, 2000.

Wonnacott, R. J., and T. H. Wonnacott, *Econometrics,* 2d ed., John Wiley & Sons, New York, 1979.

Wooldridge, Jeffrey M., *Introductory Econometrics,* 3d ed., South-Western College Publishing, 2006.

Advanced

Cameron, A. Colin, and Pravin K. Trivedi, *Microeconomics: Methods and Applications,* Cambridge University Press, New York, 2005.

Chow, Gregory C., *Econometric Methods,* McGraw-Hill, New York, 1983.

Christ, C. F., *Econometric Models and Methods,* John Wiley & Sons, New York, 1966.

Davidson, James, *Econometric Theory,* Blackwell Publishers, Oxford, U.K., 2000.

Dhrymes, P. J., *Econometrics: Statistical Foundations and Applications,* Harper & Row, New York, 1970.

Fomby, Thomas B., Carter R. Hill, and Stanley R. Johnson, *Advanced Econometric Methods,* Springer-Verlag, New York, 1984.

Goldberger, A. S., *Econometric Theory,* John Wiley & Sons, New York, 1964.

Goldberger, A. S., *A Course in Econometrics,* Harvard University Press, Cambridge, MA., 1991.

Greene, William H., *Econometric Analysis,* 4th ed., Prentice Hall, Englewood Cliffs, NJ, 2000.

Harvey, A. C., *The Econometric Analysis of Time Series,* 2d ed., MIT Press, Cambridge, MA., 1990.

Hayashi, Fumio, *Econometrics,* Princeton University Press, Princeton, NJ, 2000.

Johnston, J., *Econometric Methods,* 3d ed., McGraw-Hill, New York, 1984.

Judge, George G., Carter R. Hill, William E. Griffiths, Helmut Lütkepohl, and Tsoung-Chao Lee, *Theory and Practice of Econometrics,* John Wiley & Sons, New York, 1980.

Klein, Lawrence R., *A Textbook of Econometrics,* 2d ed., Prentice Hall, Englewood Cliffs, NJ, 1974.

Kmenta, Jan, *Elements of Econometrics,* 2d ed., Macmillan, New York, 1986.

Madansky, A., *Foundations of Econometrics,* North-Holland, Amsterdam, 1976.

Maddala, G. S., *Econometrics,* McGraw-Hill, New York, 1977.

Malinvaud, E., *Statistical Methods of Econometrics,* 2d ed., North-Holland, Amsterdam, 1976.

Mills, Terence C., and Kerry Patterson, *Palgrave Handbook of Econometrics, Vol. 1: Econometric Theory,* Palgrave/Macmillan, New York, 2006.

Mittelhammer, Ron C., George G. Judge, and Douglas J. Miller, *Econometric Foundations,* Cambridge University Press, New York, 2000.

Peracchi, Franco, *Econometrics,* John Wiley & Sons, New York, 2001.

Theil, Henry, *Principles of Econometrics,* John Wiley & Sons, New York, 1971.

Specialized

Belsley, David A., Edwin Kuh, and Roy E. Welsh, *Regression Diagnostics: Identifying Influential Data and Sources of Collinearity,* John Wiley & Sons, New York, 1980.

Dhrymes, P. J., *Distributed Lags: Problems of Estimation and Formulation,* Holden-Day, San Francisco, 1971.

Diebold, Francis X., *Elements of Forecasting,* 2d ed., South-Western Publishing, 2001.

Goldfeld, S. M., and R. E. Quandt, *Nonlinear Methods of Econometrics,* North-Holland, Amsterdam, 1972.

Gourieroux, Christian, *Econometrics of Qualitative Dependent Variables,* Cambridge University Press, New York, 2000.

Graybill, F. A., *An Introduction to Linear Statistical Models,* vol. 1, McGraw-Hill, New York, 1961.

Hamilton, James D., *Time Series Analysis,* Princeton University Press, Princeton, NJ, 1994.

Maddala, G. S., and Kim In-Moo, *Unit Roots, Cointegration, and Structural Change,* Cambridge University Press, New York, 1998.

Mills, T. C., *Time Series Techniques for Economists,* Cambridge University Press, 1990.

Rao, C. R., *Linear Statistical Inference and Its Applications,* 2d ed., John Wiley & Sons, New York, 1975.

Zellner, A., *An Introduction to Bayesian Inference in Econometrics,* John Wiley & Sons, New York, 1971.

Applied

Berndt, Ernst R., *The Practice of Econometrics: Classic and Contemporary,* Addison-Wesley, 1991.

Bridge, J. I., *Applied Econometrics,* North-Holland, Amsterdam, 1971.

Charemza, Wojciech W., and Derek F. Deadman, *New Directions in Econometric Practice: General to Specific Modelling, Cointegration and Vector Autoregression,* 2d ed., Edward Elgar Publisher, New York, 1997.

Cramer, J. S., *Empirical Econometrics,* North-Holland, Amsterdam, 1969.

Desai, Meghnad, *Applied Econometrics,* McGraw-Hill, New York, 1976.

Kennedy, Peter, *A Guide to Econometrics,* 4th ed., MIT Press, Cambridge, MA., 1998.

Leser, C. E. V., *Econometric Techniques and Problems,* 2d ed., Hafner, London, 1974.

Mills, T. C., *The Econometric Modelling of Financial Time Series,* Cambridge University Press, 1993.

Mukherjee, Chandan, Howard White, and Marc Wuyts, *Econometrics and Data Analysis for Developing Countries,* Routledge, New York, 1998.

Patterson, Kerry, *An Introduction to Applied Econometrics: A Time Series Approach,* St. Martin's Press, New York, 2000.

Rao, Potluri, and Roger LeRoy Miller, *Applied Econometrics,* Wadsworth, Belmont, CA., 1971.

Note: For a list of the seminal articles on the various topics discussed in this book, please refer to the extensive bibliography given at the end of each chapter in Fomby et al., cited above.

Name Index

Page numbers followed by n indicate material found in notes.

Subject Index

Page numbers followed by n indicate material found in notes.

B

C

P

Q

U

V

W

X

Y

Z